CAMBRIDGE
EDUCATIONAL SERVICES®

EDUCATORS' #1 CHOICE FOR SCHOOL IMPROVEMENT

SAT* • PSAT* Victory

Classroom Text

SAT • PSAT • SAT II • ACT • PLAN • EXPLORE • GRE • GMAT • LSAT • MCAT • TOEFL • GED • PRAXIS • PSAE • ITBS • CollegePrep™

About Cambridge Educational Services:

Cambridge Educational Services was founded in order to help all students, regardless of income, meet standards and perform to the best of their abilities on standardized tests and in the classroom. Our mission is to provide assessment services and program materials that make quality school improvement programs possible for a wide range of student ability levels. Our goal is to help students achieve test scores that reflect their true potential and ability. Our programs help thousands of students each year reach their goals, such as becoming National Merit Scholars, gaining admission to the colleges of their choice, and earning valuable scholarships. Cambridge publishes a variety of school improvement and preparation titles and products including textbooks, teacher's guides, skills review manuals, software, and assessment services.

Cambridge Publishing, Inc., Chicago National Headquarters, Des Plaines, IL 60018

© 1994, 1995, 1996, 1997, 2000, 2003, 2004, 2005 by Cambridge Publishing, Inc.
All rights reserved. First edition 1994
Ninth edition 2005

Printed in the United States of America
11 10 09 08   3 4 5

ISBN-13: 978-1-58894-019-3

Portions reprinted from SAT
© 2005 by Thomas H. Martinson
All rights reserved

CAMBRIDGE
EDUCATIONAL SERVICES®

EDUCATORS' #1 CHOICE FOR SCHOOL IMPROVEMENT

Dear Student,

The fact that you are reading this book means just one thing: you have a big, important test ahead of you. You want to do well, and we can help you. This course will enable you to succeed on the SAT and PSAT and improve your all-around academic performance.

Since you began going to school, you have been taught thousands of things. No one expects you to remember every single concept that you have learned since you were five years old. However, the SAT and PSAT are cumulative tests, which means that you might be tested on concepts that you have forgotten or that you never learned. Not only that, but the SAT and PSAT tests you differently than you are tested in your academic classes.

Your Cambridge SAT Student Textbook contains all of the materials that you need in order to: (1) refresh or build your understanding of important skills; (2) apply those skills in the particular context of the SAT; and (3) reduce test anxiety through practice.

You have the tools to succeed. Attend class, participate in learning, do all of your homework, and maintain a positive attitude. You can do it, we have confidence in you.

Good Luck!

The Cambridge Curriculum Committee

TABLE OF CONTENTS

HOW TO USE THIS BOOK

This book is organized into six parts:

1) information to help you make sense of the results of your pre-assessment (Step One);
2) five skills review chapters (Step Two);
3) problems resembling the real SAT and PSAT that your instructor will use to teach tested concepts and applicable strategies (Step Three);
4) four full-length SAT practice tests (Step Four);
5) forms that help you make sense of the results of your post-test (Step Five);
6) recommendations for continuing your study after the course is done (Step Six).

The following introduction will briefly explain how to use each part of this textbook.

MAKING SENSE OF YOUR OFFICIAL PRE-TEST RESULTS

In order to know where to begin preparing for the SAT or PSAT, you have to find out what you already do well and what you could learn to do better. The pre-assessment serves this purpose. First, you will take an official, retired SAT or PSAT under actual testing conditions. Then, with the help of your instructor, you will use the results of those tests to determine exactly which topics to review, for how long, and in what order.

Three Winning Strategies sections found in this step will help get you started with Applying for College, Overcoming Test Anxiety, and Time Management.

TARGETED SKILLS REVIEW

The Skills Review section of this book contains problems that will enable you to do three things: (1) review material that you may have forgotten; (2) learn material that you may never have learned; and (3) master the skills required to answer the more difficult multiple-choice questions on the SAT and PSAT.

The Skills Review is divided into five areas:

- Reading
- Math
- Math Express
- Grammar and Mechanics
- Writing

Each chapter contains concept lessons and corresponding review exercises. For example, the lessons in the Math Skills Review cover the following topics: whole numbers; fractions; signed numbers; decimals; percents; mean, median, and mode; ratios and proportions; exponents and radicals; algebraic operations; algebraic equations and inequalities; geometry; functions, graphs, and coordinate geometry; and story problems. The other Skills Review chapters cover a similar range of topics that are appropriate to each subject.

These exercises do not necessarily contain problems that mimic SAT or PSAT items. The problems are designed to help you learn a concept—not necessarily to help you learn about how the concepts appear on the actual exam. After you have mastered the skills, you will be able to take full advantage of the test-taking strategies that are developed in the Problem-Solving, Concepts, and Strategies section of the book. Your instructor may either review the Skills Review material in class or have you complete the exercises as homework.

SOLVING PROBLEMS THAT LOOK LIKE THOSE FOUND ON THE TEST

Problem-Solving, Concepts, and Strategies make up the heart of this course and, in particular, this textbook. This part of the book contains items that look like those found on the real SAT and PSAT. When compared with items on the real tests, the items in this part of the book have similar content, represent the same difficulty levels, and can be solved by using the same problem-solving skills and alternative test-taking strategies.

There are five chapters in the Problem-Solving, Concepts, and Strategies section, each representing a major component of the SAT/PSAT:

- Critical Reading: Passages
- Critical Reading: Sentence Completions
- Math: Multiple-Choice
- Math: Student-Produced Responses
- Writing

At the beginning of each of the above chapters, there is a Cambridge Course Concept Outline. These outlines act as course syllabi and list the concepts that are tested for each item-type over a two-year testing cycle. The items in each chapter are organized to correspond with the respective course concept outline. For each concept in the outline, there are various clusters of items. A cluster contains a greater number of items if the item-type appears with great frequency on the real test, and it contains a lesser number of items if the item-type appears with less frequency. Although the concepts are not arranged in clusters on the real SAT or PSAT, we organize the problems in clusters so that the concepts are emphasized and reinforced. After you learn the concepts, you will be able to practice applying this conceptual knowledge on the practice tests.

TAKING PRACTICE TESTS

In the practice test section of the book, there are four full-length SAT practice tests. In these tests, the items not only mimic the real test in content and difficulty level, but they are also arranged in an order and with a frequency that simulates the real SAT and PSAT.

Your instructor will ask you to either complete some or all of these items in class, or he or she will assign them as homework. If you are taking these four tests at home, you should take two with time restrictions and two without time restrictions. Taking the test without time restrictions will help you get a sense of how long it would take for you to comfortably and accurately solve an item. Applying the time pressure then forces you to pace yourself as you would on the real test. If you complete all four of the practice tests, any test anxiety you may have will be greatly reduced.

MAKING SENSE OF YOUR OFFICIAL POST-TEST RESULTS

In order to know how far you've come since the pre-test, you have to take another official retired SAT or PSAT. You will take a second official, retired SAT or PSAT under actual testing conditions. You will use the results to evaluate your progress and to determine exactly what topics would be the most beneficial for you to review.

FIGURING OUT WHAT TO DO NEXT

Step Six contains a short guide to help you devise a personal study plan for the days or weeks between the end of the course and the official test. You will practice what you learned in the Winning Strategies sections (Step One) to make the most of your remaining study time.

1

Step One: Pre-Assessment and Course Planning

Step One Overview:

You start your course with an official test so that you know where you stand on the SAT or PSAT. This diagnostic test tells you and your instructor where you need to focus to see the greatest improvement. You should complete this test under real testing conditions so you know what to expect on the day of the actual test. Course instruction hinges on your pre-test performance, so try hard, but it's just a pre-test so don't be too discouraged if you don't perform as well as you hoped. You'll soon be learning tips and core curricular skills to boost your score.

Winning Strategies

CAMBRIDGE
EDUCATORS' SERVICES®
C

EDUCATORS' #1 CHOICE FOR SCHOOL IMPROVEMENT

Cambridge Course Concept Outline
WINNING STRATEGIES

Following the Winning Strategies chapters are the Essay Response and Bubble Sheets for use when taking the SAT Pre-Test.

APPLYING TO COLLEGE
–*Winning Strategies*–

The goal of this section is to help you get into the college of your choice. We have advised tens of thousands of students, interviewed college admissions officers across the country, and attended annual advisors' conferences. In the following pages, we have compiled the most valuable statistics and advice from a variety of sources.

This section is designed for a range of students—from those who are already actively working on their applications to those who are only starting to think about applying to college. Therefore, some of the points that are made are very general, while other points are very specific. You may already be familiar with some of the information, while other points and tips may even surprise you. Whatever your current stage in the college application process, the following will be helpful for both applying to and getting into the college of your choice.

A. INTRODUCTION

In order to create the most effective application possible, you must understand and appreciate the function of the admissions process as both a social and an economic process. Many prospective applicants view the process of filing a college application only from their own individual perspectives, not realizing that they play a very instrumental role in the process. Those students who share this view often believe that:

> *"Colleges only care about your standardized test score."*
> *"You can't get into a really good school unless you know someone."*
> *"They really don't read your personal statement."*

Such beliefs reflect an attitude that is based on a misinterpretation of the admissions process—not taking into consideration the social and economic factors. Let us examine this process from both your perspective and the college's perspective..

From your perspective, you must keep in mind that the college admissions process is much more than merely answering a few questions about your educational background and employment history. Rather, the application process is just the first step on a career path that will last for a good portion of your life. Decisions that you make at this stage of the game may have implications on your life 30 or 40 years from now. An easy way to realize that this is true is to imagine the different courses that your life might follow depending on whether you do or do not get into college; you may also compare your career prospects depending on whether you are or are not accepted by your first-choice school.

Now, this is not to say that not getting into a certain school spells disaster. Obviously, becoming a psychologist, engineer, biochemist, computer scientist, economist, chemist, teacher, historian, musician, physicist, geologist, political scientist, or sociologist is not for everyone. Nor is it necessary to receive a degree in such subjects from the very best schools. Rather, we are simply trying to stress the importance of the admissions process to you as an individual. Indeed, you do not have to look far into the future to appreciate the effect that the admissions process will have on your everyday life. Your decisions at this point will determine, at the very least, where you are likely to live for the next four years.

Additionally, you must appreciate the financial commitment that you are making to go to college. First of all, the cost of the application process alone could easily exceed $200. The fees that you pay Educational Testing Services to take the Scholastic Aptitude Test with score reports could be as much as $100. Furthermore, schools charge application fees that typically run between $25 and $40. Assuming that you apply to ten schools, you could easily spend $350 on application fees. In addition, you would probably spend at least $100 on administrative details, such as document preparation, copying, postage, and long distance telephone calls. When you add approximately $300 for test preparation, you could easily be committed to a total of $1,000 or more.

On top of the application expenses, most schools require a non-refundable deposit to be sent along with your response to an acceptance offer by a certain deadline. You may find yourself in the uncomfortable position of having to pay such a

deposit in order to ensure that you have a college seat even though you have not yet heard from some other schools. These initial sums, however, pale in comparison to the cost of tuition, which can amount to as much as $35,000 each year. When the expense of room and board for four years is taken into account, the entire expense to obtain your college degree could easily exceed $140,000.

Do not let these numbers frighten you. We are not trying to dissuade you from pursuing a college degree. We are simply trying to dramatize a point: The decision to apply to college has significant social and economic implications for you as an individual.

From the perspective of the college, there are also social and economic implications that are taken into consideration. A college, like any other educational institution, is a corporate entity, and its admissions decisions reflect social and economic policies that are adopted by the corporation. First, consider some of the economic implications that a college must weigh when deciding to either accept or reject an applicant.

A college has to be run in the same way as any other business. It has paid employees, it owns or rents property, it operates a library, it buys furniture and office equipment, it pays utility bills, *etc*. A large part of these expenses is paid with student tuition. A college, therefore, is absolutely dependent upon a steady flow of tuition income. So, admissions decisions must be made in the context of budgetary constraints. A college simply cannot afford to have large numbers of students dropping out of school. Therefore, one of the primary concerns of a college admissions officer is to ensure that those applicants who are accepted are committed to completing a course of study. In addition, colleges rely heavily on alumni donations. So, even though this may not be an explicit concern of the admissions office, it would not be surprising to learn that an applicant who shows considerable professional promise would be considered more favorably than others. Likewise, a school that graduates successful B.A. and B.S. students gets a reputation for being a good school, and such a reputation tends to attract highly qualified applicants.

It would be far from the truth, however, to imply that an admissions decision is made based solely on economic considerations. Colleges also have a sense of the social responsibility that they bear as educators of B.A. and B.S. students—one of the most influential groups of people in our society. They meet this responsibility in some fairly obvious ways, such as by actively seeking applicants from groups who are under-represented in the professional community and by establishing programs to train professionals for positions of special need.

Ultimately, the admissions process is the interface between these two perspectives: that of the student and that of the college. The process is ideally designed to create a mutual relationship between students and institutions.. This mutual function, however, is somewhat skewed. For decades, there have been more people who are interested in pursuing professional careers than there are seats available at accredited colleges. In recent times, there have actually been more than two applicants for each available seat. Given the mismatch between the number of available seats and the number of applicants, the application process has turned into a rigorous competition.

In order to successfully compete with your peers, you must portray yourself as an attractive candidate; you must convince the admissions committee that you will help them satisfy their economic and social needs. This persuasive approach to acceptance must be a guiding force as you create your application.

With the information provided in this section, you will create an application that will place you in a good position for college acceptance—that is, an application that will give a college an affirmative reason for accepting you. In addition to this student textbook, you may also want to consider some other sources. For general information about the accredited colleges in the United States, you should refer to the *College Handbook*. This book can be found in either your school's library, or your local bookstore. The *College Handbook* is published by the College Entrance Examination Board and contains summaries of approximately 3,200 two- and four-year colleges. Use this handbook for general guidance. Additionally, request an information bulletin from each school in which you have even a passing interest. Read those bulletins carefully; they provide listings of faculty members and their qualifications, descriptions of any special programs, information about student activities and campus life, financial aid catalogues, and much more.

B. HOW THE ADMISSIONS PROCESS WORKS

There is no singularly definable admissions process. Rather, each college has its own customized admissions process, which differs from that of every other college in the country.

There are approximately 3,200 U.S. colleges and universities, and each college offers hundreds of individualized degree programs. We are unable to talk about the details of the admissions process because all schools regard the mechanics of the decision-making process as a highly sensitive matter. As a result, they refrain from sharing the details of that process with outsiders. We can, however, help clarify this seemingly random process with a few important generalizations that are made below. You can also help yourself by researching the admissions policies and statistics of different schools. In any event, you are ultimately incapable of exercising any control over the way a college makes its decision. The good news, as you will see, is that you do not need "inside" information to create an effective application.

Faculty committees may be required to make their decisions by majority vote or unanimous agreement before an applicant is accepted. A professional admissions officer; officers who may not themselves have B.A.s, B.S.s, or Ph.D.s; or a Dean of Admissions (who has a graduate degree but is not a faculty member) may make the decisions. A committee of members drawn from both administration and faculty may make the decisions. Finally, other students may even have some input into the decisions. However, we will not dwell on these different possibilities for two reasons. First, they are outside of your control. Second, regardless of the formal structure of the admissions process, it is designed to satisfy the institution's social and economic goals—as previously explained.

Despite the variety of formal structures, one generalization is possible:

> *"Every college relies to some extent on an applicant's Grade Point Average (GPA)*
> *and SAT score, but there are few (if any) colleges that rely solely on these quantitative*
> *factors."*

This statement contains two important ideas; let us examine each of them.

First of all, most colleges do use a student's Grade Point Average and SAT score to help determine his or her viability. However, the exact reliance on these numbers varies from school to school, with many schools even using a formula that combines the two together into an index. This formula is designed to weigh the two numbers so that they give admissions officers some idea of how the applicants stack up against each other.

The SAT is now scored on a scale from 600 (the minimum) to 2,400 (the maximum). You will receive three separate scores, each ranging from 200 to 800 points. These three scores will correspond to the Critical Reading, Math, and Writing exam components. Some schools will add all three scores together for a cumulative index. If you are quoted a required SAT index at a specific school, it is important that you inquire as to whether that index is the average or the total of the three separate scores.

The "200 to 800" point scale has a direct relationship to the "0 to 4" grading system that is used by most colleges: $200 \cdot 4 = 800$. This relationship enables the use of a formula that combines the three measures into an index. A typical index formula would read as follows:

$$\text{(Average SAT Score)} + (200 \cdot \text{GPA}) = \text{Index}$$

Let us now look at an example to demonstrate how the formula works. A student with a 3.5 GPA and SAT scores of 700 (Critical Reading), 700 (Math), and 700 (Writing) would receive the following index:

$$\frac{700 + 700 + 700}{3} + (200 \cdot 3.5) = 700 + 700 = 1,400$$

The significance of this index varies from school to school. Some schools have a fairly mechanical admissions process that places great emphasis on the index or some variation on its form. For example, a school may choose to set a minimum index, below which applications receive little or no consideration. Such schools may also have a second, higher minimum that triggers an automatic acceptance. In this case, students with indices that exceed the higher

minimum are accepted unless there is some glaring weakness in the application that otherwise disqualifies them. On the other hand, there are schools that claim to minimize the importance of the SAT and the GPA. They claim that the SAT is the very last factor at which they look when making decisions. Such schools tend to have a very flexible admissions process.

Most schools fall between the two ends of the spectrum. In varying degrees, many schools use the test scores and grades as a screening device to determine how much attention will be given to an application. Applications with very low test scores and grades will receive little attention. The schools reason that unless there is something obvious and compelling in the application to offset the low numbers, the applicant should be rejected. Applications with very high test scores and grades will also receive little attention. The reasoning is that unless there is something obvious and compelling in the application to reject the applicant, he or she should be accepted. Based on this theory, the applications with average test scores and grades will receive the greatest attention. These applications are provided by candidates who are at least competitive enough for that particular school but do not command an automatic acceptance. It is in this pool of candidates that competition is the most severe.

Below is a table that illustrates what happens at most colleges. The fractions represent the total number of accepted applicants divided by the total number of applicants.

	SAT SCORE (Percentile)			
GPA	61-70%	71-80%	81-90%	91-100%
3.75+	$\frac{2}{19}$	$\frac{49}{101}$	$\frac{102}{116}$	$\frac{72}{79}$
3.5-3.74	$\frac{6}{112}$	$\frac{75}{275}$	$\frac{301}{361}$	$\frac{120}{129}$
0-3.49	$\frac{10}{160}$	$\frac{90}{601}$	$\frac{375}{666}$	$\frac{201}{250}$

The twelve categories in the table show how this particular college responded to applications with certain SAT scores (shown in percentile terms) and GPAs. The category in the upper right-hand corner represents candidates who scored above the 90th percentile with GPAs above 3.75. The table shows that 72 of the 79 applicants who satisfy these conditions were accepted and seven were rejected.

What is obvious from the table is that some candidates with higher numbers were rejected in favor of candidates with lower numbers. For example, of those candidates with scores between the 81st and 90th percentiles, 74 more candidates were accepted with a GPA below 3.50 than were accepted with a GPA between 3.50 and 3.74.

Why would a college reject an applicant with higher numbers for one with lower numbers? The answer lies in our analysis of the admissions process. Apparently, there were factors in the applications of those who were accepted that suggested to the admissions committee that such applicants would better meet the social and economic goals of the institution. Those factors are unquantifiable—motivation, commitment, leadership, experience, and so on.

As you prepare your applications, you are, of course, saddled with your GPA and your SAT score. Aside from hard work, there is nothing that you can do to change those factors. (Below, however, we take up the question of re-taking the SAT.) Therefore, the only real control you will have over your application will be those unquantifiable factors, and we will advise you on how to maximize their impact.

There is one final point about the mechanics of the application process: rolling admissions. Rolling admissions is a device used by many colleges to regulate the release of acceptances. A typical college application season opens in October and closes in May or June. Applications are received throughout this season, and decisions are made on an ongoing basis with the intent of targeting an entering class. Based on its admissions history, a college will estimate the expected range of SAT scores and GPAs of the students that it will accept in the upcoming year. Then, as it receives applications (e.g., on a monthly basis), it will act on them accordingly. Students with very strong applications compared with the target group receive acceptances; students with weak applications receive rejections. Applications in the middle are carried over, and the applicants will receive either an application pending notification or no notification at all.

The rolling admissions process has advantages for both the college and the applicant. From the applicant's point of view, the earlier you know the decision about an application, the better. Once you know whether you have been accepted or rejected, you can begin to make important decisions about your future. From the college's point of view, the entering class and therefore the stability of the budget begin to take shape as early as possible.

The rolling admissions process is also a tool that you can use to your advantage: apply early. Obviously, schools have greater flexibility and there are more seats available earlier in the admissions season rather than later. We do not mean to imply that you will be rejected if you apply late in the season. In fact, it is impossible to exactly quantify the advantage that earlier applications may have over later applications. Still, if you want to maximize your chances of acceptance, apply early.

C. WHERE TO APPLY

Given the economic commitment that you will be making, one of the most obvious questions in your mind will be "Where should I apply?" You should apply to a group of schools that, given your economic resources, will maximize your chances of gaining admission.

To apply to a college, you must remit a non-refundable application fee. Essentially, you are gambling with your money. You pay the application fee in advance of knowing whether you will win or lose. So, hedge your bets. In such a gambling situation, a person has several choices. Some options will be long shots; other options will be almost sure things; and still other options will lie somewhere in between these two extremes. The long shots will pay handsome dividends, and the sure things will pay a reasonable return. The other options will obviously pay somewhere in between.

Given these considerations, you should select two or perhaps three "long shot" schools. As the term "long shot" implies, the odds of your being accepted to these schools are not very good, but the potential payoff justifies the gamble. On the other hand, you should also select one or two "sure thing" schools. In this case, you may have to apply to either a school in your geographical area that does not enjoy a particularly good reputation or a school that is located in another part of the country. The rest of your applications should go to your "good bet" schools—schools for which the chances for acceptance are 40% to 75%.

Now, let us assume that you have the resources to apply to ten schools and that you have both an above average GPA and an above average SAT score. Depending on the exact numbers, you may very well have a chance at one of the top colleges. But those colleges are your "long shot" schools. You are almost a "sure thing" at many schools, and there is a long list of schools in the middle at which your application will likely receive serious consideration but is not guaranteed for acceptance.

This strategy of "stacking" your applications will maximize your chances of acceptance at one of your desired schools, while minimizing your chances of not getting into any school at all. Of course, the details of this strategy will be unique for each individual person. For students who are lucky enough to have a high GPA and a top SAT score, the middle- and bottom-tier schools collapse into a single tier. At the other extreme, those students who are unlucky enough to have a GPA and SAT score that are below what most schools accept will have to work with the second and third tiers.

As you prepare to implement this strategy, make a realistic assessment of your chances. Candidates unfortunately tend to overestimate the importance of what they believe to be their own interesting or unique factors. For example, we often hear candidates who make such statements as, "Well sure my GPA is a little low, but I had to work part-time while I was in school," and "I know my SAT score is not that good, but I was a member of the high school Student Council." These points are valid and are usually taken into consideration by admissions officers. However, the most important concern is to how much weight these points will be given since such statements are true of most everyone who is applying to college. For example, if you are thinking of applying to a program that requires an average GPA of 3.8 and an average SAT score in the 90th percentile and you do not meet these requirements, then it will be difficult for you to obtain admission to that program unless your application has some other strikingly unique characteristics.

As you consider where to apply, you will probably want to know which undergraduate schools are the best in the country. Since there is no single criterion for "best school" that would be accepted by everyone, it is arguable whether this classification can be made objectively. However, even though no unequivocal classification can be made, it is

possible to make an approximation as to the best schools in the nation. The "U.S. News & World Report" Year 2005 survey of college school deans lists the top 25 national universities and top 25 national colleges for that year. (Entries on the list may change each year, as may the rankings.)

TOP 25 NATIONAL UNIVERSITIES

1. Harvard University	9. Columbia University (NY)	18. University of Notre Dame (IN)
Princeton University (NJ)	Dartmouth College (NH)	Vanderbilt University (TN)
3. Yale University (CT)	11. Northwestern University (IL)	20. Emory University (GA)
4. University of Pennsylvania	Washington Univ. in St. Louis	21. University of California – Berkeley
5. Duke University (NC)	13. Brown University (RI)	22. Carnegie Mellon University (PA)
Massachusetts Inst. of Technology	14. Cornell University (NY)	Univ. of Michigan – Ann Arbor
Stanford University (CA)	Johns Hopkins University (MD)	University of Virginia
8. California Institute of Technology	University of Chicago	25. Georgetown University (DC)
	17. Rice University (TX)	Univ. of California – Los Angeles

TOP 25 NATIONAL LIBERAL ARTS COLLEGES

1. Williams College (MA)	9. Haverford College (PA)	19. Colby College (ME)
2. Amherst College (MA)	Wesleyan University (CT)	Hamilton College (NY)
Swarthmore College (PA)	11. Middlebury College (VT)	21. Bryn Mawr College (PA)
4. Wellesley College (MA)	12. Vassar College (NY)	22. Bates College (ME)
5. Carleton College (MN)	13. Claremont McKenna College (CA)	23. Oberlin College (OH)
Pomona College (CA)	Smith College (MA)	24. Mount Holyoke College (MA)
7. Bowdoin College (ME)	Washington and Lee Univ. (VA)	Trinity College (CT)
Davidson College (NC)	16. Colgate University (NY)	
	Grinnell College (IA)	
	Harvey Mudd College (CA)	

D. CREATING YOUR APPLICATION

The title of this section echoes our previous analysis of the admissions process. To reiterate, you must create an application that satisfies the needs of the school to which you are applying in order to maximize your chances of success. This approach does not mean that you need to create a fictitious or over-embellished application, but it does mean that you should organize and present your experiences in a way that depicts you in the most favorable light.

Most of the questions that you will be asked require only short answers. For example: "Did you work while you were in school?", "What clubs did you join?", and "What honors or awards did you receive?" When answering such questions, you do not have much room to maneuver, but you should try to communicate as much information as possible in your short answers. Compare the following pairs of descriptions:

Member of Orchestra	*Second Violinist of the Orchestra*
Played Intra-Mural Volleyball	*Co-captain of the Volleyball Team*
Member of the AD's CSL	*One of three members on the Associate Dean's Committee on Student Life*
Worked at Billy's Burger Barn	*Assistant Manager at Billy's Burger Barn (25 hours per week)*

In addition to the short-answer questions, most applications invite you to make a personal statement. Some applications ask for very little. For example: "In a paragraph, explain to us why you want to go to college." Other applications are open-ended: "On a separate sheet of paper, tell us anything else you think we need to know about you." The point of the personal statement is for you to give the admissions committee any information that might not be available from your test scores, GPA, and short-answer questions.

You should consider the personal statement to be the most important part of your application for two reasons. First, this statement should be your argument to the admissions committee for your acceptance. It should give them all of the reasons why they should accept you. Second, the personal statement is the one aspect of the application over which you can exercise any real control. Your work experience was accumulated over the years, your GPA is already settled, and your SAT has been scored. Those aspects of the application cannot easily be manipulated. The personal statement, however, is completely under your present control.

What information should be included in a personal statement? You should devise arguments that interpret your academic, employment, and personal histories in such a way as to indicate that you have the ability to complete college and that you are committed to studying and later to pursuing a career in your chosen area of study. Most importantly, the personal statement must not be a simple restatement of facts that are already in the application. Imagine, for example, a personal statement that reads as follows:

> *I went to high school where I got a 3.5 GPA. I was a member of the Associate Dean's Committee on Student Life, and I worked as the assistant manager on the night shift at Billy's Burger Barn. Then, I took the SAT and got a 1250. I know that I will make a really good B.A. candidate and will enjoy my job.*

This personal statement is not very interesting. Furthermore, all of that information is redundant because it is already included in the answers to the standard questions on the application.

Instead, describe the facts of your life in such a way that they will be interpreted as good reasons for accepting you. Let's start with the GPA. Try to highlight certain academic facts that would suggest that your abilities exceed and are therefore not reflective of your overall GPA. Did you have a particularly challenging academic schedule that included honors or advanced placement classes? Did you have one particularly bad semester (during which you took physics, calculus, and Latin) that pulled your average down? Did you participate in any unusual courses such as field research? Also, try to emphasize any non-academic facts that would be legitimately considered "important distractions" from your studies. Was there a death in the family or some other difficult set of circumstances that interfered with your studies? How many hours did you work in an average week? What extracurricular or family commitments took time away from your studies?

These points are significant and will have an impact on the admissions committee. For example:

> *The committee will see that my final GPA is 3.5. I should point out that the average would have been higher had I not needed to work 20 hours each week to save for my college education. Additionally, my grades in the first semester of my junior year were disappointing because my grandmother, who lived with my family and with whom I was very close, died. Finally, in order to fulfill the requirements for the honors program, I wrote a 20-page honors thesis on the Dutch fishing industry of the 18th century. I have included a copy of the introduction to my thesis with this application.*

You should also take the same approach to your work experience. For example:

> *During my junior and senior years in high school, I worked an average of 20 hours per week at Billy's Burger Barn as the manager on the night shift. I would report to work at midnight and get off at four a.m. As night manager, I supervised eight other employees and was responsible for making emergency repairs on kitchen equipment. For example, once I was able to keep the deep fryer in operation by using a length of telephone cable to repair a faulty thermostat. The night manager was also responsible for maintaining order. It's no easy job to convince intoxicated students who become too rowdy to leave without calling the police. Also, we were robbed at gunpoint not once but twice.*

Of course, if you have considerable work experience (*e.g.*, if you graduated from high school several years ago rather than just recently), you will want to describe that experience in more detail.

Can you say anything about your SAT score? Probably not much—the SAT score is fairly simple and not usually open to interpretation. However, there are certain exceptions that may be taken into consideration, such as a history of poor scores on standardized exams. For example:

> *I believe that my SAT score of 1250 understates my real ability for I have never had much success on aptitude tests. Yet, I finished high school with a 3.6 GPA. The committee will see that I have two SAT scores, 1100 and 1250. During the first test, I had the flu and a fever and simply could not concentrate.*

History of poor test performance and illness are the two most common types of excuses for a disappointing SAT score.

Finally, you must also persuade the admissions committee that you are serious about obtaining your college degree. You must be able to give an example of something in your background that explains why you want to go to college. Also, it will help your case if you can suggest what you might do with a college degree. For example:

> *As a prospective environmental science major, I interned with the Student Environmental Association. Working with private company executives, whom had themselves satisfied E.P.A. emissions standards, we convinced the University to stop polluting the Ten-Mile Run Creek. From this experience, I learned how business helps to protect our environment. I plan to make environmental resources my area of study, and I hope to work for the government or a private agency to protect the environment.*

A word of warning is in order regarding your career objectives: They must be believable. It will not be sufficient to write: "I plan to solve the environmental problems of American industry." Such a statement is much too abstract. College admissions officers are also not interested in a general discourse on the advantages of democracy or the hardship of poverty. If you write, "I want to eliminate damage to the planet and to help private industries help themselves environmentally," then there had better be something in your experience that makes this statement believable.

Finally, with regard to motivation, do not imagine that there is a preferred political position that you should adopt. College admissions officers span the political spectrum.

Thus far, we have discussed the issues of ability and motivation. You may also wish to include information in your personal statement that demonstrates to the school how you would help create a diverse student body. This additional information can be something dramatic:

> *One morning, a patron choked on a burger and lost consciousness. I used the Heimlich maneuver to dislodge the food and performed CPR until a team of paramedics arrived. The patron recovered fully, in large part, according to her doctors, because of my first aid.*

Or the information may not be dramatic:

> *My parents are Armenian immigrants, so I am fluent in Armenian as well as English. I would enjoy meeting others who share an interest in the politics, legal developments, and culture of that part of the world.*

However, do not overestimate the value of this kind of information. It is, so to speak, the icing on the cake. These details about your life make you a more interesting individual and might tip the scale in your favor when all other things are equal. Although, keep in mind that it will not get you accepted into a school for which you would not otherwise be competitive in terms of SAT and GPA.

Now, we turn our attention to matters of style. Your arguments for acceptance need to be presented in an organized fashion. There is no single preferred format, but you might start with the following outline:

I. I have the ability to succeed in college.
   A. My high school studies are good.
      1. I had one bad semester due to an illness in the family.
      2. I was in the accelerated program.
      3. I wrote a comprehensive term paper.
   B. My work experience is good.
      1. I worked during three years of high school.
      2. I was promoted to shift leader at my job.
II. I have the desire to earn a college degree.
   A. During my internship, I worked with Ph.D. recipients on the pollution problem.
   B. I want to become a specialist in environmental chemistry.
III. I have unique characteristics.

The prose that you use should display your own natural style of writing. Do not write something that appears contrived. Admissions officers do not want to read essays that are written as manuscripts, with footnoted "documentary evidence." You should create your outline using as many arguments as possible. Then, you must begin to edit. For most people, the final document should not be more than a page to a page and a half in length—typed, of course! During the editing process, you should strive for an economy of language so that you can convey as much information as possible. Additionally, you will be forced to make considered judgments about the relative importance of various points. You will be forced to delete those ideas that are not really very compelling. In order to compose a really good personal statement, it may be necessary to reduce five or six pages to a single page, and the process may require more than 20 drafts. Make sure that you have at least one other person look at your essay—a teacher, counselor, or parent would be a good resource.

E. LETTERS OF RECOMMENDATION

Perhaps the best advice that we can give you about so-called "letters of recommendation" is that you should think of them as evaluations rather than recommendations. Indeed, many admissions officers refer to letter-writers as evaluators. These letters can be very important factors in an application, so who should actually write them?

First of all, some schools require a letter from the dean of students (or some similar functionary) at your high school. Essentially, this requirement serves as an inquiry into your behavior. However, colleges do not really expect that this person will have much to say on the matter since in many cases students do not become acquainted with their deans. This letter is merely intended to evoke any information about disciplinary problems that might not otherwise surface. So, the best response from a dean, and the one that most people tend to receive, is just a statement to the effect that there is nothing much to say regarding your behavior. In addition to the dean's letter, most schools require, or at least permit, you to submit two or three letters of evaluation from other sources. Who should write these letters? Remember that a letter of evaluation does not necessarily have to come from a famous person. How effective is the following letter?

Francis Scott
Chairperson of the Board

To the Admissions Committee:

I am recommending Susan Roberts for college. Her mother is a member of our board of directors. Susan's mother earned her doctorate at the University of Chicago and she regularly makes significant contributions to our corporate meetings. Susan, following in her mother's footsteps, will make a fine college candidate.

Sincerely,
Francis Scott

The letterhead holds great promise, but the body of the letter is worthless. It is obvious that Francis Scott does not really have any basis for his conclusion that Susan Roberts "will make a fine college candidate."

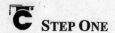

The best letters of evaluation will be written by people who know you very well (*e.g.*, a teacher with whom you took several courses, your intern supervisor, or an associate with whom you have worked closely). A good evaluation will incorporate personal knowledge into the letter and will make references to specific events and activities. For example:

Mary P. Weiss
White, Waste, and Blanche

To the Admissions Committee:

White, Waste, and Blanche is a consulting firm that advises corporations on environmental concerns. Susan Roberts has worked for us as an intern for the past two summers. Her work is outstanding, and she is an intelligent and genial person.

Last summer, as my assistant, Susan wrote a 5-page report that outlined a way of altering a client's exhaust stack to reduce sulfur emissions. The report was organized so that it was easy to follow and written in a style that was clear and easy to understand. Additionally, Susan assisted with a live presentation during a meeting with the client's board of directors and engineers. She was confident and handled some very difficult questions in an easy manner.

Finally, Susan made an important contribution to our company softball team. The team finished in last place, but Susan played in every game. Her batting average wasn't anything to brag about, but her enthusiasm more than made up for it.

Sincerely,
Mary Weiss

F. TAKING THE SAT

We have already emphasized the important role that the SAT plays in the admissions process. Therefore, it is only common sense that you do everything you can to maximize your score. You should not take the SAT until you are certain that you are capable of performing at to the best of your abilities. Colleges receive all of your SAT test scores (not just your best score), and many colleges will average multiple scores. You are already heading in the right direction by taking the *Cambridge SAT • PSAT Review Course*—we will provide you with everything you need to succeed on the SAT. The rest is up to you. Good luck!

OVERCOMING TEST ANXIETY
—Winning Strategies—

Test anxiety can manifest itself in various forms—from the common occurrences of "butterflies" in the stomach, mild sweating, or nervous laughter, to the more extreme occurrences of overwhelming fear, anxiety attacks, and unmanageable worry. It is quite normal for students to experience some mild anxiety before or during testing without being greatly affected. On the other hand, more intense worry, fear, or tension can prevent students from performing successfully on standardized tests. Some experts who study human performance propose that light stress may actually help to focus a person's concentration on the task at hand. However, stress that reaches beyond minimum levels and remains for a long period of time can block a student's ability to quickly recall facts, remember strategies, analyze complex problems, and creatively approach difficult items. When taking a test, being calm and collected promotes clear and logical thinking. Therefore, a relaxed state of mind is not only important to you as a test-taker, but it is also essential. The following strategies provide practical hints and methods to help alleviate debilitating test anxiety.

A. PLAN—HAVE A STUDY PLAN AND STICK TO IT

Putting off important test review assignments until the last minute naturally causes high stress for anyone who is seriously anxious about test day. Even the brightest student experiences nervousness when he or she walks into a test site without being fully prepared. Therefore, stress reduction methods should begin weeks or even months in advance. Prepared test-takers are more relaxed, confident, and focused, so you should begin to review materials earlier rather than later in order to reduce anxiety.

Be warned that it is almost impossible to successfully cram for standardized tests, such as the SAT, ACT, GRE, GMAT, or LSAT. Waiting until the day or week before the test to begin studying will only serve to elevate your anxiety level. Cramming at the last minute, which may have worked for you in the past with quizzes or less comprehensive tests, will not work to prepare you for long, comprehensive, standardized tests. Such comprehensive tests require extended and intensive study methods. Trying to cram will leave you feeling frustrated, unprepared, overwhelmed, and nervous about the pending test day.

So, the key to combating test anxiety is to plan ahead so that you are not unprepared. Do not procrastinate—develop a study plan, start early, and stick to it. A study plan is a written set of daily goals that will help you track the content and the sequence of your test review. This plan will help you tell yourself what, when, where, and how much you will study. (See the Time Management section on page 25 for a further description on how to organize your time effectively.)

By planning your work and working your plan, you can alleviate any unnecessary anxiety. Here are some tips on how to produce your study plan.

➤ *Record a Plan on Paper*

A written study plan is more concrete and dependable than one that simply rattles around in your head. So, you should use a piece of paper and a pencil to write out a plan for reviewing all of the materials that are necessary to succeed on the test. Record important items and dates on your calendar (Time Management), and post the study plan in a place where you will see it often (*e.g.*, your bedroom door or your refrigerator). When you accomplish one of the goals on your plan (*e.g.*, taking a timed practice exam or reviewing a certain number of items), designate its completion with a checkmark. This system of recording your goals will give you a sense of achievement.

➤ *Break the Test into Pieces*

Standardized tests are segmented into multiple sections according to subject area. However, you should not try to learn all of the material related to a particular subject area in one sitting. The subject matter that is covered is far too broad to

learn in a few short minutes, so you should not try to learn every test strategy at once or review the whole test in one day. Instead, you should break the test into smaller portions and then study a portion until you are confident that you can move on to another. You should also vary the sections that you study in order to ward off boredom. For example, on Monday, study a Math section, and on Tuesday, study a Reading section.

In addition to breaking the test into smaller portions, you should always remember to review sections that you have already studied. This review will keep all of the sections fresh in your mind for test day. No two students are capable of learning at an identical rate. Some students can learn huge chunks of information at once, while other students need to review smaller amounts of information over a greater period of time. Determine the amount of material that you can comfortably and adequately cover in one day; then, attack that amount of material on each day.

For most students, the study plan is determined by the Cambridge Review Course schedule. The class schedule and sequence have been developed to help you improve your test score. So, follow the guidance of your class instructor and mold your personal study plan around the schedule.

> ### Do Some Studying or Preparation Every Day

Yes. It is very important that you study something every single day. Once you get the "study snowball" rolling, the momentum will help you overcome the temptation to quit. Be consistent. It is far better to study sixty minutes per day for seven straight days than to study seven straight hours only once per week.

> ### Study at the Same Time and Place

Find somewhere quiet to study, where there are few distractions, the lighting is good, and you feel comfortable. Since most tests are given either at desks, tables, or computer terminals, avoid studying in bed or in a lounge chair. Simulate the test conditions by studying at a desk or table. Turn off the television or the radio. Shut down the computer, unless of course you are using it as a study tool. Give yourself uninterrupted quality time to study. Find a consistent time when you can study and lock it into your schedule. Do not let yourself off the hook. Study each day at the same time and place so that you can become accustomed to your work environment.

> ### Set Goals and Reward Yourself

Set a weekly goal for the amount of time that you will study and the amount of material that you will review. When you meet these weekly goals, reward yourself. Offer yourself special incentives that will motivate you to reach your next goal.

> ### Find a Study Partner or Someone to Hold You Accountable for Your Progress

There really is strength in numbers. Find at least one person who will help you stay on course with your goals. Have this person ask you, every few days, whether or not you are sticking to your plan. Consider finding a "study buddy." Push each other to set and reach high test preparation goals.

Early and consistent test preparation means that you will walk calmly and confidently into the testing center on test day, knowing that you have done your very best to prepare for the test.

B. PREPARE POSITIVELY—REPLACE ANXIETY WITH POSITIVITY

Positive thinking helps overcome test anxiety. For years, psychologists have studied how attitudes affect and alter achievement. These studies suggest that students with positive attitudes consistently score higher than students with negative attitudes.

Here are some practical ways to create a positive mindset:

➢ *Talk Positively to Yourself*

Success comes in a "can," not a "cannot." So, learn to think positively by mentally replacing "cannot" with "can." Negative statements such as, "I will never pass this test," "I know I can't get this," or "I'm not smart enough to get a good score," are counterproductive, and they hinder both studying and the test-taking process. In order to eliminate negative thoughts, you must first take note of them when they occur and then take steps to remove them from your mind. As soon as you recognize a negative thought, immediately replace it with a positive thought. It is quite easy. Whenever you hear phrases such as "I can't do this," or "I'm not smart enough," think to yourself, "I can do this," "I will understand this," or "I am smart enough." Furthermore, as you walk into the classroom on the day of the test, repeatedly say to yourself, "I have studied, I will do my best, and I will succeed."

➢ *Think Positively About Yourself*

Think positively with the help of visualization. Try this: While in a relaxed mood, close your eyes and envision yourself walking into the test room, perfectly calm and confident. Now, imagine yourself taking each section of the test without any difficulty and with great calmness. See yourself answering the items quickly and correctly. Watch yourself exiting the test area with confidence because you know that you performed extremely well. With these visualization techniques, you can mentally and emotionally practice taking the test in a confident and calm manner. You can practice visualizing yourself at any time and for any given situation. Many students find that it works well close to bedtime. Coaches encourage their peak performing athletes to use daily visualization exercises in order to increase their abilities in running, jumping, shooting, *etc.* Every single day, from now until the test day, practice visualization and picture yourself taking the test quickly, easily, confidently, and calmly. Visualization can help you exude a positive attitude and overcome test anxiety. Get the picture?

➢ *Act Positively Toward Yourself*

On the day of the test, act positively. Even if you do not "feel" completely confident, you should stride into the test site with your head held high and a bounce in your step. Show both yourself and your peers that you are at ease and in complete control of the situation. Present yourself as someone who knows that he or she will be successful. Acting confidently will actually help you feel confident.

Practice these strategies in order to instill a positive mental attitude. Positive thinking means believing in yourself. Believe that you can achieve your highest goal under any circumstances. Know that you can do it. Dare to try.

C. PUT AWAY NEGATIVE THOUGHTS—THEY FUEL TEST ANXIETY

Since you will be practicing positive thinking, you should also learn to recognize and eliminate distorted, or twisted, thinking. Avoid thinking any of the following distorted things about yourself:

"I must always be perfect." The reality is that everyone makes mistakes. In testing situations, perfectionists mentally fuss and fume about a single mistake instead of celebrating all of the items that they answered correctly. Dwelling on mistakes wastes time and creates more tension. Push mistakes behind you and move forward to the next set of items. Remember that we all reserve the right to learn and grow.

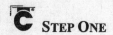

"I failed the last time, so I'll fail this time." Past failure does not lead to future failure. People do get better the more that they practice. Because you did poorly on something in the past does not guarantee a poor performance either this time or in the future. Use this test as an opportunity for a fresh start. Forget yesterday's failures and realize that today is a brand new beginning.

"People won't like me if I do poorly." It is preferable to have good relations with people and to have them approve of you or even to love you—but it is not necessary. You will not be unhappy unless you make yourself unhappy. Rely on self-approval, not on the approval of others. Do your best because you want to and you can, not because you want to please someone else.

"I have been anxious when taking tests before; therefore, I'll always be anxious." This twisted logic implies that you have no control over your behavior; however, that is not the case. You can change and learn to control your anxiety. It might take time and hard work to build calmness and confidence, but it is certainly within your reach.

D. POWER UP PHYSICALLY—RELEASE STRESS WITH PHYSICAL EXERCISE

Physical exercise is an excellent way to both reduce anxiety levels and cope with the effects of stress. Start a regular program of physical fitness that includes stretching and cardiovascular activities. If necessary, check with a doctor or a health professional in order to develop a customized fitness program.

E. PRACTICE BEING CALM—LEARN TO MENTALLY AND PHYSICALLY RELAX

You may not realize that mental and physical relaxation play significant parts in the studying process. By setting aside time for clearing your mind and body of stress and anxiety, you will refresh your mental and physical energy reserves. Spend quality time studying and reviewing for the test. Then, spend time relaxing your mind and body so that you are re-energized for your next study session.

Practice the following relaxation exercises to calm the body and mind.

➤ *Physical Relaxation Exercise*

Pick a quiet room where there are few distractions. Shut off all intrusive lights. Sit in a chair or lie down in a bed. If you wear glasses, take them off. Get comfortable, loosening any tight or binding clothing. Close your eyes, and take a deep breath. Blow out all of the air in your lungs, and then breathe in deeply. Now, focus on your tense muscles and consciously relax them. Start by focusing on your toes, your feet, and your calves. Tense and release your muscles to fully relax them. Move upward through each muscle group in your body, up to and including your facial muscles. Continue to breathe slowly, steadily, and fully during this exercise. Repeat this process, while consciously relaxing tense muscles, until you relax your entire body. Rest in this state for a few minutes. When you are finished, open your eyes, and remain still for another minute or two before rising.

➤ *Breathing Exercise*

Deep and relaxed breathing will calm your nerves and reduce stress. Whenever you start feeling anxious, take time out to perform this simple breathing exercise. Place you hands upon your stomach and breathe in slowly and deeply through your nose, feeling your rib cage rise. Pause and hold your breath for a second, thinking to yourself, "I am calm." Release your breath slowly and fully, blowing it out through your mouth. Repeat this exercise eight to ten times. Perform this exercise whenever you feel nervous or anxious.

> *Mental Relaxation Exercise*

Meditation, in various forms, has been practiced to allow the mind to release stressful thoughts. Many types of meditation can be learned and then practiced on a regular basis. A popular type of meditation is the passive form. Begin meditating after your body is in a relaxed state. Concentrate on something monotonous until your mind becomes quiet. You may choose to concentrate on a sound, a word, or an object. Observe your thoughts without controlling them. Gently refocus on the sound, word, or object. Passively observe your thoughts when they come, then gently refocus back upon the sound, word, or object.

F. PREPARE—DO NOT LEAVE IMPORTANT ITEMS UNTIL THE LAST MINUTE

You are going to want to remain as relaxed as possible on the day of the test. In order to eliminate the last-minute, frantic rush to find that "one thing" that you cannot locate, make a list of the items that you need for the day of the test. Set out those important items the night before in order to efficiently and effectively speed you on your way toward the testing center.

> *Determine the Items that You Are Expected to Bring*

Carefully read the test packet materials so that you know exactly what you should and should not bring to the test center. You may need to bring an eraser, personal I.D., calculator, or pencils. However, some test centers do not allow food, scratch paper, or alarms. Therefore, determine what things to bring and what things to leave at home.

> *Check the Working Condition of Your Calculator, Watch, etc.*

Okay, this might sound silly, but make sure that your watch and calculator (if allowed) are in good working condition. Replace old calculator batteries with new batteries. Sharpen pencils before arriving at the test center.

> *Gather the Items that You Need*

On the night before the test, gather all of the necessary items so that you can avoid the anxiety of trying to find them at the last minute.

> *Know the Directions to the Test Center*

If you have not been to the test center before, make sure that you are provided with clear and specific directions as soon as possible. If you are at all confused about how to get to the test center, call the center immediately and clarify the directions.

> *Decide Whether to Study the Night Before the Test*

Should you study the night before the test? Well, as mentioned earlier, you certainly should not attempt to cram for the test. You may want to review a few strategies, but you do not want to attempt to learn large amounts of new material. Instead, take some time to review, and then find some entertaining activity to occupy your time. Go to the gym or see a movie with friends. Laughing is always a great way to reduce stress, so you may want to find something humorous to do or watch.

> *Sleep Well*

A good night of sleep will help reduce stress on the test day. Do not stay out late on the night before the test.

> ### *Get to the Test Site Early*

Your anxiety level will increase if you arrive at the test center late, stand in line to register, run to a seat, and then immediately begin to take the test. So, arrive at the test center early enough to find the room, register, find your seat, set out necessary items (pencil, calculator, *etc.*), and still have a few minutes to relax and compose yourself. You may also need time to locate the restrooms and drinking fountains. However, do not arrive at the test center too early. Students typically get nervous and anxious when they have to wait for a long period of time with nothing to do except think about the upcoming test. So, find the balance between "too early" and "too late" that works best for you.

> ### *Watch Your Diet*

What you choose to eat can be a physical cause of stress. Therefore, control your eating habits in order to maintain lower stress levels. Eat a healthy breakfast on the day of the test. Restrict your intake of sugar, salt, and caffeine. Remember that sugar and caffeine are found in coffee, cola, cocoa, and tea. These substances trigger a stress response in your body. High levels of sugar and caffeine are associated with nervousness, dizziness, irritability, headaches, and insomnia. Additionally, smoking has been found to decrease a person's ability to handle stress. Cigarettes act as a stimulant because of their nicotine content and will serve to increase stress levels.

> ### *Dress Comfortably*

The good news is that you are going to a test, not a fashion show. So, wear comfortable clothes to the testing center; choose clothes that are not overly binding or tight. Dressing in layers is always a good idea since testing rooms are notoriously either too hot or too cold.

G. PAUSE—RELEASE PHYSICAL AND MENTAL ANXIETY BEFORE THE TEST

As already stated, relaxation allows you to focus your full attention and energy on the task at hand, rather than be distracted by tension and stress. Release as much tension and anxiety as possible right before taking the test.

> ### *Release and Relax*

Having arrived early at the test site, take the last few minutes to relax. Do not attempt to study or review at this point. Instead, use a simple relaxation technique. Close your eyes, and breathe in deeply through your nose. Hold that breath for a few seconds. Next, release that breath through your mouth. Repeat this "in-and-out" breathing cycle. Try to gradually slow the pace of the "in-and-out" motion of your breathing. Visualize yourself at a place that you find peaceful and relaxing, such as the beach, the woods, or some other favorite spot. Continue this technique for a few minutes until you feel yourself becoming relaxed and calm.

> ### *Do Some Low-Level Physical Exercise*

Take a brisk walk. For many people, walking helps lower high stress levels, while positively easing the mind from worrying about the upcoming test. Others find that stretching exercises help loosen tense muscles. Just be sure to return to the site with plenty of time to register and sit down for the test.

> ### *Massage Tension Away*

While waiting for the test, sit comfortably in your chair. Notice places in your body that feel tense—generally the shoulders, neck, or back. Gently massage tense areas for a few minutes.

H. PRESS ON—CONCENTRATE ON THE CURRENT ITEM, NOT THE LAST OR NEXT

Dwelling on answers to previous items will only elevate test anxiety, so do not worry about those sections or items that you have finished.

➤ *Focus on One Item at a Time*

Your task on any test is to correctly answer each item, one item at a time. Good test-takers focus only on the item to which they are currently working. Poor test-takers worry about items that they just completed or about items in the upcoming section. Try to stay "in the moment" by concentrating on one item at a time.

I. PROUDLY DEPART—WALK OUT WITH YOUR HEAD HELD HIGH

➤ *Know that You Have Done Your Best*

If you have followed the strategies listed in this section, attended test preparation classes, and spent time reviewing and studying on your own, you have most likely done your very best to prepare for the test. As you walk out of the test site, remind yourself that you have indeed put forth your best effort.

➤ *Watch the Labels*

After the test, never label yourself as a "failure," "loser," or "under-achiever." Instead, if you do not feel that you did as well as you expected, use the experience to learn about the test and about yourself. Students are able to re-take standardized tests, so reflect upon what you can do better next time, not upon how poorly you think you did this time.

J. PERSPECTIVE—KEEP LIFE IN PERSPECTIVE

Yes, the test you will take is important, but other things in life are important too. Remember that this test is a means to an end—getting into college, graduate school, or a profession—and not the end itself.

NOTE: Some test-takers, even after applying all of the above strategies, still experience debilitating stress. Intense anxiety or stress that causes nausea, headaches, overwhelming emotional fears, or other severe symptoms may need special attention and care that goes beyond the strategies in these pages. If you suffer from these debilitating stress symptoms, ask your high school or university counseling office what resources are available to help overcome severe test anxiety.

TIME MANAGEMENT
–Winning Strategies–

A. INTRODUCTION

High school students live hectic and exciting lives. In order to succeed in high school, you must learn how to manage your time, which really means that you must learn how to manage yourself by becoming a proactive student. To be proactive means to act assertively and decisively in order to prepare for upcoming events or situations. To be proactive also means to make wise decisions about how to plan the use of your time. Therefore, a proactive student is a well-prepared student.

School classes and homework take up a great deal of the day, but there are also opportunities for recreation, extracurricular activity, and personal development. While jobs, athletics, friends, clubs, concerts, *etc.* may take time away from your academic life, learning to manage your time and juggle multiple responsibilities is essential for succeeding in high school. This section focuses on how to better manage your time by using such powerful tools as the PLAN method and pyramid scheduling.

B. SCHEDULING FOR SUCCESS—HAVE A PLAN

The PLAN method presents four elements for maximizing your time:

> *PRIORITIZE* tasks according to their long-term benefit.
> *LIST* those tasks according to their priority.
> *ARRANGE* those tasks on a schedule.
> *NEGOTIATE* your schedule if those tasks become overwhelming.

1. P...PRIORITIZE

Though many high school activities are important, it is necessary to determine which of these activities are the most important. Students who *prioritize* their tasks arrange them in an optimum order that is based on level of importance: More important tasks take precedence over less important tasks. So, in order to prioritize, you need to identify activities that will benefit you most in the long-run.

Different students have different priorities. While most students do not study during all of their free time, successful students generally prioritize academics over other activities. These students devote a majority of their free time to studying so that they can reinforce what they have already learned in class. In order to effectively prioritize your tasks, you must first identify your own long-term goals. With a better understanding of your goals for the future, you can more effectively prioritize your activities in the present.

Here are some questions that you should ask yourself in order to better determine your long-term goals:

- What clubs would I like to join?
- What sports would I like to play?
- What social service groups would I like to join?
- With whom do I want to be friends?
- What type of impact would I like to have on my community?
- What special accomplishments do I want to achieve?
- What types of positive things do I want people to say about me?
- Who do I want to impress? How will I impress them?
- What will make me a happy and fulfilled person?
- Do I want to go to college? If so, which college and what major might I choose?
- What career would I like to pursue?

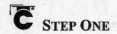

2. L...LIST

Every week, make a *list* of the tasks that you want to accomplish, placing the most important tasks at the top of your list.

3. A...ARRANGE

Each day, *arrange* all of your tasks on a daily schedule, prioritizing the most important tasks over tasks that are less important. The key to prioritization is to maintain a clear understanding of what is most important so that you can remain focused on the most significant tasks at hand.

4. N...NEGOTIATE

In any given high school quarter, there are weeks that are especially busy and may prove to be overwhelming. Typically, chapter tests and final exams require considerable amounts of study time. The following are seven tips on how to better *negotiate* the details of your schedule in accordance with the potential added pressures of exam time.

1. Anticipate weeks with heavy workloads and note them on your schedule.
2. Meet with your teachers to discuss any problems that you might have with completing class work.
3. Form a study group to help prepare for tests.
4. Get plenty of rest; you will need rest and energy during stressful times.
5. Do not wait until the last week of the quarter to complete major projects; procrastination is unproductive.
6. Attempt to get time off from your job during the most hectic times.
7. Say no to distractions such as watching television and reading books or magazines.

C. MANAGE YOUR TIME BY USING PYRAMID SCHEDULING

A pyramid consists of a large base, or foundation, which transitions into progressively narrower levels until finally reaching a small point at the top. In a similar fashion, pyramid scheduling begins with organizing your long-term projects and then moves on to your more immediate tasks until finally reaching your daily schedule. Purchase an annual calendar or planner so that you can schedule months, weeks, and days, approaching your scheduling process in the following manner:

1. SCHEDULE THE ENTIRE QUARTER

During the first week of each quarter (typically running nine weeks in length), organize all of your major assignments and responsibilities on the calendar. After you have received a syllabus for each of your classes, reference all important dates that coincide with any of the following:

- Class assignments, such as reading selections and projects
- Tests and exams
- Quizzes
- Holidays and vacations
- Personal obligations, such as birthdays and family gatherings
- Job commitments
- Extracurricular activities, such as athletic events and student government meetings

2. SCHEDULE EACH MONTH

Two days before the beginning of each month, review your monthly schedule for all assignments, tests, and quizzes. Then, reference any important dates for monthly activities that do not already appear on your calendar, such as:

- Additional assignments
- Sporting events or concerts that you plan to attend
- Personal commitments, such as work schedule and social engagements
- Study blocks for major projects, exams, tests, or quizzes

3. SCHEDULE EACH WEEK

On Sunday night of each week, review your weekly schedule for all assignments, tests, and quizzes. Look for any personal appointments or special commitments that may be scheduled for the upcoming week. Then, on a weekly calendar, outline a schedule for that upcoming week so that you will have sufficient time for studying and completing assignments. Each day of the weekly schedule should be divided up into mornings, afternoons, and evenings so that you can reference the most important times for certain daily activities, such as:

- Classes
- Class assignments, such as reading selections and projects
- Tests and exams
- Quizzes
- Holidays and vacation days
- Personal commitments, such as work schedule and social engagements
- Employment commitments
- Extracurricular activities, such as athletic events and student government meetings
- Study sessions

4. SCHEDULE EACH DAY

On the night before each school day, create a schedule that outlines important times for the following daily activities:

- Class schedule
- Study times
- Job schedule
- Free time
- Additional appointments, tasks, or responsibilities

5. FINALLY, REMEMBER TO STICK TO YOUR SCHEDULE

Unless emergencies arise, stick to your schedule. Do not change your schedule unless it is absolutely necessary to accommodate and prioritize new activities. Remember that time management is really about self-management. So, remain disciplined so that you can follow your schedule without falling prey to distractions.

D. CONCLUSION

Successful students are able to self-manage themselves by learning and using valuable time management tools. If you start to use these tools now, you can be successful in high school and beyond. Always remember to schedule your work and work your schedule!

Name: _____ Date: _____

Student ID Number: _____

SAT PRE-TEST

Section 1

Begin your essay on this page. If you need more space, continue on the next page.

_____

_____

_____

_____

_____

_____

_____

_____

_____

_____

_____

_____

_____

_____

_____

_____

_____

_____

_____

_____

_____

_____

_____

Name: ______________________ Date: ______________

Student ID Number: ______________________

SAT PRE-TEST

Start with number 1 for each new section. If a section has fewer questions than answer spaces, leave the extra answer spaces blank. Be sure to erase any errors or stray marks completely.

Section 2

1 Ⓐ Ⓑ Ⓒ Ⓓ Ⓔ	10 Ⓐ Ⓑ Ⓒ Ⓓ Ⓔ	19 Ⓐ Ⓑ Ⓒ Ⓓ Ⓔ	28 Ⓐ Ⓑ Ⓒ Ⓓ Ⓔ
2 Ⓐ Ⓑ Ⓒ Ⓓ Ⓔ	11 Ⓐ Ⓑ Ⓒ Ⓓ Ⓔ	20 Ⓐ Ⓑ Ⓒ Ⓓ Ⓔ	29 Ⓐ Ⓑ Ⓒ Ⓓ Ⓔ
3 Ⓐ Ⓑ Ⓒ Ⓓ Ⓔ	12 Ⓐ Ⓑ Ⓒ Ⓓ Ⓔ	21 Ⓐ Ⓑ Ⓒ Ⓓ Ⓔ	30 Ⓐ Ⓑ Ⓒ Ⓓ Ⓔ
4 Ⓐ Ⓑ Ⓒ Ⓓ Ⓔ	13 Ⓐ Ⓑ Ⓒ Ⓓ Ⓔ	22 Ⓐ Ⓑ Ⓒ Ⓓ Ⓔ	31 Ⓐ Ⓑ Ⓒ Ⓓ Ⓔ
5 Ⓐ Ⓑ Ⓒ Ⓓ Ⓔ	14 Ⓐ Ⓑ Ⓒ Ⓓ Ⓔ	23 Ⓐ Ⓑ Ⓒ Ⓓ Ⓔ	32 Ⓐ Ⓑ Ⓒ Ⓓ Ⓔ
6 Ⓐ Ⓑ Ⓒ Ⓓ Ⓔ	15 Ⓐ Ⓑ Ⓒ Ⓓ Ⓔ	24 Ⓐ Ⓑ Ⓒ Ⓓ Ⓔ	33 Ⓐ Ⓑ Ⓒ Ⓓ Ⓔ
7 Ⓐ Ⓑ Ⓒ Ⓓ Ⓔ	16 Ⓐ Ⓑ Ⓒ Ⓓ Ⓔ	25 Ⓐ Ⓑ Ⓒ Ⓓ Ⓔ	34 Ⓐ Ⓑ Ⓒ Ⓓ Ⓔ
8 Ⓐ Ⓑ Ⓒ Ⓓ Ⓔ	17 Ⓐ Ⓑ Ⓒ Ⓓ Ⓔ	26 Ⓐ Ⓑ Ⓒ Ⓓ Ⓔ	35 Ⓐ Ⓑ Ⓒ Ⓓ Ⓔ
9 Ⓐ Ⓑ Ⓒ Ⓓ Ⓔ	18 Ⓐ Ⓑ Ⓒ Ⓓ Ⓔ	27 Ⓐ Ⓑ Ⓒ Ⓓ Ⓔ	36 Ⓐ Ⓑ Ⓒ Ⓓ Ⓔ

Section 3

1 Ⓐ Ⓑ Ⓒ Ⓓ Ⓔ	10 Ⓐ Ⓑ Ⓒ Ⓓ Ⓔ	19 Ⓐ Ⓑ Ⓒ Ⓓ Ⓔ	28 Ⓐ Ⓑ Ⓒ Ⓓ Ⓔ
2 Ⓐ Ⓑ Ⓒ Ⓓ Ⓔ	11 Ⓐ Ⓑ Ⓒ Ⓓ Ⓔ	20 Ⓐ Ⓑ Ⓒ Ⓓ Ⓔ	29 Ⓐ Ⓑ Ⓒ Ⓓ Ⓔ
3 Ⓐ Ⓑ Ⓒ Ⓓ Ⓔ	12 Ⓐ Ⓑ Ⓒ Ⓓ Ⓔ	21 Ⓐ Ⓑ Ⓒ Ⓓ Ⓔ	30 Ⓐ Ⓑ Ⓒ Ⓓ Ⓔ
4 Ⓐ Ⓑ Ⓒ Ⓓ Ⓔ	13 Ⓐ Ⓑ Ⓒ Ⓓ Ⓔ	22 Ⓐ Ⓑ Ⓒ Ⓓ Ⓔ	31 Ⓐ Ⓑ Ⓒ Ⓓ Ⓔ
5 Ⓐ Ⓑ Ⓒ Ⓓ Ⓔ	14 Ⓐ Ⓑ Ⓒ Ⓓ Ⓔ	23 Ⓐ Ⓑ Ⓒ Ⓓ Ⓔ	32 Ⓐ Ⓑ Ⓒ Ⓓ Ⓔ
6 Ⓐ Ⓑ Ⓒ Ⓓ Ⓔ	15 Ⓐ Ⓑ Ⓒ Ⓓ Ⓔ	24 Ⓐ Ⓑ Ⓒ Ⓓ Ⓔ	33 Ⓐ Ⓑ Ⓒ Ⓓ Ⓔ
7 Ⓐ Ⓑ Ⓒ Ⓓ Ⓔ	16 Ⓐ Ⓑ Ⓒ Ⓓ Ⓔ	25 Ⓐ Ⓑ Ⓒ Ⓓ Ⓔ	34 Ⓐ Ⓑ Ⓒ Ⓓ Ⓔ
8 Ⓐ Ⓑ Ⓒ Ⓓ Ⓔ	17 Ⓐ Ⓑ Ⓒ Ⓓ Ⓔ	26 Ⓐ Ⓑ Ⓒ Ⓓ Ⓔ	35 Ⓐ Ⓑ Ⓒ Ⓓ Ⓔ
9 Ⓐ Ⓑ Ⓒ Ⓓ Ⓔ	18 Ⓐ Ⓑ Ⓒ Ⓓ Ⓔ	27 Ⓐ Ⓑ Ⓒ Ⓓ Ⓔ	36 Ⓐ Ⓑ Ⓒ Ⓓ Ⓔ

Section 4/5

1 Ⓐ Ⓑ Ⓒ Ⓓ Ⓔ	10 Ⓐ Ⓑ Ⓒ Ⓓ Ⓔ	19 Ⓐ Ⓑ Ⓒ Ⓓ Ⓔ	28 Ⓐ Ⓑ Ⓒ Ⓓ Ⓔ
2 Ⓐ Ⓑ Ⓒ Ⓓ Ⓔ	11 Ⓐ Ⓑ Ⓒ Ⓓ Ⓔ	20 Ⓐ Ⓑ Ⓒ Ⓓ Ⓔ	29 Ⓐ Ⓑ Ⓒ Ⓓ Ⓔ
3 Ⓐ Ⓑ Ⓒ Ⓓ Ⓔ	12 Ⓐ Ⓑ Ⓒ Ⓓ Ⓔ	21 Ⓐ Ⓑ Ⓒ Ⓓ Ⓔ	30 Ⓐ Ⓑ Ⓒ Ⓓ Ⓔ
4 Ⓐ Ⓑ Ⓒ Ⓓ Ⓔ	13 Ⓐ Ⓑ Ⓒ Ⓓ Ⓔ	22 Ⓐ Ⓑ Ⓒ Ⓓ Ⓔ	31 Ⓐ Ⓑ Ⓒ Ⓓ Ⓔ
5 Ⓐ Ⓑ Ⓒ Ⓓ Ⓔ	14 Ⓐ Ⓑ Ⓒ Ⓓ Ⓔ	23 Ⓐ Ⓑ Ⓒ Ⓓ Ⓔ	32 Ⓐ Ⓑ Ⓒ Ⓓ Ⓔ
6 Ⓐ Ⓑ Ⓒ Ⓓ Ⓔ	15 Ⓐ Ⓑ Ⓒ Ⓓ Ⓔ	24 Ⓐ Ⓑ Ⓒ Ⓓ Ⓔ	33 Ⓐ Ⓑ Ⓒ Ⓓ Ⓔ
7 Ⓐ Ⓑ Ⓒ Ⓓ Ⓔ	16 Ⓐ Ⓑ Ⓒ Ⓓ Ⓔ	25 Ⓐ Ⓑ Ⓒ Ⓓ Ⓔ	34 Ⓐ Ⓑ Ⓒ Ⓓ Ⓔ
8 Ⓐ Ⓑ Ⓒ Ⓓ Ⓔ	17 Ⓐ Ⓑ Ⓒ Ⓓ Ⓔ	26 Ⓐ Ⓑ Ⓒ Ⓓ Ⓔ	35 Ⓐ Ⓑ Ⓒ Ⓓ Ⓔ
9 Ⓐ Ⓑ Ⓒ Ⓓ Ⓔ	18 Ⓐ Ⓑ Ⓒ Ⓓ Ⓔ	27 Ⓐ Ⓑ Ⓒ Ⓓ Ⓔ	36 Ⓐ Ⓑ Ⓒ Ⓓ Ⓔ

Section 5/6

1 Ⓐ Ⓑ Ⓒ Ⓓ Ⓔ	10 Ⓐ Ⓑ Ⓒ Ⓓ Ⓔ	19 Ⓐ Ⓑ Ⓒ Ⓓ Ⓔ	28 Ⓐ Ⓑ Ⓒ Ⓓ Ⓔ
2 Ⓐ Ⓑ Ⓒ Ⓓ Ⓔ	11 Ⓐ Ⓑ Ⓒ Ⓓ Ⓔ	20 Ⓐ Ⓑ Ⓒ Ⓓ Ⓔ	29 Ⓐ Ⓑ Ⓒ Ⓓ Ⓔ
3 Ⓐ Ⓑ Ⓒ Ⓓ Ⓔ	12 Ⓐ Ⓑ Ⓒ Ⓓ Ⓔ	21 Ⓐ Ⓑ Ⓒ Ⓓ Ⓔ	30 Ⓐ Ⓑ Ⓒ Ⓓ Ⓔ
4 Ⓐ Ⓑ Ⓒ Ⓓ Ⓔ	13 Ⓐ Ⓑ Ⓒ Ⓓ Ⓔ	22 Ⓐ Ⓑ Ⓒ Ⓓ Ⓔ	31 Ⓐ Ⓑ Ⓒ Ⓓ Ⓔ
5 Ⓐ Ⓑ Ⓒ Ⓓ Ⓔ	14 Ⓐ Ⓑ Ⓒ Ⓓ Ⓔ	23 Ⓐ Ⓑ Ⓒ Ⓓ Ⓔ	32 Ⓐ Ⓑ Ⓒ Ⓓ Ⓔ
6 Ⓐ Ⓑ Ⓒ Ⓓ Ⓔ	15 Ⓐ Ⓑ Ⓒ Ⓓ Ⓔ	24 Ⓐ Ⓑ Ⓒ Ⓓ Ⓔ	33 Ⓐ Ⓑ Ⓒ Ⓓ Ⓔ
7 Ⓐ Ⓑ Ⓒ Ⓓ Ⓔ	16 Ⓐ Ⓑ Ⓒ Ⓓ Ⓔ	25 Ⓐ Ⓑ Ⓒ Ⓓ Ⓔ	34 Ⓐ Ⓑ Ⓒ Ⓓ Ⓔ
8 Ⓐ Ⓑ Ⓒ Ⓓ Ⓔ	17 Ⓐ Ⓑ Ⓒ Ⓓ Ⓔ	26 Ⓐ Ⓑ Ⓒ Ⓓ Ⓔ	35 Ⓐ Ⓑ Ⓒ Ⓓ Ⓔ
9 Ⓐ Ⓑ Ⓒ Ⓓ Ⓔ	18 Ⓐ Ⓑ Ⓒ Ⓓ Ⓔ	27 Ⓐ Ⓑ Ⓒ Ⓓ Ⓔ	36 Ⓐ Ⓑ Ⓒ Ⓓ Ⓔ

Section 6/7

1 Ⓐ Ⓑ Ⓒ Ⓓ Ⓔ	10 Ⓐ Ⓑ Ⓒ Ⓓ Ⓔ	19 Ⓐ Ⓑ Ⓒ Ⓓ Ⓔ	28 Ⓐ Ⓑ Ⓒ Ⓓ Ⓔ
2 Ⓐ Ⓑ Ⓒ Ⓓ Ⓔ	11 Ⓐ Ⓑ Ⓒ Ⓓ Ⓔ	20 Ⓐ Ⓑ Ⓒ Ⓓ Ⓔ	29 Ⓐ Ⓑ Ⓒ Ⓓ Ⓔ
3 Ⓐ Ⓑ Ⓒ Ⓓ Ⓔ	12 Ⓐ Ⓑ Ⓒ Ⓓ Ⓔ	21 Ⓐ Ⓑ Ⓒ Ⓓ Ⓔ	30 Ⓐ Ⓑ Ⓒ Ⓓ Ⓔ
4 Ⓐ Ⓑ Ⓒ Ⓓ Ⓔ	13 Ⓐ Ⓑ Ⓒ Ⓓ Ⓔ	22 Ⓐ Ⓑ Ⓒ Ⓓ Ⓔ	31 Ⓐ Ⓑ Ⓒ Ⓓ Ⓔ
5 Ⓐ Ⓑ Ⓒ Ⓓ Ⓔ	14 Ⓐ Ⓑ Ⓒ Ⓓ Ⓔ	23 Ⓐ Ⓑ Ⓒ Ⓓ Ⓔ	32 Ⓐ Ⓑ Ⓒ Ⓓ Ⓔ
6 Ⓐ Ⓑ Ⓒ Ⓓ Ⓔ	15 Ⓐ Ⓑ Ⓒ Ⓓ Ⓔ	24 Ⓐ Ⓑ Ⓒ Ⓓ Ⓔ	33 Ⓐ Ⓑ Ⓒ Ⓓ Ⓔ
7 Ⓐ Ⓑ Ⓒ Ⓓ Ⓔ	16 Ⓐ Ⓑ Ⓒ Ⓓ Ⓔ	25 Ⓐ Ⓑ Ⓒ Ⓓ Ⓔ	34 Ⓐ Ⓑ Ⓒ Ⓓ Ⓔ
8 Ⓐ Ⓑ Ⓒ Ⓓ Ⓔ	17 Ⓐ Ⓑ Ⓒ Ⓓ Ⓔ	26 Ⓐ Ⓑ Ⓒ Ⓓ Ⓔ	35 Ⓐ Ⓑ Ⓒ Ⓓ Ⓔ
9 Ⓐ Ⓑ Ⓒ Ⓓ Ⓔ	18 Ⓐ Ⓑ Ⓒ Ⓓ Ⓔ	27 Ⓐ Ⓑ Ⓒ Ⓓ Ⓔ	36 Ⓐ Ⓑ Ⓒ Ⓓ Ⓔ

Section 7/8

1 Ⓐ Ⓑ Ⓒ Ⓓ Ⓔ	6 Ⓐ Ⓑ Ⓒ Ⓓ Ⓔ	11 Ⓐ Ⓑ Ⓒ Ⓓ Ⓔ	16 Ⓐ Ⓑ Ⓒ Ⓓ Ⓔ
2 Ⓐ Ⓑ Ⓒ Ⓓ Ⓔ	7 Ⓐ Ⓑ Ⓒ Ⓓ Ⓔ	12 Ⓐ Ⓑ Ⓒ Ⓓ Ⓔ	17 Ⓐ Ⓑ Ⓒ Ⓓ Ⓔ
3 Ⓐ Ⓑ Ⓒ Ⓓ Ⓔ	8 Ⓐ Ⓑ Ⓒ Ⓓ Ⓔ	13 Ⓐ Ⓑ Ⓒ Ⓓ Ⓔ	18 Ⓐ Ⓑ Ⓒ Ⓓ Ⓔ
4 Ⓐ Ⓑ Ⓒ Ⓓ Ⓔ	9 Ⓐ Ⓑ Ⓒ Ⓓ Ⓔ	14 Ⓐ Ⓑ Ⓒ Ⓓ Ⓔ	19 Ⓐ Ⓑ Ⓒ Ⓓ Ⓔ
5 Ⓐ Ⓑ Ⓒ Ⓓ Ⓔ	10 Ⓐ Ⓑ Ⓒ Ⓓ Ⓔ	15 Ⓐ Ⓑ Ⓒ Ⓓ Ⓔ	20 Ⓐ Ⓑ Ⓒ Ⓓ Ⓔ

Section 8/9

1 Ⓐ Ⓑ Ⓒ Ⓓ Ⓔ	6 Ⓐ Ⓑ Ⓒ Ⓓ Ⓔ	11 Ⓐ Ⓑ Ⓒ Ⓓ Ⓔ	16 Ⓐ Ⓑ Ⓒ Ⓓ Ⓔ
2 Ⓐ Ⓑ Ⓒ Ⓓ Ⓔ	7 Ⓐ Ⓑ Ⓒ Ⓓ Ⓔ	12 Ⓐ Ⓑ Ⓒ Ⓓ Ⓔ	17 Ⓐ Ⓑ Ⓒ Ⓓ Ⓔ
3 Ⓐ Ⓑ Ⓒ Ⓓ Ⓔ	8 Ⓐ Ⓑ Ⓒ Ⓓ Ⓔ	13 Ⓐ Ⓑ Ⓒ Ⓓ Ⓔ	18 Ⓐ Ⓑ Ⓒ Ⓓ Ⓔ
4 Ⓐ Ⓑ Ⓒ Ⓓ Ⓔ	9 Ⓐ Ⓑ Ⓒ Ⓓ Ⓔ	14 Ⓐ Ⓑ Ⓒ Ⓓ Ⓔ	19 Ⓐ Ⓑ Ⓒ Ⓓ Ⓔ
5 Ⓐ Ⓑ Ⓒ Ⓓ Ⓔ	10 Ⓐ Ⓑ Ⓒ Ⓓ Ⓔ	15 Ⓐ Ⓑ Ⓒ Ⓓ Ⓔ	20 Ⓐ Ⓑ Ⓒ Ⓓ Ⓔ

Section 10

1 Ⓐ Ⓑ Ⓒ Ⓓ Ⓔ	6 Ⓐ Ⓑ Ⓒ Ⓓ Ⓔ	11 Ⓐ Ⓑ Ⓒ Ⓓ Ⓔ	16 Ⓐ Ⓑ Ⓒ Ⓓ Ⓔ
2 Ⓐ Ⓑ Ⓒ Ⓓ Ⓔ	7 Ⓐ Ⓑ Ⓒ Ⓓ Ⓔ	12 Ⓐ Ⓑ Ⓒ Ⓓ Ⓔ	17 Ⓐ Ⓑ Ⓒ Ⓓ Ⓔ
3 Ⓐ Ⓑ Ⓒ Ⓓ Ⓔ	8 Ⓐ Ⓑ Ⓒ Ⓓ Ⓔ	13 Ⓐ Ⓑ Ⓒ Ⓓ Ⓔ	18 Ⓐ Ⓑ Ⓒ Ⓓ Ⓔ
4 Ⓐ Ⓑ Ⓒ Ⓓ Ⓔ	9 Ⓐ Ⓑ Ⓒ Ⓓ Ⓔ	14 Ⓐ Ⓑ Ⓒ Ⓓ Ⓔ	19 Ⓐ Ⓑ Ⓒ Ⓓ Ⓔ
5 Ⓐ Ⓑ Ⓒ Ⓓ Ⓔ	10 Ⓐ Ⓑ Ⓒ Ⓓ Ⓔ	15 Ⓐ Ⓑ Ⓒ Ⓓ Ⓔ	20 Ⓐ Ⓑ Ⓒ Ⓓ Ⓔ

Student-Produced Responses

Only answers entered in the circles in each grid will be scored. You will not receive credit for anything written in the boxes above the circles.

9   10   11   12   13

14   15   16   17   18

Step Two: Targeted Skills Review

Step Two Highlights:

Discover careful reading techniques applicable to each section of the test in the Reading Skills Review.

Review the most commonly tested math concepts in the Math Skills Review, and use the Math Express Skills Review for quick reference.

Build a strong foundation of verbal basics in the Grammar and Mechanics Skills Review.

With the Writing Skills Review, practice the components of solid essay writing.

Step Two Overview:

Before learning specific test-taking strategies in Step Three, you may first be asked to complete part or all of the items in this step. The lessons and corresponding items in this section of the textbook are designed to reinforce the standards-based skills that you have already learned in school. Mastery of these skills will boost your performance on the SAT, the PSAT, and in the classroom. Focus your efforts on the Skills Review chapters that you find the most challenging. Grammar and Mechanics, Math, Reading, and Writing Skills Reviews are all included in this chapter.

Reading Skills Review

EDUCATORS' #1 CHOICE FOR SCHOOL IMPROVEMENT

Cambridge Course Concept Outline
READING SKILLS REVIEW

Careful Reading of Item Stems

After surveying thousands of students, we found that up to one-third of the time, an item was answered incorrectly because the student misinterpreted the item. In other words, students could have answered the item correctly had they understood what the test writers were really asking. You must read the item carefully and correctly, or you will get it wrong.

It may seem that this sort of error would only affect your ability to correctly answer Critical Reading items. In fact, if you cannot read with enough precision to comprehend the exact item that is being asked, you are also limiting your potential to correctly answer Math and Writing items. An inability to focus on the actual question means that you would most likely have problems in all sections of the exam.

The following exercises are designed to reinforce careful reading of the item stems on the actual test. Although some of the items in this exercise may seem to require knowledge of basic math and verbal concepts, it will not be necessary to "solve" an item. Do not be confused by distracting terminology or by an answer that "might" qualify as a correct restatement of the item stem. The correct answer choice to a Careful Reading item is the most specifically accurate, and therefore the *best*, restatement of the question that is being asked by the test-writers.

For each item in this section, you are asked to determine which of the given answer choices is the best restatement of the original item stem. The following Careful Reading item stems are representative of the four areas that are tested in this Skills Review.

Note: ✔ = correct, ✘ = wrong.

Critical Reading: Passages:	According to the passage, which of the following statements is true?
	According to the passage, what is true? ✔
	According to the passage, what is not true? ✘
Math: Multiple-Choice:	After the area of a given figure is increased, what is the percent increase in the area of the figure?
	What is the percentage change in area? ✔
	What is the new total area after the increase in area? ✘
Math: Student-Produced Responses:	What is the perimeter of square *ABCD*?
	What is the sum of the square's four sides? ✔
	What is the product of the square's four sides? ✘
Writing:	Which of the following would be the best revision for sentence 8?
	Which sentence would be the best replacement for the eighth sentence? ✔
	Which sentence would be the best replacement for the fifth sentence? ✘

Careful Reading of Critical Reading: Passages Item Stems

Critical Reading: Passages items appear on both the SAT and the PSAT; these items correspond to one of four passage formats: short single-paragraph, short double-paragraph, long single-passage, and long double-passage. The following exercise will help you focus on the exact question that is being asked by Critical Reading: Passages item stems that correspond to the short format selections. There is no need for you to see the entire selection as it would appear on the actual exam. When you have become proficient at careful reading, you will no longer waste valuable time on an individual item trying to determine exactly what the item is asking.

DIRECTIONS: Choose the *best* restatement of the item stem. Answers are on page 863.

1. What is the main idea of the passage?

    (A) What is the central theme of the passage?
    (B) Which specific detail is mentioned in the first sentence of the passage?
    (C) Which idea is always stated in the last sentence of the passage?
    (D) Which idea is a supporting detail in the passage?

2. The author of the passage would most likely agree with which of the following statements about words and art?

    (A) How do words relate to art?
    (B) Which statement pertains to words and art?
    (C) Which of the author's statements about words is not necessarily true of art?
    (D) Which statement does the author hold to be true about both words and art?

3. As used in this context, "address" most nearly means

    (A) What is the most common definition of "address"?
    (B) What is the only definition of "address"?
    (C) How would "address" be defined as it is used in the passage?
    (D) Who does the author address in the passage?

4. The primary purpose of the passage is to

    (A) What is the first specific detail?
    (B) What is the author's tone in the passage?
    (C) How does this passage make you feel?
    (D) What is the main objective of the passage?

5. The main point of the storyteller's interpretation is that

    (A) How does the storyteller interpret the main point of the passage?
    (B) Which of the storyteller's interpretations addresses the main point of the passage?
    (C) What is the central focus of the storyteller's interpretation?
    (D) Which of the following is not included in the storyteller's interpretation?

6. It can be inferred from the passage that the term "Monocrats" means

    (A) What does the term "Monocrats" mean?
    (B) What does the author infer about Monocrats?
    (C) Why does the author refer to Monocrats?
    (D) Where does the author refer to Monocrats in the passage?

7. It can be inferred that the author regards the Hudson Bay Company as a

    (A) Why does the author refer to the Hudson Bay Company?
    (B) What are the author's feelings about the Hudson Bay Company?
    (C) In what way is the author associated with the Hudson Bay Company?
    (D) What can you infer about the Hudson Bay Company?

8. According to the author of Passage 1, it is difficult to formulate a general historical law about revolution because

(A) Why does the author of Passage 1 find it difficult to formulate plans for a revolution?

(B) Why is it difficult to formulate a general historical law about revolution?

(C) Why does the author of Passage 1 formulate a general law?

(D) Why is it easy to formulate a general law?

9. In line 17, the phrase "adequately articulated" means

(A) What does "adequately articulated" mean in general?

(B) Which phrase adequately articulates line 17 in the passage?

(C) What does "adequately articulated" mean in the context of the passage?

(D) Which phrase is adequately articulated in the passage?

10. According to Passage 2, any disappointment at the failure of general laws to explain historical events is due to

(A) Which laws explain historical events?

(B) Why don't the general laws fail to explain historical events?

(C) What causes the disappointment at the failure of general laws to explain events?

(D) What causes the failure of general laws to explain historical events?

11. Passage 2 explains that the technique of Verstehen is used to enable the historian to study

(A) Which historian in Passage 2 explains the technique of Verstehen?

(B) According to Passage 2, what can historians study by means of the Verstehen technique?

(C) According to Passage 2, what can't historians study by means of the Verstehen technique?

(D) Which technique do historians use to study Verstehen?

12. In order to account for what Passage 2 calls the "inside" of a historical event, the author of Passage 1 would most likely refer to

(A) Why does the author of Passage 1 refer to the "inside" of a historical event?

(B) What would the author of Passage 1 refer to in order to account for the "inside" of a historical event?

(C) Why does the author of Passage 2 refer to the "inside" of a historical event?

(D) What would the author of Passage 2 refer to in order to account for the "inside" of a historical event?

13. The author's list of regions through which the cultivation of maize spread assumes that

(A) Why does the author's list pertain to the cultivation of maize?

(B) What assumption can be made by the author's list of regions?

(C) The cultivation of maize spread through which of the regions listed by the author?

(D) What assumption can be made about the cultivation of maize?

14. The author introduces the examples of wheat and barley in order to

(A) Wheat and barley are examples of what?

(B) In what order does the author refer to wheat and barley?

(C) Where does the author refer to wheat and barley in the passage?

(D) For what reason does the author mention wheat and barley?

15. What is the author's primary purpose?

(A) Which of the author's purposes is listed in the first sentence of the passage?

(B) Which purpose may be considered secondary to the author's purpose?

(C) As a reader, which of the author's purposes do you first detect when reading the passage?

(D) Which of the following is the author's primary reason for writing the passage?

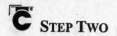
Careful Reading of Critical Reading: Passages Item Stems

Critical Reading: Passages items appear on both the SAT and the PSAT; these items correspond to one of four passage formats: short single-paragraph, short double-paragraph, long single-passage, and long double-passage. The following exercise will help you focus on the exact question that is being asked by Critical Reading: Passages item stems that correspond to the long format selections. There is no need for you to see the entire selection as it would appear on the actual exam. When you have become proficient at careful reading, you will no longer waste valuable time on an individual item trying to determine exactly what the item is asking.

DIRECTIONS: Choose the *best* restatement of the actual item that is being asked. Answers are on page 865.

1. The word "tacitly" in line 19 means

   (A) What is the tacit meaning of line 19?
   (B) In the context of line 19, what does the word "tacitly" mean?
   (C) In the context of line 19, what does the word "tacit" mean?
   (D) What is the tacit meaning of the first word in line 19?

2. Between the first and second paragraphs, Stanton changes her tone from

   (A) How does Stanton's tone in the second paragraph differ from that in the first?
   (B) What is Stanton's initial tone?
   (C) Why is Stanton's tone in the second paragraph more negative than in the first?
   (D) In what way does Stanton's tone remain unchanged?

3. Unlike Dante, Madame de Staël is

   (A) In what way is Madame de Staël like Dante?
   (B) In what way is Dante disliked by Madame de Staël?
   (C) Does Madame de Staël like Dante?
   (D) In what way is Madame de Staël unlike Dante?

4. Sun Yat-sen uses the example of Hong Kong to show

   (A) Is Sun Yat-sen from Hong Kong?
   (B) Why does Sun Yat-sen use Hong Kong as an example?
   (C) Why does Sun Yat-sen use Hong Kong as an example of Chinese culture?
   (D) Which statement is an example of Sun Yat-sen's relationship to Hong Kong?

5. How does Gandhi feel about the charge leveled against him?

   (A) Are Gandhi's charges on the level?
   (B) How does Gandhi exhibit his opposition to the charges leveled against him?
   (C) How does Gandhi feel about leveling charges against others?
   (D) What are Gandhi's feelings about the charge leveled against him?

6. Madame d'Épinay feels that Rousseau's complaints are

   (A) Why does Rousseau complain to Madame d'Epinay?
   (B) How does Rousseau feel about Madame d'Epinay's complaints?
   (C) How does Madame d'Epinay feel about Rousseau's complaints?
   (D) In what way does Madame d'Epinay feel that Rousseau's complaints are similar to her own?

7. Which of these best summarizes the difference between Rousseau's and Madame d'Épinay's philosophy of friendship?

(A) Which statement summarizes Rousseau's feelings toward Madame d'Épinay's philosophy of friendship?

(B) Which statement summarizes how Rousseau's and Madame d'Épinay's philosophies of friendship are distinct from one another?

(C) How are Rousseau's and Madame d'Épinay's philosophies of friendship similar to one another?

(D) What is the difference between Rousseau's philosophy of friendship and Madame d'Épinay's philosophy of rivalry?

8. Galileo includes the second paragraph in order to

(A) For what reason does Galileo include the second paragraph?

(B) How does the second paragraph relate to the rest of the passage?

(C) In the second paragraph, why are the sentences arranged in that particular order?

(D) Why is Galileo mentioned in the second paragraph?

9. Chekhov expresses definite opinions on each of the following points EXCEPT

(A) Which of the following points made by Chekhov is not based on fact?

(B) On which of the following points does Chekhov express a definite opinion?

(C) On which of the following points does Chekhov not express a definite opinion?

(D) Which of the following points made by Chekhov is based only on opinion?

10. The narrative of Sojourner Truth implies that slaveholders' cruelty is based on

(A) How is Sojourner Truth's cruelty implied in the narrative between slaves and slaveholders?

(B) How do Sojourner Truth's slaveholders express their cruelty?

(C) According to Sojourner Truth, what is the basis for justifying the cruelty of slaveholders?

(D) What does Sojourner Truth imply as the basis for slaveholders' cruelty?

11. Would you expect Sojourner Truth to approve of the Declaration of Sentiments?

(A) Did Sojourner Truth approve of the Declaration of Sentiments?

(B) Did Sojourner Truth expect the Declaration of Sentiments to be approved?

(C) Would Sojourner Truth approve of the Declaration of Sentience?

(D) Would Sojourner Truth approve of the Declaration of Sentiments?

12. Which of the following most accurately summarizes the main idea of the passage?

(A) What is the main point of the second paragraph?

(B) What is the main idea of the passage?

(C) Which point is a specific detail in the passage?

(D) Which of the following points is not mentioned in the passage?

13. The author of the passage seems to value the Vignes/Wolfskill site most for

(A) Why is the Vignes site valued more highly than the Wolfskill site?

(B) Why is the Vignes/Wolfskill site not valued as highly as other sites listed by the author?

(C) What is the most significant reason for why the author values the Vignes/Wolfskill site?

(D) For what reason does the author most value the Vignes/Wolfskill site?

14. In line 52, "appropriate" most nearly means

(A) Is the quote included by the author appropriate to the passage?

(B) What word in line 52 most nearly means the same thing as "appropriate"?

(C) Is line 52 appropriate to the passage?

(D) What is the best definition for the word "appropriate" as it is used in the context of line 52?

15. The chief characteristic of Lady Bertram exposed in this excerpt is her

(A) What main quality of Lady Bertram's is exposed in this excerpt?

(B) Is Lady Bertram the main character in this excerpt?

(C) Does Lady Bertram expose the main character's chief characteristic in this excerpt?

(D) Which of Lady Bertram's characteristics is not exposed in this excerpt?

16. The author of Passage 1 creates an analogy between a novel and a(n)

    (A) What does the author of Passage 1 contrast to a novel?
    (B) What does the author of Passage 2 make analogous to a novel?
    (C) What does the author of Passage 1 make analogous to a novel?
    (D) The author of Passage 1 creates an analogy between which two novels?

17. The authors of both passages would be most likely to agree with which of the following statements?

    (A) With which statement would neither author agree?
    (B) With which statement would both authors agree?
    (C) With which statement would only one of the two authors agree?
    (D) With which statement would both authors disagree?

18. According to the third paragraph, an "allergen" differs from "antigens" in that an allergen

    (A) How are "antigens" different from an "allergen"?
    (B) How are "antigens" similar to an "allergen"?
    (C) How is an "antigen" similar to "allergens"?
    (D) How is an "allergen" different from "antigens"?

19. Austen's description of Mrs. Norris's many occupations (third paragraph) depicts her as a

    (A) In describing Austen's many occupations, how does Mrs. Norris depict her?
    (B) Which of Mrs. Norris's occupations does Austen describe in the third paragraph?
    (C) How many of Mrs. Norris's occupations are described in the third paragraph?
    (D) In describing Mrs. Norris's many occupations, how does Austen depict her?

20. The passage relies upon an extended metaphor of an immune response as a

    (A) To what does the passage metaphorically compare an immune response?
    (B) What is the best definition of an immune response as it is referred to in the passage?
    (C) The metaphor of an immune response extends through how many paragraphs?
    (D) How does the author of the passage respond to commonly accepted metaphorical explanation as it is used to describe an immune response?

21. The passage suggests that which of the following would deter a child from regarding an incident of television violence as real?

    (A) What would convince a child that television violence is real?
    (B) What would prevent a child from accepting the reality of violence on television?
    (C) What type of television violence would children be most likely to regard as real?
    (D) Under what conditions would a child not be deterred from watching television violence?

22. Which of the following best describes the function of the final paragraph?

    (A) Which statement best summarizes the content of the final paragraph?
    (B) What is the function of the paragraph that precedes the final paragraph?
    (C) What purpose does the final paragraph serve?
    (D) What is the function of the first paragraph?

23. With which of the following statements about the use of dialogue in novels would the author of Passage 2 most likely agree?

    (A) With which statement about dialogue would the author of Passage 2 agree?
    (B) With which statement about dialogue would the author of Passage 2 disagree?
    (C) With which statement about dialogue would the author of Passage 1 disagree?
    (D) With which statement about dialogue in novels would the author of Passage 2 agree?

24. Austen undercuts her description of the lovely Miss Bertrams by pointing out that they

    (A) How do the Miss Bertrams undercut their description of Austen?
    (B) How do the Miss Bertrams undercut Austen's description of them?
    (C) How does Austen undermine her description of the Miss Bertrams?
    (D) How does Austen undermine the Miss Bertrams description of her?

25. The word "asserting" in line 30 means

    (A) Which of the following statements is asserted in line 30?
    (B) What is the most common definition of the word "asserting"?
    (C) Which definition of the word "asserting" is mentioned in line 30?
    (D) What is the word "asserting" intended to mean in the context of line 30?

26. In quoting Gertrude Stein's saying, "There's no there, there" (lines 8-9), Dolores Hayden most likely means to say that

    (A) What is the meaning behind Gertrude Stein's saying?
    (B) What is the meaning behind Dolores Hayden's saying?
    (C) What is the meaning behind Dolores Hayden's use of Gertrude Stein's saying?
    (D) What is the meaning behind Gertrude Stein's use of Dolores Hayden's saying?

27. The author is primarily concerned with

    (A) What does the author suggest in the first paragraph of the passage?
    (B) What idea does the author chiefly regard in the passage?
    (C) Toward what dilemma does the author exhibit genuine concern?
    (D) Which topic does the author refer to before any other in the passage?

Careful Reading of Math: Multiple-Choice Item Stems

It may seem strange to talk about reading carefully on the Math sections of the SAT and PSAT, but it is an important skill that will help you to identify the exact question that is being asked. In order to receive points for a correct answer, you must first be able to understand exactly what the test-writer is asking in each item stem. When you have become proficient at careful reading, you will no longer waste valuable time on an individual item trying to determine exactly what the item is asking. It is not necessary to worry about your math skills; these skills are addressed in the Math Skills Review. In this exercise, focus on the actual question that is being asked by the Math: Multiple-Choice item stems.

DIRECTIONS: Choose the *best* restatement of the item stem. Answers are on page 869.

1. If a machine produces 240 thingamabobs per hour, how many minutes are needed for the machine to produce 30 thingamabobs?

   (A) How many minutes does it take to make 270 thingamabobs?
   (B) How many minutes does it take to make 8 sets of 30 thingamabobs each?
   (C) How many minutes does it take to make 240 thingamabobs at 30 thingamabobs per hour?
   (D) How many minutes does it take to make 30 thingamabobs at 240 thingamabobs per hour?

2. After a 20-percent decrease in price, the cost of an item is D dollars. What was the price of the item before the decrease?

   (A) What was the original price of the item?
   (B) What was the price before the 80-percent decrease?
   (C) What was the price before the $20 decrease?
   (D) What was the price before the 80-percent increase?

3. If the price of candy increases from 5 pounds for $7 to 3 pounds for $7, how much *less* candy, in pounds, can be purchased for $3.50 at the new price than at the old price?

   (A) How much less candy can be purchased for $3.50 at the old price?
   (B) How much candy can be purchased for $3.50 at the new price?
   (C) How much less candy can be purchased for $3.50 at the new price?
   (D) How much candy can be purchased for $3.50 at the old price?

4. A jar contains 24 white marbles and 48 black marbles. What percent of the marbles in the jar are black?

   (A) What percent of the 72 marbles in the jar are white?
   (B) How many more black marbles than white marbles are in the jar?
   (C) What percent of all the marbles in the jar are not black?
   (D) Of the 72 white and black marbles in the jar, what percent are not white?

5. Twenty students attended Professor Rodriguez's class on Monday and twenty-five students attended on Tuesday. The number of students who attended on Tuesday was what percent of the number of students who attended on Monday?

   (A) 45 students are what percent of 20 students?
   (B) 45 students are what percent of 25 students?
   (C) 25 students are what percent of 20 students?
   (D) 20 students are what percent of 25 students?

6. Willie's monthly electric bills for last year were as follows: $40, $38, $36, $38, $34, $34, $30, $32, $34, $37, $39, and $40. What was the mode?

   (A) What number is the average of the series?
   (B) What number occurs least frequently?
   (C) What number occurs most frequently?
   (D) What number is the median of the series?

7. If 4.5 pounds of chocolate cost $10, how many pounds of chocolate can be purchased for $12?

   (A) At the given price, how much more chocolate can be purchased for $12 than $10?
   (B) At the given price, what is the cost of 12 pounds of chocolate?
   (C) At the given price, how many pounds can be purchased for $12?
   (D) At the given price, how many pounds can be purchased for $10?

8. At Star Lake Middle School, 45 percent of the students bought a yearbook. If 540 students bought yearbooks, how many students did NOT buy a yearbook?

   (A) How many students bought a yearbook?
   (B) How many students did not buy a yearbook if 45% bought yearbooks?
   (C) How many of the 540 students bought a yearbook if 45% bought yearbooks?
   (D) How many of the 540 students did not buy a yearbook?

9. Walking at a constant rate of 4 miles per hour, it took Jill exactly 1 hour to walk home from school. If she walked at a constant rate of 5 miles per hour, how many minutes did the trip take?

   (A) How long was the trip if Jill walked at a rate of 1 mile per hour when it takes 4 hours to walk home at a rate of 5 miles per hour?
   (B) How long was the trip if Jill walked at a rate of 4 miles per hour when it takes 1 hour to walk home at a rate of 5 miles per hour?
   (C) How long was the trip if Jill walked at a rate of 5 miles per hour when it takes 1 hour to walk home at a rate of 4 miles per hour?
   (D) How long was the trip if Jill walked at a rate of 5 miles per hour when it takes 4 hours to walk home at a rate of 1 mile per hour?

10. If the sum of 5 consecutive integers is 40, what is the smallest of the 5 integers?

    (A) What is the smallest of 5 integers that equal 40 when added together?
    (B) What is the smallest of 10 consecutive integers that equal 40 when added together?
    (C) What is the largest of 5 consecutive integers that equal 40 when added together?
    (D) What is the smallest of 5 consecutive integers that equal 40 when added together?

11. Which of the following equations correctly describes the relationship between the values x and y in the table?

    (A) According to the table, what is the relationship between x and y as expressed in an equation?
    (B) How much larger than x is y?
    (C) How much smaller than x is y?
    (D) According to the table, what is the relationship between x and z?

12. The quadratic equation $x^2 - 3x = 4$ can be solved by factoring. Which of the following states the complete solution?

    (A) What is the complete solution to the quadratic equation $x^2 - 4x = 3$?
    (B) What is the complete solution to the quadratic formula?
    (C) What is the complete solution to the quadratic equation $x^2 - 3x = 4$?
    (D) What is one of the values of x for the given quadratic equation?

13. In a card game, a player had 5 successful turns in a row, and after each one, the number of points added to his total score was double what was added the preceding turn. If the player scored a total of 465 points, how many points did he score on the first turn?

    (A) How many points did he score on the fifth turn?
    (B) How many total points did he score after all five turns?
    (C) How many points did he score after the first turn?
    (D) On the first turn, how many points did the player score?

14. At a certain firm, d gallons of fuel are needed per day for each truck. At this rate, g gallons of fuel will supply t trucks for how many days?

    (A) How many t trucks will g gallons supply for d days?
    (B) d gallons will supply t trucks for how many days if g gallons of fuel are needed per day for each truck?
    (C) g gallons will supply t trucks for how many days if d gallons of fuel are needed per day for each truck?
    (D) g gallons and d gallons together will supply t trucks for how many days?

15. A merchant increased the price of a $25 item by 10 percent. If she then reduces the new price by 10 percent, the final result is equal to which of the following?

    (A) What is the final price of a $25 item after its price has been decreased by 10% and the resulting price is then increased by 10%?
    (B) What is 10% of ten $25 items?
    (C) What is the final price of a $25 item after its price has been increased by 10% and the resulting price is then decreased by 10%?
    (D) How much is 20% of a $25 item?

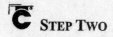

16. If a train travels m miles in h hours and 45 minutes, what is its average speed in miles per hour?

    (A) How long does it take the train to travel 45 miles?
    (B) What is the average speed if a train travels h miles in m hours and 45 minutes?
    (C) What is the average speed, in miles per hour, if a train travels 45 miles in h hours and m minutes?
    (D) What is the average speed if a train travels m miles in h hours and 45 minutes?

17. In a right isosceles triangle, the hypotenuse is equal to which of the following?

    (A) What is the hypotenuse of a right triangle?
    (B) What is the hypotenuse of a right triangle in which two sides are equal?
    (C) What is the hypotenuse of an isosceles triangle in which all three sides are equal?
    (D) What is the hypotenuse of a 30°-60°-90° triangle?

18. If a line intersects two points that are plotted at (3, 6) and (7, 9), what is its slope?

    (A) What are the slopes of two lines that include points (3, 6) and (7, 9), respectively?
    (B) What is the slope of a line that includes points (3, 6) and (7, -9)?
    (C) What is the slope of a line that includes points (6, 3) and (9, 7)?
    (D) What is the slope of a line that includes points (3, 6) and (7, 9)?

19. The average of 8 numbers is 6; the average of 6 other numbers is 8. What is the average of all 14 numbers?

    (A) What is the average of 8 numbers?
    (B) What is the average of 14 numbers?
    (C) What is the average of 8 numbers plus the other average of 6 numbers?
    (D) What is the average of the other 6 numbers?

20. If the fourth term in a geometric sequence is 125 and the sixth term is 3,125, what is the second term of the sequence?

    (A) What is the second term in the periodic sequence?
    (B) What value is represented between the first and third terms in the geometric sequence?
    (C) What geometric term represents the process that is necessary to determine the value of the given sequence?
    (D) What is the difference between 3,125 and 125?

EXERCISE **4**

Careful Reading of Math: Student-Produced Responses Item Stems

It may seem strange to talk about reading carefully on the Math sections of the SAT and PSAT, but it is an important skill that will help you to identify the exact question that is being asked. In order to receive points for a correct answer, you must first be able to understand exactly what the test-writer is asking in each item stem. When you have become proficient at careful reading, you will no longer waste valuable time on an individual item trying to determine exactly what the item is asking. It is not necessary to worry about your math skills; these skills are addressed in the Math Skills Review. In this exercise, focus on the actual question that is being asked by the Math: Student-Produced Responses item stems.

DIRECTIONS: Choose the *best* restatement of the item stem. Answers are on page 872.

1. What number increased by 25 equals twice the number?
   (A) What number is twice 25?
   (B) 25 is two times what number?
   (C) What number provides the same result when either increased by 25 or multiplied by 2?
   (D) What number provides the same result when either increased by 2 or multiplied by 25?

2. At State College, one-fourth of the students are from abroad. Of those, one-eighth are from China. What fraction of the student body is from China?
   (A) What fraction of the students are Chinese if they make up $\frac{1}{4} \div \frac{1}{8}$ of the student body?
   (B) What fraction of the students are Chinese if they make up $\frac{1}{8} \cdot \frac{1}{4}$ of the student body?
   (C) What fraction of the students are Chinese if they make up $\frac{1}{8} \div \frac{1}{4}$ of the student body?
   (D) What fraction of the students are Chinese if they make up $\frac{1}{4} + \frac{1}{8}$ of the student body?

3. If the average of 8, 10, 15, 20, and x is 11, what is x?
   (A) What is x if the average of 15, 20, 8, 10, and y is 11?
   (B) What is x if the average of 15, 20, 8, 10, and x is 15?
   (C) What is x if the average of 15, 20, 10, 8, and x is 11?
   (D) What is x if the average of 11, 20, 8, 10, and x is 11?

4. Jane and Hector have the same birthday. When Hector was 36, Jane was 30. How old was Jane when Hector was twice her age?
   (A) How old was Jane when Hector was 12?
   (B) How old will Jane be when Hector is 60?
   (C) How old was Jane when Hector was 36?
   (D) How old was Hector when Jane was 12?

5. If the price of a book increases from $10.00 to $12.50, what is the percent increase in price?
   (A) What is the percent decrease in price of a book that originally cost $12.50 and now costs $10.00?
   (B) What is the percent increase in price of a book that originally cost $10.00 and now costs $22.50?
   (C) The difference in price between a book that had cost $10.00 and now costs $12.50 is what percentage of the new price?
   (D) The difference in price between a book that had cost $10.00 and now costs $12.50 is what percentage of the old price?

6. Boys and girls belong to the chess club. There are 36 people in the club, 15 of whom are girls. In lowest terms, what fraction of the club is boys?

   (A) With 15 girls in a club of 51 total people, what fraction (in lowest terms) of the club is boys?
   (B) With 21 boys in a club of 36 people, what fraction (in lowest terms) of the club is not girls?
   (C) With 15 girls in a club of 36 people, what fraction (in lowest terms) of the club is girls?
   (D) With 21 boys in a club of 36 people, what fraction (in lowest terms) of the club is girls?

7. If the sum of two consecutive integers is 29, what is the least of these integers?

   (A) What is the smaller of two consecutive integers that when added together total 29?
   (B) What is the smaller of two non-consecutive integers that when subtracted from the larger of those two integers results in 29?
   (C) What is the larger of two consecutive integers that when added together total 29?
   (D) What is the smaller of two consecutive integers that when added together total 92?

8. If a jar of 300 black and white marbles contains 156 white marbles, what percent of the marbles is black?

   (A) 156 is what percent of 300?
   (B) 144 is what percent of 300?
   (C) 300 is what percent of 456?
   (D) 144 is what percent of 456?

9. If 0.129914 is rounded off to the nearest hundredth, how many of its digits change?

   (A) How many digits change in 0.129914 if it is rounded off to the nearest tenth?
   (B) How many digits change in 0.129414 if it is rounded off to the nearest thousandth?
   (C) How many digits change in 0.129941 if it is rounded off to the nearest hundredth?
   (D) How many digits change in 0.129914 if it is rounded off to the nearest hundredth?

10. Ray is now 10 years older than Cindy. If in 8 years Ray will be twice as old as Cindy, how old is Cindy now?

   (A) How old will Cindy be in 8 years?
   (B) What is Cindy's current age?
   (C) If Ray is currently 8 years older than Cindy, what is Cindy's current age?
   (D) When Ray is 16 years older than Cindy, how old will Cindy be?

11. Let the "JOSH" of a number be defined as 3 less than 3 times the number. What number is equal to its "JOSH"?

   (A) What value for x is equal to $3x - 3$?
   (B) What value for x is equal to $3x + 3$?
   (C) What value for y is equal to $3x + 3$?
   (D) What value for y is equal to $3x - 3$?

12. What is the area of a circle with center O?

   (A) What is the area of circle O?
   (B) The circle with center O has an area of what value?
   (C) Circle O has a center with an area of what value?
   (D) What is the circumference of circle O?

13. In the country of Glup, 1 glop is 3 glips, and 4 glips are 5 globs. How many globs are 2 glops?

   (A) 4 glips are how many globs?
   (B) 2 glops are how many glups?
   (C) 2 glops are how many globs?
   (D) 3 glips are how many globs?

14. If $\frac{4}{5}$ is subtracted from its reciprocal, then what value is the result?

   (A) What is the result of $\frac{4}{5} - \frac{5}{4}$?
   (B) What is the result of $\frac{4}{5} - \frac{4}{5}$?
   (C) What is the result of $\frac{5}{4} - \frac{4}{5}$?
   (D) What is the result of $\frac{1}{5} - \frac{4}{5}$?

15. What is the value of $\frac{2}{3} - \frac{5}{8}$?

   (A) In decimal form, what is the result of $\frac{2}{3} - \frac{5}{8}$?
   (B) By subtracting $\frac{5}{8}$ from $\frac{2}{3}$, what value is yielded?
   (C) By subtracting $\frac{2}{3}$ from $\frac{5}{8}$, what value is yielded?
   (D) By subtracting $\frac{8}{5}$ from $\frac{3}{2}$, what value is yielded?

16. What is the average of 8.5, 7.8, and 7.7?

   (A) When 8.5, 7.8, and 7.7 are placed in sequential order, which number would be in the middle?
   (B) After dividing the sum total of 8.5, 7.7, and 7.5 by 3, what is the result?
   (C) After multiplying the sum total of 8.5, 7.8, and 7.7 by 3, what is the result?
   (D) After dividing the sum total of 7.7, 8.5, and 7.8 by 3, what is the result?

17. What is the area of square $PQRS$?

   (A) What is the area of square $QSPR$?
   (B) What is the area of parallelogram $PQRS$?
   (C) What is the area of rectangle $PQRS$?
   (D) What is the area of square $SRQP$?

18. The average of 4, 5, x, and y is 6, and the average of x, z, 8, and 9 is 8. What is the value of $z - y$?

    (A) What is the value of $z - y$ if 8 is the average of 9, x, 8, and z, and 6 is the average of 5, y, x, and 4?

    (B) What is the value of $z - y$ if the average of 4, 5, x, and y is 8, and the average of x, z, 8, and 9 is 6?

    (C) What is the value of , $- y$ if 6 is the average of 9, x, 8, and z, and 8 is the average of 5, y, x, and 4?

    (D) What is the value of $y - z$ if the average of 4, 5, x, and y is 6, and the average of x, z, 8, and 9 is 8?

19. 0.01 is the ratio of 0.1 to what number?

    (A) What is the value of x if $0.01 : x$ is 0.1?
    (B) What is the value of $0.01 \div 0.1$?
    (C) What is the value of x if $.1 : x$ is $.01$?
    (D) What is the value of $.001 \div 0.1$?

20. Line segment AB is parallel to line segment ED and line segment AC is equal to line segment BC. If $\angle BED$ is $50°$, then what is the value of x?

    (A) What is the value of x if $\angle BED = 50°$, line segment CB is parallel to line segment CA, and line segment DE is equal to line segment BA?

    (B) What is the value of x if $\angle EDB = 50°$, line segment AB is parallel to line segment ED, and line segment AC is equal to line segment BC?

    (C) What is the value of x if $\angle BED = 50°$, line segment AB is parallel to line segment AC, and line segment ED is equal to line segment BC?

    (D) What is the value of x if $\angle DEB = 50°$, line segment CB is equal to line segment CA, and line segment DE is parallel to line segment BA?

Careful Reading of Writing Item Stems

The Writing portions of the SAT and PSAT are made up of Identifying Sentence Errors, Improving Sentences, Improving Paragraphs, and Essay items. The following exercise will help you focus on the exact question that is being asked by Improving Paragraphs item stems and Essay prompts. (Identifying Sentence Errors and Improving Sentences item stems do not apply.) For Improving Paragraph items, there is no need for you to see the corresponding passage as it would appear on the actual exam. When you have become proficient at careful reading, you will no longer waste valuable time on an individual item trying to determine exactly what the item is asking. Do not worry about your writing skills; these skills are addressed in the Writing Skills Review. In this exercise, focus on the actual question that is being asked by the Writing item stems.

DIRECTIONS: Choose the *best* restatement of the item stem. Answers are on page 875.

1. In context, which of the following would be best to insert at the beginning of sentence 9?

   (A) Which statement should be inserted before sentence 9?

   (B) Which statement should be inserted after sentence 9?

   (C) Which answer choice should be inserted at the end of the eighth sentence in the passage?

   (D) Which answer choice should be inserted at the beginning of the ninth sentence in the passage?

2. Which of the following best describes the overall organization of the passage?

   (A) What describes the best way in which the passage should be organized?

   (B) What describes the way in which the passage is organized?

   (C) Which passage describes the best overall method of organization?

   (D) Which type of passage would most likely follow the given passage based on its overall organization?

3. Which of the following would be the best substitute for "this" in sentence 9?

   (A) Which answer choice could be used in place of the word "this" in the ninth sentence of the passage?

   (B) The pronoun "this" is substituted for which of the following nouns that can be found in the ninth sentence of the passage?

   (C) Where would the word "this" be more appropriately inserted in sentence 9?

   (D) Which of the following sentences would be the best substitute for sentence 9?

4. Which of the following is the LEAST appropriate revision of the underlined part of sentence 11?

   (A) Which answer choice would be the best replacement for the underlined portion of the eleventh sentence in the passage?

   (B) Which answer choice would not be the worst replacement for the underlined portion of the eleventh sentence in the passage?

   (C) Which answer choice would be the worst replacement for the underlined portion of the eleventh sentence in the passage?

   (D) Which answer choice would be the worst replacement for the underlined portion of the seventh sentence in the passage?

5. The passage makes use of all of the following techniques EXCEPT

   (A) Which technique is used in the passage?

   (B) Which techniques are used in the passage?

   (C) Which technique is not used in the passage?

   (D) Which three techniques are not used in the passage?

6. Name one way in which technology benefits humankind using an example taken from history, current affairs, literature, or your own experience.

   (A) Taken from current affairs, history, literature, or someone else's experience, name two ways in which technology does not benefit humankind.

   (B) Taken from history, current affairs, or your own experience, name one way in which literature benefits humankind.

   (C) Taken from literature, current affairs, history, or your own experience, name a way in which technology aids humankind.

   (D) Taken from current affairs, history, or literature, name one way in which your own experience reflects how technology benefits humankind.

7. In your opinion, what has been the greatest technological advancement of the past 125 years?

   (A) Over the last century, which technological advancement has proven to be the most important?

   (B) Over the last one and one-quarter centuries, which technological achievement has been advanced upon more significantly than any other?

   (C) Over the last one and one-quarter centuries, which technological achievement has been advanced upon more significantly than any other (in your opinion)?

   (D) Over the last one and one-quarter centuries, which technological advancement has proven to be the most important (in your opinion)?

8. Does violence in the media lead to additional violence or is it harmless?

   (A) Is media violence harmless violence?

   (B) Does initially harmless media violence lead to harmful media violence?

   (C) Does media violence propagate harmless activity?

   (D) Is media violence harmless or does it propagate more violent activity?

9. Is the United States more of a cultural "Melting Pot," where cultures have merged into a greater whole, or a "Salad Bowl," where cultures are mixed but still distinct?

   (A) Do America's representative cultures blend into one as do the ingredients in a melting pot or are they mixed yet distinct as are the ingredients in a salad bowl?

   (B) Do America's representative cultures blend into one as do the ingredients of a salad bowl or are they mixed yet distinct as are the ingredients of a melting pot?

   (C) Do America's representative cultures mix and initially interact distinctly before eventually blending into a greater whole?

   (D) Do America's representative cultures initially merge into one before eventually distinguishing themselves as separate entities?

10. Which do you find more compelling, the belief that the quality of life was better thirty or forty years ago or that it is better today?

   (A) Do you agree with the idea that the quality of life was better thirty years ago or that it was better forty years ago?

   (B) Do you agree with the idea that the quality of life was better approximately thirty to forty years ago or that it is better today?

   (C) Do you agree with the idea that there was a compelling difference between the quality of life thirty years ago and the quality of life forty years ago?

   (D) Do you agree with the idea that the quality of life is better today than it was thirty years ago or that it is better today than it was forty years ago?

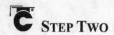

Coding of Item Stems

Most students are pressed for time on the Critical Reading: Passages items. You can save time by looking for the correct answers to items as you read the passage for the first time. Reading a passage and answering several corresponding items at the rate of less than one item per minute requires a very different skill than what you would typically use when reading a book, newspaper, or magazine.

For Critical Reading: Passages items, you must not only read the item correctly, but you must also correctly identify the item-type. Every Critical Reading: Passages item, regardless of the corresponding passage format, will be from one of seven basic types. You can avoid memorizing information that is not needed to answer an item by focusing only on information that is needed to answer the question that is being asked by that specific item-type. Remember that many more questions could be asked on any given passage than are actually asked. If you do not identify the correct item-type, then there is a good chance that you will not use the appropriate strategy for finding the correct answer. You must therefore know the characteristics of the correct answer that are associated with each item-type.

Critical Reading: Passages items are designed to test three levels of reading comprehension: appreciation of the general theme, understanding of specific points, and evaluation of the text. This section will help you to immediately recognize both the item-type and the level of reading comprehension that are being tested based on the wording of the item stem.

SEVEN TYPES OF CRITICAL READING: PASSAGES ITEMS

(1) **Main Idea** – What is the unifying theme?

(2) **Explicit Detail** – What is explicitly mentioned?

(3) **Vocabulary** – How are certain words used?

(4) **Development** – How are the ideas constructed and arranged?

(5) **Implied Idea** – What can be inferred?

(6) **Application** – How can the information be applied to new situations?

(7) **Voice** – What does the writer reveal through attitude, tone, or voice?

Refer to the Core Lesson section of the Critical Reading: Passages Lesson in Step Three for a more detailed description of the seven item-types.

Each of the three levels of reading comprehension is represented by at least one of the aforementioned seven types of Critical Reading: Passages items as follows:

Comprehension Level	Item-Type
General Theme	Main Idea
Specific Points	Explicit Detail Vocabulary Development
Evaluation	Implied Idea Application Voice

GENERAL THEME

The first level of reading, appreciation of the general theme, is the most basic. Main Idea items and items about the overall development of the selection test whether you understand the passage at the most general level. The first sentence of a paragraph—often the topic sentence—may provide a summary of the content of that paragraph. Also, the last sentence of a paragraph usually provides concluding material that may also be helpful in understanding the general theme of the passage.

SPECIFIC POINTS

The second level of reading, understanding specific points, takes you deeper into the selection. Explicit Detail items, items about the meanings of words, and items about the logical role of details all test your ability to read carefully. Since this is an "open-book" test, you can always return to the selection. Therefore, if something is highly technical or difficult to understand, do not dwell on it for too long—come back to the item later if necessary.

EVALUATION

The third level of reading, evaluation of the text, takes you even deeper into the selection. Implied Idea, Application, and Voice items requires, in addition to an understanding of the material, a judgment or an evaluation of what you have read. This is why these items are usually the most difficult.

When taking the test, approach the Critical Reading: Passages items in the following way: First, preview the item; second, identify the item-type; third, code each item according to its respective level of reading comprehension; and finally, think of the characteristics of the correct answer before you begin to read the passage. Read each passage slowly and carefully as you search for clues that will help answer each item. Also, do not "speed-read" or skim through the passage. The faster you read the passage, the less likely you are to pick the correct answer choice. Most answer choices require careful reading, analysis, and an application of the facts to the exact question that is being asked.

Coding of Item Stems

DIRECTIONS: Code each item stem according to one of the three levels of reading comprehension: General Theme (GT), Specific Points (SP), and Evaluation (E). Answers are on page 876.

1. According to the passage, tears and laughter have all of the following in common EXCEPT

   ~~evaluation~~.

   specific point (explicit detail)

2. The author implies that animals lack the ability to

   ~~general~~

   evaluation (implied idea)

3. The word "ludicrous" in line # most nearly means

   GT

   specific point (vocabulary)

4. The author develops the passage primarily by

   E

   specific point

5. In the second paragraph, the author

   GM

   specific point

6. Which of the following titles best describes the content of the selection?

   general theme

7. The author is primarily concerned with discussing the

   SP general theme

8. The passage states that the open government statute is intended to accomplish all of the following EXCEPT

9. The passage most strongly supports which of the following conclusions about a decision that is within the authority of the executive director of an agency?

   evaluation

10. In the final paragraph, the author discusses

11. The author makes all of the following points about the rules governing the commission EXCEPT

12. It can be inferred from the passage that the executive director is authorized to make certain purchases costing less than $5,000 in order to

   evaluation

13. Which of the following statements about a "review and comment" session can be inferred from the selection?

14. According to the passage, all of the following are true of metamorphic rock EXCEPT

15. As described by the selection, the sequence of events leading to the present landscape was

16. The author regards the explanation he gives as

   evaluation (application)

17. The author provides information that defines which of the following terms?

18. The author would most likely agree with which of the following statements?

19. The passage supports which of the following conclusions about the writings of Yevgeny Zamyatin?

_____

_____

20. The author's treatment of James Burnham's writing can best be described as

evaluation

21. The statement that Burnham inverted the logical priority of the individual over the state means that Burnham believed that

_____

_____

22. The author criticized Burnham for

_____

23. According to Burnham, in the completely autocratic state, history will have come to an end because

_____

_____

24. It can be inferred from the passage that the physical features of a galaxy that do not belong to a rich cluster are determined primarily by the

_____

_____

25. The author implies that the currently accepted theories on galaxy formation are

_____

_____

26. According to the passage, a cluster with a central, supergiant galaxy will

_____

_____

27. According to the passage, the outcome of a collision between galaxies depends on which of the following?

_____

_____

28. According to the passage, as a galaxy falls inward toward the center of a cluster, it

_____

_____

29. According to the passage, a star such as our Sun would probably not be found in a cluster such as Virgo because

_____

30. The phrase "Nature never became a toy to the wise spirit" means which of the following?

_____

31. The author implies that the difference between farms and the landscape is primarily a matter of

_____

_____

32. The author uses the word "property" in the phrase "property in the horizon" (line #) to mean

specific point

33. The phrase "color of the spirit" in line # means

_____

_____

34. The main purpose of this passage is to

_____

35. Which of the following best explains the distinction between a life circumstance and a life event?

_____

36. The author uses all of the following techniques EXCEPT

specific point

37. Which of the following best explains the relationship between the first paragraph and the second paragraph of the passage?

_____

38. The passage provides information that defines which of the following terms?

_____

39. According to the passage, Wineland was characterized by which of the following geographical features?

_____

_____

40. It can be inferred from the passage that scholars who doubt the authenticity of the Biarni narrative make all of the following objections EXCEPT

_____

_____

41. The author mentions the two high mountains in order to show that it is unlikely to be true that

_____

_____

42. All of the following are mentioned as similarities between Leif Erikson's voyage and Biarni's voyage EXCEPT

_____

_____

43. It can be inferred that the author regards the historicity of the Biarni narrative as

_____

_____

Vocabulary

Students often believe that if they do not know what a certain word means, then they will not be able to correctly answer an item that requires them to understand the meaning of that word. This section helps you focus on recognizing word parts, becoming more familiar with challenging vocabulary words, and using context clues to determine what difficult words mean. In addition to understanding context, this section emphasizes the importance of understanding the logical structure of a sentence and applying that understanding to anticipate appropriate words in succeeding on vocabulary related items.

Word Parts List

While memorizing vocabulary words is not the key to succeeding on vocabulary-related items, greater familiarity with the Word Parts List can only improve your chances of answering items correctly.

Prefix	Meaning	Examples
a	in, on, of, to	abed—in bed
a, ab, abs	from, away	abrade—wear off
		absent—away, not present
a, an	lacking, not	asymptomatic—showing no symptoms
		anaerobic—able to live without air
ad, ac, af, ag, al, an	to, toward	accost—approach and speak to
ap, ar, as, at		adjunct—something added to
		aggregate—bring together
ambi, amphi	around, both	ambidextrous—using both hands equally
		amphibious—living both in water and on land
ana	up, again, anew, throughout	analyze—loosen up, break up into parts
		anagram—word spelled from letters of other word
ante	before	antediluvian—before the Flood
anti	against	anti-war—against war
arch	first, chief	archetype—first model
auto	self	automobile—self-moving vehicle
bene, ben	good, well	benefactor—one who does good deeds
circum	around	circumnavigate—sail around
com, co, col, con, cor	with, together	concentrate—bring closer together
		cooperate—work together
		collapse—fall together
contra, contro, counter	against	contradict—speak against
		counterclockwise—against the clock
de	away from, down, opposite of	detract—draw away from
di	twice, double	dichromatic—having two colors
dia	across, through	diameter—measurement across
dis, di	not, away from	dislike—to not like
		digress—turn away from the subject
dys	bad, poor	dyslexia—poor reading
equi	equal	equivalent—of equal value
ex, e, ef	from, out	expatriate—one living outside native country
		emit—send out
extra	outside, beyond	extraterrestrial—from beyond the earth
fore	in front of, previous	forecast—tell ahead of time
		foreleg—front leg
homo	same, like	homophonic—sounding the same
hyper	too much, over	hyperactive—overly active
hypo	too little, under	hypothermia—having too little body heat
in, il, ig, im, ir	not	innocent—not guilty
		ignorant—not knowing
		irresponsible—not responsible
in, il, im, ir	on, into, in	impose—place on
		invade—go into

intra, intro	within, inside	intrastate—within a state
mal, male	bad, wrong, poor	maladjusted—poorly adjusted
		malevolent—ill-wishing
mis	badly, wrongly	misunderstand—understand incorrectly
mis, miso	hatred	misogyny—hatred of women
mono	single, one	monorail—train that runs on a single rail
neo	new	Neolithic—of the New Stone Age
non	not	nonentity—a nobody
ob	over, against, toward	obstruct—stand against
omni	all	omnipresent—present in all places
pan	all	panorama—a complete view
peri	around, near	periscope—device for seeing all around
poly	many	polygonal—many-sided
post	after	postmortem—after death
pre	before, earlier than	prejudice—judgment in advance
pro	in favor of, forward, in front of	proceed—go forward
		pro-war—in favor of war
re	back, again	rethink—think again
		reimburse—pay back
retro	backward	retrospective—looking backward
se	apart, away	seclude—keep away
semi	half	semiconscious—half conscious
sub, suc, suf, sug, sus	under, beneath	subscribe—write underneath
		suspend—hang down
		suffer—undergo
super	above, greater	superfluous—beyond what is needed
syn, sym, syl, sys	with, at the same time	synthesis—a putting together
		sympathy—a feeling with
tele	far	television—machine for seeing far
trans	across	transport—carry across a distance
un.	not	uninformed—not informed
vice	acting for, next in rank to	vice president—second in command

Suffix	*Meaning*	*Examples*
able, ble	able, capable	acceptable—able to be accepted
acious, cious	characterized by, having the quality of	spacious—having the quality of space
age	sum, total	mileage—total number of miles
al	of, like, suitable for	theatrical—suitable for theater
ance, ancy	act or state of	disturbance—act of disturbing
ant, ent	one who	defendant—one who defends himself
ary, ar	having the nature of, concerning	military—relating to soldiers
		polar—state of being raised
cy	act, state, or position of	presidency—position of president
		ascendancy—state of being raised up
dom	state, rank, that which belongs to	wisdom—state of being wise
ence	act, state, or quality of	dependence—state of depending
er, or	one who, that which	doer—one who does
		conductor—that which conducts
escent	becoming	obsolescent—becoming obsolete
fy	to make	pacify—make peaceful
ic, ac	of, like	demonic—of or like a demon
il, ile	having to do with, like, suitable for	civil—having to do with citizens
		tactile—having to do with touch
ion	act or condition of	operation—act of operating
ious	having, characterized by	anxious—characterized by anxiety
ish	like, somewhat	foolish—like a fool
ism	belief or practice of	racism—belief in racial superiority
ist	one who does, makes, or is concerned with	scientist—one concerned with science
ity, ty, y	character or state of being	amity—friendship
		jealousy—state of being jealous

ive	of, relating to, tending to	destructive—tending to destroy
logue, loquy	speech or writing	monologue—speech by one person
		colloquy—conversation
logy	speech, study of	geology—study of the earth
ment	act or state of	abandonment—act of abandoning
mony	a resulting thing, condition, or state	patrimony—trait inherited from one's dad
ness	act or quality	kindness—quality of being kind
ory	having the quality of	compensatory—quality of compensation
	a place or thing for	lavatory—place for washing
ous, ose	full of, having	glamorous—full of glamour
ship	skill, state of being	horsemanship—skill in riding
		ownership—state of being an owner
some	full of, like	frolicsome—playful
tude	state or quality of	rectitude—state of being morally upright
ward	in the direction of	homeward—in the direction of home
y	full of, like, somewhat	wily—full of wiles

Root	Meaning	Examples
acr	bitter	acrid, acrimony
act, ag	do, act, drive	action, react, agitate, agent
acu	sharp, keen	acute, acumen
agog	leader	pedagogue, demagogic
agr	field	agronomy, agriculture
ali	other	alias, alienate, inalienable
alt	high	altitude, contralto
alter, altr	other, change	alternative, altercation, altruism
am, amic	love, friend	amorous, amiable
anim	mind, life, spirit	animism, animate, animosity
annu, enni	year	annual, superannuated, biennial
anthrop	man	anthropoid, misanthropy
apt, ept	fit	apt, adapt, ineptitude
aqu	water	aquatic, aquamarine
arbit	judge	arbiter, arbitrary
arch	chief	anarchy, matriarch
arm	arm, weapon	army, armature, disarm
art	skill, a fitting together	artisan, artifact, articulate
aster, astr	star	asteroid, disaster, astral
aud, audit, aur	hear	auditorium, audition, auricle
aur	gold	aureate, aureomycin
aut	self	autism, autograph
bell	war	anti-bellum, belligerent
brev	short	brevity, abbreviation, abbreviate
cad, cas, cid	fall	cadence, casualty, accident
cand	white, shining	candid, candle, incandescent
cant, chant	sing, charm	cantor, recant, enchant
cap, capt, cept, ceipt, cept, cip	take, seize, hold	capable, captive, accept, incipient
capit	head	capital, decapitate, recapitulate
cede, ceed, cess	go, yield	secede, exceed, process, intercession
cent	hundred	century, percentage, centimeter
cern, cert	perceive, make certain, decide	concern, certificate, certain
chrom	color	monochrome, chromatic
chron	time	chronometer, anachronism
cide, cis	cut, kill	genocide, incision, suicide
cit	summon, impel	cite, excite, incitement
civ	citizen	uncivil, civilization
clam, claim	shout	clamorous, proclaim, claimant
clar	clear	clarity, clarion, declare
clin	slope, lean	inclination, recline
clud, clus, clos	close, shut	seclude, recluse, closet
cogn	know	recognize, incognito
col, cul	prepare	colony, cultivate, agriculture

corp	body	incorporate, corpse
cosm	order, world	cosmetic, cosmos, cosmopolitan
crac, crat	power, rule	democrat, theocracy
cre, cresc, cret	grow	increase, crescent, accretion
cred	trust, believe	credit, incredible
crux, cruc	cross	crux, crucial, crucifix
crypt	hidden	cryptic, cryptography
cur, curr, curs	run, course	occur, current, incursion
cura	care	curator, accurate
dem	people	demographic, demagogue
dent	tooth	dental, indentation
derm	skin	dermatitis, pachyderm
di, dia	day	diary, quotidian
dic, dict	say, speak	indicative, edict, dictation
dign	worthy	dignified, dignitary
doc, doct	teach, prove	indoctrinate, docile, doctor
domin	rule	predominate, domineer, dominion
dorm	sleep	dormitory, dormant
du	two	duo, duplicity, dual
duc, duct	lead	educate, abduct, ductile
dur	hard, lasting	endure, obdurate, duration
dyn	force, power	dynamo, dynamite
equ	equal	equation, equitable
erg, urg	work, power	energetic, metallurgy, demiurge
err	wander	error, aberrant
ev	time, age	coeval, longevity
fac, fact, fect, fic	do, make	facility, factual, perfect, artifice
fer	bear, carry	prefer, refer, conifer, fertility
ferv	boil	fervid, effervesce
fid	belief, faith	infidelity, confidant, perfidious
fin	end, limit	finite, confine
firm	strong	reaffirm, infirmity
flect, flex	bend	reflex, inflection
flor	blossom	florescent, floral
flu, fluct, flux	flow	fluid, fluctuation, influx
form	shape	formative, reform, formation
fort	strong	effort, fortitude
frag, fract	break	fragility, infraction
fug	flee	refuge, fugitive
gam	marry	exogamy, polygamous
ge, geo	earth	geology, geode, perigee
gen	birth, kind, race	engender, general, generation
gest	carry, bear	gestation, ingest, digest
gon	angle	hexagonal, trigonometry
grad, gress	step, go	regress, gradation
gram, graph	writing	cryptogram, telegraph
grat	pleasing, agreeable	congratulate
grav	weight, heavy	grave (situation), gravity
greg	flock, crowd	gregarious, segregate
habit, hibit	have, hold	habitation, inhibit, habitual
heli	sun	helium, heliocentric, aphelion
her, hes	stick, cling	adherent, cohesive
hydr	water	dehydration, hydrofoil
iatr	heal, cure	pediatrics, psychiatry
iso	same, equal	isotope, isometric
it	journey, go	itinerary, exit
ject	throw	reject, subjective, projection
jud	judge	judicial, adjudicate
jug, junct	join	conjugal, juncture, conjunction
jur	swear	perjure, jurisprudence
labor	work	laborious, belabor

leg	law	legal, illegitimate
leg, lig, lect	choose, gather, read	illegible, eligible, select, lecture
lev	light, rise	levity, alleviate
liber	free	liberal, libertine
liter	letter	literate, alliterative
lith	rock, stone	Neolithic, lithograph
loc	place	locale, locus, allocate
log	word, study	logic, biology, dialogue
loqu, locut	talk, speech	colloquial, loquacious, interlocutor
luc, lum	light	translucent, pellucid, illumine
lud, lus	play	allusion, ludicrous, interlude
magn	large, great	magnificent, magnitude
mal	bad, ill	malodorous, malady
man, manu	hand	manifest, manicure, manuscript
mar	sea	maritime, submarine
mater, matr	mother	matrilocal, maternal
medi	middle	intermediary, medieval
ment	mind	demented, mental
merg, mers	plunge, dip	emerge, submersion
meter, metr, mens	measure	chronometer, metronome, geometry
micr	small	microfilm, micron
min	little	minimum, minute
mit, miss	send	remit, admission, missive
mon, monit	warn	admonish, monument, monitor
mor	custom	mores, immoral
mor, mort	death	mortify, mortician
morph	shape	amorphous, anthropomorphic
mov, mob, mot	move	removal, automobile, motility
mut	change	mutable, transmute, mutation
nasc, nat	born	native, natural, nascent, innate
necr	dead, die	necropolis, necrosis
neg	deny	renege, negative
nom, noun, nown,	name, order, rule	anonymous, antinomy, misnomer
nam, nym, nomen, nomin	name	nomenclature, cognomen, nominate
nomy	law, rule	astronomy, antinomy
nov	new	novice, innovation
ocul	eye	binocular, oculist
onym	name	pseudonym, antonym
oper	work	operate, cooperation, inoperable
ora	speak, pray	oracle, oratory
orn	decorate	adorn, ornate
orth	straight, correct	orthodox, orthopedic
pan	all	panacea, pantheon
pater, patr	father	patriot, paternity
path, pat, pass	feel, suffer	telepathy, patient, compassion
ped	child	pedagogue, pediatrics
ped, pod	foot	pedestrian, impede, tripod
pel, puls	drive, push	impel, propulsion
pend, pens	hang	pendulous, suspense
pet, peat	seek	petition, impetus, repeat
phil	love	philosopher, Anglophile
phob	fear	phobic, agoraphobia
phon	sound	phonograph, symphony
phor	bearing	semaphore, metaphor
phot	light	photograph, photoelectric
pon, pos	place, put	component, repose, postpone
port	carry	report, portable, deportation
pot	power	potency, potential
press	press	pressure, impression
prim, proto, prot	first	primal, proton, protagonist
psych	mind	psychic, metempsychosis

quer, quir, quis, ques	ask, seek	query, inquiry, inquisitive, quest
reg, rig, rect	straight, rule	regulate, dirigible, corrective
rid, ris	laugh	deride, risible, ridiculous
rog	ask	rogation, interrogate
rupt	break	erupt, interruption, rupture
sanct	holy	sacrosanct, sanctify, sanction
sci, scio	know	nescient, conscious, omniscience
scop	watch, view	horoscope, telescopic
scrib, script	write	scribble, proscribe, description
sed, sid, sess	sit, seat	sediment, sedate, session
seg, sect	cut	segment, section, intersect
sent, sens	feel, think	nonsense, sensitive, sentient
sequ, secut	follow	sequel, consequence, consecutive
sol	alone	solitary, solo, desolate
solv, solu, solut	loosen	dissolve, soluble, absolution
somn	sleep	insomnia, somnolent
son	sound	sonorous, unison
soph	wise, wisdom	philosophy, sophisticated
spec, spic, spect	look	specimen, conspicuous, spectacle
spir	breathe	spirit, conspire, respiration
stab, stat	stand	unstable, status, station
stead	place	instead, steadfast
string, strict	bind	astringent, stricture, restrict
stru, struct	build	construe, structure, destructive
sum, sumpt	take	presume, consumer, assumption
tang, ting, tact, tig	touch	tangent, contingency, contact
tax, tac	arrange, arrangement	taxonomy, tactic
techn	skill, art	technique, technician
tele	far	teletype, telekinesis
tempor	time	temporize, extemporaneous
ten, tain, tent	hold	tenant, tenacity, retention
tend, tens, tent	stretch	contend, extensive, intent
tenu	thin	tenuous, attenuate
test	witness	attest, testify
the	god	polytheism, theologist
tom	cut	atomic, appendectomy
tort, tors	twist	tortuous, torsion, contort
tract	pull, draw	traction, attract, protract
trib	assign, pay	attribute, tribute, retribution
trud, trus	thrust	obtrude, intrusive
turb	agitate	perturb, turbulent, disturb
umbr	shade	umbrella, penumbra
urb	city	urbane, suburb, urban
vac	empty	vacuous, evacuation
vad, vas	go	invade, evasive
val, vail	strength, worth	valid, avail, prevalent
ven, vent	come	advent, convene, prevention
ver	true	aver, veracity, verity
verb	word	verbose, adverb, verbatim
vert, vers	turn	revert, perversion, versatile
vest	dress	vestment
vid, vis	see	video, evidence, vision, revise
vinc, vict	conquer	evince, convict, victim
viv, vit	life	vivid, revive, vital
vo, voc, vok, vow	call	vociferous, provocative, equivocate
vol	wish	involuntary, volition
volv, volut	roll, turn	involve, convoluted, revolution
vulg	common	divulge, vulgarity
zo	animal	zoologist, Paleozoic

Vocabulary List

The following list is composed of words that students may find challenging on standardized tests. The list is divided into two difficulty levels. Familiarity with the Vocabulary List can only improve your chances of answering items correctly.

—Difficulty Level 1—

abacus—a frame with beads or balls used for doing or teaching arithmetic

abash—disconcert; to make embarrassed and ill at ease

abate—to deduct; to make less

abduction—to carry off by force

aberration—a deviation from the normal or the typical

abeyance—temporary suspension

abhor—detest; to shrink from in disgust or hatred

abhorrence—loathing; detestation

abide—to stay; stand fast; remain

abjure—recant; to give up (opinions) publicly

abominate—loathe; to dislike very much

abrade—to scrape or rub off

abridge—shorten; to reduce in scope or extent

abrogate—cancel; call off

abscond—to go away hastily and secretly

absolve—acquit; to pronounce free from guilt or blame

abstinence—the act of voluntarily doing without pleasures

abstruse—hard to understand; deep; recondite

absurdity—nonsense

abyss—chasm; a deep fissure in the earth; bottomless gulf

acclaim—to greet with loud applause or approval

accretion—growth in size by addition or accumulation

acerbic—sharp, bitter, or harsh in temper and language

acquisition—something or someone acquired or added

acrimony—asperity; bitterness or harshness of temper, manner, or speech

acute—shrewd; keen or quick of mind

adapt—adjust; to make fit or suitable by changing

adjunct—connected or attached in a secondary or subordinate way

adorn—ornament; to put decorations on something

adroit—expert; clever; skillful in a physical or mental way

adulterate—not genuine; to make inferior or impure

adversary—opponent; a person who opposes or fights against another

advocate—a person who pleads another's cause

aesthete—a person who artificially cultivates artistic sensitivity or makes a cult of art and beauty

aesthetic—artistic; sensitive to art and beauty

affable—gentle and kindly

affinity—connection; close relationship

afflict—to cause pain or suffering to; distress very much

affluent—plentiful; abundant; flowing freely

aggrandize—to make seem greater

alias—assumed name

allegiance—loyalty or devotion

alleviate—to reduce or decrease; lighten or relieve

allocate—allot; to distribute in shares or according to a plan

alloy—the relative purity of gold or silver; fineness

allude—to refer in a casual or indirect way

altercation—an angry or heated argument

amalgamate—unite; combine

ambiguous—not clear; having two or more possible meanings

ambivalence—simultaneously conflicting feelings toward a person or thing

amble—to go easily and unhurriedly

ameliorate—improve; to make or become better

amenable—willing to follow advice or suggestion; answerable

amiable—good-natured; having a pleasant and friendly disposition

amicable—peaceable; showing good will

amphibious—can live both on land and in water

anagram—a word or phrase made from another by rearranging its letters

analogy—partial resemblance; similarity in some respects between things otherwise unlike

anarchy—the complete absence of government

anathema—a thing or person greatly detested

anatomist—a person who analyzes in great detail

anecdote—a short, entertaining account of some happening

anhydrous—without water

animosity—hostility; a feeling of strong dislike or hatred

annexation—attachment; adding on

anomalous—abnormal; deviating from the regular arrangement, general rule, or usual method

anthology—a collection of poems, stories, songs, or excerpts

antidote—a remedy to counteract a poison

antigen—a protein, toxin, or other substance to which the body reacts by producing antibodies

antipathy—strong or deep-rooted dislike

anvil—an iron or steel block on which metal objects are hammered into shape

apathetic—feeling little or no emotion; unmoved

apocryphal—not genuine; spurious; counterfeit; of doubtful authorship or authenticity

appease—to satisfy or relieve

appraise—to set a price for; decide the value of

apprehension—an anxious feeling of foreboding; dread

apprentice—novice; any learner or beginner

arabesque—a complex and elaborate decorative design

arbitrary—unreasonable; unregulated; despotic

arbitrate—to decide a dispute

arboreal—of or like a tree

arcane—hidden or secret

ardor—passion; emotional warmth

arduous—difficult to do; laborious; onerous

arid—dry and barren; lacking enough water for things to grow

aromatic—smelling sweet or spicy; fragrant or pungent

arouse—to awaken, as from sleep

articulate—expressing oneself easily and clearly

artisan—craftsman; a worker in a skilled trade
aspiration—strong desire or ambition
assail—assault; to attack physically and violently
assay—an examination or testing
assert—to state positively; declare; affirm
assimilate—to absorb and incorporate into one's thinking
astound—amaze; to bewilder with sudden surprise
astute—cunning; having or showing a clever or shrewd mind
atrocity—brutality; a very displeasing or tasteless thing
auditor—a hearer or listener
augment—enlarge; to make greater, as in size, quantity, or strength
auspicious—successful; favored by fortune
austere—forbidding; having a severe or stern look or manner
avid—eager and enthusiastic
avow—to declare openly or admit frankly

ballad—a romantic or sentimental song
banal—commonplace; dull or stale because of overuse
bane—ruin; death; deadly harm
barrage—a heavy, prolonged attack of words or blows
barren—empty; devoid
barrio—in Spanish-speaking countries, a district or suburb of a city
bask—to warm oneself pleasantly, as in the sunlight
baste—to sew with long, loose stitches
beacon—any light for warning or guiding
bedazzle—to dazzle thoroughly
bedizen—to dress or decorate in a cheap, showy way
belated—tardy; late or too late
belligerent—at war; showing a readiness to fight or quarrel
beneficent—doing good
benevolence—a kindly, charitable act or gift
benign—good-natured; kindly
bequeath—to hand down; pass on
berate—to scold or rebuke severely
bewilder—puzzle; to confuse hopelessly
bias—a mental leaning or inclination; partiality; bent
bilge—the bulge of a barrel or cask
bilk—to cheat or swindle; defraud
blandishment—a flattering act or remark meant to persuade
blatant—disagreeably loud or boisterous
blithe—carefree; showing a gay, cheerful disposition
boisterous—rowdy; noisy and unruly
bolster—a long, narrow cushion or pillow; to support
boon—blessing; welcome benefit
boor—a rude, awkward, or ill-mannered person
bourgeois—a person whose beliefs, attitudes, and practices are conventionally middle-class
brazen—like brass in color, quality, or hardness; impudent
breach—a breaking or being broken
breadth—width; lack of narrowness
brevity—the quality of being brief
buttress—a projecting structure built against a wall to support or reinforce it

cadet—a student at a military school; younger son or brother
cadge—to beg or get by begging
cajole—to coax with flattery and insincere talk
calk—a part of a horseshoe that projects downward to prevent slipping

callous—unfeeling; lacking pity or mercy
camaraderie—loyal, warm, and friendly feeling among comrades
candid—honest or frank
capacious—roomy; spacious
caprice—whim; a sudden, impulsive change
capricious—erratic; flighty; tending to change abruptly
caption—a heading or title, as of an article
carping—tending to find fault
cartographer—a person whose work is making maps or charts
castigate—to punish or rebuke severely
catalyst—a person or thing acting as the stimulus in bringing about or hastening a result
catapult—a slingshot or type of launcher
catastrophe—any great and sudden disaster or misfortune
caustic—corrosive; that which can destroy tissue by chemical action
cavern—a cave
cerebral—intellectual; appealing to the intellect rather than the emotions
charlatan—a person who pretends to have expert knowledge or skill
chary—careful; cautious
chasten—to punish; to refine; to make purer in style
chide—to scold
chivalrous—gallant; courteous; honorable
circuitous—roundabout; indirect; devious
circumlocution—an indirect way of expressing something
circumspect—cautious; careful
circumvent—entrap; to surround or encircle with evils
citizenry—all citizens as a group
clairvoyant—having the power to perceive that which is outside of the human senses
clamor—a loud outcry; uproar
clamorous—noisy; loudly demanding or complaining
clandestine—kept secret or hidden
cleave—split; to divide by a blow
cliché—an expression or idea that has become trite
coalesce—to grow together; to unite or merge
coddle—to treat tenderly
codicil—an appendix or supplement
coerce—enforce; to bring about by using force
coeval—of the same age or period
cognizance—perception or knowledge
cognizant—aware or informed
coherent—clearly articulated; capable of logical, intelligible speech and thought
colloquial—conversational; having to do with or like conversation
combustion—the act or process of burning
commend—praise; to express approval of
commensurate—proportionate; corresponding in extent or degree
commingle—intermix; blend; to mingle together
commodity—anything bought and sold
communicable—that which can be communicated
compassion—deep sympathy; sorrow for the sufferings of others
compatible—that which can work well together, get along well together, combine well

compelling—captivating; irresistibly interesting

competent—well qualified; capable; fit

complacency—quiet satisfaction; contentment

complacent—self-satisfied; smug

complaisant—willing to please; obliging

compliance—a tendency to give in readily to others

compliant—yielding; submissive

comprehensive—able to understand fully

comprise—to include; contain

compulsion—that which compels; driving force

computation—calculation; a method of computing

concession—an act or instance of granting or yielding

conciliatory—tending to reconcile

concise—brief and to the point; short and clear

concoct—devise; invent; plan

condemn—censure; disapprove of strongly

condescension—a patronizing manner or behavior

condolence—expression of sympathy with another in grief

condone—forgive; pardon; overlook

conduit—a channel conveying fluids; a tube or protected trough for electric wires

confiscate—to seize by authority

conformity—action in accordance with customs, rules, and prevailing opinion

congregation—a gathering of people or things

congruent—in agreement; corresponding; harmonious

conjoin—to join together; unite; combine

conjunction—a joining together or being joined together

consensus—an opinion held by all or most

conspire—to plan and act together secretly

consternation—great fear or shock that makes one feel helpless or bewildered

constituent—component; a necessary part or element

consummate—supreme; complete or perfect in every way

contemn—scorn; to view with contempt

contemporaneous—existing or happening in the same period of time

contemptuous—scornful; disdainful

contentious—always ready to argue; quarrelsome

contentment—the state of being satisfied

context—the whole situation, background, or environment relevant to a particular event, personality, creation, *etc.*

contrite—penitent; feeling sorry for sins

contumacious—disobedient; obstinately resisting authority

conventional—customary; of, sanctioned by, or growing out of custom or usage

conversion—a change from one belief, religion, doctrine, opinion, *etc.* to another

convey—to make known

conviction—a strong belief

convoluted—extremely involved; intricate; complicated

copious—very plentiful; abundant

coronation—act or ceremony of crowning a sovereign

corpuscle—a very small particle

corroborate—confirm; to make more certain the validity of

countenance—facial expression; composure

coup—a sudden, successful move or action

covert—concealed; hidden; disguised

covet—to want ardently; long for with envy

crass—tasteless; insensitive; coarse

craven—very cowardly; abjectly afraid

credence—belief, especially in the reports or testimony of another

credulity—a tendency to believe too readily

crescendo—any gradual increase in force, intensity

criterion—a standard on which judgment can be based

critique—a critical analysis or evaluation

cryptic—mysterious; having a hidden or ambiguous meaning

culmination—climax; the highest point

culpable—deserving blame; blameworthy

cultivate—to promote development or growth

cumulative—accumulated; increasing in effect, size, quantity, *etc.*

cunning—skillful or clever

curator—a person in charge of a museum, library, *etc.*

cynical—sarcastic; sneering

daunt—intimidate; to make afraid or discouraged

dearth—any scarcity or lack

debacle—an overwhelming defeat

debase—cheapen; to make lower in value, quality, character, or dignity

debilitate—to make weak or feeble

decelerate—to reduce speed; slow down

decipher—decode; to make out the meaning of

decisive—showing determination or firmness

decry—denounce; to speak out against strongly and openly

deference—courteous regard or respect

defiance—open, bold resistance to authority or opposition

defiant—openly and boldly resisting

defunct—no longer living or existing; dead or extinct

defuse—to render harmless

degenerate—having sunk below a former or normal condition

delegate—to send from one place to another; appoint; assign

deleterious—injurious; harmful to health or well-being

delineate—describe; to depict in words

delirium—uncontrollably wild excitement or emotion

demagogue—a leader who gains power using popular prejudices and false claims; a leader of the common people in ancient times

demise—a ceasing to exist; death

demure—affectedly modest or shy; coy

denouement—the outcome, solution, unraveling, or clarification of a plot in a drama, story

denounce—to condemn strongly

despotic—of or like a despot; autocratic; tyrannical

destitute—living in complete poverty

desuetude—disuse; the condition of not being used

detonate—to explode violently and noisily

detumescence—a gradual shrinking of a swelling

devastate—to make helpless; overwhelm

devious—not straightforward or frank

diction—manner of expression in words

diminutive—very small; tiny

disabuse—to rid of false ideas or misconceptions

discern—make out clearly

discombobulate—upset the composure of

discomfit—make uneasy

disconcert—embarrass; confuse

discord—disagreement; conflict

discordant—disagreeing; conflicting

discourteous—impolite; rude; ill-mannered
discrepancy—difference; inconsistency
disinter—bring to light
disparage—show disrespect for; belittle
dissident—not agreeing
distillate—the essence; purified form
distraught—extremely troubled
divergence—separating; branching off
divergent—deviating; different
diverse—different; dissimilar
diversion—distraction of attention
divination—the art of foretelling future events; clever
    conjecture
doggerel—trivial, awkward, satirical verse
dogma—a doctrine; tenet; belief
dolt—a stupid, slow-witted person; blockhead
dormant—as if asleep; quiet; still
dross—waste matter; worthless stuff; rubbish
drub—to defeat soundly in a fight or contest
dubious—feeling doubt; hesitating; skeptical
dulcet—sweet-sounding; melodious
duress—constraint by threat; imprisonment

eccentricity—irregularity; oddity
eclectic—selecting from various systems, doctrines, or
    sources
efficacious—having the intended result; effective
effusive—expressing excessive emotion
embellish—decorate by adding detail; ornament
embodiment—concrete expression of an idea
emend—correct or improve
eminent—rising above other things or places
emissary—a person sent on a specific mission
emollient—softening; soothing
empathy—ability to share in another's emotions, thoughts,
    or feelings
emulate—imitate
enamor—fill with love and desire; charm
encroach—trespass or intrude
endow—provide with some talent or quality
enigma—riddle; a perplexing and ambiguous statement
enmity—hostility; antagonism
enthrall—captivate; fascinate
enumerate—count; determine the number of
epigram—a short poem with a witty point
epithet—a descriptive name or title
epitome—a person or thing that shows typical qualities of
    something
equipoise—state of balance or equilibrium
equivocal—having two or more meanings
equivocate—to be deliberately ambiguous
eradicate—wipe out; destroy; to get rid of
erroneous—mistaken; wrong
espionage—the act of spying
espouse—support or advocate
euphoria—feeling of vigor or well-being
evocation—calling forth
ewe—female sheep
exalt—elevate; to praise; glorify
exasperate—irritate or annoy very much; aggravate
excoriate—denounce harshly

exemplary—serving as a model or example
expunge—erase or remove completely
extant—still existing; not extinct
extol—praise highly
extrapolate—arrive at conclusions or results
exuberance—feeling of high spirits

faddish—having the nature of a fad
fallacious—misleading or deceptive
famine—hunger; a withering away
feckless—weak; ineffective
feint—a false show; sham
feral—untamed; wild
fervent—hot; burning; glowing
fervid—impassioned; fervent
finite—having measurable or definable limits; not infinite
fissure—a long, narrow, deep cleft or crack
flippant—frivolous and disrespectful; saucy
florid—highly decorated; gaudy; showy; ornate
flout—show scorn or contempt
forage—search for food or provisions
forbearance—patience
forbid—not permit; prohibit
forensics—debate or formal argumentation
forge—a furnace for heating metal to be wrought; to advance
forlorn—without hope; desperate
formidable—causing fear or dread
forthright—straightforward; direct; frank
fortify—strengthen
fracas—a noisy fight or loud quarrel; brawl
fractious—hard to manage; unruly
fraught—emotional; tense; anxious; distressing
frenetic—frantic; frenzied
frieze—ornamental band formed by a series of decorations
froward—not easily controlled; stubbornly willful
fulsome—offensively flattering
futile—ineffectual; trifling or unimportant

genial—cheerful; friendly; sympathetic
germinate—start developing or growing
glib—done in a smooth, offhand fashion
goad—driving impulse; spur
gouge—scrape or hollow out
gourmand—a glutton; one who indulges to excess
gregarious—fond of the company of others; sociable
gristle—cartilage found in meat
grouse—complain; grumble
grovel—behave humbly or abjectly

hackney—make trite by overuse
hapless—unfortunate; unlucky; luckless
haste—the act of hurrying; quickness of motion
haughty—proud; arrogant
heed—take careful notice of
hence—thereafter; subsequently
herbaceous—like a green leaf in texture, color, shape
heroine—girl or woman of outstanding courage and nobility
hew—chop or cut with an ax or knife; hack; gash
hierarchy—an arrangement in order of rank, grade, class
hindsight—ability to see, after the event, what should have
    been done

hirsute—hairy; shaggy; bristly
homogeneous—of the same race or kind
hone—to perfect; sharpen; yearn
hoodwink—mislead or confuse by trickery
hue—a particular shade or tint of a given color
humble—not proud; not self-assertive; modest
humdrum—lacking variety; dull; monotonous
humility—absence of pride or self-assertion
hybrid—anything of mixed origin; unlike parts
hypocrisy—pretending to be what one is not
hypothesis—unproved theory

idealist—visionary or dreamer
idiosyncrasy—personal peculiarity or mannerism
idol—object of worship; false god
idolatrous—given to idolatry or blind adoration
idolatry—worship of idols
immaculate—perfectly clean; unsoiled
impart—make known; tell; reveal
impeccable—without defect or error; flawless
impede—obstruct or delay
impenitent—without regret, shame, or remorse
imperturbable—cannot be disconcerted, disturbed, or
　　excited; impassive
impervious—not affected
impetuous—moving with great, sudden energy
impinge—to make inroads or encroach
impious—lacking respect or dutifulness
implacable—unable to be appeased or pacified; relentless
implicate—to involve or concern
imposture—fraud; deception
inadvertent—not attentive or observant; heedless
incantation—chanted words or formula
incarcerate—imprison; confine
incessant—continual; never ceasing
incinerate—burn up; cremate
incongruous—lacking harmony or agreement
incontrovertible—not disputable or debatable
incorrigible—unable to be corrected, improved, or reformed
incumbent—lying, resting on something; imposed as a duty
indignation—righteous anger
indignity—unworthiness or disgrace
indiscernible—imperceptible
indiscriminate—confused; random
indispensable—absolutely necessary or required
indomitable—not easily discouraged, defeated, or subdued
industrious—diligent; skillful
ineffable—too overwhelming to be expressed in words
inefficacious—unable to produce the desired effect
infallible—incapable of error; never wrong
infamy—bad reputation; notoriety; disgrace
ingratiate—to achieve one's good graces by conscious effort
inimical—hostile; unfriendly
innate—existing naturally rather than through acquisition
innocuous—harmless; not controversial, offensive, or
　　stimulating
inquisitor—harsh or prying questioner
insipid—not exciting or interesting; dull
insouciant—calm and untroubled; carefree
insularity—detachment; isolation
intelligible—clear; comprehensible

intemperate—lacking restraint; excessive
interstellar—between or among the stars
inveterate—habitual; of long standing; deep-rooted
irascible—easily angered; quick-tempered

jaunty—gay and carefree; sprightly; perky
jubilant—joyful and triumphant; elated; rejoicing
jurisprudence—a part or division of law

kernel—the most central part; a grain

lackluster—lacking energy or vitality
lambaste—scold or denounce severely
lament—mourn; grieve
languid—without vigor or vitality; drooping; weak
laudable—praiseworthy; commendable
laudatory—expressing praise
legion—a large number; multitude
lethargic—abnormally drowsy or dull; sluggish
limerick—nonsense poem of five anapestic lines
limn—describe
lionize—treat as a celebrity
listless—spiritless; languid
literati—scholarly or learned people
lithe—bending easily; flexible; supple
litigant—a party to a lawsuit
liturgy—ritual for public worship in any of various religions
　　or churches
livid—grayish-blue; extremely angry
loquacious—fond of talking
loquacity—talkativeness
lucid—transparent
lummox—a clumsy, stupid person

magnanimous—noble in mind
magnitude—greatness; importance or influence
malevolence—malice; spitefulness; ill will
malfeasance—wrongdoing or misconduct
malinger—pretend to be ill to escape duty or work; shirk
masque—dramatic composition
maverick—a person who takes an independent stand
maxim—statement of a general truth
mazurka—a lively Polish folk dance
meager—thin; lean; emaciated
medieval—characteristic of the Middle Ages
mellifluous—sounding sweet and smooth; honeyed
menace—threaten harm or evil
mercenary—motivated by a desire for money or other gain
merriment—gaiety and fun
metamorphose—transform
metaphor—a figure of speech containing an implied
　　comparison
methodology—system of procedures
meticulous—extremely careful about details
minatory—menacing; threatening
miser—a greedy, stingy person
mitigate—make less rigorous or less painful; moderate
mnemonic—helping, or meant to help, the memory
modicum—small amount
monarch—hereditary head of a state
mordant—biting; cutting; caustic; sarcastic

morose—ill-tempered; gloomy
myriad—indefinitely large number
mythical—imaginary; fictitious

narcissism—self-love
negate—make ineffective
nexus—a connected group or series
nib—point of a pen
nocturnal—active during the night
noisome—having a bad odor; foul-smelling
nomad—one who has no permanent home, who moves about constantly
nostalgia—longing for things of the past
notoriety—prominence or renown, often unfavorable
novice—apprentice; beginner
nuance—a slight or delicate variation

obliterate—erase; efface
obsequious—compliant; dutiful; servile
obsolete—no longer in use or practice
obstinate—unreasonably determined to have one's own way; stubborn
obtuse—not sharp or pointed; blunt
occult—secret; esoteric
odium—disgrace brought on by hateful action
officious—ready to serve; obliging
ominous—threatening; sinister
omnipotent—unlimited in power or authority
onerous—burdensome; laborious
opulent—very wealthy or rich
oration—a formal public speech
orator—eloquent public speaker
ornate—heavily ornamented or adorned
orthodox—strictly conforming to the traditional
oscillate—to be indecisive in purpose or opinion; vacillate
ossify—settle or fix rigidly
ostracism—rejection or exclusion by general consent
overwrought—overworked; fatigued

paean—a song of joy, triumph, praise
palliate—relieve without curing; make less severe
pallid—faint in color; pale
palpable—tangible; easily perceived by the senses
pantomime—action or gestures without words as a means of expression
paradigm—example or model
paradox—a statement that seems contradictory
paramount—ranking higher than any other
parch—dry up with heat
pariah—outcast
parody—a poor or weak imitation
pathology—conditions, processes, or results of a particular disease
peccadillo—minor or petty sin; slight fault
pellucid—transparent or translucent; clear
penchant—strong liking or fondness
penitent—truly sorry for having sinned and willing to atone
peremptory—intolerantly positive or assured
peril—exposure to harm or injury; danger
peripheral—outer; external; lying at the outside
pervade—to become prevalent throughout

petrous—of or like rock; hard
petulant—peevish; impatient or irritable
philistine—a person smugly narrow and conventional in views and tastes
pinion—confine or shackle
placate—stop from being angry; appease
platitude—commonplace, flat, or dull quality
plethora—overabundance; excess
poignant—emotionally touching or moving
poseur—a person who assumes attitudes or manners merely for their effect upon others
postulate—claim; demand; require
pragmatic—busy or active in a meddlesome way; practical
preclude—shut out; prevent
precocious—exhibiting premature development
predilection—preconceived liking; partiality or preference
presage—sign or warning of a future event; omen
prescience—foreknowledge
preside—exercise control or authority
prig—annoyingly pedantic person
proclivity—natural or habitual inclination
procure—obtain; secure
profane—show disrespect for sacred things; irreverent
profuse—generous, often to excess
proliferate—to reproduce (new parts) in quick succession
prolific—turning out many products of the mind
prolix—wordy; long-winded
propagate—reproduce; multiply
propinquity—nearness of relationship; kinship
propriety—properness; suitability
prosaic—matter of fact; ordinary
prose—ordinary speech; dull
protuberance—projection; bulge
provocative—stimulating; erotic
prudence—careful management
pugnacious—eager and ready to fight; quarrelsome
pundit—actual or self-professed authority
punitive—inflicting, concerned with, or directed toward punishment

quaff—drink deeply in a hearty or thirsty way
quell—crush; subdue; put an end to
querulous—full of complaint; peevish
quotidian—everyday; usual or ordinary

ramify—divide or spread out into branches
rancor—deep spite or malice
rapacious—taking by force; plundering
rasp—rough, grating tone
ratify—approve or confirm
raucous—loud and rowdy
reciprocate—cause to move alternately back and forth
recluse—secluded; solitary
recompense—repay; compensate
regale—delight with something pleasing or amusing
relegate—exile or banish
relinquish—give up; abandon
remedial—providing a remedy
reparation—restoration to good condition
replete—well-filled or plentifully supplied
reprieve—give temporary relief to, as from trouble or pain

reprobate—disapprove of strongly

repugnant—contradictory; inconsistent

requiem—musical service for the dead

resplendent—dazzling; splendid

restitution—return to a former condition or situation

reticent—habitually silent; reserved

rhapsodize—to describe in an extravagantly enthusiastic manner

rogue—a rascal; scoundrel

rubric—a category or section heading, often in red; any rule or explanatory comment

ruffian—brutal, violent, lawless person

ruse—trick or artifice

sacred—holy; of or connected with religion

salutary—healthful; beneficial

salutation—greeting, addressing, or welcoming by gestures or words

salve—balm that soothes or heals

sanctimonious—pretending to be very holy

sanction—support; encouragement; approval

savant—learned person; eminent scholar

scrupulous—having principles; extremely conscientious

scurvy—low; mean; vile; contemptible

semaphore—system of signaling

seminal—of reproduction; germinal; originative

serene—calm; peaceful; tranquil

servile—humbly yielding or submissive; of a slave or slaves

shroud—covers, protects, or screens; veil; shelter

signatory—joined in the signing of something

sinister—wicked; evil; dishonest

sinuous—not straightforward; devious

slake—make less intense by satisfying

snide—slyly malicious or derisive

sodden—filled with moisture; soaked

solace—comfort; consolation; relief

soluble—able to be dissolved

somber—dark and gloomy or dull

soporific—pertaining to sleep or sleepiness

sporadic—occasional; not constant or regular

spurious—not true or genuine; false

squalid—foul or unclean

stealth—secret, furtive, or artfully sly behavior

stigma—mark or sign indicating something not considered normal or standard

stint—restrict or limit

stolid—unexcitable; impassive

stymie—situation in which one is obstructed or frustrated

subliminal—on the threshold of consciousness; under the surface

submission—resignation; obedience; meekness

suffice—be adequate

sully—soil; stain; tarnish by disgracing

sunder—break apart; separate; split

superfluous—excessive

supine—sluggish; listless; passive

surfeit—too great an amount or supply; excess

surreptitious—acting in a secret, stealthy way

symbiosis—relationship of mutual interdependence

syntax—orderly or systematic arrangement of words

tactile—perceived by touch; tangible

tangible—having actual form and substance

tawdry—cheap and showy; gaudy; sleazy

tedium—tediousness

tempt—persuade; induce; entice

tenet—principle, doctrine, or belief held as a truth

tenuous—slender or fine; not dense

terrestrial—worldly; earthly

throng—crowd

timorous—subject to fear; timid

toupee—a man's wig

tractable—easily worked; obedient; malleable

tranquil—calm; serene; peaceful

transcend—exceed; surpass; excel

transgress—go beyond a limit

translucent—partially transparent or clear

transmute—transform; convert

treacherous—untrustworthy or insecure

treachery—perfidy; disloyalty; treason

trepidation—fearful uncertainty; anxiety

trite—no longer having originality

troubadour—minstrel or singer

truncate—cut short

tumultuous—wild and noisy; uproarious

turgid—swollen; distended

turmoil—commotion; uproar; confusion

tyranny—very cruel and unjust use of power or authority

uncanny—inexplicable; preternaturally strange; weird

underling—one in a subordinate position; inferior

unfeigned—genuine; real; sincere

unfetter—free from restraint; liberate

unification—state of being unified

unintelligible—unable to be understood; incomprehensible

unity—oneness; singleness

univocal—unambiguous

unscrupulous—not restrained by ideas of right and wrong

untenable—incapable of being occupied

untoward—inappropriate; improper

unwitting—not knowing; unaware

upbraid—rebuke severely or bitterly

uproarious—loud and boisterous

usury—interest at a high rate

utilitarian—stressing usefulness over beauty

utopia—idealized place

vacillate—sway to and fro; waver; totter

vacuum—completely empty space

vagabond—wandering; moving from place to place

vagrant—a person who lives a wandering life

valiant—brave

vapid—tasteless; flavorless; flat

variegate—vary; diversify

veer—change direction; shift

vehement—acting or moving with great force

venerate—show feelings of deep respect; revere

vengeance—revenge

vestige—a trace of something that once existed

vex—distress; afflict; plague

vicarious—serving as a substitute

villainous—evil; wicked

vitiate—spoil; corrupt
vivacious—full of life and animation; lively
vocation—trade; profession; occupation
volatile—flying or able to fly
voluble—talkative
voluminous—large; bulky; full
voracious—ravenous; gluttonous

waft—float, as on the wind
wane—grow dim or faint
wary—cautious; on one's guard
welter—to become soaked; stained; bathed
wheedle—coax; influence or persuade by flattery
whet—make keen; stimulate

wile—sly trick
wither—shrivel; wilt
witty—cleverly amusing
wrath—intense anger; rage; fury
wrench—sudden, sharp twist or pull

yacht—small vessel for pleasure cruises or racing
yearn—to have longing or desire
yielding—submissive; obedient

zeal—intense enthusiasm
zenith—highest point; peak

—Difficulty Level 2—

abstemious—exercising moderation; self-restraint
aggregation—gathered together; accumulated
alacrity—cheerful promptness; eagerness
ambient—surrounding
amorphous—shapeless; formless
antediluvian—before the flood; antiquated
apostate—fallen from the faith
arrogate—to claim or seize as one's own
ascetic—practicing self-denial; austere
ascribe—attribute to a cause
asperity—having a harsh temper; roughness
assuage—lessen; soothe
assiduous—diligent
attenuation—a thinning out
august—great dignity or grandeur
aver—affirm; declare to be true

bacchanalian—drunken
baleful—menacing; deadly
beguile—to deceive; cheat; charm; coax
beleaguer—besiege or attack; harass
bellicose—belligerent; pugnacious; warlike
belie—misrepresent; be false to
bombastic—pompous; puffed up with conceit; using inflated
    language
bovine—resembling a cow; placid or dull
bucolic—rustic; pastoral
burgeon—grow forth; send out buds

cacophony—harsh or discordant sound; dissonance
calumny—slander
capitulate—surrender
cathartic—purgative; inducing a figurative cleansing
cavil—disagree; nit-pick; make frivolous objections
celerity—swiftness
chassis—framework and working parts of an automobile
chimerical—fantastically improbable; highly unrealistic
churlish—rude; surly
circumscribe—limit
cogent—convincing
collusion—conspiring in a fraudulent scheme
comely—attractive; agreeable
compendium—brief, comprehensive summary

concord—harmony
confluence—flowing or coming together
consecrate—induct into a religious office; declare sacred
consonance—agreement; harmony
contrite—penitent; repentant; feeling sorry for sins
contumely—insult; contemptuous treatment
conundrum—riddle; difficult problem
cosset—pamper
cupidity—excessive desire for money; avarice
cursory—hasty; done without care

decimate—destroy a great number
defer—yield; delay
demur—to take exception; object
denigrate—blacken someone's reputation or character
derision—ridicule
desiccate—dry up; drain
desultory—aimless; unmethodical; unfocused
diaphanous—translucent; see-through
diatribe—speech full of bitterness
didactic—intended primarily to instruct
diffidence—modesty; shyness; lack of confidence
dilatory—given to delay or procrastination
dilettante—aimless follower of the arts; amateur; dabbler
din—loud confusing noise
disaffection—lack of trust; to cause discontent
disarming—deprive of resentment; peaceable or friendly;
    win over
discursive—rambling; passing from one topic to another
disingenuous—deceitful; lacking in candor; not frank
disparate—basically different; unrelated
disputatious—argumentative
disquietude—uneasiness; anxiety
dissemble—conceal true motives; pretend
dissolute—loose in morals or conduct
dissonant—lacking in harmony; discordant
dogmatic—adhering to a tenet
dolorous—sorrowful; having mental anguish
duplicity—deception by pretending to feel and act one way
    while acting another; bad faith; double dealing

ebullient—greatly excited
edify—instruct; correct morally

efface—erase; obliterate as if by rubbing it out
efficacy—power to produce desired effect
effrontery—shameless boldness; impudence; temerity
egregious—notorious; shocking
encomium—glowing praise
encumber—hinder
endemic—prevailing among a specific group
enervate—weaken; debilitate
engender—cause; produce
ensconce—settle in; hide; conceal
ephemeral—fleeting; short-lived
equanimity—calmness; composure
erudite—learned; scholarly
eschew—shun
esoteric—hard to understand
etymology—study of word parts
evanescent—tending to vanish like vapor
evince—show clearly
exacerbate—worsen; embitter
exculpate—clear from blame
execrable—detestable
exegesis—explanation, especially of biblical passages
exhort—urge
exigency—urgent situation
expatriate—one choosing to live abroad

facile—easily accomplished; ready or fluent
fatuous—foolish or inane
fealty—loyalty; allegiance
felicitous—well chosen; apt; suitable
ferment—agitation; commotion
fetid—malodorous
filial—pertaining to a son or daughter
flaccid—flabby
foment—stir up; instigate
fortuitous—accidental; by chance
fulminate—to thunder; explode
fungible—capable of being used in place of something else

gainsay—contradict; speak or act against
galvanize—stimulate by shock; stir up; revitalize
gambol—romp; to skip about
garrulous—loquacious; wordy; talkative
gossamer—sheer, like cobwebs
gratuitous—given freely; unwarranted
guile—slyness and cunning

hackles—hairs on back and neck
halcyon—calm; peaceful
harbinger—one that announces or foreshadows what is
    coming; precursor; portent
hummock—small hill
hedonist—one who believes pleasure is sole aim in life
hegemony—dominance, especially of one nation over
    another
heinous—atrocious; hatefully bad
hermetic—obscure and mysterious; relating to the occult
hubris—arrogance; excessive self-conceit
humus—substance formed by decaying vegetable matter

iconoclastic—attacking cherished traditions

ignominious—dishonorable; disgraceful
imbroglio—complicated situation
immolate—offer as a sacrifice
immutable—unchangeable
impalpable—imperceptible; intangible
impecunious—without money
importune—repeatedly urge
impuissance—powerlessness; feebleness
impunity—freedom from punishment or harm
inchoate—recently begun; rudimentary
incipient—becoming apparent; beginning
incisive—sharply expressive
inculcate—impress on the mind by admonition
incursion—temporary invasion
indelible—not able to be removed or erased
indemnify—make secure against loss
indigent—poor
indite—write; compose
indolent—lazy
ineluctable—irresistible; not to be escaped
inexorable—not to be moved by entreaty; unyielding;
    relentless
iniquitous—wicked; immoral
insidious—deceitful; treacherous
internecine—mutually destructive
interpolate—insert between other things
intractable—stubborn
intransigence—refusal to compromise
intrepid—brave
inure—make accustomed to something difficult
invective—abuse
inveigh—condemn; censure

jaundice—prejudice; envious; yellow
jettison—throw overboard
jocose—given to joking
jocund—merry
juggernaut—irresistible, crushing force
juxtapose—place side by side

ken—range of knowledge
kinetic—producing motion
kismet—fate
knell—tolling of a bell
knoll—little round hill

lachrymose—producing tears
laconic—using few words
largess—liberal giving; generous gift
lascivious—lustful
lassitude—weariness; debility
latent—potential but undeveloped; dormant
laxity—carelessness
legerdemain—sleight of hand
licentious—amoral; lewd and lascivious
Lilliputian—extremely small
limpid—clear
lugubrious—mournful, often to an excessive degree

maelstrom—whirlpool
maladroit—clumsy; bungling

malediction—curse
malleable—capable of being shaped
malignant—growing worse
maraud—rove in search of plunder
martinet—one who issues orders
masticate—chew
maudlin—effusively sentimental
megalomania—mania for doing grandiose things
melee—fight
mendacity—untruthfulness
mendicant—beggar
mercurial—volatile; changeable; fickle
meretricious—flashy; tawdry
miasma—a poisonous atmosphere
misanthrope—a person who hates mankind
miscreant—villain
mollify—soothe
monolithic—consisting of a single character; uniform; unyielding
moribund—dying
myopic—nearsighted; lacking foresight
munificent—generous

nadir—lowest point
nascent—incipient; coming into being
nebulous—unclear; vague; hazy; cloudy
necromancy—black magic; dealing with the dead
nefarious—wicked
nostrum—questionable medicine
nubile—marriageable
nugatory—futile; worthless

obdurate—stubborn; unyielding
obfuscate—make obscure; confuse
obloquy—slander; disgrace; infamy
obstreperous—unruly; boisterous; noisy
obviate—make unnecessary
occlude—shut; close
odious—hateful; vile
oligarchy—government by a privileged few
opprobrium—infamy; vilification
ostensible—apparent; showing outwardly; professed

panegyric—formal praise
paragon—model of perfection
parlance—language; idiom
parlay—exploit successfully
parsimonious—stingy
paucity—scarcity
pecuniary—obsessed by money
pedantic—bookish
pejorative—negative in connotation; having a tendency to make worse; disparaging
penurious—marked by penury; stingy
perdition—eternal damnation; complete ruin
perfidy—treacherous; betrayal of trust
perfunctory—indifferent; done merely as a duty; superficial
pernicious—fatal; very destructive or injurious
perspicacious—having insight; penetrating; astute
perspicuous—plainly expressed
phlegmatic—calm; not easily disturbed

piebald—of different colors; mottled; spotted
piety—devoutness; reverence for God
pillory—criticize or ridicule
piquancy—something that stimulates taste; tartness
pithy—essential; brief and to the point
polemic—controversy; argument in support of a point of view
polyglot—speaking several languages
portent—sign; omen; something that foreshadows a coming event
precipitous—abrupt or hasty
probity—honesty; integrity
prodigal—wasteful; reckless with money
prodigious—marvelous; enormous
profligate—dissolute; reckless; loose in morals; wanton
profundity—intellectual depth
promulgate—proclaim; make public; put into effect
propitious—favorable; timely
proscribe—outlaw; ostracize; banish
protract—prolong in time or space; extend; lengthen
puerile—childish; lacking in maturity
pungent—stinging; sharp in taste; caustic
pusillanimous—cowardly

quiescent—at rest; dormant; temporarily inactive
quixotic—idealistic but impractical

raconteur—someone who is skilled at telling stories or anecdotes
raffish—vulgar; crude
raiment—clothing
recalcitrant—stubborn; refractory; reluctant; unwilling; refusing to submit
recidivism—habitual return to crime
recondite—abstruse; profound; secret
recumbent—reclining; lying down
redolent—suggestive of an odor; fragrant
redoubtable—formidable; causing fear
refractory—stubborn; obstinate
remand—order back; return to service
remonstrate—object; protest
remunerative—compensating; rewarding for service
repine—complain; mourn; fret
ribald—wanton; profane or coarse; joking or mocking

sagacious—perceptive; shrewd; having insight
salacious—lustful; lecherous; lascivious
salient—standing out conspicuously; prominent
salubrious—healthful
sanguine—having a ruddy complexion; cheerful; hopeful
sardonic—sneering; sarcastic; cynical
sartorial—tailored
saturnine—sullen; sardonic; gloomy
sedition—resistance to authority
sedulous—diligent; persevering
sententious—terse; concise; aphoristic
sophistry—seemingly plausible but fallacious reasoning
specious—seeming reasonable but incorrect
spendthrift—one who spends money extravagantly
splenetic—bad-tempered; irritable
static—showing a lack of motion

stentorian—powerful in sound; extremely loud
stringent—vigorous; rigid; binding
succor—aid; assistance; comfort
supercilious—contemptuous; arrogant
sycophant—one who seeks favor by flattering; a parasite

taciturn—quiet; habitually silent
tangential—peripheral; only slightly connected
temerity—foolish or rash boldness
temporal—not lasting forever; limited by time
tenacity—holding fast
toady—servile flatterer; a "yes man"
tome—large book
torpor—lack of activity; lethargy
tortuous—winding; full of curves
traduce—to speak falsely
transcendent—exceeding usual limits; incomparable;
    beyond ordinary existence; peerless
trenchant—effective; thorough; cutting; keen
truculent—threatening; aggressively self-assertive; savage
turbid—muddy
turpitude—depravity

ubiquitous—being everywhere; omnipresent
unctuous—oily; suave
undulating—moving with a wavelike motion
unequivocal—plain; obvious

vacuity—emptiness
vainglorious—boastful
vanguard—forerunner; advance forces
venal—capable of being bribed
venial—forgivable; trivial
veracious—truthful
verbose—wordy
verdant—green; lush in vegetation
verisimilitude—appearance of truth
veritable—actual; being truly so
vicissitude—change of fortune
viscid—having a cohesive and sticky fluid
vitriolic—corrosive; sarcastic
vituperative—abusive; scolding
vociferous—clamorous; noisy
vouchsafe—bestow condescendingly; guarantee

waggish—mischievous; humorous; tricky
wanton—excessively merry; frolicsome; having no regard
    for others
winnow—sift; separate good parts from bad
winsome—agreeable; gracious
wizen—wither; shrivel

xenophobia—fear or hatred of foreigners

zealous—fervent; enthusiastic
zephyr—gentle breeze; west wind

Vocabulary: Passages

DIRECTIONS: The following is a vocabulary exercise. After reading the passage, choose the *best* answer to each item. Answer all items on the basis of what is either *explicitly stated* or *implied* in the passage. Answers are on page 879.

Items1-10 are based on the following passage.

The following passage is an excerpt from a history of the political career of Thomas Jefferson, the author of the "Declaration of Independence."

"Heartily tired" from the brutal, almost daily conflicts that erupted over questions of national policy between himself and Alexander Hamilton, Thomas Jefferson resigned his position as Secretary of State in 1793. Although his
5 Federalist opponents were convinced that this was merely a strategic withdrawal to allow him an opportunity to plan and promote his candidacy for the Presidency should Washington step down in 1796, Jefferson insisted that this retirement from public life was to be final.

10 But even in retirement, the world of politics pursued him. As the election grew nearer and it became apparent that Washington would not seek a third term, rumors of Jefferson's Presidential ambitions grew in intensity. Reacting to these continuous insinuations in a letter to James Madison,
15 Jefferson allowed that while the idea that he coveted the office of chief executive had been originated by his enemies to impugn his political motives, he had been forced to examine his true feelings on the subject for his own peace of mind. In so doing he concluded that his reasons for
20 retirement—the desire for privacy, and the delight of family life—coupled with his now failing health were insuperable barriers to public service. The "little spice of ambition" he had in his younger days had long since evaporated and the question of his Presidency was forever closed.

25 Jefferson did not actively engage in the campaign on his own behalf. The Republican party, anticipating modern campaign tactics, created grass roots sentiment for their candidate by directing their efforts toward the general populace. In newspapers, Jefferson was presented as the
30 uniform advocate of equal rights among the citizens while Adams was portrayed as the champion of rank, titles, heredity, and distinctions. Jefferson was not certain of the outcome of the election until the end of December. Under the original electoral system established by the Constitution, each
35 Presidential elector cast his ballot for two men without designating between them as to office. The candidate who received the greater number of votes became the President; the second highest, the Vice President. Jefferson foresaw on the basis of his own calculations that the electoral vote would

40 be close. He wrote to Madison that in the event of a tie, he wished for the choice to be in favor of Adams. In public life, the New Englander had always been senior to Jefferson; and so, he explained, the expression of public will being equal, Adams should be preferred for the higher honor. Jefferson, a
45 shrewd politician, realized that the transition of power from the nearly mythical Washington to a lesser luminary in the midst of the deep and bitter political divisions facing the nation could be perilous, and he had no desire to be caught in the storm that had been brewing for four years and was about
50 to break. "This is certainly not a moment to covet the helm," he wrote to Edward Rutledge. When the electoral vote was tallied, Adams emerged the victor. Rejoicing at his "escape," Jefferson was completely satisfied with the decision. Despite their obvious and basic political differences, Jefferson
55 genuinely respected John Adams as a friend and compatriot. Although Jefferson believed that Adams had deviated from the course set in 1776, in Jefferson's eyes he never suffered diminution; and Jefferson was quite confident that Adams would not steer the nation too far from its Republican tack.
60 Within two years, Jefferson's views would be drastically altered as measures such as the Alien and Sedition Acts of 1798 convinced him of the need to wrest control of the government from the Federalists.

1. In line 1, the word "heartily" most nearly means
   - (A) sincerely
   - (B) vigorously
   - (C) zealously
   - (D) gladly
   - (E) completely

2. In line 9, the word "public" most nearly means
   - (A) communal
   - (B) open
   - (C) official
   - (D) people
   - (E) popular

3. In line 9, the word "final" most nearly means
   - (A) last
   - (B) closing
   - (C) ultimate
   - (D) eventual
   - (E) conclusive

4. In line 15, the word "allowed" most nearly means

   (A) permitted
   (B) admitted
   (C) tolerated
   (D) granted
   (E) gave

5. In line 26, the word "anticipating" most nearly means

   (A) expecting
   (B) presaging
   (C) awaiting
   (D) inviting
   (E) hoping

6. In line 30, the word "uniform" most nearly means

   (A) standard
   (B) unchanging
   (C) militant
   (D) popular
   (E) honest

7. In line 31, the word "champion" most nearly means

   (A) victor
   (B) opponent
   (C) colleague
   (D) embodiment
   (E) defender

8. In line 42, the word "senior" most nearly means

   (A) older in age
   (B) higher in rank
   (C) graduate
   (D) mentor
   (E) director

9. In line 46, the word "luminary" most nearly means

   (A) bright object
   (B) famous person
   (C) office holder
   (D) candidate
   (E) winner

10. In line 58, the word "diminution" most nearly means

   (A) foreshortening
   (B) shrinkage
   (C) abatement
   (D) ill health
   (E) degradation

Vocabulary: Sentence Completions

DIRECTIONS: Select an appropriate completion for each blank in the following paragraph from the corresponding numbered lists provided below. Answers are on page 880.

Today, the Surgeon General announced the

findings of a new —— that concludes that smoking

1

represents a serious —— to non-smokers as well as to

2

——. According to the Surgeon General, disease risk

3

due to —— of tobacco smoke is not limited to the

4

—— who is smoking, but it can also extend to those

5

who —— tobacco smoke in the same room. Simple

6

—— of smokers and non-smokers within the same

7

airspace may reduce, but does not ——, exposure of

8

non-smokers to environmental smoke. A spokesperson

for the tobacco industry —— the report, saying the

9

available —— does not support the conclusion that

10

environmental tobacco smoke is a hazard to non-

smokers. On the other hand, the Coalition for

Smoking on Health, an anti-smoking organization,

—— the report and called for —— government action

11   12

to ensure a smoke-free environment for all non-smokers.

1. (A) movie
   (B) election
   (C) report
   (D) advertisement
   (E) plan

2. (A) consciousness
   (B) hazard
   (C) remedy
   (D) possibility
   (E) treatment

3. (A) cigarettes
   (B) fumes
   (C) alcoholics
   (D) pipes
   (E) smokers

4. (A) observation
   (B) criticism
   (C) improvement
   (D) inhalation
   (E) cessation

5. (A) individual
   (B) doctor
   (C) campaign
   (D) reporter
   (E) objector

6. (A) create
   (B) breathe
   (C) enjoy
   (D) ban
   (E) control

7. (A) encouragement
   (B) prohibition
   (C) separation
   (D) intermingling
   (E) prosecution

8. (A) imagine
   (B) increase
   (C) prepare
   (D) eliminate
   (E) satisfy

9. (A) purchased
   (B) prepared
   (C) understood
   (D) criticized
   (E) worshipped

10. (A) alibi
    (B) publicity
    (C) evidence
    (D) reaction
    (E) resources

11. (A) praised
    (B) rejected
    (C) prolonged
    (D) denied
    (E) proclaimed

12. (A) minimal
    (B) immediate
    (C) reactionary
    (D) uncontrolled
    (E) theoretical

DIRECTIONS: Each of the following items contains one blank. Write down a few *possible* words that you anticipate could be used to complete the sentence. Answers are on page 880.

13. Stress is the reaction an individual feels when he believes the demands of a situation —— his ability to meet them.

     exceed

     surpass

14. The —— of his career, capturing the coveted "Most Valuable Player" award, came at a time of deep personal sadness.

     zenith

     high point

     climax

15. Martin's opponent is a(n) —— speaker who is unable to elicit a reaction from a crowd on even the most emotional of issues.

16. The cold weather caused —— damage to the Florida citrus crop, prompting growers to warn that the reduced yield is likely to result in much higher prices.

17. The report is so —— that it covers all of the main points in detail and at least touches on everything that is even remotely connected with its topic.

18. The Constitution sets up a system of checks and balances among the executive, the legislative, and the judicial branches to ensure that no one branch can establish —— control over the government.

19. The females of many common species of birds have dull coloring that —— them when they are sitting on a nest in a tree or other foliage.

20. She was one of the most —— criminals of the 1930s, her name a household word and her face in every post office.

21. Although he had not been physically injured by the explosion, the violence of the shock left him temporarily ——.

22. Good teachers know that study habits learned as a youngster stay with a student for life, so they try to find ways to —— enthusiasm for studies.

DIRECTIONS: Analyze each item, underlining a few word or phrase clues that indicate whether the sentence is a "thought-extender," a "thought-reverser," or a "combined reasoning" item. There are different approaches to solving Sentence Completions items, so the labeled clues may vary. Then, label each item accordingly as "TE," "TR," or "CR." Finally, anticipate and write down a few *possible* words that could be used to complete the sentence. Answers are on page 880.

23. The survivors had been drifting for days in the lifeboat, and in their weakness, they appeared to be —— rather than living beings.

_____

_____

24. The guillotine was introduced during the French Revolution as a(n) ——, an alternative to other less humane means of execution.

_____

_____

_____

25. Because of the —— nature of the chemical, it cannot be used near an open flame.

_____

_____

26. The Mayor's proposal for a new subway line, although a(n) ——, is not a final solution to the city's transportation needs.

_____

_____

_____

27. In a pluralistic society, policies are the result of compromise, so political leaders must be —— and must accommodate the views of others.

_____

_____

_____

28. The committee report vigorously expounded the bill's strengths but also acknowledged its ——.

_____

_____

_____

29. Because there is always the danger of a power failure and disruption of elevator service, high-rise buildings, while suitable for younger persons, are not recommended for ——.

_____

_____

_____

30. For a child to be happy, his day must be very structured; when his routine is ——, he becomes nervous and irritable.

_____

_____

31. The current spirit of —— among different religions has led to a number of meetings that their leaders hope will lead to better understanding.

_____

_____

32. Our modern industrialized societies have been responsible for the greatest destruction of nature and life; indeed, it seems that more civilization results in greater ——.

_____

_____

_____

Math Skills Review

EDUCATORS' #1 CHOICE FOR SCHOOL IMPROVEMENT

Cambridge Course Concept Outline
MATH SKILLS REVIEW

Whole Numbers

Real Number System

The following diagram outlines the subsets of the *real number system*. You should be familiar with the terminology and numbers contained in several of these subsets. Each set is a subset of the one above it; for example, the set of natural numbers is a subset of the set of whole numbers, integers, rational numbers, and real numbers. Natural numbers are whole numbers, integers, rational numbers, and real numbers. Refer back to this diagram as often as necessary.

Real Numbers

Real numbers are all the numbers on the number line including fractions, integers, radicals, negatives, and zero.

Rational Numbers

Rational numbers can be expressed as a ratio of two integers ($e.g., \frac{2}{7}, -\frac{8}{2}, \frac{9}{10}$). A rational number can be expressed as a number that terminates ($e.g., -1, 0, 35, -5.25, 8.0262$) or as a non-terminating decimal with a pattern ($e.g., 4.333..., 3.2525..., -0.19621962...$). Also, $\sqrt{4}$ is a rational number since it can be expressed as $\frac{2}{1}$, or 2.

Irrational Numbers

Irrational numbers cannot be expressed as a ratio of two integers. No pattern exists when irrational numbers are expressed as decimals and they do not terminate ($e.g., \sqrt{2}, -\sqrt{3}, \pi$).

Integers

Integers are signed (positive and negative) whole numbers and the number zero: $\{..., -2, -1, 0, 1, ...\}$.

Whole Numbers

Whole numbers are the numbers used for counting and the number zero: $\{0, 1, 2, 3, ...\}$.

Natural or Counting Numbers

Natural numbers are the numbers used for counting: $\{1, 2, 3, ...\}$.

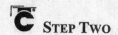
Terms and Operations

For simplicity, we will introduce the terms and operational concepts associated with all numbers using **whole numbers**. **Whole numbers** are the numbers used for counting, plus the number zero: {0, 1, 2, 3, 4, ...}. Later we will return to the other numbers of the real number system, including fractions, signed numbers, and irrational numbers.

1. Basic Terms

sum (total): The result of adding numbers together. The **sum**, or total, of 2 and 3 is 5: $2 + 3 = 5$.
difference: The result of subtracting one number from another. The **difference** between 5 and 2 is 3: $5 - 2 = 3$.
product: The result of multiplying numbers together. The **product** of 2 and 3 is 6: $2 \cdot 3 = 6$.
quotient: The result of dividing one number by another. The **quotient** when 6 is divided by 2 is 3: $6 \div 2 = 3$.
remainder: In division, if the quotient is not itself a whole number, the result can be written as a whole number quotient plus a whole number remainder. For example, $7 \div 3 = 2$, plus a **remainder** of 1.

2. Symbols of Inclusion

Sets of **parentheses**, **brackets**, and **braces** indicate the order in which operations are to be performed. The innermost symbol of inclusion indicates which operation should be executed first. Generally, operations in parentheses are done first, operations in brackets are done second, and operations in braces are done third. Parentheses, brackets, and braces have the same meaning—three different symbols are used for clarity.

Examples:

1. $(2 + 3) \cdot 4 = 20$
2. $2 + (3 \cdot 4) = 14$
3. $\frac{(2 \cdot 3) \cdot (2 + 1)}{3 \cdot (5 - 4)} = \frac{(6) \cdot (3)}{3 \cdot (1)} = \frac{18}{3} = 6$

A particularly complex statement might use parentheses, brackets, and even braces if necessary. With problems such as these, work from the inside out. Start with the operations within parentheses; then do the operations within the brackets; and finally complete the indicated operations.

Example:

$$\{[(2 \cdot 3) - 5] \cdot 1\} + [2 \cdot (4 - 1)] = (6 - 5) + (2 \cdot 3) = 1 + 6 = 7$$

3. Order of Operations

Parentheses, brackets, and braces eliminate ambiguity, but they do not always dictate the order in which operations must be done. Use this mnemonic to remember the order of operations for simplifying expressions: *Please Excuse My Dear Aunt Sally.*

Please: Parentheses, brackets, braces
Excuse: Exponents, radicals
My: Multiplication*
Dear: Division*
Aunt: Addition*
Sally: Subtraction*

*Remember: add/subtract and multiply/divide in expressions as the operations occur from left to right.

Examples:

1. $6 + 4 \cdot 3 - 5 = 6 + 12 - 5 = 18 - 5 = 13$
2. $[2(3 + 4)](3 \cdot 2) = [2(7)](6) = (14)(6) = 84$
3. $\{(2 + 7) - [(8 \cdot 6) \div 2] + 25\}\{[2 + 3(2 - 1)] \div 5\} = [(2 + 7) - (48 \div 2) + 25]\{[2 + 3(1)] \div 5\} = [(2 + 7) - 24 + 25]$
   $(5 \div 5) = (9 + 25 - 24)(1) = (9 + 1) = 10$

4. *Factoring and Canceling*

An important point to make is that even when multiplication and addition are combined, you have a choice about order of operations. In the following example, most people would probably do the addition first and then the multiplication. It is also permissible, however, to do the multiplication first.

Example:

$$5(2 + 3 + 4) = 5(9) = 45$$
$$5(2 + 3 + 4) = 5(2) + 5(3) + 5(4) = 10 + 15 + 20 = 45$$

Thus, $10 + 15 + 20$ is equal to $5(2) + 5(3) + 5(4)$, which in turn equals $5(2 + 3 + 4)$. This reverse multiplication process is called *factoring*. Factoring can be a tremendous labor-saving device. While you may be tempted to carry out the operations as indicated using a calculator, it is almost always more efficient to first simplify expressions by factoring.

Example:

$$(723)(34) - (723)(33) = 24,582 - 23,859 = 723$$
$$(723)(34) - (723)(33) = 723(34 - 33) = 723(1) = 723$$

Factoring can be combined with division for even greater simplifying power. Division of factors common to both the numerator and the denominator is called *canceling*.

Example:

$$\frac{24 + 36}{12} = \frac{12(2 + 3)}{12} = (1)(2 + 3) = 5$$

In this case, 12 can be factored from both 24 and 36. It is then possible to divide 12 by 12, which is 1.

Factors, Multiples, and Primes

Numbers that evenly divide another number are called the *factors* of that number. If a number is evenly divisible by another number, it is considered a *multiple* of that number. 1, 2, 3, 4, 6, and 12 are all factors of 12: 12 is a multiple of 2, a multiple of 3, and so on. Some numbers are not evenly divisible except by 1 and themselves. A number such as this is called a *prime* number. For example, 13 is evenly divisible by 1 and 13 but not by 2 through 12. Note: 1 is NOT considered a prime number even though it is not evenly divisible by any other number. The following are examples of prime numbers: 2, 3, 5, 7, 11, 13, 17, 19, and 23.

Example:

Let $D = 120$. How many positive factors, including 1 and 120, does D have?
➤ Express 120 using prime factors: $120 = 2(2)(2)(3)(5) = 2^3(3)(5)$. The exponents of the prime factors 2, 3, and 5, are 3, 1, and 1, respectively. Add 1 to each exponent and multiple the results together: $(3 + 1)(1 + 1)(1 + 1) = (4)(2)(2) = 16$.

Odd and Even Numbers

An *odd number* is not evenly divisible by 2; an *even number* is a number that is divisible by 2. Any number with a last digit that is 0, 2, 4, 6, or 8 is divisible by 2 and is even. Any number with a last digit that is 1, 3, 5, 7, or 9 is not evenly divisible by 2 and is odd. Zero is considered an even number. The following are important principles that govern the behavior of odd and even numbers.

PRINCIPLES OF ODD AND EVEN NUMBERS

1. EVEN ± EVEN = EVEN
2. EVEN ± ODD = ODD
3. ODD ± EVEN = ODD
4. ODD ± ODD = EVEN
5. EVEN • EVEN = EVEN
6. EVEN • ODD = EVEN
7. ODD • EVEN = EVEN
8. ODD • ODD = ODD

Examples:

1. $2 + 4 = 6$; $2 - 4 = -2$
2. $4 + 3 = 7$; $4 - 3 = 1$
3. $3 + 4 = 7$; $3 - 4 = -1$
4. $3 + 5 = 8$; $3 - 5 = -2$
5. $2 \cdot 4 = 8$
6. $2 \cdot 3 = 6$
7. $3 \cdot 2 = 6$
8. $3 \cdot 5 = 15$

The rules for multiplication do NOT apply to division. For example, if you divide the even number 4 by the even number 8, the result is $\frac{1}{2}$. Odd and even are characteristics of whole numbers and negative integers, but not fractions. A fraction is neither odd nor even.

Consecutive Integers

Consecutive integers immediately follow one another. For example, 3, 4, 5, and 6 are consecutive integers, but 3, 7, 21, and 45 are not. In a string of consecutive integers, the next number is always one more than the preceding number. Thus, if n is the first number in a string of consecutive integers, the second number is $n + 1$, the fourth number is $n + 3$, and so on.

1st	2nd	3rd	4th
n	$n + 1$	$n + 2$	$n + 3$
3	4	5	6

We can also speak of *consecutive even integers* and *consecutive odd integers*. 2, 4, 6, and 8 are consecutive even integers; 3, 5, 7, and 9 are consecutive odd integers. If n is the first number in a string of consecutive even or odd integers, the second number is $n + 2$, the third number is $n + 4$, the fourth number is $n + 6$, and so on.

1st	2nd	3rd	4th
n	$n + 2$	$n + 4$	$n + 6$
3	5	7	9
4	6	8	10

Do not be confused by the fact that the sequence for consecutive odd integers proceeds as n, $n + 2$, $n + 4$, *etc.* Even though 2, 4, *etc.* are even numbers, $n + 2$, $n + 4$, *etc.* will be odd numbers when the starting point, n, is odd.

NOTE: The SAT and PSAT allow calculators. Therefore, it is important that you learn how to use a calculator and bring the same calculator with you to the exam. Using a calculator provides greater accuracy and often saves valuable test time.

Whole Numbers

DIRECTIONS: Choose the correct answer to each of the following items. Answers are on page 882.

1. Subtracting 1 from which digit in the number 12,345 will decrease the value of the number by 1,000?

    A. 1   C. 3   E. 5
    B. 2   D. 4

2. Adding 3 to which digit in the number 736,124 will increase the value of the number by 30,000?

    A. 7   C. 6   E. 4
    B. 3   D. 2

3. Adding 1 to each digit of the number 222,222 will increase the value of the number by how much?

    A. 333,333   C. 100,000   E. 1
    B. 111,111   D. 10

4. $(1 \cdot 10,000) + (2 \cdot 1,000) + (3 \cdot 100) + (4 \cdot 10) + (5 \cdot 1) = ?$

    A. 5,000   C. 12,345   E. 543,210
    B. 15,000   D. 54,321

5. $(1 \cdot 1) + (1 \cdot 10) + (1 \cdot 100) + (1 \cdot 1,000) + (1 \cdot 10,000) = ?$

    A. 5   C. 11,111   E. 1,111,100
    B. 5,000   D. 111,110

6. $(1 \cdot 100,000) + (2 \cdot 10,000) + (3 \cdot 1,000) = ?$

    A. 123   C. 12,300   E. 1,230,000
    B. 1,230   D. 123,000

7. $(2 \cdot 1,000) + (3 \cdot 100) + (1 \cdot 10,000) + (2 \cdot 10) + 1 = ?$

    A. 11,223   C. 12,321   E. 32,121
    B. 12,132   D. 23,121

8. $(9 \cdot 10,000) + (9 \cdot 100) = ?$

    A. 99   C. 90,009   E. 90,900
    B. 9,090   D. 90,090

9. $(2 \cdot 10,000) + (8 \cdot 1,000) + (4 \cdot 10) = ?$

    A. 284   C. 2,084   E. 28,040
    B. 482   D. 2,840

10. What is the sum of 2 and 3?

    A. 1   C. 6   E. 10
    B. 5   D. 8

11. What is the sum of 5, 7, and 8?

    A. 12   C. 20   E. 28
    B. 15   D. 25

12. What is the sum of 20, 30, and 40?

    A. 60   C. 80   E. 100
    B. 70   D. 90

13. What is the difference between 8 and 3?

    A. 24   C. 8   E. 3
    B. 11   D. 5

14. What is the difference between 28 and 14?

    A. 2   C. 14   E. 392
    B. 7   D. 42

15. What is the product of 2 and 8?

    A. 4   C. 10   E. 24
    B. 6   D. 16

16. What is the product of 20 and 50?

    A. 70   C. 1,000   E. 100,000
    B. 100   D. 10,000

17. What is the product of 12 and 10?

    A. 2   C. 120   E. 300
    B. 22   D. 240

18. What is the sum of $(5 + 1)$ and $(2 + 3)$?

    A. 4   C. 24   E. 40
    B. 11   D. 33

19. What is the difference between $(5 + 2)$ and $(3 \cdot 2)$?

    A. 0   C. 3   E. 14
    B. 1   D. 10

20. What is the product of the sum of 2 and 3 and the sum of 3 and 4?

    A. 6   C. 35   E. 72
    B. 12   D. 48

21. What is the sum of the product of 2 and 3 and the product of 3 and 4?

    A. 6   C. 18   E. 72
    B. 12   D. 35

22. What is the difference between the product of 3 and 4 and the product of 2 and 3?

    A. 2   C. 6   E. 36
    B. 3   D. 12

23. What is the remainder when 12 is divided by 7?
    A. 1   C. 3   E. 5
    B. 2   D. 4

24. What is the remainder when 18 is divided by 2?
    A. 0   C. 3   E. 9
    B. 1   D. 6

25. What is the remainder when 50 is divided by 2?
    A. 0   C. 3   E. 50
    B. 1   D. 25

26. What is the remainder when 15 is divided by 8?
    A. 0   C. 4   E. 89
    B. 1   D. 7

27. What is the remainder when 15 is divided by 2?
    A. 0   C. 7   E. 14
    B. 1   D. 8

28. When both 8 and 13 are divided by a certain number, the remainder is 3. What is the number?
    A. 4   C. 6   E. 8
    B. 5   D. 7

29. When both 33 and 37 are divided by a certain number, the remainder is 1. What is the number?
    A. 4   C. 10   E. 18
    B. 9   D. 16

30. When both 12 and 19 are divided by a certain number, the remainder is 5. What is the number?
    A. 3   C. 5   E. 9
    B. 4   D. 7

31. $(4 \cdot 3) + 2 = ?$
    A. 6   C. 12   E. 26
    B. 9   D. 14

32. $(2 \cdot 3) \div (2 + 1) = ?$
    A. 0   C. 2   E. 6
    B. 1   D. 3

33. $[2 \cdot (12 \div 4)] + [6 \div (1 + 2)] = ?$
    A. 4   C. 8   E. 24
    B. 6   D. 18

34. $[(36 \div 12) \cdot (24 \div 3)] \div [(1 \cdot 3) - (18 \div 9)] = ?$
    A. 3   C. 16   E. 24
    B. 8   D. 20

35. $[(12 \cdot 3) - (3 \cdot 12)] + [(8 \div 2) \div 4] = ?$
    A. 0   C. 4   E. 16
    B. 1   D. 8

36. $(1 \cdot 2 \cdot 3 \cdot 4) - [(2 \cdot 3) + (3 \cdot 6)] = ?$
    A. 0   C. 6   E. 24
    B. 1   D. 16

37. Which of the following statements is (are) true?
    I. $(4 + 3) - 6 = 4 + (6 - 2)$
    II. $3(4 + 5) = (3 \cdot 4) + (3 \cdot 5)$
    III. $(3 + 5) \cdot 4 = 4 \cdot (5 + 3)$
    A. I only   D. II and III only
    B. II only   E. I, II, and III
    C. III only

38. $12 + 24 + 36 = ?$
    A. $3 \cdot 12$ D. $6(2) + 6(3) + 6(4)$
    B. $12(1 + 2 + 3)$ E. $12 \cdot 24 \cdot 36$
    C. $12(3 + 4 + 5)$

39. $25 + 50 + 100 = ?$
    A. $5(1 + 2 + 3)$ D. $25(1 + 2 + 4)$
    B. $5(1 + 2 + 4)$ E. $25(1 + 5 + 10)$
    C. $25(1 + 2 + 3)$

40. $\frac{99(121) - 99(120)}{33} = ?$
    A. 1   C. 33   E. 120
    B. 3   D. 99

41. $1,234(96) - 1,234(48) = ?$
    A. $1,234 \cdot 48$ D. $(1,234 \cdot 1,234)$
    B. $1,234 \cdot 96$ E. $2 \cdot 1,234$
    C. $1,234(48 + 96)$

42. How many prime numbers are greater than 20 but less than 30?
    A. 0   C. 2   E. 4
    B. 1   D. 3

43. How many prime numbers are greater that 50 but less than 60?
    A. 0   C. 2   E. 4
    B. 1   D. 3

44. Which of the following numbers is (are) prime?
    I.   11
    II. 111
    III. 1,111
    A. I only   D. I and III only
    B. II only   E. I, II, and III
    C. I and II only

45. Which of the following numbers is (are) prime?
    I.   12,345
    II. 999,999,999
    III. 1,000,000,002
    A. I only   D. I, II, and III
    B. III only   E. Neither I, II, nor III
    C. I and II only

46. What is the largest factor of both 25 and 40?
   A. 5   C. 10   E. 25
   B. 8   D. 15

47. What is the largest factor of both 6 and 9?
   A. 1   C. 6   E. 12
   B. 3   D. 9

48. What is the largest factor of both 12 and 18?
   A. 6   C. 36   E. 216
   B. 24   D. 48

49. What is the largest factor of 18, 24, and 36?
   A. 6   C. 12   E. 18
   B. 9   D. 15

50. What is the largest factor of 7, 14, and 21?
   A. 1   C. 14   E. 35
   B. 7   D. 21

51. What is the smallest multiple of both 5 and 2?
   A. 7   C. 20   E. 40
   B. 10   D. 30

52. What is the smallest multiple of both 12 and 18?
   A. 36   C. 72   E. 216
   B. 48   D. 128

53. Which of the following is (are) even?
   I.   12
   II. 36
   III. 101

   A. I only   D. I and III only
   B. II only   E. I, II, and III
   C. I and II only

54. Which of the following is (are) odd?
   I.   24 · 31
   II. 22 · 49
   III. 33 · 101

   A. I only   D. I and III only
   B. II only   E. I, II, and III
   C. III only

55. Which of the following is (are) even?
   I.   333,332 · 333,333
   II. 999,999 + 101,101
   III. 22,221 · 44,441

   A. I only   D. I and III only
   B. II only   E. I, II, and III
   C. I and II only

56. If n is an even number, then which of the following MAY NOT be even?
   A. $(n \cdot n) + n$ C. $n + 2$ E. $\frac{n}{2}$
   B. $n \cdot n - n$ D. $3(n + 2)$

57. For any whole number n, which of the following MUST be odd?
   I. $3(n + 1)$
   II. $3n + 2n$
   III. $2n - 1$

   A. I only   D. I and II only
   B. II only   E. I, II, and III
   C. III only

58. If 8 is the third number in a series of three consecutive whole numbers, what is the first number in the series?
   A. 0   C. 6   E. 11
   B. 1   D. 7

59. If 15 is the fifth number in a series of five consecutive odd numbers, what is the third number in the series?
   A. 5   C. 9   E. 13
   B. 7   D. 11

60. If m, n, and o are consecutive whole numbers that total 15, what is the largest of the three numbers?
   A. 4   C. 6   E. 17
   B. 5   D. 14

61. If $A = 2^2(3)(7) = 84$, how many positive factors, including 1 and 84, does A have?
   A. 12   C. 36   E. 84
   B. 24   D. 42

62. If $B = 5(8)(11) = 440$, how many positive factors, including 1 and 440, does B have?
   A. 8   C. 12   E. 24
   B. 10   D. 16

63. If $ab(c - d + 2e) = -6$, which of the numbers a, b, c, d, and e CANNOT be 0?
   A. a and b only   D. d only
   B. b only   E. c and d only
   C. c only

64. If $[a - 2(b + c - 3d)]e = 3$, which of the numbers a, b, c, d, and e CANNOT be 0?
   A. a C. c E. e
   B. b D. d

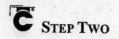

Fractions

When one whole number is divided by another whole number and the result is not a third whole number, the result is a *fraction*. For example, when 2 is divided by 3, the result is not a whole number, but rather it is the fraction $\frac{2}{3}$. Note that any whole number can also be expressed as a fraction; *e.g.*, $\frac{12}{3} = 4$, $7 = \frac{7}{1}$.

The number above the division line in the fraction is called the *numerator*; the number below the line is called the *denominator*. In a *proper fraction*, the numerator is less than the denominator, so the fraction has a value of less than 1, *e.g.*, $\frac{1}{2}$ and $\frac{3}{4}$, which are both less than 1. In an *improper fraction*, the numerator is greater than the denominator, so the fraction has a value greater than 1, *e.g.*, $\frac{3}{2}$ and $\frac{4}{3}$, which are both greater than 1. A *mixed number* consists of both a whole number and a fraction written together. For example, $2\frac{1}{2}$ is equivalent to $2 + \frac{1}{2}$, and $3\frac{4}{5}$ is equivalent to $3 + \frac{4}{5}$.

Converting Mixed Numbers to Improper Fractions

Before you add, subtract, multiply, or divide, convert *mixed numbers* to *improper fractions*. To convert a mixed number to an improper fraction, use the following procedure.

Step 1:   Use the denominator of the old fractional part of the mixed number as the new denominator.

Step 2:   Multiply the whole number part of the mixed number by the denominator of the old fractional part and add to that product the numerator of the old fractional part. This is the new numerator.

Examples:

1. Rewrite $2\frac{3}{7}$ as an improper fraction.

    ➤ The denominator of the improper fraction is 7. The numerator is determined by multiplying 7 by 2 and adding 3 to the result. To summarize: $2\frac{3}{7} \Rightarrow \frac{(2 \cdot 7) + 3}{7} = \frac{14 + 3}{7} = \frac{17}{7}$.

2. $3\frac{1}{4} = \frac{(3 \cdot 4) + 1}{4} = \frac{13}{4}$

3. $6\frac{2}{5} = \frac{(6 \cdot 5) + 2}{5} = \frac{32}{5}$

4. $2\frac{12}{13} = \frac{(2 \cdot 13) + 12}{13} = \frac{38}{13}$

Converting Improper Fractions to Mixed Numbers

To convert an improper fraction to a mixed number, reverse the process described above.

Step 1:   Divide the denominator into the numerator. The quotient becomes the whole number part of the mixed number.

Step 2:   Use the same denominator for the fraction; the numerator is the remainder of the division process in Step 1.

Examples:

1. Convert $\frac{30}{7}$ into a mixed number.

    ➤ Divide 7 into 30; the result is 4 with a remainder of 2. The 4 is the whole number part of the mixed number. Next, the numerator of the fraction is the remainder 2, and the denominator is 7. Therefore, $\frac{30}{7} = 4\frac{2}{7}$.

2. $\frac{29}{5} = 29 \div 5 = 5$ with a remainder of $4 = 5\frac{4}{5}$

3. $\frac{31}{6} = 31 \div 6 = 5$ with a remainder of $1 = 5\frac{1}{6}$

4. $\frac{43}{13} = 43 \div 13 = 3$ with a remainder of $4 = 3\frac{4}{13}$

Reducing Fractions to Lowest Terms

For reasons of convenience, it is customary to reduce all fractions to their lowest terms. When you reduce a fraction to lowest terms, you really are doing nothing but rewriting it in an equivalent form. This is accomplished by eliminating common factors in both the numerator and the denominator of the fraction.

Example:

$$\frac{8}{16} = \frac{1(8)}{2(8)} = \frac{1}{2}$$

➤ There are various ways of describing what goes on when you reduce a fraction. You might think of taking out a common factor, such as 8 in this example, and then dividing 8 into 8 (canceling). It is also possible to think of the process as dividing both the numerator and the denominator by the same number: $\frac{8}{16} = \frac{8 \div 8}{16 \div 8} = \frac{1}{2}$.

It does not matter how you describe the process, so long as you know how to reduce a fraction to its lowest terms. A fraction is expressed in lowest terms when there is no number (other than 1) that can be evenly divided into both the numerator and the denominator. For example, the fraction $\frac{8}{15}$ is in lowest terms, since there is no number (other than 1) that evenly goes into 8 that also evenly goes into 15. On the other hand, the fraction $\frac{8}{12}$ is not in lowest terms, since both 8 and 12 can be evenly divided by 4. Reducing $\frac{8}{12}$ by a factor of 4 gives $\frac{2}{3}$, which is in lowest terms since nothing (other than 1) evenly divides into both 2 and 3.

Examples:

1. $\frac{12}{36} = \frac{1 \cdot 12}{3 \cdot 12} = \frac{1}{3}$

2. $\frac{42}{48} = \frac{7 \cdot 6}{8 \cdot 6} = \frac{7}{8}$

3. $\frac{50}{125} = \frac{2 \cdot 25}{5 \cdot 25} = \frac{2}{5}$

If a fraction is particularly large, you may need to reduce it in steps. The process is largely a matter of trial and error, but there are a couple of rules that can guide you. Remember that if both the numerator and the denominator are even numbers, you can reduce the fraction by a factor of 2. Finally, if both the numerator and the denominator end in either 0 or 5, they are both divisible by 5.

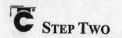

Examples:

1. $\frac{32}{64} = \frac{16(2)}{32(2)} = \frac{8(2)}{16(2)} = \frac{4(2)}{8(2)} = \frac{2(2)}{4(2)} = \frac{1(2)}{2(2)} = \frac{1}{2}$

2. $\frac{55}{100} = \frac{11(5)}{20(5)} = \frac{11}{20}$

Common Denominators

A ***common denominator*** is a number that is a multiple of the denominators of two or more fractions. For example, 12 is a multiple of both 3 and 4 (both 3 and 4 divide evenly into 12), so it is a suitable common denominator for $\frac{1}{3}$ and $\frac{1}{4}$. Converting a fraction to one with another denominator is the reverse of reducing it to lowest terms. When you multiply both the numerator and the denominator by the same number, you are really just multiplying the fraction by 1, so its value is not changed; *e.g.*, $\frac{3}{3} = 1$.

In grade school, you were taught to find the lowest common denominator for fractions. In truth, any common denominator will work. The easiest way to find a common denominator is to multiply the different denominators together. For example, a common denominator for 2 and 3 is 2 • 3, or 6; a common denominator for 3 and 4 is 3 • 4, or 12; a common denominator for 2 and 5 is 2 • 5, or 10.

What was the big deal about lowest common denominators? It is the same as reducing fractions to lowest terms: It is easier to work with smaller numbers. A common denominator for 2 and 8 is 16, but 8 is also a possibility. It is easier to deal with a fraction of denominator 8 than 16. In the final analysis, you can use any common denominator, because you can always reduce a fraction to its lowest terms.

Operations of Fractions

1. Adding Fractions

The procedure for adding fractions depends on whether or not the fractions share the same denominator. To add fractions with the same denominator, create a new fraction using that denominator. The new numerator is the sum of the old numerators.

Examples:

1. $\frac{3}{7} + \frac{2}{7} = \frac{5}{7}$

2. $\frac{2}{5} + \frac{2}{5} = \frac{4}{5}$

3. $\frac{1}{7} + \frac{2}{7} + \frac{3}{7} = \frac{6}{7}$

To add fractions with different denominators, you must first find a common denominator and convert the fractions in the manner described above. For example, $\frac{1}{3}$ and $\frac{1}{5}$. Since these fractions have unlike denominators, you must find a common denominator such as 15. Next, you convert each fraction to a fraction with a denominator of 15.

Examples:

1. $\frac{1}{3} + \frac{1}{5} = \frac{1(5)}{3(5)} + \frac{1(3)}{5(3)} = \frac{5}{15} + \frac{3}{15} = \frac{8}{15}$

2. $\frac{1}{3} + \frac{2}{7} = \frac{1(7)}{3(7)} + \frac{2(3)}{7(3)} = \frac{7}{21} + \frac{6}{21} = \frac{13}{21}$

3. $\frac{2}{9} + \frac{4}{5} = \frac{2(5)}{9(5)} + \frac{4(9)}{5(9)} = \frac{10}{45} + \frac{36}{45} = \frac{46}{45}$

To add a fraction and a whole number, you can treat the whole number as a fraction with a denominator of 1.

Example:

$$2 + \frac{1}{5} + \frac{1}{2} = \frac{2}{1} + \frac{1}{5} + \frac{1}{2} = \frac{2(10)}{1(10)} + \frac{1(2)}{5(2)} + \frac{1(5)}{2(5)} = \frac{20}{10} + \frac{2}{10} + \frac{5}{10} = \frac{27}{10}$$

To add a fraction and a mixed number, change the mixed number to an improper fraction and add together the two fractions.

Example:

$$2\frac{1}{3} + \frac{1}{3} = \frac{7}{3} + \frac{1}{3} = \frac{8}{3} = 2\frac{2}{3}$$

2. Subtracting Fractions

Follow the same procedures for subtraction of fractions as for addition, except subtract rather than add. When the fractions have the same denominators, simply subtract one numerator from the other.

Examples:

1. $\frac{5}{7} - \frac{2}{7} = \frac{3}{7}$

2. $\frac{4}{5} - \frac{3}{5} = \frac{1}{5}$

When fractions have different denominators, it is first necessary to find a common denominator.

Examples:

1. $\frac{7}{8} - \frac{3}{5} = \frac{7(5)}{8(5)} - \frac{3(8)}{5(8)} = \frac{35}{40} - \frac{24}{40} = \frac{11}{40}$

2. $\frac{5}{6} - \frac{1}{5} = \frac{5(5)}{6(5)} - \frac{1(6)}{5(6)} = \frac{25}{30} - \frac{6}{30} = \frac{19}{30}$

3. $2 - \frac{7}{6} = \frac{2}{1} - \frac{7}{6} = \frac{2(6)}{1(6)} - \frac{7(1)}{6(1)} = \frac{12}{6} - \frac{7}{6} = \frac{5}{6}$

3. Flying-X Shortcut

You do not need to worry about finding a lowest common denominator as long as you remember to reduce the result of an operation to lowest terms. This sets up a little trick for adding and subtracting fractions that makes the process a purely mechanical one—one you do not even have to think about. The trick is called the *flying-x*.

To add (or subtract) any two fractions with unlike denominators use the following procedure.

Step 1: Multiply the denominators to get a new denominator.
Step 2: Multiply the numerator of the first fraction by the denominator of the second.
Step 3: Multiply the denominator of the first fraction by the numerator of the second.
Step 4: The new numerator is the sum (or difference) of the results of Steps 2 and 3.

Once again, it is more difficult to describe the process than it is to do it. Perhaps the easiest way to learn it is to see it done. To add two fractions: $\frac{a}{b} + \frac{c}{d} = \frac{a}{b} \diagdown \!\!\!\! + \!\!\!\! \diagup \frac{c}{d} = \frac{ad + bc}{bd}$.

Example:

$$\frac{2}{7} + \frac{1}{5} = \frac{2}{7} \diagdown \!\!\!\! + \!\!\!\! \diagup \frac{1}{5} = \frac{10 + 7}{35} = \frac{17}{35}$$

As you can see, the connecting arrows make a figure that looks like an *x* floating above the ground, or a "flying-*x*."

The flying-*x* method also works for subtracting fractions.

Examples:

1. $\frac{3}{5} - \frac{1}{3} = \frac{3}{5} \gtrless \frac{1}{3} = \frac{9-5}{15} = \frac{4}{15}$

2. $\frac{6}{7} - \frac{5}{6} = \frac{6}{7} \gtrless \frac{5}{6} = \frac{36-35}{42} = \frac{1}{42}$

Of course, this may not give you the lowest terms of the fractions, so it may be necessary to reduce.

Examples:

1. $\frac{3}{4} - \frac{1}{8} = \frac{3}{4} \gtrless \frac{1}{8} = \frac{24-4}{32} = \frac{20}{32} = \frac{5}{8}$

2. $\frac{2}{3} - \frac{1}{6} = \frac{2}{3} \gtrless \frac{1}{6} = \frac{12-3}{18} = \frac{9}{18} = \frac{1}{2}$

4. *Multiplying Fractions*

Multiplication of fractions does not require a common denominator. To multiply fractions, just multiply numerators to create a new numerator, and multiply denominators to create a new denominator.

Examples:

1. $\frac{3}{4} \cdot \frac{1}{5} = \frac{3 \cdot 1}{4 \cdot 5} = \frac{3}{20}$

2. $\frac{2}{3} \cdot \frac{2}{5} = \frac{2 \cdot 2}{3 \cdot 5} = \frac{4}{15}$

5. *Dividing Fractions*

Division of fractions is the opposite of multiplication. To divide by a fraction, you invert the divisor (the fraction by which you are dividing) and then multiply the two together.

Examples:

1. $2 \div \frac{1}{4} = \frac{2}{1} \cdot \frac{4}{1} = \frac{8}{1} = 8$

2. $\frac{\frac{2}{3}}{\frac{5}{6}} = \frac{2}{3} \cdot \frac{6}{5} = \frac{12}{15} = \frac{4}{5}$

3. $\frac{1}{3} \div \frac{5}{6} = \frac{1}{3} \cdot \frac{6}{5} = \frac{6}{15} = \frac{2}{5}$

4. $\frac{2}{7} \div 2 = \frac{2}{7} \div \frac{2}{1} = \frac{2}{7} \cdot \frac{1}{2} = \frac{2}{14} = \frac{1}{7}$

5. $\frac{1}{5} \div \frac{1}{2} = \frac{1}{5} \cdot \frac{2}{1} = \frac{2}{5}$

6. $3 \div \frac{1}{5} = \frac{3}{1} \cdot \frac{5}{1} = \frac{15}{1} = 15$

Comparing Fractions

1. *Comparing Decimal Equivalents*

We can compare the values of fractions in several different ways. The first method is the one most commonly used but which often takes up valuable time. Convert the fractions to decimal equivalents and compare these values.

Example:

Find the largest value of the following fractions: $\frac{1}{2}, \frac{2}{3}, \frac{1}{8},$ and $\frac{2}{11}$.

➤ Convert the fractions to decimal equivalents: 0.5, $0.6\overline{6}$, 0.125, and $0.181\overline{8}$. Compare the values: $0.6\overline{6}$ is the largest.

2. Upward Cross-Multiplication

The second method of comparing fractions is often faster. We use *upward cross-multiplication*—multiply the denominator of the one fraction with the numerator of the other fraction in an upward direction. The fraction with the greatest product above it has the greatest value.

Example:

Find the largest value of the following fractions: $\frac{1}{2}, \frac{2}{3}, \frac{1}{8},$ and $\frac{2}{11}$.

➤ Compare $\frac{1}{2}$ with $\frac{2}{3}$ by multiplying (3)(1) and (2)(2) and place the value above each fraction: ③$\frac{1}{2} \bowtie \frac{2}{3}$④ $\Rightarrow$ 4 is larger

than 3, so $\frac{2}{3}$ is larger than $\frac{1}{2}$. Now, compare $\frac{2}{3}$ with the other two remaining fractions: ⑯$\frac{2}{3} \bowtie \frac{1}{8}$③ $\Rightarrow \frac{2}{3}$ is larger.

㉒$\frac{2}{3} \bowtie \frac{2}{11}$⑥ $\Rightarrow \frac{2}{3}$ is larger. Therefore, $\frac{2}{3}$ is the largest value.

Alternatively, you can directly compare fractions by converting all of the fractions to fractions with the same denominator. The fraction with the largest numerator is then the largest value.

Example:

Find the smallest value of the following fractions: $\frac{1}{4}, \frac{5}{14}, \frac{3}{7},$ and $\frac{1}{2}$.

➤ Convert the fractions to fractions with the same denominator: $\frac{1}{4} \cdot \frac{7}{7} = \frac{7}{28}, \frac{5}{14} \cdot \frac{2}{2} = \frac{10}{28}, \frac{3}{7} \cdot \frac{4}{4} = \frac{12}{28}, \frac{1}{2} \cdot \frac{14}{14} = \frac{14}{28}$. Since $\frac{7}{28}$ is the rewritten fraction with the smallest numerator, the fraction equivalent $\frac{1}{4}$ is the smallest value of the given fractions.

NOTE: The SAT and PSAT allow calculators. Therefore, it is important that you learn how to use a calculator and bring the same calculator with you to the exam. Using a calculator provides greater accuracy and often saves valuable test time.

Fractions

DIRECTIONS: Choose the correct answer to each of the following items. Use a calculator when necessary. Answers are on page 885.

1. $5\frac{3}{8} = ?$

   A. 1   C. $\frac{23}{8}$ E. $\frac{43}{8}$

   B. $\frac{15}{8}$ D. $\frac{35}{8}$

2. $2\frac{3}{4} = ?$

   A. $\frac{1}{4}$ C. $\frac{9}{4}$ E. $\frac{15}{4}$

   B. $\frac{3}{4}$ D. $\frac{11}{4}$

3. $3\frac{1}{12} = ?$

   A. $\frac{13}{12}$ C. $\frac{41}{12}$ E. $\frac{71}{12}$

   B. $\frac{37}{12}$ D. $\frac{53}{12}$

4. $1\frac{1}{65} = ?$

   A. $\frac{64}{65}$ C. $\frac{66}{65}$ E. $\frac{67}{66}$

   B. $\frac{65}{66}$ D. $\frac{66}{64}$

5. $5\frac{2}{7} = ?$

   A. $\frac{5}{14}$ C. $\frac{37}{7}$ E. $\frac{110}{7}$

   B. $\frac{35}{7}$ D. $\frac{70}{7}$

6. $\frac{12}{8} = ?$

   A. 4   C. $2\frac{1}{2}$ E. $1\frac{1}{4}$

   B. 3   D. $1\frac{1}{2}$

7. $\frac{20}{6} = ?$

   A. $3\frac{1}{3}$ C. $4\frac{1}{6}$ E. 6

   B. $3\frac{2}{3}$ D. $4\frac{1}{3}$

8. $\frac{23}{13} = ?$

   A. 10   C. $1\frac{10}{13}$ E. $\frac{7}{13}$

   B. $7\frac{7}{13}$ D. $\frac{13}{23}$

9. $\frac{25}{4} = ?$

   A. $\frac{4}{25}$ C. $1\frac{1}{8}$ E. $6\frac{1}{4}$

   B. $\frac{4}{12}$ D. $1\frac{1}{4}$

10. $\frac{201}{100} = ?$

   A. $1\frac{1}{100}$ C. $2\frac{1}{100}$ E. 101

   B. $1\frac{1}{50}$ D. $2\frac{1}{50}$

11. $\frac{3}{12} = ?$

   A. $\frac{1}{6}$ C. $\frac{1}{3}$ E. $\frac{3}{4}$

   B. $\frac{1}{4}$ D. $\frac{1}{2}$

12. $\frac{27}{81} = ?$

   A. $\frac{1}{9}$ C. $\frac{1}{3}$ E. $\frac{2}{3}$

   B. $\frac{2}{9}$ D. $\frac{4}{9}$

13. $\frac{125}{625} = ?$

   A. $\frac{1}{10}$ C. $\frac{2}{5}$ E. $\frac{4}{5}$

   B. $\frac{1}{5}$ D. $\frac{7}{10}$

14. $\frac{39}{52} = ?$

   A. $\frac{1}{5}$ C. $\frac{1}{3}$ E. $\frac{3}{4}$

   B. $\frac{1}{4}$ D. $\frac{1}{2}$

15. $\frac{121}{132} = ?$

   A. $\frac{1}{11}$ C. $\frac{9}{10}$ E. $\frac{11}{12}$

   B. $\frac{1}{10}$ D. $\frac{10}{11}$

16. Which of the following is equal to $\frac{4}{25}$?

 A. $\frac{8}{50}$ C. $\frac{12}{150}$ E. $\frac{200}{250}$

 B. $\frac{8}{100}$ D. $\frac{160}{200}$

17. Which of the following is NOT equal to $\frac{3}{8}$?

 A. $\frac{6}{16}$ C. $\frac{31}{81}$ E. $\frac{120}{320}$

 B. $\frac{15}{40}$ D. $\frac{33}{88}$

18. Which of the following is NOT equal to $\frac{3}{4}$?

 A. $\frac{6}{8}$ C. $\frac{20}{24}$ E. $\frac{300}{400}$

 B. $\frac{12}{16}$ D. $\frac{36}{48}$

19. Which of the following is NOT equal to $\frac{5}{6}$?

 A. $\frac{25}{30}$ C. $\frac{50}{60}$ E. $\frac{100}{120}$

 B. $\frac{45}{50}$ D. $\frac{55}{66}$

20. Which of the following is NOT equal to $\frac{1}{6}$?

 A. $\frac{2}{12}$ C. $\frac{4}{24}$ E. $\frac{6}{40}$

 B. $\frac{3}{18}$ D. $\frac{5}{30}$

21. $\frac{1}{7}+\frac{2}{7}=?$

 A. $\frac{2}{7}$ C. $\frac{6}{7}$ E. $\frac{12}{7}$

 B. $\frac{3}{7}$ D. $\frac{8}{7}$

22. $\frac{5}{8}+\frac{1}{8}=?$

 A. $\frac{1}{2}$ C. $\frac{7}{8}$ E. $\frac{4}{3}$

 B. $\frac{3}{4}$ D. $\frac{8}{5}$

23. $\frac{12}{13}+\frac{12}{13}=?$

 A. 0 C. $\frac{12}{26}$ E. $\frac{26}{13}$

 B. 1 D. $\frac{24}{13}$

24. $\frac{3}{8}+\frac{5}{8}=?$

 A. $\frac{2}{8}$ C. $\frac{5}{4}$ E. $\frac{12}{5}$

 B. 1 D. $\frac{8}{5}$

25. $\frac{1}{11}+\frac{2}{11}+\frac{7}{11}=?$

 A. $\frac{4}{11}$ C. $\frac{10}{11}$ E. $\frac{11}{7}$

 B. $\frac{7}{11}$ D. $\frac{11}{10}$

26. $\frac{3}{8}+\frac{5}{6}=?$

 A. $\frac{8}{48}$ C. $\frac{29}{24}$ E. $\frac{14}{8}$

 B. $\frac{8}{14}$ D. $\frac{3}{2}$

27. $\frac{1}{8}+\frac{1}{7}=?$

 A. $\frac{1}{56}$ C. $\frac{1}{15}$ E. $\frac{15}{56}$

 B. $\frac{1}{27}$ D. $\frac{1}{5}$

28. $\frac{1}{12}+\frac{1}{7}=?$

 A. $\frac{19}{84}$ C. $\frac{10}{19}$ E. $\frac{5}{4}$

 B. $\frac{19}{42}$ D. $\frac{20}{19}$

29. $\frac{3}{5}+\frac{2}{11}=?$

 A. $\frac{43}{110}$ C. $\frac{54}{55}$ E. $\frac{100}{43}$

 B. $\frac{43}{55}$ D. $\frac{55}{54}$

30. $\frac{1}{2}+\frac{1}{3}+\frac{1}{6}=?$

 A. $\frac{1}{36}$ C. 1 E. $\frac{7}{3}$

 B. $\frac{1}{12}$ D. $\frac{7}{6}$

31. $\frac{2}{3}+\frac{3}{6}+\frac{4}{6}=?$

 A. $\frac{9}{20}$ C. $\frac{7}{6}$ E. $\frac{16}{3}$

 B. $\frac{6}{7}$ D. $\frac{11}{6}$

32. $\frac{2}{3}-\frac{1}{3}=?$

 A. $\frac{1}{6}$ C. $\frac{2}{3}$ E. $\frac{6}{3}$

 B. $\frac{1}{3}$ D. $\frac{4}{3}$

33. $\frac{5}{7}-\frac{4}{7}=?$

 A. $\frac{9}{7}$ C. $\frac{5}{7}$ E. $\frac{1}{49}$

 B. 1 D. $\frac{1}{7}$

34. $\frac{9}{10}-\frac{1}{5}=?$

 A. $\frac{7}{10}$ C. $\frac{10}{7}$ E. $\frac{20}{7}$

 B. $\frac{7}{5}$ D. $\frac{18}{7}$

35. $\frac{3}{2}-\frac{1}{4}=?$

 A. $\frac{5}{4}$ C. $\frac{3}{4}$ E. $\frac{1}{3}$

 B. $\frac{4}{5}$ D. $\frac{2}{3}$

36. $2\frac{1}{2} - \frac{7}{8} = ?$

   A. $\frac{9}{2}$ C. $\frac{13}{8}$ E. $\frac{4}{5}$

   B. $\frac{5}{2}$ D. $\frac{5}{4}$

37. $2\frac{2}{3} - 1\frac{1}{6} = ?$

   A. $1\frac{1}{6}$ C. $1\frac{1}{2}$ E. 2

   B. $1\frac{1}{3}$ D. $1\frac{2}{3}$

38. $\frac{1}{2} \cdot \frac{2}{3} = ?$

   A. $\frac{1}{6}$ C. $\frac{1}{2}$ E. $\frac{3}{4}$

   B. $\frac{1}{3}$ D. $\frac{2}{3}$

39. $\frac{2}{7} \cdot \frac{1}{4} = ?$

   A. $\frac{1}{63}$ C. $\frac{1}{4}$ E. $\frac{5}{9}$

   B. $\frac{1}{14}$ D. $\frac{3}{8}$

40. $\frac{1}{3} \cdot \frac{1}{3} = ?$

   A. $\frac{1}{9}$ C. $\frac{1}{3}$ E. $\frac{3}{2}$

   B. $\frac{1}{6}$ D. $\frac{2}{3}$

41. $\frac{1}{2} \cdot \frac{1}{2} \cdot \frac{1}{2} = ?$

   A. $\frac{1}{16}$ C. $\frac{3}{16}$ E. $\frac{2}{3}$

   B. $\frac{1}{8}$ D. $\frac{3}{8}$

42. $\frac{2}{3} \cdot \frac{3}{4} \cdot \frac{4}{5} = ?$

   A. $\frac{2}{5}$ C. $\frac{2}{3}$ E. $\frac{4}{5}$

   B. $\frac{3}{5}$ D. $\frac{3}{4}$

43. $\frac{1}{4} \cdot \frac{1}{8} \cdot 3 = ?$

   A. $\frac{3}{32}$ C. $\frac{1}{4}$ E. $\frac{3}{4}$

   B. $\frac{1}{8}$ D. $\frac{1}{2}$

44. $\frac{1}{3} \cdot \frac{1}{6} \cdot 12 = ?$

   A. $\frac{1}{3}$ C. 1   E. 2

   B. $\frac{2}{3}$ D. $\frac{3}{2}$

45. $\frac{7}{8} \div \frac{3}{4} = ?$

   A. $\frac{7}{6}$ C. $\frac{3}{4}$ E. $\frac{1}{8}$

   B. 1   D. $\frac{1}{3}$

46. $\frac{5}{7} \div \frac{1}{7} = ?$

   A. $\frac{1}{7}$ C. 5   E. 12

   B. $\frac{1}{5}$ D. 7

47. $\frac{1}{12} \div \frac{1}{12} = ?$

   A. $\frac{1}{144}$ C. 12   E. 144

   B. 1   D. 18

48. $2 \div \frac{1}{11} = ?$

   A. 22   C. $\frac{11}{2}$ E. $\frac{1}{22}$

   B. 11   D. $\frac{11}{22}$

49. $\frac{8}{9} \div \frac{7}{8} = ?$

   A. $\frac{64}{63}$ C. $\frac{7}{9}$ E. $\frac{1}{3}$

   B. $\frac{9}{7}$ D. $\frac{1}{2}$

50. $\frac{1}{10} \div \frac{3}{5} = ?$

   A. $\frac{1}{6}$ C. $\frac{3}{10}$ E. $\frac{5}{3}$

   B. $\frac{1}{5}$ D. $\frac{3}{5}$

51. $\left(\frac{1}{4} + \frac{2}{3}\right) \cdot \left(\frac{3}{2} + \frac{1}{4}\right) = ?$

   A. $\frac{21}{47}$ C. $\frac{51}{48}$ E. $\frac{105}{51}$

   B. $\frac{33}{49}$ D. $\frac{77}{48}$

52. $\left(\frac{2}{3} \cdot \frac{1}{6}\right) \div \left(\frac{1}{2} \cdot \frac{1}{4}\right) = ?$

   A. $\frac{1}{18}$ C. $\frac{8}{9}$ E. $\frac{15}{75}$

   B. $\frac{2}{9}$ D. $\frac{11}{8}$

53. $\left[\left(\frac{1}{3} + \frac{1}{2}\right) \cdot \left(\frac{2}{3} - \frac{1}{3}\right)\right] \cdot 18 = ?$

   A. 5   C. $\frac{5}{6}$ E. $\frac{2}{3}$

   B. $\frac{7}{8}$ D. $\frac{4}{5}$

54. $\left[\left(\frac{1}{3} \div \frac{1}{6}\right) \cdot \left(\frac{2}{3} \div \frac{1}{3}\right)\right] \cdot \left(\frac{1}{2} + \frac{3}{4}\right) = ?$

   A. 5   C. 3   E. 1

   B. 4   D. 2

55. Simplify: $8\left(\frac{1}{3} + \frac{3}{4}\right)$.

   A. $\frac{1}{3}$ C. $\frac{16}{3}$ E. $\frac{26}{3}$

   B. $\frac{4}{3}$ D. $\frac{19}{3}$

56. Simplify: $\frac{1}{4} - \frac{1}{5}$.

   A. $\frac{1}{5}$ C. $\frac{1}{20}$ E. $\frac{4}{5}$

   B. $\frac{1}{3}$ D. $\frac{3}{4}$

57. Simplify: $\frac{\frac{4}{9}}{\frac{2}{5}}$.

   A. $\frac{1}{2}$ C. $\frac{8}{45}$ E. $1\frac{1}{9}$

   B. $\frac{3}{4}$ D. $\frac{11}{9}$

58. Simplify: $\left(-\frac{1}{2}\right)^2 + \left(\frac{1}{4}\right)^2 + (-2)\left(\frac{1}{2}\right)^2$.

   A. $-\frac{3}{16}$ C. $\frac{1}{3}$ E. $\frac{4}{5}$

   B. $-\frac{1}{5}$ D. $\frac{3}{4}$

59. Which fraction is the largest?

   A. $\frac{9}{16}$ C. $\frac{5}{8}$ E. $\frac{1}{2}$

   B. $\frac{7}{10}$ D. $\frac{4}{5}$

60. Jughead eats $\frac{2}{5}$ of a pound of cake each day. How many pounds of cake does Jughead eat in 3 weeks?

   A. $4\frac{1}{2}$ C. $5\frac{1}{5}$ E. 10

   B. $5\frac{3}{4}$ D. $8\frac{2}{5}$

61. Chompa eats $\frac{3}{8}$ of a bag of candy per day. How many weeks will 42 bags of candy last Chompa?

   A. 4   C. 9   E. 16

   B. 5   D. 12

62. If Chiquita can eat $2\frac{1}{2}$ bananas per day, how many bananas can Chiquita eat in 4 weeks?

   A. 70   C. 80   E. 90

   B. 75   D. 85

63. One brass rod measures $3\frac{5}{16}$ inches long and another brass rod measures $2\frac{3}{4}$ inches long. What is the total length, in inches, of the two rods combined?

   A. $6\frac{9}{16}$ C. $5\frac{1}{2}$ E. $5\frac{1}{32}$

   B. $6\frac{1}{16}$ D. $5\frac{1}{16}$

64. Which of the following equals the number of half-pound packages of tea that can be taken out of a box that holds $10\frac{1}{2}$ pounds of tea?

   A. 5   C. 11   E. 21

   B. $10\frac{1}{2}$ D. $20\frac{1}{122}$

65. If each bag of tokens weighs $5\frac{3}{4}$ pounds, how many pounds do 3 bags weigh?

   A. $7\frac{1}{4}$ C. $16\frac{1}{2}$ E. $17\frac{1}{2}$

   B. $15\frac{3}{4}$ D. $17\frac{1}{4}$

66. During one week, a man traveled $3\frac{1}{2}$, $1\frac{1}{4}$, $1\frac{1}{6}$, and $2\frac{3}{8}$ miles. The next week, he traveled $\frac{1}{4}$, $\frac{3}{8}$, $\frac{9}{16}$, $3\frac{1}{16}$, $2\frac{5}{8}$, and $3\frac{3}{16}$ miles. How many more miles did he travel the second week than the first week?

   A. $1\frac{37}{48}$ C. $1\frac{3}{4}$ E. $\frac{47}{48}$

   B. $1\frac{1}{2}$ D. 1

67. A certain type of board is sold only in lengths of multiples of 2 feet. The shortest board sold is 6 feet and the longest is 24 feet. A builder needs a large quantity of this type of board in $5\frac{1}{2}$-foot lengths. To minimize waste, which of the following board lengths should be ordered?

   A. 6-ft.   C. 22-ft.   E. 26-ft.

   B. 12-ft.   D. 24-ft.

68. A man spent $\frac{15}{16}$ of his entire fortune in buying a car for $7,500. How much money did he possess?

   A. $6,000   C. $7,000   E. $8,500

   B. $6,500   D. $8,000

69. The population of a town was 54,000 in the last census. Since then it has increased $\frac{2}{3}$. Which of the following equals its present population?

   A. 18,000   C. 72,000   E. 108,000

   B. 36,000   D. 90,000

70. $\frac{1}{3}$ of the liquid contents of a can evaporates on the first day and $\frac{3}{4}$ of the remainder evaporates on the second day. Which of the following equals the fractional part of the original contents remaining at the close of the second day?

   A. $\frac{5}{12}$ C. $\frac{1}{6}$ E. $\frac{4}{7}$

   B. $\frac{7}{12}$ D. $\frac{1}{2}$

71. A car is run until the gas tank is $\frac{1}{8}$ full. The tank is then filled to capacity by putting in 14 gallons. What is the the gas tank's capacity, in gallons?

   A. 14   C. 16   E. 18

   B. 15   D. 17

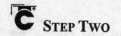

Signed Numbers

Numbers are just positions in a linear system. Each number is one greater than the number to its left and one less than the number to its right. The following number line represents the *integer number system*, which consists of the signed (positive and negative) whole numbers and zero:

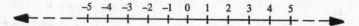

With both positive and negative integers, each position is one more than the position before it and one less than the position after it: −1 is one less than zero and one more than −2; −2 is one less than −1 and one more than −3. The minus sign indicates the direction in which the number system is moving with reference to zero. If you move to the right, you are going in the positive direction; to the left, in the negative direction.

It is natural to use negative numbers in everyday situations, such as games and banking: An overdrawn checking account results in a minus balance. You can manipulate negative numbers using the basic operations (addition, subtraction, multiplication, and division). To help explain these operations, we introduce the concept of absolute value.

Absolute Value

The *absolute value* of a number is its value without any sign and so it is always a positive numerical value: $|x| \geq 0$. Therefore, $|x| = x$ if $x \geq 0$ and $|x| = -x$ if $x < 0$. A number's absolute value is its distance on the number line from the origin, without regard to direction: $|x| = |-x|$.

Examples:

1. $|4| = 4$
2. $|-10| = 10$
3. $|5| - |3| = 5 - 3 = 2$
4. $|-2| + |-3| = 2 + 3 = 5$

This idea of value, without regard to direction, helps to clarify negative number operations.

Adding Negative Numbers

To add negative numbers to other numbers, subtract the absolute value of the negative numbers.

Example:

$10 + (-4) = 10 - |-4| = 10 - 4 = 6$

➤ The number line illustrates the logic: Start at 10 and move the counter four units in the negative direction. The result is 6:

Follow this procedure even if you wind up with a negative result, as illustrated in the following example.

Example:

$10 + (-12) = 10 - |-12| = 10 - 12 = -2$

➤ Start at 10 and move the counter 12 units in a negative direction. The result is two units to the left of zero, or −2:

Similarly, the procedure works when you add a negative number to another negative number.

Example:

$-3 + -2 = -3 - |-2| = -3 - 2 = -5$

➤ Begin at −3, and move the counter two units in the negative direction. The result is −5:

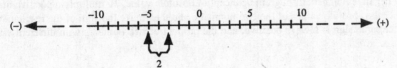

Any addition of a negative number is equivalent to subtraction of a positive number.

Examples:

1. $5 + (-2) = 5 - 2 = 3$
2. $7 + (-7) = 7 - 7 = 0$

Subtracting Negative Numbers

Subtracting negative numbers is a little different. When you subtract a negative number, you are really adding, since the number itself has a negative value. It is like a double negative: "It is not true that Bob's not here" means that Bob is here. To subtract a negative number from another quantity, add the absolute value of the negative number to the other quantity.

Example:

$10 - (-5) = 10 + |-5| = 10 + 5 = 15$

➤ Start at 10: Since the minus signs cancel each other out, move the counter in the positive direction. The result is 15:

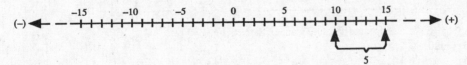

Follow this procedure no matter where you start, even if you are subtracting a negative number from zero or from another negative number.

Example:

$-5 - (-10) = -5 + |-10| = -5 + 10 = 5$

➤ Start at −5: Since the minus signs cancel each other out, move the counter in the positive direction. The result is 5:

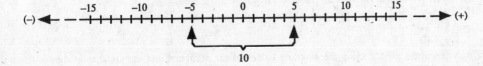

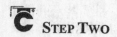

Any subtraction of a negative number is equivalent to addition of a positive number.

Examples:

1. $4 - (-4) = 4 + 4 = 8$
2. $0 - (-7) = 0 + 7 = 7$
3. $-8 - (-4) = -8 + 4 = -4$

Multiplying Negative Numbers

We can also explain the rules for multiplying negative numbers through the concept of absolute value. To multiply a positive number by a negative number, simply multiply together the absolute values of the two numbers, and then make the sign of the resultant value negative. The product of two numbers with the same sign is always positive, and the product of two numbers with different signs is always negative.

Examples:

1. $3 \cdot -6 = -(|3| \cdot |-6|) = -(3 \cdot 6) = -18$
2. $-2 \cdot 4 = -(|-2| \cdot |4|) = -(2 \cdot 4) = -8$

A way of remembering this is to think that the minus sign has "tainted" the problem, so the result must be negative.

To multiply a negative number by a negative number, multiply together the absolute values of the two numbers, and then make the sign of this value positive. The product of two negative numbers is always positive.

Example:

$-3 \cdot -6 = |-3| \cdot |-6| = 3 \cdot 6 = 18$

This is like saying that two wrongs DO make a right—a negative times a negative produces a positive.

Any product involving an odd number of negatives will always be negative. Any product involving an even number of negatives will always be positive.

Examples:

1. $-1 \cdot -2 = 2$
2. $-1 \cdot -2 \cdot -3 = -6$
3. $-1 \cdot -2 \cdot -3 \cdot -4 \cdot = 24$
4. $-1 \cdot -2 \cdot -3 \cdot -4 \cdot -5 = -120$

Dividing Negative Numbers

When dividing negative numbers, the same rules apply as with multiplication. If the division involves a positive number and a negative number, divide using the absolute values of the numbers, and then make the sign of the resultant value negative.

Examples:

1. $6 \div -3 = -(|6| \div |-3|) = -(6 \div 3) = -2$
2. $-8 \div 2 = -(|-8| \div |2|) = -(8 \div 2) = -4$

For division involving two negative numbers, divide using the absolute values of the numbers, and then make the sign of this value positive.

Example:

$$-8 \div -4 = |-8| \div |-4| = 8 \div 4 = 2$$

Any quotient involving an odd number of negatives will always be negative. Any quotient involving an even number of negatives will always be positive.

Examples:

1. $\frac{4}{-2} = -2$

2. $\frac{(-2)(6)}{-4} = \frac{-12}{-4} = 3$

3. $\frac{(3)(-2)(-4)}{(-1)(2)} = -(3 \cdot 4) = -12$

Summary of Signed Numbers

PRINCIPLES FOR WORKING WITH NEGATIVE NUMBERS

1. *Subtraction* of a *negative* number is equivalent to *addition* of a *positive* number.

2. *Addition* of a *negative* number is equivalent to *subtraction* of a *positive* number.

3. *Multiplication* or *division* involving an *odd* number of *negative* numbers always results in a *negative* number.

4. *Multiplication* or *division* involving an *even* number of *negative* numbers always results in a *positive* number.

These rules govern operations with all signed numbers. Be careful how you apply the rules to complicated expressions; just take each item step by step.

Example:

$$\frac{(2 \cdot -3) - (-2 + -12)}{(-8 \div 2) \cdot (2 + -4)} = \frac{(-6) - (-14)}{(-4) \cdot (-2)} = \frac{-6 + 14}{4 \cdot 2} = \frac{14 - 6}{8} = \frac{8}{8} = 1$$

NOTE: The SAT and PSAT allow calculators. Therefore, it is important that you learn how to use a calculator and bring the same calculator with you to the exam. Using a calculator provides greater accuracy and often saves valuable test time.

Signed Numbers

DIRECTIONS: Choose the correct answer to each of the following items. Use a calculator when necessary. Answers are on page 888.

Items #1-15: Each of the following items include a number line and a counter. Select the letter of the correct position for the counter after the indicated operations.

Example:
2 + 3 = ?

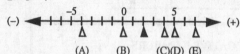

The original position of the counter is 2. If you move it three units in the positive direction, the result is 5, (D).

1. 3 + 1 = ?

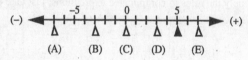

2. 5 − 2 = ?

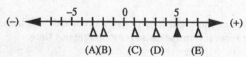

3. 5 + (−2) = ?

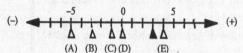

4. 3 + 2 + (−7) = ?

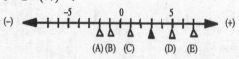

5. 2 + (−4) = ?

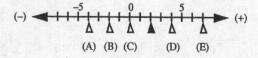

6. −2 + (−2) = ?

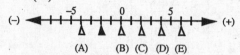

7. 4 + (−2) + (−2) = ?

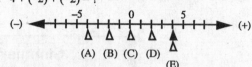

8. −4 + (−1) + (−1) = ?

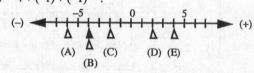

9. −4 + 8 = ?

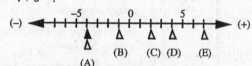

10. −2 + 2 + (−1) = ?

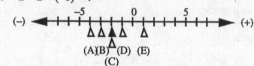

11. 2 − (−1) = ?

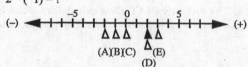

12. 5 − (−2) = ?

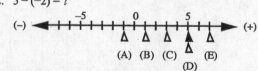

13. 0 − (−4) = ?

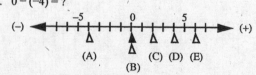

14. $-2 - (-1) = ?$

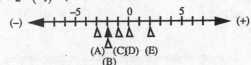

15. $-3 - (-1) - (-2) = ?$

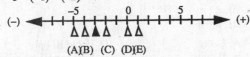

<u>Items #16-60:</u> Determine the correct answer for each of these problems without the aid of a number line.

16. $5 + 8 + (-2) + (-1) = ?$

   A. 3   C. 10   E. 23
   B. 7   D. 13

17. $12 - 7 + 6 + (-1) = ?$

   A. 2   C. 10   E. 18
   B. 6   D. 14

18. $3 + (-3) = ?$

   A. −6   C. 0   E. 6
   B. −3   D. 3

19. $0 + (-12) = ?$

   A. −12   C. −1   E. 12
   B. −6   D. 0

20. $-3 + 1 = ?$

   A. −4   C. 2   E. 8
   B. −2   D. 4

21. $-2 + (-6) = ?$

   A. −8   C. −2   E. 4
   B. −4   D. 2

22. $-2 + (-3) + (-4) = ?$

   A. −24   C. −6   E. 6
   B. −9   D. 0

23. $100 + (-99) = ?$

   A. −199   C. −1   E. 99
   B. −99   D. 1

24. $14 - (-2) = ?$

   A. 16   C. 4   E. −14
   B. 12   D. −2

25. $2 - (-5) = ?$

   A. 7   C. −2   E. −7
   B. 3   D. −3

26. $0 - (-4) = ?$

   A. −8   C. 0   E. 8
   B. −4   D. 4

27. $-2 - (-3) = ?$

   A. −6   C. −1   E. 3
   B. −5   D. 1

28. $-5 - (-1) - 1 = ?$

   A. −7   C. −3   E. 2
   B. −5   D. −1

29. $(5 - 1) + (1 - 5) = ?$

   A. −5   C. 0   E. 5
   B. −3   D. 3

30. $[2 - (-6)] - [-2 + (-1)] = ?$

   A. −2   C. 1   E. 11
   B. −1   D. 5

31. $1 \cdot -2 = ?$

   A. −2   C. $-\frac{1}{2}$ E. 2
   B. −1   D. 1

32. $-8 \cdot 6 = ?$

   A. −48   C. 2   E. 48
   B. −2   D. 14

33. $-10 \cdot -10 = ?$

   A. −100   C. 0   E. 100
   B. −20   D. 20

34. $-2 \cdot -1 \cdot 1 = ?$

   A. −3   C. 1   E. 4
   B. −2   D. 2

35. $-10 \cdot -10 \cdot -10 = ?$

   A. −1,000 C. −1   E. 1,000
   B. −30   D. 1

36. $-2 \cdot -2 \cdot -2 \cdot -2 = ?$

   A. −32   C. 4   E. 32
   B. −8   D. 16

37. $-1 \cdot -1 \cdot -1 \cdot -1 \cdot -1 \cdot -1 \cdot -1 \cdot -1 \cdot -1 \cdot -1 = ?$

   A. −10   C. 0   E. 10
   B. −1   D. 1

38. $4 \div -2 = ?$

   A. −8   C. $-\frac{1}{2}$ E. 8
   B. −2   D. 2

39. $-12 \div 4 = ?$

    A. -4 C. -2 E. 4
    B. -3 D. 3

40. $-12 \div -12 = ?$

    A. -144 C. 1 E. 144
    B. -1 D. 24

41. $[7 - (-6)] + [3 \cdot (2 - 4)] = ?$

    A. -2 C. 7 E. 23
    B. 0 D. 12

42. $[2 \cdot (-3)][1 \cdot (-4)][2 \cdot (-1)] = ?$

    A. -48 C. 2 E. 56
    B. -16 D. 28

43. $(6 \cdot -2) \div (3 \cdot -4) = ?$

    A. -12 C. 1 E. 24
    B. -1 D. 3

44. $\{[4 - (-3)] + [7 - (-1)]\}[-3 - (-2)] = ?$

    A. -25 C. -7 E. 8
    B. -15 D. -1

45. $[(2 \cdot -1) + (4 \div -2)][(-6 + 6) - (2 - 3)] = ?$

    A. 5 C. -2 E. -23
    B. 2 D. -4

46. $(2 - 3)(3 - 2)(4 - 3)(3 - 4)(5 - 4)(4 - 5) = ?$

    A. -625 C. 1 E. 625
    B. -1 D. 50

47. $[2(3 - 4)] + [(125 \div -25)(1 \cdot -2)] = ?$

    A. -12 C. 2 E. 125
    B. -8 D. 8

48. $-\frac{1}{2} \cdot 2 \cdot -\frac{1}{2} \cdot 2 \cdot -\frac{1}{2} \cdot 2 = ?$

    A. -16 C. -1 E. 2
    B. -8 D. 1

49. $[(2 \cdot 3) \div (-6 \cdot 1)][(21 \div 7) \cdot \frac{1}{3}] = ?$

    A. -5 C. 1 E. 36
    B. -1 D. 12

50. $(-5 \cdot -2) - (-2 \cdot -5) = ?$

    A. 0 C. 10 E. 18
    B. 2 D. 12

51. $6 \div -\frac{1}{3} = ?$

    A. -18 C. 2 E. 18
    B. $-\frac{1}{2}$ D. 3

52. $[-3 - (-3)] - [-2 - (-2)] - [-1 - (-1)] = ?$

    A. -12 C. 0 E. 12
    B. -6 D. 6

53. If n is any negative number, which of the following must also be negative?

    I. $n + n$
    II. $n \cdot n$
    III. $n - n$

    A. I only   D. II and III only
    B. II only   E. I, II, and III
    C. I and III only

54. If n is any negative number, which of the following must also be negative?

    I. $n \cdot -n$
    II. $-n \cdot -n$
    III. $-n + n$

    A. I only   D. II and III only
    B. II only   E. I, II, and III
    C. III only

55. If n is any positive number, which of the following must be negative?

    I. $n \cdot -n$
    II. $-n + -n$
    III. $n - (-n)$

    A. I only   D. I and III only
    B. II only   E. I, II, and III
    C. I and II only

56. If n is any positive number, which of the following must be positive?

    I. $-n - (-n)$
    II. $-n \cdot -n$
    III. $n \div (-n \cdot -n)$

    A. I only   D. I and III only
    B. II only   E. II and III only
    C. III only

57. Given any number such that $n \neq 0$, which of the following must be equal to 0?

    I. $-n \cdot -n \cdot -n \cdot -n \cdot -n \cdot -n$
    II. $[(n - n) - n] - [(n - n) - n]$
    III. $n \div [(n \div n) \div n]$

    A. I only   D. I and III only
    B. II only   E. I, II, and III
    C. I and II only

58. In the figure below, what point between A and B is two times as far from A as from B?

    $$\overset{\overset{A}{\bullet}}{\underset{-10}{}} \qquad\qquad \overset{\overset{B}{\bullet}}{\underset{41}{}}$$

    A. 7 C. 17 E. 31
    B. 10 D. 24

59. In the figure below, what point between A and B is three times as far from A as from B?

$$\underset{-12}{\overset{A}{\bullet}} \qquad \underset{28}{\overset{B}{\bullet}}$$

   A. 12   C. 20   E. 24
   B. 18   D. 21

60. $|1| + |-2| + |3| + |-4| + |5| + |-6| + |7| + |-8| + |9| + |-10| + |11| + |-12| = ?$

   A. −12   C. 6   E. 78
   B. −6   D. 12

Decimals

A *decimal* is nothing more than a special way of writing fractions using a denominator of ten, or one hundred, or one thousand, and so on. Decimals are written with a decimal point to the left of the decimal digits in order to distinguish them from whole numbers.

Examples:

1. The fraction $\frac{3}{10}$ written as a decimal is 0.3.
2. The fraction $\frac{72}{100}$ written as a decimal is 0.72.

The positions to the right of the decimal point are called decimal places. Decimal places are analogous to the positions of the digits in whole numbers (units column, tens column, *etc.*). The number of decimal places indicates the denominator of the fraction. One decimal place indicates a denominator of 10; two places indicate a denominator of 100; three indicate a denominator of 1,000; and so on. 0.335 is read as three hundred thirty-five thousandths and 0.12345 as twelve thousand three hundred forty-five hundred thousandths.

$$0 \quad . \quad 1 \quad 2 \quad 3 \quad 4 \quad 5$$

| | | TENTHS | HUNDREDTHS | THOUSANDTHS | TEN THOUSANDTHS | HUNDRED THOUSANDTHS |

When a decimal does not include a positive or negative whole number, a zero is placed to the left of the decimal point. This has no mathematical significance; it is there just to make the decimals more readable. Without the zero, someone might fail to see the decimal and read .335 as 335. On the exam, all decimals that do not include a positive or negative whole number are written with a zero to the left of the decimal point.

Converting Fractions to Decimals

If the fraction already has a denominator that is ten, one hundred, one thousand, *etc.*, the conversion is very easy. The numerator of the fraction becomes the decimal. The number of zeros in the denominator governs the placement of the decimal point. Starting just to the right of the last digit of the numerator, you count over one digit to the left for each zero in the denominator. For example, to express $\frac{127}{1,000}$ in decimal form, take the numerator, 127, as the decimal. Then, starting just to the right of the 7, count over three places to the left (one for each zero in 1,000). The decimal equivalent is 0.127.

Examples:

1. $\frac{3}{10} = 0.3$ (One zero in the denominator indicates one decimal place.)
2. $\frac{13}{100} = 0.13$ (Two zeros in the denominator indicate two decimal places.)
3. $\frac{522}{1,000} = 0.522$ (Three zeros in the denominator indicate three decimal places.)

If there are fewer digits in the numerator than zeros in the denominator, add zeros to the left of the number until you have enough decimal places. For example, consider $\frac{53}{1,000}$: the denominator contains three zeros, but 53 is only a two-digit number. Therefore, add one zero to the left of the 5: $\frac{53}{1,000} = 0.053$.

Examples:

1. $\frac{3}{100} = 0.03$ (Two zeros mean two decimal places.)

2. $\frac{71}{10,000} = 0.0071$ (Four zeros mean four decimal places.)

3. $\frac{9}{100,000} = 0.00009$ (Five zeros mean five decimal places.)

To convert a proper fraction with a denominator other than 10, 100, *etc.*, convert the fraction to an equivalent form using a denominator such as ten, one hundred, *etc.* For example, to convert $\frac{3}{4}$ to a decimal, change it into a fraction with a denominator of 100: $\frac{3}{4} = \frac{3 \cdot 25}{4 \cdot 25} = \frac{75}{100}$. Then, $\frac{75}{100}$ is written as 0.75, as described in the previous section.

Examples:

1. $\frac{2}{5} = \frac{2 \cdot 2}{5 \cdot 2} = \frac{4}{10} = 0.4$

2. $\frac{1}{4} = \frac{1 \cdot 25}{4 \cdot 25} = \frac{25}{100} = 0.25$

3. $\frac{3}{8} = \frac{3 \cdot 125}{8 \cdot 125} = \frac{375}{1,000} = 0.375$

4. $\frac{1}{50} = \frac{1 \cdot 2}{50 \cdot 2} = \frac{2}{100} = 0.02$

To determine which denominator you should use, divide the denominator of the fraction into 10, then into 100, then into 1,000, until you find the first denominator that is evenly divisible by the denominator of the fraction. For example, $\frac{3}{8}$ does not have an equivalent form with a denominator of 10, but it does have an equivalent form with a denominator of 1,000. This is the same process used above to find common denominators for fractions. (Note: You can also convert a fraction into a decimal by dividing the numerator of the fraction by its denominator. However, this method obviously presupposes that you know how to divide decimals. We will come back to the topic of converting to decimals when we discuss how to divide decimals.)

Converting Mixed Numbers to Decimals

To change a mixed number to a decimal, convert the fractional part of the mixed number to a decimal as discussed above, and then place the whole number part of the mixed number to the left of the decimal point.

Examples:

1. Convert the mixed number $2\frac{3}{4}$ to a decimal.

    ➤ First, convert $\frac{3}{4}$ to a decimal: $\frac{3}{4} = 0.75$. Then, place the whole-number part to the left of the decimal point: 2.75. Notice that the extra zero is dropped—there is no reason to write 02.75.

2. $6\frac{1}{10} = 6.1$

3. $12\frac{1}{2} = 12.5$

4. $3\frac{7}{8} = 3.875$

Converting Improper Fractions to Decimals

To convert an improper fraction to a decimal, just treat the improper fraction as a mixed number and follow the procedure just outlined.

Examples:

1. $\frac{9}{4} = 2\frac{1}{4} = 2.25$

2. $\frac{7}{2} = 3\frac{1}{2} = 3.5$

3. $\frac{8}{5} = 1\frac{3}{5} = 1.6$

It is also possible, and often easier, to convert fractions to decimals by dividing the numerator by the denominator. Again, we will postpone this part of the discussion until we have studied division of decimals.

Converting Decimals to Fractions and Mixed Numbers

To convert a decimal back to a fraction, it is necessary only to create a fraction using the digits of the decimal number as a numerator and a denominator of 1 followed by a number of zeros equal to the number of decimal places.

Examples:

1. Convert 0.125 to a fraction.
   ➢ Use 125 as the numerator and 1,000 as the denominator: $\frac{125}{1,000}$. Reduce the fraction to lowest terms: $\frac{125}{1,000} = \frac{1}{8}$.

2. $0.04 = \frac{4}{100} = \frac{1}{25}$

3. $0.25 = \frac{25}{100} = \frac{1}{4}$

4. $0.005 = \frac{5}{1,000} = \frac{1}{200}$

Finally, if the decimal consists of both a whole part and a fraction, the conversion will result in a mixed number. The whole part of the mixed number will be the whole part of the decimal. Then, convert the fractional part of the decimal as just shown.

Examples:

1. Convert 2.05 to a mixed number.
   ➢ Write 0.05 as a fraction: $0.05 = \frac{5}{100} = \frac{1}{20}$. The whole number part is 2, so $2.05 = 2\frac{1}{20}$.

2. $1.75 = 1 + \frac{75}{100} = 1 + \frac{3}{4} = 1\frac{3}{4}$

3. $32.6 = 32 + \frac{6}{10} = 32 + \frac{3}{5} = 32\frac{3}{5}$

4. $2.05 = 2 + \frac{5}{100} = 2 + \frac{1}{20} = 2\frac{1}{20}$

5. $357.125 = 357 + \frac{125}{1,000} = 357 + \frac{1}{8} = 357\frac{1}{8}$

Operations of Decimals

1. Adding and Subtracting Decimals

Decimals can be manipulated in very much the same way as whole numbers. You can add and subtract decimals.

Examples:

1. $0.2 + 0.3 + 0.1 = 0.6$
2. $0.7 - 0.2 = 0.5$

Adding zeros to the end of a decimal number does not change the value of that number. If the decimals do not have the same number of decimal places, add zeros to the right of those that do not until every number has the same number of decimal places. Then, line up the decimal points and combine the decimals as indicated. Follow the same process for subtracting decimals.

Examples:

1. $0.75 - 0.1125 = 0.7500$
   $$\begin{array}{r} - 0.1125 \\ \hline 0.6375 \end{array}$$

2. $0.125 + 0.6 + 0.115 = 0.125$
   $$\begin{array}{r} 0.600 \\ + 0.115 \\ \hline 0.840 \end{array}$$

3. $0.999 - 0.000001 = 0.999000$
   $$\begin{array}{r} - 0.000001 \\ \hline 0.998999 \end{array}$$

4. $2.14 + 0.125 + 0.0005 = 2.1400$
   $$\begin{array}{r} 0.1250 \\ + 0.0005 \\ \hline 2.2655 \end{array}$$

5. $0.8 - 0.1111 = 0.8000$
   $$\begin{array}{r} - 0.1111 \\ \hline 0.6889 \end{array}$$

6. $0.11 + 0.9 + 0.033 = 0.110$
   $$\begin{array}{r} 0.900 \\ + 0.033 \\ \hline 1.043 \end{array}$$

2. Multiplying Decimals

As with fractions, there is no need to find a common denominator when multiplying decimals: The multiplication process generates its own. Simply multiply as with whole numbers and then adjust the decimal point. To find the correct position for the decimal point first, count the total number of decimal places in the numbers that are being multiplied. Then, in the final product, place the decimal point that many places to the left, counting from the right side of the last digit.

Examples:

1. $0.25 \cdot 0.2 = ?$

   ➤ Ignore the decimals and multiply: $25 \cdot 2 = 50$. Now, adjust the decimal point. Since 0.25 has two decimal places, and 0.2 has one decimal place, count three places to the left, starting at the right side of the 0 in 50; the final product is $0.050 = 0.05$.

2. $0.1 \cdot 0.2 \cdot 0.3 = 0.006$ ($1 \cdot 2 \cdot 3 = 6$, and there are three decimal places in the multiplication.)
3. $0.02 \cdot 0.008 = 0.00016$ ($2 \cdot 8 = 16$, and there are five decimal places in the multiplication.)
4. $2 \cdot 0.5 = 1$ ($2 \cdot 5 = 10$, and there is one decimal place in the multiplication.)
5. $2.5 \cdot 2.5 = 6.25$ ($25 \cdot 25 = 625$, and there are two decimal places in the multiplication.)
6. $0.10 \cdot 0.10 \cdot 0.10 = 0.001000 = 0.001$ ($10 \cdot 10 \cdot 10 = 1,000$, and there are six decimal places in the multiplication.)

To simplify the process of multiplying decimals, drop any final zeros before multiplying. Thus, in the case of the last example, $0.10 \cdot 0.10 \cdot 0.10 = 0.1 \cdot 0.1 \cdot 0.1 = 0.001$ since there are three decimal places in the multiplication.

3. Dividing Decimals

Like multiplication, division generates a common denominator by a suitable adjustment of zeros. However, there are two situations in which division of decimals is a little tricky. Let's review them one at a time.

First, when the divisor (the number doing the dividing) is a whole number, place the decimal point in the quotient (result of division) immediately above the decimal point in the dividend (the number being divided). Then, keep dividing until there is no remainder, adding zeros as needed to the right of the dividend. This is the procedure whenever the divisor is a whole number—even if the dividend is also a whole number.

Examples:

1. $0.25 \div 5 = 5\overline{)0.25}$ $\dfrac{0.05}{}$ $\dfrac{-25}{0}$

3. $1.75 \div 25 = 25\overline{)1.75}$ $\dfrac{0.07}{}$ $\dfrac{-175}{0}$

5. $0.1 \div 250 = 250\overline{)0.1000}$ $\dfrac{0.0004}{}$ $\dfrac{-1000}{0}$

2. $2.5 \div 2 = 2\overline{)2.50}$ $\dfrac{1.25}{}$

$\dfrac{-2}{05}$
$\dfrac{-4}{10}$
$\dfrac{-10}{0}$

4. $1.44 \div 12 = 12\overline{)1.44}$ $\dfrac{0.12}{}$ $\dfrac{-144}{0}$

6. $9 \div 2 = 2\overline{)9.0}$ $\dfrac{4.5}{}$

$\dfrac{-8}{10}$
$\dfrac{-10}{0}$

The second tricky situation occurs when the divisor is a decimal. In these cases, "clear" the fractional part of the decimal by moving the decimal point to the right. For example, if dividing by 0.1, change 0.1 to 1; if dividing by 2.11, convert that to 211 by moving the decimal point two places to the right. However, you must also move the decimal point of the dividend by the same number of places to ensure that their relative values are not changed. Notice that in the following examples both decimal points are moved the same number of places to the right.

Examples:

1. $5 \div 2.5 = 2.5\overline{)50.}$ $\dfrac{2.}{}$ $\dfrac{-50}{0}$

2. $10 \div 1.25 = 1.25\overline{)10.00.}$ $\dfrac{8.}{}$ $\dfrac{-1000}{0}$

3. $50 \div 0.05 = 0.05\overline{)50.00.}$ $\dfrac{1000.}{}$ $\dfrac{-5000}{0}$

There are two final things to say about dividing decimals. First, as mentioned previously, you can use division of decimals to convert fractions to decimals. For example, to convert $\frac{9}{2}$ to a decimal number, simply divide 9 by 2.

Examples:

1. $\dfrac{9}{2} = 2\overline{)9} = 2\overline{)9.0}$ $\dfrac{4.5}{}$

$\dfrac{-8}{10}$
$\dfrac{-10}{0}$

2. $\dfrac{3}{4} = 4\overline{)3} = 4\overline{)3.00}$ $\dfrac{0.75}{}$

$\dfrac{-28}{20}$
$\dfrac{-20}{0}$

Second, some fractions do not have exact decimal equivalents. Try converting $\frac{1}{3}$ to a decimal using the division route. You will be at it forever, because you get an endless succession of "3"s. Try converting $\frac{1}{9}$ to a decimal using the division method. Again, you will get an endless succession, this time of repeating "1"s. By convention, repeating decimals are indicated using an overbar: $0.1\overline{1}$.

NOTE: The SAT and PSAT allow calculators. Therefore, it is important that you learn how to use a calculator and bring the same calculator with you to the exam. Using a calculator provides greater accuracy and often saves valuable test time.

Decimals

DIRECTIONS: Choose the correct answer to each of the following items. Use a calculator when necessary. Answers are on page 891.

1. What is $\frac{7}{10}$ expressed as a decimal?

   A. 70   C. 0.7   E. 0.0007
   B. 7   D. 0.007

2. What is $\frac{73}{100}$ expressed as a decimal?

   A. 73   C. 0.73   E. 0.0073
   B. 7.3   D. 0.073

3. What is $\frac{21}{1,000}$ expressed as a decimal?

   A. 0.21   C. 0.0021   E. 0.000021
   B. 0.021   D. 0.00021

4. What is $\frac{557}{1,000}$ expressed as a decimal?

   A. 5.57   C. 0.0557   E. 0.00057
   B. 0.557   D. 0.0057

5. What is $\frac{34}{10,000}$ expressed as a decimal?

   A. 0.00034   C. 0.034   E. 3.4
   B. 0.0034   D. 0.34

6. What is $\frac{1}{1,000,000}$ expressed as a decimal?

   A. 0.01   C. 0.0001   E. 0.000001
   B. 0.001   D. 0.00001

7. What is $\frac{30}{100}$ expressed as a decimal?

   A. 3   C. 0.03   E. 0.0003
   B. 0.3   D. 0.003

8. What is $\frac{1,000}{4,000}$ expressed as a decimal?

   A. 0.25   C. 0.0025   E. 0.000025
   B. 0.025   D. 0.00025

9. Which of the following is (are) equal to $\frac{1}{10}$?

   I. 1.0
   II. 0.1
   III. 0.1000

   A. I only   D. I and III only
   B. II only   E. II and III only
   C. III only

10. Which of the following is (are) equal to $\frac{25}{100}$?

    I. 0.25
    II. 0.025
    III. 0.0025

    A. I only   D. II and III only
    B. I and II only   E. I, II, and III
    C. I and III only

11. What is $\frac{257}{100}$ expressed as a decimal?

    A. 25.7   C. 0.257   E. 0.00257
    B. 2.57   D. 0.0257

12. What is $\frac{57}{10}$ expressed as a decimal?

    A. 57   C. 0.57   E. 0.0057
    B. 5.7   D. 0.057

13. What is $\frac{5}{8}$ expressed as a decimal?

    A. 0.125   C. 0.850   E. 5.80
    B. 0.625   D. 1.25

14. What is $\frac{4}{5}$ expressed as a decimal?

    A. 0.4   C. 0.8   E. 2.4
    B. 0.6   D. 1.2

15. What is $\frac{1}{20}$ expressed as a decimal?

    A. 0.05   C. 0.0005   E. 0.000005
    B. 0.005   D. 0.00005

16. What is $\frac{1}{50}$ expressed as a decimal?

    A. 0.2   C. 0.002   E. 0.00002
    B. 0.02   D. 0.0002

17. What is $\frac{3}{200}$ expressed as a decimal?

    A. 0.15   C. 0.0015   E. 0.000015
    B. 0.015   D. 0.00015

18. What is $\frac{9}{500}$ expressed as a decimal?

    A. 0.000018   C. 0.0018   E. 0.18
    B. 0.00018   D. 0.018

19. What is $\frac{17}{500}$ expressed as a decimal?

    A. 0.175   C. 0.0175   E. 0.00034
    B. 0.034   D. 0.0034

20. What is $\frac{123}{200}$ expressed as a decimal?

    A. 0.615   C. 0.0615   E. 0.00615
    B. 0.256   D. 0.0256

21. $0.1 + 0.1 = ?$

    A. 0.002   C. 0.2   E. 20
    B. 0.02   D. 2

22. $0.27 + 0.13 + 0.55 = ?$

    A. 0.21   C. 0.47   E. 0.95
    B. 0.36   D. 0.85

23. $0.528 + 0.116 + 0.227 = ?$

    A. 0.871   C. 0.243   E. 0.0012
    B. 0.583   D. 0.112

24. $0.7 + 0.013 + 0.028 = ?$

    A. 0.741   C. 1.02   E. 2.553
    B. 0.988   D. 1.224

25. $1.23 + 0.00001 = ?$

    A. 1.24   C. 1.23001   E. 1.230000001
    B. 1.2301   D. 1.2300001

26. $57.1 + 23.3 + 35.012 = ?$

    A. 412.115   C. 115.0412   E. 1.15412
    B. 115.412   D. 11.5412

27. $0.01 + 0.001 + 0.0001 + 0.00001 = ?$

    A. 1   C. 0.1111   E. 0.001111
    B. 0.10   D. 0.01111

28. $0.9 + 0.09 + 0.009 + 0.0009 = ?$

    A. 0.9999   C. 0.009999   E. 0.0000999
    B. 0.09999   D. 0.0009999

29. $0.27 + 0.36 + 2.1117 + 3.77777 + 1.42 = ?$

    A. 5.44   C. 8.11143   E. 14.002785
    B. 7.93947   D. 12.223479

30. $12,279.1 + 3,428.01 + 3,444.99 = ?$

    A. 19,151.99   C. 19,152.09   E. 19,152.11
    B. 19,152   D. 19,152.1

31. $0.7 - 0.3 = ?$

    A. 0.004   C. 0.04   E. 0.4
    B. 0.021   D. 0.21

32. $0.75 - 0.25 = ?$

    A. 5   C. 0.5   E. 0.005
    B. 1   D. 0.25

33. $1.35 - 0.35 = ?$

    A. 1   C. 0.1   E. 0.00001
    B. 0.35   D. 0.0035

34. $25.125 - 5.357 = ?$

    A. 19.768   C. 12.115   E. 2.288
    B. 15.432   D. 4.108

35. $1 - 0.00001 = ?$

    A. 0.9   C. 0.999   E. 0.99999
    B. 0.99   D. 0.9999

36. $0.2 \cdot 0.1 = ?$

    A. 0.3   C. 0.1   E. 0.006
    B. 0.2   D. 0.02

37. $0.1 \cdot 0.1 \cdot 0.1 = ?$

    A. 0.3   C. 0.01   E. 0.0001
    B. 0.1   D. 0.001

38. $1.1 \cdot 1.1 \cdot 1.1 = ?$

    A. 1.331   C. 0.111   E. 0.00111
    B. 1.111   D. 0.0111

39. $0.11 \cdot 0.33 = ?$

    A. 0.363   C. 0.00363   E. 0.0000363
    B. 0.0363   D. 0.000363

40. $0.2 \cdot 0.5 \cdot 0.2 \cdot 0.5 = ?$

    A. 0.1   C. 0.001   E. 0.00001
    B. 0.01   D. 0.0001

41. $5 \cdot 0.25 = ?$

    A. 1.25   C. 0.0125   E. 0.000125
    B. 0.125   D. 0.00125

42. $10 \cdot 0.000001 = ?$

    A. 0.00001   C. 0.001   E. 0.1
    B. 0.0001   D. 0.01

43. $100 \cdot 0.00052 = ?$

    A. 0.0052   C. 5.2   E. 520
    B. 0.052   D. 52

44. $1.2 \cdot 1.2 = ?$

    A. 0.144   C. 14.4   E. 1,444
    B. 1.44   D. 144

45. $1.000 \cdot 1.000 \cdot 1.000 \cdot 1.000 = ?$

    A. 1   C. 0.01   E. 0.0001
    B. 0.1   D. 0.001

46. $6 \div 0.2 = ?$

    A. 0.03   C. 3   E. 300
    B. 0.3   D. 30

47. $0.2 \div 5 = ?$

    A. 0.4   C. 0.004   E. 0.00004
    B. 0.04   D. 0.0004

48. $1 \div 0.001 = ?$

   A. 10,000   C. 100   E. 0.0001
   B. 1,000   D. 0.001

49. $25.1 \div 2.51 = ?$

   A. 100   C. 0.1   E. 0.001
   B. 10   D. 0.01

50. $0.25 \div 8 = ?$

   A. 4   C. 0.03125   E. 0.003125
   B. 0.4   D. 0.004

51. $0.005 \div 0.005 = ?$

   A. 1   C. 0.005   E. 0.00005
   B. 0.5   D. 0.0005

52. $2 \div 2.5 = ?$

   A. 8   C. 0.8   E. 0.008
   B. 5   D. 0.5

53. $111 \div 0.111 = ?$

   A. 1   C. 11   E. 1,000
   B. 10   D. 110

54. $0.12345 \div 0.012345 = ?$

   A. 100   C. 1   E. 0.01
   B. 10   D. 0.1

55. $0.002 \div 0.00002 = ?$

   A. 100   C. 0.1   E. 0.001
   B. 10   D. 0.01

56. Express as a decimal: $\frac{3}{5} + \frac{5}{8}$.

   A. 1.00   C. 1.225   E. 1.75
   B. 1.115   D. 1.50

57. Find the average of $\frac{2}{3}$ and 0.75.

   A. $\frac{9}{24}$ C. $\frac{17}{24}$ E. $\frac{23}{24}$
   B. $\frac{14}{24}$ D. $\frac{21}{24}$

58. Find the average of 0.1, 0.01, and $\frac{1}{4}$.

   A. 0.10   C. 0.50   E. 1.0
   B. 0.12   D. 0.75

59. Simplify: $\frac{12\frac{1}{3}}{0.2}$.

   A. $\frac{1}{50}$ C. $\frac{85}{2}$ E. $\frac{225}{4}$
   B. $\frac{3}{40}$ D. $\frac{185}{3}$

60. Simplify: $0.1\left[\frac{1}{3} - 2\left(\frac{1}{2} - \frac{1}{4}\right)\right]$.

   A. $-\frac{2}{15}$ C. $-\frac{1}{90}$ E. $\frac{3}{4}$
   B. $-\frac{1}{60}$ D. $\frac{1}{2}$

61. For three months, Pete saved part of his monthly allowance. He saved $4.56 the first month, $3.82 the second month, and $5.06 the third month. How much did Pete save altogether?

   A. $12.04   C. $13.04   E. $14.44
   B. $12.44   D. $13.44

62. The diameter of a rod is required to be 1.51 ± 0.015 inches. Which of the following represents the possible range of measurements for the rod's diameter?

   A. 1.490 inches to 1.520 inches
   B. 1.495 inches to 1.520 inches
   C. 1.495 inches to 1.525 inches
   D. 1.495 inches to 1.530 inches
   E. 1.500 inches to 1.530 inches

63. From an employee's salary of $190.57, an employer deducts $3.05 for social security and $5.68 for pension. What is the final amount of the check?

   A. $180.84   C. $181.84   E. $182.84
   B. $181.04   D. $182.04

64. If the outer radius of a metal pipe is 2.84 inches and the inner radius is 1.94 inches, what is the thickness of the metal?

   A. 0.85 in.   C. 1.00 in.   E. 1.25 in.
   B. 0.90 in.   D. 1.18 in.

65. Pete earns $20.56 on Monday, $32.90 on Tuesday, and $20.78 on Wednesday. He spends half of all that he earned during the 3 days. How much does he have left?

   A. $36.12   C. $37.12   E. $38.12
   B. $36.72   D. $37.72

66. What is the total cost of $3\frac{1}{2}$ pounds of meat at $1.69/lb. and 20 lemons at $0.60/dozen?

   A. $5.92   C. $6.92   E. $7.92
   B. $6.42   D. $7.42

67. A reel of cable weighs 1,279 pounds. If the empty reel weighs 285 pounds and the cable weighs 7.1 pounds per foot, how many feet of cable are on the reel?

   A. 140   C. 160   E. 180
   B. 150   D. 170

68. How much will 345 fasteners at $4.15 per hundred cost?

   A. $13.12   C. $14.12   E. $14.82
   B. $13.82   D. $14.32

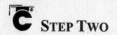

Percents

A *percent* is a special type of fraction that always has a denominator equal to 100. The percent sign, "%," is shorthand for "$\frac{x}{100}$." For example, $67\% = \frac{67}{100}$.

Converting to and from Percents

Since percents are simply a special type of fraction, both fractions and decimals can be converted to percents, and vice versa. The easiest conversion is to change a decimal to a percent: Move the decimal point two places to the right and add the percent sign.

Examples:

1. $0.27 = 27\%$
2. $0.50 = 50\%$
3. $0.275 = 27.5\%$

This substitutes "%" for two decimal places—simply a matter of changing things from one form into an equivalent form, which is a process we have already used in several ways. To change a percent back to a decimal, move the decimal point two places to the left and drop the percent sign.

Examples:

1. $27\% = 0.27$
2. $50\% = 0.50$
3. $27.5\% = 0.275$

You already know the rules for converting fractions to decimals, and vice versa. To convert a fraction to a percent, just convert the fraction to a decimal and follow the rule above.

Examples:

1. $\frac{3}{4} = 0.75 = 75\%$
2. $\frac{5}{8} = 0.625 = 62.5\%$
3. $\frac{1}{10} = 0.10 = 10\%$

To reverse the process, follow the rule given above for turning percentages back into decimals, and then use the procedure outlined in the previous section for converting decimals to fractions.

Examples:

1. $75\% = 0.75 = \frac{75}{100} = \frac{3}{4}$
2. $62.5\% = 0.625 = \frac{625}{1,000} = \frac{5}{8}$
3. $10\% = 0.1 = \frac{1}{10}$

There are two tricky types of percents: those greater than 100% and those less than 1%. First, it is possible to have a percent that is larger than 100. This would be the result of converting a mixed number, such as $2\frac{3}{4}$, to a percent: $2\frac{3}{4} = 2.75 = 275\%$. Second, percents can also be less than 1, in which case they are written with decimals; for example, 0.5%. However, these numbers follow the general rules outlined above. To convert 0.5% to a fraction: $0.5\% = 0.005 = \frac{5}{1,000} = \frac{1}{200}$. Similarly, fractions smaller than $\frac{1}{100}$ will yield a percent less than 1: $\frac{1}{2,500} = 0.0004 = 0.04\%$.

Operations of Percents

1. Adding and Subtracting Percents

Percents are fractions, so they can be manipulated like other fractions. All percents have 100 as the denominator. It is easy to add and subtract percents because you already have a common denominator.

Examples:

1. Paul originally owned 25 percent of the stock of a certain company. He purchased another 15 percent of the stock privately, and he received a gift of another 10 percent of the stock. What percent of the stock of the company does Paul now own?
   ➤ $25\% + 15\% + 10\% = 50\%$
2. In a certain election, Peter and Mary received 50 percent of all the votes that were cast. If Peter received 20 percent of the votes cast in the election, what percent of the votes did Mary receive?
   ➤ $50\% - 20\% = 30\%$

2. Multiplying Percents

To multiply percents, first convert them to decimals and then multiply. For example, $60\% \cdot 80\% = 0.60 \cdot 0.80 = 0.48$.

Example:

In a certain group, 80 percent of the people are wearing hats. If 60 percent of those wearing hats are also wearing gloves, what percent of the entire group is wearing both a hat and gloves?
➤ 60% of 80% = $60\% \cdot 80\% = 0.60 \cdot 0.80 = 0.48 = 48\%$

3. Dividing Percents

To divide percents, first convert them to decimals and then divide. For example, $100\% \div 12.5\% = 1 \div 0.125 = 8$.

Example:

Peter is purchasing an item on a lay-away plan. If he pays weekly installments of 8% of the purchase price, how many weeks will it take for Peter to payoff the entire purchase price?
➤ $100\% \div 8\% = 1 \div 0.08 = 12.5$ weeks

Percent Story Problems

Four basic variations of percent problems appear on the exam as story problems:

- What is *x* percent of something?
- This is what percent of that?
- This is a given percent of what?
- What is the percent change from this quantity to that quantity?

1. "What Is X Percent of Some Quantity?"

Percents are fractions, so in the question, "What is *x* percent of some quantity?", the *of* indicates multiplication.

Examples:

1. A certain class is made up of 125 students. If 60 percent of the students are men, how many men are in the class?
   ➤ 60% of 125 = 60% • 125 = 0.60 • 125 = 75

2. If Sam originally had $25 and gave 25 percent of that amount to his friend Samantha, how much money did Sam give to Samantha?
   ➤ 25% of $25 = 25% • 25 = 0.25 • 25 = $6.25

3. If Paula had 50 marbles and gave 20 percent of them to her friend Paul, how many marbles did Paula give to Paul?
   ➤ 20% of 50 = 20% • 50 = 0.20 • 50 = 10

2. *"What Percent Is This of That?"*

A second common item involving percents has the form, "What percent is this of that?"

Example:

What percent is 3 of 12?
➤ Convert $\frac{3}{12}$ to a decimal by dividing 3 by 12 and then change that decimal number to a percent: $\frac{3}{12} = \frac{1}{4} = 0.25 = 25\%$.

There are other ways of phrasing the same question:

- 3 is what percent of 12?
- Of 12, what percent is 3?

Note that all three of the above questions are equivalent and represent the three following general forms:

- <u>What percent is this of that</u>?
- <u>This is what percent of that</u>?
- <u>Of that, what percent is this</u>?

Although the order of words is different, these three questions ask the same thing: to express a fraction as a percent. Here is a little trick to help you avoid confusion. Notice that in each question form, there is the phrase "*of that*" and the phrase "*is this*" ("this *is*"). When you set up a fraction for the percent, always place the "*is this*" value over the "*of that*" value. We call this the "*is* over *of*" method for percents: $\frac{is}{of} = \frac{\%}{100}$.

Example:

5 is what percent of 25? Of 25, what percent is 5? What percent is 5 of 25?
➤ Notice that these questions are equivalent. $\frac{is}{of} = \frac{\%}{100} \Rightarrow \frac{5}{25} = \frac{1}{5} = 0.2 = \frac{\%}{100} \Rightarrow \% = (0.2)(100) = 20\%$.

As long as you place the "*is this*" value in the numerator and the "*of that*" value in the denominator, you cannot make a mistake.

Examples:

1. What percent is 20 of 50?
   ➤ $\frac{20}{50} = \frac{2}{5} = 0.40 = 40\%$

2. Of 125, what percent is 25?
   ➤ $\frac{25}{125} = \frac{1}{5} = 0.20 = 20\%$

3. 12 is what percent of 6?
   ➤ $\frac{12}{6} = 2 = 200\%$

The "*is* over *of*" method can be used to attack any item that presents a variation on this theme. For example, what number is 20% of 25? This is similar to the previous examples, except in this case, the percent is given and one of the two numbers is missing. Still, the "*is* over *of*" method works; "*is this*" is represented by "what number"—simply a slight variation in wording.

Examples:

1. What number is 20% of 25?

  ➤ $\frac{is}{of} = \frac{\%}{100} \Rightarrow \frac{is}{25} = \frac{20}{100} \Rightarrow is = \frac{500}{100} = 5$

2. 5 is 20% of what number?

  ➤ $\frac{is}{of} = \frac{\%}{100} \Rightarrow \frac{5}{of} = \frac{20}{100} \Rightarrow of = \frac{500}{20} = 25$

Notice that in the second example, the method still applies. No matter how wordy or otherwise difficult such items get, they are all answerable using this method.

Example:

John received a paycheck for $200. Of that amount, he paid Ed $25. What percent of the paycheck did John give Ed?

➤ $200 is the *of* value; $25 is the *is* value: $\frac{is}{of} = \frac{\%}{100} \Rightarrow \frac{25}{200} = \frac{\%}{100} \Rightarrow \% = \frac{25 \cdot 100}{200} = \frac{25}{2} = 12.5\%$.

3. *"This Is X Percent of What?"*

In the third type of percent problem, the task is to manipulate a given value and percent to determine the unknown total value. The "*is* over *of*" equation, $\frac{is}{of} = \frac{\%}{100}$, can also be used for this variation.

Examples:

1. Seven students attended a field trip. If these 7 students were $6\frac{1}{4}\%$ of all the 9th-graders, find the total number of 9th-graders.

  ➤ $\frac{is}{of} = \frac{\%}{100} \Rightarrow \frac{7}{x} = \frac{6.25\%}{100} \Rightarrow 7 \cdot 100 = 6.25 \cdot x \Rightarrow x = \frac{7 \cdot 100}{6.25} = 112.$

2. A television set discounted by 18% was sold for $459.20. What was the price of the set before the discount?

  ➤ Simplified: "$459.20 is 100% − 18%, or 82%, of what?" $\frac{459.20}{x} = \frac{82}{100} \Rightarrow 459.20 \cdot 100 = x \cdot 82 \Rightarrow x = \frac{459.20 \cdot 100}{82} = $560.

4. *Percent Change*

The fourth percent item involves a quantity change over time. This type of item asks you to express the relationship between the change and the original amount in percent terms. To solve, create a fraction that is then expressed as a percent. Think of this as the "*change* over *original*" trick, because the fraction places the change over the original amount.

Examples:

1. The price of an item increased from $20 to $25. What was the percent increase in the price?

  ➤ $\frac{Change}{Original\ Amount} = \frac{25 - 20}{20} = \frac{5}{20} = \frac{1}{4} = 0.25 = 25\%$

2. Mary was earning $16 per hour when she received a raise of $4 per hour. Her hourly wage increased by what percent?

  ➤ $\frac{Change}{Original\ Amount} = \frac{4}{16} = 0.25 = 25\%$

The "*change* over *original*" trick works for decreases as well.

Examples:

1. A stock's value declined from $50 per share to $45 per share. What was the percent decline in the value of a share?

  ➤ $\frac{Change}{Original\ Amount} = \frac{5}{50} = \frac{1}{10} = 0.10 = 10\%$

2. Student enrollment at City University dropped from 5,000 students in 1990 to 4,000 students in 2000. What was the percent drop in the number of students enrolled at City University?

  ➤ $\frac{Change}{Original\ Amount} = \frac{1,000}{5,000} = \frac{1}{5} = 0.20 = 20\%$

NOTE: The SAT and PSAT allow calculators. Therefore, it is important that you learn how to use a calculator and bring the same calculator with you to the exam. Using a calculator provides greater accuracy and often saves valuable test time.

Percents

DIRECTIONS: Choose the correct answer to each of the following items. Use a calculator when necessary. Answers are on page 894.

1. What is 0.79 expressed as a percent?
   A. 0.0079%   C. 0.79%   E. 79%
   B. 0.079%   D. 7.9%

2. What is 0.55 expressed as a percent?
   A. 55%   C. 0.55%   E. 0.0055%
   B. 5.5%   D. 0.055%

3. What is 0.111 expressed as a percent?
   A. 111%   C. 1.11%   E. 0.0111%
   B. 11.1%   D. 0.111%

4. What is 0.125 expressed as a percent?
   A. 125%   C. 1.25%   E. 0.0125%
   B. 12.5%   D. 0.125%

5. What is 0.5555 expressed as a percent?
   A. 5,555%   C. 55.55%   E. 0.555%
   B. 555.5%   D. 5.5555%

6. What is 0.3 expressed as a percent?
   A. 30%   C. 0.30%   E. 0.003%
   B. 3%   D. 0.03%

7. What is 0.7500 expressed as a percent?
   A. 7,500%   C. 75%   E. 0.75%
   B. 750%   D. 7.5%

8. What is 2.45 expressed as a percent?
   A. 2,450%   C. 24.5%   E. 0.245%
   B. 245%   D. 2.45%

9. What is 1.25 expressed as a percent?
   A. 125%   C. 1.25%   E. 0.0125%
   B. 12.5%   D. 0.125%

10. What is 10 expressed as a percent?
    A. 1,000%   C. 10%   E. 0.1%
    B. 100%   D. 1%

11. What is 0.015 expressed as a percent?
    A. 15%   C. 0.15%   E. 0.0015%
    B. 1.5%   D. 0.015%

12. What is 0.099 expressed as a percent?
    A. 99%   C. 0.99%   E. 0.0099%
    B. 9.9%   D. 0.099%

13. What is 0.0333 expressed as a percent?
    A. 3.33%   C. 0.0333%   E. 0.000333%
    B. 0.333%   D. 0.00333%

14. What is 0.001 expressed as a percent?
    A. 0.1%   C. 0.001%   E. 0.00001%
    B. 0.01%   D. 0.0001%

15. What is 0.0100 expressed as a percent?
    A. 1%   C. 0.001%   E. 0.1%
    B. 0.01%   D. 0.0001%

16. What is 25% expressed as a decimal?
    A. 25.0   C. 0.25   E. 0.0025
    B. 2.5   D. 0.025

17. What is 56% expressed as a decimal?
    A. 5.6   C. 0.056   E. 0.00056
    B. 0.56   D. 0.0056

18. What is 10% expressed as a decimal?
    A. 100.0   C. 1.0   E. 0.001
    B. 10.0   D. 0.1

19. What is 100% expressed as a decimal?
    A. 100.0   C. 1.0   E. 0.001
    B. 10.0   D. 0.1

20. What is 250% expressed as a decimal?
    A. 250.0   C. 2.5   E. 0.025
    B. 25.0   D. 0.25

21. What is 1,000% expressed as a decimal?
    A. 1,000.0   C. 10.0   E. 0.01
    B. 100.0   D. 1.0

22. What is 0.25% expressed as a decimal?
    A. 25.0   C. 0.025   E. 0.00025
    B. 0.25   D. 0.0025

23. What is 0.099% expressed as a decimal?
    A. 99   C. 0.099   E. 0.00099
    B. 0.99   D. 0.0099

24. What is 0.0988% expressed as a decimal?

    A. 0.988   C. 0.00988   E. 9.8
    B. 0.0988   D. 0.000988

25. What is 0.00100% expressed as a decimal?

    A. 0.01   C. 0.0001   E. 0.000001
    B. 0.001   D. 0.00001

26. What is $\frac{1}{10}$ expressed as a percent?

    A. 100%   C. 1%   E. 0.01%
    B. 10%   D. 0.1%

27. What is $\frac{3}{100}$ expressed as a percent?

    A. 300%   C. 3%   E. 0.03%
    B. 30%   D. 0.3%

28. What is $\frac{99}{100}$ expressed as a percent?

    A. 99%   C. 0.99%   E. 0.0099%
    B. 9.9%   D. 0.099%

29. What is $\frac{100}{1,000}$ expressed as a percent?

    A. 0.1%   C. 10%   E. 1,000%
    B. 1.0%   D. 100%

30. What is $\frac{333}{100}$ expressed as a percent?

    A. 333%   C. 3.33%   E. 0.0333%
    B. 33.3%   D. 0.333%

31. What is $\frac{9}{1,000}$ expressed as a percent?

    A. 9%   C. 0.09%   E. 0.0009%
    B. 0.9%   D. 0.009%

32. What is $\frac{3}{4}$ expressed as a percent?

    A. 0.0075%   C. 0.75%   E. 75%
    B. 0.075%   D. 7.5%

33. What is $\frac{4}{5}$ expressed as a percent?

    A. 4.5%   C. 45%   E. 450%
    B. 8%   D. 80%

34. What is $\frac{3}{50}$ expressed as a percent?

    A. 60%   C. 0.6%   E. 0.0006%
    B. 6%   D. 0.006%

35. What is $\frac{3}{75}$ expressed as a percent?

    A. 0.004%   C. 0.4%   E. 40%
    B. 0.04%   D. 4%

36. What is $\frac{6}{500}$ expressed as a percent?

    A. 0.012%   C. 1.2%   E. 120%
    B. 0.12%   D. 12%

37. What is $\frac{111}{555}$ expressed as a percent?

    A. 222%   C. 22%   E. 2%
    B. 200%   D. 20%

38. What is $\frac{8}{5,000}$ expressed as a percent?

    A. 16%   C. 0.016%   E. 0.00016%
    B. 0.16%   D. 0.0016%

39. What is $1\frac{1}{10}$ expressed as a percent?

    A. 110%   C. 1.1%   E. 0.011%
    B. 11%   D. 0.11%

40. What is $9\frac{99}{100}$ expressed as a percent?

    A. 999%   C. 9.99%   E. 0.0999%
    B. 99.9%   D. 0.999%

41. What is $3\frac{1}{2}$ expressed as a percent?

    A. 0.35%   C. 35%   E. 3,500%
    B. 3.5%   D. 350%

42. What is $1\frac{3}{4}$ expressed as a percent?

    A. 175%   C. 17.5%   E. 1.75%
    B. 134%   D. 13.4%

43. What is $10\frac{1}{5}$ expressed as a percent?

    A. 10.02%   C. 100.2%   E. 1,020%
    B. 10.2%   D. 102%

44. What is $3\frac{1}{50}$ expressed as a percent?

    A. 302%   C. 3.02%   E. 0.00302%
    B. 30.2%   D. 0.0302%

45. What is $\frac{111}{100}$ expressed as a percent?

    A. 1,110%   C. 11.1%   E. 0.0111%
    B. 111%   D. 1.11%

46. What is $\frac{7}{2}$ expressed as a percent?

    A. 0.35%   C. 35%   E. 3,500%
    B. 3.5%   D. 350%

47. What is $\frac{13}{5}$ expressed as a percent?

    A. 260%   C. 2.6%   E. 0.026%
    B. 26%   D. 0.26%

48. What is $\frac{9}{8}$ expressed as a percent?

  A. 1,125%   C. 11.25%   E. 0.1125%
  B. 112.5%   D. 1.125%

49. What is $\frac{22}{5}$ expressed as a percent?

  A. 440%   C. 4.4%   E. 0.044
  B. 44%   D. 0.44%

50. What is $\frac{33}{6}$ expressed as a percent?

  A. 550%   C. 5.5%   E. 0.55%
  B. 53%   D. 5.3%

51. Which of the following is equal to 18%?

  A. $\frac{18}{1}$ C. $\frac{18}{100}$ E. $\frac{18}{10,000}$
  B. $\frac{18}{10}$ D. $\frac{18}{1,000}$

52. Which of the following is equal to 80%?

  A. 80   C. 0.8   E. 0.008
  B. 8   D. 0.08

53. Which of the following is equal to 45%?

  A. $\frac{1}{9}$ C. $\frac{11}{19}$ E. $\frac{9}{10}$
  B. $\frac{9}{20}$ D. $\frac{3}{4}$

54. Which of the following is equal to 7%?

  A. 0.007   C. 0.7   E. 70
  B. 0.07   D. 7

55. Which of the following is equal to 13.2%?

  A. 0.0132   C. 1.32   E. 132
  B. 0.132   D. 13.2

56. Which of the following is equal to 1.111%?

  A. 0.001111   C. 0.11111   E. 11.11
  B. 0.01111   D. 1.111

57. Which of the following is equal to 10.101%?

  A. 0.0010101   C. 0.10101   E. 10.101
  B. 0.010101   D. 1.0101

58. Which of the following is equal to 33%?

  A. $\frac{1}{3}$ C. $\frac{33}{111}$ E. $\frac{333}{10,000}$
  B. $\frac{33}{100}$ D. $\frac{333}{1,000}$

59. Which of the following is equal to 80.1%?

  A. $80\frac{1}{10}$ C. $\frac{801}{1,000}$ E. 0.00801
  B. 8.01   D. 0.0801

60. Which of the following is equal to 0.02%?

  A. $\frac{1}{5}$ C. $\frac{1}{500}$ E. $\frac{1}{50,000}$
  B. $\frac{1}{50}$ D. $\frac{1}{5,000}$

61. Which of the following is equal to 250%?

  A. $\frac{25}{1,000}$ C. $\frac{1}{4}$ E. 25
  B. $\frac{25}{100}$ D. 2.5

62. Which of the following is equal to 1,000%?

  A. $\frac{1}{10}$ C. 10   E. 1,000
  B. 1   D. 100

63. 37% + 42% = ?

  A. 6%   C. 106%   E. 154%
  B. 79%   D. 110%

64. 210% + 21% = ?

  A. 21,021%   C. 23.1%   E. 0.231%
  B. 231%   D. 2.31%

65. 8% + 9% + 10% + 110% = ?

  A. 17%   C. 180%   E. 18,000%
  B. 137%   D. 1,800%

66. 254% + 166% + 342% = ?

  A. 900%   C. 432%   E. 92%
  B. 762%   D. 111%

67. 0.02% + 0.005% = ?

  A. 7%   C. 1%   E. 0.025%
  B. 2.5% D. 0.07%

68. 33% − 25% = ?

  A. 0.08%   C. 8%   E. 800%
  B. 0.8%   D. 80%

69. 100% − 0.99% = ?

  A. 1%   C. 11%   E. 99.99%
  B. 9.9%   D. 99.01%

70. 222% − 22.2% = ?

  A. 221.88%   C. 22.188%   E. 1.998%
  B. 199.8%   D. 19.98%

71. If John read 15 percent of the pages in a book on Monday and another 25 percent on Tuesday, what percent of the book did he read on Monday and Tuesday combined?

  A. 7.5%   C. 55%   E. 80%
  B. 40%   D. 75%

72. If from 9:00 a.m. to noon Mary mowed 35 percent of a lawn, and from noon to 3:00 p.m. she mowed another 50 percent of the lawn, what percent of the lawn did she mow between 9:00 a.m. and 3:00 p.m.?

A. 17.5% C. 74.3% E. 98%
B. 60%   D. 85%

Items #73-75 refer to the following table.

Schedule for Completing Project X					
	Mon.	Tues.	Wed.	Thurs.	Fri.
% of work to be completed each day	8%	17%	25%	33%	17%

73. By the end of which day is one-half of the work scheduled to be completed?

A. Monday C. Wednesday E. Friday
B. Tuesday D. Thursday

74. By the end of Tuesday, what percent of the work is scheduled to be completed?

A. 8% C. 25% E. 88%
B. 17% D. 50%

75. If production is on schedule, during which day will $\frac{2}{3}$ of the project have been completed?

A. Monday C. Wednesday E. Friday
B. Tuesday D. Thursday

76. A bucket filled to 33% of its capacity has an amount of water equal to $\frac{1}{4}$ of the bucket's capacity added to it. The bucket is filled to what percent of its capacity?

A. 8% C. 33% E. 75%
B. 25% D. 58%

77. If Edward spends 15% of his allowance on a book and another 25% on food, what percent of his allowance remains?

A. 10% C. 45% E. 80%
B. 40% D. 60%

78. 50% of 50% = ?

A. 1% C. 25% E. 250%
B. 2.5% D. 100%

79. 1% of 100% = ?

A. 0.01% C. 1% E. 100%
B. 0.1% D. 10%

80. If a jar contains 100 marbles and 66% of those marbles are red, how many marbles in the jar are red?

A. 6 C. 66 E. 6,660
B. 34 D. 660

81. If 75% of 240 cars in a certain parking lot are sedans, how many of the cars in the parking lot are sedans?

A. 18 C. 60 E. 210
B. 24 D. 180

82. If 0.1% of the 189,000 names on a certain mailing list have the initials *B.D.*, how many names on the list have the initials *B.D.*?

A. 1.89 C. 189 E. 189,000
B. 18.9 D. 18,900

83. What percent of 10 is 1?

A. 0.1% C. 10% E. 1,000%
B. 1% D. 100%

84. What percent of 12 is 3?

A. 2.5% C. 25% E. 400%
B. 3.6% D. 36%

85. 50 is what percent of 40?

A. 125% C. 80% E. 8%
B. 90% D. 12.5%

86. What number is 10% of 100?

A. 0.01 C. 1 E. 1,000
B. 0.1 D. 10

87. What number is 250% of 12?

A. 3 C. 24 E. 36
B. 15 D. 30

88. If Patty's age is 48 and Al's age is 36, then Al's age is what percent of Patty's age?

A. 7.5% C. 75% E. 175%
B. 25% D. $133\frac{1}{3}$%

89. If 25 of the employees at a bank are women and 15 are men, then what percent of the bank's employees are women?

A. 37.5% C. 60% E. 90%
B. 40% D. 62.5%

90. If the price of an item increases from $5.00 to $8.00, the new price is what percent of the old price?

A. 20% C. 62.5% E. 160%
B. 60% D. 92.5%

91. If the price of an item increases from $5.00 to $8.00, the old price is what percent of the new price?

A. 20% C. 62.5% E. 160%
B. 60% D. 92.5%

92. If the price of a share of stock drops from $200 to $160, the new price is what percent of the old price?

A. 20% C. 50% E. 125%
B. 25% D. 80%

93. If the price of a share of stock drops from $200 to $160, the old price is what percent of the new price?
    A. 20% C. 50% E. 125%
    B. 25% D. 80%

94. If the price of a share of stock drops from $200 to $160, what was the percent decline in the price?
    A. 20% C. 50% E. 125%
    B. 25% D. 80%

Items #95-99 refer to the following table.

Enrollments for a One-Week Seminar	
Week Number	Number of Enrollees
1	10
2	25
3	20
4	15
5	30

95. The number of people who enrolled for the seminar in Week 1 was what percent of the number of people who enrolled in Week 2?
    A. 5% C. 50% E. 250%
    B. 40% D. 80%

96. The number of people who enrolled for the seminar in Week 4 was what percent of the number of people who enrolled in Week 5?
    A. 15% C. 50% E. 200%
    B. 25% D. 100%

97. The number of people who enrolled for the seminar in Week 5 was what percent of the number of people who enrolled in Week 4?
    A. 15% C. 50% E. 200%
    B. 25% D. 100%

98. What was the percent increase in the number of people enrolled for the seminar from Week 1 to Week 2?
    A. 40% C. 100% E. 250%
    B. 80% D. 150%

99. What was the percent decrease in the number of people enrolled for the seminar from Week 3 to Week 4?
    A. 25% C. 75% E. $133\frac{1}{3}$%
    B. $33\frac{1}{3}$% D. 125%

100. If a textbook costs $35, what is 8% sales tax on the textbook?
    A. $1.20 C. $2.00 E. $3.20
    B. $1.80 D. $2.80

101. If a textbook costs $30 plus 8.5% sales tax, what is the total cost of one textbook?
    A. $3.55 C. $23.55 E. $33.55
    B. $12.55 D. $32.55

102. How much is 25% of 80?
    A. 2 C. 20 E. 45
    B. 8 D. 40

103. How much is 2.3% of 90?
    A. 1.07 C. 2.17 E. 2.3
    B. 2.07 D. 2.7

104. On a test that had 50 items, Gertrude got 34 out of the first 40 correct. If she received a grade of 80% on the test, how many of the last 10 items did Gertrude have correct?
    A. 6 C. 10 E. 34
    B. 8 D. 12

105. The number of the question you are now reading is what percent of 1,000?
    A. 0.1% C. 10.5% E. 1,050%
    B. 10% D. 100%

106. 40 is what percent of 50?
    A. 5% C. 80% E. 95%
    B. 25% D. 90%

107. 80 is what percent of 20?
    A. 4% C. 40% E. 400%
    B. 8% D. 200%

108. In the junior class, 300 enrolled in a test preparation course, while 500 did not. What percent of the junior class did not enroll in a test preparation course?
    A. 7% C. 62.5% E. 90%
    B. 35% D. 75%

109. Mary's factory produces pencils at a cost to her company of $0.02 per pencil. If she sells them to a wholesaler at $0.05 each, what is her percent of profit based on her cost of $0.02 per pencil?
    A. 25% C. 75% E. 150%
    B. 50% D. 100%

110. In a certain class of 30 students, 6 received A's. What percent of the class did not receive an A?
    A. 8% C. 60% E. 90%
    B. 40% D. 80%

111. If the Wildcats won 10 out of 12 games, to the nearest whole percent, what percentage of their games did the Wildcats win?
    A. 3 C. 38 E. 94
    B. 8 D. 83

112. On Thursday, Hui made 86 out of 100 free throws. On Friday, she made 46 out of 50 free throws. What was Hui's free throw percentage for the two days?
    A. 8.8% C. 28% E. 88%
    B. 12.8% D. 82%

113. A stereo was discounted by 20% and sold at the discount price of $256. Which of the following equals the price of the stereo before the discount?

    A. less than $300
    B. between $300 and $308
    C. between $308 and $316
    D. between $316 and $324
    E. more than $324

114. In a bag of red and black jellybeans, 136 are red jellybeans and the remainder are black jellybeans. If 15% of the jellybeans in the bag are black, what is the total number of jellybeans in the bag?

    A. 151   C. 175   E. 906
    B. 160   D. 200

115. The regular price of a TV set is $118.80. Which of the following equals the price of the TV set after a sale reduction of 20%?

    A. $158.60   C. $138.84   E. $29.70
    B. $148.50   D. $95.04

116. A circle graph of a budget shows the expenditure of 26.2% for housing, 28.4% for food, 12% for clothing, 12.7% for taxes, and the balance for miscellaneous items. Which of the following equals the percent for miscellaneous items?

    A. 79.3   C. 68.5   E. 20.7
    B. 70.3   D. 29.7

117. Two dozen shuttlecocks and four badminton rackets are to be purchased for a playground. The shuttlecocks are priced at $.35 each and the rackets at $2.75 each. The playground receives a discount of 30% from these prices. Which of the following equals the total cost of this equipment?

    A. $7.29   C. $13.58   E. $19.40
    B. $11.43   D. $18.60

118. A piece of wood weighing 10 ounces is found to have a weight of 8 ounces after drying. Which of the following equals the moisture content?

    A. 80%   C. $33\frac{1}{3}$%   E. 20%
    B. 40%   D. 25%

119. A bag contains 800 coins. Of these, 10 percent are dimes, 30 percent are nickels, and the rest are quarters. Which of the following equals the amount of money in the bag?

    A. less than $150
    B. between $150 and $300
    C. between $301 and $450
    D. between $450 and $800
    E. more than $800

120. Six quarts of a 20% solution of alcohol in water are mixed with 4 quarts of a 60% solution of alcohol in water. Which of the following equals the alcoholic strength of the mixture?

    A. 80%   C. 36%   E. 10%
    B. 40%   D. 25%

121. A man insures 80% of his property and pays a $2\frac{1}{2}$% premium amounting to $348. What is the total value of his property?

    A. $19,000   C. $18,000   E. $13,920
    B. $18,400   D. $17,400

122. A clerk spent his 35-hour work week as follows: $\frac{1}{5}$ of his time he sorted mail, $\frac{1}{2}$ of his time he filed letters, and $\frac{1}{7}$ of the time he did reception work. The rest of his time was devoted to messenger work. Which of the following approximately equals the percent of time spent on messenger work by the clerk during the week?

    A. 6%   C. 14%   E. 20%
    B. 10%   D. 16%

123. In a school in which 40% of the enrolled students are boys, 80% of the boys are present on a certain day. If 1,152 boys are present, which of the following equals the total school enrollment?

    A. 1,440   C. 3,600   E. 5,760
    B. 2,880   D. 5,400

124. Mrs. Morris receives a salary raise from $25,000 to $27,500. Find the percent of increase.

    A. 19%   C. 90%   E. $12\frac{1}{2}$%
    B. 10%   D. 151%

125. The population of Stormville has increased from 80,000 to 100,000 in the last 20 years. Find the percent of increase.

    A. 20%   C. 80%   E. 10%
    B. 25%   D. 60%

126. The value of Super Company Stock dropped from $25 a share to $21 a share. Find the percent of decrease.

    A. 4%   C. 12%   E. 20%
    B. 8%   D. 16%

127. The Rubins bought their home for $30,000 and sold it for $60,000. Find the percent of increase.

    A. 100%   C. 200%   E. 150%
    B 50%   D. 300%

128. During the pre-holiday rush, Martin's Department Store increased its sales staff from 150 to 200 persons. By what percent must it now decrease its sales staff to return to the usual number of salespersons?

A. 25%   C. 20%   E. 75%

B. $33\frac{1}{3}$%   D. 40%

Mean, Median, and Mode

Mean (or average), *median*, and *mode* are three types of statistics that can be determined for a given set of numbers. These statistics provide particular information about a particular set of data.

Mean

1. Calculating a Mean (Average)

To calculate an *average (arithmetic mean)*, just add the quantities contributing to the average and then divide that sum by the number of quantities involved. For example, the average of 3, 7, and 8 is 6: $3 + 7 + 8 = 18$, and $18 \div 3 = 6$. Typically, on the exam, the term "average" is used instead of "mean" or "arithmetic mean."

Example:

> A student's final grade is the average of her scores on five exams. If she receives scores of 78, 83, 82, 88, and 94, what is her final grade?
> ➤ To find the average, add the five grades and divide that sum by 5: $\frac{78 + 83 + 82 + 88 + 94}{5} = \frac{425}{5} = 85$.

It is possible that an easy item might ask that you find the average of a few numbers, as above; however, items about averages can take several other forms. The generalized formula for an average (arithmetic mean) is given by the following equation.

EQUATION FOR FINDING AN AVERAGE

  Average (Arithmetic Mean) = $\overline{x} = \dfrac{x_1 + x_2 + x_3 + \ldots + x_n}{n}$

---

2. Determining Missing Elements

Some items provide the average of a group of numbers and some—but not all—of the quantities involved. You are then asked to find the *missing element(s)*. For example, if the average of 3, 8, and x is 6, what is the value of x? Since the average of the three numbers is 6, the sum or total of the three numbers is $3 \cdot 6 = 18$. The two given numbers are equal to $3 + 8 = 11$, so the third number must be $18 - 11 = 7$. Check the solution by averaging 3, 8, and 7: $3 + 8 + 7 = 18$, and $18 \div 3 = 6$.

Examples:

1. For a certain five-day period, the average high temperature (in degrees Fahrenheit) for Chicago was 30°. If the high temperatures recorded for the first four of those days were 26°, 32°, 24°, and 35°, what was the high temperature recorded on the fifth day?
   ➤ The sum of the five numbers is $5 \cdot 30 = 150$. The sum for the four days we know about is: $26 + 32 + 24 + 35 = 117$. Thus, the fifth day must have had a high temperature of $150 - 117 = 33$.
2. The average of Jose's scores on four tests is 90. If three of those scores are 89, 92, and 94, what is his fourth score?
   ➤ The sum of all four scores must be $4 \cdot 90 = 360$. The three known scores sum to: $89 + 92 + 94 = 275$. Thus, the remaining score must be $360 - 275 = 85$.
3. The average of a group of eight numbers is 9. If one of these numbers is removed from the group, the average of the remaining numbers is 7. What is the value of the number removed?
   ➤ The sum of the original numbers is $8 \cdot 9 = 72$. The sum of the remaining numbers is $7 \cdot 7 = 49$, so the value of the number that was removed must be $72 - 49 = 23$.

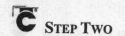

A variation on this type of an item might ask about more than one missing element.

Example:

In a group of children, three of the children are ages 7, 8, and 10, and the other two are the same age. If the average of the ages of all five children is 7, what is the age of the other two children?
➤ The total sum of the five ages must be $5 \cdot 7 = 35$. The known ages total only $7 + 8 + 10 = 25$, so the ages of the two other children must total 10. Since there are two of them, each one must be 5 years old.

3. Calculating Weighted Averages

In the average problems discussed thus far, each element in the average has been given equal weight. Sometimes, averages are created that give greater weight to one element than to another.

Example:

Cody bought 4 books that cost $6.00 each and 2 books that cost $3.00 each. What is the average cost of the 6 books?
➤ The average cost of the 6 books is not just the average of $6.00 and $3.00, which is $4.50. He bought more of the higher priced books, so the average must reflect that fact. One method is to treat each book as a separate expense: $\frac{6+6+6+6+3+3}{6} = \frac{30}{6} = 5$. Another method is to "weigh" the two different costs: $6(4) + 3(2) = 30$ and $\frac{30}{6} = 5$.

Median

The *median* of an odd number of data values is the middle value of the data set when it is arranged in ascending or descending order. The median of an even number of data values is the average of the two middle values of the data set when it is arranged in ascending or descending order.

Examples:

1. What is the median of {1, 1, 2, 3, 4, 5, 6, 7, 7, 7, 8, 8, 9}?
   ➤ The set contains an odd number of data values, so the median is the middle value: 6.
2. What is the median of {7, 9, 10, 16}?
   ➤ The set contains an even number of data values, so the median is the average of the two middle values: $\frac{9 + 10}{2} = 9.5$.

Mode

The *mode* is the value that appears most frequently in a set of data. Some data sets have multiple modes, while other data sets have no modes.

Examples:

1. The mode of {2, 4, 5, 5, 5, 6, 6, 19.2} is 5.
2. The group of numbers {−3, 5, 6, −3, −2, 7, 5, −3, 6, 5, 5, −3} is bimodal since −3 and 5 each occur four times.

NOTE: The SAT and PSAT allow calculators. Therefore, it is important that you learn how to use a calculator and bring the same calculator with you to the exam. Using a calculator provides greater accuracy and often saves valuable test time.

Mean, Median, and Mode

DIRECTIONS: Choose the correct answer to each of the following items. Use a calculator when necessary. Answers are on page 901.

1. What is the average of 8, 6, and 16?

   A. 10   C. 13   E. 18
   B. 12   D. 15

2. What is the average of 0 and 50?

   A. 0   C. 10   E. 50
   B. 5   D. 25

3. What is the average of 5, 11, 12, and 8?

   A. 6   C. 9   E. 12
   B. 8   D. 10

4. What is the average of 25, 28, 21, 30, and 36?

   A. 25   C. 29   E. 44
   B. 28   D. 34

5. What is the average of $\frac{1}{4}$, $\frac{3}{4}$, $\frac{5}{8}$, $\frac{1}{2}$, and $\frac{3}{8}$?

   A. $\frac{3}{32}$ C. $\frac{1}{2}$ E. $\frac{27}{32}$
   B. $\frac{5}{16}$ D. $\frac{5}{8}$

6. What is the average of $0.78, $0.45, $0.36, $0.98, $0.55, and $0.54?

   A. $0.49   C. $0.56   E. $0.61
   B. $0.54   D. $0.60

7. What is the average of 0.03, 0.11, 0.08, and 0.5?

   A. 0.18   C. 0.28   E. 1.0
   B. 0.25   D. 0.50

8. What is the average of 1,001, 1,002, 1,003, 1,004, and 1,005?

   A. 250   C. 1,003   E. 5,000
   B. 1,000   D. 2,500

9. What is the average of −8, −6, and −13?

   A. −18   C. −13   E. −9
   B. −15   D. −12

10. Jordan receives test scores of 79, 85, 90, 76, and 80. What is the average of these test scores?

    A. 82   C. 84   E. 86
    B. 83   D. 85

11. Mr. Whipple bought five different items costing $4.51, $6.25, $3.32, $4.48, and $2.19. What is the average cost of the five items?

    A. $3.40   C. $3.90   E. $4.15
    B. $3.80   D. $4.00

12. Nadia received scores of 8.5, 9.3, 8.2, and 9.0 in four different gymnastics events. What is the average of her scores?

    A. 8.5   C. 8.9   E. 9.1
    B. 8.75   D. 9

13. Five people have ages of 44, 33, 45, 44, and 29 years. What is the average of their ages in years?

    A. 36   C. 40   E. 43
    B. 39   D. 41

14. In a certain government office, if 360 staff hours are needed to process 120 building permit applications, on the average how long (in hours) does it take to process one application?

    A. 3   C. 12   E. 36
    B. 6   D. 24

15. In a chemical test for Substance X, a sample is divided into five equal parts. If the purity of the five parts is 84 percent, 89 percent, 87 percent, 90 percent, and 80 percent, then what is the overall purity of the sample (expressed as a percent of Substance X)?

    A. 83   C. 86   E. 88
    B. 84   D. 87

16. The average of three numbers is 24. If two of the numbers are 21 and 23, what is the third number?

    A. 20   C. 26   E. 30
    B. 24   D. 28

17. The average of three numbers is 5. If two of the numbers are zero, what is the third number?

    A. 1   C. 5   E. 15
    B. 3   D. 10

18. The average of the weight of four people is 166 pounds. If three of the people weigh 150 pounds, 200 pounds, and 180 pounds, what is the weight of the fourth person?

    A. 134   C. 155   E. 165
    B. 140   D. 161

19. For a certain student, the average of five test scores is 83. If four of the scores are 81, 79, 85, and 90, what is the fifth test score?

    A. 83   C. 81   E. 79
    B. 82   D. 80

20. Sue bought ten items at an average price of $3.60. The cost of eight of the items totaled $30. If the other two items were the same price, what was the price she paid for each?

    A. $15.00   C. $6.00   E. $1.50
    B. $7.50   D. $3.00

21. In a certain shipment, the weights of twelve books average 2.75 pounds. If one of the books is removed, the weights of the remaining books average 2.70 pounds. What was the weight, in pounds, of the book that was removed?

    A. 1.7   C. 3.0   E. 4.5
    B. 2.3   D. 3.3

22. The average of a group of seven test scores is 80. If the lowest and the highest scores are thrown out, the average of the remaining scores is 78. What is the average of the lowest and highest scores?

    A. 100   C. 90   E. 85
    B. 95   D. 88

23. In a certain group, twelve of the children are age 10, and eight are age 15. What is the average of the ages of all the children in the group?

    A. 9.5   C. 11   E. 12
    B. 10.5   D. 11.5

24. Robert made the following deposits in a savings account:

Amount	Frequency
$15	4 times
$20	2 times
$25	4 times

    What was the average of all the deposits Robert made?

    A. $18.50   C. $21.50   E. $22.50
    B. $20.00   D. $22.00

25. The average of the weights of six people sitting in a boat is 145 pounds. After a seventh person gets into the boat, the average of the weights of all seven people in the boat is 147 pounds. What is the weight, in pounds, of the seventh person?

    A. 160   C. 155   E. 147
    B. 159   D. 149

26. Find the mean of the following 5 numbers: 2, 3, 13, 15, and 1.

    A. 4.6   C. 6.8   E. 16.8
    B. 6.2   D. 8.6

27. Find the mean of the following 6 numbers: −3, 2, 6, 5, 2, and 0.

    A. 1   C. 5   E. 8
    B. 2   D. 6

28. If the mean of 6 numbers is 10, what is the sixth number if the five given numbers are −3, 5, 6, 13, and 17?

    A. 12   C. 18   E. 22
    B. 16   D. 20

29. The average of 5 numbers is 56. If two new numbers are added to the list, the average of the 7 numbers is 58. Which of the following equals the average of the two new numbers?

    A. 64   C. 62   E. 60
    B. 63   D. 61

30. Arranged in some order, $3x + 1$, $2x + 4$, and $x + 10$ represent 3 consecutive whole numbers. If x represents a whole number and the average of the 3 numbers is 13, then solve for x.

    A. 2   C. 6   E. 10
    B. 4   D. 8

31. Arthur interviewed 100 female corporate officers and found that 34 of them were 55 years old, 28 were 45 years old, 26 were 35 years old, and 12 of them were 25 years old. What was the average of the women's ages?

    A. 16   C. 43.4   E. 45
    B. 43   D. 44.3

Items #32-34 refer to the following information.
During the last 14 games, a basketball player scored the following points per game: 42, 35, 29, 42, 33, 37, 26, 38, 42, 47, 51, 33, 30, and 40.

32. What is the median score?

    A. 35.4   C. 36   E. 38
    B. 35.7   D. 37.5

33. What is the mode?

    A. 35.4   C. 38   E. 44
    B. 37.5   D. 42

34. If after one more game, the player's average for points per game is exactly 37, how many points did the player score in the fifteenth game?

    A. 30   C. 37.5   E. 44
    B. 37   D. 42

35. Find the median of the following 5 numbers: 1, 3, 7, 2, and 8.

    A. 1   C. 3   E. 7
    B. 2   D. 4.2

36. Find the median for the following data set: {2, −3, 8, 4, 9, −16, 12, 0, 4, 2, 1}.

    A. 4   C. 2   E. 0
    B. 2.1   D. 1

37. Find the median for the following data set: {2, −3, 8, 4, 9, −16, 12, 8, 4, 2}.

    A. 2   C. 3.5   E. 4.2
    B. 3   D. 4

38. Find the mode of the following 5 numbers: 4, 8, 10, 8, and 15.

    A. 4   C. 9   E. 15
    B. 8   D. 10

39. Find the mode of the following data set: {6, 8, 10, 2, −2, 2, 8, 4, 2}.

    A. 6   C. 4   E. 1
    B. 4.4   D. 2

40. A set of seven numbers contains the numbers: 1, 4, 5, and 6. The other three numbers are represented by $2x + 8$, $x − 4$, and $7x − 4$. If the mode of these seven numbers is a negative even integer, then what is a possible value for x?

    A. 0   C. 2   E. 5
    B. 1   D. 4

41. The grades received on a test by twenty students were 100, 55, 75, 80, 65, 65, 95, 90, 80, 45, 40, 50, 85, 85, 85, 80, 80, 70, 65, and 60. What is the average of these grades?

    A. 70.5   C. 77   E. 100
    B. 72.5   D. 80.3

42. Arthur purchased 75 six-inch rulers costing 15¢ each, 100 one-foot rulers costing 30¢ each, and 50 one-yard rulers costing 72¢ each. What was the average price per ruler?

    A. $26\frac{1}{8}$¢   C. 39¢   E. $77\frac{1}{4}$¢
    B. $34\frac{1}{3}$¢   D. 42¢

43. What is the average grade for a student who received 90 in English, 84 in algebra, 75 in French, and 76 in music, if the subjects have the following weights: English 4, algebra 3, French 3, and music 1?

    A. 81   C. 82   E. 83
    B. $81\frac{1}{2}$ D. $82\frac{1}{2}$

Items #44-46 refer to the following information.
A census shows that on a certain neighborhood block the number of children in each family is 3, 4, 4, 0, 1, 2, 0, 2, and 2, respectively.

44. Find the average number of children per family.

    A. 4   C. $3\frac{1}{2}$ E. $1\frac{1}{2}$
    B. 3   D. 2

45. Find the median number of children.

    A. 1   C. 3   E. 5
    B. 2   D. 4

46. Find the mode of the number of children.

    A. 0   C. 2   E. 4
    B. 1   D. 3

Ratios and Proportions

Working with Ratios

1. Two-Part Ratios

A **ratio** is a statement about the relationship between any two quantities, or we might say a ratio is a statement that compares any two quantities. Suppose that in an English class there are five girls and eight boys. We can compare those quantities by saying that the ratio of girls to boys is 5 to 8. Conversely, the ratio of boys to girls is 8 to 5. Notice that order is very important in stating a ratio. The order of the numbers in the ratio must reflect the order of the categories being compared. In our example, it would be incorrect to say that the ratio of girls to boys is 8 to 5.

A phrase such as "5 to 8" is one way of stating a ratio, but there are several other ways. A ratio can also be described using a colon: "the ratio of girls to boys is 5:8" or "the ratio of boys to girls is 8:5." Alternatively, the ratio can be written in fraction form: "the ratio $\frac{girls}{boys}$ is $\frac{5}{8}$," and "the ratio $\frac{boys}{girls}$ is $\frac{8}{5}$."

Ratios of the form $a{:}b$ or a/b can also refer to numbers instead of a number of objects. We can speak abstractly of the ratio 5:8, which is the ratio of any set of five things to any set of eight things. Consequently, ratios can be manipulated in the same way as fractions. Just as you could rewrite a fraction to get a form with a different denominator, you can convert a ratio to an equivalent form by multiplying both terms of the ratio by the same number. For example, $\frac{5}{8} = \frac{5 \cdot 2}{8 \cdot 2} = \frac{10}{16}$ and $\frac{8}{5} = \frac{8 \cdot 3}{5 \cdot 3} = \frac{24}{15}$.

It is customary to reduce a ratio to its lowest terms just as you would reduce fractions to their lowest terms. For example, in a certain classroom, there are ten girls and sixteen boys; the ratio of girls to boys is 10/16, which is 5/8. Although you may not be aware of it, you probably also use ratios informally in ordinary conversation. A common phrase that signifies a ratio is "for every (number)…there are (number)…." For example, in the classroom just described, for every 10 girls there are 16 boys, or in lowest terms, for every 5 girls there are 8 boys, and for every 8 boys there are 5 girls.

Finally, a ratio can also be stated as a rate using the word "per." If a car travels 200 miles and uses 10 gallons of fuel, the car gets 200 miles per 10 gallons, or 20 miles per gallon. Cost, too, is often described as a ratio. If it is possible to purchase a dozen greeting cards for $2.40, the cost of the cards is $2.40 per dozen, or 20 cents per card.

2. Three-Part Ratios

When three quantities are to be compared, they can be stated using ordinary ratios. For example, if a bowl of fruit contains two apples, three pears, and five oranges, the ratio of apples to pears is 2:3; the ratio of apples to oranges is 2:5; and the ratio of pears to oranges is 3:5. This same information can also be conveyed in a single statement. The ratio of apples to pears to oranges is 2:3:5.

A **three-part ratio** depends on the middle term to join the two outside terms. Above, the ratio of apples to pears is 2:3, and the ratio of pears to oranges is 3:5. Since 3 is common to both ratios, it can be the middle term. Sometimes it will be necessary to find a common middle term.

Example:

On a certain day, a bank has the following rates of exchange: $\frac{dollar}{mark} = \frac{1}{3}$ and $\frac{mark}{pound} = \frac{6}{1}$. What is the ratio of dollars to pounds?

➤ To find the ratio dollars:pounds, we will use marks as the middle term. However, the ratio of dollars to marks is 1:3, and the ratio of marks to pounds is 6:1. We must change the first ratio to express it in terms of six marks rather than three marks. This is like finding a common denominator before adding fractions: $\frac{1}{3} = \frac{1 \cdot 2}{3 \cdot 2} = \frac{2}{6}$, so the ratio of dollars to marks is 2:6, and the ratio of dollars to marks to pounds is 2:6:1. Thus, the ratio of dollars to pounds is 2:1.

3. Using Ratios to Divide Quantities

An item may require that you divide a quantity according to a certain ratio.

Examples:

1. A $100 prize is divided between two contestants according to the ratio 2:3. How much does each contestant receive?
   ➤ Add the terms of the ratio to determine by how many parts the prize is to be divided. Divide the prize by that many parts, and multiply the result by the number of parts to be given to each contestant. $2 + 3 = 5$, so the prize is to be divided into five parts. Each part is $100 \div 5 = \$20$. One contestant gets $2 \cdot \$20 = \$40$, and the other contestant receives $3 \cdot \$20 = \$60$.

2. Bronze is 16 parts tin and 9 parts copper. If a bronze ingot weighs 100 pounds, how much does the tin weigh (in pounds)?
   ➤ First, the number of parts in the ratio is $16 + 9 = 25$. Second, $100 \div 25 = 4$, so each part is worth 4 pounds. Since there are 16 parts of tin, the tin must weigh $16 \cdot 4 = 64$ pounds.

Working with Proportions

A *proportion* is the mathematical equivalent of a verbal analogy. For example, 2:3::8:12 is equivalent to "two is to three as eight is to twelve." The main difference between an analogy and a proportion is the precision. A verbal analogy depends upon words that do not have unique and precise meanings, while mathematical proportions are made up of numbers, which are very exact.

In a mathematical proportion, the first and last terms are called the "extremes" of the proportion because they are on the extreme outside, and the two middle terms are called the "means" (mean can mean "middle"). In a mathematical proportion, the product of the extremes is always equal to the product of the means. For example, 2:3::8:12 and $2 \cdot 12 = 3 \cdot 8$.

1. Determining the Missing Elements in Proportions

Since any ratio can be written as a fraction, a proportion, which states that two ratios are equivalent, can also be written in fractional forms as an equation. This is the foundation for the process called cross-multiplication, a process that is useful in solving for an unknown element in a proportion.

Examples:

1. $\frac{2}{3} = \frac{8}{12} \Rightarrow \frac{2}{3} \gtrless \frac{8}{12} \Rightarrow 2 \cdot 12 = 3 \cdot 8$

2. $\frac{6}{9} = \frac{12}{x} \Rightarrow \frac{6}{9} \gtrless \frac{12}{x} \Rightarrow 6x = 108 \Rightarrow x = \frac{108}{6} = 18$.
   ➤ After cross-multiplying, divide both sides of the equality by the numerical coefficient of the unknown. Then, check the correctness of this solution by substituting 18 back in to the original proportion: $\frac{6}{9} = \frac{12}{18} \Rightarrow \frac{6}{9} \gtrless \frac{12}{18} \Rightarrow 6 \cdot 18 = 9 \cdot 12$.

3. $\frac{3}{15} = \frac{x}{45} \Rightarrow \frac{3}{15} \gtrless \frac{x}{45} \Rightarrow 3 \cdot 45 = 15x \Rightarrow x = \frac{135}{15} = 9$
   ➤ Check the solution by substitution: $\frac{3}{15} = \frac{9}{45} \Rightarrow \frac{3}{15} \gtrless \frac{9}{45} \Rightarrow 3 \cdot 45 = 15 \cdot 9 \Rightarrow 135 = 135$.

2. Direct Proportions

The use of proportions can be a powerful problem-solving tool. *Direct proportions* equate ratios of two quantities having a direct relationship. The more there is of one quantity, the more there is of the other quantity, and vice versa.

Example:

If the cost of a dozen donuts is $3.60, what is the cost of 4 donuts? Assume there is no discount for buying in bulk.

➤ One method for solving this item is to calculate the cost of one donut ($3.60/12 = \$0.30$), and then multiply that cost by four ($\$0.30 \cdot 4 = \$1.20$). While this approach is not incorrect, the same result can be reached in a conceptually simpler way. The more donuts being purchased, the greater the total cost, and vice versa. Relate the quantities using a direct proportion: $\frac{\text{Total Cost } X}{\text{Total Cost } Y} = \frac{\text{Number } X}{\text{Number } Y} \Rightarrow \frac{\$3.60}{x} = \frac{12}{4} \Rightarrow 12x = \$3.60 \cdot 4 \Rightarrow x = \frac{\$14.40}{12} = \$1.20$.

In the previous example, we set up the proportion by grouping like terms: "cost" is on one side of the proportion and "number" is on the other side. It is equally correct to set up the proportion as $\frac{\text{Total Cost } X}{\text{Number } X} = \frac{\text{Total Cost } Y}{\text{Number } Y}$. Additionally, it does not matter which quantity is on top or bottom: $\frac{\text{Number } X}{\text{Total Cost } X} = \frac{\text{Number } Y}{\text{Total Cost } Y}$ is equally correct. However, it is generally a good idea to group like terms to avoid confusion.

The LONGER the travel time, the GREATER the distance traveled (assuming a CONSTANT speed).

Example:

If a plane moving at a constant speed flies 300 miles in 6 hours, how far will the plane fly in 8 hours?

➤ Group like terms: $\frac{\text{Time } X}{\text{Time } Y} = \frac{\text{Distance } X}{\text{Distance } Y} \Rightarrow \frac{6}{8} = \frac{300}{x} \Rightarrow \frac{6}{8} \succ\!\prec \frac{300}{x} \Rightarrow 6x = 8 \cdot 300 \Rightarrow x = \frac{2,400}{6} = 400.$

The LONGER the time of operation, the GREATER the output.

Example:

If an uninterrupted stamping machine operating at a constant rate postmarks 320 envelopes in 5 minutes, how long will it take the machine to postmark 480 envelopes?

➤ Group like terms: $\frac{\text{Time } X}{\text{Time } Y} = \frac{\text{Output } X}{\text{Output } Y} \Rightarrow \frac{5}{x} = \frac{320}{480} \Rightarrow \frac{5}{x} \succ\!\prec \frac{320}{480} \Rightarrow 5(480) = x(320) \Rightarrow x = \frac{5(480)}{320} = 7.5$ minutes.

The GREATER the number of items, the GREATER the weight.

Example:

If 20 jars of preserves weigh 25 pounds, how much do 15 jars of preserves weigh?

➤ Group like terms: $\frac{\text{Weight of Jars } X}{\text{Weight of Jars } Y} = \frac{\text{Jars } X}{\text{Jars } Y} \Rightarrow \frac{25}{x} = \frac{20}{15} \Rightarrow \frac{25}{x} \succ\!\prec \frac{20}{15} \Rightarrow 25(15) = x(20) \Rightarrow x = \frac{25(15)}{20} = 18.75$ pounds.

3. Inverse Proportions

In some situations, quantities are related inversely; that is, an increase in one results in a decrease in the other. For example, the more workers, or machines, doing a job, the less time it takes to finish. In this case, quantities are related inversely to each other. To solve problems involving inverse relationships, use the following procedure to set up an inverse proportion.

1. Set up an ordinary proportion—make sure to group like quantities.
2. Invert the right side of the proportion.
3. Cross-multiply and solve for the unknown.

Example:

Traveling at a constant rate of 150 miles per hour, a plane makes the trip from Phoenix to Grand Junction in 4 hours. How long will the trip take if the plane flies at a constant rate of 200 miles per hour?

➤ First, set up a proportion, grouping like terms: $\frac{\text{Speed } X}{\text{Speed } Y} = \frac{\text{Time } X}{\text{Time } Y} \Rightarrow \frac{150}{200} = \frac{4}{x}$. Then, invert the right side of the proportion: $\frac{150}{200} = \frac{x}{4} \Rightarrow \frac{150}{200} \succ\!\prec \frac{x}{4} \Rightarrow 150(4) = 200x \Rightarrow x = \frac{150(4)}{200} = 3$ hours.

While it is possible, though not advised, to set up a direct proportion without grouping like terms, with an inverse proportion, it is essential to group like terms. This is sufficient reasoning to always group like terms: You will not make a mistake if the item involves an inverse proportion.

NOTE: The SAT and PSAT allow calculators. Therefore, it is important that you learn how to use a calculator and bring the same calculator with you to the exam. Using a calculator provides greater accuracy and often saves valuable test time.

Ratios and Proportions

DIRECTIONS: Choose the correct answer to each of the following items. Use a calculator when necessary. Answers are on page 904.

1. If a jar contains 3 blue marbles and 8 red marbles, what is the ratio of blue marbles to red marbles?

   A. 3:11 C. 8:3 E. 4:1
   B. 3:8 D. 11:3

2. If a school has 24 teachers and 480 students, what is the ratio of teachers to students?

   A. $\frac{1}{20}$ C. $\frac{1}{48}$ E. $\frac{1}{200}$
   B. $\frac{1}{24}$ D. $\frac{1}{56}$

3. If a library contains 12,000 works of fiction and 3,000 works of nonfiction, what is the ratio of works of fiction to works of nonfiction?

   A. $\frac{1}{9}$ C. $\frac{1}{4}$ E. $\frac{5}{1}$
   B. $\frac{1}{5}$ D. $\frac{4}{1}$

4. Which of the following is (are) equivalent to $\frac{1}{3}$?

   I. $\frac{40}{120}$

   II. $\frac{75}{100}$

   III. $\frac{120}{360}$

   A. I only D. II and III only
   B. III only E. I, II, and III
   C. I and III only

Items #5-6 refer to the following table.

Students at Tyler Junior High School		
	7th Grade	8th Grade
Girls	90	80
Boys	85	75

5. What is the ratio of seventh-grade girls to the total number of girls at Tyler Junior High School?

   A. $\frac{9}{17}$ C. $\frac{18}{17}$ E. $\frac{17}{9}$
   B. $\frac{8}{9}$ D. $\frac{9}{8}$

6. What is the ratio of eighth-grade girls to the total number of students at Tyler Junior High School?

   A. $\frac{8}{33}$ C. $\frac{8}{15}$ E. $\frac{17}{30}$
   B. $\frac{9}{33}$ D. $\frac{8}{17}$

7. If an airplane flies 275 miles on 25 gallons of fuel, then what is the average fuel consumption for the entire trip expressed in miles per gallon?

   A. 25 C. 15 E. 7
   B. 18 D. 11

8. An assortment of candy includes 12 chocolates, 6 caramels, and 9 mints. What is the ratio of chocolates:caramels:mints?

   A. 4:3:2 C. 3:4:2 E. 2:4:3
   B. 4:2:3 D. 3:2:4

9. If Lucy has twice the amount of money that Ricky has, and Ricky has three times the amount of money that Ethel has, then what is the ratio of the amount of money Ethel has to the amount of money Lucy has?

   A. $\frac{1}{8}$ C. $\frac{1}{4}$ E. $\frac{2}{1}$
   B. $\frac{1}{6}$ D. $\frac{1}{2}$

10. If three farkels buy two kirns, and three kirns buy five pucks, then nine farkels buy how many pucks?

    A. 2 C. 8 E. 17
    B. 5 D. 10

11. If Machine X operates at twice the rate of Machine Y, and Machine Y operates at $\frac{2}{3}$ the rate of Machine Z, then what is the ratio of the rate of operation of Machine X to the rate of operation of Machine Z?

    A. $\frac{4}{1}$ C. $\frac{4}{3}$ E. $\frac{1}{3}$
    B. $\frac{3}{1}$ D. $\frac{3}{4}$

12. If 48 marbles are to be divided between Bill and Carl in the ratio of 3:5, how many marbles should Bill get?

    A. 6 C. 18 E. 30
    B. 8 D. 24

13. If $10 is to be divided between Janeway and Nelix so that Nelix receives $\frac{1}{4}$ of what Janeway receives, then how much should Janeway receive?

    A. $10.00   C. $7.50   E. $2.00
    B. $8.00   D. $6.00

14. If a $1,000 reward is to be divided among three people in the ratio of 2:3:5, what is the largest amount that will be given to any one of the three recipients?

    A. $200   C. $500   E. $900
    B. $300   D. $750

15. If $\frac{6}{8} = \frac{x}{4}$, then $x = ?$

    A. 12   C. 4   E. 2
    B. 6   D. 3

16. If $\frac{14}{x} = \frac{2}{7}$, then $x = ?$

    A. 7   C. 28   E. 343
    B. 14   D. 49

17. If $\frac{3}{4} = \frac{4}{x}$, then $x = ?$

    A. $\frac{3}{16}$ C. $\frac{4}{3}$ E. $\frac{16}{3}$
    B. $\frac{3}{4}$ D. $\frac{7}{3}$

18. If 240 widgets cost $36, what is the cost of 180 widgets?

    A. $8   C. $24   E. $32
    B. $16   D. $27

19. If a kilogram of a certain cheese costs $9.60, what is the cost of 450 grams of the cheese? (1 kilogram = 1,000 grams)

    A. $2.78   C. $3.88   E. $5.12
    B. $3.14   D. $4.32

20. If 50 feet of electrical wire cost $4.80, then $10.80 will buy how many feet of the wire?

    A. 60   C. 67.25   E. 112.5
    B. 62.5   D. 75

21. In a certain group of people, 100 people have red hair. If only 25 percent of the people have red hair, then how many people do not have red hair?

    A. 75   C. 300   E. 500
    B. 125   D. 400

22. If a certain fundraising project has raised $12,000, which is 20 percent of its goal, how much money will have been raised when 50 percent of the goal has been reached?

    A. $60,000   C. $18,000   E. $4,800
    B. $30,000   D. $15,000

23. If 48 liters of a certain liquid weigh 50 kilograms, then how much (in kilograms) will 72 liters of the liquid weigh?

    A. 25   C. 75   E. 120
    B. 60   D. 90

24. If the trip from Soldier Field to Wrigley Field takes two hours walking at a constant rate of four miles per hour, how long (in hours) will the same trip take walking at a constant rate of five miles per hour?

    A. 2.5   C. 1.6   E. 1.25
    B. 1.75   D. 1.5

25. A swimming pool is filled by either of two pipes. Pipe A supplies water at the rate of 200 gallons per hour and takes eight hours to fill the pool. If Pipe B can fill the pool in five hours, what is the rate (in gallons per hour) at which Pipe B supplies water?

    A. 125   C. 360   E. 575
    B. 320   D. 480

26. What is the ratio of 3 to 8 expressed as a decimal?

    A. 0.125   C. 0.375   E. 1
    B. 0.25   D. 0.50

27. If the ratio of 3 to 4 is the same as the ratio of 15 to x, find x.

    A. 5   C. 15   E. 25
    B. 10   D. 20

28. Annika can solve 10 math problems in 30 minutes. At this rate, how many math problems can she solve in 48 minutes?

    A. 8   C. 32   E. 56
    B. 16   D. 46

29. Seung can walk up 6 flights of stairs in 4 minutes. At this rate, how many flights of stairs could he walk up in 18 minutes?

    A. 4   C. 14   E. 27
    B. 10   D. 20

30. If 4 candy bars cost $1.04, how much should 6 candy bars cost?

    A. $0.96   C. $1.56   E. $2.06
    B. $1.25   D. $1.85

31. If Baby Andrew takes 8 steps to walk 2 yards, how many steps will he take to walk 5 yards?

    A. 5   C. 15   E. 25
    B. 10   D. 20

32. If a 40-inch stick is divided in a 3:5 ratio, how long (in inches) is the shorter piece?

    A. 5   C. 15   E. 25
    B. 10   D. 20

33. Orville claims that 3 bags of his popcorn will yield 28 ounces when popped. If this is the case, how many ounces will 5 bags of his popcorn yield when popped?

    A. 23   C. $54\frac{1}{2}$ E. $64\frac{2}{3}$

    B. $46\frac{2}{3}$ D. 64

34. In a poll of 1,000 people, 420 said they would vote for Mason. Based on this poll, how many people would be expected to vote for Mason if 60,000,000 people actually vote?

    A. 25,200,000   C. 26,000,000   E. 26,500,000
    B. 25,500,000   D. 26,200,000

35. In 4 days, a worm grew from 5 cm. to 12 cm. At this rate, how long will the worm be in another 6 days?

    A. 21 cm.   C. 22.25 cm.   E. 23 cm.
    B. 22 cm.   D. 22.5 cm.

36. Elan can mow 3 lawns in 85 minutes. At this rate, how long would he need to mow 5 lawns?

    A. 140 minutes, 20 seconds
    B. 141 minutes
    C. 141 minutes, 40 seconds
    D. 142 minutes
    E. 142 minutes, 50 seconds

37. Sarah does $\frac{1}{5}$ of a job in 6 minutes. At this rate, what fraction of the job will she do in 10 minutes?

    A. $\frac{1}{4}$ C. $\frac{1}{2}$ E. $\frac{3}{2}$

    B. $\frac{1}{3}$ D. $\frac{3}{4}$

38. A snapshot measures $2\frac{1}{2}$ inches by $1\frac{7}{8}$ inches. If it is enlarged so that the longer dimension is 4 inches, what is the length of the enlarged shorter dimension?

    A. $2\frac{1}{2}$ in.   C. $3\frac{3}{8}$ in.   E. 5 in.
    B. 3 in.   D. 4 in.

39. Three of the men's white handkerchiefs cost $2.29. How much will a dozen of those handkerchiefs cost?

    A. $27.48   C. $9.16   E. $4.58
    B. $13.74   D. $6.87

40. A certain pole casts a 24 foot long shadow. At the same time another pole that is 3 feet high casts a 4 foot long shadow. How high is the first pole, given that the heights and shadows are in proportion?

    A. 18 ft.   C. 20 ft.   E. 24 ft.
    B. 19 ft.   D. 21 ft.

41. If a drawing is scaled $\frac{1}{8}$ inch to the foot, what is the actual length represented by $3\frac{1}{2}$ inches on the drawing?

    A. 3.5 ft.   C. 21 ft.   E. 120 ft.
    B. 7 ft.   D. 28 ft.

42. Aluminum bronze consists of copper and aluminum, usually in the ratio of 10:1 by weight. If an object made of this alloy weighs 77 pounds, how many pounds of aluminum does it contain?

    A. 0.7   C. 7.7   E. 77.0
    B. 7.0   D. 70.7

43. It costs 31 cents/ft.^{2} to lay vinyl flooring. How much will it cost to lay 180 ft.^{2} of flooring?

    A. $16.20   C. $55.80   E. $180.00
    B. $18.60   D. $62.00

44. If Tuvak earns $352 in 16 days, how much will he earn in 117 days?

    A. $3,050   C. $2,285   E. $1,170
    B. $2,574   D. $2,080

45. Assuming that on a blueprint $\frac{1}{8}$ inch equals 12 inches of actual length, what is the actual length, in inches, of a steel bar represented on the blueprint by a line $3\frac{3}{4}$ inches long?

    A. $3\frac{3}{4}$ C. 36   E. 450

    B. 30   D. 360

46. Blake, James, and Staunton invested $9,000, $7,000, and $6,000, respectively. Their profits were to be divided according to the ratio of their investments. If James uses his share of the firm's profit of $825 to pay a personal debt of $230, how much will he have left?

    A. $30.50   C. $34.50   E. $37.50
    B. $32.50   D. $36.50

47. If on a road map $1\frac{5}{8}$ inches represents 10 miles, how many miles does 2.25 inches represent?

    A. $\frac{180}{13}$ miles   C. $\frac{57}{4}$ miles   E. 3 miles

    B. $\frac{53}{4}$ miles   D. $\frac{27}{2}$ miles

48. Jake and Jessie are standing next to each other in the sun. If Jake's shadow is 48 inches long, and he is 72 inches tall, how long is Jessie's shadow, in inches, if she is 66 inches tall?

    A. 42   C. 44   E. 46
    B. 43   D. 45

49. A blueprint allows 1 inch for every 12 feet. At that rate, 7 inches represents how many yards?

    A. $\frac{28}{3}$ C. 84   E. 336

    B. 28   D. 252

50. A bug crawls clockwise around the outside rim of a clock from the 12 to the 4 and travels 7 inches. If a second bug crawls around the outside rim from the 6 to the 11, in the same direction, how many inches did the bug travel?

    A. 7.75   C. 8.25   E. 8.75
    B. 8   D. 8.5

Exponents and Radicals

Powers and Exponents

1. Powers of Numbers

A *power* of a number indicates repeated multiplication. For example, "3 to the fifth power" means $3 \cdot 3 \cdot 3 \cdot 3 \cdot 3$, which equals 243. Therefore, 3 raised to the fifth power is 243.

Examples:

1. 2 to the second power $= 2 \cdot 2 = 4$.

2. 2 to the third power $= 2 \cdot 2 \cdot 2 = 8$.

3. 2 to the fourth power $= 2 \cdot 2 \cdot 2 \cdot 2 = 16$.

4. 3 to the second power $= 3 \cdot 3 = 9$.

5. 3 to the third power $= 3 \cdot 3 \cdot 3 = 27$.

The second power of a number is also called the square of the number. This refers to a square with sides equal in length to the number; the square of the number is equal to the area of the aforementioned square.

$$3 \cdot 3 = 9$$

The third power of a number is also called the cube of the number, which refers to a cube with sides equal in length to the number; the cube of the number is equal to the volume of the cube with sides equal in length to that number.

$$2 \cdot 2 \cdot 2 = 8$$

Beyond the square and the cube, powers are referred to by their numerical names, *e.g.*, fourth, fifth, sixth, and so on.

2. Exponential Notation

The notation system for designating the power of a number is a superscript following the number. The number being multiplied is the *base,* and the superscript is the *exponent*. The exponent indicates the operation of repeated multiplication.

Examples:

1. The third power of 2 is written as 2^3: base $\rightarrow 2^{3 \leftarrow \text{exponent}} = 2 \cdot 2 \cdot 2$.

2. The fifth power of 2 is written as 3^5: base $\rightarrow 3^{5 \leftarrow \text{exponent}} = 3 \cdot 3 \cdot 3 \cdot 3 \cdot 3$.

A base without an exponent is unchanged and represents the *first power* of the number. Since $x^1 = x$, the exponent 1 is not explicitly noted.

Examples:

1. $2^1 = 2$

2. $1,000^1 = 1,000$

Operations Involving Exponents

There are special rules that apply to operations involving exponents. When you begin working with radicals (fractional exponents) and algebraic expressions, these same rules will apply.

1. Multiplication Involving Exponents

The **product rule** is used to multiply two identical bases with similar or different exponents. To multiply powers of the same base, add the exponents: $x^m \cdot x^n = x^{m+n}$. To better understand this rule, explicitly write out the multiplication indicated by the exponents.

Example:

$$2^2 \cdot 2^3 = 2^{2+3} = 2^5 = (2 \cdot 2)(2 \cdot 2 \cdot 2)$$
➤ Writing out the expression and using the product rule give you the same result, but it is much faster to apply the latter.

Therefore, the product rule provides an easy shortcut for multiplying identical bases with exponents.

Examples:

1. $3^2 \cdot 3^5 = 3^{(2+5)} = 3^7$
2. $5^2 \cdot 5^3 \cdot 5^5 = 5^{(2+3+5)} = 5^{10}$
3. $x^3 \cdot x^4 = x^{(3+4)} = x^7$
4. $y^7 \cdot y^2 \cdot y^4 = y^{(7+2+4)} = y^{13}$

Notice that each of these examples has only one base. The product rule does NOT apply to terms with different bases.

Example:

$$2^4 \cdot 3^4 = ?$$
➤ The product rule cannot be used since 2 and 3 are not equal bases. You must explicitly multiply all of the numbers: $2^4 \cdot 3^4 = (2 \cdot 2 \cdot 2 \cdot 2)(3 \cdot 3 \cdot 3 \cdot 3) = 16 \cdot 81 = 1,296$.

Finally, the product rule does NOT apply to addition or subtraction of bases with exponents, even if the bases are identical.

Example:

$2^2 + 2^3 \neq 2^5$, since $2^2 + 2^3 = (2 \cdot 2) + (2 \cdot 2 \cdot 2) = 4 + 8 = 12$ and $2^5 = 2 \cdot 2 \cdot 2 \cdot 2 \cdot 2 = 32$.

2. Division Involving Exponents

The **quotient rule** is used for division involving identical bases with exponents. When dividing similar bases, subtract the exponent in the denominator from the exponent in the numerator: $\frac{x^m}{x^n} = x^{m-n}$. As with the product rule, the quotient rule can be verified by explicitly carrying out the indicated operations, as illustrated in the first of the following examples.

Examples:

1. $\frac{2^5}{2^3} = 2^{(5-3)} = 2^2$

    ➤ Writing out the expression and using the quotient rule give you the same result: $\frac{2^5}{2^3} = \frac{2 \cdot 2 \cdot 2 \cdot 2 \cdot 2}{2 \cdot 2 \cdot 2} = \frac{32}{8} = 4 = 2^2$.

2. $\frac{5^{10}}{5^9} = 5^{(10-9)} = 5^1 = 5$

3. $\frac{x^8}{x^6} = x^{(8-6)} = x^2$

4. $\frac{y^3}{y^2} = y^{(3-2)} = y^1 = y$

An *exponent of zero* results whenever a quantity is divided into itself. Since a quantity divided into itself is equal to 1, any base (except zero) with an exponent of zero is also equal to 1: $x^0 = 1$ if $x \neq 0$. 0^0 is an undefined operation in math.

Examples:

1. $\frac{5^3}{5^3} = 5^{(3-3)} = 5^0 = 1$

2. $\frac{x^{12}}{x^{12}} = x^{(12-12)} = x^0 = 1$

3. Raising a Power to a Power

The *power rule* is used when a power of a number is raised to another power. This is done by multiplying the exponents together: $(x^m)^n = x^{mn}$. Again, we can prove the validity of this shortcut by explicitly carrying out the indicated multiplications.

Examples:

1. $(2^2)^3 = 2^{(2 \cdot 3)} = 2^6$

   ➤ Writing out the expression and using the power rule give you the same result: $(2^2)^3 = (2 \cdot 2)^3 = 4^3 = 4 \cdot 4 \cdot 4 = 64 = 2^6$.

2. $(x^3)^4 = x^{(3 \cdot 4)} = x^{12}$

4. Raising a Product to a Power

The *product power rule* is used when a product with exponents is raised to a power. The exponent outside the parentheses governs all the factors inside the parentheses. When raising a product to a power, first multiply the exponent on the outside by each exponent on the inside: $(x^m \cdot y^p)^n = x^{mn} \cdot y^{pn}$.

Examples:

1. $(2 \cdot 3)^2 = 2^2 \cdot 3^2 = 4 \cdot 9 = 36$

   ➤ Writing out the expression and using the product power rule give you the same result: $(2 \cdot 3)^2 = (6)^2 = 36$.

2. $(2^2 \cdot 3^3)^2 = 2^{(2 \cdot 2)} \cdot 3^{(3 \cdot 2)} = (2^4)(3^6) = (16)(729) = 11,664$

3. $(x^2 \cdot y^3)^4 = x^{(2 \cdot 4)} \cdot y^{(3 \cdot 4)} = x^8 y^{12}$

5. Raising a Quotient to a Power

The *quotient power rule* is used when a quotient with exponents is raised to a power. It is essentially the same as the previous rule for determining the power of a product. The exponent outside the parentheses governs all the factors inside the parentheses. Determine the power of a quotient by multiplying the exponent on the outside by each exponent on the inside:

$$\left(\frac{x^m}{y^p}\right)^n = \frac{x^{mn}}{y^{pn}}.$$

Examples:

1. $\left(\frac{2}{3}\right)^3 = \frac{2^3}{3^3} = \frac{8}{27}$

   ➤ Writing out the expression and using the quotient power rule give you the same result: $\left(\frac{2}{3}\right)^3 = \frac{2}{3} \cdot \frac{2}{3} \cdot \frac{2}{3} = \frac{2 \cdot 2 \cdot 2}{3 \cdot 3 \cdot 3} = \frac{8}{27}$.

2. $\left(\frac{1^2}{3^3}\right)^2 = \frac{1^{(2 \cdot 2)}}{3^{(3 \cdot 2)}} = \frac{1^4}{3^6} = \frac{1}{729}$

3. $\left(\frac{x^2}{y^3}\right)^2 = \frac{x^{(2 \cdot 2)}}{y^{(3 \cdot 2)}} = \frac{x^4}{y^6}$

6. Negative Exponents

Negative exponents do not signify negative numbers. Instead, they signify fractions. Specifically, a negative exponent indicates the power of the *reciprocal* of the base: $x^{-n} = \frac{1}{x^n}$.

Examples:

1. $\frac{2^2}{2^3} = 2^{(2-3)} = 2^{-1} = \frac{1}{2^1} = \frac{1}{2}$ or $\frac{2^2}{2^3} = \frac{2 \cdot 2}{2 \cdot 2 \cdot 2} = \frac{4}{8} = \frac{1}{2}$

2. $3^{-2} = \left(\frac{1}{3}\right)^2 = \frac{1}{9}$

3. $x^{-3} = \left(\frac{1}{x}\right)^3 = \frac{1}{x^3}$

7. Rational (Fractional) Exponents

Exponents are not restricted to integer values. *Rational (fractional) exponents* are also possible. Later in this chapter, we will use rational exponents when working with radicals. Rational exponents also appear in algebraic expressions, functions, and equations. The rules for working with rational exponents are the same as those for integer exponents.

Examples:

1. $2^{1/2} \cdot 2^{1/2} = 2^1 = 2$

2. $(x^2 y^4)^{1/4} = x^{1/2} y$

8. Working with Exponents

Complex expressions may require the application of two or more operations involving exponents. No matter how complex an item gets, it can be solved by a series of simple steps following the five rules that are explained above for working with exponents. Remember to follow the rules for order of operations. Also, be careful when negative signs are involved.

Examples:

1. $(2^3 \cdot 3^2)^2 = 2^{3 \cdot 2} \cdot 3^{2 \cdot 2} = 2^6 \cdot 3^4$

2. $\left(\frac{3^3 \cdot 5^5}{3^2 \cdot 5^2}\right)^2 = (3^{3-2} \cdot 5^{5-2})^2 = (3^1 \cdot 5^3)^2 = 3^2 \cdot 5^6$

3. $\left(\frac{x^2 \cdot y^3}{x \cdot y^2}\right)^2 = (x^{2-1} \cdot y^{3-2})^2 = (x \cdot y)^2 = x^2 y^2$

4. $(-3)^3 (-2)^6 = (-27)(64) = -1,728$

5. $-2^4 (-3)^2 = -(2^4)(-3)^2 = -(16)(9) = -144$

These rules for working with exponents provide simple shortcuts, as verified by explicitly executing all indicated operations. When you begin to manipulate algebraic expressions, not only will these same shortcuts apply, but they will become indispensable.

SUMMARY OF OPERATIONS INVOLVING EXPONENTS

$$x^1 = x; \; x^0 = 1$$

Product Rule: $x^m \cdot x^n = x^{m+n}$

Quotient Rule: $\frac{x^m}{x^n} = x^{m-n}$

Power Rule: $(x^m)^n = x^{mn}$

Product Power Rule: $(x^m \cdot y^p)^n = x^{mn} \cdot y^{pn}$

Quotient Power Rule: $\left(\frac{x^m}{y^p}\right)^n = \frac{x^{mn}}{y^{pn}}$

Negative Exponents: $x^{-n} = \left(\frac{1}{x}\right)^n = \frac{1}{x^n}$

Roots and Radicals

1. Roots of Numbers

A **square root** of a number x is a solution to the equation $\sqrt{x} = b$, in which $x = b^2$. When you perform the multiplication indicated by an exponent, you are in effect answering the question, "What do I get when I multiply this number by itself so many times?" Now ask the opposite question, "What number, when multiplied by itself so many times, will give me a certain value?" For example, when you raise 2 to the third power, you find out that $2^3 = 8$. Now, ask the question in the other direction. What number, when raised to the third, is equal to 8?

This reverse process is called "finding the root of a number." Why roots? Look at the following diagram; since $2^6 = 64$, the sixth root of 64 is 2. The picture resembles plant roots.

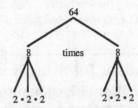

Of course, we rarely deal with sixth roots. Mostly, we deal with two roots: $2 \cdot 2 = 4$, so the second or **square root** of 4 is 2; and occasionally with numbers having three roots: $2 \cdot 2 \cdot 2 = 8$, so the third or **cube root** of 8 is 2.

The operation of taking a square root of a number is signaled by the **radical** sign, $\sqrt{}$. **Radical** comes from the Latin word "rad," which means "root."

Examples:

1. $\sqrt{1} = 1$	3. $\sqrt{9} = 3$	5. $\sqrt{25} = 5$	7. $\sqrt{49} = 7$	9. $\sqrt{81} = 9$	11. $\sqrt{121} = 11$
2. $\sqrt{4} = 2$	4. $\sqrt{16} = 4$	6. $\sqrt{36} = 6$	8. $\sqrt{64} = 8$	10. $\sqrt{100} = 10$	12. $\sqrt{144} = 12$

The symbol $\sqrt{}$ always denotes a positive number. Later, when we get to the topic of quadratic equations in algebra, we will run across a "$\pm$" sign preceding the radical; this signifies both the positive and negative values of the root.

If a radical sign is preceded by a superscript number, then the number, or **index**, indicates a root other than the square root. In the notation $\sqrt[n]{a}$, n is the root or index, $\sqrt{}$ is the radical, and a is the radicand.

Examples:

1. $\sqrt[3]{8} = 2 \Rightarrow$ The cube root of 8 is 2.

2. $\sqrt[4]{81} = 3 \Rightarrow$ The fourth root of 81 is 3.

3. $\sqrt[6]{64} = 2 \Rightarrow$ The sixth root of 64 is 2.

2. Determining Square Roots

If a number is a perfect square (*e.g.*, 4, 9, 16, *etc.*), then extracting its square root is easy. Simply use the values given in the examples of square roots above. Not every number, however, has an exact square root. In such cases, you can do one of two things. First, you may be able to find in the number a factor that does have an exact square root and extract that factor from under the radical sign.

Examples:

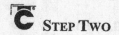
1. $\sqrt{125} = ?$

   ➢ 125 does not have a perfect square root. However, 25 has a perfect square and is a factor of 125, so factor 125 into 25 and 5: $\sqrt{125} = \sqrt{25 \cdot 5}$. Then, take the square root of 25, which is 5; $\sqrt{25} \cdot \sqrt{5} = 5 \cdot \sqrt{5}$. The final expression is $5\sqrt{5}$, which means 5 multiplied by the square root of 5: $\sqrt{125} = 5\sqrt{5}$.

2. $\sqrt{27} = \sqrt{9 \cdot 3} = \sqrt{9} \cdot \sqrt{3} = 3 \cdot \sqrt{3} = 3\sqrt{3}$

3. $\sqrt{32} = \sqrt{16 \cdot 2} = \sqrt{16} \cdot \sqrt{2} = 4 \cdot \sqrt{2} = 4\sqrt{2}$

4. $\sqrt{52} = \sqrt{4 \cdot 13} = \sqrt{4} \cdot \sqrt{13} = 2 \cdot \sqrt{13} = 2\sqrt{13}$

For the purposes of the exam, knowledge of the approximate values for common square roots may save valuable test time. For example, it is useful to know that $\sqrt{2}$ is approximately 1.4 and that $\sqrt{3}$ is approximately 1.7. Other values can be approximated by using ranges; *e.g.,* $\sqrt{7}$ must be between 2 and 3 ($\sqrt{4} < \sqrt{7} < \sqrt{9}$). Since 7 is closer to 9 than to 4, a good approximation of $\sqrt{7}$ is 2.6 to 2.7. Note that the knowledgeable use of a calculator when applicable can be quite helpful.

Operations Involving Radicals
(Rational Exponents)

Radicals can be rewritten using ***rational (fractional) exponents***. This simplifies the process of working with radicals, since all of the rules for exponents apply to fractional exponents and thus to radicals. The relationship between a rational exponent and the radical representing a given root is: $\sqrt[n]{x^m} = x^{m/n}$, where m and n are integers, and $n \neq 0$.

Examples:

1. $\sqrt{4} = 4^{1/2} = 2$
2. $\sqrt[3]{8} = 8^{1/3} = 2$

When you multiply a square root by itself, the result is the radicand: $(\sqrt{x})(\sqrt{x}) = x$. This can be explained using the product rule for exponents as illustrated in the following example.

Example:

$$(\sqrt{2})(\sqrt{2}) = 2^{1/2} \cdot 2^{1/2} = 2^1 = 2$$

The power rules for working with exponents are the ones you are most likely to use when working with radicals. The following example illustrates how the product power rule applies to radicals.

Example:

$$\sqrt{125} = 125^{1/2} = (25 \cdot 5)^{1/2} = 25^{1/2} \cdot 5^{1/2} = (\sqrt{25})(\sqrt{5}) = 5\sqrt{5}$$

Notice that this is just the process of extracting a square root by finding a factor, but what makes this process work is the product power rule of exponents. The quotient power rule is used in the following example.

Example:

$$\sqrt{\frac{4}{9}} = \left(\frac{4}{9}\right)^{1/2} = \frac{4^{1/2}}{9^{1/2}} = \frac{\sqrt{4}}{\sqrt{9}} = \frac{2}{3}$$

Importantly, since radicals are fractional exponents and obey the rules for exponents, you cannot simply add radicals. $\sqrt{4} + \sqrt{9}$ is not equal to $\sqrt{13}$, and you can prove this by taking the square root of 4, which is 2, and the square root of 9, which is 3. 2 + 3 is 5, which does not equal $\sqrt{13}$.

OPERATIONS INVOLVING RADICALS (RATIONAL EXPONENTS)

Product Rule: $\sqrt{x} \cdot \sqrt{x} = x^{1/2} x^{1/2} = x^1 = x$

Quotient Rule: $\dfrac{\sqrt[m]{x}}{\sqrt[n]{x}} = \dfrac{x^{1/m}}{x^{1/n}} = x^{(1/m - 1/n)}$

Power Rule: $\left(\sqrt[m]{x}\right)^n = \left(x^{1/m}\right)^n = x^{n/m}$

Product Power Rule: $\sqrt[m]{x^n y^p} = (x^n y^p)^{1/m} = x^{n/m} y^{p/m} = \sqrt[m]{x^n} \cdot \sqrt[m]{y^p}$

Quotient Power Rule: $\sqrt[m]{\dfrac{x^n}{y^p}} = \left(\dfrac{x^n}{y^p}\right)^{1/m} = \dfrac{x^{n/m}}{y^{p/m}} = \dfrac{\sqrt[m]{x^n}}{\sqrt[m]{y^p}}$

NOTE: The SAT and PSAT allow calculators. Therefore, it is important that you learn how to use a calculator and bring the same calculator with you to the exam. Using a calculator provides greater accuracy and often saves valuable test time.

Exponents and Radicals

DIRECTIONS: Choose the correct answer to each of the following items. Use a calculator when necessary. Answers are on page 906.

1. What is the third power of 3?

   A. 1   C. 9   E. 27
   B. 3   D. 15

2. What is the fourth power of 2?

   A. 2   C. 8   E. 32
   B. 4   D. 16

3. What is the first power of 1,000,000?

   A. 0   C. 1   E. 1,000,000
   B. $\frac{1}{1,000,000}$ D. 10

4. $100^0 = ?$

   A. 0   C. 10   E. 100,000
   B. 1   D. 100

5. $2^3 \cdot 2^2 = ?$

   A. 6   C. 2^5 E. 4^6
   B. 8   D. 2^6

6. $3^{10} \cdot 10^3 = ?$

   I. 30^{30}
   II. $300 \cdot 1,000$
   III. $30 + 30$

   A. I only   D. II and III only
   B. II only   E. Neither I, II, nor III
   C. I and III only

7. $5^4 \cdot 5^9 = ?$

   A. 25^{36} C. 5^{13} E. 5
   B. 5^{36} D. 5^5

8. $2^3 \cdot 2^4 \cdot 2^5 = ?$

   A. 2^{12} C. 8^{12} E. 8^{60}
   B. 2^{60} D. 4^{60}

9. $(2+3)^{20} = ?$

   A. 5^{20} C. 6^{20} E. 20^6
   B. $2^{20} + 3^{20}$ D. 20^5

10. $\frac{2^5}{2^3} = ?$

    A. 2^2 C. 2^8 E. 2^{15}
    B. 4^4 D. 4^8

11. $\frac{3^{10}}{3^8} = ?$

    A. 3   C. 9^2 E. 3^{80}
    B. 3^2 D. 3^{18}

12. $\frac{5^2}{5^2} = ?$

    I. 0
    II. 1
    III. 5^0

    A. I and II only   D. III only
    B. I and III only   E. Neither I, II, nor III
    C. II and III only

13. $\frac{3^2}{3^3} = ?$

    I. 3^{-1}
    II. $\frac{1}{3}$
    III. -1

    A. I only   D. I and III only
    B. II only   E. I, II, and III
    C. I and II only

14. $(2^2)^3 = ?$

    A. 2^5 C. 4^5 E. 6^5
    B. 2^6 D. 4^6

15. $(5^2)^6 = ?$

    A. 5^8 C. 10^4 E. 10^{12}
    B. 5^{12} D. 10^8

16. $(7^7)^7 = ?$

    A. 21   C. 7^{49} E. 49^{49}
    B. 7^{14} D. 21^7

17. $(3 \cdot 2)^2 = ?$

    I. 36
    II. $3 \cdot 3 \cdot 2 \cdot 2$
    III. $3^2 \cdot 2^2$

    A. I only   D. I and III only
    B. II only   E. I, II, and III
    C. III only

18. $(5 \cdot 3)^2 = ?$

    I. 15^2
    II. $5^2 \cdot 3^2$
    III. 8^2

    A. I only
    B. II only
    C. III only
    D. I and II only
    E. I, II, and III

19. $\left(\frac{8}{3}\right)^2 = ?$

    I. $\frac{64}{9}$
    II. $\frac{8^2}{3^2}$
    III. 11^2

    A. I only
    B. II only
    C. I and II only
    D. I and III only
    E. I, II, and III

20. $\left(\frac{4}{9}\right)^2 = ?$

    A. $\frac{2}{3}$
    B. $\frac{4}{9}$
    C. $\frac{16}{81}$
    D. $\frac{4^2}{9}$
    E. $\frac{4}{9^2}$

21. $(2 \cdot 2^2 \cdot 2^3)^2 = ?$

    A. 2^8
    B. 2^{10}
    C. 2^{12}
    D. 2^{16}
    E. 2^{18}

22. $\left(\frac{2^4 \cdot 5^4}{2^2 \cdot 5^2}\right)^2 = ?$

    A. $2^4 \cdot 5^4$
    B. $2^6 \cdot 2^6$
    C. 4^6
    D. 4^8
    E. 24

23. $\frac{3^6 \cdot 5^3 \cdot 7^9}{3^4 \cdot 5^3 \cdot 7^8} = ?$

    A. $3^2 \cdot 5 \cdot 7$
    B. $3^2 \cdot 5 \cdot 7^2$
    C. $3 \cdot 5 \cdot 7$
    D. $3^2 \cdot 5$
    E. $3^2 \cdot 7$

24. $\left(\frac{5^{12} \cdot 7^5}{5^{11} \cdot 7^5}\right)^2 = ?$

    A. 25
    B. 49
    C. 5^7
    D. 5^{11}
    E. 7^5

25. $\left(\frac{12^{12} \cdot 11^{11} \cdot 10^{10}}{12^{12} \cdot 11^{11} \cdot 10^9}\right)^2 = ?$

    A. 0
    B. 1
    C. 10
    D. 100
    E. $1,000$

26. $\sqrt{36} = ?$

    I. 6
    II. -6
    III. $3\sqrt{3}$

    A. I only
    B. I and II only
    C. I and III only
    D. II and III only
    E. I, II, and III

27. $\sqrt{81} + \sqrt{4} = ?$

    I. $\sqrt{85}$
    II. $\sqrt{9} + \sqrt{2}$
    III. 11

    A. I only
    B. II only
    C. III only
    D. I and II only
    E. II and III only

28. $\sqrt{27} = ?$

    A. 3
    B. $3\sqrt{3}$
    C. $3\sqrt{9}$
    D. 27
    E. 81

29. $\sqrt{52} = ?$

    A. $\sqrt{5} + \sqrt{2}$
    B. 7
    C. $2\sqrt{13}$
    D. $13\sqrt{4}$
    E. 13^2

30. $\sqrt{\frac{9}{4}} = ?$

    A. $\frac{\sqrt{3}}{2}$
    B. $\frac{3}{\sqrt{2}}$
    C. $\frac{3}{2}$
    D. 5
    E. $\sqrt{5}$

31. $\frac{\sqrt{81}}{\sqrt{27}} = ?$

    A. $\sqrt{3}$
    B. 3
    C. $3\sqrt{3}$
    D. 9
    E. $9\sqrt{3}$

32. $2\sqrt{2}$ is most nearly equal to which of the following?

    A. 2.8
    B. 3.4
    C. 4
    D. 7
    E. 12

33. $\sqrt{27}$ is approximately equal to which of the following?

    A. 3
    B. 4
    C. 4.5
    D. 5.1
    E. 9

34. $\sqrt{12}$ is approximately equal to which of the following?

    A. 2
    B. 3.4
    C. 4
    D. 6
    E. 8

35. $\sqrt{23}$ is approximately equal to which of the following?

    A. 4
    B. 4.8
    C. 6
    D. 7
    E. 8

36. $\sqrt{45}$ is approximately equal to which of the following?

    A. 5
    B. 5.5
    C. 6.6
    D. 7
    E. 7.5

37. Simplify: $(7 + \sqrt{5})(3 - \sqrt{5})$.

    A. $4 + 4\sqrt{5}$
    B. $4 - \sqrt{5}$
    C. $16 + 4\sqrt{5}$
    D. $16 - 4\sqrt{5}$
    E. 16

38. Simplify: $(5 - \sqrt{2})(3 - \sqrt{2})$.
   A. $17 + \sqrt{2}$ C. $17 + \sqrt{8}$ E. 25
   B. $17 - 8\sqrt{2}$ D. $17 + 8\sqrt{2}$

39. Simplify: $(\sqrt{3} + 1)(2 - \sqrt{3})$.
   A. -1 C. $-1 + \sqrt{3}$ E. $1 + \sqrt{3}$
   B. $-1 - \sqrt{3}$ D. 1

40. Simplify: $\sqrt{2} \cdot 2\sqrt{3}$.
   A. $-2\sqrt{6}$ C. 2   E. $2\sqrt{6}$
   B. $-\sqrt{6}$ D. $\sqrt{6}$

41. Simplify: $\sqrt{8} + \sqrt{50}$.
   A. $-7\sqrt{2}$ C. $\sqrt{2}$ E. 7
   B. $-\sqrt{2}$ D. $7\sqrt{2}$

42. Simplify: $\sqrt{3^2 + 5^2}$.
   A. 6   C. 7   E. 8
   B. $\sqrt{34}$ D. $\sqrt{51}$

43. Simplify: $\sqrt{(2\sqrt{3})^2 + 2^2}$.
   A. 1   C. 3   E. 5
   B. 2   D. 4

44. Is $(5 + \sqrt{2})(5 - \sqrt{2})$ rational?
   A. Yes
   B. No
   C. Cannot be determined from the given information

45. Is $\frac{(5 + \sqrt{2})}{(5 - \sqrt{2})}$ rational?
   A. Yes
   B. No
   C. Cannot be determined from the given information

46. Multiply and simplify: $\frac{\sqrt{2}}{2}\left(\sqrt{6} + \frac{\sqrt{2}}{2}\right)$.
   A. $\sqrt{3} + \frac{1}{2}$ C. $\sqrt{6} + 1$ E. $\sqrt{6} + 2$
   B. $\frac{\sqrt{3}}{2}$ D. $\sqrt{6} + 1$

47. Divide and simplify: $\frac{15\sqrt{96}}{5\sqrt{2}}$.
   A. $7\sqrt{3}$ C. $11\sqrt{3}$ E. $40\sqrt{3}$
   B. $7\sqrt{12}$ D. $12\sqrt{3}$

48. Which of the following radicals is a perfect square?
   A. $\sqrt{0.4}$ C. $\sqrt{0.09}$ E. $\sqrt{0.025}$
   B. $\sqrt{0.9}$ D. $\sqrt{0.02}$

49. $\left(-\frac{1}{3}\right)^4 = ?$
   A. $-\frac{1}{81}$ C. $-\frac{1}{12}$ E. $-\frac{1}{64}$
   B. $\frac{1}{81}$ D. $\frac{1}{12}$

50. $-4^4 = ?$
   A. -256 C. -16 E. -8
   B. 256   D. 16

51. $\sqrt[12]{x^6} = ?$
   A. x^6 C. x^2 E. x^{-2}
   B. x^{-6} D. $x^{1/2}$

52. $\sqrt[k]{6^{2km}}$ MUST be a positive integer if:
   A. k is a positive integer
   B. k is a multiple of 3
   C. $k < 0$
   D. m is a non-negative common fraction
   E. m is a non-negative integer

Algebraic Operations

Algebra is the branch of mathematics that uses letter symbols to represent numbers. The letter symbols are, in essence, placeholders. They function somewhat like "someone" or "somewhere." For example, in the sentence "Someone took the book and put it somewhere," neither the identity of the person in question nor the new location of the book is known. We can rewrite this sentence in algebraic terms: "x put the book in y place." The identity of x is unknown, and the new location of the book is unknown. It is for this reason that letter symbols in algebra are often referred to as "unknowns."

Algebra, like English, is a language, and for making certain statements, algebra is much better than English. For example, the English statement "There is a number such that, when you add 3 to it, the result is 8" can be rendered more easily in algebraic notation: $x + 3 = 8$. In fact, learning the rules of algebra is really very much like learning the grammar of any language. Keeping this analogy between algebra and English in mind, let's begin by studying the components of the algebraic language.

Elements of Algebra

1. Algebraic Terms

The basic unit of the English language is the word. The basic unit of algebra is the **term**. In English, a word consists of one or more letters. In algebra, a term consists of one or more letters or numbers. For example, x, $2z$, xy, N, 2, $\sqrt{7}$, and π are all algebraic terms. A term can be a product, quotient, or single symbol.

In English, a word may have a root, a prefix, a suffix, an ending, and so on. In algebra, a term may have a coefficient, an exponent, and a sign, etc. Of course, algebraic terms also include a variable, also referred to as the base.

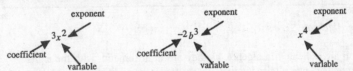

Just as with numbers, when the sign of an algebraic term is positive, the "+" is not written; *e.g.*, $3x$ is equivalent to $+3x$. Additionally, when the coefficient is 1, it is understood to be included and is not written out; *e.g.*, x rather than $1x$.

The elements in an algebraic term are all joined by the operation of multiplication. The coefficient and its sign are multiplied by the variable. For example: $-3x = (-3)(x)$; $5a = (+5)(a)$; and $\frac{1}{2}N = \left(+\frac{1}{2}\right)(N)$.

The exponent, as you have already learned, also indicates multiplication. Thus, x^2 means x times x; a^3 means a times a times a; and N^5 means N times N times N times N times N. Be careful not to confuse the coefficient with the exponent. $3x$ means "$+3$ times x," while x^3 means "x times x times x." Of course, many terms have both a coefficient and an exponent. Thus, $3x^2$ means "$+3$ times x times x," and $-5a^3$ means "-5 times a times a times a."

2. Algebraic Expressions

In English, words are organized into phrases. In algebra, terms are grouped together in **expressions**. An expression is a collection of algebraic terms that are joined by addition, subtraction, or both.

Examples:

1. $x + y$
2. $-2x + 3y + z$
3. $3x^2 - 2y^2$
4. $x^2 + y^{20}$

A **rational expression** is a fraction containing algebraic terms. In other words, rational expressions are algebraic fractions.

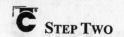

Examples:

1. $\dfrac{1}{x}$

2. $\dfrac{x^2}{xy - y^2}$

3. $\dfrac{3 + \frac{1}{x}}{9 - \frac{1}{x^2}}$

Algebraic expressions are classified according to the number of terms the expression contains. A *monomial* is an algebraic expression with exactly one term. A *polynomial* is an algebraic expression with more than one term. A *binomial* is a polynomial with exactly two terms. A *trinomial* is a polynomial with exactly three terms.

3. Algebraic Equations

In algebra, a complete sentence is called an equation. An equation asserts that two algebraic expressions are equal. Equations involving rational expressions are called *rational equations*.

Examples:

1. $2x + 4 = 3x - 2$

2. $\dfrac{y^2 - 5y}{y^2 - 4y - 5} = \dfrac{y}{y + 1}$

Operations of Algebraic Terms

1. Adding and Subtracting Algebraic Terms

Addition and subtraction are indicated in algebra, as they are in arithmetic, with the signs "+" and "−." In arithmetic, these operations combine the numbers into a third number. For example, the addition of 2 and 3 is equivalent to combining 2 and 3 to form the number 5: $2 + 3 = 5$.

In algebra, however, only *similar (like) terms* may be combined. Similar terms are terms with the same variables having the same exponent values. Coefficients do not factor into whether or not terms are similar.

Examples:

1. $3x^2$, $40x^2$, $-2x^2$, and $\sqrt{2}x^2$ are similar terms.

2. xy, $5xy$, $-23xy$, and πxy are similar terms.

3. $10xyz$, $-xyz$, and xyz are similar terms.

4. $3x$ and $3x^2$ are NOT similar terms.

5. xy and x^2y are NOT similar terms.

6. xy, yz, and xz are NOT similar terms.

To simplify an algebraic expression, group similar terms and add/subtract the numerical coefficients of each group. Variables and exponents of combined similar terms remain unchanged.

Examples:

1. $x^2 + 2x^2 + 3x^2 = ?$

   ➤ All three terms are similar since each includes x^2. Combine the terms by adding the coefficients: $1 + 2 + 3 = 6$. Thus, the result is 6x2.

2. $y + 2x + 3y - x = ?$

   ➤ With two different types of terms, group the similar terms together: $(2x - x) + (y + 3y)$. Add the coefficients for each type of term. For the x terms, the combined coefficient is $2 - 1 = 1$; for the y terms, $1 + 3 = 4$. The result is $x + 4y$.

3. $x - 3x + 5x - 2x = (1 - 3 + 5 - 2)x = x$

4. $2x - y - 3x + 4y + 5x = (2x - 3x + 5x) + (4y - y) = 4x + 3y$

5. $5x^2 + 3x^3 - 2x^2 + 4x^3 = (5x^2 - 2x^2) + (3x^3 + 4x^3) = 3x^2 + 7x^3$

Notice that when you have combined all similar terms, it is not possible to carry the addition or subtraction any further.

2. *Multiplying and Dividing Algebraic Terms*

Use the arithmetic *rules of exponents* to multiply or divide algebraic terms. Remember that $x^0 = 1$ when $x \neq 0$, and $x^1 = x$.

OPERATIONS OF ALGEBRAIC TERMS

Product Rule: $x^m \cdot x^n = x^{m+n}$
$$ax^m \cdot bx^n = abx^{m+n}$$

Quotient Rule: $\dfrac{x^m}{x^n} = x^{m-n}$

Power Rule: $(x^m)^n = x^{mn}$

Product Power Rule: $(x^m \cdot y^p)^n = x^{mn} \cdot y^{pn}$

Quotient Power Rule: $\left(\dfrac{x^m}{y^p}\right)^n = \dfrac{x^{mn}}{y^{pn}}$

Negative Exponents: $x^{-n} = \dfrac{1}{x^n}$

Examples:

Product Rule:
$$(x^2)(x^3) = x^{(2+3)} = x^5$$
$$(3x^2)(xy) = (3 \cdot 1)(x^2 \cdot xy) = 3 \cdot x^{(2+1)} \cdot y = 3x^3y$$
$$(2xyz)(3xy)(4yz) = (2 \cdot 3 \cdot 4)(xyz \cdot xy \cdot yz) = 24 \cdot x^{(1+1)} \cdot y^{(1+1+1)} \cdot z^{(1+1)} = 24x^2y^3z^2$$

Quotient Rule:
$$\frac{x^3}{x^2} = x^{(3-2)} = x^1 = x$$
$$\frac{2x^4y^3}{x^2z} = \frac{2}{1} \cdot \frac{x^4y^3}{x^2z} = 2 \cdot \frac{x^{(4-2)}y^3}{z} = \frac{2x^2y^3}{z}$$

Power Rule:
$$(x^2)^3 = x^{(2)(3)} = x^6$$

Product Power Rule:
$$(x^2y^3)^2 = x^{(2)(2)}y^{(3)(2)} = x^4y^6$$

Quotient Power Rule:
$$\left(\frac{x^2}{y^3}\right)^2 = \frac{x^{(2)(2)}}{y^{(3)(2)}} = \frac{x^4}{y^6}$$

Operations of Algebraic Fractions

1. *Adding and Subtracting Algebraic Fractions*

Adding and subtracting algebraic fractions, like adding and subtracting numerical fractions, require common denominators. If the denominators are the same, simply add/subtract the numerators: $\dfrac{a}{x} \pm \dfrac{b}{x} = \dfrac{a \pm b}{x}$.

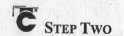
Examples:

1. $\dfrac{5}{x}+\dfrac{3}{x}=\dfrac{5+3}{x}=\dfrac{8}{x}$

2. $\dfrac{2x}{y}-\dfrac{x}{y}=\dfrac{2x-x}{y}=\dfrac{x}{y}$

3. $\dfrac{a}{cd}+\dfrac{x}{cd}=\dfrac{a+x}{cd}$

To add or subtract algebraic fractions with unlike denominators, you must first find a common denominator. Usually, this can be accomplished by using the same "flying x" method as with numerical fractions: $\dfrac{a}{x}\pm\dfrac{b}{y}=\dfrac{ay}{xy}\pm\dfrac{bx}{yx}=\dfrac{ay\pm bx}{xy}$.

Example:

$$\dfrac{2x}{y}+\dfrac{3y}{x}=\dfrac{2x}{y}\!\diagdown\!+\!\diagdown\!\dfrac{3y}{x}=\dfrac{2x^2+3y^2}{xy}$$

2. Multiplying and Dividing Algebraic Fractions

To multiply algebraic fractions, follow the rule for multiplying numeric fractions. Multiply terms in the numerators to create a new numerator, and multiply terms in the denominator to create a new denominator: $\dfrac{a}{c}\bullet\dfrac{b}{d}=\dfrac{ab}{cd}$.

Examples:

1. $\dfrac{2}{x}\bullet\dfrac{3}{y}=\dfrac{6}{xy}$

2. $\dfrac{x^2y^3}{z}\bullet\dfrac{x^3y^2}{wz}=\dfrac{x^5y^5}{wz^2}$

To divide algebraic fractions, follow the rule for dividing numeric fractions. Invert the divisor, or second fraction, and multiply: $\dfrac{a}{c}\div\dfrac{b}{d}=\dfrac{a}{c}\bullet\dfrac{d}{b}=\dfrac{ad}{cb}$.

Examples:

1. $\dfrac{2}{y}\div\dfrac{3}{x}=\dfrac{2}{y}\bullet\dfrac{x}{3}=\dfrac{2x}{3y}$

2. $\dfrac{2x^2}{y}\div\dfrac{y}{x}=\dfrac{2x^2}{y}\bullet\dfrac{x}{y}=\dfrac{2x^3}{y^2}$

Multiplying Algebraic Expressions

A *polynomial* is an algebraic expression with one or more terms involving only the operations of addition, subtraction, and multiplication of variables. Polynomial means "many terms," although it is possible to get a monomial by adding two polynomials. A multiplication item such as $(x + y)(x + y)$ requires a special procedure. The fundamental rule for multiplying is that every term of one expression must be multiplied by every term of the other expression.

1. Distributive Property

First, let's look at the case in which a polynomial is to be multiplied by a single term. One way of solving the item is to first add and then multiply. Alternatively, we can use the *distributive property* to multiply every term inside the parentheses by the term outside the parentheses, and then we can add the terms: $x(y + z) = xy + xz$. The result is the same regardless of the method used. The following example illustrates these two methods using real numbers.

Example:

$2(3 + 4 + 5) = 2(12) = 24$
➢ The distributive property returns the same result: $2(3 + 4 + 5) = (2 \cdot 3) + (2 \cdot 4) + (2 \cdot 5) = 6 + 8 + 10 = 24$.

When working with algebraic expressions, use the distributive property, since you cannot add unlike terms. The following examples apply the distributive property to algebraic expressions.

Examples:

1. $x(y + z) = xy + xz$
2. $a(b + c + d) = ab + ac + ad$

To multiply two polynomials, either add the polynomials before multiplying them, or reverse the order of operations using the distributive property.

Example:

$(2 + 3)(1 + 3 + 4) = (5)(8) = 40$
➢ The distributive property returns the same result: $(2 + 3)(1 + 3 + 4) = (2 \cdot 1) + (2 \cdot 3) + (2 \cdot 4) + (3 \cdot 1) + (3 \cdot 3) + (3 \cdot 4) = 2 + 6 + 8 + 3 + 9 + 12 = 40$.

2. *FOIL Method*

To multiply two binomials using the ***FOIL method***, follow these steps for combining the binomial terms: (1) multiply the first terms, (2) multiply the outer terms, (3) multiply the inner terms, (4) multiply the last terms, and (5) combine like terms. The FOIL method is simply a mnemonic shortcut derived from the distributive property. The following diagram illustrates application of the FOIL method.

MULTIPLYING TWO BINOMIALS
(FOIL: First, Outer, Inner, Last)

$(x + y)\ (x + y) = x^2 + xy + xy + y^2 = x^2 + 2xy + y^2$

Examples:

1. $(x + y)(x + y) = ?$
    ➢ First: $(x)(x) = x^2$; Outer: $(x)(y) = xy$; Inner: $(y)(x) = xy$; Last: $(y)(y) = y^2$. Add: $x^2 + xy + xy + y^2 = x^2 + 2xy + y^2$.
2. $(x - y)(x - y) = ?$
    ➢ First: $(x)(x) = x^2$; Outer: $(x)(-y) = -xy$; Inner: $(-y)(x) = -xy$; Last: $(-y)(-y) = y^2$. Add: $x^2 - xy - xy + y^2 = x^2 - 2xy + y^2$.

Three situations, one in addition to the two illustrated in the previous examples, arise with such frequency that you should memorize the results to simplify the calculation.

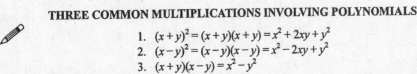

THREE COMMON MULTIPLICATIONS INVOLVING POLYNOMIALS

1. $(x + y)^2 = (x + y)(x + y) = x^2 + 2xy + y^2$
2. $(x - y)^2 = (x - y)(x - y) = x^2 - 2xy + y^2$
3. $(x + y)(x - y) = x^2 - y^2$

You might be asked to multiply something more complex than two binomials. The process is tedious and time-consuming, but ultimately it is executed the same way.

Example:

$(x + y)^3 = ?$

➤ Apply the FOIL method to the first two binomials, then multiply the last binomial to the resultant trinomial of the first two binomials: $(x + y)^3 = (x + y)(x + y)(x + y) = (x^2 + 2xy + y^2)(x + y) =$
$x(x^2) + x(2xy) + x(y^2) + y(x^2) + y(2xy) + y(y^2) = x^3 + 2x^2y + xy^2 + x^2y + 2xy^2 + y^3 = x^3 + 3x^2y + 3xy^2 + y^3$.

Factoring Algebraic Expressions

Although the term *factoring* intimidates many students, factoring is really nothing more than reverse multiplication. For example, if $(x + y)(x + y) = x^2 + 2xy + y^2$, then $x^2 + 2xy + y^2$ can be factored into $(x + y)(x + y)$. Fortunately, for the purposes of taking the test, any factoring you might need to do will fall into one of three categories.

1. Finding a Common Factor

If all the terms of an algebraic expression contain a common factor, then that term can be factored out of the expression.

Examples:

1. $ab + ac + ad = a(b + c + d)$
2. $abx + aby + abz = ab(x + y + z)$
3. $x^2 + x^3 + x^4 = x^2(1 + x + x^2)$
4. $3a + 6a^2 + 9a^3 = 3a(1 + 2a + 3a^2)$

2. Reversing a Known Polynomial Multiplication Process

Three patterns recur with such frequency on the exam that you should memorize them. These patterns are the same as the ones you were encouraged to memorize in the discussion of the FOIL method.

> **THREE COMMON POLYNOMIAL MULTIPLICATION REVERSALS**
> 1. Perfect square trinomial: $x^2 + 2xy + y^2 = (x + y)(x + y)$
> 2. Perfect square trinomial: $x^2 - 2xy + y^2 = (x - y)(x - y)$
> 3. Difference of two squares: $x^2 - y^2 = (x + y)(x - y)$

3. Reversing an Unknown Polynomial Multiplication Process

Occasionally, you may find it necessary to factor an expression that does not fall into one of the three categories presented above. The expression will most likely have the form $ax^2 + bx + c$; e.g., $x^2 + 2x + 1$. To factor such expressions, set up a blank diagram: (   )(   ). Then, fill in the diagram by answering the following series of questions.

1. What factors will produce the first term, ax^2?
2. What possible factors will produce the last term, c?
3. Which of the possible factors from step 2, when added together, will produce the middle term, bx?

Examples:

1. Factor $x^2 + 3x + 2$.
    >   • What factors will produce the first term, ax^2? x times x yields x^2, so the factors, in part, are $(x\quad)(x\quad)$.
        • What possible factors will produce the last term? The possibilities are $\{2, 1\}$ and $\{-2, -1\}$.
        • Which of the two sets of factors just mentioned, when added together, will produce a result of $+3x$?
    The answer is $\{2, 1\}$: $2 + 1 = 3$, as the FOIL method confirms: $(x + 2)(x + 1) = x^2 + x + 2x + 2 = x^2 + 3x + 2$.

2. Factor $x^2 + 4x - 12$.
    >   • What factors will generate ax^2? $(x\quad)(x\quad)$.
        • What factors will generate -12? $\{1, -12\}$, $\{12, -1\}$, $\{2, -6\}$ $\{6, -2\}$, $\{3, -4\}$, and $\{4, -3\}$.
        • Which factors, when added together, will produce the middle term of $+ 4x$? The answer is $\{6, -2\}$: $6 + (-2) = 4$.
    Thus, the factors are $(x + 6)$ and $(x - 2)$, as the FOIL method confirms: $(x + 6)(x - 2) = x^2 - 2x + 6x - 12 = x^2 + 4x - 12$.

Absolute Value in Algebraic Expressions

Algebraic terms involving absolute values are treated the same way as numeric absolute values. Remember that the absolute value of any term is always a positive numerical value.

PRINCIPLES OF ABSOLUTE VALUE

1. $|x| = x$ if $x \geq 0$; $|x| = -x$ if $x < 0$
2. $|x| = |-x|$
3. $|x| \geq 0$
4. $|x - y| = |y - x|$

Examples:

1. If $w = -3$, $|w| = ?$
    > Since the value of w is less than zero, $|w| = -w = -(-3) = 3$.

2. Let x be a member of the following set: $\{-11, -10, -9, -8, -7, -6, -5, -4, -3, -2, -1, 0, 1, 2, 3, 4\}$. $\frac{|2x - |x||}{3}$ is a positive integer for how many different numbers in the set?
    > If $x < 0$, then $|x| = -x$: $\frac{|2x - |x||}{3} = \frac{|2x - (-x)|}{3} = \frac{|2x + x|}{3} = \frac{|3x|}{3} = |x|$, which is always a positive. Therefore, $\frac{|2x - |x||}{3}$ is a positive integer for all numbers in the set less than zero. If $x \geq 0$, then $|x| = x$: $\frac{|2x - |x||}{3} = \frac{|2x - x|}{3} = \frac{|x|}{3} = \frac{x}{3}$. Thus, the only other number in the set that returns a positive integer is 3. The total number of values in the set that satisfy the condition is: $11 + 1 = 12$.

Radicals in Algebraic Expressions

Radicals in algebraic expressions are manipulated in the same way as numeric radicals using the rules of exponents.

Example:

Does $\frac{3\sqrt{x} + \sqrt{x^3}}{x} = \frac{3}{\sqrt{x}} + \sqrt{x}$?

> $\frac{3\sqrt{x} + \sqrt{x^3}}{x} = \frac{3\sqrt{x}}{x} + \frac{\sqrt{x^3}}{x} = \frac{3x^{1/2}}{x} + \frac{x^{3/2}}{x} = 3x^{(1/2 - 1)} + x^{(3/2 - 1)} = 3x^{-1/2} + x^{1/2} = \frac{3}{\sqrt{x}} + \sqrt{x}$.

When simplifying expressions containing roots and radicals that are inverse operations of one another, it is important to note that the sign of the variable impacts the sign of the result. Consider $\sqrt{x^2}$. If $x \geq 0$, then $\sqrt{x^2} = x$; if $x < 0$, then $\sqrt{x^2} = -x$.

Examples:

1. $\sqrt{2^2} = 2$
2. $\sqrt{(-2)^2} = -(-2) = 2$

NOTE: The SAT and PSAT allow calculators. Therefore, it is important that you learn how to use a calculator and bring the same calculator with you to the exam. Using a calculator provides greater accuracy and often saves valuable test time.

Algebraic Operations

DIRECTIONS: Choose the correct answer to each of the following items. Use a calculator when necessary. Answers are on page 909.

1. Which of the following is (are) like terms?

   I. $34x$ and $-18x$
   II. $2x$ and $2xy$
   III. x^3 and $3x$

   A. I only
   B. II only
   C. I and III only
   D. II and III only
   E. I, II, and III

2. Which of the following is (are) like terms?

   I. $\sqrt{2}x$ and $\sqrt{3}x$
   II. π and 10
   III. x^2 and $2x^2$

   A. I only
   B. II only
   C. I and II only
   D. I and III only
   E. I, II, and III

3. $x + 2x + 3x = ?$

   A. $6x^6$
   B. x^6
   C. $6x$
   D. $x + 6$
   E. $x - 6$

4. $2x + 3x - x + 4x = ?$

   A. $8x^8$
   B. x^8
   C. $8x$
   D. $x + 8$
   E. $x - 8$

5. $a^3 + a^2 + a = ?$

   A. $3a^3$
   B. a^3
   C. $2a^2$
   D. a^2
   E. $a^3 + a^2 + a$

6. $z^2 + 2z^2 - 5z^2 = ?$

   A. $-9z^2$
   B. $-2z^2$
   C. 0
   D. $2z^2$
   E. $5z^2$

7. $a^3 - 12a^3 + 15a^3 + 2a^3 = ?$

   A. $6a^3$
   B. $2a^2$
   C. $6a$
   D. $3a$
   E. a

8. $3c + 2a - 1 + 4c - 2a + 1 = ?$

   A. $2a + 4c + 1$
   B. $4a + 3c - 2$
   C. $a + c - 1$
   D. $2a + 1$
   E. $7c$

9. $-7nx + 2nx + 2n + 7x = ?$

   A. 0
   B. $-5nx + 2n + 7x$
   C. $18nx$
   D. $9nx + 9xn$
   E. $4nx$

10. $c^2 + 2c^2d^2 - c^2 = ?$

    A. $4c^2d^2$
    B. $2c^2d^2$
    C. c^2d^2
    D. $2cd$
    E. cd

11. $2x^2 + 2x^2 + 2x^2 = ?$

    A. $6x^6$
    B. $2x^6$
    C. $6x^2$
    D. $6x$
    E. 6

12. $3xy + 3x^2y - 2xy + y = ?$

    A. $6xy - y$
    B. $x + xy + y$
    C. $3x^2y + xy + y$
    D. $x^2y^2 + xy$
    E. $3xy + x$

13. $x^2 + 2xy - 3x + 4xy - 6y + 2y^2 + 3x - 2xy + 6y = ?$

    A. $x^2 - 2xy + y^2$
    B. $x^2 + y^2 + 3x + 2y$
    C. $x^2 + 2y^2 + 4xy + 6x + 6y$
    D. $x^2 + 2y^2 + 4xy + 6x$
    E. $x^2 + 2y^2 + 4xy$

14. $8p + 2p^2 + pq - 4p^2 - 14p - pq = ?$

    A. $-2p^2 - 6p$
    B. $-p^2 + 6p$
    C. $2p^2 + 6p$
    D. $p^2 + 3p$
    E. $3p^2 - pq$

15. $pqr + qrs + rst + stu = ?$

    A. $pqrst$
    B. $pq + qr + rs + st + tu$
    C. $pqr + rst$
    D. $4pqrst$
    E. $pqr + qrs + rst + stu$

16. $(x^2)(x^3) = ?$

    A. $x^{2/3}$
    B. x
    C. $x^{3/2}$
    D. x^5
    E. x^6

17. $(a)(a^2)(a^3)(a^4) = ?$

    A. $10a$
    B. $24a$
    C. a^5
    D. a^{10}
    E. a^{24}

18. $y^5 \div y^2 = ?$

    A. $3y$
    B. $7y$
    C. $y^{5/2}$
    D. y^3
    E. y^7

19. $(x^2y)(xy^2) = ?$

    A. $4xy$
    B. x^3y^3
    C. xy^4
    D. x^4y^4
    E. xy^{16}

20. $(abc)(a^2bc^2) = ?$

    A. $4abc$ C. $a^3b^2c^3$ E. abc^6

    B. a^2bc^2 D. $a^3b^3c^3$

21. $(xy^2)(x^2z)(y^2z) = ?$

    A. $8xyz$ C. $x^3y^4z^2$ E. $x^3y^3z^3$

    B. x^2y^4z D. $x^3y^3z^2$

22. $\dfrac{x^2y^4}{xy} = ?$

    A. y^3 C. x^2y^3 E. xy^8

    B. xy^3 D. x^3y^5

23. $\dfrac{a^3b^4c^5}{abc} = ?$

    A. $a^2b^3c^4$ C. $(abc)^3$ E. $(abc)^{60}$

    B. $a^3b^4c^5$ D. $(abc)^{12}$

24. $(x^2y^3)^4 = ?$

    A. $(xy)^9$ C. x^8y^{12} E. xy^{24}

    B. x^6y^7 D. xy^{20}

25. $\left(\dfrac{a^2}{b^3}\right)^3 = ?$

    A. $\dfrac{a^5}{b}$ C. a^5b E. a^6b^9

    B. $\dfrac{a^6}{b^9}$ D. a^6b

26. $\dfrac{x^3y^4z^5}{x^4yz} = ?$

    A. y^2z^4 C. $\dfrac{y^3z^4}{x}$ E. $\dfrac{y^6z^6}{x}$

    B. xy^2z^4 D. $\dfrac{y^3z^5}{x}$

27. $\left(\dfrac{c^4d^2}{c^2d}\right)^3 = ?$

    A. c^5d^3 C. c^6d^3 E. c^6d^6

    B. c^5d^5 D. c^6d^4

28. $\left(\dfrac{x^2y^3}{xy}\right)\left(\dfrac{x^3y^4}{xy}\right) = ?$

    A. x^2y^3 C. x^3y^5 E. x^6y^7

    B. x^3y^4 D. x^5y^6

29. $\left(\dfrac{abc^2}{abc^3}\right)\left(\dfrac{a^2b^2c}{ab}\right) = ?$

    A. $\dfrac{ab}{c}$ C. ab E. 1

    B. $\dfrac{bc}{a}$ D. c

30. $\left(\dfrac{x^3y^3z^2}{x^4y^2z}\right)^2\left(\dfrac{x^2y^3z^2}{xy^2z^4}\right)^3 = ?$

    A. xyz C. $x^5y^5z^5$ E. xyz^{12}

    B. $x^2y^2z^2$ D. $x^6y^6z^6$

31. $\dfrac{a}{c} + \dfrac{b}{c} = ?$

    A. $\dfrac{ab}{c}$ C. $\dfrac{a+b}{2c}$ E. $\dfrac{a+b}{abc}$

    B. $\dfrac{a+b}{c}$ D. $\dfrac{a+b}{c^2}$

32. $\dfrac{x}{2} + \dfrac{y}{2} + \dfrac{z}{2} = ?$

    A. $\dfrac{x+y+z}{2}$ C. $\dfrac{x+y+z}{8}$ E. $\dfrac{xyz}{8}$

    B. $\dfrac{x+y+z}{6}$ D $\dfrac{xyz}{2}$

33. $\dfrac{ab}{x} + \dfrac{bc}{x} + \dfrac{cd}{x} = ?$

    A. $\dfrac{abcd}{x}$ C. $\dfrac{ab+bc+cd}{x}$ E. $\dfrac{ab+bc+cd}{x^3}$

    B. $\dfrac{a+b+c+d}{3x}$ D. $\dfrac{ab+bc+cd}{3x}$

34. $\dfrac{x^2}{k} + \dfrac{x^3}{k} + \dfrac{x^4}{k} = ?$

    A. $\dfrac{x^9}{k}$ C. $\dfrac{x^{24}}{k}$ E. $\dfrac{x^2+x^3+x^4}{3k}$

    B. $\dfrac{x^9}{3k}$ D. $\dfrac{x^2+x^3+x^4}{k}$

35. $\dfrac{2x}{z} - \dfrac{y}{z} = ?$

    A. $\dfrac{2x-y}{z}$ C. $\dfrac{2x-y}{x^2}$ E. $\dfrac{2xy}{2z}$

    B. $\dfrac{2x-y}{2z}$ D. $\dfrac{2xy}{z}$

36. $\dfrac{x}{y} + \dfrac{y}{x} = ?$

    A. $\dfrac{xy}{x+y}$ C. $\dfrac{x+y}{xy}$ E. $\dfrac{x^2+y^2}{xy}$

    B. $\dfrac{x+y}{y+x}$ D. $\dfrac{xy+yx}{xy}$

37. $\dfrac{a}{b} - \dfrac{b}{a} = ?$

    A. $\dfrac{ab}{a-b}$ C. $\dfrac{a-b}{ab}$ E. $\dfrac{a^2-b^2}{ab}$

    B. $\dfrac{a-b}{b-a}$ D. $\dfrac{ab-ba}{ab}$

38. $\dfrac{x^2}{y} + \dfrac{x^3}{z} = ?$

    A. $\dfrac{x^2+x^3}{yz}$ C. $\dfrac{x^6}{yz}$ E. $\dfrac{x^2z+x^3y}{yz}$

    B. $\dfrac{x^5}{yz}$ D. $\dfrac{x^2+x^3}{yz}$

39. $\dfrac{x}{a} + \dfrac{y}{b} + \dfrac{z}{c} = ?$

    A. $\dfrac{xyz}{abc}$ D. $\dfrac{xbc+yac+zab}{a+b+c}$

    B. $\dfrac{x+y+z}{a+b+c}$ E. $\dfrac{xa+yb+zc}{abc}$

    C. $\dfrac{xbc+yac+zab}{abc}$

40. $\frac{x^2}{y^2} - \frac{y^3}{x^3} = ?$

   A. $\frac{x^2 - x^3}{y^5}$ C. $\frac{x^2 - y^3}{x^2 - y^2}$ E. $\frac{x^6 - y^6}{x^3 y^2}$

   B. $\frac{x^3 - x^2}{y^6}$ D. $\frac{x^5 - y^5}{x^3 y^2}$

41. $2(x + y) = ?$

   A. $2xy$ C. $2 + x + yy$ E. $2x^2 + 2y^2$
   B. $2x + 2y$ D. $4x$

42. $a(b + c) = ?$

   A. $ab + bc$ C. $2abc$ E. $ab + ac + bc$
   B. $ab + ac$ D. $ab^2 + b^2 c$

43. $3(a + b + c + d) = ?$

   A. $3abcd$
   B. $3a + b + c + d$
   C. $3a + 3b + 3c + 3d$
   D. $3ab + 3bc + 3cd$
   E. $12a + 12b + 12c + 12d$

44. $2x(3x + 4x^2) = ?$

   A. x^{10} C. $5x^2 + 6x^3$ E. $6(x^2 + x^3)$
   B. $6x + 8x^2$ D. $6x^2 + 8x^3$

45. $3a^2(ab + ac + bc) = ?$

   A. $3a^3 b^2 c$ D. $3a^3 b + 3a^3 c + 3a^2 bc$
   B. $3a^3 + 3b^2 + 3c$ E. $3a^5 b + 3a^5 c$
   C. $3a^2 b + 3a^2 c + 3a^2 bc$

46. $(x + y)(x + y) = ?$

   A. $x^2 + y^2$ D. $x^2 - 2xy + y^2$
   B. $x^2 - y^2$ E. $x^2 + 2xy + y^2$
   C. $x^2 + 2xy - y^2$

47. $(a + b)^2 = ?$

   A. $a^2 + b^2$ D. $a^2 - 2ab + b^2$
   B. $a^2 - b^2$ E. $a^2 + 2ab + b^2$
   C. $a^2 + 2ab - b^2$

48. $(x - y)^2 = ?$

   A. $x^2 + 2xy - y^2$ D. $x^2 - 2xy - y^2$
   B. $x^2 + 2xy + y^2$ E. $x^2 + y^2$
   C. $x^2 - 2xy + y^2$

49. $(a + b)(a - b) = ?$

   A. $a^2 - b^2$ D. $a^2 - 2ab + b^2$
   B. $a^2 + b^2$ E. $a^2 + 2ab - b^2$
   C. $a^2 + 2ab + b^2$

50. $(x - 2)^2 = ?$

   A. $2x$ C. $x^2 - 4$ E. $x^2 - 4x - 4$
   B. $4x$ D. $x^2 - 4x + 4$

51. $(2 - x)^2 = ?$

   A. $4 - x^2$ C. $x^2 + 4x + 4$ E. $x^2 - 4x - 4$
   B. $x^2 + 4$ D. $x^2 - 4x + 4$

52. $(ab + bc)(a + b) = ?$

   A. $a^2 b + ab^2 + b^2 c + abc$ D. $a^2 b + ab + bc + abc$
   B. $a^2 b + ab^2 + abc$ E. $a^2 + b^2 + c^2 + abc$
   C. $a^2 b + ab^2 + a^2 bc$

53. $(x - y)(x + 2) = ?$

   A. $x^2 + 2xy + 2y$ D. $x^2 - xy + 2x - 2y$
   B. $x^2 + 2xy + x + y$ E. $x^2 + 2x + 2y - 2$
   C. $x^2 + 2xy + x - 2y$

54. $(a + b)(c + d) = ?$

   A. $ab + bc + cd$ D. $ac + ad + bc + bd$
   B. $ab + bc + cd + ad$ E. $ab + ac + ad$
   C. $ac + bd$

55. $(w + x)(y - z) = ?$

   A. $wxy - z$ D. $wy + wz + xy - xz$
   B. $wy + xy - yz$ E. $wy - wz + xy - xz$
   C. $wy - wz + xy + xz$

56. $(x + y)(w + x + y) = ?$

   A. $x^2 + wx + wy + xy$
   B. $x^2 + y^2 + wx + wy + 2xy$
   C. $x^2 + y^2 + wxy$
   D. $x^2 + y^2 + wx^2 y^2$
   E. $x^2 y^2 + wxy$

57. $(2 + x)(3 + x + y) = ?$

   A. $x^2 + 6xy + 6$
   B. $x^2 + 6xy + 3x + 2y + 6$
   C. $x^2 + 2xy + 6x + 6y + 6$
   D. $x^2 + xy + 5x + 2y + 6$
   E. $x^2 + 3xy + 2x + y + 6$

58. $(x + y)^3 = ?$

   A. $x^3 + 5x^2 y + y^2 z + xyz$ D. $x^3 + 6x^2 y^2 + y^3$
   B. $x^3 + 3x^3 y + 3xy^3 + y^3$ E. $x^3 + 12x^2 y^2 + y^3$
   C. $x^3 + 3x^2 y + 3xy^2 + y^3$

59. $(x - y)^3 = ?$

   A. $x^3 - 3x^2 y + 3xy^2 - y^3$ D. $x^3 + 6x^2 y^2 + y^3$
   B. $x^3 + 3x^2 y + 3xy^2 + y^3$ E. $x^3 + 6x^2 y^2 - y^3$
   C. $x^3 + 3x^2 y - 3xy^2 - y^3$

60. $(a + b)(a - b)(a + b)(a - b) = ?$

   A. 1 D. $a^4 - 2a^2 b^2 + b^4$
   B. $a^2 - b^2$ E. $a^4 + 2a^2 b^2 + b^4$
   C. $a^2 + b^2$

61. $2a + 2b + 2c = ?$

    A. $2(a + b + c)$
    B. $2(abc)$
    C. $2(ab + bc + ca)$
    D. $6(a + b + c)$
    E. $8(a + b + c)$

62. $x + x^2 + x^3 = ?$

    A. $x(x + 2x + 3x)$
    B. $x(1 + 2x + 3x)$
    C. $x(1 + 2 + 3)$
    D. $x(1 + x + x^2)$
    E. $x(1 + 3x)$

63. $2x^2 + 4x^3 + 8x^4 = ?$

    A. $2x^2(1 + 2x + 4x^2)$
    B. $2x^2(1 + 2x + 4x^3)$
    C. $2x^2(x + 2x + 4x^2)$
    D. $2x^2(x + 2x^2 + 4x^3)$
    E. $2x^2(x^2 + 2x^3 + 4x^4)$

64. $abc + bcd + cde = ?$

    A. $ab(c + d + e)$
    B. $ac(b + e)$
    C. $b(a + c + de)$
    D. $c(ab + bd + de)$
    E. $d(a + b + c + e)$

65. $x^2y^2 + x^2y + xy^2 = ?$

    A. $(x + y)^2$
    B. $x^2 + y^2$
    C. $x^2y^2(x + y)$
    D. $xy(xy + x + y)$
    E. $xy(x + y + 1)$

66. $p^2 + 2pq + q^2 = ?$

    A. $(p + q)(p - q)$
    B. $(p + q)(p + q)$
    C. $p^2 - q^2$
    D. $p^2 + q^2$
    E. $(p - q)^2$

67. $144^2 - 121^2 = ?$

    A. 23
    B. $(144 + 121)(144 - 121)$
    C. $(144 + 121)(144 + 121)$
    D. $(23)^2$
    E. $(144 + 121)^2$

68. $x^2 - y^2 = ?$

    A. $(x + y)(x - y)$
    B. $(x + y)(x + y)$
    C. $(x - y)(x - y)$
    D. $x^2 + y^2$
    E. $2xy$

69. $x^2 + 2x + 1 = ?$

    A. $(x + 1)(x - 1)$
    B. $(x + 1)(x + 1)$
    C. $(x - 1)(x - 1)$
    D. $x^2 - 1$
    E. $x^2 + 1$

70. $x^2 - 1 = ?$

    A. $(x + 1)(x + 1)$
    B. $(x - 1)(x - 1)$
    C. $(x + 1)(x - 1)$
    D. $(x - 1)^2$
    E. $(x + 1)^2$

71. $x^2 + 3x + 2 = ?$

    A. $(x + 1)(x - 2)$
    B. $(x + 2)(x + 1)$
    C. $(x + 2)(x - 1)$
    D. $(x - 2)(x - 1)$
    E. $(x + 3)(x - 1)$

72. $a^2 - a - 2 = ?$

    A. $(a + 2)(a - 1)$
    B. $(a - 2)(a + 1)$
    C. $(a + 1)(a + 2)$
    D. $(a + 2)(a - 2)$
    E. $(a + 1)(a - 1)$

73. $p^2 + 4p + 3 = ?$

    A. $(p + 3)(p + 1)$
    B. $(p + 3)(p - 1)$
    C. $(p - 3)(p - 1)$
    D. $(p + 3)(p + 4)$
    E. $(p + 3)(p - 4)$

74. $c^2 + 6c + 8 = ?$

    A. $(c + 2)(c + 4)$
    B. $(c + 2)(c - 4)$
    C. $(c + 4)(c - 2)$
    D. $(c + 3)(c + 5)$
    E. $(c + 8)(c - 1)$

75. $x^2 + x - 20 = ?$

    A. $(x + 5)(x - 4)$
    B. $(x + 4)(x - 5)$
    C. $(x + 2)(x - 10)$
    D. $(x + 10)(x - 2)$
    E. $(x + 20)(x - 1)$

76. $p^2 + 5p + 6 = ?$

    A. $(p + 1)(p + 6)$
    B. $(p + 6)(p - 1)$
    C. $(p + 2)(p + 3)$
    D. $(p - 3)(p - 2)$
    E. $(p + 5)(p + 1)$

77. $x^2 + 8x + 16 = ?$

    A. $(x + 2)(x + 8)$
    B. $(x + 2)(x - 8)$
    C. $(x - 4)(x - 4)$
    D. $(x + 4)(x - 4)$
    E. $(x + 4)(x + 4)$

78. $x^2 - 5x - 6 = ?$

    A. $(x + 1)(x + 6)$
    B. $(x + 6)(x - 1)$
    C. $(x + 2)(x + 3)$
    D. $(x - 6)(x + 1)$
    E. $(x - 2)(x - 3)$

79. $a^2 - 3a + 2 = ?$

    A. $(a - 2)(a - 1)$
    B. $(a - 2)(a + 1)$
    C. $(a + 1)(a - 2)$
    D. $(a - 3)(a + 1)$
    E. $(a + 3)(a + 1)$

80. $x^2 + x - 12 = ?$

    A. $(x + 6)(x + 2)$
    B. $(x + 6)(x - 2)$
    C. $(x + 4)(x - 3)$
    D. $(x - 4)(x - 3)$
    E. $(x + 12)(x + 1)$

81. $x^2 - 8x + 16 = ?$

    A. $x + 2$
    B. $x + 4$
    C. $(x + 2)^2$
    D. $(x - 4)^2$
    E. $(x + 4)^3$

82. What number must be added to $12x + x^2$ to make the resulting trinomial expression a perfect square?

    A. 4
    B. 16
    C. 25
    D. 36
    E. 49

83. What number must be added to $4x^2 - 12x$ to make the resulting trinomial expression a perfect square?

   A. 2   C. 9   E. 16
   B. 4   D. 12

84. $x^2 - 8x + 15 = ?$

   A. $(x + 5)(x + 3)$ D. $(x - 5)(x - 3)$
   B. $(x - 5)(x + 3)$ E. $(x - 15)(x - 1)$
   C. $(x + 5)(x - 3)$

85. $2x^2 + 5x - 3 = ?$

   A. $(x - 1)(x + 3)$ D. $(3x + 1)(x + 3)$
   B. $(2x - 1)(x + 3)$ E. $(3x - 1)(2x + 3)$
   C. $(2x + 1)(x - 3)$

86. $21x + 10x^2 - 10 = ?$

   A. $(5x - 2)(2x + 5)$ D. $(8x + 2)(4x + 5)$
   B. $(5x + 2)(2x + 5)$ E. $(10x - 4)(2x - 5)$
   C. $(5x + 2)(2x - 5)$

87. $ax^2 + 3ax = ?$

   A. $3ax$ C. $ax(x + 3)$ E. $ax^2(x + 3)$
   B. $ax(x - 3)$ D. $ax^2(x - 3)$

88. $2x^2 - 8x + 3 - (x^2 - 3x + 9) = ?$

   A. $(x - 6)(x - 1)$ D. $(2x - 6)(x - 1)$
   B. $(x - 6)(x + 1)$ E. $(2x + 6)(x + 1)$
   C. $(x + 6)(x + 1)$

89. If $15x^2 + ax - 28 = (5x - 4)(3x + 7)$, then $a = ?$

   A. 7   C. 23   E. 33
   B. 14   D. 28

90. $x^2 - 9 = ?$

   A. $x^2 - 3$ D. $(x + 3)(x - 3)$
   B. $(x - 3)(x - 3)$ E. $x - 3$
   C. $(x + 3)(x + 3)$

91. $x^2 - 9y^4 = ?$

   A. $(x + 3y^2)(x - 3y^2)$ D. $(2x + 3y^2)(2x + 3y^2)$
   B. $(x - 3y^2)(x - 3y^2)$ E. $(2x - 3y^2)(2x - 3y^2)$
   C. $(x + 3y^2)(x + 3y^2)$

92. $x^2 + 6x - 27 = ?$

   A. $(x - 9)(x - 9)$ D. $(x + 9)(x + 3)$
   B. $(x - 9)(x - 3)$ E. $(x + 9)(x - 3)$
   C. $(x - 3)(x - 3)$

93. Simplify: $\frac{8x^{-4}}{2x}$.

   A. $\frac{2}{x^5}$ C. $\frac{3}{x^5}$ E. $\frac{8}{x^5}$
   B. $\frac{4}{x^4}$ D. $\frac{4}{x^5}$

94. Simplify: $\frac{3^{-1}x^5y^2}{2xy}$.

   A. $\frac{x^4y}{6}$ C. $\frac{x^6y^2}{8}$ E. $\frac{x^6y^2}{10}$
   B. $\frac{x^4y}{6}$ D. $\frac{x^6y^4}{6}$

95. Simplify: $\frac{6x^{-5}y^2}{3^{-1}x^{-4}y}$.

   A. $\frac{12y^4}{x^4}$ C. $\frac{16y^5}{x^4}$ E. $\frac{18y^5}{x^6}$
   B. $\frac{16y^4}{x^5}$ D. $\frac{18y}{x}$

96. Simplify: $\frac{9^2x^3y}{3^{-1}x^{-4}y}$.

   A. $243x^7$ C. $248x^7$ E. $256x$
   B. $244x^3$ D. $252x^2$

97. If $x = -2$, $x^2 = ?$

   A. -4 C. 6   E. 10
   B. 4   D. 8

98. If $x = -3$ and $y = 5$, then $x^2y = ?$

   A. -50 C. 45   E. 55
   B. -45 D. 50

99. If $x = -2$ and $y = -3$, then $x^2 - 4xy - x = ?$

   A. -24 C. -18 E. -14
   B. -20 D. -16

100. Expand and simplify: $(x - y)(x^2 - 2x + 5)$.

   A. $x^3 - 2x^2 + 5x - x^2y + 2xy - 5y$
   B. $x^3 + 2x^2 + 5x - x^2y + 2xy - 5y$
   C. $x^3 - 2x^2 - 5x - x^2y + 2xy - 5y$
   D. $x^3 - 2x^2 + 5x + x^2y + 2xy - 5y$
   E. $x^3 - 2x^2 + 5x - x^2y - 2xy - 5y$

101. Expand and simplify: $(2x + \sqrt{3})^2$.

   A. $3x^2 + 3x\sqrt{3} + 3$ D. $-4x^2 + 4x\sqrt{3} + 3$
   B. $4x^2 - 4x\sqrt{3} + 3$ E. $4x^2 + 4x\sqrt{3} + 3$
   C. $4x^2 - 4x\sqrt{3} - 3$

102. If $x = -2$ and $y = 3$, then $2x^2 - xy = ?$

   A. 10   C. 14   E. 18
   B. 12   D. 16

103. Simplify: $\left(\frac{x^2y^3x^5}{2^{-1}}\right)^2$.

   A. $4x^{12}y^4$ C. $4x^{14}y^4$ E. $4x^{14}y^6$
   B. $4x^{12}y^{66}$ D. $4x^{12}y^6$

104. Does $\sqrt{x^2 + y^2} = x + y$?

   A. Yes
   B. No
   C. Cannot be determined from the given information

105. Does $\sqrt{(x+y)^2} = \sqrt{x^2 + 2xy + y^2}$?
    A. Yes
    B. No
    C. Cannot be determined from the given information

106. Does $\dfrac{x}{\sqrt{2x-y}} = x\sqrt{2x+y}$?
    A. Yes
    B. No
    C. Cannot be determined from the given information

107. Does $\dfrac{6}{\sqrt{2a-3c}} = \dfrac{6\sqrt{2a-3c}}{(2a-3c)}$?
    A. Yes
    B. No
    C. Cannot be determined from the given information

108. Find the sum of $\dfrac{n}{6} + \dfrac{2n}{5}$.
    A. $\dfrac{13n}{30}$ C. $\dfrac{3n}{30}$ E. $\dfrac{3n}{11}$
    B. $17n$ D. $\dfrac{17n}{30}$

109. Combine into a single fraction: $1 - \dfrac{x}{y}$.
    A. $\dfrac{1-x}{y}$ C. $\dfrac{x-y}{y}$ E. $\dfrac{y-x}{xy}$
    B. $\dfrac{y-x}{y}$ D. $\dfrac{1-x}{1-y}$

110. Divide $\dfrac{x-y}{x+y}$ by $\dfrac{y-x}{y+x}$.
    A. 1 C. $\dfrac{(x-y)^2}{(x+y)^2}$ E. 0
    B. -1 D. $-\dfrac{(x-y)^2}{(x+y)^2}$

111. Simplify: $\dfrac{1 + \frac{1}{x}}{\frac{y}{x}}$.
    A. $\dfrac{x+1}{y}$ C. $\dfrac{x+1}{xy}$ E. $\dfrac{y+1}{y}$
    B. $\dfrac{x+1}{x}$ D. $\dfrac{x^2+1}{xy}$

112. Find an expression equivalent to $\left(\dfrac{2x^2}{y}\right)^3$.
    A. $\dfrac{8x^5}{3y}$ C. $\dfrac{6x^5}{y^3}$ E. $\dfrac{8x^6}{y^3}$
    B. $\dfrac{6x^6}{y^3}$ D. $\dfrac{8x^5}{y^3}$

113. Simplify: $\dfrac{\frac{1}{x} + \frac{1}{y}}{3}$.
    A. $\dfrac{3x+3y}{xy}$ C. $\dfrac{xy}{3}$ E. $\dfrac{y+x}{3}$
    B. $\dfrac{3xy}{x+7}$ D. $\dfrac{y+x}{3xy}$

114. Divide and simplify: $\dfrac{\sqrt{32b^3}}{\sqrt{8b}}$. Assume that $b \geq 0$.
    A. $2\sqrt{b}$ C. $2b$ E. $b\sqrt{2b}$
    B. $\sqrt{2b}$ D. $\sqrt{2b^2}$

115. Simplify: $\sqrt{\dfrac{x^2}{9} + \dfrac{x^2}{16}}$. Assume that $x \geq 0$.
    A. $\dfrac{25x^2}{144}$ C. $\dfrac{5x^2}{12}$ E. $\dfrac{7x}{12}$
    B. $\dfrac{5x}{12}$ D. $\dfrac{x}{7}$

116. Simplify: $\sqrt{36y^2 + 64x^2}$.
    A. $6y + 8x$ D. $10x^2y^2$
    B. $10xy$ E. Cannot be simplified
    C. $6y^2 + 8x^2$

117. Simplify: $\sqrt{\dfrac{x^2}{64} - \dfrac{x^2}{100}}$. Assume that $x \geq 0$.
    A. $\dfrac{x}{40}$ C. $\dfrac{x}{2}$ E. $\dfrac{3x}{80}$
    B. $-\dfrac{x}{2}$ D. $\dfrac{3x}{40}$

118. Simplify: $\sqrt{\dfrac{y^2}{2} - \dfrac{y^2}{18}}$. Assume that $y \geq 0$.
    A. $\dfrac{2y}{3}$ D. $\dfrac{y\sqrt{3}}{6}$
    B. $\dfrac{y\sqrt{5}}{3}$ E. Cannot be simplified
    C. $\dfrac{10y}{3}$

119. $\sqrt{a^2 + b^2}$ is equal to which of the following?
    A. $a + b$ D. $(a+b)(a-b)$
    B. $a - b$ E. None of these
    C. $\sqrt{a^2} + \sqrt{b^2}$

120. Given every pair (x, y) of negative numbers and resulting value $\dfrac{x}{|x|} + \dfrac{xy}{|xy|}$, what is the set of all numbers formed?
    A. $\{0\}$ C. $\{2\}$ E. $\{0, 2\}$
    B. $\{-2\}$ D. $\{0, -2\}$

121. When factored as completely as possible with respect to the integers, $16x^4 - 81y^{16} = ?$
    A. $(4x^2 + 9y^4)(4x^2 - 9y^4)$
    B. $(4x^2 + 9y^8)(4x^2 - 9y^8)$
    C. $(4x^2 + 9y^4)(2x + 3y)(2x - 3y)$
    D. $(4x^2 + 9y^8)(2x + 3y^4)(2x - 3y^4)$
    E. $16x^4 - 81y^{16}$

Algebraic Equations and Inequalities

Pursuing the analogy between English and algebra as a language, the algebraic analogue of a complete sentence in English (with subject and verb) is an equation. An **algebraic equation** is a statement that two algebraic expressions are equivalent.

Examples:

English	*Algebra*
Ed is three years older than Paul	$E = P + 3$
Paul is twice as old as Mary.	$P = 2M$
Ned has $2 more than Ed.	$N = E + \$2$
Bill has three times as much money as does Ted	$B = 3T$

Solving Algebraic Formulas

An **algebraic formula** is an equation that typically involves a relationship between literal quantities. Problems that involve formulas often ask you to solve for a particular unknown (variable) using substitution. Algebraic formulas can take many different forms, including function math, scientific equations, geometric formulas, and story-problems. Regardless of the format, the concept is the same: Replace the variables for which values are given and solve for the unknown variable.

Examples:

1. For all real numbers x and y, $x \oplus y = 2x + y^2$. What is the value of $3 \oplus 7$?
   ➤ Substitute 3 for x and 7 for y in the given expression: $x \oplus y = 2x + y^2 \Rightarrow 3 \oplus 7 = 2(3) + (7)^2 = 6 + 49 = 55$.

2. The formula that relates Fahrenheit temperature to Celsius temperature is: $F = 1.8C + 32$, where F is Fahrenheit degrees (°F) and C is Celsius degrees (°C). What is the temperature, in Fahrenheit degrees, if the temperature is 25°C?
   ➤ Substitute 25 for C in the given equation and solve for F: $F = 1.8C + 32 = 1.8(25) + 32 = 45 + 32 = 77°F$.

3. The volume of a sphere is: $V = \frac{4\pi r^3}{3}$, where r is the radius of the sphere. Find the volume of a sphere with a radius of 6.
   ➤ Substitute 6 for r in the given formula and solve for V: $V = \frac{4\pi r^3}{3} = \frac{4\pi(6)^3}{3} = \frac{4\pi(216)}{3} = 4\pi \cdot 72 = 288\pi$.

4. If a person must pick one object from a group of x objects and then one object from a group of y objects, the number of possible combinations is xy. Jan must select 1 candy bar from 7 different candy bars and 1 pack of gum from 3 different packs of gum. What is the maximum number of combinations available to Jan?
   ➤ Substitute 7 for x and 3 for y in the given expression: # of combinations $= xy = (7)(3) = 21$.

Formulas that represent real-life situations often involve variables with units of measure, such as inches or gallons. You must ensure that all variables have similar units on both sides of the equation in order for the equality to remain true. To maintain consistency, it may be necessary to convert units using equivalent expressions (*e.g.*, 12 inches/foot, 1foot/12 inches, 60 minutes/hour, 1 hour/60 minutes). Thus, when dealing with quantities given in units of any type, it helps to explicitly write out the units in the expressions.

Example:

If string costs k cents per foot at the hardware store, how much will w feet and j inches of the string cost?
   ➤ Cost of string $(\cent) = \frac{k\,\text{cents}}{1\,\text{ft. of string}} \cdot$ length of string (ft.) $= \frac{k\,\text{cents}}{1\,\text{ft.}} \cdot \left[w\,\text{ft.} + \left(j\,\text{in.} \cdot \frac{1\,\text{ft.}}{12\,\text{in.}} \right) \right] = \frac{k\,\text{cents}}{1\,\text{ft.}} \cdot \left[w\,\text{ft.} + \left(j\,\text{in.} \cdot \frac{1\,\text{ft.}}{12\,\text{in.}} \right) \right] = \frac{k\,\text{cents}}{1\,\text{ft.}} \cdot \left(w + \frac{j}{12} \right)(\text{ft.})$. Therefore, the cost of the string, in cents, is: $k\left(w + \frac{j}{12} \right)$.

Basic Principle of Equations

The fundamental rule for working with any equation is: Whatever you do to one side of an equation, you must do exactly the same thing to the other side of the equation. This rule implies that you can add, subtract, multiply, and divide both sides of the equality by any value without changing the statement of equality. The only exception is that you cannot divide by zero. The following example illustrates the validity of this principle using an equation containing only real numbers.

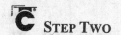

Example:

$5 = 5$

➤ This is obviously a true statement. You can add any value to both sides of the equation, say 10, and the statement will remain true. Add 10: $5 + 10 = 5 + 10 \Rightarrow 15 = 15$. You can also subtract the same value from both sides, *e.g.*, 7: $15 - 7 = 15 - 7 \Rightarrow 8 = 8$. You can multiply both sides by the same value, *e.g.*, -2: $8 \cdot -2 = 8 \cdot -2 \Rightarrow -16 = -16$. Finally, you can divide both sides by the same value (except zero); *e.g.*, -4: $-16 \div -4 = -16 \div -4 \Rightarrow 4 = 4$.

This principle for manipulating equations applies to algebraic equations with variables, as the following example illustrates.

Example:

$5 + x = 5 + x$

➤ Add x: $5 + x + x = 5 + x + x \Rightarrow 5 + 2x = 5 + 2x$. Whatever x is, since it appears on both sides of the equation, both sides of the equation must still be equal. Now, subtract a value, *e.g.*, y: $5 + 2x - y = 5 + 2x - y$. Again, since y appears on both sides of the equation, the statement that the two expressions are equal remains true.

Do NOT multiply both sides of an equation by zero if the equation contains a variable. You may lose special characteristics of the variable. For example, the equation $2x = 8$ is true only if $x = 4$. However, the equation $0(2x) = 0(8)$ is true for any value of x.

Solving Linear Equations

Equations that have only variables of the first power are called equations of the first degree or ***linear equations***. While a linear equation can have any number of different variables, equations with one or two variables are most common on the exam.

The fundamental rule of equations is the key to solving linear equations. To solve for an unknown variable, identically manipulate both sides of the equation to isolate the variable on one side. Be sure to reduce the other side of the equation by combining similar terms.

Examples:

1. If $2x + 3 = x + 1$, then what is the value of x?
    ➤ To solve for x, manipulate the equation to isolate x. Subtract x from both sides: $2x + 3 - x = x + 1 - x \Rightarrow x + 3 = 1$. Next, subtract 3 from both sides: $x + 3 - 3 = 1 - 3 \Rightarrow x = -2$.

2. If $4x + 2 = 2x + 10$, then what is the value of x?
    ➤ Subtract $2x$ from both sides of the equation: $4x + 2 - 2x = 2x + 10 - 2x \Rightarrow 2x + 2 = 10$. Then, subtract 2 from both sides: $2x + 2 - 2 = 10 - 2 \Rightarrow 2x = 8$. Divide both sides by 2: $2x \div 2 = 8 \div 2 \Rightarrow x = 4$.

3. If $3y - 2x = 12$, then what is the value of y?
    ➤ Add $2x$ to both sides of the equation: $3y - 2x + 2x = 12 + 2x \Rightarrow 3y = 12 + 2x$. Divide both sides by 3: $y = \frac{2x}{3} + 4$.

So far, we have been very formal in following the fundamental rule for working with equations. The process is simplified using a shortcut called ***transposition***. Transposing is the process of moving a term or a factor from one side of the equation to the other by changing it into its mirror image. Perform these "inverse operations" until the variable is isolated. Note that this shortcut does not change the fundamental rule or its outcome: it simply bypasses the formal steps.

To transpose a term that is added or subtracted, move it to the other side of the equation and change its sign. Thus, a term with a positive sign on one side is moved to the other side and becomes negative, and vice versa. It is imperative when using transposition that you do not forget to change signs when terms change sides.

Examples:

1. $x + 5 = 10$
    ➤ Rather than going through the formal steps of subtracting 5 from both sides of the equality, simply transpose the 5: move it from the left side to the right side and change its sign from "+" to "−": $x = 10 - 5 \Rightarrow x = 5$.

2. $x - 5 = 10 \Rightarrow x = 10 + 5 \Rightarrow x = 15$

3. $3x = 5 + 2x \Rightarrow 3x - 2x = 5 \Rightarrow x = 5$

To transpose a multiplicative factor, move the factor to the opposite side of the equation and invert it; that is, replace it with its reciprocal.

Example:

$\frac{2x+5}{3} = 9$

➢ $2x$ and 5 are both divided by 3; in other words, they are both multiplied by $\frac{1}{3}$. Therefore, the $\frac{1}{3}$ must be transposed first. Move it to the opposite side of the equation and invert it: $2x + 5 = 9(3) = 27$. Now the 5 can be transposed: $2x = 27 - 5 = 22$. Finally, solve for x by transposing the 2: $x = 22 \cdot \frac{1}{2} = 11$.

Solving Simultaneous Equations

Ordinarily, if an equation has more than one variable, it is not possible to determine the unique numeric solution for any individual variable. For example, the equation $x + y = 10$ does not have one unique solution set for x and y: x and y could be 1 and 9, 5 and 5, −2 and 12, and so on. However, if there are as many equations as there are variables, the equations can be manipulated as a system to determine the value of each variable. This technique is called *solving simultaneous equations* because the equations are taken to be true at the same time, or simultaneously, in order to determine the variable value. On the exam, simultaneous equations are typically limited to two equations and two unknowns.

Example:

Given $x + y = 10$ and $x - y = 6$, solve for x and y.
➢ If we treat both of the equations as making true statements at the same time, then there is only one solution set for x and y, for there is only one pair of numbers that will satisfy both equations, $x = 8$ and $y = 2$.

It is easy to see the answer to the previous example, but solutions will not always be this obvious. How do you find the specific solution for a given set of equations? There are three methods for solving simultaneous equations: substitution, linear combination (elimination), and graphing using a calculator.

1. Substitution

The steps for *substitution* are as follows:

1. Pick one of the two given equations and define one variable in terms of the other.
2. Substitute the defined variable into the other equation and solve.
3. Substitute the solution back into either equation and solve for the remaining variable.

Examples:

1. If $2x + y = 13$ and $x - y = 2$, what are the values of x and y?
   ➢ Redefine one variable in terms of the other. Since y is already a single variable in both equations, define y in terms of x: $y = 13 - 2x$. Substitute $13 - 2x$ for y in the second equation and solve for x: $x - (13 - 2x) = 2 \Rightarrow 3x = 15 \Rightarrow x = 5$. Finally, solve for y by substituting 5 for x in either equation: $2x + y = 13 \Rightarrow 2(5) + y = 13 \Rightarrow y = 3$.

2. If $3x + 2y = 16$ and $2x - y = 6$, what are the values of x and y?
   ➢ Since y is a simple term in the second equation, define y in terms of x: $2x - y = 6 \Rightarrow y = 2x - 6$. Substitute this expression for y in the first equation and solve for x: $3x + 2(2x - 6) = 16 \Rightarrow 7x = 28 \Rightarrow x = 4$. Finally, solve for y by substituting 4 for x in either equation: $2x - y = 6 \Rightarrow 2(4) - y = 6 \Rightarrow y = 2$.

3. If $y = 7 + x$ and $3x + 2y = 4$, what are the values of x and y?
   ➢ Substitute $7 + x$ for y in the second equation and solve for x: $3x + 2y = 4 \Rightarrow 3x + 2(7 + x) = 4 \Rightarrow 5x = -10 \Rightarrow x = -2$. Substitute −2 for x in the first equation and solve for y: $y = 7 + x = 7 - 2 = 5$.

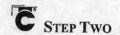

2. Linear Combination (Elimination)

The second method for solving simultaneous equations is *linear combination* or *elimination*. Eliminate one of the two variables by adding or subtracting the two equations. If necessary, division of one equation by another may eliminate one of two variables. This is the case when solving equations containing variables with exponents.

Examples:

1. If $2x + y = 8$ and $x - y = 1$, what are the values of x and y?
   ➤ In this pair of simultaneous equations, there is a "$+y$" term in one equation and a "$-y$" term in the other. Since $+y$ and $-y$ added together yields zero, eliminate the y term by adding the two equations together. (Actually, you will be adding the left side of the second equation to the left side of the first equation and the right side of the second to the right side of the first, but it is easier to speak of the process as "adding equations.") $[2x + y = 8] + [(x - y = 1)] = [3x = 9] \Rightarrow x = 3$. Find the value of y by substituting 3 for x in either equation: $2x + y = 8 \Rightarrow 2(3) + y = 8 \Rightarrow y = 8 - 6 = 2$.

2. If $4x + 3y = 17$ and $2x + 3y = 13$, what are the values of x and y?
   ➤ In this pair, each equation has a $+3y$ term, which you can eliminate by subtracting the second equation from the first. $[4x + 3y = 17] - [2x + 3y = 13] = [2x = 4] \Rightarrow x = 2$. Solve for y by substituting 2 for x in either equation: $4x + 3y = 17 \Rightarrow 4(2) + 3y = 17 \Rightarrow 8 + 3y = 17 \Rightarrow 3y = 9 \Rightarrow y = 3$.

3. $x^5 = 6y$ and $x^4 = 2y$; x is a real number such that $x \neq 0$ and y is a real number. Solve for x.
   ➤ The system of equations is reduced to one equation and one variable by dividing the first equation by the second equation: $\frac{x^5}{x^4} = \frac{6y}{2y} \Rightarrow x = 3$.

If a system of equations has more variables than equations, then not every variable value can be determined. Instead, you will be asked to solve for one or more variables in terms of another variable.

Examples:

1. If $y = 2a$ and $3x + 8y = 28a$, find x in terms of a.
   ➤ Substitute $2a$ for y and solve for x: $3x + 8y = 28a \Rightarrow 3x + 8(2a) = 28a \Rightarrow 3x = 28a - 16a \Rightarrow x = \frac{12a}{3} = 4a$.

2. In terms of a, solve the following pair of equations for x and y: $3x - 4y = 10a$ and $5x + 2y = 8a$.
   ➤ First, solve for either x or y in terms of a alone. To find x in terms of a, multiply the second equation by 2 and add the result to the first equation. $[2(5x + 2y = 8a)] + [3x - 4y = 10a] = [13x = 26a] \Rightarrow x = 2a$. To find y in terms of a, substitute $2a$ for x in either equation: $5x + 2y = 8a \Rightarrow y = \frac{8a - 5(2a)}{2} \Rightarrow y = \frac{-2a}{2} = -a$.

3. Graphing with a Calculator

The SAT and PSAT allow calculators: A graphing calculator may be used to solve simultaneous equations quickly. There are several methods to solve a system of simultaneous equations using a calculator: (1) use a calculator's system solver program; (2) in each equation, define y in terms of x and graph these equations for y simultaneously to find the point of intersection, (x, y); (3) use inverse matrices, and (4) write a special program for certain types of problems.

Example:

Given $2x - y = 6$ and $3x + 2y = 16$, solve for x and y.

➤ A calculator graphs equations in y-form. Therefore, solve each equation for y before entering the equations into the graphing calculator. $2x - y = 6 \Rightarrow y = \frac{(6 - 2x)}{-1}$. $3x + 2y = 16 \Rightarrow y = \frac{(16 - 3x)}{2}$. Graph both equations—the point of intersection is (4, 2). Note that if your calculator has a system solver program, then rewriting the equations in y-form and explicitly graphing them is unnecessary.

Solving Quadratic Equations

Equations that involve variables of the second power (*e.g.*, x^2) are called *quadratic equations*. Unlike a linear equation with a single variable, which has a single solution, a quadratic may have two solutions. By convention, quadratic equations are written so that the right side of the equation is equal to zero. The general form is: $ax^2 + bx + c = 0$.

Example:

Solve for x: $x^2 + x - 2 = 0$.
➤ To solve the quadratic equation, factor the left side of the equation: $x^2 + x - 2 = 0 \Rightarrow (x + 2)(x - 1) = 0$. For the equality to hold true, $x + 2$ or $x - 1$ must equal zero. Therefore, $x = -2$ or 1, so this quadratic equation has two solutions.

This last example illustrates the *zero product property*: if $xy = 0$, then $x = 0$ or $y = 0$.

Example:

$x^2 - 3x - 4 = 0$
➤ Factor the left side of the equation: $(x + 1)(x - 4) = 0$. Either $x + 1 = 0$, in which case $x = -1$, or $x - 4 = 0$, in which case $x = 4$. Therefore, the solution set for this quadratic equation is $\{-1, 4\}$.

However, not every quadratic equation has two different solutions.

Example:

$x^2 + 2x + 1 = 0$
➤ Factor the left side of the equation: $(x + 1)(x + 1) = 0$. Since the two factors are the same, the equation has one solution: -1.

For quadratic equations not in standard form, you must first group like terms and rearrange the equation into standard form.

Examples:

1. Solve for x: $2x^2 + 12 - 3x = x^2 + 2x + 18$.
    ➤ Rewrite the equation: $2x^2 + 12 - 3x = x^2 + 2x + 18 \Rightarrow (2x^2 - x^2) + (-3x - 2x) + (12 - 18) = 0 \Rightarrow x^2 - 5x - 6 = 0$. Factor the left side: $(x - 6)(x + 1) = 0$. Either $x - 6 = 0$ and $x = 6$, or $x + 1 = 0$ and $x = -1$. Therefore, $x = 6$ or -1.

2. Solve for x: $x(8 + x) = 2x + 36 + 6x$.
    ➤ Group like terms: $x(8 + x) = 2x + 36 + 6x \Rightarrow 8x + x^2 = 8x + 36 \Rightarrow x^2 = 36$. Since squaring a negative number yields a positive and squaring a positive number yields a positive, there are two answers for x. Thus, $x = 6$ or -6.

Some higher degree equations can also be solved if they can be written in quadratic form.

Example:

Solve for x: $x^4 - 13x^2 + 36 = 0$.
➤ Factor: $(x^2 - 9)(x^2 - 4) = 0$. Factor again: $(x + 3)(x - 3)(x + 2)(x - 2) = 0$. To find the four possible values of x, set each factor equal to zero and solve for x: $x + 3 = 0 \Rightarrow x = -3$; $x - 3 = 0 \Rightarrow x = 3$; $x + 2 = 0 \Rightarrow x = -2$; and $x - 2 = 0 \Rightarrow x = 2$. Therefore, the solution set is: $\{-3, 3, -2, 2\}$.

Alternatively, you can use the quadratic formula, $x = \dfrac{-b \pm \sqrt{b^2 - 4ac}}{2a}$, to solve quadratic equations.

Example:

Solve for x: $3 - x = 2x^2$.
➤ $3 - x = 2x^2 \Rightarrow 2x^2 + x - 3 = 0$. $a = 2$, $b = 1$, $c = -3$. $x = \dfrac{-b \pm \sqrt{b^2 - 4ac}}{2a} = \dfrac{-1 \pm \sqrt{1^2 - 4(2)(-3)}}{2(2)} = \dfrac{-1 \pm \sqrt{1 + 24}}{4} = \dfrac{-1 \pm 5}{4}$. $x = \{1, -\frac{3}{2}\}$.

Algebraic Inequalities

An *inequality* is very much like an equation except, as the name implies, it is a statement that two quantities are not equal. Four different symbols are used to make statements of inequality:

- \> greater than
- \< less than
- ≥ greater than or equal to
- ≤ less than or equal to

Examples:

$5 > 1$ .... 5 is greater than 1.
$2 > -2$ .... 2 is greater than -2.
$x > 0$ .... x is greater than zero.
$x > y$ .... x is greater than y.
$8 < 9$ .... 8 is less than 9.
$-4 < -1$ .... -4 is less than -1.
$x < 0$ .... x is less than zero.
$y < x$ .... y is less than x.
$x \geq 0$ .... x is greater than or equal to zero. (x could be zero or any number larger than zero.)
$x \geq y$ .... x is greater than or equal to y. (Either x is greater than y, or x and y are equal.)
$x \leq 0$ .... x is less than or equal to zero. (x could be zero or any number less than zero.)
$x \leq y$ .... x is less than or equal to y. (Either x is less than y, or x and y are equal.)

The fundamental rule for working with inequalities is similar to that for working with equalities: Treat each side of the inequality exactly the same. You can add or subtract the same value to each side of an inequality without changing the inequality, and you can multiply or divide each side of an inequality by any *positive* value without changing the inequality.

Example:

$5 > 2$ (Add 25 to both sides.)
$5 + 25 > 2 + 25 \Rightarrow$
$30 > 27$ (Subtract 6 from both sides.)
$30 - 6 > 27 - 6 \Rightarrow$
$24 > 21$ (Multiply both sides by 2.)
$24(2) > 21(2) \Rightarrow$
$48 > 42$ (Divide both sides by 6.)
$48 \div 6 > 42 \div 6 \Rightarrow$
$8 > 7$

However, if you multiply or divide an inequality by a *negative* number, the direction of the inequality is reversed. Therefore, remember to change the direction of the inequality when multiplying or dividing by a negative number.

Example:

$4 > 3$ (Multiply both sides by -2.)
$4(-2) < 3(-2) \Rightarrow$
$-8 < -6$

These properties hold true for inequalities containing variables, as the following two examples illustrate.

Examples:

1. For what values of x is $3(2-x) + 7x > 30$?
   ➤ Solve for x: $3(2-x) + 7x > 30 \Rightarrow 6 - 3x + 7x > 30 \Rightarrow 6 + 4x > 30 \Rightarrow 4x > 24 \Rightarrow x > 6$.

2. For what values of x is $3(2-x) + x > 30$?
   ➤ Solve for x: $3(2-x) + x > 30 \Rightarrow 6 - 3x + x > 30 \Rightarrow 6 - 2x > 30 \Rightarrow -2x > 24 \Rightarrow x < -12$.

Exponents in Equations and Inequalities

1. Integer and Rational Exponents

Algebraic equations and inequalities can include terms with integer and rational exponents. The rules of exponents apply when manipulating these terms.

Examples:

1. If $x = 2$, then what is the value of $(x^{-2x})^{x^{-x}}$?
   ➤ Substitute $x = 2$ into the given expression: $(x^{-2x})^{x^{-x}} = [(2)^{-2(2)}]^{2^{-2}} = [(2)^{-4}]^{1/2^2} = 2^{(-4)(1/4)} = 2^{-1} = \frac{1}{2}$.

2. Find the value of $2x^0 + x^{2/3} + x^{-2/3}$ when $x = 27$.
   ➤ Substitute $x = 27$: $2x^0 + x^{2/3} + x^{-2/3} = 2(27)^0 + (27)^{2/3} + (27)^{-2/3} = 2(1) + (\sqrt[3]{27})^2 + \frac{1}{27^{2/3}} = 2 + 9 + \frac{1}{9} = 11\frac{1}{9}$.

2. Algebraic Exponentials

When solving equations that involve algebraic exponential terms, try to find a common base to use throughout the problem.

Example:

Solve for x: $4^{x+2} = 8^{3x-6}$
➤ Since $4 = 2^2$ and $8 = 2^3$, the common base in this item is 2. Thus: $4^{x+2} = 8^{3x-6} \Rightarrow (2^2)^{x+2} = (2^3)^{3x-6} \Rightarrow 2^{2x+4} = 2^{9x-18}$.
Now, drop the common base and solve for x: $2x + 4 = 9x - 18 \Rightarrow 22 = 7x \Rightarrow x = \frac{22}{7}$.

3. Exponential Growth

Items that involve exponential growth test knowledge of exponential growth sequences, also called geometric sequences. In a geometric sequence, the *ratio*, r, of any term to its preceding term is constant. If the terms of a geometric sequence are designated by $a_1, a_2, a_3 \ldots a_n$, then $a_n = a_1 r^{n-1}$. Sequences that involve exponential growth have real-life applications, such as determining population growth over a specific period.

Examples:

1. Find the 5th term of the geometric sequence: 4, 12, 36....
   ➤ In this geometric sequence, the ratio between the terms is 3. Therefore, the 5th term is: $a_n = a_1 r^{n-1} \Rightarrow a_5 = 4(3)^{5-1} = 4(3)^4 = 4 \cdot 81 = 324$.

2. On June 1, 1990, the population of Grouenphast was 50,250. If the population is increasing at an annual rate of 8.4%, what is the approximate population of Grouenphast on June 1, 2010?
   ➤ An annual increase of 8.4% means that each year the population will be 108.4% of the previous year's population. Thus, the ratio between terms, r, is 1.084. The population on June 1, 1990 is the starting term: $a_1 = 50,250$. Since June 1, 2010 is 20 years later, the population at that time is the 21st term in the sequence: $n = 21$. Therefore, the population on June 1, 2010 is: $a_n = a_1 r^{n-1} \Rightarrow a_{21} = 50,250(1.084)^{21-1} = 50,250(1.084)^{20} \approx 252,186$.

The previous example involving growth over time suggests an alternate form of the geometric sequence equation called the **exponential growth equation**: $a_t = a_0 r^{t/T}$. In this equation, a_t is the amount after time t; a_0 is the initial amount ($t = 0$), r is the proportionality constant, t is the total period of growth, and T is the time per cycle of growth. Note that this equation also applies to exponential decay, where the initial amount is larger than the amount after time t.

Example:

The number of rabbits in a certain population doubles every 3 months. Currently, there are 5 rabbits in the population. How many rabbits will there be 3 years from now?

➤ In this case, the total time of growth is 3 years. Since the population doubles every 3 months, the time per cycle of growth is one-fourth of a year. Using the formula for exponential growth: $a_t = a_0 r^{t/T} \Rightarrow a_3 = (5)(2)^{3/0.25} = (5)(2)^{12} = 20,450$. We can verify this solution by working out the values, allowing the population to double every 3 months.

Period (months)	0	3	6	9	12	15	18	21	24	27	30	33	36
Population Size	5	10	20	40	80	160	320	640	1,280	2,560	5,120	10,240	20,480

Rational Equations and Inequalities

Algebraic equations and inequalities may include rational (fractional) expressions. When manipulating rational expressions, follow the same rules as discussed with equations, inequalities, and algebraic fractions.

Example:

1. If $\dfrac{x}{x+6} = \dfrac{y^3 - 1}{(y+1)(y^2 - y + 1) + 4}$, then $x = ?$

➤ $\dfrac{x}{x+6} = \dfrac{y^3 - 1}{y^3 - y^2 + y + y^2 - y + 1 + 4} = \dfrac{y^3 - 1}{y^3 + 5} = \dfrac{y^3 - 1}{y^3 - 1 + 6} = \dfrac{y^3 - 1}{(y^3 - 1) + 6}$. Therefore, $x = y^3 - 1$.

2. Let x represent a positive whole number. Given the two inequalities, $\dfrac{1}{x} > \dfrac{1}{4}$ and $\dfrac{x-3}{(x^2 - 3x)} < \dfrac{1}{7}$, how many more values for x satisfy the second equality than satisfy the first inequality?

➤ For the first inequality: $\dfrac{1}{x} > \dfrac{1}{4} \Rightarrow x < 4$. Thus, the set of satisfying values for x is $\{1, 2, 3\}$. For the second inequality, $\dfrac{x-3}{x(x-3)} < \dfrac{1}{7}$, since it is not possible to divide by zero, $x \neq 3$. Reduce the equation: $\dfrac{x-3}{x(x-3)} < \dfrac{1}{7} \Rightarrow \dfrac{1}{x} < \dfrac{1}{7} \Rightarrow 7 > x$. Since $x < 7$ and $x \neq 3$, the set of satisfying values for the second inequality is $\{1, 2, 4, 5, 6\}$. Thus, two more whole numbers satisfy the second inequality than the first.

Radical Equations and Inequalities

Expressions in algebraic equations and inequalities may include radicals. The same principles for working with equations and inequalities apply when manipulating radicals.

Example:

$5\sqrt{x-4} - 28 = 12$ for what value of x?

➤ $5\sqrt{x-4} - 28 = 12 \Rightarrow 5\sqrt{x-4} = 40 \Rightarrow \sqrt{x-4} = 8 \Rightarrow x - 4 = 64 \Rightarrow x = 68$.

Absolute Value in Equations and Inequalities

Expressions in algebraic equations and inequalities may include absolute values. The same principles for working with equations and inequalities apply when manipulating absolute values.

Example:

1. What is the sum of all different integers that can be substituted for x such that $|x| + |x-3| = 3$?
   ➤ The absolute value of any real number, including integers, is always zero or more. Therefore, try only $-3, -2, -1, 0, 1, 2,$ 3. The last four work in the equality: $|0| + |0-3| = 0 + 3 = 3$; $|1| + |1-3| = 1 + 2 = 3$; $|2| + |2-3| = 2 + 1 = 3$; $|3| + |3-3| = 3 + 0 = 3$. Thus, $0 + 1 + 2 + 3 = 6$.

2. If x represents an integer, $|x-3| + |x+2| < 7$ for how many different values of x?
   ➤ Absolute values are always equal to or greater than zero. Thus, if $x = -4$, $|x-3| = |-4-3| = 7$; there is no need to try any integers less than -3. Similarly, if $x = 5$, $|x+2| = |5+2| = 7$, there is no need to try any integers greater than 4. Therefore, test only the integers between -3 and 4. Six integers satisfy the inequality: $-2, -1, 0, 1, 2, 3$. Alternatively, a graphing calculator could be used to solve this problem.

The SAT and PSAT allow calculators. A graphing calculator can be used to solve quadratic equations quickly. Depending on the type of calculator, you may need to write a quadratic formula program for your calculator.

Algebraic Equations and Inequalities

DIRECTIONS: Choose the correct answer to each of the following items. Use a calculator when necessary. Answers are on page 914.

1. If $3x = 12$, then $x = ?$
   A. 2   C. 4   E. 10
   B. 3   D. 6

2. If $2x + x = 9$, then $x = ?$
   A. 0   C. 3   E. 9
   B. 1   D. 6

3. If $7x - 5x = 12 - 8$, then $x = ?$
   A. 0   C. 2   E. 4
   B. 1   D. 3

4. If $3x + 2x = 15$, then $x = ?$
   A. 2   C. 5   E. 9
   B. 3   D. 6

5. If $a - 8 = 10 - 2a$, then $a = ?$
   A. −2   C. 2   E. 6
   B. 0   D. 4

6. If $p - 11 - 2p = 13 - 5p$, then $p = ?$
   A. −4   C. 1   E. 6
   B. −1   D. 2

7. If $12x + 3 - 4x - 3 = 8$, then $x = ?$
   A. −5   C. 0   E. 5
   B. −1   D. 1

8. If $5x - 2 + 3x - 4 = 2x - 8 + x + 2$, then $x = ?$
   A. −5   C. 1   E. 6
   B. 0   D. 3

9. If $a + 2b - 3 + 3a = 2a + b + 3 + b$, then $a = ?$
   A. −1   C. 2   E. 6
   B. 0   D. 3

10. If $4y + 10 = 5 + 7y + 5$, then $y = ?$
    A. −2   C. 0   E. 8
    B. −1   D. 4

11. If $-4 - x = 12 + x$, then $x = ?$
    A. −8   C. 1   E. 4
    B. −2   D. 2

12. If $\frac{x}{2} + x = 3$, then $x = ?$
    A. $\frac{1}{2}$ C. 1   E. 3
    B. $\frac{2}{3}$ D. 2

13. If $\frac{2x}{3} + \frac{x}{4} + 4 = \frac{x}{6} + 10$, then $x = ?$
    A. $\frac{11}{12}$ C. 5   E. 20
    B. $\frac{3}{2}$ D. 8

14. If $\frac{a}{2} - \frac{a}{4} = 1$, then $a = ?$
    A. $\frac{1}{2}$ C. 1   E. 4
    B. $\frac{2}{3}$ D. 2

15. If $\frac{1}{p} + \frac{2}{p} + \frac{3}{p} = 1$, then $p = ?$
    A. $\frac{2}{3}$ C. 1   E. 6
    B. $\frac{3}{4}$ D. 2

16. If $\frac{2x - 6}{3} = 8$, then $x = ?$
    A. 1   C. 6   E. 18
    B. 3   D. 15

17. If $\frac{5 - x}{5} = 1$, then $x = ?$
    A. −5   C. 0   E. 5
    B. −1   D. 1

18. If $\frac{2 - x}{10} = 1$, then $x = ?$
    A. −8   C. $-\frac{1}{5}$ E. 5
    B. −1   D. 1

19. If $\frac{5}{x + 1} + 2 = 5$, then $x = ?$
    A. $-\frac{2}{7}$ C. $\frac{7}{2}$ E. 10
    B. $\frac{2}{3}$ D. 7

20. If $\frac{x}{2} + \frac{x}{3} = \frac{1}{2} + \frac{1}{3}$, then $x = ?$
    A. $\frac{1}{3}$ C. 1   E. 3
    B. $\frac{2}{3}$ D. 2

21. If $3x + y = 10$ and $x + y = 6$, then $x = ?$
    A. 1   C. 3   E. 5
    B. 2   D. 4

22. If $2x + y = 10$ and $x + y = 7$, then $y = ?$
    A. 3   C. 5   E. 9
    B. 4   D. 6

23. If $x + 3y = 5$ and $2x - y = 3$, then $x = ?$
    A. 2   C. 5   E. 9
    B. 4   D. 6

24. If $x + y = 2$ and $x - y = 2$, then $y = ?$
    A. −2   C. 0   E. 2
    B. −1   D. 1

25. If $a + b = 5$ and $2a + 3b = 12$, then $b = ?$
    A. 1   C. 3   E. 6
    B. 2   D. 4

26. If $5x + 3y = 13$ and $2x = 4$, then $y = ?$
    A. 1   C. 3   E. 5
    B. 2   D. 4

27. If $k - n = 5$, and $2k + n = 16$, then $k = ?$
    A. −3   C. 1   E. 7
    B. 0   D. 5

28. If $t = k - 5$ and $k + t = 11$, then $k = ?$
    A. 2   C. 8   E. 14
    B. 3   D. 11

29. If $a + 5b = 9$ and $a - b = 3$, then $a = ?$
    A. 1   C. 5   E. 11
    B. 4   D. 7

30. If $8 + x = y$ and $2y + x = 28$, then $x = ?$
    A. 2   C. 6   E. 18
    B. 4   D. 12

31. If $\frac{x+y}{2} = 4$ and $x - y = 4$, then $x = ?$
    A. 1   C. 4   E. 8
    B. 2   D. 6

32. If $\frac{x+y}{2} = 7$ and $\frac{x-y}{3} = 2$, then $x = ?$
    A. 2   C. 8   E. 14
    B. 4   D. 10

33. If $x + y + z = 10$ and $x - y - z = 4$, then $x = ?$
    A. 2   C. 6   E. 12
    B. 3   D. 7

34. If $x + 2y - z = 4$ and $2x - 2y + z = 8$, then $x = ?$
    A. −2   C. 4   E. 8
    B. 0   D. 6

35. If $x + y + z = 6$, $x + y - z = 4$, and $x - y = 3$, then $x = ?$
    A. −2   C. 4   E. 8
    B. 0   D. 6

36. If $x^2 - 5x + 4 = 0$, then $x = ?$
    A. −2 or 1   C. −1 or 2   E. 4 or 2
    B. 4 or 1   D. −4 or −1

37. If $x^2 - 3x - 4 = 0$, then $x = ?$
    A. −4 or 1   C. −1 or 2   E. 6 or −1
    B. −2 or 2   D. 4 or −1

38. If $x^2 + 5x + 6 = 0$, then $x = ?$
    A. −3 or −2   C. −1 or 6   E. 6 or −2
    B. −3 or 2   D. 1 or −6

39. If $x^2 - 3x + 2 = 0$, then $x = ?$
    A. −2 or −1   C. 1 or 2   E. 3 or 5
    B. −1 or 2   D. 2 or 3

40. If $x^2 + 3x + 2 = 0$, then which of the following values is (are) possible for x?
    I. 1
    II. −1
    III. −2
    A. I only   D. I and II only
    B. II only   E. II and III only
    C. III only

41. If $x^2 + 5x = -4$, then $x = ?$
    A. −1 or −4   C. 1 or 2   E. 2 or 6
    B. −1 or −2   D. 1 or 4

42. If $x^2 - 8 = 7x$, then $x = ?$
    A. −8 and −1   C. −1 and 8   E. 1 and 8
    B. −4 and 1   D. 1 and 4

43. If $k^2 - 10 = -3k$, then $k = ?$
    A. −10 and −1   C. −5 and 3   E. 2 and −5
    B. −10 and 1   D. −3 and 5

44. If $x^2 = 12 - x$, then $x = ?$
    A. −4 and −3   C. −3 and 4   E. 1 and 6
    B. −4 and 3   D. −2 and 6

45. If $3x^2 = 12x$, then $x = ?$
    A. 0 or 3   C. −2 or 2   E. 3 or 12
    B. 0 or 4   D. 2 or 4

46. If $4(5 - x) = 2(10 - x^2)$, then $x = ?$
    A. 0 or 2   C. −2 or 4   E. 4 or 5
    B. 2 or 4   D. 0 or −2

47. For what values of x is $3 + 4x < 28$?

    A. $x < 4$ C. $x < 6.25$ E. $x \geq 0$
    B. $x > 4$ D. $x > 6.25$

48. For what values of x is $5(3x - 2) \geq 50$?

    A. $x \geq 4$ C. $x \geq 10$ E. $x > 8$
    B. $x \leq 4$ D. $x \leq 10$

49. For what values of x is $8 - 3x > 35$?

    A. $x > 0$ C. $x \geq 0$ E. $x \geq 9$
    B. $x > -3$ D. $x < -9$

50. If $x^2 = 6x - 8$, then $x = ?$

    A. -8 and -2 C. -2 and 2 E. 2 and 8
    B. -4 and -2 D. 2 and 4

51. If $(x - 8)(x + 2) = 0$, then $x = ?$

    A. -8 or -2 C. 4 or -2 E. 10 or -5
    B. -4 or -2 D. 8 or -2

52. If $9 - 3(6 - x) = 12$, then $x = ?$

    A. 4 or -2 C. 4 E. 7
    B. 7 or -2 D. 6

53. If $\frac{x + 5}{4} = 17$, then $x = ?$

    A. 13 or 25 C. 63 E. 124
    B. 54 D. 75 or -24

54. If $\frac{x}{2} - \frac{x - 2}{3} = 0.4$, then $x = ?$

    A. -1 or 1.4 C. 2 or -1.6 E. 2.6
    B. -1.6 D. 2.4

55. If $0.02x + 1.44 = x - 16.2$, then $x = ?$

    A. 18 C. 14 E. 10
    B. 16 D. 12

56. If $3 - 2(x - 5) = 3x + 4$, then $x = ?$

    A. $\frac{1}{2}$ or $\frac{1}{4}$ C. $\frac{9}{5}$ E. 5
    B. $-\frac{9}{5}$ D. 1 or 3

57. If $x^2 - 9x = 22$, then $x = ?$

    A. -11 or 2 C. 2 or 3 E. 11
    B. 3 D. 11 or -2

58. If $(x + 8)(x + 1) = 78$, then $x^2 + 9x = ?$

    A. 50 C. 60 E. 70
    B. 55 D. 65

59. If $2x + 3y = 12$ and $x = -6$, then $y = ?$

    A. 2 C. 8 E. 12
    B. 4 D. 10

60. At what point does the line $5x + 2y = 20$ intersect the x-axis? (Hint: What must the y-coordinate be?)

    A. $(-4, 0)$ C. $(0, 0)$ E. $(4, 2)$
    B. $(-2, 0)$ D. $(4, 0)$

61. If $3x + 5y = 10$, then $y = ?$

    A. $-0.6x - 2$ C. $0.5x - 4$ E. $-0.6x + 2$
    B. $-0.4x + 2$ D. $0.6x - 2$

62. If $x = ay + 3$, then $y = ?$

    A. $\frac{x - 2}{4a}$ C. $\frac{a}{x - 3}$ E. $\frac{a}{3x}$
    B. $\frac{x - 3}{a}$ D. $\frac{x + a}{3}$

63. If $8x + 16 = (x + 2)(x + 5)$, then $x = ?$

    A. 3 or -2 C. -2 E. 3
    B. -3 D. 2 or 3

64. If $\frac{x + 5}{0.2} = 0.3x$, then $x = ?$

    A. $-\frac{125}{23}$ C. $-\frac{250}{47}$ E. $\frac{250}{47}$
    B. -76 D. $\frac{47}{250}$

65. If $\frac{0.2 + x}{3} = \frac{\frac{5}{6}}{4}$, then $x = ?$

    A. $-\frac{40}{17}$ C. 0 E. $\frac{40}{17}$
    B. $-\frac{17}{40}$ D. $\frac{17}{40}$

66. If x is an integer and $6 < x < 8$, then what is the value of x?

    A. 4 C. 7 E. 10
    B. 5 D. 9

67. If x is an integer and $5 \leq x \leq 7$, then which of the following values is (are) possible for x?

    I. 5
    II. 6
    III. 7

    A. II only   D. II and III only
    B. I and II only   E. I, II, and III
    C. I and III only

68. If x and y are integers, $2 < x < 4$, and $8 > y > 6$, then what is the value of xy?

    A. 12 C. 21 E. 32
    B. 16 D. 24

69. If x and y are integers, $5 > x \geq 2$, and $6 < y \leq 9$, then which of the following is the *minimum* value of xy?

    A. 14 C. 20 E. 54
    B. 18 D. 45

70. If $1 \le x \le 3$, then which of the following values is (are) possible for x?

   I. $\frac{5}{2}$

   II. $\frac{7}{2}$

   III. $\frac{3}{2}$

   A. I only
          D. I and III only
   B. II only
          E. I, II, and III
   C. I and II only

71. If $3^{8x+4} = 27^{2x+12}$, then $x = ?$

   A. $\frac{1}{4}$
          C. 4
          E. 16

   B. $\frac{1}{9}$
          D. 9

72. If $(3+x)x = 2x + x + 16$, then which of the following is (are) the possible value(s) for x?

   A. 2
          C. 2 or -2
          E. 8 or -8
   B. 4
          D. 4 or -4

73. If $10x^2 = 30$ and $(6+y)y = 6y + 52$, then $2x^2 + 2y^2 = ?$

   A. 110
          C. 82
          E. 55
   B. 96
          D. 72

74. If $|x| = 5$, then $x = ?$

   A. 5
   B. 5 or -5
   C. Any real number less than 5
   D. No real number
   E. Any real number greater than zero

75. The commutative property states that if a final result involves two procedures or objects, then the final result is the same regardless of which procedure or object is taken first and which is taken second. Which of the following is an example of the commutative property of addition?

   A. $xy = yx$
          D. $7 - 3 = 3 - 7$

   B. $5 + 4 = 4 + 5$
          E. $\frac{x}{y} = \frac{y}{x}$

   C. $2a + b = 2b + a$

76. The probability that an event will happen can be shown by the fraction $\frac{winning\ events}{total\ events}$ or $\frac{favorable\ events}{total\ events}$. From the 8 digit number 12,344,362, Helen selects a digit at random. What is the probability that she selected 4?

   A. $\frac{1}{8}$
          C. $\frac{1}{4}$
          E. $\frac{4}{1}$

   B. $\frac{1}{5}$
          D. $\frac{1}{2}$

77. The perimeter of a regular hexagon is given by the formula $P = 6s$, where P is the perimeter and s is the length of one side. If one side of a regular hexagon has a length of 3, what is the perimeter?

   A. 12
          C. 18
          E. 30
   B. 15
          D. 21

78. The simple interest earned on an investment is given by the formula $I = prt$, where I is the amount of interest, p is the amount invested, r is the yearly percentage rate of interest, and t is the number of years for the investment. What is the simple interest earned on an investment of \$1,000 for 2 years at a yearly percentage rate of interest of 6%?

   A. \$6
          C. \$60
          E. \$600
   B. \$12
          D. \$120

79. If $x = 3a$ and $y = 5x + 6$, then $y = ?$

   A. 21
          C. $6a + 15$
          E. $21a$
   B. $15a + 6$
          D. $3a + 15$

80. If $2(x+3) = 18a + 10$, then $x = ?$

   A. $9a + 2$
          C. $16a + 4$
          E. 11
   B. $9a + 5$
          D. $9a + 3.5$

81. The formula that relates Fahrenheit temperature to Celsius temperature is $F = 1.8C + 32$, where F is the temperature in Fahrenheit degrees and C is the temperature in Celsius degrees. What is the temperature, in Celsius degrees, if the temperature in Fahrenheit degrees is 41°?

   A. 5
          C. 9
          E. 73
   B. 7.2
          D. 10.8

82. If x is a real number such that $x \ne 0$, y is a real number, $x^5 = 8y$, and $x^4 = y$, then which of the following is true?

   A. $x = 7y$
          C. $x = 8y^2$
          E. $x = 8$
   B. $x = 8y$
          D. $x = 7y^2$

83. George must select 1 pencil from 6 different pencils and 1 pen from 5 different pens. How many different combinations can George make?

   A. 5
          C. 30
          E. 65
   B. 11
          D. 56

84. The commutative property states that if a final result involves two procedures or objects, then the final result is the same regardless of which procedure or object is taken first and which is taken second. Which of the following is an example of the commutative property of multiplication?

   A. $xy = yx$
          D. $7 - 3 = 3 - 7$

   B. $5 + 4 = 4 + 5$
          E. $\frac{x}{y} = \frac{y}{x}$

   C. $2a + b = 2b + a$

85. A geometric sequence is a sequence of numbers formed by continually multiplying by the same number; *e.g.*, {81, 27, 9, 3, ...} is a geometric sequence formed by continually multiplying by $\frac{1}{3}$. What is the next term in the geometric sequence of {2, 8, 32, 128, ...}?

   A. 132   C. 384   E. 1,024
   B. 256   D. 512

86. A sequence is formed by substituting consecutive whole numbers in the expression $x^3 + x^2 - 2x + 1$. What is the next term in the sequence of {1, 9, 31, 73, ...}?

   A. 115   C. 135   E. 141
   B. 125   D. 137

87. A letter is selected at random from the word "DAVID." What is the probability that the letter selected is "D"?

   A. $\frac{1}{5}$
   B. $\frac{1}{4}$
   C. $\frac{1}{3}$
   D. $\frac{2}{5}$
   E. $\frac{3}{5}$

88. Which of the following values for c returns two distinct real solutions to the equation $x^2 - 8x + c = 0$?

   A. −20   C. 18   E. 20
   B. 17   D. 19

89. Which of the following values for b returns two distinct real solutions to the equation $x^2 + bx + 8 = 0$?

   A. 6   C. 4   E. 1
   B. 5   D. $\sqrt{2}$

90. The cost of buying a certain material is k cents per yard. What is the cost, in cents, of x yards and y inches of the material?

   A. $kx + y$ C. $x + 36y$ E. $xk + 36yk$
   B. $36x + y$ D. $xk + \frac{yk}{36}$

91. The volume of a cone is $\frac{\pi r^2 h}{3}$, where r is the radius of the cone base and h is the cone height. What is the volume, in cubic inches, of a cone of height 12 inches that has a base of radius 3 inches?

   A. 144π C. 72π E. 36π
   B. 108π D. 54π

92. If $x^2 - 14k^2 = 5kx$, what are the 2 solutions for x in terms of k?

   A. $2k$ and $7k$ C. k and $5k$ E. k and $-5k$
   B. $-2k$ and $7k$ D. $-k$ and $5k$

93. An arithmetic sequence is a sequence of numbers formed by continually adding the same number; *e.g.*, {1, 3, 5, 7, 9, 11, ...} is an arithmetic sequence formed by continually adding 2. What is the ninth term in the arithmetic sequence of {1, 4, 7, 10, 13, ...}?

   A. 16   C. 19   E. 25
   B. 17   D. 21

94. One of the letters in the alphabet is selected at random. What is the probability that the letter selected is a letter found in the word "MATHEMATICS"?

   A. $\frac{1}{26}$
   B. $\frac{4}{13}$
   C. $\frac{5}{13}$
   D. $\frac{11}{26}$
   E. $\frac{6}{13}$

95. $\frac{1}{a} + \frac{1}{b} = 7$ and $\frac{1}{a} - \frac{1}{b} = 3$. Find $\frac{1}{a^2} - \frac{1}{b^2}$.

   A. 10   C. 3   E. 4
   B. 7   D. 21

96. If $\frac{3x}{4} = 1$, then $\frac{2x}{3} = ?$

   A. $\frac{1}{3}$ C. $\frac{2}{3}$ E. 2
   B. $\frac{1}{2}$ D. $\frac{8}{9}$

97. If $x = \frac{y}{7}$ and $7x = 12$, then $y = ?$

   A. 3   C. 7   E. 72
   B. 5   D. 12

98. If $x = k + \frac{1}{2} = \frac{k+3}{2}$, then $x = ?$

   A. $\frac{1}{3}$ C. 1   E. $\frac{5}{2}$
   B. $\frac{1}{2}$ D. 2

99. If $7 - x = 0$, then $10 - x = ?$

   A. −3   C. 3   E. 10
   B. 0   D. 7

100. If $x = 7 - \sqrt{3}$ and $y = 7 + \sqrt{3}$, which of the following must be rational?

   I. xy
   II. $x + y$
   III. $\frac{x}{y}$

   A. I only   D. I and II only
   B. III only   E. I, II, and III
   C. I and III only

101. Find the value, in simplest form, of the fraction $\frac{2^{x+4}-2(2^x)}{2(2^{x+3})}$.

    A. $\frac{1}{2}$ C. $\frac{3}{4}$ E. $\frac{7}{8}$

    B. $\frac{1}{4}$ D. $\frac{5}{8}$

102. Let $y = 2^x$ and $w = 8^x$. For what value of x does $w = 2y$?

    A. a rational number between 0 and 2
    B. a whole number between 2 and 8
    C. a irrational number between 2 and 8
    D. no such value of x exists
    E. more than one such value of x exists

103. Assume that the growth/decay formula is $y = kc^{t/T}$, in which y is the remaining amount after time t, k is the initial amount, c is the constant of proportionality, and T is the time per cycle of c. The half-life of a certain radioisotope is 9 days. Initially, there was 7.68 grams of the radioisotope. After how many days will less than 1 gram of the radioisotope be left?

    A. 23   C. 31   E. 33
    B. 27   D. 32

104. A population that starts at 16 and doubles every 30 months can be expressed as $16(2^{2x/5})$, where x is the number of elapsed years. What is the approximate population size after 105 months have elapsed?

    A. 11   C. 56   E. 192
    B. 27   D. 181

105. Let n be a member of the set $\{5, 6, 7, 8, 9, 10, 11, 12, 13, 14, 15, 16\}$. For how many different values of n is the following equation true?

$$\frac{1+2+\ldots+n}{2+4+\ldots+2n}=\frac{1}{2}$$

    A. 0   C. 6   E. 12
    B. 1   D. 11

106. Which of the following statements is always correct?

    A. If $x < 0$, then $x^2 > -x$
    B. If $x > 0$, then $(x + 3)(x + 2) > x^2 + 4x + 3$
    C. If $x > 0$, then $x^3 + 8 > (x + 2)(x^2 - 2x + 4)$
    D. If $x = 8$, then $1 + 2 + 3 + \ldots + x > x(x + 1)$
    E. If $x = 6$, then $\frac{2^x}{2^{x-1}} > 4$.

107. A prime number is defined as a whole number that is greater than 1 whose only divisors are 1 and the number itself. Examples of prime numbers are 13, 17, and 29. What is the smallest prime number that divides the sum of $3^3 + 5^5 + 7^7 + 11^{11}$ is:

    A. 2   C. 5   E. 11
    B. 3   D. 7

108. Let x represent a positive odd integer. The smallest value of x such that $(3^{1/4})(3^{3/4})(3^{5/4})\ldots(3^{x/4})$ is greater than 2^x is:

    A. a multiple of 3
    B. a multiple of 5 but not a multiple of 3
    C. a multiple of 7 but not a multiple of either 3 or 5
    D. 11
    E. 13

109. If x represents a real number, how many different values of x satisfy the equation $x^{128} = 16^{32}$?

    A. 0
    B. 1
    C. 2
    D. more than 2, but infinite
    E. infinite

110. How many of the following five numerical expressions represent whole numbers?

$$8^0, \; 9^{-2}, \; \left(\tfrac{1}{9}\right)^{-2}, \; \left(\tfrac{1}{8}\right)^{2/3}, \; \left(\tfrac{1}{16}\right)^{-1/4}$$

    A. 0   C. 3   E. 4
    B. 2   D. 4

111. If $y = 3^x$, $3^{x+2} = ?$

    A. y^2 C. $y + 3$ E. $y + 9$
    B. 2^y D. $9y$

112. How many real values of x exist such that $x = \sqrt{x} + 20$?

    A. 0
    B. 1
    C. 2
    D. more than 2, but not infinite
    E. infinite

113. Let x be an element of $\{-6, -5, -4, -3, -2, -1, 0, 2, 4, 6, 8, 10, 12\}$ and $x = 3k$, where k is an integer. Find the sum of all different values of x such that $\sqrt{2x + 8} = \sqrt{y}$ for some value of y if y is an element of $\{-2, 0, 2, 4, 6, 8, 10, 12, 14, 16, 18, 20, 22, 24, 26, 28\}$.

    A. 3   C. 9   E. 15
    B. 6   D. 12

114. Let k be a positive whole number such that $11 < k < 15$. If $\sqrt{8x} + k = 18$, for how many different values of k will the solution set for x contain an even integer?

    A. 0   C. 2   E. 4
    B. 1   D. 3

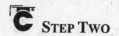

Geometry

If you have ever taken a basic course in geometry, you probably remember having to memorize theorems and do formal proofs. Fortunately, you will not be asked to do any formal proofs on the exam, and the formulas you need to know are few and relatively simple. Most often, test items ask you to find the measure of an angle, the length of a line, or the area of a figure.

Geometric Notation

You should be familiar with basic geometric notation. The line segment with points P and Q as endpoints is represented by $\overline{PQ}$. PQ represents the length of $\overline{PQ}$. A line passing through points P and Q is represented by $\overleftrightarrow{PQ}$. $\overrightarrow{PQ}$ represents the ray beginning at point P and passing through point Q. Finally, the symbol "≅" is used to represent the term "congruent."

Example:

If $\overleftrightarrow{AB}$ does not contain point C, but it does contain point D, what is the maximum number of points in the intersection of $\overleftrightarrow{AB}$ and $\overleftrightarrow{CD}$?

➤ $\overleftrightarrow{AB}$ and $\overleftrightarrow{CD}$ are different lines, so the maximum number of points at which they can intersect is one point, point D.

Line and Angle Properties

For the purposes of this review and the test, the word ***line*** means a straight line:

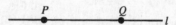

The line above is designated line l. The portion of line l from point P to point Q is called "line segment $\overline{PQ}$."

When two lines intersect, they form an ***angle***, and their point of intersection is called the ***vertex*** of that angle.

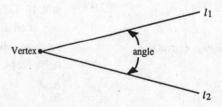

The size of an angle is measured in ***degrees***. Degrees are defined in reference to a circle. By convention, a circle is divided into 360 equal parts, or degrees.

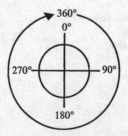

A 90° angle is also called a *right angle*. A right angle is often indicated in the following way:

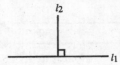

Two right angles form a straight line:

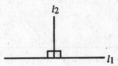

Since two right angles form a straight line, the degree measure of the angle of a straight line is 90° + 90° = 180°:

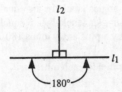

An angle that is less than 90° is called an *acute angle*:

In the figure above, $\angle PQR$ is an acute angle.

An angle that is greater than 90° but less than 180° is called an *obtuse angle*:

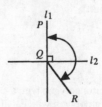

In the figure above, $\angle PQR$ is an obtuse angle.

When two lines intersect, the opposite (or vertical) angles created by their intersection are congruent, or equal:

$$w = y$$
$$x = z$$

Two lines that do not intersect regardless of how far they are extended are *parallel* to each other. In the following figure, the symbol ‖ indicates that l_1 and l_2 are parallel.

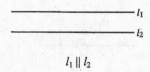

$$l_1 \parallel l_2$$

When parallel lines are intersected by a third line, a *transversal*, the following angle relationships are created:

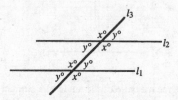

All angles labeled *x* are equal.
All angles labeled *y* are equal.
Any *x* plus any *y* totals 180.

Two lines that are *perpendicular* to the same line are parallel to each other:

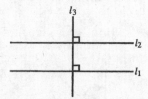

Since l_1 and l_2 are both perpendicular to l_3, we can conclude that l_1 and l_2 are parallel to each other.

Polygon Properties

- A *polygon* is a closed figure created by three or more lines.
- A *triangle* is any polygon with exactly three sides.
- A *quadrilateral* is any polygon with exactly four sides.
- A *pentagon* is any polygon with exactly five sides.
- A *hexagon* is any polygon with exactly six sides.

A polygon with more than six sides is usually referred to as a polygon with a certain number of sides; for example, a polygon with ten sides is called a ten-sided polygon. A *regular polygon* is a polygon with equal sides and equal angles (*e.g.*, a square). The sum of the degree measures of the *exterior angles* of a polygon is 360. The sum of the degree measures of the *interior angles* of a polygon can be expressed as $180(n-2)$, where n is the number of sides in the polygon.

Triangle Properties and Formulas

1. Properties of Triangles

A *triangle* is a three-sided figure. Within a given triangle, the larger an angle is, the longer the opposite side of the angle is; conversely, the longer a side is, the larger the opposite angle is.

Examples:

1. In the figure below, since $\overline{PR} > \overline{QR} > \overline{PQ}$, $\angle Q > \angle P > \angle R$.

2. In the figure below, since $\angle P > \angle Q > \angle R$, $\overline{QR} > \overline{PR} > \overline{PQ}$.

Within a given triangle, if two sides are equal, then the angles opposite the two sides are equal, and vice versa:

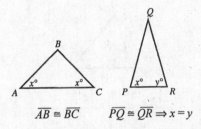

$$\overline{AB} \cong \overline{BC} \qquad \overline{PQ} \cong \overline{QR} \Rightarrow x = y$$

A triangle with exactly two equal sides is called an *isosceles triangle*. A triangle with exactly three equal sides is called an *equilateral triangle*.

Example:

> An equilateral triangle has three equal sides and therefore three equal angles: $x = y = z$. Thus, each angle must be 60°.

A triangle with a right angle is called a *right triangle*. The longest side of the right triangle, which is opposite the 90° angle, is called the *hypotenuse*.

2. *Pythagorean Theorem*

The sides of every right triangle fit a special relationship called the *Pythagorean theorem*: the square of the hypotenuse is equal to the sum of the squares of the other two sides. This is easier to understand when it is summarized in a formula.

Pythagorean theorem: $c^2 = a^2 + b^2$

3. *Formulas of Triangles*

The *perimeter* of a triangle is the sum of the lengths of the three sides:

$$Perimeter = P = a + b + c$$

The *altitude* of a triangle is a line drawn from a vertex perpendicular to the opposite side. The formula for finding the *area* of a triangle is equal to one-half multiplied by the altitude and the base.

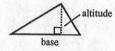

$$Area = \frac{ab}{2}$$

Example:

In the figure below, what is the area of the triangle?

➢ $A_{\text{triangle}} = \frac{ab}{2} = \frac{4 \cdot 5}{2} = 10.$

30°-60°-90° and 45°-45°-90° Triangles

1. Basic Trigonometric Identities

Two right triangles deserve special mention: 30°-60°-90° and 45°-45°-90° triangles. These triangles have special properties that are derived from basic trigonometry. While trigonometry may be used as a method for finding the solution, items on these types of triangles can also be answered using an alternative method based on these special properties.

The basic trigonometric identities—*sine*, *cosine*, and *tangent*—relate the sides and angles of right triangles. These identities are defined in terms of hypotenuse, side opposite, and side adjacent. The *hypotenuse* is the side opposite the right angle. *Side opposite* refers to the side opposite a referenced angle. The *side adjacent* is the side next to the referenced angle other than the hypotenuse. The three basic trigonometric functions are defined as follows:

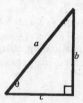

sine: $\quad \sin \theta = \dfrac{\text{side Opposite } \angle\theta}{\text{Hypotenuse}} = \dfrac{b}{a}$

cosine: $\quad \cos \theta = \dfrac{\text{side Adjacent } \angle\theta}{\text{Hypotenuse}} = \dfrac{c}{a}$

tangent: $\quad \tan \theta = \dfrac{\text{side Opposite } \angle\theta}{\text{side Adjacent } \angle\theta} = \dfrac{b}{c}$

Note that the mnemonic "SOH-CAH-TOA" can be used to memorize the three definitions of sine, cosine, and tangent.

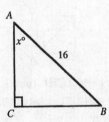

Example:

Find the values of sin A, sin C, cos A, cos C, tan A, and tan C in the triangle below.

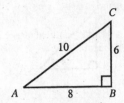

➤ $\sin A = \dfrac{\text{side opposite } \angle A}{\text{hypotenuse}} = \dfrac{6}{10} = \dfrac{3}{5},$ $\quad \sin C = \dfrac{\text{side opposite } \angle C}{\text{hypotenuse}} = \dfrac{8}{10} = \dfrac{4}{5},$ $\quad \cos A = \dfrac{\text{side adjacent } \angle A}{\text{hypotenuse}} = \dfrac{8}{10} = \dfrac{4}{5},$

$\cos C = \dfrac{\text{side adjacent } \angle C}{\text{hypotenuse}} = \dfrac{6}{10} = \dfrac{3}{5},$ $\quad \tan A = \dfrac{\text{side opposite } \angle A}{\text{side adjacent } \angle A} = \dfrac{6}{8} = \dfrac{3}{4},$ $\quad \tan C = \dfrac{\text{side opposite } \angle C}{\text{side adjacent } \angle C} = \dfrac{8}{6} = \dfrac{4}{3}.$

2. Trigonometry and the Pythagorean Theorem

Using the basic trigonometric identities in conjunction with the Pythagorean theorem allows us to solve for the measure of any angle or side in a right triangle. Specifically, if we know the values of any two angles or sides, we can solve for any unknown angle or side. The following example illustrates this strategy.

Example:

In the right triangle below, $\sin x = \frac{3}{4}$. What is the length of $\overline{AC}$?

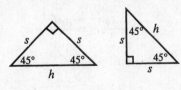

➤ Determine the length of $\overline{BC}$ from the given value for sin x: $\sin x = \dfrac{3}{4} = \dfrac{\text{side opposite } \angle x}{\text{hypotenuse}} = \dfrac{BC}{16} \Rightarrow BC = \dfrac{3(16)}{4} = 12$. Next, use the Pythagorean theorem to find the length of $\overline{AC}$: $(AB)^2 = (AC)^2 + (BC)^2 \Rightarrow 16^2 = (AC)^2 + 12^2 \Rightarrow (AC)^2 = 16^2 - 12^2 = 256 - 144 = 112 \Rightarrow AC = \sqrt{112} = \sqrt{16(7)} = 4\sqrt{7}$.

3. Special Properties of 45°-45°-90° Triangles

The values of the sine, cosine, and tangent identities for 45°-45°-90° triangles, when applied to the Pythagorean theorem, provide us with a shortcut for relating the lengths of the sides of these special triangles. In a triangle with angles of 45°-45°-90°, the length of the hypotenuse is equal to the length of either side multiplied by the square root of two. Conversely, the length of each of the two sides is equal to one-half the length of the hypotenuse multiplied by the square root of two.

$$h = s\sqrt{2} \Leftrightarrow s = \frac{h\sqrt{2}}{2}$$

Examples:

1. In $\triangle ABC$, both $\angle A$ and $\angle C$ are 45°. If the length of $\overline{AB}$ is 3, what is the length of $\overline{AC}$?

➤ $h = s\sqrt{2} \Rightarrow AC = AB(\sqrt{2}) = 3\sqrt{2}$.

2. In $\triangle LMN$, both $\angle L$ and $\angle N$ are 45°. If the length of $\overline{LN}$ is 4, what is the length of $\overline{MN}$?

➤ $s = \dfrac{h\sqrt{2}}{2} \Rightarrow MN = LN\left(\dfrac{\sqrt{2}}{2}\right) = (4)\left(\dfrac{\sqrt{2}}{2}\right) = 2\sqrt{2}$.

3. In the figure below, FGHJ is a square. What is the value of sin $\angle$FHJ?

➤ In the square, diagonal $\overline{FH}$ bisects right angle $\angle GHJ$. Thus, $\angle FHJ = 45°$. Use the properties of 45°-45°-90° triangles: let $FJ = x$; then, $JH = x$, and $FH = x\sqrt{2}$. Thus, sin $\angle FHJ = \dfrac{FJ}{FH} = \dfrac{x}{x\sqrt{2}} = \dfrac{1}{\sqrt{2}}$.

4. *Special Properties of 30°-60°-90° Triangles*

Similarly, the sides of 30°-60°-90° triangles also share special relationships based on the trigonometric functions and the Pythagorean theorem. In triangles with angles of 30°-60°-90°, the length of the side opposite the 30° angle is equal to one-half the length of the hypotenuse, and the length of the side opposite the 60° angle is equal to one-half the length of the hypotenuse multiplied by $\sqrt{3}$.

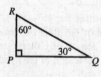

$$PR = \frac{QR}{2}, \ PQ = \frac{QR\sqrt{3}}{2}.$$

Examples:

1. In $\triangle ABC$, $\angle A = 60°$ and $\angle C = 40°$. If the length of $\overline{AC}$ is 6, what are the lengths of $\overline{AB}$ and $\overline{BC}$?

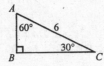

> $AB = \frac{AC}{2} = \frac{6}{2} = 3$. $BC = \frac{AC\sqrt{3}}{2} = \frac{6\sqrt{3}}{2} = 3\sqrt{3}$.

2. In $\triangle FGH$, $\angle F = 60°$. If the length of $\overline{FH}$ is 14, what is the length of $\overline{FG}$?

> The length of the side opposite the 30° angle, $\overline{FG}$, is equal to one-half the length of the side opposite the 90° angle, $\overline{FH}$: $FG = \frac{FH}{2} = \frac{14}{2} = 7$. Alternatively, use the trigonometry identities: $\sin 30° = \frac{FG}{FH} = \frac{FG}{14}$. Since $\sin 30° = \frac{1}{2}$, $\frac{1}{2} = \frac{FG}{14} \Rightarrow FG = 7$.

Similar Triangles

"Real world" items such as blueprints, scale drawings, microscopes, and photo enlargements involve similar figures. *Similar triangles* are frequently encountered on the exams. The symbol for similarity is "~." If two triangles are similar, the corresponding sides have the same ratio, and their matching angles are *congruent*; that is, they have the same number of degrees. The symbol for congruency is "≅."

Examples:

1. In the figure below, $\triangle ABC \sim \triangle DEF$. Find the length of $\overline{AC}$.

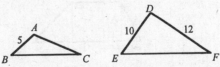

> The triangles are similar, so create a proportion relating the similar sides: $\frac{AC}{5} = \frac{12}{10} \Rightarrow 10(AC) = 5(12) = 60 \Rightarrow AC = 6$.

2. Right triangle PQR is similar to right triangle STV. The hypotenuse of $\triangle PQR$ is 12 units long and one of the legs is 6 units long. Find the smallest angle of $\triangle STV$.
> Any right triangle in which one leg is equal to one-half the hypotenuse must be a 30°-60°-90° triangle. Since the two triangles are similar, the matching angles are congruent. Therefore, the smallest angle of $\triangle STV$ is 30°.

Quadrilateral Properties and Formulas

A *quadrilateral* is a closed, four-sided figure in two dimensions. Common quadrilaterals are the parallelogram, rectangle, and square. The sum of the four angles of a quadrilateral is 360°. A *parallelogram* is a quadrilateral in which both pairs of opposite sides are parallel. Opposite sides of a parallelogram are equal, or congruent. Similarly, opposite angles of a parallelogram are also equal, or congruent. Again, the symbol for congruency is "≅."

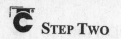

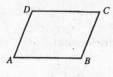

$$\overline{DC} \cong \overline{AB}; \ \overline{DA} \cong \overline{CB}$$
$$\angle D \cong \angle B; \ \angle A \cong \angle C$$

The area of a parallelogram is found by multiplying the base times its height. The height must be measured at a right angle.

Example:

In the figure below, find the area of the parallelogram.

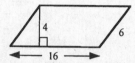

➤ The base of the parallelogram is 16 and the height is 4 (not 6). Remember, the height must be measured at a right angle to the base. Therefore, the area = 16 • 4 = 64.

A *trapezoid* is a quadrilateral with only two parallel sides. The area of a trapezoid is equal to one-half of the height times the sum of the two bases, which are the two parallel sides. Alternatively, a trapezoid can be broken down into triangles and rectangles, and the sum of these areas equals the trapezoid's area. The following example illustrates both methods.

Example:

In the figure below, find the area of the trapezoid.

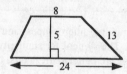

➤ The area of a trapezoid $= \frac{(b_1 + b_2)h}{2} = \frac{(8 + 24)(5)}{2} = 80$. However, if you do not remember the formula, simply break down the trapezoid into two triangles and a rectangle:

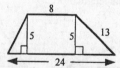

Use the Pythagorean theorem to find the base of the right-hand triangle: $x^2 + 5^2 = 13^2 \Rightarrow x = \sqrt{169 - 25} = \sqrt{144} = 12$. This implies that the base of the left-hand triangle is: $24 - 12 - 8 = 4$. Thus, the left-hand triangle's area is: $\frac{4 \cdot 5}{2} = 10$; the right-hand triangle's area is: $\frac{12 \cdot 5}{2} = 30$; and the rectangle's area $= 8 \cdot 5 = 40$. The trapezoid area is: $10 + 30 + 40 = 80$.

FORMULAS FOR PARALLELOGRAMS AND TRAPEZOIDS

$$Parallelogram \ Area = b \cdot h$$
$$Trapezoid \ Area = \frac{(b_1 + b_2)h}{2}$$

A *rectangle* is any four-sided figure that has four right angles. Since the opposite sides of a rectangle are congruent, it is customary to speak of the two dimensions of a rectangle: width and length. A *square* is a rectangle with four congruent sides.

To find the *perimeter* of either a rectangle or a square, simply add the lengths of the four sides. To find the *area* of a rectangle, multiply the width times the length. In a square, the sides are all congruent, so there is no difference between length and width. To find the area of a square, just square the length of one side.

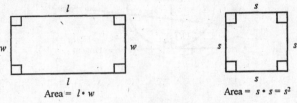

FORMULAS FOR RECTANGLES AND SQUARES

$$\text{Rectangle Perimeter} = 2(\text{width}) + 2(\text{length})$$
$$= 2w + 2l = 2(w + l)$$
$$\text{Rectangle Area} = w \cdot l$$

$$\text{Square Perimeter} = 4(\text{side}) = 4s$$
$$\text{Square Area} = s \cdot s = s^2$$

Circle Properties and Formulas

1. Properties of Circles

A *circle* is a closed plane curve, all points of which are equidistant from the center. A complete circle contains 360°, and a semicircle contains 180°. The distance from the center of the circle to any point on the circle is called the *radius*:

A line segment that passes through the center of the circle and that has endpoints on the circle is called the *diameter*. The diameter of a circle is twice the radius.

A *chord* is a line segment that connects any two points on a circle. A *secant* is a chord that extends in either one or both directions. A *tangent* is a line that touches a circle at one and only one point. A line that is tangent to a circle is perpendicular to a radius drawn to the point of tangency. The *circumference*, or perimeter, is the curved line that bounds the circle. An *arc* of a circle is any part of the circumference.

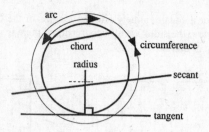

Example:

Two different circles lie in a flat plane. The circles may or may not intersect, but neither circle lies entirely within the other. What is the difference between the minimum and maximum number of lines that could be common tangents to both circles?

➤ Three cases are possible for the orientation of the two circles:

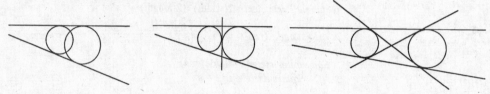

The difference between the minimum and maximum number of tangents that could be common to both circles is $4 - 2 = 2$.

A *central angle*, such as $\angle AOB$ in the next figure, is an angle with a vertex at the center of the circle and with sides that are radii. A central angle is equal to, or has the same number of degrees as, its intercepted arc. An *inscribed angle*, such as $\angle MNP$, is an angle with a vertex on the circle and with sides that are chords. An inscribed angle has half the number of degrees of its intercepted arc. $\angle MNP$ intercepts arc $\overline{MP}$ and has half the degrees of arc $\overline{MP}$.

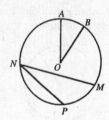

2. *Formulas for Circles*

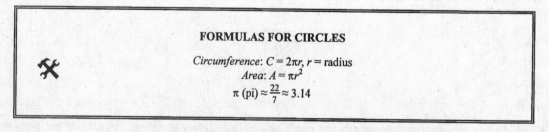

FORMULAS FOR CIRCLES

Circumference: $C = 2\pi r$, r = radius
Area: $A = \pi r^2$
π (pi) $\approx \frac{22}{7} \approx 3.14$

Surface Area and Volume of Solids

In a three-dimensional figure, the total space contained within the figure is called the *volume*; it is expressed in *cubic denominations* (*e.g.*, cm.³). The total outside surface is called the *surface area*; it is expressed in *square denominations* (*e.g.*, cm.²). In computing volume and surface area, express all dimensions in the same denomination.

A *rectangular solid* is a figure of three dimensions having six rectangular faces that meet each other at right angles. The three dimensions are length, width, and height. A *cube* is a rectangular solid whose edges are equal. Soda cans, poles, and fire extinguishers all are *cylinders*.

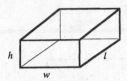

Volume = $w \cdot l \cdot h$

Cube Volume = s^3

Cylinder Volume = $h\pi r^2$

FORMULAS FOR RECTANGULAR SOLIDS, CUBES, AND CYLINDERS

Rectangular Solid Volume = width • length • height = $w \cdot l \cdot h$
Rectangular Solid Surface Area = $2(w \cdot l) + 2(l \cdot h) + 2(h \cdot w)$

Cube Volume = $side^3 = s^3$
Cube Surface Area = $6s^2$

Cylinder Volume = height • end area = $h(\pi r^2)$
Cylinder Surface Area = $(2\pi r \cdot h) + 2(\pi r^2)$

Examples:

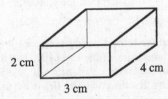

Volume = 3 cm • 4 cm • 2 cm = 24 cm³
Surface Area = 2(3 cm • 4 cm)
 + 2(4 cm • 2 cm)
 + 2(2cm • 3 cm)
 = 24 cm² + 16 cm² + 12 cm²
 = 52 cm²

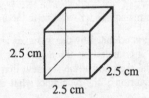

Volume = $(2.5 \text{ cm})^3 = 15.625 \text{ cm}^3$
Surface Area = 6(2.5 cm²) = 37.5 cm²

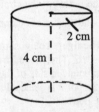

Volume = 4 cm • $\pi(2 \text{ cm})^2 \approx 50.27 \text{ cm}^3$
Surface Area = [2π(2 cm) • 4 cm]
 + 2π(2 cm)²
 = π(16 cm²) + π(8 cm²)
 = π(24 cm²)
 $\approx$ 75.4 cm²

The *surface area of a sphere* is 4π multiplied by the radius squared. The *volume of a sphere* is $\frac{4\pi}{3}$ multiplied by the radius cubed.

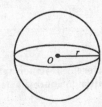

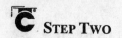

FORMULAS FOR SPHERES

$$\text{Sphere Surface Area} = 4\pi r^2$$
$$\text{Sphere Volume} = \frac{4\pi r^3}{3}$$

Geometric Probability

Some items on the exam may involve geometric probability. For example, if a point is to be chosen at random from the interior of a region, part of which is shaded, you might be asked to find the probability that the point chosen will be from the shaded portion of the region. Such an item might be presented in a specific context, such as throwing darts at a target.

Examples:

1. The figure below shows a circle inscribed in a square. The area of the square is 324. If a point is selected at random in the interior of the square, what is the approximate probability that the point also lies in the interior of the circle?

> Since the area of the square is 324, $A_{square} = s^2 \Rightarrow s = 18$. The side of the square is equal to the diameter of the circle, so the radius of the circle is $18 \div 2 = 9$. The area of the circle is: $A_{circle} = \pi r^2 = \pi(9)^2 = 81\pi$. Therefore, the probability that a point chosen at random in the interior of the square will also be in the interior of the circle is: $\frac{A_{circle}}{A_{square}} = \frac{81\pi}{324} = \frac{\pi}{4} \approx 0.785$.

2. The figure below shows a rectangle that is bounded by the two axes and two lines whose respective equations are $y = 8$ and $x = 6$. The shaded trapezoidal region is bounded on three sides by portions of three sides of the rectangle. The fourth unbounded side of the shaded trapezoidal region is a line segment that is a portion of the line whose equation is $2y = x + 4$. If a point is selected at random in the interior of the rectangle, what is the probability that the point also lies in the shaded region?

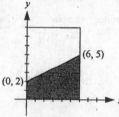

> For the line $2y = x + 4$, substitute values for x and solve for y. If $x = 0$, $2y = 0 + 4 \Rightarrow y = 2$. If $x = 6$, $2y = 6 + 4 \Rightarrow y = 5$. The parallel sides of the trapezoid have lengths of 2 and 5; the altitude of the trapezoid is 6. Therefore, the probability that the point will be in both the interior of the rectangle and the interior of the shaded region is:

$$\frac{A_{shaded}}{A_{rectangle}} = \frac{\frac{6(2 + 5)}{2}}{6 \cdot 8} = \frac{3 \cdot 7}{48} = \frac{21}{48} = \frac{7}{16}.$$

NOTE: The SAT and PSAT allow calculators. Therefore, it is important that you learn how to use a calculator and bring the same calculator with you to the exam. Use the "π" button to approximate and save valuable test time.

Geometry

DIRECTIONS: Choose the correct answer to each of the following items. Use a calculator when necessary. Answers are on page 921.

1. In the figure below, $x = ?$

    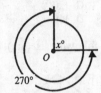

    O is the center of the circle.

    A. 30   C. 90   E. 270
    B. 60   D. 120

2. In the figure below, $x = ?$

    O is the center of the circle.

    A. 45   C. 90   E. 150
    B. 60   D. 120

3. In the figure below, $x = ?$

    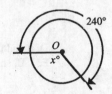

    O is the center of the circle.

    A. 60   C. 120   E. 180
    B. 90   D. 150

4. In the figure below, $x = ?$

    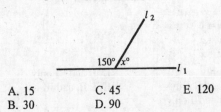

    A. 15   C. 45   E. 120
    B. 30   D. 90

5. In the figure below, $x = ?$

    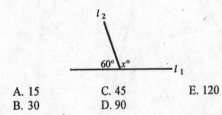

    A. 15   C. 45   E. 120
    B. 30   D. 90

6. In the figure below, $x = ?$

    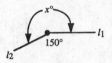

    A. 210   C. 150   E. 120
    B. 180   D. 135

7. In the figure below, $x = ?$

    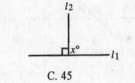

    A. 15   C. 45   E. 90
    B. 30   D. 60

8. In the figure below, $x = ?$

    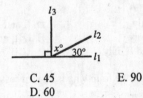

    A. 15   C. 45   E. 90
    B. 30   D. 60

9. In the figure below, $x = ?$

    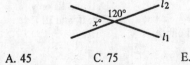

    A. 45   C. 75   E. 120
    B. 60   D. 90

10. In the figure below, $x = ?$

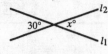

    A. 30   C. 55   E. 80
    B. 45   D. 65

11. Which of the following is (are) true of the figure below?

    I. $\overline{AB} \cong \overline{BC}$
    II. $\overline{BC} \cong \overline{AC}$
    III. $\overline{AC} \cong \overline{AB}$

    A. I only   D. I and III only
    B. II only   E. I, II, and III
    C. I and II only

Items #12-16 are based on the following figure.

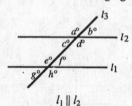

$l_1 \parallel l_2$

12. Which of the following is (are) necessarily true?
    I. $a = b$
    II. $b = c$
    III. $g = h$
    A. I only   D. II and III only
    B. II only   E. I, II, and III
    C. I and II only

13. Which of the following is (are) necessarily true?
    I. $b = c$
    II. $d = c$
    III. $g = e$
    A. I only   D. II and III only
    B. III only   E. I, II, and III
    C. I and III only

14. Which of the following is (are) necessarily true?
    I. $c + d = 180$
    II. $c + a = 180$
    III. $b + g = 180$
    A. I only   D. II and III only
    B. III only   E. I, II, and III
    C. I and II only

15. If $e = 120$, then $g = ?$
    A. 60   C. 120   E. 180
    B. 90   D. 150

16. If $h = 60$, then $d = ?$
    A. 60   C. 120   E. 180
    B. 90   D. 150

17. Which of the following is (are) true of the figure below?

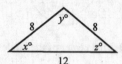

    I. $x = y$
    II. $y = z$
    III. $z = x$
    A. I only   D. I and II only
    B. II only   E. I, II, and III
    C. III only

18. Which of the following is (are) true of the figure below?

    I. $\overline{PQ} \cong \overline{QR}$
    II. $\overline{QR} \cong \overline{PR}$
    III. $\overline{PR} \cong \overline{PQ}$
    A. I only   D. II and III only
    B. III only   E. I, II, and III
    C. I and II only

19. Which of the following is (are) true of the figure below?

    I. $x = y$
    II. $y = z$
    III. $z = x$
    A. I only   D. II and III only
    B. I and II only   E. I, II, and III
    C. I and III only

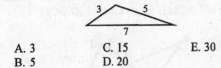

20. What is the perimeter of the triangle below?

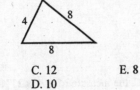

A. 3   C. 15   E. 30
B. 5   D. 20

21. What is the perimeter of the triangle below?

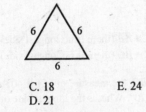

A. 20   C. 12   E. 8
B. 18   D. 10

22. What is the perimeter of the triangle below?

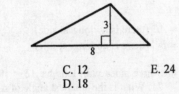

A. 6   C. 18   E. 24
B. 12   D. 21

23. What is the area of the triangle below?

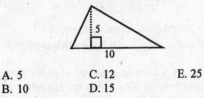

A. 3   C. 12   E. 24
B. 6   D. 18

24. What is the area of the triangle below?

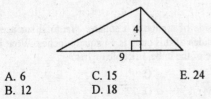

A. 5   C. 12   E. 25
B. 10   D. 15

25. What is the area of the triangle below?

A. 6   C. 15   E. 24
B. 12   D. 18

26. In the figure below, what is the length of $\overline{RS}$?

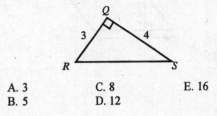

A. 3   C. 8   E. 16
B. 5   D. 12

27. In the figure below, what is the length of $\overline{AB}$?

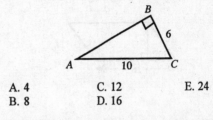

A. 4   C. 12   E. 24
B. 8   D. 16

28. In the figure below, what is the length of $\overline{PR}$?

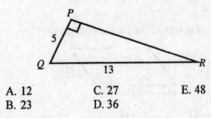

A. 12   C. 27   E. 48
B. 23   D. 36

29. In the figure below, what is the length of $\overline{AC}$?

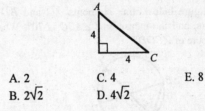

A. 2   C. 4   E. 8
B. $2\sqrt{2}$ D. $4\sqrt{2}$

30. In the figure below, what is the length of $\overline{JL}$?

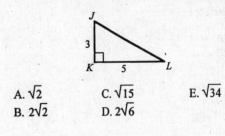

A. $\sqrt{2}$ C. $\sqrt{15}$ E. $\sqrt{34}$
B. $2\sqrt{2}$ D. $2\sqrt{6}$

31. What is the area of the parallelogram below?

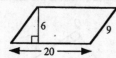

A. 180
B. 120
C. 58
D. 29
E. 15

32. What is the area of the parallelogram below?

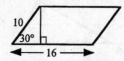

A. 160
B. 80
C. 52
D. 26
E. 16

33. What is the area of the parallelogram below?

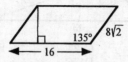

A. $128\sqrt{3}$ C. 128   E. 64
B. $128\sqrt{2}$ D. $64\sqrt{2}$

34. In the figure below, line segments $\overline{AC}$ and $\overline{BD}$ are diameters, and the measure of $\angle ABO$ is 70°. What is the measure of $\angle COD$?

A. 110°
B. 70°
C. 40°
D. 35°
E. 30°

35. In the figure below, $\overline{AC}$ and $\overline{DE}$ bisect each other at point B. The measure of $\angle A$ is 20° and the measure of $\angle D$ is 86°. What is the measure of $\angle DBC$?

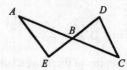

A. 106°
B. 74°
C. 66°
D. 45°
E. 33°

36. In $\triangle ABC$, the measure of $\angle A$ is 23° and the measure of $\angle B$ is 84°. What is the longest side of $\triangle ABC$?

A. $\overline{AC}$
B. $\overline{AB}$
C. $\overline{BC}$
D. $\overline{AC} \cong \overline{AB}$ (there is no longest side)
E. $\overline{AC} \cong \overline{BC}$ (there is no longest side)

37. In $\triangle ABC$, the measure of $\angle A$ is 40° and the measure of $\angle B$ is 70°. What is the longest side of $\triangle ABC$?

A. $\overline{AC}$
B. $\overline{AB}$
C. $\overline{BC}$
D. $\overline{AC} \cong \overline{AB}$ (there is no longest side)
E. $\overline{AC} \cong \overline{BC}$ (there is no longest side)

38. $\triangle ABC$ has three sides with lengths $AB = 19$, $BC = 20$, and $AC = 21$. What is the smallest angle of $\triangle ABC$?

A. $\angle A$
B. $\angle B$
C. $\angle C$
D. $\angle A \cong \angle B$ (there is no smallest angle)
E. $\angle A \cong \angle B \cong \angle C$ (there is no smallest angle)

39. Each side of a cube is a square with an area of 49 square centimeters. What is the volume of the cube, in cubic centimeters?

A. 49   C. 7^4 E. 7^{49}
B. 7^3 D. 49^7

40. Each side of a cube is a square. The total surface area of all sides of this cube is 54 square inches. What is the volume of the cube, in cubic inches?

A. 54^3 C. 9^3 E. 9
B. $(\sqrt{54})^3$ D. 27

41. What is the area of the trapezoid below?

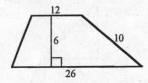

   A. 260   C. 130   E. 58
   B. 130   D. 114

42. What is the perimeter of the trapezoid below?

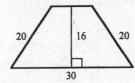

   A. 70   C. 80   E. 100
   B. 76   D. 90

43. The volume of a sphere is $V = \frac{4}{3}\pi r^3$, where r is the radius of the sphere. If the surface area of the sphere is 324π cm.^{2}, what is the sphere's volume, in cm.^{3}.

   A. 243π
   B. 324π
   C. 729π
   D. 972π
   E. $1,296\ \pi$

44. What is the perimeter of the figure below?

   A. 6   C. 10   E. 16
   B. 8   D. 12

45. What is the perimeter of the figure below?

   A. 8   C. 14   E. 16
   B. 12   D. 15

46. What is the area of the figure below?

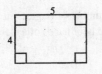

   A. 10   C. 16   E. 20
   B. 15   D. 18

47. What is the area of the figure below?

   A. 6   C. 12   E. 24
   B. 8   D. 16

48. What is the area of the figure below?

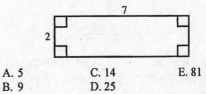

   A. 5   C. 14   E. 81
   B. 9   D. 25

49. In the figure below, $AB = 5$. What is the area of square $ABCD$?

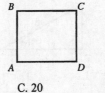

   A. 5   C. 20   E. 40
   B. 10   D. 25

50. If the radius of a circle is 2, what is the diameter?
   A. 1   C. 3   E. 8
   B. 2   D. 4

51. If the diameter of a circle is 10, what is the radius?
   A. 2   C. 8   E. 20
   B. 5   D. 15

52. If the radius of a circle is 3, what is the circumference?
   A. 2π C. 6π E. 12π
   B. 3π D. 9π

53. If the radius of a circle is 5, what is the circumference?
   A. 5π C. 15π E. 24π
   B. 10π D. 20π

54. If the diameter of a circle is 8, what is the circumference?
   A. 8π C. 4π E. π
   B. 6π D. 2π

55. If the radius of a circle is 3, what is the area?
   A. π C. 6π E. 12π
   B. 3π D. 9π

56. If the radius of a circle is 5, what is the area?
   A. 25π C. 18π E. π
   B. 21π D. 2π

57. If the diameter of a circle is 8, what is the area?
  A. 16π C. 10π E. 4π
  B. 12π D. 8π

58. If the diameter of a circle is 12, what is the area?
  A. 18π C. 30π E. 36π
  B. 24π D. 32π

59. In the figure below, what are a and b?

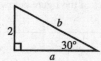

  A. $a=\sqrt{3}, b=2$ D. $a=4, b=2\sqrt{3}$
  B. $a=2\sqrt{3}, b=4$ E. $a=4, b=4\sqrt{3}$
  C. $a=2, b=2$

60. In the figure below, what are c and d?

  A. $c=2, d=\sqrt{3}$ D. $c=4\sqrt{2}, d=2$
  B. $c=2\sqrt{2}, d=3$ E. $c=3, d=2\sqrt{3}$
  C. $c=4, d=4\sqrt{3}$

61. In the figure below, what are e and f?

  A. $e=2, f=6$ D. $e=7, f=10$
  B. $e=\sqrt{2}, f=8$ E. $e=7, f=14$
  C. $e=4, f=3\sqrt{5}$

62. In the figure below, what are g and h?

  A. $g=\sqrt{3}, h=\sqrt{3}$ D. $g=4, h=4\sqrt{3}$
  B. $g=2\sqrt{2}, h=2\sqrt{3}$ E. $g=6, h=7$
  C. $g=2\sqrt{3}, h=4\sqrt{3}$

63. What is the altitude of an equilateral triangle with a perimeter of 24?
  A. $2\sqrt{3}$ C. 6   E. 8
  B. $4\sqrt{3}$ D. $4\sqrt{5}$

64. In the figure below, what are i and j?

  A. $i=3, j=3\sqrt{2}$ D. $i=5, j=3\sqrt{3}$
  B. $i=3, j=3$ E. $i=4, j=5$
  C. $i=4\sqrt{2}, j=4$

65. In the figure below, what are k and m?

  A. $k=3, m=3$ D. $k=9, m=9$
  B. $k=2\sqrt{3}, m=3$ E. $k=3, m=9$
  C. $k=4, m=6$

66. In the figure below, $AB = BC = \sqrt{6}$. What is the length of $\overline{AC}$? Note that the triangle is not drawn to scale.

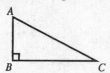

  A. 2   C. 3   E. 4
  B. $2\sqrt{3}$ D. $3\sqrt{2}$

67. If the perimeter of a square is equal to 40, what is the length of the diagonal?
  A. $10\sqrt{2}$ C. 10   E. 14
  B. $5\sqrt{3}$ D. $3\sqrt{5}$

68. In the figure below, what is p equal to?

  A. $2\sqrt{2}$ C. $10\sqrt{2}$ E. $24\sqrt{2}$
  B. $2\sqrt{3}$ D. $20\sqrt{3}$

69. What is the number of degrees in the angle formed by the minute and hour hands of a clock at 2:20?
  A. $90°$ C. $60°$ E. $30°$
  B. $70°$ D. $50°$

70. What is the radius of a circle with an area of 49?

   A. 7   C. $\frac{7}{\sqrt{\pi}}$ E. π^2

   B. 7π D. $\frac{7}{\pi}$

71. What is the area of a circle with a circumference of $\frac{22\pi}{3}$?

   A. $\frac{484\pi}{9}$ C. $\frac{121\pi}{3}$ E. $\frac{556\pi}{4}$

   B. $\frac{121\pi}{9}$ D. $\frac{484\pi}{3}$

72. A circle has an area of $36\pi^3$. What is the radius of the circle?

   A. 6   C. $6\pi^2$ E. $6\pi^4$

   B. 6π D. $6\pi^3$

73. If the radius of a circle is 8, what is the circumference of the circle?

   A. 4π C. 12π E. 16π

   B. 8π D. 14π

74. In the figure below, what is the value of the shaded area?

   A. 16π C. 64π E. $16\pi^2$

   B. 32π D. 66π

75. In the figure below, the length of $\overline{OA}$ is 2 and the length of $\overline{OB}$ is 3. What is the area between the two circles?

   A. 4π C. 6π E. 8π

   B. 5π D. 7π

76. In the figure below, a circle with an area of 144π is inscribed in a square. What is the area of the shaded region?

   A. $576 - 144\pi$ D. $1{,}728 - 144\pi$

   B. $216 - 72\pi$ E. $256 - 24\pi$

   C. $144 - 24\pi$

77. A square has a perimeter of 40. A second square has an inscribed circle with an area of 64π. What is the ratio of the length of a side of the first square to the length of a side of the second square?

   A. 5:8   C. 5:16   E. 12:π

   B. 5:4   D. 10:8π

78. The area of a square is $64x^2y^{16}$. What is the length of a side of the square?

   A. $8xy^8$ C. $8x^2y^{16}$ E. $20x^2y^4$

   B. $8xy^4$ D. $16x^2y^{16}$

79. In the figure below, what is the area of square $BCDE$?

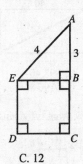

   A. 5   C. 12   E. 49

   B. 7   D. 24

80. What is the area of a right triangle with legs of lengths 4 and 5?

   A. 6   C. 12   E. 24

   B. 10   D. 20

81. In the figure below, assume O is the center of the circle. If $\angle OAB$ is 45°, then what is the area of the shaded segment?

   A. $32\pi - 16\sqrt{2}$ C. $4\pi - 8$ E. $8\pi - 8$

   B. $32\pi - 8$ D. $8\pi - 16$

82. In the figure below, rectangle $ABCD$ has an area of 15. What is the length of the diagonal $\overline{AC}$?

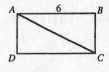

   A. 4   C. 6.5   E. 7.5

   B. 5   D. 7

83. Regarding the figure below, which one of the following statements is true?

A. $a^2 + b^2 = c^2$ C. $b + c = a$ E. $a + c = b$
B. $a + b = c$ D. $b^2 + c^2 = a^2$

84. At 12 cents per square foot, how much will it cost to paint the rectangular slab in the figure below?

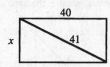

A. $43.20   C. $98.40   E. $201.50
B. $46.40   D. $196.80

85. In the figure below, what is the length of $\overline{BC}$?

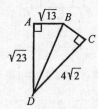

A. 1   C. 3   E. 5
B. 2   D. 4

86. If the diagonal of a square is $5\sqrt{2}$, what is the area of the square?

A. 10   C. 25   E. 35
B. 20   D. 30

87. What is the area of the rectangle in the figure below?

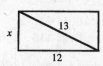

A. 156   C. 72   E. 60
B. 78   D. 66

88. In the figure below, what is x equal to?

A. $\sqrt{29} - 5$ C. 24   E. $\sqrt{2}$
B. $\sqrt{24}$ D. 2

89. If $2\sqrt{3}$ is the diagonal of a square, then what is the perimeter of the square?

A. $4\sqrt{6}$ C. $6\sqrt{3}$ E. 14
B. 8   D. 12

90. In the figures below, what is the ratio of the perimeter of $\triangle ABC$ to the perimeter of $\triangle DEF$?

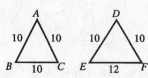

A. 1:1   C. 15:16   E. 7:3
B. 5:6   D. 6:5

91. In terms of π, what is the area of a circle whose radius is $2\sqrt{5}$?

A. π C. 10π E. 40π
B. 4π D. 20π

92. What is the radius of a circle whose area is 12π?

A. $\sqrt{3}$ C. $2\sqrt{3}$ E. 3
B. 1   D. 2

93. What is the radius of a circle if the distance to walk halfway around the rim of the circle is $\sqrt{6\pi}$?

A. $\sqrt{2}$ C. 2   E. 3
B. $\sqrt{3}$ D. $\sqrt{6}$

94. If the legs of a right triangle are 2 and 5, what is the hypotenuse?

A. $\sqrt{22}$ C. $5\sqrt{2}$ E. 6
B. $\sqrt{29}$ D. $\sqrt{35}$

95. If the hypotenuse of a right triangle is 37 and one leg is 35, what is the length of the other leg?

A. $4\sqrt{3}$ C. 12   E. 16
B. $6\sqrt{2}$ D. $14\sqrt{2}$

96. If $2\sqrt{12}$, $3\sqrt{6}$, and $4\sqrt{3}$ are the dimensions of a rectangular solid, what is the volume of the solid?

A. $216\sqrt{24}$ C. $144\sqrt{6}$ E. $\sqrt{24}$
B. $\sqrt{5,184}$ D. 5,184

97. What is the volume of a cylinder with an altitude of 10 and a circumference of $\sqrt{128\pi}$?

    A. $\sqrt{1,280}\pi$ C. 640π E. $3,460\pi$
    B. 320π D. $1,280\pi$

98. In the figure below, what is x equal to?

    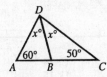

    A. 30   C. 35   E. 70
    B. 32   D. 40

99. If the ratio of the sides of a triangle are $x:x\sqrt{3}:2x$, and the length of the smallest side is 5, what is the length of the largest side?

    A. 10   C. $8\sqrt{3}$ E. 20
    B. 12   D. 15

100. In the figure below, what is the length of $\overline{JK}$?

    A. $6m\sqrt{3}$ C. $12m$ E. $14m$
    B. $9m$ D. $12m\sqrt{3}$

101. In the figure below, $\triangle DEF$ is an isosceles triangle. What is the length of $\overline{DF}$?

    A. $2\sqrt{6}$ C. $\sqrt{3}$ E. $12\sqrt{2}$
    B. $6\sqrt{2}$ D. 12

102. If the longest side of a 30°-60°-90° triangle is $2\sqrt{3}$, what is the area of the triangle?

    A. 8   C. $1.5\sqrt{3}$ E. 1
    B. 4   D. 2

103. In the figure below, what is the length of the diagonal $\overline{AC}$ of square $ABCD$?

    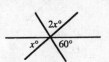

    A. $4\sqrt{2}$ C. $8\sqrt{2}$ E. $32\sqrt{2}$
    B. 8   D. 16

104. In the figure below, if arc BC equals 60°, then what is the area of $\triangle ABC$?

    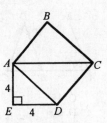

    A. 16   C. $8\sqrt{3}$ E. $10\sqrt{2}$
    B. $4\sqrt{3}$ D. 12

105. In the figure below, what is $2x° - 60°$ equal to?

    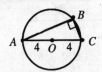

    A. 80°   C. 30°   E. 10°
    B. 40°   D. 20°

106. In the figure below, a equals all of the following EXCEPT

    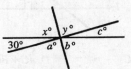

    A. y C. $180 - b - c$ E. $180 - x - y$
    B. $150 - x$ D. $150 - b$

107. In the figure below, $\overline{EC} \parallel \overline{AB}$ and $\overline{AD} \cong \overline{BD}$. What is the sum of the degree measures of $\angle A + \angle B + \angle BCE$?

    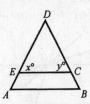

    A. $x + y$ C. $180 + x$ E. $90 - y$
    B. $3x$ D. $-2x$

108. In the figure below, if $\overline{AE} \parallel \overline{BD}$ and $\overline{BD} \cong \overline{DC}$, then what is $\angle BDC$ equal to?

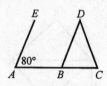

A. 10°   C. 18°   E. 24°
B. 15°   D. 20°

109. In the figure below, if $l_1 \parallel l_2$ and $\angle 7 = 117°$, which other angles must also equal 117°?

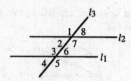

A. 1, 3, 5   C. 2, 3, 6   E. 1, 2, 3, 4
B. 1, 2, 8   D. 5, 6, 8

110. In the figure below, what is the value of x?

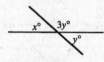

A. 30°   C. 60°   E. 80°
B. 45°   D. 65°

111. In the figure below, which of the following statements is true?

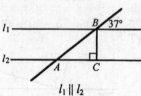

$l_1 \parallel l_2$

A. $AC > BC$ D. $AC + BC = AB$
B. $AC < BC$ E. $AC - BC = AB$
C. $AC = BC$

112. In the figure below, $\overline{OM} \parallel \overline{PJ}$, and $\overline{FG}$ and $\overline{EG}$ divide $\angle CGO$ into 3 congruent angles. What is the degree measure of $\angle EGC$?

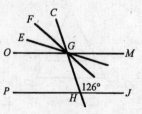

A. 18°   C. 42°   E. 63°
B. 36°   D. 54°

113. In the figure below, $\triangle ABE \sim \triangle ACD$. What is the length of $\overline{CD}$?

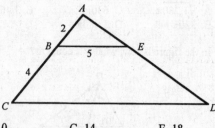

A. 10   C. 14   E. 18
B. 12   D. 15

114. A triangle with sides of 12, 14, and 20 is similar to a second triangle that has one side with a length of 40. What is the smallest possible perimeter of the second triangle?

A. 48   C. 120   E. 180
B. 92   D. 160

115. A right circular cylinder has a base whose diameter is $8x$; the height of the cylinder is $3y$. What is the volume of the cylinder?

A. $24xy$ C. $48\pi xy$ E. $48\pi x^2 y$
B. $24\pi x^2 y$ D. $96\pi xy$

116. If the perimeter of a rectangle is 68 yd. and the width is 48 ft., what is the length?

A. 10 yd.   C. 20 ft.   E. 54 ft.
B. 18 ft.   D. 46 ft.

117. What is the total length of fencing needed to enclose a rectangular area 46 ft. × 34 ft.?

A. $26\frac{1}{3}$ yd.   C. 48 yd.   E. $53\frac{1}{3}$ yd.
B. $26\frac{2}{3}$ yd.   D. $52\frac{2}{3}$ yd.

118. An umbrella 50" long can lie diagonally on the bottom of a trunk with a length and width that are which of the following, respectively?

A. 26", 30"   C. 31", 31"   E. 40", 30"
B. 30", 36"   D. 40", 21"

119. A road runs 1,200 ft. from point A to point B, and then makes a right angle going to point C, a distance of 500 ft. A new road is being built directly from A to C. How much shorter will the new road be than the old road?

A. 400 ft.   C. 850 ft.   E. 1,300 ft.
B. 609 ft.   D. 1,000 ft.

120. A certain triangle has sides of lengths 6", 8", and 10". A rectangle equal in area to that of the triangle has a width of 3". What is the perimeter, in inches, of the rectangle?

A. 11   C. 22   E. 30
B. 16   D. 24

121. A ladder 65 ft. long is leaning against a wall. Its lower end is 25 ft. away from the wall. How much farther away will it be if the upper end is moved down 8 ft.?

    A. 60 ft.   C. 14 ft.   E. 8 ft.
    B. 52 ft.   D. 10 ft.

122. A rectangular bin 4 ft. long, 3 ft. wide, and 2 ft. high is solidly packed with bricks whose dimensions are 8 in. × 4 in. × 2 in. What is the number of bricks in the bin?

    A. 54
    B. 320
    C. 648
    D. 848
    E Cannot be determined from the given information

123. If the cost of digging a trench is $2.12/yd.^{3}, what would be the cost of digging a trench $2 \times 5 \times 4$ yd.^{3}?

    A. $21.20   C. $64.00   E. $104.80
    B. $40.00   D. $84.80

124. A piece of wire is shaped to enclose a square, whose area is 121 square inches. It is then reshaped to enclose a rectangle whose length is 13 inches. What is the area of the rectangle, in square inches?

    A. 64   C. 117   E. 234
    B. 96   D. 144

125. What is the area of a 2-foot-wide walk around the outside of a garden that is 30 feet long and 20 feet wide?

    A. 104 ft.^{2} C. 680 ft.^{2} E. 1,416 ft.^{2}
    B. 216 ft.^{2} D. 704 ft.^{2}

126. The area of a circle is 49π. What is its circumference, in terms of π?

    A. 14π C. 49π E. 147π
    B. 28π D. 98π

127. In two hours, the minute hand of a clock rotates through an angle equal to which of the following?

    A. 90°   C. 360°   E. 1,080°
    B. 180°   D. 720°

128. A box is 12 inches in width, 16 inches in length, and 6 inches in height. How many square inches of paper would be required to cover it on all sides?

    A. 192   C. 720   E. 1,440
    B. 360   D. 900

129. If the volume of a cube is 64 cubic inches, what is the sum of the lengths of its edges?

    A. 48 in.   C. 24 in.   E. 12 in.
    B. 32 in.   D. 16 in.

130. In the figure below, $x = ?$

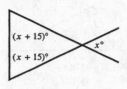

    A. 20   C. 50   E. 90
    B. 35   D. 65

131. What is the difference of the areas of two squares with sides of 5 and 4, respectively?

    A. 3   C. 9   E. 91
    B. 4   D. 16

132. A triangle with sides of 4, 6, and 8 has the same perimeter as an equilateral triangle with sides of length equal to which of the following?

    A. 2   C. 3   E. 8
    B. $\frac{3}{2}$ D. 6

133. In the figure below, $x = ?$

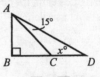

    $\overline{AB} \cong \overline{BC}$

    A. 15   C. 40   E. 75
    B. 30   D. 60

134. If the area of the rectangle shown below is equal to 1, then $l = ?$

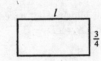

    A. $\frac{4}{9}$ C. $\frac{4}{3}$ E. 2
    B. 1   D. $\frac{9}{4}$

135. A semicircle is divided into three arcs with respective lengths 2π, 6π, and 14π. The semicircle is a part of a circle with which of the following radii?

    A. 44
    B. 33
    C. 22
    D. 11
    E. 6

136. In the figure below, $x = ?$

A. 15   C. 45   E. 90
B. 30   D. 60

137. In the figure below, $\angle A \cong \angle B$.

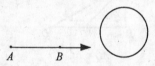

Which of the following statements must be true?

A. $\angle A \cong \angle B \cong \angle C$
B. $\angle A \ncong \angle C$
C. $\overline{AC} \cong \overline{BC}$
D. $\overline{BC} \cong \overline{AB}$
E. $\overline{AB} \cong \overline{AC}$

138. In the incomplete figure below, the circle and $\overrightarrow{AB}$ have how many points of intersection?

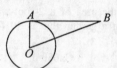

A. 0
B. 1
C. 2
D. 3
E. An infinite number

139. In the figure below, which is not necessarily drawn to scale, $\angle A \cong \angle C$ and $\angle B \cong \angle D$.

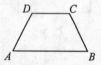

How many of the following four statements of congruence must be true?

$\angle A \cong \angle B$
$\overline{AB} \cong \overline{DC}$
$\overline{AD} \cong \overline{BC}$
$\overline{AB} \cong \overline{BC} \cong \overline{CD} \cong \overline{AD}$

A. 0   C. 2   E. 4
B. 1   D. 3

140. In the diagram below, $\overline{AD} \cong \overline{AE}$, $\overline{AB} \cong \overline{BF}$, $\overline{BF} \cong \overline{CF}$, and $\overline{CE} \cong \overline{DE}$.

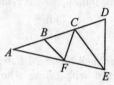

What is the number of degrees in $\angle DAE$?

A. 20   C. 25   E. 35
B. 24   D. 30

141. In the diagram below, $\angle ABC = 90°$, $AC = 10\sqrt{2}$, and $AB + BC = 3\sqrt{38}$. What is the area of $\triangle ABC$?

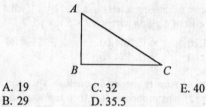

A. 19   C. 32   E. 40
B. 29   D. 35.5

142. In the figure below, $\triangle ABC$ intersects a circle with center O. $\overline{AB}$ is tangent to the circle at A. If $AB = 8$ and $BO = 10$, what is the area of the circle?

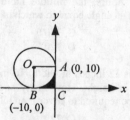

A. 4π C. 36π E. 100π
B. 6π D. 64π

143. The figure below shows a circle with center O, two radii $\overline{OA}$ and $\overline{OB}$, and two tangents $\overline{AC}$ and $\overline{BC}$. What is the area of the shaded region?

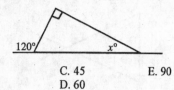

A. $100 - 100\pi$ C. $50 - 50\pi$ E. $100 - 25\pi$
B. $50 - 100\pi$ D. $50 - 25\pi$

144. The figure below shows two circles lying in the same plane with respective centers at O and P. $\overline{AB}$ is a common external tangent segment to the two circles at A and B, respectively. If $OA = 13$, $PB = 3$, and $OP = 26$, then what is the length of $\overline{AB}$?

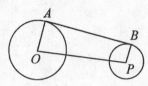

A. 26   C. 24   E. 18
B. 25   D. 20

145. The figure below shows a circle of area 144π square inches with a radius drawn to the point of tangency of the circle on the x-axis.

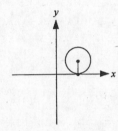

If this point of tangency is 16 inches from the origin, then the number of inches from the origin to the center of the circle is:

A. 12   C. 16   E. 20
B. $12\sqrt{2}$ D. $16\sqrt{2}$

146. In the figure below, $\overline{TP} \cong \overline{RA}$, and $\overline{TR} \parallel \overline{PA}$. $TR = 12$, $PA = 44$. If $\angle P = 45°$, what is the area of $TRAP$?

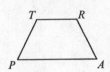

A. 448   C. 520   E. 1,792
B. 464   D. 896

147. In the figure below, B and E lie on $\overline{AC}$ and $\overline{AD}$, respectively, of $\triangle ACD$, such that $\overline{BE} \parallel \overline{CD}$. $\overline{BD} \perp \overline{AC}$, and $\overline{BC} \cong \overline{ED}$. If $BC = 10$ and $CD = 20$, what is the area of $\triangle ABE$?

A. 100
B. $50\sqrt{3}$
C. 50
D. $25\sqrt{3}$
E. Cannot be determined from the given information

148. In the figure below, which is not necessarily drawn to scale, $\angle ABC = 90°$, $AB = 10$, and $\tan \angle ACB = 1$. What is the length of $\overline{AC}$?

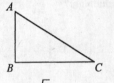

A. 10   C. $10\sqrt{2}$ E. $20\sqrt{3}$
B. 20   D. $10\sqrt{3}$

149. In the figure below, two sides of the rectangle $ABGF$ lie on two sides of the square $ACDE$. $AF = 9$, $BC = 8$, and $FE = 1$.

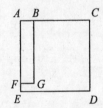

If a point is chosen at random in the interior of the square, what is the probability that the point also lies in the interior of the rectangle?

A. $\frac{1}{50}$ C. $\frac{7}{50}$ E. $\frac{11}{50}$
B. $\frac{3}{50}$ D. $\frac{9}{50}$

150. The figure below shows three acute angles and two obtuse angles.

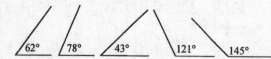

If two different angles are created randomly using the five angles shown, what is the probability that both angles are acute?

A. $\frac{1}{10}$ C. $\frac{2}{5}$ E. $\frac{3}{10}$

B. $\frac{1}{5}$ D. $\frac{3}{5}$

151. Last night, Dave and Kathy both arrived at Pizza Palace at two different random times between 10:00 p.m. and midnight. They had agreed to wait exactly 15 minutes for each other to arrive before leaving. What is the probability that Dave and Kathy were together at Pizza Palace last night between 10:00 p.m. and midnight?

A. $\frac{1}{8}$ C. $\frac{15}{64}$ E. $\frac{31}{64}$

B. $\frac{1}{4}$ D. $\frac{3}{8}$

Functions, Graphs, and Coordinate Geometry

Coordinate Axis System

The easiest way to understand the coordinate axis system is as an analog to the points of the compass. If we take a plot of land, we can divide it into quadrants:

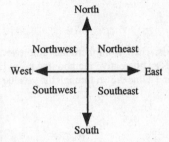

Now, if we add measuring units along each of the directional axes, we can actually describe any location on this piece of land by two numbers.

Example:

Point *P* is located at 4 units East and 5 units North. Point *Q* is located at 4 units West and 5 units North. Point *R* is located at 4 units West and 2 units South. Point *T* is located at 3 units East and 4 units South.

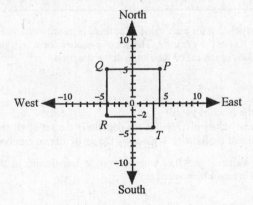

The coordinate system used in coordinate geometry differs from our map of a plot of land in that it uses *x*- and *y*-axes divided into negative and positive regions.

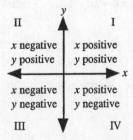

It is easy to see that ***Quadrant I*** corresponds to our Northeast quarter, in which the measurements on both the *x*- and *y*-axes are positive. ***Quadrant II*** corresponds to our Northwest quarter, in which the measurements on the *x*-axis are negative and the measurements on the *y*-axis are positive. ***Quadrant III*** corresponds to our Southwest quarter, in which both the *x*-axis measurements

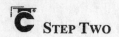
and the y-axis measurements are negative. Finally, **Quadrant IV** corresponds to our Southeast quarter, in which the x-values are positive while the y-values are negative.

Ordered Pairs

An **ordered pair** of coordinates has the general form (x, y). The first element refers to the **x-coordinate**: the distance left or right of the **origin**, or intersection of the axes. The second element gives the **y-coordinate**: the distance up or down from the origin.

Example:

Plot $(3, 2)$.
➤ Move to the positive 3 value on the x-axis. Then, from there move up two units on the y-axis, as illustrated by the graph on the left. The graph on the right demonstrates an alternative method: the point $(3, 2)$ is located at the intersection of a line drawn through the x-value 3 parallel to the y-axis and a line drawn through the y-value 2 parallel to the x-axis.

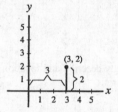 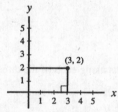

Properties of Functions

A function is a set of ordered pairs (x, y) such that for each value of x, there is exactly one value of y. By convention, we say that "y is a function of x," which is written as: $y = f(x)$ or $y = g(x)$, *etc.* The set of x-values for which the set is defined is called the **domain** of the function. The set of corresponding values of y is called the **range** of the function.

Example:

What are the domain and range of the function $y = |x|$?
➤ The function is defined for all real values of x. Hence the domain is the set of all real numbers. Since $y = |x|$ can only be a positive number or zero, the range of the function is given by the set of all real numbers equal to or greater than zero.

When we speak of $f(a)$, we mean the value of $y = f(x)$ when $x = a$ is substituted in the expression for $f(x)$. If $z = f(y)$ and $y = g(x)$, we say that $z = f[g(x)]$. Thus, z is in turn a function of x.

Examples:

1. If $f(x) = 2x^x - 3x$, find the value of $f(3)$.
   ➤ Substitute 3 for x in the given expression: $f(x) = 2x^x - 3x \Rightarrow f(3) = 2(3)^3 - 3(3) = 2(27) - 9 = 54 - 9 = 45$.

2. If $f(x) = 2x - 9^{1/x}$, what is $f(-2)$?
   ➤ $f(-2) = 2(-2) - 9^{-1/2} = -4 - \dfrac{1}{\sqrt{9}} = -4 - \dfrac{1}{3} = -\dfrac{13}{3}$.

3. If $z = f(y) = 3y + 2$ and $y = g(x) = x + 2$, then $z = ?$
   ➤ $z = f[g(x)] = 3[g(x)] + 2 = 3(x + 2) + 2 = 3x + 6 + 2 = 3x + 8$.

Plotting Equations

The coordinate axis system provides a framework for plotting equations. Simply plot several pairs of points for the given equation.

Examples:

1. Plot the equation $x = y$.
   ➤ This equation has an infinite number of solutions:

x	1	2	3	5	0	-3	-5	...
y	1	2	3	5	0	-3	-5	...

   Plot these pairs of x and y on the axis system. Draw a line through them to produce a plot of the original equation. The complete picture of the equation $x = y$ is a straight line including all the real numbers such that x is equal to y.

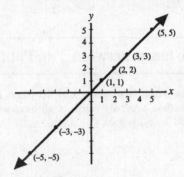

2. Plot the equation $y = 2x$.
   ➤ This equation has an infinite number of solutions:

x	-4	-2	-1	0	1	2	4	...
y	-8	-4	-2	0	2	4	8	...

   After entering the points on the graph, complete the picture. It is a straight line, but it rises more rapidly than does $x = y$.

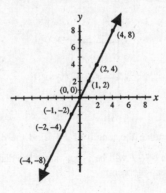

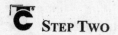

Midpoint of Line Segments

For a line segment between two points, (x_1, y_1) and (x_2, y_2), the **midpoint** $= \left(\frac{x_1 + x_2}{2}, \frac{y_1 + y_2}{2}\right)$. The x-coordinate of the midpoint is the average of the two x-axis endpoints and the y-coordinate of the midpoint is the average of the two y-axis endpoints.

Examples:

1. Find the midpoint between $(-5, 8)$ and $(11, 34)$.
    ➤ The midpoint is $\left(\frac{x_1 + x_2}{2}, \frac{y_1 + y_2}{2}\right) = \left(\frac{-5 + 11}{2}, \frac{8 + 34}{2}\right) = \left(\frac{6}{2}, \frac{42}{2}\right) = (3, 21)$.

2. One endpoint of a circle diameter is located at $(13, 1)$. If the center of the circle is $(15, 10)$, find the other endpoint.
    ➤ The midpoint of the diameter is $(15, 10)$, so $15 = \frac{x_1 + x_2}{2} = \frac{13 + x_2}{2}$ and $10 = \frac{y_1 + y_2}{2} = \frac{1 + y_2}{2}$. $x_2 = (15 \cdot 2) - 13 = 17$ and $y_2 = (10 \cdot 2) - 1 = 19$. Thus, $(x_2, y_2) = (17, 19)$.

Distance Between Two Points

To determine the distance between two points on a coordinate graph, consider points P and Q. For simplicity's sake, we will confine the discussion to the first quadrant, but the method generally works in all quadrants and even with lines covering two or more quadrants. Assign the value (x_1, y_1) to point P and (x_2, y_2) to point Q:

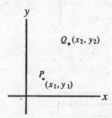

To find distance between points P and Q, construct a triangle:

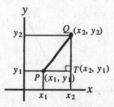

Point T now has the coordinates (x_2, y_1). To calculate the length of $\overline{PT}$, find the distance moved on the x-axis: $x_2 - x_1$ units. The y-coordinate does not change. Similarly, the length of $\overline{QT}$ will be $y_2 - y_1$ since the distance is purely vertical, moving up from y_1 to y_2, with no change in the x-value. Apply the Pythagorean theorem:

$$(PQ)^2 = (PT)^2 + (QT)^2 = (x_2 - x_1)^2 + (y_2 - y_1)^2$$
$$PQ = \sqrt{(x_2 - x_1)^2 + (y_2 - y_1)^2}$$

Example:

In the figure below, what is the length of $\overline{PQ}$?

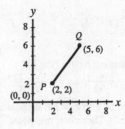

➤ Find the length of $\overline{PQ}$ by constructing a triangle:

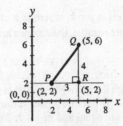

$\overline{QR}$ runs from (5, 6) to (5, 2), so it must be 4 units long. $\overline{PR}$ runs from (2, 2) to (5, 2), so it is 3 units long. Use the Pythagorean theorem: $(PQ)^2 = (QR)^2 + (PR)^2 = 4^2 + 3^2 = 16 + 9 = 25$. Therefore, $PQ = \sqrt{25} = 5$.

Therefore, you can find the length of any line segment drawn in a coordinate axis system between points (x_1, y_1) and (x_2, y_2) using this ***distance formula***: $d = \sqrt{(x_2 - x_1)^2 + (y_2 - y_1)^2}$. Notice that it does not actually matter which point is considered the start of the line and the end of the line, since the change in each coordinate is squared in the distance formula.

Example:

In the figure below, what is the distance between P and Q?

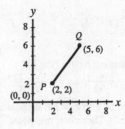

➤ The distance between P and Q is: $\sqrt{(x_2 - x_1)^2 + (y_2 - y_1)^2} = \sqrt{(10 - 2)^2 + (9 - 3)^2} = \sqrt{64 + 36} = \sqrt{100} = 10$.

Linear Functions

1. Slope-Intercept Form

If x and y are related by a linear equation, then y is a ***linear function***. Except for a vertical line, every line equation is a linear function that can be represented in ***slope-intercept form***: $y = mx + b$. m is the slope of the line and b is the y-intercept. The y-intercept is the y-coordinate of the point where the line intersects the y-axis, or where $x = 0$. The ***slope***, m, of a line describes

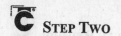

the steepness of the line. It is defined as the change in y-values divided by the change in x-values, or rise over run: **slope** $= m = \frac{y_2 - y_1}{x_2 - x_1} = \frac{rise}{run}$.

Examples:

1. Find the slope of the line containing (3, 2) and (8, 22).
   ➤ $m = \frac{y_2 - y_1}{x_2 - x_1} = \frac{22 - 2}{8 - 3} = \frac{20}{5} = 4$.

2. Find the slope of the line given by the equation $6x + 12y = 13$.
   ➤ $6x + 12y = 13 \Rightarrow 12y = -6x + 13 \Rightarrow y = \frac{-6x + 13}{12} \Rightarrow y = -\frac{x}{2} + \frac{13}{12}$. Therefore, the slope is $-\frac{1}{2}$.

3. The points $(-5, 12)$, $(0, 7)$ and $(10, -3)$ lie on a line. What is the y-intercept of this line?
   ➤ The x-coordinate of the second point is 0. Therefore, this point's y-coordinate, 7, is the y-intercept of the line.

2. Parallel Lines

The equation of a line that is parallel to the x-axis is $y = k$, where is a constant. The equation of a line that is parallel to the y-axis is $x = c$, where c is a constant. If two lines are parallel, their slopes are equal and vice versa.

Example:

Find the equation for a line that passes through the point $(0, 12)$ and is parallel to the line $y = 7x - 15$.
➤ A line has slope-intercept form $y = mx + b$. If the line passes through the y-axis at $(0, 12)$, then the y-intercept $b = +12$. If the two lines are parallel, then the slopes are equal and $m = +7$. Therefore, the line equation is $y = mx + b \Rightarrow y = 7x + 12$.

3. Perpendicular Lines

If two perpendicular lines have slopes m_1 and m_2, then $m_1 = -\frac{1}{m_2}$ and vice versa.

Example:

The equation of a line is $y = \frac{x}{4} + 10$. If a second line is perpendicular to the line, what is the slope of this line?

➤ If two lines are perpendicular to one another, their slopes are opposite reciprocals of one another. Thus, if a line has slope of $\frac{1}{4}$, then the line perpendicular to it has a slope of -4.

Quadratic Functions

If y is expressed in the form $y = ax^2 + bx + c$, where $a \neq 0$ and b is any real number, y is a **quadratic function**. Graphs of quadratic functions are called parabolas. The basic graph that you need to know is $f(x) = x^2$, as illustrated in the first of the following examples.

Examples:

1. Which of the following graphs depicts a quadratic function?

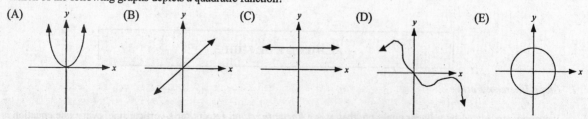

➤ All quadratic equations can be written in the form $y = ax^2 + bx + c$. (B) is a linear plot with the y-intercept equal to 0: $y = ax$. (C) is a constant value for y: $y = k$. (E) is a plot of a circle: $x^2 + y^2 = k$, where k is a constant. (D) is a complicated function without a standard form of equation. Only (A) is a quadratic equation: $y = ax^2$.

2. A quadratic function of the form $y = ax^2 + bx + c$ includes the following ordered pairs of (x, y): (1, 17), (5, 61), and (7, 95). What is the value of c for this quadratic function?

➢ Solve the system of three simultaneous equations that are generated by the three ordered pairs: $17 = a(1)^2 + b(1) + c$, $61 = a(5)^2 + b(5) + c$, and $95 = a(7)^2 + b(7) + c$. The quadratic function is $y = x^2 + 5x + 11$. Alternatively, the value of c can be determined by entering the three ordered pairs into a graphing calculator and using the quadratic regression feature.

Functions as Models

Functions can be mathematical models of real-life situations. For example, an item might present information about the projected sales of a product at various prices and ask for a mathematical model in the form of a graph or equation that represents projected sales as a function of price. Alternatively, you may be asked simply to identify graphs of linear and quadratic functions.

Example:

The line of best fit for $y = f(x)$ for the ordered pairs (−4, −18), (1, 3), (2, 6), (3, 8), and (4, 14) is best represented by which of the following graphs?

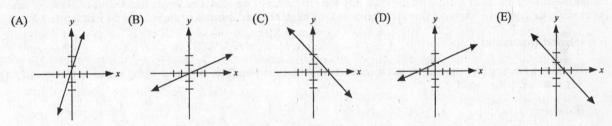

(A)   (B)   (C)   (D)   (E)

➢ The correct answer is (A). Both x and y increase in value for each ordered pair, so eliminate (C) and (E). You can eliminate (B) since the values of x and y in the given ordered pairs clearly indicate that $x \neq y$. Finally, eliminate (D) because when $x = 1$, $y = 3$, whereas in the graph of (D), $y < 3$ when $x = 1$.

Qualitative Behavior of Graphs

You should also understand how the graphs of functions behave qualitatively. Items on the exam might show the graph of a function in the xy-coordinate plane and ask for the number of values of x for which $f(x)$ equals a particular value. Alternatively, an item may present a graph with numerical values, requiring you to recognize the form of the graphed function.

Examples:

1. The figure below shows a graph of the function $y = x^2 + 2x + 6$. What is the smallest possible integer value of y?

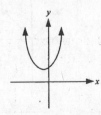

➢ The lowest point on the function occurs when $x < 0$. Find the symmetry by substitution: if $x = 1$, $y = 9$; if $x = 0$, $y = 6$; if $x = -1$, $y = 5$; if $x = -2$, $y = 6$; if $x = -3$, $y = 9$. The coordinates of these points are (−3, 9), (−2, 6), (−1, 5), (0, 6), and (1, 9), respectively. Thus, the lowest point occurs at (−1, 5). Alternatively, solve for the vertex using the properties of parabolas. The standard form of a parabola is: $y = a(x - h)^2 + k$, where the vertex is at (h, k). Write the equation in standard form: $y = (x^2 + 2x + 1) + 6 - 1 = (x + 1)^2 + 5 = [x - (-1)]^2 + 5$. Therefore, the vertex is at (−1, 5).

2. What is the sum of all distinct integer y-values for the graph of the absolute value function in the figure below?

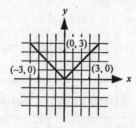

➤ Each negative y-value has a canceling positive y-value. Therefore, the answer is zero.

Transformation Effects on Graphs

When you alter a graph, you transform it. If you transform a graph without changing its shape, you translate it. Vertical and horizontal transformations are translations. Items on the exam may test knowledge of the effects of simple translations of graphs of functions. For example, the graph of a function $f(x)$ could be given and you might be asked items about the graph of the function $f(x + 2)$.

1. *Vertical Translations*

   To move a function up or down, you add or subtract outside the function. That is, $f(x) + b$ is $f(x)$ moved up b units, and $f(x) - b$ is $f(x)$ moved down b units.

   Example:

   In order to obtain the graph of $y = (x + 2)^2 + 6$ from the graph of $y = x^2 + 4x + 11$, how should the graph of $y = x^2 + 4x + 11$ be moved?

   ➤ Rewrite the original function in the form $f(x) + b$: $y = x^2 + 4x + 11 \Rightarrow y = x^2 + 4x + 4 + 7 = (x + 2)^2 + 7$. Therefore, to obtain the graph of $y = (x + 2)^2 + 6$ from the graph of $y = (x + 2)^2 + 7$, the graph must be moved one unit down.

2. *Horizontal Translations*

   To shift a function to the left or to the right, add or subtract inside the function. That is, $f(x + b)$ is $f(x)$ shifted b units to the left, and $f(x - b)$ is $f(x)$ shifted b units to the right.

   Example:

   The graph below is of the function $y = |x|$.

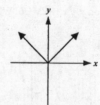

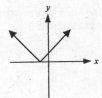
Which of the following is a graph of the function $y = |x + 3|$?

(A)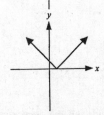

(B)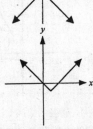

(C)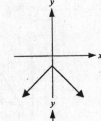

(D)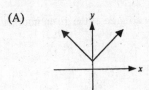

(E)

➤ By translation of the original graph from $y = |x|$ to $y = |x + 3|$, the original graph is moved three units to the left, (C). Alternatively, substitute values for x and y: $y = 0$ for $x = -3$. (C) is the only graph that contains the point $(-3, 0)$.

Graphing Geometric Figures

You can also use the coordinate system for graphing geometric figures. The following figure is a graph of a square whose vertices are at coordinates $(0, 0)$, $(4, 0)$, $(4, 4)$, and $(0, 4)$.

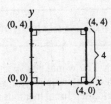

Each side of the square is equal to 4 since each side is 4 units long and parallel to either the x- or y-axis. Since every coordinate point is the perpendicular intersection of two lines, it is possible to measure distances in the coordinate system.

Examples:

1. In the figure below, what is the area of the circle?

➤ To solve this problem, find the radius of the circle. The center of the circle is located at the intersection of $x = 2$ and $y = 2$, or the point $(2, 2)$. Thus, the radius is 2 units long and the area is 4π.

2. △*ABC* has coordinates *A*, *B*, and *C* equal to (5, 3), (19, 7), and (17, 25), respectively. By how much does the largest slope for any median of △*ABC* exceed the largest slope for any altitude of △*ABC*?

➢ The largest slope occurs for the steepest ascent for increasing values of *x*. Draw a figure of the given information in the coordinate plane:

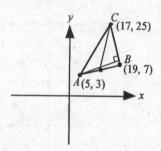

A median is drawn from one angle of a triangle to the midpoint of the opposite side. Of the three possible medians, the median that connects *C* to the midpoint of $\overline{AB}$ has the largest slope. The midpoint of $\overline{AB}$ is $\left(\frac{5+19}{2}, \frac{7+3}{2}\right) = (12, 5)$. Therefore, the slope of the median is $\frac{25-5}{17-12} = 4$. An altitude is drawn from one angle of a triangle to the opposite side at a right angle. Of the three possible altitudes, the altitude that connects *A* to $\overline{BC}$ has the largest slope. Since this altitude is perpendicular to $\overline{BC}$, its slope is the opposite reciprocal of the slope of $\overline{BC}$. The slope of $\overline{BC}$ is $\frac{25-7}{17-19} = \frac{18}{-2} = -9$, so the slope of the altitude $\frac{1}{9}$. Therefore, the amount by which the slope of the median is larger than the slope of the altitude is: $4 - \frac{1}{9} = \frac{36}{9} - \frac{1}{9} = \frac{35}{9}$.

Data Interpretation, Scatterplots, and Matrices

The test may ask about the line of best fit for a scatterplot. You would be expected to identify the general characteristics of the line of best fit by looking at the scatterplot. For example, an item may require you to identify that a line of best fit for a scatterplot has a slope that is positive but less than 1. You are not expected to use formal methods for finding the equation of a line of best fit.

Example:

The points in the scatter plot below show the relationship between 14 students' test scores on a mid-term test and a final test. What is the approximate average (arithmetic mean) of the scores on the final test for all students who scored above 90 on the midterm test?

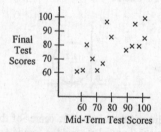

➢ Five students scored above 90 on the mid-term. Their marks are the five to the right on the scatterplot. The five corresponding scores on the final are approximately 80, 80, 85, 95, and 100. The average of these scores is approximately 88.

You are also expected to be able to interpret data displayed in tables, charts, and graphs.

Example:

The tables below show the number, type, and cost of candy bars bought during one week at two local drugstores.

	Number of Candy Bars Bought					
	Type A		Type B		Type C	
	Large	Giant	Large	Giant	Large	Giant
Drugstore *P*	60	20	69	21	43	17
Drugstore *Q*	44	18	59	25	38	13

Cost per Candy Bar		
	Large	Giant
Type A	$0.45	$0.69
Type B	$0.45	$0.79
Type C	$0.55	$0.99

What is the total cost of all Type B candy bars bought at these two drugstores during the week?

➤ Total the cost of all Type B bars bought at the two drugstores: $69(0.45) + 21(0.79) + 59(0.45) + 25(0.79) = \$93.94$.

Functions, Graphs, and Coordinate Geometry

DIRECTIONS: Choose the correct answer to each of the following items. Use a calculator when necessary. Answers are on page 930.

1. Let $f(x) = \frac{x-2}{2x-13}$. If x represents a whole number, what is the largest value of x such that $f(x) < 0$?

    A. −1   C. 1   E. 8
    B. 0   D. 6

2. If $f(x) = 8$ when $x = 2$ and $f(x) = 20$ when $x = 6$, then $f(x) = kx + w$. The value of $k + w$ is:

    A. 2   C. 5   E. 20
    B. 4   D. 8

3. If $-5 < x < -1$, and $f(x) = |14 - |1 + 2x||$, then $f(x)$ equals:

    A. $13 - 2x$ C. $13 + 2x$ E. $13 + 3x$
    B. $15 + 2x$ D. $2x - 13$

4. If $f(x) = \frac{kx}{3x+5}$, $x \neq -\frac{5}{3}$, k is a constant, and $f(x)$ satisfies the equation $f(f(x)) = x$ for all real values of x except for $x = -\frac{5}{3}$, what is the value of k?

    A. k cannot be uniquely determined.
    B. k does not equal any real value.
    C. $k = -\frac{5}{3}$
    D. $k = -\frac{3}{5}$
    E. $k = -5$

5. If $f(x) = 3 + 2^x$ and $g(x) = (2 + 3)^x$, then what is the value of $f(2) + g(3)$?

    A. 36   C. 150   E. 300
    B. 132   D. 225

6. Which of the following graphs represents a relation of which the domain is the set of all real numbers and the range is the set of all non-negative real numbers?

    A.
    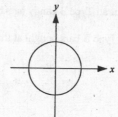

    B.
    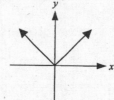

    C.
    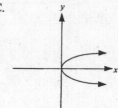

    D.
    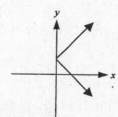

    E.
    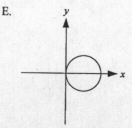

7. The range of the relation $\{(x, y) \mid y^2 = 4x\}$ is $\{0, 9, 16\}$. Which of the following is the domain?

A. $\{0, 20.25, 64\}$
B. $\{0, 3, 4\}$
C. $\{0, 36, 64\}$
D. $\{-4, -3, 0, 3, 4\}$
E. $\{0, 2.25, 4\}$

8. If $y = 2x + 1$ and the domain for x is the set of all non-negative integers, then the range for y is the set of which of the following?

A. non-negative integers
B. non-negative even integers
C. odd integers
D. positive odd integers
E. real numbers equal to or greater than 1.

9. If $7x + 4y = 218$, and both x and y are positive integers, what is the sum of the two largest values in the range of y?

A. 433   C. 427   E. 95
B. 428   D. 101

10. How many whole numbers are not in the domain of values for x if $y = \frac{(x-1)(x-2)(x-3)}{\sqrt{x^2 - 11x + 30}}$?

A. 1   C. 3   E. 5
B. 2   D. 4

11. Which of the lettered points on the number line below could represent the result when the coordinate of point F is divided by the coordinate of point X?

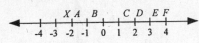

A. A C. C E. E
B. B D. D

12. $\overline{AB}$ is the diameter of a circle whose center is point O. If the coordinates of point A are $(2, 6)$ and the coordinates of point B are $(6, 2)$, find the coordinates of point O.

A. $(4, 4)$ C. $(2, -2)$ E. $(2, 2)$
B. $(4, -4)$ D. $(0, 0)$

13. $\overline{AB}$ is the diameter of a circle whose center is point O. If the coordinates of point O are $(2, 1)$ and the coordinates of point B are $(4, 6)$, find the coordinates of point A.

A. $\left(3, 3\frac{1}{2}\right)$ C. $\left(0, -4\right)$ E. $\left(-1, -2\frac{1}{2}\right)$
B. $\left(1, 2\frac{1}{2}\right)$ D. $\left(2\frac{1}{2}, 1\right)$

14. Find the distance from the point whose coordinates are $(4, 3)$ to the point whose coordinates are $(8, 6)$.

A. 5   C. $\sqrt{7}$ E. 15
B. 25   D. $\sqrt{67}$

15. The vertices of a triangle are $(2, 1)$, $(2, 5)$, and $(5, 1)$. What is the area of the triangle?

A. 12   C. 8   E. 5
B. 10   D. 6

16. The area of a circle whose center is at $(0, 0)$ is 16π. The circle does NOT pass through which of the following points?

A. $(4, 4)$ C. $(4, 0)$ E. $(0, -4)$
B. $(0, 4)$ D. $(-4, 0)$

17. What is the slope of a line that passes through $(0, -5)$ and $(8, 27)$?

A. 4   C. $\frac{8}{32}$ E. -4
B. 2   D. $-\frac{8}{32}$

18. The slope of a line that passes through points $(3, 7)$ and $(12, y)$ is $\frac{1}{3}$. What is the value of y?

A. 2   C. $6\frac{2}{3}$ E. 10
B. 4   D. $7\frac{1}{3}$

19. What is the slope of the line $y = 5x + 7$?

A. 7   C. 2   E. $\frac{1}{5}$
B. 5   D. $\frac{7}{5}$

20. A line passes through points $(3, 8)$ and $(w, 2k)$. If $w \neq 3$, what is the slope of the line?

A. $\frac{8 - 2k}{3 + w}$ C. $\frac{2k - 8}{w - 3}$ E. $\frac{3}{8}$
B. $\frac{2k + 8}{w + 3}$ D. $\frac{w - 3}{2k - 8}$

21. What is the equation of the line that passes through the point $(0, 13)$ and is parallel to the line $4x + 2y = 17$?

A. $4x + 2y = 13$
B. $4x + 2y = -13$
C. $y = -2x + 13$
D. $y = 2x + 13$
E. Cannot be determined from the given information

22. A line passes through the point $(0, -5)$ and is perpendicular to the line $y = -\frac{x}{2} + 5$. What is the equation of the line?

 A. $y = -\frac{x}{2} - 5$

 B. $y = 2x - 5$

 C. $y = -2x - 5$

 D. $y = -\frac{x}{2} + 13$

 E. Cannot be determined from the given information

23. If point P has coordinates $(-2, 2)$ and point Q has coordinates $(2, 0)$, what is the distance from point P to point Q?

 A. -4 C. $4\sqrt{5}$ E. 6

 B. $2\sqrt{5}$ D. 4

24. If point R has coordinates (x, y) and point S has coordinates $(x + 1, y + 1)$, what is the distance between point R and point S?

 A. $\sqrt{2}$ C. $\sqrt{x^2 + y^2}$ E. $x + y + 1$

 B. 2   D. $\sqrt{x^2 + y^2 + 2}$

25. Will is standing 40 yards due north of point P. Grace is standing 60 yards due west of point P. What is the shortest distance between Will and Grace?

 A. 20 yards   C. $20\sqrt{13}$ yards   E. $80\sqrt{13}$ yards

 B. $4\sqrt{13}$ yards   D. 80 yards

26. On a coordinate graph, what is the distance between points $(5, 6)$ and $(6, 7)$?

 A. $\sqrt{2}$ C. 2   E. $6\sqrt{2}$

 B. 1   D. 4

27. On a coordinate plane, point B is located 7 units to the left of point A. The x-coordinate of point A is x, and the y-coordinate of point A is y. What is the x-coordinate of point B?

 A. $x - 7$

 B. $x + 7$

 C $y + 7$

 D. $y - 7$

 E. Cannot be determined from the given information

28. Point R is represented on the coordinate plane by (x, y). The vertical coordinate of point S is three times the vertical coordinate of point R and the two points have the same horizontal coordinate. The ordered pair that represents point S is:

 A. $(3x, y)$ C. $(x, y - 3)$ E. $(x, 3y)$

 B. $(x, y + 3)$ D. $(3x, 3y)$

29. A square is drawn in a coordinate plane. Which of the following transformations of the square will shift the square 7 units to the right and 5 units downward?

 A. Add 7 to each x-coordinate and add 5 to each y-coordinate.

 B. Multiply each x-coordinate by 7 and divide each y-coordinate by 5.

 C. Add 7 to each x-coordinate and subtract 5 from each y-coordinate.

 D. Subtract 7 from each x-coordinate and subtract 5 from each y-coordinate.

 E. Subtract 7 from each x-coordinate and add 5 to each y-coordinate.

30. In the rectangular coordinate system below, if $x = 4.2$, then y equals which of the following?

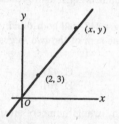

 A. 2.8   C. 4.8   E. 6.3

 B. 3.4   D. 6.2

31. Points $(x, -4)$ and $(-1, y)$ (not shown in the figure below) are in Quadrants III and II, respectively. If x and $y \neq 0$, in which quadrant is point (x, y)?

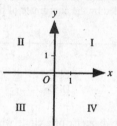

 A. I

 B. II

 C. III

 D. IV

 E. Cannot be determined from the given information

32. If Sam lives 8 miles west of Jeni, and Molly lives 10 miles north of Jeni, approximately how many miles less would Molly walk if she walks directly to Sam's house, rather than first to Jeni's house and then to Sam's house?

 A. 1   C. 3   E. 5

 B. 2   D. 4

33. If point B (not shown in the figure below) lies below the x-axis at point $(4, -4)$, what is the area of $\triangle ABC$?

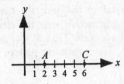

A. 2   C. 6   E. 16
B. 4   D. 8

34. On a coordinate graph, what is the distance between points $(-1, 4)$ and $(2, 8)$?
A. 3   C. 5   E. 8
B. 4   D. 6

35. In the figure below, $\overline{AB}$ is the base of a water ski ramp and is 18 feet long. The slope (rise divided by run) of the ramp is m. If the ramp is y feet high, then what is the value of y?

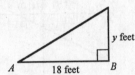

A. $\frac{m}{18}$ C. $18 - m$ E. $m + 18$
B. $18m$ D. $m - 18$

36. What is the midpoint between $(-2, 15)$ and $(8, 17)$?
A. $(6, 16)$ C. $(5, 16)$ E. $(6, 32)$
B. $(3, 16)$ D. $(5, 32)$

37. In the figure below, $\overline{AB}$ is the diameter of a circle whose center is at point P. What are the coordinates for point B?

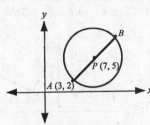

A. $(10, 7)$ C. $(12, 7)$ E. $(11, 7)$
B. $(5, 2.5)$ D. $(11, 8)$

38. If $f(x) = 17x + 14$, then $f(2) + f(3) + f(4)$ is:
A. 195   C. 126   E. 51
B. 153   D. 102

39. How many of the following graphs are graphs of linear functions?

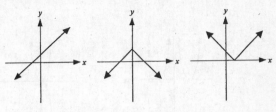

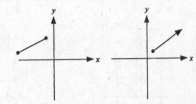

A. 1   C. 3   E. 5
B. 2   D. 4

40. $f(x)$ and $g(x)$ represent linear functions. If $f(x) = 5$ for $x = 1$, $g(x) = 3x + 8$, and $f(x) = g(x)$ for $x = 2$, then what is the value of $f(4)$?
A. 12   C. 20   E. 32
B. 16   D. 24

41. In each of the following four sets, the three ordered pairs belong to a linear function. In how many of the four sets is the value of the variable x less than zero?

$\{(0, 1), (-4, -7), (x, 0)\}$
$\{(0, 2), (-5, 52), (x, 12)\}$
$\{(2, -5), (-2, -17), (x, 13)\}$
$\{(6, 17), (8, 25), (x, 4)\}$

A. 0   C. 2   E. 4
B. 1   D. 3

42. If $y = mx + b$, $x = 5$ for $y = 20$, and $x = 9$ for $y = 32$, then $m + b$ is:
A. 76   C. 14   E. 3
B. 52   D. 8

43. Which of the following graphs depicts the quadratic functions $y = \frac{x^2}{2}$ and $y = -\frac{x^2}{2}$?

A.

D.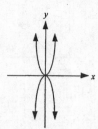

B.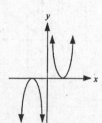

E.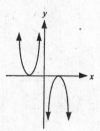

C.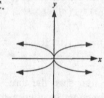

44. If $y = -2x^2 + 16x - 1$, what is the largest possible value for y?

A. −1
B. 13
C. 31
D. 32
E. Cannot be determined from the given information

45. The graph of $y = 4x^2$ intersects the graph of $y = x^2 + 3x$ at how many points?

A. 0   C. 2   E. 4
B. 1   D. 3

46. A student noted that the graph of the following ordered points for (x, y) appeared to approximate a parabolic curve: $(1, 7)$, $(-1, 0)$, $(2, 12)$, $(4, 29)$, $(5, 42)$. Which of the following equations best represents the curve?

A. $y = x^2 + 6$
B. $y = x^2 + 3x + 2$
C. $y = 2x^2 + x + 4$
D. $y = x^2 - x + 8$
E. $y = 2x^2 + x + 4$

47. The graph of the following ordered pairs for (x, y) is approximately a straight line of the form $y = mx + b$: $(1, 18)$, $(2, 23)$, $(3, 27)$, $(4, 32)$, $(5, 38)$. Which of the following best approximates the value of b?

A. 13   C. 20   E. 25
B. 18   D. 23

48. A scientist studying insect movement observes that in a day, each insect travels a particular geometric pattern and the distance traveled by each insect is directly proportional to the insect's length. The values for insect length and distance traveled in a day, in inches, for four insects are: $(1, 1.57)$, $(1.5, 2.36)$, $(2, 3.14)$, and $(3, 4.71)$. The geometric pattern traveled by the four insects is a:

A. square
B. equilateral triangle
C. circle
D. semicircle
E. regular polygon of five sides

49. The figure below shows two parallel lines with coordinates of points as shown. What is the slope of the line passing through point $(0, 6)$?

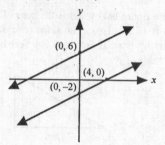

A. $\frac{1}{2}$ C. $\frac{1}{4}$ E. $\frac{1}{6}$
B. $\frac{1}{3}$ D. $\frac{1}{5}$

50. The center of a circle is located at $(19, 7)$. One end of a diameter of the circle is located at $(4, 6)$. The second end of the diameter is located at:

A. $(11.5, 6.5)$ C. $(34, 8)$ E. $(38, 8)$
B. $(11.5, 13)$ D. $(38, 14)$

51. In the figure below, which is not necessarily drawn to scale, $ABCD$ is a square and $\angle FGH \cong \angle A$.

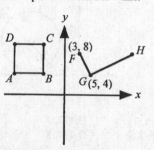

If points F and G have the coordinates as indicated in the figure, how many of the following four ordered pairs could possibly represent point H?

$(8, 6)$, $(9, 6)$, $(11, 7)$, $(13, 8)$

A. 0   C. 2   D. 3
B. 1   E. 4

52. The line that passes through (1, 5) and (−2, 17) is parallel to the line that passes through (17, 6) and (13, y). What is the value of y?

    A. 10   C. 16   E. 22
    B. 14   D. 18

53. What is the distance from the point (−2, 5) to the point (7, −7)?

    A. 9   C. 15   E. 24
    B. 12   D. 18

54. The figure below shows a circle with an area of 9π.

    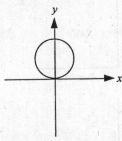

    The circle is tangent to the x-axis at (0, 0) and the center of the circle lies on the y-axis. The constant function $y = k$ intersects the circle at exactly one point. If $k > 0$, what is the value of k?

    A. 1   C. 3   E. 9
    B. 2   D. 6

55. The figure below shows a graph of $y = \dfrac{12}{x^2 + 6x + 7}$. How many different integers for y are not a part of the graph of $y = \dfrac{12}{x^2 + 6x + 7}$?

    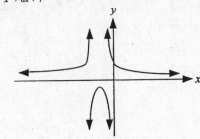

    A. 2   C. 7   E. 13
    B. 6   D. 12

56. The graph below shows two different parabola functions: $y = (x − 1)^2 + 4$ and $y − 2 = −(x + 5)^2$.

    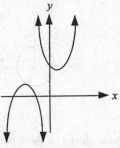

    The values of y that are not on either of the parabolas are all values of y such that:

    A. $−5 \leq y \leq 1$ C. $1 < y < 4$ E. $4 < y < 5$
    B. $2 < y < 4$ D. $1 \leq y \leq 5$

57. The graph below is of the function $y = (x − 2)^2 + 3$.

    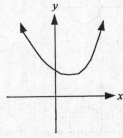

    If a horizontal shift of four units to the left were performed on the original graph, at what point (x, y) would the transformed graph intersect the original graph?

    A. (2, 7)   C. (6, 3)   E. (0, 3)
    B. (2, −1)   D. (−2, 3)

58. The graph of $y = 3x^2$ can be produced from the graph of $y = x^2$ by performing a vertical stretch by a factor of three. The graph of $y = 2x^2 + 12x + 1$ can be produced from the graph of $y = x^2$ by performing a vertical stretch by a factor of two, a horizontal shift of three units to the left, and a vertical shift of:

    A. 17 units down.
    B. 12 units down.
    C. 1 unit down.
    D. 1 unit up.
    E. 12 units up.

59. The graph below shows a circle whose equation is $x^2 + y^2 = 16$.

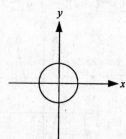

The graph is moved by the following transformations: four units to the right and two units up. Which of the following is the correctly transformed graph?

A.

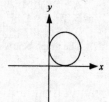

B.

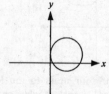

C.

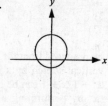

D.

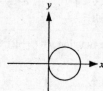

E.

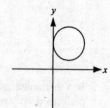

60. The stronger the relationship between two variables, the more closely the points on a scatter plot will approach some linear or curvilinear pattern. Which of the scatter plots below represents the strongest relationship between the two variables?

A.

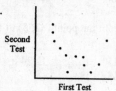

B.

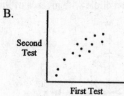

C.

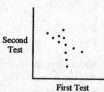

D.

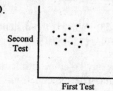

E.

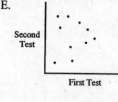

61. The following ordered pairs for (x, y) represent points on a graph: (5, 15), (10, 28), (11, 27), (25, 47), (40, 76), (50, 111), and (60, 129). Which of the following equations represents the line of best fit (the line that most closely approximates the set of points)?

A. $y = \frac{x}{3}$ C. $y = 3x - 6$ E. $y = 5x - 4$

B. $y = \frac{x}{3} - 2$ D. $y = 2x + 3$

Solving Story Problems

Story problems may test arithmetic, algebra, or geometry in the context of a "story." You should have everything you need to solve these problems. However, remember that if a math story item stumps you, you have the answer at hand. Simply work backwards from the answer choices—the right answer has to be one of the choices. Since quantitative (*i.e.*, numerical value) choices are arranged in size order, starting with the middle answer choice will result in the fewest calculations.

In solving story problems, the most important technique is to read accurately. Be sure you clearly understand what you are asked to find. Then, evaluate the item in common sense terms and to eliminate answer choices. For example, if two people are working together, their combined speed is greater than either individual speed, but not more than twice as fast as the fastest speed. Finally, be alert for the "hidden equation"—some necessary information so obvious that the item assumes that you know it.

Examples:

1. boys plus girls = total class
2. imported wine plus domestic wine = all wine
3. wall and floor make a right angle (Pythagorean theorem)

Some of the frequently encountered types of problem-solving problems are described in this section, although not every item you may encounter will fall into one of these categories. However, thoroughly familiarizing yourself with the types of problems that follow will help you to develop the skills to translate and solve all kinds of verbal problems.

Coin Problems

For coin *problems*, change the value of all monies involved to cents before writing an equation. The number of nickels must be multiplied by 5 to give their value in cents; dimes must be multiplied by 10; quarters by 25; half-dollars by 50; and dollars by 100.

Example:

Richard has $3.50 consisting of nickels and dimes. If he has 5 more dimes than nickels, how many dimes does he have?
➤ Let x = the number of nickels; $x + 5$ = the number of dimes; $5x$ = the value of the nickels in cents; $10x + 50$ = the value of the dimes in cents; and 350 = the value of the money he has in cents. Thus: $5x + 10x + 50 = 350 \Rightarrow 15x = 300 \Rightarrow x = 20$. Therefore, Richard has 20 nickels and 25 dimes.

In an item such as this, you can be sure that 20 would be among the multiple-choice answers. You must be sure to read carefully what you are asked to find and then continue until you have found the quantity sought.

Number and Set Problems

Number problems can be story problems that require knowledge of the properties of numbers in order to solve the item. Typically, number problems involve *consecutive integers* or *consecutive odd/even numbers*. Consecutive integers are one number apart and can be represented by x, $x + 1$, $x + 2$, *etc.* Consecutive even or odd integers are two numbers apart and can be represented by x, $x + 2$, $x + 4$, *etc.*

Example:

Three consecutive odd integers have a sum of 33. Find the average of these integers.
➤ Represent the integers as x, $x + 2$, and $x + 4$. Write an equation indicating the sum is 33: $3x + 6 = 33 \Rightarrow 3x = 27 \Rightarrow x = 9$. Thus, the integers are 9, 11, and 13. In the case of evenly spaced numbers such as these, the average is the middle number, 11. Since the sum of the three numbers was given originally, all we really had to do was to divide this sum by 3 to find the average, without ever knowing what the numbers were.

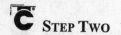

Set problems test understanding of relationships between different sets of numbers or *elements*. A *set* is a collection of things; *e.g.*, the set of positive integers.

DEFINITIONS FOR WORKING WITH SETS

The *number of elements* in set P is: $n(P)$.

The *union* of two sets P and Q is the set of all elements in *either* P or Q, or both: $P \cup Q$.
The *intersection* of two sets P and Q is the set of all elements in *both* P and Q: $P \cap Q$.

The *cardinal number theorem* is used find the number of elements in a union of two sets.
$$n(P \cup Q) = n(P) + n(Q) - n(P \cap Q)$$

Examples:

1. Let $S = \{3, 5, x\}$. If exactly one subset of S contains two different elements whose sum is 12, what value(s) can x be?
   ➤ Since either $3 + x = 12$ or $5 + x = 12$, then $x = 9$ or $x = 7$.

2. In a class of 30 students, 15 students are learning French, 11 students are learning Spanish, and 7 students are learning neither French nor Spanish. How many students in the class are learning both French and Spanish?
   ➤ Use the cardinal number theorem: $n(F \cup S) = n(F) + n(S) - n(F \cap S) \Rightarrow 30 - 7 = 15 + 11 - n(F \cap S) \Rightarrow n(F \cap S) = 3$.

A *Venn diagram* may help to solve problems involving sets that overlap.

Example:

Two circles are drawn on a floor. 20 people are standing in circle A. 15 people are standing in circle B. 9 people are standing in both circles. Find the total number of people standing in the two circles.
➤ The item can be symbolized with a Venn diagram:

From the diagram, it can be seen that there are a total of $11 + 9 + 6$ or 26 people.

Age Problems

Age problems involve a comparison of ages at the present time, several years from now, or several years ago. A person's age x years from now is found by adding x to his present age. A person's age x years ago is found by subtracting x from his present age.

Example:

Michelle was 12 years old y years ago. What is her age b years from now?
➤ Michelle's present age is $12 + y$. In b years, her age will be $12 + y + b$.

Interest Problems

To calculate the annual amount of interest paid on an investment, multiply the principal invested by the rate (percent) of interest paid: *Interest income = principal · rate.*

Example:

Mr. Krecker invests $4,000, part at 6% and part at 7%; the first year return is $250. Find the amount invested at 7%.

➤ Let x equal the amount invested at 7%. Thus, $4,000 - x$ equals the amount invested at 6%; $0.07x$ equals the income from the 7% investment; and $0.06(4,000 - x)$ equals the income from the 6% investment. Therefore: $0.07x + 0.06(4,000 - x) = 250 \Rightarrow 7x + 6(4,000 - x) = 25,000 \Rightarrow 7x + 24,000 - 6x = 25,000 \Rightarrow x = 1,000$ ($1,000 invested at 7%).

Mixture Problems

You should be familiar with two kinds of *mixture problems*. The first type is sometimes referred to as dry mixture, in which dry ingredients of different values, such as nuts or coffee, are mixed. The second type of mixture item deals with different priced tickets. For this type of problem, it is best to organize the data in a chart of three rows and three columns labeled as illustrated in the following problem.

Example:

A dealer wishes to mix 20 pounds of nuts selling for 45 cents per pound with some more expensive nuts selling for 60 cents per pound to make a mixture that will sell for 50 cents per pound. How many pounds of the more expensive nuts should he use?

➤ Create table summarizing the provided information:

	No. of lbs. ×	Price/lb. =	Total Value
Original	20	0.45	0.45(20)
Added	x	0.60	0.60(x)
Mixture	$20 + x$	0.50	0.50($20 + x$)

The value of the original nuts plus the value of the added nuts must equal the value of the mixture: $0.45(20) + 0.60(x) = 0.50(20 + x) \Rightarrow 45(20) + 60(x) = 50(20 + x) \Rightarrow 900 + 60x = 1,000 + 50x \Rightarrow 10x = 100 \Rightarrow x = 10$. Therefore, he should use 10 lbs. of 60-cent nuts.

The second type of mixture item deals with percents and amounts rather than prices and value.

Example:

How much water must be added to 20 gallons of solution that is 30% alcohol to dilute it to a solution that is only 25% alcohol?

➤ Create a table summarizing the provided information:

	No. of gals. ×	% alcohol =	Amt. alcohol
Original	20	0.30	0.30(20)
Added	x	0	0
Mixture	$20 + x$	0.25	0.25($20 + x$)

Note that the percent of alcohol in water is zero. Had pure alcohol been added to strengthen the solution, the percent would have been 100. Thus, the amount of alcohol added (none) plus the original amount must equal the amount of alcohol in the new solution: $0.30(20) = 0.25(20 + x) \Rightarrow 30(20) = 25(20 + x) \Rightarrow 600 = 500 + 25x \Rightarrow 100 = 25x \Rightarrow x = 4$ gallons.

Motion Problems

The fundamental relationship in all *motion problems* is *distance = rate • time*. The problems at the level of this examination usually derive their equation from a relationship concerning distance. Most problems fall into one of three types.

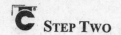

1. Motion in Opposite Directions

When two objects moving at the same speed start at the same time and move in opposite directions, or when two objects start at points at a given distance apart and move toward each other until they meet, then the distance the second travels will equal one-half the total distance covered. Either way, the total distance $= d_1 + d_2$:

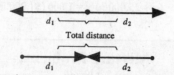

2. Motion in the Same Direction

This type of item is sometimes called the "catch-up" problem. Two objects leave the same place in the same direction at different times and at different rates, but one "catches up" to the other. In such a case, the two distances must be equal.

3. Round Trip

In this type of problem, the rate going is usually different from the rate returning. The times are also different. But if we go somewhere and then return to the starting point, the distances must be the same.

To solve any motion problem, it is helpful to organize the data in a box with columns for rate, time, and distance. A separate line should be used for each moving object. Remember that if the rate is given in *miles per hour*, the time must be in *hours* and the distance in *miles*.

Examples:

1. Two cars leave a restaurant at 1 p.m., with one car traveling east at 60 miles per hour and the other west at 40 miles per hour along a straight highway. At what time will they be 350 miles apart?

   ➢ Create a table summarizing the provided information:

	Rate	×	Time	=	Distance
Eastbound	60		x		$60x$
Westbound	40		x		$40x$

   Notice that the time is unknown, since we must determine the number of hours traveled. However, since the cars start at the same time and stop when they are 350 miles apart, their times are the same: $60x + 40x = 350 \Rightarrow 100x = 350 \Rightarrow x = 3.5$. Therefore, in 3.5 hours, it will be 4:30 p.m.

2. Gloria leaves home for school, riding her bicycle at a rate of 12 m.p.h. Twenty minutes after she leaves, her mother sees Gloria's English paper on her bed and leaves to bring it to her. If her mother drives at 36 m.p.h, how far must she drive before she reaches Gloria?

   ➢ Create a table summarizing the provided information:

	Rate	×	Time	=	Distance
Gloria	12		x		$12x$
Mother	36		$x - \frac{1}{3}$		$36\left(x - \frac{1}{3}\right)$

   The 20 minutes has been converted to $\frac{1}{3}$ of an hour. In this problem, the times are not equal, but the distances are: $12x = 36\left(x - \frac{1}{3}\right) = 36x - 12 \Rightarrow 12 = 24x \Rightarrow x = \frac{1}{2}$. Thus, if Gloria rode for $\frac{1}{2}$ hour at 12 m.p.h., the distance covered was 6 miles.

3. Nisha leaves home at 11 a.m. and rides to Andrea's house to return her bicycle. She travels at 12 miles per hour and arrives at 11:30 a.m. She turns right around and walks home. How fast does she walk if she returns home at 1 p.m.?

➤ Create a table summarizing the provided information:

	Rate $\times$	Time	= Distance
Going	12	$\frac{1}{2}$	6
Return	x	$1\frac{1}{2}$	$\frac{3x}{2}$

The distances are equal: $6 = \frac{3x}{2} \Rightarrow 12 = 3x \Rightarrow x = 4$ m.p.h.

Variation Problems

Variation in mathematics refers to the interrelationship of variables in such a manner that a change of value for one variable produces a corresponding change in another. There are three basic types of variation: *direct*, *inverse*, and *joint*.

1. Direct Variation

The expression "x varies directly with y" can be described by any of the following equations.

DIRECT VARIATION RELATIONSHIPS

$y = kx$, k is a constant $\frac{x_1}{y_1} = \frac{x_2}{y_2}$

Two quantities are said to vary directly if they change in the same direction. As one increases, the other increases and their ratio is equal to the positive constant.

For example, the amount you must pay for milk varies directly with the number of quarts of milk you buy. The amount of sugar needed in a recipe varies directly with the amount of butter used. The number of inches between two cities on a map varies directly with the number of miles between these cities.

Example:

If x varies directly as y^2, and $x = 12$ when $y = 2$, what is the value of x when $y = 3$?

➤ Notice that the variation involves the square of y. Therefore: $\frac{x_1}{y_1^2} = \frac{x_2}{y_2^2} \Rightarrow \frac{12}{2^2} = \frac{x}{3^2} \Rightarrow \frac{12}{4} = \frac{x}{9} \Rightarrow 3 = \frac{x}{9} \Rightarrow x = 27$.

2. Inverse Variation

The expression "x varies inversely as y" can be described by any of the following equations.

INVERSE VARIATION RELATIONSHIPS

$xy = k$, k is a constant $\frac{x_1}{y_2} = \frac{x_2}{y_1}$

Two quantities vary inversely if they change in opposite directions. As one quantity increases, the other quantity decreases.

For example, the number of people hired to paint a house varies inversely with the number of days the job will take. A doctor's stock of flu vaccine varies inversely with the number of patients she injects. The number of days a given supply of cat food lasts varies inversely with the number of cats being fed.

Example:

The time t to empty a container varies inversely with the square root of the number of men m working on the job. If it takes 3 hours for 16 men to do the job, how long will it take 4 men working at the same rate to empty the container?

➤ $\dfrac{t_1}{\sqrt{m_2}} = \dfrac{t_2}{\sqrt{m_1}} \Rightarrow t_1\sqrt{m_1} = t_2\sqrt{m_2} \Rightarrow 3\sqrt{16} = t\sqrt{4} \Rightarrow t = 3 \cdot \dfrac{\sqrt{16}}{\sqrt{4}} = 3(\sqrt{4}) = 3 \cdot 2 = 6.$

3. *Joint Variation*

The expression "x varies jointly as y and z" can be described by any of the following equations.

JOINT VARIATION RELATIONSHIPS

$\dfrac{x}{yz} = k$, k is a constant $\dfrac{x_1}{y_1z_1} = \dfrac{x_2}{y_2z_2}$ $\dfrac{x_1}{x_2} = \left(\dfrac{y_1}{y_2}\right)\left(\dfrac{z_1}{z_2}\right)$

Example:

The area, A, of a triangle varies jointly as the base b and the height h. If $A = 20$ when $b = 10$ and $h = 4$, what is the value of A when $b = 6$ and $h = 7$?

➤ $\dfrac{A_1}{b_1h_1} = \dfrac{A_2}{b_2h_2} \Rightarrow \dfrac{20}{(10)(4)} = \dfrac{A_2}{(6)(7)} \Rightarrow A_2 = 21.$

Percent Problems

Many problem-solving items involve percents as they apply to certain types of business situations.

1. *Percent Increase or Decrease*

Percent increase or decrease is found by putting the amount of increase or decrease over the original amount and changing this fraction to a percent.

Example:

A company normally employs 100 people. During a slow spell, it fired 20% of its employees. By what percent must it now increase its staff to return to full capacity?

➤ $20\% = \dfrac{1}{5} \cdot 100 = 20$. The company now has $100 - 20 = 80$ employees. If it then increases by 20 employees, the percent of increase is $\dfrac{20}{80} = \dfrac{1}{4}$, or 25%.

2. Discounts

A discount is expressed as a percent of the original price that will be deducted from that price to determine the sale price.

Examples:

1. Bill's Hardware offers a 20% discount on all appliances during a sale week. How much must Mrs. Russell pay for a washing machine marked at $280?

➤ $20\% = \frac{1}{5} \Rightarrow \frac{1}{5} \cdot \$280 = \$56$ discount $\Rightarrow \$280 - \$56 = \$224$ sale price. Alternatively, the following shortcut simplifies the solution: if there is a 20% discount, Mrs. Russell will pay 80% of the marked price: $80\% = \frac{4}{5} \Rightarrow \frac{4}{5} \cdot \$280 = \$224$ sale price.

2. A store offers a television set marked at $340 less consecutive discounts of 10% and 5%. Another store offers the same set with a single discount of 15%. How much does the buyer save buying at the better price?

➤ In the first store, the initial discount means the buyer pays 90%, or $\frac{9}{10}$ of $340, which is $306. The second discount must be figured on the first sale price. The additional 5% discount means the buyer pays 95% of $306, or $290.70. A 5% discount on $306 is less than an additional 5% discount on $340. Thus, the second store will have a lower sale price. In the second store, the buyer will pay 85% of $340, or $289—$1.70 less than the price at the first store.

3. Commission

Many salespeople earn money on a commission basis. In order to inspire sales, they are paid a percentage of the value of goods that they personally sell. This amount is called a commission.

Examples:

1. Mr. Saunders works at Brown's Department Store, where he is paid $80 per week in salary plus a 4% commission on all his sales. How much does he earn in a week in which he sells $4,032 worth of merchandise?

➤ Find 4% of $4,032 and add this amount to $80: $\$4,032 \cdot 0.04 = \$161.28 \Rightarrow \$161.28 + \$80 = \$241.28$.

2. Bill Olson delivers newspapers for a dealer and keeps 8% of all money collected. In one month, he was able to keep $16. How much did he forward to the dealer?

➤ First, find how much he collected by asking $16 is 8% of what number: $\$16 = 0.08x \Rightarrow \$1,600 = 8x \Rightarrow x = \$200$. Then, subtract the amount Bill kept ($16) from the total collected ($200). Therefore, Bill forwarded $184 to the dealer.

4. Taxes

Taxes are a percent of money spent or money earned.

Examples:

1. Dane County collects a 7% sales tax on automobiles. If the price of a used Ford is $5,832 before taxes, what will it cost when the sales tax is added in?

➤ Find 7% of $5,832 to determine the amount of tax and then add that amount to $5,832. This can be done in one step by finding 107% of $5,832: $\$5,832 \cdot 1.07 = \$6,240.24$.

2. If income is taxed at the rate of 10% for the first $10,000 of earned income, 15% for the next $10,000, 20% for the next $10,000, and 25% for all earnings over $30,000, how much income tax must be paid on a yearly income of $36,500?

➤ Find the income tax collected at each percentage rate and add them:

```
      10% of first $10,000  = $1,000
      15% of next $10,000   = $1,500
      20% of next $10,000   = $2,000
    + 25% of $6,500         = $1,625
             Total tax      = $6,125
```

EXERCISE **13**

Solving Story Problems

DIRECTIONS: Choose the correct answer to each of the following items. Use a calculator when necessary. Answers are on page 935.

1. A suit is sold for $68 while marked at $80. What is the rate of discount?

   A. 15%   C. $17\frac{11}{17}$%   E. 24%
   B. 17%   D. 20%

2. Lilian left home with $60 in her wallet. She spent $\frac{1}{3}$ of that amount at the supermarket, and she spent $\frac{1}{2}$ of what remained at the drugstore. If Lilian made no other expenditures, how much money did she have when she returned home?

   A. $10   C. $20   E. $50
   B. $15   D. $40

3. In the figure below, circle O and circle P are tangent to each other. If the circle with center O has a diameter of 8 and the circle with center P has a diameter of 6, what is the length of segment $\overline{OP}$?

   A. 7   C. 14   E. 28
   B. 10   D. 20

4. A man buys a radio for $70 after receiving a discount of 20%. What was the marked price?

   A. $56   C. $87.50   E. $92
   B. $84.50   D. $90

5. Colin and Shaina wish to buy a gift for a friend. They combine their money and find they have $4.00, consisting of quarters, dimes, and nickels. If they have 35 coins and the number of quarters is half the number of nickels, how many quarters do they have?

   A. 5   C. 20   E. 36
   B. 10   D. 23

6. Willie receives r% commission on a sale of s dollars. How many dollars does he receive?

   A. rs C. $100rs$ E. $\frac{rs}{100}$
   B. $\frac{r}{s}$ D. $\frac{r}{100s}$

7. Three times the smallest of three consecutive odd integers is 3 more than twice the largest. Find the largest integer.

   A. 9   C. 13   E. 17
   B. 11   D. 15

8. A refrigerator was sold for $273, yielding a 30% profit on the cost. For how much should it be sold to yield only a 10% profit on the cost?

   A. $210   C. $235   E. $241
   B. $231   D. $240

9. If 60 feet of uniform wire weigh 80 pounds, what is the weight, in pounds, of 2 yards of the same wire?

   A. $2\frac{2}{3}$ C. 80   E. 2,400
   B. 8   D. 120

10. What single discount is equivalent to two successive discounts of 10% and 15%?

    A. 25%   C. 24%   E. 22%
    B. 24.5%   D. 23.5%

11. Robert is 15 years older than Stan. However, y years ago Robert was twice as old as Stan. If Stan is now b years old and $b > y$, find the value of $b - y$.

    A. 13   C. 15   E. 17
    B. 14   D. 16

12. The net price of a certain article is $306 after successive discounts of 15% and 10% are taken off the marked price. What is the marked price?

    A. $408   C. $382.50   E. None of these
    B. $400   D. $234.09

13. A gear 50 inches in diameter turns a smaller gear 30 inches in diameter. If the larger gear makes 15 revolutions, how many revolutions does the smaller gear make in that time?

    A. 9   C. 20   E. 30
    B. 12   D. 25

14. If a merchant makes a profit of 20% based on the selling price of an article, what percent does he make on the cost?

    A. 15   C. 25   E. 45
    B. 20   D. 40

15. How many ounces of pure acid must be added to 20 ounces of a solution that is 5% acid to strengthen it to a solution that is 24% acid?

A. $2\frac{1}{2}$ C. 6   E. 10

B. 5   D. $7\frac{1}{2}$

16. If x men can do a job in h days, how long would y men take to do the same job?

A. $\frac{x}{h}$ C. $\frac{hy}{x}$ E. $\frac{x}{y}$

B. $\frac{xh}{y}$ D. xyh

17. A certain radio costs a merchant $72. At what price must he sell it if he is to make a profit of 20% of the selling price?

A. $86.40   C. $90   E. $148

B. $88   D. $144

18. A dealer mixes a pounds of nuts that cost b cents per pound with c pounds of nuts that cost d cents per pound. At what price should he sell a pound of the mixture if he wishes to make a profit of 10 cents per pound?

A. $\frac{ab+cd}{a+c}+10$ D. $\frac{b+d}{a+c}+0.10$

B. $\frac{ab+cd}{a+c}+0.10$ E. $\frac{b+d+10}{a+c}$

C. $\frac{b+d}{a+c}+10$

19. If a furnace uses 40 gallons of oil in a week, how many gallons, to the nearest gallon, does it use in 10 days?

A. 57   C. 28   E. 4

B. 44   D. 20

20. Nell invests $2,400 in the Security National Bank at 5%. How much additional money must she invest at 8% so that the total annual income will be equal to 6% of her entire investment?

A. $4,400   C. $3,000   E. $1,200

B. $3,600   D. $2,400

21. A baseball team has won 40 games out of 60 played. It has 32 more games to play. How many of these must the team win to make its record 75% for the season?

A. 28   C. 30   E. 34

B. 29   D. 32

22. A recipe requires 13 oz. of sugar and 18 oz. of flour. If only 10 oz. of sugar are used, how much flour, to the nearest ounce, should be used?

A. 11   C. 13   E. 15

B. 12   D. 14

23. Ivan left Austin to drive to Boxville at 6:15 p.m. and arrived at 11:45 p.m. If he averaged 30 miles per hour and stopped one hour for dinner, how many miles is Boxville from Austin?

A. 120   C. 180   E. 190

B. 135   D. 185

24. If prices are reduced 25% and sales increase 20%, what is the net effect on gross receipts?

A. They increase by 5%.   D. They increase by 10%.

B. They decrease by 5%.   E. They decrease by 10%.

C. They remain the same.

25. If a car can drive 25 miles on two gallons of gasoline, how many gallons will be needed for a trip of 150 miles?

A. 12   C. 16   E. 20

B. 13   D. 17

26. A plane traveling 600 miles per hour is 30 miles from Kennedy Airport at 4:58 p.m. At what time will it arrive at the airport?

A. 5:00 p.m.   C. 5:02 p.m.   E. 5:23 p.m.

B. 5:01 p.m.   D. 5:20 p.m.

27. A salesperson earns a commission of 5% on all sales between $200 and $600, and 8% on all sales over $600. What is the commission earned in a week in which sales total $800?

A. $20   C. $48   E. $88

B. $36   D. $78

28. A school has enough bread to last 30 children 4 days. If 10 children are added, how many days will the bread last?

A. $\frac{1}{3}$ C. $2\frac{1}{3}$ E. 3

B. $1\frac{1}{3}$ D. $2\frac{2}{3}$

29. Mr. Bridges can wash his car in 15 minutes, while his son Dave takes twice as long to do the same job. If they work together, how many minutes will the job take them?

A. 5   C. 10   E. 30

B. $7\frac{1}{2}$ D. $22\frac{1}{2}$

30. At c cents per pound, what is the cost of a ounces of salami?

A. $\frac{c}{a}$ C. ac E. $\frac{16c}{a}$

B. $\frac{a}{c}$ D. $\frac{ac}{16}$

31. If 3 miles are equivalent to 4.83 kilometers, then 11.27 kilometers are equivalent to how many miles?

A. $2\frac{1}{3}$ C. 7   E. $7\frac{1}{2}$

B. 5   D. $7\frac{1}{3}$

32. If enrollment at City University grew from 3,000 to 12,000 in the last 10 years, what was the percent of increase in enrollment?

   A. 25%   C. 300%   E. 400%
   B. 125%   D. 330%

33. At a certain printing plant, each of m machines prints 6 newspapers every s seconds. If all machines work together but independently without interruption, how many minutes will it take to print an entire run of 18,000 newspapers?

   A. $\frac{180s}{m}$ C. $50ms$ E. $\frac{300m}{s}$
   B. $\frac{50s}{m}$ D. $\frac{ms}{50}$

34. If p pencils cost d dollars, how many pencils can be bought for c cents?

   A. $\frac{100pc}{d}$ C. $\frac{pd}{c}$ E. $\frac{cd}{p}$
   B. $\frac{pc}{100d}$ D. $\frac{pc}{d}$

35. A car dealer who gives a customer a 20% discount on the list price of a car still realizes a net profit of 25% of cost. If the dealer's cost is $4,800, what is the usual list price of the car?

   A. $6,000   C. $7,200   E. $8,001
   B. $6,180   D. $7,500

36. The variable m varies directly as the square of t. If m is 7 when $t = 1$, what is the value of m when $t = 2$?

   A. 28   C. 7   E. 2
   B. 14   D. $3\frac{1}{2}$

37. 6 students in a class failed algebra, representing $16\frac{2}{3}\%$ of the class. How many students passed the course?

   A. 48   C. 33   E. 28
   B. 36   D. 30

38. If the value of a piece of property decreases by 10% while the tax rate on the property increases by 10%, what is the effect on taxes?

   A. Taxes increase by 10%.
   B. Taxes increase by 1%.
   C. There is no change in taxes.
   D. Taxes decrease by 1%.
   E. Taxes decrease by 10%.

39. The variable m varies jointly as r and l. If m is 8 when r and l are each 1, what is the value of m when r and l are each 2?

   A. 64   C. 16   E. 2
   B. 32   D. 4

40. 95% of the residents of Coral Estates live in private homes. 40% of those live in air-conditioned homes. What percent of the residents of Coral Estates live in air-conditioned homes?

   A. 3%   C. 30%   E. 38%
   B. 3.8%   D. 34%

41. Exactly three years before the year in which Anna was born, the year was $1980 - x$. In terms of x, what is the year of Anna's twentieth birthday?

   A. $1977 + x$ C. $2003 - x$ E. $2006 + x$
   B. $1997 + x$ D. $2003 + x$

42. Mr. Carlson receives a salary of $500 a month and a commission of 5% on all sales. What must be the amount of his sales in July so that his total monthly income is $2,400?

   A. $48,000   C. $7,600   E. $2,000
   B. $38,000   D. $3,800

43. John can wax his car in 3 hours. Jim can do the same job in 5 hours. How long will it take them if they work together?

   A. $\frac{1}{2}$ hour   C. 2 hours   E. 8 hours
   B. $1\frac{7}{8}$ hours   D. $2\frac{7}{8}$ hours

44. In the junior class at Shawnee High School, 168 students took the SAT, 175 students took the ACT, 80 students took both, and 27 students did not take either one. What is the total number of students in the junior class at Shawnee High School?

   A. 440   C. 290   E. 248
   B. 343   D. 282

45. Let $R = \{3, 5, 6, 7, 9\}$. How many different subsets of R with 1, 2, 3, or 4 elements contain one or more odd numbers?

   A. 31   C. 29   E. 27
   B. 30   D. 28

46. A survey of 51 students was conducted concerning each student's favorite flavors of ice cream. Of the 51 students, 10 students liked only vanilla, 12 students liked only strawberry, and 15 students liked only chocolate. Every student liked at least one of the three flavors. 7 students liked both vanilla and strawberry, and 9 students liked both vanilla and chocolate. The largest possible number of students who could have liked both chocolate and strawberry is:

   A. 2   C. 7   E. 14
   B. 3   D. 12

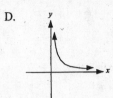

47. Set X is the set of all positive integral multiples of 8: $X = \{8, 16, 24, 32, ...\}$. Set Y is the set of all positive integral multiples of 6: $Y = \{6, 12, 18, 24, ...\}$. The intersection of these two sets is the set of all positive integral multiples of:

   A. 2   C. 14   E. 48
   B. 4   D. 24

48. If y varies directly with x and the constant of variation is 3, then $y = 12.3$ when $x = 4.1$. If y varies directly with x and $y = 6.72$ when $x = 4.2$, then what is the constant of variation?

   A. 3.1   C. 2.52   E. 2.50
   B. 4.2   D. 1.6

49. Each of the following choices is comprised of three equations relating x and y. Identify the set of equations that demonstrates direct variation, inverse variation, and neither direct nor inverse variation, respectively?

   A. $y = 3x; x^2 + y^2 = x + 5; y = \frac{4}{x}$

   B. $y = 3x; x^2 + y^2 = x + 5; y = \frac{x}{4}$

   C. $x = \frac{y}{3}; xy = 7; x^2 + y^2 = \frac{x}{5}$

   D. $y = 3x; y = \frac{4}{x}; x = 5y$

   E. $y = \frac{2x}{3}; x = 5y; x^2 + y^2 = x + 7$

50. At a constant temperature, the resistance of a wire varies directly with length and inversely with the square of the wire diameter. A piece of wire that is 0.1 inch in diameter and 50 feet long has a resistance of 0.1 ohm. What is the resistance, in ohms, of a wire of the same material that is 9000 feet long and 0.3 inches in diameter?

   A. 0.3   C. 2   E. 9
   B. 0.9   D. 3

51. Let y vary directly as x, and let w vary directly as the square of x. If $y = 10$ for $x = 1.25$ and $w = 8$ for $x = \sqrt{2}$, then for what positive value of x will $y = w$?

   A. 1   C. 2   E. 5
   B. $1\frac{1}{2}$ D. 4

52. The perimeter of a square varies directly as the length of one side of the square with a constant of variation of 4. The circumference of a circle varies directly as the circle's radius and a constant of variation equal to:

   A. π C. 1   E. $\frac{1}{\pi}$
   B. 2π D. 2

53. If x and y vary inversely, then for any ordered pair (x, y), the value of xy is a constant number. The ordered pairs $(-12, -3)$ and $(6, 6)$ represent an example of inverse variation for x and y. Which of the following graphs represents a possible inverse variation relationship between x and y?

A.   D.
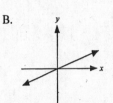   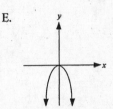

B.   E.
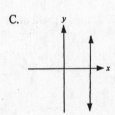

C.

54. The formula for compound interest is $A = P\left(1 + \frac{r}{n}\right)^{nt}$, where A is the final amount, P is the initial investment, r is the annual percentage interest rate, t is the time period, and n is the number of times per year that the interest is compounded. If an initial investment of \$10,000 accrues compound interest at a percentage rate of 4.16% and is worth \$10,424.02, \$10,866.03, \$11,326.77, and \$11,807.06 after 1, 2, 3, and 4 years, respectively, then n is approximately equal to:

   A. 1   C. 4   E. 12
   B. 2   D. 6

Math Express Skills Review

CAMBRIDGE
EDUCATIONAL SERVICES®

EDUCATORS' #1 CHOICE FOR SCHOOL IMPROVEMENT

Cambridge Course Concept Outline
MATH EXPRESS SKILLS REVIEW

Arithmetic Summary

1. **Real Numbers:** Real numbers are all the numbers on the number line, including integers, decimals, fractions, and radical numbers.

   e.g., $-\frac{1}{2}, 0, \frac{2}{3}, \sqrt{2}, \pi$

   A real number is *rational* if it can be written as the ratio of two integers where the denominator does not equal zero. Natural numbers, whole numbers, integers, common fractions, and repeating decimals are some examples of rational numbers.

   e.g., $-\frac{1}{2}, 0, 0.75, \frac{2}{3}$

   A real number is *irrational* if it cannot be written as the ratio of two integers. Irrational numbers have infinite non-repeating decimal representations.

   e.g., $\sqrt{2}, \pi$

   Properties of real numbers:
   $(+)(+) = (+)$
   $(-)(-) = (+)$
   $(+)(-) = (-)$
   $(-)^2 = (+)$
   $m + 0 = m$, where m is a real number
   $m \cdot 0 = 0$, where m is a real number

   e.g., 1. $\left(\frac{1}{2}\right)(4) = 2$
   2. $(-2)\left(-\frac{4}{5}\right) = \frac{8}{5}$
   3. $(2)(-4) = -8$
   4. $\left(-\frac{3}{4}\right)(4) = -3$
   5. $(-2)^2 = 4$
   6. $2 + 0 = 2$
   7. $(2)(0) = 0$

2. **Natural Numbers:** *Natural* numbers are the set of positive integers and are also referred to as counting numbers: 1, 2, 3, 4, 5, ...

3. **Whole Numbers:** *Whole* numbers are the numbers used for counting, plus the number zero: 0, 1, 2, 3, ...

   e.g., 0, 5, 56, 490

4. **Integers:** *Integers* are positive or negative whole numbers.

   e.g., $-568, -45, 0, 6, 67, \frac{16}{2}, 345$

5. **Positive and Negative Integers:** If the signs of the two numbers being added or subtracted are *different*, disregard the signs temporarily, subtract the smaller number from the larger number, and keep the sign attached to the larger number.

   e.g., $-3 + 2 = -1$
   $-4 + 6 = 2$

   If the signs of the two numbers being added or subtracted are the *same*, disregard the signs temporarily, add the two numbers, and keep the sign attached to each number.

   e.g., 1. $-5 - 3 = -8$
   2. $4 + 8 = 12$

6. **Even and Odd Integers:** An *even* integer is evenly divisible by 2, whereas an *odd* integer is not evenly divisible by 2. 0 is an even integer.

   e.g., Even integers: $-50, -4, 0, 2, 34$
   Odd integers: $-45, -3, 9, 15$

   Important properties of even and odd integers:
   even + even = even   *e.g.,* $2 + 4 = 6$
   even + odd = odd $4 + 3 = 7$
   odd + odd = even $3 + 5 = 8$
   odd + even = odd $3 + 4 = 7$
   even • even = even $2 \cdot 4 = 8$
   even • odd = even $2 \cdot 3 = 6$
   odd • odd = odd $3 \cdot 5 = 15$
   odd • even = even $3 \cdot 2 = 6$

7. **Factor:** A *factor* is a number that divides evenly into another number.

   e.g., 1, 2, 3, 4, 6, and 12 are factors of 12

8. **Prime:** A *prime* number is any natural number (except 1) that is divisible only by 1 and itself.

   e.g., 2, 3, 5, 7, 11, 13, 17, and 19 are all prime numbers

9. **Prime Factors:** All natural numbers can be expressed as the product of prime numbers, which are called the *prime factors* of that number.

   e.g., 1. $3 = (3)(1)$
   2. $12 = (2)(2)(3)$

10. **Consecutive Integers:** *Consecutive* integers are in continuous sequence. If the first integer of a consecutive sequence is m, the sequence is $m, m + 1, m + 2$, *etc.*

    e.g., 1. $\{4, 5, 6, 7, ...\}$
    2. $\{-10, -9, -8, -7, ...\}$

    Consecutive *even* or *odd* integers are in continuous sequence of even or odd integers, respectively. An even or odd sequence is $m, m + 2, m + 4, m + 6$, *etc.*

    e.g., 1. $\{-4, -2, 0, 2, ...\}$
    2. $\{7, 9, 11, 13, ...\}$

11. Miscellaneous Symbols:

$=$ ⇔ is equal to
$\neq$ ⇔ is not equal to
$<$ ⇔ is less than
$>$ ⇔ is greater than
$\leq$ ⇔ is less than or equal to
$\geq$ ⇔ is greater than or equal to
$|x|$ ⇔ absolute value of x (always non-negative)

e.g.,   1. $3 = 3$
      2. $\frac{3}{4} \neq \frac{5}{6}$
      3. $-3 < 6$
      4. $5 > 4$
      5. $m - 3 \leq -3$, for $m = ..., -3, -2, -1, 0$
      6. $m + 3 \geq 3$, for $m = 0, 1, 2, 3, ...$
      7. $|-5| = 5$

12. Terms: The *sum* or *total* is the result of adding numbers together. The *difference* is the result of subtracting one number from another. The *product* is the result of multiplying numbers together. The *quotient* is the result of dividing one number by another. The *remainder* is the number remaining after one number is divided into another number.

e.g.,   1. The sum (or total) of 2 and 3 is 5: $2 + 3 = 5$.
      2. The difference between 5 and 2 is 3: $5 - 2 = 3$.
      3. The product of 2 and 3 is 6: $(2)(3) = 6$.
      4. The quotient of 6 divided by 2 is 3: $6 \div 2 = 3$.
      5. The remainder of 7 divided by 3 is 1: $7 \div 3 = 2$ plus a remainder of 1.

13. Fractions: When one whole integer is divided by another whole integer (other than zero) and the result is not a third whole integer, the result is a fraction, or ratio. The top number is called the *numerator*; the bottom number is called the *denominator*.

e.g.,   2 divided by 3 results in a fraction, not a whole number: $2 \div 3 = \frac{2}{3}$.

Proper fractions have a numerator of lower value than the denominator and thus have a value less than 1.

e.g., $\frac{1}{2}$ and $\frac{3}{4}$ are both < 1.

Improper fractions have a numerator of greater value than the denominator, and thus have a value greater than 1.

e.g., $\frac{3}{2}$ and $\frac{4}{3}$ are both > 1.

A *mixed number* consists of both a whole number and a fraction written together.

e.g.,   1. $2\frac{1}{2} = 2 + \frac{1}{2}$
      2. $3\frac{4}{5} = 3 + \frac{4}{5}$

To add, subtract, multiply, or divide fractions, convert mixed numbers to improper fractions as follows:

a. The new denominator is the denominator of the fractional part of the mixed number.
b. The new numerator is the whole number of the mixed number multiplied by the denominator of the fractional part and then added to its numerator.

e.g.,   1. $3\frac{1}{4} = \frac{(3 \cdot 4) + 1}{4} = \frac{13}{4}$
      2. $6\frac{2}{5} = \frac{(6 \cdot 5) + 2}{5} = \frac{32}{5}$
      3. $2\frac{12}{13} = \frac{(2 \cdot 13) + 12}{13} = \frac{38}{13}$

To convert an improper fraction to a mixed number, reverse the process as follows:

a. Divide the denominator into the numerator. The integer part of the quotient becomes the whole number part of the mixed number.
b. With the same denominator, create a fraction with the numerator equal to the remainder of the first step.

e.g.,   1. $\frac{29}{5} = 29 \div 5 = 5$ with a remainder of $4 = 5\frac{4}{5}$.
      2. $\frac{31}{6} = 31 \div 6 = 5$ with a remainder of $1 = 5\frac{1}{6}$.
      3. $\frac{43}{13} = 43 \div 13 = 3$ with a remainder of $4 = 3\frac{4}{13}$.

14. Reducing Fractions: It is conventional to reduce all fractions to lowest terms. To reduce a fraction to lowest terms, eliminate redundant factors that are in both the numerator and the denominator. Either factor or divide out the redundant factors from both.

e.g., $\frac{8}{16} = \frac{1(8)}{2(8)} = \frac{1}{2}$, or $\frac{8}{16} = \frac{8 \div 8}{16 \div 8} = \frac{1}{2}$.

A fraction is expressed in *lowest terms* when there is no natural number (other than 1) that can be divided evenly into both the numerator and the denominator.

e.g., $\frac{8}{15}$ is in lowest terms, as there is no natural number (other than 1) that divides evenly into 8 and 15.

15. Complex Fractions: A *complex fraction* is a fraction in which either the numerator or the denominator, or both, contains fractions. There are two methods for simplifying complex fractions.

Method 1: Multiply the numerator by the reciprocal of the denominator and simplify.

e.g., $\dfrac{\frac{1}{2}}{\frac{3}{4}} = \left(\frac{1}{2}\right)\left(\frac{4}{3}\right) = \frac{4}{6} = \frac{2}{3}$

Method 2: Multiply both the numerator and the denominator by the least common denominator for the terms in the numerator and the denominator of the complex fraction and simplify.

e.g., $\dfrac{\frac{1}{2}}{\frac{3}{4}} \cdot \dfrac{(4)}{(4)} = \dfrac{\frac{4}{2}}{\frac{12}{4}} = \frac{2}{3}$

16. **Common Denominators:** A *common denominator* is a number that is a multiple of the denominators of two or more fractions.

    e.g., Since 12 is an even multiple of both 3 and 4, it is a common denominator for $\frac{1}{3}$ and $\frac{1}{4}$.

    Converting a fraction to another denominator is the reverse of reducing it to lowest terms. Multiplying the numerator and the denominator of a fraction by the same number is equal to multiplying it by 1—the value is unchanged.

    e.g., 1. $\frac{1}{4} = \frac{(1)(3)}{(4)(3)} = \frac{3}{12}$

       2. $\frac{2}{3} = \frac{(2)(4)}{(3)(4)} = \frac{8}{12}$

17. **Adding Fractions:** The procedure for adding fractions varies depending on whether or not the fractions already share the same denominator.

    To add fractions with the same denominator, create a new fraction using the common denominator. The new numerator is the sum of the old numerators.

    e.g., $\frac{3}{7} + \frac{2}{7} = \frac{5}{7}$

    To add fractions with different denominators, find a common denominator and convert the fractions.

    e.g., 1. $\frac{1}{3} + \frac{1}{5} = \frac{1(5)}{3(5)} + \frac{1(3)}{5(3)} = \frac{5}{15} + \frac{3}{15} = \frac{8}{15}$

       2. $\frac{1}{3} + \frac{2}{7} = \frac{1(7)}{3(7)} + \frac{2(3)}{7(3)} = \frac{7}{21} + \frac{6}{21} = \frac{13}{21}$

    To add a fraction and a whole number, treat the whole number as a fraction with a denominator of 1.

    e.g., $2 + \frac{1}{5} + \frac{1}{2} = \frac{2}{1} + \frac{1}{5} + \frac{1}{2} = \frac{2(10)}{1(10)} + \frac{1(2)}{5(2)} + \frac{1(5)}{2(5)}$
    $= \frac{20}{10} + \frac{2}{10} + \frac{5}{10} = \frac{27}{10}$

    To add a fraction and a mixed number, change the mixed number to an improper fraction and then add.

    e.g., $2\frac{1}{3} + \frac{1}{3} = \frac{7}{3} + \frac{1}{3} = \frac{8}{3} = 2\frac{2}{3}$

18. **Subtracting Fractions:** Follow the same procedure for addition, except subtract rather than add.

    To subtract fractions with the same denominator, simply subtract the second numerator from the first.

    e.g., $\frac{5}{7} - \frac{2}{7} = \frac{3}{7}$

    To subtract fractions with different denominators, first find a common denominator.

    e.g., $\frac{7}{8} - \frac{3}{5} = \frac{7(5)}{8(5)} - \frac{3(8)}{5(8)} = \frac{35}{40} - \frac{24}{40} = \frac{11}{40}$

19. **"Flying-X" Method for Adding and Subtracting Fractions:** It is not necessary to find the least common denominator when adding or subtracting fractions if you reduce the result to lowest terms. Any common denominator will work—simply use the *flying-x* method.

$$\frac{a}{b} + \frac{c}{d} = \frac{a}{b} \gtrless \frac{c}{d} = \frac{ad + bc}{bd}$$

a. Multiply the denominators together to get a new denominator.

b. Multiply the numerator of the first fraction by the denominator of the second.

c. Multiply the denominator of the first fraction by the numerator of the second.

d. The new numerator is the sum (or difference) of the results of steps 2 and 3.

e.g., 1. $\frac{2}{7} + \frac{1}{5} = \frac{2}{7} \gtrless \frac{1}{5} = \frac{10 + 7}{35} = \frac{17}{35}$

   2. $\frac{3}{5} + \frac{1}{3} = \frac{3}{5} \gtrless \frac{1}{3} = \frac{9 + 5}{15} = \frac{14}{15}$

20. **Multiplying Fractions:** Multiplication of fractions does not require a common denominator. Just multiply numerators to create a new numerator, and multiply denominators to create a new denominator.

    e.g., 1. $\frac{3}{4} \cdot \frac{1}{2} = \frac{(3)(1)}{(4)(2)} = \frac{3}{8}$

       2. $\frac{2}{3} \cdot \frac{2}{5} = \frac{(2)(2)}{(3)(5)} = \frac{4}{15}$

21. **Dividing Fractions:** To divide by a fraction, take the reciprocal of the divisor (the fraction doing the dividing) and then multiply the two terms.

    e.g., 1. $2 \div \frac{1}{4} = 2 \cdot \frac{4}{1} = \frac{8}{1} = 8$

       2. $\frac{\frac{2}{5}}{6} = \frac{2}{3} \cdot \frac{6}{5} = \frac{12}{15} = \frac{4}{5}$

22. **Converting Fractions to Decimals:** If the fraction already has a denominator that is 10, 100, 1,000, *etc.*, the conversion is easy. The numerator of the fraction becomes the decimal. The placement of the decimal point is governed by the number of zeros in the denominator.

    e.g., Express $\frac{127}{1,000}$ in decimal form.

    In the numerator, count three places to the left of the 7—one for each zero in 1,000: $\frac{127}{1,000} = 0.127$.

    If there are fewer numbers in the numerator than there are decimal places, add zeros to the left of the number until there are enough decimal places.

    e.g., $\frac{3}{100} = 0.03$

    To convert a proper fraction with a denominator other than 10, 100, etc., first convert the fraction to the equivalent form using a denominator such as 10, 100, *etc.* To determine which denominator to use, divide the denominator of the fraction into 10, then into 100, then into 1,000, until a denominator that is evenly divisible by the denominator of the original fraction is found.

    e.g., 1. $\frac{2}{5} = \frac{(2)(2)}{(5)(2)} = \frac{4}{10} = 0.4$

       2. $\frac{1}{4} = \frac{(1)(25)}{(4)(25)} = \frac{25}{100} = 0.25$

       3. $\frac{3}{8} = \frac{(3)(125)}{(8)(125)} = \frac{375}{1,000} = 0.375$

To convert proper fractions to decimals, dividing the denominator into the numerator is usually easier.

e.g., 1. $\frac{2}{5} = 5\overline{)2.0}^{0.4} = 0.4$

2. $\frac{3}{8} = 8\overline{)3.000}^{0.375} = 0.375$

To convert a mixed number into a decimal, convert the fractional part of the mixed number to a decimal as just discussed, and then place the whole number part of the mixed number to the left of the decimal point.

e.g., 1. $6\frac{1}{10} = 6.1$ (Convert $\frac{1}{10}$ to 0.1 and then place the 6 to the left of the decimal point.)

2. $3\frac{7}{8} = 3.875$ (Convert $\frac{7}{8}$ to 0.875 and then place the 3 to the left of the decimal point.)

To convert an improper fraction to a decimal, convert it to a mixed number and follow the procedure just outlined.

e.g., $\frac{9}{4} = 2\frac{1}{4} = 2.25$

23. **Converting Decimals to Fractions:** The numerator of the fraction is the digit(s) to the right of the decimal point. The denominator is a 1 followed by the same number of zeros as the number of decimal places to the right of the decimal point.

e.g., $0.005 = \frac{5}{1,000} = \frac{1}{200}$ (0.005 has three decimal places, so the new denominator is 1 followed by 3 zeros.)

If a decimal has numbers to both the right and left of the decimal point, the conversion to a fraction results in a mixed number. The whole part of the mixed number is the whole part of the decimal.

e.g., 1. $1.75 = 1$ plus $\frac{75}{100} = 1$ plus $\frac{3}{4} = 1\frac{3}{4}$

2. $357.125 = 357$ plus $\frac{125}{1,000} = 357$ plus $\frac{1}{8} = 357\frac{1}{8}$

Memorize these decimal equivalents:

$\frac{1}{2} = 0.5 \qquad \frac{1}{3} = 0.3\overline{3} \qquad \frac{1}{4} = 0.25 \qquad \frac{1}{5} = 0.20$

$\frac{1}{6} = 0.166\overline{6} \qquad \frac{1}{7} = 0.\overline{142857} \qquad \frac{1}{8} = 0.125 \qquad \frac{1}{9} = 0.1\overline{1}$

Note: A bar over a digit or digits indicates that the digit or group of digits repeats.

24. **Adding and Subtracting Decimals:** To add or subtract decimals, line up the decimal points, fill in the appropriate number of zeros, and then add or subtract.

e.g., $0.25 + 0.1 + 0.825 = $

$$
\begin{array}{r}
0.25 \\
0.1 \\
+\ 0.825 \\
\hline
= 0.250 \\
0.100 \\
+\ 0.825 \\
\hline
1.175
\end{array}
$$

25. **Multiplying Decimals:** To multiply decimals, first multiply as with whole numbers and then adjust the decimal point. Count the total number of decimal places in the numbers being multiplied, count that many places to the left from the right of the final number in the product, and put the decimal point there.

e.g., 1. $(0.1)(0.2)(0.3) = 0.006$ ($1 \cdot 2 \cdot 3 = 6$, and there are three decimal places in the multiplication.)

2. $(0.10)(0.10)(0.10) = 0.001000 = 0.001$ ($10 \cdot 10 \cdot 10 = 1,000$, and there are six decimal places in the problem.)

26. **Dividing Decimals:** When the divisor is a whole number, place a decimal point in the quotient immediately above the decimal point in the dividend. Keep dividing until there is no remainder, adding zeros as needed to the right of the divisor.

e.g., $2.5 \div 2 = 2\overline{)2.50}$

$$
\begin{array}{r}
1.25 \\
2\,\overline{)2.50} \\
-2 \\
\hline
0\,5 \\
-4 \\
\hline
10 \\
-10 \\
\hline
0
\end{array}
$$

When the divisor is a *decimal,* "clear" the fractional part of the decimal by moving both the divisor and dividend decimal points the same number of spaces to the right.

e.g., $5 \div 2.5 = 2.5\overline{)50.}$

$$
\begin{array}{r}
2. \\
2.5\,\overline{)50.} \\
-5\,0 \\
\hline
0
\end{array}
$$

27. **Ratios:** A *ratio* is a statement about the relationship between two quantities. The ratio of two quantities, x and y, can be expressed as $x \div y$, x/y, or $x{:}y$.

e.g., 1. $\frac{2}{5} = 2{:}5$

2. $\frac{boys}{girls} = $ boys:girls = ratio of boys to girls

3. $\frac{miles}{hour} = $ miles:hour = miles/hour = miles per hour

28. **Proportions:** A *proportion* is a statement of equality between two ratios.

e.g., $\frac{3}{4} = \frac{9}{12}$

With *direct variation,* ratios are directly related: The more of one quantity, the more of the other, and vice versa.

e.g., If 12 donuts cost \$3.60, how much do 4 donuts cost?

$\frac{\text{Total Cost for } X}{\text{Total Cost for } Y} = \frac{X}{Y} \Rightarrow \frac{\$3.60}{Y} = \frac{12}{4} \Rightarrow \$3.60(4) = 12Y$

$Y = 3.60(4) \div 12 = \$1.20$

With *inverse variation,* ratios are inversely related: An increase in one quantity is a decrease in the other. Use this method to solve inverse variation problems: first, set up an ordinary proportion, making sure that you group like quantities; then, take the reciprocal of the proportion's right side; and finally, cross-multiply and solve for the unknown.

e.g., Traveling at a constant rate of 150 m.p.h., a plane makes the trip from City P to City Q in four hours. How long will the trip take if the plane flies at a constant rate of 200 m.p.h.?

$$\frac{\text{Speed } X}{\text{Speed } Y} = \frac{\text{Time } X}{\text{Time } Y} \Rightarrow \frac{150 \text{ mph}}{200 \text{ mph}} = \frac{4 \text{ hours}}{Y \text{ hours}} \Rightarrow \frac{150}{200} = \frac{Y}{4}$$
$$Y = 4(150) \div 200 = 3 \text{ hours}$$

29. **Percentage Conversions:** *To change any decimal to a percent*, move the decimal point two places to the right and add a percent sign. To change a percent to a decimal, reverse the process.

   e.g., 1. $0.275 = 27.5\%$
   2. $0.03 = 3\%$
   3. $0.02\% = 0.0002$
   4. $120\% = 1.20$

   To convert a fraction to a percent, first convert the fraction to a decimal. Reverse the process for converting percents to fractions.

   e.g., 1. $\frac{3}{4} = 0.75 = 75\% = 0.75 = \frac{75}{100} = \frac{3}{4}$
   2. $\frac{5}{8} = 0.625 = 62.5\% = 0.625 = \frac{625}{1,000} = \frac{5}{8}$

30. **Common Percent Problems:** All percent problems have the same three components: *is*, *of*, and *%*. Depending on the form of the question, one of these three components is the unknown variable.

   "What is x% of that?"
   "This is what percent of that?"
   "This is x% of what?"

   Percentage problems can be solved using several different methods. Two methods are outlined below.

   Method 1: Write the statement as an equation, rewrite the percent as $\frac{\%}{100}$, and solve for the unknown.

   e.g., 5 is 20% of what number?
   $5 = \frac{20x}{100} \Rightarrow x = \frac{(5)(100)}{20} = 25$. Thus, 5 is 20% of 25.

   Method 2: Since there are three parts to all percent problems (*is*, *of*, and *%*), use the following equation to solve for the unknown: $\frac{is}{of} = \frac{\%}{100}$.

   e.g., 1. 20 is what percent of 50?
   $\% = x$, $is = 20$, $of = 50$
   $\frac{is}{of} = \frac{\%}{100} \Rightarrow \frac{20}{50} = \frac{x}{100} \Rightarrow \frac{(20)(100)}{50} = 40\%$

   2. What number is 20% of 25?
   $\% = 20$, $is = x$, $of = 25$
   $\frac{is}{of} = \frac{\%}{100} \Rightarrow \frac{x}{25} = \frac{20}{100} \Rightarrow x = \frac{(20)(25)}{(100)} = 5$

   Another common percent item is *change in price*.

   $$\% \text{ Price Change} = \frac{|\text{New Price} - \text{Old Price}|}{\text{Old Price}}$$

   The absolute value allows for price decreases as well.

e.g., An item's price is increased from \$20 to \$25. What is the percent increase in the price?
$\frac{|\text{New Price} - \text{Old Price}|}{\text{Old Price}} = \frac{25 - 20}{20} = \frac{5}{20} = \frac{1}{4} = 25\%$

31. **Averages:** To calculate an *average* (or mean), add together the quantities to be averaged; then divide that sum by the number of quantities added.

   e.g., The average of 3, 7, and 8 is 6: $3 + 7 + 8 = 18$ and $18 \div 3 = 6$.

   If solving for a *missing element* of an average, set up the average equation and solve for the unknown.

   e.g., The average score on four tests is 90. If three scores are 89, 92, and 94, what is the fourth score?
   $\frac{89 + 92 + 94 + x}{4} = 90 \Rightarrow x = 85$

   In *weighted averages*, greater weight is given to one element than to another.

   e.g., Four books cost \$6.00 each and two books cost \$3.00 each. What is the average cost of a book?
   $\frac{(4)(6) + (2)(3)}{4 + 2} = \frac{24 + 6}{6} = \frac{30}{6} = 5$

32. **Median:** The *median* is the middle value of a number set when arranged in ascending or descending order. The median of an even numbered set is the average of the two middle values, when the numbers are arranged in ascending or descending order.

   e.g., The median of $\{8, 6, 34, 5, 17, 23\}$ is: $\frac{8 + 17}{2} = 12.5$.

33. **Mode:** The value that appears most frequently in a set of numbers is the *mode*.

   e.g., The mode of 4, 5, 3, 4, 5, 1, 2, 3, 6, 4, and 6, is 4.

34. **Counting Principle:** To determine the number of ways that particular events can occur, multiply the number of ways that each event can occur.

   e.g., 1. How many ways can you select one boy and one girl from a class of 15 girls and 13 boys?
   $(15)(13) = 195$ ways

   2. In how many ways can 5 students sit in a row with 5 chairs?
   $(5)(4)(3)(2)(1) = 120$ ways

   3. In how many ways can you fill three chairs given five students?
   $(5)(4)(3) = 60$ ways

35. **Probability Principle:** The probability that an event will happen can be found from the fraction $\frac{\text{winning events}}{\text{total events}}$ or $\frac{\text{favorable events}}{\text{total events}}$

e.g., From the set {−4, −3, −2, 0, 1, 6, 8, 1002}, a number is selected at random. Find the probability that the selected number is an even integer.

There are 6 even integers (−4, −2, 0, 6, 8, 1002) out of a total of 8 integers, so the probability is: $\frac{6}{8} = \frac{3}{4}$.

Algebra Summary

1. Basic Operations:

Addition: $n + n = 2n$
$n + m = n + m$

Subtraction: $3n - 2n = n$
$n - m = n - m$

Multiplication: n times $m = (n)(m) = nm$
$(n)(0) = 0$

Division: n divided by $m = n \div m = \frac{n}{m}$
$n \div 0 = $ undefined

2. Powers: A *power* of a number indicates repeated multiplication.

e.g., 3 raised to the fifth power is $(3)(3)(3)(3)(3) = 243$.

3. Exponents: An *exponent* is a number that indicates the operation of repeated multiplication. Exponents are notated as superscripts. The number being multiplied is the *base*.

e.g., 1. $2^3 = (2)(2)(2) = 8$
2. $5^4 = (5)(5)(5)(5) = 625$

Exponent Rules:

1. $x^m \cdot x^n = x^{m+n}$
2. $x^m \div x^n = x^{m-n}$
3. $(x^m)^n = x^{mn}$
4. $(xy)^m = x^m y^m$
5. $\left(\frac{x}{y}\right)^m = \frac{x^m}{y^m}$
6. $x^1 = x$, for any number x
7. $x^0 = 1$, for any number x, such that $x \neq 0$
8. 0^0 is undefined.

e.g., 1. $(2^3)(2^2) = (2 \cdot 2 \cdot 2)(2 \cdot 2) = 2^{3+2} = 2^5$
$(3^2)(3^3)(3^5) = 3^{2+3+5} = 3^{10}$
2. $2^4 \div 2^2 = \frac{(2)(2)(2)(2)}{(2)(2)} = 2^{4-2} = 2^2$

$5^3 \div 5^5 = 5^{3-5} = 5^{-2} = \left(\frac{1}{5}\right)^2 = \frac{1}{25}$
3. $(2^2)^3 = (2 \cdot 2)^3 = (2 \cdot 2)(2 \cdot 2)(2 \cdot 2) = 2^{2 \cdot 3} = 2^6$
4. $(2 \cdot 3)^2 = (2 \cdot 3)(2 \cdot 3) = (2 \cdot 2)(3 \cdot 3) = 2^2 \cdot 3^2$
$= 4 \cdot 9 = 36$
$(2^3 \cdot 3^2)^2 = 2^{3 \cdot 2} \cdot 3^{2 \cdot 2} = 2^6 \cdot 3^4$
5. $\left(\frac{2}{3}\right)^2 = \frac{2^2}{3^2} = \frac{4}{9}$

$\left(\frac{3^3 \cdot 5^5}{3^2 \cdot 5^2}\right)^2 = (3^{3-2} \cdot 5^{5-2})^2 = (3^1 \cdot 5^3)^2 = (3^2)(5^6)$

A negative exponent signifies a fraction, indicating the *reciprocal* of the base.

e.g., 1. $x^{-1} = \frac{1}{x}$
2. $2x^{-1} = 2\left(\frac{1}{x}\right) = \frac{2}{x}$
3. $4^{-2} = \left(\frac{1}{4}\right)^2 = \frac{1}{16}$

4. Roots: The *root* of a number is a number that is multiplied a specified number of times to give the original number. Square root $= m^{1/2} = \sqrt{m}$. Cube root $= m^{1/3} = \sqrt[3]{m}$.

e.g., 1. $\sqrt{4} = 4^{1/2} = 2$
2. $\sqrt[3]{8} = 8^{1/3} = 2$
3. $\sqrt{125} = 125^{1/2} = (25 \cdot 5)^{1/2} = (25^{1/2})(5^{1/2}) = (\sqrt{25})(\sqrt{5}) = 5\sqrt{5}$
4. $\sqrt{\frac{4}{9}} = \left(\frac{4}{9}\right)^{1/2} = \frac{4^{1/2}}{9^{1/2}} = \frac{\sqrt{4}}{\sqrt{9}} = \frac{2}{3}$

5. Basic Algebraic Operations: Algebraic operations are the same as for arithmetic, with the addition of unknown quantities. Manipulate operations in the same way, combining (adding and subtracting) only like terms. Like terms have the same variables with the same exponents.

e.g., 1. $x^2 - 3x + 5x - 3x^2 = -2x^2 + 2x$
2. $(x^2)(x^3) = x^{2+3} = x^5$
3. $4x^3 y^4 \div 2xy^3 = 2x^2 y$
4. $\frac{5}{x} + \frac{3}{x} = \frac{5+3}{x} = \frac{8}{x}$
5. $\left(\frac{x^2 y^3}{z}\right)\left(\frac{x^3 y^2}{wz}\right) = \frac{x^5 y^5}{wz^2}$

6. Multiplying Polynomials: A *polynomial* is an algebraic expression with more than one term. A binomial is a polynomial consisting of exactly two terms. When multiplying two binomials, use the *FOIL* (*F*irst, *O*uter, *I*nner, *L*ast) *method*:

$(x + y)(x + y) = ?$
Multiply the *first* terms: $x \cdot x = x^2$
Multiply the *outer* terms: $x \cdot y = xy$
Multiply the *inner* terms: $y \cdot x = yx = xy$
Multiply the *last* terms: $y \cdot y = y^2$
Combine like terms: $(x + y)(x + y) = x^2 + 2xy + y^2$

e.g., $(x - y)(x - y) = ?$
First: $(x)(x) = x^2$
Outer: $(x)(-y) = -xy$
Inner: $(-y)(x) = -xy$
Last: $(-y)(-y) = y^2$
Combine: $x^2 - xy - xy + y^2 = x^2 - 2xy + y^2$

If the two polynomials are not binomials, do the following:

e.g., $(x+y)(x^2+2xy+y^2)$
$= x(x^2) + x(2xy) + x(y^2) + y(x^2) + y(2xy) + y(y^2)$
$= x^3 + 2x^2y + xy^2 + x^2y + 21xy^2 + y^3$
$= x^3 + 3x^2y + 3xy^2 + y^3$

Memorize these common patterns:
$(x+y)^2 = (x+y)(x+y) = x^2 + 2xy + y^2$
$(x-y)^2 = (x-y)(x-y) = x^2 - 2xy + y^2$
$(x+y)(x-y) = x^2 - y^2$

7. **Factoring:** *Factoring* is the reverse of multiplication. There are three factoring situations.

a. If all of the terms in an expression contain a common factor, then it can be factored out of each term. Do this first, if possible.

e.g., 1. $ab + ac + ad = a(b + c + d)$
2. $x^2 + x^3 + x^4 = x^2(1 + x + x^2)$
3. $3xy + xz + 4x = x(3y + z + 4)$

b. Algebraic expressions are often one of three common patterns.

e.g., 1. $x^2 + 2xy + y^2 = (x+y)(x+y) = (x+y)^2$
2. $x^2 - 2xy + y^2 = (x-y)(x-y) = (x-y)^2$
3. $x^2 - y^2 = (x-y)(x+y)$

c. Occasionally, expressions do not fall into one of the two categories above. To factor the expression, which is usually in the form $ax^2 + bx + c$, set up the following blank diagram: ( )( ). Fill in the diagram by answering the following questions:

- What factors produce the first term, ax^2?
- What factors produce the last term, c?
- Which of the possible factors, when added together, produce the middle term, bx?

e.g., 1. $x^2 + 3x + 2 = (x+2)(x+1)$
2. $x^2 + 4x - 12 = (x+6)(x-2)$

8. **Solving Linear Equations:** An equation that contains variables only of the first power is a linear equation. You can add, subtract, multiply, and divide both sides of an equation by the same value without changing the statement of equality. (You cannot multiply or divide by zero.) To find the value of a variable, isolate the variable on one side of the equation and solve.

e.g., 1. $4x + 2 = 2x + 10$
$4x + 2 - 2x = 2x + 10 - 2x$
$2x + 2 = 10$
$2x + 2 - 2 = 10 - 2$
$2x = 8$
$\frac{2x}{2} = \frac{8}{2}$
$x = 4$

2. $\frac{2x+6}{2} = 9$
$x = \frac{9(2)-6}{2} = 6$

9. **Solving Quadratic Equations:** Equations that involve variables of the second power are called quadratic equations and may have zero, one, or two real solutions.

a. If possible, take the square root of both sides.

e.g., $x^2 = 25 \Rightarrow x = \pm 5$

b. Otherwise, arrange all terms on the left side of equation so that the right side of equation is zero: $ax^2 + bx + c = 0$. Factor the left side of the equation and set each binomial equal to zero. Solve for the unknown.

e.g., 1. Solve for x: $x^2 - 2x = 3$.
$x^2 - 2x - 3 = 0 \Rightarrow (x-3)(x+1) = 0$
$x = 3$ or $x = -1$

2. Solve for x: $x^2 - 3x = 4$.
$x^2 - 3x - 4 = 0 \Rightarrow (x-4)(x+1) = 0$
$x = 4$ or $x = -1$

c. The quadratic formula, $x = \frac{-b \pm \sqrt{b^2 - 4ac}}{2a}$, may also be used to solve quadratic equations.

e.g., Solve for x: $3 - x = 2x^2$.
$3 - x = 2x^2 \Rightarrow 2x^2 + x - 3 = 0$
$a = 2; b = 1; c = -3$.
$x = \frac{-b \pm \sqrt{b^2 - 4ac}}{2a} = \frac{-1 \pm \sqrt{1^2 - 4(2)(-3)}}{2(2)} = \frac{-1 \pm \sqrt{1 + 24}}{4}$
$= \frac{-1 \pm 5}{4} = 1$ or $-\frac{3}{2}$

d. The SAT and PSAT allow calculators. A graphing calculator may be used to quickly solve quadratic equations if it has a quadratic formula program.

10. **Solving Simultaneous Equations:** Given two equations with two variables, the equations may be solved simultaneously for the values of the two variables. There are several methods for solving simultaneous equations.

Method 1—Substitution: Solve one equation for one variable and substitute this into the other equation to find the other variable. Plug back into the first equation.

e.g., If $2x - y = 6$ and $3x + 2y = 16$, solve for x and y.

Solve for y: $2x - y = 6$
$$y = 6 - 2x = 2x - 6$$

Substitute: $3x + 2y = 16$
$$3x + 2(2x - 6) = 16$$
$$3x + 4x - 12 = 16$$
$$7x = 28$$
$$x = 4$$

Substitute: $y = 2x - 6 = 2(4) - 6 = 2$

Method 2—Elimination: Make the coefficients of one variable equal and then add (or subtract) the two equations to eliminate one variable.

e.g., If $2x - y = 6$ and $3x + 2y = 16$, solve for x and y.

Combine: $2[2x - y = 6]$
$$\underline{+ \ 3x + 2y = 16}$$
$$7x = 28 \Rightarrow x = 4$$

Substitute: $2x - y = 6$
$$2(4) - y = 6$$
$$y = 2$$

Method 3—Graphing Calculator: The SAT and PSAT allow calculators: a graphing calculator may be used to quickly solve simultaneous equations. In each equation, solve for y in terms of x. Graph both equations simultaneously; the point of intersection, (x, y), is the solution. Some calculators may have a built-in program to solve simultaneous equations.

e.g., If $2x - y = 6$ and $3x + 2y = 16$, solve for x and y.

Solve each equation for y as a function of x.

$$2x - y = 6$$
$$-y = 6 - 2x$$
$$y = \frac{(6 - 2x)}{-1}$$
$$3x + 2y = 16$$
$$2y = 16 - 3x$$
$$y = \frac{(16 - 3x)}{2}$$

Graph both equations for y—the intersection is found at $(4, 2)$.

Method 4—Calculator System Solver Program: A graphing calculator with a system solver program may also be used to solve simultaneous equations. Graphing the equations to find the point of intersection is not necessary using a system solver program.

11. Inequalities: The fundamental rule for working with inequalities is similar to that for working with equalities. The same value may be added or subtracted to each side of an inequality without changing the inequality. Each side may be multiplied or divided by the same *positive* value without changing the direction of the inequality.

e.g.,
1. $5 > 2$
   $$5 + 25 > 2 + 25$$
   $$30 > 27$$

2. $24 > 20$
   $$24(2) > 20(2)$$
   $$48 > 40$$

3. $24 > 20$
   $$24 \div 4 > 20 \div 4$$
   $$6 > 5$$

To multiply or divide by a *negative* number, reverse the direction of the inequality.

e.g.,
1. $4 > 2$
   $$4(-2) < 2(-2)$$
   $$-8 < -4$$

2. $4 > 2$
   $$4 \div (-2) < 2 \div (-2)$$
   $$-2 < -1$$

12. Slope: The *slope*, m, of a line describes its steepness. It is defined as the change in y-values divided by the change in x-values, or rise over run.

$$m = \frac{\Delta y}{\Delta x} = \frac{y_2 - y_1}{x_2 - x_1} = \frac{\text{rise}}{\text{run}}$$

e.g., The slope of the line that contains points $(-3, 5)$ and $(2, 7)$ is: $m = \frac{y_2 - y_1}{x_2 - x_1} = \frac{7 - 5}{2 - (-3)} = \frac{2}{5}$.

13. Linear Equations:

Slope-Intercept Form: $y = mx + b$; $m = \text{slope} = \frac{\Delta y}{\Delta x} = \frac{y_2 - y_1}{x_2 - x_1}$

Point-Slope Form: $y - y_1 = m(x - x_1)$

Standard Form: $Ax + By = C$; $m = -\frac{A}{B}$

14. Distance Formula: The distance between two points can be found using the *distance formula*:

$$d = \sqrt{(x_2 - x_1)^2 + (y_2 - y_1)^2}$$

where (x_1, y_1) and (x_2, y_2) are the given points.

e.g., The distance between $(-1, 4)$ and $(7, 3)$ is equal to:
$$d = \sqrt{(7 - (-1))^2 + (3 - 4)^2} = \sqrt{64 + 1} = \sqrt{65}.$$

15. **Midpoint Formula:** The midpoint between two points, (x_1, y_1) and (x_2, y_2), is found using the *midpoint formula*:

$$\text{midpoint} = \left(\frac{x_1 + x_2}{2}, \frac{y_1 + y_2}{2}\right)$$

e.g., The midpoint between points $(-3, 6)$ and $(4, -9)$ is:

$$\left(\frac{x_1 + x_2}{2}, \frac{y_1 + y_2}{2}\right) = \left(\frac{-3 + 4}{2}, \frac{6 + -9}{2}\right) = \left(\frac{1}{2}, -\frac{3}{2}\right).$$

16. **Functions:** A function is a set of ordered pairs (x, y) such that for each value of x, there is exactly one value of y. The set of x-values for which the set is defined is called the domain of the function. The set of corresponding values of y is called the range of the function.

e.g., What is the domain and range for $f(x) = x^2$?

f represents the function. x represents values in the domain of the function. $f(x)$ represents values in the range of the function. Since x can be any real number, the domain is the set of all real numbers. We square the value of x to obtain $f(x)$. Squaring any real number yields a number of zero or more. Thus, the range is the set of all non-negative numbers.

Common Equations Summary

1. **Distance:** $Distance = (Rate)(Time)$. Given two of the three values, any unknown may be solved for by rearranging the equation.

   e.g., After driving constantly for four hours, Olivia reached her destination—200 miles from where she started. What was her average rate of travel?

   Distance = (Rate)(Time)

   $Rate = \frac{Distance}{Time} = \frac{200 \text{ miles}}{4 \text{ hours}} = 50 \text{ mph}$

2. **Simple Interest:** $I_s = Prt$, where P is the principal, r is the rate, and t is the time period.

   e.g., With a principal of $1,200 and a rate of 10% per year, what was the interest earned over one month?

   $I_s = Prt = (\$1,200)\left(\frac{0.10}{\text{year}}\right)\left(\frac{1 \text{ year}}{12 \text{ months}}\right) = \$10$

3. **Compound Interest:** $I_c = P(1 + r)^n - P$, where P is the principal, r is the rate, and n is the number of periods.

   e.g., With a principal of $1,000 and a compound interest rate of 15% per year, how much compound interest was earned over 5 years?

   $I_c = P(1 + r)^n - P$
   $= (\$1,000)(1 + 0.15)^5 - (\$1,000)$
   $\approx \$2,011 - \$1,000 = \$1,011$

4. **Combined Work Rates:** $Rate_1 + Rate_2 = Rate_3$

   e.g., Machine I washes four loads in 60 minutes and Machine II washes one load in 30 minutes. How many loads will both machines working together wash in 20 minutes?

   $\frac{x \text{ loads}}{20 \text{ min.}} = \frac{4 \text{ loads}}{60 \text{ min.}} + \frac{1 \text{ load}}{30 \text{ min.}} = \frac{4 \text{ loads}}{60 \text{ min.}} + \frac{2 \text{ loads}}{60 \text{ min.}}$

   $x = 20\left(\frac{4}{60} + \frac{2}{60}\right) = \frac{6(20)}{60} = 2 \text{ loads}$

5. **Mixed Denominations:** When an item gives information that involves *mixed denominations* (*e.g.*, different prices for same item, tickets, colors, *etc.*), set up simultaneous equations and solve the system of equations for the desired unknown quantity.

   e.g., The store sold apples for $0.20 and oranges for $0.50 each. A total of 50 apples and oranges were bought for $19. How many apples and how many oranges were bought?

   $x = \text{\# of apples}; y = \text{\# of oranges}$
   $x + y = 50 \Rightarrow x = 50 - y$

   $(0.20)x + (0.50)y = 19$
   $0.2(50 - y) + 0.5y = 19$
   $10 - 0.2y + 0.5y = 19$
   $0.3y = 9$
   $y = 30 \text{ oranges}$
   $x = 50 - y = 50 - 30 = 20 \text{ apples}$

6. **Mixture of Concentrations or Values:** A *mixture item* is one in which two quantities of different items with different concentrations or values are mixed together and a new quantity (the sum of the two) and concentration or value are created.

   $$Q_1C_1 + Q_2C_2 = (Q_1 + Q_2)C_3$$

   e.g., How many liters of a juice that is 10% orange juice must be added to three liters of another juice that is 15% orange juice to produce a mixture that is 12% orange juice?

   $Q_1C_1 + Q_2C_2 = (Q_1 + Q_2)C_3$
   $Q(0.10) + (3)(0.15) = (Q + 3)(0.12)$
   $0.1Q + 0.45 = 0.12Q + 0.36$
   $0.45 - 0.36 = 0.12Q - 0.1Q$
   $0.09 = 0.02Q$
   $Q = 4.5$

7. **Markup, Cost, and Revenue:** $R = (1 + M)C$, where R is the revenue, M is the markup, and C is the cost.

   e.g., The revenue from an item is $120. With a markup in cost of 25%, what is the original cost?

   $C = \frac{R}{1 + M} = \frac{120}{1 + 0.25} = \$96$

Geometry Summary

1. Lines and Angles:

a. Symbols:

$\overline{AB}$: line segment with endpoints A and B
$\overrightarrow{AB}$: infinite ray from A through B
$\overleftrightarrow{AB}$: infinite line through A and B
$l_1 \parallel l_2$: parallel lines
$\perp$: perpendicular
$\square$: right angle

b. Facts About Lines and Angles:

Vertical angles are equal:

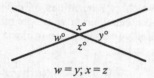

$$w = y;\ x = z$$

Two extended lines that do not intersect regardless of length are *parallel* to each other:

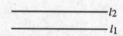

Parallel lines intersected by a third line, the transversal, create the following angles:

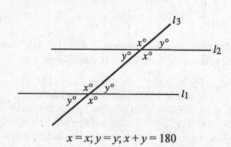

$$x = x;\ y = y;\ x + y = 180$$

Two lines *perpendicular* to the same line are parallel to each other:

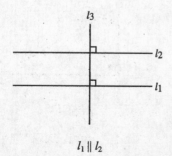

$$l_1 \parallel l_2$$

There are 180° in a *straight line*:

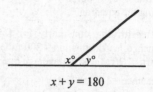

$$x + y = 180$$

There are 90° in a *right angle* and two right angles form a straight line:

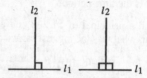

An angle less than 90° is an *acute angle*. In the following figure, $\angle PQR$ is an acute angle:

An angle greater than 90° is an *obtuse angle*. In the following figure, $\angle PQR$ is an obtuse angle:

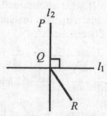

2. Polygons: A *polygon* is a closed figure created by three or more lines. The sum of the interior angles of any polygon is $180(n - 2)$, where n = the number of sides of the polygon. The sum of the measures of the exterior angles of a polygon is 360° for all polygons.

A *triangle* is any polygon with exactly three sides.

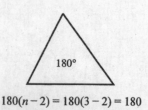

$$180(n - 2) = 180(3 - 2) = 180$$

A *quadrilateral* is any polygon with exactly four sides. Opposite sides of a *parallelogram* are equal and parallel.

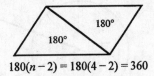

$$180(n-2) = 180(4-2) = 360$$

A *pentagon* is any polygon with exactly five sides.

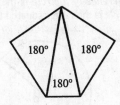

$$180(n-2) = 180(5-2) = 540$$

A *hexagon* is any polygon with exactly six sides.

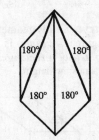

$$180(n-2) = 180(6-2) = 720$$

3. **Triangles:** A *triangle* is a 3-sided figure. Within a given triangle, the larger the angle, the longer the opposite side; conversely, the longer the side, the larger the opposite angle.

A triangle with two equal sides is an *isosceles* triangle. A triangle with three equal sides is an *equilateral* triangle.

Within a given triangle, if two sides are equal, their opposite angles are equal, and vice versa:

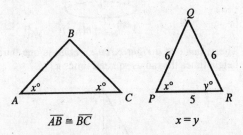

$$\overline{AB} \cong \overline{BC} \qquad\qquad x = y$$

The sides of every right triangle follow the *Pythagorean theorem*: the square of the hypotenuse is equal to the sum of the squares of the other two sides.

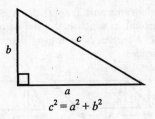

$$c^2 = a^2 + b^2$$

The *perimeter of a triangle* is the sum of the lengths of the three sides:

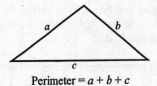

$$\text{Perimeter} = a + b + c$$

The *area of a triangle* is one-half times the base times the height:

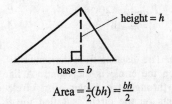

$$\text{Area} = \frac{1}{2}(bh) = \frac{bh}{2}$$

In a *45°-45°-90° triangle*, the length of the hypotenuse is equal to the length of either side multiplied by the square root of two:

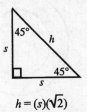

$$h = (s)(\sqrt{2})$$

In a *30°-60°-90° triangle*, the length of the side opposite the 30° angle is equal to one-half the length of the hypotenuse and the length of the side opposite the 60° angle is equal to one-half the length of the hypotenuse multiplied by $\sqrt{3}$:

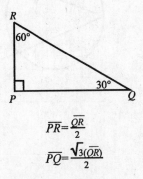

$$\overline{PR} = \frac{\overline{QR}}{2}$$

$$\overline{PQ} = \frac{\sqrt{3}(\overline{QR})}{2}$$

4. **Parallelograms and Trapezoids:** A *parallelogram* is a quadrilateral in which both pairs of opposite sides are parallel. A *trapezoid* is a quadrilateral with only two parallel sides.

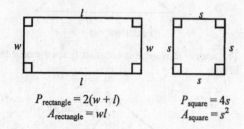

$$A_{\text{parallelogram}} = bh$$

$$A_{\text{trapezoid}} = \frac{h(b_1 + b_2)}{2}$$

5. **Rectangles and Squares:** A *rectangle* is any four-sided figure that has four right angles. A *square* is a rectangle with four equal sides:

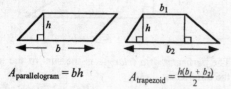

$$P_{\text{rectangle}} = 2(w + l) \qquad P_{\text{square}} = 4s$$
$$A_{\text{rectangle}} = wl \qquad A_{\text{square}} = s^2$$

6. **Circles:** The distance from the center of a circle to any point on the circle is the *radius*. A line segment that passes through the center of a circle and that has endpoints on the circle is called the *diameter*. The diameter of a circle is twice the radius. There are 360° of *arc* in a circle:

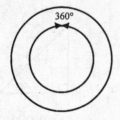

An angle inscribed in a circle intercepts an arc that is twice its measure:

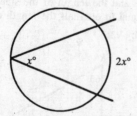

An angle whose vertex is at the center of a circle intercepts an arc of the same measure:

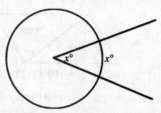

The *circumference of a circle* is the radius times 2π. The *area of a circle* is the radius squared times π.

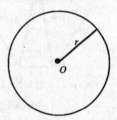

$$C_{\text{circle}} = 2\pi r; \; A_{\text{circle}} = \pi r^2$$

7. **Solid Geometry:** Solid geometry refers to three-dimensional figures. *Volume* is a three-dimensional quantity. The *volume of a rectangular solid* is the length times the width times the height:

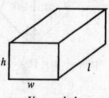

$$V_{\text{solid}} = lwh$$

The *volume of a cylinder* is the height times the radius squared times π.

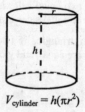

$$V_{\text{cylinder}} = h(\pi r^2)$$

The *volume of a right circular cone* is one-third of the height times the radius squared times π.

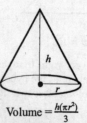

$$\text{Volume} = \frac{h(\pi r^2)}{3}$$

The *surface area of a sphere* is four times π times the radius squared. The *volume of a sphere* is four-thirds times π times the radius cubed.

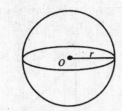

$$A_{\text{sphere surface}} = 4\pi r^2; \quad V_{\text{sphere}} = \frac{4\pi r^3}{3}$$

Trigonometry Summary

1. **Basic Trigonometric Functions:** The three basic trigonometric functions are sine, cosine, and tangent. The functions can be viewed in relationship to a right triangle.

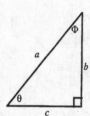

The *hypotenuse* is the side opposite the right angle. The *side opposite* is the side opposite the referenced angle. The *side adjacent* is the side next to the referenced angle, but not the hypotenuse.

Memorize these trigonometric definitions:

sine: $\sin \theta = \dfrac{\text{side Opposite } \angle\theta}{\text{Hypotenuse}} = \dfrac{b}{a}$

cosine: $\cos \theta = \dfrac{\text{side Adjacent } \angle\theta}{\text{Hypotenuse}} = \dfrac{c}{a}$

tangent: $\tan \theta = \dfrac{\text{side Opposite } \angle\theta}{\text{side Adjacent } \angle\theta} = \dfrac{b}{c}$

cosecant: $\csc \theta = \dfrac{1}{\sin \theta} = \dfrac{\text{Hypotenuse}}{\text{side Opposite } \angle\theta} = \dfrac{a}{b}$

secant: $\sec \theta = \dfrac{1}{\cos \theta} = \dfrac{\text{Hypotenuse}}{\text{side Adjacent } \angle\theta} = \dfrac{a}{c}$

cotangent: $\cot \theta = \dfrac{1}{\tan \theta} = \dfrac{\text{side Adjacent } \angle\theta}{\text{side Opposite } \angle\theta} = \dfrac{c}{b}$

SOH-CAH-TOA can be used to memorize the sine, cosine, and tangent ratios.

e.g., Find the values of sin A, cos A, tan A, csc A, sec A, cot A, sin C, cos C, tan C, csc C, sec C, and cot C in the triangle below.

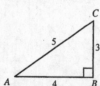

$\sin A = \dfrac{\text{side opp. } \angle A}{\text{hyp.}} = \dfrac{3}{5}$, $\sin C = \dfrac{\text{side opp. } \angle C}{\text{hyp.}} = \dfrac{4}{5}$

$\cos A = \dfrac{\text{side adj. } \angle A}{\text{hyp.}} = \dfrac{4}{5}$, $\cos C = \dfrac{\text{side adj. } \angle C}{\text{hyp.}} = \dfrac{3}{5}$

$\tan A = \dfrac{\text{side opp. } \angle A}{\text{side adj. } \angle A} = \dfrac{3}{4}$, $\tan C = \dfrac{\text{side opp. } \angle C}{\text{side adj. } \angle C} = \dfrac{4}{3}$

$\csc A = \dfrac{\text{hyp.}}{\text{side opp. } \angle A} = \dfrac{5}{3}$, $\csc C = \dfrac{\text{hyp.}}{\text{side opp. } \angle C} = \dfrac{5}{4}$

$\sec A = \dfrac{\text{hyp.}}{\text{side adj. } \angle A} = \dfrac{5}{4}$, $\sec C = \dfrac{\text{hyp.}}{\text{side adj. } \angle C} = \dfrac{5}{3}$

$\cot A = \dfrac{\text{side adj. } \angle A}{\text{side opp. } \angle A} = \dfrac{4}{3}$, $\cot C = \dfrac{\text{side adj. } \angle C}{\text{side opp. } \angle C} = \dfrac{3}{4}$

e.g., In the right triangle below, sin $x = 0.75$. What is the length of $\overline{AC}$?

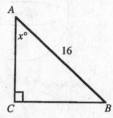

$\sin x = \dfrac{\text{side opposite } \angle x}{\text{hypotenuse}} \Rightarrow \dfrac{3}{4} = \dfrac{\overline{BC}}{16} \Rightarrow \overline{BC} = \dfrac{3(16)}{4} = 12$.

Therefore, using the Pythagorean theorem: $(\overline{AB})^2 = (\overline{AC})^2 + (\overline{BC})^2 \Rightarrow 16^2 = (\overline{AC})^2 + 12^2 \Rightarrow (\overline{AC})^2 = 256 - 144 = 112 \Rightarrow \overline{AC} = \sqrt{112} = \sqrt{16(7)} = 4\sqrt{7}$.

2. **Useful Trigonometric Relationships:**

$\sin x = \dfrac{1}{\csc x}$, $\cos x = \dfrac{1}{\sec x}$, $\tan x = \dfrac{1}{\cot x}$, $\tan x = \dfrac{\sin x}{\cos x}$,

$\sin^2 x + \cos^2 x = 1$; $1 + \cot^2 x = \csc^2 x$; $\tan^2 x + 1 = \sec^2 x$

Note: $\sin^2 x$ is the equivalent of $(\sin x)^2$.

e.g., If $\sin x = \dfrac{3}{5}$ and $\cos x = \dfrac{4}{5}$, what is the value of tan x, csc x, sec x, and cot x?

$\tan x = \dfrac{\sin x}{\cos x} = \dfrac{\frac{3}{5}}{\frac{4}{5}} = \dfrac{3}{4}$, $\csc x = \dfrac{1}{\sin x} = \dfrac{1}{\frac{3}{5}} = \dfrac{5}{3}$

$\sec x = \dfrac{1}{\cos x} = \dfrac{1}{\frac{4}{5}} = \dfrac{5}{4}$, $\cot x = \dfrac{1}{\tan x} = \dfrac{1}{\frac{3}{4}} = \dfrac{4}{3}$

e.g., If $\sin^2 x = \dfrac{1}{4}$, what is the value of $\cos^2 x$?

$\cos^2 x = 1 - \sin^2 x = 1 - \dfrac{1}{4} = \dfrac{3}{4}$.

3. **Graphing Using Trigonometry:** Frequently, trigonometry is used in graphing. Angles on a graph are customarily measured in a counterclockwise manner from the positive *x*-axis.

e.g., 1. In the figure below, the angle shown has a measure of 210°: 90° + 90° + 30° = 210°.

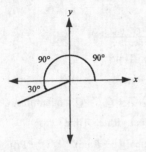

2. Without using a calculator, determine the values of cos 300° and sin 300°.

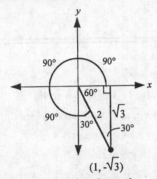

$(1, -\sqrt{3})$

Notice that after drawing the angle, we create a right triangle by drawing a perpendicular from the end of the angle to the *x*-axis. The hypotenuse of any such triangle is always considered to be positive. However, the point at the end of the original angle may not always have positive coordinates. You may make up any length desired for one side of the triangle. Then, use geometry or trigonometry with the angles inside the triangle to get the remaining lengths. In this example, we let the hypotenuse equal 2 and used geometry or trigonometry to get 1 and $\sqrt{3}$ as shown on the figure. Notice that the point at the end of our original 300° angle has a positive *x*-coordinate, 1, and a negative *y*-coordinate, $-\sqrt{3}$. We must use those signed values. The 300° angle leaves us 60° from the closer *x*-axis. Thus, cos 300° uses the 60° angle: cos 300° = $\frac{\text{side adj.}}{\text{hyp.}} = \frac{1}{2}$, and sin 300° = $\frac{\text{side opp.}}{\text{hyp.}} = -\frac{\sqrt{3}}{2}$.

ARITHMETIC, ALGEBRA, AND COORDINATE GEOMETRY FORMULAS

Averages: $A = \frac{x_1 + x_2 + x_3 + \ldots + x_n}{n}$; $x_1, x_2, x_3 \ldots x_n =$ values, $n =$ total numbers

Percentage Problems: $\frac{is}{of} = \frac{\%}{100}$

Price Percentage Change: $\Delta\% = \frac{|\text{New Price} - \text{Old Price}|}{\text{Old Price}}$

Distance Problems: Distance = Rate • Time

Combined Work Rate Problems: $\text{Rate}_3 = \text{Rate}_1 + \text{Rate}_2$

Mixture Problems: $(Q_1 + Q_2)C_3 = Q_1C_1 + Q_2C_2$; $Q =$ quantities, $C =$ concentrations

Simple Interest Problems: Interest = Principal • Rate • Time

Compound Interest Problems: Interest = $(\text{Principal})(1 + \text{Rate})^{\text{\# of periods}} -$ Principal

Revenue Problems: Revenue = $(1 + \text{Markup})(\text{Cost})$

Slope-Intercept Linear Equation: $y = mx + b$

Slope of a Line: $m = \frac{y_2 - y_1}{x_2 - x_1}$

GEOMETRY FORMULAS

Perimeter of a Square: $P_{\text{square}} = 4s$; $s =$ side

Perimeter of a Rectangle: $P_{\text{rectangle}} = 2l + 2w$; $l =$ length, $w =$ width

Perimeter of a Triangle: $P_{\text{triangle}} = a + b + c$; a, b, and c are the sides

Circumference of a Circle: $C_{\text{circle}} = 2\pi r$; $\pi \approx 3.14$, $r =$ radius

Area of a Square: $A_{\text{square}} = s^2$; $s =$ length of side

Area of a Rectangle: $A_{\text{rectangle}} = lw$; $l =$ length, $w =$ width

Area of Parallelogram: $A_{\text{parallelogram}} = bh$; $b =$ base, $h =$ height

Area of Trapezoid: $A_{\text{trapezoid}} = \frac{(b_1 + b_2)h}{2}$, $b =$ base, $h =$ height

Area of a Triangle: $A_{\text{triangle}} = \frac{bh}{2}$; $b =$ base, $h =$ height

Area of a Circle: $A_{\text{circle}} = \pi r^2$; $r =$ radius, $\pi \approx 3.14$

Volume of a Cube: $V_{\text{cube}} = s^3$; $s =$ side

Volume of a Rectangle Solid: $V_{\text{solid}} = lwh$; $l =$ length, $w =$ width, $h =$ height

Volume of a Cylinder: $V_{\text{cylinder}} = \pi r^2 h$; $h =$ height, $\pi \approx 3.14$, $r =$ radius

Volume of a Cone: $V_{\text{cone}} = \frac{\pi r^2 h}{3}$, $h =$ height, $\pi \approx 3.14$, $r =$ radius

Surface Area of a Sphere: $A_{\text{sphere surface}} = 4\pi r^2$; $\pi \approx 3.14$, $r =$ radius

Volume of a Sphere: $V_{\text{sphere}} = \frac{4\pi r^3}{3}$; $\pi \approx 3.14$, $r =$ radius

POLYGON FORMULAS

45°-45°-90° Triangle: $h = s\sqrt{2}$; $h =$ hypotenuse, $s =$ length of either leg

30°-60°-90° Triangle: $a = \frac{h}{2}$, $a =$ side opposite $\angle 30°$, $h =$ hypotenuse

$b = \frac{\sqrt{3}(h)}{2}$; $b =$ side opposite $\angle 60°$, $h =$ hypotenuse

Pythagorean Theorem (Right Triangles): $c^2 = a^2 + b^2$; $c =$ hypotenuse, a and $b =$ legs

Sum of Interior Angles of Polygon: $S = 180(n - 2)$; $n =$ number of sides of the polygon

TRIGONOMETRY FORMULAS

$\sin A = \frac{\text{opp}}{\text{hyp}}$ $\cos A = \frac{\text{adj}}{\text{hyp}}$ $\tan A = \frac{\text{opp}}{\text{adj}}$ $\csc A = \frac{\text{hyp}}{\text{opp}}$ $\sec A = \frac{\text{hyp}}{\text{adj}}$ $\cot A = \frac{\text{adj}}{\text{opp}}$

$\sin^2 A + \cos^2 A = 1$ $1 + \cot^2 A = \csc^2 A$ $\tan^2 A + 1 = \sec^2 A$

GLOSSARY OF TERMS

Absolute Value—the value of a number when the sign is not considered

Acute Angle—an angle with a measure of less than 90°

Adjacent Angles—angles that share a common side and a common vertex

Area—the space within a closed plane figure, measured in square units

Binomial—an algebraic expression with two terms

Circle—the set of all points in a plane that are equidistant from a center point

Circumference—the distance around a circle

Coefficient—the number in front of a term

Complementary Angles—two angles with a sum of 90°

Composite Numbers—a number that can be divided evenly by more than itself and one

Cube (1)—a six-sided solid with all six faces being equal-sized squares

Cube (2)—the result when a number is multiplied by itself twice

Cube Root—a number that when raised to the third power will yield a second given number

Denominator—the bottom term of a fraction

Diameter—a line segment extending from one side of a circle to the opposite, through the center point

Difference—the result of subtraction

Domain—the set of all x-values for a function

Equilateral Triangle—a triangle with all three sides equal and all three angles being 60°

Evaluate—to determine the value of an expression

Exponent—used to indicate the operation of repeated multiplication

Factor—an integer that divides into another equally

Function—ordered pairs (x, y) with exactly one y-value for any x-value

Hypotenuse—the side opposite the right angle of a right triangle

Improper Fraction—a fraction where the numerator is larger than the denominator

Integers—the set of numbers divisible by one without producing a remainder

Irrational Numbers—any number that cannot be expressed as a fraction

Isosceles Triangle—a triangle with two equal sides and equal opposite angles

Least Common Denominator—the smallest natural number that can be divided evenly by all denominators in the equation

Legs—in a right triangle, the two sides that are not the hypotenuse

Mean—the sum of all items divided by the number of items

Median—in a set of numbers arranged in order, the middle value or the mean of the two middle values

Mixed Number—a term that has both a whole number part and a fractional part

Mode—the most commonly occurring value in a set of values

Monomial—an algebraic expression with only one term

Natural Numbers—the set of positive integers starting with 1

Numerator—the top term of a fraction

Obtuse Angle—an angle with a measure between 90° and 180°

Origin—the intersection between the x- and y-axes of a coordinate graph

Parallel Lines—lines that never intersect regardless of how far they are extended

Parallelogram—a four-sided closed figure with opposite sides that are parallel and of equal length

Percentage—a fraction with a denominator of 100

Perimeter—the total distance around the outside of a polygon

Perpendicular Lines—two lines that intersect at a 90° angle

Polygon—a multi-sided plane closed figure

Polynomial—an algebraic expression with two or more terms

Power—used to indicate repeated multiplication

Prime Numbers—numbers that are evenly divisible only by themselves and one

Product—the result of multiplication

Proper Fraction—a fraction where the denominator is larger than the numerator

Quadrants—the four sections of a coordinate graph

Quadrilateral—a four-sided plane closed figure

Quotient—the result of division

Radius—a line segment extending from the center of a circle to any point on the circle

Range (1)—the difference between the largest and smallest numbers in a set

Range (2)—the set of all y-values for a function

Rational Number—any number that can be expressed as a fraction

Real Numbers—the set of rational and irrational numbers

Rectangle—a four-sided plane closed figure with opposite sides equal and 90° angles

Right Triangle—a triangle with a 90° angle

Root—a number that when raised to a certain power will yield a second given number

Scientific Notation—a number written as the product of a real number between 1 and 10 and a power of 10

Set—a group of numbers, elements, objects, *etc.*

Square (1)—the result when a number is multiplied by itself

Square (2)—a four-sided plane closed figure with all four sides equal and 90° angles

Square Root—a number that when raised to the second power will yield a second given number

Sum—the result of addition

Supplementary Angles—two angles with a sum of 180°

Term—an expression, either numerical or literal

Triangle—a three-sided plane closed figure

Variable—a symbol that is used to stand for a number

Vertex—a point at which two rays or sides of a polygon meet to form an angle

Volume—the space inside a solid, measured in cubic units

Whole Numbers—the set of positive integers including zero

X-axis—the horizontal axis of a coordinate graph

Y-axis—the vertical axis of a coordinate graph

Grammar and Mechanics Skills Review

EDUCATORS' #1 CHOICE FOR SCHOOL IMPROVEMENT

Cambridge Course Concept Outline
GRAMMAR AND MECHANICS SKILLS REVIEW

Parts of Speech

Nouns

A *noun* is a word that refers to any one of the following items: persons, animals, plants, objects, times, places, and ideas.

Examples:

Persons:	Bob, woman, niece, student, doctor, men, brothers, teachers
Animals:	dog, mouse, cow, cats, elephants, birds
Plants:	grass, tree, bushes, oaks
Objects:	glove, car, building, sidewalk, desks, buses
Times:	hour, 8 o'clock, Thanksgiving, Mondays, weekends
Places:	home, office, city, Puerto Rico, Poland, Africa
Ideas:	democracy, love, youth, sisterhood, dreams

Pronouns

A *pronoun* is a word that can substitute for a noun.

Examples:

Hernandez hit a home run. He waved to the crowd.
The woman went into the store. She bought a book.
My sisters live in St. Louis. They are coming to visit.
The bull escaped from the pasture. The farmer caught him.
The plant seems dry. Julie should water it.

Verbs

A *verb* is a word that expresses activity, change, feeling, or existence.

Examples:

The dog is running down the street.
Mary wrote a letter.
Kevin sewed a button on the shirt.
The weather became cold.
The sky darkened.
John likes Mary.
Carl worries that he might not pass the test.
The house is green.
The letter was several days late.

Modifiers

A *modifier* gives further detail to nouns and verbs.

Examples:

The <u>blue</u> car ran into the <u>red</u> car.
The <u>tall</u> woman was carrying an <u>expensive</u> umbrella.
The farmer <u>patiently</u> waited for the cows.
Margaret walked <u>quickly</u> into the kitchen.

Conjunctions

A *conjunction* joins together nouns or ideas.

Examples:

Paul <u>and</u> Mary ate dinner.
I like coffee, <u>but</u> George likes tea.
You can take the subway <u>or</u> the bus.
Harry played <u>while</u> Sam sang.
<u>Although</u> Ed had not arrived, we ate anyway.

Prepositions

A *preposition* shows the relationship between an idea and a noun in the sentence.

Examples:

Patty sat <u>on</u> the chair.
Cliff gave the apples <u>to</u> Tom.
Geneva is the owner <u>of</u> the diner.
The mop is <u>in</u> the closet <u>beside</u> the broom.

You can't end a sentence with a preposition.

Parts of Speech

DIRECTIONS: In Items #1-20, identify each underlined word's part of speech. Use the following key:

N = Noun	V = Verb
Pro = Pronoun	M = Modifier
C = Conjunction	Prep = Preposition

Answers are on page 939.

1. The <u>ambulance</u> weaved in and out of <u>traffic</u> as <u>it</u> <u>hurried</u> to the <u>hospital</u>.

   ambulance **N**   traffic **N**   it **Pro**
   hurried **V**   hospital **N**

2. The movers <u>unloaded</u> the sofa <u>and</u> put <u>it</u> <u>in</u> the living room.

   movers **N**   unloaded **V** and **C**
   it **Pro**   in **Prep**

3. The <u>dark</u> <u>clouds</u> completely <u>blocked</u> <u>our</u> view of the mountains <u>and</u> the lake.

   dark **M**   clouds **N**   blocked **V**
   our **Pro**   and **C**

4. After <u>dinner</u>, we <u>cleared</u> the dishes from the <u>table</u>, put them in the kitchen sink, <u>and</u> <u>sat</u> down to watch the game.

   dinner **N**   cleared **V**   table **N**
   and **C**   sat **V**

5. One <u>room</u> in the library <u>was filled</u> <u>with</u> books written by <u>authors</u> of <u>Polish</u> ancestry.

   room **N**   was filled **V**   with **Prep**
   authors **N**   Polish **M**

6. Some of the <u>first</u> television <u>shows</u> <u>were</u> adaptations of <u>earlier</u> radio versions of the same <u>programs</u>.

   first ____   shows ____   were ____
   earlier ____   programs ____

7. When the <u>waiter</u> <u>arrived</u>, <u>Victor</u> <u>ordered</u> pie with ice cream, chocolate syrup, <u>and</u> a cherry.

   waiter ____   arrived ____   Victor ____
   ordered ____   and ____

8. The building <u>inspector</u> <u>finally</u> <u>approved</u> the plans <u>and</u> <u>allowed</u> the construction to continue.

   inspector ____   finally ____   approved ____
   and ____   allowed ____

9. The superintendent <u>notified</u> the tenants <u>in</u> the building that the <u>water</u> <u>would be</u> off for two <u>hours</u>.

   notified ____   in ____   water ____
   would be ____   hours ____

10. Just as the <u>band</u> <u>finished</u> the number, the <u>crowd</u> <u>burst</u> into <u>loud</u> applause.

    band ____   finished ____   crowd ____
    burst ____   loud ____

11. Carlos <u>telephoned</u> Iris to tell <u>her</u> that he <u>would be</u> late for <u>their</u> <u>date</u>.

    telephoned ____   her ____   would be ____
    their ____   date ____

12. The <u>cat</u> <u>was sleeping</u> on the windowsill in the <u>warmth</u> <u>of</u> the afternoon <u>sun</u>.

    cat ____   was sleeping ____   warmth ____
    of ____   sun ____

13. As the <u>train</u> <u>pulled</u> into each station, the conductor <u>called</u> out the <u>name</u> of that station <u>and</u> the name of the next station.

    train ____   pulled ____   called ____
    name ____   and ____

14. By the time <u>we</u> got to Woodstock, the <u>children</u> <u>were</u> sound asleep <u>in</u> the <u>rear</u> of the car.

    we ____   children ____   were ____
    in ____   rear ____

15. Before <u>they</u> <u>leave</u> the camp, the guides <u>teach</u> the <u>hikers</u> how to identify poison ivy <u>and</u> warn them to avoid it.

    they ____   leave ____   teach ____
    hikers ____   and ____

16. Chuck <u>covered</u> the steaming hot pancakes with plenty of <u>melted</u> butter and sweet, <u>sticky</u> <u>syrup</u>.

    covered ____   steaming ____   melted ____
    sticky ____   syrup ____

17. Last weekend, we <u>made</u> a <u>special</u> trip to the mountains to see the <u>brilliant</u> colors of the <u>beautiful</u> fall leaves.

    weekend ____   made ____   special ____
    brilliant ____   beautiful ____

18. After that eventful afternoon, Art <u>wrote</u> to Cathy several times, <u>but</u> <u>his</u> letters all came back <u>unopened</u>.

    eventful ____   wrote ____   but ____
    his ____   unopened ____

19. Through the morning mist, we could just <u>barely</u> <u>make out</u> the headlights of the <u>bus</u> <u>as</u> <u>it</u> turned off the highway.

   barely _____   make out _____   bus _____

   as _____   it _____

20. Our host <u>offered</u> <u>us</u> a choice of coffee <u>or</u> tea and served some little cakes, which <u>were</u> <u>delicious</u>.

   offered _____   us _____   or _____

   were _____   delicious _____

DIRECTIONS: In Items #21-36, correct the underlined preposition if necessary. If the original sentence is correct, choose (A); if the sentence requires no preposition, choose (D). Answers are on page 939.

21. This class is different <u>than</u> the other.
   - A. NO CHANGE
   - B. of
   - C. from
   - D. OMIT the underlined portion.

22. Where are you going <u>to</u>?
   - A. NO CHANGE
   - B. from
   - C. in
   - D. OMIT the underlined portion.

23. He has not yet taken advantage <u>off</u> the sale.
   - A. NO CHANGE
   - B. of
   - C. from
   - D. OMIT the underlined portion.

24. The teacher broke the news <u>to</u> the student.
   - A. NO CHANGE
   - B. too
   - C. two
   - D. OMIT the underlined portion.

25. Due to decreased sales, the workers were laid <u>off</u> by the company.
   - A. NO CHANGE
   - B. of
   - C. down
   - D. OMIT the underlined portion.

26. The manager promised to look <u>in to</u> the customer's complaint.
   - A. NO CHANGE
   - B. into
   - C. unto
   - D. OMIT the underlined portion.

27. He took it <u>up on</u> himself to schedule the meeting.
   - A. NO CHANGE
   - B. on
   - C. upon
   - D. OMIT the underlined portion.

28. She found it <u>below</u> her to clean her own house.
   - A. NO CHANGE
   - B. beneath
   - C. be neat
   - D. OMIT the underlined portion.

29. The office will open sometime <u>in</u> a half hour.
   - A. NO CHANGE
   - B. within
   - C. inside
   - D. OMIT the underlined portion.

30. Are you under the weather?
   - A. NO CHANGE
   - B. below
   - C. beneath
   - D. OMIT the underlined portion.

31. There are many students waiting <u>on</u> the instructor during her office hours.
   - A. NO CHANGE
   - B. for
   - C. to
   - D. OMIT the underlined portion.

32. Please save energy by turning <u>of</u> the lights before you leave the house.
   - A. NO CHANGE
   - B. off
   - C. in
   - D. OMIT the underlined portion.

33. The dancers swung <u>in</u> motion when the music started.
   - A. NO CHANGE
   - B. in to
   - C. into
   - D. OMIT the underlined portion.

34. I work at the bank <u>in</u> the corner of Main and Packard.
   - A. NO CHANGE
   - B. on
   - C. around
   - D. OMIT the underlined portion.

35. The lawyer voiced his objection <u>on</u> the recount of the votes.
   - A. NO CHANGE
   - B. to
   - C. about
   - D. OMIT the underlined portion.

36. Ralph had difficulty getting to sleep <u>till</u> very late.
   - A. NO CHANGE
   - B. up to
   - C. until
   - D. OMIT the underlined portion.

Common Grammatical Errors

Subject-Verb Agreement

One common grammatical error is lack of agreement between subject and verb. The simplest subject-verb disagreements are usually obvious, as in the following examples. Note: ✓ = correct, ✗ = wrong.

Examples:

> The books <u>is</u> on the shelf. ✗
>
> The books <u>are</u> on the shelf. ✓
>
> The teacher <u>admonish</u> the class to calm down. ✗
>
> The teacher <u>admonished</u> the class to calm down. ✓

In order to test your ability to spot such errors, test-writers may use one of the three following tricks:

> **WHAT OBSCURES SUBJECT-VERB AGREEMENT**
>
> 1. Material Inserted Between Subject and Verb
> 2. Inverted Sentence Structure
> 3. Use of Compound Subjects

1. *Material Inserted Between Subject and Verb*

The test-writers insert material between the subject and verb to obscure their connection. If you are not careful, by the time you reach the verb, you will have forgotten the subject; as a result, it will not be easy to determine whether the verb agrees with the subject. Consider the following examples:

Examples:

> Star <u>performers</u> in the movies or on television usually <u>earns</u> *(earn)* substantial income from royalties. ✗
>
> One school of thought maintains that the federal <u>deficit</u>, not exorbitant corporate profits or excessively high wages, <u>cause</u> *(caused)* most of the inflation we are now experiencing. ✗
>
> A recent survey shows that a <u>household</u> in which both the wife and the husband are pursuing careers <u>stand</u> *(stands)* a better chance of surviving intact than one in which only the husband works. ✗

In each of these three sentences, the subject and verb do not agree: "performers...earns," "deficit...cause," and "household...stand." However, the errors may not be immediately evident because of the intervening material. In the first sentence, the subject is separated from the verb by prepositional phrases. In the second sentence, the subject and the verb are separated by a parenthetical expression. In the third sentence, a clause intervenes between the subject and the verb.

The plausibility of the incorrect verb choice, and therefore the chance that the error will go unnoticed, is strengthened when test-writers place a word or phrase near the verb that might be mistaken for the subject: "television...earns," "profits and wages...cause," and "careers...stand." If the first word of each of these pairs had been the subject, then there would have been no failure of agreement.

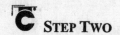

2. Inverted Sentence Structure

A second common problem of subject-verb agreement is *inverted sentence structure*. In an inverted sentence, the verb precedes the subject. You should pay careful attention to the agreement between subject and verb, no matter how those elements are ordered.

Examples:

Although the first amendment to the Constitution does guarantee freedom of speech, the Supreme Court has long recog-
~~have~~
nized that there <u>has</u> to be some <u>restrictions</u> on the exercise of this right. ✗

Jennifer must have been doubly pleased that day, for seated in the gallery to watch her receive the award <u>was</u> her brother,
~~were~~
her parents, and her husband. ✗

In both of these sentences, the subjects and verbs do not agree. The relationships are obscured by the order in which the elements appear in the sentence—the verbs come before the subjects. These sentences should read:

Although the first amendment to the Constitution does guarantee freedom of speech, the Supreme Court has long recognized that there <u>have</u> to be some restrictions on the exercise of this right. ✓

Jennifer must have been doubly pleased that day, for seated in the gallery to watch her receive the award <u>were</u> her brother, her parents, and her husband. ✓

WATCH FOR INVERTED SENTENCE STRUCTURES

Regardless of the order of the sentence—subject-verb or verb-subject—the verb must always agree with its subject. If a sentence has a complex structure, it often helps to look at each element in isolation.

---

3. Use of Compound Subjects

Finally, be alert for *compound subjects*. Usually, when the subject of a sentence consists of two or more elements joined by the conjunction "and," the subject is considered plural and requires a plural verb. Consider the following example:

Example:

were
Of the seven candidates, only John, Bill, and Jim <u>was</u> past office holders. ✗

The subject, "John, Bill, and Jim," is compound (joined by "and") and requires the plural verb "were"—even though the individual nouns are singular.

WATCH FOR COMPOUND SUBJECTS

Compound subjects, typically two or more subjects joined by "and," are plural and need a plural verb.

Be careful not to confuse the compound subject with the disjunctive subject. When elements of the subject are joined by "or," the verb must agree with the element nearest to it. Replacing "and" with "or" changes our previous example:

Example:

Of the seven candidates, John, Bill, or Jim <u>is</u> likely to win. ✓

The elements are joined by "or," so the verb must agree with "John" or "Bill" or "Jim." The verb "is" correctly agrees with the disjunctive subject.

Additionally, watch out for subjects that are designed to look like compound subjects but which are actually singular. Typically, these subjects are disguised using pronouns.

Example:

Neither one of those fools even <u>know</u> how to change a light bulb. ✘

The subject is not "those fools"; instead, it is the singular subject "Neither one." Thus, the singular verb "knows" is required

---

WATCH FOR DISJUNCTIVE AND SINGULAR SUBJECTS

1. If the elements of the subject are joined by "or," the subject is disjunctive. The verb must agree with the closest element of the subject.

2. Be alert for singular subjects that appear to be plural (typically pronouns).

Pronoun Usage

The rules for *pronoun usage* are summarized below. Note: ✔ = correct, ✘ = wrong.

PRONOUN USAGE RULES

1. A pronoun must have an antecedent (referent) to which it refers.

2. The pronoun must refer clearly to the antecedent.

3. The pronoun and antecedent must agree.

4. The pronoun must have the proper case.

---

1. Pronouns Must Have Antecedents

A *pronoun* is used as a substitute for a noun. The noun that it replaces is called the *antecedent* (referent). With the exception of certain idioms such as "It is raining," a pronoun that does not have an antecedent is used incorrectly.

Examples:

Although Glen is president of the student body, he has not yet passed his English exam, and because of <u>it</u>, he will not graduate with the rest of his class. ✘

The damage done by Senator Smith's opposition to the policy of equal employment is undeniable, but <u>that</u> is exactly what he attempted to do in his speech on Thursday. ✘

In the first example, what is the antecedent of "it"? It is not "he has not yet passed his English exam," because that is a complete thought, or clause, not just a noun. "It" is not a pronoun substitute for that entire thought. Rather, "it" refers to Glen's "failure" to pass the exam, thereby providing "it" with the required antecedent. However, "failure" does not appear in noun form in the sentence. In other words, "it" wants to refer to a noun, but there is no noun to function as its point of reference. The sentence must be rewritten: "because of that fact, he will not graduate...."

In the second example, "that" functions as a relative pronoun—it relates something in the first clause to the second clause. However, to what does "that" refer? Test possibilities by substituting them for "that" in the second clause. The sentence should make sense when you replace the pronoun with its antecedent. Is the antecedent "damage"?

but <u>damage</u> is exactly what he attempted to do.... ✘

Perhaps, then, the antecedent is <u>opposition</u> or <u>undeniable</u>:

but <u>opposition</u> is exactly what he attempted to do.... ✘

but <u>undeniable</u> is exactly what he attempted to do.... ✘

There are no other candidates for the antecedent, so we must conclude that the use of "that" is incorrect. Most likely, what the writer intended to say was that the Senator attempted to deny the damage:

The damage done by Senator Smith's opposition to the policy of equal employment is undeniable, but he attempted to deny that damage in his speech on Thursday. ✔

PRONOUNS MUST HAVE ANTECEDENTS

 Except for a few idiomatic expressions ("It" is getting late, "It" will be sunny today), every pronoun must have an antecedent. An antecedent must be a noun, not a thought or phrase. Identify a pronoun's antecedent and then check that it is correct by substituting it for the pronoun in the sentence.

---

2. *Antecedents Must Be Clear*

The antecedent of a pronoun must be made clear from the structure of the sentence. Consider these examples:

Examples:

Edward's father died before <u>he</u> reached his 20th birthday, so <u>he</u> never finished his education. ✘

In 1980, the University Council voted to rescind Provision 3, <u>which</u> made it easier for some students to graduate. ✘

In the first example, it is not clear whether the father died before he reached the age of 20 or before Edward reached the age of 20. Furthermore, it is not clear whose education remained unfinished. Similarly, in the second example, the antecedent of "which" is not clear. "Which" may refer to Provision 3 or it may refer to the University Council's vote to rescind Provision 3.

WATCH FOR UNCLEAR ANTECEDENTS

 The antecedent of a pronoun must be clearly identified by the structure of the sentence.

Example:

The letter is on the desk <u>that</u> we received yesterday. ✘

The letter <u>that</u> we received yesterday is on the desk. ✔

Finally, the impersonal use of "it," "they," and "you" tends to produce vague, wordy sentences.

Examples:

In the manual <u>it</u> says to make three copies. ✘

The manual says to make three copies. ✔

<u>They</u> predict we are in for a cold, wet winter. ✘

The almanac predicts a cold, wet winter. ✔

3. Pronoun-Antecedent Agreement

The pronoun must agree with its antecedent. Consider the following example:

Example:

> Historically, the college dean was also a professor, but today <u>they</u> are usually administrators. ✘

In the example, "they" must refer to "dean," but "dean" is singular and "they" is plural. The sentence can be corrected in one of two ways: by changing the first clause to the plural or by changing the second clause to the singular.

> Historically, college deans were also professors, but today they are usually administrators. ✓

> Historically, the college dean was also a professor, but today the dean is usually an administrator. ✓

WATCH FOR PRONOUN-ANTECEDENT AGREEMENT

If the antecedent is singular, the pronoun must be singular; if the antecedent is plural, the pronoun must be plural.

Finally, it is incorrect to use different forms of the same pronoun to refer to an antecedent. This error results in the sentence having different antecedents and therefore a *shifting subject*.

WATCH FOR SHIFTING SUBJECTS

Watch for shifting subject errors. These errors occur if different forms of the same pronoun are used to refer to the antecedent.

Example:

> The teacher told John that <u>he</u> thought <u>his</u> work was improving. ✘

Does the teacher think that his own work is improving or that John's work is improving? The correct sentence reads: "The teacher told John that John's work was improving."

4. Pronouns Must Have Proper Case

A pronoun must agree with its antecedent in case, number, and person. The pronoun's function in a sentence determines which case should be used. You should be familiar with the following three categories of pronoun case: nominative (or subjective), objective, and possessive.

TYPES OF PRONOUN CASE

> ✎ *Nominative* (*subjective*) case pronouns are used as subjects of sentences.
>
> ✎ *Objective* case pronouns are used as objects: direct objects, indirect objects, and objects of prepositions. If a prepositional phrase ends with a pronoun, it must be an objective pronoun.
>
> ✎ *Possessive* case pronouns are used to show possession. Use a possessive pronoun preceding a gerund. A gerund is the "-ing" form of a verb that is used as a noun.
>
> ✎ *Interrogative* pronouns stand in for the answer to a question.

The following examples illustrate correct usage of pronoun case.

Examples:

(subjective)

Nominative: I thought <u>he</u> would like the gift <u>we</u> bought. ✓

Objective: The choice for the part is between Bob and <u>me</u>. ✓ (The object pronoun <u>me</u> follows the preposition <u>between</u>.)

Possessive: Do you mind <u>my</u> using your computer? ✓ (The possessive pronoun <u>my</u> precedes the gerund <u>using</u>.)

Interrogative: <u>Who</u> is the starting pitcher for the Orioles today? ✓

📖 EXAMPLES OF PRONOUN CASE 📖

	Nominative Case Singular	Nominative Case Plural	Objective Case Singular	Objective Case Plural	Possessive Case Singular	Possessive Case Plural
1st Person:	I	we	me	us	my	our
2nd Person:	you	you	you	you	your	your
3rd Person:	he, she, it	they	him, her, it	them	his, her, its	their
Interrogative:	who	who	whom	whom	whose	whose

The following are additional examples of the *nominative*, or <u>subjective</u>, pronoun case.

Examples:

<u>John</u> and <u>him</u> were chosen. ✗

John and <u>he</u> were chosen. ✓ (<u>He</u> is the subject of the verb; we certainly would not say that <u>him</u> was chosen.)

It was <u>her</u> who was chosen. ✗

<u>She</u> was chosen. ✓

<u>Us</u> student-workers decided to organize into a union. ✗

<u>We</u> student-workers decided to organize into a union. ✓

He is as witty as <u>her</u>. ✗

He is as witty as <u>she</u> is. ✓

<u>Whom</u> do you suppose will win the election? ✗

<u>Who</u> do you suppose will win the election? ✓

The following are additional examples of the *objective* pronoun case.

Examples:

They accused Tom and <u>he</u> of stealing. ✘

They accused Tom and <u>him</u> of stealing. ✔ (*Him* is the object of the verb <u>accused</u>; they accused <u>him</u>, not <u>he</u>.)

The tickets were given to Bill and <u>I</u>. ✘

The tickets were given to Bill and <u>me</u>. ✔ (<u>Me</u> is the object of <u>to</u>; the tickets were given to <u>me</u>, not to <u>I</u>.)

<u>Who</u> did you see? ✘

<u>Whom</u> did you see? ✔ (Hint: Make this a declarative sentence: "You saw <u>him</u>." You would not say, "You saw <u>he</u>.")

An easy way to remember when to use "who" versus "whom" is that in those situations that "him" (or "her") would be appropriate, "whom" should be used; in those situations that "he" (or "she") would be appropriate, "who" should be used.

Finally, personal pronouns that express ownership never require an apostrophe. Also, a pronoun that precedes a gerund ("-ing" verb form used as a noun) is usually the possessive case.

Examples:

This book is <u>your's</u>, not <u>her's</u>. ✘

This book is <u>yours</u>, not <u>hers</u>. ✔

He rejoiced at <u>him</u> going to the party. ✘

He rejoiced at <u>his</u> going to the party. ✔

Some pronouns are either singular or plural, while others can be both. The structure and intended meaning of the sentence indicate whether the pronoun is singular or plural.

 SINGULAR AND/OR PLURAL PRONOUNS

Singular: anybody, another, everybody, everything, somebody, something, nobody, one, anyone, everyone, someone, no one, each, every, neither, either, much

Plural: both, few, many, most, several

Singular & Plural: all, any, half, more, none, some

Technically, pronouns are divided into eight formal categories:

📖 **FORMAL CATEGORIES OF PRONOUNS** 📖

Personal: I, we, my, mine, our, ours, me, us, you, your, yours, he, she, it, they, his, hers, its, their, theirs, him, her, them

Demonstrative: this, these, that, those

Indefinite: all, any, anything, both, each, either, one, everyone, everybody, everything, few, many, more, neither, none, somebody, someone, something

Relative: who, whose, whom, which, of which, that, of that, what, of what

Interrogative: who, whose, whom, which, of which, what, of what

Numerical: one, two, three, first, second, third

Reflexive/Intensive: myself, ourselves, yourself, yourselves, himself, herself, itself, themselves

Reciprocal: each other, one another

For the test, it is not necessary to know the names of the individual categories and which pronouns belong in which categories. However, through your experience in conversation and writing, you should be able to correctly use each type of pronoun, and you should have the ability to spot when each type of pronoun is used incorrectly.

Example:

Many of the students <u>which</u> were participating in the spelling bee had been finalists last year. ✖

In the above example, the pronoun "which" refers to "Many of the students" and it is the incorrect pronoun choice. Instead, the sentence should read: "Many…who were participating…."

Adjectives vs. Adverbs

Note: ✓ = correct, ✖ = wrong.

⭐ **1. *Adjectives Modify Nouns, Adverbs Modify Verbs***

Adjectives are used to modify nouns, while *adverbs* are used to modify verbs, adjectives, or other adverbs.

Example: adverb → quickly

No matter how <u>quick</u> he played, Rich never beat Julie when playing the card game "speed." ✖

In the above example, "quick" is intended to modify the speed with which Rich played cards. However, "quick" is an adjective and therefore cannot be used to modify a verb. By adding "-ly" to the end of "quick," we can transform it into an adverb and the sentence reads: "No matter how quickly he played…."

The following examples further illustrate the proper use of adjectives and adverbs.

Examples:

Adjectives: Mr. Jackson is a <u>good</u> teacher. ✓
He is a <u>bad</u> driver. ✓
There has been a <u>considerable</u> change in the weather. ✓
My sister is a <u>superb</u> dancer. ✓
The teacher gave a <u>quick</u> explanation of the problem. ✓
This is a <u>slow</u> exercise. ✓

Adverbs: Mr. Jackson teaches <u>well</u>. ✓
He drives <u>badly</u>. ✓
The weather has changed <u>considerably</u>. ✓
My sister dances <u>superbly</u>. ✓
The teacher explained the problem <u>quickly</u>. ✓
This exercise must be done <u>slowly</u>. ✓

The first three of the following examples underscore that adjectives, not adverbs, must be used to modify nouns. The remaining examples show that adverbs, not adjectives, must be used to modify verbs and adjectives.

Examples:

He said that the medicine tasted <u>terribly</u>. ✗
He said that the medicine tasted <u>terrible</u>. ✓

The dog remained <u>faithfully</u> to its master until the end. ✗
The dog remained <u>faithful</u> to its master until the end. ✓

I felt <u>badly</u> about forgetting the appointment. ✗
I felt <u>bad</u> about forgetting the appointment. ✓

He can do the job <u>easier</u> than you can. ✗
He can do the job more <u>easily</u> than you can. ✓

The problem seemed <u>exceeding</u> complex to me. ✗
The problem seemed <u>exceedingly</u> complex to me. ✓

It rained <u>steady</u> all day yesterday. ✗
It rained <u>steadily</u> all day yesterday. ✓

The professor presented an <u>obvious</u> important point in class. ✗
The professor presented an <u>obviously</u> important point in class. ✓

We all agreed that the new film was <u>real</u> funny. ✗
We all agreed that the new film was <u>really</u> funny. ✓

The students found the physics examination <u>extreme</u> difficult. ✗
The students found the physics examination <u>extremely</u> difficult. ✓

If you speak <u>firm</u>, he will listen to you. ✗
If you speak <u>firmly</u>, he will listen to you. ✓

He made <u>considerable</u> more progress than I did. ✗
He made <u>considerably</u> more progress than I did. ✓

2. Linking Verbs

Linking verbs are followed by adjectives, not adverbs. The following is a list of common linking verbs.

COMMON LINKING VERBS				
be	become	appear	look	seem
remain	feel	smell	sound	taste

Note that some of the verbs listed as linking verbs may sometimes function as verbs of action. The following examples illustrate this point.

Examples:

Adjectives: I feel <u>tired</u>. ✔
He looked <u>angry</u>. ✔
The pie tastes <u>delicious</u>. ✔

Adverbs: I felt my way <u>slowly</u> in the darkness. ✔
He looked about the room <u>angrily</u>. ✔
She tasted the pie <u>cautiously</u>. ✔

3. Watch for Adjectives Posing as Adverbs

WATCH FOR ADJECTIVE-ADVERB SWITCHING

Be alert for adjectives posing in place of adverbs and vice versa. Adjectives can usually be transformed into adverbs by adding "-ly." However, verbs must be modified by adverbs, not simply an adjective posing as an adverb.

Examples:

The girl looks <u>intelligently</u>. ✘
The girl looks <u>intelligent</u>. ✔

That perfume smells <u>sweetly</u>, doesn't it? ✘
That perfume smells <u>sweet</u>, doesn't it? ✔

The physician appeared <u>nervously</u> when he talked to the patient. ✘
The physician appeared <u>nervous</u> when he talked to the patient. ✔

This bed seems very <u>comfortably</u>. ✘
This bed seems very <u>comfortable</u>. ✔

Several people arrived too <u>lately</u> to be admitted to the performance. ✘ ("Lately" is not an adverb for "late." Instead, "lately" means "as of late.")
Several people arrived too <u>late</u> to be admitted to the performance. ✔

The horse ran <u>fastly</u> enough to win the race. ✘ ("Fastly" is not a word!)
The horse ran <u>fast</u> enough to win the race. ✔

The architect worked <u>hardly</u> to finish his drawings by the next day. ✘ ("Hardly" is not an adverb for "hard." Instead, "hardly" means "barely.")
The architect worked <u>hard</u> to finish his drawings by the next day. ✔

Double Negatives

It is true that we all hear and sometimes say *double negatives* in daily conversation. However, double negatives are NOT acceptable in standard written English.

Note: ✗ = wrong.

Example:

I <u>hadn't hardly</u> begun to understand Spanish when I had to move again. ✗

The phrase "hadn't hardly" is a double negative. The sentence should read: "I had hardly begun to understand...."

WATCH FOR DOUBLE NEGATIVES

 Watch for double negatives ("not barely," "hardly nothing")—they are always incorrect.

Nouns and Noun Clauses

Nouns are names of people, places, things, or ideas; they are used to indicate the subject of a sentence. Like pronouns, nouns have a case. Note: ✓ = correct, ✗ = wrong.

TYPES OF NOUN CASE

 Nominative (Subjective) case is used when the noun is the subject of the sentence.

 Objective case is used when the noun is an indirect or direct object or is the object of a preposition.

 Possessive case is used when nouns are intended to show possession.

Sometimes the place of the noun in a sentence is filled by a *noun clause* instead of a single noun. A noun clause is a dependent clause.

Example:

<u>That Judy was chosen for the promotion</u> is not surprising. ✓

The failure to properly introduce a noun clause is an error of sentence structure. "That" by itself is not the noun, nor is "Judy was chosen for the promotion" a noun. However, the two combined create a noun clause and function as the noun.

RULE FOR INTRODUCING NOUN CLAUSES

 A noun clause is a group of words that functions as the subject (or another noun usage) of a sentence. "That" is often the best word to use to introduce noun clauses.

Examples:

> The reason the saxophone is a popular jazz instrument is <u>because</u> its timbre can approximate that of the human voice. ✘
> The reason the saxophone is a popular jazz instrument is <u>that</u> its timbre can approximate that of the human voice. ✓

> <u>Why</u> American car manufacturers did not reduce car sizes earlier than they did is a mystery to most market experts. ✘
> <u>That</u> American car manufacturers did not reduce car sizes earlier than they did is a mystery to most market experts. ✓

The above examples make the error of introducing noun clauses with <u>because</u> and <u>why</u>. In both sentences, a noun clause is required; <u>that</u> should be used in both cases.

 WATCH FOR "BECAUSE" AND "WHY" AS NOUN CLAUSE INTRODUCTIONS

Noun clauses must be introduced by "that," not "because" or "why."

Additionally, do NOT use "where" for "that" in object clauses.

Example:

> I saw in the bulletin <u>where</u> Mrs. Wagner's retirement was announced. ✘
> I saw in the bulletin <u>that</u> Mrs. Wagner's retirement was announced. ✓

However, if the subject of the sentence actually is about where something is, then use "where."

Examples:

> <u>Where</u> the wedding had initially been scheduled is not where it ended up being held. ✓
> All I want to know is <u>where</u> we are supposed to go for homeroom attendance. ✓

never assume!

Common Grammatical Errors

DIRECTIONS: For Items #1-25, circle the letter of the underlined part of the sentence containing the grammatical error. Answers are on page 940.

1. The professor deals harsh *harshly* with students who are not
   A   B
   prepared, and he is even more severe with those who
   B   C   D
   plagiarize.

2. A recent study indicates that the average person ignores
             A   B
   most commercial advertising and does not buy
                             C
   products because of them. *because of it*
           D

3. Despite the fact that New York City is one of the most
        A   B
   densely populated areas in the world, there are many
                          C
   parks where one can sit on a bench under the trees and
   you can read a book. *one can*
   D

4. Charles Dickens wrote about the horrifying conditions
                  A   B
   in the English boarding schools that he learned about
                        C
   on one of his trips to Yorkshire.
          D

5. André Breton initiated the Surrealist movement with
               A   B
   the publication of a manifesto, and it incorporated the
       B   C
   theories of Freud as well as his own.
              D

6. The review of the concert published in the morning's
                       A
   paper mentioned that the soloist is a very promising
                         B
   talent and that the orchestra played capable.
            C   D

7. During the war, there were many people in the Polish
         A
   countryside that sheltered those who had escaped from
             B   C   D
   concentration camps.

8. The dean lectured to we students on the privilege and
             A   B   C
   responsibility of attending the university.
               D

9. You taking the initiative in the negotiations will profit
      A   B   C
   the company to a great degree.
             D

10. The members of the club insisted that I be the
                   A   B
    representative of the organization at the conference
                              C
    which was something I had hoped to avoid.
      C   D

11. No one knows for sure whether there was a real person
      A   B   C
    about which Shakespeare wrote his sonnets.
       C   D

12. Although the director of the zoo takes great pains to
      A   B   C
    recreate the natural habitats of the animals, few of the
      C
    exhibits is completely accurate in every detail.
             D

13. Climatic differences between the north and south of
    some countries helps to account for the differences in
      A   B   C
    temperament of the inhabitants of the two regions.
                       D

14. The month of August was particularly cold; hardly no
                    A   B
    daily temperatures were recorded above 80 degrees,
        B   C
    and only one was recorded above 90 degrees.
          D

15. The diaries of Stendhal, which make entertaining
                      A
    reading, also provides a great wealth of information
      A   B
    about musical taste and performance practice in the last
          C   D
    century.
      D

16. <u>Given the evidence</u> of the existence of a complicated
    A
    system of communication <u>used by whales</u>, it is
    B
    <u>necessary to</u> acknowledge <u>its</u> intelligence.
    C   **D**

17. <u>Him being at the rally</u> <u>does not necessarily mean</u> <u>that</u>
    A   **B**   **C**
    the congressman <u>agrees</u> with the president's entire
    D
    platform.

18. Although there is no perfect form of government,
    representative democracy, <u>as it is practiced in America</u>,
    A
    <u>is a system</u> that is <u>working well</u> and <u>more than</u>
    B   **C**   **D**
    <u>satisfactory</u>.
    D

19. George <u>hired</u> a caterer, <u>who</u> <u>he</u> <u>later recommended</u>,
    A   **B** **C** **D**
    after tasting her specialty—spring rolls.

20. <u>After driving past Trinity Church</u>, the bus <u>stopped at</u>
    A   **B**
    <u>the recent constructed</u> Exposition Tower, the <u>tallest</u>
    B   **C**
    building in the city, <u>to allow the passengers to take</u> the
    D
    special elevators to the observation tower.

21. The student senate <u>passed</u> the resolution <u>banning</u>
    A   **B**
    <u>smoking in the cafeteria</u> <u>with scarcely any</u> dissenting
    B   **C**
    votes <u>which angered</u> many members of the faculty.
    D

22. Most employers <u>assume</u> that <u>one's</u> professional
    A
    personality and work habits <u>are formed</u> <u>as a result of</u>
    B   **C**
    <u>your</u> early work experience.
    D

23. <u>Only a small number</u> of taxi drivers <u>fail to insure</u> their
    A   **B**
    vehicles, but usually <u>these are the ones</u> who need <u>it</u>
    C   **D**
    most.

24. <u>Angered</u> by the <u>double</u> standard society <u>imposed on</u>
    A   **A**   **B**
    women, Edna St. Vincent Millay <u>wrote candid about</u>
    C
    <u>her</u> opinions and her personal life.
    D

25. Unless <u>they hire players</u> <u>who</u> <u>are</u> better hitters, the fans
    A   **B** **C**
    <u>will gradually lose</u> interest in the team despite the fine
    efforts of the pitching staff.

DIRECTIONS: For Items #26-41, after identifying each answer choice as an adjective or adverb, determine whether the blank should be filled in with the adjective choice or the adverb choice. Answers are on page 941.

26. Kathy <u>does her</u> homework _____. *verb*
    slow _____   slowly ____✓____

27. We <u>understand each other</u> _____.
    really well ____✓____ real good _____

28. <u>Students</u> should be _____ to their professors at
    all times.
    polite ____✓____   politely _____

29. Paula has adjusted to her new school. She is doing
    _____.
    good _____   well ____✓____

30. I think the <u>cake</u> is done. It smells _____.
    good ____✓____   well _____

31. Your room is a _____ mess. Clean it up at once!
    terrible ____✓____   terribly _____

32. When I found out that the accident was my fault, I felt _____.

    awfully _____   awful _____

33. The movie we saw last night wasn't _____ exciting.

    terrible _____   terribly _____

34. Doing a job _____ right away saves time in the long run.

    well _____   good _____

35. Cats have a developed sense of smell. They can smell _____.

    well _____   good _____

36. "Mrs. Chang, your son works _____ in class. You can be proud of him."

    hard _____   hardly _____

37. In order to deliver the package on time, the messenger biked _____.

    fast _____   quick _____

38. The college I will be attending in September is _____.

    nearly _____   near _____

39. After contracting the disease, Marc's symptoms appeared _____.

    slow _____   slowly _____

40. Doctors need to remain _____ even during an epidemic.

    healthy _____   healthily _____

41. Leo's stomach felt _____ after the terrific Thanksgiving feast.

    heavy _____   heavily _____

Analyzing Sentence Structure

When analyzing the structure of a sentence, ask yourself the following four questions.

> **CHECKLIST FOR ANALYZING SENTENCE STRUCTURE**
>
> 1. Is the sentence a run-on sentence?
>
> 2. Are the elements of the sentence parallel?
>
> 3. Are there any incomplete split constructions?
>
> 4. Do the verb tenses correctly reflect the sequence of events?

Run-on Sentences

Be aware of sentences that carelessly run main clauses together without appropriate punctuation or connectors. *Run-on sentences* can be corrected in one of three ways: "end-stop" punctuation, a semicolon, or a connector. Note: ✓ = correct, ✗ = wrong.

The most common way to correct a run-on sentence is to divide the sentence using "end-stop" punctuation.

Examples:

The lecture was dull you almost fell asleep. ✗
The lecture was dull. You almost fell asleep. ✓

Was the lecture dull you almost fell asleep. ✗
Was the lecture dull? You almost fell asleep. ✓

The lecture was incredibly dull you almost fell asleep. ✗
The lecture was incredibly dull! You almost fell asleep. ✓

The comma is not an end-mark. Do NOT use a comma by itself to separate two sentences.

Example:

Close the window, there is a draft in the room. ✗
Close the window. There is a draft in the room. ✓

Sometimes, two sentences are very closely related in meaning, and full "end-stop" punctuation may seem too strong. A semicolon can then be used to divide the two sentences.

Example:

It was a beautiful day there was not a cloud in the sky. ✗
It was a beautiful day; there was not a cloud in the sky. ✓

A third way to correct the run-on is to use a connector (conjunction) such as "and," "but," "for," "or," and "nor" if the two sentences are equally important. It is usually advisable to place a comma before these connectors.

Example:

I like to ski, my friend prefers to sit by the fire. ✗
I like to ski, but my friend prefers to sit by the fire. ✓

Particular problem words that may cause run-ons are "however," "therefore," "consequently," and "moreover." These words are not sentence connectors, and when they follow a complete thought, either a period or a semicolon should precede them.

Faulty Parallelism

Faulty parallelism is a common grammatical error for writers. Whenever elements of a sentence perform similar or equal functions, they should have the same form. Consider the following faulty sentences; they are missing necessary words. Note: ✓ = correct, ✗ = wrong.

Examples:

At most colleges, the dominant attitude among students is that <u>gaining</u> admission to professional graduate school is more important than <u>to obtain</u> a well-rounded education. ✗ *obtaining*

To demand that additional seasonings be placed on the table is <u>insulting</u> the chef's judgment on the proper balance of ingredients. ✗ *4 to insult*

The review was very critical of the film, citing the poor photography, the weak plot, and the dialogue <u>was stilted</u>. ✗ *4 the stilted dialogue*

In the first example, "gaining admission" and "to obtain" must both have the same form. Either both must be in the gerund form or both must be in the infinitive form. For example: "gaining admission…is more important than obtaining…."

In the second example, the subject ("to demand") and the predicated complement ("insulting") must both have the same form: "To demand…is to insult…."

In the last example, the last element of the list of film criticisms is not of the same form as the other two elements. The sentence should read: "…citing the poor photography, the weak plot, and the stilted dialogue."

CHECK THAT ALL ELEMENTS OF A SENTENCE ARE PARALLEL

 Check that all elements of a sentence are parallel—including verb forms, noun forms, and word pairs such as "this…that," "either…or," and "neither…nor."

Examples:

He spends his time playing cards, swimming, going to the theater, and at school. ✗
He spends his time playing cards, swimming, going to the theater, and <u>going to</u> school. ✓

He manages his business affairs with knowledge, ease, and confidently. ✗
He manages his business affairs with knowledge, ease, and <u>confidence</u>. ✓

He was required by the instructor to go to the library, to take out several books on the Vietnam War, and that he should report to the class on what he had learned. ✗
He was required by the instructor to go to the library, to take out several books on the Vietnam War, and <u>to report</u> to the class on what he had learned. ✓

I am studying the sources of educational theory and how educational theory has evolved. ✗
I am studying the sources and <u>the evolution</u> of educational theory. ✓

He was not only sympathetic but also knew when to be considerate. ✗
He was not only sympathetic but also <u>considerate</u>. ✓

Not only did he enjoy the movie but also the play. ✗
<u>He enjoyed</u> not only the movie but also the play. ✓

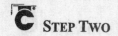
I was concerned about the price of the car and if it was comfortable. ✘
I was concerned about the price and <u>the comfort</u> of the car. ✔

Neither does he speak Spanish nor Helen. ✘
Neither he nor Helen <u>speaks</u> Spanish. ✔

Incomplete Split Constructions

Split constructions refer to phrases in which a thought, interrupted by intervening material, is completed later in the sentence. Note: ✔ = correct, ✘ = wrong.

Example:

The officials were not only aware of, but actually encouraged, the misreporting of scores. ✔

This sentence contains a perfectly acceptable split construction. Ordinarily, the object of a preposition closely follows the preposition: "aware of the misreporting." Here, the object of the preposition is separated from the preposition by the phrase "but actually encouraged." This is unobjectionable as long as the thought is properly completed. There is a danger, however, that the intervening material will throw something off in the sentence.

CHECK THAT SPLIT CONSTRUCTIONS ARE COMPLETED

A split construction is a sentence structure in which two otherwise separate ideas are joined together by a later element. Be alert for split constructions and check that any interrupted thought is correctly completed.

Consider the following faulty sentences; they are incomplete split constructions.

Examples:

Her colleagues always speak of Professor Collins as a person who has and will always be sensitive to the needs of younger students. ✘
Judging from the pricing policies of many large corporations, maintaining a stable share of the market is as important, if not more important than, making a large profit. ✘

In the first sentence, the error is in the verb. The auxiliary verb "has" needs the verb "been," but "been" does not appear in the sentence. The sentence could be corrected by completing the construction: "…has been and will always be…."
In the second sentence, the error is an incomplete comparison. The sentence should read: "…as important as, if not more important than,…."

RULE FOR CHECKING FOR SPLIT CONSTRUCTIONS

The intervening material makes it difficult to spot errors of split construction. Therefore, when checking for split constructions, read the sentence without the intervening material—it should make sense, be grammatically correct, and be a complete sentence.

Verb Tense

The same *verb tense* should be used whenever possible within a sentence or paragraph. Avoid shifts in ~~~~ valid reason. Note: ✓ = correct, ✗ = wrong.

Example:

Joan <u>came</u> home last week and <u>goes</u> to her home in the country where she <u>spends</u> the last weekend of her vacation. ✗
Joan <u>came</u> home last week and <u>went</u> to her home in the country where she <u>spent</u> the last weekend of her vacation. ✓

1. Principal Parts of Verbs

Verb tense is indicated by changing the verb or by combining certain verb forms with auxiliary verbs. The ***principal parts*** are the verb tenses from which all verb forms are derived: present, past, present perfect, future perfect, and past perfect.

VERB PRINCIPAL PARTS

1. *Present Tense:* talk, write

2. *Past Tense:* talked, wrote

3. *Present Perfect Tense:* have talked, has written

4. *Future Perfect Tense:* will have talked, will have written

5. *Past Perfect Tense:* had talked, had written

Verbs are classified as regular (or weak) and irregular (or strong), according to the way in which their principal parts are formed. Regular verbs form their past, present perfect, future perfect, and past perfect tenses by the addition of "-ed" to the infinitive.

Examples:

Present Tense	Past Tense	Present Perfect Tense	Future Perfect Tense	Past Perfect Tense
talk	talked	has (have) talked	will have talked	had talked
help	helped	has (have) helped	will have helped	had helped
walk	walked	has (have) walked	will have walked	had walked

The principal parts of irregular verbs are formed by changes in the verb itself:

Examples:

Present Tense	Past Tense	Present Perfect Tense	Future Perfect Tense	Past Perfect Tense
see	saw	has (have) seen	will have seen	had seen
say	said	has (have) said	will have said	had said
go	went	has (have) gone	will have gone	had gone

Examples:

Present Tense

We were taught that vitamins <u>were</u> important for our well-being. ✗
We were taught that vitamins <u>are</u> important for our well-being. ✓

Past Tense

When he spoke, all the people <u>cheer</u> him. ✗
When he spoke, all the people <u>cheered</u> him. ✓

Since he <u>is</u> late, he did not receive a gift. ✗
Since he <u>was</u> late, he did not receive a gift. ✓

Present Perfect Tense

I am told that you <u>had completed</u> the job. ✗
I am told that you <u>have completed</u> the job. ✓

Future Perfect Tense

I <u>have</u> earned enough money for the car by the end of the month. ✗
I <u>will have earned</u> enough money for the car by the end of the month. ✓

Past Perfect Tense

I was told that you <u>have completed</u> the job before you left. ✗
I was told that you <u>had completed</u> the job before you left. ✓

In the first example, the verb tense "are" is used because when expressing a permanent fact, the present tense is used.

The following page contains a summary of the present tense, past tense, and past participles of many common irregular verbs. The past participle is a word that typically expresses completed action, that is traditionally one of the principal parts of the verb, and that is traditionally used in the formation of the perfect tenses in the active voice and of all tenses in the passive voice.

PRINCIPAL PARTS OF COMMON IRREGULAR VERBS

Present	Past	Past Participle
arise	arose	arisen
be	was, were	been
bear	bore	borne
become	became	become
begin	began	begun
bid	bade	bid, bidden
blow	blew	blown
break	broke	broken
bring	brought	brought
build	built	built
buy	bought	bought
catch	caught	caught
choose	chose	chosen
cling	clung	clung
come	came	come
cut	cut	cut
do	did	done
draw	drew	drawn
drink	drank	drunk
drive	drove	driven
eat	ate	eaten
fall	fell	fallen
feed	fed	fed
feel	felt	felt
fight	fought	fought
find	found	found
flee	fled	fled
fling	flung	flung
fly	flew	flown
forget	forgot	forgotten
forgive	forgave	forgiven
freeze	froze	frozen
get	got	gotten
give	gave	given
go	went	gone
grow	grew	grown
hang (a person)	hanged	hanged
hang (an object)	hung	hung
hear	heard	heard
hide	hid	hidden
hold	held	held
hurt	hurt	hurt
keep	kept	kept
know	knew	known
lay	laid	laid

Present	Past	Past Participle
lead	led	led
leave	left	left
lend	lent	lent
lie	lay	lain
light	lit, lighted	lit, lighted
lose	lost	lost
make	made	made
meet	met	met
read	read	read
ride	rode	ridden
ring	rang	rung
rise	rose	risen
run	ran	run
see	saw	seen
send	sent	sent
sew	sewed	sewn
shake	shook	shaken
sit	sat	sat
shoot	shot	shot
shrink	shrank, shrunk	shrunk, shrunken
slay	slew	slain
sleep	slept	slept
slide	slid	slid
speak	spoke	spoken
spend	spent	spent
spin	spun	spun
spring	sprang, sprung	sprung
stand	stood	stood
steal	stole	stolen
sting	stung	stung
swear	swore	sworn
swing	swung	swung
swim	swam	swum
take	took	taken
teach	taught	taught
tear	tore	torn
tell	told	told
think	thought	thought
throw	threw	thrown
wake	waked, woke	waked, woken
wear	wore	worn
weave	wove	woven
win	won	won
wring	wrung	wrung
write	wrote	written

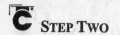

2. When to Use the Perfect Tenses

Use the **present perfect** for an action begun in the past and extended to the present.

Example:

> I cannot have any more turkey or stuffing; already I <u>have eaten</u> too much food. ✓
> In this case, <u>ate</u> would be incorrect. The action <u>have eaten</u> (present perfect) began in the past and extended to the present.

Use the **past perfect** for an action begun and completed in the past before some other past action.

Example:

> The foreman asked what <u>had happened</u> to my eye. ✓

In this case, "happened" would be incorrect. The action "asked" and the action "had happened" (past perfect) are used because one action (regarding the speaker's eye) is "more past" than the other action (the foreman's asking).

Use the **future perfect** for an action begun at any time and completed in the future. When there are two future actions, the action completed first is expressed in the future perfect tense.

Example:

> When I reach Chicago tonight, my uncle <u>will have left</u> for Los Angeles. ✓

The action "will have left" is going to take place before the action "reach," although both actions will occur in the future.

3. The Subjunctive Mood

The **subjunctive** expresses a condition contrary to a fact, a wish, a supposition, or an indirect command.

WHEN TO USE THE SUBJUNCTIVE MOOD

1. To express a wish not likely to be fulfilled or impossible to realize

:) 2. In a subordinate clause after a verb that expresses a command, a request, or a suggestion

3. To express a condition known or supposed to be contrary to fact

4. After "as if" or "as though"

The most common subjunctives are "were" and "be." "Were" is used instead of the indicative form "was," and "be" is used instead of the indicative form "am."

Examples:

> I wish it <u>were</u> possible for us to approve his transfer at this time. ✓
> If I <u>were</u> in St. Louis, I should be glad to attend. ✓
> If this <u>were</u> a simple case, we would easily agree on a solution. ✓
> If I <u>were</u> you, I should not mind the assignment. ✓
> He asked <u>that</u> the report <u>be</u> submitted in duplicate. ✓
> It is recommended <u>that</u> this office <u>be</u> responsible for preparing the statements. ✓
> We suggest <u>that</u> he <u>be</u> relieved of the assignment. ✓

In formal writing and speech, "as if" and "as though" are followed by the subjunctive since they introduce as supposition something not factual. In informal writing and speaking, the indicative is sometimes used.

Examples:

He talked <u>as if</u> he <u>were</u> an expert on taxation. (He is not.) ✓
This report looks <u>as though</u> it <u>were</u> the work of a college freshman. ✓

Avoid shifts in mood. Once you have decided on the mood that properly expresses your message, use that mood throughout the sentence or the paragraph. A shift in mood is confusing to the listener or reader; it indicates that the speaker or writer himself has changed his way of looking at the conditions.

Example:

It is requested that a report of the proceedings <u>be</u> prepared and copies <u>should be</u> distributed to all members. ("Be" is subjunctive; "should be" is indicative.) ✗
It is requested that a report of the proceedings <u>be</u> prepared and that copies <u>be</u> distributed to all members. ✓

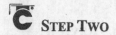

EXERCISE **3**

Analyzing Sentence Structure

DIRECTIONS: In Sentences #1-30, circle the correct verb choice. Answers are on page 942.

1. Each year, many people who did not graduate from high school (receive, receives) GED diplomas.

2. The books on the top shelf (was, were) all written by Emily Brontë.

3. The stores in the downtown sector's newly renovated mall (offer, offers) brand name fashions at reduced prices.

4. Only a few dust-covered bottles of the vintage wine (remain, remains) in the cellar.

5. Each tourist who visits the caverns (is, are) given a guidebook.

6. Underneath the leaf covering (was, were) several different species of insects.

7. The young boys, who had never before been in trouble with the law, (was, were) worried about what their parents would say.

8. Several barrels containing a highly toxic liquid (has, have) been discovered at the abandoned factory.

9. The sponsors of the arts and crafts fair (hope, hopes) that it will attract several thousand visitors.

10. Dawn, Harriet, and Gloria, who have formed their own singing group, (is, are) auditioning for jobs.

11. According to insiders, the mayor, whose administration has been rocked by several crises, (worry, worries) that more layoffs are inevitable.

12. There (has, have) been several acts of vandalism in the cemetery in recent months.

13. Rock musicians who perform in front of large speakers often (loses, lose) part of their hearing.

14. The leaves from the branches of the tree that hang over the fence (falls, fall) into the neighbor's yard.

15. The computer and the printer, which are sitting on James' desk, (has, have) never been used.

16. Theresa, wearing her hip-length waders, (was, were) fishing in the middle of the stream.

17. The film critic for the *New York Times* (write, writes) that the film is very funny and entertaining.

18. Several of the ingredients that are used in the dish (has, have) to be prepared in advance.

19. The computer that controls the temperature of the living quarters of the ship (was, were) malfunctioning.

20. There (has, have) been some support for a proposal to build a new courthouse in the center of town.

21. Bill and Jean (is, are) going to the game tomorrow.

22. There (was, were) several students absent last week.

23. I hope that no one has left (his or her, their) homework at home.

24. Each of the sisters celebrated (her, their) birthday at the Plaza.

25. The music of Verdi's operas (is, are) filled with dramatic sweep.

26. All the musicians tuned (his, their) instruments.

27. Either Mrs. Martinez or Carlos (go, goes) to church each week.

28. I told you to (have, have had) the dog walked and fed by the time I got home from work.

29. Last month, the storekeeper, having lost most of his business to a conglomerate retail store, (can, could) not pay the monthly rent bill.

30. Once the weather (became, becomes) cold, Jim could no longer ride his bicycle to work.

DIRECTIONS: For Items #31-58, choose the verb form that completes the sentence correctly. Answers are on page 944.

31. A gentleman is _____ to see you.

    A. comes
    B. came
    C. come
    D. coming
    E. will come

32. Bill was _____ to telephone you last night.

    A. to suppose
    B. supposed
    C. suppose
    D. supposing
    E. will suppose

33. My friend has _____ to get impatient.

    A. to begin
    B. began
    C. begin
    D. beginning
    E. begun

34. He has _____ a serious cold.

    A. catched
    B. caught
    C. catch
    D. catching
    E. will catch

35. He could _____ before large groups if he were asked.

    A. sing
    B. sang
    C. sung
    D. singed
    E. singing

36. She has _____ before large groups several times.

    A. sing
    B. sang
    C. sung
    D. singed
    E. singing

37. They have already _____ to the theater.

    A. go
    B. goes
    C. going
    D. gone
    E. will go

38. He has _____ me excellent advice.

    A. give
    B. gave
    C. gived
    D. giving
    E. given

39. He is _____ to his parents.

    A. to devote
    B. devote
    C. devoted
    D. devoting
    E. will devote

40. The engineer has designed and _____ his own home.

    A. to build
    B. builds
    C. building
    D. built
    E. had built

41. He _____ as he ran onto the stage following the clown and the magician.

    A. to laugh
    B. laughing
    C. laughed
    D. laughs
    E. had laughed

42. She _____ the high-jump so well at trials that she is going to the Olympics this summer.

    A. had jumped
    B. to jump
    C. jumping
    D. jumps
    E. jumped

43. It _____ that she continued to blame me even after she knew it wasn't my fault.

    A. hurt
    B. hurts
    C. has hurt
    D. hurting
    E. will hurt

44. The man _____ the murder occur if he had really been on that street corner when he said he was.

    A. see
    B. sees
    C. would have saw
    D. seen
    E. would have seen

45. The child _____ everywhere now that she is able to stand up by herself.
    A. to walk
    B. walks
    C. walked
    D. walking
    E. had walked

46. Tomorrow morning, Sam _____ his sister.
    A. was calling
    B. called
    C. calling
    D. has called
    E. will call

47. After she had completed her investigation, the state trooper _____ her report.
    A. was writing
    B. wrote
    C. has written
    D. writes
    E. will write

48. When I was growing up, we _____ every summer at my grandmother's home in the country.
    A. spend
    B. will spend
    C. have spent
    D. were spending
    E. spent

49. Whenever we get a craving for a late night snack, we _____ a pizza.
    A. order
    B. ordered
    C. had ordered
    D. have ordered
    E. were ordering

50. For years now, John _____ his milk at the corner grocery.
    A. buys
    B. will buy
    C. has bought
    D. is buying
    E. bought

51. We were just leaving when the telephone _____.
    A. rang
    B. will ring
    C. was ringing
    D. has rung
    E. had rung

52. We arrived at the house by noon, but the wedding _____ over.
    A. is
    B. will be
    C. had been
    D. has been
    E. was

53. We _____ to drive to the game, but the car stalled.
    A. plan
    B. will plan
    C. had planned
    D. are planning
    E. have planned

54. The roofers were putting the last shingles on the house while the plumber _____ the water lines.
    A. is testing
    B. was testing
    C. tests
    D. will test
    E. had tested

55. A large flock of Canadian Geese _____ over the meadow and landed in the pond.
    A. will fly
    B. were flying
    C. fly
    D. flew
    E. are flying

56. Hui worked very hard to complete her coursework before the baby _____ due.
    A. is
    B. are
    C. was
    D. will be
    E. were

57. We _____ to drive from Wisconsin to Washington in two days, but we were late.
    A. want
    B. are wanting
    C. were wanted
    D. wants
    E. had wanted

58. Earl and I _____ to eat lunch together outside if it doesn't rain.
    A. will hope
    B. had hoped
    C. hope
    D. did hope
    E. hoped

DIRECTIONS: For Items #59-81, circle the letter of the underlined part of the sentence containing the error. Answers are on page 946.

59. The owner of the collection <u>requested that</u> the museum
A
<u>require</u> <u>all people with a camera</u> <u>to leave</u> them at the
B   C   D
door.   *all people with cameras*

60. The young comic <u>found</u> that capturing the audience's
A
attention was easy, <u>but to maintain</u> <u>their</u> interest <u>was</u>
B   C   D
difficult.   *maintaining*

61. The whale had been <u>laying</u> on the beach for over two
A
hours before the rescue teams <u>were able to begin</u>
B
<u>moving</u> it <u>back into</u> the water.   *lying*
C   D

62. The praying mantis <u>is welcomed by</u> homeowners for <u>its</u>
A   B
ability <u>to control</u> destructive garden pests, <u>unlike the</u>
C   D
<u>cockroach, which serves no useful function.</u>
D

63. The <u>newly</u> <u>purchased</u> picture was <u>hanged</u> on the back
A   B   C
wall <u>nearest</u> the bay window.   *hung*
D

64. The <u>opening scene</u> of the film was a <u>grainy, black-and-</u>
A   B
<u>white</u> shot of an empty town square <u>in which</u> an outlaw
B   C
was <u>hung</u>.
D

65. <u>We spent</u> an exhausting day <u>shopping we</u> <u>could hardly</u>
A   B   C
wait <u>to get</u> home.
D

66. The fact that she is bright, articulate, and <u>has charisma</u>
A
<u>will serve</u> her well in her campaign for governor,
B
<u>particularly</u> since her opponent <u>has none</u> of those
C   D
qualities.

67. Puritans such as William Bradford <u>displaying</u> the
A
courage and piety <u>needed to survive</u> in the New World,
B
a world <u>both</u> promising and threatening, <u>which</u> offered
C   D
unique challenges to their faith.

68. The woman to <u>whom</u> I take my clothes <u>for tailoring</u> has
A   B
<u>sewed</u> the hem on this skirt <u>perfectly</u>.
C   D

69. Unfortunately, <u>before</u> cures are found for diseases such
A
as cancer, many lives <u>would have been</u> lost and
B
million of dollars in medical services <u>spent to</u> treat
C
symptoms <u>rather than</u> to provide a cure.
D

70. The <u>house on</u> the corner was <u>completely</u> <u>empty, no</u>
A   B   C
one <u>came</u> to the door.
D

71. For many people, it is difficult <u>to accept</u> compliments
A
graciously and <u>even more difficult</u> <u>taking</u> criticism
B   C
<u>graciously</u>.
D

72. <u>Due to the</u> <u>extremely warm</u> weather this winter, the
A   B
water has not <u>froze</u> on the pond <u>sufficiently</u>.
C   D

73. The French poet Artaud <u>believed</u> <u>that,</u> <u>following</u> the
A   B   C
climax of a drama, the audience <u>experienced</u> a violent
D
catharsis and is thereby "reborn."

74. <u>Where</u> had <u>everyone</u> <u>gone all</u> the lights were <u>off</u>.
A   B   C   D

75. <u>Rather</u> than <u>declaring</u> bankruptcy, he <u>applied</u> for a loan
A   B   C
and the bank <u>loaned</u> him the money.
D

76. <u>Wagering</u> on the Kentucky Derby favorite <u>is</u> a bad
A   B
<u>betting</u> proposition, for in the last fifteen years, the
C
horse that has been the crowd favorite at post time of
the Kentucky Derby <u>loses</u> the race.
D

77. We entered the cave <u>very</u> <u>slowly almost</u> afraid of what
    A   B
    we <u>might find</u> <u>there</u>.
    C   D

78. After he <u>had learned</u> <u>of</u> her suicide, he <u>drunk</u> all of the
    A   B   C
    poison <u>from the vial</u>.
    D

79. <u>During the years</u> she spent <u>searching for a cure</u> for the
    A   B
    disease, Dr. Thompson interviewed hundreds of
    patients, ran thousands of tests, and <u>cross-checking</u>
    C
    <u>millions of bits of data</u>.
    D

80. <u>After struggling with the problem</u> for most of the
    A
    afternoon, he finally <u>flinged</u> the papers <u>on</u> the desk and
    B   C
    <u>ran out of the room</u>.
    D

81. <u>Suddenly</u>, I felt that something <u>was going to</u> <u>happen</u>
    A   B   C
    <u>my</u> heart began to <u>beat furiously</u>.
    C   D

DIRECTIONS: For Sentences #82-96, correct the faulty parallelism if one exists. Answers are on page 947.

82. When at school, he studies, goes to the library, and he
    works on the computer.
    ... he studies, goes to the library and works on the computer

83. In order to get eight hours of sleep, the student prefers
    to sleep sleeping in late in the morning to go to bed early in the
    evening. *+ or + 4 going*
    In order to get eight hours of

84. I still need to pass Math 252, English 301, and return
    two overdue books before I am allowed to graduate.
    pass Math 252 and English 301
    and return ...

85. You need to talk to either the teacher or the counselor.
    CORRECT

86. Dr. Smydra is not only a captivating lecturer, but also
    an engaging conversationalist.
    CORRECT

87. I will either graduate this fall or lose out on a great
    opportunity with IBM.

88. Our instructor suggested that we study the assignment
    carefully, go to the library to research the topic
    extensively, and we should conduct a survey among 20
    subjects.

89. The increase of attrition among community college
    students is caused by a lack of family support and
    students have a limited income while attending school.

90. Many non-smokers complained about the health risks
    associated with second-hand smoke; as a result,
    smoking is banned in the library, in the cafeteria, and
    smokers have to leave the building to light a cigarette.

91. After talking to financial aid and see your advisor,
    return to the registrar's office.

92. Professor Walker not only helped me, but many of my
    classmates as well.

93. In his communications class, he can either work in
    groups or in pairs.

94. I prefer that other geography textbook because of the
    clear explanations, numerous exercises, and Mrs.
    Patrick's vivid teaching style.

95. The question is whether to study tonight or should I get
    up earlier tomorrow morning?

96. Reasons for the latest tuition increase are the upgraded
    computers, new library and, last but not least, inflation
    has increased to 6.5%.

Problems of Logical Expression

Ask yourself the following five questions when checking the logical expression of a sentence.

CHECKLIST FOR LOGICAL EXPRESSION ERRORS

1. Does the sentence contain a faulty or illogical comparison?

2. Does the sentence maintain consistent verb tenses?

3. Does the sentence actually convey the intended meaning?

4. Is the sentence clear and concise?

5. Does the sentence contain any misplaced modifiers?

Faulty or Illogical Comparisons

One problem of logical expression is faulty or illogical comparisons. A faulty comparison is the attempt to compare two things that cannot logically be compared. Consider the following faulty examples. Note: ✓ = correct, ✗ = wrong.

Examples:

> Today, life expectancies of both men and women are much higher compared to the turn of the century when living conditions were much harsher. ✗
> The average salary of a professional basketball player is higher than the top-level management of most corporations. ✗

A comparison can only be made between like items. Yet, in the first sentence we see an attempt to compare "life expectancies" with "the turn of the century"—two dissimilar concepts. The sentence is corrected by simply adding the phrase "those of" before "the turn of the century." Now we have life expectancies compared to life expectancies, and that is a logical comparison.

The same error occurs in the second sentence. An attempt is made to compare "average salary" to "management." The error can be corrected in the same way as in the first example: "…is higher than those of the top-level management…."

WATCH FOR ILLOGICAL COMPARISONS

Be alert for sentences that attempt to make an illogical comparison between two dissimilar concepts.

When two things are being compared, the comparative form of the adjective is used. The comparative is formed in one of the two following ways.

RULES FOR COMPARISONS BETWEEN TWO OBJECTS

1. Two objects can be compared by adding "-er" to the adjective.

2. Two objects can be compared by placing "more" before the adjective.

Examples:

She is <u>more prettier</u> than her sister. ✗
She is <u>more pretty</u> than her sister. ✓
She is <u>prettier</u> than her sister. ✓

Jeremy is <u>more wiser</u> than we know. ✗
Jeremy is <u>wiser</u> than we know. ✓
Jeremy is <u>more wise</u> than we know. ✓

If three or more things are being compared, then the superlative form of the adjective is used. The superlative is formed in one of the two following ways.

RULES FOR COMPARISONS AMONG THREE OR MORE OBJECTS

1. Three or more objects can be compared by adding "-est" to the adjective.

2. Three or more objects can be compared by placing "most" before the adjective.

Examples:

Mary is the <u>shorter</u> of all of her friends. ✗
Mary is the <u>shortest</u> of all of her friends. ✓

This is the <u>most sharpest</u> knife I have. ✗
This is the <u>sharpest</u> knife I have. ✓

Calculus is the <u>most difficult</u> class that I have this year. ✓

Some comparative and superlative modifiers require changing the words themselves. A few of these irregular comparisons are given below; consult your dictionary whenever you are in doubt about the comparisons of any adjective or adverb.

MODIFIERS THAT DO CHANGE

Positive	Comparative	Superlative
good	better	best
well	better	best
bad (evil, ill)	worse	worst
badly	worse	worst
far	farther, further	farthest, furthest
late	later, latter	latest, last
little	less, lesser	least
many, much	more	most

Some adjectives and adverbs express qualities that go beyond comparison. They represent the highest degree of a given quality and, as a result, they cannot be improved. Some of these words are listed below.

MODIFIERS THAT DO <u>NOT</u> CHANGE

complete	preferable	horizontally	supreme	totally
correct	round	secondly	immortally	unique
dead	deadly	square	infinitely	uniquely
perfectly	exact	squarely	perfect	universally
perpendicularly				

The use of the comparative in such an expression as "This thing is better than any other" implies that "this thing" is separate from the group or class to which it is being compared. In these expressions, a word such as "other" or "else" is required to separate the thing being compared from the rest of the group of which it is a part.

Example:

Our house is cooler than any house on the block. ✗
Since "our house" is one of the houses on the block, it should not be included in the comparison. The sentence should read:
Our house is cooler than any other house on the block. ✓

Example:

He has a better record than any salesman in our group. ✗

Since "he" is himself one of the salesmen in the group, the comparison must separate him from the group. The sentence should read:

He has a better record than any <u>other</u> salesman in our group. ✓

Finally, be aware of incomplete comparisons. The result is illogical and confusing.

Examples:

The plays of Shakespeare are as good as Marlowe. ✗
The plays of Shakespeare are as good as <u>those</u> of Marlowe. ✓

His skill in tennis is far better than other athletes his age. ✗
His skill in tennis is far better than <u>that</u> of other athletes his age. ✓

His poetry is as exciting, if not more exciting than, the poetry of his instructor. ✗
His poetry is as exciting <u>as</u>, if not more exciting than, the poetry of his instructor. ✓

Sequence and Verb Tense

A second common problem of logical expression is poor choice of verb tense. The choice of *verb tense* in a correctly written sentence reflects the *sequence* of events described. The following examples contain verb tense errors. Note: ✓ = correct, ✗ = wrong.

Examples:

As soon as Linda finished writing her dissertation, she <u>will take</u> a well-earned vacation in Paris. ✗
A recent study shows that many mothers re-enter the labor force after their children <u>left</u> home. ✗

In the first example, both "writing" and "vacation" must be placed in the same time frame. As written, the sentence places the two actions in different, unconnected time frames. Depending on whether Linda has already completed the dissertation, the sentence could be corrected in either of two ways:

As soon as Linda <u>finishes</u> writing her dissertation, she will take a well-earned vacation in Paris. ✓
As soon as Linda finished writing her dissertation, she <u>took</u> a well-earned vacation in Paris. ✓

The first corrected version of the first example states that neither event has yet occurred and that the writing will precede the vacation. The second corrected version of the first example states that the events are completed and that the writing preceded the vacation.

In the second example, the verb "left" is incorrect because the verb "re-enter" is describing a present, ongoing action. The sentence can be corrected by making it clear that "children leaving home" is also a present phenomenon:

A recent study shows that many mothers re-enter the labor force after their children <u>leave</u> home. ✓
A recent study shows that many mothers re-enter the labor force after their children <u>have left</u> home. ✓

Either sentence is acceptable since both make it clear that leaving home is not a completed past action but an ongoing phenomenon.

 WATCH FOR SHIFTING VERB TENSES

Make sure that verb tenses properly reflect the sequence, as well as the duration, of any action described in the sentence.

Examples:

Charles came to town last week and <u>goes</u> to a resort where he <u>rests</u> for three days. ✘
Charles came to town last week and <u>went</u> to a resort where he <u>rested</u> for three days. ✔

Joan came home last week and <u>goes</u> to her home in the country where she <u>spends</u> the last weekend of her vacation. ✘
Joan came home last week and <u>went</u> to her home in the country where she <u>spent</u> the last weekend of her vacation. ✔

Unintended Meanings

Another problem in the category of logical expression relates to whether the sentence actually says what it intends to say. Often, sentences will intend to say one thing but actually say another. Note: ✘ = wrong.

Examples:

A childless charwoman's daughter, Dr. Roberts was a self-made woman. ✘
If the present interest rates fall, the dollar will lose some of its value on the foreign exchange. ✘

At first, both of these sentences may seem plausible, but a closer reading will show that each contains an error of logical expression. The first example is actually self-contradictory. As written, it asserts that Dr. Roberts was the daughter of a childless charwoman. In that case, Dr. Roberts would indeed have been a self-made woman! The sentence intends to say that Dr. Roberts was both childless and the daughter of a charwoman: "A charwoman's daughter and childless, Dr. Roberts was a self-made woman."

The second example is a bit subtler. It suggests that present interest rates can change, but that is internally inconsistent, since if the interest rate changes, the result is a new interest rate, not a changed "present" rate. The sentence is corrected by deleting the word "present."

In this category, there are as many possible examples as there are possible errors in human reasoning. Therefore, when checking for intended meaning, just ask yourself what the logic of the sentence implies.

CHECK THAT THE SENTENCE STRUCTURE HAS INTENDED MEANING

 Determine if the sentence says what it intends to say from the sentence's logical structure.

Conciseness

There are endless possibilities for conciseness errors. Several examples are illustrated below. Note: ✔ = correct, ✘ = wrong.

1. Avoid Awkward Sentences and Passive Verbs

A sentence may be grammatically and logically correct yet be in need of correction because it is awkward.

Examples:

> The giant condor is able to spread its wings up to 25 feet. ✗
> The giant condor has a wingspan of up to 25 feet. ✔
>
> Although most students would benefit from further study of the sciences, doing so is frightening to most of them in that science courses are more difficult than liberal arts courses. ✗
> Although most students would benefit from further study of the sciences, most of them are afraid to take science courses because they are more difficult than liberal arts courses. ✔
>
> Given that the Incas lacked the wheel, the buildings at Machu Picchu are more astonishing than any Greek temples that are comparable as an achievement. ✗
> Given that the Incas lacked the wheel, the buildings at Machu Picchu are more astonishing than any comparable Greek temple. ✔

In each case, the second sentence is less awkward and more clearly renders the intended thought by being more direct and concise.

A common error among writers is the use of the passive verb. Each of the following examples illustrates that by replacing weak passive verbs, sentences are rendered both clear and concise.

Examples:

> One-fourth of the market <u>was captured</u> by the new computer firm. ✗
> The new computer firm <u>captured</u> one-fourth of the market. ✔
> The lottery prize <u>being</u> $110 million, there are almost as many tickets sold as there are prize dollars. ✗
> When the lottery prize <u>is</u> $110 million, there are almost as many tickets sold as there are prize dollars. ✔
> The teacher, <u>having finished</u> the day's lesson, let us leave class early. ✗
> Because the teacher <u>finished</u> the day's lesson, she let us leave class early. ✔

AVOID PASSIVE VERBS

 Any verb construction using a form of the verb "be" or "have" in addition to the active verb is called a passive verb. Passive verbs are not often used and should be avoided. The active voice is stronger and more direct.

---

2. *Avoid Needlessly Wordy Sentences*

Occasionally, an original sentence will be incorrect simply because it is needlessly wordy.

Examples:

> The protracted discussion over what route to take continued for a long time. ✗
> The discussion over what route to take continued for a long time. ✔
>
> An aim of the proposal is chiefly to ensure and guarantee the academic freedom of students. ✗
> An aim of the proposal is to guarantee the academic freedom of students. ✔

To be protracted is to be continued for a long time; an aim is a chief concern, and to ensure is to guarantee. Therefore, each original is needlessly wordy.

Misplaced Modifiers

Another error of logical expression is the infamous misplaced modifier. Generally, a modifier should be placed as close to what it modifies as possible. A modifier that is too far from that which it intends to modify, or too close to some other important element, will seem to modify the wrong part of the sentence. Consider the following faulty sentences. Note: ✔ = correct, ✗ = wrong.

Examples:

> Stuffed with herb dressing, trussed neatly, and baked to a golden hue, Aunt Fannie served her famous holiday turkey. ✖

> The doctor said gently to the patient that there was nothing wrong with a smile. ✖

> At the party, Fred served cold lemonade to his thirsty guests in paper cups. ✖

Consider the first example—poor Aunt Fannie! The proximity of the introductory modifier to Aunt Fannie suggests that she was stuffed, trussed, and baked. The sentence can be corrected by relocating the modifying phrase: "Aunt Fannie served her famous holiday turkey, stuffed with herb dressing, trussed neatly, and baked to a golden hue."

The second example is ambiguous and it could mean either that there is nothing wrong with smiling or that the doctor said, with a smile, that nothing was wrong with the patient. The corrected sentence reads: "With a smile, the doctor said gently to the patient that there was nothing wrong."

Finally, in the third example, the location of the prepositional phrase "in paper cups" implies that the guests are actually inside the paper cups! The sentence is corrected by moving the modifying phrase so that it is closer to what it is intended to modify: "At the party, Fred served cold lemonade in paper cups to his thirsty guests."

WATCH FOR MISPLACED MODIFIERS

 Be alert for sentences with ambiguous or incorrect modification. Correct misplaced modifiers by placing them as close as possible to what they modify.

Examples:

> I bought a piano from an old lady with intricate carvings. ✖
> I bought a piano with intricate carvings from an old lady. ✓
> I read about the destruction of Rome in my history class. ✖
> In my history class, I read about the destruction of Rome. ✓

The word "only" often causes confusion. Examine the following confusing sentences.

Examples:

> <u>Only</u> he kissed her. ✓
> He <u>only</u> kissed her. ✓
> He kissed <u>only</u> her. ✓

All three sentences are possible, but a different meaning is conveyed in each, depending on the positioning of "only."

Finally, problems may be created by the placement of a participle phrase.

Example:

> Answering the doorbell, the cake remained in the oven. ✖

It sounds as though the cake answered the doorbell! Correct this sentence by adding a subject to which the phrase can refer:

Answering the doorbell, we forgot to take the cake from the oven. ✓

Example:

Falling on the roof, we heard the sound of the rain. ✗
We heard the sound of the rain falling on the roof. ✓

Problems of Logical Expression

DIRECTIONS: Read the following passage. In Items #1-14, choose the best answer that corrects the sentence without changing its meaning or intent. When correcting the sentences, look at the sentence in the context of the passage in order to check for consistency and logical expression. If the sentence is correct as written, choose (A). Answers are on page 948.

(1) When I was a child, my grandmother's kitchen was the scene of feverish activity during the early fall. (2) Each morning, she would go to the farmers' market and returns with baskets of fruits and vegetables. (3) Then, she would spend the rest of the day preparing the food for the wide-mouthed canning jars that would preserve them through the winter. (4) By late fall, the pantry shelves are lined with rows of jars containing pickled peaches, creamed corn, and many varieties of jams and jellies.

(5) Today, we are able to buy fresh fruits and vegetables at the local grocery store even during the winter. (6) Indeed, years ago, home-canning was a practical solution to one of nature's dilemmas. (7) On the one hand, the harvest produced more fruits and vegetables than could be consumed immediately, so without some way to preserve the produce, they would spoil. (8) On the other hand, during the winter months, fresh produce was not available, so it was important to have preserved foods available.

(9) There are nothing mysterious about home-canning. (10) Fruits or vegetables are packed into special canning jars, fitted with self-sealing lids, and you submerge them in boiling water. (11) The sustained high heat kills dangerous organisms causing the food to spoil. (12) As it gradually cools, a vacuum pulls the lid down against the mouth of the jar to make an airtight seal. (13) Unless the seal is broken, no organisms can enter the jar to cause spoilage.

(14) Although we no longer depend on home-canning, home-canning can be fun. (15) Jams and jellies spread over hot toast on a cold winter morning seems to taste better when you have made them yourself. (16) You also enjoy giving homemade preserves to friends and relatives as gifts. (17) All one needs to do to get started is to find a book about home-canning at the local library or bookstore and follow the directions.

1. Sentence (2): Each morning, she would go to the farmers' market and <u>returns</u> with baskets of fruits and vegetables.
   A. NO CHANGE
   B. is returning
   C. would return
   D. was returning
   E. have returned

2. Sentence (3): Then, she would spend the rest of the day preparing the food for the wide-mouthed canning jars that <u>would preserve them</u> through the winter.
   A. NO CHANGE
   B. would preserve it
   C. preserved them
   D. was preserving them
   E. preserves it

3. Sentence (4): By late fall, the pantry shelves <u>are lined</u> with rows of jars containing pickled peaches, creamed corn, and many varieties of jams and jellies.
   A. NO CHANGE
   B. is lined
   C. were lined
   D. was lined
   E. might be lined

4. Sentence (6): <u>Indeed,</u> years ago, home-canning was a practical solution to one of nature's dilemmas.
   A. NO CHANGE
   B. Indeed
   C. Furthermore,
   D. Moreover,
   E. However,

5. Sentence (7): On the one hand, the harvest produced more fruits and vegetables than could be consumed immediately, so without some way to preserve the produce, <u>they would spoil</u>.
   A. NO CHANGE
   B. it would spoil
   C. they spoil
   D. it spoils
   E. it spoiled

6. Sentence (8): On the other hand, during the winter months, fresh produce was not available, so it <u>was</u> important to have preserved foods available.

A. NO CHANGE
B. is
C. has been
D. could be
E. can be

7. Sentence (9): There <u>are</u> nothing mysterious about home-canning.

A. NO CHANGE
B. is
C. was
D. were
E. has been

8. Sentence (10): Fruits or vegetables are packed into special canning jars, fitted with self-sealing lids, and <u>you submerge them</u> in boiling water.

A. NO CHANGE
B. you submerge it
C. you submerged them
D. you submerged it
E. submerged

9. Sentence (11): The sustained high heat kills dangerous organisms <u>causing</u> the food to spoil.

A. NO CHANGE
B. that caused
C. that could cause
D. to cause
E. which caused

10. Sentence (12): <u>As it gradually cools,</u> a vacuum pulls the lid down against the mouth of the jar to make an airtight seal.

A. NO CHANGE
B. As they gradually cool,
C. Gradually cooling,
D. Gradually cooled,
E. As the jars gradually cool,

11. Sentence (13): Unless the seal is broken, no organisms <u>can enter</u> the jar to cause spoilage.

A. NO CHANGE
B. are entering
C. entered
D. have entered
E. had entered

12. Sentence (15): Jams and jellies spread over hot toast on a cold winter morning <u>seems to taste</u> better when you have made them yourself.

A. NO CHANGE
B. seem to taste
C. seems tasting
D. will seem to taste
E. seemed to taste

13. Sentence (16): You also enjoy giving homemade preserves to friends and relatives as gifts.

A. NO CHANGE
B. will enjoy giving
C. enjoyed giving
D. enjoy to give
E. enjoys giving

14. Sentence (17): All <u>one needs</u> to do to get started is to find a book about home-canning at the local library or bookstore and follow the directions.

A. NO CHANGE
B. your needs
C. you need
D. people need
E. the reader needs

DIRECTIONS: In Items #15-29, circle the letter of the underlined part of the sentence containing the error. Answers are on page 950.

15. <u>Written in almost total isolation from the world</u>, Emily
    (A)
    Dickinson <u>spoke of</u> love <u>and</u> death in <u>her</u> poems.
        B   C   D

16. <u>Early in his career</u>, the pianist entertained thoughts
        A
    <u>of becoming</u> a composer; but after receiving bad
        B
    reviews for his own work, <u>he</u> <u>had given up</u>.
                               C   D

    gave up

17. The baseball game was halted <u>due to rain and</u>
        A
    <u>rescheduled</u> for the following day, <u>even though</u> <u>the fans</u>
        B   C   D
    <u>would not leave</u> the stadium.
        D

    but

18. Being highly qualified for the position, the bank

    president will conduct a final interview of the new

    candidate tomorrow, after which he will make her a

    job offer.

19. The literature of Native Americans has been

    overlooked by most scholars, and the reason is because

    most university courses in literature are taught in

    departments that also teach a language, such as French.

20. In broken English, the police officer patiently listened

    to the tourist ask for directions to Radio City Music

    Hall, after which she motioned the tourist and his

    family into the squad car and drove them to their

    destination.

21. Bullfighting remains a controversial sport and many

    are repulsed by it, since Hemingway was an aficionado

    of the sport and glorified it in his writing.

22. Following the recent crash of the stock market, Peter

    bought a book on portfolio management in order to

    learn methods to protect his investments from a well-

    known investment banker.

23. Since we have a broader technological base, American

    scientists believe that our space program will

    ultimately prove superior to the Soviet Union.

24. Although a person may always represent himself in a

    judicial proceeding, licensed lawyers only may

    represent others in such proceedings for a fee.

25. Unlike the pale and delicately built ballerinas of

    romantic ballet, Judith Jamison's movement seems

    more African than European-American, and her

    physical appearance reinforces the contrast.

26. Market experts predict that in ten years, when the

    harmful effects of caffeine become more generally

    known, the number of tons of decaffeinated coffee

    consumed by Americans each year will exceed coffee

    containing caffeine.

27. Illiteracy, a widespread problem in the United States,

    undermines productivity because many mistakes are

    made by workers who do not know how to read on

    the job.

28. As sailors are often assigned to ships that remain at sea

    for months at a time, men in the Navy spend more time

    away from home than any branch of the service.

29. Like A.J. Ayer, much of Gilbert Ryle's philosophical

    argumentation relies on analysis of the way people

    ordinarily use language.

DIRECTIONS: For Sentences #30-44, correct the faulty comparison if one exists. Answers are on page 951.

30. The life of my generation is easier than my parents.

... than that of my parents.

31. My two daughters enjoy different TV shows; the oldest watches game shows, while the youngest prefers talk shows.

when there's only two subjects don't use "est"

the older one watch..., while the younger ...

32. Her present instructor is better of all the ones she has had so far.

instructor is the best of all the ones ...

33. In the technology lab, I choose the computer with the more greater memory. *omit more*

Or

greatest

34. According to the counselor, taking these classes in this order is much beneficial than the other way around.

more

35. Our school is very unique in many aspects.

Our school is ~~very~~ unique ...

36. The fraternity he joined is better than all fraternities.

37. Professor Baker's explanations are not as clear as Professor Thomas' explanations.

38. You can learn just as much, if not more, online as in a regular classroom.

39. Which of these three sections is better?

40. I am spending more time on the assignments in my management class than all my other classes combined.

41. You will receive your grades no latest than tomorrow at 2 p.m.

42. There is no need for farther negotiation.

43. She is doing so badly in her art class that she could not do any worst.

44. This exercise seems more difficult than all of them.

DIRECTIONS: Rewrite Sentences #45-54 so that the modified word in each is clear. Answers are on page 952.

45. He tripped on a crack in the pavement going to school.

Going to school, he tripped on a crack in the pavement.

46. Mary only failed the test; everyone else in her class passed.

Only Mary ....

47. Did you see the film about the five people on the boat on television?

Did you see the film on television ...

48. The police officer ordered the man to stop in his patrol car.

The police officer, in his patrol car, ordered the man to stop.

49. Upon picking up the phone, the noise became muted.

When you picked up the phone, the noise became muted.

50. While swimming, a fish nibbled on my toe.

While I was swimming, ...

51. He went to the old church to pray for the people on Cemetery Hill.

52. Of all his admirers, his wife only loved him.

_____

_____

53. Upon entering the class, the blackboard came into view.

_____

_____

54. The baby was pushed by his mother in a stroller.

_____

_____

DIRECTIONS: Some of Sentences #55-64 are correct, but most are incorrect. Rewrite each incorrect sentence correctly. Answers are on page 953.

55. She likes tennis, golf, and to go swimming.

She likes tennis, golf and
swimming.

56. He could not deliver the supplies. Because the roads had not yet been plowed.

. . . the supplies because . . .

_____

57. If you want to succeed, one must be willing to work hard.   _y you_

_____

_____

58. Jeff is taller than any boy in his class.

. . . ~~teh~~ than any
other boy . . .

59. To get to school, we nearly walked two miles.   _had_

~~nearhea~~ . . . we walked nearly . . .

_____

60. The heroine was unbelievable naive.   _ly_

. . . unbelievably . . .

_____

61. Drive carefully. There may be ice on the roads.

_____

_____

62. Leaning out the window, the garden could be seen below.

_____

_____

63. The hotel room was clean and comfortable that we had reserved.

_____

_____

64. This book is heavier in weight than that one.

_____

_____

Idioms and Clarity of Expression

Standard English contains numerous idioms and two-word verbs that are perfectly acceptable to use. The following is a list of commonly accepted idioms and two-word verbs.

IDIOMS AND TWO-WORD VERBS

about time, about to
above all
act up
add up (*make sense*)
a good deal of
an arm and a leg
at the drop of a hat
back out (of)
bank on
be about to
be an old hand (at)
be a question of
beat around the bush
be bound to
be broke
be fed up (with)
be off
be out of something
be out of the question
be over
be short for, be short of
be the picture of
be up to someone
be warm
bite off more than one can chew
break down, break the ice
break the news (to)
bring about
broken English
brush up on
by and large
by heart, by no means
call off
call on
care for
catch on, catch up (with)
come across, come down with
come out smelling like a rose
cost an arm and a leg
count on, count out
cut down on, cut it close
cut out, cut out for
day in and day out
die down
do over, do with, do without
dream up
drop in (on), drop off
size up
sleep on it
snap out of
speak up (*say something, speak more loudly*)
spell out (for)
stand a chance
stand for
stand out
start up
stay out, stay up
a stone's throw (from)
straighten up
take a chance, take advantage (of)
take after, take in, take into account

every other
fall behind, fall through
a far cry from
feel free
feel like a million bucks
feel up to
few and far between
fill in (for)
fly off the handle
follow in someone's footsteps
for good
get the hang of
get in one's blood
get in the way
get off, get on, get over, get to
get rid of
get the better of
get under way
give a hand (to, with)
go on (with)
go without saying
hand in, hand out
hang up
have a heart
have in mind
have over
hear first hand (from)
hear from, hear of
hit it off
hold on (to), hold still, hold up
how come?
in the dark, in hot water
in the long run, in no time
jump to conclusions
keep an eye on, keep an eye out (for)
keep from, keep on one's toes
keep on (with), keep up (with)
knock it off
lay off
learn the ropes
leave out
let (somebody) alone, let (somebody) know
let go of
look after, look for, look forward to
look into, look out (for)
look up (to)
make a difference, make a point of
make ends meet, make out
take it easy, take off (*leave*)
take one's mind off, take one's time
take over, take pains, take turns
talk over
tangle with
tell apart
think much of
think over
throw cold water on
tie up, tie into
trade in
turn down, turn up, turn into
turn off, turn on, turn out, turn in
under the weather

make sense of, make way for
make up, make up one's mind
mark up, mark down
may as well, might as well
mean to
move on, move up
next to nothing
nose something out
now and then
odds and ends
on a shoestring, on its last leg
on the go
on one's last leg, on one's toes
on pins and needles
on second thought
on the mend, on the road, on the run
on the tip of one's tongue
on the whole
open up
out of order, out of sorts
out of this world, out to win
over and over
part with
pass up
pat oneself on the back
pay off, pay someone a visit
pick out, pick up (learn)
pick up the tab (for)
a piece of cake
play by ear
point out
pull one's leg
put aside, put off
put one's best foot forward
put together, put up (with)
rave about
rough it
rule out
run into, run out of, run short (of)
save one's breath
search me
see off, see to
serve one right
set out
settle down, settle on
sing another tune
show around, show up
shut down
up against
ups and downs
up-to-date
use up
wait for, wait on
warm up (to)
watch out (for)
wear out
a whole new ballgame
with flying colors
without a hitch
work out (*exercise, solve*)
write out
zero in (on)

...pression that is not idiomatic is one that is not acceptable standard written English for any of the following reasons.

```
┌──────────────────────────────────────────────────────┐
│      CHECKLIST FOR IDIOMATIC EXPRESSION ERRORS         │
│     1. Wrong Prepositions                              │
│     2. Diction                                         │
│     3. Gerunds vs. Infinitives                         │
│     4. Ambiguity in Scope                              │
│     5. Low-Level Usage                                 │
└──────────────────────────────────────────────────────┘
```

Wrong Prepositions

In standard written English, only certain prepositions can be used with certain verbs. You should know which prepositions to use with which verbs as a result of daily conversation and writing in standard written English. Note: ✘ = wrong.

Example:

I asked him repeatedly if he was from <u>about</u> here, but he never answered me. ✘

The phrase "was from about here" is not correct. You should recognize the correct phrase from daily conversation: "he was from around here."

Diction

The second category of idiomatic expression errors involves diction, i.e., word choice. Sometimes, a word is used incorrectly, which leads to a construction that is simply not idiomatic or not acceptable according to standard usage. Note: ✔ = correct, ✘ = wrong.

Example:

The techniques of empirical observation in the social sciences are different <u>than</u> those in the physical sciences. ✘

This example is improved by replacing "than" with "from." Rewritten, the sentence reads: "The techniques of empirical observation in the social sciences are different "from" those in the physical sciences."

A variation on this theme uses pairs of words that are often incorrectly used, as the following examples illustrate.

Examples:

John expressed his intention to make the trip, but <u>if</u> he will actually go is doubtful. ✘

John expressed his intention to make the trip, but <u>whether</u> he will actually go is doubtful. ✓

Herbert divided the cake <u>among</u> Mary and Sally. ✘

Herbert divided the cake <u>between</u> Mary and Sally. ✓

Herbert divided the cake <u>between</u> Mary, Sally, and himself. ✘

Herbert divided the cake <u>among</u> Mary, Sally, and himself. ✓

The <u>amount</u> of students in the class declined as the semester progressed. ✘

The <u>number</u> of students in the class declined as the semester progressed. ✓

There are <u>less</u> students in Professor Smith's class than there are in Professor Jones' class. ✘

There are <u>fewer</u> students in Professor Smith's class than there are in Professor Jones' class. ✓

Some sentences are incorrect because they use a word that does not convey the intended meaning. The confusion is understandable because of the similarity between the correct word and the chosen word.

WATCH FOR INAPPROPRIATE DICTION

Be alert for non-idiomatic usage and commonly misused words.

The following list is an extended summary of commonly confused word groups.

CONFUSING WORD GROUPS

accede—*to agree with* .... They will *accede* to your request for more information.
exceed—*to be more than* .... Unfortunately, her expenditures now *exceed* her income.
concede—*to yield* (not necessarily in agreement) .... They *concede* that more information is necessary.

accept—*to receive*, or .... I'll *accept* the gift from you.
    to agree to something .... I will lend you the money if you *accept* my conditions.
except—*to exclude or excluding* .... Everyone *except* my uncle went home.

access—*availability*, or .... The lawyer was given *access* to the grand jury records.
    to get at .... I could not *access* the files without the proper password.
excess—*state of surpassing specified limits* (noun), or .... Expenditures this month are far in *excess* of income.
    more than usual (adjective) .... The airline charged him fifty dollars for *excess* baggage.

adapt—*to adjust or change* .... Children can *adapt* to changing conditions very easily.
adept—*skillful* .... Proper instruction makes children *adept* in various games.
adopt—*to take as one's own* .... The war orphan was *adopted* by the general and his wife.

adapted to—*original or natural suitability* .... The gills of the fish are *adapted to* underwater breathing.
adapted for—*created suitability* .... Atomic energy is constantly being *adapted for* new uses.
adapted from—*changed to be made suitable* .... Many of Wagner's librettos were *adapted from* Norse sagas.

addition—*the act or process of adding* .... In *addition* to a dictionary, he always used a thesaurus.
edition—*a printing of a publication* .... The first *edition* of Shakespeare's plays appeared in 1623.

advantage—*a superior position* .... He had an *advantage* in experience over his opponent.
benefit—*a favor conferred or earned* .... The rules were changed for his *benefit*.

adverse—*unfavorable* .... He was very upset by the *adverse* decision.
averse—*having a feeling of repugnance or dislike* .... Many writers are *averse* to criticism of their work.

advice—*counsel, opinion* (noun) .... Let me give you some free *advice*.
advise—*to offer advice* (verb) .... I'd *advise* you to see your doctor.

affect—*to influence* (verb) .... The pollution *affected* our health.
effect—*to cause or bring about* (verb), or .... Our lawsuit *effected* a change in the law.
    a result (noun) .... The *effect* of the storm could not be measured.

all ready—*everybody or everything ready* .... They were *all ready* to write when the test began.
already—*previously* .... They had *already* written the letter.

all together—*everybody or everything together* .... The boys and girls stood *all together* in line.
altogether—*completely* .... His action was *altogether* strange for a person of his type.

allude—*to make a reference to* .... In his essay, he *alludes* to Shakespeare's puns.
elude—*to escape from* .... The burglar *eluded* the police.

allusion—*an indirect reference* .... The poem is an *allusion* to one of Shakespeare's sonnets.
illusion—*an erroneous concept or perception* .... My mirror created the *illusion* of space in the narrow hall.

alongside of—*side by side with* .... Bill stood *alongside of* Henry.
alongside—*parallel to the side* .... Park the car *alongside* the curb.

among—*a term used with more than two persons or things* .... The inheritance was equally divided *among* the four kids.
between—*a term used with two persons or things* .... The inheritance was divided *between* the two kids.

angel—*a heavenly creature* .... She has been an *angel* in these difficult times.
angle—*a point at which two lines meet*, or .... A line perpendicular to another line forms a right *angle*.
    an aspect seen from a particular point of view .... From that *angle*, the picture looks completely different.

ante—*a prefix meaning before* .... The *antechamber* is the small room before the main room.
anti—*a prefix meaning against* .... He is known to be *anti*-American.

assistance—*the act of assisting, aid* .... I needed his *assistance* when I repaired the roof.
assistants—*helpers, aides* .... The chief surgeon has four *assistants*.

breadth—*width* .... The canvas was twice greater in length than in *breadth*.
breath—*an intake of air* .... Before you dive in, take a very deep *breath*.
breathe—*to draw air in and give it out* .... It is difficult to *breathe* when you have a bad cold.

CONFUSING WORD GROUPS

build—*to erect, construct (verb), or* .... I want to *build* a sandcastle.
the physical makeup of a person (noun) .... She has a very athletic *build*.
built—*the past tense of build*.. We *built* a moat around the sandcastle.

buy—*to purchase*... I want to *buy* a new tie.
by—*near,* .... My bloodhound likes to sleep *by* the door at night.
by means of, or.. He comes to school *by* public transportation.
not later than .... Mary said that she would be back at work *by* noon.
bye—*free pass to next round*.. She had a *bye* in the tournament.

canvas—*a heavy, coarse material*.. The *canvas* sails were very heavy.
canvass—*to solicit, conduct a survey*... The politicians are going to *canvass* our neighborhood.

capital—*place of government, or*.. Paris is the *capital* of France.
wealth .... It takes substantial *capital* to open a restaurant.
capitol—*building that houses legislatures* .... Congress convenes in the *Capitol* in Washington, D.C.

carat—*a unit of weight*... The movie star wears a ten-*carat* diamond ring.
caret—*a proofreading symbol, indicating where* .... He added a phrase in the space above the *caret*.
something is to be inserted
carrot—*a vegetable* .... Does he feed his pet rabbit a *carrot* every other day?

click—*a brief, sharp sound* .... The detective drew his gun when he heard the lock *click*.
clique—*an exclusive group of people or set* .... In high school, I was not part of any *clique*.

cease—*to end* .... Please *cease* making those sounds.
seize—*to take hold of*... *Seize* him by the collar as he comes around the corner.

choice—*a selection* .... My *choice* for a career is teaching.
choose—*to select* .... We may *choose* our own advisors.
chose—*the past tense of choose* .... I finally *chose* my wedding dress.

cite—*to quote*... He enjoys *citing* Shakespeare to illustrate his views.
sight—*seeing, what is seen*.. The *sight* of the accident was appalling.
site—*a place where something is located or occurs* .... We are seeking a new *site* for the baseball field.

cloth—*fabric or material* .... The seats were covered with *cloth*, not vinyl.
clothe—*to put on clothes, to dress* .... Her job is to *clothe* the actors for each scene.

coarse—*vulgar, or*.. He was shunned because of his *coarse* behavior.
harsh .... The sandpaper was very *coarse*.
course—*a path, or*... The ship took its usual *course*.
a plan of study .... How many *courses* are you taking this term?

complement—*a completing part* .... His wit was a *complement* to her beauty.
compliment—*an expression of praise or admiration* .... He received many *compliments* for his fine work.

confidant—*one to whom private* .... His priest was his only *confidant*.
matters are confided (noun)
confidence—*a feeling of assurance or certainty (noun)* .... The ballplayer is developing *confidence* in his ability.
confident—*having confidence in oneself (adjective)*............... Her success in business has given her a *confident* manner.

conscience—*the ability to recognize the difference* .... The attorney said the criminal lacked a *conscience*.
between right and wrong
conscious—*aware*... He was *conscious* that his actions had consequences.

consul—*a government representative* .... Americans abroad should keep in touch with the *consuls*.
council—*an assembly that meets for deliberation*..................... The student *council* met to discuss a campus dress code.
counsel—*advice (counselor)*.. The defendant heeded the *counsel* of his friends.

decent—*suitable* .... The *decent* thing to do is to admit your error.
descent—*going down* .... The *descent* into the cave was dangerous.
dissent—*disagreement* .... Two of the justices filed a *dissenting* opinion.

desert (DEZZ-ert)—*an arid area*... I have seen several movies set in the Sahara *desert*.
desert (di-ZERT)—*abandon, or* .... The soldier was warned not to *desert* his company.
a reward or punishment .... We're certain that execution is a just *desert* for his crime.
dessert (di-ZERT)—*the final course of a meal* .... We had strawberry shortcake for *dessert*.

disburse—*to pay out* .... This week the bank has *disbursed* a million dollars.
disperse—*to scatter, distribute widely* .... The defeated army began to *disperse*.

discomfit—*to upset* .... The general's plan was designed to *discomfit* the enemy.
discomfort—*lack of ease* .... This starched collar causes *discomfort*.

dual—*double* .... Dr. Jekyll had a *dual* personality.
duel—*a contest between two persons or groups* .... Aaron Burr and Alexander Hamilton engaged in a *duel*.

elicit—*to draw forth, evoke*.. Her performance *elicited* tears from the audience.
illicit—*illegal, unlawful* .... He was arrested because of his *illicit* business dealings.

emigrate—*to leave a country* .... They *emigrated* from Norway in the nineteenth century.
immigrate—*to enter a country* .... Many Irish *immigrated* to the United States.

CONFUSING WORD GROUPS

eminent—*of high rank, prominent, outstanding* .... He was the most *eminent* physician of his time.
imminent—*about to occur, impending* .... His nomination to the board of directors is *imminent*.

epitaph—*an inscription on a tombstone or monument* .... His *epitaph* was taken from a section of the Bible.
epithet—*a term used to describe or characterize* .... The drunk was shouting *epithets* at the passersby.
    the nature of a person or thing

expand—*to spread out* .... As the staff increases, we can *expand* our office space.
expend—*to use up* .... Don't *expend* all your energy on one project.

fair—*light in color*, ... I have a very *fair* complexion.
    reasonable, or .... Your attitude is not a *fair* one.
    beauty .... The *fair* princess rode her horse off into the sunset.
fare—*a set price* .... The *fare* is reduced for senior citizens.

farther—*used to express* distance .... John ran *farther* than Bill walked.
further—*used to express* time or degree .... Please go no *further* in your argument.

faze—*to worry or disturb* .... I tried not to let his mean look *faze* me.
phase—*an aspect* .... A crescent is a *phase* of the moon.

find—*to locate* .... Can you *find* the keys?
fine—*good*, ... He is a *fine* cook.
    well, ... After being very sick for two weeks, now I feel absolutely *fine*.
    precise, or .... The calibration of the scale requires very *fine* measurements.
    a penalty .... I received a parking *fine* for an expired meter.
fined—*penalized* .... The judge *fined* him twenty dollars.

formally—*in a formal way* .... He was dressed *formally* for the dinner party.
formerly—*at an earlier time* .... He was *formerly* a delegate to the convention.

fort (fort)—*a fortified place* .... A small garrison was able to hold the *fort*.
forte (FOR-tay)—*a strong point* .... Conducting Wagner's music was Toscanini's *forte*.
forte (FOR-tay)—*a musical term that means loudly* .... The musical composition was meant to be played *forte*.

idle—*unemployed or unoccupied* .... He didn't enjoy remaining *idle* while he recuperated.
idol—*image or object of worship* .... Rock musicians are the *idols* of many teenagers.

in—*indicates* inclusion or location, or .... The spoons are *in* the drawer.
    motion within limits .... We were walking *in* the room.
into—*motion toward one place from another* .... I put the spoons *into* the drawer.

incidence—*to the extent or frequency of an occurrence* .... The *incidence* of rabies has decreased since last year.
incidents—*occurrences, events* .... Luckily, the accidents were just minor *incidents*.

it's—*the contraction of* it is, or .... *It's* a very difficult assignment.
    the contraction of it has .... *It's* been a very long day.
its—*possessive pronoun meaning* belonging to it .... We tried to analyze *its* meaning.

knew—*the past tense of* know .... I *knew* her many years ago.
new—*of recent origin* .... I received a *new* bicycle for my birthday.

know—*to have knowledge or understanding* .... I *know* your brother.
no—*a negative used to express* denial or refusal .... There are *no* more books available.

later—*after a certain time* .... I'll see you *later*.
latter—*the second of two* .... Of the two speakers, the *latter* was more interesting.

lay—*to put* .... I (*lay, laid, have laid*) the gift on the table.
lie—*to recline* .... I (*lie, lay, have lain*) on my blanket on the beach.

lets—*the third person singular present of* let .... He *lets* me park my car in his garage.
let's—*contraction for* let us .... *Let's* go home early today.

lightening—*making less heavy* .... Removing the books will succeed in *lightening* your bag.
lightning—*electric discharge in the atmosphere*, or .... Thunderstorms often produce startling *lightning* bolts.
    moving with great speed .... The horse raced *lightning* fast.

loose—*not fastened or restrained*, or .... The dog got *loose* from the leash.
    not tight-fitting .... After my diet, the new pants were too *loose* on me.
lose—*to mislay*, ... Try not to *lose* your umbrella.
    to be unable to keep, or .... She *lost* her mind.
    to be defeated .... They can't *lose* with their new strategy.

mind—*human consciousness* (noun), ... Make up your *mind* which record you want.
    to object (verb), or .... We don't *mind* if you bring a friend.
    to watch out for .... I cannot go to the movies because I have to *mind* the children.
mine—*a possessive, showing ownership* .... Use your own sled; that one is *mine*.

moral—*good or ethical* (adjective), or .... The trust administrator had a *moral* obligation to the heirs.
    a lesson to be drawn (noun) .... The *moral* of the story is that it pays to be honest.
morale—*spirit* .... The team's *morale* improved after the coach's speech.

passed—*the past tense of* to pass .... The week *passed* very quickly.
past—*just preceding or an earlier time*, or .... The *past* week was a very exciting one.
    in a direction going close to and then beyond .... We walked down the block and *past* the old mansion.

CONFUSING WORD GROUPS

patience—*enduring calmly with tolerant understanding* .... He has very little *patience* with fools.
patients—*people under medical treatment* .... There are twenty *patients* waiting to see the doctor.

personal—*used to describe an individual's character, conduct, or private affairs* .... He took a *personal* interest in each of the students.
personnel—*an organized body of individuals* .... The store's *personnel* department is on the third floor.

precede—*to come before* .... What events *preceded* the fight?
proceed—*to go ahead* .... We can *proceed* with our next plan.

principal—*chief or main* (adjective), ... His *principal* support comes from the real estate industry.
    a leader, or .... The school *principal* called a meeting of the faculty.
    a sum of money (noun) .... He earned 10% interest on the *principal* he invested.
principle—*a fundamental truth or belief* .... As a matter of *principle*, he didn't register for the draft.

prophecy—*prediction* (noun, rhymes with *sea*) .... What is the fortune-teller's *prophecy*?
prophesy—*to predict* (verb, rhymes with *sigh*) .... What did the witches *prophesy*?

quiet—*silent, still* .... My brother is very shy and *quiet*.
quit—*to give up or discontinue* .... I *quit* the team last week.
quite—*very, exactly, or to the greatest extent* .... His analysis is *quite* correct.

raise—*to lift, to erect* .... The neighbors helped him *raise* a new barn.
raze—*to tear down* .... The demolition crew *razed* the old building.
rise—*to increase in value*, or .... The price of silver will *rise* again this month.
    to get up or move from a lower to a higher position .... If a judge enters a room, everyone must *rise* from their seats.

seem—*to appear* .... He *seems* to be sleeping.
seen—*the past participle of see* .... Have you *seen* your sister lately?

set—*to place something down* (mainly) .... He (*sets, set, has set*) the lamp on the table.
sit—*to seat oneself* (mainly) .... He (*sits, sat, has sat*) on the chair.

stationary—*standing still* .... Long ago, people thought that the earth was *stationary*.
stationery—*writing material* .... We bought our school supplies at the *stationery* store.

suppose—*to assume or guess* .... I *suppose* you will be home early.
supposed—*past tense and past participle of suppose* .... I (*supposed, had supposed*) you would be home early.
supposed—*ought to or should* (followed by *to*) .... I am *supposed* to be in school tomorrow.

than—*used to express comparison* .... Jim ate more *than* we could put on the large plate.
then—*used to express time*, or .... I knocked on the door, and *then* I entered.
    a result or consequence .... If you go, *then* I will go too.

their—*belonging to them* .... We took *their* books home with us.
there—*in that place* .... Your books are over *there* on the desk.
they're—*the contraction of they are* .... *They're* coming over for dinner.

though—*although* or .... *Though* he's my friend, I can't recommend him.
    as if (preceded by *as*) .... He acted *as though* nothing had happened.
thought—*past tense of to think* (verb), or .... I *thought* you were serious!
    an idea (noun) .... It is the *thought* that counts.
through—*in one side and out another*, ... We enjoyed running *through* the snow.
    by way of, or .... They met each other *through* a mutual friend.
    finished .... My boyfriend and I are completely *through* with one another.

to—*in the direction of* (preposition), or .... We shall go *to* school.
    used before a verb to indicate the *infinitive* .... I like *to* swim.
too—*very, also* .... It is *too* hot today.
two—*the numeral 2* .... I ate *two* sandwiches for lunch.

use—*to employ or put into service* .... I want to *use* your chair.
used—*past tense and the past participle of to use* .... I *used* your chair.
used—*in the habit of or accustomed to*, ... I am *used* to your comments.
    (followed by *to*)
used—*an adjective meaning not new* .... I bought a *used* car.

weather—*atmospheric conditions* .... I don't like the *weather* in San Francisco.
whether—*introduces a choice* .... He inquired *whether* we were going to the dance.
    (*whether* should not be preceded by *of* or *as to*)

were—*a past tense of to be* .... They *were* there yesterday.
we're—*the contraction of we are* .... *We're* in charge of the decorations.
where—*place or location* .... *Where* are we meeting your brother?

who's—*the contraction of who is*, or .... *Who's* the next batter?
    the contraction of who has .... *Who's* already gone to this movie?
whose—*of whom, implying ownership* .... *Whose* notebook is on the desk?

your—*a possessive showing ownership* .... Please give him *your* notebook.
you're—*the contraction of you are* .... *You're* very sweet.

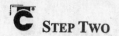

Gerunds vs. Infinitives

The *infinitive* is the "to" form of a verb and the *gerund* is the "-ing" form of a verb. Both the infinitive and the gerund forms of a verb may be used as nouns. In some circumstances, use of either verb form is correct.

Examples:

<u>Adding</u> an extra room to the house is the next project.
<u>To add</u> an extra room to the house is the next project.

In this example, each sentence is correct. However, in some circumstances, gerunds and infinitives are NOT interchangeable.

WATCH FOR GERUND-INFINITIVE SWITCHING

Watch for situations in which the infinitive form of the verb has been switched with the gerund form, or vice versa, when it is not appropriate usage in standard written English.

The following list is a summary of common verbs that are often followed by infinitives.

VERBS OFTEN FOLLOWED BY "TO" VERB FORMS

advise**	care	encourage**	implore**	prefer*	teach**
afford	cause**	endeavor	instruct**	prepare	teach...how**
agree	caution**	expect*	intend*	pretend	tell**
allow**	challenge**	fail	invite**	proceed	tend
appear	claim	forbid**	learn	promise*	threaten
appoint**	come	force**	manage	prove	urge**
arrange	command**	forget	mean	refuse	use**
ask*	compel**	get (manage,	motivate**	remind**	volunteer
attempt	consent	have the opportunity)	need*	request**	wait
be	convince**	get** (persuade)	oblige**	require**	want*
be supposed	dare*	happen	offer	seem	warn**
beg*	decide	help*	order**	serve	wish*
begin	demand	hesitate	pay*	show...how**	would like*
believe**	deserve	hire**	permit**	struggle	would love*
can't afford	direct**	hope	persuade**	swear	would prefer*
can't wait	enable**	hurry	plan		

* verb + infinitive, or verb + (noun *or* pronoun) + infinitive   ** verb + (noun *or* pronoun) + infinitive

---

Examples:

Our new physics professor <u>prefers to teach</u> by example; that is, by laboratory experience, rather than by theory.
Our dinner reservations were at such an exclusive restaurant, the host <u>required</u> my date <u>to wear</u> a coat and tie.

The following list is a summary of common verbs that are often followed by gerunds.

 VERBS OFTEN FOLLOWED BY "-*ING*" VERB FORMS

acknowledge	defer	escape	keep (continue)	recommend
admit	delay	excuse	mention	regret
anticipate	deny	explain	mind (object to)	report
appreciate	detest	feel like	miss	resent
avoid	discontinue	finish	postpone	risk
be worth	discuss	forgive	practice	spend time
cannot help	dislike	give up (stop)	prevent	suggest
cannot stand	dispute	go	prohibit	tolerate
celebrate	dread	imagine	quit	understand
complete	endure	involve	recall	
consider	enjoy	justify		

Examples:

My brother <u>recommended bicycling</u> to relieve the knee pain normally caused by running.
In the final written settlement, the company agreed to <u>discontinue testing</u> on animals.

Either infinitives or gerunds may follow certain verbs without changing the original meaning of the verb.

 VERBS FOLLOWED BY EITHER INFINITIVES OR GERUNDS WITHOUT CHANGE IN MEANING

attempt	cannot stand	intend	neglect
begin	continue	like	prefer
cannot bear	hate	love	start

Examples:

Following the divorce, she <u>attempted to bring</u> her ex-husband to court on charges of failure to pay alimony.
I had to admit, I <u>preferred eating</u> at a restaurant rather than eating at home when he was cooking!

However, the meanings of certain other verbs do change when followed by infinitives or gerunds.

 VERBS FOLLOWED BY EITHER INFINITIVES OR GERUNDS WITH CHANGE IN MEANING

forget	propose	regret	stop
mean	quit	remember	try

Examples:

You can <u>forget having</u> the party here.
I <u>forgot to have</u> the electricity connected by the time we moved into the new house.

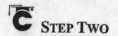

Ambiguity in Scope

Watch for **ambiguity in scope**. This occurs when there is no clear division between two ideas, so that the ideas seem to merge. Note: ✘ = wrong.

Examples:

> After the arrest, the accused was charged with resisting arrest and criminal fraud. ✘
> The recent changes in the tax law will primarily affect workers who wait tables in restaurants, operate concessions in public places, and drive taxis. ✘

In the first example, the scope of "resisting" is not clear. The sentence can be interpreted to mean that the accused was charged with resisting criminal fraud. The intended scope is made clear by inserting "with": "…charged with resisting arrest and with criminal fraud." The corrected sentence indicates that there are two separate ideas, not one.

In the second example, the use of "and" seems to tie three separate ideas together; that is, it is those workers who do all three jobs who will be affected—clearly not the intent of the sentence. These are three separate ideas that can be clarified by changing "and" to "or," or by making a series of parallel ideas: "…workers who wait tables in restaurants, workers who operate concessions in public places, and workers who drive taxis."

WATCH FOR AMBIGUITY IN SCOPE

 Be alert for sentences that run two or more ideas together. Usually the error can be corrected by adding words to clarify the two ideas as distinct and to separate them from one another.

Low-Level Usage

There are a few expressions heard frequently in conversation that are regarded as **low-level usage** and are unacceptable in standard written English. The exam measures the ability to recognize the difference between standard and non-standard writing. Note: ✔ = correct, ✘ = wrong.

Example:

> She <u>sure</u> is pretty! ✘
> She <u>certainly</u> is pretty! ✔

AVOID LOW-LEVEL USAGE

Instead of:	*Say*:	*Instead of*:	*Say*:
ain't	am not; are not; is not	would of	would have
aren't I	am I not	may of	may have
around (2 p.m.)	about (2 p.m.)	might of	might have
being that	since	must of	must have
between you and I	between you and me	off of	off
bunch (of people)	group (of people)	on account of	because
but that	that	plan on	plan to
cannot seem	seems unable	put in	spend, make, or devote
different than	different from	quite a few	many
else than	other than	same as	in the same way as; just as
equally as good	equally good; just as good	sort of	somewhat; rather
have got	have	theirselves	themselves
having took	having taken	try and	try to
in back of	behind	unbeknownst to	without the knowledge of
kind of	somewhat; rather	upwards of	more than
worst kind	very badly	should of	should have

Idioms and Clarity of Expression

DIRECTIONS: In Sentences #1-104, circle the correct word choice. Answers are on page 955.

1. He is the (principal, principle) backer of the play.

2. I hope your company will (accept, except) our offer.

3. We hope to have good (weather, whether) when we are on vacation.

4. Put the rabbit back (in, into) the hat.

5. The attorney will (advice, advise) you of your rights.

6. She is far taller (than, then) I imagined.

7. Are they (all ready, already) to go?

8. She answered the letter on shocking pink (stationary, stationery).

9. What is the (affect, effect) you are trying to achieve?

10. I want to (set, sit) next to my grandfather.

11. He's going to (lay, lie) down for a nap.

12. I'm (all together, altogether) tired of his excuses.

13. He saluted when the flag (passed, past) by.

14. I'd like another portion of (desert, dessert).

15. Try not to (loose, lose) your good reputation.

16. How much will the final examination (effect, affect) my grade?

17. What is it (you're, your) trying to suggest?

18. She's not (use, used) to such cold weather.

19. The cost of the coat will (raise, rise) again.

20. You are (suppose, supposed) to be home at six o'clock.

21. Her cat ran straight for (its, it's) bowl of food.

22. Are you (conscience, conscious) of what you are doing?

23. It will (seen, seem) that we are afraid.

24. His essays are filled with literary (allusions, illusions).

25. This wine will be a good (complement, compliment) to the meal.

26. It's (later, latter) than you think!

27. My cousin has a swimmer's (build, built).

28. I never (knew, new) him before today.

29. She asked her a (personal, personnel) question.

30. The golf (coarse, course) was very crowded.

31. The costume was made from old (cloth, clothe) napkins.

32. The ball carrier was trying to (allude, elude) the tacklers.

33. There are (know, no) more exhibitions planned.

34. I will wait for you in the (ante, anti) room.

35. Her (moral, morale) is very low.

36. Begin the sentence with a (capital, capitol) letter.

37. The fact that he nearly had an accident did not even (faze, phase) him.

38. He earns royalties in (access, excess) of a million dollars a year.

39. Now, may we (precede, proceed) with the debate?

40. Her (fort, forte) is writing lyrics for musical comedy.

41. They wondered how they were going to (disburse, disperse) the huge crowd.

42. Everyone was dressed (formally, formerly) for the dinner party.

43. I am not (adverse, averse) to continuing the discussion at another time.

44. Can something be done to retard the (incidence, incidents) of influenza in that area?

45. "Seeing the film in class will serve a (dual, duel) purpose," he explained.

46. I'm not sure I want to (expand, expend) so much energy on that project.

47. Imagine my (discomfit, discomfort) when she showed up at the party too!

48. He was a famous matinee (idle, idol) many years ago.

49. When did they (emigrate, immigrate) from New York to Paris?

50. I think she is part of a (click, clique) of snobs and creeps.

51. She paid little attention to the fortune-teller's (prophecy, prophesy).

52. The lights went out when the (lightning, lightening) hit the house.

53. I'll provide you (what ever, whatever) assistance you require.

54. We are in (eminent, imminent) danger of losing our reservations.

55. Will she be able to (adapt, adopt) to our way of performing the operation?

56. As we went through the old cemetery, we were fascinated by some of the (epitaphs, epithets).

57. He shared the riches (between, among) Laura, Millie, and Ernestine.

58. The housing law was rewritten for his (advantage, benefit).

59. (Alot, A lot) of the time, he falls asleep at nine o'clock.

60. It was difficult to keep track of the (amount, number) of people who visited him last week.

61. I see him in the park (almost, most) every day.

62. Are you certain that he is (alright, all right) now?

63. She is just beginning to (aggravate, annoy) her mother.

64. He is the school's oldest living (alumni, alumnus).

65. He spotted the riverbank and then guided the canoe up (alongside, alongside of).

66. (Being as, Since) it is Wednesday, we are going to a Broadway matinee.

67. He is (anxious, eager) to be finished with the dental treatment.

68. Where do you want to (meet, meet at)?

69. My aunt just went inside to rest (awhile, a while).

70. It was (about, around) noon when we met for lunch.

71. I brought a (couple, couple of) books for you; both are historical novels.

72. Between (you and I, you and me), I think that her hat is very unbecoming.

73. The (continual, continuous) ticking of the clock was very disconcerting.

74. She (cannot seem, seems unable) to get up early enough to eat breakfast with him.

75. I (assume, expect) that you really earned your salary today.

76. I'm (disinterested, uninterested) in seeing that movie.

77. You must be (every bit as, just as) sleepy as I am.

78. I doubt (that, whether) it will snow today.

79. Sam, Joe, Lou, and Artie have worked with (each other, one another) before.

80. She asked him (if, whether) he wanted to have lunch with her or with her sister.

81. All (humans, human beings) need to take a certain amount of water into their bodies every week.

82. We hope to (conclude, finalize) the deal this month.

83. We were upset when she (flaunted, flouted) her mother's orders.

84. His girlfriend only eats (healthful, healthy) foods.

85. He said such terrible things about her that she is suing him for (libel, slander).

86. I would like to see you in (regard, regards) to the apartment you plan to rent.

87. She is always late for work, (irregardless, regardless) of how early she wakes up in the morning.

88. He'll (loan, lend) you a hand carrying the groceries.

89. The media (are, is) doing the job poorly.

90. The art director was taken (off, off of) the most profitable gallery show.

91. I hope that she will (quit, stop) sending us the job applications.

92. The reason the baby is crying is (because, that) she is hungry.

93. Does he (manage, run) the department efficiently?

94. Anyone who wants to have (his or her, their) conference with me today is invited to meet in my office at ten o'clock.

95. She scored more points than (any, any other) player on the team.

96. His room is very neat (but, while) hers is very messy.

97. He will (try and, try to) be more pleasant to his sister.

98. I shall give it to (whoever, whomever) arrives first.

99. This time, we will not wait (for, on) you for more than ten minutes.

DIRECTIONS: In Sentences #100-114, determine whether the gerund choice (A), the infinitive choice (B), or BOTH the gerund and the infinitive (C), is the correct answer to fill in the blank. Answers are on page 962.

100. After the break, the teacher continued _____.
    A. lecturing
    B. to lecture
    C. BOTH

101. He forgot _____ me at the party last year, so he introduced himself again.
    A. meeting
    B. to meet
    C. BOTH

102. Please remember _____ five minutes early on the day of the test.
    A. arriving
    B. to arrive
    C. BOTH

103. He hesitated _____ for the assignment.
    A. volunteering
    B. to volunteer
    C. BOTH

104. After her speech, the lecturer proceeded _____ questions.
    A. taking
    B. to take
    C. BOTH

105. The politician continued _____ soft money contributions during his campaign.
    A. accepting
    B. to accept
    C. BOTH

106. "I will not tolerate _____," the professor said.
    A. talking
    B. to talk
    C. BOTH

107. Taking sixteen credit hours, the student has neglected _____ some of her essays.
    A. writing
    B. to write
    C. BOTH

108. She has not even begun _____ for the exam even though it is tomorrow.
    A. preparing
    B. to prepare
    C. BOTH

109. The applicant tried _____ for an extension of the deadline, but his request was turned down.
    A. asking
    B. to ask
    C. BOTH

110. The class has been warned not _____.
    A. cheating
    B. to cheat
    C. BOTH

111. The senior anticipates _____ next month.
    A. graduating
    B. to graduate
    C. BOTH

112. Knowing that the deadline is tomorrow has forced me _____ on the project.
    A. concentrating
    B. to concentrate
    C. BOTH

113. Cats cannot stand _____ the sound of a vacuum cleaner.
    A. hearing
    B. to hear
    C. BOTH

114. I do not want to spend any more time _____ these equations.
    A. solving
    B. to solve
    C. BOTH

DIRECTIONS: For Items #115-129, circle the letter of the underlined part of the sentence containing the error and write the correct word or phrase. Answers are on page 962.

115. Economists have established that there is a relation—
     A   (B)
     albeit an indirect one—between the amount of oil
                                        C
     imported into this country and the number of traffic
                                        D
     accidents.

     Correct Word/Phrase: ___relationship___

116. Ironically, today Elizabeth I and her rival for the
                                       A
     English throne, Mary Stuart, whom Elizabeth had
                                   B   C
     executed, lay side by side in Westminster Abbey.
               (D)
     Correct Word/Phrase: ___lie___

117. Although the script is interesting and well-written, it
     is not clear whether it can be adopted for television
                    A   (B)
     since the original story contains scenes that could not
                                                  C
     be broadcast over the public airwaves.
     C   D
     Correct Word/Phrase: ___adapted___

118. If he had known how difficult law school would be, he
           A
     would of chosen a different profession or perhaps even
     (B)
     have followed the tradition of going into the family
     C   D
     business.   would of > never acceptable!
     Correct Word/Phrase: ___would have___

119. When shopping malls and business complexes get
                                                 A
     built, quite often the needs of the handicapped are not
     A   B
     considered; as a result, it later becomes necessary to
     make costly modifications to structures to make them
          C
     accessible to persons of impaired mobility.
     D
     Correct Word/Phrase: _____

120. Researchers have found that children experience twice
                    A   B
     as much deep sleep than adults, a fact which may teach
                         C   D
     us something about the connection between age and
     learning ability.

     Correct Word/Phrase: _____

121. Despite the ample evidence that smoking is hazardous
     A   B
     to one's health, many people seem to find the warnings
                      C
     neither frightening or convincing.
                         D
     Correct Word/Phrase: _____

122. No matter how many encores the audience demands,
                    A
     Helen Walker is always willing to sing yet another
                  B   C
     song which pleases the audience.
          D
     Correct Word/Phrase: _____

123. In light of recent translations of stone carvings
                 A
     depicting scenes of carnage, scholars are now
     B
     questioning as to whether the Incas were really a
                 C   D
     peace-loving civilization.

     Correct Word/Phrase: _____

124. In galleries containing works of both Gauguin and
     Cézanne, you will find an equal number of admirers
                                     A
     in front of the works of each, but most art critics agree
     B   C
     that Gauguin is not of the same artistic stature with
                                                        D
     Cézanne.

     Correct Word/Phrase: _____

125. The Board of Education will never be fully responsive
                           A   B   C
     to the needs of Hispanic children in the school system
     so long that the mayor refuses to appoint a Hispanic
            D
     educator to the Board.

     Correct Word/Phrase: _____

126. The judge <u>sentenced</u> the president of the corporation
     A

     to ten years in prison for <u>embezzling</u> corporate funds
                                  B

     but <u>gave</u> his partner in crime <u>less of a sentence</u>.
          C   D

     Correct Word/Phrase: _____

127. Scientists <u>have recently discovered</u> that mussels <u>secrete</u>
                  A   B

     a powerful adhesive that allows them <u>attaching</u>
                                            C

     themselves to rocks, concrete pilings, and <u>other</u> stone
                                                  D

     or masonry structures.

     Correct Word/Phrase: _____

128. Wall paintings found recently in the caves of Brazil

     are <u>convincing</u> evidence that cave art <u>developed</u> in
          A   B

     the Americas at an earlier time <u>as</u> <u>it</u> did on other
                                      C   D

     continents.

     Correct Word/Phrase: _____

129. The <u>drop</u> in oil prices and the slump in the computer
          A

     industry <u>account for</u> the recent <u>raise</u> in unemployment
               B   C

     in Texas and the <u>associated</u> decline in the value of real
                        D

     estate in the region.

     Correct Word/Phrase: _____

Punctuation

Although *punctuation* is stressed less than other aspects of standard written English on the exam, it is important to be aware of the principal rules governing punctuation. This section is not intended to give the definitive set of punctuation rules, but rather to provide a basic framework for correct usage.

Commas

USE A COMMA BEFORE COORDINATING CONJUNCTIONS

 Coordinating conjunctions ("and," "but," "nor," "or," "for," "yet," "so") join two independent clauses. Use a comma before coordinating conjunctions unless the two clauses are very short.

Note: ✓ = correct, ✗ = wrong.

Examples:

The boy wanted to borrow a book from the library, <u>but</u> the librarian would not allow him to take it until he had paid his fines. ✓

Joe has been very diligent about completing his work, <u>but</u> he has had many problems concerning his punctuality. ✓

I sincerely hope that these exercises prove to be of assistance to you, <u>and</u> I believe that they will help you to make a better showing on your examinations. ✓

Generally, a comma is not used before a subordinate clause that ends a sentence. However, in long, unwieldy sentences, it is acceptable.

If there is no subject following the conjunction, then a comma cannot be used, as this would create a sentence fragment. If there is a subject following the conjunction, but the two clauses are very short, the separating comma may be omitted.

Examples:

She went to the cafe <u>and</u> bought a cup of coffee. ✓

Roy washed the dishes <u>and</u> Helen dried them. ✓

I saw him <u>and</u> I spoke to him. ✓

A restrictive phrase or clause is vital to the meaning of a sentence and cannot be omitted. Do NOT set apart restrictive phrases or clauses with commas.

Example:

A sailboat, without sails, is useless. ✗

A sailboat without sails is useless. ✓

USE COMMAS FOR CLARITY

1. Use a comma if the sentence might be subject to different interpretations without it.

2. Use a comma if a pause would make the sentence clearer and easier to read.

The following examples show how commas change the interpretation of the sentences.

Examples:

The banks that closed yesterday are in serious financial trouble. (Some banks closed yesterday, and those banks are in trouble.)
The banks, which closed yesterday, are in serious financial trouble. (All banks closed yesterday, and all banks are in trouble.)
My cat Leo fell down the laundry chute. (The implication is that I have more than one cat.)
My cat, Leo, fell down the laundry chute. (Here, Leo is an appositive. Presumably, he is the only cat.)

Inside the people were dancing. ✗

Inside, the people were dancing. ✓

After all crime must be punished. ✗

After all, crime must be punished. ✓

Pausing is not infallible, but it is the best resort when all other rules governing use of the comma seem to fail.

USE COMMAS TO SEPARATE COORDINATE ADJECTIVES, WORDS IN A SERIES, AND NOUNS IN DIRECT ADDRESS

1. Coordinate adjectives are adjectives of equal importance that precede the noun that they describe. If the word "and" can be added between the adjectives without changing the sense of the sentence, then use commas.

 2. Use a comma between words in a series when three or more elements are present. In such a series, use a comma before "and" or "or." If the series ends in *etc.,* use a comma before *etc.* Do not use a comma after *etc.* in a series, even if the sentence continues.

3. Use commas to set off nouns in direct address. The name of the person addressed is separated from the rest of the sentence by commas.

Examples:

The jolly, fat man stood at the top of the stairs. ✓

He is a wise, charming man. ✓

She is a slow, careful reader. ✓

Coats, umbrellas, and boots should be placed in the closet at the end of the hall. ✓

Pencils, scissors, paper clips, *etc.* belong in your top desk drawer. ✓

Bob, please close the door. ✓

I think, José, you are the one who was chosen. ✓

USE A COMMA TO SEPARATE QUOTATIONS AND INTRODUCTORY PHRASES

1. Use a comma to separate a short, direct quotation from the speaker.

2. Use a comma after an introductory phrase of two or more words.

3. Use a comma after an introductory phrase whenever the comma would aid clarity.

4. Use a comma after introductory gerunds, participles, and infinitives, regardless of their length.

On the other hand, if the subordinate clause follows the main clause, it is not necessary to set it off with a comma.

Examples:

She said, "I must leave work on time today." ✓

"Tomorrow I begin my summer job," he told us. ✓

As a child, she was a tomboy. ✓

She was a tomboy as a child. ✓

To Dan, Phil was a friend as well as a brother. ✓

Phil was a friend as well as a brother to Dan. ✓

In 1998, 300 people lost their lives in an earthquake. ✓

300 people lost their lives in an earthquake in 1998. ✓

When you come home, please ring the bell before opening the door. ✓

Please ring the bell before opening the door when you come home. ✓

Because the prisoner had a history of attempted jailbreaks, he was put under heavy guard. ✓

The prisoner was put under heavy guard because he had a history of attempted jailbreaks. ✓

Finally, commas must be used to set off a phrase or to interrupt the flow of the sentence.

USE PAIRS OF COMMAS TO SET OFF
APPOSITIVE, PARENTHETICAL, AND NON-RESTRICTIVE ELEMENTS

1. An appositive phrase follows a noun or pronoun and has the same meaning as that noun or pronoun.

 2. Parenthetical expressions are words that interrupt the flow of the sentence ("however," "though," "for instance," "by the way," "to tell the truth," "believe me," "it appears to me," "I am sure," "as a matter of fact") without changing the meaning of the sentence.

3. A non-restrictive element introduces material that is not essential to the sentence and, if removed, will not change the meaning of the original sentence.

Examples:

Mr. Dias, <u>our lawyer</u>, gave us some great advice. ✓

Bob, <u>an industrious and hard-working student</u>, will run for class treasurer. ✓

This book, <u>I believe</u>, is the best of its kind. ✓

Julie and her three dogs, <u>I am sure</u>, will not easily find an apartment to rent. ✓

Sam, <u>who is a very well behaved dog</u>, never strays from the front yard. ✓

Millie, <u>who is a fine student</u>, has a perfect attendance record. ✓

Test for placement of commas in a parenthetical expression by reading the sentence aloud. If you would pause before and after such an expression, then commas should set it off. In general, if you can omit the material without changing the meaning of the main clause, then the material is non-restrictive and it should be set off by commas.

USE COMMAS TO SEPARATE DATES, ADDRESSES, AND SPECIFIC LOCATIONS

 Commas, including a comma after the last item, separate the different parts of a date and address.

Examples:

The train will arrive on Friday, February 13, 2003, if it is on schedule. ✔

My new address is: 2040 Winnebago Ave., Apt. #2, Madison, WI. ✔

My daughter traveled from Cambridge, Massachusetts, to Albany, New York, in three hours. ✔

The above rules summarize the most important uses of commas. If you use them in just these situations, then you will not make a serious comma usage mistake.

SITUATIONS IN WHICH NOT TO USE COMMAS

1. Do not use a comma to separate a subject from its verb.

2. Do not use commas to set off restrictive or necessary clauses or phrases.

3. Do not use a comma in place of a conjunction.

Semicolons

Note: ✔ = correct, ✘ = wrong.

USE A SEMICOLON TO SEPARATE TWO COMPLETE IDEAS

 A semicolon may be used to separate two complete ideas (independent clauses) in a sentence when the two ideas have a close relationship, and they are NOT connected with a coordinating conjunction.

Example:

The setting sun caused the fields to take on a special glow; all was bathed in a pale light. ✔

The **semicolon** is often used between two or more independent clauses connected by conjunctive adverbs such as "consequently," "therefore," "also," "furthermore," "for example," "however," "nevertheless," "still," "yet," "moreover," and "otherwise." (Note: A comma must follow the adverb.)

USE SEMICOLONS ONLY FOR INDEPENDENT CLAUSES

 Unless each clause can function as an independent sentence, it is probably wrong to use a semicolon.

Examples:

He waited at the station for well over an hour; however, no one appeared. ✓

He waited at the station for well over an hour. However, no one appeared. ✓

Anne is working at the front desk on Monday; Ernie will take over on Tuesday. ✓

Anne is working at the front desk on Monday. Ernie will take over on Tuesday. ✓

She waited for her check to arrive in the mail for two weeks; however, the check never appeared. ✓

She waited for her check to arrive in the mail for two weeks. However, the check never appeared. ✓

However, do NOT use a semicolon between an independent clause and a phrase or subordinate clause.

Example:

She worked extra hours every night; yet, was not able to finish the project on time. ✗

She worked extra hours every night yet was not able to finish the project on time. ✓

To summarize, two main clauses should be separated by a conjunction, by a semicolon, or by a period (two sentences). The same two clauses may be written in any one of three ways, as the following example shows.

Example:

Autumn had come and the trees were almost bare. ✓

Autumn had come; the trees were almost bare. ✓

Autumn had come. The trees were almost bare. ✓

If you are uncertain about how to use a semicolon to connect independent clauses, write two sentences instead.

**USE A SEMICOLON TO SEPARATE A SERIES OF
PHRASES CONTAINING COMMAS OR A SERIES OF NUMBERS**

1. Use a semicolon to separate a series of phrases or clauses, each of which contains commas.

2. Use a semicolon to avoid confusion with numbers.

Examples:

The old gentleman's heirs were Margaret Whitlock, his half-sister; James Bagley, the butler; William Frame, companion to his late cousin, Robert Bone; and his favorite charity, the Salvation Army. ✓

Add the following prices: $.25; $7.50; and $12.89. ✓

Colons

The *colon* is always used in the following situations. Note: ✓ = correct, ✗ = wrong.

RULES FOR SITUATIONS REQUIRING A COLON

1. A colon should be placed after the salutation in a business letter.

2. Use a colon to separate hours from minutes.

3. The colon is used to precede a list of three or more items or a long quotation.

4. A colon should be used to introduce a question.

5. A colon is generally used in places where a full stop would leave the beginning of the sentence unchanged in meaning.

Examples:

Dear Board Member: ✓

The eclipse occurred at 10:36 A.M. ✓

Many people refer to four, rather than three, branches of government: executive, judicial, legislative, and media. ✓

My question is this: are you willing to punch a time clock? ✓

Avoid using the colon directly after a verb or when it interrupts the natural flow of language.

Examples:

We played: volleyball, badminton, football, and tag. ✗

We played volleyball, badminton, football, and tag. ✓

We purchased: apples, pears, bananas, and grapes. ✗

We purchased apples, pears, bananas, and grapes. ✓

DO NOT USE COLONS TO CALL ATTENTION IF ALREADY SIGNALED

 A colon may be used to introduce or to call attention to elaboration or explanation. However, do not use colons after expressions such as "like," "for example," "such as," and "that is." In fact, colons are intended to replace these terms.

Be careful not to use a colon to introduce or call attention to material that is already signaled by some other element of the sentence.

Example:

We did many different things on our vacation, such as: hiking, camping, biking, canoeing, and kayaking. ✗

We did many different things on our vacation, such as hiking, camping, biking, canoeing, and kayaking. ✓

We did many different things on our vacation: hiking, camping, biking, canoeing, and kayaking. ✓

Periods

RULES FOR SITUATIONS REQUIRING A PERIOD

1. Use a period at the end of a sentence that makes a statement, gives a command, or makes a "polite request" in the form of a question that does not require an answer.

2. Use a period after an abbreviation and after the initial in a person's name.

Examples:

He is my best friend.
There are thirty days in September.
Would you please hold the script so that I may see if I have memorized my lines.
Gen. Robert E. Lee led the Confederate forces.

Note: Do NOT use a period in postal service name abbreviations such as AZ (Arizona) or MI (Michigan).

Exclamation and Question Marks

RULES FOR SITUATIONS REQUIRING EXCLAMATION MARKS

Use exclamation marks after expressions showing strong emotion or issuing a command. Use an exclamation mark only to express strong feeling or emotion or to imply urgency.

Examples:

Wonderful! You won the lottery!
Oh no! I won't go!

RULES FOR SITUATIONS REQUIRING QUESTION MARKS

Use a question mark after a request for information. A question mark is used only after a direct question. A period is used after an indirect question.

Note: A question must end with a *question mark* even if the question does not encompass the entire sentence.

Examples:

At what time does the last bus leave?
"Daddy, are we there yet?" the child asked.
Did you take the examination on Friday?
The instructor wanted to know if you took the examination on Friday.

Dashes

The material following the *dash* usually directs the reader's attention to the content that precedes it. Unless this material ends a sentence, dashes, like parentheses, must be used in pairs.

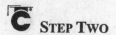

RULES FOR SITUATIONS REQUIRING A DASH

1. Use a dash for emphasis or to set off an explanatory group of words.

 2. Use a dash before a word or group of words that indicates a summation or reversal of what preceded it.

3. Use a dash to mark a sudden break in thought that leaves a sentence unfinished.

Examples:

The tools of his trade—probe, mirror, and cotton swabs—were neatly arranged on the dentist's tray.
Patience, sensitivity, understanding, and empathy—these are the marks of a friend.
He was not pleased with—in fact, he was completely hostile toward—the takeover.

Dashes in sentences have a function that is similar to commas when they are used to set off parenthetical remarks. The difference between the two is a matter of emphasis. The dashes mark a more dramatic shift or interruption of thought. Do not mix dashes and commas.

Hyphens

RULES FOR SITUATIONS REQUIRING A HYPHEN

 1. Use a hyphen with a compound modifier that precedes the noun.

2. Use a hyphen with fractions that serve as adjectives or adverbs.

The following examples demonstrate situations in which it is correct to use a *hyphen* and situations in which it is NOT correct to use a hyphen.

Examples:

There was a <u>sit-in</u> demonstration at the office.
We will <u>sit in</u> the auditorium.
I purchased a <u>four-cylinder</u> car.
I purchased a car with <u>four cylinders</u>.

Quotation Marks

Note: ✓ = correct, ✗ = wrong.

WHEN TO USE QUOTATION MARKS

1. Use quotation marks to enclose the actual words of the speaker or writer.

 2. Use quotation marks to emphasize words used in a special or unusual sense.

3. Use quotation marks to set off titles of short themes or parts of a larger work.

Examples:

Jane said, "There will be many people at the party." ✓

He kept using the phrase "you know" throughout his conversation. ✓

"Within You, Without You" is my favorite song on the *Sgt. Pepper's Lonely Hearts Club Band* album by The Beatles. ✓

WHEN NOT TO USE QUOTATION MARKS

1. Do not use quotation marks for indirect quotations.
2. Do not use quotation marks to justify a poor choice of words.

Examples:

He said that "he would be happy to attend the meeting." ✗

He said that he would be happy to attend the meeting. ✓

I gave her research summary article a low score because I didn't think she "got it right." ✗

I gave her research summary article a low score because I didn't think she understood the methods or results. ✓

PUNCTUATION RULES FOR SITUATIONS WITH QUOTATIONS

1. Always place periods and commas inside quotation marks.

2. Place question marks inside quotation marks if it is part of a quotation. If the entire sentence, including the quotation, is a question, place the question mark outside the quotation marks.

3. Place exclamation marks inside quotation marks if it is part of a quotation. If the entire sentence, including the quotation, is an exclamation, place the exclamation mark outside the quotation marks.

4. Always place colons and semicolons outside quotation marks.

Examples:

The principal said, "Cars parked in the fire lane will be ticketed." ✓

The first chapter of *The Andromeda Strain* is entitled "The Country of Lost Borders." ✓

My favorite poem is "My Last Duchess," a dramatic monologue written by Robert Browning. ✓

Three stories in Kurt Vonnegut's *Welcome to the Monkey House* are "Harrison Bergeron," "Next Door," and "Epicac." ✓

Mother asked earlier tonight, "Did you take out the garbage?" ✓

Do you want to go to the movies and see "Jurassic Park"? ✓

The sentry shouted, "Drop your gun!" ✓

Save us from our "friends"! ✓

My favorite poem is "My Last Duchess"; this poem is a dramatic monologue written by Robert Browning. ✓

He was quoted as supporting the investigation in the "Washington Post": "I don't know of any proof of misappropriation of funds; however, I support a full investigation into any possible wrongdoing by government officials." ✓

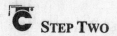

Apostrophes

Errors of *apostrophe* usage usually occur when a paper isn't proofread or when a writer isn't sure how to use an apostrophe correctly. The apostrophe is used for possession and contraction. Note: ✓ = correct, ✗ = wrong.

USE APOSTROPHES FOR POSSESSION

 Use apostrophes to indicate the possessive case of nouns. Do NOT use apostrophes with possessive pronouns (*e.g.,* "yours," "hers," "ours," "theirs," and "whose").

Examples:

> lady's = belonging to the lady ✓
> ladies' = belonging to the ladies ✓

To test for correct placement of the apostrophe, read the apostrophe as "of the."

Examples:

> childrens' = of the childrens ✗
> children's = of the children ✓

The placement rule applies at all times, even with regard to compound nouns separated by hyphens and with regard to entities made up of two or more names.

Examples:

> Lansdale, Jackson, and Smith's law firm = the law firm belonging to Lansdale, Jackson, and Smith ✓
> Brown and Sons' delivery truck = the delivery truck of Brown and Sons ✓

If the noun does not end in "s"—whether singular or plural—add "'s"; if the noun ends in "s," simply add the apostrophe.

Examples:

> Socrates's philosophy ✗
> Socrates' philosophy ✓
> Johnsons's house ✗
> Johnsons' house ✓

USE APOSTROPHES FOR CONTRACTIONS

 Use an apostrophe to indicate a contraction; insert the apostrophe in place of the omitted letter(s). It is NOT acceptable in standard written English to begin a paragraph with a contraction.

Examples:

haven't = have not ✓

o'clock = of the clock ✓

class of '85 = class of 1985 ✓

Be careful with "its" and "it's." "It's" is the contraction of "it is." "Its" is the third person possessive pronoun. Also, do NOT confuse "they're" ("they are"), "their" (possessive), and "there" (preposition).

Example:

The cat knows when <u>it's</u> time for <u>its</u> bath. ✓

They're happy to be done with <u>their</u> work. ✓

punctuations go inside quotes!

m-dash (——) pg. 338

Punctuation

DIRECTIONS: Punctuate Sentences #1-55 with additional commas, semicolons, periods, exclamation marks, question marks, quotation marks, dashes, hyphens, and apostrophes *if necessary*. Answers are on page 963.

1. He was not aware that you had lost your passport

2. Did you report the loss to the proper authorities

3. I suppose you had to fill out many forms .

4. What a nuisance !

5. I hate doing so much paper work

6. Did you ever discover where the wallet was

7. I imagine you wondered how it was misplaced

8. Good for you

9. At least you now have your passport

10. What will you do if it happens again

11. I dont know if they are coming, though I sent them an invitation weeks ago .

12. Neurology is the science that deals with the anatomy, physiology, and pathology of the nervous system .

13. Nursery lore, like everything human, has been subject to many changes over long periods of time

14. Bob read Joyces Ulysses to the class; everyone seemed to enjoy the reading .

15. In order to provide more living space we converted an attached garage into a den

16. Because he is such an industrious student, he has many friends .

17. I dont recall who wrote A Midsummer Nights Dream

18. In the writing class students learned about coordinating conjunctions and but so or yet for and nor

19. Those who do not complain are never pitied is a familiar quotation by Jane Austen

20. Howard and his ex-wife are on amicable terms .

21. Her last words were, call me on Sunday, and she jumped on the train

22. He is an out of work carpenter

23. This is what is called a pregnant chad

24. Come early on Monday the teacher said to take the exit exam

25. The dog mans best friend is a companion to many

26. The winner of the horse race is to the best of my knowledge Silver

27. Every time I see him the dentist asks me how often I floss

28. The officer was off duty when he witnessed the crime

29. Anna Karenina is my favorite movie

30. Red white and blue are the colors of the American flag

31. Stop using stuff in your essays its too informal

32. She was a self made millionaire

33. The Smiths who are the best neighbors anyone could ask for have moved out

34. My eighteen year old daughter will graduate this spring

35. Dracula lived in Transylvania

36. The students were told to put away their books

37. Begun while Dickens was still at work on Pickwick Papers Oliver Twist was published in 1837 and is now one of the authors most widely read works

38. Given the great difficulties of making soundings in very deep water it is not surprising that few such soundings were made until the middle of this century

39. Did you finishing writing your thesis prospectus on time

40. The root of modern Dutch was once supposed to be Old Frisian but the general view now is that the characteristic forms of Dutch are at least as old as those of Old Frisian

41. Moose once scarce because of indiscriminate hunting are protected by law and the number of moose is once again increasing

42. He ordered a set of books several records and a film almost a month ago

43. Perhaps the most interesting section of New Orleans is the French Quarter which extends from North Rampart Street to the Mississippi River

44. Writing for a skeptical and rationalizing age Shaftesbury was primarily concerned with showing that goodness and beauty are not determined by revelation authority opinion or fashion

45. We tried our best to purchase the books but we were completely unsuccessful even though we went to every bookstore in town

46. A great deal of information regarding the nutritional requirements of farm animals has been accumulated over countless generations by trial and error however most recent advances have come as the result of systematic studies at schools of animal husbandry

47. Omoo Melvilles sequel to Typee appeared in 1847 and went through five printings in that year alone

48. Go to Florence for the best gelato in all of Italy said the old man to the young tourist

49. Although the first school for African Americans was a public school established in Virginia in 1620 most educational opportunities for African Americans before the Civil War were provided by private agencies

50. As the climate of Europe changed the population became too dense for the supply of food obtained by hunting and other means of securing food such as the domestication of animals were necessary

51. In Faulkners poetic realism the grotesque is somber violent and often inexplicable in Caldwells writing it is lightened by a ballad like humorous sophisticated detachment

52. The valley of the Loire a northern tributary of the Loire at Angers abounds in rock villages they occur in many other places in France Spain and northern Italy

53. The telephone rang several times as a result his sleep was interrupted

54. He has forty three thousand dollars to spend however once that is gone he will be penniless

55. Before an examination do the following review your work get a good nights sleep eat a balanced breakfast and arrive on time to take the test

Capitalization and Spelling

Capitalization

**CAPITALIZE FIRST WORD OF SENTENCES,
PROPER NAMES, DAYS, MONTHS, AND HOLIDAYS**

 Capitalize the first word of a sentence, all proper names, the days of the week, the months of the year, and holidays.

Note that the seasons are NOT capitalized.

Examples:

With cooperation, a depression can be avoided.
America, General Motors, Abraham Lincoln, First Congregational Church
The check was mailed on Thursday, the day before Christmas.
In Florida, winter is mild.

CAPITALIZE FIRST WORD AND NOUNS IN SALUTATIONS

 Capitalize the first word and all nouns in the salutation of a letter and the first word of the complimentary close of a letter.

Examples:

Dear Mr. Jones,
My dear Mr. Jones,
Truly yours,
Very truly yours,

CAPITALIZE FIRST AND IMPORTANT WORDS IN TITLES

 Capitalize the first and all other important words in a title.

Example:

The Art of Salesmanship

CAPITALIZE WORDS WHEN PART OF A PROPER NAME

 Capitalize a word used as part of a proper name.

Examples:

William Street
That street is narrow.
Morningside Terrace
We have a terrace apartment.

CAPITALIZE TITLES WHEN REFERRING TO A PARTICULAR PERSON

 Capitalize titles when they refer to a particular official or family member.

Examples:

The report was read by Secretary Marshall.
Our secretary, Miss Shaw, is ill.
Let's visit Uncle Harry.
I have three uncles.

CAPITALIZE "NORTH," "SOUTH," "WEST," AND "EAST" WHEN REFERRING TO A PARTICULAR REGION

 Capitalize points of a compass when they refer to particular regions of a country but not when they refer to direction in general

---

Examples:

We're going to the South next week.
New York is south of Albany.
They honeymooned in the Far East.
She transferred here from a university in the Middle East.

CAPITALIZE FIRST WORD IN QUOTATIONS

 Capitalize the first word of a direct quotation.

Example:

Alexander Pope wrote, "A little learning is a dangerous thing."

When a direct quotation sentence is broken, the first word of the second half of the sentence is not capitalized.

Example:

"Don't phone," Lilly told me, "because it will be too late."

CAPITALIZE LANGUAGES

 Capitalize languages, but do NOT capitalize the names of other school subjects.

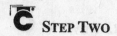

Example:

I am enrolled in English, math, history, and French.

Class titles, however, are still titles, so capitalize the first and important words.

Example:

I need four math credits, so I will take Euclidian Geometry.

Spelling

1. *"I" Before "E" Rule*

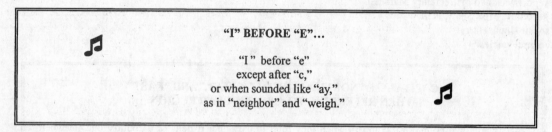

"I" BEFORE "E"...

"I " before "e"
except after "c,"
or when sounded like "ay,"
as in "neighbor" and "weigh."

Examples:

grieve, relief, believe, chief, piece, briefcase
receive, deceive, receipt
neighbor, weight, reign, freight

The "i" before "e" rule has the following three exceptions.

WATCH FOR EXCEPTIONS TO THE "I" BEFORE "E" RULE

1. Words in which both vowels are pronounced use "ie" after "c," as in "society."

2. Words with a "shen" sound use "ie" after "c," as in "sufficient."

3. Other exceptions are: "either" or "neither," "foreign," "height," "seize," "their," and "weird."

---

2. *Adding Suffixes*

It is important to know when to double consonants when adding suffixes such as "-ing" and "-ed."

> ### RULES FOR DOUBLING CONSONANTS WHEN ADDING SUFFIXES
>
> 1. Double the final consonant of a one-syllable word when the final consonant is preceded by a single vowel.
>
> 2. For words with more than one syllable, follow the first rule only when the accent is on the last syllable.
>
> 3. Do NOT double the final consonant when the word already ends in two consonants.
>
> 4. Do NOT double the final consonant if the consonant is preceded by two vowels.
>
> 5. For words ending with "c," add a "k" before adding a suffix.

These rules apply only when the added suffix begins with a vowel. If the suffix begins with a consonant, do NOT double the last letter of the word. Note: If the suffix begins with a vowel and the word ends with a vowel, the last letter of the word should be dropped when the suffix is added.

Examples:

> stop ⇒ stopped; pin ⇒ pinned; fit ⇒ fitter; sit ⇒ sitting; nag ⇒ nagging; fat ⇒ fatten
> infer ⇒ inferred; permit ⇒ permitted; bellow ⇒ bellowed; frighten ⇒ frightened; commit ⇒ committing
> bark ⇒ barked; wink ⇒ winked; work ⇒ worked
> soil ⇒ soiled; fail ⇒ failed; heat ⇒ heated
> picnic ⇒ picnicking

3. Forming Plurals

> ### RULES FOR FORMING PLURALS OF WORDS
>
> 1. Add "-s."
>
> 2. Change "y" to "i" and add "-es" for words in which "y" is preceded by a consonant.
>
> 3. Add "-s" for words ending in "y" when "y" is preceded by a vowel.
>
> 4. For nouns ending in "-ess," add "-es."

Examples:

> walnut ⇒ walnuts; salad ⇒ salads
> lady ⇒ ladies; enemy ⇒ enemies; policy ⇒ policies; city ⇒ cities
> valley ⇒ valleys; play ⇒ plays
> princess ⇒ princesses; hostess ⇒ hostesses

Capitalization and Spelling

DIRECTIONS: Indicate whether Words #1-25 should be capitalized. Answers are on page 971.

1. thanksgiving	☑ Yes	☐ No		14. michael jordan	☑ Yes	☐ No
2. flower	☐ Yes	☑ No		15. arsonist	☐ Yes	☑ No
3. airplane	☐ Yes	☑ No		16. uncle	☐ Yes	☑ No
4. ohio	☑ Yes	☐ No		17. token	☐ Yes	☑ No
5. france	☑ Yes	☐ No		18. hamburger	☐ Yes	☑ No
6. muhammad ali	☑ Yes	☐ No		19. halloween	☑ Yes	☐ No
7. magician	☐ Yes	☑ No		20. morning	☐ Yes	☑ No
8. tin can	☐ Yes	☑ No		21. central park	☑ Yes	☐ No
9. rocky mountains	☑ Yes	☐ No		22. ten o'clock	☐ Yes	☑ No
10. governor davis	☑ Yes	☐ No		23. january	☑ Yes	☐ No
11. pine tree	☐ Yes	☑ No		24. afternoon	☐ Yes	☑ No
12. overcoat	☐ Yes	☑ No		25. monday	☑ Yes	☐ No
13. television	☐ Yes	☑ No				

DIRECTIONS: For Words #26-35, fill in the missing letters, "*i*" and "*e*," in the appropriate order. Answers are on page 972.

26. f _ie_ ld   ★ 29. v _ei_ n   ★ 32. sc _ie_ ntific   ★ 34. consc _ie_ ntious

27. conc _ei_ t   30. c _ei_ ling   33. s _ei_ zure   ★ 35. anc _ie_ nt

★ 28. sl _ei_ gh   31. n _ie_ ce

DIRECTIONS: For Words #36-55, add the appropriate suffix. Answers are on page 972.

36. fib + ing = fibbing
37. beg + ing = begging
38. control + able = controllable
39. commit + ment = commitment
40. color + ful = colourful
41. stop + ing = stopping
42. big + est = biggest
43. quit + ing = ~~quitting~~ quitting

44. rob + ing = robbing
45. glad + ly = gradly
46. bride + al = bridal
47. force + ible = forcible
48. force + ful = forceful
49. imagine + ary = imaginiry
50. hope + less = hopeless
51. true + ly = truly

52. remove + ing = *removing*

53. life + like = *lifelike*

54. like + ly = *likely*

55. service + able = *serviceable*

DIRECTIONS: For each group of Words #56-85, there is one misspelling. Find the misspelled word and spell it correctly on the line provided. Answers are on page 973.

56. carriage, consceince, association   *conscience*

57. achievement, chief, aviater   *aviator*

58. alltogether, almost, already   *al together*

59. annual, desireable, despair   *desirable*

60. independance, ninety, nevertheless   _____

61. billian, weather, rhyme   _____

62. quiet, lying, naturaly   _____

63. speach, straight, valleys   _____

64. transfered, tragedy, reference   _____

65. received, reciept, reception   _____

66. calender, appropriately, casualties   _____

67. affidavid, colossal, development   _____

68. diptheria, competent, bigoted   _____

69. prevelent, precipice, nauseous   _____

70. fundamentally, obedience, bookeeper   _____

71. tenant, repetetious, serviceable   _____

72. cloudiness, donkies, babyish   _____

73. wholly, wirey, strenuous   _____

74. successfully, renowned, propagander   _____

75. recuperate, vacuum, specificaly   _____

76. innoculate, aeronautics, saboteur   _____

77. prejudice, panacea, amethist   _____

78. laringytis, recipe, psychological   _____

79. scissors, supremacy, cinamon   _____

80. rarify, resind, thousandth   _____

81. superstitious, surgeon, irresistably   _____

82. sophomore, brocoli, synonym   _____

83. questionnaire, mayonaise, prophecy   _mayonnaise_

84. jeoperdy, narrative, monotonous   _____

85. primitive, obedience, mocassin   _____

Writing Skills Review

CAMBRIDGE
EDUCATIONAL SERVICES®

EDUCATORS' #1 CHOICE FOR SCHOOL IMPROVEMENT

Cambridge Course Concept Outline
WRITING SKILLS REVIEW

Planning an Essay

Understand the Assignment

1. Let the Prompt Be Your Topic

When presented with a prompt, always read it several times until you are completely familiar with the material. Sometimes it may be helpful to underline key words or phrases that are important.

Usually, the prompt is intended to be your topic and an inspiration to writing. If you pay careful attention to the language of the prompt, it can actually help you to get started.

Consider this sample essay prompt:

> *Human beings are often cruel, but they also have the capacity for kindness and compassion. In my opinion, an example that demonstrates this capacity is ——.*

Assignment: Complete the statement above with an example from current affairs, history, literature, or your own personal experience. Then write a well-organized essay explaining why you regard that event favorably.

This topic explicitly invites you to choose an example of kindness or compassion from history, current events, literature, or even personal experience. Thus, you could write about the end of a war (history), a mission of humanitarian aid (current events), the self-sacrifice of a fictional character (literature), or even about the day that your family helped a stranded motorist (personal experience). Remember that what you have to say is not as important as how you say it.

2. Develop a Point of View

Sometimes an essay prompt will invite you to present your opinion on an issue. When you encounter such prompts, you must decide whether you are in agreement or disagreement with the statement given.

3. Write Only on the Assigned Topic

While the types of prompts may differ among assignments or tests, the directions all agree on this point: You must write on the assigned topic. The assigned topic is often "open-ended," so you should have no problem coming up with something to write.

Organize Your Thoughts

1. Limit the Scope of Your Essay

The requirements of your writing assignment should determine the length and scope of your essay. Always remember to define the coverage of an essay before setting pen to paper; this will improve the focus of an essay so that the essay sets out to accomplish only the assigned task, whether it is to defend a controversial position or to define a definition. The more limited and specific your topic, the more successful your essay is likely to be: You will be able to supply the specific details that add depth and sophistication to an essay. You will also reduce the possibility of straying onto a tangent point or under-developing a specific claim.

2. Develop a Thesis

A thesis statement solidifies the scope, purpose, and direction of an essay in a clear and focused statement. This thesis statement usually includes your claims or assertions and the reasoning and evidence that support them. If possible, try to formulate the thesis of your composition in a single sentence during the pre-writing stage. When developing a thesis, keep in mind the following ideas:

IMPORTANT POINTS FOR DEVELOPING A THESIS

1. The thesis must not be too broad or too narrow.

2. The thesis must be clear to both you and the essay reader.

3. Everything in the essay must support your thesis.

4. Use specific details and examples rather than generalizations to support your thesis.

---

3. Identify Key Points

Identify the two or three (perhaps four) important points that you want to make. Then, decide on the order of presentation for those points.

4. Write an Outline

Once you gain a clear understanding of the assignment and its requirements, it is then important to organize the major points of your essay in a written outline. The purpose of outline is to develop a logical structure to your arguments and to streamline the focus of your essay. An outline should include your thesis statement, the key points of your argument, and the concluding statement of your essay. A sample outline structure is presented below for your reference.

SAMPLE OUTLINE

I.   Introduction
   A. Thesis Statement

II. First Key Point.
   A. Subpoint 1
   B. Subpoint 2
   C. Subpoint 3

III. Second Key Point
   A. Subpoint 1
   B. Subpoint 2

IV. Third Key Point
   A. Subpoint 1
   B. Subpoint 2
   C. Subpoint 3

V.   Conclusion
   A. Restatement of Thesis

Composition

Organize Ideas into Paragraphs

It is the hallmark of a good writer to use paragraphs effectively. Paragraphs are important because they provide a structure through which the writer can convey meaning. To illustrate this point with an analogy, imagine a grocery store in which items are not organized into sections. In this store, there is no fresh produce section, no canned goods section, no baked goods section, and no frozen foods section. Consequently, a single bin holds bunches of bananas, cans of beans, loaves of bread, and frozen turkeys; this disorganization characterizes every bin, shelf, rack, and refrigerated case in the store, making shopping in our imaginary store very difficult. Likewise, essays without paragraphs, or with poorly organized paragraphs, are very difficult—if not impossible—to understand.

Decide on how many paragraphs you are going to write. Your essay should contain two to four important points that develop or illustrate your thesis. Each important point should be treated in its own paragraph.

Do not write simply to fill up pages and make it seem that you have many ideas. This approach can result in repetition and wordiness, which is a sign of disorganization and unclear thinking. Write enough to sufficiently demonstrate your writing ability and to prove your thesis. Five paragraphs (an introduction paragraph, three main body paragraphs, and a concluding paragraph) are usually sufficient.

Write the Essay

Many students get frustrated before they even begin to write. They sit and stare at the blank page and complain that they are "blocked": They can't think of anything to write. The secret to successfully beginning an essay is to simply start writing after you have completed the pre-writing stage, even if the first few sentences of the essay may need revision. Follow this simple essay structure:

BASIC ESSAY STRUCTURE

Introduction: State what you are going to elaborate in the essay.
State your position clearly.
State the elements that you will be using to support your position.

Body: Each paragraph in the body of your essay will be devoted to one of the supporting elements that are introduced in the introduction.
Elaborate on the element in the paragraph by using examples.

Conclusion: Summarize your position and the reasons for your position.

---

1. The Introduction

You have already analyzed the question in your pre-writing stage. Now, you will use the introduction (first paragraph) to write clear and concise sentences, describing the topic that you are writing about and indicating to the reader what you plan to say in your essay to back up your position or to illustrate, with examples, the main point. The general idea of the introduction is to indicate to the reader the direction that your essay will take. However, do not spend too much time on the introduction. This is not the place to expound on the ideas and examples.

When writing your introduction, keep in mind these points:

WRITING INTRODUCTORY PARAGRAPHS

1. Always remain focused on the essay prompt. Never stray from the intended essay thesis.

2. Avoid being cute or funny, ironic or satiric, overly emotional or too dramatic. Set the tone or attitude in your first sentence. Your writing should be sincere, clear, and straightforward.

3. Do not repeat the question word for word. A paraphrase in your own words is far better than just copying the words of the exam question.

4. In your first paragraph, tell the reader the topic of your essay and the ideas that will guide the essay's development and organization. A clear topic sentence accomplishes this task.

5. Each sentence should advance your topic and be interesting to your reader.

An effective introduction often refers to the subject of the essay, explains the value of the topic, or attracts the attention of the reader by giving a pertinent illustration. Ineffective beginnings often contain unrelated material, ramble, and lack clarity.

2. The Body

The heart of the essay is the development, or the middle paragraph(s). Here, the writer must attempt, in paragraph form, to support the main idea of the essay through illustrations, details, and examples. The developmental paragraphs must serve as a link in the chain of ideas and contribute directly to the essay's central thought. All the sentences of the development must explain the essential truth of the thesis or topic sentence without digression.

Each paragraph should start with a transitional statement or phrase that describes the relationship of the paragraph to the previous paragraphs. The length of any one of these body paragraphs can be variable, but each paragraph should only cover one main idea with adequate detail. You may do this through a style that is descriptive, narrative, or expository, using a factual or an anecdotal approach. Whatever approach you choose and whatever style you adopt, your writing must be coherent, logical, unified, and well-ordered.

When writing your essay, avoid the following common mistakes:

AVOID THESE COMPOSITION ERRORS

1. Don't use sentences that are irrelevant and contain extraneous material.

2. Don't use sentences that have no sequence of thought or logical development of ideas.

3. Don't use sentences that do not relate to the topic sentence or do not flow from the preceding sentence.

---

3. Transitions

The good writer makes use of transitional words or phrases to connect thoughts, to provide for a logical sequence of ideas, and to link paragraphs. On the next page is a list of some of these transitions and the logical relationships that they indicate.

TRANSITIONAL WORDS AND PHRASES FOR ESSAY DEV

Addition:	also	in addition	first, second,	
	moreover	similarly	furthermore	
	again	and	not only...bu	
	both...and			
	finally			
Alternation:	or	nor	either...or	neither......
Cause/effect/ purpose:	therefore	as	consequently	because
	since	for	accordingly	hence
	so that	so	as a consequence	for this purpose
	as a result			
Conditions:	if	as if (as though)	once...then	unless
Contrast:	however	still	all the same	although
	but	on the other hand	on the contrary	nevertheless
	even though	yet	instead	otherwise
	though			
Space:	here	opposite to	next to	where
	there	to the left/right	wherever	nearby
	in the middle			
Support:	for example	such as	for instance	in fact
	in general			
Summary:	as shown above	to sum up	in other words	in short
	in brief	in conclusion	in summary	in general
Time:	later	after (noun)	meanwhile	finally
	since (clause)	until (clause)	while (clause)	before (noun)
	then	during	after (clause)	whenever
	as soon as	at the present time	in (month, year)	eventually
	when	before (clause)		

4. The Conclusion

The successful writer must know when and how to end an essay. To effectively conclude your essay, you should draw together comments in a strong, clear concluding paragraph. This paragraph should give the reader the feeling that the essay has made its point, that the thesis has been explained, or that a point of view has been established. This can be accomplished in about three to six sentences in one of the following ways:

EFFECTIVE METHODS FOR CONCLUDING AN ESSAY

1. Restate the main idea.

2. Summarize the material covered in the essay.

3. Conclude with a clear statement of your opinion on the issue(s) involved and discussed in the essay.

There are good techniques, and there are some very ineffective methods for drawing a composition to a close. Avoid the following mistakes:

> ## INEFFECTIVE METHODS FOR CONCLUDING AN ESSAY
>
> 1. DO NOT apologize for your inability to discuss all the issues in the allotted time.
>
> 2. DO NOT complain that the topic did not interest you or that you don't think it was fair to be asked to write on so broad a topic.
>
> 3. DO NOT introduce material that you will not develop, ramble on about non-pertinent matters, or use material that is trite or unrelated.

Keep in mind that a good conclusion is related to the thesis of the essay and is an integral part of the essay. It may be a review or a restatement, or it may lead the reader to do his or her own thinking, but the conclusion must be strong, clear, and effective.

An effective concluding paragraph may restate the thesis statement, summarize the main idea of the essay, draw a logical conclusion, or offer a strong opinion of what the future holds. An ineffective final paragraph often introduces new material in a scanty fashion, apologizes for the ineffectiveness of the material presented, or is illogical or unclear.

Principles of Good Writing

While writing, keep the three principles of good writing in mind: write grammatically, punctuate and spell correctly, and write concisely, clearly, and legibly. Following these conventions will allow you to communicate your ideas clearly and effectively, improving the overall quality of your essay.

1. Write Grammatically

The principles of grammar covered in the Grammar and Mechanics Skills Review should be used when writing your essay. At a minimum, you should be sure of the following when writing your essay:

> ## CORRECT GRAMMAR IS A MUST FOR EFFECTIVE ESSAYS
>
> 1. Does each sentence have a conjugated (main) verb that agrees with its subject?
>
> 2. Does each pronoun have a referent (antecedent) with which it agrees?
>
> 3. Do similar elements in each sentence have parallel form?
>
> 4. Do the modifiers make sense?
>
> 5. Does each sentence say what it means to say in a direct and concise way?

Your checklist should also include the other writing principles reviewed in the Grammar and Mechanics Skills Review.

2. Punctuate and Spell Correctly

In addition to writing grammatically, concisely, and formally (without using slang and other low-level usage language), you must punctuate and spell correctly. Refer to the Grammar and Mechanics Skills Review for an in-depth punctuation and spelling review.

Since you are in charge of writing the essay, you can choose to avoid punctuation and spelling errors. If you are unsure about how to punctuate a particular construction or spell a particular word, choose an alternative.

3. Write Concisely, Clearly, and Legibly

Simple, direct sentences are less likely to get you into trouble than complex, convoluted ones. In writing an essay for a standardized test, any sentence that is more complicated than a sentence with two independent clauses joined by a conjunction such as "and" or "but" or a sentence with one dependent and one independent clause joined by a conjunction such as "while" or

"although" is an invitation to error. Unless you are confident in your ability to keep all of the _____ sentence under control, use a simpler method of expression.

Additionally, avoid using unnecessary and wordy phrases, such as those illustrated in the char_____

AVOID THESE UNNECESSARY AND WORDY PHRASES

Instead of:	Say:
In my opinion, I believe that	I believe that
In the event of an emergency	In an emergency
On the possibility that it may	Since it may
close to the point of	close to
have need for	need
with a view to	to
in view of the fact that	because
give consideration to	consider
mean to imply	imply
disappear from view	disappear
in this day and age	today
the issue in question	issue

Also, while neatness is not graded, it is almost certainly true that an illegible essay will not receive a good grade. Even if you cannot perform calligraphy, you should at least be able to write legibly.

Revision

Proofread Your Essay

Proofreading is an essential part of the writing process. The first draft of an essay usually will not be free of errors. This means that you will need to reread the essay and correct any grammatical errors or logical inconsistencies in your paper. There are two categories of errors that generally manifest in essays: structural errors and mechanics and usage errors.

1. Proofread for Structural Errors

When proofreading, first consider the structural elements of an essay, as these are of primary importance in establishing your argument. The three most important structural factors that should be considered when editing an essay are unity, coherence, and support. Essays are judged by how well they meet these three basic requirements. To improve your essay, ask yourself the following questions:

UNITY, COHERENCE, AND SUPPORT ARE
VITAL FOR AN EFFECTIVE ESSAY

1. Do all of the details in the essay support and develop the main thesis?

2. Do all of the illustrations relate to the main point and add to the general effectiveness of the essay?

3. Have irrelevant ideas been deleted?

4. Does the essay show a sense of organization?

5. Is the material presented logically?

6. Does the essay include transitional words or phrases that allow the reader to move easily from one idea to the next?

7. Does the essay use details that make it interesting and vivid?

8. Is the main idea supported with concrete and specific illustrations?

9. Does the essay contain sufficient supporting details to clarify and persuade?

---

2. Proofread for Mechanics and Usage Errors

Next, look for any mechanics and usage errors. Although these errors are less important than structural errors, they may distract the reader from the substance of your arguments, decreasing the overall ease and readability of your essay. As you proofread, you may also consider altering a word or adjusting a phrase to make your essay more effective.

COMMON WRITING ERRORS ELIMINATED BY PROOFREADING

1. Omission of words—especially "the," "a," and, "an"

2. Omission of final letters on words

3. Careless spelling errors

4. Incorrect use of capital letters

5. Faulty punctuation

Scoring Rubric

The following rubric (scoring guide) summarizes how your essay will likely be graded by the essay reader:

ESSAY SCORE QUALIFICATIONS

Score   *Essay Qualities*

Outstanding
- demonstrates *clear and consistent competence* though it may have occasional errors
- effectively and insightfully addresses the writing task
- is well-organized and fully developed
- uses appropriate and innovative examples to support ideas
- demonstrates a superior grasp of grammar and style, varies sentence structure, and uses a wide range of vocabulary

Superior
- demonstrates *reasonably consistent competence* with occasional errors or lapses in quality
- effectively addresses the writing task
- is generally well-organized and adequately developed
- uses appropriate examples to support ideas
- demonstrates a competent grasp of grammar and style, employs some syntactic variety, and uses appropriate vocabulary

Good
- demonstrates *adequate competence* with occasional errors and lapses in quality
- addresses the writing task
- is organized and somewhat developed
- uses examples to support ideas
- demonstrates an adequate but inconsistent grasp of grammar and style with minor errors in grammar and diction
- displays minimal sentence variety

Average
- demonstrates *developing competence*
- may contain one or more of the following weaknesses: inadequate organization or development; inappropriate or insufficient details to support ideas; and an accumulation of errors in grammar, diction, or sentence structure

Below Average
- demonstrates *some incompetence*
- is flawed by one or more of the following weaknesses: poor organization; thin development; little or inappropriate detail to support ideas; and frequent errors in grammar, diction, and sentence structure

Weak
- demonstrates *incompetence*
- is seriously flawed by one or more of the following weaknesses: very poor organization, very thin development, and usage or syntactical errors so severe that meaning is somewhat obscured

---

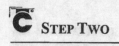

Sample Essay 1

DIRECTIONS: You have 25 minutes to plan and write an essay on the topic assigned below. DO NOT WRITE ON ANY OTHER TOPIC. AN ESSAY ON ANOTHER TOPIC IS NOT ACCEPTABLE. Think carefully about the issue presented in the following excerpt and the assignment below. Sample essays and analyses are on page 975.

then make the conclusion.

Residents of rural areas often wonder why people would voluntarily choose to live in a large city and insist that rural life—with its open spaces, relative freedom from worries about crime, and healthful living conditions—is preferable. Conversely, residents of urban areas say that city life—with access to public transportation, cultural amenities, and many entertainment opportunities—is preferable.

& agree w/ either urban or rural. supporting details.

Assignment: Which do you find more compelling, the belief that the quality of life is greater in urban areas or the belief that the quality of life is greater in rural areas? Plan and write an essay in which you develop your point of view on this issue. Support your position with reasoning and examples taken from your reading, studies, experience, and observations.

Sample Essay 2

DIRECTIONS: You have 25 minutes to plan and write an essay on the topic assigned below. DO NOT WRITE ON ANY OTHER TOPIC. AN ESSAY ON ANOTHER TOPIC IS NOT ACCEPTABLE. Think carefully about the issue presented in the following excerpt and the assignment below. Sample essays and analyses are on page 976.

> *The Internet, originally seen as a savior to many, is now seen as an unexpected plague. Media companies are losing millions in revenue to Internet pirates. Cyber thieves are stealing identities and ruining lives. Companies have overextended themselves by pouring capital down the drain with nothing in return. The Internet has not lived up to its initial billing.*

Assignment: Has the Internet been a positive technological advance or have its negative effects on society outweighed the positives? Plan and write an essay in which you develop your point of view on this issue. Support your position with reasoning and examples taken from your reading, studies, experience, and observations.

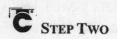

Sample Essay 3

DIRECTIONS: You have 25 minutes to plan and write an essay on the topic assigned below. DO NOT WRITE ON ANY OTHER TOPIC. AN ESSAY ON ANOTHER TOPIC IS NOT ACCEPTABLE. Think carefully about the issue presented in the following excerpt and the assignment below. Sample essays and analyses are on page 978.

> *Although there is a strong push around the globe to eliminate so-called "Frankenfoods," agricultural products that have been bio-engineered, these protests are by and large unfounded. Through advances in food technology, famine and world hunger will some day be a thing of the past.*

Assignment: In your view, should bio-engineered foods have a greater access to the marketplace or should these foods be kept from the public awaiting more testing? Plan and write an essay in which you develop your point of view on this issue. Support your position with reasoning and examples taken from your reading, studies, experience, and observations.

3

Step Three: Problem-Solving, Concepts, and Strategies

Step Three Highlights:

Review the most commonly-tested concepts for each SAT and PSAT section.

Learn everything you need to know about the three test sections: Critical Reading, Mathematics, and Writing.

Discover the powerful alternative test-taking strategies that will give you an edge when taking the SAT or PSAT.

Measure progress on tested concepts with quizzes and advanced "upper-quartile" items.

Step Three Overview:

This section of the textbook contains many items that look like those found on the real SAT and PSAT. When compared with items on the real test, these problems have the same content, represent similar difficulty levels, and are solved by using the same problem-solving and alternative test-taking strategies. You will go over these items with your instructor in class. Use the "Notes and Strategies" sheets located throughout this section to record the alternative test-taking strategies taught during these lessons.

Critical Reading:
Passages

Cambridge Course Concept Outline
CRITICAL READING: PASSAGES

I. CORE LESSON (p. 377)
- **A. ITEM-TYPES**
  - **1. APPLYING ITEM-TYPES TO LONG PASSAGES**
    - **a. MAIN IDEA** (Items #1-2, p. 378)
    - **b. EXPLICIT DETAIL** (Items #3-5, p. 379)
    - **c. VOCABULARY** (Item #6, p. 379)
    - **d. DEVELOPMENT** (Items #7-8, p. 379)
    - **e. IMPLIED IDEA** (Items #9-11, p. 379)
    - **f. APPLICATION** (Items #12-13, p. 380)
    - **g. VOICE** (Items #14-15, p. 380)
  - **2. APPLYING ITEM-TYPES TO SHORT PASSAGES** (Items #16-29, p. 382)
- **B. STRATEGIES**
  - **1. THREE READING COMPREHENSION LEVELS**
    - **a. GENERAL THEME**
    - **b. SPECIFIC POINTS**
    - **c. EVALUATION**
  - **2. USING THE THREE COMPREHENSION LEVELS**
  - **3. FIVE STEPS TO APPROACHING PASSAGES**
    - **a. LABEL PASSAGES AS "EASY" OR "HARD"**
    - **b. PREVIEW FIRST AND LAST SENTENCES OF SELECTION**
    - **c. PREVIEW ITEM STEMS**
    - **d. READ THE PASSAGE**
    - **e. ANSWER THE ITEMS** (Items #30-41, p. 384)
  - **4. ITEM-TYPE STRATEGIES**
    - **a. MAIN IDEA CLUES** (Items #42-44, p. 388)
    - **b. EXPLICIT DETAIL CLUES** (Item #45, p. 389)
    - **c. VOCABULARY CLUES** (Items #46-50, p. 389)
    - **d. DEVELOPMENT CLUES** (Items #51-52, p. 389)
    - **e. IMPLIED IDEA CLUES** (Items #53-54, p. 390)
    - **f. APPLICATION CLUES** (Item #55, p. 390)
    - **g. VOICE CLUES** (Item #56, p. 390)

II. EXTENDED LESSON (p. 392)
- **A. NATURAL SCIENCES** (Items #1-15, p. 392)
- **B. SOCIAL STUDIES** (Items #16-22, p. 396)
- **C. HUMANITIES** (Items #23-42, p. 398)
- **D. LITERARY FICTION** (Items #43-57, p. 405)

III. CHALLENGE ITEMS (Items #1-60, p. 408)

CORE LESSON

The passages and items in this section accompany the Core Lesson of the Critical Reading: Passages Lesson. You will work through the items with your instructor in class. Use the included Notes and Strategies pages to record the problem-solving strategies that are discussed in class.

The first passage begins on the following page.

DIRECTIONS: Each passage below is followed by one or more items based on its content. Answer the items on the basis of what is stated or implied in the corresponding passage. Answers are on page 983.

Items 1-15 are based on the following passage.

To broaden their voting appeal in the Presidential election of 1796, the Federalists selected Thomas Pinckney, a leading South Carolinian, as running mate
Line for the New Englander John Adams. But Pinckney's
5 Southern friends chose to ignore their party's intentions and regarded Pinckney as a Presidential candidate, creating a political situation that Alexander Hamilton was determined to exploit. Hamilton had long been wary of Adams' stubbornly independent brand of
10 politics and preferred to see his running mate, who was more pliant and over whom Hamilton could exert more control, in the President's chair.

The election was held under the system originally established by the Constitution. At that time, there was
15 but a single tally, with the candidate receiving the largest number of electoral votes declared President and the candidate with the second largest number declared Vice President. Hamilton anticipated that all the Federalists in the North would vote for Adams and
20 Pinckney equally in an attempt to ensure that Jefferson would not be either first or second in the voting. Pinckney would be solidly supported in the South while Adams would not. Hamilton concluded if it were possible to divert a few electoral votes from Adams to
25 Pinckney, Pinckney would receive more than Adams, yet both Federalists would outpoll Jefferson.

Various methods were used to persuade the electors to vote as Hamilton wished. In the press, anonymous articles were published attacking Adams
30 for his monarchical tendencies and Jefferson for being overly democratic, while pushing Pinckney as the only suitable candidate. In private correspondence with state party leaders, the Hamiltonians encouraged the idea that Adams' popularity was slipping, that he could not
35 win the election, and that the Federalists could defeat Jefferson only by supporting Pinckney.

Had sectional pride and loyalty not run as high in New England as in the deep South, Pinckney might well have become Washington's successor. New
40 Englanders, however, realized that equal votes for Adams and Pinckney in their states would defeat Adams; therefore, eighteen electors scratched Pinckney's name from their ballots and deliberately threw away their second votes to men who were not
45 even running. It was fortunate for Adams that they did, for the electors from South Carolina completely

abandoned him, giving eight votes to Pinckney and eight to Jefferson.

In the end, Hamilton's interference in Pinckney's
50 candidacy lost him even the Vice Presidency. Without New England's support, Pinckney received only 59 electoral votes, finishing third to Adams and Jefferson. He might have been President in 1797, or as Vice President a serious contender for the Presidency in
55 1800; instead, stigmatized by a plot he had not devised, he served a brief term in the United States Senate and then dropped from sight as a national influence.

1. The main purpose of the passage is to

    (A) propose ~~reforms~~ of the procedures for electing the President and Vice President
    (B) condemn Alexander Hamilton for interfering in the election of 1796
    (C) describe the political events that led to John Adams' victory in the 1796 Presidential election
    (D) contrast the political philosophy of the Federalists to that of Thomas Jefferson
    (E) praise Thomas Pinckney for his refusal to participate in Hamilton's scheme to have him elected President

2. Which of the following titles best describes the content of the passage?

    (A) The Failure of Alexander Hamilton's Plan for Thomas Pinckney to Win the 1796 Presidential Election
    (B) The Roots of Alexander Hamilton's Distrust of John Adams and New England's Politics
    (C) Important Issues in the 1796 Presidential Campaign as Presented by the Federalist Candidates
    (D) The Political Careers of Alexander Hamilton, John Adams, and Thomas Pinckney
    (E) Political and Sectional Differences between New England and the South in the Late 1700s

3. According to the passage, which of the following was true of the Presidential election of 1796?

(A) Thomas Jefferson received more electoral votes than did Thomas Pinckney.
(B) John Adams received strong support from the electors of South Carolina.
(C) Alexander Hamilton received most of the electoral votes of New England.
(D) Thomas Pinckney was selected by Federalist party leaders to be the party's Presidential candidate.
(E) Thomas Pinckney received all 16 of South Carolina's electoral votes.

4. According to the passage, Hamilton's plan included all of the following EXCEPT

(A) Articles published in newspapers to create opposition to John Adams
(B) South Carolina's loyalty to Thomas Pinckney
(C) Private contact with state officials urging them to support Thomas Pinckney
(D) John Adams' reputation as a stubborn and independent New Englander
(E) Support that the New England states would give to John Adams

5. The passage supplies information that answers which of the following questions?

(A) How many electoral votes were cast for John Adams in the 1796 Presidential election?
(B) Under the voting system originally set up by the Constitution, how many votes did each elector cast?
(C) Who was Jefferson's running mate in the 1796 Presidential election?
(D) What became of Alexander Hamilton after his plan to have Thomas Pinckney elected President failed?
(E) How many more electoral votes did Jefferson receive in the 1796 Presidential election than Pinckney?

6. In line 11, the word "pliant" most nearly means

(A) assertive
(B) public
(C) national
(D) popular
(E) yielding

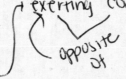 exerting contra
opposite of

7. Why does the author refer to the election procedure established by the original Constitution?

(A) To prove to the reader that New England as a whole had more electoral votes than the state of South Carolina
(B) To persuade the reader that Thomas Pinckney's defeat could have been avoided
(C) To alert the reader that the procedure used in 1796 was unlike that presently used
(D) To encourage the reader to study Constitutional history
(E) To remind the reader that the President and Vice President of the United States are chosen democratically

8. The overall development of the passage can best be described as

(A) refuting possible explanations for certain phenomena
(B) documenting a thesis with specific examples
(C) offering an explanation of a series of events
(D) making particular proposals to solve a problem
(E) attacking the assumption of an argument

9. The passage implies that some electors voted for John Adams because they were

(A) in favor of a monarchy
(B) persuaded to do so by Hamilton
(C) afraid South Carolina would not vote for Pinckney
(D) concerned about New England's influence over the South
(E) anxious to have a President from their geographical region

10. Which of the following can be inferred from the passage?

(A) Thomas Pinckney had a personal dislike for Jefferson's politics.
(B) The Federalists regarded themselves as more democratic than Jefferson.
(C) The Hamiltonians contacted key Southern leaders to persuade them to vote for Adams.
(D) Electors were likely to vote for candidates from their own geographical region.
(E) New England states cast more electoral votes for Jefferson than did the South.

11. It can be inferred that had South Carolina not cast any electoral votes for Jefferson, the outcome of the 1796 election would have been a

(A) larger margin of victory for John Adams
(B) victory for Thomas Jefferson
(C) Federalist defeat in the Senate
(D) victory for Thomas Pinckney
(E) defeat of the Federalist Presidential candidate

12. The electors who scratched Pinckney's name from their ballots behaved most like which of the following people?

(A) A newspaper publisher who adds a special section to the Sunday edition to review the week's political events
(B) A member of the clergy who encourages members of other faiths to meet to discuss solutions to the community's problems
(C) An artist who saves preliminary sketches of an important work even after the work is finally completed
(D) A general who orders his retreating troops to destroy supplies they must leave behind so the enemy cannot use the supplies
(E) A runner who sets too fast a pace during the early stages of a race and has no energy left for the finish

13. Hamilton's strategy can best be summarized as

(A) divide and conquer
(B) retreat and regroup
(C) feint and counterattack
(D) hit and run
(E) camouflage and conceal

14. The tone of the passage can best be described as

(A) witty
(B) comical
(C) scholarly
(D) frivolous
(E) morose

15. The author's attitude toward Hamilton's plan can be described as

(A) angry
(B) approving
(C) analytical
(D) regretful
(E) disinterested

NOTES AND STRATEGIES

Items 16-22 are based on the following passage.

Line

5

10

15

The 16th-century revival of learning was naturalistic, a rejection of the dominant supernaturalistic strain of thought. Perhaps the influence of classic Greek literature has been overestimated by some historians, and undoubtedly the change in thinking was mainly a product of contemporary conditions; but there can be no doubt that educated people, enamored of the new viewpoint, turned eagerly to Greek literature. This interest in Greek thought was not in literature for its own sake, but in the spirit it expressed. The mental freedom that animated Greek expression aroused new readers to think and observe in a similar untrammeled fashion. 16th-century history of science shows that the young physical sciences borrowed points of departure from the new interest in Greek literature. As Windelband said, "the new science of nature was the offspring of humanism."

16. The author's primary purpose is to

(A) connect 16th-century science and Greek thought
(B) distinguish modern thinking from Greek thinking
(C) contrast Greek naturalism with Greek supernaturalism
(D) show the relevance of Greek thinking to modern science
(E) demonstrate that 16th-century science utilized Greek myths

17. According to the author, the most important influence on the revival of learning in the 16th century was

(A) ancient Greek literature
(B) 16th-century scientific thought
(C) existing historical conditions
(D) supernaturalistic thinking
(E) humanistic interpretation of Greek thought

18. In line 13, the word "untrammeled" most nearly means

(A) unhistorical
(B) uninteresting
(C) irresponsible
(D) unrestricted
(E) irreverent

19. The author cites Windelband as an authority on

(A) ancient Greek life
(B) classical Greek texts
(C) modern science
(D) 16th-century thought
(E) supernaturalism

20. The author implies that scholars have debated the extent to which

(A) ancient Greek thought was truly characterized by intellectual freedom
(B) supernaturalism in the 16th century interfered with scientific progress
(C) humanism represented a radical departure from earlier supernaturalistic thinking
(D) renewed interest in Greek thinking valued ancient literature for its own merits
(E) Greek literature inspired the 16th-century revival in learning

21. The discussion of ancient Greek literature presupposes that it is possible to

(A) distinguish the "spirit" of literature from actual written words
(B) be influenced by literature without having to read the texts
(C) trace the roots of any intellectual movement back to ancient times
(D) analyze a scientific question without the history that gave rise to the question
(E) find direct influences of ancient writings in all modern writings

22. It can be inferred that the author's attitude toward Windelband's conclusion is one of

(A) condemnation
(B) indifference
(C) mistrust
(D) approval
(E) regret

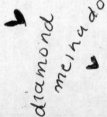

Items 23-29 are based on the following passage.

Are republics less likely than monarchies to make war? Sparta, Rome, and Carthage, all republics, often engaged in war. Sparta was little better than a well
Line regulated camp, and Rome never tired of conquest.
5 Carthage was the aggressor in the very war that destroyed it. In later times, Venice figured often in wars of ambition, until Pope Julius II gave a deadly blow to the power and pride of that haughty republic. In Britain, the representatives of the people compose
10 one branch of the national legislature. Few nations have been more frequently engaged in war, and there have been almost as many popular as royal wars. The cries nations and representatives have forced monarchs to enter and continue wars contrary to their
15 inclinations. Is any of this surprising? Are not the former administered by humans as well as the latter?

23. The author's primary purpose is to

(A) demonstrate that republics do not ordinarily engage in war
(B) deny that war is a valid instrument of foreign policy
(C) condemn several ancient republics for their aggressive tendencies
(D) criticize Britain for allowing its monarchs to initiate wars
(E) show that republics are as likely as monarchies to wage war

24. In line 16, the word "former" refers to

(A) nations
(B) people
(C) republics
(D) representatives
(E) monarchies

25. In line 12, the word "popular" most nearly means

(A) very well-liked
(B) completely victorious
(C) supported by people
(D) brutally devastating
(E) cautiously started

26. The author develops the thesis of the passage primarily by

(A) citing examples to answer a question
(B) finding a contradiction in a theory
(C) personally attacking the proponent of a claim
(D) challenging the evidence presented for a conclusion
(E) redefining key terms in the discussion

27. The author implies that republics are

(A) more likely than monarchies to wage war
(B) less likely than monarchies to initiate a war
(C) equally as likely as monarchies to act defensively
(D) just as likely as monarchies to be involved in war
(E) more likely than monarchies to fight a war of aggression

28. Which of the following would be most appropriate for the author to take up in a continuation of the selection?

(A) contrasting different military tactics used by republics and monarchies
(B) studying the changing value over time of war as a tool of national policy
(C) analyzing moral implications of initiating a war without adequate reason
(D) reviewing some examples of unjust wars started by monarchies
(E) comparing justifications given by republics and monarchies for war

29. It can be inferred that the author's attitude toward the actions of Venice is

(A) laudatory   *giving praise*
(B) neutral
(C) disapproving
(D) indifferent
(E) speculative

haughty → conceited

diamond

Items 30-34 are based on the following passage.

The liberal view of democratic citizenship that developed in the 17th and 18th centuries was fundamentally different from that of the classical Greeks. The pursuit of private interests with as little interference as possible from government was seen as the road to human happiness and progress rather than the public obligations and involvement in the collective community that were emphasized by the Greeks. Freedom was to be realized by limiting the scope of governmental activity and political obligation and not through immersion in the collective life of the *polis*. The basic role of the citizen was to select governmental leaders and keep the powers and scope of public authority in check. On the liberal view, the rights of citizens against the state were the focus of special emphasis.

Over time, the liberal democratic notion of citizenship developed in two directions. First, there was a movement to increase the proportion of members of society who were eligible to participate as citizens—especially through extending the right of suffrage—and to ensure the basic political equality of all. Second, there was a broadening of the legitimate activities of government and a use of governmental power to redress imbalances in social and economic life. Political citizenship became an instrument through which groups and classes with sufficient numbers of votes could use the state's power to enhance their social and economic well-being.

Within the general liberal view of democratic citizenship, tensions have developed over the degree to which government can and should be used as an instrument for promoting happiness and well-being. Political philosopher Martin Diamond has categorized two views of democracy as follows. On the one hand, there is the "libertarian" perspective that stresses the private pursuit of happiness and emphasizes the necessity for restraint on government and protection of individual liberties. On the other hand, there is the "majoritarian" view that emphasizes the "task of the government to uplift and aid the common man against the malefactors of great wealth." The tensions between these two views are very evident today. Taxpayer revolts and calls for smaller government and less government regulation clash with demands for greater government involvement in the economic marketplace and the social sphere.

30. The author's primary purpose is to

(A) study ancient concepts of citizenship
(B) contrast different notions of citizenship
(C) criticize modern libertarian democracy
(D) describe the importance of universal suffrage
(E) introduce means of redressing an imbalance of power

31. It can be inferred from the passage that the Greek word "polis" means

(A) family life
(B) military service
(C) marriage
(D) private club
(E) political community

32. The author cites Martin Diamond in the last paragraph because the author

(A) regards Martin Diamond as an authority on political philosophy
(B) wishes to refute Martin Diamond's views on citizenship
(C) needs a definition of the term "citizenship"
(D) is unfamiliar with the distinction between libertarian and majoritarian concepts of democracy
(E) wants voters to support Martin Diamond as a candidate for public office

33. According to the passage, all of the following are characteristics that would distinguish the liberal idea of government from the Greek idea of government EXCEPT

(A) The emphasis on the rights of private citizens
(B) The activities that government may legitimately pursue
(C) The obligation of citizens to participate in government
(D) The size of the geographical area controlled by a government
(E) The definition of human happiness

34. A majoritarian would be most likely to favor
legislation that would

(A) eliminate all restrictions on individual liberty
(B) cut spending for social welfare programs
(C) provide greater protection for consumers
(D) lower taxes on the wealthy and raise taxes on
the average worker
(E) raise taxes on the average worker and cut
taxes on business

Items 35-41 are based on the following passage.

Park Service strategies to restore natural quiet to the Grand Canyon include both short-term and long-term actions. A limit has been imposed on the number
Line
5 of aircraft operating in the park, and a curfew has been enacted in the Zuni and Dragon corridors. The immediate benefit will be a dramatic reduction in noise levels in some of the most scenic and most sensitive park areas. The Park Service has also increased the number of flight-free zones in the park. In the long-
10 term, the air tour industry must be encouraged to conduct operations using quieter aircraft. Many of the current air tour craft will be phased out and replaced with more noise-efficient designs that incorporate quiet aircraft technology. Additional encouragement will be
15 provided by rewarding companies that invest in new technology. For example, special air tour routes will be established where only quiet aircraft would be permitted to operate.

35. The author's primary concern is to

(A) debate the impact of governmental financial incentives
(B) describe strategies for reducing noise levels in the Grand Canyon
(C) discourage the operation of air tours over the Grand Canyon
(D) discredit the motives of those who oppose noise pollution control
(E) dispute the effectiveness of government noise reduction plans

36. The passage mentions all of the following as strategies for controlling noise pollution in the Grand Canyon EXCEPT

(A) economic incentives for tour companies to buy new aircraft
(B) a curfew on flights over especially sensitive park areas
(C) a total ban on tour flights over the park areas
(D) restrictions on the number of flights over the park
(E) establishment of more flight-free zones in the park

37. In line 6, the word "dramatic" most nearly means

(A) theatrical
(B) suddenly noticeable
(C) slowly developing
(D) permanent
(E) speculative

38. The author mentions the Zuni corridor in order to

(A) illustrate the impact of a flight-free zone
(B) demonstrate the effect of curfews on critical areas
(C) highlight the value of phasing out older aircraft equipment
(D) underscore the advantage of providing incentives
(E) prove the importance of reducing park noise levels

39. The passage implies that the Park Service believes that

(A) tourism is more important than controlling noise
(B) some reduction in park noise levels is desirable
(C) curfews are more effective than flight-free zones
(D) quieter air tour equipment is not presently available
(E) only natural noise levels in the park are acceptable

40. Which of the following would most interfere with the plan to control noise by offering financial incentives to air tour operators?

(A) Special air tour routes would not be sufficiently profitable to pay for the cost of purchasing quiet technology.
(B) The availability of air tours attracts numerous visitors to the Grand Canyon who would not visit were the tours not offered.
(C) The air tourism industry has indicated a willingness to adopt new technology if it is profitable to do so.
(D) Special air tour routes ordinarily include some of the park's most remote and most beautiful scenery.
(E) Many tourists who visit the park on foot or as members of horseback tours complain about the noise of overflights.

41. The author's attitude toward the proposals for
    reducing noise pollution in the park is one of

    (A) skepticism
    (B) reluctance
    (C) approval
    (D) enthusiasm
    (E) ignorance

Items 42-56 are based on the following passage.

The Aleuts, residing on several islands of the Aleutian Chain, the Pribilof Islands, and the Alaskan Peninsula, have possessed a written language since 1825, when the Russian missionary Ivan Veniaminov selected appropriate characters of the Cyrillic alphabet to represent Aleut speech sounds, recorded the main body of Aleut vocabulary, and formulated grammatical rules. The Czarist Russian conquest of the proud, independent sea hunters was so devastatingly thorough that tribal traditions, even tribal memories, were almost obliterated. The slaughter of the majority of an adult generation was sufficient to destroy the continuity of tribal knowledge, which was dependent upon oral transmission. Consequently, the Aleuts developed a fanatical devotion to their language as their only cultural heritage.

The Russian occupation placed a heavy linguistic burden on the Aleuts. Not only were they compelled to learn Russian to converse with their overseers and governors, but they had to learn Old Slavonic to take an active part in church services as well as to master the skill of reading and writing their own tongue. In 1867, when the United States purchased Alaska, the Aleuts were unable to break sharply with their immediate past and substitute English for any one of their three languages.

To communicants of the Russian Orthodox Church, knowledge of Slavonic remained vital, as did Russian, the language in which one conversed with the clergy. The Aleuts came to regard English education as a device to wean them from their religious faith. The introduction of compulsory English schooling caused a minor renaissance of Russian culture as the Aleut parents sought to counteract the influence of the schoolroom. The harsh life of the Russian colonial rule began to appear more happy and beautiful in retrospect.

Regulations forbidding instruction in any language other than English increased its unpopularity. The superficial alphabetical resemblance of Russian and Aleut linked the two tongues so closely that every restriction against teaching Russian was interpreted as an attempt to eradicate the Aleut tongue. From the wording of many regulations, it appears that American administrators often had not the slightest idea that the Aleuts were clandestinely reading and writing in their own tongue or that they even had a written language of their own. To too many officials, anything in Cyrillic letters was Russian and something to be stamped out. Bitterness bred by abuses and the exploitations that the Aleuts suffered from predatory American traders and adventurers kept alive the Aleut resentment against the language spoken by Americans.

Gradually, despite the failure to emancipate the Aleuts from a sterile past by relating the Aleut and English languages more closely, the passage of years has assuaged the bitter misunderstandings and caused an orientation away from Russian toward English as their second language, but Aleut continues to be the language that molds their thought and expression.

42. The author is primarily concerned with describing

(A) the Aleuts' loyalty to their language and American failure to understand the language
(B) Russian and American treatment of Alaskan inhabitants both before and after 1867
(C) how the Czarist Russian occupation of Alaska created a written language for the Aleuts
(D) American government attempts to persuade the Aleuts to use English as a second language
(E) the atrocities committed by Russia against the Aleuts during the Czarist Russian occupation

43. The author is primarily concerned with

(A) describing the Aleuts' loyalty to their language and American failure to understand the language
(B) criticizing Russia and the United States for their mistreatment of the Aleuts
(C) praising the Russians for creating a written language for the Aleuts
(D) condemning Russia for its mistreatment of the Aleuts during the Czarist Russian occupation
(E) ridiculing American efforts to persuade the Aleuts to adopt English as a second language

44. Which of the following titles best fits the passage?

(A) Aleut Loyalty to Their Language: An American Misunderstanding
(B) Failure of Russian and American Policies in Alaska
(C) Russia's Gift to the Aleuts: A Written Language
(D) Mistreatment of Aleuts During Russian Occupation
(E) The Folly of American Attempts to Teach Aleuts English

45. According to the passage, which of the following was the most important reason for the Aleuts' devotion to their language?

(A) Invention of a written version of their language
(B) Introduction of Old Slavonic for worship
(C) Disruption of oral transmission of tribal knowledge
(D) Institution of compulsory English education
(E) Prohibition against writing or reading Russian

46. In line 17, the word "linguistic" infers relation to

(A) orthodoxy
(B) commerce
(C) language
(D) laws
(E) culture

47. In line 33, the word "renaissance" most nearly means

(A) resurgence
(B) rejection
(C) repeal
(D) reassessment
(E) reminder

48. In line 45, the word "clandestinely" most nearly means

(A) secretly
(B) reliably
(C) openly
(D) casually
(E) exactly

49. In line 54, the word "sterile" most nearly means

(A) germ-free
(B) unproductive
(C) fortunate
(D) ill-timed
(E) dominant

50. In line 56, the word "assuaged" most nearly means

(A) failed
(B) created
(C) intensified
(D) eased
(E) formed

51. The passage is developed primarily by

(A) testing the evidence supporting a theory
(B) describing causes and effects of events
(C) weighing the pros and cons of a plan
(D) projecting the future consequences of a decision
(E) debating both sides of a moral issue

52. Why does the author mention that the Russians killed the majority of adult Aleuts?

(A) To call attention to the immorality of foreign conquest
(B) To urge Russia to make restitution to the children of those killed
(C) To stir up outrage against the Russians for committing such atrocities
(D) To explain the extreme loyalty that Aleuts feel to their language
(E) To prove that the Aleuts have a written language

53. Which of the following statements about the religious beliefs of the Aleuts can be inferred from the passage?

    (A) Prior to the Russian occupation they had no religious beliefs
    (B) American traders and adventurers forced them to abandon all religious beliefs
    (C) At no time in their history have the Aleuts had an organized religion
    (D) Aleut leaders adopted the religious beliefs of the American officials following the 1867 purchase
    (E) The Russians forced Aleuts to become members of the Russian Orthodox Church

54. The passage implies that

    (A) the Cyrillic alphabet was invented for the Aleut language
    (B) all of the Cyrillic characters were used in writing the Aleut language
    (C) Russian and the Aleut language have some similar speech sounds
    (D) English is also written using the Cyrillic alphabet
    (E) the Cyrillic alphabet displaced the original Aleut alphabet

55. Distributing which of the following publications would be most likely to encourage Aleuts to make more use of English?

    (A) Russian translations of English novels
    (B) English translations of Russian novels
    (C) An English-Russian bilingual text devoted to important aspects of Aleutian culture
    (D) An Aleut-English bilingual text devoted to important aspects of Aleutian culture
    (E) A treatise about religions other than the Russian Orthodox Church written in English

56. The author's attitude toward the Aleuts can best be described as one of

    (A) understanding and sympathy
    (B) callousness and indifference
    (C) condemnation and reproof
    (D) ridicule and disparagement
    (E) awe and admiration

NOTES AND STRATEGIES

EXTENDED LESSON

DIRECTIONS: The passages and items in this section accompany the Extended Lesson of the Critical Reading: Passages Lesson. You will work through the items with your instructor in class. Each passage below is followed by one or more items based on its content. Answer the items on the basis of what is stated or implied in the corresponding passage(s). Answers are on page 983.

Items 1-7 are based on the following passage.

Like tropical reef corals, deep-sea corals have hard skeletons built from calcium and carbonate ions extracted from seawater. Oxygen and oxygen isotopes in carbonate ions can be used to determine the water temperature when the skeleton was formed. The absolute abundance of an isotope is difficult to measure, so studies focus on the ratio of the rare oxygen isotope ^{18}O to the common isotope ^{16}O. This ratio is inversely related to water temperature during formation of carbonates, so higher ratios mean lower temperatures. Some corals live for decades or centuries, so their skeletons contain a natural record of climate variability, like tree rings and ice cores. The ratio can be used as a proxy for data that cannot be obtained by direct measurement. The information gathered would be useful in determining the extent to which global warming may be a problem.

Line
5

10

15

1. The passage is primarily a discussion of how

    (A) scientists use proxies to study changing climate conditions
    (B) natural climate records generate data about global warming
    (C) coral reefs extract chemicals from the ocean to build reefs
    (D) deep-sea coral reefs can provide information about climate change
    (E) global warming threatens deep-sea and tropical corals

2. In line 14, the word "proxy" most nearly means

    (A) conclusion
    (B) substitute
    (C) theory
    (D) instrument
    (E) proof

3. A finding that the ratio of the ^{18}O isotope to the ^{16}O had been increasing for a certain period would most strongly support the conclusion that

    (A) the water temperature in the surrounding area had decreased
    (B) global warming had intensified for those years
    (C) climate variations for the period were insignificant
    (D) ocean water temperature around the reef had increased
    (E) other natural records show increases as well

4. The author mentions tropical reef corals in line 1 in order to

    (A) prevent a possible misunderstanding
    (B) provide the reader with a point of reference
    (C) highlight an important difference for the reader
    (D) introduce the reader to a key distinction
    (E) indicate for the reader the main thesis of the passage

5. The author's attitude toward climate change can best be described as

    (A) alarmed
    (B) complacent
    (C) concerned
    (D) fearful
    (E) optimistic

6. According to the passage, studies use the ratio of the ^{18}O isotope to the ^{16}O isotope because

    (A) it is difficult to determine how much of any given isotope was in the environment
    (B) direct measurements of ocean temperatures cannot be taken at great depths
    (C) rare oxygen isotopes are found with sufficient frequency to permit direct measurements
    (D) carbonate ions can absorb either the oxygen isotope ^{18}O isotope to the ^{16}O isotope
    (E) deep-sea corals do not lie at or near the surface but at the bottom of the ocean

7. It can be inferred that scientists determine the approximate years in which various parts of a deep-sea coral were formed

    (A) without referring to the oxygen isotope content of carbonate ions

    (B) by relying on the ratio of the ^{18}O isotope to the ^{16}O isotope

    (C) by calculating the availability of the ^{18}O isotope in the environment

    (D) by calculating the availability of the ^{16}O isotope in the environment

    (E) by relying on the ratio of the ^{16}O isotope to the ^{18}O isotope in the skeleton

Items 8-15 are based on the following passage.

Galaxies come in a variety of sizes and shapes: majestic spirals, ruddy disks, elliptically shaped dwarfs and giants, and a menagerie of other, more bizarre
Line forms. Most currently, popular theories suggest that
5 conditions prior to birth—mass of the protogalactic cloud, its size, its rotation—determine whether a galaxy will be large or small, spiral or elliptical; but about ten percent of all galaxies are members of rich clusters of thousands of galaxies. The gravitational forces of fields
10 of nearby galaxies constantly distort galaxies in the crowded central region of rich clusters. In addition, rich clusters of galaxies are pervaded by a tenuous gas with a temperature of up to 100 million degrees. Galaxies are blasted and scoured by a hot wind created by their
15 motion through the gas. In crowded conditions such as these, environment becomes a more important determinant of the size and shape of a galaxy than heredity. In fact, if our galaxy had happened to form well within the core of a cluster such as Virgo, the Sun
20 would probably never have formed, because the Sun, a second- or third-generation star located in the disk of the galaxy, was formed from leftover gas five billion years or so after the initial period of star formation. By that time, in a rich cluster, the galaxy may well have
25 already been stripped of its gas.

As a galaxy moves through the core of a rich cluster, it is not only scoured by hot gas; it encounters other galaxies as well. If the collision is one-on-one at moderate to high speeds of galaxies of approximately
30 the same size, both galaxies will emerge relatively intact, if a little distorted and ragged about the edges. If, however, a galaxy coasts by a much larger one in a slow, grazing collision, the smaller one can be completely disrupted and assimilated by the larger.
35 Under the right conditions, these cosmic cannibals can consume 50 to 100 galaxies. The accumulative effect of these collisions is to produce a dynamic friction on the large galaxy, slowing it down. As a result, it gradually spirals in toward the center of the
40 cluster. Eventually, the gravitational forces that bind the stars to the infalling galaxy are overwhelmed by the combined gravity of the galaxies in the core of the cluster—just as the ocean is pulled away from the shore at ebb tide by the Moon, the stars are pulled away from
45 their infalling parent galaxy. If there is a large galaxy at the center of the cluster, it may ultimately capture these stars. With the passage of time, many galaxies will be torn asunder in the depths of this gravitational maelstrom and be swallowed up in the ever-expanding
50 envelope of the central cannibal galaxy.

Galactic cannibalism also explains why there are few if any bright galaxies in these clusters other than the central supergiant galaxy. That is because the bright galaxies, which are the most massive, experience the
55 greatest dynamical friction. They are the first to go down to the gravitational well and be swallowed up by the central galaxies.

Over the course of several billion years, 50 or so galaxies may be swallowed up, leaving only the central
60 supergiant and the 51st, the 52nd, etc., brightest galaxies. Given time, all the massive galaxies in the cluster will be absorbed, leaving a sparse cluster of a supergiant galaxy surrounded by clouds of small, dim galaxies.

8. In line 3, the word "menagerie" most nearly means

(A) odd mixture
(B) open environment
(C) uniform collection
(D) flat area
(E) simple structure

9. It can be inferred from the passage that the physical features of a galaxy that does not belong to a rich cluster are determined primarily by the

(A) size and rotation of the protogalactic cloud
(B) intensity of light emanating from the galaxy
(C) temperature of the interstellar gas
(D) age of the protogalactic cloud
(E) speed at which the protogalactic cloud is moving through space

10. The author implies that the currently accepted theories on galaxy formation are

(A) completely incorrect and misguided
(B) naive and out-of-date
(C) speculative and unsupported by observation
(D) substantially correct but in need of modification
(E) accurate and adequate to explain all known observations

11. According to the passage, a cluster with a central, supergiant galaxy will

(A) contain no intermediately bright galaxies
(B) have 50-100 galaxies of all sizes and intensities
(C) consist solely of third- and fourth-generation stars
(D) produce only spiral and disk-shaped galaxies
(E) be surrounded by galaxies of all sizes and shapes

12. According to the passage, the outcome of a collision between galaxies depends on which of the following?

   (A) The relative velocities of the galaxies
   (B) The relative ages of the galaxies
   (C) The relative sizes of the galaxies
   (D) The relative velocities and ages of the galaxies
   (E) The relative velocities and sizes of the galaxies

13. According to the passage, as a galaxy falls inward toward the center of a cluster, it

   (A) collides with the central core and emerges relatively intact
   (B) absorbs superheated gases from the interstellar medium
   (C) is broken apart by the gravitational forces of the core
   (D) is transformed by collisions into a large, spiral galaxy
   (E) captures unattached stars that have been ejected from the galaxy's core

14. The passage provides information that will answer which of the following questions?

   (A) What is the age of our sun?
   (B) What proportion of all galaxies are found in clusters?
   (C) Approximately how many galaxies would be found in a rich cluster?
   (D) What type of galaxy is ours?
   (E) At what velocity does our solar system travel?

15. The tone of the passage can best be described as

   (A) light-hearted and amused
   (B) objective but concerned
   (C) detached and unconcerned
   (D) cautious but sincere
   (E) enthusiastic and enlightened

Items 16-22 are based on to the following passage.

Considerable advances have been made in healthcare services since World War II. These include better access to healthcare (particularly for the poor and minorities), improvements in physical plants, and increased numbers of physicians and other health personnel. All have played a part in the recent improvement in life expectancy. But there is mounting criticism of the large remaining gaps in access, unbridled cost inflation, the further fragmentation of service, excessive indulgence in wasteful high-technology "gadgeteering," and breakdowns in doctor-patient relationships. In recent years, proposed panaceas and new programs, small and large, have proliferated at a feverish pace and disappointments have multiplied at almost the same rate. This has led to an increased pessimism—"everything has been tried and nothing works"—that sometimes borders on cynicism or even nihilism.

It is true that the automatic "pass through" of rapidly spiraling costs to government and insurance carriers produced for a time a sense of unlimited resources and allowed a mood to develop whereby every practitioner and institution could "do his own thing" without undue concern for the "Medical Commons." The practice of full-cost reimbursement encouraged capital investment and now the industry is overcapitalized. Many cities have hundreds of excess hospital beds; hospitals have proliferated a superabundance of high-technology equipment; and structural ostentation and luxury were the order of the day. In any given day, one-fourth of all community beds are vacant; expensive equipment is underused or, worse, used unnecessarily. Capital investment brings rapidly rising operating costs.

Yet, in part, this pessimism derives from expecting too much of healthcare. Care is often a painful experience accompanied by fear and unwelcome results; although there is room for improvement, it will always retain some unpleasantness and frustration. Moreover, the capacities of medical science are limited. Humpty Dumpty cannot always be put back together again. Too many physicians are reluctant to admit their limitations to patients; too many patients and families are unwilling to accept such realities. Nor is it true that everything has been tried and nothing works, as shown by the prepaid group practice plans at the Kaiser Foundation and Puget Sound. However, typically such undertakings have been drowned by a veritable flood of public and private moneys that have supported and encouraged the continuation of conventional practices and subsidized their shortcomings on a massive, almost unrestricted scale. Except for the most idealistic and dedicated, there were no incentives to seek change or to practice self-restraint or frugality. In this atmosphere, it is not fair to condemn as failures all attempted experiments; it may be more accurate to say that many never had a fair trial.

16. In line 14, the word "feverish" most nearly means

(A) diseased
(B) rapid
(C) controlled
(D) timed
(E) temperate

17. According to author, the "pessimism" mentioned in line 34 is partly attributable to the fact that

(A) there has been little real improvement in healthcare services
(B) expectations about healthcare services are sometimes unrealistic
(C) large segments of the population find it impossible to get access to healthcare services
(D) advances in technology have made healthcare service unaffordable
(E) doctors are now less concerned with patient care

18. The author cites the prepaid plans (lines 45-46) as

(A) counterexamples to the claim that nothing has worked
(B) examples of healthcare plans that were overfunded
(C) evidence that healthcare services are fragmented
(D) proof of the theory that no plan has been successful
(E) experiments that yielded disappointing results

19. It can be inferred that the sentence "Humpty Dumpty cannot always be put back together again" means that

(A) the cost of healthcare services will not decline
(B) some people should not become doctors
(C) medical care is not really essential to good health
(D) illness is often unpleasant and even painful
(E) medical science cannot cure every ill

20. With which of the following descriptions of the system for the delivery of healthcare services would the author most likely agree?

(A) It is biased in favor of doctors and against patients.
(B) It is highly fragmented and completely ineffective.
(C) It has not embraced new technology rapidly enough.
(D) It is generally effective but can be improved.
(E) It discourages people from seeking medical care.

21. Which of the following best describes the logical structure of the selection?

(A) The third paragraph is intended as a refutation of the first and second paragraphs.
(B) The second and third paragraphs are intended as a refutation of the first paragraph.
(C) The second and third paragraphs explain and put into perspective the points made in the first paragraph.
(D) The first paragraph describes a problem, and the second and third paragraphs present two horns of a dilemma.
(E) The first paragraph describes a problem, the second its causes, and the third a possible solution.

22. The author's primary concern is to

(A) criticize physicians and healthcare administrators for investing in technologically advanced equipment
(B) examine some problems affecting delivery of healthcare services and assess the severity of those problems
(C) defend the medical community from charges that healthcare has not improved since World War II
(D) analyze the reasons for the healthcare industry's inability to provide quality care to all segments of the population
(E) describe the peculiar economic features of the healthcare industry that are the causes of spiraling medical costs

Items 23-29 are based on the following passage.

The figure dangling from the electric sign or propped against the side of the ticket-booth is quintessentially Charlie Chaplin, and the splayed feet, moustache, derby hat, and rattan cane make up a
Line
5 universal symbol of laughter. It is impossible to dissociate Chaplin from Keystone comedy where he began. The Keystone touch is evident in all his later work, often as its most precious element. He enters from a corner of the screen and becomes entangled in a
10 force greater than himself. He advances to the center where he spins like a marionette in a whirlpool until the madness of the action ejects him at the opposite end of the screen. He wanders in a stranger and exits unchanged. "I am here today" was his legend. With its
15 emotional overtone of "gone tomorrow," it was both faintly ironic and exactly right. There is always something about Chaplin and his characters that slips away.

23. The author's attitude toward Chaplin can best be described as

(A) condescending
(B) admiring
(C) judgmental
(D) inconsistent
(E) unflattering

24. In line 14, the word "legend" most nearly means

(A) endearing habit
(B) personal history
(C) exaggerated story
(D) descriptive caption
(E) peculiar character

25. The author implies that Chaplin's movie characters are

(A) independent and heroic
(B) similar from film to film
(C) borrowed from other actors
(D) wooden and lifeless
(E) minor role players

26. With which of the following statements would the author most likely agree?

(A) It is possible to detect the influences of an artist's earlier work in later works.
(B) An artist's earlier work is a more important indicator of talent than later work.
(C) Chaplin's work at Keystone represents the most important accomplishments of his career.
(D) The number of times a character can appear in films is limited, as people will eventually tire of the character.
(E) Chaplin appeals primarily to unsophisticated movie-goers who are amused by stock characters.

27. The passage mentions all of the following as helping to define Chaplin's movie character EXCEPT

(A) mode of dress
(B) color themes
(C) body posture
(D) on-screen antics
(E) action sequence

28. The author's primary concern is to

(A) introduce the reader to Chaplin's most important films
(B) analyze audience reaction to Chaplin's film characters
(C) explore the effect of Chaplin's personal life on his work
(D) compare Chaplin's work with that of other comic actors
(E) discuss some of the important features of Chaplin's work

29. The author compares Chaplin's movie character to a marionette (line 11) in order to

(A) suggest that Chaplin was not aware of his role
(B) demonstrate that Chaplin once worked at Keystone
(C) emphasize that the character was not in control
(D) illustrate the variety of roles played by Chaplin
(E) elicit sympathy for the character from the reader

NOTES AND STRATEGIES

Items 30-38 are based on the following passage.

When we speak casually, we call *Nineteen Eighty-Four* a novel, but to be more exact we should call it a political fable. This requirement is not refuted by the
Line fact that the book is preoccupied with an individual,
5 Winston Smith, who suffers from a varicose ulcer, or by the fact that it takes account of other individuals, including Julia, Mr. Charrington, Mrs. Parsons, Syme, and O'Brien. The figures claim our attention, but they exist mainly in their relation to the political system that
10 determines them. It would indeed be possible to think of them as figures in a novel, though in that case they would have to be imagined in a far more diverse set of relations. They would no longer inhabit or sustain a fable, because a fable is a narrative relieved of much
15 contingent detail so that it may stand forth in an unusual degree of clarity and simplicity. A fable is a structure of types, each of them deliberately simplified lest a sense of difference and heterogeneity reduce the force of the typical. Let us say, then, that *Nineteen Eighty-Four* is a
20 political fable, projected into a near future and incorporating historical references mainly to document a canceled past.

Since a fable is predicated upon a typology, it must be written from a certain distance. The author
25 cannot afford the sense of familiarity that is induced by detail and differentiation. A fable, in this respect, asks to be compared to a caricature, not to a photograph. It follows that in a political fable there is bound to be some tension between a political sense dealing in the
30 multiplicity of social and personal life, and a fable sense committed to simplicity of form and feature. If the political sense were to prevail, the narrative would be drawn away from fable into the novel, at some cost to its simplicity. If the sense of fable were to prevail, the
35 fabulist would station himself at such a distance from any imaginary conditions in the case that his narrative would appear unmediated, free or bereft of conditions. The risk would be considerable: a reader might feel that the fabulist has lost interest in the variety of human life
40 and fallen back upon an unconditioned sense of its types, that he has become less interested in lives than in a particular idea of life. The risk is greater still if the fabulist projects his narrative into the future: The reader cannot question by appealing to life conditions already
45 known. He is asked to believe that the future is another country and that "they just do things differently there."

In a powerful fable, the reader's feeling is likely to be mostly fear: He is afraid that the fabulist's vision of any life that could arise may be accurate. The fabulist's
50 feeling may be more various. A fable such as *Nineteen Eighty-Four* might arise from disgust, despair, or world-weariness induced by evidence that nothing, despite

one's best efforts, has changed and that it is too late now to hope for the change one wants.

30. In line 15, the word "contingent" most nearly means

   (A) dependent
   (B) essential
   (C) boring
   (D) unnecessary
   (E) compelling

31. In drawing an analogy between a fable and a caricature (lines 26-27), the author would most likely regard which of the following pairs of ideas as also analogous?

   (A) The subject of a caricature and the topic of a fable
   (B) The subject of a caricature and the main character in *Nineteen Eighty-Four*
   (C) The subject of a fable and the artist who draws the caricature
   (D) The artist who draws the caricature and a novelist
   (E) The minor characters in a fable and a photographer

32. Which of the following would be the most appropriate title for the passage?

   (A) A Critical Study of the Use of Characters in *Nineteen Eighty-Four*
   (B) *Nineteen Eighty-Four*: Political Fable Rather Than Novel
   (C) *Nineteen Eighty-Four*: Reflections on the Relationship of the Individual to Society
   (D) The Use of Typology in the Literature of Political Fables
   (E) Distinguishing a Political Fable from a Novel

33. According to the passage, which of the following are characteristics of a political fable?

   (A) It is widely popular at its time of development.
   (B) The reader is unlikely to experience fear as his reaction to the political situation described.
   (C) Its time frame must treat events that occur at some point in the future.
   (D) Its characters are defined primarily by their relationship to the social order.
   (E) It is similar to a caricature.

34. Which of the following best explains why the author mentions that Winston Smith suffers from a varicose ulcer?

(A) To demonstrate that a political fable must emphasize type over detail
(B) To show that Winston Smith has some characteristics that distinguish him as an individual
(C) To argue that Winston Smith is no more important than any other character in *Nineteen Eighty-Four*
(D) To illustrate one of the features of the political situation described in *Nineteen Eighty-Four*
(E) To suggest that *Nineteen Eighty-Four* is too realistic to be considered a work of fiction

35. The "tension" that the author mentions in line 29 refers to the

(A) necessity of striking a balance between the need to describe a political situation in simple terms and the need to make the description realistic
(B) reaction the reader feels because he is drawn to the characters of the fable as individuals but repulsed by the political situation
(C) delicate task faced by a literary critic who must interpret the text of a work while attempting to describe accurately the intentions of the author
(D) danger that too realistic a description of a key character will make the reader feel that the fable is actually a description of his own situation
(E) conflict of aspirations and interests between characters that an author creates to motivate the action of the narrative

36. The author's attitude toward *Nineteen Eighty-Four* can best be described as

(A) condescending
(B) laudatory
(C) disparaging
(D) scholarly
(E) ironic

37. The author uses the phrase "another country" to describe a political fable in which

(A) political events described in a fable occur in a place other than the country of national origin of the author
(B) a lack of detail makes it difficult for a reader to see the connection between his own situation and the one described in the book
(C) too many minor characters create the impression of complete disorganization, leading the reader to believe he is in a foreign country
(D) the author has allowed his personal political convictions to infect his description of the political situation
(E) an overabundance of detail prevents the reader from appreciating the real possibility that such a political situation could develop

38. The author's primary concern is to

(A) define and clarify a concept
(B) point out a logical inconsistency
(C) trace the connection between a cause and an effect
(D) illustrate a general statement with examples
(E) outline a proposal for future action

Items 39-42 are based on the following two passages.

Passage 1

    Comedy appeals only to the intelligence, for laughter is incompatible with emotion. Depict some fault, however trifling, in such a way as to arouse
Line sympathy, fear, or pity, and it is impossible to laugh.
5 On the other hand, a vice—even one that is, generally speaking, of an odious nature—can be made ludicrous by a suitable contrivance. So long as it leaves our emotions unaffected, it is funny. This is not to say that the vice itself is ludicrous but only that the vice, as
10 embodied in a particular character, is ludicrous. The only requirement is that it must not engage our feelings.

Passage 2

    Absentmindedness is always comical. Indeed, the deeper the absentmindedness the higher the comedy.
15 Systematic absentmindedness, like that of Don Quixote, is the most comical thing imaginable; it is the comic itself, drawn as nearly as possible from its very source. Take any other comic character, however unconscious he may be of what he says or does: He
20 cannot be comical unless there is some aspect of his person of which he is unaware, one side of his nature which he overlooks. On that account alone does he make us laugh.

39. The author of Passage 1 implies that laughter

    (A) is not an emotional reaction
    (B) counteracts feelings of dread
    (C) vice can be corrected by laughter
    (D) is triggered only by a vice
    (E) endures longer than emotion

40. The author of Passage 1 discusses vice primarily in order to

    (A) advise the reader on how to avoid certain behavior
    (B) make it clear that comedy does engage the emotions
    (C) provide an example that the reader will find amusing
    (D) demonstrate that emotions are more powerful than intelligence
    (E) argue that vice becomes more acceptable if it is portrayed in a humorous fashion

41. In context, "deeper" (line 14) means

    (A) complete
    (B) complex
    (C) courageous
    (D) futile
    (E) insignificant

42. Which of the following best describes the logical connection between the views expressed in the two passages?

    (A) Passage 2 provides examples that show that the views of Passage 1 are incorrect.
    (B) Passage 2 redefines a key term that is used by the author of Passage 1.
    (C) The two passages reach the same conclusion based on different evidence.
    (D) The two passages both cite systematic research for their conclusions.
    (E) The two passages discuss different aspects of the topic.

NOTES AND STRATEGIES

Items 43-57 are based on the following two passages.

Passage 1

Shortly after sunrise, just as the light was beginning to come streaming through the trees, I caught the big bright eyes of a deer gazing at me through the garden hedge. The expressive eyes, the slim black-tipped muzzle, and the large ears were perfectly visible, as if placed there at just the right distance to be seen. She continued to gaze while I gazed back with equal steadiness, motionless as a rock. In a few minutes she ventured forward a step, exposing her fine arching neck and forelegs, then snorted and withdrew.

Trembling sprays indicated her return, and her head came into view; several steps later, she stood wholly exposed inside the garden hedge, gazed eagerly around, and again withdrew, but returned a moment afterward, this time advancing into the middle of the garden. Behind her I noticed other pairs of eyes.

It then occurred to me that I might possibly steal up to one of them and catch it, not with any intention of killing it, but only to run my hand along its beautiful curving limbs. They seemed, however, to penetrate my conceit and bounded off with loud, shrill snorts, vanishing into the forest.

I have often tried to understand how so many deer, wild sheep, bears, and grouse—nature's cattle and poultry—could be allowed to run at large through the mountain gardens without in any way marring the beauty of their surroundings. I was, therefore, all the more watchful of this feeding flock, and carefully examined the garden after they left, to see what flowers had suffered; I could not, however, detect the slightest disorder, much less destruction. It seemed rather that, like gardeners, they had been keeping it in order. I could not see one crushed flower, nor a single blade of grass that was bent or broken down. Nor among the daisy, gentian, or bryanthus gardens of the Alps, where the wild sheep roam at will, have I ever noticed the effects of destructive feeding or trampling. Even the burly, shuffling bears beautify the ground on which they walk, decorating it with their awe-inspiring tracks, and writing poetry on the soft sequoia bark in boldly drawn hieroglyphics. But, strange to say, man, the crown, the sequoia of nature, brings confusion with all his best gifts and with the overabundant, misbegotten animals that he breeds, sweeps away the beauty of the wilderness like a fire.

Passage 2

The night was intolerable for Antoine. The buffalo were about him in countless numbers, regarding him with vicious glances. It was only due to the natural offensiveness of man that they gave him any space. The bellowing of the bulls became louder, and there was a marked uneasiness on the part of the herd. This was a sign of an approaching storm.

Upon the western horizon were seen flashes of lightning. The cloud that had been a mere speck had now become an ominous thunderhead. Suddenly the wind came, and lightning flashes became more frequent, showing the ungainly forms of the animals like strange monsters in the white light. The colossal herd was again in violent motion. It was a blind rush for shelter, and no heed was paid to buffalo wallows or even deep gulches. All was in the deepest of darkness. There seemed to be groaning in heaven and earth—millions of hoofs and throats roaring in unison.

As a shipwrecked sailor clings to a mere fragment of wood, so Antoine, although almost exhausted with fatigue, stuck to the saddle of his pony. As the mad rush continued, every flash displayed heaps of bison in death's struggle under the hoofs of their companions.

When he awoke and looked around him again it was morning. The herd had entered the strip of timber which lay on both sides of the river, and it was here that Antoine conceived his first distinct hope of saving himself.

"Waw, waw, waw!" was the hoarse cry that came to his ears, apparently from a human being in distress. Antoine strained his eyes and craned his neck to see who it could be. Through an opening in the branches ahead he perceived a large grizzly bear lying along an inclined limb and hugging it desperately to maintain his position. The herd had now thoroughly pervaded the timber, and the bear was likewise hemmed in. He had taken his unaccustomed refuge after making a brave stand against several bulls, one of which lay dead near by, while he himself was bleeding from several wounds.

Antoine had been assiduously looking for a friendly tree, by means of which he hoped to escape from captivity. His horse, by chance, made his way directly under the very box-elder that was sustaining the bear and there was a convenient branch just within his reach. He saw at a glance that the occupant of the tree would not interfere with him. They were, in fact, companions in distress. Antoine sprang desperately from the pony's back and seized the cross-limb with both his hands.

By the middle of the afternoon the main body of the herd had passed, and Antoine was sure that his captivity had at last come to an end. Then he swung himself from his limb to the ground, and walked stiffly

to the carcass of the nearest cow, which he dressed, and
prepared himself a meal. But first he took a piece of
100 liver on a long pole to the bear!

43. The word "sprays" (line 11) refers to

(A) minute droplets
(B) light mist
(C) thin legs
(D) heavy showers
(E) small branches

44. In context, "steal up" (lines 17-18) means

(A) acquire unlawfully
(B) prepare for action
(C) promise faithfully
(D) approach undetected
(E) confine within a boundary

45. In the first two paragraphs, the author of Passage
1 is primarily concerned to

(A) recount an experience
(B) explore a theory
(C) teach a lesson
(D) offer an opinion
(E) criticize a plan

46. In context, "conceit" (line 21) means

(A) arrogance
(B) selfishness
(C) fanciful notion
(D) dissatisfaction
(E) clever plan

47. According to the passage, the deer and the sheep
are alike in that they both

(A) are wary of human beings
(B) inhabit remote Alpine gardens
(C) feed without causing destruction
(D) live untamed in wilderness regions
(E) strike beautiful and dramatic poses

48. The "boldly drawn hieroglyphics" (line 40) are
probably

(A) claw marks
(B) park signs
(C) rare flowers
(D) hoofprints
(E) graffiti

49. The author compares the deer to gardeners (lines
31-34) in order to

(A) encourage the reader to learn more about
deer
(B) refute the idea that deer are aggressive
(C) illustrate the similarity between deer and
humans
(D) emphasize that deer are not destructive
(E) dramatize the need for wildlife protection

50. In context, "wallows" (line 59) means

(A) shallow depression
(B) deep cave
(C) rugged cliff
(D) low hill
(E) open plain

51. By "the natural offensiveness of man" (lines 47-
48), the author of Passage 2 probably refers to
man's

(A) frequent rudeness
(B) disagreeable odor
(C) uncontrolled aggression
(D) distasteful behavior
(E) primitive nature

52. All of the following are true of the comparison drawn in the third paragraph of Passage 2 EXCEPT

    (A) Antoine, like a shipwrecked sailor, is in a desperate situation.
    (B) The herd of buffalo are like the storm driven sea.
    (C) Antoine's pony supports him the way that debris might support a shipwrecked sailor.
    (D) The struggle to survive leaves both Antoine and the shipwrecked sailor exhausted.
    (E) The environment is filled with dangerous creatures that threaten a sailor the way Antoine fears the buffalo.

53. The tone of the first two paragraphs of Passage 2 is

    (A) frivolous
    (B) suspenseful
    (C) animated
    (D) reserved
    (E) lighthearted

54. The phrase "unaccustomed refuge" (line 81) suggests that the bear

    (A) preferred open areas to confined spaces
    (B) rarely climbed a tree for safety
    (C) did not often encounter buffalo
    (D) was fearful of the presence of a human
    (E) had been surprised by the storm

55. In context, "dressed" (line 98) means

    (A) adorned
    (B) clothed
    (C) bound
    (D) embellished
    (E) prepared

56. The mood of Passage 2 moves from

    (A) joy to despair
    (B) hopelessness to hope
    (C) happiness to gloom
    (D) excitement to torpor
    (E) apprehension to courageousness

57. The information provided in Passage 2 most directly challenges Passage 1 is its description of

    (A) wild animals as gentle and non-destructive
    (B) human beings as able to survive dangerous threats
    (C) gardens as suitable habitats for wild animals
    (D) bears as being unable to climb trees
    (E) the effect of storms on fragile landscapes

NOTES AND STRATEGIES

CHALLENGE ITEMS

DIRECTIONS: This section contains advanced level Critical Reading: Passages items. Each passage below is followed by items based on its content. Answer the items on the basis of what is stated or implied in the passage(s). Answers are on page 983.

Item 1 is based on the following passage.

What nutrition is to physiological life, education is to social life. As societies become more complex in structure and resources, the need for formal or
Line intentional teaching and learning increases. As formal
5 teaching and training grow in extent, there is the danger of creating an undesirable split between the experience gained in direct associations and what is acquired in school. This danger was never greater than presently, due to the rapid growth of technical modes
10 of skill.

1. In the passage, the author draws an analogy between

   (A) school and family
   (B) teaching and life
   (C) nutrition and education
   (D) experience and ignorance
   (E) intentionality and learning

Items 2-3 are based on the following passage.

It is useful to distinguish between "life events" and "life circumstances" when analyzing depression-inducing factors, as life circumstances and events
Line promote stress in different ways. Stressful life events
5 include the death of a spouse, divorce, or job loss; stressful life circumstances include single parenthood, low income, and poor education. Depression usually includes elements from both categories, though stressful life events most often afflict single mothers. In
10 fact, epidemiological studies show that more women than men exhibit signs of depression. However, the sex difference in rates of depression can also be explained by a condition of learned helplessness, as society encourages women to trust and nurture others rather
15 than to be aggressive and to seek power. Thus, any particular incident of depression in women or men may include a history of learned helplessness as well as an immediate environmental agent of depression.

2. The main purpose of this passage is to

   (A) describe the behavior of depressed people
   (B) explain the biochemical causes of depression
   (C) discuss the factors that contribute to depression
   (D) analyze the different rates of depression in men and women
   (E) identify the family situations that lead to depression

3. Which of the following best explains the distinction between a life circumstance and a life event?

   (A) A life circumstance is a long-term condition, while a life event is a sudden change.
   (B) Life circumstances occur less frequently than but are more serious than life events.
   (C) A life circumstance is a learned behavior and a life event is caused by an outside agent.
   (D) A life circumstance can easily be controlled but a life event cannot be.
   (E) A life circumstance is more likely to cause depression in women; a life event is more likely to cause depression in men.

Items 4-5 are based on the following passage.

Historically, the socialization process in America
has been characterized by the interaction of structured
groups that share both a sense of mission about the
nation's future and codes of behavior rooted in
Line
5 common principles. Communities were bound by
religious beliefs, ethnic backgrounds, and strong family
relationships. However, this configuration of
socializing institutions no longer functions as it once
did. Mobility is one factor in the changing picture.
10 One-fifth of Americans change residence each year,
but they do not "pack" their culture; they simply move,
breaking old community ties. A second factor in the
breakdown of the socialization process is
depersonalization. Emerson once wrote that an
15 institution is the lengthened shadow of one man.
Today's institution is more likely to be the lengthened
shadow of itself. By now the process of social
decompression may be irreversible.

4. The author cites Emerson (lines 14-15) in order to

(A) dramatize the power of institutions in our
society
(B) explain the importance of individual freedom
(C) demonstrate the need for the study of
humanities in American schools
(D) highlight the progress that society has made
since Emerson
(E) argue that all institutions should be run by an
individual

5. The tone of the passage can best be described as

(A) tentative but worried
(B) scholarly but optimistic
(C) passionate but controlled
(D) angry but calm
(E) analytical but concerned

Item 6 is based on the following passage.

A constitution consists of many particulars, and
there will be different combinations of opinions on the
different points. The majority on one question may be the
minority on a second, and a different group altogether
Line
5 may constitute the majority on a third. To establish a
constitution, it is necessary to satisfy all parties. But an
amendment to a constitution, once established, is a single
proposition. There is need to compromise in relation to
any other point. The will of the requisite number would at
10 once bring the matter to a decisive issue.

6. The primary purpose of the passage is to

(A) persuade voters that a constitutional
amendment is needed
(B) show that a constitutional amendment need
not require unanimous consent
(C) explain why it is more difficult to establish
than to amend a constitution
(D) illustrate the difficulties inherent in
establishing a constitution
(E) compare governments with and without
written constitutions.

Items 7-14 are based on the following passage.

A fundamental principle of pharmacology is that all drugs have multiple actions. Actions that are desirable in the treatment of disease are considered therapeutic, while those that are undesirable or pose
5 risks to the patient are called "effects." Adverse drug effects range from the trivial, for example, nausea or dry mouth, to the serious, such as massive gastrointestinal bleeding or thromboembolism; and some drugs can be lethal. Therefore, an effective
10 system for the detection of adverse drug effects is an important component of the healthcare system of any advanced nation. Much of the research conducted on new drugs aims at identifying the conditions of use that maximize beneficial effects and minimize the risk of
15 adverse effects. The intent of drug labeling is to reflect this body of knowledge accurately so that physicians can properly prescribe the drug or, if it is to be sold without prescription, so that consumers can properly use the drug.
20 The current system of drug investigation in the United States has proved very useful and accurate in identifying the common side effects associated with new prescription drugs. By the time a new drug is approved by the Food and Drug Administration, its
25 side effects are usually well described in the package insert for physicians. The investigational process, however, cannot be counted on to detect all adverse effects because of the relatively small number of patients involved in pre-marketing studies and the
30 relatively short duration of the studies. Animal toxicology studies are, of course, done before marketing in an attempt to identify any potential for toxicity, but negative results do not guarantee the safety of a drug in humans, as evidenced by such well
35 known examples as the birth deformities due to thalidomide.
This recognition prompted the establishment in many countries of programs to which physicians report adverse drug effects. The United States and other
40 countries also send reports to an international program operated by the World Health Organization. These programs, however, are voluntary reporting programs and are intended to serve a limited goal: alerting a government or private agency to adverse drug effects
45 detected by physicians in the course of practice. Other approaches must be used to confirm suspected drug reactions and to estimate incidence rates. These other approaches include conducting retrospective control studies, for example, the studies associating
50 endometrial cancer with estrogen use, and systematically monitoring hospitalized patients to determine the incidence of acute common side effects,

as typified by the Boston Collaborative Drug Surveillance Program.
55 Thus, the overall drug surveillance system of the United States is composed of a set of information bases, special studies, and monitoring programs, each contributing in its own way to our knowledge about marketed drugs. The system is decentralized among a
60 number of governmental units and is not administered as a coordinated function. Still, it would be inappropriate at this time to attempt to unite all of the disparate elements into a comprehensive surveillance program. Instead, the challenge is to improve each
65 segment of the system and to take advantage of new computer strategies to improve coordination and communication.

7. In line 63, the word "disparate" most nearly means

(A) useless
(B) expensive
(C) temporary
(D) educational
(E) unconnected

8. The author's primary concern is to discuss

(A) methods for testing the effects of new drugs on humans
(B) the importance of having accurate information about the effects of drugs
(C) procedures for determining the long-term effects of new drugs
(D) attempts to curb the abuse of prescription drugs
(E) the difference between the therapeutic and non-therapeutic actions of drugs

9. The author implies that a drug with adverse side effects

(A) will not be approved for use by consumers without a doctor's prescription
(B) must wait for approval until lengthy studies prove the effects are not permanent
(C) should be used only if its therapeutic value out-weighs its adverse effects
(D) should be withdrawn from the marketplace pending a government investigation
(E) could be used in foreign countries even though it is not approved for use in the United States

10. Which of the following can be inferred from the passage?

(A) The decentralization of the overall drug surveillance system results in it being completely ineffective in any attempts to provide information about adverse drug effects.
(B) Drugs with serious adverse side effects are never approved for distribution.
(C) Some adverse drug effects are discovered during testing because they are very rare.
(D) Some adverse drug effects cannot be detected prior to approval because they take a long time to develop.
(E) None of the above.

11. The author introduces the example of thalidomide in the last sentence of the second paragraph to show that some

(A) drugs do not have the same actions in humans that they do in animals
(B) drug testing procedures are ignored by careless laboratory workers
(C) drugs have no therapeutic value for humans
(D) drugs have adverse side effects as well as beneficial actions
(E) physicians prescribe drugs without first reading the manufacturer's recommendations

12. It can be inferred that the estrogen study mentioned in the last sentence of the third paragraph

(A) uncovered long-term side effects of a drug that had already been approved for sale by the Food and Drug Administration
(B) discovered potential side effects of a drug that was still awaiting approval for sale by the Food and Drug Administration
(C) revealed possible new applications of a drug that had previously been approved for a different treatment
(D) is an example of a study that could be more efficiently conducted by a centralized authority than by volunteer reporting
(E) proved that the use of the drug estrogen was not associated with side effects such as thromboembolism

13. The author is most probably leading up to a discussion of some suggestions about how to

(A) centralize authority for drug surveillance in the United States
(B) centralize authority for drug surveillance among international agencies
(C) coordinate better the sharing of information among the drug surveillance agencies
(D) eliminate the availability and sale of certain drugs now on the market
(E) improve drug-testing procedures to detect dangerous effects before drugs are approved

14. The author makes use of which of the following devices in the passage?

(A) Definition of terms
(B) Examples
(C) Analogy
(D) Definition of terms and example
(E) Definition of terms and analogy

Item 15 is based on the following passage.

The day was extremely hot, and we rode without seeing a tree or a bush or a drop of water. Our horses and mules suffered, but at sunset they pricked up their *Line* ears and mended their pace. Water was near. We came
5 to a shallow valley with a stream, and along its banks were tents. Troops and wagons were moving over the opposite ridge. In order to find an unoccupied camping ground, we had to pass a quarter mile upstream. In the morning, the country was covered with mist, and we
10 saw through the obscurity that tents were falling and ranks rapidly forming. Almost every day, we met long trains of wagons crawling at a snail's pace toward Santa Fe.

15. The passage states that it was necessary to cross upstream in order to

   (A) get a clearer view of the military encampment
   (B) find clean water for the horses and mules
   (C) join the wagons on the journey to Santa Fe
   (D) avoid others who had already made a camp
   (E) ford at the shallowest point available

Item 16 is based on the following passage.

If we had to demonstrate for ourselves all the facts that we use every day, the task would never be complete. Life is too short, and we don't have the *Line* capacity to test every one of them. Consequently, we
5 trust various opinions that we have neither the time nor the power to verify for ourselves. On this groundwork, we raise the structure of our own thoughts, not by choice, but by the inflexible law of our nature. And it is a good thing too, for society would not otherwise exist.
10 Society presupposes that citizens are held together by common beliefs.

16. The passage implies that if everyone insisted upon testing every proposition for himself or herself

   (A) people would eventually reach the same conclusion
   (B) citizens would lack the common beliefs necessary for society
   (C) only the most intelligent people would possess knowledge
   (D) common beliefs would be more firmly founded on truth
   (E) factual errors could be eliminated from widely held opinions

NOTES AND STRATEGIES

Items 17-23 are based on the following passage.

Lightning is an electrical discharge of immense proportions. Some 80% of lightning occurs within clouds; about 20% is cloud-to-ground lightning; and an
Line extremely small percentage is cloud-to-sky lightning.
5 Cloud-to-ground lightning begins when complex meteorological processes cause a tremendous electrostatic charge to build up within a cloud. Typically, the bottom of the cloud is negatively charged. When the charge reaches 50 to 100 million
10 volts, air is no longer an effective insulator, and lightning occurs within the cloud itself. Ten to 30 minutes after the onset of intracloud lightning, negative charges called stepped leaders emerge from the bottom of the cloud, moving toward the earth in 50-meter
15 intervals at speeds of 100 to 200 kilometers per second and creating an ionized channel. As the leaders near the Earth, their strong electric field causes streamers of positively charged ions to develop at the tips of pointed objects that are connected directly or indirectly to the
20 ground. These positively charged streamers flow upward.
When the distance, known as the striking distance, between a stepped leader and one of the streamers reaches 30 to 100 meters, the intervening air
25 breaks down completely and the leader is joined to the Earth via the streamer. Now a pulse of current known as a return stroke ranging from thousands to hundreds of thousands of amperes moves at one tenth to one third the speed of light from the Earth through the
30 object from which the streamer emanated and up the ionized channel to the charge center within the cloud. An ionized channel remains in the air and additional negative charges called dart leaders will quickly move down this path resulting in further return strokes. This
35 multiplicity causes the flash to flicker. The entire event typically lasts about one second.
The return stroke's extremely high temperature creates the visible lightning and produces thunder by instantly turning moisture into steam. Most direct
40 damage results from the heavy return stroke current because it produces high temperatures in the channel, or from arcing at the point of ground contact. If the lightning current is carried by an enclosed conductor (*e.g.*, within a jacketed cable, through a concrete wall,
45 or beneath a painted surface), entrapped moisture is turned into high-pressure steam that can cause a cable, wall, or painted object to explode. Arcing frequently ignites combustibles.
Lightning causes hundreds of millions of dollars
50 in property losses annually and the majority of forest fires. Lightning is also the leading weather-related killer in the U.S., causing from 100 to 200 deaths each year.

17. In line 12, the word "intracloud" most nearly means

(A) between clouds
(B) within a cloud
(C) from cloud to sky
(D) from ground to cloud
(E) from leader to cloud

18. The selection defines the striking distance as the distance between

(A) the ground and the cloud
(B) a stepped leader and a dart leader
(C) a dart leader and a return stroke
(D) a streamer and a stepped leader
(E) two clouds

19. According to the selection, the flickering appearance of a lightning strike is created by

(A) the stepped movement of leaders
(B) multiple return strokes
(C) water being vaporized
(D) arcing at ground contact
(E) unstable negative leaders

20. What topic might the author logically address in a continuation of the passage?

(A) Precautions to minimize lightning damage
(B) Other weather phenomena that cause injury
(C) Basic principles governing electricity
(D) Identifying different types of clouds
(E) History of scientific theory about lightning

21. According to the passage, which of the following is NOT true of stepped leaders?

(A) They develop 10 to 30 minutes after intracloud lightning.
(B) As they traverse the distance from cloud to ground, they create an ionized channel.
(C) Their powerful positive charge causes streamers to develop in grounded objects.
(D) They emerge from the bottom of the cloud and move downward in intervals of 50 meters.
(E) Their rate of progress is 100 to 200 kilometers per second.

22. The passage answers which of the following questions?

(A) How does lightning produce the associated thunder?
(B) How far above the ground is the bottom of the typical lightning-producing cloud?
(C) How frequently will lightning strike a given object?
(D) How long does it take a cloud to build up an electrostatic charge?
(E) How does intracloud lightning cross from one area of a cloud to another?

23. The author's primary concern is to

(A) warn about the dangers posed by lightning strikes
(B) describe the sequence of events that make up a lightning strike
(C) discuss fundamental scientific laws pertaining to electricity
(D) support the commonly held view that lightning strikes the ground
(E) prove that lightning occurs because of a charge imbalance between a cloud and the ground

Items 24-25 are based on the following passage.

Human beings are the only animals that laugh and weep, for they are the only animals that are struck with the difference between what things are and what they
Line ought to be. We weep at what exceeds our expectations
5 in serious matters; we laugh at what disappoints our expectations in trifles. We shed tears from sympathy with real and necessary distress; we burst into laughter from want of sympathy with that which is unreasonable and unnecessary. Tears are the natural and involuntary
10 response of the mind overcome by some sudden and violent emotions. Laughter is the same sort of convulsive and involuntary movement, occasioned by mere surprise or contrast.

24. According to the passage, tears and laughter have all of the following in common EXCEPT

(A) They are both involuntary reactions.
(B) They are both the result of violent emotions.
(C) They both depend on prior expectations.
(D) They are both natural emotions.
(E) They are both reactions to experiences of the world.

25. The author implies that animals lack the ability to

(A) perceive emotional changes in humans
(B) feel pain or pleasure
(C) evoke sorrow or laughter in humans
(D) respond strongly to external stimuli
(E) imagine things other than as they are

Items 26-27 are based on the following passage.

One continuing problem in labor-management relations is the "us/them" mentality. In addition to fiscal constraints, continuing problems with the Fair
Line Labor Standards Act, bad faith negotiations, bad
5 management practices, poor union leadership, and a continued loss of management prerogatives will all combine to produce forces that will cause a significant increase in disruptive job actions in the near future. Neither side is blameless. The tragedy of the situation
10 is that the impact of poor labor-management relations is relatively predictable and is thus avoidable. Since the economic situation will not improve significantly in the next few years, the pressure on the part of union leaders to obtain more benefits for their members will
15 be frustrated, setting the stage for confrontation between labor and management.

26. The author's discussion of labor-management relations can best be described as

(A) extremely pro-labor
(B) mildly pro-labor
(C) neutral
(D) mildly pro-management
(E) extremely pro-management

27. The author implies that if the economic conditions improve

(A) management will lose much of its power
(B) labor leaders will not seek more benefits
(C) labor-management tensions will decline
(D) the Fair Labor Standards Act will be repealed
(E) labor will win a voice in management

NOTES AND STRATEGIES

Items 28-36 are based on the following passage.

Public general hospitals originated in the almshouse infirmaries established as early as colonial times by local governments to care for the poor. Later, in the late eighteenth and early nineteenth centuries, the infirmary separated from the almshouse and became an independent institution supported by local tax money. At the same time, private charity hospitals began to develop. Both private and public hospitals mainly provided food and shelter for the impoverished sick, since there was little that medicine could actually do to cure illness, and the middle class was treated at home by private physicians.

Late in the nineteenth century, private charity hospitals began trying to attract middle-class patients. Although the depression of 1890 stimulated the growth of charitable institutions and an expanding urban population became dependent on assistance, there was a decline in private contributions to these organizations that forced them to look to local government for financial support. Since private institutions had also lost benefactors, they began to charge patients. In order to attract middle-class patients, private institutions provided services and amenities that distinguished between paying and nonpaying patients, making the hospital a desirable place for private physicians to treat their own patients. As paying patients became more necessary to the survival of the private hospital, the public hospitals slowly became the only place for the poor to get treatment. By the end of the nineteenth century, cities were reimbursing private hospitals for their care of indigent patients and the public hospitals remained dependent on the tax dollars.

The advent of private hospital health insurance, which provided middle-class patients with the purchasing power to pay for private hospital services, guaranteed the private hospital a regular source of income. Private hospitals restricted themselves to revenue-generating patients, leaving the public hospitals to care for the poor. Although public hospitals continued to provide services for patients with communicable diseases and outpatient and emergency services, the Blue Cross plans developed around the needs of the private hospitals and the inpatients they served. Thus, reimbursement for ambulatory care has been minimal under most Blue Cross plans, and provision of outpatient care has not been a major function of the private hospital, in part because private patients can afford to pay for the services of private physicians. Additionally, since World War II, there has been a tremendous influx of federal money into private medical schools and the hospitals associated with them. Further, large private medical centers with expensive research equipment and programs have attracted the best administrators, physicians, and researchers. Because of the greater resources available to the private medical centers, public hospitals have increasing problems attracting highly qualified research and medical personnel. With the mainstream of health care firmly established in the private medical sector, the public hospital has become a "dumping ground."

28. In line 31, the word "indigent" most nearly means

(A) without the means to pay
(B) having emergency medical needs
(C) lacking health insurance
(D) reimbursed by the government
(E) treated by a private doctor

29. According to the passage, the very first private hospitals

(A) developed from almshouse infirmaries
(B) provided better care than public infirmaries
(C) were established mainly to service the poor
(D) were supported by government revenues
(E) catered primarily to middle-class patients

30. It can be inferred that the author believes the differences that currently exist between public and private hospitals are primarily the result of

(A) political considerations
(B) economic factors
(C) ethical concerns
(D) legislative requirements
(E) technological developments

31. It can be inferred that the growth of private health insurance

(A) relieved local governments of the need to fund public hospitals
(B) guaranteed that the poor would have access to medical care
(C) forced middle-class patients to use public hospitals
(D) prompted the closing of many charitable institutions
(E) reinforced the distinction between public and private hospitals

32. Which of the following would be the most logical topic for the author to introduce in the next paragraph?

(A) A plan to improve the quality of public hospitals
(B) An analysis of the profit structure of health insurance companies
(C) A proposal to raise taxes on the middle class
(D) A discussion of recent developments in medical technology
(E) A list of the subjects studied by students in medical school

33. The author's primary concern is to

(A) describe the financial structure of the healthcare industry
(B) demonstrate the importance of government support for healthcare institutions
(C) criticize wealthy institutions for refusing to provide services to the poor
(D) identify the historical causes of the division between private and public hospitals
(E) praise public hospitals for their willingness to provide health care for the poor

34. The author cites all of the following as factors contributing to the decline of public hospitals EXCEPT

(A) Government money was used to subsidize private medical schools and hospitals to the detriment of public hospitals.
(B) Public hospitals are not able to compete with private institutions for top-flight managers and doctors.
(C) Large private medical centers have better research facilities and more extensive research programs than public hospitals.
(D) Public hospitals accepted the responsibility for treating patients with certain diseases.
(E) Blue Cross insurance coverage does not reimburse subscribers for medical expenses incurred in a public hospital.

35. The author's attitude toward public hospitals can best be described as

(A) contemptuous and prejudiced
(B) apprehensive and distrustful
(C) concerned and understanding
(D) enthusiastic and supportive
(E) unsympathetic and annoyed

36. The author implies that any outpatient care provided by a hospital is

(A) paid for by private insurance
(B) provided in lieu of treatment by a private physician
(C) supplied primarily by private hospitals
(D) a source of revenue for public hospitals
(E) no longer provided by hospitals, public or private

<u>Item 37</u> is based on the following passage.

A belief in luck is only one element in the
psychology of gambling. Betting on contests of speed
or strength or skill also includes a desire to heighten
the intensity of a win by imposing an additional cost
that is proportional to the wager lost. The third element
is one that is not put into words nor that is even
recognized by the bettor: enhancing the chances of
success for the contestant on which the bet is made. At
some very primitive level, the bettor feels that the
effort expended must somehow matter, like a sacrifice
to a god for a bountiful harvest. There is an instinctual
feeling that events will inherently favor the side that
has offered the sacrifice.

Line
5
10

37. The reasoning above presupposes that it is
possible for a bettor to

(A) win a wager and yet lose money on a contest
of skill
(B) make a gamble fully expecting to lose the
wager
(C) place a bet on a contest in which luck is not a
factor
(D) lose a gamble yet enjoy the victory of the
winning side
(E) act upon motives of which he or she is not
aware

NOTES AND STRATEGIES

Items 38-45 are based on the following passage.

The National Security Act of 1947 created a national military establishment headed by a single Secretary of Defense. The legislation had been a year-
Line and-a-half in the making—beginning when President
5 Truman first recommended that the armed services be reorganized into a single department. During that period, the President's concept of a unified armed service was torn apart and put back together several times; the final measure to emerge from Congress was
10 a compromise. Most of the opposition to the bill came from the Navy and its numerous civilian spokesmen, including Secretary of the Navy James Forrestal. In support of unification (and a separate air force that was part of the unification package) were the Army air
15 forces, the Army, and, most importantly, the President of the United States.

Passage of the bill did not end the bitter interservice disputes. Rather than unify, the act served only to federate the military services. It neither halted
20 the rapid demobilization of the armed forces that followed World War II nor brought to the new national military establishment the loyalties of officers steeped in the traditions of the separate services. At a time when the balance of power in Europe and Asia was
25 rapidly shifting, the services lacked any precise statement of United States foreign policy from the National Security Council on which to base future programs. The services bickered unceasingly over their respective roles and missions, already complicated by
30 the Soviet nuclear capability that, for the first time, made the United States subject to devastating attack. Not even the appointment of Forrestal as First Secretary of Defense allayed the suspicions of naval officers and their supporters that the role of the U.S.
35 Navy was threatened with permanent eclipse. Before the war of words died down, Forrestal himself was driven to resignation and then suicide.

By 1948, the United States military establishment was forced to make do with a budget approximately 10
40 percent of what it had been at its wartime peak. Meanwhile, the cost of weapons procurement was rising geometrically as the nation came to put more and more reliance on the atomic bomb and its delivery systems. These two factors inevitably made adversaries
45 of the Navy and the Air Force as the battle between advocates of the B-36 and the supercarrier so amply demonstrates. Given severe fiscal restraints on the one hand, and on the other the nation's increasing reliance on strategic nuclear deterrence, the conflict between
50 these two services over roles and missions was essentially a contest over slices of an ever-diminishing pie.

Yet if in the end neither service was the obvious victor, the principle of civilian dominance over the
55 military clearly was. If there had ever been any danger that the United States military establishment might exploit, to the detriment of civilian control, the goodwill it enjoyed as a result of its victories in World War II, that danger disappeared in the interservice
60 animosities engendered by the battle over unification.

38. In line 20, the word "demobilization" most nearly means

(A) shift to a unified military
(B) realignment of allies
(C) change from war to peace
(D) adoption of new technology
(E) adjustment to a renewed threat

39. According to the passage, the interservice strife that followed unification occurred primarily between the

(A) Army and Army air forces
(B) Army and Navy
(C) Army air forces and Navy
(D) Air Force and Army
(E) Air Force and Navy

40. It can be inferred from the passage that Forrestal's appointment as Secretary of Defense was expected to

(A) placate members of the Navy
(B) result in decreased levels of defense spending
(C) outrage advocates of the Army air forces
(D) win Congressional approval of the unification plan
(E) make Forrestal a Presidential candidate against Truman

41. According to the passage, President Truman supported which of the following?

(A) Elimination of the Navy
(B) A unified military service
(C) Establishment of a separate air force
(D) Elimination of the Navy and establishment of a separate air force
(E) A unified military service and establishment of a separate air force

42. With which of the following statements about defense unification would the author most likely agree?

   (A) Unification ultimately undermined United States military capability by inciting interservice rivalry.
   (B) The unification legislation was necessitated by the drastic decline in appropriations for the military services.
   (C) Although the unification was not entirely successful, it had the unexpected result of ensuring civilian control of the military.
   (D) In spite of the attempted unification, each service was still able to pursue its own objectives without interference from the other branches.
   (E) Unification was in the first place unwarranted, and in the second place ineffective.

43. According to the selection, the political situation following the passage of the National Security Act of 1947 was characterized by all of the following EXCEPT

   (A) a shifting balance of power in Europe and in Asia
   (B) fierce interservice rivalries
   (C) lack of strong leadership by the National Security Council
   (D) shrinking postwar military budgets
   (E) a lame-duck President who was unable to unify the legislature

44. The author cites the resignation and suicide of Forrestal in order to

   (A) underscore the bitterness of the interservice rivalry surrounding the passage of the National Security Act of 1947
   (B) demonstrate that the Navy eventually emerged as the dominant branch of service after the passage of the National Security Act of 1947
   (C) suggest that the nation would be better served by a unified armed service under a single command
   (D) provide an example of a military leader who preferred to serve his country in war rather than in peace
   (E) persuade the reader that Forrestal was a victim of political opportunists and an unscrupulous press

45. The author is primarily concerned with

   (A) discussing the influence of personalities on political events
   (B) describing the administration of a powerful leader
   (C) criticizing a piece of legislation
   (D) analyzing a political development
   (E) suggesting methods for controlling the military

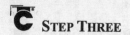

Items 46-47 are based on the following passage.

The Puerto Rican community is an ethnic
subgroup with its own unique character. Puerto Rico
was "discovered" and colonized by Spanish
Line conquistadors, and the Taino Indians eventually
5 disappeared. Some Indian features are found among
Puerto Ricans today, though for all practical purposes
their culture was completely destroyed. As the Indian
population dwindled, black slaves were transported
from Africa in large numbers; these slaves brought
10 elements of their own culture, many of which remain
evident in Puerto Rico today. By the 19th century, the
Puerto Rican had emerged as a distinct personality and
could be one of a number of colors: white, black,
Indian, or mixed. The pride of the Indian, the
15 "hidalguismo" (flamboyancy and idealism) of the
Spaniard, and the fatalism of the African blacks are all
aspects of this personality.

46. The passage is primarily concerned with the

   (A) evolution of the Puerto Rican character
   (B) expeditions of the Spanish conquistadors
   (C) African customs that are still practiced in
       Puerto Rico
   (D) disappearance of the Taino Indians
   (E) colonization of Puerto Rico

47. Which of the following best explains why the
    author places the word "discovered" (line 3) in
    quotation marks?

   (A) to show that he is quoting from another
       source
   (B) to show his admiration for Spanish culture
   (C) to underscore the fact that the island had
       been an uninhabited paradise
   (D) to acknowledge, ironically, that Puerto Rico
       was already inhabited
   (E) to emphasize the importance of Spanish
       contributions to Puerto Rican culture

NOTES AND STRATEGIES

Items 48-55 are based on the following passage.

The founders of the American Republic viewed their revolution primarily in political rather than economic or social terms. Furthermore, they talked about education as essential to the public good—a goal that took precedence over knowledge as occupational training or as a means to self-fulfillment or self-improvement. Over and over again, the Revolutionary generation, both liberal and conservative in outlook, asserted its conviction that the welfare of the Republic rested upon an educated citizenry and that schools, especially free public schools, would be the best means of educating the citizenry in civic values and the obligations required of everyone in a democratic republican society. All agreed that the principal ingredients of a civic education were literacy and the inculcation of patriotic and moral virtues, some others adding the study of history and the study of principles of the republican government itself.

The founders, as was the case with almost all their successors, were long on exhortation and rhetoric regarding the value of civic education, but they left it to the textbook writers to distill the essence of those values for schoolchildren. Texts in American history and government appeared as early as the 1790s. The textbook writers turned out to be largely of conservative persuasion, more likely Federalist in outlook than Jeffersonian, and they almost universally agreed that political virtue must rest upon moral and religious precepts. Since most textbook writers were New Englanders, this meant that the texts were infused with Protestant, and above all Puritan, outlooks.

In the first half of the Republic, civic education in the schools emphasized the inculcation of civic values and made little attempt to develop participatory political skills. That was a task left to incipient political parties, town meetings, churches, and the coffee or ale houses where men gathered for conversation. Additionally, as a reading of certain Federalist papers of the period would demonstrate, the press probably did more to disseminate realistic as well as partisan knowledge of government than the schools. The goal of education, however, was to achieve a higher form of *unum* for the new Republic. In the middle half of the nineteenth century, the political values taught in the public and private schools did not change substantially from those celebrated in the first fifty years of the Republic. In the textbooks of the day, their rosy hues if anything became golden. To the resplendent values of liberty, equality, and a benevolent Christian morality were now added the middle-class virtues—especially of New England—of hard work, honesty, integrity, the rewards of individual effort, and obedience to parents and legitimate authority. But of all the political values taught in school, patriotism was preeminent; and whenever teachers explained to schoolchildren why they should love their country above all else, the idea of liberty assumed pride of place.

48. In line 5, the phrase "took precedence over" most nearly means

(A) set an example for
(B) formulated a policy of
(C) enlightened someone on
(D) had greater importance than
(E) taught only practical skills

49. The passage deals primarily with the

(A) content of textbooks used in early American schools
(B) role of education in late eighteenth- and early to mid-nineteenth-century America
(C) influence of New England Puritanism on early American values
(D) origin and development of the Protestant work ethic in modern America
(E) establishment of universal, free public education in America

50. According to the passage, the founders of the Republic regarded education primarily as

(A) a religious obligation
(B) a private matter
(C) an unnecessary luxury
(D) a matter of individual choice
(E) a political necessity

51. The author states that textbooks written in the middle part of the nineteenth century

(A) departed radically in tone and style from earlier textbooks
(B) mentioned for the first time the value of liberty
(C) treated traditional civic virtues with even greater reverence
(D) were commissioned by government agencies
(E) contained no reference to conservative ideas

52. Which of the following would LEAST likely
have been the subject of an early American
textbook?

    (A) Basic rules of English grammar
    (B) The American Revolution
    (C) Patriotism and other civic virtues
    (D) Vocational education
    (E) Principles of American government

53. The author's attitude toward the educational
system discussed in the passage can best be
described as

    (A) cynical and unpatriotic
    (B) realistic and analytical
    (C) pragmatic and frustrated
    (D) disenchanted and bitter
    (E) idealistic and naive

54. The passage provides information that would be
helpful in answering which of the following
questions?

    (A) Why was a disproportionate share of early
American textbooks written by New England
authors?
    (B) Was the Federalist party primarily a liberal or
conservative force in early American
politics?
    (C) How many years of education did the
founders believe were sufficient to instruct
young citizens in civic virtue?
    (D) What were the names of some of the Puritan
authors who wrote early American
textbooks?
    (E) Did most citizens of the early Republic agree
with the founders that public education was
essential to the welfare of the Republic?

55. The author implies that an early American Puritan
would likely insist that

    (A) moral and religious values are the foundation
of civic virtue
    (B) textbooks should instruct students in political
issues of vital concern to the community
    (C) textbooks should give greater emphasis to the
value of individual liberty than to the duties
of patriotism
    (D) private schools with a particular religious
focus are preferable to public schools with no
religious instruction
    (E) government and religion are separate
institutions and the church should not
interfere in political affairs

Item 56 is based on the following passage.

Icing occurs when an aircraft penetrates a cloud of small, supercooled water droplets. When ice accumulates on flying surfaces, the result is loss of control and even loss of lift. One approach to the problem of icing is the use of anti-icing and de-icing systems. This approach requires the installation of complex mechanical or thermal systems. A second approach is to design components in ways that eliminate, or at least minimize, adverse effects of ice accretion. This method requires no external power; systems are less costly to build and to maintain, and there is no chance of failure. While components that are completely unaffected by ice may not be possible, reducing the adverse effects of icing by proper aerodynamic design is feasible.

56. It can be inferred that the author regards anti-icing and de-icing systems as

(A) the preferred approach to the problem of icing
(B) a second best approach to the problem of icing
(C) cost effective when compared to the design approach
(D) more practicable than attempts to design away the problem
(E) safer than design changes intended to minimize the effects of ice

Items 57-58 are based on the following passage.

A sprain is a stretching or a tearing injury to a ligament; a strain is an injury to a muscle or a tendon that is caused by twisting or pulling. The severity of a sprain depends on the extent of injury (whether the tear is partial or complete) and the number of ligaments involved. A strain, depending on the severity of the injury, may be a simple overstretching of the muscle or tendon, or it can result in a partial or complete tear. A sprain usually results from a fall or a sudden twist. Typically, sprains occur when people fall on an outstretched arm, land on the side of the foot, or twist a knee. The usual symptoms include pain, swelling, bruising and inability to use the joint. A strain is usually caused by overstressing the muscles. Typically, people with a strain experience pain, muscle spasm, and muscle weakness.

57. The primary purpose of the passage is to

(A) explain how to treat sprains and strains
(B) analyze the common causes of sprains and strains
(C) identify the symptoms of injuries to ligaments, muscles, and tendons
(D) explain how to avoid sprains and strains
(E) distinguish sprains and strains as injuries

58. An injury that results from a sudden twist during a fall and causes a purple swelling and the complete inability to move the joint would most likely be called

(A) acute strain
(B) chronic strain
(C) severe sprain
(D) mild sprain
(E) inflammation

Items 59-60 are based on the following two passages.

Passage 1

    An E. coli outbreak at a county fair sickened hundreds of people. Epidemiologists concluded that individuals with culture-confirmed cases of E. coli
Line infection were exposed on August 28 by consuming
5 beverages sold by vendors supplied with water from Well 6. A dye study performed in late September showed a hydraulic connection between the septic system of a nearby 4-H dormitory and Well 6. Tests of a cattle manure storage area suspected as a possible
10 contamination source did not show a hydraulic connection with Well 6 nor with the presence of the relevant strain of E. Coli. Therefore, the outbreak was caused by leakage from the dormitory septic system.

Passage 2

    Manure runoff from the nearby cattle barn cannot
15 be ruled out as a cause of the outbreak because exact environmental conditions, including drought followed by heavy rain, could not be replicated during the later study. Additionally, manure in the storage area was removed daily. Thus, it can never be known if manure-
20 contaminated water percolated from the manure storage area to Well 6.

59. In line 20, the word "percolated" most nearly means

    (A) boiled
    (B) infected
    (C) tested
    (D) was consumed
    (E) seeped

60. Which of the following best describes the relationship between the two passages?

    (A) The two speakers agree that E. coli caused the illnesses but believe that two different strains were involved.
    (B) The two speakers agree that E. coli caused the illnesses but disagree about the source of the contamination.
    (C) The two speakers agree that the same strain of E. coli caused the outbreak and agree that the dormitory septic system was the source.
    (D) Speaker 1 maintains that E. coli was the cause of the outbreak of illness, but Speaker 2 thinks that some other agent might have been involved.
    (E) Speaker 2 argues that that several sources contributed to the contamination, while Speaker 1 says that the only source was the dormitory septic system.

TIMED-PRACTICE QUIZZES

DIRECTIONS: This section contains three quizzes in the long single-passage selection format and three quizzes in the short single-paragraph selection format. Under timed conditions, answer the items in each quiz on the basis of what is stated or implied in the passage(s). Answers are on page 983.

A. QUIZ I (Long Single-Passage; 8 items; 15 minutes)

Items 1-8 are based on the following passage.

The healthcare economy is replete with unusual and even unique economic relationships. One of the least understood involves the peculiar roles of producer or "provider" and purchaser or "consumer" in the
Line typical doctor-patient relationship. In most sectors of
5 the economy, the seller attempts to attract a potential buyer with various inducements of price, quality, and utility, and the buyer makes the decision. Where circumstances permit the buyer no choice because there
10 is effectively only one seller and the product is relatively essential, government usually asserts monopoly and places the industry under price and other regulations. Neither of these conditions prevails in most of the healthcare industry.
15 In the healthcare industry, the doctor-patient relationship is the mirror image of the ordinary relationship between producer and consumer. Once an individual has chosen to see a physician—and even then there may be no real choice—it is the physician
20 who usually makes all significant purchasing decisions: whether the patient should return "next Wednesday," whether x-rays are needed, whether drugs should be prescribed, *etc.* It is a rare and sophisticated patient who will challenge such professional decisions or raise
25 in advance questions about price, especially when the ailment is regarded as serious.
This is particularly significant in relation to hospital care. The physician must certify the need for hospitalization, determine what procedures will be
30 performed, and announce when the patient may be discharged. The patient may be consulted about some of these decisions, but in the main it is the doctor's judgments that are final. Little wonder, then, that in the eyes of the hospital, the physician is the real
35 "consumer." Consequently, the medical staff represents the "power center" in hospital policy and decision-making, not the administration.

Although usually there are in this situation four identifiable participants—the physician, the hospital,
40 the patient, and the payer (generally an insurance carrier or government)—the physician makes the essential decisions for all of them. The hospital becomes an extension of the physician; the payer generally meets most of the bona fide bills generated
45 by the physician/hospital; and for the most part the patient plays a passive role. In routine or minor illnesses, or just plain worries, the patient's options are, of course, much greater with respect to use and price. In illnesses that are of some significance, however,
50 such choices tend to evaporate, and it is for these illnesses that the bulk of the healthcare dollar is spent. We estimate that about 75 to 80 percent of healthcare expenditures are determined by physicians, not patients. For this reason, economy measures directed at
55 patients or the public are relatively ineffective.

1. In line 1, the phrase "replete with" most nearly means

   (A) filled with
   (B) restricted by
   (C) enriched by
   (D) damaged by
   (E) devoid of

2. The author's primary purpose is to

   (A) speculate about the relationship between a patient's ability to pay and the treatment received
   (B) criticize doctors for exercising too much control over patients
   (C) analyze some important economic factors in healthcare
   (D) urge hospitals to reclaim their decision-making authority
   (E) inform potential patients of their healthcare rights

3. It can be inferred that doctors are able to determine hospital policies because

   (A) it is doctors who generate income for the hospital
   (B) most of a patient's bills are paid by health insurance
   (C) hospital administrators lack the expertise to question medical decisions
   (D) a doctor is ultimately responsible for a patient's health
   (E) some patients might refuse to accept their physician's advice

4. According to the author, when a doctor tells a patient to "return next Wednesday," the doctor is in effect

   (A) taking advantage of the patient's concern for his health
   (B) instructing the patient to buy more medical services
   (C) warning the patient that a hospital stay might be necessary
   (D) advising the patient to seek a second opinion
   (E) admitting that the initial visit was ineffective

5. The author is most probably leading up to

   (A) a proposal to control medical costs
   (B) a discussion of a new medical treatment
   (C) an analysis of the causes of inflation in the United States
   (D) a study of lawsuits against doctors for malpractice
   (E) a comparison of hospitals and factories

6. The tone of the passage can best be described as

   (A) whimsical
   (B) cautious
   (C) analytical
   (D) inquisitive
   (E) defiant

7. With which of the following statements would the author be likely to agree?

   (A) Few patients are reluctant to object to the course of treatment prescribed by a doctor or to question the cost of the services.
   (B) The payer, whether an insurance carrier or the government, is less likely to acquiesce to demands for payment when the illness of the patient is regarded as serious.
   (C) Today's patients are more informed as to what services and procedures they will need from their healthcare providers.
   (D) The more serious the illness of a patient, the less likely it is that the patient will object to the course of treatment prescribed or to question the cost of services.
   (E) None of the above

8. The author's primary concern is to

   (A) define a term
   (B) clarify a misunderstanding
   (C) refute a theory — to go against !
   (D) discuss a problem
   (E) announce a new discovery

B. QUIZ II (Long Single-Passage; 7 items; 15 minutes)

Items 1-7 are based on the following passage.

Man, so the truism goes, lives increasingly in a man-made environment. This puts a special burden on human immaturity, for it is plain that adapting to such
Line variable conditions must depend very heavily on
5 opportunities for learning, or whatever the processes are that are operative during immaturity. It must also mean that during immaturity, man must master knowledge and skills that are neither stored in the gene pool nor learned by direct encounter, but that are
10 contained in the culture pool—knowledge about values and history, skills as varied as an obligatory natural language or an optional mathematical one, as mute as levers or as articulate as myth telling.
Yet, it would be a mistake to leap to the
15 conclusion that because human immaturity makes possible high flexibility, therefore anything is possible for the species. Human traits were selected for their survival value over a four- to five-million-year period with a great acceleration of the selection process during
20 the last half of that period. There were crucial, irreversible changes during that final man-making period: the recession of formidable dentition, a 50-percent increase in brain volume, the obstetrical paradox—bipedalism and strong pelvic girdle, larger
25 brain through a smaller birth canal—an immature brain at birth, and creation of what Washburn has called a "technical-social way of life," involving tool and symbol use.
Note, however, that hominidization consisted
30 principally of adaptations to conditions in the Pleistocene.
These preadaptations, shaped in response to earlier habitat demands, are part of man's evolutionary inheritance. This is not to say that close beneath the
35 skin of man is a naked ape, that civilization is only a veneer. The technical-social way of life is a deep feature of the species adaptation. But we would err if we assumed a priori that man's inheritance placed no constraint on his power to adapt. Some of the
40 preadaptations can be shown to be presently maladaptive. Man's inordinate fondness for fats and sweets no longer serves his individual survival well. Furthermore, the human obsession with sexuality is plainly not fitted for survival of the species now,
45 however well it might have served to populate the upper Pliocene and the Pleistocene. Nevertheless, note that the species responds typically to these challenges by technical innovation rather than by morphological

or behavioral change. Contraception dissociates
50 sexuality from reproduction. Of course, we do not know what kinds and what range of stresses are produced by successive rounds of such technical innovation. Dissociating sexuality and reproduction, for example, surely produces changes in the structure
55 of the family, which in turn redefine the role of women, which in turn alters the authority pattern affecting the child, etc. Continuing and possibly accelerating change seems inherent in such adaptation. This, of course, places an enormous pressure on man's
60 uses of immaturity, preparing the young for unforeseeable change—the more so if there are severe restraints imposed by human preadaptations to earlier conditions of life.

1. The primary purpose of the passage is to

   (A) refute some misconceptions about the importance of human immaturity
   (B) introduce a new theory of the origins of the human species
   (C) describe the evolutionary forces that formed the physical appearance of modern humans
   (D) discuss the importance of human immaturity as an adaptive mechanism
   (E) outline the process by which humans mature into social beings

2. It can be inferred that the obstetrical paradox is puzzling because

   (A) it occurred very late during the evolution of the species
   (B) evolutionary forces seemed to work at cross purposes to each other
   (C) technological innovations have made the process of birth easier
   (D) an increase in brain size is not an ordinary evolutionary event
   (E) a strong pelvic girdle is no longer necessary to the survival of the species

3. Which of the following statements can be inferred from the passage?

(A) Human beings are today less sexually active than were our ancestors during the Pleistocene era.

(B) During the Pleistocene era, a fondness for fats and sweets was a trait that contributed to survival of humans.

(C) Mathematics was invented by human beings during the latter half of the Pleistocene era.

(D) The use of language and tools is a trait that is genetically transmitted from one generation to the next.

(E) During immaturity, human beings gain knowledge and learn skills primarily through the process of direct encounter.

4. As used in line 32, the term "preadaptations" refers to traits that

(A) were useful to earlier human beings but have since lost their utility

(B) appeared in response to the need to learn a natural language and the use of tools

(C) humans currently exhibit but that developed in response to conditions of an earlier age

(D) are disadvantageous to creatures whose way of life is primarily technical and social

(E) continue to exist despite evolutionary pressures that threaten to erase them

5. The author mentions contraception to demonstrate that

(A) human beings may adapt to new conditions by technological invention rather than by changing their behavior

(B) sexual promiscuity is no longer an aid to the survival of the human species

(C) technological innovation is a more important adaptive mechanism than either heredity or direct encounter

(D) conditions during the upper Pliocene and Pleistocene eras no longer affect the course of human evolution

(E) morphological change is a common response to new demands placed on a creature by its environment

6. With which of the following statements would the author LEAST likely agree?

(A) The technical-social way of life of humans is an adaptive mechanism that arose in response to environmental pressures.

(B) The possibility of technical innovation makes it unlikely that the physical appearance of humans will change radically in a short time.

(C) Technological innovations can result in changes in the social structures in which humans live.

(D) New demands created by changes in the social structure are sometimes met by technological innovation.

(E) The fact that humans have a technical-social way of life makes the species immune from evolutionary pressures.

7. The author is most probably addressing which of the following audiences?

(A) Medical students in a course on human anatomy

(B) College students in an introductory course on archaeology

(C) Psychologists investigating the uses of human immaturity

(D) Biologists trying to trace the course of human evolution

(E) Linguists doing research on the origins of natural languages

C. QUIZ III (Long Single-Passage; 8 items; 15 minutes)

<u>Items 1-8</u> are based on the following passage.

The uniqueness of the Japanese character is the result of two, seemingly contradictory forces: the strength of traditions, and selective receptivity to
Line foreign achievements and inventions. As early as the
5 1860s, there were counter movements to the traditional orientation. Yukichi Fukuzawa, the most eloquent spokesman of Japan's "Enlightenment," claimed "The Confucian civilization of the East seems to me to lack two things possessed by Western civilization: science
10 in the material sphere and a sense of independence in the spiritual sphere." Fukuzawa's great influence is found in the free and individualistic philosophy of the Education Code of 1872, but he was not able to prevent the government from turning back to the canons of
15 Confucian thought in the Imperial Rescript of 1890. Another interlude of relative liberalism followed World War I, when the democratic idealism of President Woodrow Wilson had an important impact on Japanese intellectuals and, especially, students; but more
20 important was the Leninist ideology of the 1917 Bolshevik Revolution. Again, in the early 1930s, nationalism and militarism became dominant, largely because of failing economic conditions.
Following the end of World War II, substantial
25 changes were undertaken in Japan to liberate the individual from authoritarian restraints. The new democratic value system was accepted by many teachers, students, intellectuals, and old liberals, but it was not immediately embraced by the society as a
30 whole. Japanese traditions were dominated by group values, and notions of personal freedom and individual rights were unfamiliar.
Today, democratic processes are evident in the widespread participation of the Japanese people in
35 social and political life; yet, there is no universally accepted and stable value system. Values are constantly modified by strong infusions of Western ideas, both democratic and Marxist. School textbooks espouse democratic principles, emphasizing equality
40 over hierarchy and rationalism over tradition; but in practice these values are often misinterpreted and distorted, particularly by youth who translate the individualistic and humanistic goals of democracy into egoistic and materialistic ones.
45 Most Japanese people have consciously rejected Confucianism, but vestiges of the old order remain. An important feature of relationships in many institutions such as political parties, large corporations, and

university faculties is the *oyabun-kobun* or parent-child relation. A party leader, supervisor, or professor, in
50 return for loyalty, protects those subordinate to him and takes general responsibility for their interests throughout their entire lives, an obligation that sometimes even extends to arranging marriages. The corresponding loyalty of the individual to his patron
55 reinforces his allegiance to the group to which they both belong. A willingness to cooperate with other members of the group and to support without qualification the interests of the group in all its external relations is still a widely respected virtue. The *oyabun-*
60 *kobun* creates ladders of mobility that an individual can ascend, rising as far as abilities permit, so long as he maintains successful personal ties with a superior in the vertical channel, the latter requirement usually taking precedence over a need for exceptional competence.
65 Consequently, there is little horizontal relationship between people even within the same profession.

1. As used in line 46, the word "vestiges" most nearly means

   (A) institutions
   (B) superiors
   (C) traces
   (D) subordinates
   (E) virtues

2. Which of the following is most like the relationship of the *oyabun-kobun* described in the passage?

   (A) A political candidate and the voting public
   (B) A gifted scientist and his protégé
   (C) Two brothers who are partners in a business
   (D) A judge presiding at the trial of a criminal defendant
   (E) A leader of a musical ensemble who is also a musician in the group

3. According to the passage, Japanese attitudes are NOT influenced by which of the following?

   (A) Democratic ideals
   (B) Elements of modern Western culture
   (C) Remnants of an earlier social structure
   (D) Marxist ideals
   (E) Confucianism

4. The author implies that

(A) decisions about promotions within the vertical channel are often based on personal feelings
(B) students and intellectuals do not understand the basic tenets of Western democracy
(C) Western values have completely overwhelmed traditional Japanese attitudes
(D) respect for authority was introduced into Japan following World War II
(E) most Japanese workers are members of a single political party

5. In developing the passage, the author does which of the following?

(A) Introduces an analogy
(B) Defines a term
(C) Presents statistics
(D) Cites an authority
(E) Issues a challenge

6. It can be inferred that the Imperial Rescript of 1890

(A) was a protest by liberals against the lack of individual liberty in Japan
(B) marked a return in government policies to conservative values
(C) implemented the ideals set forth in the Education Code of 1872
(D) was influenced by the Leninist ideology of the Bolshevik Revolution
(E) prohibited the teaching of Western ideas in Japanese schools

7. Which of the following is the most accurate description of the organization of the passage?

(A) A sequence of inferences in which the conclusion of each successive step becomes a premise in the next argument
(B) A list of generalizations, most of which are supported by only a single example
(C) A chronological analysis of historical events leading up to a description of the current situation
(D) A statement of a commonly accepted theory that is then subjected to a critical analysis
(E) An introduction of a key term that is then defined by giving examples

8. Which of the following best states the central thesis of the passage?

(A) The value system of Japan is based upon traditional and conservative values that have, in modern times, been modified by Western and other liberal values.
(B) Students and radicals in Japan have used Leninist ideology to distort the meaning of democratic, Western values.
(C) The notions of personal freedom and individual liberty did not find immediate acceptance in Japan because of the predominance of traditional group values.
(D) Modern Japanese society is characterized by hierarchical relationships in which a personal tie to a superior is often more important than merit.
(E) The influence on Japanese values of the American ideals of personal freedom and individual rights is less important than the influence of Leninist ideology.

D. QUIZ IV (Short Single-Paragraph; 10 items; 15 minutes)

<u>Item 1</u> is based on the following passage.

In 1800, after two thousand years of public and private construction projects, travel in Europe had hardly improved at all. A few bridges had been built, and a post-road extended from Madrid to St. Petersburg; but the diligence that rumbled from Calais to Paris required three days to cover the one hundred and fifty miles. Travelers to Marseilles met with rough roads and hardships like those of the Middle Ages. Italy was almost as remote from the north of Europe as when carriage-roads were first built. Indeed, because of the violence of revolutionary wars during the last ten years of the eighteenth century, conditions had actually deteriorated.

Line
5

10

1. As used in line 5, the word "diligence" refers to a

    (A) positive mental attitude
    (B) heavy wheeled conveyance
    (C) unimproved roadway
    (D) lengthy journey
    (E) perseverance in adversity

<u>Item 2</u> is based on the following passage.

Before there was a Federal Constitution, an Articles of Confederation provided for a union of the former British colonies of what is now called the United States. From the beginning, however, many Americans recognized the inadequacies of the Articles as a national government, and a movement for a new national government began outside the Congress. Representatives of Maryland and Virginia, meeting at Mt. Vernon to discuss trade problems between the two States, agreed to invite delegates from all States to discuss commercial affairs at a meeting in Annapolis, Maryland, in September 1786. Although delegates from only five States reached the Annapolis Convention, that group issued a call for a meeting of all States to discuss necessary revisions of the Articles of Confederation. Responding to this call, every State except Rhode Island selected delegates for the Federal Convention at Philadelphia.

Line
5

10

15

2. The author states that the convention to create a new national government was primarily a response to

    (A) the Annapolis Convention
    (B) a trade meeting at Mt. Vernon
    (C) the Federal Convention
    (D) the Continental Congress
    (E) Rhode Island's delegates

Item 3 is based on the following passage.

    In America today, most people are living longer.
The reasons are simple: advances in medicine and
healthcare, better nutrition and healthier lifestyles, and
Line a major reduction in environmental pollutants. By the
5 year 2020, one in six Americans—53 million men and
women—will be age 65 or older. This is the same
generation that overloaded schools, challenged the
healthcare system, and overburdened the transportation
network. The nation is not ready for this surge in the
10 senior population. Many of these seniors will need
housing and healthcare services that may be neither
available nor affordable unless the nation acts now. If
the situation is dire now, it will be desperate in the year
2020.

E 3. The author regards the situation created by the
    aging population as a

    (A) passing phenomenon
    (B) historical precedent
    (C) long-term challenge
    (D) fortunate development
    (E) governmental crisis

Item 4 is based on the following passage.

    Manufactured homes evolved from the mobile
home and tend to have certain distinctive features such
as a lower pitch to the roof because they are built in the
Line factory and towed to a final location. They have little
5 or no roof overhangs because of highway width
limitations and are long and narrow due to hauling
restrictions. However, many of the differences between
manufactured and site-built homes are disappearing.
Manufacturers are using siding and roofing that are the
10 same as those used on other types of housing. They
have developed hinged roofs that can be delivered flat
and set up on site with a normal roof pitch and
overhangs. Newer manufactured homes can also be set
on permanent foundations, thereby avoiding the
15 skirting that is usually associated with manufactured
housing. Furthermore, manufactured homes are larger
than ever, as multi-section units have become
available.

 4. The author implies that the feature of
    manufactured homes that is LEAST likely to
    change is the

    (A) overhangs at the edges of the roofs
    (B) quality of the siding material used
    (C) type of foundation used for support
    (D) size and shape of individual sections
    (E) pitch of the roof of the finished home

Item 5 is based on the following passage.

Many volcanoes are associated with movement of tectonic plates. Where the plates move apart, as along the Atlantic mid-ocean ridge, a rift forms allowing magma to escape from deep within the Earth. The temperature of the magma is about 1200° C; but due to the cold deep ocean water, the magma solidifies into a mixture of minerals and volcanic glass. The resulting basalt formations are slowly broken down due to "weathering." Once believed to be a chemical process, new evidence suggests that microbial organisms may partly be responsible for "weathering." Microscopic examinations of weathered basalts show pits, channels, and other patterns that are unlike chemical weathering. These weathered rocks also contain large amounts of carbon, phosphorus, and nitrogen, byproducts of biological activity, as well as traces of nucleic acids. No living cells have been discovered in the rocks, but objects have been found that resemble cellular structures.

Line
5

10

15

5. It can be inferred that the pits and channels in the basalt (line 12)

(A) were created when the basalt was cooled by ocean water
(B) are generally the products of organic activity
(C) resulted from chemical processes at high temperatures
(D) exhibit the size and shape of cellular structures
(E) inhibit the functioning of chemical processes

Item 6 is based on the following passage.

Imagine the telecommunication cables of a large city: Millions of calls flash down fiber optic cables at incredible speeds. Multiply that many-fold and that's the brain. As a neuron receives messages from surrounding cells, an electrical charge builds up. This charge travels down the axon to the end, where it triggers the release of chemical messengers that are called neurotransmitters, which move from the axon across a tiny gap to the dendrites or cell bodies of other neurons. There, they bind to specific receptor sites on the receiving end of dendrites of nearby neurons and open channels through the cell membrane into the receiving nerve cell's interior or start other processes that determine what the receiving nerve cell will do.

Line
5

10

6. The author's primary purpose in the passage is to

(A) present new scientific findings
(B) describe the ~~structure~~ of the brain
(C) discuss methods of improving brain function
(D) propose a model for telecommunications
(E) outline a biochemical process

Item 7 is based on the following passage.

About 50% of nitrogen that is applied to crops as fertilizer is taken up by plants; the remainder washes off or is blown off the soil. Run-off of nitrogen and
Line
phosphate from fertilizers results in "eutrophication" of
5   surface waters. Eutrophication is a natural process in which a water body is enriched by the addition of excessive nutrients, which causes excessive algae growth and depletes oxygen. Many species cannot survive in these conditions, and large "dead zones"
10 appear from decaying matter undergoing anaerobic degradation.

7. The author uses the word "excessive" (line 7) to describe nutrients that are

   (A) present in fertilizers and that cannot be absorbed by crops
   (B) in surface water above what is needed to maintain a balance of life
   (C) applied to crops only to be blown off later
   (D) present in surface water and that are not absorbed by algae
   (E) made from chemicals and that pollute water and create dead zones

Item 8 is based on the following passage.

It is sometimes more noble to be wrong than to be right. We feel respect for consistency, even in error, and we lament the virtue that is debauched into a vice.
Line
At least the person who acts consistently but wrongly
5   can be said to have a measure of integrity, while the person who acts virtuously one day and villainously the next is at best weak and at worst hypocritical. And is that not what it means to have integrity? The word echoes its root: a whole. The person who has integrity
10 consistently values virtue even though it may be unattainable.

8. The author would most likely accept which of the following as an example of integrity?

   (A) an enemy soldier who fights bravely and fairly
   (B) a professor who teaches that all morals are relative
   (C) a merchant who donates to charity to generate goodwill
   (D) a lawmaker who supports a bill only to please voters
   (E) an artist who paints portraits that flatter the subject

Items 9-10 are based on the following passage.

As a debater, Abraham Lincoln was consistently
an actor, a caricaturist, and a satirist. In an early
political debate, he mimicked his opponent so
Line   accurately and with such bitter ridicule that the man
5   was reduced to tears. At the bar, his famous "Skin the
defendant alive" meant an outpouring of personal
ridicule. Personal ridicule was usually presented with a
guileless air. As he rose to respond to Douglas in one
of those rightly famous debates, Lincoln deadpanned,
10   "I was not aware until now that Mr. Douglas's father
was a cooper. And I have no doubt that he was a very
good one." Lincoln bowed gravely to Douglas and
continued, "He has made one of the best whiskey casks
I have ever seen."

9. In line 11, the word "cooper" most nearly means

   (A) satirist
   (B) debater
   (C) barrel maker
   (D) defendant
   (E) offspring

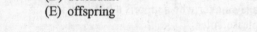

10. In lines 13-14, Lincoln implies that Douglas

    (A) was an excellent debater
    (B) had the intelligence of a cask
    (C) deserved to be skinned alive
    (D) was not as famous as his father
    (E) should not have used personal ridicule

E. QUIZ V (Short Single-Paragraph; 10 items; 15 minutes)

Item 1 is based on the following passage.

The French are great optimists. They seize upon every good thing as soon as it appears and revel in even fleeting pleasure. The English, on the other hand, are
Line apt to neglect the present good in preparing for the
5 possible evil. However badly things may be going otherwise, if the sun breaks through the clouds for even a moment, the French are out in holiday dress and spirits, carefree as butterflies, as though the sun will shine forever. But no matter how brightly the sun is
10 shining, if there is wisp of cloud on the horizon, the English venture forth distrustfully with umbrellas in hand.

1. The author of the passage uses weather as

   (A) an example of a force of nature
   (B) an illustration of pleasant and unpleasant traits
   (C) an excuse to write about French and English habits
   (D) a symbol of good and bad fortune
   (E) a measure of a society's values

Item 2 is based on the following passage.

It has been half a century since nuclear energy was introduced to the public in a most dramatic, but unfortunately, most destructive way—through the use
Line of a nuclear weapon. Since then, enormous strides have
5 been made in developing the peaceful applications of this great and versatile force. Because these strides have always been overshadowed by the focus of public attention on military uses, the public has never fully understood or appreciated the gains and status of the
10 peaceful atom.

2. The author implies that had a nuclear weapon not been used

   (A) people would be more receptive to peaceful uses of nuclear power
   (B) governments would be less likely to deploy nuclear weapons
   (C) public support for nuclear weaponry would be undermined
   (D) the security of nations having nuclear arsenals would be weakened
   (E) military and non-military uses of nuclear power would be limited

Item 3 is based on the following passage.

In 1964, the Surgeon General announced that cigarette smoking was a significant health hazard, yet smoking still kills over 400,000 people annually in the United States alone—more deaths each year than from AIDS, alcohol, cocaine, heroin, homicide, suicide, motor vehicle crashes, and fires combined. We have made gains in preventing and controlling tobacco use; but despite the massive education campaigns and years of litigation, as well as substantial price hikes designed to curb smoking, the incidence of smoking has increased. There is no disagreement that the best option for any person using tobacco products is to stop; and when asked, most smokers say they want to quit. Unfortunately very few of them are able to break the habit.

3. The author cites deaths from non-smoking causes (lines 5-6) primarily to

(A) show that smoking is not as serious a problem as many people believe
(B) demonstrate that many health hazards other than smoking require attention
(C) illustrate the variety of diseases that pose a danger in modern society
(D) dramatize the seriousness of the health problem presented by the use of tobacco
(E) stress the importance of encouraging people to discontinue the use of tobacco

Item 4 is based on the following passage.

We think of invasive non-native plants as overgrowing an entire ecosystem, but plants can also change entire ecosystems by modifying ecosystem traits and processes. In Florida, Australian paperbark trees, with spongy outer bark and highly flammable leaves and litter, have increased the frequency of fire. This has helped paperbark replace native plants on at least 400,000 acres. In the arid Southwest, the deep roots of Mediterranean salt cedars deplete soil water. On the island of Hawaii, the nitrogen-fixing firebush has invaded nitrogen-poor areas. As there are no native nitrogen-fixers, native plants have adapted to the nitrogen-poor soil, while introduced species cannot tolerate it, so a wave of invasive plants are taking over areas that are prepared by the firebush.

4. Which of the following best summarizes the main point of the passage?

(A) Non-native plant species can devastate an ecosystem by overgrowing native plant species.
(B) Non-native plants can change an ecosystem without directly displacing native species.
(C) Native plant species are often unable to adapt to significant changes in an ecosystem.
(D) The introduction of non-native plant species carries a significant environmental risk.
(E) Plants such as the Australian paperbark tree are not able to survive in their native habitats.

Item 5 is based on the following passage.

For indigenous people of the United States, the continuance of cultural values and traditions depends on the transmission of language, but many languages are dying and many more have become extinct already.
Line
5 Of the 85-100 indigenous languages that used to exist in California, half are gone. As for the other half, the vast majority have 5 or fewer speakers, all over 70 years old. The languages are silent at home and in the community, and so the most effective way to get a
10 critical mass of new fluent speakers of an endangered language is through the school, the same institution that was used to destroy those very languages in the past.

5. Which of the following most nearly captures the meaning of "critical mass" (line 10)?

(A) A sufficient number
(B) At least five of more
(C) Five or fewer
(D) Eighty-five to 100
(E) More than 70

Item 6 is based on the following passage.

In 1986, a Wall Street Journal article used the phrase "glass ceiling" to refer to an invisible, but impenetrable, barrier preventing women from reaching the highest level of business. Subsequent research
Line
5 confirmed the existence of such a barrier. Ninety-seven percent of the senior managers of Fortune 500 companies are male. Where there are women in high places, their compensation is lower than that of men in comparable positions. Nor is the glass ceiling likely to
10 disappear soon. There are relatively few women in the "pipeline," the positions most likely to lead to the top. In short, the world at the top of the corporate hierarchy does not look anything like America.

6. The author regards the existence of the "glass ceiling" as

(A) well-documented
(B) theoretically possible
(C) relatively unlikely
(D) entirely speculative
(E) virtually impossible

Item 7 is based on the following passage.

In politics, the hero does not live happily ever after. The last chapter is merely a place where the writer imagines that the polite reader has begun to look furtively at the clock. When Plato came to the point where it was fitting to sum up, his assurance turned into stage-fright. Those sentences in the Republic are so absurd that it is impossible either to live by them or to forget them: "Until philosophers are kings, or kings have the spirit of philosophy, and political greatness and wisdom meet in one, cities will never cease from ill." Whenever we make an appeal to reason in politics, the difficulty in this parable recurs, for there is an inherent difficulty about using reason to deal with an unreasoning world.

7. The author uses the phrase "inherent difficulty" (line 13) to indicate that

(A) Plato's instructions in the Republic have no application to current events
(B) it is unrealistic to expect that political leaders will be philosophers
(C) political leaders rarely have the personal characteristics to be heroic
(D) the practical world can only be ordered according to the principles of reason
(E) political greatness and wisdom coexist only when a political leader is also a philosopher

Item 8 is based on the following passage.

Zora Neale Hurston, author of four novels, a folk opera, and nearly 100 short stories, loved a good lie. When her late-model car aroused suspicion among poor country folk whose lives she was researching, she pretended to be a bootlegger. She lied on official documents like marriage licenses, giving her age at the time of her second marriage as 31 rather than 48. Her letters sometimes seem to be written by different people, and her autobiography, in which she claims to have been born in Eatonville, Florida rather than Notasulga, Alabama, is full of misinformation. So, Hurston's own statements and writings are not likely to settle any of the debates over the details of her life.

8. The author implies that Hurston's writings are not a good source of information about the details of her life because

(A) details of an author's personal life are not usually available
(B) autobiographical information cannot be independently verified
(C) writers of fiction cannot be trusted to portray events accurately
(D) official documents are more reliable than family histories
(E) Hurston's descriptions of the details of her life are unreliable

Items 9-10 are based on the following passage.

Recently, six Magellanic penguins that were taken from the wild arrived at the San Francisco Zoo. The 46 long-time resident Magellanic penguins, which had spent relatively sedentary lives of grooming and staying in burrows, began to simulate migratory behavior when they watched the new penguins swimming around the 130 × 40-foot pool. All 52 birds now swim almost all of the time, resting on the artificial island in the middle of the pool only at night. Indeed, when the pool is drained for cleaning, the penguins refuse to leave, walking around it instead of swimming.

Line

5

10

9. In line 4, the word "sedentary" most nearly means

(A) sheltered
(B) aquatic
(C) uninteresting
(D) inactive
(E) spontaneous

10. Which of the following conclusions can be most reliably drawn from the information above?

(A) Migratory behavior in animals is acquired rather than innate.
(B) Animals in zoo environments rarely exhibit active behavior.
(C) Magellanic penguins in the wild spend most of their time swimming.
(D) The close quarters of a zoo environment suppress animal migratory behavior.
(E) Animals sometimes mimic the behavior they see in other animals.

F. QUIZ VI (Short Single-Paragraph; 10 items; 15 minutes)

Items 1-2 are based on the following passage.

A democracy is beyond question the freest government because everyone is equally protected by the laws and equally has a voice in making them. I do
Line
5 not say an equal voice. Some people have stronger lungs than others and can express more forcibly their opinions of public affairs. Others may not speak very loudly, yet they have a faculty of saying more in a short time; and in the case of others, who speak little or not at all, what they do say contains good sense and so
10 carries a lot of weight. So, all things considered, every citizen has not, in this sense of the word, an equal voice. But the right being equal, what is the problem if it is unequally exercised?

1. Which of the following best describes the relationship between the question posed in lines 12-13 and the rest of the paragraph?

   (A) The question is rhetorical in that the author believes that it has already been answered.
   (B) The question is unanswerable because the author has failed to define key terms.
   (C) The question is open-ended, and the answer depends on how one defines "democracy."
   (D) The question is ambiguous because the answer depends on the reader's preference.
   (E) The question is unfair because it presupposes that the reader accepts the author's position.

2. In line 7, the word "faculty" most nearly means

   (A) ability
   (B) teachers
   (C) tendency
   (D) language
   (E) conclusion

Item 3 is based on the following passage.

A dictionary, while it sets forth the spelling, pronunciation, and meaning of individual words, does not serve as a model of style for good writing. I think it
Line
5 was Jonathan Swift who proposed forming an academy of learned scholars who would settle the true spelling, accentuation and proper meaning of words and the purest, most simple, and perfect phraseology of language. It has always seemed to me, however, that if some great master of style could give an example of
10 good composition, which might serve as a model to future speakers and writers, it would do more to fix the orthography, idiomatic usage, and sentence structure than all the dictionaries and institutes that have been ever made.

3. Which of the following best describes the main point of the passage?

   (A) Good writers know instinctively how to use words to create clear and unambiguous sentences.
   (B) An academy of scholars would provide more authoritative guidance to writers than a dictionary.
   (C) An example of good writing would serve as a reference for spelling, meaning, and sentence structure.
   (D) Examples of good writing by accomplished authors would make the use of dictionaries unnecessary.
   (E) Dictionaries do not include models of good writing for authors to follow.

Item 4 is based on the following passage.

Goethe's *Faust* can hardly be said to be a play designed primarily for the galleries. In general, it might be ranked with *Macbeth* or *She Stoops to Conquer* or
Line *Richelieu.* One never sees it fail, however, that "Faust"
5 will fill the gallery with people who would never dream of going to see one of the other plays just mentioned; and the applause never leaves one in doubt as to the reasons for Goethe's popularity. It is the suggestiveness of the love scenes, the red costume of
10 Mephistopheles, the electrical effects, and the rain of fire, that give the desired thrill—all pure melodrama of course. *Faust* is a good show as well as a good play.

4. The author implies that the people mentioned in line 5 would not attend a performance of *Macbeth* because

(A) *Macbeth* is considered to be inferior to *Faust* as a work of literature
(B) the production of *Macbeth* would not include suggestive scenes and special effects
(C) the galleries would be filled with theatergoers who do not understand the play
(D) melodrama is not intended to appeal to people who are hoping to be entertained
(E) certain themes in *Macbeth* might not be suitable for all audiences

Items 5-6 are based on the following passage.

The transportation sector is responsible for a large majority of air pollutants in urban areas. Biofuels, because of the oxygen they contain, can reduce carbon monoxide emissions that result from incomplete
Line combustion. Ground-level ozone (smog) is a result of a
5 complex reaction triggered by ultraviolet radiation, but the principal ingredients are carbon monoxide, hydrocarbons, and nitrogen oxides. The addition of biofuels to gasoline products reduces incomplete combustion and therefore carbon monoxide and
10 unburned tailpipe hydrocarbon emissions. On the other hand, a 10%-ethanol gasoline is more volatile than pure gasoline or ethanol, so hydrocarbon evaporation from the fuel system may be higher. Furthermore, nitrogen oxide formation increases with combustion
15 temperature, so its production increases slightly with oxygenated fuels. However, the overall impact of using biofuels is to substantially reduce pollutant emissions.

5. The author regards the use of biofuels as

(A) entailing some environmental costs but on the balance beneficial
(B) preferable in every regard to conventional fuels such as gasoline
(C) inefficient and actually likely to result in an increase in pollution
(D) able to do little to reduce pollution but likely to cause no environmental harm
(E) able to reduce pollution but that any reductions would likely be insignificant

6. In line 12, the word "volatile" most nearly means

(A) extremely unstable
(B) evaporating quickly
(C) environmentally favorable
(D) completely burned
(E) chemically complex

Item 7 is based on the following passage.

Unlike most cells, which have a short lifespan, nerve cells, which are generated during gestation or a short time after birth, live a long time. Brain neurons can live over 100 years. In an adult, when neurons die
Line 5 because of disease or injury, they are not usually replaced. However, recent research shows that in a few brain regions, new neurons can be born. In general, though, to prevent their own death, living neurons must constantly maintain and remodel themselves. If cell
10 cleanup and repair slows down or stops for any reason, nerve cells cannot function well and eventually die.

7. The author mentions the findings of recent research (lines 6-7) primarily as

(A) proof of the theory that nerve cells are formed during gestation or shortly after birth
(B) an example of the kind of cell cleanup and repair that is needed to preserve nerve cells
(C) further evidence for the notion that neurons are susceptible to disease and injury
(D) a qualification on the general rule that neurons are not replaced
(E) a counter-example to the principle that nerve cells live a long time

Items 8-9 are based on the following passage.

In the decade following World War I, millions of Americans believed that there existed a radical conspiracy to overthrow the United States government and that a "Red revolution" might begin at any
Line 5 moment. Newspaper headlines shouted news of strikes and Bolshevist riots. Properly elected members of the Assembly of New York State were expelled because they had been elected as members of the Socialist Party. The Vice-President cited as a dangerous
10 manifestation of radicalism in women's colleges the fact that Radcliffe debaters upheld the affirmative in a debate that labor unions are essential to successful collective bargaining. It was an era of lawless and disorderly defense of law and order, of unconstitutional
15 defense of the Constitution, of suspicion and civil conflict—literally, a reign of terror.

8. The most important feature of the logical development of the passage is the

(A) presentation of competing theories
(B) use of examples
(C) definition of important terms
(D) introduction of statistics
(E) refutation of an argument

9. By the use of the word "shouted" (line 5), the author intends to suggest that the newspapers

(A) accurately reported important events
(B) overlooked evidence of a conspiracy
(C) incited strikes and civil unrest
(D) invented stories about Bolsheviks
(E) exaggerated the danger of revolution

Item 10 is based on the following passage.

    Chukar partridge chicks can run up a tree by
flapping their wings. The beating wings serve the same
purpose as spoilers on racecars: to provide better
Line traction. Similarly, feathered dinosaurs may have
5 flapped their primitive wings to better run up inclines,
helping them to catch prey. Thus, the "proto-wing"
may have offered a non-flight-related survival benefit,
and only later did this wing-beating behavior lead to
the aerial possibilities of wings. This evolutionary path
10 of primitive birds toward flight is different from two
previous models: the arboreal model, in which birds
first launched themselves from trees, and the cursorial
model, in which they took off from the ground.

10. The author of the passage primarily intends to

    (A) offer a third alternative to an either/or
        challenge
    (B) provide a counterexample to refute a popular
        theory
    (C) point out a contradiction in a competing
        position
    (D) attack the proponent of a plan rather than its
        merits
    (E) shift the burden of proof to an opponent of a
        plan

EDUCATORS' #1 CHOICE FOR SCHOOL IMPROVEMENT

Strategy Summary Sheet
CRITICAL READING: PASSAGES

STRUCTURE OF CRITICAL READING: PASSAGES: There are four types of Critical Reading: Passages formats: long single-passage selections (400-500 words, followed by 10 items), long double-passage selections (750-850 words between two passages, followed by 12 items), short single-paragraph selections (100 words, followed by 2 items), and short double-paragraph selections (200 words between two single-paragraph passages, followed by 4 items). Items that follow the long double-passage and the short double-paragraph formats will be based on the two provided passages and the relationship between them. The long double-passage selection and the short double-paragraph selection occur only once per exam. The SAT contains Critical Reading: Passages items in three Critical Reading test sections. The PSAT contains 35 Critical Reading: Passages items that are distributed between two 25-minute Critical Reading test sections.

ITEM-TYPES: Knowing the seven item-types can help you to quickly identify what an item is asking.

1. *Main Idea*: Main Idea items ask about the central theme that unifies the passage(s).

    EXAMPLES: *Which of the following is the main point of the passage?*
    The primary purpose of the passage is to....

2. *Explicit Detail*: Explicit Detail items ask about details that are specifically mentioned in the passage. This type of item differs from a Main Idea item in that explicit details are points provided by the author in developing the main idea of the passage. Explicit Detail items provide "locator words" that identify the required information in the passage.

    EXAMPLES: *The author mentions which of the following?*
    According to the passage,...?

3. *Vocabulary*: Vocabulary items test the understanding of a word or phrase in context. In addition to testing vocabulary, these items incorporate elements that are similar to Critical Reading: Sentence Completions items. The nature of the Vocabulary items indicates two points. First, the correct answer choice will make sense when it is substituted for the referenced word. Second, the correct answer choice may not be the most commonly used meaning of the word; in fact, if it were, then what would be the point of including the item on the test? Thus, the general strategy for this type of item is to favor the less commonly used meaning.

    EXAMPLES: *The word —— in line ## means....*
    In line ##, what is the best definition of —— ?

4. *Development*: Development items ask about the overall structure of the passage or about the logical role played by a specific part of the passage.

    EXAMPLES: *The author develops the passage primarily by....*
    The author mentions...in order to....

5. *Implied Idea*: Rather than ask about what is specifically stated in the passage, Implied Idea items ask about what can be logically inferred from what is stated in the passage. For example, the passage might explain that a certain

organism (*X*) is found only in the presence of another organism (*Y*). An accompanying Implied Idea item might ask the following question: "If organism *Y* is not present, what can be inferred?" Since the passage implies that in the absence of *Y*, *X* cannot be present, the answer would be "*X* is not present." Since this type of item generally builds on a specific detail, "locator words" for identifying information in the passage are often provided in the item stem.

> EXAMPLES: *The passage implies that....*
> *The author uses the phrase "..." to mean....*

6. *Application*: Application items are similar to Implied Idea items, but they go one step further: Examinees must apply what they have learned from the passage to a new situation.

> EXAMPLES: *With which of the following statements would the author most likely agree?*
> *The passage is most probably taken from which of the following sources?*

7. *Voice*: Voice items ask about the author's attitude toward a specific detail or the overall tone of the passage.

> EXAMPLES: *The tone of the passage can best be described as....*
> *The author regards...as....*

GENERAL STRATEGY: This is not an exact science. Practice is essential to mastering the following techniques:

1. *Read the first two sentences of each passage in the test section.* There is usually an introductory paragraph for excerpted passages that identifies the author and provides a brief description of the selection. Read this introductory material to gauge interest, and read the first two sentences of each passage to determine its difficulty-level. Label each passage as either "Easy" or "Hard" based on your initial understanding of the material and your level of interest. Analyze the easier passages first.

2. *Preview the first and last sentences of the selection.* If the selection is more than one paragraph long, begin with a preview of the first and last sentences of each paragraph.

3. *Preview the item stems for a given passage.* Code each item stem as one of the following three levels of reading comprehension:

   a. *Level 1—Appreciation of the General Theme*: The first level of reading, appreciation of the general theme, is the most basic. Main Idea items and items about the overall development of the selection test whether you understand the passage at the most general level. The first sentence of a paragraph—often the topic sentence—may provide a summary of the content of that paragraph. Also, the last sentence of a paragraph usually provides concluding material that may also be helpful in understanding the general theme of the passage.

   > EXAMPLE: Main Idea items

   b. *Level 2—Understanding of Specific Points*: The second level of reading, understanding specific points, takes you deeper into the selection. Explicit Detail items, items about the meanings of words, and items about the logical role of details all test your ability to read carefully. Since this is an "open-book" test, you can always return to the selection. Therefore, if something is highly technical or difficult to understand, do not dwell on it for too long—come back later if necessary.

   > EXAMPLES: Explicit Detail items
   > Vocabulary items
   > Development items

   c. *Level 3—Evaluation of the text*: The third level of reading, evaluation of the text, takes you even deeper into the selection. Implied Idea, Application, and Voice items ask not just for understanding, but require a judgment or an evaluation of what you have read. This is why these items are usually the most difficult.

EXAMPLES: Implied Idea items
Application items
Voice items

4. *Read the passage.* Ask what the author is attempting to describe, especially in the case of Evaluation items. Also, read the first sentence in each paragraph prior to reading the entire selection. This step is optional, depending on the ease of the selection, your personal preference, and the time available. Bracket difficult material, either mentally or with some sort of a mark, and then simply revisit it if necessary or if time permits. Instead of wasting time re-reading, attempt to understand the context in which the author introduces a particular concept.

5. *Circle the answers to the items in the test booklet, and transcribe the answers to all the items for a passage to the answer sheet after finishing each passage.* Circle the answers to the items in the test booklet. This approach helps increase accuracy and makes checking your work easier and more efficient. For each selection, transcribe the answers to the answer sheet together as a group. Only when the time limit approaches should you transcribe the answers individually.

ADDITIONAL STRATEGIES FROM IN-CLASS DISCUSSION: _____

_____

_____

_____

_____

_____

_____

_____

_____

_____

_____

_____

_____

_____

_____

_____

_____

_____

_____

Critical Reading:
Sentence Completions

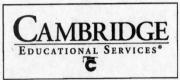

CAMBRIDGE
EDUCATIONAL SERVICES®

EDUCATORS' #1 CHOICE FOR SCHOOL IMPROVEMENT

Cambridge Course Concept Outline
CRITICAL READING: SENTENCE COMPLETIONS

CORE LESSON

DIRECTIONS: The items in this section accompany the in-class review of the Sentence Completions concepts and skills tested by the SAT and PSAT/NMSQT. You will work through the items with your instructor in class. Each sentence below has one or two blanks, each blank indicating that something has been omitted. Beneath the sentence are five lettered words or sets of words. Choose the word or set of words that, when inserted in the sentence, *best* fits the meaning of the sentence as a whole. Answers are on page 984.

1. His —— should not be confused with cowardice; during the war, I saw him on several occasions risk his own life while rescuing members of his unit.

   (A) heroism
   (B) indifference
   (C) caution
   (D) notoriety → official, that witnesses (publically known)
   (E) confidence

2. Although critics denounced the film as silly and inane, people flocked to the theater to see it, guaranteeing its —— success.

   (A) scholarly
   (B) hypothetical
   (C) critical
   (D) financial
   (E) eventual

3. Even the most arbitrary and —— corporation today must be aware of the attitudes of its employees; management may at times be more or less ——, but all must respect the power of an organized work force.

   (A) influential. .outraged
   (B) prosperous. .precipitous
   (C) flexible. .patronizing
   (D) authoritarian. .responsive
   (E) susceptible. .permanent

4. The ease with which the candidate answers difficult questions creates the impression that she has been a public servant for years, but in reality she entered politics only ——.

   (A) securely
   (B) enthusiastically
   (C) frequently
   (D) needfully
   (E) recently

5. Though afflicted by headaches, nausea, and respiratory difficulties, Nietzsche refused to let his —— problems prevent him from writing.

   (A) imaginary
   (B) financial
   (C) emotional
   (D) theoretical
   (E) physical

6. The university should —— the function of the alumni fund so that its importance will be better appreciated by the school's graduates who are asked to contribute to it.

   (A) revoke
   (B) elucidate → explain
   (C) ascertain → to garner.
   (D) prescribe
   (E) entice → bribing

7. In spite of the —— of the minister's sermon, when it was finished, most of the congregation was ——.

   (A) passion. .fidgety
   (B) tedium. .fearful
   (C) understanding. .merciful
   (D) obtrusiveness. .hurt
   (E) veracity. .inspired

8. For Thomas Aquinas, the Scholastic thinker and author of the *Summa Theologica*, the question of angels dancing on a pinhead was not —— but a —— issue of vital import to his project of reconciling Aristotelean metaphysics with medieval Church doctrine.

   (A) whimsy. .profound
   (B) insightful. .complex
   (C) comical. .superficial
   (D) premeditated. .serious
   (E) caprice. .fanciful

diamond christine melhado

9. The rocket scientists had fully expected the thermothrockle to hydrolize under the intense ionizing radiation requiring the mission to be aborted; but the astronauts —— the problem by tekelating the suborbital flexion, and the mission continued.

   (A) recreated
   (B) transmitted
   (C) misjudged
   (D) circumvented
   (E) proscribed

10. The passage of the mass transit bill over the Governor's veto, despite opposition by key leaders in the legislature, was a devastating —— for the party machinery and suggests that other, much-needed legislation may receive similar treatment in the future.

    (A) victory
    (B) optimism
    (C) compromise
    (D) slap
    (E) setback

11. Since the evidence of the manuscript's —— is ——, its publication will be postponed until a team of scholars has examined it and declared it to be genuine.

    (A) authenticity. .inconclusive
    (B) truthfulness. .tarnished
    (C) veracity. .indubitable
    (D) legitimacy. .infallible
    (E) profundity. .forthcoming

12. Although Barbara argues strongly that current policies are unjust, she does not —— any particular changes.

    (A) reject
    (B) presume
    (C) advocate
    (D) remember
    (E) oppose

13. Despite the fact that they had clinched the divisional title long before the end of regular season play, the team continued to play every game as though it were ——.

    (A) superfluous
    (B) irrational
    (C) lengthy
    (D) hopeless
    (E) vital

14. Although the terms "toad" and "frog" refer to two different animals belonging to different genera, some students —— the two.

    (A) distinguish
    (B) confuse
    (C) respect
    (D) observe
    (E) mention

15. The terms "toad" and "frog" refer to two different animals belonging to different genera, and careful students —— between the two.

    (A) intermingle
    (B) ignore
    (C) distinguish
    (D) confuse
    (E) dispute

16. The ascent of the mountain is ——, but anyone who makes it to the top is rewarded by a spectacular view.

    (A) helpful
    (B) easy
    (C) unique
    (D) unpleasant
    (E) automatic

17. Although there are more female students at the college than male students, the women seem to have a(n) —— influence on the student government.

    (A) enormous
    (B) negligible
    (C) provocative
    (D) venerable
    (E) active

18. Unless we —— our water resources, there may come a time when our supplies of clean water are completely depleted.

(A) predict
(B) use
(C) conserve
(D) replace
(E) tap

19. If we continue to consume our fossil fuel supply without restraint, then someday it will be ——.

(A) replenished
(B) limited
(C) useless
(D) available
(E) exhausted

20. The critics must have detested the play, for the review was not merely ——, it was ——.

(A) unhappy. .miserable
(B) laudatory. .enthusiastic
(C) sincere. .long
(D) appreciative. .stinging
(E) critical. .scathing

21. The judge, after ruling that the article had unjustly —— the reputation of the architect, ordered the magazine to —— its libelous statements in print.

(A) praised. .communicate
(B) injured. .retract
(C) sullied. .publicize
(D) damaged. .disseminate
(E) extolled. .produce

22. Joyce's novel *Finnegan's Wake* continues to —— critics, including those who find it incomprehensible and call it ——.

(A) appall. .genial
(B) captivate. .nonsensical
(C) baffle. .transparent
(D) bore. .compelling
(E) entertain. .monotonous

23. People who use their desktop computers for writing can become almost hypnotized by the unbroken succession of letters and text; in such cases, a computer video game can supply a welcome ——.

(A) burden
(B) diversion
(C) handicap
(D) predicament
(E) insight

24. There is no necessary connection between a dollar and what can be purchased for a dollar; the value of money is —— and can be —— by supply and demand.

(A) arbitrary. .altered
(B) predetermined. .overruled
(C) conventional. .inspired
(D) lackluster. .improved
(E) optional. .prevented

25. Her acceptance speech was ——, eliciting thunderous applause at several points.

(A) tedious
(B) well-received
(C) cowardly
(D) uninteresting
(E) poorly written

26. The public debates were often ——, finally deteriorating into mudslinging contests.

(A) informative
(B) bitter
(C) theoretical
(D) inspiring
(E) insightful

27. Elementary school children, who have not yet been repeatedly disappointed by other people, are much more —— than older and more cynical high school students.

(A) inquisitive
(B) relaxed
(C) enjoyable
(D) trusting
(E) enlightened

28. Nutritionists have found that certain elements long known to be —— in large quantities are —— to life in small amounts.

    (A) lethal. .essential
    (B) deadly. .painful
    (C) healthful. .pleasurable
    (D) fatal. .unbearable
    (E) unfashionable. .important

29. It is highly characteristic of business' —— attitude that little or no interest was evinced in urban renewal until similar undertakings elsewhere proved that such projects could be ——.

    (A) prestigious. .feasible
    (B) capitalistic. .rigid
    (C) degrading. .completed
    (D) mercantile. .insensitive
    (E) pragmatic. .profitable

30. George Bernard Shaw expressed his —— for technological progress when he said that the human race is just interested in finding more —— ways of exterminating itself.

    (A) hope. .impartial
    (B) regard. .remote
    (C) preference. .violent
    (D) support. .effective
    (E) contempt. .efficient

31. Although this disease threatens the lives of several thousand people every year, the —— of supplies and equipment has —— the progress of medical research for a cure.

    (A) discontinuance. .ensured
    (B) scarcity. .hampered
    (C) rationing. .enhanced
    (D) squandering. .facilitated
    (E) financing. .neglected

32. The committee's report is not as valuable as it might have been because it addresses only the symptoms and not the —— causes of the problem.

    (A) unimpeachable
    (B) ephemeral
    (C) underlying
    (D) incipient
    (E) superficial

33. Calvin had long been known for his mendacity, but even those who knew him well were surprised at the —— explanation he gave for the shortage of funds.

    (A) elegant
    (B) disingenuous
    (C) sincere
    (D) dogmatic
    (E) bitter

NOTES AND STRATEGIES

CHALLENGE ITEMS

DIRECTIONS: This section contains Sentence Completions items in the top quartile of difficulty. Each sentence below has one or two blanks, each blank indicating that something has been omitted. Beneath the sentence are five lettered words or sets of words. Choose the word or set of words that, when inserted in the sentence, *best* fits the meaning of the sentence as a whole. Answers are on page 984.

1. The judge shouted to counsel on both sides that he would —— no argument on the issue and enjoined them to ——.

   (A) hear. .vote
   (B) accept. .speculation
   (C) brook. .silence
   (D) entertain. .toleration
   (E) contrive. .cease

2. In order to —— the deadline for submitting the research paper, the student tried to —— additional time from the professor.

   (A) extend. .wheedle
   (B) accelerate. .obtain
   (C) postpone. .forego
   (D) sustain. .imagine
   (E) conceal. .procure

3. Due to the —— of the materials needed to manufacture the product and the ever-increasing demand for it, it is highly probable that the final cost to the consumer will ——.

   (A) immensity. .evolve
   (B) paucity. .escalate
   (C) scarcity. .relax
   (D) acuity. .stabilize
   (E) certainty. .fluctuate

4. After the —— journey, the President sent a request to the Prime Minister asking that they —— their meeting until he had had an opportunity to refresh himself.

   (A) exhilarating. .commence
   (B) lengthy. .defray
   (C) exhausting. .defer
   (D) dilatory. .reschedule
   (E) leisurely. .accelerate

5. Following the aborted Bay of Pigs invasion, Congressional opinion about the CIA shifted from almost universal —— of the agency as both essential and highly professional to widespread —— its value as a national policy tool and the integrity of its members.

   (A) endorsement. .skepticism about
   (B) acceptance. .control over
   (C) knowledge. .doubt about
   (D) condemnation. .destruction of
   (E) praise. .victimization of

6. Jazz is an American art form that is now —— in Europe through the determined efforts of —— in France, Scandinavia, and Germany.

   (A) foundering. .governments
   (B) diminishing. .musicians
   (C) appreciated. .opponents
   (D) waning. .novices
   (E) flourishing. .expatriates

7. One of the kidnappers, when left alone with the hostage, attempted to persuade him that they were neither —— nor ——, but only interested in calling international attention to their cause.

   (A) impeccable. .sincere
   (B) redoubtable. .condescending
   (C) antagonistic. .vindictive
   (D) recalcitrant. .clandestine
   (E) intrepid. .compliant

8. Although the comedian was very clever, many of his remarks were —— and —— lawsuits against him for slander.

   (A) derogatory. .resulted in
   (B) pithy. .came upon
   (C) protracted. .forestalled
   (D) depraved. .assuaged
   (E) recanted. .sparked

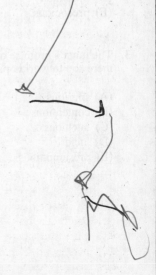

NOTES AND STRATEGIES

idk!
stupid boy..

9. Because the disease is relatively rare and doctors know little about it, any treatment prescribed can —— the pain but cannot —— the patient.

   (A) alleviate. .infect
   (B) palliate. .cure
   (C) abate. .affect
   (D) minimize. .revive
   (E) intensify. .rejuvenate

10. The —— customer was —— by the manager's prompt action and apology.

    (A) pecuniary. .appalled
    (B) weary. .enervated
    (C) sedulous. .consoled
    (D) intrepid. .mortified
    (E) irate. .mollified

11. You must act with —— if you want to buy your airline ticket before tomorrow's price increase.

    (A) celerity
    (B) clemency
    (C) facility
    (D) lassitude
    (E) laxity

12. The —— background music hinted of the dangers threatening the movie's heroine.

    (A) trenchant
    (B) ebullient
    (C) sardonic
    (D) portentous
    (E) precocious

13. The junta's promise of free elections was ——, a mere sop to world opinion.

    (A) spurious
    (B) contentious
    (C) unctuous
    (D) lucid
    (E) presumptuous

14. His —— manner served to hide the fact that he secretly indulged in the very vices he publicly ——.

    (A) sedulous. .dispelled
    (B) sanctimonious. .condemned
    (C) dogmatic. .espoused
    (D) stentorian. .prescribed
    (E) candid. .promulgated

15. The Eighteenth Amendment, often called the Prohibition Act, —— the sale of alcoholic beverages.

    (A) prolonged
    (B) preempted
    (C) sanctioned
    (D) proscribed
    (E) encouraged

16. The —— attitudes politicians have today cause them to —— at the slightest hint of controversy.

    (A) dauntless. .recoil
    (B) craven. .cower
    (C) pusillanimous. .prevail
    (D) undaunted. .quail
    (E) fractious. .grovel

17. Mrs. Jenkins, upon hearing that her arm was broken, looked —— at the doctor.

    (A) jovially
    (B) plaintively
    (C) fortuitously
    (D) serendipitously
    (E) opportunely

18. Even —— pleasures may leave —— memories.

    (A) ephemeral. .lasting
    (B) emphatic. .stalwart
    (C) transitory. .fleeting
    (D) surreptitious. .secret
    (E) enigmatic. .mysterious

19. Unsure of her skills in English, the young girl was —— when called on to speak in class.

   (A) remunerative
   (B) transient
   (C) reticent
   (D) sartorial
   (E) resilient

20. Each spring, the —— tree put out fewer and fewer leaves.

   (A) ambient
   (B) malignant
   (C) desultory
   (D) moribund
   (E) reclusive

21. The bully's menacing, —— manner was actually just for show; in reality, it was entirely ——.

   (A) imperturbable. .vapid
   (B) truculent. .affected
   (C) stringent. .credulous
   (D) supercilious. .blatant
   (E) parsimonious. .contentious

22. A public official must be —— in all his or her actions to avoid even the appearance of impropriety.

   (A) redolent
   (B) unctuous
   (C) baleful
   (D) circumspect
   (E) propitious

23. She was —— as a child, accepting without question everything she was told.

   (A) obstreperous
   (B) recalcitrant
   (C) credulous
   (D) truculent
   (E) tearful

24. Warned by smoke alarms that a widespread fire was ——, the ushers —— the theatre immediately.

   (A) expected. .filled
   (B) ubiquitous. .purged
   (C) eminent. .checked
   (D) imminent. .evacuated
   (E) insidious. .obviated

25. The municipality attracted the country's scientific elite and —— them, insulating them entirely from the problems of ordinary civilian life.

   (A) cajoled
   (B) muted
   (C) mused
   (D) cosseted
   (E) impeded

26. Although the bank executive gave the appearance of a(n) —— businessman, he was really a ——.

   (A) dedicated. .capitalist
   (B) respectable. .reprobate
   (C) depraved. .profligate
   (D) empathetic. .philanthropist
   (E) churlish. .miscreant

27. During a campaign, politicians often engage in —— debate, attacking each other's proposals in a torrent of —— words.

   (A) acerbic. .amiable
   (B) acrimonious. .malicious
   (C) intensive. .nebulous
   (D) garrulous. .inarticulate
   (E) impassioned. .vapid

28. —— by her family, the woman finally agreed to sell the farm.

   (A) Decimated
   (B) Importuned
   (C) Encumbered
   (D) Interpolated
   (E) Designated

29. The ghost of his royal father —— the young Hamlet to avenge his murder.

   (A) enervates
   (B) parlays
   (C) marauds
   (D) exhorts
   (E) inculcates

30. A life of hardship and poverty has —— them to petty physical discomforts.

   (A) ascribed
   (B) inured
   (C) remonstrated
   (D) deferred
   (E) impugned

31. Although he was known as a —— old miser, his anonymous gifts to charity were always ——.

   (A) grasping. .tasteless
   (B) spendthrift. .gracious
   (C) gregarious. .selfish
   (D) penurious. .generous
   (E) stingy. .mangy

32. The composer was —— enough to praise the work of a musician he detested.

   (A) magnanimous
   (B) loquacious
   (C) munificent
   (D) parsimonious
   (E) surreptitious

33. Though the law's —— purpose was to curtail false advertising, its actual result was to —— free speech.

   (A) potential. .preclude
   (B) mendacious. .eschew
   (C) ostensible. .circumscribe
   (D) illicit. .reconcile
   (E) recalcitrant. .repress

34. The royal astrologers were commanded to determine the most —— date for the king's coronation.

   (A) propitious
   (B) ostensible
   (C) aberrant
   (D) resplendent
   (E) obsequious

35. The poem by the great satirist was dripping with venom and was —— with scorn.

   (A) contentious
   (B) discordant
   (C) redolent
   (D) sardonic
   (E) vicarious

36. The new regime immediately —— laws implementing the promised reforms.

   (A) vouchsafed
   (B) ensconced
   (C) augmented
   (D) promulgated
   (E) parlayed

37. A long illness can —— even the strongest constitution.

   (A) obviate
   (B) inculcate
   (C) bolster
   (D) enervate
   (E) disparage

38. The city —— to the advancing invaders without firing a single shot.

   (A) extolled
   (B) regressed
   (C) equivocated
   (D) dissembled
   (E) capitulated

39. If you find peeling potatoes to be ——, perhaps you'd prefer to scrub the floors?

    (A) felicitous
    (B) remunerative
    (C) onerous
    (D) vilifying
    (E) redundant

40. To strengthen her client's case, the lawyer sought to put the —— of the witness in doubt.

    (A) laxity
    (B) posterity
    (C) probity
    (D) onus
    (E) sensitivity

41. His —— CD collection included everything from Bach to rock.

    (A) divisive
    (B) effusive
    (C) eclectic
    (D) intrinsic
    (E) laconic

42. Her statements were so —— that we were left in doubt as to her real intentions.

    (A) equitable
    (B) equivocal
    (C) innocuous
    (D) dogmatic
    (E) incisive

43. Blue whales grow to —— size and must eat tons of plankton to —— their huge appetites.

    (A) prodigious. .satiate
    (B) effusive. .assuage
    (C) colossal. .deplete
    (D) fortuitous. .exhort
    (E) obstreperous. .vanquish

44. Both coffee and tea have beneficial as well as —— side-effects; while they stimulate the heart and help overcome fatigue, they also —— insomnia and other nervous disorders.

    (A) injurious. .exacerbate
    (B) malignant. .interrupt
    (C) salutary. .heighten
    (D) negligible. .forestall
    (E) specious. .prevent

45. The Parks Department claims that there is a —— of wildlife in the New York City area, and that species that have not lived in the area for most of the century are once again being sighted.

    (A) resurgence
    (B) paucity
    (C) superstructure
    (D) prototype
    (E) compendium

46. Although he had inherited a substantial amount of money, his —— soon led to his filing for bankruptcy.

    (A) prodigality
    (B) volubility
    (C) tenacity
    (D) fastidiousness
    (E) animosity

47. The sonatas of Beethoven represent the —— of classicism, but they also contain the seeds of its destruction, romanticism, which —— the sonata form by allowing emotion rather than tradition to shape the music.

    (A) denigration. .perpetuates
    (B) pinnacle. .shatters
    (C) plethora. .heightens
    (D) fruition. .restores
    (E) ignorance. .encumbers

48. In the Middle Ages, the Benedictine monasteries were often —— of civilization and a refuge for science in an otherwise —— and superstitious world.

   (A) arbiters. .scholarly
   (B) brethren. .sanctimonious
   (C) forerunners. .erudite
   (D) conservators. .barbarous
   (E) advocates. .rarefied

49. Recent studies demonstrate that personal memory is actually quite ——, subject to contamination and reshaping so that aspects of a person's memory are apt to be —— or erroneous.

   (A) implausible. .inaccurate
   (B) volatile. .subjective
   (C) malleable. .insensitive
   (D) inhibited. .recalcitrant
   (E) comprehensive. .reflective

50. It is difficult for a modern audience, accustomed to the —— of film and television, to appreciate opera with its grand spectacle and —— gestures.

   (A) irreverence. .hapless
   (B) sophistication. .monotonous
   (C) minutiae. .extravagant
   (D) plurality. .subtle
   (E) flamboyance. .inane

51. Behaviorism was a protest against the —— psychological tradition that held that the proper data of psychology were ——, which reflected one's consciousness or state of mind.

   (A) redoubtable. .superficial
   (B) moralistic. .irrelevant
   (C) rudimentary. .material
   (D) newfangled. .preposterous
   (E) orthodox. .mentalistic

52. Psychologists and science fiction writers argue that people persist in believing in extraterrestrial life, even though the federal government —— all such beliefs, because people need to feel a personal sense of —— in a godless universe.

   (A) decries. .morbidity
   (B) endorses. .despair
   (C) creates. .guilt
   (D) discourages. .spirituality
   (E) debunks. .alienation

53. Pollen grains and spores that are 200 million years old are now being extracted from shale and are —— the theory that the breakup of the continents occurred in stages; in fact, it seems that the breakups occurred almost ——.

   (A) refining. .blatantly
   (B) reshaping. .simultaneously
   (C) countermanding. .imperceptibly
   (D) forging. .vicariously
   (E) supporting. .haphazardly

54. The period of the fall of the Roman Empire was a dark period for —— as well as for the other arts, for men had forgotten how to cook; in fact, it seemed as if they had lost all interest in —— matters.

   (A) gastronomy. .culinary
   (B) astrology. .sedentary
   (C) histrionics. . scientific
   (D) numismatics. .cultural
   (E) aesthetics. .clandestine

55. Although the manager of the corporation was wrong, his stubborn refusal to —— or even to compromise —— an already tense situation.

   (A) arbitrate. .thwarted
   (B) capitulate. .exacerbated
   (C) censure. .rectified
   (D) mandate. .violated
   (E) scrutinize. .contained

56. The design of the building was magnificent, but its classical lines seemed almost —— and out of place in the business district that was —— ultramodern steel and glass skyscrapers.

   (A) garish. .beleaguered by
   (B) anachronistic. .replete with
   (C) untoward. .bereft of
   (D) grotesque. .enhanced by
   (E) sanguine. .populated by

57. Animal behaviorists theorize that dogs are more —— than cats because they are pack animals, whereas cats, which are solitary hunters, are more independent and —— and therefore less likely to try to please their owners.

   (A) precocious. .complex
   (B) aggressive. .obsequious
   (C) tractable. .obdurate
   (D) intelligent. .resilient
   (E) formidable. .reliable

NOTES AND STRATEGIES

TIMED-PRACTICE QUIZZES

A. QUIZ I (12 items; 10 minutes)

DIRECTIONS: This section contains three Sentence Completions quizzes. While being timed, complete each quiz. Each sentence below has one or two blanks, each blank indicating that something has been omitted. Beneath the sentence are five lettered words or sets of words. Choose the word or set of words that, when inserted in the sentence, *best* fits the meaning of the sentence as a whole. Answers are on page 984.

1. —— the activities of her employees, the director refused to —— their methods.

 (A) Disarming. .condone
 (B) Applauding. .question
 (C) Repudiating. .punish
 (D) Handling. .oversee
 (E) Approving. .arrogate

2. The —— soldier —— at the idea that he was to go to battle.

 (A) luckless. .rejoiced
 (B) youthful. .retired
 (C) unwilling. .recoiled
 (D) frail. .relapsed
 (E) vigorous. .repined

3. The critic thought the film was completely unrealistic; he termed the plot —— and the acting ——.

 (A) contrived. .unbelievable
 (B) imaginative. .genuine
 (C) ambitious. .courageous
 (D) artificial. .unparalleled
 (E) absorbing. .uninspiring

4. Dedicated wildlife photographers willingly travel great distances and gladly endure considerable hardship to share with audiences their —— for the natural world.

 (A) distaste
 (B) contempt
 (C) preference
 (D) expectations
 (E) enthusiasm

5. Though the story is set in a small village in a remote area of South America, the novel's themes are so —— that its events could have occurred anywhere and involved any of us at any time.

 (A) mythical
 (B) universal
 (C) overstated
 (D) anguished
 (E) complex

6. A good historian merely makes —— and accumulates facts; a great historian uses —— to understand why events occurred the way they did.

 (A) statements. .research
 (B) references. .evidence
 (C) observations. .imagination
 (D) arguments. .texts
 (E) errors. .sympathy

7. The goal of the archaeological dig is to recover as many artifacts as possible before they are —— by the construction of the new bridge.

 (A) preserved
 (B) revived
 (C) reproduced
 (D) obliterated
 (E) illustrated

8. The experienced ambassador was generally an —— person who regained her composure quickly even on those —— occasions when she was close to losing her temper.

 (A) articulate. .momentous
 (B) imperturbable. .infrequent
 (C) unforgiving. .numerous
 (D) idealistic. .rare
 (E) insistent. .trying

E 9. In Doyle's famous detective stories, Mycroft, the brother of Sherlock Holmes, is described as quite ———, going only from his apartment to his office to his club and back to his apartment.

(A) illustrious
(B) omnivorous → both meat / veggies.
(C) loquacious? → very talkative.
(D) spontaneous
(E) sedentary

C 10. Determinist philosophers have argued that our moral intuitions are ——— rather than learned and that they are dictated by genetic makeup.

(A) transcendental → to surpass
(B) fortuitous → accidental
(C) innate → born w/ us
(D) contingent → something that may occur
(E) empirical → based on observation.

learned.
genetic make-up.
pg. 470 - 471

english grammar spelling vocabulary.

B 11. The rescue workers' gnawing sense of ——— developed into concern and ultimately despair as they gradually approached the remote site of the car crash.

(A) resignation
(B) foreboding
(C) anticipation
(D) urgency
(E) duplicity

E 12. Karen was ——— in her vindictiveness, frequently feigning disarming warmth while ——— waiting for an opportunity to strike back.

(A) confident. .foolishly
(B) open. .cautiously
(C) withdrawn. .overtly
(D) secure. .immodestly
(E) ruthless. .secretly

diamond

B. QUIZ II (12 items; 10 minutes)

1. The —— treatment of the zoo animals resulted in community-wide ——.

   (A) curious. .apathy
   (B) popular. .neglect
   (C) critical. .distention
   (D) adequate. .revulsion
   (E) inhumane. .criticism

2. Unlike gold, paper money has no —— value; it is merely a representation of wealth.

   (A) financial
   (B) inveterate
   (C) economic
   (D) intrinsic
   (E) fiscal

3. As science progresses, observations that at one time seemed to conflict with one another can sometimes be —— by a more advanced theory.

   (A) established
   (B) inferred
   (C) detected
   (D) reconciled
   (E) delimited

4. Carling, a political appointee who was not really able to run the agency, tended to promote others even less —— than himself who would not question his authority.

   (A) competent
   (B) likable
   (C) honest
   (D) wholesome
   (E) envied

5. It is no longer possible to regard one nation's economy as an —— system; we are now moving toward becoming a global village with international markets.

   (A) ineffective
   (B) opportunistic
   (C) equitable
   (D) irrational
   (E) isolated

6. Attorneys would be extremely unlikely to boast that no one can hear a word they say, but some doctors seem to be quite proud of their —— handwriting.

   (A) elegant
   (B) unique
   (C) cultivated
   (D) illegible
   (E) handsome

7. The farm consisted of land that was barely —— with poor soil made —— by the almost total lack of spring rains.

   (A) cultivated. .productive
   (B) fertile. .rich
   (C) profitable. .consistent
   (D) teeming. .desirable
   (E) arable. .arid

8. The phrase "physical law" is merely a metaphor, for physical laws do not compel objects to behave in a certain way but simply —— the way they do behave.

   (A) suggest
   (B) describe
   (C) finish
   (D) become
   (E) condition

9. Because the orchestra's conductor is an intensely private person, he —— making the appearances at fund-raising functions that are part of the job.

   (A) loathes
   (B) anticipates
   (C) excuses
   (D) prepares
   (E) convenes

10. It is ironic and even tragic that people who have relatively little are generous to those who have even less while the wealthy can be totally ——.

   (A) fortunate
   (B) elite
   (C) selfish
   (D) stylish
   (E) active

11. Unfortunately, Professor Greentree has the unusual ability to transform a lively discussion on a central issue into a dreadfully boring —— on a —— point.

   (A) discourse. .significant
   (B) textbook. .single
   (C) monologue. .tangential
   (D) treatise. .useful
   (E) critique. .stimulating

12. His untimely death, at first thought to be due to a —— fever, was later —— to poison.

   (A) degenerative. .relegated
   (B) debilitating. .ascribed
   (C) raging. .reduced
   (D) sanguine. .abdicated
   (E) pernicious. .prescribed

C. QUIZ III (12 items; 10 minutes)

1. The football team was —— by injuries: of the 53 members, only 40 were fit to play.

   (A) truncated
   (B) decimated
   (C) invaded
   (D) ostracized
   (E) reviled

2. Since the city cannot ticket their cars, the diplomats can park anywhere with ——.

   (A) penury
   (B) impunity
   (C) precision
   (D) languor
   (E) ignominy

3. If you —— the charges instead of —— them, people may conclude that you are guilty.

   (A) delegate. .enumerating
   (B) preempt. .disclaiming
   (C) efface. .disavowing
   (D) reduce. .mitigating
   (E) ignore. .rebutting

4. On the narrow and —— mountain road, the truck skidded when it rounded a curve.

   (A) pejorative
   (B) salutary
   (C) propitious
   (D) sedulous
   (E) tortuous

5. Although her acting was ——, she looked so good on stage that the audience applauded anyway.

   (A) dynamic
   (B) laudable
   (C) implacable
   (D) execrable
   (E) intrepid

6. Because of her unpopular opinions, she was unable to —— broad support among the voters; however, those who did support her were exceptionally ——.

   (A) alienate. .many
   (B) survey. .divided
   (C) cut across. .quiet
   (D) amass. .loyal
   (E) evoke. .languid

7. Philosophical differences —— the unification of the two parties into one.

   (A) delegated
   (B) legislated
   (C) impeded
   (D) enacted
   (E) entrusted

8. When a job becomes too ——, workers get ——, their attention wanders, and they start to make careless errors.

   (A) diverse. .busy
   (B) hectic. .lazy
   (C) tedious. .bored
   (D) fascinating. .interested
   (E) rewarding. .sloppy

9. His —— of practical experience and his psychological acuity more than —— his lack of formal academic training.

   (A) claims. .compromise
   (B) background. .repay
   (C) breadth. .account for
   (D) wealth. .compensate for
   (E) fund. .elucidate

10. The merchant —— a small neighborhood business into a citywide chain of stores.

    (A) appraised
    (B) transferred
    (C) parlayed
    (D) redeemed
    (E) instilled

11. It is not always easy to —— one's mistakes, but it is inevitably more —— to try to hide them.

    (A) cover. .suspect
    (B) confess. .difficult
    (C) cancel. .attractive
    (D) solve. .satisfying
    (E) anticipate. .circumspect

12. A professional journalist will attempt to —— the facts learned in an interview by independent ——

    (A) endorse. .questioning
    (B) query. .study
    (C) garnish. .sources
    (D) verify. .investigation
    (E) embellish. .scrutiny

EDUCATORS' #1 CHOICE FOR SCHOOL IMPROVEMENT

Strategy Summary Sheet
CRITICAL READING: SENTENCE COMPLETIONS

STRUCTURE OF CRITICAL READING: SENTENCE COMPLETIONS: The SAT contains Sentence Completions items in two of three Critical Reading test sections. The PSAT contains 13 Sentence Completions items that are distributed between two 25-minute Critical Reading test sections. Each of the test sentences contains one or two blanks. Students are to select the term(s) that will best replace the omitted word(s) in order to complete the sentence. This exam measures their understanding of both reading comprehension and vocabulary. Virtually any subject area may be covered, but no special outside knowledge is required. Complex vocabulary and sentence structure increase item difficulty. Answer choices are incorrect when the resulting sentences are not idiomatically valid or when the overall meaning becomes illogical. While an answer choice may be eliminated because the completed sentence fails to make sense, you must not discard an alternative because of grammatical syntax because such syntax will always be correct.

GENERAL STRATEGY: The overall strategy contains five main approaches: "Anticipate and Test" Strategy, "Simplify Your Life," Logical Pattern Recognition (Thought-Extenders, Thought-Reversers, and Combined Reasoning), Be a Sentence Completions Detective (Coordinate Conjunctions, Subordinate Conjunctions, Key Adjectives and Adverbs, Punctuation, Phrases, and Various Elements), and Hard Cases ("Go to Pieces" Strategy and Difficult Answers Strategy).

1. *"Anticipate and Test" Strategy*: The students should read the sentence through for understanding, trying to imagine what word or words would effectively complete the sentence. Then, they should look at the answer choices to find the one that comes closest to their initial prediction. Occasionally, they will find the very word or words that they anticipated, but most of the time the answer choices will include words that are similar to those that came to mind when they initially read the sentence. After picking the answer choice that matches their anticipated guesses, they should insert the selection into the sentence to test it and read the sentence through to make sure that the answer choice reads smoothly and correctly. Upon reading it, examinees should be convinced that this is the correct answer choice. If that does not work, test the remaining answer choices. The anticipation part of this strategy does not apply when sentences are open-ended, that is, when they allow for multiple possible completion scenarios. In this event, the students should directly substitute the various answer choices into the blank(s) and test for validity.

2. *"Simplify Your Life"*: The difficulty of Sentence Completions items is based on the number of details that are included. In general, the more details there are in a sentence, the harder the item is to answer. Students can eliminate unnecessary details to make the item easier.

3. *Logical Pattern Recognition*: For more difficult sentences, it may be useful to analyze the underlying logical structure. While a countless number of sentences are possible, logical structure falls into two basic categories that are often signaled via key words or punctuation. One must still be careful to recognize that complex sentences may not contain pure extenders or reversers but may have a mixture of both elements.

    •   *Thought-Extenders*: An omitted term may serve to extend another thought in the sentence. In this event, look for terminology that continues or reinforces/strengthens the underlying logic. *Key Terms:* "and," "so," "therefore," "since," "because," "as a result," "if/then," "consequently." Also, look for certain thought-extending punctuation (commas or semicolons).

- *Thought-Reversers*: An omitted term may play the role of "thought-reverser" in the sentence. In this event, look for terminology that contrasts with or diminishes/weakens the underlying logic. *Key Terms:* "although," "though," "but," "else," "in spite of," "despite," "however," "unless," "large/small."

- *Combined Reasoning*: Complex sentences often contain a mixture of "thought-extenders" and "thought-reversers." To correctly answer these items, it is important to first understand the underlying logical structure of the sentence: Identify the ideas and thoughts that are extended and the ideas and thoughts that are reversed.

4. *Be a Sentence Completions Detective*: In constructing Sentence Completions items, the test-writers leave clues for students to use. The following are the most important clues:

- *Coordinate Conjunctions*: Conjunctions are words that join together words, phrases, clauses, or sentences. They indicate to the reader how the joined elements are related to each other. In Sentence Completions items, "and" and "but" are the most commonly used coordinate conjunctions.

- *Subordinate Conjunctions*: A subordinate conjunction joins together two ideas in a sentence and indicates that one idea is subordinate to, or dependent upon, the other idea. Since they have to indicate the way in which the subordinate clause depends upon the main clause, subordinate conjunctions will serve as important verbal clues. Examples of subordinate conjunctions include "although," "unless," "if," and "for."

- *Key Adjectives and Adverbs*: In many cases, the elements of the sentence that provide descriptive detail (adjectives and adverbs) are important clues.

- *Punctuation*: Sometimes, a punctuation mark will serve as an important clue. A semicolon or a colon indicates the continuation of a thought.

- *Phrases*: A phrase clue consists of any additional information that the test-writers add to make clear what is supposed to go in the blank.

- *Various Elements*: Sometimes, a single clue may not be sufficient to dispose of an item. In many cases, there are several clues and therefore several different ways of getting the right answer. Combined Reasoning items, for instance, almost always draw upon multiple clues.

5. *Hard Cases*: There are Sentence Completions items on the test that are very difficult due to complex logical structures and difficult vocabulary. While the strategies presented above will still be helpful, these items often require a more sophisticated approach. Here are two strategies for handling these "hard cases." The first strategy is for handling sentences with complex logical structures; the second strategy is for handling sentences with difficult vocabulary.

- *"Go to Pieces" Strategy*: When approaching Sentence Completions items with complex logical structures, the students should try to simplify the task by breaking the sentence into pieces and isolating a small part of the sentence that they understand; this part of the sentence must contain an omitted word. Then, test the answer choices, eliminating as many of them as possible. This strategy is useful for items that have two blanks because if either of the two resulting constructions lacks meaning, then you may discard that answer choice. As previously illustrated, an answer choice may be incorrect because it does not create an idiomatic construction.

- *Difficult Answers Strategy*: Remember that difficult items have difficult answers. The more difficult Sentence Completions items tend to be near the end of a group, but they can be anywhere, depending on the students' vocabulary skills. In fact, you may know all of the words in a more difficult item but not all of the words in an easier item. If forced to guess, the students should not choose an easy answer choice. Instead, they should choose the answer choice with the most difficult vocabulary word(s).

ADDITIONAL STRATEGIES FROM IN-CLASS DISCUSSION: _____

_____

_____

_____

_____

_____

_____

_____

_____

_____

_____

_____

_____

_____

_____

_____

_____

_____

_____

_____

_____

_____

_____

_____

_____

_____

Math:
Multiple-Choice

EDUCATORS' #1 CHOICE FOR SCHOOL IMPROVEMENT

Cambridge Course Concept Outline
MATH: MULTIPLE-CHOICE

I. CORE LESSON (p. 485)

A. ITEM-TYPES
1. ARITHMETIC AND NUMBERS (Items #1-2, p. 485)
2. ALGEBRA AND FUNCTIONS (Items #3-6, p. 485)
3. COORDINATE GEOMETRY (Item #7, p. 486)
4. GEOMETRY AND MEASUREMENT (Items #8-10, p. 486)
5. DATA ANALYSIS, STATISTICS, AND PROBABILITY (Item #11, p. 486)

B. GENERAL STRATEGIES
1. A NOTE ABOUT FIGURES (Items #12-15, p. 487)
2. IMPORTANT FACTS ABOUT THE ANSWER CHOICES
   a. ANSWER CHOICES ARE ARRANGED IN ORDER
   b. WRONG CHOICES CORRESPOND TO CONCEPTUAL ERRORS (Item #16, p. 487)
3. "SIGNAL" WORDS REQUIRE SPECIAL ATTENTION (Items #17-20, p. 487)
4. LADDER OF DIFFICULTY (Items #21-29, p. 489)
5. ADDITIONAL HELPFUL HINTS

C. ARITHMETIC REVIEW AND STRATEGIES
1. SIMPLE MANIPULATIONS—JUST DO IT! (Items #30-31, p. 490)
2. COMPLICATED MANIPULATIONS—LOOK FOR SHORTCUTS
   a. SIMPLIFYING (Item #32, p. 490)
   b. FACTORING (Items #33-34, p. 490)
   c. APPROXIMATION (Items #35-36, p. 490)
   d. THE "FLYING-X" METHOD (Item #37, p. 491)
   e. DECIMAL/FRACTION EQUIVALENTS (Item #38, p. 491)
3. SOLVING COMPLICATED ARITHMETIC APPLICATION ITEMS (Items #39-40, p. 491)
4. COMMON ARITHMETIC ITEMS
   a. PROPERTIES OF NUMBERS (Items #41-49, p. 491)
   b. SETS: UNION, INTERSECTION, AND ELEMENTS (Items #50-54, p. 493)
   c. ABSOLUTE VALUE (Items #55-57, p. 494)
   d. PERCENTS (Items #58-64, p. 494)
   e. RATIOS (Items #65-66, p. 495)
   f. PROPORTIONS AND DIRECT/INVERSE VARIATION (Items #67-73, p. 495)
5. ARITHMETIC STRATEGY: "TEST-THE-TEST" (Items #74-79, p. 497)

D. ALGEBRA REVIEW AND STRATEGIES
1. MANIPULATING ALGEBRAIC EXPRESSIONS
   a. BASIC ALGEBRAIC MANIPULATIONS (Items #80-81, p. 498)
   b. EVALUATING EXPRESSIONS (Items #82-85, p. 498)
   c. MANIPULATING EXPRESSIONS INVOLVING EXPONENTS (Items #86-87, p. 499)
   d. FACTORING EXPRESSIONS (Items #88-90, p. 499)
2. EVALUATING SEQUENCES INVOLVING EXPONENTIAL GROWTH (Items #91-94, p. 499)
3. SOLVING ALGEBRAIC EQUATIONS OR INEQUALITIES WITH ONE VARIABLE
   a. SIMPLE EQUATIONS (Item #95, p. 501)

CORE LESSON

DIRECTIONS: The items in this section demonstrate the Math: Multiple-Choice concepts and skills that are tested by the SAT and PSAT/NMSQT. You will work through the items with your instructor in class. For each item, choose the best answer. Use any available space in the section for scratch work. Answers are on page 984.

Notes:

(1) The use of a calculator is permitted. All numbers used are real numbers.

(2) Figures that accompany problems in this test are intended to provide information useful in solving the problems. They are drawn as accurately as possible EXCEPT when it is stated in a specific problem that the figure is not drawn to scale. All figures lie in a plane unless otherwise indicated.

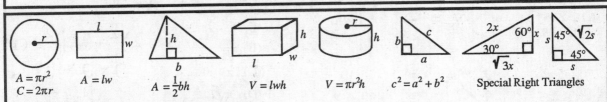

$A = \pi r^2$
$C = 2\pi r$

$A = lw$

$A = \frac{1}{2}bh$

$V = lwh$

$V = \pi r^2 h$

$c^2 = a^2 + b^2$

Special Right Triangles

The number of degrees of arc in a circle is 360.
The measure in degrees of a straight angle is 180.
The sum of the measures in degrees of the angles of a triangle is 180.

---

1. If the price of fertilizer has been decreased from 3 pounds for $2 to 5 pounds for $2, how many more pounds of fertilizer can be purchased for $10 than could have been purchased before?

   (A) 2
   (B) 8
   (C) 10
   (D) 12
   (E) 15

2. <u>Five students</u> formed a political club to support a candidate for local office. They project that club membership will <u>double every three weeks</u>. Which of the following can be used to find the number of members that the club projects to have after twelve weeks?

   (A) $5(2^{2/3})$
   (B) $5(2^{3/2})$
   (C) $5(2^{12/3})$
   (D) $5(2^{3/12})$
   (E) $5 + 5(2^4)$

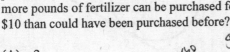

3. If $\frac{2x-5}{3} = -4x$, then $x =$

   (A) -1
   (B) $-\frac{5}{14}$
   (C) 0
   (D) $\frac{5}{14}$
   (E) 1

4. A vending machine dispenses k cups of coffee, each at a cost of c cents, every day. During a period d days long, what is the amount of money in dollars taken in by the vending machine from the sale of coffee?

   (A) $\frac{100kc}{d}$
   (B) kcd
   (C) $\frac{dk}{c}$
   (D) $\frac{kcd}{100}$
   (E) $\frac{kc}{100d}$

---

5. If $f(x) = 2x - 3$ and $g(x) = x^2 - 2$, then $f(g(2)) =$

   (A) −1
   (B) 0
   (C) 1
   (D) 4
   (E) 7

   (handwritten: $2^2 - 2$ $g(2)$, $2(2) - 3$ $f(g)$, 1)

6. If $|x + 3| = 5$, then $x =$

   (A) −8 or 2
   (B) −2 or 8
   (C) −8
   (D) −2
   (E) 2 or 8

   (handwritten: $x + 3 = 5$ $\{x + 3 = -5$, $-3 \quad -3$, $x = -8$, $x = 2\}$)

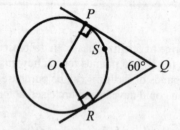

7. In the figure above, line m has a slope of 1. What is the y-intercept of the line?

   (A) −5
   (B) −3
   (C) 0
   (D) 3
   (E) 7

   (handwritten: $y = mx + b$, $4 = 1(-3) + b$, $7 = b$)

   (handwritten near figure: (−3, 4), m = 1, (had to be bigger than 4))

8. If a circle has a radius of 1, what is its area?

   (handwritten: $A = \pi r^2$)

   (A) $\frac{\pi}{2}$
   (B) π
   (C) 2π
   (D) 4π
   (E) π^2

9. In the figure above, ΔPQR is inscribed in a circle with center O. What is the area of the circle?

   (A) $\frac{\pi}{2}$
   (B) $\frac{\pi}{\sqrt{2}}$
   (C) π
   (D) $\pi\sqrt{2}$
   (E) 2π

   (handwritten: $A = \pi r^2$, $(\sqrt{2})^2 + (\sqrt{2})^2 = c^2$, $2 + 2 = c^2$, $4 = c^2$, $2 = c$)

10. In the figure above, $\overrightarrow{QP}$ is tangent to circle O at point P, and $\overrightarrow{QR}$ is tangent to circle O at point R. What is the degree measure of the minor arc PSR?

   (A) 30
   (B) 60
   (C) 90
   (D) 120
   (E) 180

   (handwritten: $90 + 90 + 60 = 240$, $360 - 240$, $= 120$)

11. What is the average of 8.5, 7.8, and 7.7?

   (A) 8.3
   (B) 8.2
   (C) 8.1
   (D) 8.0
   (E) 7.9

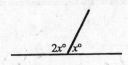

12. In the figure above, $x =$

  (A) 15
  (B) 30
  (C) 45
  (D) 60
  (E) 120

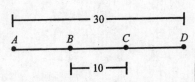

Note: Figure not drawn to scale.

13. In the figure above, what is the length of $\overline{AB} + \overline{CD}$?

  (A) 5
  (B) 10
  (C) 15
  (D) 20
  (E) 40

Items 14-15 refer to the following figure.

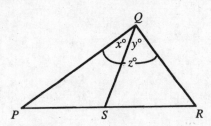

Note: Figure not drawn to scale.

14. Which of the following must be true?

  I. $PS < SR$
  II. $z = 90$
  III. $x > y$

  (A) I only
  (B) I and II only
  (C) I and III only
  (D) I, II, and III
  (E) Neither I, II, nor III

15. Which of the following must be true?

  I. $PR > PS$
  II. $z > x$
  III. $x + y = z$

  (A) I only
  (B) I and II only
  (C) I and III only
  (D) I, II, and III
  (E) Neither I, II, nor III

16. In a certain year, the number of girls who graduated from City High School was twice the number of boys. If $\frac{3}{4}$ of the girls and $\frac{5}{6}$ of the boys went to college immediately after graduation, what fraction of the graduates that year went to college immediately after graduation?

  (A) $\frac{5}{36}$
  (B) $\frac{16}{27}$
  (C) $\frac{7}{9}$
  (D) $\frac{29}{36}$
  (E) $\frac{31}{36}$

17. A jar contains black and white marbles. If there are ten marbles in the jar, then which of the following could NOT be the ratio of black to white marbles?

  (A) 9:1
  (B) 7:3
  (C) 1:1
  (D) 1:4
  (E) 1:10

18. If n is a negative number, which of the following is the least in value?

  (A) $-n$
  (B) $n - n$
  (C) $n + n$
  (D) n^2
  (E) n^4

NOTES AND STRATEGIES

19. If a machine produces 240 thingamabobs per hour, how many <u>minutes</u> are needed for the machine to produce 30 thingamabobs?

    (A) 6
    (B) 7.5
    (C) 8
    (D) 12
    (E) 12.5

    $\dfrac{240}{60} = \dfrac{30}{x}$

    $1800 = 240x$

    $x = 7.5$

20. Of the 120 people in a room, $\frac{3}{5}$ are women. If $\frac{2}{3}$ of the people are married, what is the maximum number of women in the room who could be <u>unmarried</u>?

    72 women

    24 are married

    (A) 80
    (B) 72
    (C) 48
    (D) 40
    (E) 32

    $\begin{array}{r} 72 \\ -\overline{48} \\ \hline 24 \end{array}$

21. Three friends are playing a game in which each person simultaneously displays one of three hand signs: a clenched fist, an open palm, or two extended fingers. How many unique combinations of the signs are possible?

    F → fist
    P → palm
    2 → fingers

    (A) 3
    (B) 9
    (C) 10
    (D) 12
    (E) 27

    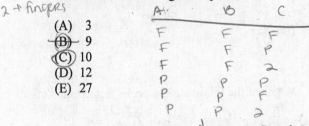

22. If $\frac{1}{3}$ of the number of girls in a school equals $\frac{1}{5}$ of the total number of students, what is the ratio of girls to boys in the school?

    (A) 5:3
    (B) 3:2
    (C) 2:5
    (D) 1:3
    (E) 1:5

    $3(\frac{1}{3})G = \frac{1}{2}P(3)$

    $G = \frac{3}{5}P$

    $B = \frac{2}{5}P$

    $3:2$

23. Peter walked from point P to point Q and back again, a total distance of 2 miles. If he averaged 4 miles per hour on the trip from P to Q and 5 miles per hour on the return trip, what was his average walking speed for the entire trip?

    (A) $2\frac{2}{9}$
    (B) 4
    (C) $4\frac{4}{9}$
    (D) $4\frac{1}{2}$
    (E) 5

24. After a 20 percent decrease in price, the cost of an item is D dollars. What was the price of the item before the decrease?

    (A) $0.75D$
    (B) $0.80D$
    (C) $1.20D$
    (D) $1.25D$
    (E) $1.5D$

25. On a certain trip, a motorist drove 10 miles at 30 miles per hour, 10 miles at 40 miles per hour, and 10 miles at 50 miles per hour. What portion of her total driving time was spent driving 50 miles per hour?

    (A) $1\frac{13}{51}$
    (B) $\frac{5}{7}$
    (C) $\frac{5}{12}$
    (D) $\frac{1}{3}$
    (E) $\frac{12}{47}$

26. What is the <u>maximum</u> number of non-overlapping sections that can be created when a circle is crossed by three straight lines?

    (A) 3
    (B) 4
    (C) 5
    (D) 6
    (E) 7

27. At Glenridge High School, 20 percent of the students are seniors. If all of the seniors attended the school play, and 60 percent of <u>all the students</u> attended the play, what percent of the <u>non-seniors</u> attended the play?

    (A) 20%
    (B) 40%
    (C) 50%
    (D) 60%
    (E) 100%

Water Usage in Cubic Feet

$$71,111$$

28. The water meter at a factory displays the reading above. What is the <u>minimum</u> number of cubic feet of water that the factory must use before four of the five digits on the meter are again the same?

    (A) 10,000
    (B) 1,000
    (C) 999
    (D) 666
    (E) 9

29. A telephone call from City X to City Y costs $1.00 for the first three minutes and $0.25 for each additional minute thereafter. What is the <u>maximum</u> length of time, in minutes, that a caller could talk for $3.00?

    (A) 8
    (B) 10
    (C) 11
    (D) 12
    (E) 13

30. $\frac{8}{9} - \frac{7}{8} =$

    (A) $\frac{1}{72}$
    (B) $\frac{1}{8}$
    (C) $\frac{1}{7}$
    (D) $\frac{15}{72}$
    (E) $\frac{15}{7}$

31. $\sqrt{1 - \left(\frac{2}{9} + \frac{1}{36} + \frac{1}{18}\right)} =$

    (A) $\frac{1}{5}$
    (B) $\sqrt{\frac{2}{3}}$
    (C) $\frac{5}{6}$
    (D) 1
    (E) $\sqrt{3}$

32. $\frac{1}{2} \cdot \frac{2}{3} \cdot \frac{3}{4} \cdot \frac{4}{5} \cdot \frac{5}{6} \cdot \frac{6}{7} \cdot \frac{7}{8} =$

    (A) $\frac{1}{56}$
    (B) $\frac{1}{8}$
    (C) $\frac{28}{37}$
    (D) $\frac{41}{43}$
    (E) $\frac{55}{56}$

33. $86(37) - 37(85) =$

    (A) 0
    (B) 1
    (C) 37
    (D) 85
    (E) 86

34. Which of the following is a prime factorization of 120?

    (A) (2)(2)(15)
    (B) (2)(3)(4)(5)
    (C) (2)(2)(3)(10)
    (D) (2)(2)(2)(3)(5)
    (E) (2)(2)(3)(3)(5)

35. $\frac{0.2521 \cdot 8.012}{1.014}$ is approximately equal to

    (A) 0.25
    (B) 0.5
    (C) 1.0
    (D) 1.5
    (E) 2.0

36. Which of the following fractions is the largest?

(A) $\frac{111}{221}$ .5022624434

(B) $\frac{75}{151}$ .4966887417

(C) $\frac{333}{998}$ .3336673347

(D) $\frac{113}{225}$ .50222...

(E) $\frac{101}{301}$ .3355

37. If $z = \frac{x+y}{x}$, $1 - z =$

(A) $\frac{1-x+y}{x}$

(B) $\frac{x+y-1}{x}$

(C) $\frac{1-x-y}{x}$

(D) $-\frac{y}{x}$

(E) $1-x-y$

38. $\frac{0.111 \cdot 0.666}{0.166 \cdot 0.125}$ is approximately equal to which of the following?

(A) 6.8

(B) 4.3

(C) 3.6

(D) 1.6

(E) 0.9

39. If the senior class has 360 students, of whom $\frac{5}{12}$ are women, and the junior class has 350 students, of whom $\frac{4}{7}$ are women, how many more women are there in the junior class than in the senior class?

(A) $(360 - 350)(\frac{4}{7} - \frac{5}{12})$

(B) $\frac{(360-350)(\frac{4}{7} - \frac{5}{12})}{2}$

(C) $(\frac{4}{7} \cdot \frac{5}{12})(360 - 350)$

(D) $(\frac{4}{7} \cdot 350) - (\frac{5}{12} \cdot 360)$

(E) $(\frac{5}{12} \cdot 360) - (\frac{4}{7} \cdot 350)$

40. If the price of candy increases from 5 pounds for $7 to 3 pounds for $7, how much less candy (in pounds) can be purchased for $3.50 at the new price than at the old price?

(A) $\frac{2}{7}$

(B) 1

(C) $1\frac{17}{35}$

(D) 2

(E) $3\frac{34}{35}$

41. If n is any integer, which of the following is always an odd integer?

(A) $n - 1$

(B) $n + 1$

(C) $n + 2$

(D) $2n + 1$

(E) $2n + 2$

42. Which of the following expressions represents the product of two consecutive integers?

(A) $2n + 1$

(B) $2n + n$

(C) $2n^2$

(D) $n^2 + 1$

(E) $n^2 + n$

43. If n is any integer, which of the following expressions must be even?

   I. $2n$
   II. $2n + n$
   III. $2n \cdot n$

(A) I only

(B) II only

(C) III only

(D) I and II only

(E) I and III only

NOTES AND STRATEGIES

44. If n is the first number in a series of three consecutive even numbers, which of the following expressions represents the sum of the three numbers?

(A) $n+2$
(B) $n+4$
(C) $n+6$
(D) $3n+6$
(E) $6(3n)$

$2 + 4 + 6$
$= 12$

45. If n is an odd number, which of the following expressions represents the third odd number following n?

$3\quad 5\quad 7\quad 9$

(A) $n+3$
(B) $n+4$
(C) $n+6$
(D) $3n+3$
(E) $4n+4$

46. If n is any odd integer, which of the following expressions must also be odd?

3

I. $n+n$
II. $n+n+n$
III. $n \cdot n \cdot n$

(A) I only
(B) II only
(C) III only
(D) II and III only
(E) I, II, and III

47. If n is a negative number, which of the following expressions must be positive?

I. $2n$
II. n^2
III. n^5

-1

(A) I only
(B) II only
(C) III only
(D) I and II only
(E) II and III only

48. If $0 < x < 1$, which of the following expressions is the largest?

(A) x
(B) $2x$
(C) x^2
(D) x^3
(E) $x+1$

49. If $-1 < x < 0$, which of the following expressions is the largest?

(A) -1
(B) x
(C) $2x$
(D) x^3
(E) $x-1$

50. If set $S = \{2, 3, 4\}$ and set P is the set of all products of different elements in set S, then set $P =$

(A) $\{6, 8, 12\}$
(B) $\{6, 8, 18\}$
(C) $\{6, 8, 12, 24\}$
(D) $\{6, 8, 12, 18, 24\}$
(E) $\{6, 8, 12, 18, 24, 36\}$

51. If set X is the set of all integers between 1 and 24, inclusive, that are evenly divisible by 3, and set Y is the set of all integers between 1 and 24, inclusive, that are evenly divisible by 4, what is the set of all elements in both sets X and Y?

(A) $\{12\}$
(B) $\{3, 4\}$
(C) $\{12, 24\}$
(D) $\{4, 12, 24\}$
(E) $\{3, 4, 12, 24\}$

52. If x is an element of set X, in which set X is the set of integers evenly divisible by 3 such that $6 < x < 11$, and y is an element of set Y, where set Y is the set of integers evenly divisible by 4 such that $7 < y < 12$, what is the intersection of sets X and Y?

    (A) {}
    (B) {8}
    (C) {9}
    (D) {12}
    (E) {8, 12}

53. If set S is the set of all positive odd integers and set T is the set of all positive even integers, then the union of sets S and T (the set of all elements that are in either set or both sets) is the set of

    (A) positive integers
    (B) integers
    (C) even integers
    (D) odd integers
    (E) real numbers

54. In a certain school, each of the 72 music students must participate in the marching band, the orchestra, or both. If only music students participate, 48 students total participate in the marching band, and 54 students total participate in the orchestra, how many students participate in both programs?

    (A) 6
    (B) 18
    (C) 24
    (D) 30
    (E) 36

55. $|-2| + 3 - |-4| =$

    (A) −5
    (B) −4
    (C) −1
    (D) 1
    (E) 9

56. $|5| - |-5| + |-3| =$

    (A) −8
    (B) −3
    (C) 3
    (D) 8
    (E) 13

57. $|-3| \cdot |-4| \cdot -5 =$

    (A) −60
    (B) −30
    (C) −7
    (D) 20
    (E) 60

58. A jar contains 24 white marbles and 48 black marbles. What percent of the marbles in the jar are black?

    (A) 10%
    (B) 25%
    (C) $33\frac{1}{3}$%
    (D) 60%
    (E) $66\frac{2}{3}$%

59. A group of 3 friends shared the cost of a tape recorder. If Andy, Barbara, and Donna each paid $12, $30, and $18, respectively, then Donna paid what percent of the cost of the tape recorder?

    (A) 10%
    (B) 30%
    (C) $33\frac{1}{3}$%
    (D) 50%
    (E) $66\frac{2}{3}$%

60. Twenty students attended Professor Rodriguez's class on Monday and 25 students attended on Tuesday. The number of students who attended on Tuesday was what percent of the number of students who attended on Monday?

(A) 5%
(B) 20%
(C) 25%
(D) 80%
(E) 125%

61. If the population of a town was 20,000 in 1990 and 16,000 in 2000, what was the percentage decline in the town's population?

(A) 50%
(B) 25%
(C) 20%
(D) 10%
(E) 5%

Items 62-64 refer to the following table.

CAPITAL CITY FIRES	
Year	Number of Fires
1992	100
1993	125
1994	140
1995	150
1996	135

62. The number of fires in 1992 was what percentage of the number of fires in 1993?

(A) 25%
(B) $66\frac{2}{3}$%
(C) 80%
(D) 100%
(E) 125%

63. The number of fires in 1996 was what percentage of the number of fires in 1995?

(A) 90%
(B) 82%
(C) 50%
(D) 25%
(E) 10%

64. What was the percent decrease in the number of fires from 1995 to 1996?

(A) 10%
(B) 25%
(C) 50%
(D) 82%
(E) 90%

65. A groom must divide 12 quarts of oats between two horses. If Dobbin is to receive twice as much as Pegasus, how many quarts of oats should the groom give to Dobbin?

(A) 4
(B) 6
(C) 8
(D) 9
(E) 10

66. If the ratio of John's allowance to Lucy's allowance is 3:2, and the ratio of Lucy's allowance to Bob's allowance is 3:4, what is the ratio of John's allowance to Bob's allowance?

(A) 1:6
(B) 2:5
(C) 1:2
(D) 3:4
(E) 9:8

67. If 4.5 pounds of chocolate cost $10, how many pounds of chocolate can be purchased for $12?

(A) $4\frac{3}{4}$
(B) $5\frac{2}{5}$
(C) $5\frac{1}{2}$
(D) $5\frac{3}{4}$
(E) 6

STEP THREE

NOTES AND STRATEGIES

68. At Star Lake Middle School, 45 percent of the students bought a yearbook. If 540 students bought yearbooks, how many students did <u>not</u> buy a yearbook?

   (A) 243
   (B) 540
   (C) 575
   (D) 660
   (E) 957

69. In the equation $y = kx$, k is the constant of variation. If y is equal to 6 when $x = 2.4$, what is the constant of variation?

   (A) 0.4
   (B) 2.5
   (C) 3.4
   (D) 3.6
   (E) 14.4

70. A train traveling at a constant speed, k, takes 90 minutes to go from point P to point Q, a distance of 45 miles. What is the value of k, in miles per hour?

   (A) 20
   (B) 30
   (C) 45
   (D) 60
   (E) 75

71. The cost of picture framing depends on the outer perimeter of the frame. If a 15" × 15" picture frame costs $35 more than a 10" × 10" picture frame, what is the cost of framing, in dollars per inch?

   (A) $3.50
   (B) $2.75
   (C) $2.25
   (D) $1.75
   (E) $1.50

72. Walking at a constant speed of 4 miles per hour, it took Jill exactly 1 hour to walk home from school. If she walked at a constant speed of 5 miles per hour, how many <u>minutes</u> did the trip take?

   (A) 48
   (B) 54
   (C) 56
   (D) 72
   (E) 112

73. Ms. Peters drove from her home to the park at an average speed of 30 miles per hour and returned home along the same route at an average speed of 40 miles per hour. If her driving time from home to the park was 20 minutes, how many minutes did it take Ms. Peters to drive from the park to her home?

   (A) 7.5
   (B) 12
   (C) 15
   (D) 24
   (E) 30

74. Which of the following is the larger of two numbers the product of which is 600 and the sum of which is five times the difference between the two?

   (A) 10
   (B) 15
   (C) 20
   (D) 30
   (E) 50

75. If $\frac{1}{3}$ of a number is 3 more than $\frac{1}{4}$ of the number, then what is the number?

   (A) 18
   (B) 24
   (C) 30
   (D) 36
   (E) 48

76. If $\frac{3}{5}$ of a number is 4 more than $\frac{1}{2}$ of the number, then what is the number?

(A) 20
(B) 28
(C) 35
(D) 40
(E) 56

77. If both 16 and 9 are divided by n, the remainder is 2. What is n?

(A) 3
(B) 4
(C) 5
(D) 6
(E) 7

78. The sum of the digits of a three-digit number is 16. If the tens digit of the number is 3 times the units digit, and the units digit is $\frac{1}{4}$ of the hundreds digit, then what is the number?

(A) 446
(B) 561
(C) 682
(D) 862
(E) 914

79. If the sum of five consecutive integers is 40, what is the smallest of the five integers?

(A) 4
(B) 5
(C) 6
(D) 7
(E) 8

80. If $a^3 + b = 3 + a^3$, then $b =$

(A) 3^3
(B) $3\sqrt{3}$
(C) 3
(D) $\sqrt[3]{3}$
(E) $-\sqrt{3}$

81. Which of the following expressions is equivalent to $4a + 3b - (-2a - 3b)$?

(A) $2a$
(B) $12ab$
(C) $2a + 6b$
(D) $6a + 6b$
(E) $8a + 9b$

82. If $x = 2$, what is the value of $x^2 + 2x - 2$?

(A) -2
(B) 0
(C) 2
(D) 4
(E) 6

83. If $x = 2$, then $\frac{1}{x^2} + \frac{1}{x} - \frac{x}{2} =$

(A) $-\frac{3}{4}$
(B) $-\frac{1}{4}$
(C) 0
(D) $\frac{1}{4}$
(E) $\frac{1}{2}$

84. If $\frac{1}{3}x = 10$, then $\frac{1}{6}x =$

(A) $\frac{1}{15}$
(B) $\frac{2}{3}$
(C) 2
(D) 5
(E) 30

85. If $p = 1$, $q = 2$, and $r = 3$, then $\frac{(q \cdot r)(r - q)}{(q - p)(p \cdot q)} =$

(A) -3
(B) -1
(C) 0
(D) 3
(E) 6

86. $\frac{9(x^2y^3)^6}{(3x^6y^9)^2}=$

(A) 1
(B) 3
(C) x^2y^3
(D) $3x^2y^3$
(E) $x^{12}y^{12}$

87. $2(4^{-1/2})-2^0+2^{3/2}+2^{-2}=$

(A) $-2\sqrt{2}-\frac{1}{4}$
(B) $2\sqrt{2}-\frac{1}{4}$
(C) $2\sqrt{2}$
(D) $2\sqrt{2}+\frac{1}{4}$
(E) $2\sqrt{2}+\frac{5}{4}$

88. Which of the following expressions is equivalent to $\frac{x^2-y^2}{x+y}$?

(A) x^2-y^2
(B) x^2+y^2
(C) x^2+y
(D) $x+y^2$
(E) $x-y$

89. Which of the following expressions is equivalent to $\frac{x^2-x-6}{x+2}$?

(A) $x^2-\frac{x}{2}-3$
(B) x^2-2
(C) $x-2$
(D) $x-3$
(E) x

90. Which of the following is the factorization of $6x^2+4x-2$?

(A) $(6x+1)(x-3)$
(B) $(6x+3)(x-1)$
(C) $(3x-1)(2x-2)$
(D) $(2x+2)(3x-1)$
(E) $(2x+4)(3x-2)$

91. In a geometric sequence of positive numbers, the fourth term is 125 and the sixth term is 3,125. What is the second term of the sequence?

(A) 1
(B) 5
(C) 10
(D) 25
(E) 50

92. City University projects that a planned expansion will increase the number of enrolled students every year for the next five years by 50 percent. If 400 students enroll in the first year of the plan, how many students are expected to enroll in the fifth year of the plan?

(A) 200
(B) 600
(C) 675
(D) 1,350
(E) 2,025

93. Jimmy's uncle deposited $1,000 into a college fund account and promised that at the start of each year, he would deposit an amount equal to 10% of the account balance. If no other deposits or withdrawals were made and no additional interest accrued, what was the account balance after three additional annual deposits were made by Jimmy's uncle?

(A) $1,030
(B) $1,300
(C) $1,331
(D) $1,500
(E) $1,830

94. A tank with a capacity of 2,400 liters is filled with water. If a valve is opened that drains 25 percent of the contents of the tank every minute, what is the volume of water (in liters) that remains in the tank after 3 minutes?

(A) 1,800
(B) 1,350
(C) 1,012.5
(D) 600
(E) 325.75

NOTES AND STRATEGIES

95. If $(2 + 3)(1 + x) = 25$, then $x =$

(A) $\frac{1}{5}$

(B) $\frac{1}{4}$

(C) 1

(D) 4

(E) 5

96. If $\frac{12}{x+1} - 1 = 2$, and $x \neq -1$, then $x =$

(A) 1
(B) 2
(C) 3
(D) 11
(E) 12

97. If $\frac{x}{x+2} = \frac{3}{4}$, and $x \neq -2$, then $x =$

(A) 6
(B) 4
(C) 3
(D) 2
(E) 1

98. If $\frac{x}{x-2} - \frac{x+2}{2(x-2)} = 8$, and $x \neq 2$, which of the following is the complete solution set for x?

(A) $\{\}$
(B) $\{-2\}$
(C) $\{2\}$
(D) $\{4\}$
(E) $\{8\}$

99. If $\frac{3}{x-2} > \frac{1}{6}$, which of the following defines the possible values for x?

(A) $x < 20$
(B) $x > 0$
(C) $x > 2$
(D) $0 < x < 20$
(E) $2 < x < 20$

100. If $\sqrt{2x + 1} - 1 = 4$, then $x =$

(A) -5
(B) -1
(C) 1
(D) 12
(E) 24

101. Which of the following is the complete solution set for $\sqrt{3x - 2} - 3 = -4$?

(A) $\{\}$
(B) $\{-1\}$
(C) $\{1\}$
(D) $\{-1, 1\}$
(E) $\{1, 2\}$

102. If $\sqrt{2x - 5} = 2\sqrt{5 - 2x}$, then $x =$

(A) 1

(B) 2

(C) $\frac{5}{2}$

(D) 10

(E) 15

103. Which of the following is the complete solution set for $\sqrt{x^2 + 9} = 5$?

(A) $\{-4, 4\}$
(B) $\{-4\}$
(C) $\{0\}$
(D) $\{4\}$
(E) $\{\}$

104. If $4^{x+2} = 64$, then $x =$

(A) 1
(B) 2
(C) 3
(D) 4
(E) 5

105. If $8^x = 2^{x+3}$, then $x =$

(A) 0

(B) 1

(C) $\frac{2}{3}$

(D) 3

(E) $\frac{3}{2}$

106. If $3^{2x} = \frac{1}{81}$, then $x =$

(A) -2

(B) $-\frac{3}{2}$

(C) $-\frac{2}{3}$

(D) $\frac{2}{3}$

(E) $\frac{3}{2}$

107. If $5^3 = (\sqrt{5})^{-2x}$, then $5^x =$

(A) $\frac{1}{125}$

(B) $\frac{1}{25}$

(C) $\frac{1}{5}$

(D) 5

(E) 25

108. Which of the following is the complete solution set for $\left|\frac{2x+1}{3}\right| = 5$?

(A) $\{-8, -7\}$

(B) $\{-8, 7\}$

(C) $\{-7, 8\}$

(D) $\{7\}$

(E) $\{8\}$

109. Which of the following is the complete solution set for $|x + 6| = 3x$?

(A) $\{-3, \frac{3}{2}\}$

(B) $\{-\frac{3}{2}, 3\}$

(C) $\{\frac{3}{2}, 3\}$

(D) $\{3\}$

(E) $\{\}$

110. Which of the following is the complete solution set for $|2x - 1| > 3$?

(A) All real numbers

(B) The null set

(C) All real numbers less than -1 or greater than 2

(D) All real numbers less than -2 or greater than 1

(E) All real numbers less than -3

111. If $|3x - 6| > 9$, then which of the following must be true?

(A) $-3 < x < 2$

(B) $-2 < x < 3$

(C) $x < -3$ or $x > 2$

(D) $x < -1$ or $x > 5$

(E) $x < -1$ or $x > 9$

112. Which of the following identifies exactly those values of x that satisfy $|-2x + 4| < 4$?

(A) $x > -4$

(B) $x < 4$

(C) $x > 0$

(D) $0 < x < 4$

(E) $-4 < x < 0$

113. If $f(x) = x^2 + x$, what is the value of $f(-2)$?

(A) -8

(B) -2

(C) 2

(D) 8

(E) 12

114. Given: $y = f(x) = \left(\frac{6x^2 - 2^{-x}}{|x|}\right)^{-1/2}$ for all integers. If $x = -1$, what is the value of y?

(A) 2

(B) $\frac{1}{2}$

(C) $\frac{1}{4}$

(D) $-\frac{1}{2}$

(E) -2

115. If $f(x) = x + 3$ and $g(x) = 2x - 5$, what is the value of $f(g(2))$?

(A) -2

(B) 0

(C) 2

(D) 4

(E) 10

116. If $f(x) = 3x + 2$ and $g(x) = x^2 + x$, what is the value of $g(f(-2))$?

(A) 15

(B) 12

(C) 6

(D) 3

(E) -2

117. If $f(x) = 2x^2 + x$ and $g(x) = f(f(x))$, what is the value of $g(1)$?

(A) 3

(B) 18

(C) 21

(D) 39

(E) 55

118. If $f(x) = 3x + 4$ and $g(x) = 2x - 1$, for what value of x does $f(x) = g(x)$?

(A) -5

(B) -2

(C) 0

(D) 3

(E) 7

119. If $x^* = x^2 - x$ for all integers, then $-2^* =$

(A) -6

(B) -2

(C) 0

(D) 4

(E) 6

120. If $x^* = x^2 - x$ for all integers, then $(3^*)^* =$

(A) 27

(B) 30

(C) 58

(D) 72

(E) 121

121. If $f(x) = 3x - 2$ and $-5 < x < 5$, which of the following defines the range of $f(x)$?

(A) $-17 < f(x) < 13$

(B) $-13 < f(x) < 17$

(C) $-5 < f(x) < 12$

(D) $0 < f(x) < 17$

(E) $3 < f(x) < 13$

122. If $f(x) = \frac{x+2}{x-1}$, for which of the following values of x is $f(x)$ undefined?

(A) -2

(B) -1

(C) $\frac{1}{2}$

(D) 1

(E) 2

123. If $f(x) = \frac{2 - 2x}{x}$, which of the following defines the range of $f(x)$?

(A) All real numbers

(B) All real numbers except -2

(C) All real numbers except 0

(D) All real numbers except 2

(E) All real numbers greater than 2

NOTES AND STRATEGIES

124. If $|4x - 8| < 12$, which of the following defines the possible values of x?

(A) $-8 < x < -4$
(B) $-4 < x < 8$
(C) $-1 < x < 5$
(D) $1 < x < 5$
(E) $4 < x < 8$

125. The cost of making a call using a phone-card is $0.15 for dialing and $0.04 per minute of connection time. Which of the following equations could be used to find the cost, y, of a call x minutes long?

(A) $y = x(0.04 + 0.15)$
(B) $y = 0.04x + 0.15$
(C) $y = 0.04 + 0.15x$
(D) $y = 0.15 - 0.04x$
(E) $y = 0.04 - 0.15x$

126. If $x + y = 3$, then $2x + 2y =$

(A) $-\frac{2}{3}$
(B) $\frac{1}{2}$
(C) $\frac{2}{3}$
(D) 6
(E) 8

127. If $7x = 2$ and $3y - 7x = 10$, then $y =$

(A) 2
(B) 3
(C) 4
(D) 5
(E) 6

128. If $2x + y = 8$ and $x - y = 1$, then $x + y =$

(A) -1
(B) 1
(C) 2
(D) 3
(E) 5

129. If $4x + 5y = 12$ and $3x + 4y = 5$, then $7(x + y) =$

(A) 7
(B) 14
(C) 49
(D) 77
(E) 91

x	-2	-1	0	1	2
y	$\frac{10}{3}$	$\frac{8}{3}$	2	$\frac{4}{3}$	$\frac{2}{3}$

130. Which of the following equations correctly describes the relationship between the values x and y in the table above?

(A) $3x + 2y = 6$
(B) $3x - 2y = 3$
(C) $3x + 3y = -6$
(D) $6x + 4y = 7$
(E) $2x + 3y = 6$

131. Which of the following is the solution set for $2x^2 - 2x = 12$?

(A) $\{-3, -2\}$
(B) $\{-2, 3\}$
(C) $\{\frac{2}{3}, 3\}$
(D) $\{\frac{3}{2}, 2\}$
(E) $\{2, 3\}$

132. If $x^2 - 3x = 4$, then which of the following shows all possible values of x?

(A) $\{4, 1\}$
(B) $\{4, -1\}$
(C) $\{-4, 1\}$
(D) $\{-4, -1\}$
(E) $\{-4, 1, 4\}$

133. If $x^2 - y^2 = 0$ and $x + y = 1$, then $x - y =$

(A) -1
(B) 0
(C) 1
(D) 2
(E) 4

134. Which of the following is the solution set for $3x^2 + 3x = 6$?

    (A) $\{1, -2\}$
    (B) $\{1, 2\}$
    (C) $\{\frac{1}{2}, 1\}$
    (D) $\{\frac{1}{2}, \frac{1}{3}\}$
    (E) $\{-1, -2\}$

135. Which of the following is the solution set for $2x^2 - 3x = 2$?

    (A) $\{\frac{1}{2}, 2\}$
    (B) $\{-\frac{1}{2}, 2\}$
    (C) $\{-\frac{1}{2}, -2\}$
    (D) $\{2, -2\}$
    (E) $\{2, 4\}$

136. Diana spent $\frac{1}{2}$ of her weekly allowance on a new book and another $3 on lunch. If she still had $\frac{1}{6}$ of her original allowance left, how much is Diana's allowance?

    (A) $24
    (B) $18
    (C) $15
    (D) $12
    (E) $9

137. In a certain game, a player had five successful turns in a row, and after each one, the number of points added to his total score was double what was added the preceding turn. If the player scored a total of 465 points, how many points did he score on the first play?

    (A) 15
    (B) 31
    (C) 93
    (D) 155
    (E) 270

138. At a certain firm, d gallons of fuel are needed per day for each truck. At this rate, g gallons of fuel will supply t trucks for how many days?

    (A) $\frac{dt}{g}$
    (B) $\frac{gt}{d}$
    (C) dgt
    (D) $\frac{t}{dg}$
    (E) $\frac{g}{dt}$

139. Y years ago, Paul was twice as old as Bob. If Bob is now 18 years old, how old is Paul today in terms of Y?

    (A) $36 + Y$
    (B) $18 + Y$
    (C) $18 - Y$
    (D) $36 - Y$
    (E) $36 - 2Y$

140. After filling the car's fuel tank, a driver drove from point P to point Q and then to point R. She used $\frac{2}{5}$ of the fuel driving from P to Q. If she used another 7 gallons to drive from Q to R and still had $\frac{1}{4}$ of a tank left, how many gallons does the tank hold?

    (A) 12
    (B) 18
    (C) 20
    (D) 21
    (E) 35

141. If pencils cost x cents each, how many pencils can be purchased for y dollars?

    (A) $\frac{100}{xy}$
    (B) $\frac{xy}{100}$
    (C) $\frac{100y}{x}$
    (D) $\frac{y}{100x}$
    (E) $100xy$

142. A merchant increased the original price of an item by 10 percent. If she then reduces the new price by 10 percent, the final price, in terms of the original price, is equal to which of the following?

(A) a decrease of 11 percent
(B) a decrease of 1 percent
(C) no net change
(D) an increase of 1 percent
(E) an increase of 11 percent

143. Harold is twice as old as Jack, who is three years older than Dan. If Harold's age is five times Dan's age, how old (in years) is Jack?

(A) 2
(B) 4
(C) 5
(D) 8
(E) 10

144. A tank with capacity T gallons is empty. If water flows into the tank from Pipe X at the rate of X gallons per minute, and water is pumped out by Pipe Y at the rate of Y gallons per minute, and X is greater than Y, in how many <u>minutes</u> will the tank be filled?

(A) $\frac{T}{Y-X}$

(B) $\frac{T}{X-Y}$

(C) $\frac{T-X}{Y}$

(D) $\frac{X-Y}{60T}$

(E) $\frac{60T}{XY}$

145. Machine X produces w widgets in five minutes. Machine X and Machine Y, working at the same time, produce w widgets in two minutes. How long will it take Machine Y working alone to produce w widgets?

(A) 2 minutes, 30 seconds
(B) 2 minutes, 40 seconds
(C) 3 minutes, 20 seconds
(D) 3 minutes, 30 seconds
(E) 3 minutes, 40 seconds

146. If a train travels m miles in h hours and 45 minutes, what is its average speed in miles per hour?

(A) $\frac{m}{h+\frac{3}{4}}$

(B) $\frac{m}{1\frac{3}{4}h}$

(C) $m\left(h+\frac{3}{4}\right)$

(D) $\frac{m+45}{h}$

(E) $\frac{h}{m+45}$

147. On a playground, there are x seesaws. If 50 children are all riding on seesaws, two to a seesaw, and five seesaws are <u>not</u> in use, what is the value of x?

(A) 15
(B) 20
(C) 25
(D) 30
(E) 35

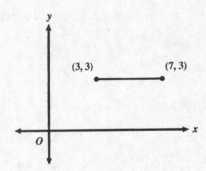

148. In the figure above, the line segment joining points (3, 3) and (7, 3) forms one side of a square. Which of the following CANNOT be the coordinates of another vertex of the square?

(A) (3, –1)
(B) (3, 7)
(C) (7, –3)
(D) (7, –1)
(E) (7, 7)

NOTES AND STRATEGIES

149. Which of the following is a graph of the line that passes through the points (–5, 3), (–1, 1), and (3, –1)?

(A)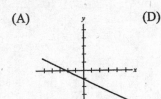

(B)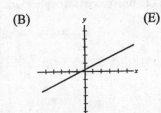

(C)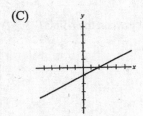

(D)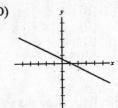

(E)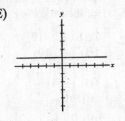

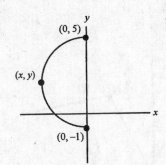

150. In the figure above, what are the coordinates, (x, y), of the point on the semicircle that is farthest from the y-axis?

(A) (–4, –4)
(B) (–3, –3)
(C) (–2, –3)
(D) (–3, 2)
(E) (3, 2)

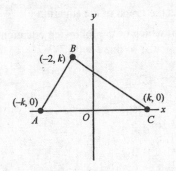

151. In the figure above, the area of △ABC is 8. What is the value of k?

(A) 2
(B) $2\sqrt{2}$
(C) 4
(D) $4\sqrt{2}$
(E) 8

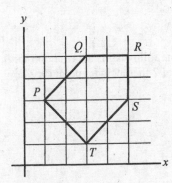

152. In the figure above, which two sides of polygon PQRST have the same slope?

(A) $\overline{PQ}$ and $\overline{QR}$
(B) $\overline{PQ}$ and $\overline{RS}$
(C) $\overline{PQ}$ and $\overline{ST}$
(D) $\overline{QR}$ and $\overline{RS}$
(E) $\overline{RS}$ and $\overline{ST}$

153. Line l is the graph of the equation $y = \frac{3x}{2} + 2$. The graph of which of the following equations is perpendicular to line l at $(0, 2)$?

   (A) $y = \frac{3x}{2} - 2$

   (B) $y = \frac{2x}{3} - 2$

   (C) $y = -\frac{2x}{3} + 2$

   (D) $y = -\frac{3x}{2} + 3$

   (E) $y = -3x + 4$

154. If Set $A = \{(-2, 3); (-1, -1); (-4, -5)\}$, and Set $B = \{(3, 4); (4, 3); (2, -1)\}$, how many lines can be drawn with a positive slope that include exactly one point from Set A and one point from Set B?

   (A) 2
   (B) 3
   (C) 4
   (D) 5
   (E) 6

155. Which of the following is the equation for the line with slope of 2 that includes point $(0, 2)$?

   (A) $y = x - 1$
   (B) $y = 2x - 1$
   (C) $y = 2x - 2$
   (D) $y = 2x + 2$
   (E) $y = x + 1$

156. Which of the following is the equation for the line that includes points $(-1, 1)$ and $(7, 5)$?

   (A) $y = \frac{x}{2} + 2$

   (B) $y = \frac{x}{2} + \frac{3}{2}$

   (C) $y = \frac{x}{2} + \frac{2}{3}$

   (D) $y = 2x + \frac{3}{2}$

   (E) $y = 2x + 2$

157. If the graph of a line in the coordinate plane includes the points $(2, 4)$ and $(8, 7)$, what is the y-intercept of the line?

   (A) 6
   (B) 4
   (C) 3
   (D) −1
   (E) −3

158. If the slope and y-intercept of a line are −2 and 3, respectively, then the line passes through which of the following points?

   (A) $(-5, -10)$
   (B) $(-5, 10)$
   (C) $(-2, 3)$
   (D) $(3, 4)$
   (E) $(4, -5)$

159. What is the distance between the points $(-3, -2)$ and $(3, 3)$?

   (A) $\sqrt{3}$

   (B) $2\sqrt{3}$

   (C) 5

   (D) $\sqrt{29}$

   (E) $\sqrt{61}$

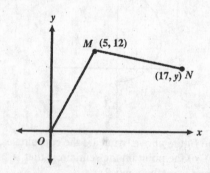

160. In the coordinate plane above, $\overline{MO} \cong \overline{MN}$ and $\overline{MO} \perp \overline{MN}$. What is the value of y?

   (A) 5
   (B) 7
   (C) 12
   (D) 13
   (E) 17

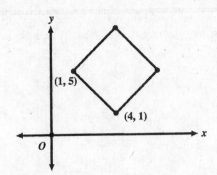

161. In the figure above, what is the area of the square region?

(A) 4

(B) 8

(C) $8\sqrt{2}$

(D) 16

(E) 25

162. In the coordinate plane, what is the midpoint of the line segment with endpoints $(-3, -5)$ and $(5, 7)$?

(A) $(1, 1)$

(B) $(1, 6)$

(C) $(3, \frac{7}{2})$

(D) $(4, 6)$

(E) $(8, 12)$

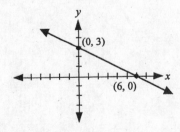

163. The figure above is the graph of which of the following equations?

(A) $x + 2y = 6$

(B) $2x + y = 6$

(C) $x + \frac{y}{2} = 6$

(D) $\frac{x}{2} + y = 2$

(E) $x - 3y = 2$

164. A school rented the ballroom of a hotel for a dance. The cost of the rental is $1,500 plus $5.00 per person who attends. Each person who attends will pay an admission charge of $12.50. If x represents the number of people who attend, which of the graphs can be used to determine how many people must attend for the admission charges to cover exactly the cost of renting the ballroom?

(A)

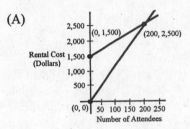

(B)

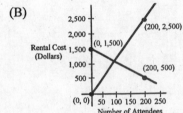

(C)

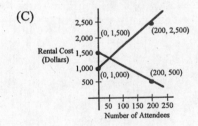

(D)

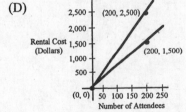

(E)

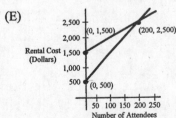

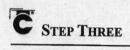

NOTES AND STRATEGIES

165. Which of the following is the graph of the inequality $y \geq 2x$?

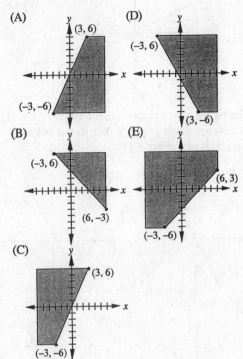

166. Which of the following is the graph of the equation $(x-1)^2 + y^2 = 4$?

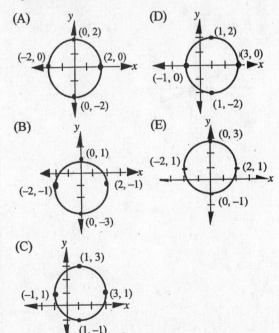

167. Which of the following is the graph of the equation $\frac{x^2}{9} + \frac{y^2}{16} = 1$?

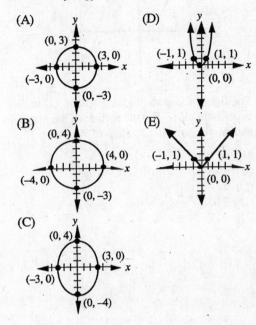

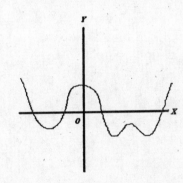

168. The figure above shows the graph of a function $g(x)$. How many times does the graph cross the x-axis?

(A) 1
(B) 2
(C) 3
(D) 4
(E) 5

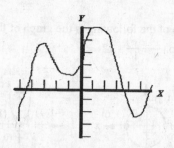

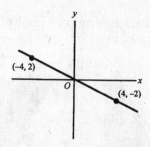

169. The figure above shows the graph of $f(x)$ in the coordinate plane. For the portion of the graph shown, for how many values of x is $f(x) = 3$?

(A) 0
(B) 1
(C) 2
(D) 3
(E) 4

170. The figure above represents the graph of $y = f(x)$ in the coordinate plane. Which of the following is the graph of $y' = f(x - 1)$?

(A)

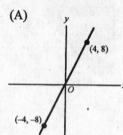

(D)

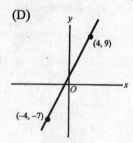

(B)

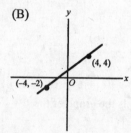

(E)

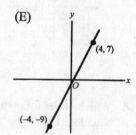

(C)

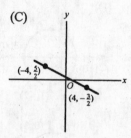

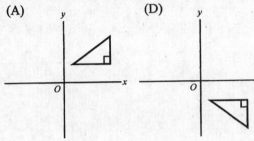

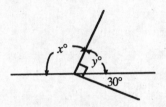

172. In the figure above, $x =$

(A) 45
(B) 60
(C) 75
(D) 90
(E) 120

171. If the triangle in the figure above is reflected across the y-axis and then reflected across the x-axis, which of the following graphs shows the resulting position of the triangle?

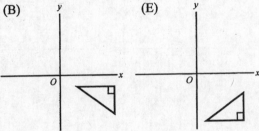

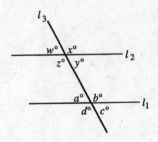

173. In the figure above, $x =$

(A) 45
(B) 60
(C) 90
(D) 105
(E) 120

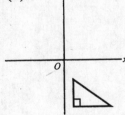

174. In the figure above, l_1 is parallel to l_2. Which of the following __must__ be true?

(A) $w = a$
(B) $y + b = 180$
(C) $w = a$ and $y + b = 180$
(D) $y + b = 180$ and $x + d = 180$
(E) $w = a$, $y + b = 180$, and $x + d = 180$

NOTES AND STRATEGIES

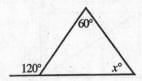

175. In the figure above, $x = ?$

    (A) 30
    (B) 45
    (C) 60
    (D) 75
    (E) 90

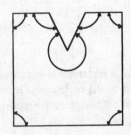

176. In the figure above, what is the sum of the indicated angles?

    (A)   540
    (B)   720
    (C)   900
    (D) 1,080
    (E) 1,260

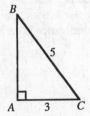

177. In the figure above, what is the length of $\overline{AB}$?

    (A) 2
    (B) $2\sqrt{3}$
    (C) 4
    (D) $4\sqrt{2}$
    (E) 8

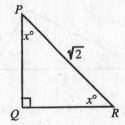

178. In the figure above, what is the length of $\overline{PQ}$?

    (A) 1
    (B) $\sqrt{2}$
    (C) $2\sqrt{2}$
    (D) 4
    (E) 5

179. In a right isosceles triangle, the hypotenuse is equal to which of the following?

    (A) Half the length of either of the other sides
    (B) The length of either of the other sides multiplied by $\sqrt{2}$
    (C) Twice the length of either of the other sides
    (D) The sum of the lengths of the other two sides
    (E) The sum of the lengths of the other two sides multiplied by $\sqrt{2}$

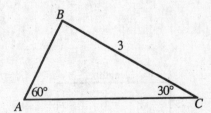

180. In the triangle above, what is the length of $\overline{AC}$?

    (A) 2
    (B) $\sqrt{3}$
    (C) $2\sqrt{3}$
    (D) $3\sqrt{3}$
    (E) 6

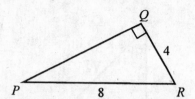

181. In the figure above, the perimeter of $\triangle PQR =$

(A) $12 + \sqrt{3}$

(B) $12 + 2\sqrt{3}$

(C) $12 + 4\sqrt{3}$

(D) 28

(E) 56

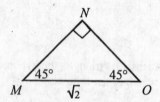

182. In the figure above, what is the area of $\triangle MNO$?

(A) $\frac{1}{2}$

(B) $\frac{\sqrt{2}}{2}$

(C) 1

(D) $\sqrt{2}$

(E) 2

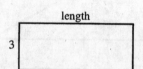

183. If the area of the rectangle above is 18, what is the perimeter?

(A) 9

(B) 12

(C) 18

(D) 24

(E) 30

184. In the figure above, $PQRS$ is a rectangle. If $\overline{PR} =$ 5 centimeters, what is the area, in square centimeters, of the rectangle?

(A) 2

(B) 3

(C) 4

(D) 8

(E) 12

185. If the width of a rectangle is increased by 10% and the length of the rectangle is increased by 20%, by what percent does the area of the rectangle <u>increase</u>?

(A) 2%

(B) 10%

(C) 15%

(D) 32%

(E) 36%

186. If the area of a circle is equal to 9π inches, which of the following is (are) true?

    I. The radius is 3 inches.

    II. The diameter is 6 inches.

    III. The circumference is 6π inches.

(A) I only

(B) II only

(C) III only

(D) I and II only

(E) I, II, and III

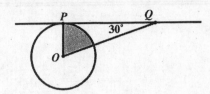

187. In the figure above, O is the center of the circle, and $\overleftrightarrow{PQ}$ is tangent to the circle at P. If the radius of circle O has a length of 6, what is the area of the shaded portion of the figure?

(A) π
(B) 3π
(C) 6π
(D) 9π
(E) 12π

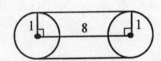

Note: Figure not drawn to scale.

188. The figure above shows two pulleys connected by a belt. If the centers of the pulleys are 8 feet apart and the pulleys each have a radius of 1 foot, what is the length, in feet, of the belt?

(A) 4π
(B) 8π
(C) $8 + \pi$
(D) $16 + \pi$
(E) $16 + 2\pi$

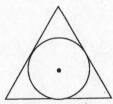

189. In the figure above, a circle is inscribed in an equilateral triangle. If the radius of the circle is 1, what is the perimeter of the triangle?

(A) $\sqrt{3}$
(B) $2\sqrt{3}$
(C) $3\sqrt{3}$
(D)   6
(E) $6\sqrt{3}$

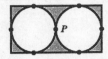

190. The figure above shows two circles of diameter 2 that are tangent to each other at point P. The line segments form a rectangle and are tangent to the circles at the points shown. What is the area of the shaded portion of the figure?

(A) $8 - 2\pi$
(B) $8 - \pi$
(C) $4 - 2\pi$
(D) $4 - \pi$
(E) 2π

191. If a circle of radius 1 foot is inscribed in a square, what is the area, in feet, of the square?

(A) $\dfrac{\sqrt{2}}{2}$
(B)   1
(C) $\sqrt{2}$
(D)   2
(E)   4

192. An isosceles right triangle is inscribed in a semicircle with a radius of 1 inch. What is the area, in square inches, of the triangle?

(A) $\dfrac{\sqrt{2}}{3}$
(B) $\dfrac{1}{2}$
(C)   1
(D) $\sqrt{2}$
(E) $2\sqrt{2}$

 **STEP THREE**

NOTES AND STRATEGIES

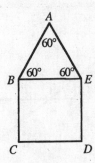

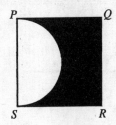

193. In the figure above, *BCDE* is a square with an area of 4. What is the perimeter of △*ABE*?

(A) 3
(B) 4
(C) 6
(D) 8
(E) 12

195. In the figure above, *PQRS* is a square, and $\overline{PS}$ is the diameter of a semicircle. If the length of $\overline{PQ}$ is 2, what is the area of the shaded portion of the diagram?

(A) $4 - 2\pi$
(B) $4 - \pi$
(C) $4 - \frac{\pi}{2}$
(D) $8 - \pi$
(E) $8 - \frac{\pi}{2}$

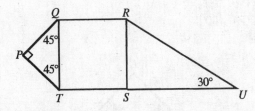

194. In the figure above, if *QRST* is a square and the length of $\overline{PQ}$ is $\sqrt{2}$, what is the length of $\overline{RU}$?

(A) $\sqrt{2}$
(B) $2\sqrt{2}$
(C) $\sqrt{6}$
(D) 4
(E) $4\sqrt{3}$

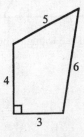

196. If the lengths of the sides, in inches, are as marked on the figure above, what is the area, in square inches, of the quadrilateral?

(A) 6
(B) $6 + \sqrt{3}$
(C) 12
(D) 18
(E) 24

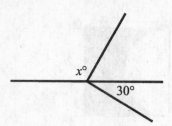

197. In the figure above, $x =$

(A) 30
(B) 65
(C) 120
(D) 150
(E) 170

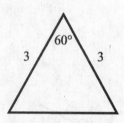

198. The perimeter of the triangle shown above is

(A) $3\sqrt{2}$
(B) 6
(C) 7.5
(D) 9
(E) 15

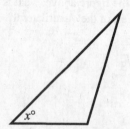

199. In the figure above, $x =$

(A) 30
(B) 45
(C) 60
(D) 75
(E) 90

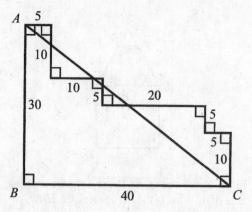

200. In the figure above, what is the length of $\overline{AC}$?

(A) $30\sqrt{2}$
(B) 50
(C) 75
(D) $60\sqrt{2}$
(E) 100

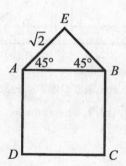

201. In the figure above, what is the area of square $ABCD$?

(A) 2
(B) $2\sqrt{2}$
(C) 4
(D) $4\sqrt{2}$
(E) 8

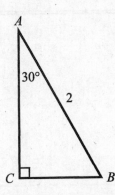

202. In the triangle above, the measure of ∠*BAC* is 30° and the length of $\overline{AB}$ is 2. Which of the following best approximates the length of $\overline{AC}$?

(A) 0.8
(B) 1.0
(C) 1.7
(D) 1.9
(E) 2.3

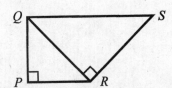

203. In the figure above, Δ*PQR* and Δ*PRS* are isosceles right triangles. If *QP* = 3, what is the length of $\overline{QS}$? (sin 45° = $\frac{\sqrt{2}}{2}$.)

(A) $\sqrt{2}$

(B) $2\sqrt{2}$

(C) 4

(D) 6

(E) 8

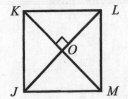

204. If the area of the square *JKLM* in the figure above is 4, what is the sum of the lengths of the diagonals $\overline{JL}$ and $\overline{KM}$? (sin 45° = $\frac{\sqrt{2}}{2}$.)

(A) $\frac{\sqrt{2}}{2}$

(B) $2 + \frac{\sqrt{2}}{2}$

(C) $4\sqrt{2}$

(D) $4 + 4\sqrt{2}$

(E) $8\sqrt{2}$

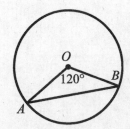

205. In the figure above, *O* is the center of the circle with radius 10. What is the area of Δ*AOB*? (sin 30° = $\frac{1}{2}$; sin 60° = $\frac{\sqrt{3}}{2}$.)

(A) $10\sqrt{3}$

(B) 10

(C) 25

(D) $25\sqrt{3}$

(E) 50

NOTES AND STRATEGIES

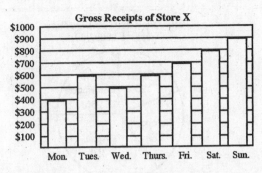

Gross Receipts of Store X

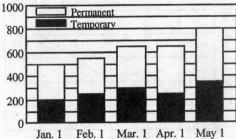

Number of Corporation X Employees

206. During the week shown in the graph above, what was the greatest increase in sales from one day to the next?

(A) $50
(B) $100
(C) $150
(D) $200
(E) $250

208. Based on the data presented above, what was the difference, if any, between the number of permanent workers employed by Corporation X on March 1st and the number of permanent workers employed by Corporation X on April 1st?

(A)   0
(B)   50
(C)   100
(D)   150
(E)   200

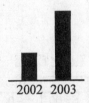

2002   2003

207. If the graph above represents expenditures by Corporation X in two different years, what was the approximate ratio of expenditures in 2002 to those in 2003?

(A) $\frac{1}{5}$

(B) $\frac{2}{5}$

(C) $\frac{1}{2}$

(D) $\frac{2}{3}$

(E) 2

COMPANY T DOMESTIC SALES
(Millions of Dollars)

209. Based on the data presented above, what was the difference in the value of foreign sales by Company T between 1983 and 1985?

(A) $1,000,000
(B) $2,000,000
(C) $3,000,000
(D) $5,000,000
(E) $6,000,000

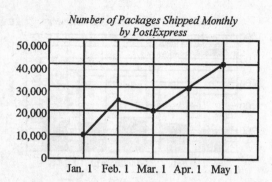

Number of Packages Shipped Monthly by PostExpress

210. Based on the data presented above, what was the approximate total number of packages shipped by PostExpress for the months January, February, and March, inclusive?

(A) 40,000
(B) 55,000
(C) 60,000
(D) 70,000
(E) 85,000

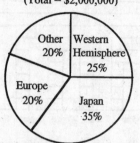

PetProducts 2002 Foreign Sales
(Total = $2,000,000)

212. Based on the data presented above, what was the dollar value of foreign sales to Europe by PetProducts in 2002?

(A) $200,000
(B) $400,000
(C) $1,200,000
(D) $1,600,000
(E) $2,000,000

GOVERNMENT EXPENDITURES
$1,000,137 = 100%

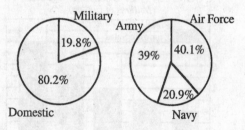

211. Based on the data presented above, approximately how much money was spent on the Air Force?

(A) $39,704
(B) $79,409
(C) $96,123
(D) $198,027
(E) $401,054

T-shirt Prices

	Blue	Red	White
Small	$5.00	$6.00	$7.00
Large	$5.75	$6.50	$7.25
Extra Large	$6.50	$7.25	$8.00

213. Based on the data presented above, what is the total cost of 5 large blue t-shirts, 8 small red t-shirts, and 4 extra large white t-shirts?

(A) $56.00
(B) $88.25
(C) $105.50
(D) $108.75
(E) $135.00

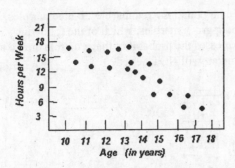

214. The above scatterplot shows the video-game playing habits of 20 students. The graph most strongly supports the conclusion that the number of hours per week spent playing video-games

(A) is constant from age 10 to age 18
(B) increases as age increases from 10 to 18
(C) decreases as age increases from 10 to 18
(D) is constant for ages 10 through 14 and then decreases
(E) is constant for ages 10 through 14 and then increases

215. If the average of 35, 38, 41, 43, and x is 37, what is x?

(A) 28
(B) 30
(C) 31
(D) 34
(E) 36

216. The average weight of 6 packages is 50 pounds per package. Another package is added, making the average weight of the 7 packages 52 pounds per package. What is the weight, in pounds, of the additional package?

(A) 2
(B) 7
(C) 52
(D) 62
(E) 64

217. The average of 10 test scores is 80. If the high and low scores are dropped, the average is 81. What is the average of the high and low scores?

(A) 76
(B) 78
(C) 80
(D) 81
(E) 82

218. In Latin 101, the final exam grade is weighted two times as heavily as the mid-term grade. If Leo received a score of 84 on his final exam and 90 on his mid-term, what was his course average?

(A) 88
(B) 87.5
(C) 86.5
(D) 86
(E) 85

219. In a group of children, three children are 10 years old and two children are 5 years old. What is the average age, in years, of the children in the group?

(A) 6
(B) 6.5
(C) 7
(D) 7.5
(E) 8

220. The number of employment applications received by All-Star Staffing each month during 2002 was as follows: 8, 3, 5, 3, 4, 3, 1, 0, 3, 4, 0, and 7. What is the median number of applications received in 2002?

(A) 3
(B) 4
(C) 5
(D) 6
(E) 7

221. William's monthly electric bills for last year were as follows: $40, 38, 36, 38, 34, 34, 30, 32, 34, 37, 39, and 40. What is the mode of the bills?

    (A) $33
    (B) $34
    (C) $35
    (D) $36
    (E) $37

222. If Set $A = \{1, 2, 3, 4, 5, 6\}$ and Set $B = \{1, 2, 3, 4, 5, 6\}$, what is the probability that the sum of one number from Set A and one number from Set B will total 7?

    (A) $\frac{1}{12}$
    (B) $\frac{5}{36}$
    (C) $\frac{1}{6}$
    (D) $\frac{1}{5}$
    (E) $\frac{1}{3}$

The Dark Night	History of Canada	Ring More Than Once	A Bright Morning		George Washington
		Mary Smith		Chemistry	C. Adams
Mary Smith	Carol Kim			Victor Brown	
			T. Jackson		
•Mystery•	•Textbook•	•Mystery•	•Mystery•	•Textbook•	•Biography•

223. If a book is selected at random from the collection shown above, which of the following has the greatest probability of being selected?

    (A) A book by Mary Smith
    (B) A textbook
    (C) A mystery
    (D) A book written by either Carol Kim or Victor Brown
    (E) A biography

224. If a jar contains r red marbles, b blue marbles, and g green marbles, which of the following expresses the probability that a marble drawn at random will NOT be red?

    (A) $\frac{-r}{r+b+g}$
    (B) $\frac{r}{r+b+g}$
    (C) $\frac{b+g-r}{b+g+r}$
    (D) $\frac{r}{b+g}$
    (E) $\frac{b+g}{b+g+r}$

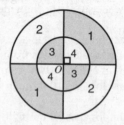

225. The figure above shows a dartboard consisting of two concentric circles with center O. The radius of the larger circle is equal to the diameter of the smaller circle. What is the probability that a randomly thrown dart striking the board will score a "3."

    (A) $\frac{1}{16}$
    (B) $\frac{1}{8}$
    (C) $\frac{1}{4}$
    (D) $\frac{1}{2}$
    (E) $\frac{3}{4}$

Note: Figure not drawn to scale.

226. An underwater salvage team is searching the ocean floor for a lost signal device using a large circular search pattern and a smaller circular search pattern with a radius equal to one-third that of the larger pattern. If the device is known to be inside the boundary of the larger search area, what is the probability that it is NOT located in the shaded portion of the figure?

(A) $\frac{1}{9}$

(B) $\frac{1}{6}$

(C) $\frac{1}{3}$

(D) $\frac{1}{2}$

(E) $\frac{8}{9}$

CHALLENGE ITEMS

DIRECTIONS: The items in this section reflect the format and difficulty range of Math: Multiple-Choice on the SAT, though difficult items are emphasized. For each item, choose the best answer. Use any available space in the section for scratch work. You may use your calculator for any items you choose, but some of the items may best be done without using a calculator. Answers are on page 985.

Notes:

(1) The use of a calculator is permitted. All numbers used are real numbers.

(2) Figures that accompany problems in this test are intended to provide information useful in solving the problems. They are drawn as accurately as possible EXCEPT when it is stated in a specific problem that the figure is not drawn to scale. All figures lie in a plane unless otherwise indicated.

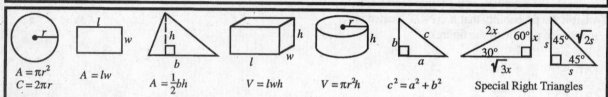

$A = \pi r^2$
$C = 2\pi r$

$A = lw$

$A = \frac{1}{2}bh$

$V = lwh$

$V = \pi r^2 h$

$c^2 = a^2 + b^2$

Special Right Triangles

The number of degrees of arc in a circle is 360.
The measure in degrees of a straight angle is 180.
The sum of the measures in degrees of the angles of a triangle is 180.

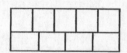

1. Nine playing cards from the same deck are placed as shown in the figure above to form a large rectangle of area 180 sq. in. How many inches are there in the perimeter of this large rectangle?

   (A) 29
   (B) 58
   (C) 64
   (D) 116
   (E) 210

2. If each of the dimensions of a rectangle is increased by 100%, by what percent is the area increased?

   (A) 100%
   (B) 200%
   (C) 300%
   (D) 400%
   (E) 500%

3. What is 10% of $\frac{1}{3}x$ if $\frac{2}{3}x$ is 10% of 60?

   (A) 0.1
   (B) 0.2
   (C) 0.3
   (D) 0.4
   (E) 0.5

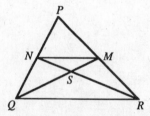

4. In the figure above, M and N are midpoints of sides $\overline{PR}$ and $\overline{PQ}$, respectively, of $\triangle PQR$. What is the ratio of the area of $\triangle MNS$ to that of $\triangle PQR$?

   (A) 2:5
   (B) 2:9
   (C) 1:4
   (D) 1:8
   (E) 1:12

NOTES AND STRATEGIES

5. A cube has an edge that is 4 inches long. If the edge is increased by 25%, by what percent is the volume increased?

(A) 25%
(B) 48%
(C) 73%
(D) 95%
(E) 122%

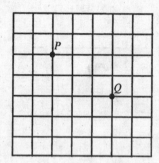

6. In the graph above, the axes and the origin are not shown. If point P has coordinates (3, 7), what are the coordinates of point Q, assuming each box is one square unit?

(A) (5, 6)
(B) (1, 10)
(C) (6, 9)
(D) (6, 5)
(E) (5, 10)

7. The average of 8 numbers is 6; the average of 6 other numbers is 8. What is the average of all 14 numbers?

(A) 6
(B) $6\frac{6}{7}$
(C) 7
(D) $7\frac{2}{7}$
(E) $8\frac{1}{7}$

8. The front wheels of a wagon are 7 feet in circumference and the back wheels are 9 feet in circumference. When the front wheels have made 10 more revolutions than the back wheels, what distance, in feet, has the wagon gone?

(A) 126
(B) 180
(C) 189
(D) 315
(E) 630

9. Doreen can wash her car in 15 minutes, while her younger brother Dave takes twice as long to do the same job. If they work together, how many minutes will the job take them?

(A) 5
(B) $7\frac{1}{2}$
(C) 10
(D) $22\frac{1}{2}$
(E) 30

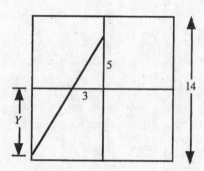

10. In the figure above, the sides of the large square are each 14 inches long. Joining the midpoints of each opposite side forms 4 smaller squares. What is the value of Y, in inches?

(A) 5
(B) 6
(C) $6\frac{5}{8}$
(D) $6\frac{2}{3}$
(E) 6.8

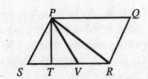

Note: Figure not drawn to scale.

11. In the figure above, $PQRS$ is a parallelogram, and $\overline{ST} = \overline{TV} = \overline{VR}$. If $\angle PTS = 90°$, what is the ratio of the area of $\triangle SPT$ to the area of the parallelogram?

(A) $\frac{1}{6}$

(B) $\frac{1}{5}$

(C) $\frac{2}{7}$

(D) $2\frac{1}{3}$

(E) $2\frac{2}{7}$

12. If $p > q$ and $r < 0$, which of the following is (are) true?

    I. $pr < qr$
    II. $p + r > q + r$
    III. $p - r < q - r$

(A) I only
(B) II only
(C) I and III only
(D) I and II only
(E) I, II, and III

13. A pound of water is evaporated from 6 pounds of seawater that is 4% salt. What is the percentage of salt in the remaining solution?

(A) 3.6%
(B) 4%
(C) 4.8%
(D) 5.2%
(E) 6%

14. John is now three times Pat's age. Four years from now, John will be x years old. In terms of x, how old is Pat now?

(A) $\frac{x+4}{3}$

(B) $3x$

(C) $x + 4$

(D) $x - 4$

(E) $\frac{x-4}{3}$

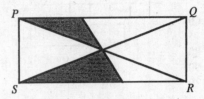

15. In the figure above, what percent of the area of rectangle $PQRS$ is shaded?

(A) 20
(B) 25
(C) 30
(D) $33\frac{1}{3}$
(E) 35

16. A cylindrical container has a diameter of 14 inches and a height of 6 inches. Since one gallon equals 231 cubic inches, what is the approximate capacity, in gallons, of the tank?

(A) $\frac{2}{3}$

(B) $1\frac{1}{7}$

(C) $2\frac{2}{7}$

(D) $2\frac{2}{3}$

(E) 4

17. A train running between two towns arrives at its destination 10 minutes late when it goes 40 miles per hour and 16 minutes late when it goes 30 miles per hour. What is the distance, in miles, between the two towns?

(A) $8\frac{6}{7}$

(B) 12

(C) 192

(D) 560

(E) 720

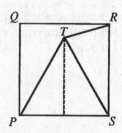

18. In the figure above, *PQRS* is a square and *PTS* is an equilateral triangle. What is the degree measure of ∠*TRS*?

(A) 60
(B) 75
(C) 80
(D) 90
(E) 120

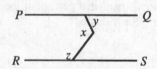

19. In the figure above, line $\overline{PQ}$ is parallel to line $\overline{RS}$, $y = 60°$, and $z = 130°$. What is the degree measure of ∠*x*?

(A) 90
(B) 100
(C) 110
(D) 120
(E) 130

20. Paul can paint a fence in 2 hours and Fred can paint the same fence in 3 hours. If Paul and Fred work together, how many hours will it take them to paint the fence?

(A) 5
(B) $2\frac{1}{2}$
(C) $1\frac{1}{5}$
(D) 1
(E) $\frac{5}{6}$

21. A motorist drives 60 miles to her destination at an average speed of 40 miles per hour and makes the return trip at an average speed of 30 miles per hour. What is her average speed, in miles per hour, for the entire trip?

(A) 17
(B) $34\frac{2}{7}$
(C) 35
(D) $43\frac{1}{3}$
(E) 70

22. An ice cream truck drives down Willy Street 4 times a week. The truck carries 5 different flavors of ice cream bars, each of which comes in 2 different designs. If the truck runs Monday through Thursday, and Monday was the first day of the month, by what day of the month could Zachary, buying 1 ice cream bar each time the truck drives down the street, purchase all of the different varieties of ice cream bars?

(A) 11th
(B) 16th
(C) 21st
(D) 24th
(E) 30th

23. If $N! = N(N-1)(N-2)\ldots[N-(N-1)]$, what does $\frac{N!}{(N-2)!}$ equal?

(A) $N^2 - N$
(B) $N^5 + N^3 - N^2 + \frac{N}{N^2}$
(C) $N + 1$
(D) 1
(E) 6

NOTES AND STRATEGIES

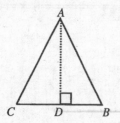

24. In the figure above, *ABC* is an equilateral triangle with a perpendicular line drawn from point *A* to point *D*. If the triangle is "folded over" on the perpendicular line so that points *B* and *C* meet, the perimeter of the new triangle is approximately what percent of the perimeter of the triangle before the fold?

    (A) 100%
    (B) 78%
    (C) 50%
    (D) 32%
    (E) 25%

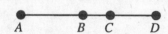

Note: Figure not drawn to scale.

25. In the figure above, segment $\overline{AB}$ is three times longer than segment $\overline{BC}$, and segment $\overline{CD}$ is two times longer than segment $\overline{BC}$. If segment $\overline{BC}$ is removed from the line and the other two segments are joined to form one line, what is the ratio of the original length of $\overline{AD}$ to the new length of $\overline{AD}$?

    (A) 3:2
    (B) 6:5
    (C) 5:4
    (D) 7:6
    (E) 11:10

26. If $(x + 1)(x - 2)$ is positive, then

    (A) $x < -1$ or $x > 2$
    (B) $x > -1$ or $x < 2$
    (C) $-1 < x < 2$
    (D) $-2 < x < 1$
    (E) $x = -1$ or $x = 2$

Annual Sale of Cassettes ABC SOUND STORES	
Year	*Number Sold*
1995	7,000
1996	9,000
1997	12,000
1998	16,000
1999	20,000
2000	24,000

27. In the above table, which yearly period had the smallest percent increase in sales?

    (A) 1995-96
    (B) 1996-97
    (C) 1997-98
    (D) 1998-99
    (E) 1999-00

28. If s, t, and u are different positive integers and $\frac{s}{t}$ and $\frac{t}{u}$ are positive integers, which of the following CANNOT be a positive integer?

    (A) $\frac{s}{u}$
    (B) $s \cdot t$
    (C) $\frac{u}{s}$
    (D) $(s + t)u$
    (E) $(s - u)t$

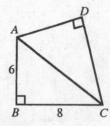

Note: Figure not drawn to scale.

29. In the figure above, $\overline{AD} = \overline{DC}$. What is the value of $\overline{AD} + \overline{DC}$?

    (A) $18\sqrt{2}$
    (B) 18
    (C) $10\sqrt{2}$
    (D) 10
    (E) $6\sqrt{2}$

TIMED-PRACTICE QUIZZES

DIRECTIONS: For each item, choose the best answer. Use any available space in the section for scratch work. You may use your calculator for any items you choose, but some of the items may best be done without using a calculator. Answers are on page 985.

Notes:

(1) The use of a calculator is permitted. All numbers used are real numbers.

(2) Figures that accompany problems in this test are intended to provide information useful in solving the problems. They are drawn as accurately as possible EXCEPT when it is stated in a specific problem that the figure is not drawn to scale. All figures lie in a plane unless otherwise indicated.

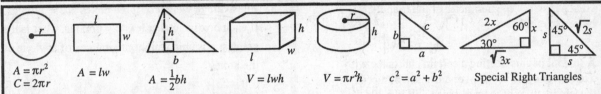

$A = \pi r^2$
$C = 2\pi r$
$A = lw$
$A = \frac{1}{2}bh$
$V = lwh$
$V = \pi r^2 h$
$c^2 = a^2 + b^2$
Special Right Triangles

The number of degrees of arc in a circle is 360.
The measure in degrees of a straight angle is 180.
The sum of the measures in degrees of the angles of a triangle is 180.

A. QUIZ I (15 items; 20 minutes)

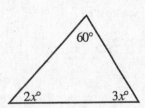

1. In the triangle above, $x =$

    (A) 24
    (B) 20
    (C) 16
    (D) 12
    (E) 10

2. A normal dozen contains 12 items, and a baker's dozen contains 13 items. If x is the number of items that could be measured either in a whole number of normal dozens or in a whole number of baker's dozens, what is the <u>minimum</u> value of x?

    (A) 1
    (B) 12
    (C) 13
    (D) 25
    (E) 156

 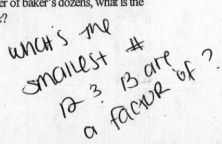

what's the smallest # 12 & 13 are a factor of?

3. In the figure above, what is the degree measure of the <u>smaller</u> of the two angles formed by the hour and minute hands of the clock?

    (A) 45
    (B) 60
    (C) 90
    (D) 120
    (E) 240

4. Starting from points that are 200 kilometers apart, two trains travel toward each other along two parallel tracks. If one train travels at 70 kilometers per hour and the other travels at 80 kilometers per hour, how much time, in hours, will elapse before the trains pass each other?

(A) $\frac{3}{4}$
(B) 1
(C) $\frac{4}{3}$
(D) $\frac{3}{2}$
(E) 2

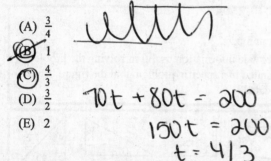

$$70t + 80t = 200$$
$$150t = 200$$
$$t = 4/3$$

5. A student begins heating a certain substance with a temperature of 50° C over a Bunsen burner. If the temperature of the substance will rise 20° C for every 24 minutes it remains over the burner, what will be the temperature, in degrees Celsius, of the substance after 18 minutes?

(A) 52
(B) 56
(C) 60
(D) 65
(E) 72

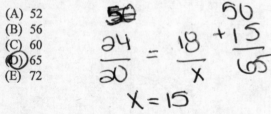

$$\frac{24}{20} = \frac{18}{x} \quad \frac{+15}{65}$$
$$x = 15$$

6. If the ratio of men to women in a meeting is 8 to 7, what fractional part of the people at the meeting is women?

(A) $\frac{1}{56}$
(B) $\frac{1}{15}$
(C) $\frac{1}{7}$
(D) $\frac{7}{15}$
(E) $\frac{8}{7}$

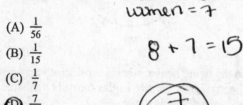

men = 8
women = 7

$$8 + 7 = 15$$
$$\frac{7}{15}$$

7. The object of a popular board game is to use clues to identify a suspect and the weapon used to commit a crime. If there are 3 suspects and 6 weapons, how many different solutions to the game are possible?

(A) 2
(B) 3
(C) 9
(D) 12
(E) 18

8. The average weight of three boxes is $25\frac{1}{3}$ pounds. If each box weighs at least 24 pounds, what is the greatest possible weight, in pounds, of any one of the boxes?

(A) 25
(B) 26
(C) 27
(D) 28
(E) 29

9. If n subtracted from $\frac{13}{2}$ is equal to n divided by $\frac{2}{13}$, what is the value of n?

(A) $\frac{2}{3}$
(B) $\frac{13}{15}$
(C) 1
(D) $\frac{13}{11}$
(E) 26

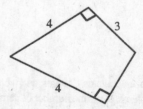

35/6

10. In the figure above, what is the area of the quadrilateral?

(A) 18
(B) 15
(C) 12
(D) 9
(E) 8

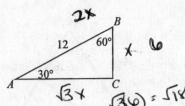

11. In the figure above, what is the length of $\overline{BC}$?
    ($\sin 30° = \frac{1}{2}$.)

    (A) 2

    (B) 3

    (C) $3\sqrt{3}$

    (D) 6

    (E) $6\sqrt{3}$

12. After being dropped from a height of h meters, a ball bounces 3 meters high on the third bounce and $\frac{4}{3}$ meters high on the fifth bounce. What is the value, in meters, of h?

    (A) $\frac{27}{8}$

    (B) $\frac{9}{2}$

    (C) $\frac{27}{4}$

    (D) $\frac{81}{8}$

    (E) $\frac{27}{2}$

13. Set $A = \{-2, -1, 0\}$, and Set $B = (-1, 0, 1\}$. If a is an element of Set A and b is an element of Set B, for how many pairs (a, b) is the product ab a member of both Set A and Set B?

    (A) 0

    (B) 2

    (C) 4

    (D) 6

    (E) 9

14. Which of the following is the complete solution set for $|2x + 4| = 12$?

    (A) $\{-8, 4\}$

    (B) $\{-4, 8\}$

    (C) $\{0, 8\}$

    (D) $\{4, 8\}$

    (E) $\{6, 8\}$

15. If $f(x) = \dfrac{(x-1)^2}{(-2-x)}$, for what value of x is $f(x)$ undefined?

    (A) -2

    (B) -1

    (C) 0

    (D) 1

    (E) 2

B. QUIZ II (20 items; 25 minutes)

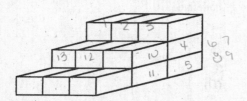

1. The figure above is a plan that shows a solid set of steps to be constructed from concrete blocks of equal size. How many blocks are needed to construct the steps?

   (A) 12
   (B) 15
   (C) 18
   (D) 21
   (E) 24

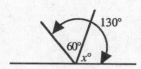

2. In the figure above, what is the value of x?

   (A) 70
   (B) 60
   (C) 50
   (D) 40
   (E) 30

3. If $2^{x+1} = 4^{x-1}$, what is the value of x?

   (A) 1
   (B) 2
   (C) 3
   (D) 4
   (E) 5

   $2^{x+1} = 2^{2(x-1)}$

   $x+1 = 2(x-1)$

   $x+1 = 2x-2$

4. Of the actors in a certain play, five actors are in Act I, 12 actors are in Act II, and 13 actors are in Act III. If 10 of the actors are in exactly two of the three acts and all of the other actors are in just one act, how many actors are in the play?

   $12 + 13 + 5$

   (A) 17
   (B) 20
   (C) 24
   (D) 30
   (E) 38

5. In the figure above, $\overline{AB} \cong \overline{BC} \cong \overline{CA}$. What is the value of y?

   (A) 20
   (B) 60
   (C) 80
   (D) 100
   (E) 120

6. Under certain conditions, a bicycle traveling k meters per second requires $\frac{k^2}{20} + k$ meters to stop. If $k = 10$, how many <u>meters</u> does the bicycle need to stop?

   (A) 10
   (B) 12
   (C) 15
   (D) 20
   (E) 30

   $\dfrac{10^2}{20} + 10$

   $\dfrac{100}{20} + 10$

   $5 + 10$

7. What is the slope of a line that passes through the origin and $(-3, -2)$?

   $(0,0)$
   $(-3,-2)$

   (A) $\frac{3}{2}$
   (B) $\frac{2}{3}$
   (C) 0
   (D) $-\frac{2}{3}$
   (E) $-\frac{3}{2}$

   $\dfrac{\Delta y}{\Delta x}$

   $\dfrac{-2-0}{-3-0} = \dfrac{2}{3}$

8. An album contains x black-and-white photographs and y color photographs. If the album contains 24 photographs, then which of the following CANNOT be true?

(A) $x = y$
(B) $x = 2y$
(C) $x = 3y$
(D) $x = 4y$
(E) $x = 5y$

9. If $2a = 3b = 4c$, then what is the average (arithmetic mean) of a, b, and c, in terms of a?

(A) $\frac{13a}{18}$
(B) $\frac{13a}{9}$
(C) $\frac{8a}{3}$
(D) $\frac{4a}{3}$
(E) $2a$

10. If $x = 6 + y$ and $4x = 3 - 2y$, what is the value of x?

(A) 4
(B) $\frac{11}{3}$
(C) $\frac{5}{2}$
(D) $-\frac{2}{3}$
(E) $-\frac{7}{2}$

11. If $\frac{2}{3}$ is written as a decimal to 101 places, what is the sum of the first 100 digits to the right of the decimal point?

(A) 66
(B) 595
(C) 599
(D) 600
(E) 601

12. In the figure above, O is the center of the circle with radius 1. What is the area of the shaded region?

(A) $\frac{3\pi}{4} + \frac{1}{2}$
(B) $\frac{3\pi}{4} - \frac{1}{2}$
(C) $\frac{\pi}{4} + \frac{1}{2}$
(D) $\frac{\pi}{4} - \frac{1}{2}$
(E) $\pi - 1$

13. If $f(3) = 5$ and $f(7) = 7$, what is the slope of graph of $f(x)$ in the coordinate plane?

(A) -2
(B) $-\frac{1}{2}$
(C) 1
(D) $\frac{1}{2}$
(E) 2

14. In a list of the first 100 positive integers, the digit 9 appears how many times?

(A) 9
(B) 10
(C) 11
(D) 19
(E) 20

15. If $\frac{x}{x+3} = \frac{3}{4}$, and $x \neq -3$, then $x =$

(A) 3
(B) 4
(C) 5
(D) 7
(E) 9

16. Which of the following is the complete solution set for $\sqrt{2x+3}+2=5$?

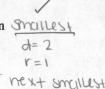

(A) {}
(B) {−1}
(C) {3}
(D) {−1, 3}
(E) {1, 2}

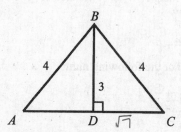

17. In the figure above, what is the length of $\overline{AC}$?
($\sin \angle ABD = \frac{\sqrt{7}}{4}$.)

(A) 5
(B) $2\sqrt{7}$
(C) $4\sqrt{3}$
(D) 7
(E) $3\sqrt{7}$

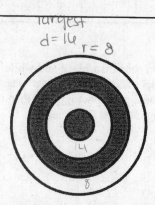

18. A dartboard has four concentric circles with the center as indicated in the figure above. If the diameter of each circle except for the smallest is twice that of the next smaller circle, what is the probability that a randomly thrown dart will strike the shaded portion of the figure?

(A) $\frac{3}{16}$
(B) $\frac{1}{4}$
(C) $\frac{13}{64}$
(D) $\frac{17}{64}$
(E) $\frac{1}{2}$

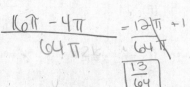

19. If $f(3) = 4$ and $f(-3) = 1$, what is the y-intercept of the graph of $f(x)$ in the coordinate plane?

(A) $-\frac{5}{2}$
(B) $-\frac{2}{5}$
(C) 0
(D) $\frac{2}{5}$
(E) $\frac{5}{2}$

Sales of Company X (in millions)

20. Which of the following pie graphs best represents the division of total sales between foreign and domestic sales for 1994?

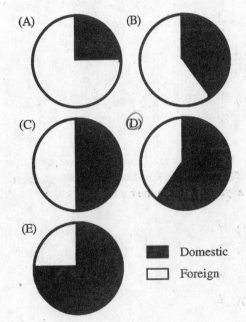

(A)

(B)

(C)

(D)

(E)

■ Domestic

☐ Foreign

C. QUIZ III (25 items; 25 minutes)

1. What is the average (arithmetic mean) of all integers 6 through 15 (including 6 and 15)?

(A) 6
(B) 9
(C) 10.5
(D) 11
(E) 21

$6 + 7 + 8 + 9 + 10 + 11 + 12 + 13$
$+ 14 + 15$

2. Which of the following numbers is the largest?

(A) 0.08
(B) 0.17
(C) 0.171
(D) 0.1077
(E) 0.10771

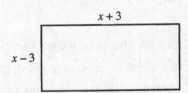

3. If the rectangle above has an area of 72, then $x =$

(A) 3
(B) 4
(C) 6
(D) 8
(E) 9

$72 = (x + 3)(x - 3)$
$72 = x^2 - 3x + 3x - 9$
$72 = x^2 - 9$
$81 = x^2 \quad x = 9$

4. Machine X produces 15 units per minute and Machine Y produces 12 units per minute. In one hour, Machine X will produce how many more units than Machine Y?

(A) 90
(B) 180
(C) 240
(D) 270
(E) 360

$\dfrac{15}{60} = \dfrac{x}{3600}$
$x = 900$

$\dfrac{12}{60} = \dfrac{x}{3600}$
$x = 720$

Team Expenses		
Transportation	$240	■
Lodging	$360	▦
Meals	$120	□

5. Which of the following pie charts represents the data shown above?

(A)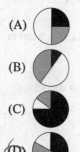

(B)

(C)

(D)

(E)

6. On the first day after being given an assignment, a student read $\frac{1}{2}$ the number of pages assigned, and on the second day, the student read 3 more pages. If the student still has 6 additional pages to read, how many pages were assigned?

(A) 15
(B) 18
(C) 24
(D) 30
(E) 36

handwritten: 1) ½ X   2) X + 3

7. The average (arithmetic mean) of Pat's scores on three tests was 80. If the average of her scores on the first two tests was 78, what was her score on the third test?

(A) 82
(B) 84
(C) 86
(D) 88
(E) 90

handwritten: 80 + 80 + 80 = 240   78 × 2 = 156   240 − 156 = 84

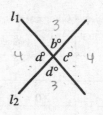

8. In the figure above, $a + c - b$ is equal to which of the following?

(A) $2a - d$
(B) $2a + d$
(C) $2d - a$
(D) $2a$
(E) 180

handwritten: 4 + 4 − 3 =   8 − 3 = 5

9. If $3a + 6b = 12$, then $a + 2b =$

(A) 1
(B) 2
(C) 3
(D) 4
(E) 6

handwritten: 3(2) + 6(1) = 12   2 + 2(1) = $\frac{3(a+2b)}{3} = \frac{12}{3}$ a + 2b = 4

10. Two circles with radii r and $r + 3$ have areas that differ by 15π. What is the radius of the <u>smaller</u> circle?

(A) 4
(B) 3
(C) 2
(D) 1
(E) $\frac{1}{2}$

handwritten: $(r+3)^2\pi - r^2\pi = 15\pi$ plug in answers into equation

11. If x, y, and z are integers, $x > y > z > 1$, and $xyz = 144$, what is the <u>greatest</u> possible value of x?

(A) 8
(B) 12
(C) 16
(D) 24
(E) 36

12. For all integers, $x \spadesuit y = 2x + 3y$. Which of the following must be true?

   I. $3 \spadesuit 2 = 12$
   II. $x \spadesuit y = y \spadesuit x$
   III. $0 \spadesuit (1 \spadesuit 2) = (0 \spadesuit 1) \spadesuit 2$

   (A) I only
   (B) I and II only
   (C) I and III only
   (D) II and III only
   (E) I, II, and III

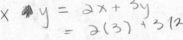

$x \spadesuit y = 2x + 3y$
$= 2(3) + 3(2)$
$= 6 + 6$
$= 12$

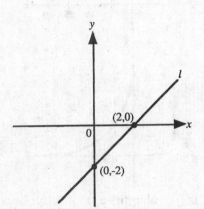

13. In the figure above, what is the slope of line l?

    (A) 1
   (B) $\frac{1}{2}$
   (C) 0
   (D) $-\frac{1}{2}$
   (E) -1

$\frac{\Delta y}{\Delta x}$

$\frac{0 - (-2)}{2 - 0} = \frac{2}{2} = 1$

14. If Yuriko is now twice as old as Lisa was 10 years ago, how old is Lisa today if Yuriko is now n years old?

   (A) $\frac{n}{2} + 10$
   (B) $\frac{n}{2} - 10$
   (C) $n - 10$
   (D) $2n + 10$
   (E) $2n - 10$

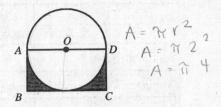

$A = \pi r^2$
$A = \pi 2^2$
$A = \pi 4$

15. In the figure above, $ABCD$ is a rectangle with sides $\overline{AB}$, $\overline{BC}$, and $\overline{CD}$ touching the circle with center O. If the radius of the circle is 2, what is the area of the shaded region?

   rectangle
   $A = 2 \cdot 4$
   $= 8$

   (A) $\frac{3\pi}{2}$
   (B) $\frac{3\pi}{4}$
   (C) $8 - 2\pi$
   (D) $2 - \pi$
   (E) $\pi - 1$

   $8 - \frac{\pi}{}$

16. The sum of two positive consecutive integers is n. In terms of n, what is the value of the larger of the two integers?

   (A) $\frac{n-1}{2}$
   (B) $\frac{n+1}{2}$
   (C) $\frac{n}{2} + 1$
   (D) $\frac{n}{2} - 1$
   (E) $\frac{n}{2}$

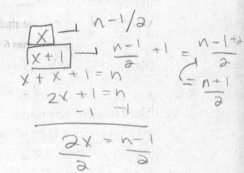

$n - 1/2$

x
$x + 1$

$\frac{n-1}{2} + 1 = \frac{n-1+2}{2}$
$= \frac{n+1}{2}$

$x + x + 1 = n$
$2x + 1 = n$
$-1 \quad -1$

$\frac{2x}{2} = \frac{n-1}{2}$

$x = \frac{n-1}{2}$

	Old Scale	New Scale
Minimum Score	0	120
Minimum Passing Score	60	?
Maximum Score	100	180

17. The table above shows a teacher how to convert scores for a test from the Old Scale to the New Scale. What is the Minimum Passing Score on the New Scale?

   (A) 108
   (B) 136
   (C) 156
   (D) 164
   (E) 208

18. If a polygon with all equal sides is inscribed in a circle, then the measure in degrees of the minor arc created by adjacent vertices of the polygon could be all of the following EXCEPT

   (A) 30
   (B) 25
   (C) 24
   (D) 20
   (E) 15

$360 \div n =$

19. A jar contains 5 blue marbles, 25 green marbles, and x red marbles. If the probability of drawing a red marble at random is $\frac{1}{4}$, what is the value of x?

   (A) 25
   (B) 20
   (C) 15
   (D) 12
   (E) 10

20. $\frac{1}{10^{25}} - \frac{1}{10^{26}} =$

   (A) $\frac{9}{10^{25}}$
   (B) $\frac{9}{10^{26}}$
   (C) $\frac{1}{10^{25}}$
   (D) $-\frac{9}{10^{25}}$
   (E) $-\frac{1}{10}$

21. When the 10-gallon tank of an emergency generator is filled to capacity, the generator operates without interruption for 20 hours, consuming fuel at a constant rate. Which of the graphs below represents the fuel consumption of the generator over time?

(A)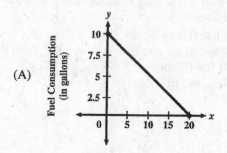

(B)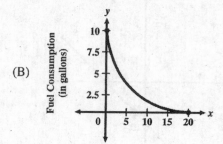

(C)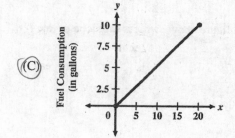

(D)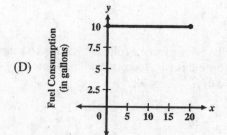

(E)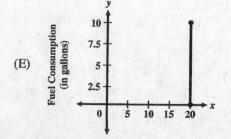

Floor Readings for the Red River

Time	1:00 pm	2:00 pm	3:00 pm	4:00 pm
Inches above Normal	0.5	1.5	?	13.5

22. The table above shows readings of water levels for the Red River at various times. If readings of the rise of the water level followed a geometric progression, the water level at 3:00 was how many inches above normal?

    (A) 4
    (B) 4.5
    (C) 4.75
    (D) 5
    (E) 5.25

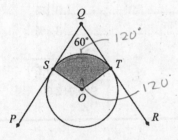

23. In the figure above, $\overline{PQ}$ is tangent to circle O at point S and $\overline{QR}$ is tangent to circle O at point T. If the radius of circle O is 2, what is the area of the shaded portion of the figure?

    (A) $\frac{\pi}{3}$
    (B) $\frac{2\pi}{3}$
    (C) π
    (D) $\frac{4\pi}{3}$
    (E) 2π

Items 24-25 refer to the following table.

ANNUAL EXPENDITURES FOR THE JONES FAMILY
(percent of disposable income)

Category	2002	2003
Rent	23.0%	19.3%
Food	17.6%	18.2%
Clothing	14.2%	15.1%
Automobile	11.3%	12.3%
Utilities	10.9%	10.2%
Savings	6.2%	5.1%
Entertainment	5.2%	5.3%
Medical and Dental Care	4.0%	3.7%
Charitable Contributions	3.2%	3.9%
Household Furnishings	2.9%	3.1%
Other	1.5%	3.8%
	+ 100.0%	+ 100.0%
Total Expenditures:	$34,987.00	$40,012.00

---

24. Approximately how much money did the Jones family spend on medical and dental care in 2002?

    (A) $1,200
    (B) $1,400
    (C) $1,520
    (D) $2,250
    (E) $4,000

25. If the categories in the table are rank ordered from one to eleven in each year, for how many categories would the rank ordering change from 2002 to 2003?

    (A) 2
    (B) 3
    (C) 4
    (D) 5
    (E) 6

EDUCATORS' #1 CHOICE FOR SCHOOL IMPROVEMENT

Strategy Summary Sheet
MATH: MULTIPLE-CHOICE

STRUCTURE OF MATH: MULTIPLE-CHOICE: The SAT has three Math sections that are presented in any order during the exam. Two SAT Math sections are 25 minutes long. The third SAT Math section is 20 minutes long. These three Math sections combined contain 54 total items, including 44 Multiple-Choice items. The PSAT/ NMSQT has two 25-minute Math sections that are presented in any order during the exam. The two PSAT Math sections combined contain 38 total items, including 28 Multiple-Choice items. All Math figures are drawn to scale unless accompanied by a note specifying otherwise. Math: Multiple-Choice answer choices are typically arranged in sequential order unless the item stem asks for the largest or smallest quantity.

GENERAL STRATEGY: When approaching a Math: Multiple-Choice item, there are several things for which you should pay careful attention:

1. *Figures:* Unless otherwise specifically noted, the figures included as illustrations are drawn to scale.

2. *Answer Choices:* Most answer choices are arranged in the order of ascending or descending value, and many incorrect answer choices correspond to conceptual errors.

3. *Signal Words:* Typically, signal words are capitalized, underlined, or sometimes italicized. Whenever an answer is asked for in specified units, those units will be underlined (or italicized). While the specific formatting of these signal words may vary, the importance they lend to correctly understanding the item is critical. When an item stem contains a thought-reverser, it is usually capitalized. Pay careful attention to any thought-reversers—"NOT," "CANNOT," and "EXCEPT"—as they reverse the intended meaning of an item.

4. *Ladder of Difficulty:* In each section of Math: Multiple-Choice items, the difficulty level increases as the item number increases. Therefore, allot less time for earlier items. When solving items that are high on the ladder of difficulty, do NOT expect obvious answers or easy solutions. It is unlikely that answers corresponding to easy solutions or to numbers in the item stem will be the correct choice. Remember to pace yourself—the difficult, time-consuming items have the same value as the easy items.

5. *Preview Item Stems:* Read the item stem first (usually it is located at the end of the item material.) Only then should examinees read the details of the item, keeping this item stem in mind.

6. *Confirm Solutions:* Double-check the solution by confirming that it answers the particular question that is being asked. When applicable, this confirmation includes verifying that the solution is given in the units specified by the item stem.

If you are unable to either find an elegant (quick) solution or solve the item directly based on subject knowledge, the following alternative solutions strategies can be extremely helpful:

1. *"Test-the-Test" Strategy:* The correct answer to any item is always one of five given choices. Many items are easier and faster to solve by simply testing each of the answer choices rather than determine the answer directly using a traditional mathematical solution strategy. The "test-the-test" strategy can mean plugging answer choices back into the item, starting with (C), to test the validity of an expression, or checking each

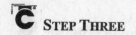
answer choice against any stated conditions. "Test-the-test" typically applies to items with numerical solutions or variables and values that meet stated conditions.

2. *"Plug-and-Chug" Strategy*: This strategy is similar to the "test-the-test" strategy in that the item stem and answer choices (rather than direct mathematical solution strategies) are used to isolate the correct answer. The difference is that rather than testing the validity of each answer choice against the item stem conditions, the item stem and/or answer choices are evaluated by plugging in chosen numbers: "plug-and-chug." This strategy is especially helpful when solving algebra problems.

3. *"Eliminate-and-Guess" Strategy*: If unable to determine the correct answer directly by using mathematical methods or indirectly by using either the "test-the-test" or "plug-and-chug" strategy, eliminate as many answer choices as possible and then guess from the remaining answer choices. For difficult mathematics items, eliminate answer choices that can be reached either by a single step or by copying a number from the item.

CHECKLIST OF CONCEPTS AND SKILLS:

ARITHMETIC
___ Simplifying: Fractions, Collecting Terms
___ Factoring
___ Approximation
___ The "Flying-X" Method
___ Decimal/Fraction Equivalents
___ Properties of Numbers (Odd, Even, Negative, Positive, Consecutive)
___ Sets (Union, Intersection, Elements)
___ Absolute Value
___ Percents (Change, Original Amount, Price Increase)
___ Ratios (Two-Part, Three-Part, Weighted)
___ Proportions (Direct, Indirect)

ALGEBRA
___ Evaluation of Expressions (Rational, Radical)
___ Exponents (Integer, Rational, Negative)
___ Factoring
___ Sequence
___ Solving Single Variable Equations and Inequalities
___ Absolute Value
___ Function (Picture) Math
___ Domain and Range
___ Solving Equations (Multi-Variable, Linear, Quadratic, Simultaneous)
___ Story Problems: Work (Joint Effort), Averages

COORDINATE GEOMETRY
___ Coordinate Plane
___ Slope of a Line
___ Slope-Intercept Form of a Linear Equation
___ Distance Formula
___ Graphing Linear Equations
___ Graphing First-Degree Inequalities
___ Graphing Quadratic Equations
___ Permutations of Equations and Graphs

GEOMETRY
___ Lines and Angles (Perpendicular, Parallel, Intersecting, Big Angle/Little Angle Theorem)
___ Triangles (Equilateral, Isosceles, Acute, Obtuse, Perimeter, Area, Altitudes, Angles, Bisectors, Pythagorean Theorem)
___ Quadrilaterals (Squares, Rectangles, Rhombuses, Parallelograms, Trapezoids, Perimeter, Area)
___ Polygons (Sum of Interior Angles)
___ Circles (Chords, Tangents, Radius, Diameter, Circumference, Area)
___ Solids (Cubes, Cylinders, Spheres, Volumes, Surface Areas)
___ Complex Figures

DATA ANALYSIS
___ Graphs (Bar, Cumulative, Line)
___ Pie Charts
___ Tables (Matrices)
___ Scatterplots
___ Averages (Simple, Weighted), Median, Mode
___ Probability (Arithmetic and Geometric)

ADDITIONAL STRATEGIES FROM IN-CLASS DISCUSSION: _____

_____

_____

_____

_____

_____

_____

_____

_____

_____

_____

_____

_____

_____

_____

_____

_____

_____

_____

_____

_____

_____

_____

_____

_____

_____

Math:
Student-Produced Responses

EDUCATORS' #1 CHOICE FOR SCHOOL IMPROVEMENT

Cambridge Course Concept Outline
MATH: STUDENT-PRODUCED RESPONSES

CORE LESSON

DIRECTIONS: The items in this section demonstrate the Math: Student-Produced Responses concepts and skills that are tested by the SAT and PSAT/NMSQT. You will work through the items with your instructor in class. For each item, enter your answer by marking the ovals in the special grid. Use any available space in the section for scratch work. Answers are on page 985.

For each item, you are required to mark your answer on a special answer grid. You should write your answer in the boxes at the top of each column and then fill in the ovals beneath each answer that you write. Here are some examples:

Answer: 3/4 or .75
(show answer either way)

Answer: 325

Note: A mixed number such as $3\frac{1}{2}$ must be gridded as 7/2 or as 3.5. If gridded as 31/2, it will be read as "thirty-one halves."

Note: Either position is correct.

Notes:

(1) The use of a calculator is permitted. All numbers used are real numbers.

(2) Figures that accompany problems in this test are intended to provide information useful in solving the problems. They are drawn as accurately as possible EXCEPT when it is stated in a specific problem that the figure is not drawn to scale. All figures lie in a plane unless otherwise indicated.

$A = \pi r^2$
$C = 2\pi r$

$A = lw$

$A = \frac{1}{2}bh$

$V = lwh$

$V = \pi r^2 h$

$c^2 = a^2 + b^2$

Special Right Triangles

The number of degrees of arc in a circle is 360.
The measure in degrees of a straight angle is 180.
The sum of the measures in degrees of the angles of a triangle is 180.

1. What number increased by 25 equals twice the number?

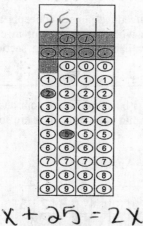

$$X + 25 = 2X$$

2. Dr. Leo's new office is 2.8 yards by 4 yards. She plans to run a decorative border around the perimeter of the office. How many yards of wallpaper border should she purchase?

3. At State College, one-fourth of the students are from abroad. Of those, one-eighth are from China. What fraction of the student body is from China?

$$100$$
$$25$$

4. What is the value of $\frac{2}{3} - \frac{5}{8}$?

$$\frac{16}{24} - \frac{15}{24}$$
$$\frac{1}{24}$$

130   195

5. What is the value of 65(1) + 65(2) + 65(3) + 65(4)?

260

650

6. A jar contains 15 pennies and 25 nickels. Expressed in lowest terms, what fraction of the coins are pennies?

7. Matinee ticket prices are $1.50 for children and $3.50 for adults. Regular ticket prices are $4.50 for children and $6.50 for adults. If 3 adults and 1 child attend a matinee, what percentage of the regular price will they pay?

8. If the average of 8, 10, 15, 20, and x is 11, what is x?

$$\frac{53 + x}{5} = $$

x = 2

9. If $x = 14$, what is the value of $2x - (2 + x)$?

$28 - (2 + x)$
$28 - (16)$

12

10. If $3x + y = 33$ and $x + y = 17$, then what is the value of x?

$3x + y = 33$
$-\ x + y = 17$
_____
$2x = 16$

$x = 8$

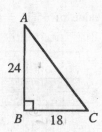

11. In the figure above, what is the length of $\overline{AC}$?

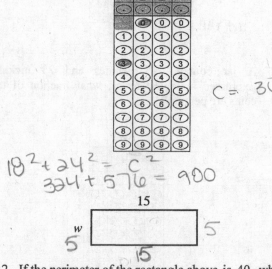

$c = 30$

$18^2 + 24^2 = c^2$
$324 + 576 = 900$

15

w 5 ⎢ ⎥ 5

15

12. If the perimeter of the rectangle above is 40, what is its area?

13. If a circle with radius 0.25 is inscribed in a square, what is the area of the square?

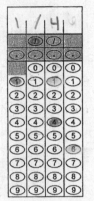

14. If the price of a book increases from $10.00 to $12.50, what is the percent increase in price?

15. Boys and girls belong to the chess club. There are 36 people in the club, 15 of whom are girls. In lowest terms, what fraction of the club is boys?

36 total
15 women
21 Boys

16. Jason built a fence around his rectangular garden. The width of the garden is 2.8 yards, and the length is twice that size. How many yards of fencing did Jason use?

perimeter

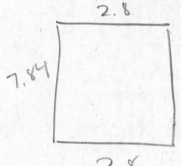

2.8

7.84

7.84

2.8

17. If $x = 9$, what is the value of $x^2 + 2x - 9$?

$9^2 + 2(9) - 9$
$81 + 18 - 9$
$99 - 9$
90

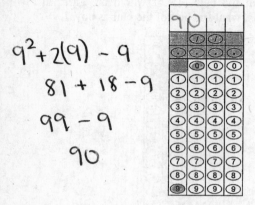

19. If $x = 3y - 1$ and $x + y = 15$, what is the value of x?

$x - 3y = -1$
$- \quad x + y = 15$
_____
$-4y = -16$
$y = 4$

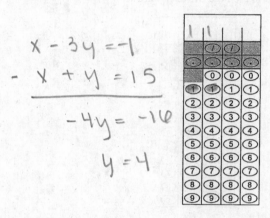

18. For all numbers, $x * y = 2xy$. What is $1.5 * 2.5$?

20. Jane and Hector have the same birthday. When Hector was 36, Jane was 30. How old was Jane when Hector was twice her age?

$x = 3(4) - 1$
$x = 11$

~~14 + 11~~

$x + 4 = 15$
$x = 11$

Hector	Jane
36	30
x+6	x
12	6

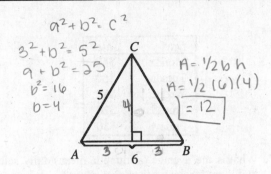

$a^2 + b^2 = c^2$
$3^2 + b^2 = 5^2$
$9 + b^2 = 25$
$b^2 = 16$
$b = 4$

$A = \frac{1}{2} b h$
$A = \frac{1}{2}(6)(4)$
$= 12$

21. What is the area of isosceles triangle *ABC*?

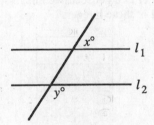

22. If lines 1 and 2 are parallel, what is $x + y$?

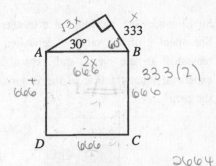

23. In this figure, what is the perimeter of square *ABCD*?

2664

333(2)

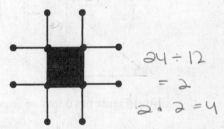

$24 \div 12$
$= 2$
$2 \cdot 2 = 4$

24. In the figure above, equally spaced points are joined by line segments that intersect each other at 90 degrees. If the total length of all line segments in the figure is 24, what is the area of the shaded part?

25. Su Li made $45 working as a mother's helper. She spent $\frac{1}{5}$ of the money, deposited $\frac{1}{3}$ of the remainder in the bank, and kept the rest for expenses. What fraction of the original $45 did she keep?

```
8 / 1 5          45
                -9
                ──
                36
                -12
                ──
                24

                24   8
                ── = ──
                45   15
```

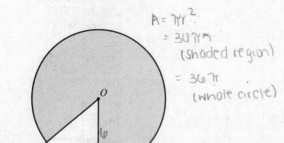

A = πr²
= 30πn
(shaded region)

= 36π
(whole circle)

Note: Figure not drawn to scale.

26. In the figure above, the circle with center O has a radius of 6. If the area of the shaded region is 30π, what is the value of x?

```
3 0
```

Day	Sales
Monday	$40
Tuesday	$60
Wednesday	$80
Thursday	$20
Friday	$50

27. What is the average (arithmetic mean) daily sales in dollars for the week shown above?

```
5 0          40 +60+80+20+50

             250
             ───
              5
             = 50
```

28. If the sum of two consecutive integers is 29, what is the least of these integers?

15+14 = 29

```
1 4
```

29. If a jar of 300 black and white marbles contains 156 white marbles, what percent of the marbles is black?

$$300$$
$$-156$$
$$\overline{144}$$

Grid answer: 48

30. Mr. Wahl spends $\frac{1}{3}$ of his day in meetings, $\frac{1}{6}$ of his day on the phone, and $\frac{1}{8}$ of his day answering questions. What fraction of his day can be devoted to other things?

Grid answer: 3/8

31. Line l, with a slope of $\frac{1}{2}$, passes through the points $(0, \frac{1}{4})$ and $(2, y)$. What is the value of y?

Grid answer: 5/4

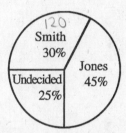

Smith 30%
Jones 45%
Undecided 25%

120

32. A total of 400 voters responded to the survey represented by the pie chart above. How many more respondents were in favor of Jones than Smith?

$$400 \quad 400$$
$$\times .30 \quad \times 45$$
$$\overline{120} \quad \overline{180}$$

$$180$$
$$-120$$
$$\overline{60}$$

Grid answer: 60

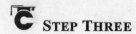

NOTES AND STRATEGIES

CHALLENGE ITEMS

DIRECTIONS: This section contains Math: Student-Produced Responses items in the top quartile of difficulty. For each item, enter your by marking the ovals in the special grid. Use any available space in the section for scratch work. Answers are on page 985.

For each item, you are required to mark your answer on a special answer grid. You should write your answer in the boxes at the top of each column and then fill in the ovals beneath each answer that you write. Here are some examples:

Answer: 3/4 or .75
(show answer either way)

Answer: 325

Note: A mixed number such as $3\frac{1}{2}$ must be gridded as 7/2 or as 3.5. If gridded as 31/2, it will be read as "thirty-one halves."

Note: Either position is correct.

Notes:

(1) The use of a calculator is permitted. All numbers used are real numbers.

(2) Figures that accompany problems in this test are intended to provide information useful in solving the problems. They are drawn as accurately as possible EXCEPT when it is stated in a specific problem that the figure is not drawn to scale. All figures lie in a plane unless otherwise indicated.

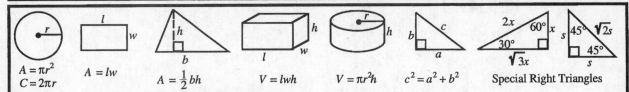

$A = \pi r^2$
$C = 2\pi r$

$A = lw$

$A = \frac{1}{2}bh$

$V = lwh$

$V = \pi r^2 h$

$c^2 = a^2 + b^2$

Special Right Triangles

The number of degrees of arc in a circle is 360.
The measure in degrees of a straight angle is 180.
The sum of the measures in degrees of the angles of a triangle is 180.

1. In a three-hour examination of 350 questions, there are 50 mathematical problems. If twice as much time should be allowed for each mathematical problem as for each of the other questions, how many minutes should be spent on the mathematical problems?

2. In a pantry, there are 28 cans of vegetables. 8 have labels with white lettering, 18 have labels with green lettering, and 8 have labels with neither white nor green lettering. How many cans have both white and green lettering?

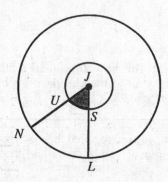

3. Given the circles above, if radius JN is 3 times line segment JU, then the ratio of the shaded area to the area of sector NJL is $1:b$. What is the value of b?

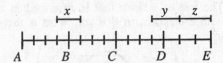

4. In the figure above, points B, C, and D divide $\overline{AE}$ into 4 equal parts. $\overline{AB}$, $\overline{BC}$, and $\overline{CD}$ are divided into 4 equal parts as shown above. $\overline{DE}$ is divided into 3 equal parts as shown. What does $\dfrac{x+z}{y}$ equal?

5. The shortest distance from the center of a circle to a chord is 5. If the length of the chord is 24, what is the length of the radius of the circle?

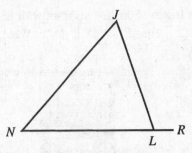

6. In the figure above, $\angle N = (9x - 40)°$, $\angle J = (4x + 30)°$, and $\angle JLR = (8x + 40)°$. What is the measure of $\angle J$? (Do not grid the degree symbol.)

7. In the figure above, two circles are tangent to each other and each is tangent to 3 sides of the rectangle. If the radius of each circle is 3, then the area of the shaded portion is $a - 18\pi$. What is the value of a?

8. The length of the line segment with end points that are (3, –2) and (–4, 5) is $b\sqrt{2}$. What is the value of b?

9. A car travels from Town A to Town B, a distance of 360 miles, in 9 hours. How many hours would the same trip have taken had the car traveled 5 mph faster?

10. The area of a circle that is inscribed in a square with a diagonal of 8 is $a\pi$. What is the value of a?

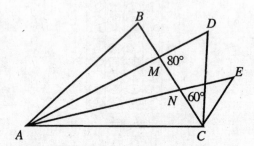

Line segments DA and EA trisect $\angle BAC$.

11. If $\angle DMC = 80°$ and $\angle ENC = 60°$, then how many degrees is $\angle BAC$? (Do not grid the degree symbol.)

12. In the junior class at Dawnville High School, 44 of 70 juniors take pre-calculus and 46 take chemistry. If 10 take neither course, how many take both pre-calculus and chemistry?

13. $a - b = b - c = c - a$. What is the value of $\frac{2a + 3b}{c}$?

NOTES AND STRATEGIES

TIMED-PRACTICE QUIZZES

DIRECTIONS: This section contains three Math: Student-Produced Responses quizzes. While being timed, solve the items using available space on the page for scratchwork, and choose the best answers. The following reference information is all you may refer to while taking these quizzes. You may use a calculator. Answers are on page 985.

For each item, you are required to mark your answer on a special answer grid. You should write your answer in the boxes at the top of each column and then fill in the ovals beneath each answer that you write. Here are some examples:

Answer: 3/4 or .75
(show answer either way)

Answer: 325

Note: A mixed number such as $3\frac{1}{2}$ must be gridded as 7/2 or as 3.5. If gridded as 31/2, it will be read as "thirty-one halves."

Note: Either position is correct.

Notes:

(1) The use of a calculator is permitted. All numbers used are real numbers.

(2) Figures that accompany problems in this test are intended to provide information useful in solving the problems. They are drawn as accurately as possible EXCEPT when it is stated in a specific problem that the figure is not drawn to scale. All figures lie in a plane unless otherwise indicated.

$A = \pi r^2$
$C = 2\pi r$

$A = lw$

$A = \frac{1}{2}bh$

$V = lwh$

$V = \pi r^2 h$

$c^2 = a^2 + b^2$

Special Right Triangles

The number of degrees of arc in a circle is 360.
The measure in degrees of a straight angle is 180.
The sum of the measures in degrees of the angles of a triangle is 180.

A. QUIZ I (10 items; 15 minutes)

1. The difference between x and $3x$ is greater than 7 but less than 11. If x is an integer, what is one possible value of x?

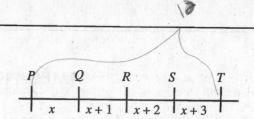

3. If line segment PT above has a length of 12, then what is the value of x?

2. If p and q are integers such that $p > q > 0$ and $p + q = 12$, what is the least possible value of $p - q$?

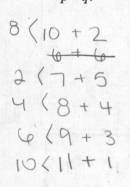

$8 < 10 + 2$

~~$6 + 6$~~

$2 < 7 + 5$

$4 < 8 + 4$

$6 < 9 + 3$

$10 < 11 + 1$

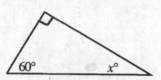

4. In the figure above, what is the value of x?

5. As part of an orienteering exercise, a hiker walks due north from point P for 3 miles to point Q and then due east for 4 miles to point R. What is the straight-line distance from point R to point P?

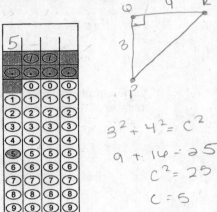

$3^2 + 4^2 = c^2$
$9 + 16 = 25$
$c^2 = 25$
$c = 5$

6. If 0.129914 is rounded off to the nearest hundredth, how many of its digits change?

7. The average of 4, 5, x, and y is 6, and the average of x, z, 8, and 9 is 8. What is the value of $z - y$?

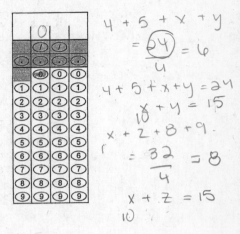

$\frac{4+5+x+y}{4} = 6$
$4+5+x+y = 24$
$x+y = 15$
$\frac{x+z+8+9}{4} = 8$
$= \frac{32}{4} = 8$
$x + z = 15$

8. Copy Machine X produces 20 copies per minute, and Copy Machine Y produces 30 copies per minute. If Y is started 1 minute after X, how many minutes after X is started will Y have produced the same number of copies as X?

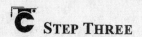
9. A triangle has sides of x, 4, and 5. If x is an integer, what is the maximum value of x?

10. Ray is now 10 years older than Cindy. If in 8 years Ray will be twice as old as Cindy, how old is Cindy now?

cindy   2 → 10
ray   12 → 20

B. QUIZ II (10 items; 15 minutes)

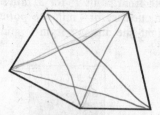

1. In the pentagon above, what is the maximum number of different diagonals that can be drawn?

2. If $4x = 2(2 + x)$ and $6y = 3(2 + y)$, then what is the value of $2x + 3y$?

$4x = 2(2+x)$
$4x = 4 + 2x$
$2x = 4$
$x = 2$
$6y = 3(2+y)$
$6y = 6 + 3y$
$3y = 6$
$y = 2$

$2(2) + 3(2)$
$4 + 6$
10

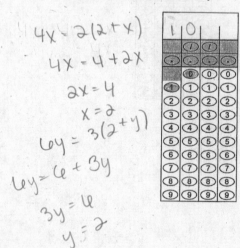

3. Let the "JOSH" of a number be defined as 3 less than 3 times the number. What number is equal to its "JOSH"?

JOSH = 3X − 3

3X − 3 = X

−3 = −2X

3/2 = X

5. 0.01 is the ratio of 0.1 to what number?

?

.1 : X = .01

$\frac{.1}{X} = .01$

4. Machine A produces flue covers at a uniform rate of 2,000 per hour. Machine B produces flue covers at a uniform rate of 5,000 in $2\frac{1}{2}$ hours. After $7\frac{1}{4}$ hours, Machine A has produced how many more flue covers than Machine B?

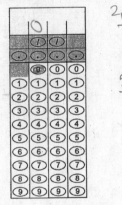

$\frac{2,000}{60}$ MAC A

$\frac{5,000}{150}$ MAC B

6. In the figure above, $\overline{AB}$ is parallel to $\overline{ED}$ and $\overline{AC} = \overline{BC}$. If ∠BED is 50°, then what is the value of x?

isoceles triangle

$\frac{2,000}{60} = \frac{X}{435}$ MAC A

X = 14500

$\frac{5,000}{150} = \frac{X}{435}$

X = 14500

7. At NJL High School, $\frac{1}{4}$ of the school's population are seniors, $\frac{1}{5}$ are juniors, and $\frac{1}{3}$ are sophomores. If there are 390 freshmen, what is the total school population?

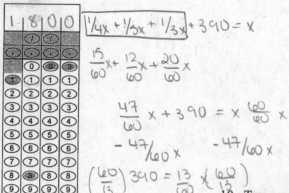

$1/4x + 1/5x + 1/3x + 390 = x$

$\frac{15}{60}x + \frac{12}{60}x + \frac{20}{60}x$

$\frac{47}{60}x + 390 = x \quad \frac{60}{60}x$

$-47/60x \qquad -47/60x$

$\left(\frac{60}{13}\right) 390 = \frac{13}{60}x \left(\frac{60}{13}\right)$

$1800 = x$

8. From the town of Williston Park to Albertson, there are 3 different roads. From the town of Albertson to Mineola, there are 5 roads. How many different paths are there to go from Willistown Park to Mineola through Albertson?

9. If 12 candies cost $1.70, how many of these candies can be bought for $10.20?

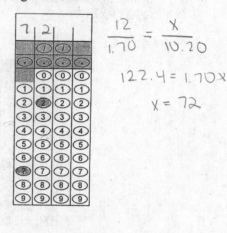

$\frac{12}{1.70} = \frac{x}{10.20}$

$122.4 = 1.70x$

$x = 72$

10. Two roads intersect at right angles. A pole is 30 meters from one road and 40 meters from the other road. How far (in meters) is the pole from the point where the roads intersect?

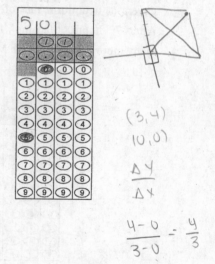

$(3,4)$

$(0,0)$

$\frac{\Delta y}{\Delta x}$

$\frac{4-0}{3-0} = \frac{4}{3}$

C. QUIZ III (10 items; 15 minutes)

1. What is the value of $(2a^2 - a^3)^2$ when $a = -1$?

$(2a^2 - a^3)(2a^2 - a^3)$

$(2(-1)^2 - (-1)^3)(2(-1)^2 - (-1)^3)$

$(2 + 1)(2 + 1)$

$4 + 2 + 2 + 1$

9

2. A jar contains 2 red marbles, 3 green marbles, and 4 orange marbles. If a marble is picked at random, what is the probability that the marble is not orange?

$2 + 3 + 4$

$= 9$

$5/9$

3. In the country of Glup, 1 glop is 3 glips, and 4 glips are 5 globs. How many globs are 2 glops?

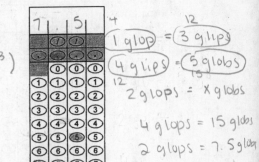

1 glop = 3 glips

4 glips = 5 globs

2 glops = x globs

4 glops = 15 globs

2 glops = 7.5 globs

4. If $\frac{k}{3} + \frac{k}{4} = 1$, then what is the value of k?

$\left(\frac{k}{3}\right) + \left(\frac{k}{4}\right) = (1)^{12}$

$\frac{4k}{12} + \frac{3k}{12} = 12$

5. If the area of a square with side x is 5, what is the area of a square with side $3x$?

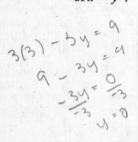

2.5

2.5

$x^2 = 5$

$3x \cdot 3x$

$3 \cdot 3 \cdot x \cdot x$

$3 \cdot 3 \cdot x^2$

$3 \cdot 3 \cdot 5$

45

6. If $2x + 2y = 6$ and $3x - 3y = 9$, what is the value of $x^2 - y^2$?

$3(3) - 3y = 9$

$9 - 3y = 9$

$\dfrac{-3y}{-3} = \dfrac{0}{-3}$

$y = 0$

$2x + 2y = 6$

$\dfrac{6 - 2x}{2} = \dfrac{2y}{2}$

$3 - x = y$

$3x - 3(3-x) = 9$

$3x - 9 + 3x = 9$

$+9 +9$

$6x = 18$

$x = 3$

$3^2 - 0^2$

$9 - 0 = 9$

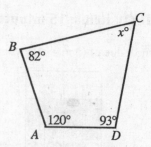

7. In quadrilateral $ABCD$ above, the measure of $\angle A = 120°$, the measure of $\angle B = 82°$, and the measure of $\angle D = 93°$. What is the value of x?

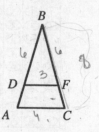

8. In the diagram above, $\triangle ABC$ is similar to $\triangle DBF$. If $DF = 3$, $BD = BF = 6$, and $AC = 4$, what is the perimeter of $\triangle ABC$?

$\dfrac{3}{4} = \dfrac{6}{x}$

$3x = 24$

$x = 8$

9. If $\frac{4}{5}$ is subtracted from its reciprocal, then what value is the result?

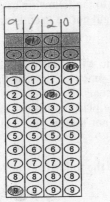

$\frac{4}{5}$

$5/4 - 4/5$

10. If the ratio of a:b is 1:5 and the ratio of b:c is 3:2, then what value is the ratio of $(a + c)$:c?

1:5 a:b

3:2 b:c

3:15 $\Big\}$ 3:10

15:10

$(a+c)$: c $\frac{13}{10} = 1.3$

CALCULATOR EXERCISE

DIRECTIONS: Label each of these items from the Math lessons according to the following categories: (1) a calculator would be very useful (saves valuable test time), (2) a calculator might or might not be useful, or (3) a calculator would be counterproductive (wastes valuable test time). Answers are on page 986.

Make sure that the calculator you bring to the SAT or PSAT/NMSQT is one with which you are thoroughly familiar. You may bring any of the following types of calculators: graphing, four-function, or scientific. Although no item requires the use of a calculator, a calculator may be helpful to answer some items. The calculator may be useful for any item that involves complex arithmetic computations, but it cannot take the place of understanding how to set up a mathematical item. This exercise is designed to illustrate when and when not to use your calculator. The degree to which you can use your calculator will depend on its features.

1. What is the average of 8.5, 7.8, and 7.7?

(1)

   (A) 8.3
   (B) 8.2
   (C) 8.1
   (D) 8.0
   (E) 7.9

2. If $0 < x < 1$, which of the following is the largest?

(3)

   (A) x
   (B) $2x$
   (C) x^2
   (D) x^3
   (E) $x + 1$

3. If 4.5 pounds of chocolate cost \$10, how many pounds of chocolate can be purchased for \$12?

(1)

   (A) $4\frac{3}{4}$
   (B) $5\frac{2}{5}$
   (C) $5\frac{1}{2}$
   (D) $5\frac{3}{4}$
   (E) 6

4. What is the value of $\frac{8}{9} - \frac{7}{8}$?

(1)

   (A) $\frac{1}{72}$
   (B) $\frac{15}{72}$
   (C) $\frac{1}{7}$
   (D) $\frac{1}{8}$
   (E) $\frac{15}{7}$

5. Which of the following fractions is the largest?

(2)

   (A) $\frac{111}{221}$ .50226244434
   (B) $\frac{75}{151}$
   (C) $\frac{333}{998}$
   (D) $\frac{113}{225}$
   (E) $\frac{101}{301}$

6. Dr. Leo's new office is 2.8 yards by 4 yards. She plans to run a decorative border around the perimeter of the office. How many yards of wallpaper border should she purchase?

(2)

11.2
13.6

7. What is the value of $\frac{2}{3} - \frac{5}{8}$?

9. If the perimeter of the rectangle above is 40, what is its area?

8. If $3x + y = 33$ and $x + y = 17$, then what is the value of x?

10. If the price of a book increases from $10.00 to $12.50, what is the percent increase in price?

$x = 17 - y$

$3(17 - y) = 33$

$51 - 3y = 33$

$51 = 3y + 33$

$18 = 3y$

$6 = y$

$x + 6 = 17$

$x = 11$

$\dfrac{2.50}{10} = \dfrac{x}{100}$

$10x = 250$

$x = 25$

EDUCATORS' #1 CHOICE FOR SCHOOL IMPROVEMENT

Strategy Summary Sheet
MATH: STUDENT-PRODUCED RESPONSES

STRUCTURE OF MATH: STUDENT-PRODUCED RESPONSES: The SAT has three Math sections that are presented in any order during the exam. Two SAT Math sections are 25 minutes long. The third SAT Math section is 20 minutes long. These three Math sections combined contain 54 total items, including 10 Student-Produced Responses items. The PSAT/NMSQT has two 25-minute Math sections that are presented in any order during the exam. The two PSAT Math sections combined contain 38 items, including 10 Student-Produced Responses items. All Math figures are drawn to scale unless accompanied by a note specifying otherwise.

GENERAL STRATEGY:

1. Assumptions regarding the grid:
   - grid answers are no more than four digits in length;
   - grid answers, if decimals (non-zero digits to the right of decimal point), are between .001 and 99.9;
   - grid answers, if fractions, are between 1/99 and 99/1; and
   - grid answers are always positive.

2. Write answers so that the final digit is on the right.

3. Make sure to fill in circles corresponding to the answer.

4. A decimal point fills one whole space, and therefore it counts as one of the four digits.

5. A fraction bar fills one whole space, and therefore it counts as one of the four digits.

6. Reduce fractions to lowest terms.

7. Omit unnecessary zeros.

8. Watch the standard of measure.

Pay attention to thought-reversers (capitalized) and underlined words. Items are arranged according to a ladder of difficulty. The material tested is the same as that for the Math: Multiple-Choice items—strategies and concepts are also the same.

ADDITIONAL STRATEGIES FROM IN-CLASS DISCUSSION: _____

_____

_____

_____

_____

Writing

CAMBRIDGE
EDUCATIONAL SERVICES®

EDUCATORS' #1 CHOICE FOR SCHOOL IMPROVEMENT

Cambridge Course Concept Outline
WRITING

CORE LESSON

DIRECTIONS: The items in this section demonstrate the Writing concepts and skills that are tested by the SAT and PSAT. You will work through the items with your instructor in class. Answers are on page 986.

IDENTIFYING SENTENCE ERRORS
DIRECTIONS: Identifying Sentence Errors items test your knowledge of grammar, usage, word choice, and idiom. Some sentences are correct. No sentence contains more than one error. You will find that the error, if there is one, is underlined and lettered. Elements of the sentence that are not underlined will not be changed. In choosing answers, follow the requirements of standard written English. If there is an error, select the one underlined part that must be changed to make the sentence correct and fill in the corresponding oval on your answer sheet. If there is no error, fill in oval (E).

IMPROVING SENTENCES DIRECTIONS: In Improving Sentences items, part or all of the sentence is underlined. Below each sentence you will find five ways of phrasing the underlined part. Select the answer that produces the most effective sentence, one that is clear and exact, without awkwardness or ambiguity, and fill in the corresponding oval on your answer sheet. In choosing answers, follow the requirements of standard written English. Choose the answer that best expresses the meaning of the original sentence. Answer (A) is always the same as the underlined part. Choose answer (A) if you think the original sentence needs no revision.

1. The professor <u>were traveling</u> in Europe <u>when</u> she
   A   B
   <u>received</u> notice of <u>her</u> promotion. <u>No error</u>
   C   D   E

2. The professor <u>voted Teacher of the Year</u> by the
   A
   students <u>were traveling</u> in Europe <u>when</u> she
   B   C
   received notice of <u>her</u> promotion. <u>No error</u>
   D   E

3. Most teachers, unless <u>they have</u> an appointment
   A
   to a prestigious university, <u>earns</u> relatively
   B
   <u>less as</u> a teacher <u>than they might</u> in business.
   C   D
   <u>No error</u>
   E

4. Many nutritionists now <u>believe</u> <u>that</u> a balanced
   A   B
   diet and not large doses of vitamins <u>are</u> the <u>best</u>
   C   D
   guarantee of health. <u>No error</u>
   E

5. Television comedies <u>in which</u> <u>there is</u> at least
   A   B
   one <u>really detestable</u> character <u>captures</u> the
   C   D
   interest of viewers. <u>No error</u>
   E

6. The opposition to smoking in public places <u>are prompting many state legislatures to consider</u> banning smoking in such locations.

   (A) are prompting many state legislatures to consider
   (B) is prompting many state legislatures to consider
   (C) are prompting many state legislatures considering
   (D) is prompting many state legislatures considering
   (E) is prompting many state legislatures' consider

C 7. Diplomats sent to an unstable region or a genuinely hostile territory usually <u>is assigned an aide or chauffeur who function</u> also as a bodyguard.

    (A) is assigned an aide or chauffeur who function

    (B) are assigned an aide or chauffeur who function

    (C) are assigned an aide or chauffeur who functions

    (D) is assigned an aide or chauffeur that function

    (E) are assigned an aide or chauffeur which functions

C 8. <u>Though</u> this is the wealthiest country in the
     A

world, within a <u>few</u> blocks of the White House
        B

<u>there is</u> scores of homeless people <u>who live</u> on
   C   D

the streets. <u>No error</u>
         E

B 9. <u>Just</u> a few miles from the factories and
    A

skyscrapers <u>stand</u> a medieval castle <u>which looks</u>
         B   C

<u>exactly as</u> it did in the 12th century. <u>No error</u>
   D   E

A 10. John, his wife, and the rest of his family <u>plans</u>
                             A

<u>to attend</u> the award dinner <u>to be given</u> by the
   B   C

company for the employees with the <u>most</u>
                           D

seniority. <u>No error</u>
        E

11. Either the governor or one of his close aides

    <u>prefer</u> <u>not to have</u> the Senator <u>seated at</u> the head
     A   B   C

    table where he <u>would be</u> conspicuous. <u>No error</u>
                D   E

12. <u>Surrounded by</u> layers of excelsior, none of the
     A

crystal goblets <u>were broken</u> <u>when</u> the workers
             B   C

<u>dropped</u> the crate. <u>No error</u>
 D   E

13. During her rise to fame, she betrayed many of her friends, <u>and because of it</u>, very few people trust her.

    (A) and because of it

    (B) and in spite of it

    (C) and because of her friends

    (D) and even though

    (E) and because of her behavior

14. In New York City, <u>they</u> are brusque and even
                 A

rude <u>but</u> quick <u>to come to</u> one another's
     B   C

assistance <u>in a time of</u> crisis. <u>No error</u>
         D   E

15. Ten years ago, the United States <u>imported</u> ten
                       A

times <u>as much</u> French wine as Italian wine, but
     B

today Americans <u>are drinking</u> more of <u>it</u>.
           C   D

<u>No error</u>
  E

16. Although a police officer <u>used to be</u> a symbol of
                  A

authority, today <u>they receive</u> <u>little</u> respect
             B   C

<u>from most</u> people. <u>No error</u>
   D   E

17. The Abbot <u>was</u> an effective administrator
         A

who <u>attempted to</u> assign each monk a task
      B

<u>particularly suited</u> to <u>their</u> talents and training.
     C   D

<u>No error</u>
  E

NOTES AND STRATEGIES

18. After three years of college education, a person

    <u>should be allowed to</u> apply to graduate school,
    　　　　A

    <u>because</u> by that time <u>you are</u> ready <u>to choose</u> a
    　　B　　　　　　　　C　　　　　　D

    profession. <u>No error</u>
    　　　　　　　　E

19. If one wishes <u>to apply for</u> a scholarship, <u>you</u>
    A　　　　　　B　　　　　　　　　　　C

    must submit a <u>completed</u> application by March 1.
    　　　　　　　　D

    <u>No error</u>
    E

20. The judges <u>were</u> unable to make a final decision
    　　　　　　A

    on a single winner, so <u>they</u> divided first prize
    　　　　　　　　　　　B

    <u>between</u> John and <u>he</u>. <u>No error</u>
    　C　　　　　　D　　　E

21. Although Peter <u>had been looking</u> <u>forward to</u> the
    　　　　　　　　A　　　　　　B

    debate for weeks, a sore throat <u>prevented him</u>
    　　　　　　　　　　　　　　　　C

    taking <u>part</u>. <u>No error</u>
    　　　D　　　E

22. Some psychologists maintain that a child <u>who</u>
    　　　　　　　　　　　　　　　　　　A

    <u>has seen</u> violence on television <u>is</u> more likely to
    　B　　　　　　　　　　　　　C

    react <u>violent</u> in situations of stress. <u>No error</u>
    　　　D　　　　　　　　　　　　E

23. The <u>recent created</u> commission <u>has done</u> nothing
    　　　A　　　　　　　　　B

    to address the problem <u>except to approve</u> the
    　　　　　　　　　　　C

    color of <u>its</u> stationary. <u>No error</u>
    　　　D　　　　　　E

24. <u>Not hardly</u> a sound <u>could be heard</u> in the
    　A　　　　　　　B

    auditorium <u>when</u> the speaker <u>approached</u> the dais
    　　　　　C　　　　　　　D

    to announce the result of the contest. <u>No error</u>
    　　　　　　　　　　　　　　　　E

25. Although she <u>had been hired</u> by the magazine
    　　　　　　A

    <u>to write</u> book reviews, <u>she knew</u> <u>scarcely nothing</u>
    　B　　　　　　　　C　　　　D

    about current fiction. <u>No error</u>
    　　　　　　　　　E

26. The reason Harriet <u>fired</u> her secretary is <u>because</u> he
    　　　　　　　A　　　　　　　　B

    <u>was</u> <u>frequently</u> late and spent too much time on
    　C　　D

    personal phone calls. <u>No error</u>
    　　　　　　　　E

27. <u>The reason the manager changed catchers was</u>
    <u>because</u> he hoped that the opposing side would
    put in a left-handed pitcher.

    (A) The reason the manager changed catchers
    　　was because
    (B) The reason that catchers were changed by the
    　　manager was because
    (C) The reason the manager changed catchers
    　　which
    (D) The manager changed catchers because
    (E) The manager changed catchers, the reason
    　　being

28. I read in a magazine <u>where</u> scientists <u>believe</u> that
    　　　　　　　　　A　　　　　　B

    <u>they</u> <u>have discovered</u> a new subatomic particle.
    　C　　D

    <u>No error</u>
    E

29. To abandon <u>their</u> homes, leave behind their
                 A
    families, and <u>traveling</u> across the ocean <u>required</u>
                   B   C
    great courage on the part of the immigrants

    <u>who moved</u> to America. <u>No error</u>
      D   E

30. The review <u>praised</u> the wit, charm, and
                  A
    <u>interpreting</u> of the recitalist <u>but never once</u>
        B   C
    <u>mentioned</u> her voice. <u>No error</u>
        D   E

31. To acknowledge that <u>one</u> <u>has</u> something to learn
                         A   B
    <u>is</u> <u>taking</u> the first step on the road to true
    C   D
    wisdom. <u>No error</u>
               E

32. The students are <u>critical of</u> the dean because he <u>is</u>
                        A   B
    either <u>unfamiliar or</u> doesn't care about the urgent
              C
    <u>need for</u> new student housing on campus.
       D
    <u>No error</u>
      E

33. Baseball <u>has and</u> probably always will be the
                A
    sport <u>that</u> <u>symbolizes</u> for people <u>in</u> other
          B   C   D
    countries the American way of life. <u>No error</u>
                                            E

34. The great pianist Vladimir Horowitz <u>plays</u> the
                                            A
    music <u>of</u> the Romantic Era <u>better than</u> <u>any pianist</u>
          B   C   D
    in history. <u>No error</u>
                    E

35. <u>Like Neil Simon, many of Tennessee Williams'</u>
    <u>plays</u> reflect a culture familiar to the playwright.

    (A) Like Neil Simon, many of Tennessee
        Williams' plays
    (B) Many of Tennessee Williams' plays, like Neil
        Simon's
    (C) Many of Tennessee Williams' plays, like Neil
        Simon
    (D) Many of Neil Simon and Tennessee
        Williams' plays
    (E) As with the plays of Neil Simon, many of
        Tennessee Williams' plays

36. Educators <u>are</u> now expressing <u>their</u> concern that
                 A   B
    American school children <u>prefer</u> watching
                                C
    television <u>to books</u>. <u>No error</u>
                  D   E

37. The novels of Nathaniel Hawthorne <u>contain</u>
                                          A
    characters who <u>are</u> every bit <u>as</u> sinister and
                      B   C
    frightening <u>as the master</u> of cinematic suspense,
                    D
    Alfred Hitchcock. <u>No error</u>
                          E

38. A Japanese firm <u>has developed</u> a computer so
                       A
    small that users <u>can carry</u> it in <u>their</u> <u>briefcase</u>.
                        B   C   D
    <u>No error</u>
      E

39. Carlos <u>has a very</u> pleasant personality and he is a
               A
    talented musician; <u>therefore</u>, <u>he gets</u> good grades
                          B   C
    <u>in</u> school. <u>No error</u>
    D   E

40. John <u>had already been</u> granted three extensions of
A

the deadline; <u>moreover,</u> the dean <u>refused</u> to grant
B   C

<u>him another.</u>   <u>No error</u>
D   E

41. A poll of students <u>shows that</u> Helen is the top
A

choice <u>for</u> student body president. Helen,
B

<u>however,</u> <u>is</u> likely to win the election.   <u>No error</u>
C   D   E

42. The producers realized the concert <u>has been a</u>
<u>success as they heard</u> the cheers and applause of
the audience.

(A) has been a success as they heard
(B) has been a success hearing
(C) was a success hearing
(D) had been a success when they heard
(E) succeeded in that they heard

43. The teacher began <u>to discuss</u> the homework
A

assignment <u>when</u> he <u>will be</u> interrupted <u>by</u> the
B   C   D

sound of the fire alarm.   <u>No error</u>
E

44. The conductor <u>announced</u> that the concert would
A

resume <u>as soon as</u> the soloist <u>replaces</u> the broken
B   C

string on <u>her</u> violin.   <u>No error</u>
D   E

45. <u>Many</u> patients begin <u>to show</u> symptoms again
A   B

after <u>they</u> <u>stopped</u> taking the drug.   <u>No error</u>
C   D   E

46. Mary Lou was awarded the gold medal because
she scored <u>more points than any child</u>
<u>participating</u> in the field day.

(A) more points than any child participating
(B) more points than any other child participating
(C) most points than any child participating
(D) more points than any child who had
participated
(E) more points as any child participating

47. <u>Appearing</u> in his first American tour, the British
singer's album rose to the top of the charts.

(A) Appearing
(B) While appearing
(C) While he was appearing
(D) When appearing
(E) Upon appearing

48. The sheriff called off the search for the escaped
convict because he doubted that <u>the convict can</u>
<u>successfully cross the river because the current</u>
<u>was so swift</u>.

(A) the convict can successfully cross the river
because the current was so swift
(B) the convict successfully crossed the river
because the current was so swift
(C) the convict successfully crossed the river
being that the current was so swift
(D) the convict would have been successful in
crossing the river, the current being so swift
(E) a successful attempt to cross the river was
made by the convict because the current was
so swift

49. Angela is hoping to save enough for a trip to
Europe, during which <u>the small village where her</u>
<u>grandparents were born will be visited</u>.

(A) the small village where her grandparents were
born will be visited
(B) the small village where her grandparents had
been born will be visited
(C) she will visit the small village where her
grandparents were born
(D) there will be a visit to the small village where
her grandparents were born
(E) a visit to the small village where her
grandparents were born will be included

NOTES AND STRATEGIES

50. <u>Finally and at long last</u> the old dog opened his eyes and noticed the intruder.

    (A) Finally and at long last
    (B) Finally
    (C) So finally
    (D) Yet at long last
    (E) Finally and long lastingly

51. The speaker declared that <u>alternative ways of utilizing</u> waterfront land ought to be explored.

    (A) alternative ways of utilizing
    (B) alternatives of use for
    (C) alternative utilizations of
    (D) alternative ways of utilization of
    (E) alternate uses of

52. After months of separation, Gauguin finally joined Van Gogh <u>in Arles in October of 1888, Gauguin left a few weeks later.</u>

    (A) in Arles in October of 1888, Gauguin left a few weeks later
    (B) in Arles; Gauguin, however, leaving a few weeks later
    (C) in Arles, while Gauguin left a few weeks later
    (D) in Arles, it was three weeks later when Gauguin was gone
    (E) in Arles, in October of 1888, but left a few weeks later

53. The nineteenth-century composers Wagner and Mahler did more than just write <u>music, they conducted</u> their own works.

    (A) music, they conducted
    (B) music, in that they conducted
    (C) music; they conducted
    (D) music, with their conducting of
    (E) music; as conductors, they did

54. <u>Since only</u> the ruling party <u>is allowed to</u> vote, <u>its</u>
        A   B   C
    members are able to maintain the <u>existing</u> status
                                        D
    quo. <u>No error</u>
           E

55. Each year, the geese <u>make</u> their <u>annual</u> <u>migration</u>
                              A   B   C
    from Northern Canada to <u>their winter habitats</u> in
                                          D
    the United States. <u>No error</u>
                           E

56. <u>Although</u> the committee met for over two weeks
        A
    and issued a 50-page report, <u>its findings</u> were
                                        B
    <u>of little</u> <u>importance</u> <u>or</u> consequence. <u>No error</u>
        C   D   E

57. <u>Letters were received by the editor of the newspaper that complained of its editorial policy.</u>

    (A) Letters were received by the editor of the newspaper that complained of its editorial policy.
    (B) Letters were received by the editor of the newspaper having complained of its editorial policy.
    (C) The editor of the newspaper received letters complaining of the newspaper's editorial policy.
    (D) Letters were received by the editor in which there were complaints to the editor of the newspaper about its editorial policy.
    (E) Letters were received by the editor complaining of the newspaper's editorial policy by the editor.

58. Riding in a coach and wearing the crown jewels, <u>the crowd cheered the royal couple.</u>

    (A) the crowd cheered the royal couple
    (B) cheering for the royal couple was done by the crowd
    (C) the royal couple was cheered by the crowd
    (D) the royal couple's cheering was done by the crowd
    (E) the royal couple, who was being cheered by crowd

59. <u>Wrapped in several thicknesses of newspaper, packed carefully in a strong cardboard carton, and bound securely with tape, the worker made sure that the fragile figurines would not be broken.</u>

   (A) Wrapped in several thicknesses of newspaper, packed carefully in a strong cardboard carton, and bound securely with tape, the worker made sure that the fragile figurines would not be broken.
   (B) Wrapped in several thicknesses of newspaper, packed carefully in a strong cardboard carton, and then binding the carton securely with tape, the worker made sure that the fragile figurines would not be broken.
   (C) The figurines, having been securely wrapped in several thicknesses of newspaper, packed carefully in a strong cardboard carton which was then securely bound with tape, the worker made sure would not be broken.
   (D) The worker, wrapping the figurines in several thicknesses of newspaper, packing them carefully in a strong cardboard carton, and securely binding the carton with tape, made sure that they would not be broken.
   (E) To make sure that the figurines would not be broken, the worker wrapped them in several thicknesses of newspaper, packed them carefully in a strong cardboard carton, and securely bound the carton with tape.

60. <u>In contrast of</u> the prevailing opinion, the
        A
    editorial <u>lays</u> the blame <u>for</u> the strike on the
              B   C
    workers and <u>their</u> representatives. <u>No error</u>
                  D   E

61. Although ballet and modern dance are both

    <u>concerned in</u> movement in space to musical
        A
    accompaniment, the training for ballet <u>is more</u>
                                             B   C
    rigorous <u>than that</u> for modern dance. <u>No error</u>
              D   E

62. By midnight the guests still <u>had not been served</u>
                                      A
    anything <u>to eat</u>, so <u>they</u> were <u>ravishing</u>. <u>No error</u>
              B   C   D   E

63. The <u>raise</u> in the number of accidents <u>attributable</u>
         A   B
    to drunk drivers <u>has prompted</u> a call for <u>stiffer</u>
                        C   D
    penalties for driving while intoxicated. <u>No error</u>
                                                E

64. The idea of trying <u>completing</u> the term paper <u>by</u>
                          A   B
    Friday <u>caused</u> Ken <u>to cancel</u> his plans for the
            C   D
    weekend. <u>No error</u>
               E

65. Psychologists <u>think</u> that many people eat
                    A
    <u>satisfying</u> <u>a need</u> for affection that is not
       B   C
    otherwise <u>fulfilled</u>. <u>No error</u>
                D   E

66. <u>Along with an end to featherbedding and no-show jobs</u>, the new head of the Transit Authority has eliminated many other inefficient employment practices.

   (A) Along with an end to featherbedding and no-show jobs
   (B) In addition to eliminating featherbedding and no-show jobs
   (C) Not only did he end featherbedding and no-shows jobs,
   (D) Besides featherbedding and no-show jobs coming to an end
   (E) Together with the ending of featherbedding and no-show jobs

67. <u>Being that</u> the hour <u>was</u> late, we <u>agreed</u> to adjourn
    A   B   C

    the meeting and <u>reconvene</u> at nine o'clock the
                        D

    following morning. <u>No error</u>
                          E

68. John, <u>having took</u> his seat at the head of the
          A

    table, <u>announced</u> <u>that</u> the dinner <u>would feature</u>
              B   C   D

    specialties from Thailand. <u>No error</u>
                                  E

69. The winter was so severe <u>that</u> <u>several</u> of Hillary's
                                A   B

    prize rose bushes <u>had sustained</u> <u>serious</u> damage
                          C   D

    from the frost. <u>No error</u>
                       E

70. I think that Dore's illustrations of Dante's *Divine
    Comedy* <u>are excellent; but my favorite drawing is
    "Don Quixote in His Library."</u>

    (A) are excellent; but my favorite drawing is
        "Don Quixote in His Library."
    (B) are excellent, but my favorite drawing is
        "Don Quixote in His Library."
    (C) are excellent and my favorite drawing is
        "Don Quixote in His Library."
    (D) are excellent in that my favorite drawing is
        "Don Quixote in His Library."
    (E) are excellent even though "Don Quixote in
        His Library" is my favorite drawing.

71. <u>Practically</u> all nitrates are crystalline and <u>readily</u>
    A   B

    <u>soluble, and</u> they are characterized by marked
    C

    decrepitation <u>when</u> heated on charcoals by a
                      D

    blowpipe. <u>No error</u>
                 E

72. The door <u>was</u> <u>ajar,</u> and the house <u>had been</u>
              A   B   C

    <u>ransacked</u>. <u>No error</u>
    D   E

73. Since many diseases and insects cause serious

    damage to <u>crops,</u> special national legislation has
              A

    been passed to provide for the quarantine of

    imported <u>plants;</u> and under provisions of various
              B

    <u>acts,</u> inspectors are placed at ports of entry to
    C

    prevent smugglers from bringing in plants

    <u>that might be</u> dangerous. <u>No error</u>
    D   E

74. <u>A full train crew consists of a motorman, a
    brakeman, a conductor, and two ticket takers.</u>

    (A) A full train crew consists of a motorman, a
        brakeman, a conductor, and two ticket takers.
    (B) A full train crew consists of a motorman, a
        brakeman, a conductor and two ticket takers.
    (C) A full train crew consists of a motorman,
        brakeman, conductor, and two ticket takers.
    (D) A full train crew consists of, a motorman, a
        brakeman, a conductor, and two ticket takers.
    (E) A full train crew consists of a motorman a
        brakeman a conductor and two ticket takers.

75. The procedure requires that you open the outer

    cover <u>plate,</u> remove the <u>thermostat,</u> replace the
          A   B

    broken <u>switch,</u> <u>and then</u> replace the thermostat.
            C   D

    <u>No error</u>
    E

76. <u>After</u> Peter finished painting the bird <u>feeder</u> he
    A   B

    <u>and</u> Jack <u>hung it</u> from a limb of the oak tree.
    C   D

    <u>No error</u>
    E

NOTES AND STRATEGIES

77. When Pat explained to his mother that ten was
    A

    the highest mark given on the entrance test she
                      B   C

    breathed a sigh of relief. No error
    D   E

78. Tim hopes to score well on the exam because he
    plans to go to an Ivy League school.

    (A) Tim hopes to score well on the exam because
        he plans to go to an Ivy League school.
    (B) Tim hopes to score well on the exam and he
        plans to go to an Ivy League school.
    (C) Tim hopes to score well on the exam,
        because he plans to go to an Ivy League
        school.
    (D) Tim hopes to score well on the exam, and he
        plans to go to an Ivy League school.
    (E) Tim hopes to score well on the exam he plans
        to go to an Ivy League school.

79. In this impoverished region with its arid soil a
    typical diet may contain only 800 calories per
    day.

    (A) In this impoverished region with its arid soil
        a typical diet may contain only 800 calories
        per day.
    (B) In this impoverished region with its arid soil;
        a typical diet may contain only 800 calories
        per day.
    (C) In this impoverished region, with its arid soil,
        a typical diet may contain only 800 calories
        per day.
    (D) In this impoverished region with its arid soil,
        a typical diet may contain only 800 calories
        per day.
    (E) In this impoverished region with its arid soil:
        a typical diet may contain only 800 calories
        per day.

80. Begun in 1981 and completed in 1985 the bridge
    A   B

    provided the first link between the island and the
    C   D

    mainland. No error
              E

81. To slow the bleeding Van tied a tourniquet
    around the lower portion of the leg.

    (A) To slow the bleeding Van tied a tourniquet
        around the lower portion of the leg.
    (B) To slow the bleeding—Van tied a tourniquet
        around the lower portion of the leg.
    (C) To slow the bleeding, Van tied a tourniquet
        around the lower portion of the leg.
    (D) To slow the bleeding, Van tied a tourniquet,
        around the lower portion of the leg.
    (E) Van tied a tourniquet, to slow the bleeding,
        around the lower portion of the leg.

82. Niagara Falls, which forms part of the border
    A   B

    between the United States and Canada, was the
                                C

    site of a saw mill built by the French in 1725.
                        D

    No error
    E

83. Secretary of State Acheson, however, made a
                       A   B

    reasoned defense of the treaty. No error
    C   D   E

84. Until the end of the 18th century, the only
                            A

    musicians in Norway, were simple
                 B

    unsophisticated peasants who traveled about.
                             C   D

    No error
    E

85. Prizes will be awarded in each event, and the
           A   B

    participant, who compiles the greatest overall total,
                C

    will receive a special prize. No error
    D   E

86. Since learning of the dangers of <u>caffeine, neither</u>
                                   A   B

    my wife <u>nor</u> I have consumed any <u>beverage,</u>
             C   D

    containing caffeine. <u>No error</u>
                            E

87. <u>After</u> months of <u>separation,</u> Gauguin finally
    A   B

    joined Van Gogh in Arles in October of

    <u>1888, Gauguin left</u> a few weeks later. <u>No error</u>
        C   D   E

88. <u>He grew up on a farm in Nebraska; he is now the captain of a Navy ship.</u>

    (A) He grew up on a farm in Nebraska; he is now the captain of a Navy ship.
    (B) He grew up on a farm in Nebraska, he is now the captain of a Navy ship.
    (C) He grew up on a farm in Nebraska he is now the captain of a Navy ship.
    (D) He grew up on a farm; in Nebraska he is now the captain of a Navy ship.
    (E) He grew up on a farm in Nebraska but he is now the captain of a Navy ship.

89. <u>The Smithtown players cheered the referee's decision; the Stonybrook players booed it.</u>

    (A) The Smithtown players cheered the referee's decision; the Stonybrook players booed it.
    (B) The Smithtown players cheered the referee's decision the Stonybrook players booed it.
    (C) The Smithtown players cheered the referee's decision, the Stonybrook players booed it.
    (D) The Smithtown players cheered the referee's decision: the Stonybrook players booed it.
    (E) The Smithtown players cheered the referee's decision, but the Stonybrook players booed it.

90. <u>When</u> John entered the <u>room; everyone</u> stood <u>up.</u>
    A   B   C   D
    <u>No error</u>
    E

91. Clem <u>announced</u> <u>that</u> the prize <u>would be</u> donated
             A   B   C

    to Harbus <u>House;</u> a well-known charity. <u>No error</u>
                D   E

92. The <u>seemingly</u> tranquil lane has been the scene of
           A

    many crimes <u>including: two</u> <u>assaults,</u> three
                     B   C

    <u>robberies,</u> and one murder. <u>No error</u>
       D   E

93. In addition to test <u>scores,</u> college admissions
                       A

    officers take into consideration many other factors

    such <u>as:</u> <u>grades,</u> extracurricular <u>activities, and</u>
        B   C   D

    letters of recommendation. <u>No error</u>
                          E

94. <u>Peter notified Elaine. The guidance counselor, that he had been accepted.</u>

    (A) Peter notified Elaine. The guidance counselor, that he had been accepted.
    (B) Peter notified Elaine the guidance counselor, that he had been accepted.
    (C) Peter notified Elaine, the guidance counselor that he had been accepted.
    (D) Peter notified Elaine, the guidance counselor, that he had been accepted.
    (E) Peter notified Elaine that the guidance counselor had been accepted.

95. <u>Peanuts—blanched or lightly roasted, add an interesting texture and taste to garden salads.</u>

    (A) Peanuts—blanched or lightly roasted, add an interesting texture and taste to garden salads.
    (B) Peanuts—blanched or lightly roasted—add an interesting texture and taste to garden salads.
    (C) Peanuts: blanched or lightly roasted, add an interesting texture and taste to garden salads.
    (D) Peanuts, blanched or lightly roasted—add an interesting texture and taste to garden salads.
    (E) Peanuts blanched or lightly roasted; add an interesting texture and taste to garden salads.

96. The optimist <u>feels that</u> his glass is <u>one-half</u> <u>full</u>;
            A   B   C

    the pessimist feels that his glass is one-half

    <u>empty.</u>   <u>No error</u>
     D   E

97. <u>The first chapter of *The Scarlet Letter* is "The
    Custom House."</u>

    (A) The first chapter of *The Scarlet Letter* is "The
    Custom House."
    (B) The first chapter of *The Scarlet Letter* is "The
    Custom House".
    (C) The first chapter of *The Scarlet Letter* is The
    Custom House.
    (D) The first chapter of *The Scarlet Letter* is *The
    Custom House.*
    (E) The first chapter of *The Scarlet Letter* is "The
    Custom House."

DIRECTIONS: Punctuate the following paragraph.

98. On Monday, Mark received a letter of
    acceptance from State College. He immediately
    called his mother, herself a graduate of State
    College, to tell her about his acceptance. When
    he told her he had also been awarded a
    scholarship; she was very excited. After
    hanging up Mark's mother decided to throw a
    surprise party for Mark. She telephoned his
    brother, his sister, and several of his friends.
    Because the party was supposed to be a
    surprise she made them all promise not to
    say anything to Mark. Mark however, had a
    similar idea, a party for his mother to
    celebrate his acceptance at her alma-mater. He
    telephoned his brother, his sister, and several
    of his parents' friends to invite them to a
    party at his house on Saturday night, and he
    made them all promise to say nothing to his
    mother. On Saturday night both Mark and his
    mother were surprised.

IMPROVING PARAGRAPHS DIRECTIONS: The
following passages are early drafts of essays. Some
parts of the passages need to be rewritten. Read each
passage and answer the items that follow. Some items
are about particular sentences or parts of sentences and
ask you to improve sentence structure and word choice.
Other items refer to parts of the essay or the entire
essay and ask you to consider organization and
development. In making your decisions, follow the
conventions of standard written English.

*Items 99-104 are based on the following essay, which
is a response to an assignment to write about a chore
for which you have a responsibility and why you like or
dislike doing the chore.*

  *(1) Each year, my family plants a vegetable
garden. (2) Both my parents work, and with this it is
the job of the children to tend the garden.*
  *(3) Work starts several weeks before the growing
season actually begins. (4) We put little pots of soil
containing seeds that must sprout before they are
planted outdoors on the sun porch. (5) Then, my father
prepares the ground with a rototiller. (6) The danger of
frost is past, it is time to plant.*
  *(7) For the first few weeks, we water the seed
beds regularly and pull weeds by hand. (8) Once the
plants are established, the leaves of the good plants
block the sunlight so weeds can't grow. (9) There are
other jobs such as staking tomatoes and tending to
running vines.*
  *(10) Then the blossoms appear and are pollinated
by bees and other insects. (11) As small vegetables
appear, the blossoms drop off. (12) They continue to
grow and later in the summer begin to ripen. (13) Up
to this point, tending the garden has been a chore, but
now it becomes a pleasure. (14) Each afternoon, we
pick the ripe ones and wash them so that they are
ready for cooking. (15) I suppose that I feel proud that
I have helped to feed my family. (16) I have to admit
that I enjoy the taste of the freshly picked vegetables.*

99. Which of the following is the best way to revise the underlined portion of sentence 2 (reproduced below)?

Both my parents work, and with this it is the job of the children to tend the garden.

(A) a situation that makes it
(B) because it is
(C) in that it is
(D) so it is
(E) making it

100. In context, which of the following is the best way to revise sentence 6 (reproduced below)?

The danger of frost is past, it is time to plant.

(A) When the danger of frost is past, it is time to plant.
(B) The danger of frost is past, when it is time to plant.
(C) The danger of frost being past, it is time to plant.
(D) Planting begins, and the danger of frost passes.
(E) The time to plant is when the danger of frost is passing.

101. In context, which of the following would be best to insert at the beginning of sentence 9?

(A) However,
(B) Further,
(C) Actually,
(D) Because
(E) Since

102. In sentence 14, the word "ones" refers to

(A) blossoms
(B) bees
(C) gardens
(D) chores
(E) vegetables

103. Which of the following is the best way to combine sentences 15 and 16 (reproduced below)?

I suppose that I feel proud that I have helped to feed my family. I have to admit that I enjoy the taste of the freshly picked vegetables.

(A) Feeling proud that I have helped to feed my family, I have to admit that I enjoy the taste of the freshly picked vegetables.
(B) I suppose that I feel proud that I have helped to feed my family, but I have to admit that I enjoy the taste of the freshly picked vegetables.
(C) Supposing that I feel proud that I have helped to feed my family, I have to admit that I enjoy the taste of the freshly picked vegetables.
(D) I have to admit that I enjoy the taste of the freshly picked vegetables, so I suppose that I feel proud that I have helped to feed my family.
(E) Helping to feed my family makes me supposedly feel proud as well as admitting that I enjoy the taste of the freshly picked vegetables.

104. Which of the following best describes the overall organization of the passage?

(A) Chronological development
(B) Presenting two sides of an issue
(C) Making a general statement and giving illustrations
(D) Posing a question and then answering it
(E) Citing an authority and then drawing a conclusion

Items 105-110 *are based on the following essay, which is a response to an assignment to write about an issue that is facing America and what might be done to resolve it.*

(1) In my mind, one of the most pressing issues facing America today is health care. (2) One aspect of the problem is going to the doctor. (3) Many people just cannot afford to pay for a visit to a doctor. (4) They avoid going to the doctor until they are really sick. (5) If they were treated in the first place, they wouldn't get so sick. (6) This practice not only causes human suffering but is wasteful. (7) Health insurance for surgery is also an issue. (8) Many people do not get adequate health insurance with their jobs and cannot afford to pay for it. (9) This also creates an unfair distribution of health care in America.

(10) An even more important aspect of the health care problem in America is the choices that people make for themselves. (11) Take smoking for example. (12) Scientific evidence proves that smoking causes lung cancer and other diseases. (13) Yet, many people continue to smoke, and young people continue to start smoking. (14) There are other health problems such as overweight and drugs that may also come from private choices.

(15) Some government assistance is needed for those who cannot afford medical care or health insurance. (16) The most important thing, however, is for people to be concerned with their own health and not expect the government to do things for them. (17) If we take care of ourselves by eating better, exercising more, and avoiding destructive choices, we will all live longer, healthier, and happier lives.

105. In context, which of the following is the best way of revising the underlined portion of sentence 2 (reproduced below)?

One aspect of the problem is <u>going to the doctor</u>.

(A) going to the doctor
(B) medicine
(C) doctors and patients
(D) getting to go to the doctor
(E) lack of access to a doctor

106. Which of the following is the best way to combine sentences 3 and 4 (reproduced below)?

Many people just cannot afford to pay for a visit to a doctor. They avoid going to the doctor until they are really sick.

(A) Because many people just cannot afford to pay for a visit to a doctor, and they avoid going until they are really sick.
(B) Because many people just cannot afford to pay for a visit to a doctor, they avoid going until they are really sick.
(C) In that many people avoid going to a doctor until they are really sick, they cannot afford to pay for a visit.
(D) When many people cannot afford to pay for a visit to a doctor, they avoid going until they are all really sick.
(E) People just cannot afford to pay for a visit to a doctor if they avoid going until they are really sick.

107. Which of the following would be the best substitute for "this" in sentence 9?

(A) Medical care and health insurance
(B) The fact that health insurance doesn't exist
(C) Health insurance
(D) The availability of health insurance
(E) The inability to pay for health insurance

108. In context, which of the following is the best way of revising sentence 11 (reproduced below)?

Take smoking for example.

(A) Take smoking for example.
(B) Smoking to take an example.
(C) An example of smoking.
(D) To smoke is an example.
(E) Taking smoking as an example.

109. Which of the following is the best way to revise the underlined portion of sentence 14 (reproduced below)?

    There are other health problems such as overweight and drugs that may also come from private choices.

    (A) such as being overweight and using drugs that may also come from private choices
    (B) such as overweightness and drug usage that may also come from private choices
    (C) like overweight and drugs that may also come from private choices
    (D) that may also come from private choices such as overweight and drugs
    (E) that may also come from private choices including overweight and drugs

110. In context, which of the following best describes the purpose of the final paragraph?

    (A) To expose faulty reasoning
    (B) To evaluate a theory set forth earlier
    (C) To provide specific illustrations
    (D) To propose a solution to a problem
    (E) To persuade the reader to change an opinion

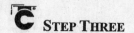

111. **DIRECTIONS:** Read the following prompt and assignment, which are written as they would appear on the SAT. Then, instead of writing an entire essay as directed by the assignment, use the space that is provided below to <u>create only an outline for an essay</u> that responds to the assignment. Include a thesis, as well as a topic sentence and a list of several examples for each part of your essay.

> *Human beings are often cruel, but they also have the capacity for kindness and compassion. In my opinion, an example that demonstrates this capacity is ——.*

Assignment: Complete the statement above with an example from current affairs, history, literature, or your own personal experience. Then write a well-organized essay explaining why you regard that event favorably.

CHALLENGE ITEMS

DIRECTIONS: This section contains Writing items in the top quartile of difficulty. Answers are on page 986.

IDENTIFYING SENTENCE ERRORS

DIRECTIONS: Identifying Sentence Errors items test your knowledge of grammar, usage, word choice, and idiom. Some sentences are correct. No sentence contains more than one error. You will find that the error, if there is one, is underlined and lettered. Elements of the sentence that are not underlined will not be changed. In choosing answers, follow the requirements of standard written English. If there is an error, select the <u>one underlined part</u> that must be changed to make the sentence correct and fill in the corresponding oval on your answer sheet. If there is no error, fill in oval (E).

(saw)

1. If Mary Outerbridge <u>would not have seen</u> English
                                    A
   officers <u>playing</u> tennis in Bermuda <u>where</u> she
            B   C
   <u>was vacationing</u> at the time, she would not have
    D
   introduced the game to America. <u>No error</u>
                                       E

2. <u>When we consider</u> the miracles of modern
    A
   science, we find it hard to imagine <u>that</u> in 1349
                                        B
   the Black Death <u>killed</u> one-third of <u>England's</u>
                    C   D
   population. <u>No error</u>
                  E

3. <u>When</u> the critics <u>wrote</u> critical reviews of the
    A   B
   Broadway <u>opening</u> of the rock star's new musical,
             C
   neither the producer nor the director <u>were</u>
                                          D
   available for an interview. <u>No error</u>
                                   E

4. Those <u>who are successful in business</u> often
           A
   discover <u>that</u> wealth and fame <u>do not guarantee</u>
             B   C
   happiness and <u>learning</u> that peace of mind is
                  D
   important. <u>No error</u>
                 E

5. About 3500 B.C., ancient Egypt made great

   it

   progress in agriculture after <u>they</u> adopted several
                                  A
   new techniques of cultivation <u>among which</u>
                                  B
   were <u>raking, plowing, and manuring</u>. <u>No error</u>
         C   E

6. <u>In</u> the southwest corner of the cemetery, where
    A
   the honeysuckle vines <u>have all but</u> covered the
                          B
   grave markers, <u>lays</u> the body of the county's
                   C
   <u>greatest</u> war hero. <u>No error</u>
    D   E

7. The final number of the musical, a duet,

   <u>was written</u> by Sue and is sung by <u>she</u> and
    A   B
   Reginald, the male lead, <u>as</u> the other members of
                            C
   the cast take <u>their</u> bows. <u>No error</u>
                  D   E

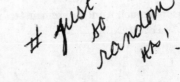

8. The owner of the property, who <u>had farmed</u> the
                                        A
   land for <u>more than</u> 40 years, <u>listened to</u> the
              B   C
   company's offer but said that he could not answer

   (definitely)

   <u>definite</u> without further consideration. <u>No error</u>
   D   E

9. Immediately after the legislators <u>freezed</u> the level
                                        A
   of benefits, citizens groups <u>began contacting</u>
                                   B
   <u>their</u> members to encourage them to write letters
     C
   of protest <u>to</u> their representatives in Congress.
               D
   <u>No error</u>
   E

10. Since the treasurer and <u>him</u> <u>had already discussed</u>
                              A   B
    the details of the financial report, Robert felt that

    it was not necessary for <u>him</u> <u>to attend</u> the budget
                              C   D
    meeting. <u>No error</u>
              E

11. The history of the ancient Egyptians, as recorded

    <u>by</u> graphic drawings <u>called</u> hieroglyphics,
     A   B
    <u>describe</u> <u>in great detail</u> the burial of King
     C   D
    Tutankhamen's body in a sarcophagus of wood

    and gold. <u>No error</u>
               E

12. The conditions <u>of</u> the subway system
                    A
    <u>having been improved</u> <u>dramatically</u> over the past
     B   C
    three years, <u>but</u> much work still remains to be
                  D
    done. <u>No error</u>
           E

13. Introduced <u>at the last moment</u> by the Scholastic
                A
    Council <u>was</u> a demand <u>that</u> the college allocate
             B   C
    funds for a day-care center and a demand that the

    college <u>hire</u> more minority faculty members.
             D
    <u>No error</u>
    E

14. <u>Summarily rejecting</u> the demands of the students
     A
    for a greater voice in determining <u>university</u>
                                         B
    policy, the dean now worries <u>that</u> her decision
                                   C
    <u>might result</u> in new student demonstrations.
     D
    <u>No error</u>
    E

15. The dog <u>has been replaced</u> by the cat as the pet of
             A
    choice for Americans <u>because</u> cats <u>are</u> more
                           B   C
    independent and require less care <u>than</u> dogs.
                                        D
    <u>No error</u>
    E

16. Because many modern actors <u>study</u> method
                                 A
    acting, <u>a system devised</u> by Stanislavsky, <u>their</u>
             B   C
    interpretations of the role of Hamlet differ

    <u>from Shakespeare's time</u>. <u>No error</u>
     D   E

17. <u>During</u> the second half of the nineteenth century,
     A

    waves of immigration <u>in</u> the United States
                          B

    <u>brought</u> hundreds of thousands of foreigners to
     C

    America's cities <u>and created</u> the condition termed
                      D

    the "melting pot." <u>No error</u>
                        E

18. The governor's oratorical skill, <u>which</u> has helped
                                      A

    him <u>to win</u> several elections, <u>comes</u> either from
        B   C

    his college debating experience <u>and</u> from an in-
                                     D

    depth knowledge of the issues. <u>No error</u>
                                    E

19. The decade of the 1920s was <u>an important one</u> for
                                 A

    English literature, for during that time a large

    <u>amount</u> of works now considered classics were
     B

    written <u>by</u> great writers <u>such as</u> Ezra Pound,
             C   D

    D.H. Lawrence, and T.S. Eliot. <u>No error</u>
                                    E

IMPROVING SENTENCES DIRECTIONS: In Improving Sentences items, part or all of the sentence is underlined. Below each sentence you will find five ways of phrasing the underlined part. Select the answer that produces the most effective sentence, one that is clear and exact, without awkwardness or ambiguity, and fill in the corresponding oval on your answer sheet. In choosing answers, follow the requirements of standard written English. Choose the answer that best expresses the meaning of the original sentence. Answer (A) is always the same as the underlined part. Choose answer (A) if you think the original sentence needs no revision.

20. Unemployed laborers ignored the picket lines set up by striking workers at the factory's only <u>entrance, and they thereby rendered it</u> ineffective.

    (A) entrance, and they thereby rendered it
    (B) entrance and therefore rendered it
    (C) entrance, by which the strike was rendered
    (D) entrance, thereby this rendered the strike
    (E) entrance, thereby rendering the strike

21. <u>Ignoring a projected decline in births over the next decade,</u> the school board allocated funds for a new elementary school based upon an increase in the infant population last year.

    (A) Ignoring a projected decline in births over the next decade,
    (B) By ignoring a projected decline in births over the next decade,
    (C) To ignore a projected decline in births over the next decade,
    (D) The next decade's projected decline in births having been ignored,
    (E) A projected decline in births over the next decade is ignored when

22. The supporters of the volunteer ambulance corps were assured <u>as to the deductibility of their donations on their tax returns</u>.

    (A) as to the deductibility of their donations on their tax returns
    (B) as to their donations being deductible on their tax returns
    (C) that their, the supporters', donations are deductible on their tax returns
    (D) that in regards to their tax returns the donations are deductible
    (E) that their donations are deductible on their tax returns

23. <u>A million dollars before his twenty-fifth birthday having been made</u>, the young entrepreneur decided to write a book instructing others in the techniques of his success.

    (A) A million dollars before his twenty-fifth birthday having been made
    (B) A million dollars before his twenty-fifth birthday made
    (C) By twenty-five, when he made a million dollars
    (D) When he made a million dollars by his twenty-fifth birthday
    (E) Having made a million dollars by his twenty-fifth birthday

24. The most frequently advanced justifications for rising physicians' fees <u>is they pay increasing malpractice insurance premiums and invest</u> in costly equipment.

    (A) is they pay increasing malpractice insurance premiums and invest
    (B) are they pay increasing malpractice insurance premiums and invest
    (C) are that physicians pay increasing malpractice insurance premiums and that they invest
    (D) is increasing malpractice insurance premiums and investing
    (E) are increasing malpractice insurance premiums and the need to invest

25. Visiting Europe as a tourist ten years after the end of the war, <u>the rapid pace of the postwar reconstruction amazed the former soldier</u>.

    (A) the rapid pace of the postwar reconstruction amazed the former soldier
    (B) the postwar reconstruction that had taken place at a rapid pace amazed the former soldier
    (C) the former soldier was amazed at the rapid pace of the postwar reconstruction
    (D) the former soldier who was amazed at the rapid pace of the postwar reconstruction
    (E) the former soldier was amazed at how rapid the postwar reconstruction was

26. Although Janice has expressed a desire to become a couture designer, <u>she lacks the necessary sewing skills and has no</u> interest in detail work.

    (A) she lacks the necessary sewing skills and has no
    (B) lacking the necessary sewing skills, she has no
    (C) she is without the necessary sewing skills and
    (D) she does not have the necessary sewing skills nor the
    (E) she is lacking in the necessary sewing skills and

27. It is distressing to many would-be teachers that the Board of Examiners in New York City has the sole power to decide <u>about licensing teachers</u>.

    (A) about licensing teachers
    (B) whether or not a teacher should be licensed
    (C) whether or not teachers' licensing
    (D) as to whether or not a teacher should be licensed
    (E) the licensing of teachers, if they so choose

28. A person's decision to pursue a career in law sometimes results <u>from a lack of any true direction rather than from</u> any commitment to the principles of justice.

    (A) from a lack of any true direction rather than from
    (B) from a lack of any true direction as from
    (C) as a lack of any true direction as much as from
    (D) from a lack of any true direction and
    (E) from a lack of any true direction but

29. Left to his own devices, a curious four-year-old can learn much from computerized <u>toys, the problem being that the learning experience</u> is devoid of any social element.

    (A) toys, the problem being that the learning experience
    (B) toys, but the problem is that using computerized toys to learn
    (C) toys; in learning from toys, one
    (D) toys, but that learning experience
    (E) toys; the problem is that in learning from them, it

30. Since some vegetables, such as tomatoes, peppers, and eggplants, are difficult to grow from seed, <u>seedlings will</u> improve your chances of a rich harvest.

    (A) seedlings will
    (B) seedlings
    (C) the use of seedlings will
    (D) to use seedlings will
    (E) using seedlings to

31. Because Ian had been wounded in the European <u>Campaign, so he was asked</u> to serve as Grand Marshal of the Memorial Day Parade.

    (A) Campaign, so he was asked
    (B) Campaign, he was asked
    (C) Campaign, they asked him
    (D) Campaign, so they asked him
    (E) Campaign, that he was asked

32. The present administration <u>has always and will continue to be</u> committed to a policy of guaranteeing a good education to every child in the district.

    (A) has always and will continue to be
    (B) has always and continues to be
    (C) has always been and will continue
    (D) has always been and will continue to be
    (E) always has been and continues

33. The gift certificate for a hot-air balloon ride gives the recipient the option <u>that you may exchange the certificate</u> for cash.

    (A) that you may exchange the certificate
    (B) that the certificate may be exchanged
    (C) of exchanging the certificate
    (D) of your exchanging the certificate
    (E) to exchange the certificate

IMPROVING PARAGRAPHS DIRECTIONS: The following passages are early drafts of essays. Some parts of the passages need to be rewritten. Read each passage and answer the items that follow. Some items are about particular sentences or parts of sentences and ask you to improve sentence structure and word choice. Other items refer to parts of the essay or the entire essay and ask you to consider organization and development. In making your decisions, follow the conventions of standard written English.

Items 34-37 *are based on the following essay, which is a response to an assignment to write about an environmental resource solution and its history.*

(1) Today, planners are looking for renewable energy sources to satisfy the growing demand for energy. (2) One idea that gets much attention in the press is generating electricity from wind power. (3) Articles in newspapers and magazines are often written as though wind power is a new idea, but it is really one of the oldest energy sources used by human beings.

(4) No records of the earliest wind machines survive, but they may have been built in China more than three thousand years ago or perhaps on the windy plains of Afghanistan. (5) Some sources hint that Egyptians during the time of the Pharaohs used wind power for drawing water for agricultural purposes. (6) Around 2,000 B.C., Hammurabi may have taken time out from developing his legal code to sponsor development of some sort of wind machine.

(7) The earliest confirmed wind machines were located in Persia. (8) Persian writers described gardens irrigated by wind-driven water lifts. (9) The Persian machines were horizontal devices, carousel-like contraptions that revolved around a center pole and that caught the wind with bundles of reeds. (10) Indeed, there is a certain engineering advantage to the carousel: it doesn't matter from which direction the wind is blowing.

(11) From the Middle East, windmachine technology may have been carried to Europe by returning Crusaders, for soon after the Crusades

windmills appeared in Northern Europe and on the British Isles. (12) Windmills flourished for awhile in Europe but gave way to steam power.

(13) Those engaged in research and development on wind power now face the same problem that caused the shift from wind to steam power: how to handle the extremes of wind velocity. (14) Wind, after all, is real iffy. (15) It can fail to blow just when it is needed, or it can blow a gale right when it isn't needed.

34. Which of the following best explains why sentence 7 should begin a new paragraph?

    (A) The writer begins to discuss wind power in Persia rather than in China, Afghanistan, or Egypt.
    (B) The writer shifts to a discussion of historical records rather than speculation.
    (C) The Persian wind machines were horizontal wheels rather than vertical ones.
    (D) It is not certain that windmachine technology was brought to Europe from the Middle East.
    (E) The Persians were the first to successfully harness the power of the wind.

35. Which of the following is the LEAST appropriate revision of the underlined part of sentence 11?

    From the Middle East, windmachine technology may have been carried to Europe by returning Crusaders, <u>for soon after the Crusades windmills appeared in Northern Europe and on the British Isles</u>.

    (A) since windmills appeared in Northern Europe and on the British Isles soon after the Crusades
    (B) in as much as windmills appeared soon after the Crusades in Northern Europe and on the British Isles
    (C) because windmills appeared in Northern Europe and on the British Isles soon after the Crusades
    (D) given that windmills appeared soon after the Crusades in Northern Europe and on the British Isles
    (E) therefore windmills appeared in Northern Europe and on the British Isles soon after the Crusades

36. Which of the following revisions is most needed?

    (A) Substitute <u>increasing</u> for <u>growing</u> in sentence 1.
    (B) Substitute <u>exist</u> for <u>survive</u> in sentence 4.
    (C) Substitute <u>built</u> for <u>located</u> in sentence 7.
    (D) Substitute <u>yielded</u> for <u>gave way</u> in sentence 12.
    (E) Substitute <u>very variable</u> for <u>real iffy</u> in sentence 14.

37. Which of the following is the best order for paragraphs 2, 3, and 4?

    (A) 2, 3, 4
    (B) 2, 4, 3
    (C) 3, 2, 4
    (D) 3, 4, 2
    (E) 4, 2, 3

38. **DIRECTIONS:** You have 25 minutes to plan and write an essay on the topic assigned below. DO NOT WRITE ON ANY OTHER TOPIC. AN ESSAY ON ANOTHER TOPIC IS NOT ACCEPTABLE. Think carefully about the issue presented in the following excerpt and the assignment below.

1. *Many people rightfully reminisce about "the good old days," insisting that the quality of life was much better thirty or forty years ago. The problems of the modern world were less then. Environmental issues were of no concern, overcrowding less of a problem, and life was simpler.*

2. *While conditions have definitely changed since "the good old days," the quality of life today is considerably improved over that of thirty or forty years ago. Modernization has brought many positive changes in the world including increased food production, faster transportation, and greatly improved global communication.*

Assignment: Which do you find more compelling, the belief that the quality of life was better thirty or forty years ago or that it is better today? Plan and write an essay in which you develop your point of view on this issue. Support your position with reasoning and examples taken from your reading, studies, experience, or observations.

NOTES AND STRATEGIES

TIMED-PRACTICE QUIZZES

DIRECTIONS: This section contains four Writing quizzes. For Identifying Sentence Errors items, choose the letter that corresponds to the underlined part of the sentence that is incorrect. If no error occurs, choose (E). For Improving Sentences items, choose the answer choice that best corrects the underlined portion of the sentence without altering the meaning of the sentence. If the original underlined part is correct, choose (A). For Improving Paragraphs items, choose the answer that best answers the item. For the essay, see the specific directions and assignment on that page. Answers are on page 986.

A. QUIZ I (16 items; 12 minutes)

C 1. <u>During</u> the televised meeting of the Senate, the
A
first issue <u>to be discussed</u> <u>were</u> Federal grants and
B   C
loans <u>for</u> higher education. <u>No error</u>
D   E

D 2. Men in the Navy <u>spend</u> more time <u>away from</u>
A   B
home <u>than</u> <u>any other branch</u> of the service.
C   D
<u>No error</u>
E

E 3. Illiteracy is a <u>widespread</u> problem in the United
A
States; many mistakes <u>are made</u> in the workplace
B
by people <u>who</u> do not know how <u>to read</u>.
C   D
<u>No error</u>
E

B 4. The <u>earliest</u> Americans originated in Northeast
A
Asia and <u>have migrated</u> <u>across</u> a land bridge
B   C
sometime <u>during</u> the Pleistocene era. <u>No error</u>
D   E

D 5. The comedian <u>found</u> that capturing the <u>audience's</u>
A   B
attention <u>was</u> easy, but <u>to maintain</u> it was
C   D
difficult. <u>No error</u>
E

D 6. <u>Because</u> the project <u>had been</u> a team effort,
A   B   *among*
we divided the bonus equally <u>between</u> the five of
C   D
us. <u>No error</u>
E

E 7. The most important food-energy source <u>of three-fourths of the world's population are grains</u>.

(A) of three-fourths of the world's population are grains
(B) for three-fourths of the world's population are grains
(C) for three-fourths of the world's population is grains
(D) for three-fourths of the worlds' population is grains
(E) for three-fourths of the world's population is grain

E 8. <u>Fluoride</u> helps protect a child's teeth while the teeth grow, <u>but it is unharmful to their bodies</u>.

(A) but it is unharmful to their bodies
(B) and it is unharmful to their bodies
(C) and it is not harmful to their bodies
(D) and it is not harmful to the bodies
(E) and it is not harmful to the body

9. Greek fire, a gelatinous, incendiary mixture, was used in warfare before gunpowder was invented.

(A) Greek fire, a gelatinous, incendiary mixture, was used in warfare before gunpowder was invented.

(B) Greek fire, a gelatinous, incendiary mixture, was used during warfare before the invention of gunpowder.

(C) Greek fire, a gelatinous, incendiary mixture before the invention of gunpowder, was used in warfare.

(D) A gelatinous, incendiary mixture, warfare involved the use of Greek fire before the invention of gunpowder.

(E) Gelatinous and incendiary, Greek fire was a mixture that was used in warfare before the invention of gunpowder.

10. After having had Ann Boleyn beheaded, the next day King Henry VIII was betrothed to Jane Seymour.

(A) After having had Ann Boleyn beheaded, the next day King Henry VIII was betrothed to Jane Seymour.

(B) After having had Ann Boleyn beheaded, King Henry VIII was betrothed to Jane Seymour the next day.

(C) Having had Ann Boleyn beheaded, King Henry VIII was betrothed to Jane Seymour the next day.

(D) On the day after he had Ann Boleyn beheaded, King Henry VIII was betrothed to Jane Seymour.

(E) On the day after having had Ann Boleyn beheaded, King Henry VIII was betrothed to Jane Seymour.

Items 11-16 are based on the following essay, which is a response to an assignment to write about the ways in which different activities serve the same function in different cultural settings.

(1) I now live in the country; but when I was younger, my family lived in Brooklyn, New York. (2) You might think of Brooklyn as nothing but high-rise buildings. (3) However, in my old neighborhood, most people lived in two- or three-family houses that were attached to each other. (4) They call these row houses. (5) Row houses have small front yards, usually covered with concrete, and somewhat larger backyards. (6) People who live in Brooklyn do many of the same things that we do in the country, only slightly differently.

(7) Cookouts are a favorite summer pastime. (8) People who do not have a backyard take their grills to the park. (9) Row houses do not have garages, but they do have front steps that are called stoops. (10) So instead of garage sales, they have stoop sales. (11) Families put used clothing and other articles for sale on their stoop, and people stop by to look and maybe buy just like at a garage sale.

(12) There is no county fair in the city, but there are feasts and festivals. (13) A street is closed down for a day or even a week. (14) Both sides are lined with stands. (15) Some stands have traditional fair games such as throwing darts at balloons. (16) Like the county fair, you can win a stuffed animal if you are lucky. (17) There are also stands serving Italian sausages and peppers, Vietnamese spring rolls, Mexican tacos, or Chinese noodles. (18) So in a different cultural setting, a county fair becomes a world's fair.

11. Which of the following is the best way to revise the underlined portion of sentence 4 (reproduced below)?

They call these row houses.

(A) They call these
(B) They call them
(C) Called
(D) These are called
(E) Defined as

12. In context, which of the following is the best way of combining sentences 7 and 8 (reproduced below)?

    Cookouts are a favorite summer pastime. People who do not have a backyard take their grills to the park.

    (A) Cookouts are a favorite summer pastime, and people who not have a backyard take their grills to the park.
    (B) Cookouts, a favorite summer pastime, are had by people in the park who do not have backyards.
    (C) A favorite summer pastime, cookouts are enjoyed by people who do not have a backyard in the park.
    (D) A favorite summer pastime, people with and without backyards enjoy cookouts, but some in the park.
    (E) People have cookouts as a favorite summer pastime, and those without backyards do it in the park.

13. In context, which of the following is the best way to revise sentence 10 (reproduced below)?

    So instead of garage sales, they have stoop sales.

    (A) (As it is now)
    (B) So instead of garage sales, stoop sales are held.
    (C) So instead of garage sales, people have stoops sales.
    (D) They have stoop sales instead of garage sales.
    (E) They have stoop sales, but they do not have garage sales.

14. In context, which of the following is the best way of revising sentence 16 (reproduced below)?

    Like the county fair, you can win a stuffed animal if you are lucky.

    (A) As the county fair, you can win a stuffed animal if you are lucky.
    (B) As at the county fair, you can win a stuffed animal if you are lucky.
    (C) You can win a stuffed animal at the county fair if you are lucky.
    (D) If you are lucky, like the county fair, you can win a stuffed animal.
    (E) If you are lucky, as the county fair, you can win a stuffed animal.

15. The passage makes use of all of the following techniques EXCEPT

    (A) defining a term for the reader
    (B) comparing different situations
    (C) contrasting different situations
    (D) providing examples for the reader
    (E) relying on a noted authority

16. A discussion of which of the following would be the most appropriate continuation of the passage?

    (A) techniques used in the construction of row houses
    (B) fire department regulations for grilling in the park
    (C) aspects of holiday celebrations that are unique to the city
    (D) methods for cooking various types of the dishes mentioned
    (E) more details on the types of games played at county fairs

B. QUIZ II (16 items; 12 minutes)

1. Although the script <u>is interesting</u> and well-
                              A

   written, <u>it</u> will <u>have to be</u> <u>adopted</u> for television.
             B   C   D

   <u>No error</u>
       E

2. The differences in climate <u>accounts</u> for the <u>marked</u>
                                    A   B

   distinction <u>between</u> the north and south <u>of</u> some
                   C   D

   countries. <u>No error</u>
                   E

3. The conductor <u>would like to have been</u> a
                         A

   composer <u>but</u> after years of <u>unsuccessful</u>
                B   C

   attempts, he <u>has given</u> it up. <u>No error</u>
                     D   E

4. The judge <u>sentenced</u> the president of the
                   A

   corporation to ten years in prison <u>for embezzling</u>
                                            B

   funds, but he <u>gave</u> his partner <u>less of a</u> sentence.
                     C   D

   <u>No error</u>
       E

5. <u>You taking</u> the <u>initiative</u> in the negotiations
        A   B

   <u>will profit</u> the company to a <u>great degree</u>.
        C   D

   <u>No error</u>
       E

6. The princess, <u>along with</u> her entourage, <u>travel</u> by
                      A   B

   ship because <u>she is</u> afraid <u>to fly</u>. <u>No error</u>
                     C   D   E

7. The possibility of massive earthquakes <u>are</u>
   <u>regarded by most area residents with</u> a mixture of
   skepticism and caution.

   (A) are regarded by most area residents with
   (B) is regarded by most area residents with
   (C) is regarded by most area residents as
   (D) is mostly regarded by area residents with
   (E) by most area residents is regarded with

8. Certain infections are <u>made up by both viral and</u>
   <u>bacterial elements which makes</u> treatment of these
   infections difficult.

   (A) made up by both viral and bacterial elements
       which makes
   (B) composed of both viral and bacterial
       elements; this combination makes
   (C) composed of both viral and bacterial
       elements which make
   (D) composed by viral as well as bacterial
       elements and they make
   (E) including both viral as well as bacterial
       elements that make

9. <u>When it rains outside, most parents prefer small</u>
   <u>children to play indoors.</u>

   (A) When it rains outside, most parents prefer
       small children to play indoors.
   (B) Most parents prefer the indoors for their
       children's play when it rains.
   (C) Most parents prefer that small children play
       indoors when it rains.
   (D) When raining outside, most parents prefer
       small children to play indoors.
   (E) When raining, most parents prefer small
       children to play indoors.

10. <u>Opening the door to the street, the heat waves distorted the lamppost causing it to shimmy like a mirage.</u>

    (A) Opening the door to the street, the heat waves distorted the lamppost causing it to shimmy like a mirage.

    (B) The heat waves distorted the lamppost causing it to shimmy like a mirage through the open door to the street.

    (C) Through the open door to the street, one could see the lamppost, distorted by the heat waves, shimmying like a mirage.

    (D) Through the door which opened to the street, one could see the lamppost shimmying, distorted by the heat waves.

    (E) The heat waves distorted the lamppost, causing it to shimmy through the door like a mirage which opened to the street.

<u>Items 11-16</u> *are based on the following essay, which is a response to an assignment to write about a country that you would like to visit and why.*

(1) The country that I would most like to visit is France. (2) I have taken two years of French in school. (3) I would like to practice what I have learned.

(4) Like everyone else, I want to visit Paris. (5) Many movies have been made about that city, such as the classic "An American in Paris," and it seems very glamorous. (6) I would walk along the Seine River, and then stop into a sidewalk cafe for a "limonade" (lemonade). (7) I would see historical places such as the site where the Bastille once stood and the Tomb of Napoleon as well as other points of interest such as Montmartre and the Eiffel Tower. (8) The Eiffel Tower was designed by Gustav Eiffel for the Exposition of 1889.

(9) Most of all, however, I would like to visit the beaches of Normandy, where allied troops landed in 1944. (10) My grandfather, who lived with my family when I was growing up, was a soldier at Normandy on D-Day. (11) As his only granddaughter, we were very close. (12) He used to tell me about the landing and where the army went as they moved inland. (13) I know he won medals, but he always talked about how brave the others were (14) He never talked about war, but he talked a lot about how happy the French were when the Allied forces arrived. (15) Before he died, he gave me the diary he kept during that time. (16) I want to start at the beach and following the route that he took.

11. Which of the following is the best way to revise the underlined portions of sentences 2 and 3 (reproduced below) in order to combine the two sentences?

I have taken two years of French in <u>school. I would like to</u> practice what I have learned.

    (A) school, but I would like to

    (B) school, and I would like to

    (C) school, being able to

    (D) school, so I

    (E) school, while I

12. In context, which of the following is the best way of revising sentence 5 (reproduced below)?

Many movies have been made about that city, such as the classic "An American in Paris," and it seems very glamorous.

    (A) (As it is now)

    (B) Many classic movies, such as "An American in Paris," have been made about that city, and it seems very glamorous.

    (C) "An American in Paris," a classic movie, was made about that city, and it seems very glamorous.

    (D) Many classic movies have been made about that city, such as "An American in Paris," and it seems very glamorous.

    (E) Many movies, such as the classic "An American in Paris," have been made about that city, and they seem very glamorous.

13. In context, the most appropriate revision of sentence 8 is to

    (A) make it the first sentence of paragraph 2

    (B) make it the first sentence of paragraph 3

    (C) make it the last sentence of the passage

    (D) place it in parentheses

    (E) delete it entirely

14. In context, which of the following is the best revision of sentence 11 (reproduced below)?

As his only granddaughter, we were very close.

(A) His only granddaughter was very close to him.
(B) I was his only granddaughter, so we were very close.
(C) We were very close, being his only granddaughter.
(D) We were very close, and I was his only granddaughter.
(E) Being an only granddaughter, we were very close.

15. In context, which of the following is the best revision of sentence 16 (reproduced below)?

I want to start at the beach and following the route that he took.

(A) I want to start at the beach and follow the route that he took.
(B) Starting at the beach and following the route that he took.
(C) In order to start at the beach, I want to follow the route that he took.
(D) Following the route that he took, I want to start at the beach.
(E) The route that he took I want to follow starting at the beach.

16. Which of the following best describes the structure of the essay?

(A) An answer to a question with two reasons
(B) An answer to a question with three reasons
(C) Two answers to a single question
(D) Three answers to a single question
(E) Two theories about a single event

C. QUIZ III (16 items; 12 minutes)

1. Alfred Stieglitz <u>launched</u> the career of Georgia
   A
   O'Keeffe, <u>who</u> he later married, <u>by exhibiting</u> her
   B   C
   paintings <u>in</u> his gallery. <u>No error</u>
   D   E

2. A recent study <u>indicates</u> that the average person
   A
   <u>ignores</u> most commercial advertising and
   B
   <u>does not buy</u> products because of <u>them</u>. <u>No error</u>
   C   D   E

3. The dean <u>lectured</u> <u>us students</u> <u>on</u> the privilege and
   A   B   C
   responsibility <u>of attending</u> the university.
   D
   <u>No error</u>
   E

4. Only one of the animals in the zoo <u>is</u> in <u>their</u>
   A   B
   natural <u>habitat</u>, but there are plans <u>to remedy</u> the
   C   D
   situation. <u>No error</u>
   E

5. <u>Feeling guilty about raising his voice,</u>
   A
   <u>Webster sought out</u> his friend in the local tavern
   B
   and <u>tried to assuage</u> his friend's bitterness
   C
   <u>by offering him</u> a glass of port. <u>No error</u>
   D   E

6. Eleanor <u>was</u> undecided <u>whether to go</u> to the
   A   B
   authorities with the money or <u>if she should keep it;</u>
   C
   but finally <u>greed got</u> the better of her. <u>No error</u>
   D   E

7. All of the students except George and <u>she intends</u>
   <u>on ordering</u> the newest edition of the textbook.

   (A) she intends on ordering
   (B) her intends on ordering
   (C) her intends to order
   (D) her intend to order
   (E) she intend to order

8. <u>According to tradition</u>, Vishnu appeared as
   Krishna to rid the world of a tyrannical king
   named Kamsa, the son of a demon.

   (A) According to tradition
   (B) Due to tradition
   (C) Because of tradition
   (D) Tradition has it that
   (E) Traditionally

9. Scholars recognized immediately after <u>publication</u>
   <u>that the language experiments in *Finnegan's*</u>
   <u>*Wake* are different than</u> any other novel.

   (A) publication that the language experiments in
       Finnegan's Wake are different than
   (B) publication that the language experiments in
       Finnegan's Wake are different from
   (C) publication that the language experiments in
       Finnegan's Wake are different from those of
   (D) its publication that the language experiments
       in *Finnegan's Wake* differ from
   (E) its publication that the language experiments
       in *Finnegan's Wake* are different from those
       of

10. He had few redeeming virtues and those were obscured by his acerbic personality, and I was extremely fond of him.

    (A) He had few redeeming virtues and those were obscured by his acerbic personality, and
    (B) He had few redeeming virtues, which were obscured by his acerbic personality, and
    (C) Although he had few redeeming virtues and those were obscured by his acerbic personality,
    (D) Although he had few redeeming virtues, which were obscured by his acerbic personality,
    (E) Although he had few redeeming virtues, and those obscured by his acerbic personality,

Items 11-16 are based on the following essay, which is a response to an assignment to write about a current issue facing the United States.

(1) Human beings are using more and more energy. (2) One reason is that the world's population is growing, so there is more demand for energy. (3) Another is that people, especially those whose standard of living is beginning to improve, want to consume more and more energy. (4) However, it is creating new threats to the environment.

(5) Nuclear power plants produce electricity for people to use. (6) What should be done with the spent reactor fuel? (7) Some experts say to put it deep into abandoned salt mines, but other experts say to store it temporarily until a better solution is found. (8) Additionally, it has been known for over 30 years that smog caused by cars is a health hazard. (9) We haven't been able to solve the problem. (10) Some experts say we have come a long way, but others say that we haven't even begun. (11) Some scientists say that global warming will cause the polar ice caps to melt, with the result of massive flooding. (12) Other scientists say this will not happen.

(13) I am not a scientist, so I cannot say who is right. (14) However, I would argue more attention needs to be paid to the common cause of all these problems. (15) Perhaps then, an overall solution would be arrived at by the experts.

11. In context, the word "it" in sentence 4 refers to

    (A) A higher standard of living
    (B) The increase in the world's population
    (C) The demand for energy
    (D) The increased consumption of energy
    (E) New environmental problems

12. Which of the following is the most effective way to combine sentences 5 and 6 (reproduced below)?

    Nuclear power plants produce electricity for people to use. What should be done with the spent reactor fuel?

    (A) Nuclear power plants produce electricity, so what should be done with the spent reactor fuel?
    (B) Nuclear power plants produce electricity, but what should be done with the spent reactor fuel?
    (C) What should be done with the spent reactor fuel because nuclear power plants produce electricity?
    (D) How should the spent reactor fuel from the nuclear power plants producing electricity be disposed of?
    (E) What should be done with the spent reactor fuel as it produces electricity as a nuclear power plant?

13. In context, which of the following would be the most effective word to introduce sentence 8?

    (A) Because
    (B) Now,
    (C) Still,
    (D) Also,
    (E) Fortunately,

14. In context, which of the following would be the best revision of the underlined portion of sentence 11 (reproduced below)?

Some scientists say that global warming will cause the polar ice caps to melt, with the result of massive flooding.

(A) to melt, resulting in massive flooding
(B) to melt, to result in massive flooding
(C) melting, with the result of massive flooding
(D) to melt and to flood massively
(E) to melt and resulting with massive floods

15. In context, which of the following is the best revision of sentence 15 (reproduced below)?

Perhaps then, an overall solution would be arrived at by the experts.

(A) Perhaps then, an overall solution would be arrived at by the experts.
(B) Perhaps then, an overall solution will be arrived at by the experts.
(C) Perhaps then, the experts would arrive at an overall solution.
(D) The experts, perhaps then, would arrive at an overall solution.
(E) An overall solution would, then, perhaps be arrived at by the experts.

16. The author develops the essay primarily by

(A) posing a question and answering it
(B) citing statistics
(C) criticizing experts and scientists
(D) offering a solution
(E) contrasting expert opinions

D. QUIZ IV (1 Essay item; 25 minutes)

DIRECTIONS: You have 25 minutes to plan and write an essay on the topic assigned below. DO NOT WRITE ON ANY OTHER TOPIC. AN ESSAY ON ANOTHER TOPIC IS NOT ACCEPTABLE. Think carefully about the issue presented in the following excerpt and the assignment below.

1. *Actors and athletes, or anyone in the public eye, should not be surprised that the public is interested in their private lives. Having a public profession, and all the rewards that come with that occupation, means that public figures must contend with diminished privacy.*

2. *Just because someone works in a so-called public profession does not necessarily mean that they should not expect a degree of privacy. Signing a contract to play professional sports is not signing away a private life. Just because an athlete might play before a crowd of thousands, she should not have to contend with intrusive fans and media members.*

Assignment: Should anyone with a profession that puts them in the public eye expect to live a private life? Plan and write an essay in which you develop your point of view on this issue. Support your position with reasoning and examples taken from your reading, studies, experience, or observations.

Strategy Summary Sheet
WRITING

STRUCTURE OF WRITING ITEMS: The Writing section of the SAT and PSAT has three types of multiple-choice Writing items: Identifying Sentence Errors, Improving Sentences, and Improving Paragraphs. The SAT has three Writing sections: two 25-minute sections and one 10-minute section. These three Writing sections combined contain 49 total Multiple-Choice items and one Essay item. The PSAT has one 30-minute Writing test section (the fifth and last section), which contains 14 Identifying Sentence Errors items, 20 Improving Sentences items, and 5 Improving Paragraphs items. The Multiple-Choice items are designed to measure a student's ability to identify effective expressions in standard written English, to recognize faults in usage and structure, and to choose effective revisions in sentences and paragraphs. The Essay item is intended to measure a student's ability to develop and support a position on a topic.

GENERAL STRATEGY: After memorizing the directions, they can be safely ignored; therefore, do not waste valuable test time by re-reading instructions. However, do not ignore the essay prompt for the Improving Paragraphs items. The Writing: Multiple-Choice items should be answered according to difficulty level—from easiest to hardest. The Identifying Sentence Errors items are generally the easiest of the three types, followed by the Improving Sentences items, and lastly the Improving Paragraphs items. Each Writing item-type counts the same towards the Writing score.

STRATEGY FOR IDENTIFYING SENTENCE ERRORS ITEMS:

1. Read the entire sentence once quickly. Look for obvious errors.

2. Take a closer look at the underlined parts of the sentence. Remember that answer choice (E) is always "No error." Look for obvious errors in the underlined parts.

3. Look for errors in usage—when an underlined part of the sentence is not properly connected to another part of the sentence that is not underlined.

4. Do not be afraid to choose answer choice (E). Approximately one-fifth of the correct answer choices will be (E).

5. Use the *Checklist for Possible Writing Errors*, presented on the following page, when searching for errors.

STRATEGY FOR IMPROVING SENTENCES ITEMS:

1. Read the entire sentence for comprehension of the overall meaning. Look for possible errors. Mentally note how to correct possible errors.

2. Study answer choices for one that matches your anticipated answer. Do not read answer choice (A) because it is always the same as the underlined part of the original sentence.

3. Compare answer choices. What makes them different? Is the difference good or bad?

4. Do not choose answer choices that introduce new errors or change the meaning of the sentence.

5. Do not be afraid to choose answer choice (A). Approximately one-fifth of the correct answer choices will be (A).

6. Use the *Checklist for Possible Writing Errors*, presented below, when searching for errors.

STRATEGY FOR IMPROVING PARAGRAPHS ITEMS:

1. Do not ignore the essay prompt—it may provide valuable information about the overall point of the essay.

2. Remember that all revisions must be made in context—changes to the original sentences and structure of the essay cannot change the original meaning.

3. Read the entire essay first. Develop a mental picture of the main point, development, and organization.

4. Pay attention to the development and organization—the relationships between and among sentences.

5. Use the *Checklist for Possible Writing Errors*, presented below, when revising sentences.

6. When revising sentences, be sure that the new sentence structure follows all rules for standard written English and maintains consistency in the verb tense, pronoun case, tone, *etc.* with the overall essay.

7. When revising the essay, make sure that the new revisions maintain the logical development and organization of the essay. Make sure that the revised paragraphs refer to only one main topic.

CHECKLIST FOR POSSIBLE WRITING ERRORS:

1. *Verbs:* Does the sentence have a main verb? Do all verbs agree with their subjects? Are they in the correct tense?

2. *Pronouns:* Do all pronouns have clearly identifiable referents? Do they agree with their referents? Are they in the proper case?

3. *Adjectives and Adverbs:* Do all adjectives or adverbs correctly modify verbs or other adjectives? Is the use of a specific adjective or adverb appropriate?

4. *Prepositions:* Are all prepositions used idiomatically?

5. *Conjunctions:* Are all conjunctions consistent with the logic of the sentence?

6. *Modifier:* If the sentence has a modifier, is it close to what it modifies? Is the idea clearly and logically presented?

7. *Comparisons:* If the sentence makes a comparison, are like things being compared? Is the idea clearly and logically presented?

8. *Parallelism:* If the sentence includes a series of ideas, are the ideas presented in the same form?

9. *Diction:* Do the words mean what the sentence intends for them to mean?

10. *Conciseness:* Does the sentence use more words than necessary? For Improving Sentences and Improving Paragraphs items, does the proposed answer choice eliminate unnecessary wordiness without introducing additional errors?

11. *Directness:* Can the sentence be worded more directly? For Improving Sentences and Improving Paragraphs items, does the proposed answer choice eliminate unnecessary indirectness without introducing additional errors?

STRATEGY FOR THE ESSAY:

1. Begin with the prompt.

2. Write only on the assigned topic. Writing on any other topic will result in a score of 0.

3. Do not try to do too much. Try to mentally limit the scope of your topic.

4. Organize your thoughts and write an outline before beginning the essay. Do not spend more than two minutes writing the outline.

   a. Familiarize yourself with the essay prompt and assignment.

   b. Develop a point of view.

   c. Develop a thesis.

   d. Identify two to four important points.

   e. Decide on the order of presentation of the major points.

5. Organize ideas into paragraphs.

   a. Introduction

   b. Two to Four Body Paragraphs

   c. Conclusion

6. Write grammatically.

7. Write clearly, concisely, and legibly.

8. Punctuate and spell correctly.

9. Spend at least four minutes proofreading your essay.

ADDITIONAL STRATEGIES FROM IN-CLASS DISCUSSION: _____

_____

_____

_____

_____

_____

_____

_____

_____

_____

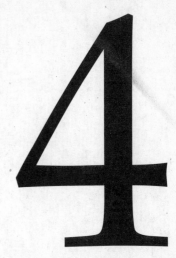

Step Four: Practice Test Reinforcement

Step Four Highlights:

Complete the four, full-length SAT tests to reinforce everything you've learned in your course.

Work through the tests either all at once or by section to highlight specific skills and concepts.

Step Four Overview:

In this section, you will have the opportunity to apply everything that you have learned throughout the Cambridge Course. Each of the four practice tests has been arranged in an order and with a frequency that approximates the real SAT. Completing these practice tests will help reinforce the test content, help you become more comfortable with timing and pacing, reduce your test anxiety, and give you the chance to practice using alternative test-taking strategies. If you're working on these on your own, complete the first two tests without timing restrictions to practice the application of the concepts you've learned this far. Then, complete the second two tests with the appropriate timing to practice your pacing.

Practice Test I

CAMBRIDGE
EDUCATION

EDUCATORS' #1 CHOICE

Cambridge Course Concept Outline
PRACTICE TEST I

When completing Practice Test I, use the Essay Response and Bubble Sheet beginning on page 637, unless otherwise directed by your instructor.

Name: _____   Date: _____

Student ID Number: _____

PRACTICE TEST I

Section 1

Begin your essay on this page. If you need more space, continue on the next page.

_____

_____

_____

_____

_____

_____

_____

_____

_____

_____

_____

_____

_____

_____

_____

_____

_____

_____

_____

_____

_____

_____

_____

_____

_____

_____

Name: _____ Date: _____

Student ID Number: _____

PRACTICE TEST I

Start with number 1 for each new section. If a section has fewer questions than answer spaces, leave the extra answer spaces blank. Be sure to erase any errors or stray marks completely.

Section 2

1 Ⓐ Ⓑ Ⓒ Ⓓ Ⓔ	10 Ⓐ Ⓑ Ⓒ Ⓓ Ⓔ	19 Ⓐ Ⓑ Ⓒ Ⓓ Ⓔ	28 Ⓐ Ⓑ Ⓒ Ⓓ Ⓔ
2 Ⓐ Ⓑ Ⓒ Ⓓ Ⓔ	11 Ⓐ Ⓑ Ⓒ Ⓓ Ⓔ	20 Ⓐ Ⓑ Ⓒ Ⓓ Ⓔ	29 Ⓐ Ⓑ Ⓒ Ⓓ Ⓔ
3 Ⓐ Ⓑ Ⓒ Ⓓ Ⓔ	12 Ⓐ Ⓑ Ⓒ Ⓓ Ⓔ	21 Ⓐ Ⓑ Ⓒ Ⓓ Ⓔ	30 Ⓐ Ⓑ Ⓒ Ⓓ Ⓔ
4 Ⓐ Ⓑ Ⓒ Ⓓ Ⓔ	13 Ⓐ Ⓑ Ⓒ Ⓓ Ⓔ	22 Ⓐ Ⓑ Ⓒ Ⓓ Ⓔ	31 Ⓐ Ⓑ Ⓒ Ⓓ Ⓔ
5 Ⓐ Ⓑ Ⓒ Ⓓ Ⓔ	14 Ⓐ Ⓑ Ⓒ Ⓓ Ⓔ	23 Ⓐ Ⓑ Ⓒ Ⓓ Ⓔ	32 Ⓐ Ⓑ Ⓒ Ⓓ Ⓔ
6 Ⓐ Ⓑ Ⓒ Ⓓ Ⓔ	15 Ⓐ Ⓑ Ⓒ Ⓓ Ⓔ	24 Ⓐ Ⓑ Ⓒ Ⓓ Ⓔ	33 Ⓐ Ⓑ Ⓒ Ⓓ Ⓔ
7 Ⓐ Ⓑ Ⓒ Ⓓ Ⓔ	16 Ⓐ Ⓑ Ⓒ Ⓓ Ⓔ	25 Ⓐ Ⓑ Ⓒ Ⓓ Ⓔ	34 Ⓐ Ⓑ Ⓒ Ⓓ Ⓔ
8 Ⓐ Ⓑ Ⓒ Ⓓ Ⓔ	17 Ⓐ Ⓑ Ⓒ Ⓓ Ⓔ	26 Ⓐ Ⓑ Ⓒ Ⓓ Ⓔ	35 Ⓐ Ⓑ Ⓒ Ⓓ Ⓔ
9 Ⓐ Ⓑ Ⓒ Ⓓ Ⓔ	18 Ⓐ Ⓑ Ⓒ Ⓓ Ⓔ	27 Ⓐ Ⓑ Ⓒ Ⓓ Ⓔ	36 Ⓐ Ⓑ Ⓒ Ⓓ Ⓔ

Section 3

1 Ⓐ Ⓑ Ⓒ Ⓓ Ⓔ	10 Ⓐ Ⓑ Ⓒ Ⓓ Ⓔ	19 Ⓐ Ⓑ Ⓒ Ⓓ Ⓔ	28 Ⓐ Ⓑ Ⓒ Ⓓ Ⓔ
2 Ⓐ Ⓑ Ⓒ Ⓓ Ⓔ	11 Ⓐ Ⓑ Ⓒ Ⓓ Ⓔ	20 Ⓐ Ⓑ Ⓒ Ⓓ Ⓔ	29 Ⓐ Ⓑ Ⓒ Ⓓ Ⓔ
3 Ⓐ Ⓑ Ⓒ Ⓓ Ⓔ	12 Ⓐ Ⓑ Ⓒ Ⓓ Ⓔ	21 Ⓐ Ⓑ Ⓒ Ⓓ Ⓔ	30 Ⓐ Ⓑ Ⓒ Ⓓ Ⓔ
4 Ⓐ Ⓑ Ⓒ Ⓓ Ⓔ	13 Ⓐ Ⓑ Ⓒ Ⓓ Ⓔ	22 Ⓐ Ⓑ Ⓒ Ⓓ Ⓔ	31 Ⓐ Ⓑ Ⓒ Ⓓ Ⓔ
5 Ⓐ Ⓑ Ⓒ Ⓓ Ⓔ	14 Ⓐ Ⓑ Ⓒ Ⓓ Ⓔ	23 Ⓐ Ⓑ Ⓒ Ⓓ Ⓔ	32 Ⓐ Ⓑ Ⓒ Ⓓ Ⓔ
6 Ⓐ Ⓑ Ⓒ Ⓓ Ⓔ	15 Ⓐ Ⓑ Ⓒ Ⓓ Ⓔ	24 Ⓐ Ⓑ Ⓒ Ⓓ Ⓔ	33 Ⓐ Ⓑ Ⓒ Ⓓ Ⓔ
7 Ⓐ Ⓑ Ⓒ Ⓓ Ⓔ	16 Ⓐ Ⓑ Ⓒ Ⓓ Ⓔ	25 Ⓐ Ⓑ Ⓒ Ⓓ Ⓔ	34 Ⓐ Ⓑ Ⓒ Ⓓ Ⓔ
8 Ⓐ Ⓑ Ⓒ Ⓓ Ⓔ	17 Ⓐ Ⓑ Ⓒ Ⓓ Ⓔ	26 Ⓐ Ⓑ Ⓒ Ⓓ Ⓔ	35 Ⓐ Ⓑ Ⓒ Ⓓ Ⓔ
9 Ⓐ Ⓑ Ⓒ Ⓓ Ⓔ	18 Ⓐ Ⓑ Ⓒ Ⓓ Ⓔ	27 Ⓐ Ⓑ Ⓒ Ⓓ Ⓔ	36 Ⓐ Ⓑ Ⓒ Ⓓ Ⓔ

Section 4/5

1 Ⓐ Ⓑ Ⓒ Ⓓ Ⓔ	10 Ⓐ Ⓑ Ⓒ Ⓓ Ⓔ	19 Ⓐ Ⓑ Ⓒ Ⓓ Ⓔ	28 Ⓐ Ⓑ Ⓒ Ⓓ Ⓔ
2 Ⓐ Ⓑ Ⓒ Ⓓ Ⓔ	11 Ⓐ Ⓑ Ⓒ Ⓓ Ⓔ	20 Ⓐ Ⓑ Ⓒ Ⓓ Ⓔ	29 Ⓐ Ⓑ Ⓒ Ⓓ Ⓔ
3 Ⓐ Ⓑ Ⓒ Ⓓ Ⓔ	12 Ⓐ Ⓑ Ⓒ Ⓓ Ⓔ	21 Ⓐ Ⓑ Ⓒ Ⓓ Ⓔ	30 Ⓐ Ⓑ Ⓒ Ⓓ Ⓔ
4 Ⓐ Ⓑ Ⓒ Ⓓ Ⓔ	13 Ⓐ Ⓑ Ⓒ Ⓓ Ⓔ	22 Ⓐ Ⓑ Ⓒ Ⓓ Ⓔ	31 Ⓐ Ⓑ Ⓒ Ⓓ Ⓔ
5 Ⓐ Ⓑ Ⓒ Ⓓ Ⓔ	14 Ⓐ Ⓑ Ⓒ Ⓓ Ⓔ	23 Ⓐ Ⓑ Ⓒ Ⓓ Ⓔ	32 Ⓐ Ⓑ Ⓒ Ⓓ Ⓔ
6 Ⓐ Ⓑ Ⓒ Ⓓ Ⓔ	15 Ⓐ Ⓑ Ⓒ Ⓓ Ⓔ	24 Ⓐ Ⓑ Ⓒ Ⓓ Ⓔ	33 Ⓐ Ⓑ Ⓒ Ⓓ Ⓔ
7 Ⓐ Ⓑ Ⓒ Ⓓ Ⓔ	16 Ⓐ Ⓑ Ⓒ Ⓓ Ⓔ	25 Ⓐ Ⓑ Ⓒ Ⓓ Ⓔ	34 Ⓐ Ⓑ Ⓒ Ⓓ Ⓔ
8 Ⓐ Ⓑ Ⓒ Ⓓ Ⓔ	17 Ⓐ Ⓑ Ⓒ Ⓓ Ⓔ	26 Ⓐ Ⓑ Ⓒ Ⓓ Ⓔ	35 Ⓐ Ⓑ Ⓒ Ⓓ Ⓔ
9 Ⓐ Ⓑ Ⓒ Ⓓ Ⓔ	18 Ⓐ Ⓑ Ⓒ Ⓓ Ⓔ	27 Ⓐ Ⓑ Ⓒ Ⓓ Ⓔ	36 Ⓐ Ⓑ Ⓒ Ⓓ Ⓔ

Section 5/6

1 Ⓐ Ⓑ Ⓒ Ⓓ Ⓔ	10 Ⓐ Ⓑ Ⓒ Ⓓ Ⓔ	19 Ⓐ Ⓑ Ⓒ Ⓓ Ⓔ	28 Ⓐ Ⓑ Ⓒ Ⓓ Ⓔ
2 Ⓐ Ⓑ Ⓒ Ⓓ Ⓔ	11 Ⓐ Ⓑ Ⓒ Ⓓ Ⓔ	20 Ⓐ Ⓑ Ⓒ Ⓓ Ⓔ	29 Ⓐ Ⓑ Ⓒ Ⓓ Ⓔ
3 Ⓐ Ⓑ Ⓒ Ⓓ Ⓔ	12 Ⓐ Ⓑ Ⓒ Ⓓ Ⓔ	21 Ⓐ Ⓑ Ⓒ Ⓓ Ⓔ	30 Ⓐ Ⓑ Ⓒ Ⓓ Ⓔ
4 Ⓐ Ⓑ Ⓒ Ⓓ Ⓔ	13 Ⓐ Ⓑ Ⓒ Ⓓ Ⓔ	22 Ⓐ Ⓑ Ⓒ Ⓓ Ⓔ	31 Ⓐ Ⓑ Ⓒ Ⓓ Ⓔ
5 Ⓐ Ⓑ Ⓒ Ⓓ Ⓔ	14 Ⓐ Ⓑ Ⓒ Ⓓ Ⓔ	23 Ⓐ Ⓑ Ⓒ Ⓓ Ⓔ	32 Ⓐ Ⓑ Ⓒ Ⓓ Ⓔ
6 Ⓐ Ⓑ Ⓒ Ⓓ Ⓔ	15 Ⓐ Ⓑ Ⓒ Ⓓ Ⓔ	24 Ⓐ Ⓑ Ⓒ Ⓓ Ⓔ	33 Ⓐ Ⓑ Ⓒ Ⓓ Ⓔ
7 Ⓐ Ⓑ Ⓒ Ⓓ Ⓔ	16 Ⓐ Ⓑ Ⓒ Ⓓ Ⓔ	25 Ⓐ Ⓑ Ⓒ Ⓓ Ⓔ	34 Ⓐ Ⓑ Ⓒ Ⓓ Ⓔ
8 Ⓐ Ⓑ Ⓒ Ⓓ Ⓔ	17 Ⓐ Ⓑ Ⓒ Ⓓ Ⓔ	26 Ⓐ Ⓑ Ⓒ Ⓓ Ⓔ	35 Ⓐ Ⓑ Ⓒ Ⓓ Ⓔ
9 Ⓐ Ⓑ Ⓒ Ⓓ Ⓔ	18 Ⓐ Ⓑ Ⓒ Ⓓ Ⓔ	27 Ⓐ Ⓑ Ⓒ Ⓓ Ⓔ	36 Ⓐ Ⓑ Ⓒ Ⓓ Ⓔ

Section 6/7

1 Ⓐ Ⓑ Ⓒ Ⓓ Ⓔ	10 Ⓐ Ⓑ Ⓒ Ⓓ Ⓔ	19 Ⓐ Ⓑ Ⓒ Ⓓ Ⓔ	28 Ⓐ Ⓑ Ⓒ Ⓓ Ⓔ
2 Ⓐ Ⓑ Ⓒ Ⓓ Ⓔ	11 Ⓐ Ⓑ Ⓒ Ⓓ Ⓔ	20 Ⓐ Ⓑ Ⓒ Ⓓ Ⓔ	29 Ⓐ Ⓑ Ⓒ Ⓓ Ⓔ
3 Ⓐ Ⓑ Ⓒ Ⓓ Ⓔ	12 Ⓐ Ⓑ Ⓒ Ⓓ Ⓔ	21 Ⓐ Ⓑ Ⓒ Ⓓ Ⓔ	30 Ⓐ Ⓑ Ⓒ Ⓓ Ⓔ
4 Ⓐ Ⓑ Ⓒ Ⓓ Ⓔ	13 Ⓐ Ⓑ Ⓒ Ⓓ Ⓔ	22 Ⓐ Ⓑ Ⓒ Ⓓ Ⓔ	31 Ⓐ Ⓑ Ⓒ Ⓓ Ⓔ
5 Ⓐ Ⓑ Ⓒ Ⓓ Ⓔ	14 Ⓐ Ⓑ Ⓒ Ⓓ Ⓔ	23 Ⓐ Ⓑ Ⓒ Ⓓ Ⓔ	32 Ⓐ Ⓑ Ⓒ Ⓓ Ⓔ
6 Ⓐ Ⓑ Ⓒ Ⓓ Ⓔ	15 Ⓐ Ⓑ Ⓒ Ⓓ Ⓔ	24 Ⓐ Ⓑ Ⓒ Ⓓ Ⓔ	33 Ⓐ Ⓑ Ⓒ Ⓓ Ⓔ
7 Ⓐ Ⓑ Ⓒ Ⓓ Ⓔ	16 Ⓐ Ⓑ Ⓒ Ⓓ Ⓔ	25 Ⓐ Ⓑ Ⓒ Ⓓ Ⓔ	34 Ⓐ Ⓑ Ⓒ Ⓓ Ⓔ
8 Ⓐ Ⓑ Ⓒ Ⓓ Ⓔ	17 Ⓐ Ⓑ Ⓒ Ⓓ Ⓔ	26 Ⓐ Ⓑ Ⓒ Ⓓ Ⓔ	35 Ⓐ Ⓑ Ⓒ Ⓓ Ⓔ
9 Ⓐ Ⓑ Ⓒ Ⓓ Ⓔ	18 Ⓐ Ⓑ Ⓒ Ⓓ Ⓔ	27 Ⓐ Ⓑ Ⓒ Ⓓ Ⓔ	36 Ⓐ Ⓑ Ⓒ Ⓓ Ⓔ

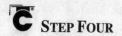

Section 7/8

1 Ⓐ Ⓑ Ⓒ Ⓓ Ⓔ	6 Ⓐ Ⓑ Ⓒ Ⓓ Ⓔ	11 Ⓐ Ⓑ Ⓒ Ⓓ Ⓔ	16 Ⓐ Ⓑ Ⓒ Ⓓ Ⓔ
2 Ⓐ Ⓑ Ⓒ Ⓓ Ⓔ	7 Ⓐ Ⓑ Ⓒ Ⓓ Ⓔ	12 Ⓐ Ⓑ Ⓒ Ⓓ Ⓔ	17 Ⓐ Ⓑ Ⓒ Ⓓ Ⓔ
3 Ⓐ Ⓑ Ⓒ Ⓓ Ⓔ	8 Ⓐ Ⓑ Ⓒ Ⓓ Ⓔ	13 Ⓐ Ⓑ Ⓒ Ⓓ Ⓔ	18 Ⓐ Ⓑ Ⓒ Ⓓ Ⓔ
4 Ⓐ Ⓑ Ⓒ Ⓓ Ⓔ	9 Ⓐ Ⓑ Ⓒ Ⓓ Ⓔ	14 Ⓐ Ⓑ Ⓒ Ⓓ Ⓔ	19 Ⓐ Ⓑ Ⓒ Ⓓ Ⓔ
5 Ⓐ Ⓑ Ⓒ Ⓓ Ⓔ	10 Ⓐ Ⓑ Ⓒ Ⓓ Ⓔ	15 Ⓐ Ⓑ Ⓒ Ⓓ Ⓔ	20 Ⓐ Ⓑ Ⓒ Ⓓ Ⓔ

Section 8/9

1 Ⓐ Ⓑ Ⓒ Ⓓ Ⓔ	6 Ⓐ Ⓑ Ⓒ Ⓓ Ⓔ	11 Ⓐ Ⓑ Ⓒ Ⓓ Ⓔ	16 Ⓐ Ⓑ Ⓒ Ⓓ Ⓔ
2 Ⓐ Ⓑ Ⓒ Ⓓ Ⓔ	7 Ⓐ Ⓑ Ⓒ Ⓓ Ⓔ	12 Ⓐ Ⓑ Ⓒ Ⓓ Ⓔ	17 Ⓐ Ⓑ Ⓒ Ⓓ Ⓔ
3 Ⓐ Ⓑ Ⓒ Ⓓ Ⓔ	8 Ⓐ Ⓑ Ⓒ Ⓓ Ⓔ	13 Ⓐ Ⓑ Ⓒ Ⓓ Ⓔ	18 Ⓐ Ⓑ Ⓒ Ⓓ Ⓔ
4 Ⓐ Ⓑ Ⓒ Ⓓ Ⓔ	9 Ⓐ Ⓑ Ⓒ Ⓓ Ⓔ	14 Ⓐ Ⓑ Ⓒ Ⓓ Ⓔ	19 Ⓐ Ⓑ Ⓒ Ⓓ Ⓔ
5 Ⓐ Ⓑ Ⓒ Ⓓ Ⓔ	10 Ⓐ Ⓑ Ⓒ Ⓓ Ⓔ	15 Ⓐ Ⓑ Ⓒ Ⓓ Ⓔ	20 Ⓐ Ⓑ Ⓒ Ⓓ Ⓔ

Section 10

1 Ⓐ Ⓑ Ⓒ Ⓓ Ⓔ	6 Ⓐ Ⓑ Ⓒ Ⓓ Ⓔ	11 Ⓐ Ⓑ Ⓒ Ⓓ Ⓔ	16 Ⓐ Ⓑ Ⓒ Ⓓ Ⓔ
2 Ⓐ Ⓑ Ⓒ Ⓓ Ⓔ	7 Ⓐ Ⓑ Ⓒ Ⓓ Ⓔ	12 Ⓐ Ⓑ Ⓒ Ⓓ Ⓔ	17 Ⓐ Ⓑ Ⓒ Ⓓ Ⓔ
3 Ⓐ Ⓑ Ⓒ Ⓓ Ⓔ	8 Ⓐ Ⓑ Ⓒ Ⓓ Ⓔ	13 Ⓐ Ⓑ Ⓒ Ⓓ Ⓔ	18 Ⓐ Ⓑ Ⓒ Ⓓ Ⓔ
4 Ⓐ Ⓑ Ⓒ Ⓓ Ⓔ	9 Ⓐ Ⓑ Ⓒ Ⓓ Ⓔ	14 Ⓐ Ⓑ Ⓒ Ⓓ Ⓔ	19 Ⓐ Ⓑ Ⓒ Ⓓ Ⓔ
5 Ⓐ Ⓑ Ⓒ Ⓓ Ⓔ	10 Ⓐ Ⓑ Ⓒ Ⓓ Ⓔ	15 Ⓐ Ⓑ Ⓒ Ⓓ Ⓔ	20 Ⓐ Ⓑ Ⓒ Ⓓ Ⓔ

Student-Produced Responses

Only answers entered in the circles in each grid will be scored. You will not receive credit for anything written in the boxes above the circles.

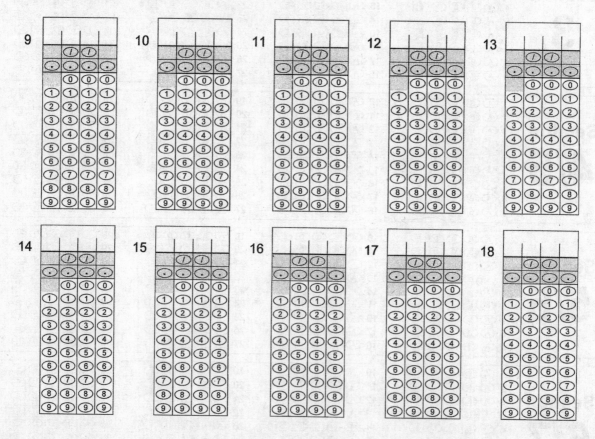

1 1 1 1 1 1 1 1 1 1 1 1 1

Time—25 Minutes 1 Essay	Think carefully about the issue presented in the following excerpt and the assignment below.

DIRECTIONS: You have 25 minutes to plan and write an essay on the topic assigned below. DO NOT WRITE ON ANY OTHER TOPIC. AN ESSAY ON ANOTHER TOPIC IS NOT ACCEPTABLE. Think carefully about the issue presented in the following excerpt and the assignment below.

> A 98-year-old farmer was recently asked what he thought was the greatest technological advancement of the past 125 years. He responded: "electricity, since it made so many chores much easier and faster." A 35-year-old executive was asked the same question, and she responded: "computers, since they made so many chores much easier and faster."

Assignment: In your opinion, what has been the greatest technological advancement of the past 125 years? Plan and write an essay in which you develop your point of view on this issue. Support your position with reasoning and examples taken from your reading, studies, experience, and observations.

thesis: The greatest technological advancement ~~tenmore~~ in the past 125 years would be the internet. The internet gives many people freedom to search and learn new things quickly & easily.

introduction → thesis ⌐
                   why ─┘

1st ¶ → How internet have made generations more advance?
        positive effects   Why is it
        negative effects.   considered a tech. advance?

2nd ¶ → How the importance of technology differs among different age groups?

conclusion → restate thesis
             positive / negative
                  effects of tech. (internet)

IF YOU FINISH BEFORE TIME IS CALLED, YOU MAY CHECK YOUR WORK ON THIS TEST ONLY. DO NOT WORK ON ANY OTHER TEST SECTION.	**STOP**

2 2 2 2 2 2 2 2 2 2 2 2

Time—25 Minutes 18 Items	In this section, solve each item, using any available space on the page for scratchwork. Then, decide which is the best of the choices given and fill in the corresponding oval on the answer sheet.

Notes: The figures accompanying the items are drawn as accurately as possible unless otherwise stated in specific items. Again, unless otherwise stated, all figures lie in the same plane. All numbers used in these items are real numbers. Calculators are permitted for this test.

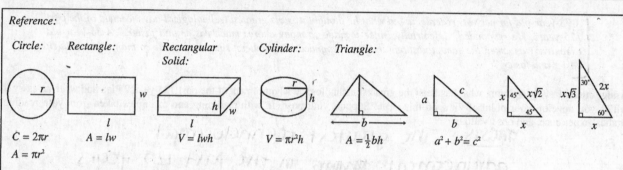

Reference:

Circle: $C = 2\pi r$, $A = \pi r^2$

Rectangle: $A = lw$

Rectangular Solid: $V = lwh$

Cylinder: $V = \pi r^2 h$

Triangle: $A = \frac{1}{2}bh$, $a^2 + b^2 = c^2$

- The measure in degrees of a straight angle is 180.
- The number of degrees of arc in a circle is 360.
- The sum of the measure of the angles of a triangle is 180.

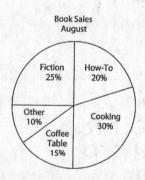

Book Sales August

Fiction 25%
How-To 20%
Other 10%
Cooking 30%
Coffee Table 15%

1. The circle graph above shows all of the books, categorized by type, that were sold by a store in the month of August. If the store sold 150 Fiction books, how many books did it sell for the entire month?

   (A) 25
   (B) 300
   (C) 450
   (D) 600
   (E) 750

2. In the xy-coordinate system, $(m, 0)$ is one of the points of intersection of the graphs of $y = x^2 - 4$ and $y = -x^2 - 4$. If $m > 0$, what is the value of m?

   (A) 2
   (B) 4
   (C) 8
   (D) 16
   (E) 32

GO ON TO THE NEXT PAGE

ENTRIES FOR THE DOG SHOW

Number of Dogs	Number of Owners
1	3
2	4
3	X
4	1

3. The table above shows the number of dogs entered per owner and the number of owners that entered that number of dogs. If the average (arithmetic mean) number of dogs entered by each owner is 2, what is the value of X?

$$\frac{1(3) + 2(4) + 3(x) + 4(1)}{8 + x} = 2$$

(A) 1
(B) 2
(C) 3
(D) 4
(E) 5

4. After the first term of a series, each term in the sequence is $\frac{1}{2}$ the sum of the preceding term and 4. If n is the first term of the sequence and $n \neq 0$, what is the ratio of the first term to the second term?

$$n, \; \tfrac{1}{2}(n+4)$$

(A) $\dfrac{2}{n+4}$

(B) $\dfrac{2}{n+2}$

$$\frac{n}{\frac{1}{2}(n+4)} = $$

(C) $\dfrac{2n}{n+4}$

$$= \frac{1}{2}n + 2$$

(D) $\dfrac{2n}{n+2}$

$$= \frac{n}{1} \cdot \frac{2}{n+4}$$

(E) $\dfrac{2}{4-n}$

$$= \frac{2n}{n+4}$$

5. If the radius of circle O is 20 percent less than the radius of circle P, the area of circle O is what percent of the area of circle P?

(A) 60%
(B) 64%
(C) 72%
(D) 80%
(E) 120%

6. If the average (arithmetic mean) of 20, 23, 24, x, and y is 26, and $\frac{x}{y} = \frac{3}{4}$, then $x =$

$$\frac{20 + 23 + 24 + x + y}{5} = 26$$

(A) 25
(B) 27
(C) 36
(D) 41
(E) 63

$$\frac{x}{y} = 3/4$$

$$3y = 4x$$
$$y = 4/3x$$

putin

7. The price of 5 boxes of candy is d dollars. If each box contains 30 pieces of candy, what is the price, in *cents*, of 12 pieces of candy?

(A) $8d$
(B) $12d$
(C) $\dfrac{25d}{2}$
(D) $50d$
(E) $72d$

$$\frac{100d}{30(5)} \cdot 12$$

8. If a cube has a side of length 2, what is the distance from any vertex to the center of the cube?

(A) $\dfrac{\sqrt{2}}{2}$
(B) $\sqrt{3}$
(C) $2\sqrt{2}$
(D) $2\sqrt{3}$
(E) $\dfrac{3}{2}$

GO ON TO THE NEXT PAGE

Directions for Student-Produced Responses Items

Items 9-18 each require you to solve an item and mark your answer on a special answer grid. For each item, you should write your answer in the boxes at the top of each column and then fill in the ovals beneath each answer you write. Here are some examples.

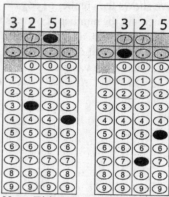

Answer: 3/4 or .75
(show answer either way)

Answer: 325

Note: A mixed number such as $3\frac{1}{2}$ must be gridded as 7/2 or as 3.5. If gridded as "31/2," it will be read as "thirty-one halves."

Note: Either position is correct.

9. If $x + 1 + 2x + 2 + 3x + 3 = 6$, then $x =$

$$x+1+2x+2+3x+3=6$$
$$6x+6=6$$
$$\quad\quad -6 \quad -6$$
$$\overline{\quad 6x = 0 \quad x = 0}$$

10. If a horse gallops at an average speed of 40 feet per second, how many seconds will it take for the horse to gallop 500 feet?

$40f = 1sec$
$500f = 12\frac{1}{2}sec$
$40 \times 12\frac{1}{2} = 500$

$12.5secs$

11. If n is a positive integer greater than 6, and if the remainder is the same when 13 and 21 are divided by n, then $n =$

$$\frac{13}{n} \quad \frac{21}{n}$$

guest and check

$n = 8$

12. If $\frac{64}{x} - 6 = 2$, then $x =$

$$\frac{64}{x} - 6 = 2$$
$$\quad\quad +6 \quad +6$$
$$\overline{\quad \frac{64}{x} = 8}$$

$x = 8$

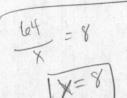 GO ON TO THE NEXT PAGE

13. If x, y, and z are consecutive integers, and $x > y > z$, then $(x-y)(x-z)(y-z) =$

$$x > y > z$$
$$(4) \quad (3) \quad (2)$$

$$(x-y)(x-z)(y-z)$$
$$4-3 \quad 4-2 \quad 3-2$$
$$1 \cdot 2 \cdot 1 \boxed{= 2}$$

14. If x is a positive odd number less than 10, and y is a positive even number less than 10, what is the greatest number that xy can equal?

$$x < 10 \qquad x = 1, 3, 5, 7, 9$$
$$y < 10 \qquad y = 2, 4, 6, 8$$
$$9 \times 8 = 72$$
$$\boxed{= 72}$$

15. Cyrus worked 8 hours on Monday. On each successive day, he worked half as long as he did on the previous day. How many total hours had he worked by the end of the day on Friday?

$$\boxed{15 \tfrac{1}{2} \text{ hr}}$$

16. Imagine a right triangle ABC with $\overline{AB}$ congruent to $\overline{BC}$. What is the measure, in degrees, of $\angle BAC$?

$$\boxed{45°}$$

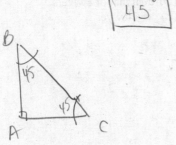

17. At Auburn Mills High, 80% of the graduating seniors go on to college. Of those college-bound seniors, 75% will attend school in-state. If there are 150 graduating seniors in all, how many will attend college out-of-state?

30

18. Danielle sliced a pizza into sixths. She then sliced each slice into thirds. She served 4 of the small slices to Pete. In lowest terms, what fraction of the whole pizza did Pete have?

$$\boxed{2/9}$$

$$\frac{1}{6} \cdot \frac{1}{3} = \tfrac{1}{18} \cdot 4$$
$$= \frac{4}{18} = \frac{2}{9}$$

and = multiply

3 3 3 3 3 3 3 3 3 3 3 3

| Time—25 Minutes 35 Items | For each item in this section, choose the best answer and blacken the corresponding space on the answer sheet. |

Directions: The following sentences test correctness and effectiveness of expression. In choosing answers, follow the requirements of standard written English; that is, pay attention to grammar, choice of words, sentence construction, and punctuation.

In each of the following sentences, part of the sentence or the entire sentence is underlined. Beneath each sentence you will find five ways of phrasing the underlined part. Choice A repeats the original; the other four are different.

Choose the answer that best expresses the meaning of the original sentence. If you think the original is better than any of the alternatives, choose it; otherwise choose one of the others. Your choice should produce the most effective sentence—clear and precise, without awkwardness or ambiguity.

Example: Answer

Allen visiting his cousin in France last summer.

(A) visiting
(B) visited
(C) does visit
(D) a visit
(E) is visiting

(A) ● (C) (D) (E)

1. A horse's chance of winning a race depends not so much on the final times of previous races but instead on class, a measurable factor that is the horse's determination to win.

(A) but instead
(B) rather than
(C) so much as
(D) than
(E) As

2. The average starting salary of a lawyer in a firm in New York City is about 25% higher than a lawyer in a firm in Chicago.

(A) than a lawyer
(B) than that of a lawyer
(C) than lawyers
(D) than that of lawyers
(E) as a lawyer

GO ON TO THE NEXT PAGE

3. People in show business say that you should be careful how you treat people on your way up <u>because one meets</u> the same people on the way back down.

    (A) because one meets
    (B) being that one meets
    (C) because you meet
    (D) because we meet
    (E) for you to meet

4. Trying to make the streets safer, many neighborhood committees have asked the police to install surveillance cameras on light <u>posts, for it will record</u> any criminal activities.

    (A) posts, for it will record
    (B) posts, in that it will record
    (C) posts in order to record
    (D) posts for the recording of
    (E) posts to be able to record

5. Of all of the introductory courses offered by the biology department, <u>only Professor Collins devotes</u> several class periods to the effects of Global Warming on the extinction of species in the rain forest.

    (A) only Professor Collins devotes
    (B) Professor Collins only devotes
    (C) Professor Collins devotes only
    (D) only Professor Collins is the teacher who devotes
    (E) only that taught by Professors Collins devotes

GO ON TO THE NEXT PAGE

Directions: The following sentences test your knowledge of grammar, usage, diction (choices of words) and idiom.

    Some sentences are correct.
    No sentence contains more than one error.

You will find that the error, if there is one, is underlined and lettered. Elements of the sentence that are not underlined will not be changed. In choosing answers, follow the requirements of standard written English.

If there is an error, select the <u>one underlined part</u> that must be changed to make the sentence correct and fill in the corresponding oval on your answer sheet.

If there is no error, fill in answer oval (**E**).

Example:

<u>Answer</u>

The principal <u>asked</u> ten of <u>we</u> students
          A   B

<u>to enter</u> the <u>public speaking</u> contest. <u>No error</u>
   C   D   E

Ⓐ ● Ⓒ Ⓓ Ⓔ

---

6. The Everglades, located on the <u>southern</u> tip of
                              A

   Florida, is a soggy, low-lying <u>tropical</u> area of
                           B

   <u>solidly</u> packed muck, saw grass, and
    C

   <u>having marshy knolls.</u> <u>No error</u>
         D   E

7. Sir Edward Elgar was an English composer <u>who</u>
                                 A

   lived from 1857 to 1934 and is best known for <u>his</u>
                                      B

   Pomp and Circumstance marches that <u>are</u> most
                             C

   often associated <u>with</u> graduation ceremonies.
                  D

   <u>No error</u>
      E

8. An electrolyte <u>is</u> any electrical conductor <u>such as</u>
               A   B

   a solution of salt in water <u>where</u> the current is
                         C

   carried by ions <u>instead of</u> free electrons.
                 D

   <u>No error</u>
      E

9. <u>During</u> World War II, over 300,000 Allied troops
    A

   were stranded at Dunkirk and cut off from

   <u>land retreat</u> by the Germans; <u>however,</u> a fleet of
        B   C

   British ships and boats <u>will rescue</u> most of them.
                         D

   <u>No error</u>
      E

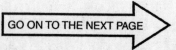
GO ON TO THE NEXT PAGE

10. Though dragonflies have elongated bodies that
       A   B

    today reach five inches, during the Permian

    period, one species it had a wingspan of more than
                  C   D

    two feet. No error
            E

11. The eagle, a large, predatory bird, is solitude; but
                             A B

    when it mates, it mates for life. No error
        C   D   E

12. The Embargo Act of 1807, which was in force
                        A

    until 1809, prohibits international shipping
              B   C

    to and from all United States ports. No error
      D   E

13. The Chunnel, consisting of a central service tube
              A   B

    and two railway tubes, run beneath the English
                   C   D

    Channel between England and France. No error
                             E

14. Calling Aurora by the Romans, Eos was the
      A   B   C
    Greek goddess of dawn and the mother of the

    winds. No error
     D   E

15. Enzymes are proteins that accelerate chemical
          A   B   C
    reactions in a cell that would otherwise proceed

    imperceptible or not at all. No error
        D   E

16. Since ancient times, days have arbitrarily been
      A   B

    inserted into calendars because the solar year
     C

    not being evenly divisible into months and days.
     D

    No error
     E

17. The Hopi, a people of the Southwest United
                 A

    States, they resisted European influence more
          B   C

    successfully than other Pueblo tribes. No error
               D   E

18. Hokusai was a Japanese painter and wood
          A

    engraver whose prodigious output included book
          B   C

    illustrations, printed cards, and landscapes in a
                           D

    variety of styles. No error
              E

19. Dramatic theater developed in ancient Greece
              A

    from religious rituals in which the actors
                 B

    were believed to participate directly in the events
       C

    that were depicted and not merely represent
          D

    characters in the action. No error
                 E

20. Although both are elected to national office,
           A

    members of the House of Representatives are
      B

    typically more attentive to local issues than
      C

    the Senate. No error
        D   E

GO ON TO THE NEXT PAGE

21. The Dean stressed that the university depends

    upon donations by <u>their</u> graduates <u>to help</u>
                A   B

    students <u>who</u> might <u>otherwise</u> not be able to
          C   D

    afford the tuition. <u>No error</u>
                    E

22. The New England aster, which <u>has</u> a long straight
                       A

    stalk and rayed flowers that <u>varies</u> in color from
                      B

    deep purple to pale pink, normally <u>grows</u> along
                       C

    roadsides and drainage ditches <u>and</u> blooms in the
                      D

    early autumn. <u>No error</u>
                E

23. <u>Calling it</u> the "Gateway to the West," the city of
      A

    St. Louis <u>was</u> the starting point for <u>many</u> of the
           B   C

    important trails that were <u>used</u> during the great
                    D

    westward migration. <u>No error</u>
                    E

24. <u>Most</u> recreational hot air ballooning is restricted
      A

    to short day trips over terrain that <u>has been</u>
                       B

    <u>mapped</u> out ahead of time, so there <u>is hardly no</u>
     C   D

    need for navigational instruments. <u>No error</u>
                       E

25. The company's most valuable asset is <u>its</u>
                            A

    engineers for <u>he or she</u> is willing to work long
              B

    hours for no additional pay <u>just</u> for the
                    C

    intellectual reward <u>of solving</u> a difficult problem.
                 D

    <u>No error</u>
     E

GO ON TO THE NEXT PAGE

Directions: The following passages are early drafts of essays. Some parts of the passages need to be rewritten.

Read the passages and answer the items that follow. Some items are about particular sentences or parts of sentences and ask you to improve sentence structure and word choice. Other items refer to parts of the essays or the entire essays and ask you to consider organization and development. In making your decisions, follow the conventions of standard written English. After you have chosen your answer, fill in the corresponding oval on your answer sheet.

Items 26-30 refer to the following passage.

(1) I have been an amateur astronomer for years. (2) My first telescope was a gift from my uncle. (3) He taught astronomy at the local college. (4) I was only nine years old.

(5) One of the advantages of astronomy as a hobby is that you did not have to be an expert to enjoy it. (6) With even an inexpensive telescope, you can step outside on a clear night and see thousands of stars. (7) How many are there?

(8) We know that our solar system is part of a much larger system of hundreds of billions of stars. (9) As such, this system is the Milky Way Galaxy, a huge disk of stars and gas.

(10) We also know that ours is not the only galaxy in the universe. (11) As far as the largest telescopes in the world can see, there are galaxies in every direction. (12) The nearest large galaxy to the Milky Way is the Andromeda Galaxy, which is about two million light years away. (13) Andromeda is a giant spiral galaxy, much like our own in size, shape, and number and type of stars. (14) This nearby sister galaxy provides us an opportunity to get a good view of a galaxy much like our own.

26. What is the best way to deal with sentence 3?

    (A) (As it is now.)
    (B) Connect it to sentence 2 with the word "who."
    (C) Place it before sentence 2.
    (D) Connect it to sentence 2 with the word "and."
    (E) Delete it.

27. In the context, which is the best version of "that you did not have to be" in sentence 5?

    (A) (As it is now.)
    (B) that you do not have to be
    (C) that you not being
    (D) which you did not have to be
    (E) your not being

28. Which is the best way to deal with the phrase "As such" in sentence 9?

    (A) (As it is now.)
    (B) Move it to the end of the sentence.
    (C) Replace it with "Actually."
    (D) Replace it with "As a matter of fact."
    (E) Delete it.

GO ON TO THE NEXT PAGE

29. The writer wishes to add the following parenthetical sentence to the last paragraph:

    (*A light year is the distance traveled by light in a year, almost ten million, million kilometers.*)

    The sentence would best fit the context if inserted

    (A) before sentence 10
    (B) between sentences 10 and 11
    (C) between sentences 11 and 12
    (D) between sentences 12 and 13
    (E) between sentences 13 and 14

30. Which of the following, if placed after sentence 14, would be the most effective concluding sentence for the essay?

    (A) However, astronomy may not be suitable for very young children.
    (B) Finally, you can learn more about galaxies by becoming an amateur astronomer yourself.
    (C) Therefore, think about the Andromeda Galaxy the next time you look at the night sky.
    (D) The Mellagenic Clouds are my favorite galaxies, but they are seen only in the southern skies.
    (E) In effect, we get to see ourselves as others would see us.

GO ON TO THE NEXT PAGE

Items 31 - 35 refer to the following passage.

(1) My favorite American artist is Georgia O'Keeffe. (2) Her parents were dairy farmers, but Georgia knew she was going to be an artist from early on. (3) She studied and taught art in Chicago, Virginia, Texas, and South Carolina.

(4) After years of teaching, Georgia did a series of abstract charcoals. (5) She sent the drawings to a friend who in turn showed them to Alfred Stieglitz, a well-known photographer and gallery owner in New York. (6) Stieglitz exhibited the drawings without first consulting Georgia. (7) This angered her, and she went to New York with the intention of removing the drawings. (8) After meeting Stieglitz, she agreed to let him show her work.

(9) This began a relationship that was to result in their marrying. (10) Georgia painted cityscapes inspired by the spectacular view from their 30th floor apartment. (11) Stieglitz and O'Keeffe also spent a lot of time in the Adirondack Mountains, where she created many paintings of the Lake George area.

(12) After 12 years, Georgia had had enough of the city as a subject and felt the need to travel again and took a trip to New Mexico. (13) She was inspired by the mountains and deserts of the region and the mysterious aura of the place. (14) She referred to landscape as "the faraway" and would travel dusty roads in a Model A Ford to find scenes to paint. (15) After Stieglitz's death in 1946, Georgia established permanent residence in New Mexico, so she could paint her famous images of sun-bleached skulls.

(16) With eyesight failing, she spent her final years in Santa Fe. (17) She died on March 6, 1986, at the age of 98, and her ashes were scattered over her "faraway."

31. Which of the following would be the most suitable sentence to insert immediately after sentence 1?

(A) Georgia graduated from the Chatham Episcopal Institute in 1905.
(B) In 1985, she was awarded the National Medal of Arts.
(C) She was born in Wisconsin in 1887.
(D) My favorite European artist is Vincent Van Gogh.
(E) Her family moved from the dairy farm to Virginia.

32. To best connect sentence 8 with the rest of the second paragraph, which is the best word or phrase to insert following the underlined portion of sentence 8 (reproduced below)?

After meeting Stieglitz, she agreed to let him show her work.

(A) however,
(B) naturally,
(C) you see,
(D) certainly,
(E) for that reason,

33. In context, sentence 9 could be made more precise by adding which of the following words after "This"?

(A) teaching
(B) trip
(C) incident
(D) example
(E) friend

34. Which of the following versions of the underlined portion of sentence 15 (reproduced below) best suits the context?

After Stieglitz's death in 1946, Georgia established permanent residence in New Mexico, so she could paint her famous images of sun-bleached skulls.

(A) (As it is now.)
(B) so she could be painting
(C) and she painted
(D) though she painted
(E) where she painted

35. The author uses the phrase "faraway" in sentence 17 to

   (A) set up a contrast between the discussion of O'Keeffe's landscapes and her cityscapes

   (B) reinforce the idea that O'Keeffe felt a strong personal connection to New Mexico

   (C) show the tragedy of O'Keeffe's death after a lengthy career as an artist

   (D) remind the reader that O'Keeffe knew from an early age that she wanted to be an artist

   (E) plant doubts in the reader's mind about the mysterious circumstances of O'Keeffe's death

IF YOU FINISH BEFORE TIME IS CALLED, YOU MAY CHECK YOUR WORK ON THIS TEST ONLY. DO NOT WORK ON ANY OTHER TEST SECTION. **STOP**

4 4 4 4 4 4 4 4 4 4 4 4

| **Time—25 Minutes** | For each item in this section, choose the best answer and blacken the |
| **24 Items** | corresponding space on the answer sheet. |

Each item below has one or two blanks, each blank indicating that something has been omitted. Beneath the sentence are five lettered words or sets of words. Choose the word or set of words that <u>best</u> fits the meaning of the sentence as a whole.

Example:

Although its publicity has been ----, the film itself is intelligent, well acted, handsomely produced, and altogether ----.

(A) tasteless..respectable
(B) extensive..moderate
(C) sophisticated..amateur
(D) risqué..crude
(E) perfect..spectacular ● Ⓑ Ⓒ Ⓓ Ⓔ

---

1. All attempts to keep the cabin warm were ---- due to the frigid weather and the fact that the cabin was ----.

(A) delegated..well-constructed
(B) futile..poorly insulated
(C) successful..well-appointed
(D) punctual..well-situated
(E) profitable..extremely spacious

2. Although the candidate is ---- and a popular media figure, her platform is not ---- the general populace, and she will probably lose the election.

(A) reclusive..accessible to
(B) distressed..opposed by
(C) personable..supported by
(D) diminutive..injurious to
(E) rabid..relevant to

3. Traditionally, clubs with ---- membership are ---- admit new members without a thorough investigation of their backgrounds.

(A) a raucous..anxious to
(B) an elite..reluctant to
(C) a turgid..fearful to
(D) a sensible..urged to
(E) a disruptive..elated to

4. The ability to compose music depends on a solid background in theory, but the musical talent is essentially ---- and cannot be taught.

(A) destroyed
(B) experienced
(C) innate
(D) forgotten
(E) assured

5. Although the professor had ---- support from the faculty who were either indifferent or downright hostile, he continued to teach using his ---- methods.

(A) adequate..similar
(B) minimal..idiosyncratic
(C) resounding..archaic
(D) adverse..popular
(E) bracing..suspicious

GO ON TO THE NEXT PAGE

6. Van Gogh's shapes and colors are so ---- that some art historians have attributed his view of the world to illness or to madness.

    (A) inaccessible
    (B) startling
    (C) intermediate
    (D) corrupt
    (E) trivial

7. Although he was usually ----, he ---- the hostess and was never invited back.

    (A) tidy..flattered
    (B) disinterested..suspected
    (C) forgetful..enchanted
    (D) tactful..insulted
    (E) careful..concealed

8. The will was ---- according to the law because there was ---- evidence that the deceased had been mentally incompetent.

    (A) sanctimonious..chronological
    (B) invalid..overwhelming
    (C) punitive..subsequent
    (D) signed..irrefutable
    (E) suspect..inadequate

Each passage below is followed by one or more items based on its content. Answer the items following each passage on the basis of what is <u>stated</u> or <u>implied</u> in the passage.

Item 9 is based on the following passage.

Art, like words, is a form of communication. Words—spoken and written—make available to each new generation the knowledge discovered through the experience and reflection of preceding generations. Art *(Line 5)* makes available to each new generation the feelings and emotions of preceding generations. Just as the evolution of knowledge proceeds by dislodging and replacing mistaken beliefs, so too the evolution of feeling proceeds through art. Feelings that are not *(10)* beneficial to humankind are replaced by others that aid human well-being. This is the purpose of art.

9. The author of the passage would most likely agree with which of the following statements about words and art?

    (A) The function of both art and words is to depict the world as accurately as possible.
    (B) Art and words—in their respective spheres—are both cumulative and progressive.
    (C) As an activity, art is more important for improving the human condition than communication.
    (D) Art is less necessary to the advancement of human ideals than word communication.
    (E) Art is dependant on word communication since ultimately words must be used to explain the significance of art.

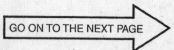
GO ON TO THE NEXT PAGE

Item 10 is based on the following passage.

The omnipresent television set is the American's personal sensory deprivation kit. It deprives the viewer of stereoscopic sight, fully dimensional sounds, and the taste, smell, and feel of the action. Furthermore, there is no personal involvement in the content presented. Reality TV, were it truly a depiction of reality, would use a camera to film the back of a television viewer's upper body and head. Over the viewer's shoulder would be a television showing the same scene. Thus, the experience of the viewer would be identical to that of the "viewer:" the same visually flat and thin auditory experiences and completely lacking any experiences of taste, smell, or feel.

10. The author's primary purpose is to

(A) suggest ways in which television programming might be improved
(B) describe the differences between reality and television programming
(C) demonstrate that television cannot convey a sense of reality
(D) illustrate the harmful effects of television on society at large
(E) propose rules to regulate the content of television programming

Items 11-12 are based on the following passage.

In the presidential election of 1792, George Washington received the unanimous vote of Federalist and Republicans electors alike. However, Southern planters, who in 1789 were ready to cooperate with the moneyed men of the North, parted with them when they realized that policies designed to benefit the Northern merchants and bankers brought no profit to the Southern planters. While willing to support Washington in 1792, they would not accept Vice-President John Adams, as he represented the commerce, shipbuilding, fisheries, and banking institutions of New England and the North. Appealing to shopkeepers, artisans, laboring men, and farmers of the North because of their sympathy with the French Revolution and to Southern landowners with their agrarian bias, the Republicans waged a gallant but losing campaign to have their leader, Thomas Jefferson, elected Vice-President. Then, in 1793, England declared war on republican France over the guillotining of Louis XVI. The following year, John Jay authored a treaty that was suggestive of a sympathetic policy toward monarchical and conservative England over republican, liberty-loving France. The treaty intensified the Republicans' spirit and gave the party—originally known by the uninspiring term Anti-Federalists—a unified sense of mission for the 1796 election: the Republican lovers of liberty against the Monocrats.

11. It can be inferred from the passage that the term "Monocrats" (line 28) was

(A) used by John Jay in his treaty to refer to France's King Louis XVI
(B) invented by the Federalists to refer to the landowners of the South
(C) coined by Republicans to disparage the Federalists' support of England
(D) employed by Republicans to describe their leader, Thomas Jefferson
(E) suggested by the Federalists as an appropriate description of John Adams

GO ON TO THE NEXT PAGE

12. The primary purpose of the passage is to

   (A) discuss the origins of Jefferson's Republican party
   (B) describe Jefferson's defeat in the 1792 election
   (C) theorize about the effects of wealth on political parties
   (D) criticize England's foreign policy toward France in the 1790s
   (E) correct a misunderstanding about political debate in the 1790s

Item 13 is based on the following passage.

In 1969, the United States landed astronauts on the moon, and television and newspapers showed images of the astronauts on the barren moonscape. The
Line following week, a storyteller in rural northwest
5 Tanzania interpreted the event for a gathering of Hayan elders. The storyteller sang of Kisha Lishno, who enticed a vain monarch to invade a nearby "land without a ruler." The glory-hungry king set out with his army. When they arrived, the army, tired and bleary-
10 eyed from a forced march, did not realize the newfound territory was a lake. The army marched into the lake and nearly everyone drowned. The few men that escaped returned to a homeland ruled by a new king: Kisha Lishno.

13. The main point of the storyteller's moon landing interpretation is that

   (A) the United States did not really land astronauts on the moon
   (B) it would be unwise for Tanzania to fund a space program
   (C) Kisha Lishno assumed control as the result of a power vacuum
   (D) the moon landing was a wasteful undertaking inspired by vanity
   (E) the military of the United States is a significant threat

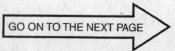
GO ON TO THE NEXT PAGE

Item 14 is based on the following passage.

Throughout history, successful organizations have recognized people as their most important institutional resource. Thus, religious organizations, educational
Line institutions, and even businesses have worked to recruit
5 and train highly qualified people, who in serving the purposes of their employment have contributed more or less directly to the solutions of more significant problems. Organizations such as the Jesuit order, Oxford University, and the Hudson Bay Company
10 provide outstanding examples. These groups have created management atmospheres that foster the growth of people by allowing them the freedom to apply their mental talents to larger problems. By doing so, the emergence of new intellectual and social
15 paradigms is possible.

14. It can be inferred that the author regards the Hudson Bay Company as a

(A) successful business that developed sound management practices
(B) wealthy corporation unable to develop strong leadership talent
(C) short-lived institution with little historical significance
(D) profitable enterprise founded upon religious principles
(E) typical corporation following accepted business practices

GO ON TO THE NEXT PAGE

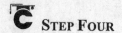

Items 15-24 are based on the following passage.

Traditional strategies for controlling insect-pests tend to rely on the use of nonselective insecticides that cause extensive ecological disruption. The alternative
Line sterile-insect technique, in which members of the target
5 species are irradiated to cause sterility, has enjoyed some modest success. When released into an infested area, the sterile insects mate with normal insects but produce no offspring. Unfortunately, the irradiation weakens the insects, making it less likely that they will
10 mate; and, in any event, sterile insects do not search selectively for non-sterile mates. A third, newly developed strategy is based on parasite release.

Pest hosts and their associated parasites have evolved biological and behavioral characteristics that
15 virtually ensure that the relative numbers of hosts and parasites in the ecosystem they inhabit remain within relatively narrow limits—even though coexisting populations may fluctuate up to 100-fold during a single season. The close numerical relationships are
20 entirely consistent with nature's balancing mechanisms, which permit closely associated organisms to live together in harmony. Thus, in natural populations, the ratios of parasites to hosts are not high enough to result in dependable control. However, it is
25 possible to mass-rear parasites so that they can be released at strategic times and in numbers that result in parasite-to-host ratios sufficient to control host populations.

Biosteres tryoni, for example, has a strong
30 affinity for medfly larvae. Let us assume that a new medfly infestation is discovered. It is likely to have originated from a single female and, even in an area with a good surveillance program, to be in the third reproductive cycle. The rate of population increase is
35 tenfold per generation; so at the time the infestation comes to light, about 1,000 males and 1,000 females are emerging and will produce a total of approximately 80,000 larvae. Reproduction will be concentrated in an area of about one square mile, but scattered
40 reproduction will occur anywhere within a 25-square-mile area. At first glance, the odds of controlling the infestation by parasite release seem low; but with new techniques for mass-producing parasites, it is possible to release one million males and one million females
45 into the infested area. This would mean an average of 62 females per acre, and the average female parasitizes about 30 host larvae during its lifetime. Additionally, the parasites actively search for host habitats by using the kairomone signals emanating from infested fruit.
50 Even assuming that only ten percent of the released females are successful and, further, that they parasitize

an average of only ten larvae, they could still parasitize one million larvae. Only 80,000 larvae are available, however; so the actual ratio would be 12.5:1. A ratio as
55 low as 5:1 results in 99 percent parasitism.

This method of pest eradication presents no health or environmental problems and is actually cheaper. The cost of mass-rearing and distributing *B. tryoni* is about $2,000 per million. So even if six million parasites of
60 both sexes are released during a period corresponding to three medfly reproductive cycles, the total cost of the treatment would be $12,000—compared to $25,000 for a single insecticide spray application to the same 25-square mile area.

15. The author implies that the sterile insect release strategy is not completely effective because

   (A) some sterile insects mate with other sterile insects
   (B) weakened sterile insects refuse to mate with healthy insects
   (C) the cost of producing a sufficient number of sterile insects is prohibitive
   (D) sterile insects are incapable of producing offspring
   (E) irradiation leaves a radioactive residue offensive to healthy insects

16. Which of the following words, when substituted for "strategic" in line 26, would best preserve the meaning of the original sentence?

   (A) military
   (B) random
   (C) critical
   (D) ill-advised
   (E) frequent

17. According to the passage, *Biosteres tryoni* is effective in controlling medfly infestations because

   (A) female *B. tryoni* feed on adult medflies
   (B) male and female *B. tryoni* parasitize medfly larvae
   (C) male and female *B. tryoni* mate with medflies
   (D) male *B. tryoni* prevent male medflies from mating
   (E) female *B. tryoni* parasitize medfly larvae

18. It can be inferred that if *B. tryoni* were not attracted by kairomone signals from medfly-infested fruit that the parasite release strategy would be

   (A) less effective because some *B. tryoni* would remain in areas not infested
   (B) less effective because none of the *B. tryoni* would parasitize medfly larvae
   (C) equally as effective because *B. tryoni* do not damage fruit crops
   (D) more effective because some *B. tryoni* would fail to reproduce
   (E) more effective because the *B. tryoni* would remain more widely dispersed

19. In the development of the passage, the author

   (A) explains a scientific theory and then offers evidence to refute it
   (B) cites statistics to compare the relative effectiveness of different strategies
   (C) speculates on the probable course of scientific developments
   (D) states a general principle and then provides an example of its application
   (E) poses a question and then provides a detailed answer to it

20. Which of the following statements about medfly reproduction can be inferred from the passage?

   (A) The medfly is capable of reproducing asexually.
   (B) A typical generation contains ten times as many females as males.
   (C) A new generation of medfly is produced once a year.
   (D) A medfly colony will reproduce for only three generations.
   (E) Only about 25 percent of larvae reach adulthood.

21. It can be inferred that an insecticide application for the hypothetical infestation would treat a 25-square mile area because

   (A) the cost for a single spray application to the area is $25,000
   (B) *B. tryoni* would tend to concentrate themselves in infested areas
   (C) medfly reproduction might occur anywhere within that region
   (D) the spray would repel medflies from fruit not already infested
   (E) medflies from another, yet undiscovered infestation might be in the area

22. In the final paragraph, the phrase "even if" (line 59) indicates that the author is

   (A) making an unproved assumption about the effectiveness of parasite pest control programs
   (B) providing evidence of the ecological harm done by indiscriminate use of pesticides
   (C) responding to a point about program cost that was specifically developed in the previous paragraph
   (D) offering proof that parasite-release programs actually destroy the host pest insects
   (E) considering the strongest possible objection against the cost of the parasite release strategy

23. The author is primarily concerned with

   (A) criticizing the use of nonselective insecticides
   (B) defending the use of parasite release programs
   (C) explaining the workings of a new pest-control method
   (D) refuting the suggestion that parasite release is costly
   (E) analyzing the reproductive habits of the medfly

GO ON TO THE NEXT PAGE

24. It can be inferred that the author regards the release of parasites to control pests as

    (A) reasonably effective
    (B) prohibitively expensive
    (C) environmentally reckless
    (D) highly experimental
    (E) unnecessarily complex

IF YOU FINISH BEFORE TIME IS CALLED, YOU MAY CHECK YOUR WORK ON THIS TEST ONLY. DO NOT WORK ON ANY OTHER TEST SECTION.

STOP

—662—

5 5 5 5 5 5 5 5 5 5 5 5

| Time—25 Minutes 20 Items | In this section, solve each item, using any available space on the page for scratchwork. Then, decide which is the best of the choices given and fill in the corresponding oval on the answer sheet. |

Notes: The figures accompanying the items are drawn as accurately as possible unless otherwise stated in specific items. Again, unless otherwise stated, all figures lie in the same plane. All numbers used in these items are real numbers. Calculators are permitted for this test.

Reference:

Circle: Rectangle: Rectangular Solid: 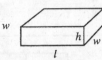 Cylinder: 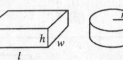 Triangle:

$C = 2\pi r$ $A = lw$ $V = lwh$ $V = \pi r^2 h$ $A = \frac{1}{2}bh$ $a^2 + b^2 = c^2$

$A = \pi r^2$

- The measure in degrees of a straight angle is 180.
- The number of degrees of arc in a circle is 360.
- The sum of the measure of the angles of a triangle is 180.

---

1. If $\frac{1}{2N} + \frac{1}{2N} = \frac{1}{4}$, then $N =$

   (A) 4
   (B) 2
   (C) 1
   (D) $\frac{1}{2}$
   (E) $\frac{1}{4}$

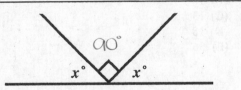

2. In the figure above, $x =$

   (A) 30
   (B) 45
   (C) 60
   (D) 75
   (E) 90

3. In a certain game, a person's age is multiplied by 2 and then the product is divided by 3. If the result of performing the operations on John's age is 12, what is John's age?

   (A) 2
   (B) 8
   (C) 12
   (D) 18
   (E) 36

   $12 \cdot 3 = \frac{36}{2}$
   $= 18$

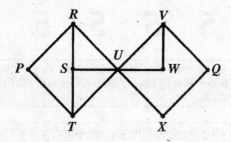

4. The figure above is a map showing the stations and connecting subway lines for a city's subway system. If a man wishes to travel by subway from station P to station Q without passing through any station more than once, which of the following MUST be true?

    (A) If he passes through T, he must next pass through S.
    (B) If he passes through S, he must next pass through U.
    (C) If he passes through U, he must next pass through V.
    (D) If he passes through R, he cannot later pass through T.
    (E) If he passes through V, he cannot later pass through W.

5. A helper must load 38 bricks onto a truck. Given that she can carry at most 4 bricks at a time, what is the fewest number of trips that she must make to move all of the bricks from the brick pile onto the truck?

    (A) 9
    (B) 9.5
    (C) 10
    (D) 10.5
    (E) 12

6. For all numbers, $(a - b)(b - c) - (b - a)(c - b) =$

    (A) −2
    (B) −1
    (C) 0
    (D) $ab - ac - bc$
    (E) $2ab - 2ac - 2bc$

7. n is a positive integer. If n is a multiple of both 6 and 9, what is the least possible value of n?

    (A) 12
    (B) 18
    (C) 27
    (D) 36
    (E) 54

8. If $f(x) = x^2 - x$, what is the value of $f(f(2))$?

    (A) 0
    (B) 1
    (C) 2
    (D) 4
    (E) 8

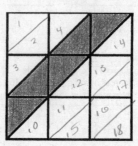

9. The figure above shows a square piece of land that is divided into 9 smaller square lots. The shaded portion is a railroad right-of-way. If the area of the shaded portion of the figure is 5 square miles, what is the area, in square miles, of the entire piece of land?

    (A) 9
    (B) 10
    (C) 13
    (D) 18
    (E) 36

GO ON TO THE NEXT PAGE

10. Set $X = \{1, 2, 3, 4\}$
    Set $Y = \{1, 2, 3, 4\}$

    For how many different ordered pairs (a, b) in which a is an element of X and b is an element of Y is $a - b > 0$?

    (A) 24
    (B) 18
    (C) 15
    (D) 12
    (E) 6

11. If x and y are negative integers, and $x > y$, which of the following is the greatest?

    (A) $-(xy)^2$
    (B) x^2y
    (C) xy
    (D) $x + y$
    (E) $y - x$

12. A student receives an average of 75 on three exams that are scored on a scale from 0 to 100. If one of her test scores was 75, what is the lowest possible score that she could have received on any of the three tests?

    (A) 0
    (B) 1
    (C) 25
    (D) 40
    (E) 50

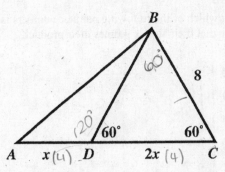

13. In $\triangle ABC$ above, what is the length of side $\overline{AC}$?

    (A) 4
    (B) 8
    (C) 12 $4 + 2(4) = 12$
    (D) 18
    (E) 22

14. During a certain shift, a quality control inspector inspects 6 out of every 30 items produced. What was the ratio of inspected items to uninspected items during that shift?

    (A) 1:4 $\frac{6}{30}$ $\frac{24}{30}$
    (B) 1:5
    (C) 1:6
    (D) 5:1 $6:24$
    (E) 6:1 $1:4$

GO ON TO THE NEXT PAGE

15. For which of the following pairs of numbers is it true that their sum is 9 times their product?

    (A) $1, \frac{1}{19}$

    (B) $1, \frac{1}{9}$

    (C) $1, \frac{1}{8}$

    (D) 1, 8

    (E) 1, 9

16. $\frac{1}{2^{-3}} \cdot \frac{1}{3^{-2}} =$

    (A) -36

    (B) -6

    (C) 2

    (D) 9

    (E) 72

17. What is the solution set for $\left|\frac{x-2}{3}\right| = 4$?

    (A) {14, -10}

    (B) {14, 10}

    (C) {10, -14}

    (D) {10, 10}

    (E) {10, -10}

18. If $f(-1) = 1$ and $f(2) = 7$, what is the slope of the graph of $f(x)$ in the coordinate system?

    (A) -3

    (B) $-\frac{1}{2}$

    (C) $\frac{1}{2}$

    (D) 2

    (E) $\frac{5}{2}$

STUDENT POPULATION AT SCHOOL X

	Juniors	Seniors	Total
Women	124		
Men			280
Total			880

19. The table above shows the Junior/Senior student population at School X according to gender and class standing. Which of the following quantities is NOT, in and of itself, sufficient to complete the matrix?

    (A) The number of women who are seniors
    (B) The number of men who are seniors
    (C) The number of juniors who are men
    (D) The number of juniors
    (E) The number of seniors

20. The cost of a taxi ride is $1.50 for hiring the cab and $0.40 per mile or any part of a mile of distance traveled. Which of the following equations can be used to find the cost, y, of a ride of exactly x miles, in which x is an integer?

    (A) $y = x(0.4 + 1.5)$
    (B) $y = 0.4x + 1.5$
    (C) $y = 0.4 + 1.5x$
    (D) $y = 1.5 - 0.4x$
    (E) $y = 0.4 - 1.5x$

IF YOU FINISH BEFORE TIME IS CALLED, YOU MAY CHECK YOUR WORK ON THIS TEST ONLY. DO NOT WORK ON ANY OTHER TEST SECTION.

STOP

6 6 6 6 6 6 6 6 6 6 6 6 6 6

| **Time—25 Minutes** **24 Items** | For each item in this section, choose the best answer and blacken the corresponding space on the answer sheet. |

Each item below has one or two blanks, each blank indicating that something has been omitted. Beneath the sentence are five lettered words or sets of words. Choose the word or set of words that <u>best</u> fits the meaning of the sentence as a whole.

Example:

Although its publicity has been ----, the film itself is intelligent, well acted, handsomely produced, and altogether ----.

(A) tasteless..respectable
(B) extensive..moderate
(C) sophisticated..amateur
(D) risqué..crude
(E) perfect..spectacular

---

1. The manuscripts of Thomas Wolfe were so ---- that the publisher was forced to ---- them in order to make them coherent and concise.

(A) obscure..expand
(B) lengthy..edit
(C) unpopular..recall
(D) interesting..organize
(E) depressing..inspire

2. The changes in the organization were so gradual that they seemed almost ----.

(A) hasty
(B) spontaneous
(C) imperceptible
(D) distorted
(E) omitted

3. Although it is difficult to be ---- the plight of one's adversary, it is not necessary to be ---- or cruel.

(A) sympathetic to..callous
(B) excited about..capricious
(C) pessimistic about..dilatory
(D) jealous of..rigorous
(E) ignorant of..esoteric

4. Professor Gray's translation of the work is so ---- that it completely ---- the material and renders it incomprehensible.

(A) thematic..retards
(B) grandiose..obviates
(C) accurate..obscures
(D) ubiquitous..transforms
(E) idiosyncratic..distorts

5. The customers were so incensed at the obvious ---- of the waiter that they could not be ---- and refused to pay their check.

(A) exigence..disconcerted
(B) volubility..condoned
(C) ineptitude..assuaged
(D) lassitude..thwarted
(E) fortitude..mollified

6. The poetry of Mallarmé, like the poetry of most of the symbolists, is not clear and easily accessible but rather vague and ----.

(A) opaque
(B) redundant
(C) lucid
(D) straightforward
(E) concrete

GO ON TO THE NEXT PAGE

7. Mary was very annoyed that her secretary did not meet her deadlines, and she warned her that her laziness and ---- could result in her dismissal.

   (A) procrastination
   (B) ambition
   (C) zeal
   (D) veracity
   (E) fortitude

8. Although a solemn tone was appropriate to the seriousness of the occasion, the speaker lapsed into ----, which was depressing rather than moving.

   (A) reverence
   (B) frankness
   (C) loquaciousness
   (D) levity
   (E) morbidity

Each passage below is followed by one or more items based on its content. Answer the items following each passage on the basis of what is <u>stated</u> or <u>implied</u> in the passage.

Item 9 is based on the following passage.

Biologists have discovered a new species of fairy shrimp that live in the dry lakebeds of Idaho's desert. Though these shrimp look delicate enough to indicate their name, their eggs are hard enough to survive for years in the baking heat of summer and the frozen cold of winter until enough rain falls to create the pools of water in which the shrimp live. A few weeks after hatching, the shrimp mate, leaving behind tiny cyst-like offspring, and then die.

Line
5

9. According to the passage, the fairy shrimp spends the active phase of its life in

   (A) frozen ground
   (B) standing water
   (C) dry sand
   (D) running streams
   (E) underground niches

Item 10 is based on the following passage.

The prospect of an avian flu pandemic reminds us all that the forces of nature can be far more lethal than anything created by humans. While the U.S. is not on
Line the brink of such an epidemic, experts agree that it is
5 only a matter of time before some new, virulent strain of influenza will threaten the world. The government is already testing the first doses of an experimental vaccine and closely monitoring a variety of disease indicators.

10. The tone of the passage can best be described as

(A) alarmed
(B) concerned
(C) dismissive
(D) irreverent
(E) optimistic

Items 11-12 are based on the following passage.

Having grown up in the liberal culture of King Henry VIII's court, Elizabeth was a bold horsewoman, an expert shot, a graceful dancer, a skilled musician,
Line and an accomplished scholar. She spoke Italian and
5 French as fluently as English and read Greek. From her father, Henry VIII, Elizabeth inherited her frank and hardy address, her courage, and her self-confidence. Her sensuous and self-indulgent nature she inherited from her mother, Ann Boleyn. She loved gaiety,
10 laughter, and wit, but her vanity and caprice played no part in the affairs of state. No nobler group of ministers ever gathered round the council-board than those of Queen Elizabeth, but she was the instrument of none. Her policy, founded on good common sense, was her
15 own.

11. The primary purpose of the passage is to

(A) describe an interesting personality
(B) discuss important historical events
(C) appraise the policies of a leader
(D) criticize monarchy as a type of government
(E) provide a family history

12. In line 7, "address" most nearly means

(A) geographical location
(B) artistic talent
(C) title of honor
(D) manner of speaking
(E) physical prowess

GO ON TO THE NEXT PAGE

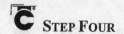

Items 13-14 are based on the following passage.

Some botanists believe that maize evolved
independently in Asia and in the Americas. However, it
is more likely that maize originated first in the
Line Americas: Columbus brought maize back to Spain
5 following his 1492 voyage. It was then distributed
throughout Europe and carried along trade routes,
ultimately reaching China within 60 years. This rapid
spread of cultivation from west to east was the result of
maize being particularly well-suited to the climates of
10 those regions in Eurasia where it was introduced. The
Bahamas encompass the same latitudes as Egypt, Saudi
Arabia, Pakistan, Nepal, Bangladesh, and Yunnan in
southwestern China. This model for the geographical
evolution of maize follows a pattern similar to the well-
15 established spread of wheat and barley several
thousand years earlier from the Middle East to Ireland
in the west and to Japan in the east.

13. The author introduces the examples of wheat and
    barley in order to

    (A) demonstrate that wheat and barley are more
        important foods than maize
    (B) support the thesis that maize appeared
        independently in both China and the
        Americas
    (C) prove that wheat and barley also originated
        in the Americas and then spread to Europe
        and Asia
    (D) refute the claim that new plant species
        generally propagate in a west to east
        direction
    (E) illustrate that maize could also have spread
        across the various regions as argued

14. The author's list of regions through which the
    cultivation of maize spread assumes that

    (A) maize could have originated exclusively in
        Asia
    (B) regions at the same latitudes have similar
        climates
    (C) maize is a hardier crop than either wheat or
        barley
    (D) maize was introduced to Spain no later than
        1493
    (E) Columbus visited no islands other than the
        Bahamas

Items 15-24 are based on the following passage.

The following passage discusses certain aspects of the evolution of stars.

The theory of stellar evolution predicts that when the core of a star has used up its nuclear fuel, the core will collapse. If the star is about the size of the Sun, it will turn into a degenerate dwarf star. If it is somewhat larger, it may undergo a supernova explosion that leaves behind a neutron star. However, if the stellar core has a mass greater than about three solar masses, gravitational forces overwhelm nuclear forces and the core will collapse. Since nuclear forces are the strongest repulsive forces known, nothing can stop the continued collapse of the star. A black hole in space is formed.

Because of the intense gravitational forces near the black hole, nothing can escape from it, not even light. If we were to send a probe toward an isolated black hole, the probe would detect no radiation from the black hole. Yet, it would sense a gravitational field like the one that would be produced by a normal star of the same mass. As the probe approached the black hole, the gravitational forces would increase inexorably. At a distance of a few thousand kilometers, the gravitational forces would be so great that the side of the probe closest to the black hole would literally be torn away from the side furthest away from the black hole. Eventually, at a distance of a few kilometers from the black hole, the particles that made up the probe would be lost forever down the black hole. This point of no return is called the gravitational radius of the black hole.

Given this, how can we hope to observe such an object? Nature, herself, could conceivably provide us with a "probe" of a black hole: a binary star system in which one of the stars has become a black hole and is absorbing the mass of its companion star. As the matter of the companion star falls into the black hole, it would accelerate. This increased energy of motion would be changed into heat energy. Near the gravitational radius the matter would move at speeds close to the speed of light, and temperatures would range from tens of millions of degrees to perhaps as much as a billion degrees. At these temperatures, X- and gamma radiation are produced. Further, since the matter near the gravitational radius would be orbiting the black hole about once every millisecond, the X-radiation should show erratic, short-term variability unlike the regular or periodic variability associated with neutron stars and degenerate dwarfs.

The X-ray source Cygnus X-1 fulfills these "experimental" conditions. It is part of a binary star system, in which a blue supergiant star is orbiting an invisible companion star. This invisible companion has a mass greater than about nine times the mass of the Sun, and it is a strong X-ray source with rapid variations in the intensity of its X-ray flux. Most astronomers believe that Cygnus X-1 is a black hole; but this belief is tempered with a dose of caution. The idea of a black hole is still difficult to swallow, but theorists can think of no other object that could explain the phenomenon of Cygnus X-1. For this reason, in most scientific papers, Cygnus X-1 is referred to simply as a black hole "candidate."

15. The primary concern of the passage is to

(A) present a theory and describe the kind of evidence that would prove it correct
(B) outline a widely accepted theory and offer evidence that refutes that theory
(C) describe a phenomenon and present a theory to explain the phenomenon
(D) advance a theory and then supply a specific example as proof of the theory
(E) describe the result of an experiment that was conducted to prove a theory

16. The passage indicates that a neutron star (line 6) originated as a

(A) degenerate dwarf star of any size
(B) normal star with a mass less than one-third that of our sun
(C) normal star with a mass greater than that of our sun but less than three times that of our sun
(D) normal star with a mass at least three times greater than that of our sun
(E) supernova with a mass at least three times greater than that of our sun

17. In line 10, the word "repulsive" most nearly means

(A) forbidding
(B) disgusting
(C) offensive
(D) disagreeable
(E) repellent

GO ON TO THE NEXT PAGE

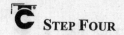

18. The passage suggests that the mass of a black hole would be

(A) negligible
(B) about one-third that of the normal star from which it was formed
(C) approximately the same mass as the normal star from which it was formed
(D) approximately equal to the mass of two binary stars
(E) just about equal to the mass of our star

19. The passage defines the "gravitational radius" of a black hole as the

(A) orbital distance separating a visible star from a black hole in a binary star system
(B) distance at which matter is irreversibly drawn into the black hole by gravitational forces
(C) distance from the black hole at which an approaching rocket would first start to disintegrate
(D) radius of the massive star that created the black hole when it collapsed in upon itself
(E) scale for measuring the short-term variability of X-radiation emitted by a black hole

20. In line 55, the word "tempered" most nearly means

(A) moderated
(B) hardened
(C) kneaded
(D) cooled
(E) proved

21. The passage indicates that a black hole would be

(A) most likely to develop in a binary star system
(B) a source of large quantities of X- and gamma rays
(C) observable through a powerful telescope
(D) formed from a degenerate dwarf star
(E) invisible even at close range

22. In line 60, the word "candidate" most nearly means

(A) pretender
(B) possibility
(C) official
(D) office-seeker
(E) scientist

23. Which of the following is NOT mentioned by the author as evidence to suggest that the Cygnus X-1 source might be a black hole?

(A) Cygnus X-1 is a source of powerful X-ray radiation.
(B) The companion star of Cygnus X-1 has a mass sufficiently large enough to create a black hole.
(C) The intensity of the X-rays emanating from Cygnus X-1 exhibits short-term variability.
(D) The star around which the visible star of Cygnus X-1 is orbiting is not itself visible.
(E) The visible star of the Cygnus X-1 system is a blue supergiant.

24. The author regards the existence of black holes as

(A) in principle unprovable
(B) theoretically possible
(C) extremely unlikely
(D) experimentally confirmed
(E) a logical contradiction

IF YOU FINISH BEFORE TIME IS CALLED, YOU MAY CHECK YOUR WORK ON THIS TEST ONLY. DO NOT WORK ON ANY OTHER TEST SECTION. **STOP**

8 8 8 8 8 8 8 8 8 8 8 8

| Time—20 Minutes 16 Items | In this section, solve each item, using any available space on the page for scratchwork. Then, decide which is the best of the choices given and fill in the corresponding oval on the answer sheet. |

Notes: The figures accompanying the items are drawn as accurately as possible unless otherwise stated in specific items. Again, unless otherwise stated, all figures lie in the same plane. All numbers used in these items are real numbers. Calculators are permitted for this test.

Reference:

Circle: Rectangle: Rectangular Solid: Cylinder: Triangle:

 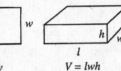

$C = 2\pi r$ $A = lw$ $V = lwh$ $V = \pi r^2 h$ $A = \frac{1}{2}bh$ $a^2 + b^2 = c^2$

$A = \pi r^2$

- The measure in degrees of a straight angle is 180.
- The number of degrees of arc in a circle is 360.
- The sum of the measure of the angles of a triangle is 180.

---

1. If 1 mil = 0.1 cents, how many mils are there in $3.13?

   (A)   0.313
   (B)   3.13
   (C)   31.3
   (D)   313
   (E)   3,130

   $\frac{1}{.1} = \frac{x}{313}$

2. Which of the following is a pair of numbers that are not equal?

   (A) $\frac{63}{6}, \frac{21}{2}$
   (B) 0.3%, 0.003
   (C) $\frac{44}{77}, \frac{4}{7}$
   (D) $\frac{3}{8}, 0.375$
   (E) $\sqrt{3^2}, 9$

3. If x and y are different positive integers and $\frac{x}{y}$ is an integer, then which of the following must be true?

   I. $x > y$
   II. $xy > 0$
   III. $y - x < 0$

   (A) I only
   (B) II only
   (C) III only
   (D) I and II only
   (E) I, II, and III

GO ON TO THE NEXT PAGE

Items 4-5 refer to the following information.

For all positive integers n:

$\boxed{n} = 2n$ if n is even.

$\boxed{n} = 3n$ if n is odd.

4. If n is a prime number greater than 2, then $\boxed{n-1} =$

(A) $3n$
(B) $2n$
(C) $3n - 3$
(D) $2n - 2$
(E) n

[handwritten: y odd #, 2(n-1), 2n-2]

5. $\boxed{3} \cdot \boxed{4} =$

[handwritten: 3(3), 4(2), 3n · 2n, n · 8]

(A) $\boxed{6}$

(B) $\boxed{7}$

(C) $\boxed{12}$

(D) $\boxed{18}$

(E) $\boxed{36}$

[handwritten: 36 · 2 = 72]

6. Which of the following is the equation for the line that includes points $(-1, 1)$ and $(7, 5)$?

(A) $y = \frac{x}{2} + 2$

(B) $y = \frac{x}{2} + \frac{2}{3}$

(C) $y = \frac{x}{2} + \frac{3}{2}$

(D) $y = 2x + \frac{3}{2}$

(E) $y = 2x + 2$

[handwritten near figure: small circle diameter = 4, $\pi r^2 = 4\pi$; big circle diameter = 8, πr^2, 16π; shaded $16\pi - 4\pi = 12\pi$]

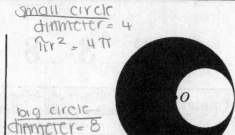

7. In the figure above, O is the center of the circle. What is the ratio of the shaded area in the figure to the unshaded area in the figure?

(A) $\frac{4}{1}$

(B) $\frac{\pi}{1}$

(C) $\frac{3}{1}$

(D) $\frac{5}{2}$

(E) $\frac{2}{1}$

[handwritten: $\frac{12\pi}{4\pi} = \frac{3}{1}$]

8. If a cube has a surface area of $54x^2$, what is its volume?

(A) $3x$
(B) $3x^2$
(C) $3x^3$
(D) $9x^3$
(E) $27x^3$

[handwritten: $\frac{6s^2}{6} = \frac{54x^2}{6}$, $\sqrt{s^2} = \sqrt{9x^2}$, $s = 3x$, $s = 3x \cdot 3x \cdot 3x = 27x^3$]

GO ON TO THE NEXT PAGE

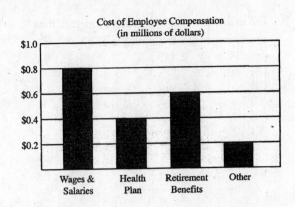

Cost of Employee Compensation
(in millions of dollars)

9. In the graph above, Wages & Salaries account for what percent of employee compensation?

(A) 40%
(B) 25%
(C) $12\frac{1}{2}$%
(D) 10%
(E) 8%

10. If x is an integer that is a multiple of both 9 and 5, which of the following must be true?

   I. x is equal to 45.
   II. x is a multiple of 15.
   III. x is odd.

(A) I only
(B) II only
(C) III only
(D) II and III only
(E) I, II, and III

11. Initially, 24 people apply for jobs with a firm, and $\frac{1}{3}$ of those people are turned down without being given an interview. If $\frac{1}{4}$ of the remaining applicants are hired, how many applicants are given jobs?

(A) 2
(B) 4
(C) 6
(D) 8
(E) 12

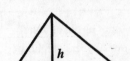

12. In the figures above, if the area of the rectangle is equal to the area of the triangle, then $h =$

(A) 2
(B) 3
(C) 4
(D) 6
(E) 9

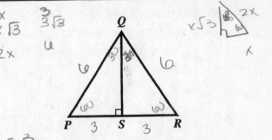

13. In the figure above, $\overline{PQ} = \overline{QR} = \overline{PR}$. If $\overline{PS} = 3$, what is the area of $\triangle PQR$?

$$\left(\cos 30° = \frac{\sqrt{3}}{2}\right)$$

(A) 3
(B) $3\sqrt{3}$ (approximately 5.2)
(C) 6
(D) $6\sqrt{3}$ (approximately 10.39)
(E) $9\sqrt{3}$ (approximately 15.59)

GO ON TO THE NEXT PAGE

14. The price of a book, after it was reduced by $\frac{1}{3}$, is B dollars. What was the price of the book, in dollars, before the reduction?

   (A) $\frac{2B}{3}$

   (B) $\frac{3B}{4}$

   (C) $\frac{6B}{5}$

   (D) $\frac{4B}{3}$

   (E) $\frac{3B}{2}$

15. Y years ago, Tom was three times as old as Julie was at the time. If Julie is now 20 years old, how old is Tom in terms of Y?

   (A) $60 + 2Y$

   (B) $30 + 2Y$

   (C) $30 - 2Y$

   (D) $60 - 2Y$

   (E) $60 - 3Y$

16. If S is the sum of x consecutive integers, then S must be even if x is a multiple of

   (A) 6

   (B) 5

   (C) 4

   (D) 3

   (E) 2

IF YOU FINISH BEFORE TIME IS CALLED, YOU MAY CHECK YOUR WORK ON THIS TEST ONLY. DO NOT WORK ON ANY OTHER TEST SECTION.

STOP

9 9 9 9 9 9 9 9 9 9 9 9 9

Time—20 Minutes 19 Items	For each item in this section, choose the best answer and blacken the corresponding space on the answer sheet.

Each item below has one or two blanks, each blank indicating that something has been omitted. Beneath the sentence are five lettered words or sets of w ords. Choose the word or set of words that <u>best</u> fits the meaning of the sentence as a whole.

Example:

Although its publicity has been ----, the film itself is intelligent, well acted, handsomely produced, and altogether ----.

(A) tasteless..respectable
(B) extensive..moderate
(C) sophisticated..amateur
(D) risqué..crude
(E) perfect..spectacular

1. The treatment of the mental illnesses for which there is no cure can only ---- the symptoms, not ---- the disease.

   (A) defend..eradicate
   (B) disrupt..deflate
   (C) ameliorate..eliminate
   (D) confine..restore
   (E) augment..delineate

2. Although Senator Jones had the ---- needed to run for office, it was his ---- that the party considered his greatest asset.

   (A) credentials..charisma
   (B) experience..apathy
   (C) esteem..wrongdoing
   (D) greed..altruism
   (E) serenity..haughtiness

3. Due to the ---- of the materials needed to manufacture the product and the ever-increasing demand for it, it is highly probable that the final cost to the consumer will ----.

   (A) immensity..evolve
   (B) paucity..escalate
   (C) scarcity..relax
   (D) acuity..stabilize
   (E) certainty..fluctuate

4. Although the comedian was very clever, many of his remarks were ---- and ---- lawsuits against him for slander.

   (A) derogatory..resulted in
   (B) pithy..came upon
   (C) protracted..forestalled
   (D) depraved..assuaged
   (E) recanted..sparked

GO ON TO THE NEXT PAGE

The two passages below are followed by items based on their content and the relationship between the two passages. Answer the items on the basis of what is <u>stated</u> or <u>implied</u> in the passages and in any introductory material that may be provided.

Items 5-19 are based on the following pair of passages.

The following passages are excerpts from two different sources that discuss particular approaches to history.

Passage 1

As Carl Hempel demonstrates in his seminal essay "The Function of General Laws in History," a general law plays the same role in both history and the
Line natural sciences. According to Hempel's deductive-
5 nomological model, proper scientific explanation—whether for history or the natural sciences—includes three sorts of statements:

(A) A set of statements about conditions (that can be designated as C1, C2, and so on) that are true at a
10 particular place and time.

(B) A set of universal hypotheses connecting events of type C with events of type E.

(C) A statement asserting that E is logically deducible from the statements of A and B.

15 The "C" events are, of course, causes, while the "E" events are effects. Given a sufficiently precise description of background conditions by Set A and an adequately articulated set of empirical laws in Set B, a conclusion such as "A popular uprising overthrew the
20 government" can be logically deduced with as much certainty as that of a syllogism.†

The notion that a historian cannot study past events in the same way that a chemist studies reactions or a physicist studies falling objects is due to a
25 misunderstanding. Historical explanations intentionally omit from Set A statements about human nature that are well known to the sciences of psychology and sociology because they are too numerous to mention. Further, many of the general laws used by historians do
30 not seem susceptible to easy confirmation in the way that laboratory experiments are. It is difficult to find a sufficiently large number of revolutions to assess the validity of the assertion that a drop of a certain magnitude in a population's standard of living will
35 inevitably be followed by revolution.

Thus, we should more accurately speak not of scientific explanations of historical events but of "sketches" of history. This terminology would call attention to the incompleteness and the imprecision in

40 historical explanation, while at the same time reminding us that the form of explanation is the same as that of the natural sciences.

†A syllogism is a form of reasoning in which a conclusion is drawn from two statements:

Major Premise: All ruminants are quadrupeds.
Minor Premise: All cows are ruminants.
Conclusion: Therefore, all cows are quadrupeds.

Passage 2

The obvious distinction between history and the natural sciences is that history is concerned with
45 human actions. The historian makes a distinction between what may be called the outside and the inside of an event. The outside of the event is everything belonging to it that can be described in terms of bodies and their movements: the passage of Caesar across a
50 river called the Rubicon on a certain date or the spilling of Caesar's blood on the senate-house floor on another. The inside of the event can only be described in terms of thought: Caesar's defiance of Republican law or the clash of constitutional policy between Caesar and
55 Caesar's assassins. The historian is not investigating mere events (a mere event is one that has only an outside and no inside) but actions, and an action is the unity of the outside and inside of an event.

The task of the historian is thus distinguished
60 from that of the natural scientist in two ways. On the one hand, the historian must undertake an additional investigation that is neither needed by nor available to the natural scientist. The historian must inquire after the "why" of an event, that is, the thought behind it. On
65 the other hand, the task of the historian is somewhat simpler than that of the natural scientist because once that question has been answered there is no further question to be raised. There is no reason to look behind the thought associated with the event for a supervening
70 general law.

Since the questions that the historian asks are different from those posed by the natural scientist, the historian will employ a different method. The historian penetrates to the inner aspect of the event by the
75 technique of "Verstehen."† To be sure, the historian will study whatever documents and other physical evidence are available, but these are important only insofar as they provide an access to the inside of the event.

80 A purely physical event can only be understood as a particular occurrence governed by a universal or

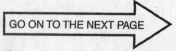

general law, but the inside of an event is a thought—unique, and as such, not subject to a law-like explanation. Nor is this reason for disappointment. It is
85 not the case that there are historical laws but the techniques just do not yet exist to find them. Rather, the laws just do not exist to be found. To expect to find causal explanation in history and to demand of history predictions about the course of future events is an
90 illegitimate expectation conceived and fostered by the false analogy of history to the natural sciences and the incorrect assumption that the natural sciences are the paradigm for all human knowledge.

The positivist will object that this means that
95 history is, in principle, less rigorous than natural science, but this objection ignores the point that there simply are no historical laws to be discovered. In fact, because an historical event has both an inside and an outside, it is the events of natural science that are, in a
100 sense, deficient. As R. G. Collingwood wrote so boldly in the concluding section of *The Idea of History*, "Natural science...depends on historical thought for its existence." In history, there are no general scientific laws to be uncovered, and the search for them is the
105 foolish pursuit of a will'o-the-wisp that exists only in the fables of positivist literature.

†*Verstehen* is the German word for "understanding."

5. As used in line 5, the word "nomological" most nearly means

(A) law-like
(B) historical
(C) accurate
(D) logical
(E) scientific

6. In line 18, the phrase "adequately articulated" means

(A) verbally presented
(B) only preliminary
(C) confidently denoted
(D) precisely defined
(E) sufficiently detailed

7. In the second paragraph of Passage 1, the author suggests that a series of historical events could serve the same scientific function as

(A) eyewitness accounts
(B) general laws
(C) laboratory experiments
(D) historical sketches
(E) syllogisms

8. According to the author of Passage 1, it is difficult to formulate a general historical law about revolution because

(A) revolutions, by definition, involve the overthrow of an existing government
(B) too few revolutions are available for study to yield valid conclusions
(C) details about a revolution are generally only known to a few key participants
(D) historical events ordinarily involve a large number of unidentified actors
(E) the intentions of the leaders of a revolution cannot be determined

9. The attitude of the author of Passage 1 toward psychology and sociology is one of

(A) skepticism
(B) indifference
(C) confidence
(D) outrage
(E) disappointment

10. Passage 1 is primarily an argument against the position that

(A) revolutions are caused by factors that can be identified
(B) history is not a science like physics or chemistry
(C) science is an undertaking requiring the use of logic
(D) history is more important than the physical sciences
(E) laboratory experiments produce conclusions that are scientifically reliable

GO ON TO THE NEXT PAGE

11. Passage 2 explains that the technique of Verstehen is used to enable the historian to study

    (A) the outside of historical events
    (B) motives and intentions of historical actors
    (C) psychology and sociology
    (D) historical laws
    (E) natural events in a historical context

12. According to Passage 2, any "disappointment" at the failure of general laws to explain historical events (line 84) is due to

    (A) failure to correctly apply the deductive-nomological model
    (B) the inability to make meaningful statements about historical events
    (C) the complexity of historical events when compared to natural occurrences
    (D) inadequate facts to support a legitimate conclusion about the events
    (E) an unreasonable expectation about the universality of natural sciences

13. In line 93, the word "paradigm" most nearly means

    (A) logic
    (B) understanding
    (C) foundation
    (D) model
    (E) goal

14. Which of the following would most likely be a "positivist," as that term is used in line 94?

    (A) the author of Passage 1
    (B) the author of Passage 2
    (C) any natural scientist
    (D) any historical figure
    (E) R. G. Collingwood

15. According to Passage 2, what is the main difference between history and the natural sciences?

    (A) History explains events that have occurred in the past, while natural sciences predict the future.
    (B) The natural sciences produce true knowledge of actual events, while history consists of subjective opinions.
    (C) The natural sciences require the use of logic, while history depends solely upon Verstehen.
    (D) Natural sciences depend upon experimental data, while history relies solely upon recollection.
    (E) The natural sciences study purely physical events, while history is concerned with reasons for human actions.

16. In line 106, the word "fables" most nearly means

    (A) ancient folklore
    (B) moral stories
    (C) fictitious narratives
    (D) plot lines
    (E) misconceptions

17. The author of Passage 1 and the author of Passage 2 would be most likely to agree with which of the following statements?

    (A) Psychology and sociology use the same methodology as the natural sciences.
    (B) Scientific historians should construct their explanations in the same way that the physicist does.
    (C) The inability of historians to conduct laboratory testing shows that history is not a science.
    (D) Syllogistic reasoning is an important tool for historical research.
    (E) Events that have no element of thought are governed by law-like regularities.

GO ON TO THE NEXT PAGE

18. Which statement best expresses the objection that the Passage 2 author would be most likely to make to Hempel's theory of history?

(A) It is incomplete because it fails to include information from disciplines such as psychology and sociology.
(B) It is misguided because it ignores the fact that human actions have a mental as well as a physical component.
(C) It is weak because historians are not able to use experiments to test the validity of their theories.
(D) It is not particularly useful because historical events are too complex to be predicted successfully.
(E) It is incorrect because it relies upon the syllogism, an outmoded form of reasoning.

19. In order to account for what Passage 2 calls the "inside" of a historical event, the author of Passage 1 would most likely refer to

(A) various principles of psychology and sociology
(B) well-known laws of physical science
(C) experiments conducted in a laboratory
(D) documents written by a key actor
(E) authoritative historical writings

10 10 10 10 10 10 10 10 10

Time—10 Minutes
14 Items

For each item in this section, choose the best answer and blacken the corresponding space on the answer sheet.

<u>Directions:</u> The following sentences test correctness and effectiveness of expression. In choosing answers, follow the requirements of standard written English; that is, pay attention to grammar, choice of words, sentence construction, and punctuation.

In each of the following sentences, part of the sentence or the entire sentence is underlined. Beneath each sentence you will find five ways of phrasing the underlined part. Choice A repeats the original; the other four are different.

Choose the answer that best expresses the meaning of the original sentence. If you think the original is better than any of the alternatives, choose it; otherwise choose one of the others. Your choice should produce the most effective sentence—clear and precise, without awkwardness or ambiguity.

Example:

Allen <u>visiting</u> his cousin in France last summer.

(A) visiting
(B) visited
(C) does visit
(D) a visit
(E) is visiting

<u>Answer</u>

Ⓐ ● Ⓒ Ⓓ Ⓔ

---

1. Three hundred years ago, famine was a periodic experience that came so <u>regular that people accepted periods of extreme hunger as normal</u>.

   (A) regular that people accepted periods of extreme hunger as normal
   (B) regularly that people accepted periods of extreme hunger as normal
   (C) regularly that people normally accepted periods of extreme hunger
   (D) regularly as people accepted periods of extreme hunger as normal
   (E) regularly since people accepted periods of extreme hunger as normal

2. The Puritan was composed of two different persons: <u>the one all self-abasement and penitence;</u> the other, proud and inflexible.

   (A) the one all self-abasement and penitence
   (B) one of them all self-abasement and penitence
   (C) the one self-abasing and penitent
   (D) the one self-abasement and penitence
   (E) self-abasing and penitent

GO ON TO THE NEXT PAGE →

3. <u>In 1896, when she began studying the effects of radium</u>, Marie Curie was building on the work of Roentgen and Becquerel.

(A) In 1896, when she began studying the effects of radium
(B) In 1896, beginning to study the effects of radium
(C) Beginning to study the effects of radium in 1896
(D) Since she began to study the effects of radium in 1896
(E) In order to begin to study the effects of radium in 1896

4. <u>Having been forbidden by Church law to marry, it was not unusual for a priest during the Middle Ages to sire a family.</u>

(A) Having been forbidden by Church law to marry, it was not unusual for a priest during the Middle Ages to sire a family.
(B) Forbidden by Church law to marry, it was not unusual for a priest during the Middle Ages to sire a family.
(C) Although they were forbidden by Church law to marry, it was not unusual for a priest during the Middle Ages to sire a family.
(D) Although a priest was forbidden by Church law to marry, it was not unusual for him during the Middle Ages to sire a family.
(E) Although they were forbidden by Church law to marry, it was not unusual for priests during the Middle Ages to sire families.

5. The singing teachers of the old Italian school taught <u>little more but</u> breath control because they believed that with proper breath control, all other technical problems could be easily solved.

(A) little more but
(B) little more than
(C) little more as
(D) more than a little
(E) rather than

6. In the early stages of the development of the common law, <u>equitable remedies were available only in the courts of the Chancery and not in the courts of law, such as injunctions</u>.

(A) equitable remedies were available only in the courts of the Chancery and not in the courts of law, such as injunctions
(B) equitable remedies, such as injunctions, were available only in the courts of the Chancery and not in the courts of law
(C) only equitable remedies, such as injunctions, were available in the courts of Chancery and not in the courts of law
(D) the availability of equitable remedies, such as injunctions, was restricted to the courts of Chancery and not to the courts of law
(E) equitable remedies, such as injunctions, were not available in the courts of law but only in the courts of Chancery

7. These extensive forest reserves must be defended from the acquisitive hands of those whose ruthless axes <u>would destroy the trees and</u> expose the land to the ravages of sun and rain.

(A) would destroy the trees and
(B) will destroy the trees and
(C) would destroy the trees to
(D) would destroy the trees which would
(E) would destroy the trees that could

8. Good American English is simply good English; that of London and Sydney <u>differ no more from</u> Boston and Chicago than the types of houses in which people live.

(A) differ no more from
(B) differs no more from
(C) differ no more than
(D) differs no more from that of
(E) differ no more from those of

GO ON TO THE NEXT PAGE

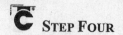

9. Concrete is an artificial engineering material made from a mixture of portland cement, water, fine and coarse aggregates, <u>having a small</u> amount of air.

   (A) having a small
   (B) having added a small
   (C) adding a small
   (D) and a little
   (E) and a small

10. During the Middle Ages, literacy was defined as <u>one who could read and write</u> Latin.

   (A) one who could read and write
   (B) one who would read and write
   (C) reading and writing
   (D) those who could read and write
   (E) the ability to read and write

11. Ballet dancers warm up before each performance by doing a series of pliés and stretching <u>exercises, and it reduces</u> the chance of injury.

   (A) exercises, and it reduces
   (B) exercises, which reduces
   (C) exercises, reducing
   (D) exercises; the routine reduces
   (E) exercises, so the routine reduces

12. An airline may overbook a flight <u>to ensure a full passenger load, but it is required to pay compensation to</u> any passenger who cannot be accommodated on that flight.

   (A) to ensure a full passenger load, but it is required to pay compensation to
   (B) ensuring a full passenger load, but it is required to pay compensation to
   (C) to ensure a full passenger load, since compensation is required to
   (D) to ensure a full passenger load, which is required to pay compensation to
   (E) to ensure a full passenger load and pay compensation

13. It is typical of the high soprano voice, <u>like</u> the highest voices within each vocal range, to be lighter in weight and more flexible.

   (A) like
   (B) as
   (C) like it is of
   (D) as it is of
   (E) similar to

14. After her admission to the bar, <u>Margaret, herself a childless attorney's only daughter</u>, specialized in adoption and family law.

   (A) Margaret, herself a childless attorney's only daughter
   (B) Margaret herself, a childless attorney's only daughter
   (C) Margaret, herself the childless and only daughter of an attorney
   (D) Margaret, only a childless attorney's daughter herself
   (E) Margaret herself, only a daughter of a childless attorney

Practice Test II

CAMBRIDGE
EDUCATIONAL SERVICES®

EDUCATORS' #1 CHOICE FOR SCHOOL IMPROVEMENT

Cambridge Course Concept Outline
PRACTICE TEST II

When completing Practice Test II, use the Essay Response and Bubble Sheets beginning on page 689, unless otherwise directed by your instructor.

Name: _____   Date: _____

Student ID Number: _____

PRACTICE TEST II

Section 1

Begin your essay on this page. If you need more space, continue on the next page.

_____

_____

_____

_____

_____

_____

_____

_____

_____

_____

_____

_____

_____

_____

_____

_____

_____

_____

_____

_____

_____

_____

_____

_____

_____

_____

_____

Name: _____   Date: _____

Student ID Number: _____

PRACTICE TEST II

Start with number 1 for each new section. If a section has fewer questions than answer spaces, leave the extra answer spaces blank. Be sure to erase any errors or stray marks completely.

Section 2

1 Ⓐ Ⓑ Ⓒ Ⓓ Ⓔ	10 Ⓐ Ⓑ Ⓒ Ⓓ Ⓔ	19 Ⓐ Ⓑ Ⓒ Ⓓ Ⓔ	28 Ⓐ Ⓑ Ⓒ Ⓓ Ⓔ
2 Ⓐ Ⓑ Ⓒ Ⓓ Ⓔ	11 Ⓐ Ⓑ Ⓒ Ⓓ Ⓔ	20 Ⓐ Ⓑ Ⓒ Ⓓ Ⓔ	29 Ⓐ Ⓑ Ⓒ Ⓓ Ⓔ
3 Ⓐ Ⓑ Ⓒ Ⓓ Ⓔ	12 Ⓐ Ⓑ Ⓒ Ⓓ Ⓔ	21 Ⓐ Ⓑ Ⓒ Ⓓ Ⓔ	30 Ⓐ Ⓑ Ⓒ Ⓓ Ⓔ
4 Ⓐ Ⓑ Ⓒ Ⓓ Ⓔ	13 Ⓐ Ⓑ Ⓒ Ⓓ Ⓔ	22 Ⓐ Ⓑ Ⓒ Ⓓ Ⓔ	31 Ⓐ Ⓑ Ⓒ Ⓓ Ⓔ
5 Ⓐ Ⓑ Ⓒ Ⓓ Ⓔ	14 Ⓐ Ⓑ Ⓒ Ⓓ Ⓔ	23 Ⓐ Ⓑ Ⓒ Ⓓ Ⓔ	32 Ⓐ Ⓑ Ⓒ Ⓓ Ⓔ
6 Ⓐ Ⓑ Ⓒ Ⓓ Ⓔ	15 Ⓐ Ⓑ Ⓒ Ⓓ Ⓔ	24 Ⓐ Ⓑ Ⓒ Ⓓ Ⓔ	33 Ⓐ Ⓑ Ⓒ Ⓓ Ⓔ
7 Ⓐ Ⓑ Ⓒ Ⓓ Ⓔ	16 Ⓐ Ⓑ Ⓒ Ⓓ Ⓔ	25 Ⓐ Ⓑ Ⓒ Ⓓ Ⓔ	34 Ⓐ Ⓑ Ⓒ Ⓓ Ⓔ
8 Ⓐ Ⓑ Ⓒ Ⓓ Ⓔ	17 Ⓐ Ⓑ Ⓒ Ⓓ Ⓔ	26 Ⓐ Ⓑ Ⓒ Ⓓ Ⓔ	35 Ⓐ Ⓑ Ⓒ Ⓓ Ⓔ
9 Ⓐ Ⓑ Ⓒ Ⓓ Ⓔ	18 Ⓐ Ⓑ Ⓒ Ⓓ Ⓔ	27 Ⓐ Ⓑ Ⓒ Ⓓ Ⓔ	36 Ⓐ Ⓑ Ⓒ Ⓓ Ⓔ

Section 3

1 Ⓐ Ⓑ Ⓒ Ⓓ Ⓔ	10 Ⓐ Ⓑ Ⓒ Ⓓ Ⓔ	19 Ⓐ Ⓑ Ⓒ Ⓓ Ⓔ	28 Ⓐ Ⓑ Ⓒ Ⓓ Ⓔ
2 Ⓐ Ⓑ Ⓒ Ⓓ Ⓔ	11 Ⓐ Ⓑ Ⓒ Ⓓ Ⓔ	20 Ⓐ Ⓑ Ⓒ Ⓓ Ⓔ	29 Ⓐ Ⓑ Ⓒ Ⓓ Ⓔ
3 Ⓐ Ⓑ Ⓒ Ⓓ Ⓔ	12 Ⓐ Ⓑ Ⓒ Ⓓ Ⓔ	21 Ⓐ Ⓑ Ⓒ Ⓓ Ⓔ	30 Ⓐ Ⓑ Ⓒ Ⓓ Ⓔ
4 Ⓐ Ⓑ Ⓒ Ⓓ Ⓔ	13 Ⓐ Ⓑ Ⓒ Ⓓ Ⓔ	22 Ⓐ Ⓑ Ⓒ Ⓓ Ⓔ	31 Ⓐ Ⓑ Ⓒ Ⓓ Ⓔ
5 Ⓐ Ⓑ Ⓒ Ⓓ Ⓔ	14 Ⓐ Ⓑ Ⓒ Ⓓ Ⓔ	23 Ⓐ Ⓑ Ⓒ Ⓓ Ⓔ	32 Ⓐ Ⓑ Ⓒ Ⓓ Ⓔ
6 Ⓐ Ⓑ Ⓒ Ⓓ Ⓔ	15 Ⓐ Ⓑ Ⓒ Ⓓ Ⓔ	24 Ⓐ Ⓑ Ⓒ Ⓓ Ⓔ	33 Ⓐ Ⓑ Ⓒ Ⓓ Ⓔ
7 Ⓐ Ⓑ Ⓒ Ⓓ Ⓔ	16 Ⓐ Ⓑ Ⓒ Ⓓ Ⓔ	25 Ⓐ Ⓑ Ⓒ Ⓓ Ⓔ	34 Ⓐ Ⓑ Ⓒ Ⓓ Ⓔ
8 Ⓐ Ⓑ Ⓒ Ⓓ Ⓔ	17 Ⓐ Ⓑ Ⓒ Ⓓ Ⓔ	26 Ⓐ Ⓑ Ⓒ Ⓓ Ⓔ	35 Ⓐ Ⓑ Ⓒ Ⓓ Ⓔ
9 Ⓐ Ⓑ Ⓒ Ⓓ Ⓔ	18 Ⓐ Ⓑ Ⓒ Ⓓ Ⓔ	27 Ⓐ Ⓑ Ⓒ Ⓓ Ⓔ	36 Ⓐ Ⓑ Ⓒ Ⓓ Ⓔ

Section 4/5

1 Ⓐ Ⓑ Ⓒ Ⓓ Ⓔ	10 Ⓐ Ⓑ Ⓒ Ⓓ Ⓔ	19 Ⓐ Ⓑ Ⓒ Ⓓ Ⓔ	28 Ⓐ Ⓑ Ⓒ Ⓓ Ⓔ
2 Ⓐ Ⓑ Ⓒ Ⓓ Ⓔ	11 Ⓐ Ⓑ Ⓒ Ⓓ Ⓔ	20 Ⓐ Ⓑ Ⓒ Ⓓ Ⓔ	29 Ⓐ Ⓑ Ⓒ Ⓓ Ⓔ
3 Ⓐ Ⓑ Ⓒ Ⓓ Ⓔ	12 Ⓐ Ⓑ Ⓒ Ⓓ Ⓔ	21 Ⓐ Ⓑ Ⓒ Ⓓ Ⓔ	30 Ⓐ Ⓑ Ⓒ Ⓓ Ⓔ
4 Ⓐ Ⓑ Ⓒ Ⓓ Ⓔ	13 Ⓐ Ⓑ Ⓒ Ⓓ Ⓔ	22 Ⓐ Ⓑ Ⓒ Ⓓ Ⓔ	31 Ⓐ Ⓑ Ⓒ Ⓓ Ⓔ
5 Ⓐ Ⓑ Ⓒ Ⓓ Ⓔ	14 Ⓐ Ⓑ Ⓒ Ⓓ Ⓔ	23 Ⓐ Ⓑ Ⓒ Ⓓ Ⓔ	32 Ⓐ Ⓑ Ⓒ Ⓓ Ⓔ
6 Ⓐ Ⓑ Ⓒ Ⓓ Ⓔ	15 Ⓐ Ⓑ Ⓒ Ⓓ Ⓔ	24 Ⓐ Ⓑ Ⓒ Ⓓ Ⓔ	33 Ⓐ Ⓑ Ⓒ Ⓓ Ⓔ
7 Ⓐ Ⓑ Ⓒ Ⓓ Ⓔ	16 Ⓐ Ⓑ Ⓒ Ⓓ Ⓔ	25 Ⓐ Ⓑ Ⓒ Ⓓ Ⓔ	34 Ⓐ Ⓑ Ⓒ Ⓓ Ⓔ
8 Ⓐ Ⓑ Ⓒ Ⓓ Ⓔ	17 Ⓐ Ⓑ Ⓒ Ⓓ Ⓔ	26 Ⓐ Ⓑ Ⓒ Ⓓ Ⓔ	35 Ⓐ Ⓑ Ⓒ Ⓓ Ⓔ
9 Ⓐ Ⓑ Ⓒ Ⓓ Ⓔ	18 Ⓐ Ⓑ Ⓒ Ⓓ Ⓔ	27 Ⓐ Ⓑ Ⓒ Ⓓ Ⓔ	36 Ⓐ Ⓑ Ⓒ Ⓓ Ⓔ

Section 5/6

1 Ⓐ Ⓑ Ⓒ Ⓓ Ⓔ	10 Ⓐ Ⓑ Ⓒ Ⓓ Ⓔ	19 Ⓐ Ⓑ Ⓒ Ⓓ Ⓔ	28 Ⓐ Ⓑ Ⓒ Ⓓ Ⓔ
2 Ⓐ Ⓑ Ⓒ Ⓓ Ⓔ	11 Ⓐ Ⓑ Ⓒ Ⓓ Ⓔ	20 Ⓐ Ⓑ Ⓒ Ⓓ Ⓔ	29 Ⓐ Ⓑ Ⓒ Ⓓ Ⓔ
3 Ⓐ Ⓑ Ⓒ Ⓓ Ⓔ	12 Ⓐ Ⓑ Ⓒ Ⓓ Ⓔ	21 Ⓐ Ⓑ Ⓒ Ⓓ Ⓔ	30 Ⓐ Ⓑ Ⓒ Ⓓ Ⓔ
4 Ⓐ Ⓑ Ⓒ Ⓓ Ⓔ	13 Ⓐ Ⓑ Ⓒ Ⓓ Ⓔ	22 Ⓐ Ⓑ Ⓒ Ⓓ Ⓔ	31 Ⓐ Ⓑ Ⓒ Ⓓ Ⓔ
5 Ⓐ Ⓑ Ⓒ Ⓓ Ⓔ	14 Ⓐ Ⓑ Ⓒ Ⓓ Ⓔ	23 Ⓐ Ⓑ Ⓒ Ⓓ Ⓔ	32 Ⓐ Ⓑ Ⓒ Ⓓ Ⓔ
6 Ⓐ Ⓑ Ⓒ Ⓓ Ⓔ	15 Ⓐ Ⓑ Ⓒ Ⓓ Ⓔ	24 Ⓐ Ⓑ Ⓒ Ⓓ Ⓔ	33 Ⓐ Ⓑ Ⓒ Ⓓ Ⓔ
7 Ⓐ Ⓑ Ⓒ Ⓓ Ⓔ	16 Ⓐ Ⓑ Ⓒ Ⓓ Ⓔ	25 Ⓐ Ⓑ Ⓒ Ⓓ Ⓔ	34 Ⓐ Ⓑ Ⓒ Ⓓ Ⓔ
8 Ⓐ Ⓑ Ⓒ Ⓓ Ⓔ	17 Ⓐ Ⓑ Ⓒ Ⓓ Ⓔ	26 Ⓐ Ⓑ Ⓒ Ⓓ Ⓔ	35 Ⓐ Ⓑ Ⓒ Ⓓ Ⓔ
9 Ⓐ Ⓑ Ⓒ Ⓓ Ⓔ	18 Ⓐ Ⓑ Ⓒ Ⓓ Ⓔ	27 Ⓐ Ⓑ Ⓒ Ⓓ Ⓔ	36 Ⓐ Ⓑ Ⓒ Ⓓ Ⓔ

Section 6/7

1 Ⓐ Ⓑ Ⓒ Ⓓ Ⓔ	10 Ⓐ Ⓑ Ⓒ Ⓓ Ⓔ	19 Ⓐ Ⓑ Ⓒ Ⓓ Ⓔ	28 Ⓐ Ⓑ Ⓒ Ⓓ Ⓔ
2 Ⓐ Ⓑ Ⓒ Ⓓ Ⓔ	11 Ⓐ Ⓑ Ⓒ Ⓓ Ⓔ	20 Ⓐ Ⓑ Ⓒ Ⓓ Ⓔ	29 Ⓐ Ⓑ Ⓒ Ⓓ Ⓔ
3 Ⓐ Ⓑ Ⓒ Ⓓ Ⓔ	12 Ⓐ Ⓑ Ⓒ Ⓓ Ⓔ	21 Ⓐ Ⓑ Ⓒ Ⓓ Ⓔ	30 Ⓐ Ⓑ Ⓒ Ⓓ Ⓔ
4 Ⓐ Ⓑ Ⓒ Ⓓ Ⓔ	13 Ⓐ Ⓑ Ⓒ Ⓓ Ⓔ	22 Ⓐ Ⓑ Ⓒ Ⓓ Ⓔ	31 Ⓐ Ⓑ Ⓒ Ⓓ Ⓔ
5 Ⓐ Ⓑ Ⓒ Ⓓ Ⓔ	14 Ⓐ Ⓑ Ⓒ Ⓓ Ⓔ	23 Ⓐ Ⓑ Ⓒ Ⓓ Ⓔ	32 Ⓐ Ⓑ Ⓒ Ⓓ Ⓔ
6 Ⓐ Ⓑ Ⓒ Ⓓ Ⓔ	15 Ⓐ Ⓑ Ⓒ Ⓓ Ⓔ	24 Ⓐ Ⓑ Ⓒ Ⓓ Ⓔ	33 Ⓐ Ⓑ Ⓒ Ⓓ Ⓔ
7 Ⓐ Ⓑ Ⓒ Ⓓ Ⓔ	16 Ⓐ Ⓑ Ⓒ Ⓓ Ⓔ	25 Ⓐ Ⓑ Ⓒ Ⓓ Ⓔ	34 Ⓐ Ⓑ Ⓒ Ⓓ Ⓔ
8 Ⓐ Ⓑ Ⓒ Ⓓ Ⓔ	17 Ⓐ Ⓑ Ⓒ Ⓓ Ⓔ	26 Ⓐ Ⓑ Ⓒ Ⓓ Ⓔ	35 Ⓐ Ⓑ Ⓒ Ⓓ Ⓔ
9 Ⓐ Ⓑ Ⓒ Ⓓ Ⓔ	18 Ⓐ Ⓑ Ⓒ Ⓓ Ⓔ	27 Ⓐ Ⓑ Ⓒ Ⓓ Ⓔ	36 Ⓐ Ⓑ Ⓒ Ⓓ Ⓔ

Section 7/8

1 Ⓐ Ⓑ Ⓒ Ⓓ Ⓔ	6 Ⓐ Ⓑ Ⓒ Ⓓ Ⓔ	11 Ⓐ Ⓑ Ⓒ Ⓓ Ⓔ	16 Ⓐ Ⓑ Ⓒ Ⓓ Ⓔ
2 Ⓐ Ⓑ Ⓒ Ⓓ Ⓔ	7 Ⓐ Ⓑ Ⓒ Ⓓ Ⓔ	12 Ⓐ Ⓑ Ⓒ Ⓓ Ⓔ	17 Ⓐ Ⓑ Ⓒ Ⓓ Ⓔ
3 Ⓐ Ⓑ Ⓒ Ⓓ Ⓔ	8 Ⓐ Ⓑ Ⓒ Ⓓ Ⓔ	13 Ⓐ Ⓑ Ⓒ Ⓓ Ⓔ	18 Ⓐ Ⓑ Ⓒ Ⓓ Ⓔ
4 Ⓐ Ⓑ Ⓒ Ⓓ Ⓔ	9 Ⓐ Ⓑ Ⓒ Ⓓ Ⓔ	14 Ⓐ Ⓑ Ⓒ Ⓓ Ⓔ	19 Ⓐ Ⓑ Ⓒ Ⓓ Ⓔ
5 Ⓐ Ⓑ Ⓒ Ⓓ Ⓔ	10 Ⓐ Ⓑ Ⓒ Ⓓ Ⓔ	15 Ⓐ Ⓑ Ⓒ Ⓓ Ⓔ	20 Ⓐ Ⓑ Ⓒ Ⓓ Ⓔ

Section 8/9

1 Ⓐ Ⓑ Ⓒ Ⓓ Ⓔ	6 Ⓐ Ⓑ Ⓒ Ⓓ Ⓔ	11 Ⓐ Ⓑ Ⓒ Ⓓ Ⓔ	16 Ⓐ Ⓑ Ⓒ Ⓓ Ⓔ
2 Ⓐ Ⓑ Ⓒ Ⓓ Ⓔ	7 Ⓐ Ⓑ Ⓒ Ⓓ Ⓔ	12 Ⓐ Ⓑ Ⓒ Ⓓ Ⓔ	17 Ⓐ Ⓑ Ⓒ Ⓓ Ⓔ
3 Ⓐ Ⓑ Ⓒ Ⓓ Ⓔ	8 Ⓐ Ⓑ Ⓒ Ⓓ Ⓔ	13 Ⓐ Ⓑ Ⓒ Ⓓ Ⓔ	18 Ⓐ Ⓑ Ⓒ Ⓓ Ⓔ
4 Ⓐ Ⓑ Ⓒ Ⓓ Ⓔ	9 Ⓐ Ⓑ Ⓒ Ⓓ Ⓔ	14 Ⓐ Ⓑ Ⓒ Ⓓ Ⓔ	19 Ⓐ Ⓑ Ⓒ Ⓓ Ⓔ
5 Ⓐ Ⓑ Ⓒ Ⓓ Ⓔ	10 Ⓐ Ⓑ Ⓒ Ⓓ Ⓔ	15 Ⓐ Ⓑ Ⓒ Ⓓ Ⓔ	20 Ⓐ Ⓑ Ⓒ Ⓓ Ⓔ

Section 10

1 Ⓐ Ⓑ Ⓒ Ⓓ Ⓔ	6 Ⓐ Ⓑ Ⓒ Ⓓ Ⓔ	11 Ⓐ Ⓑ Ⓒ Ⓓ Ⓔ	16 Ⓐ Ⓑ Ⓒ Ⓓ Ⓔ
2 Ⓐ Ⓑ Ⓒ Ⓓ Ⓔ	7 Ⓐ Ⓑ Ⓒ Ⓓ Ⓔ	12 Ⓐ Ⓑ Ⓒ Ⓓ Ⓔ	17 Ⓐ Ⓑ Ⓒ Ⓓ Ⓔ
3 Ⓐ Ⓑ Ⓒ Ⓓ Ⓔ	8 Ⓐ Ⓑ Ⓒ Ⓓ Ⓔ	13 Ⓐ Ⓑ Ⓒ Ⓓ Ⓔ	18 Ⓐ Ⓑ Ⓒ Ⓓ Ⓔ
4 Ⓐ Ⓑ Ⓒ Ⓓ Ⓔ	9 Ⓐ Ⓑ Ⓒ Ⓓ Ⓔ	14 Ⓐ Ⓑ Ⓒ Ⓓ Ⓔ	19 Ⓐ Ⓑ Ⓒ Ⓓ Ⓔ
5 Ⓐ Ⓑ Ⓒ Ⓓ Ⓔ	10 Ⓐ Ⓑ Ⓒ Ⓓ Ⓔ	15 Ⓐ Ⓑ Ⓒ Ⓓ Ⓔ	20 Ⓐ Ⓑ Ⓒ Ⓓ Ⓔ

Student-Produced Responses

Only answers entered in the circles in each grid will be scored. You will not receive credit for anything written in the boxes above the circles.

9   10   11   12   13

14   15   16   17   18

1 1 1 1 1 1 1 1 1 1 1 1 1

Time—25 Minutes 1 Essay	Think carefully about the issue presented in the following excerpt and the assignment below.

DIRECTIONS: You have 25 minutes to plan and write an essay on the topic assigned below. DO NOT WRITE ON ANY OTHER TOPIC. AN ESSAY ON ANOTHER TOPIC IS NOT ACCEPTABLE. Think carefully about the issue presented in the following excerpt and the assignment below.

Stockbrokers in New York can trade on the London Stock Exchange as easily as they can on Wall Street. Scrap metal from an alley in Chicago is helping fuel a boom in China. The world is shrinking because of advances in transportation and communication. This allows for increased trade, stronger world and local economies, and less poverty on a global scale—all extremely positive effects of a global economy.

Globalization has some positive benefits, but the negatives far outweigh these. For one, globalization has led to a loss of native and indigenous cultures. Tribes in Brazil's Amazon rain forest are being forced out of their ancestral lands because of the world's insatiable demand for building materials and land for crops or livestock. Keeping up with a world market has bankrupted countries that cannot keep up leading to famine and political unrest.

Assignment: Have globalization's positive or negative effects been dominate? Plan and write an essay in which you develop your point of view on this issue. Support your position with reasoning and examples taken from your reading, studies, experience, and observations.

IF YOU FINISH BEFORE TIME IS CALLED, YOU MAY CHECK YOUR WORK ON THIS TEST ONLY. DO NOT WORK ON ANY OTHER TEST SECTION. **STOP**

2 2 2 2 2 2 2 2 2 2 2 2

Time—25 Minutes 18 Items	In this section, solve each item, using any available space on the page for scratchwork. Then, decide which is the best of the choices given and fill in the corresponding oval on the answer sheet.

Notes: The figures accompanying the items are drawn as accurately as possible unless otherwise stated in specific items. Again, unless otherwise stated, all figures lie in the same plane. All numbers used in these items are real numbers. Calculators are permitted for this test.

Reference:

Circle: Rectangle: Rectangular   Cylinder: Triangle:
                                     Solid:

$C = 2\pi r$ $A = lw$ $V = lwh$ $V = \pi r^2 h$ $A = \frac{1}{2}bh$ $a^2 + b^2 = c^2$

$A = \pi r^2$

- The measure in degrees of a straight angle is 180.
- The number of degrees of arc in a circle is 360.
- The sum of the measure of the angles of a triangle is 180.

---

1. If the average (arithmetic mean) of 5, 5, 10, 12, and x is equal to x, what is the value of x?

    (A) 6
    (B) 8
    (C) 10
    (D) 12
    (E) 16

    $$\frac{5 + 5 + 10 + 12 + x}{6}$$
    $$= x$$

2. If $(3x + 3)(3x + 3) = 0$, what are all the possible values of x?

    (A) -1 only
    (B) 1/3 only
    (C) -1 and 1 only
    (D) 3 only
    (E) -3 and 3 only

    $(3(-1) + 3)(3(-1) + 3)$
    $(-3 + 3)(-3 + 3)$
    $(0)(0)$
    0

GO ON TO THE NEXT PAGE

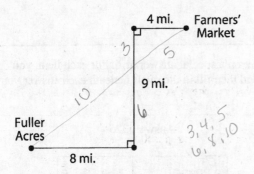

4 mi.   Farmers'
Market

9 mi.

Fuller
Acres

8 mi.

3. The figure above shows the roads that connect Fuller Acres with Farmers' Market. If there existed a direct and straight path from Fuller Acres to Farmers' Market, how much shorter, in miles, would the trip be from Fuller Acres to Farmers' Market?

(A) 1
(B) 3
(C) 4
(D) 6
(E) 8

4. Let $[x]$ be defined as $[x] = x^2 + x$ for all values of x. If $[n] = [n+2]$, what is the value of n?

(A) -3/2
(B) -2/3
(C) 2/3
(D) 2
(E) 3

$[(n+2)^2 + (n+2)]$

plug in answers

5. If $\frac{13t}{7}$ is an integer, then t could be any of the following EXCEPT

(A) -91
(B) -7
(C) 3
(D) 70
(E) 91

6. If $\frac{(x+y)}{x} = 4$ and $\frac{(y+z)}{z} = 5$, what is the value of $\frac{x}{z}$?

(A) $\frac{1}{4}$
(B) $\frac{1}{3}$
(C) $\frac{3}{4}$
(D) $\frac{4}{3}$
(E) $\frac{3}{1}$

$\frac{(x+y)}{x} = 4$ $\frac{(y+z)}{z} = 5$

$4x = x + y$ $5z = y + z$
$\quad -x \quad -x$

$3x = y$ $4z = y$

$x = y/3$ $z = \frac{y}{4}$

$\frac{x}{z}$ $\frac{y/3}{y/4}$ $\frac{y}{3} \cdot \frac{4}{y}$ $\boxed{\frac{4}{3}}$

7. On Monday, Juan withdraws $\frac{1}{2}$ of the money in his savings account. On Tuesday, he withdraws another $60, leaving $\frac{1}{5}$ of the original amount in the account. How much money was originally in Juan's savings account?

(A) $600
(B) $300
(C) $200
(D) $150
(E) $120

8. A painter is planning to paint a row of three houses, using the colors red, gray, and white. If each house is to be painted a single color, and if the painter must use each of the three colors, how many different ways are there of painting the three houses?

(A) 1
(B) 2
(C) 3
(D) 6
(E) 9

GO ON TO THE NEXT PAGE

Directions for Student-Produced Responses Items

Items 9-18 each require you to solve an item and mark your answer on a special answer grid. For each item, you should write your answer in the boxes at the top of each column and then fill in the ovals beneath each answer you write. Here are some examples.

Answer: 3/4 or .75
(show answer either way)

Answer: 325

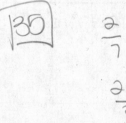

Note: A mixed number such as $3\frac{1}{2}$ must be gridded as 7/2 or as 3.5. If gridded as "31/2," it will be read as "thirty-one halves."

Note: Either position is correct.

9. If $x = 2$, then $x^2 - 2x =$

$x = 2$

$2^2 - 2(2) =$

$4 - 2(2) =$

$4 - 4 = 0$

$\boxed{0}$

10. If 2 pounds of coffee make exactly 7 pots of coffee, how many pots of coffee can be made from a 10-pound bag of coffee?

$\boxed{35}$

$\dfrac{2}{7} = \dfrac{10}{x}$

$\dfrac{2x}{2} = \dfrac{70}{2}$

$x = 35$

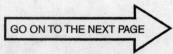 GO ON TO THE NEXT PAGE

11. If roses cost $1.00 each and carnations cost $0.50 each, how many more carnations than roses can be purchased for $10.00?

$1.00 R 10
$0.50 C 20

10 more.

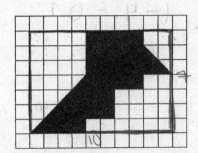

12. In the figure above, each of the small squares has a side of length 1. What is the area of the shaded region?

30

13. If $(x + y)^2 = (x - y)^2 + 4$, then $xy =$

$(x+y)(x+y) = (x-y)(x-y) + 4$
$x^2 + 2xy + y^2 = x^2 - 2xy + y^2 + 4$
$4xy = 4$
$\boxed{xy = 1}$

14. If the points (-3,-3), (-2, 2), and (3,-3) are the vertices of a triangle, what is the area of the triangle?

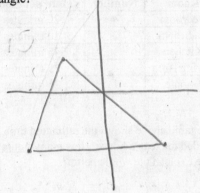

15

GO ON TO THE NEXT PAGE

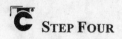

15. What is the smallest of 5 consecutive integers if the sum of the integers is 55?

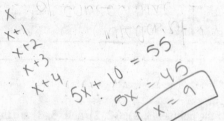

x
$x+1$
$x+2$
$x+3$
$x+4$ $5x+10=55$
$5x=45$
$x=9$

ESTIMATED TIME OF CLEANING

Room	Number	Time per Room
Bedroom	4	20 minutes
Bathroom	2	30 minutes
Kitchen	1	45 minutes
Living Area	4	25 minutes
Garage	1	75 minutes

16. The table above shows the estimated time by area needed to clean a house. How many <u>hours</u> will it take to clean the whole house?

$20+20+20+20 = 80$
$30+30 = 60$
45
$25+25+25+25 = 100$
75 $360 \div 60 = 6$
$\boxed{6 \text{ hours}}$

17. If $f(x) = 2x - 5$ and $g(x) = x - 2$, for what value of x does $f(x) = g(x)$?

$2x - 5 = x - 2$
$-x \quad\quad -x$
$x - 5 = -2$
$+5 \quad +5$
$\boxed{x = 3}$

18. If the slope of the line that passes through the points $(x, 0)$ and $(3, -4)$ is 2, what is the value of x?

$\dfrac{\Delta y}{\Delta x}$

$\dfrac{(-4 - 0)}{(3 - x)} = \dfrac{2}{1}$

$-4 - 0 = 6 - 2x$
$-4 = 6 - 2x$
$+2x \quad\quad +2x$
$2x - 4 = 6$
$+4 \quad +4$
$\dfrac{2x}{2} = \dfrac{10}{2}$
$\boxed{x = 5}$

IF YOU FINISH BEFORE TIME IS CALLED, YOU MAY CHECK YOUR WORK ON THIS TEST ONLY. DO NOT WORK ON ANY OTHER TEST SECTION.   **STOP**

3 3 3 3 3 3 3 3 3 3 3 3

Time—25 Minutes 35 Items	For each item in this section, choose the best answer and blacken the corresponding space on the answer sheet.

Directions: The following sentences test correctness and effectiveness of expression. In choosing answers, follow the requirements of standard written English; that is, pay attention to grammar, choice of words, sentence construction, and punctuation.

In each of the following sentences, part of the sentence or the entire sentence is underlined. Beneath each sentence you will find five ways of phrasing the underlined part. Choice A repeats the original; the other four are different.

Choose the answer that best expresses the meaning of the original sentence. If you think the original is better than any of the alternatives, choose it; otherwise choose one of the others. Your choice should produce the most effective sentence—clear and precise, without awkwardness or ambiguity.

Example: Answer

Allen <u>visiting</u> his cousin in France last summer.

(A) visiting
(B) visited
(C) does visit
(D) a visit
(E) is visiting

Ⓐ ● Ⓒ Ⓓ Ⓔ

1. Personal style depends not so much on the actual clothing you wear <u>but one's choice of</u> items such as jewelry and make-up.

   (A) but one's choice of
   (B) but one's choosing
   (C) but your choice of
   (D) as your choice of
   (E) as your choosing

2. Kevin has been accepted by the nation's top engineering school, but <u>the tuition cannot be afforded by his family</u>.

   (A) the tuition cannot be afforded by his family
   (B) his family cannot afford to do so
   (C) his family cannot afford to pay the tuition
   (D) his family cannot afford to do it
   (E) affording the tuition is something his family cannot do

3. In Irish step dancing, the peculiar juxtaposition of the rigid torso and arms with rapidly tapping feet <u>is attributed to</u> the concern of parish priests about overly sensual displays.

   (A) is attributed to
   (B) are attributed to
   (C) is attributable for
   (D) attributed to
   (E) attribute

GO ON TO THE NEXT PAGE

4. One of the thrills of bird-watching is catching a fleeting glimpse of <u>a very rare specimen including the Northern Bobwhite or</u> the Red-shouldered Hawk.

   (A) a very rare specimen including the Northern Bobwhite or
   (B) a very rare specimen such as the Northern Bobwhite or
   (C) a very rare specimen such as the Northern Bobwhite and
   (D) very rare specimens including the Northern Bobwhite or
   (E) very rare specimens such as the Northern Bobwhite or

5. The cause of the declining number of frogs in the swamp is <u>unknown, nor is it known</u> why amphibians in the area exhibit congenital malformations.

   (A) unknown, nor is it known
   (B) unknown, neither do they know
   (C) not known, nor do they know
   (D) not known, unknown too is
   (E) not known, neither do they

GO ON TO THE NEXT PAGE

6. <u>Being called</u> etymology, the study of word
   A

<u>origins</u> can provide archaeologists with
   B

information <u>about</u> the migration of <u>ancient</u>
        C   D

populations. <u>No error</u>
        E

7. The <u>most important</u> of <u>all</u> economic indicators of
     A   B

prosperity and growth <u>in</u> a given region <u>are</u> new
             C   D

construction. <u>No error</u>
        E

8. The <u>development</u> of new software tools <u>made</u> it
    A   B

possible to communicate <u>easy</u> over the internet,
             C

and now virtually everyone <u>is</u> connected to the
                 D

web. <u>No error</u>
    E

9. Of the many environmental problems <u>threatening</u>
                  A

animals and plants on various endangered species

<u>lists</u>, destruction of habitat by humans <u>is</u> usually
 B   C

the <u>greatest</u>. <u>No error</u>
   D   E

GO ON TO THE NEXT PAGE

10. <u>By studying</u> the observed color shift of light
  A
emitted by stars, astronomers <u>can determine</u> the
          B
speed <u>at which</u> a galaxy <u>is</u> traveling. <u>No error</u>
   C   D   E

11. Large-scale withdrawal of savings from banks

<u>occur</u> <u>when</u> interest rates offered by banks <u>are</u> not
 A B   C
competitive with financial returns

<u>on other investments</u> and savers look for higher
   D
returns elsewhere. <u>No error</u>
       E

12. The runners from the Downtown Athletic Club

<u>who</u> competed in Monday's track meet <u>were</u> not
 A   B
only faster <u>but</u> better conditioned than
    C
<u>the Greater City Track Club</u>. <u>No error</u>
   D   E

13. The Democrats and the Republicans now

<u>dominate</u> the political landscape of <u>America, but</u>
 A   B
European democracies <u>have</u> numerous smaller
        C
<u>ones</u>. <u>No error</u>
 D E

14. <u>Ceremonial</u> versions of the flag of the United
  A
States <u>are</u> <u>trimmed</u> <u>with</u> a decorative fringe
   B   C
<u>resembling some</u> oriental rugs. <u>No error</u>
   D   E

15. A subsidiary of a large corporation <u>that becomes</u>
              A
an independent company may initially be <u>less</u>
               B
profitable because <u>it</u> must cover expenses
       C
<u>formally</u> paid by the parent corporation. <u>No error</u>
 D   E

16. <u>In order to</u> be effective as a team, <u>both oxen</u> in a
 A   B
yoke <u>must pull</u> in the same direction with
   C
<u>approximate</u> equal force. <u>No error</u>
 D   E

17. <u>Not only</u> is the Granny Smith apple <u>among</u> the
 A   B
most versatile apples produced today, but <u>they are</u>
              C
<u>also</u> among the most widely cultivated. <u>No error</u>
 D   E

18. An olive, when picked from the <u>trees</u>, <u>is</u> not
         A B
edible and must first <u>be cured</u> in brine or lye
       C
before it <u>can be eaten</u>. <u>No error</u>
   D   E

19. Abraham Lincoln, <u>largely</u> on the strength of <u>their</u>
       A   B
performance in the famous Lincoln-Douglas
debates, <u>became known</u> as one of the greatest
    C
orators <u>in</u> American history. <u>No error</u>
   D   E

20. Monkfish is sometimes <u>called</u> the "poor man's
        A
lobster" <u>because</u> the texture and taste of the fish
   B
<u>resemble</u> the <u>more expensive crustacean</u>.
 C   D
<u>No error</u>
 E

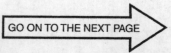

21. After <u>everyone</u> had been eliminated from the
        A

    contest except <u>Jim and I</u>, the judge <u>announced</u> a
                    B   C

    ten-minute break <u>before the final round</u> would
                        D

    begin. <u>No error</u>
            E

22. After <u>decisively</u> winning several crucial battles
        A

    during the early part of the war, the general

    <u>was appointed</u> commander of the entire combined
        B

    armed forces, but he <u>was</u> less successful as a
                            C

    commanding general <u>than his earlier campaigns</u>.
                            D

    <u>No error</u>
        E

23. In 1970, the United States <u>passed</u> a law <u>required</u>
                                  A   B

    all men eighteen years <u>or older</u> <u>to register</u> with
                            C   D

    the Selective Service System. <u>No error</u>
                                    E

24. <u>During</u> the Golden Age of the City College of
        A

    New York, when the school <u>produced</u>
                                B

    <u>several Nobel Prize winners</u>, seven out of every
        C

    ten students enrolled at the school <u>had been born</u>
                                            D

    outside the United States. <u>No error</u>
                                    E

25. George Gershwin <u>composed</u> the soundtracks for
                        A

    several <u>films</u>, <u>including</u> *Shall We Dance*, <u>which</u>
            B   C   D

    his brother, Ira, wrote the lyrics. <u>No error</u>
                                        E

GO ON TO THE NEXT PAGE

Directions: The following passages are early drafts of essays. Some parts of the passages need to be rewritten.

Read the passages and answer the items that follow. Some items are about particular sentences or parts of sentences and ask you to improve sentence structure and word choice. Other items refer to parts of the essays or the entire essays and ask you to consider organization and development. In making your decisions, follow the conventions of standard written English. After you have chosen your answer, fill in the corresponding oval on your answer sheet.

Items 26 - 30 refer to the following passage.

(1) Uranus is a strange planet. (2) It lies tipped over on its side. (3) Instead of spinning like a top, it rolls like a ball along the path of its orbit. (4) The geographic poles are located on either side, one pointing toward the Sun and the other pointing away. (5) The clouds in the Uranian atmosphere move in the same direction that the planet rotates.

(6) The moons of Uranus are equally as strange. (7) Miranda, the one closest to the planet, has huge markings where terrains of totally different types appear to have been jammed together. (8) On Ariel, the next moon out, the landscape has huge faults; however, there is no evidence of any geologic activity on Ariel. (9) Umbriel, the third moon, seems to be painted with a dark substance. (10) On one side is the "doughnut," it being a bright, round indentation caused by the impact of a large object. (11) Between the orbit of Miranda and the planet's surface are up to one hundred charcoal-colored rings, ringlets, and bands of dust.

(12) Like the clouds in the planet's atmosphere, they circle Uranus in the same direction as the planet rotates. (13) That is, they orbit over the top and bottom of the planet rather than around the sides, as the Earth's atmosphere does.

(14) Scientists are confident that they will discover additional planets in our Solar System. (15) Until they do it, Uranus will remain the strangest of all.

26. The sentence that best states the main idea of the passage is

(A) sentence 1
(B) sentence 5
(C) sentence 6
(D) sentence 8
(E) sentence 15

27. In context, which of the following is the best version of sentence 4 (reproduced below)?
The geographic poles are located on either side, one pointing toward the Sun and the other pointing away.

(A) (As it is now.)
(B) Located on either side, the geographic poles are pointing, one toward the Sun and the other away.
(C) On either side, the geographic poles are located pointing toward the Sun or away.
(D) The geographic poles are pointing toward and away from the Sun with one being on each side.
(E) Pointing toward the Sun and away from it are the geographic poles located on either side.

28. In the context of the second paragraph, which revision is most needed in sentence 10?

(A) Insert "Nevertheless" at the beginning.
(B) Omit the phrase "the impact of."
(C) Omit the words "it being."
(D) Change the first comma to a semicolon.
(E) Insert "was" before the word "caused."

GO ON TO THE NEXT PAGE

29. Which of the following revisions would most improve the organization of paragraphs two and three?

   (A) Make a new paragraph following sentence 7.
   (B) Make a new paragraph following sentence 9.
   (C) Make sentence 11 the first sentence of paragraph three.
   (D) Make sentence 12 the last sentence of paragraph two.
   (E) Combine paragraphs two and three.

30. Which of the following is the best version of the underlined portion of sentence 15 (reproduced below)?

   Until they do it, Uranus will remain the strangest of all.

   (A) (As it is now.)
   (B) Until the discovery, Uranus
   (C) Until others are discovered, Uranus
   (D) Regardless of it, Uranus
   (E) Regardless of that, Uranus

Items 31 - 35 refer to the following passage.

(1) Do you like music, art, sports or some similar activity? (2) Then you would enjoy stamp collecting. (3) Stamps offer a look at the major cultural trends that shape our world. (4) Plus they honor individual artists, musicians, athletes, and others whose have made important contributions to their fields.

(5) It's easy to start a stamp collection. (6) Simply save stamps from letters, packages and postcards, and ask friends and family to save stamps from their mail. (8) Neighborhood businesses that get a lot of mail might save their envelopes for you, too.

(9) At some point in your collecting, you'll find an old stamp and wonder whether it might be valuable. (10) That depends on how rare the stamp is and what condition it is in.

(11) Then, as to condition, a cancelled stamp is one which has been through the postal system and bears a postmark. (12) Cancelled stamps are usually the least valuable. (13) An unused stamp has no cancellation but may not have any gum on the back. (14) A stamp in mint condition is the same as it was when purchased from the post office. (15) Mint stamps are usually worth more than unused stamps.

(16) You probably will not find a rare stamp on an envelope that has just been through the mail, but you might find one in the attic or garage in a box with old records and papers. (17) Even if you don't find a stamp that is worth a lot of money, you are sure to have a good time looking for them.

31. The function of sentence 1 is to

   (A) ask a rhetorical question to get the reader's attention
   (B) tell the reader the order in which topics will appear
   (C) inform the reader what position the author will take
   (D) show puzzlement about various cultural activities
   (E) assure the reader that the topic is a suitable one

GO ON TO THE NEXT PAGE

32. In context, sentence 10 could be made more precise by changing

    (A) "that" to "which"
    (B) "that" to "value"
    (C) "that" to "collecting"
    (D) "it" to "they"
    (E) "it" to "them"

33. Which of the following would be the most suitable sentence to insert immediately after sentence 10?

    (A) The value of items such as paintings and books as well as stamps depends on how rare they are.
    (B) Commemorative stamps are issued by the Post Office to celebrate a particular event such as the first moon landing.
    (C) You can get an idea of how rare the stamp is by consulting a buyer's guide at your local library.
    (D) The most valuable stamps are usually sold at auction to wealthy collectors.
    (E) The first postage stamp issued by the United States was a five cent stamp showing Benjamin Franklin.

34. Of the following, which is the best version of sentence 12 (reproduced below)?

Cancelled stamps are usually the least valuable.

    (A) (As it is now.)
    (B) Cancelled stamps are usually the less valuable.
    (C) Cancelled stamps are usually less valuable than the others.
    (D) Of other stamps, cancelled ones are usually less valuable.
    (E) Of all stamps, cancelled ones are usually less valuable.

35. In the context of the final paragraph, which revision is most needed in sentence 17?

    (A) Change "them" to "one."
    (B) Change "them" to "it."
    (C) Change "if" to "though."
    (D) Change "sure" to "surely."
    (E) Omit "Even."

IF YOU FINISH BEFORE TIME IS CALLED, YOU MAY CHECK YOUR WORK ON THIS TEST ONLY. DO NOT WORK ON ANY OTHER TEST SECTION.   **STOP**

–706–

4 4 4 4 4 4 4 4 4 4 4 4

Time—25 Minutes 24 Items	For each item in this section, choose the best answer and blacken the corresponding space on the answer sheet.

Each item below has one or two blanks, each blank indicating that something has been omitted. Beneath the sentence are five lettered words or sets of words. Choose the word or set of words that **best** fits the meaning of the sentence as a whole.

Example:

Although its publicity has been ----, the film itself is intelligent, well acted, handsomely produced, and altogether ----.

(A) tasteless..respectable
(B) extensive..moderate
(C) sophisticated..amateur
(D) risqué..crude
(E) perfect..spectacular   ● Ⓑ Ⓒ Ⓓ Ⓔ

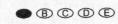

1. Since there are so few conservative thinkers on the committee, their influence on its recommendations is ----.

   (A) monumental
   (B) negligible
   (C) discriminatory
   (D) impractical
   (E) cathartic

2. Laboratory tests that often maim animals and depend solely upon observation to determine results are not only ---- but highly ---- since no two people see the same thing.

   (A) safe..consistent
   (B) patented..conclusive
   (C) controversial..valuable
   (D) gratifying..explosive
   (E) cruel..unreliable

3. Execution by lethal injection, although horrifying, is certainly more civilized than the ---- penalty of death by torture or dismemberment.

   (A) pervasive
   (B) viler
   (C) humane
   (D) prolific
   (E) complacent

4. Although vitamins are helpful for maintaining good health, alcohol, caffeine, and other drugs severely ---- their effectiveness, leaving the body's defenses ----.

   (A) augment..weakened
   (B) reduce..indelible
   (C) inhibit..impaired
   (D) confuse..allied
   (E) duplicate..activated

5. To understand a work of art, it is necessary to place it in ---- context to capture its ---- significance as well as its present meaning.

   (A) a specious..referential
   (B) a random..cumulative
   (C) an inventive..partial
   (D) a historical..original
   (E) a sophisticated..international

6. The victim confronted his attacker in the courtroom calmly, with ---- and without apparent ---- although he had been severely traumatized by the incident.

   (A) woe..composure
   (B) ineptitude..obstinacy
   (C) tempering..philanthropy
   (D) equanimity..rancor
   (E) scorn..malingering

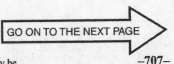
GO ON TO THE NEXT PAGE

7. The politician hungered for power; as a result of his ----, he succeeded in winning the election but ----his closest friends and supporters.

    (A) furtiveness..dissuaded
    (B) winsomeness..disgruntled
    (C) malevolence..mesmerized
    (D) acerbity..seduced
    (E) cupidity..alienated

8. With the evidence ---- from numerous X-ray studies, scientists are beginning to form a picture of the atomic structure of the cell.

    (A) remanded
    (B) gleaned
    (C) pilfered
    (D) atrophied
    (E) implored

Each passage below is followed by one or more items based on its content. Answer the items following each passage on the basis of what is stated or implied in the passage.

Item 9 is based on following passage.

Technology has the potential to help public television better fulfill its mission to provide programming that emphasizes education, innovation, diversity, and local relevance. Multicasting will make
5 available additional channels for thematically linked program series that are designed for specific segments of the population. For example, a channel for Hispanic families will include local, regional, and national programs and services in Spanish as well as English. A
10 discrete children's service will feature an expanded line-up of Ready-to-Learn programs. With enhanced television, viewers with interactive keypads or remote controls will be able to navigate seamlessly through program elements for additional resources, text,
15 graphics, animation, or audio clips. The possibilities are infinite—limited only by producer and educator imaginations.

9. The author's attitude toward the possibility of using technology to improve public television programming is

    (A) untrusting and skeptical
    (B) indifferent and unsupportive
    (C) cautious and noncommittal
    (D) concerned and wary
    (E) optimistic and enthusiastic

GO ON TO THE NEXT PAGE

Item 10 is based on the following passage.

Mayors, though usually nowhere nearly as powerful, are more important to local residents than either a governor or the President. A mayor works in
Line closer physical proximity to citizens than either the
5 governor or the President. City Hall is no farther from home than the grocery store or place of employment, and it is still possible to reach a mayor or at least a staff member by telephone. Moreover, most citizens have seen and even spoken to the mayor, who spends a lot of
10 time in public; and local newspapers often report on the activities of the mayor, nearly all of which take place in the community and concern local residents. The President may be the Commander-in-Chief, but the mayor is the person who makes sure that the garbage is
15 picked up every week.

10. The author refers to garbage collection in the final sentence in order to

   (A) minimize the importance of a mayor's role in international affairs
   (B) remind readers that government should serve the needs of the citizens
   (C) underscore the importance of the mayor's role as a local official
   (D) express skepticism about the ability of local government to function effectively
   (E) clarify the distinction among local, state, and national levels of government

Item 11 is based on the following passage.

About 190 million acres of Federal forest and rangeland in the lower forty-eight States face a high risk of large-scale insect or disease epidemics and
Line catastrophic fire due to deteriorating ecosystem health
5 and drought. While some experts blame the increased risk of catastrophic wildland fire on long-term drought or on expansion of the wildland-urban interface in the Western United States, the underlying cause is the buildup of forest fuel and changes in vegetation composition over the last century. Unnaturally dense
10 stands competing for limited water and nutrients are at increased risk of unnaturally intense wildland fires and insect or disease epidemic.

11. It can be inferred that the author of the passage disagrees with other experts over the

   (A) extent of forest and rangeland that is at risk
   (B) threat posed to forest and rangeland by fire, insects, and disease
   (C) source of the danger to threatened forest and rangeland
   (D) advisability of avoiding insects and disease and unnecessary fires
   (E) cost of implementing a program to save threatened forests and rangeland

GO ON TO THE NEXT PAGE

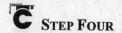

Item 12 is based on the following passage.

Historical records contain relatively few accounts of ship-whale collisions before 1950. It seems unlikely that collisions were ignored, as the few such incidents
Line that were reported were treated as great curiosities. For
5 example, a whale carried into Baltimore harbor by a tanker in 1940 attracted a crowd of 10,000. The low number of collisions recorded before 1950 might be due to three factors: the depleted whale populations caused by commercial overexploitation; limited traffic
10 in areas frequented by whales; and the small number of ships that were large enough to seriously injure or kill an animal the size of whale. Additionally, historical records suggest that ship strikes fatal to whales only first occurred late in the 1800s as ships began to reach
15 speeds of 13 to 15 knots. These strikes remained infrequent until about 1950 and then became more frequent through the 1970s as the speed of ships increased.

12. The author believes that all of the following have contributed to the increased number of ship-whale collisions in modern times EXCEPT

   (A) faster speeds at which modern ships operate
   (B) an increase in the number of ships in whale habitats
   (C) a greater number of large ships
   (D) a resurgence in the population of whales
   (E) a lack of accurate record keeping about collisions

Items 13-14 are based on the following passage.

While the potential benefits of genetic research may seem obvious to the scientific community, it is important to realize that non-scientists may not be
Line aware of these benefits. By being open with
5 communities about the goals and process of their research before it is conducted, scientists can better design studies to yield meaningful data while working within distinct social and cultural contexts. By sharing results with a community after a study has been
10 completed, research participants are more likely to know what to do to seek treatment or how to implement preventive measures to improve their health. In general, well-informed communities that have a window into the research process are likely to
15 maintain a more positive attitude about scientific research—not only about how research is conducted but about what great benefits science can offer humankind.

13. The primary purpose of the passage is to

   (A) suggest some ideas to make genetic research more acceptable to the public
   (B) describe the public health advantages of engaging in genetic research
   (C) outline the negative consequences of invading the privacy of patients
   (D) encourage members of the public to participate in scientific research
   (E) familiarize laypersons with the design of important scientific studies

14. The author implies (lines 8-13) that research participants who are unfamiliar with the results of a scientific study will be

   (A) more likely to work closely with the scientists
   (B) less likely to enjoy health benefits from the study
   (C) better able to participate in the scientific inquiry
   (D) reluctant to volunteer information about personal identity
   (E) adequately prepared to make health care decisions for others

GO ON TO THE NEXT PAGE

Items 15-24 are based on the following passage.

There has been considerable debate on the issue of violence in television and in motion pictures. The following passage explores the question of whether violence in television commercials directed at children is a serious problem.

The violence employed in television commercials directed specifically at children usually appears in the context of fantasy. The impact of the violent portrayals varies according to the number of fantasy cues present in the portrayal. Cartoon violence generally has three such cues (animation, humor, and a remote setting); make-believe violence generally has two cues (humor and a remote setting) and realistic, acted violence generally has only one cue (the viewer's knowledge that the portrayal is fictional).

Most children as young as four years can distinguish these three contexts; however, about one-quarter of four- to eight-year-olds define cartoon violence as a depiction of violence *per se*; about half also perceive make-believe violence in this way; and over half see realistic (acted) violence as violence. Children appear to make these distinctions solely on the basis of the physical fantasy cues. There is no support for the idea that children, especially young children, can differentiate types of violence on a cognitive or rational basis—for example, by justification of the motives for the violent behavior or the goodness of its consequences.

Still, there is very little evidence of direct imitation of television violence by children, though there is evidence that fantasy violence, as well as portrayals of real-life violence, can energize previously learned aggressive responses such as a physical attack on another child during play. It is by no means clear, however, that the violence in a portrayal is solely responsible for this energizing effect. Rather, the evidence suggests that any exciting material triggers subsequent aggressive behavior and that it is the effect of violence that instigates or energizes any subsequent violent behavior.

Moreover, this type of "violent" behavior demonstrated in experiments with children is more likely to reflect either novel play activities or, more typically, a lowering of previously learned play inhibitions, than an increase in socially threatening aggression. In short, cold imitation of violence by children is extremely rare, and the very occasional evidence of direct, imitative associations between television violence and aggressive behavior has been limited to extremely novel and violent acts by teenagers or adults with already established patterns of deviant behavior.

The instigational effect means, in the short term, that exposure to violent portrayals could be dangerous to a child if shortly after the exposure (within 15 to 20 minutes) the child happens to be in a situation that calls for interpersonal aggression as an appropriate response, *e.g.,* an argument between siblings or among peers. This same instigational effect, however, could be produced by other exciting but non-violent television content or by any other excitational source, including, ironically enough, television failure or a parent's turning off the set.

So, there is no convincing causal evidence of any cumulative instigational effects such as more aggressive or violent dispositions in children. In fact, passivity is a more likely long-term result of heavy viewing of television violence. Any instigation of deviant behavior by children seems to be confined to short-term circumstantial effects.

All of this implies that an indictment of fantasy violence in children's programming must rest mainly on a very slight risk that the violent portrayal may be imitated and a somewhat greater risk that the violence may have a short-term instigational effect when circumstances suggest aggression as an appropriate response. The evidence does not warrant the strong conclusions advanced by many critics who tend to use television violence as a scapegoat to draw public attention away from the real causes of violence—causes like abusive spouses and parents and a culture that celebrates violence generally. The violent acts depicted in these television commercials are rarely imitable and the duration of the violence is much too short to have an instigational effect.

15. The primary purpose of the passage is to

   (A) correct a popular misconception
   (B) outline the history of a phenomenon
   (C) propose a solution to a social problem
   (D) criticize the work of earlier researchers
   (E) offer a theory of criminal behavior

GO ON TO THE NEXT PAGE

16. The passage suggests that which of the following would deter a child from regarding an incident of television violence as real?

    I. Including easily recognized cartoon characters
    II. Setting the action far into the future or past
    III. Having characters laugh at their misfortunes

    (A) I only
    (B) II only
    (C) I and II only
    (D) II and III only
    (E) I, II, and III

17. In line 41, "cold" most nearly means

    (A) chilling
    (B) wrongful
    (C) dangerous
    (D) exact
    (E) crafty

18. In line 52, "appropriate" most nearly means

    (A) acceptable
    (B) desirable
    (C) normal
    (D) learned
    (E) violent

19. It can be inferred that a child who has an argument with a sibling two to three hours after watching fantasy violence on television would

    (A) almost surely be more aggressive than usual
    (B) tend to act out the fantasy violence on the sibling
    (C) probably not be unusually violent or aggressive
    (D) likely lapse into a state of total passivity
    (E) generally, but not always, be more violent

20. The information provided in the second paragraph most strongly supports which of the following conclusions?

    (A) Children judge the morality of an action according to the motives of the actor.
    (B) Realistic, acted violence is more likely than fantasy to trigger violent behavior.
    (C) People are born with a sense of right and wrong but later learn to be violent.
    (D) Children who are unable to distinguish fantasy from reality are more likely to be aggressive.
    (E) Some children are not always able to distinguish between fantasy and reality.

21. In line 57, the author uses the word "ironically" to indicate that

    (A) the outcome of an action may be the opposite of what might be expected
    (B) the moral consequences of an action do not depend on its effects on others
    (C) personal expectations about someone's personality may be wrong
    (D) it is not possible to predict reliably how children will behave
    (E) different theories of child behavior reach contradictory conclusions

22. Which of the following best describes the author's attitude about critics who say that television is an important cause of violent behavior in children?

    (A) qualified endorsement
    (B) contemptuous dismissal
    (C) enthusiastic acceptance
    (D) moderate skepticism
    (E) cautious criticism

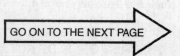

GO ON TO THE NEXT PAGE

23. The discussion in lines 11-16 implies that
children are more likely to perceive realistic
violence than make-believe violence as violence
per se because of

(A) a predisposition to react violently to more
violent situations
(B) an inability to recognize the significance of
cartoon figures
(C) the lack of contextual clues accompanying
realistic violence
(D) the failure to appreciate the importance of
humor
(E) a natural inclination to feel a sense of
identity with victims

24. In line 60, "cumulative" means

(A) short-term
(B) added together
(C) concealed
(D) predetermined
(E) inventive

5 5 5 5 5 5 5 5 5 5 5 5

| Time—25 Minutes 20 Items | In this section, solve each item, using any available space on the page for scratchwork. Then, decide which is the best of the choices given and fill in the corresponding oval on the answer sheet. |

Notes: The figures accompanying the items are drawn as accurately as possible unless otherwise stated in specific items. Again, unless otherwise stated, all figures lie in the same plane. All numbers used in these items are real numbers. Calculators are permitted for this test.

Reference:

Circle: Rectangle: Rectangular Solid: Cylinder: Triangle:

$C = 2\pi r$ $A = lw$ $V = lwh$ $V = \pi r^2 h$ $A = \frac{1}{2}bh$ $a^2 + b^2 = c^2$

$A = \pi r^2$

- The measure in degrees of a straight angle is 180.
- The number of degrees of arc in a circle is 360.
- The sum of the measure of the angles of a triangle is 180.

1. If $x + 2 = 7$ and $x + y = 11$, then $y =$

   (A) 2
   (B) 4
   (C) 6
   (D) 7
   (E) 9

   $x + 2 = 7$
   $x + 2 \quad -2$
   $x = 5$

   $5 + y = 11$
   $-5 \qquad -5$
   $y = 6$

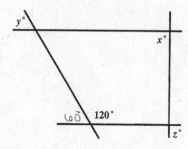

2. In the figure above, if $y + z = 150$, then $x =$

   (A) 30
   (B) 45
   (C) 75
   (D) 90
   (E) 120

GO ON TO THE NEXT PAGE

$x(5) = 3x + 3/2$

The product of x and 5 is equal to one-half of the sum of $3x$ and 3.

3. Which of the following equations correctly expresses the relationship described above?

(A) $5x = \frac{9x}{2}$

(B) $5x = 2(3x + 3)$

(C) $5x = \frac{(3x + 3)}{2}$

(D) $\frac{x}{5} = 2(3x + 3)$

(E) $\frac{x}{5} = \frac{(3x + 3)}{2}$

4. If $f(x) = -2x^2 + 2$, then $f(3) =$

(A) 16
(B) 4
(C) 0
(D) -4
(E) -16

$-2(3)^2 + 2$
$-2(9) + 2$
$-18 + 2$
-16

5. During a sale, 3 of a certain item can be purchased for the usual cost of 2 of the items. If John buys 36 of the items at the sale price, how many of the items could he have bought at the regular price?

(A) 18
(B) 24
(C) 30
(D) 48
(E) 72

3·2
36·24

$\frac{3}{2} = \frac{36}{x}$

$3x = 72$

$x = 24$

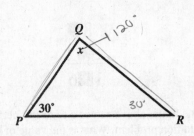

Note: Figure not drawn to scale.

6. In $\triangle PQR$ above, if $\overline{PQ} \cong \overline{QR}$, then $x =$

(A) 30
(B) 60
(C) 90
(D) 120
(E) 150

7. If $px + 2 = 8$ and $qx + 3 = 10$, what is the value of $\frac{p}{q}$?

(A) $\frac{3}{5}$

(B) $\frac{8}{15}$

(C) $\frac{10}{13}$

(D) $\frac{6}{7}$

(E) $\frac{16}{13}$

$px + 2 = 8$
$px = 6$
$qx + 3 = 10$
$qx = 7$
$x = 1$
$\frac{6}{7} = \frac{p}{q}$

8. If $2^x = 16$ and $x = \frac{y}{2}$, then $y =$

(A) 2
(B) 3
(C) 4
(D) 6
(E) 8

$2^4 = 16$

$\frac{4}{1} = \frac{y}{2}$

$y = 8$

GO ON TO THE NEXT PAGE

$$8\bullet$$
$$+\bullet 2$$
$$\overline{1\blacksquare 6}$$

9. The figure above shows a correctly performed addition problem. What is the value of ■?

(A) 2
(B) 4
(C) 6
(D) 8
(E) 9

84 ● = 4
+ 42 ■ = 2
1 2 6

10. If $\sqrt{5x} + 4 = 9$, $x =$

(A) -5
(B) -3
(C) 0
(D) 3
(E) 5

$\sqrt{25} + 4 = 9$
$5 + 4 = 9$
$x = 5$

11. If a triangle has a height of $\frac{1}{x}$ and an area of 2, what is the length of the base of the triangle?

(A) $4x$
(B) x
(C) $\frac{1}{2x}$
(D) $\frac{1}{4x}$
(E) x^2

$a = \frac{1}{2} bh$

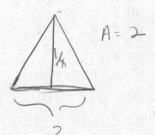

$A = 2$

$2 = \frac{1}{2} b \left(\frac{1}{x}\right)$

$2 = \frac{1}{2} \cdot \frac{b}{x}$

$x \cdot 4 = \frac{b}{x} \cdot x$

$b = 4x$

12. If the sum of three numbers is $4x$ and the sum of four other numbers is $3x$, then the average (arithmetic mean) of all seven numbers is

(A) $7x$
(B) x
(C) $\frac{x}{7}$
(D) 7
(E) 1

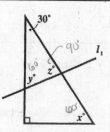

13. In the figure above, if $x = y$, then $z =$

(A) 30
(B) 45
(C) 60
(D) 75
(E) 90

14. If $6 \le x \le 30$, $3 \le y \le 12$, and $2 \le z \le 10$, then what is the least possible value of $\frac{x+y}{z}$?

(A) $\frac{9}{10}$
(B) $\frac{9}{5}$
(C) $\frac{21}{5}$
(D) $\frac{9}{2}$
(E) 21

GO ON TO THE NEXT PAGE

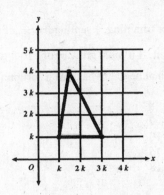

15. $(-3x)^3\left(\dfrac{-3x^3}{27}\right) =$

(A) -1
(B) 3
(C) 9
(D) 27
(E) $27x^3$

$\left(-\dfrac{9x^3}{1}\right)\left(-\dfrac{3x^3}{27}\right) = 1$

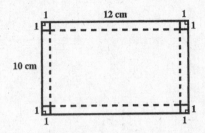

16. The figure above shows a rectangular piece of cardboard with sides of 10 centimeters and 12 centimeters. From each of the four corners, a 1 centimeter by 1 centimeter square is cut out. If an open rectangular box is then formed by folding along the dotted lines, what is the volume of the box in cubic centimeters?

(A) 80
(B) 96
(C) 99
(D) 120
(E) 168

17. If the area of the triangle in the figure above is 12, then $k =$

(A) 1
(B) 2
(C) 3
(D) 4
(E) 6

$a = \frac{1}{2}bh$

$12 = \frac{1}{2}(2k)(3k)$

$\dfrac{12}{3} = \dfrac{3k^2}{3}$

$4 = k^2$ $k = 2$

18. For the numbers a, b, c, and d, the average (arithmetic mean) is twice the median. If

$a < b < c < d$, $a = -2c$, $b = 0$, and $d = nc$, what is the value of n?

(A) -5
(B) -3
(C) 0
(D) 3
(E) 5

$\dfrac{a+b+c+d}{4} = 2 \text{ (median)}$

$\dfrac{-2c + 0 + c = nc}{4} = 2 \text{median}$

19. If x and y are two different positive integers and $x^3 y^2 = 200$, then $xy =$

(A) 5
(B) 6
(C) 10
(D) 25
(E) 40

$x^3 y^2 = 200$

$2^3 5^2 = 200$

$xy = 10$

$5(2) = 10$

GO ON TO THE NEXT PAGE

20. After trimming, a sapling has $\frac{9}{10}$ of its original height. If it must grow $\frac{9}{10}$ of a foot to regain its original height, what was its original height?

    (A) 8
    (B) 9
    (C) 10
    (D) 16
    (E) 18

IF YOU FINISH BEFORE TIME IS CALLED, YOU MAY CHECK YOUR WORK ON THIS TEST ONLY. DO NOT WORK ON ANY OTHER TEST SECTION. **STOP**

–718–
Copyright © 2005 by Cambridge Publishing, Inc. No part of this book may be reproduced in any form without the written permission of Cambridge.

6 6 6 6 6 6 6 6 6 6 6 6

| Time—25 Minutes
24 Items | For each item in this section, choose the best answer and blacken the corresponding space on the answer sheet. |

Each item below has one or two blanks, each blank indicating that something has been omitted. Beneath the sentence are five lettered words or sets of words. Choose the word or set of words that <u>best</u> fits the meaning of the sentence as a whole.

Example:

Although its publicity has been ----, the film itself is intelligent, well acted, handsomely produced, and altogether ----.

(A) tasteless..respectable
(B) extensive..moderate
(C) sophisticated..amateur
(D) risqué..crude
(E) perfect..spectacular   ● Ⓑ Ⓒ Ⓓ Ⓔ

1. His seemingly casual and ---- tone ---- a serious concern for the welfare of his clients.

    (A) flippant..belied
    (B) worried..displayed
    (C) effective..disputed
    (D) callous..betrayed
    (E) contentious..minimized

2. The actress owed her reputation to her ---- public and not to the ---- reviews that bordered on being cruel.

    (A) diffident..approbatory
    (B) congenial..simpering
    (C) trusting..didactic
    (D) adoring..scathing
    (E) innocent..deferential

3. Treason is punishable by death because ---- constitutes a threat to the very ---- of the state.

    (A) perfidy..survival
    (B) grief..existence
    (C) veracity..foundation
    (D) pacifism..dismantling
    (E) patriotism..well-being

4. Although scientists have sought to measure time, only writers and poets have truly ---- its quality and our ---- experience of it.

    (A) neglected..uniform
    (B) understood..benign
    (C) captured..ephemeral
    (D) belied..credulous
    (E) devised..fractious

5. Although a gala performance, the conducting was ----, and the orchestra less than enthusiastic, but the audience seemed ---- the defects and was enthralled.

    (A) auspicious..sensitive to
    (B) perfunctory..oblivious to
    (C) decimated..mindful of
    (D) voracious..excited by
    (E) animated..impaired by

6. Although the language was ---- and considered to be inferior to standard English, Robert Burns wrote his love poetry in the dialect of the Scots.

    (A) interpreted
    (B) belittled
    (C) distinguished
    (D) appreciated
    (E) elevated

GO ON TO THE NEXT PAGE ➡

7. Given the Secretary of State's ---- the President's foreign policies, he has no choice but to resign.

   (A) reliance upon
   (B) antipathy toward
   (C) pretense of
   (D) support for
   (E) concurrence with

8. In order to ---- the deadline for submitting the research paper, the student tried to ---- additional time from the professor.

   (A) extend..wheedle
   (B) accelerate..obtain
   (C) postpone..forego
   (D) sustain..imagine
   (E) conceal..procure

GO ON TO THE NEXT PAGE

Each passage below is followed by one or more items based on its content. Answer the items following each passage on the basis of what is <u>stated</u> or <u>implied</u> in the passage.

Item 9 is based on the following passage.

The Constitutional Convention of 1787 kept its proceedings secret in order to avoid any premature public disclosure of its deliberations. Many historians
Line view that secrecy was the key to the convention's
5 success. Often, we reflexively insist that government should be completely transparent; however, U.S. democracy, the most successful government in all of history, was born behind closed doors.

9. In this context, "transparent" means

    (A) simplistic
    (B) uncontroversial
    (C) civilian
    (D) perfect
    (E) open to public view

Item 10 is based on the following passage.

You can tell a lot about a neighborhood by looking at its sidewalks. My sidewalk is not in bad shape, but its lifespan probably caught a huge break
Line this past winter when the jet stream developed a kink
5 and sent much of our usual northwest precipitation south to California.

Concrete is often a symbol of permanence, but rain and ice have an amazing capacity to erode and eventually destroy any kind of mineral-based slab. The
10 ground has a tendency to settle. Trees that are planted too closely to pavement will cause the pavement to shift or snap as the roots grow. Recently, I decided to clean my sidewalk using a power washer. The sidewalk is definitely cleaner, but the high-pressure spray also
15 blasted grit and dirt from every nook and cranny, which makes obvious even the smallest cracks. As the old saying goes: "No good deed goes unpunished."

10. The author of the passage would most likely apply the "old saying" to which of the following?

    (A) Purchasing a new washing machine that makes laundry cleaner and brighter
    (B) Depositing money into a savings account that pays a fixed rate of interest each year
    (C) Lowering the value of an antique table by stripping and refinishing the piece
    (D) Substituting milk in a recipe that calls for cream, thereby lowering the fat content
    (E) Redesigning a roadway so that traffic will flow more smoothly

GO ON TO THE NEXT PAGE

Item 11 is based on the following passage.

The Africanized honeybee, popularly known as the "killer bee," is moving into the southern United States. Scientists are not certain how far north the bee
Line will spread, but they do know that it will cause
5 problems wherever it resides in large numbers. This insect, which has been migrating from South America since the 1950s, looks just like a domestic honeybee, but the Africanized bee is a wild bee that is not comfortable being around people or animals. Any
10 colony of bees will defend its hive, but Africanized bees are more likely to sense a threat at greater distances, become more upset with less reason, and sting in much greater numbers.

11. The author implies that the most important difference between the Africanized honeybee and the domestic honey is the Africanized bee's

   (A) migratory habits
   (B) natural range
   (C) aggressiveness
   (D) ability to sting
   (E) reproductive rate

Item 12 is based on the following passage.

Protecting solar access is not a new concept. The Roman Empire had solar access laws, and the Doctrine of Lights protected landowners' rights to light in
Line nineteenth-century Britain. Some U.S. communities
5 adopted solar access regulations in response to the 1970s energy crisis, and many others are now considering solar access protection. The definition of solar access varies slightly from one jurisdiction to another. In San Jose, for instance, solar access is
10 defined as the unobstructed availability of direct sunlight at solar noon on December 21st. In Boulder, Colorado, sunlight must not be obstructed between 10 a.m. and 2 p.m. on December 21st. Other laws specify the percentage of wall area, glazing, or roof that can be
15 shaded by buildings or mature vegetation, and some guidelines even allow for "solar friendly vegetation," such as deciduous trees with branching patterns that allow a maximum amount of winter sunlight to reach the building.

12. The discussion in lines 1-7 is intended primarily to

   (A) demonstrate the importance of national leadership on environmental issues
   (B) provide the reader with historical background on solar access
   (C) point out limitations with proposals to use solar energy devices
   (D) correct a common misunderstanding about the distribution of sunlight
   (E) start a debate over the need to conserve scarce energy resources

GO ON TO THE NEXT PAGE

Items 13-14 are based on the following passage.

Line

5

10

15

Amphibian malformations have been reported in 44 states since 1996. These deformities include extra legs, extra eyes, misshapen or incompletely formed limbs, limb formation in anatomically inappropriate places, missing limbs, and missing eyes. While anatomical deformities are a natural phenomenon within virtually all species, the widespread occurrence of these deformities and the relatively high frequency of malformations within local populations concern wildlife biologists. Most agree that the rates of deformities far exceed what can be considered natural, and these biologists are currently investigating several factors—including parasites, contaminants, and UV radiation—which may be causing the deformities. It is important to keep in mind that the cause of deformities in one region may, or may not, be responsible for those in another area. Alternatively, a combination of factors may be the cause of malformation occurrences across the country.

13. The author regards the research on the causes of amphibian malformations as

    (A) haphazard
    (B) exhaustive
    (C) contradictory
    (D) unreliable
    (E) inconclusive

14. Which of the following words, when substituted for "natural" in line 11 best preserves the meaning of the original?

    (A) elevated
    (B) uncontrived
    (C) normal
    (D) insignificant
    (E) frequent

GO ON TO THE NEXT PAGE

Items 15-24 are based on the following passage.

The following passage discusses the effects of microwave radiation on the body temperature of an organism.

Behavior is one of two general responses available to endothermic (warm-blooded) species for the regulation of body temperature, the other being
Line innate mechanisms of heat production and heat loss.
5 Human beings rely primarily on the first to provide a hospitable thermal microclimate for themselves in which the transfer of heat between the body and the environment is accomplished with minimal involvement of innate mechanisms of heat production
10 and loss. Thermoregulatory behavior *anticipates* hyperthermia, and the organism adjusts its behavior to avoid becoming hyperthermic: it removes layers of clothing, it goes for a cool swim, etc. The organism can also respond to changes in the temperature of the body
15 core, as is the case during exercise; but such responses result from the direct stimulation of thermorecptors distributed widely within the central nervous system, and the ability of these mechanisms to help the organism adjust to gross changes in its environment is
20 limited.

Until recently, it was assumed that organisms respond to microwave radiation in the same way that they respond to temperature changes that are caused by other forms of radiation. After all, the argument runs,
25 microwaves are radiation and heat body tissues. This theory ignores the fact that the stimulus to a behavioral response is normally a temperature change that occurs at the surface of the organism. The thermoreceptors that prompt behavioral changes are located within the
30 first millimeter of the skin's surface, but the energy of a microwave field may be selectively deposited in deep tissues, effectively bypassing these thermorecptors, particularly if the field is at near-resonant frequencies. The resulting temperature profile may well be a kind of
35 reverse thermal gradient in which the deep tissues are warmed more than those of the surface. Since the heat is not conducted outward to the surface to stimulate the appropriate receptors, the organism does not appreciate this stimulation in the same way that it does heating
40 and cooling of the skin. In theory, the internal organs of a human being or an animal could be quite literally cooked well-done before the animal even realizes that the balance of its thermomicroclimate has been disturbed.
45 Until a few years ago, microwave irradiations at equivalent plane-wave power densities of about 100 mW/cm^2 were considered unequivocally to produce "thermal" effects; irradiations within the range of 10 to 100 mW/cm^2 might or might not produce "thermal"
50 effects; while effects observed at power densities below 10 mW/cm^2 were assumed to be "nonthermal" in nature. Experiments have shown this to be an oversimplification, and a recent report suggests that fields as weak as 1mW/cm^2 can be thermogenic. When
55 the heat generated in the tissues by an imposed radio frequency (plus the heat generated by metabolism) exceeds the heat-loss capabilities of the organism, the thermoregulatory system has been compromised. Yet, surprisingly, not long ago, an increase in the internal
60 body temperature was regarded merely as "evidence" of a thermal effect.

15. The author is primarily concerned with

(A) showing that behavior is a more effective way of controlling bodily temperature than innate mechanisms
(B) criticizing researchers who will not discard their theories about the effects of microwave radiation on organisms
(C) demonstrating that effects of microwave radiation are different from those of other forms of radiation
(D) analyzing the mechanism by which an organism maintains its bodily temperature in a changing thermal environment
(E) discussing the importance of thermoreceptors in the control of the internal temperature of an organism

16. In line 4, the word "innate" most nearly means

(A) natural
(B) voluntary
(C) reflexive
(D) acquired
(E) reproductive

GO ON TO THE NEXT PAGE

17. The author makes which of the following points about innate mechanisms for heat production?

  I. They are governed by thermorecptors inside the body of the organism rather than at the surface.
  II. They are a less effective means of compensating for gross changes in temperature than behavioral strategies.
  III. They are not affected by microwave radiation.

(A) I only
(B) I and II only
(C) I and III only
(D) II and III only
(E) I, II, and III

18. The author suggests that the proponents of the theory that microwave radiation acts on organisms in the same way as other forms of radiation based their conclusions primarily on

(A) laboratory research
(B) unfounded assumption
(C) control group surveys
(D) deductive reasoning
(E) causal investigation

19. In line 38, the word "appreciate" most nearly means

(A) esteem
(B) prefer
(C) enjoy
(D) notice
(E) regard

20. The author's strategy in lines 40-44 is to

(A) introduce a hypothetical example to dramatize a point
(B) propose an experiment to test a scientific hypothesis
(C) cite a case study to illustrate a general contention
(D) produce a counterexample to disprove an opponent's theory
(E) speculate about the probable consequences of a scientific phenomenon

21. In line 58, the word "compromised" most nearly means

(A) agreed
(B) permitted
(C) endangered
(D) settled
(E) adjusted

22. The tone of the passage can best be described as

(A) genial and conversational
(B) alarmed and disparaging
(C) facetious and cynical
(D) scholarly and noncommittal
(E) analytical and concerned

23. The author is primarily concerned with

(A) pointing out weaknesses in a popular scientific theory
(B) developing a hypothesis to explain a scientific phenomenon
(C) reporting on new research on the effects of microwave radiation
(D) criticizing the research methods of earlier investigators
(E) clarifying ambiguities in the terminology used to describe a phenomenon

24. Which of the following would be the most logical topic for the author to take up in the paragraph following the final paragraph of the selection?

(A) A suggestion for new research to be done on the effects of microwaves on animals and human beings
(B) An analysis of the differences between microwave radiation and other forms of radiation
(C) A proposal that the use of microwave radiation be prohibited because it is dangerous
(D) A survey of the literature on the effects of microwave radiation on human beings
(E) A discussion of the strategies used by various species to control hyperthermia

IF YOU FINISH BEFORE TIME IS CALLED, YOU MAY CHECK YOUR WORK ON THIS TEST ONLY. DO NOT WORK ON ANY OTHER TEST SECTION.

STOP

8 8 8 8 8 8 8 8 8 8 8 8

| Time—20 Minutes 16 Items | In this section, solve each item, using any available space on the page for scratchwork. Then, decide which is the best of the choices given and fill in the corresponding oval on the answer sheet. |

Notes: The figures accompanying the items are drawn as accurately as possible unless otherwise stated in specific items. Again, unless otherwise stated, all figures lie in the same plane. All numbers used in these items are real numbers. Calculators are permitted for this test.

Reference:

Circle: Rectangle: Rectangular Solid: 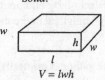 Cylinder: Triangle:

$C = 2\pi r$ $A = lw$ $V = lwh$ $V = \pi r^2 h$ $A = \frac{1}{2}bh$ $a^2 + b^2 = c^2$

$A = \pi r^2$

- The measure in degrees of a straight angle is 180.
- The number of degrees of arc in a circle is 360.
- The sum of the measure of the angles of a triangle is 180.

Dimensions of 5 different boxes	
Box A:	2 x 3 x 4 24
Box B:	2 x 3 x 3 18
Box C:	3 x 4 x 5 60
Box D:	5 x 4 x 2 40
Box E:	4 x 4 x 2 32

1. Which box has the greatest volume?

    BOX C = 60

    (A) A
    (B) B
    (C) C
    (D) D
    (E) E

2. The product of an even, positive number and an odd, negative number is

    (A) negative and even
    (B) negative and odd
    (C) negative and either even or odd
    (D) positive and odd
    (E) positive and even

3. If w, x, y, and z are positive numbers, each of the following expressions equals $w(x + y + z)$ EXCEPT

    $wxy + wyz$

    $\neq$

    (A) $wx + wy + wz$
    (B) $wx + w(y + z)$
    (C) $w(x + y) + wz$
    (D) $w(x + z) + wy$
    (E) $w(xy) + w(yz)$

4. Originally, a group of 11 students was supposed to equally share a cash prize. If 1 more student is added to the group and the 12 students share the prize equally, then each new share is worth what fraction of each original share?

    (A) $\frac{1}{12}$
    (B) $\frac{1}{11}$
    (C) $\frac{1}{10}$
    (D) $\frac{10}{11}$
    (E) $\frac{11}{12}$

GO ON TO THE NEXT PAGE

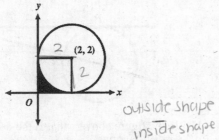

outside shape
inside shape.

5. In the figure above, the center of the circle has coordinates (2, 2). What is the area of the shaded portion of the figure?

Area of the
square = 4

4 − π

(A) $2 - \pi$
(B) $4 - \pi$
(C) $8 - 2\pi$
(D) $8 - \pi$
(E) $16 - 4\pi$

	Having Y	Not Having Y	
Having X	10	30	40
Not Having X	40	20	50

6. The table above gives the distribution of two genetic characteristics, X and Y, in a population of 100 subjects. What is the ratio of the number of people having characteristic X to the number of people having characteristic Y?

(A) 1:3
(B) 1:2
(C) 2:3
(D) 4:5   40:50
(E) 3:2   4:5

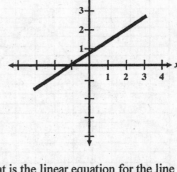

7. What is the linear equation for the line through points $(-1, 0)$ and $(2, 2)$ in the coordinate graph above?

(A) $y = -\frac{2x}{3} - \frac{2}{3}$
(B) $y = 2x - 3$
(C) $y = \frac{2x}{3} + \frac{2}{3}$
(D) $y = x + \frac{2}{3}$
(E) $y = 3x + 2$

8. A 10,000 bushel shipping compartment is being filled with grain by a pipe at a constant rate. After 20 minutes, the container is filled to 40 percent of its capacity. After another 15 minutes, the container will be filled to what percent of its capacity?

(A) 55%
(B) 60%
(C) $66\frac{2}{3}$%
(D) 70%
(E) 75%

9. A bowling team has 5 members, 40% of whom averaged over 230 this fall. Of those over-230 scorers, 50% had scores averaging 250 or better. How many people had scores averaging below 250?

(A) 1
(B) 2
(C) 3
(D) 4
(E) 5

GO ON TO THE NEXT PAGE

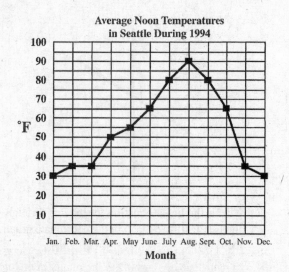

Average Noon Temperatures in Seattle During 1994

10. The above graph depicts the average monthly temperatures in Seattle during 1994. Which of the following is true of the temperatures?

  I. The average (arithmetic mean) is greater than 50°F.
  II. The median is greater than 50°F.
  III. The mode is greater than 50°F.

(A) I only
(B) II only
(C) I and II only
(D) II and III only
(E) I, II, and III

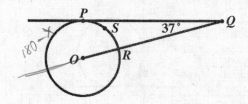

11. In the figure above, what is the degree measure of minor arc PSR?

(A) 30°
(B) 43°
(C) 53°
(D) 86°
(E) 90°

½ difference of two arcs.

$37 = \frac{1}{2}(180 - x - x)$

$74 = 180 - 2x$

$x = 53°$

12. What is the solution set for k in the equation

$$\left| k - \frac{1}{8} \right| = \left| \frac{1}{3} - \frac{1}{2} \right|?$$

(A) $\left\{ -\frac{1}{24}, \frac{7}{24} \right\}$

(B) $\left\{ -\frac{1}{24}, \frac{1}{8} \right\}$

(C) $\left\{ \frac{1}{8}, \frac{1}{24} \right\}$

(D) $\left\{ \frac{7}{24}, \frac{1}{24} \right\}$

(E) $\left\{ \frac{1}{3}, \frac{1}{7} \right\}$

$\left| k - \frac{1}{8} \right| = \left| \frac{1}{3} - \frac{1}{2} \right|$

$\left| k - \frac{1}{8} \right| = \left| -\frac{1}{6} \right|$

$\left| k - \frac{1}{8} \right| = \frac{1}{6}$

I. $k - \frac{1}{8} = \frac{1}{6}$
  $k = \frac{7}{24}$

II. $k - \frac{1}{8} = -\frac{1}{6}$
  $k = -\frac{1}{24}$

GO ON TO THE NEXT PAGE

AGE DIFFERENCE FOR CHILDREN IN FIVE FAMILIES

Family	Oldest	Age	Youngest	Age	Difference
LaTours	Joan	15	Ed	12	
Pickett	Harold	17	Claire	8	
Thibault	Rene	16	Henri	3	
Barber	Fred	9	Gloria	7	
Newcomb	Danny	12	Syd	8	

13. The table above shows the ages for the oldest and youngest children in five different families. If "Difference" is defined as the age of the oldest child minus the age of the youngest child, then what is the median of the missing values in the column labeled "Difference"?

    (A) 1
    (B) 3
    (C) 4
    (D) 9
    (E) 13

14. If $x^{1/4} = 20$, then $x =$

    (A) $\sqrt[4]{20}$
    (B) 5
    (C) 80
    (D) 2,000
    (E) 160,000

15. In the coordinate plane, the graph of which of the following lines is perpendicular to the graph of line $y = \frac{3}{2}x + 1$?

    (A) $y = \frac{3}{2}x - 1$
    (B) $y = \frac{3}{4}x + 1$
    (C) $y = \frac{3}{4}x - 1$
    (D) $y = -\frac{2}{3}x + 2$
    (E) $y = -\frac{3}{2}x - 1$

16. A tank contains g gallons of water. Water flows into the tank by one pipe at the rate of m gallons per minute, and water flows out by another pipe at the rate of n gallons per minute. If $n > m$, how many minutes will it take to empty the tank?

    (A) $\frac{(g-m)}{n}$
    (B) $\frac{g}{(m-n)}$
    (C) $\frac{(n-g)}{m}$
    (D) $\frac{(n-m)}{g}$
    (E) $\frac{g}{(n-m)}$

IF YOU FINISH BEFORE TIME IS CALLED, YOU MAY CHECK YOUR WORK ON THIS TEST ONLY. DO NOT WORK ON ANY OTHER TEST SECTION.

STOP

9 9 9 9 9 9 9 9 9 9 9 9

Time—20 Minutes 19 Items	For each item in this section, choose the best answer and blacken the corresponding space on the answer sheet.

Each item below has one or two blanks, each blank indicating that something has been omitted. Beneath the sentence are five lettered words or sets of words. Choose the word or set of words that <u>best</u> fits the meaning of the sentence as a whole.

Example:

Although its publicity has been ----, the film itself is intelligent, well acted, handsomely produced, and altogether ----.

(A) tasteless..respectable
(B) extensive..moderate
(C) sophisticated..amateur
(D) risqué..crude
(E) perfect..spectacular

1. According to recent studies, prices in supermarkets are considerably higher in the inner city, thus ---- the poor who receive assistance to buy the food.

   (A) reprimanding
   (B) intimidating
   (C) alleviating
   (D) assuaging
   (E) exploiting

2. Legislation to stop smoking in public places has been ---- by some as a move to save lives, while it is ---- by the tobacco industry, which calls the action "alarmist."

   (A) heralded..condemned
   (B) thwarted..buffered
   (C) initiated..condoned
   (D) prejudiced..supported
   (E) extolled..elicited

3. Joyce's novel *Finnegan's Wake* continues to ---- critics, including those who find it incomprehensible and call it ----.

   (A) appall..genial
   (B) enthrall..nonsensical
   (C) baffle..transparent
   (D) bore..compelling
   (E) entertain..monotonous

4. Jazz is an American art form that is now ---- in Europe through the determined efforts of ---- in France, Scandinavia, and Germany.

   (A) foundering..governments
   (B) diminishing..musicians
   (C) appreciated..opponents
   (D) waning..novices
   (E) flourishing..expatriates

GO ON TO THE NEXT PAGE

> The two passages below are followed by items based on their content and the relationship between the two passages. Answer the items on the basis of what is <u>stated</u> or <u>implied</u> in the passages and in any introductory material that may be provided.

Items 5-19 are based on the following pair of passages.

The passages are adapted from remarks by college professors and experts in the Tibetan language and culture made during a round table discussion on the political, linguistic, and cultural challenges faced by Tibet.

Passage 1

There is a real threat of extinction of the Tibetan language and the Tibetan culture within two or, at the most, three generations. Languages convey very
Line specific social and cultural behaviors and ways of
5 thinking. As a result, the extinction of the Tibetan language would have tremendous consequences for the Tibetan culture. The culture cannot be preserved without it.

Why is it important to preserve the language and
10 its culture? Tibetan language and culture are original. Along side Sanskrit, Chinese, and Japanese literatures, Tibetan literature is one of the oldest, most original, and greatest in volume. Language is also important for the economic survival of Tibetans. Many rural
15 Tibetans, whether nomads or peasants, are almost like foreigners in their own country; they do not have the linguistic ability to find jobs. When they come to the cities, their culture is marginalized and devalued. This leads also to the marginalization and devaluation of the
20 people themselves. The language and culture are also extremely important for the secularization and modernization of Tibetan society. Right now, many young Tibetans go to monasteries because that is one of the few places left for traditional study. If they could
25 study their own culture in middle school, a lot of them would prefer to study in lay schools.

Think about 5 million Tibetan people surrounded by more than 1.5 billion Chinese-speaking people, and you will understand the nature of the threat. Right now,
30 the Tibetan people are not really allowed to have meetings in Tibetan. Even when 20 or more Tibetans are meeting together, they speak in Chinese. All middle school education is in Chinese. Even though Tibetan books and manuals exist for mathematics, physics, and
35 chemistry, teachers will not use them. The Chinese Government is not unaware of this situation and has enacted regulations protecting the Tibetan language, a

so-called "minority language," within the People's Republic of China. This is encouraging, but at the same
40 time, it shows that the need to act is urgent.

The goal is to promote the Tibetan language and culture in the educational system and to establish a real Tibetan-Chinese bilingual society, not as it is now: a monolingual Chinese society. This goal implies a need
45 for advertising the new Chinese law and exerting pressure so that it is really implemented. Promoting standard, spoken Tibetan is also extremely important because there is a high rate of unemployment and an incredible level of illiteracy. It is important to promote
50 standard, spoken Tibetan by funding projects that will publish classical texts in the vernacular. There are some very concrete ways in which people form Western countries can contribute to the promotion of the Tibetan language and culture. For example,
55 universities and arts foundations should sponsor literary prizes and awards for Tibetan writers. Artists and writers who live in Western countries should travel to Tibet, interacting with the people and organizing cultural festivals. Other ways to promote Tibetan
60 language and culture include: donating to public radio stations and encouraging stations to broadcast the classics of Tibetan and foreign literature; paying Tibetan teachers to compile tapes of traditional music and folk tales that have not yet been recorded; and
65 developing calligraphy and Tibetan spelling competitions. These are all very concrete step that will encourage Tibetans to believe that their language and culture are not only alive but thriving.

Passage 2

In the first place, it is important to understand that
70 Tibetan is not a language in the way that modern English is a language, with a range of dialects so that speakers easily understand each other in accordance with common vocabulary, grammar, and so forth. There is no standard Tibetan. There is, however, an
75 emergent proto-standard Tibetan that is spoken widely in the diasporic community.† This language derives from the Lhasa language, a good basis for a standard Tibetan that could be used across Tibet in addition to regional dialects.
80 Second, literary Tibetan, typically referred to as classical Tibetan, has a long and distinguished tradition going back at least to the seventh century. Classical

GO ON TO THE NEXT PAGE

Tibetan is remarkably conservative in terms of
spelling, grammar usage, and vocabulary. Someone
85 who is conversant in modern classical Tibetan can
actually pick up 10th century texts and read them
fluently, something which is not at all true of English.
Unfortunately, most Tibetan dialects are not equally
conservative in pronunciation and vocabulary. As a
90 result, classical Tibetan is dramatically divergent from
spoken Tibetan, which makes classical Tibetan
unnecessarily difficult to learn. Also, many standard
colloquial spoken terms have no standardized spelling
or use in literary Tibetan. A modern literary Tibetan
100 language has begun to emerge in creative writing,
newspapers, and the like, but this modern literary
Tibetan has yet to become a fully transregional
vernacular: a literary Tibetan that can be easily
understood, easily learned, and used for daily
105 communications

Third, Tibetans who are fluent in spoken Tibetan
often lack specific colloquial competencies not because
they are pressured to switch over to Chinese, but
because often they are actually unable to use Tibetan in
110 specific professional or intellectual environments. They
do not know the vocabulary. When speaking of
computer science, mathematics, biology, or certain
governmental activities, they literally do not know how
to talk. Thus, it is important to promote the use of
115 Tibetan equivalents to Chinese terms in these
professional areas.

Consequently, why do the Tibetans not give up
Tibetan altogether and simply speak Chinese?
Everyone could become, in two or three generations,
120 native speakers of Chinese. This shift to Chinese would
be damaging because it would create a traumatic rift
between the way of life for modern Tibetans and their
1,300-year literary and cultural history. A people's
sense of identity, place, and time is inextricably bound
125 up with their language. By losing the Tibetan language,
the specifically Tibetan identity and world with its
culture, insights, values and behaviors, is essentially
consigned to the past.

Within two or three decades, it is possible that the
130 Tibetan language will be all but extinct, surviving only
as the province of a few isolated monasteries. There is,
however, another possibility in which standard Tibetan
could become widely spoken and again become a
medium for educational and commercial context. A
135 newly generated vernacular Tibetan could become one
that is meaningful in educational and personal context.

[†]A diasporic community refers to Tibetans and their descendants
living outside of Tibet.

5. The author develops Passage 1 primarily by

(A) asking a question and then exploring several
possible answers
(B) posing a dilemma and then showing that one
of its assumptions is false
(C) outlining a problem and then revealing that it
is worse than thought
(D) proposing a plan of action and then
criticizing the plan
(E) describing a situation and its causes and
suggesting some solutions

6. According to Passage 1, many rural Tibetans have
difficulty finding jobs because

(A) the unemployment rate in the cities is higher
than in the rural areas
(B) they lack any skills that would make them
employable
(C) they are not able to speak a language that is
understood by employers
(D) they insist on preserving traditional Tibetan
values
(E) employers are primarily interested in hiring
Chinese workers

7. It can be inferred from the comparison of lay
middle schools and monasteries as educational
centers (lines 22-25) that

(A) monasteries are better equipped to provide
students with valuable job skills than lay
schools
(B) the preference of many students for
monastery schools retards the secularization
of Tibetan society
(C) monasteries in Tibet are do a better job than
lay schools of teaching mathematics and
physical sciences
(D) monasteries are a powerful force in Tibet for
the secularization and modernization of the
country
(E) lay schools have become less popular as
monasteries have strengthened their cultural
studies programs

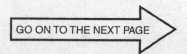

GO ON TO THE NEXT PAGE

8. The author of Passage 1 thinks that the regulations passed by the Chinese government to protect the Tibetan language

    (A) are unlikely to be effective in encouraging the use of Tibetan rather than Chinese
    (B) will almost certainly prevent Chinese from replacing Tibetan as the dominant culture
    (C) were secretly intended to undermine the use of Tibet in public discourse
    (D) could help preserve Tibetan culture if aggressively implemented
    (E) should be repealed in favor of laws intended to promote a monolingual society

9. In line 51, the word "vernacular" means

    (A) bilingualism
    (B) classical text
    (C) ordinary language
    (D) unpublished works
    (E) handwritten documents

10. The suggestions by author of Passage 1 for moving toward a bilingual society in Tibet include all of the following EXCEPT

    (A) programs to lower the unemployment rate
    (B) awards for Tibetan writers
    (C) paying teachers to preserve folk culture
    (D) competitions centered on Tibetan language
    (E) organizing cultural festivals

11. In line 75, the word "emergent" most nearly means

    (A) uniform
    (B) widespread
    (C) modern
    (D) developing
    (E) flexible

12. In Passage 2, the comparison of English and Tibetan suggests that that written English

    (A) is a more difficult language to learn than classical Tibetan
    (B) consists of fewer distinct dialects than modern Tibetan
    (C) displays greater variation of regional form than proto-Tibetan
    (D) has changed more over the centuries than classical Tibetan
    (E) is not directly related to modern culture in English speaking regions

13. As used in this context, the word "conservative" (line 83) means

    (A) illiterate
    (B) limited
    (C) subordinate
    (D) collective
    (E) stable

14. The author of Passage 2 develops the first three paragraphs by

    (A) listing the advantages of classical Tibetan over more modern versions
    (B) describing a series of problems that affect Tibetan and possible solutions to each
    (C) discussing various attempts to restore Tibetan to the status it enjoyed in classical times
    (D) providing examples of features of the Tibetan language that make its mastery difficult
    (E) challenging members of the diasporic Tibetan community to modernize Tibetan

GO ON TO THE NEXT PAGE

15. The author of Passage 2 poses the question at the beginning of the fourth paragraph to

(A) suggest that the problems outlined earlier are less pressing than they might otherwise seem
(B) show the similar roles played by Chinese and Tibetan in Tibetan society
(C) introduce a discussion of what could happen to Tibetan culture if the language is simply abandoned
(D) shift the discussion from Tibetan language to Tibetan culture
(E) signal a shift from a discussion of abstract concerns to specific problems

16. It can be inferred that both authors agree that

(A) the classical form of a language is more important than its modern version
(B) it is possible to study language without learning about culture
(C) language is essential to the survival of a culture
(D) Tibetan and Chinese express similar social and cultural norms
(E) certain languages are better suited to modern discourse than others

17. The attitude of the two authors toward the possibility of the continued survival of Tibetan is best summarized by which of the following?

(A) Both believe that Tibetan and its culture are most likely to disappear entirely within a relatively few years.
(B) Both believe that Tibetan and its culture are threatened but could survive if steps are taken to preserve them.
(C) The author of Passage 1 believes that Tibetan language and culture cannot survive while the author of Passage 2 believes that they can.
(D) The author of Passage 2 believes that Tibetan language and culture cannot survive while the author of Passage 1 believes that they can.
(E) The authors agree that Tibetan language and culture are still vital and will continue as they have for centuries regardless of other events.

18. Both authors provide information to help answer each of the following questions EXCEPT

(A) What would be the consequences of Tibetans abandoning their language?
(B) What is the significance of Tibetan language and culture?
(C) What events or actions might help preserve Tibetan as a language?
(D) How long is Tibetan likely to survive as a viable language?
(E) How does the Tibetan language compare in various ways with English?

19. Which of the following best describes the relationship between the analyses of Tibetan presented by the two authors?

(A) The author of Passage 1 emphasizes the political problems facing Tibetan while the author of Passage 2 focuses on features of the language itself.
(B) The author of Passage 1 highlights the strengths of Classical Tibetan while the author of Passage 2 describes the advantages of modern Tibetan.
(C) The author of Passage 1 writes about the development of written Tibetan while the author of Passage 2 is primarily concerned with the spoken version of the language.
(D) The author of Passage 1 treats language as a manifestation of culture while the author of Passage 2 regards language as existing independently of culture.
(E) The author of Passage 1 identifies several misunderstandings about the Tibetan language while the author of Passage 2 advocates specific plans to improve Tibetan.

IF YOU FINISH BEFORE TIME IS CALLED, YOU MAY CHECK YOUR WORK ON THIS TEST ONLY. DO NOT WORK ON ANY OTHER TEST SECTION.

STOP

10 10 10 10 10 10 10 10 10

Time—10 Minutes 14 Items	For each item in this section, choose the best answer and blacken the corresponding space on the answer sheet.

<u>Directions:</u> The following sentences test correctness and effectiveness of expression. In choosing answers, follow the requirements of standard written English; that is, pay attention to grammar, choice of words, sentence construction, and punctuation.

In each of the following sentences, part of the sentence or the entire sentence is underlined. Beneath each sentence you will find five ways of phrasing the underlined part. Choice A repeats the original; the other four are different.

Choose the answer that best expresses the meaning of the original sentence. If you think the original is better than any of the alternatives, choose it; otherwise choose one of the others. Your choice should produce the most effective sentence—clear and precise, without awkwardness or ambiguity.

Example:

Allen <u>visiting</u> his cousin in France last summer.

(A) visiting
(B) visited
(C) does visit
(D) a visit
(E) is visiting

Answer

Ⓐ ● Ⓒ Ⓓ Ⓔ

1. More and more fashion-conscious dressers are asking themselves <u>if it is</u> moral to wear clothing made from the skin of an animal.

   (A) if it is
   (B) about if it is
   (C) whether it is
   (D) as to whether or not it is
   (E) about whether it is

2. The compact disc will soon become the most common form of recorded <u>music, eventually replacing</u> records and tapes altogether.

   (A) music, eventually replacing
   (B) music, and eventually replacing
   (C) music that eventually replaces
   (D) music by eventually replacing
   (E) music to eventually replace

GO ON TO THE NEXT PAGE

3. <u>When used together, the cosmetic company claims that its products enhance the appearance of the skin by preventing blemishes and reducing signs of aging.</u>

(A) When used together, the cosmetic company claims that its products enhance the appearance of the skin by preventing blemishes and reducing signs of aging.
(B) The cosmetic company claims that, when used together, the appearance of the skin will be enhanced by the products by their preventing blemishes and reducing signs of aging.
(C) When used together, the products will enhance the appearance of the skin, also preventing blemishes and reducing signs of aging, or so the company claims.
(D) According to the cosmetic company, when its products are used together, they will enhance the appearance of the skin, prevent blemishes, and reduce signs of aging.
(E) According to the cosmetic company, when its products are used together, the appearance of the skin will be enhanced and blemishes will be prevented reducing the signs of aging.

4. <u>Appearing to be</u> the only candidate whose views would be acceptable to its membership, the Youth Caucus finally endorsed George Avery for City Council.

(A) Appearing to be
(B) Seeming to be
(C) Because he appeared to be
(D) Because he seemed
(E) Being

5. <u>Arturo Toscanini, well known for his sharp tongue as well as his musical genius, once cowed a famous singer</u> with the remark that there were for him no stars except those in the heavens.

(A) Arturo Toscanini, well known for his sharp tongue as well as his musical genius, once cowed a famous singer
(B) Arturo Toscanini, well known for his sharp tongue as well than his musical genius, cowed once a famous singer
(C) Arturo Toscanini's well-known sharp tongue as well as his musical genius once cowed a famous singer
(D) Arturo Toscanini, who had a well-known sharp tongue as well as musical genius, once cowed a famous singer
(E) Well known for his sharp tongue as well as his musical genius, a famous singer was once cowed by Arturo Toscanini

6. Although Beverly Sills never achieved superstar status in Europe or at the Metropolitan Opera, <u>yet she was singing major roles at the City Opera during 20 years.</u>

(A) yet she was singing major roles at the City Opera during 20 years
(B) she did sing major roles at the City Opera during 20 years
(C) she sang major roles at the City Opera for 20 years
(D) but she sang major roles at the City Opera for 20 years
(E) yet for 20 years major roles had been sung by her at the City Opera

GO ON TO THE NEXT PAGE

7. Although Mary Ann is not a great <u>scholar, neither has she published any books, she has and always will be</u> a great teacher and well-loved by her students.

(A) scholar, neither has she published any books, she has and always will be
(B) scholar, nor having published any books, she has been and always will be
(C) scholar and she hasn't published any books, she has been and always will be
(D) scholar nor published any books, still she had been and always will be
(E) scholar nor has she published any books, but she has been and always will be

8. Puritan fanatics brought to civil and military affairs a coolness of judgment and mutability of purpose that some writers have thought inconsistent with their religious zeal, <u>but which was in fact a natural outgrowth of it</u>.

(A) but which was in fact a natural outgrowth of it
(B) but which were in fact a natural outgrowth of it
(C) but which were in fact natural outgrowths of it
(D) but it was in fact a natural outgrowth of them
(E) which was in fact a natural outgrowth of it

9. <u>Unlike the French, the German art songs are dramatic and sometimes almost operatic.</u>

(A) Unlike the French, the German art songs are dramatic and sometimes almost operatic.
(B) Unlike the French art songs, the German art songs are dramatic and sometimes almost operatic.
(C) The German art songs, unlike the French, are dramatic and sometimes almost operatic.
(D) The German art songs are dramatic and sometimes almost operatic, unlike the French.
(E) The German art songs, which are dramatic and sometimes almost operatic, are unlike the French.

10. The earliest texts in cuneiform script are about 5,000 years <u>old, having antedated the use</u> of the first alphabets by some 1,500 years.

(A) old, having antedated the use
(B) old, having antedated the invention
(C) old, antedating the use
(D) old and antedate the use
(E) old and antedate the invention

11. Henry David Thoreau was a philosopher as well as a naturalist; Gandhi <u>read *Civil Disobedience* in 1906 and made it</u> a major document in his struggle for Indian independence.

(A) read *Civil Disobedience* in 1906 and made it
(B) read *Civil Disobedience* in 1906 in order to make it into
(C) read *Civil Disobedience* and, in 1906, made it
(D) would have read *Civil Disobedience* in 1906 and would have made it
(E) reading *Civil Disobedience* in 1906 and making it

12. Some homeowners prefer gas heat to <u>oil because there is no need for deliveries or no large storage tanks, with its being cheaper in most places</u>.

(A) oil because there is no need for deliveries or no large storage tanks, with its being cheaper in most places
(B) oil because there is no need for deliveries or large storage tanks, and in most places gas is cheaper
(C) oil, being that there are no deliveries, no large storage tanks, and it is cheaper in most places
(D) oil, needing no deliveries or large storage tanks, and anyways gas is cheaper in most places
(E) oil, since gas is cheaper in most places and has no need of deliveries or large storage tanks

GO ON TO THE NEXT PAGE

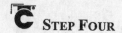

13. <u>Although we now blame most catastrophes on "nature,"</u> thinkers in the Middle Ages thought every fire, earthquake, and disease to be the result of divine anger.

    (A) Although we now blame most catastrophes on "nature,"
    (B) Most catastrophes are now blamed on "nature" by us, and
    (C) We now blame "nature" for catastrophes, moreover,
    (D) Although "nature" is now blamed for most catastrophes by us,
    (E) Now blaming most catastrophes on "nature,"

14. A survey of over 1,000 people conducted by a marketing firm determined that people over the age of 40 do not like cherry cola as <u>well as people under the age of 20.</u>

    (A) well as people under the age of 20
    (B) much as people under the age of 20
    (C) many people under the age of 20 do
    (D) well than people under the age of 20 do
    (E) much as people under the age of 20

IF YOU FINISH BEFORE TIME IS CALLED, YOU MAY CHECK YOUR WORK ON THIS TEST ONLY. DO NOT WORK ON ANY OTHER TEST SECTION.   **S T O P**

Practice Test III

CAMBRIDGE
EDUCATIONAL SERVICES®

EDUCATORS' #1 CHOICE FOR SCHOOL IMPROVEMENT

Cambridge Course Concept Outline
PRACTICE TEST III

When completing Practice Test III, use the Essay Response and Bubble Sheets beginning on page 743, unless otherwise directed by your instructor.

Name: _____ Date: _____

Student ID Number: _____

PRACTICE TEST III

Section 1

Begin your essay on this page. If you need more space, continue on the next page.

_____

_____

_____

_____

_____

_____

_____

_____

_____

_____

_____

_____

_____

_____

_____

_____

_____

_____

_____

_____

_____

_____

_____

_____

Name: _____   Date: _____

Student ID Number: _____

PRACTICE TEST III

Start with number 1 for each new section. If a section has fewer questions than answer spaces, leave the extra answer spaces blank. Be sure to erase any errors or stray marks completely.

Section 2

1 ⒶⒷⒸⒹⒺ	10 ⒶⒷⒸⒹⒺ	19 ⒶⒷⒸⒹⒺ	28 ⒶⒷⒸⒹⒺ
2 ⒶⒷⒸⒹⒺ	11 ⒶⒷⒸⒹⒺ	20 ⒶⒷⒸⒹⒺ	29 ⒶⒷⒸⒹⒺ
3 ⒶⒷⒸⒹⒺ	12 ⒶⒷⒸⒹⒺ	21 ⒶⒷⒸⒹⒺ	30 ⒶⒷⒸⒹⒺ
4 ⒶⒷⒸⒹⒺ	13 ⒶⒷⒸⒹⒺ	22 ⒶⒷⒸⒹⒺ	31 ⒶⒷⒸⒹⒺ
5 ⒶⒷⒸⒹⒺ	14 ⒶⒷⒸⒹⒺ	23 ⒶⒷⒸⒹⒺ	32 ⒶⒷⒸⒹⒺ
6 ⒶⒷⒸⒹⒺ	15 ⒶⒷⒸⒹⒺ	24 ⒶⒷⒸⒹⒺ	33 ⒶⒷⒸⒹⒺ
7 ⒶⒷⒸⒹⒺ	16 ⒶⒷⒸⒹⒺ	25 ⒶⒷⒸⒹⒺ	34 ⒶⒷⒸⒹⒺ
8 ⒶⒷⒸⒹⒺ	17 ⒶⒷⒸⒹⒺ	26 ⒶⒷⒸⒹⒺ	35 ⒶⒷⒸⒹⒺ
9 ⒶⒷⒸⒹⒺ	18 ⒶⒷⒸⒹⒺ	27 ⒶⒷⒸⒹⒺ	36 ⒶⒷⒸⒹⒺ

Section 3

1 ⒶⒷⒸⒹⒺ	10 ⒶⒷⒸⒹⒺ	19 ⒶⒷⒸⒹⒺ	28 ⒶⒷⒸⒹⒺ
2 ⒶⒷⒸⒹⒺ	11 ⒶⒷⒸⒹⒺ	20 ⒶⒷⒸⒹⒺ	29 ⒶⒷⒸⒹⒺ
3 ⒶⒷⒸⒹⒺ	12 ⒶⒷⒸⒹⒺ	21 ⒶⒷⒸⒹⒺ	30 ⒶⒷⒸⒹⒺ
4 ⒶⒷⒸⒹⒺ	13 ⒶⒷⒸⒹⒺ	22 ⒶⒷⒸⒹⒺ	31 ⒶⒷⒸⒹⒺ
5 ⒶⒷⒸⒹⒺ	14 ⒶⒷⒸⒹⒺ	23 ⒶⒷⒸⒹⒺ	32 ⒶⒷⒸⒹⒺ
6 ⒶⒷⒸⒹⒺ	15 ⒶⒷⒸⒹⒺ	24 ⒶⒷⒸⒹⒺ	33 ⒶⒷⒸⒹⒺ
7 ⒶⒷⒸⒹⒺ	16 ⒶⒷⒸⒹⒺ	25 ⒶⒷⒸⒹⒺ	34 ⒶⒷⒸⒹⒺ
8 ⒶⒷⒸⒹⒺ	17 ⒶⒷⒸⒹⒺ	26 ⒶⒷⒸⒹⒺ	35 ⒶⒷⒸⒹⒺ
9 ⒶⒷⒸⒹⒺ	18 ⒶⒷⒸⒹⒺ	27 ⒶⒷⒸⒹⒺ	36 ⒶⒷⒸⒹⒺ

Section 4/5

1 ⒶⒷⒸⒹⒺ	10 ⒶⒷⒸⒹⒺ	19 ⒶⒷⒸⒹⒺ	28 ⒶⒷⒸⒹⒺ
2 ⒶⒷⒸⒹⒺ	11 ⒶⒷⒸⒹⒺ	20 ⒶⒷⒸⒹⒺ	29 ⒶⒷⒸⒹⒺ
3 ⒶⒷⒸⒹⒺ	12 ⒶⒷⒸⒹⒺ	21 ⒶⒷⒸⒹⒺ	30 ⒶⒷⒸⒹⒺ
4 ⒶⒷⒸⒹⒺ	13 ⒶⒷⒸⒹⒺ	22 ⒶⒷⒸⒹⒺ	31 ⒶⒷⒸⒹⒺ
5 ⒶⒷⒸⒹⒺ	14 ⒶⒷⒸⒹⒺ	23 ⒶⒷⒸⒹⒺ	32 ⒶⒷⒸⒹⒺ
6 ⒶⒷⒸⒹⒺ	15 ⒶⒷⒸⒹⒺ	24 ⒶⒷⒸⒹⒺ	33 ⒶⒷⒸⒹⒺ
7 ⒶⒷⒸⒹⒺ	16 ⒶⒷⒸⒹⒺ	25 ⒶⒷⒸⒹⒺ	34 ⒶⒷⒸⒹⒺ
8 ⒶⒷⒸⒹⒺ	17 ⒶⒷⒸⒹⒺ	26 ⒶⒷⒸⒹⒺ	35 ⒶⒷⒸⒹⒺ
9 ⒶⒷⒸⒹⒺ	18 ⒶⒷⒸⒹⒺ	27 ⒶⒷⒸⒹⒺ	36 ⒶⒷⒸⒹⒺ

Section 5/6

1 ⒶⒷⒸⒹⒺ	10 ⒶⒷⒸⒹⒺ	19 ⒶⒷⒸⒹⒺ	28 ⒶⒷⒸⒹⒺ
2 ⒶⒷⒸⒹⒺ	11 ⒶⒷⒸⒹⒺ	20 ⒶⒷⒸⒹⒺ	29 ⒶⒷⒸⒹⒺ
3 ⒶⒷⒸⒹⒺ	12 ⒶⒷⒸⒹⒺ	21 ⒶⒷⒸⒹⒺ	30 ⒶⒷⒸⒹⒺ
4 ⒶⒷⒸⒹⒺ	13 ⒶⒷⒸⒹⒺ	22 ⒶⒷⒸⒹⒺ	31 ⒶⒷⒸⒹⒺ
5 ⒶⒷⒸⒹⒺ	14 ⒶⒷⒸⒹⒺ	23 ⒶⒷⒸⒹⒺ	32 ⒶⒷⒸⒹⒺ
6 ⒶⒷⒸⒹⒺ	15 ⒶⒷⒸⒹⒺ	24 ⒶⒷⒸⒹⒺ	33 ⒶⒷⒸⒹⒺ
7 ⒶⒷⒸⒹⒺ	16 ⒶⒷⒸⒹⒺ	25 ⒶⒷⒸⒹⒺ	34 ⒶⒷⒸⒹⒺ
8 ⒶⒷⒸⒹⒺ	17 ⒶⒷⒸⒹⒺ	26 ⒶⒷⒸⒹⒺ	35 ⒶⒷⒸⒹⒺ
9 ⒶⒷⒸⒹⒺ	18 ⒶⒷⒸⒹⒺ	27 ⒶⒷⒸⒹⒺ	36 ⒶⒷⒸⒹⒺ

Section 6/7

1 ⒶⒷⒸⒹⒺ	10 ⒶⒷⒸⒹⒺ	19 ⒶⒷⒸⒹⒺ	28 ⒶⒷⒸⒹⒺ
2 ⒶⒷⒸⒹⒺ	11 ⒶⒷⒸⒹⒺ	20 ⒶⒷⒸⒹⒺ	29 ⒶⒷⒸⒹⒺ
3 ⒶⒷⒸⒹⒺ	12 ⒶⒷⒸⒹⒺ	21 ⒶⒷⒸⒹⒺ	30 ⒶⒷⒸⒹⒺ
4 ⒶⒷⒸⒹⒺ	13 ⒶⒷⒸⒹⒺ	22 ⒶⒷⒸⒹⒺ	31 ⒶⒷⒸⒹⒺ
5 ⒶⒷⒸⒹⒺ	14 ⒶⒷⒸⒹⒺ	23 ⒶⒷⒸⒹⒺ	32 ⒶⒷⒸⒹⒺ
6 ⒶⒷⒸⒹⒺ	15 ⒶⒷⒸⒹⒺ	24 ⒶⒷⒸⒹⒺ	33 ⒶⒷⒸⒹⒺ
7 ⒶⒷⒸⒹⒺ	16 ⒶⒷⒸⒹⒺ	25 ⒶⒷⒸⒹⒺ	34 ⒶⒷⒸⒹⒺ
8 ⒶⒷⒸⒹⒺ	17 ⒶⒷⒸⒹⒺ	26 ⒶⒷⒸⒹⒺ	35 ⒶⒷⒸⒹⒺ
9 ⒶⒷⒸⒹⒺ	18 ⒶⒷⒸⒹⒺ	27 ⒶⒷⒸⒹⒺ	36 ⒶⒷⒸⒹⒺ

 **STEP FOUR**

Section 7/8

1 Ⓐ Ⓑ Ⓒ Ⓓ Ⓔ	6 Ⓐ Ⓑ Ⓒ Ⓓ Ⓔ	11 Ⓐ Ⓑ Ⓒ Ⓓ Ⓔ	16 Ⓐ Ⓑ Ⓒ Ⓓ Ⓔ
2 Ⓐ Ⓑ Ⓒ Ⓓ Ⓔ	7 Ⓐ Ⓑ Ⓒ Ⓓ Ⓔ	12 Ⓐ Ⓑ Ⓒ Ⓓ Ⓔ	17 Ⓐ Ⓑ Ⓒ Ⓓ Ⓔ
3 Ⓐ Ⓑ Ⓒ Ⓓ Ⓔ	8 Ⓐ Ⓑ Ⓒ Ⓓ Ⓔ	13 Ⓐ Ⓑ Ⓒ Ⓓ Ⓔ	18 Ⓐ Ⓑ Ⓒ Ⓓ Ⓔ
4 Ⓐ Ⓑ Ⓒ Ⓓ Ⓔ	9 Ⓐ Ⓑ Ⓒ Ⓓ Ⓔ	14 Ⓐ Ⓑ Ⓒ Ⓓ Ⓔ	19 Ⓐ Ⓑ Ⓒ Ⓓ Ⓔ
5 Ⓐ Ⓑ Ⓒ Ⓓ Ⓔ	10 Ⓐ Ⓑ Ⓒ Ⓓ Ⓔ	15 Ⓐ Ⓑ Ⓒ Ⓓ Ⓔ	20 Ⓐ Ⓑ Ⓒ Ⓓ Ⓔ

Section 8/9

1 Ⓐ Ⓑ Ⓒ Ⓓ Ⓔ	6 Ⓐ Ⓑ Ⓒ Ⓓ Ⓔ	11 Ⓐ Ⓑ Ⓒ Ⓓ Ⓔ	16 Ⓐ Ⓑ Ⓒ Ⓓ Ⓔ
2 Ⓐ Ⓑ Ⓒ Ⓓ Ⓔ	7 Ⓐ Ⓑ Ⓒ Ⓓ Ⓔ	12 Ⓐ Ⓑ Ⓒ Ⓓ Ⓔ	17 Ⓐ Ⓑ Ⓒ Ⓓ Ⓔ
3 Ⓐ Ⓑ Ⓒ Ⓓ Ⓔ	8 Ⓐ Ⓑ Ⓒ Ⓓ Ⓔ	13 Ⓐ Ⓑ Ⓒ Ⓓ Ⓔ	18 Ⓐ Ⓑ Ⓒ Ⓓ Ⓔ
4 Ⓐ Ⓑ Ⓒ Ⓓ Ⓔ	9 Ⓐ Ⓑ Ⓒ Ⓓ Ⓔ	14 Ⓐ Ⓑ Ⓒ Ⓓ Ⓔ	19 Ⓐ Ⓑ Ⓒ Ⓓ Ⓔ
5 Ⓐ Ⓑ Ⓒ Ⓓ Ⓔ	10 Ⓐ Ⓑ Ⓒ Ⓓ Ⓔ	15 Ⓐ Ⓑ Ⓒ Ⓓ Ⓔ	20 Ⓐ Ⓑ Ⓒ Ⓓ Ⓔ

Section 10

1 Ⓐ Ⓑ Ⓒ Ⓓ Ⓔ	6 Ⓐ Ⓑ Ⓒ Ⓓ Ⓔ	11 Ⓐ Ⓑ Ⓒ Ⓓ Ⓔ	16 Ⓐ Ⓑ Ⓒ Ⓓ Ⓔ
2 Ⓐ Ⓑ Ⓒ Ⓓ Ⓔ	7 Ⓐ Ⓑ Ⓒ Ⓓ Ⓔ	12 Ⓐ Ⓑ Ⓒ Ⓓ Ⓔ	17 Ⓐ Ⓑ Ⓒ Ⓓ Ⓔ
3 Ⓐ Ⓑ Ⓒ Ⓓ Ⓔ	8 Ⓐ Ⓑ Ⓒ Ⓓ Ⓔ	13 Ⓐ Ⓑ Ⓒ Ⓓ Ⓔ	18 Ⓐ Ⓑ Ⓒ Ⓓ Ⓔ
4 Ⓐ Ⓑ Ⓒ Ⓓ Ⓔ	9 Ⓐ Ⓑ Ⓒ Ⓓ Ⓔ	14 Ⓐ Ⓑ Ⓒ Ⓓ Ⓔ	19 Ⓐ Ⓑ Ⓒ Ⓓ Ⓔ
5 Ⓐ Ⓑ Ⓒ Ⓓ Ⓔ	10 Ⓐ Ⓑ Ⓒ Ⓓ Ⓔ	15 Ⓐ Ⓑ Ⓒ Ⓓ Ⓔ	20 Ⓐ Ⓑ Ⓒ Ⓓ Ⓔ

Student-Produced Responses

Only answers entered in the circles in each grid will be scored. You will not receive credit for anything written in the boxes above the circles.

9   10   11   12   13

14   15   16   17   18

1 1 1 1 1 1 1 1 1 1 1 1

Time—25 Minutes
1 Essay

Think carefully about the issue presented in the following excerpt and the assignment below.

DIRECTIONS: You have 25 minutes to plan and write an essay on the topic assigned below. DO NOT WRITE ON ANY OTHER TOPIC. AN ESSAY ON ANOTHER TOPIC IS NOT ACCEPTABLE. Think carefully about the issue presented in the following excerpt and the assignment below.

> *Some schools and districts have eliminated study hall for their students. The primary drive behind this elimination is to allow students to take additional electives and substantive subjects. Though students might have slightly more work to complete at home, they will leave school much more well-rounded with their added knowledge.*

Assignment: Should schools eliminate study hall? Plan and write an essay in which you develop your point of view on this issue. Support your position with reasoning and examples taken from your reading, studies, experience, and observations.

2 2 2 2 2 2 2 2 2 2 2

Time—25 Minutes 18 Items	In this section, solve each item, using any available space on the page for scratchwork. Then, decide which is the best of the choices given and fill in the corresponding oval on the answer sheet.

Notes: The figures accompanying the items are drawn as accurately as possible unless otherwise stated in specific items. Again, unless otherwise stated, all figures lie in the same plane. All numbers used in these items are real numbers. Calculators are permitted for this test.

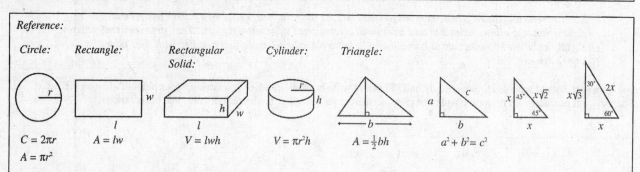

Reference:

Circle: Rectangle: Rectangular Solid: Cylinder: Triangle:

$C = 2\pi r$ $A = lw$ $V = lwh$ $V = \pi r^2 h$ $A = \frac{1}{2}bh$ $a^2 + b^2 = c^2$

$A = \pi r^2$

- The measure in degrees of a straight angle is 180.
- The number of degrees of arc in a circle is 360.
- The sum of the measure of the angles of a triangle is 180.

1. If $5,454 = 54(x+1)$, then $x =$

   (A) 10
   (B) 11
   (C) 100
   (D) 101
   (E) 1001

[handwritten: $5454 = 54x + 54$; $5400 = 54x$; $100 = x$]

2. If $k^x \cdot k^9 = k^{21}$ and $(m^y)^3 = m^{18}$, then $(x - y) =$

   (A) 3
   (B) 6
   (C) 9
   (D) 12
   (E) 15

[handwritten: $(m^y)^3 = m^{18}$; $x = 12$; $y = 6$; $12 - 6 = 6$]

3. At the ABC Bulk Mail Center, an old machine stuffs and seals envelopes at a rate of 150 envelopes per minute, and a new machine stuffs and seals envelopes at a rate of 350 envelopes per minute. How many minutes will it take both machines working together to seal and stuff a total of 750 envelopes?

   (A) 0.80
   (B) 1.25
   (C) 1.50
   (D) 1.60
   (E) 2.10

[handwritten: $\frac{150}{60}$; $\frac{350}{60}$; $\frac{150}{60} = \frac{750}{x}$; $x = 30$; $x = 1.28$]

4. If $x = \frac{3y^2}{z}$, what is the result of doubling both y and z?

   (A) x is not changed.
   (B) x is doubled.
   (C) x is tripled.
   (D) x is multiplied by 2.
   (E) x is multiplied by 6.

[handwritten: let $y = 2$, $z = 3$; $x = \frac{3(4)^2}{6}$; $x = 4$; $x = 8$]

GO ON TO THE NEXT PAGE

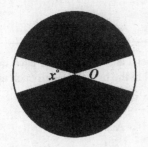

5. The circle with center O has a radius of length 2. If the total area of the shaded regions is 3π, then $x =$

$A = \pi r^2$
$A = 4\pi$

$4\pi - 3\pi$
Area of non-shaded region $= \pi$

(A) 270
(B) 180
(C) 120
(D) 90
(E) 45

$= 90/2$ ☒ $\boxed{45}$

6. If a bar of metal alloy consists of 100 grams of tin and 150 grams of lead, what percent of the entire bar, by weight, is tin?

(A) 10%
(B) 15%
(C) $33\frac{1}{3}\%$
(D) 40%
(E) $66\frac{2}{3}\%$

$\dfrac{100\,gr}{250} = \dfrac{x}{100}$

$x = 40 \%$

7. If $\dfrac{1}{x} + \dfrac{1}{y} = \dfrac{1}{z}$, then $z =$

(A) $\dfrac{1}{xy}$

(B) xy

(C) $\dfrac{x+y}{xy}$

(D) $\dfrac{xy}{x+y}$

(E) $\dfrac{2xy}{x+y}$

$\dfrac{y+x}{xy} = \dfrac{1}{z}$

$\dfrac{z(y+x)}{y+x} = \dfrac{xy}{y+x}$

$z = \dfrac{xy}{y+x}$

8. In a certain clothing store, 60% of all the articles are imported and 20% of all the articles are priced at $100 or more. If 40% of the total articles priced at $100 or more are imported, what percent of the articles are priced under $100 and are not imported?

(A) 28%
(B) 12%
(C) 8%
(D) 4.8%
(E) 2%

100 articles

60 imported
20 priced @ $100 or more
   8 priced @ $100 or more imported
12 priced @ $100 or more but NOT imported

$40 - 12 = \boxed{28}$ → less than $100 and NOT imported

GO ON TO THE NEXT PAGE

Rest of this

Directions for Student-Produced Responses Items

Items 9-18 each require you to solve an item and mark your answer on a special answer grid. For each item, you should write your answer in the boxes at the top of each column and then fill in the ovals beneath each answer you write. Here are some examples.

Answer: 3/4 or .75
(show answer either way)

Answer: 325

Note: A mixed number such as $3\frac{1}{2}$ must be gridded as 7/2 or as 3.5. If gridded as "31/2," it will be read as "thirty-one halves."

Note: Either position is correct.

9. If $3x + 2 = 8$, then $6x =$

10. Members of a civic organization purchase boxes of candy for $1 each and sell them for $2 each. If no other expenses are incurred, how many boxes of candy must they sell to earn a net profit of $500?

GO ON TO THE NEXT PAGE

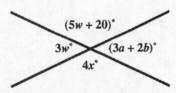

11. In a school with a total enrollment of 360 students, 90 students are seniors. What percent of all students enrolled in the school are seniors?

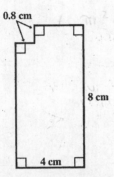

12. The figure above is a scale drawing of the floor of a dining hall. If 1 centimeter on the drawing represents 5 meters, what is the area, in square meters, of the floor?

13. If two straight lines intersect as shown, what is the value of x?

14. A school club spent $\frac{2}{5}$ of its budget for one project and $\frac{1}{3}$ of what remained for another project. If the club's entire budget was equal to $300, how much of the budget, in dollars, was left after the two projects?

15. The average of the following six numbers is 16: 10, 12, 15.1, 15.2, 28, and x. What is the value of x?

16. At the zoo, 25% of the animals are birds, 30% are reptiles or amphibians, and the rest are mammals. If there are 12 geese, representing 20% of the birds, how many mammals are there at the zoo?

17. Jerry grew 5 inches in 1993 and 2 inches more in 1994, before reaching his final height of 5 feet 10 inches. What percentage of his final height did his 1993-1994 growth represent?

GO ON TO THE NEXT PAGE

18. A circle with a radius of 2 is superimposed upon a square with sides measuring 5 so that the center of the circle and the center of the square are identical. At how many points will the square and circle intersect?

IF YOU FINISH BEFORE TIME IS CALLED, YOU MAY CHECK YOUR WORK ON THIS TEST ONLY. DO NOT WORK ON ANY OTHER TEST SECTION. **STOP**

—752—

3 3 3 3 3 3 3 3 3 3 3 3

Time—25 Minutes	For each item in this section, choose the best answer and blacken the
35 Items	corresponding space on the answer sheet.

Directions: The following sentences test correctness and effectiveness of expression. In choosing answers, follow the requirements of standard written English; that is, pay attention to grammar, choice of words, sentence construction, and punctuation.

In each of the following sentences, part of the sentence or the entire sentence is underlined. Beneath each sentence you will find five ways of phrasing the underlined part. Choice A repeats the original; the other four are different.

Choose the answer that best expresses the meaning of the original sentence. If you think the original is better than any of the alternatives, choose it; otherwise choose one of the others. Your choice should produce the most effective sentence—clear and precise, without awkwardness or ambiguity.

Example: Answer

Allen <u>visiting</u> his cousin in France last summer.

(A) visiting
(B) visited
(C) does visit
(D) a visit
(E) is visiting

Ⓐ ● Ⓒ Ⓓ Ⓔ

1. Before the invention of television, <u>radio was the chief form of at-home entertainment</u>.

   (A) radio was the chief form of at-home entertainment
   (B) radio has been the chief form of at-home entertainment
   (C) radio, having been the chief form of at home entertainment
   (D) the chief form of at-home entertainment is the radio
   (E) radio, a form of at-home entertainment, was the chief

2. Once she determined that the muddy conditions <u>will pose</u> a hazard to the players, the athletic director postponed the game.

   (A) will pose
   (B) would pose
   (C) posing
   (D) had posed
   (E) are posing

GO ON TO THE NEXT PAGE

3. The sustained decline in student enrollment raises doubts about <u>if the highly technical course of instruction is a viable</u> college program.

   (A) if the highly technical course of instruction is a viable
   (B) if there is viability in the highly technical course of instruction as
   (C) whether the highly technical course of instruction is a viable
   (D) the highly technical course of instruction as a viable
   (E) the viability of the highly technical course of instruction as

4. <u>In a panicked tone, the duty nurse heard the mother asking for help for her injured child.</u>

   (A) In a panicked tone, the duty nurse heard the mother asking for help for her injured child.
   (B) The duty nurse heard the mother asking for help for her injured child, who spoke in a panicked tone.
   (C) Her tone being panicked, the mother asked the duty nurse for help for her injured child.
   (D) The duty nurse, in a panicked tone, heard the mother asking for help for her injured child.
   (E) The duty nurse heard the mother asking in a panicked tone for help for her injured child.

5. The CEO of the firm was <u>accused by a group of opposition shareholders of diverting company funds to his private account and with sexual harassment</u> of other employees.

   (A) accused by a group of opposition shareholders of diverting company funds to his private account and with sexual harassment
   (B) accused by a group of opposition shareholders of diverting company funds to his private account and sexual harassment
   (C) being accused by a group of opposition shareholders of diverting company funds to his private account and with sexual harassment
   (D) accused by a group of opposition shareholders of diverting both company funds to his private account and sexual harassment
   (E) diverting company funds to his private account and sexual harassment as accused by a group of opposition shareholders

GO ON TO THE NEXT PAGE ⇒

6. Khartoum, the <u>capital</u> of Sudan, <u>is</u> situated <u>at</u> the
           A   B   C
   confluence of the Blue Nile and White Nile <u>river</u>.
                                       D

   <u>No error</u>
    E

7. Hieroglyphics and the alphabet <u>are</u> forms of
                       A
   writing <u>that</u> date to the Middle Kingdom of
         B
   Egypt, <u>though</u> the first was fading from use while
        C
   the second was <u>only developing</u>. <u>No error</u>
                 D   E

8. Several of the <u>most influential</u> <u>economists</u> in the
               A   B
   United States <u>are</u> <u>graduates or</u> teachers at the
             C   D
   University of Chicago. <u>No error</u>
                    E

9. <u>During</u> his first and <u>only</u> trip to Pennsylvania,
   A   B
   William Penn, Quaker leader and founder of the
   colony, drew up a liberal Frame of Government
   and <u>establishes</u> friendly relations <u>with</u> the
        C   D
   indigenous people. <u>No error</u>
                E

GO ON TO THE NEXT PAGE

10. Dynamite, an explosive <u>made from</u> nitroglycerine
                          A
    and various inert fillers, <u>were invented</u> by Alfred
                                B
    Nobel, the Swedish chemist <u>who</u> <u>endowed</u> the
                                 C   D
    Nobel prizes. <u>No error</u>
                     E

11. <u>When</u> you listen to the music of Khachaturian, a
    A
    Russian composer of Armenian <u>heritage,</u> <u>one</u>
                                    B   C
    <u>can hear</u> elements of Armenian and Asian folk
      D
    music. <u>No error</u>
              E

12. A considerable <u>improvement</u> over the Bessemer
                     A
    Process, the open-hearth process of <u>producing</u>
                                          B
    steel can use up to 100 percent scrap metal, refine

    pig iron with a <u>high</u> phosphorus content, and
                      C
    <u>production of</u> less brittle steels. <u>No error</u>
      D   E

13. <u>Usually</u> nocturnal and <u>feeds</u> on small animals
    A   B
    such as insects, the salamander <u>is found</u> in <u>damp</u>
                                       C   D
    regions of the northern temperate zone. <u>No error</u>
                                                E

14. The first of Kepler's <u>law</u> states <u>that</u> the shape of
                            A   B
    <u>each</u> planet's orbit <u>is</u> an ellipse with the sun at
    C   D
    one focus. <u>No error</u>
                 E

15. <u>For</u> someone who enjoys eating in restaurants,
    A
    New York City <u>offers</u> a variety of ethnic cuisines,
                    B
    each with <u>their</u> <u>own</u> flavors. <u>No error</u>
              C   D   E

GO ON TO THE NEXT PAGE

16. While rowing, the direction and speed of the boat
    ‾‾‾‾‾‾‾‾‾‾‾
    A
    or shell are controlled by the coxswain, who also
             ‾‾‾   ‾‾‾
             B   C
    calls the rhythms of the rowers' strokes. No error
                                     ‾‾‾‾‾‾‾ ‾‾‾‾‾‾‾‾
                                     D   E

17. Rayon, one of the oldest synthetic fibers, is made
           ‾‾‾   ‾‾‾‾‾‾ ‾‾‾‾‾‾‾
           A   B   C
    from cellulose, chiefly derived from wood pulp.
    ‾‾‾‾   ‾‾‾‾‾‾‾
    D
    No error
    ‾‾‾‾‾‾‾
    E

18. George Bernard Shaw, the Irish playwright and

    critic, was a popular speaker who writes five
                  ‾‾‾‾‾‾‾   ‾‾‾ ‾‾‾‾‾‾
                  A   B   C
    novels before becoming a music critic for London
                            ‾‾‾‾‾
                            D
    newspaper in the late 1890s. No error
                                 ‾‾‾‾‾‾‾‾
                                 E

19. In the 1760s, Adam Smith traveled to France
                              ‾‾‾‾‾‾‾‾
                              A
    where he met some of the Physiocrats and started
    ‾‾‾‾‾   ‾‾‾‾‾‾‾
    B   C
    to writing his masterpiece, *The Wealth of*
    ‾‾‾‾‾‾‾‾‾
    D
    Nations. No error
              ‾‾‾‾‾‾‾‾
              E

20. In order to guide a smart bomb, an aircraft pilot
            ‾‾‾‾‾‾‾‾
            A
    aims a laser beam to the target, which then
                      ‾‾   ‾‾‾‾‾
                      B   C
    reflects the beam back to a computer in the

    weapon itself. No error
           ‾‾‾‾‾‾ ‾‾‾‾‾‾‾‾
           D   E

21. Chivalry was the system of ethical ideals that
             ‾‾‾
             A
    grew out of feudalism and that reached their high
         ‾‾‾‾‾‾   ‾‾‾‾‾
         B   C
    point in the 12ᵗʰ and 13ᵗʰ centuries. No error
                                ‾‾‾‾‾‾‾‾‾ ‾‾‾‾‾‾‾‾
                                D   E

22. The area that is now Portugal was added to the
                 ‾‾‾‾   ‾‾
                 A   B
    Roman Empire around 5 A.D., later overrun
                 ‾‾‾‾‾‾
                 C
    by Germanic tribes in the 5ᵗʰ century, and finally

    conquested by the Moors in 711. No error
    ‾‾‾‾‾‾‾‾‾   ‾‾‾‾‾‾‾‾
    D   E

23. Valedictorian of his Rutgers class, an Olympic

    gold medalist, and he was an internationally
                       ‾‾‾‾‾‾   ‾‾‾‾‾‾‾‾‾‾‾‾‾‾‾
                       A   B
    renowned singer, Paul Robeson was a man of
                                  ‾‾‾
                                  C
    many talents. No error
    ‾‾‾‾   ‾‾‾‾‾‾‾‾
    D   E

24. The cavities of the internal nose, which are lined
                                       ‾‾‾‾‾
                                       A
    with a mucous membrane, is covered with fine
                            ‾‾‾‾‾‾‾‾‾‾
                            B
    hairs that help to filter dust and impurities from
                    ‾‾   ‾‾‾‾
                    C   D
    the air. No error
            ‾‾‾‾‾‾‾‾
            E

25. It has been noted that when one of the senses
                            ‾‾‾‾
                            A
    such as sight, hear, or smell, is seriously degraded
                  ‾‾‾‾   ‾‾‾‾‾‾‾‾
                  B   C
    the other two become more acute. No error
                         ‾‾‾‾   ‾‾‾‾‾‾‾‾
                         D   D

GO ON TO THE NEXT PAGE

Directions: The following passages are early drafts of essays. Some parts of the passages need to be rewritten.

Read the passages and answer the items that follow. Some items are about particular sentences or parts of sentences and ask you to improve sentence structure and word choice. Other items refer to parts of the essays or the entire essays and ask you to consider organization and development. In making your decisions, follow the conventions of standard written English. After you have chosen your answer, fill in the corresponding oval on your answer sheet.

Items 26 - 30 refer to the following passage.

(1) My favorite opera is La Bohème by Puccini. (2) Why is La Bohème my favorite? (3) The action of the opera takes place on the Left Bank of Paris in the 1830s. (4) The Left Bank is where the struggling artists and students lived. (5) Four of the main characters in the opera are a painter, a philosopher, a musician, and, most important for me, a poet. (6) The sets include a sidewalk café and a garret room. (7) They even have a passionate romance with a tragic ending.

(8) The opera is based on Scènes de la Vie de Bohème written by Henri Murger. (9) When Murger wrote this novel, he himself was a poor writer living in the Latin Quarter in the 1840s. (10) The book is a collection of short, funny stories about Henri and his friends.

(11) The individual scenes, on which the novel is based, first appeared as a series of stories in a Parisian newspaper. (12) The group of struggling artists that made up Henri's group loved to eat and drink in cafés, but they hardly ever had any money to pay the check. (13) They were all very poor, but they will make the most of the present without worrying about the future.

(14) Legend has it that someone once came to visit Murger in his tiny apartment and found Murger in bed. (15) When the visitor suggested that Murger get dressed go to a café, Murger said that he couldn't because he'd lent his only pair of pants to a friend. (16) I like to think of this story and imagine myself as Murger, being that he is the struggling writer.

26. The function of sentence 2 is to

(A) pose a question that the writer will answer
(B) invite the reader to answer to the question
(C) signal the writer's confidence about the topic
(D) imply that "favorite" is a matter of personal choice
(E) express the writer's doubt about the selection

27. If the writer wanted to add that the Left Bank is also called the Latin Quarter, that purpose could best be accomplished by inserting

(A) "The Latin Quarter is another name for the Left Bank." after sentence 3
(B) "The Latin Quarter and the Left Bank are the same thing." after sentence 3
(C) "(also called the Latin Quarter)" after "Left Bank" in sentence 4
(D) "The Left Bank is also called the Latin Quarter." after sentence 4
(E) "The Latin Quarter is another name for the Left Bank." after sentence 4

28. Which of the following is the best revision of the underlined portion of sentence 7 (reproduced below)?

They even have a passionate romance with a tragic ending.

(A) Fortunately, they even have
(B) As a matter of fact, they even have
(C) It is even that they have
(D) The opera even has
(E) It even has

29. In the context of the third paragraph, which revision is most needed in sentence 13?

(A) Omit "but."
(B) Change "they" to "struggling artists."
(C) Change "will make" to "made."
(D) Start a new sentence with "they."
(E) Change "but" to "and."

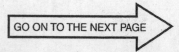
GO ON TO THE NEXT PAGE

30. In the context of the last paragraph, which revision is most needed in sentence 16?

    (A) Insert "In point of fact" at the beginning
    (B) Omit the word "story."
    (C) Omit the words "being that he is."
    (D) Change the comma to a semicolon
    (E) Change "is" to "was."

Items 31 - 35 refer to the following passage.

(1) In 1928, a National Flag Conference adopted the National Flag Code. (2) The Code established principles of flag etiquette based upon the practices of the military. (3) These principles were eventually enacted into law. (4) The Flag Code law does not impose penalties for misuse of the United States Flag, but it is the guide for the proper handling and display of the Stars and Stripes. (5) Generally, you should display the flag only from sunrise to sunset on buildings and on stationary flagstaffs in the open. (6) You can, however, display the flag twenty-four hours a day if it is properly illuminated during the hours of darkness. (7) It is appropriate to display the flag on any day of the year but especially on important holidays such as Memorial Day, Independence Day and Veterans Day. (8) The flag should not be displayed on days when the weather is inclement, unless they're all-weather flags.

(9) When raising the flag, it should be hoisted briskly. (10) When you take it down, it should be lowered ceremoniously. (11) Take care not to let it touch the ground. (12) It should be neatly folded and carefully stored away.

(13) It is all right to clean and mend your flag. (14) However, when it becomes so worn that it no longer serves as a proper symbol of the United States, it should be replaced. (15) The old flag should be destroyed, preferably by burning.

(16) You may think that displaying the flag just means buying a flag and hanging it on a pole. (17) Because the Flag Code covers many other points that you probably don't know about, this will surprise you. (18) If you rally want to show your patriotism by displaying the flag, then you should be familiar with the rules of flag etiquette.

31. The main idea of the essay is expressed by

    (A) sentence 1
    (B) sentence 8
    (C) sentence 15
    (D) sentence 16
    (E) sentence 18

GO ON TO THE NEXT PAGE

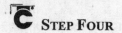

32. The overall development of the thesis would be made clearer by beginning a new paragraph with

   (A) sentence 2
   (B) sentence 3
   (C) sentence 5
   (D) sentence 6
   (E) sentence 8

33. In the context of the first paragraph, which revision is most needed in sentence 8?

   (A) Omit the word "unless."
   (B) Change "flag" to "flags."
   (C) Change "they're" to "it's an" and "flags" to "flag."
   (D) Omit the word "when."
   (E) Change the comma to a semicolon

34. Which of the following is the best revision of sentence 9 (reproduced below)?

   When raising the flag, it should be hoisted briskly.

   (A) (As it is now.)
   (B) When raising, the flag should be hoisted briskly.
   (C) When the flag is rising, it should be done briskly.
   (D) When raising the flag, you should hoist it briskly.
   (E) When briskly raising the flag, it should be hoisted.

35. Which of the following, in context, is the best way of revising sentence 17 (reproduced below)?

   Because the Flag Code covers many other points that you probably don't know about, this will surprise you.

   (A) The Flag Code covers many other points that may surprise you.
   (B) Because the Flag Code covers many other points that may surprise you.
   (C) You may be surprised that the Flag Code covers many other points.
   (D) Surprising you, the Flag Code probably covers many other points you don't know about.
   (E) Many other points are covered by the Flag Cole that may surprise you.

IF YOU FINISH BEFORE TIME IS CALLED, YOU MAY CHECK YOUR WORK ON THIS TEST ONLY. DO NOT WORK ON ANY OTHER TEST SECTION. **STOP**

−760−

4 4 4 4 4 4 4 4 4 4 4 4

Time—25 Minutes
24 Items

For each item in this section, choose the best answer and blacken the corresponding space on the answer sheet.

Each item below has one or two blanks, each blank indicating that something has been omitted. Beneath the sentence are five lettered words or sets of words. Choose the word or set of words that <u>best</u> fits the meaning of the sentence as a whole.

Example:

Although its publicity has been ----, the film itself is intelligent, well acted, handsomely produced, and altogether ----.

(A) tasteless..respectable
(B) extensive..moderate
(C) sophisticated..amateur
(D) risqué..crude
(E) perfect..spectacular

1. The history book, written in 1880, was tremendously ----, unfairly blaming the South for the Civil War.

(A) biased
(B) objective
(C) suppressed
(D) questionable
(E) complicated

2. In the Middle Ages, scientists and clergymen thought the universe was well-ordered and ----; today scientists are more likely to see the world as ----.

(A) baffling..dogmatic
(B) harmonious..chaotic
(C) transient..predictable
(D) emancipated..intriguing
(E) divergent..galling

3. Hot milk has long been a standard cure for insomnia because of its ---- quality.

(A) malevolent
(B) amorphous
(C) soporific
(D) plaintive
(E) desultory

4. Since the results of the experiment were ---- the body of research already completed, the committee considered the results to be ----.

(A) similar to..speculative
(B) inconsistent with..anomalous
(C) compounded by..heretical
(D) dispelled by..convincing
(E) contradicted by..redundant

5. Psychologists believe that modern life ---- neurosis because of the ---- of traditional values that define acceptable behavior.

(A) copes with..inundation
(B) strives for..condoning
(C) concentrates on..plethora
(D) fosters..disappearance
(E) corroborates..dispelling

6. Peter, ---- by the repeated rejections of his novel, ---- to submit his manuscript to other publishers.

(A) encouraged..declined
(B) elated..planned
(C) undaunted..continued
(D) inspired..complied
(E) undeterred..refused

GO ON TO THE NEXT PAGE

7. All ---- artists must struggle with the conflict
   between ---- their own talent and knowledge that
   very few are great enough to succeed.

   (A) great..neglect of
   (B) aspiring..faith in
   (C) ambitious..indifference to
   (D) prophetic..dissolution of
   (E) serious..disregard of

GO ON TO THE NEXT PAGE

Each passage below is followed by one or more items based on its content. Answer the items following each passage on the basis of what is <u>stated</u> or <u>implied</u> in the passage.

Item 8 is based on the following passage.

The use of balls probably originated in the Middle East, as an aspect of religious ceremonies. Their use was apparently introduced into Europe by the
Line Moors during the time of their occupation of Spain.
5 The earliest written references to balls of the sort that we associate with games are found in the writings of Christian theologians dating from the period shortly after the Moorish invasion of Europe. These theologians condemned the use of balls as a form of
10 Saturnalia, a pagan festival.

8. The author assumes that the

(A) initial appearance of balls in Europe would have been noted in contemporary writings
(B) use of balls in Europe was originally restricted to religious rites
(C) practices of one religion are often adopted by other religions in the region
(D) games associated with a culture are spread when the influence of that culture grows
(E) writings of a religious movement accurately reflect the practices of its adherents

Item 9 is based on the following passage

Nicholas Nickleby, the second novel of Charles Dickens, has been referred to by some commentators as romantic, but the novel is actually highly realistic.
Line Dickens collected material for his novel on a journey
5 through Yorkshire, during which he investigated for himself the deplorable conditions of the cheap boarding schools that produced broken bones and deformed minds in the name of education.

9. The author's primary purpose is to

(A) expose a pattern of long-standing abuse
(B) prove that novels are either romantic or realistic
(C) revise major commentary of the works of Dickens
(D) propose a new literary theory of the novel
(E) correct a misunderstanding about Nicholas Nickleby

GO ON TO THE NEXT PAGE

Item 10 is based on the following passage.

We tend to think of air pollution as a modern problem, but in 1257, when the Queen of England visited Nottingham, she found the smoke so bad that
Line she left for fear of her life. The culprit was soot and
5 smoke that came from the burning of coal. By the 19th Century, London and other industrialized cities already had serious air pollution problems. By the start of the 20th Century, bronchitis was called the "British disease." England got 30% less sunshine than 50 years
10 earlier, and a prominent art critic noted a darkening in the colors used by artists of the time. The Sherlock Holmes stories mention frequently the swirling, yellow-gray fog that enveloped London, and historical records show that buildings were coated with soot
15 almost as soon as they were cleaned and repainted.

10. In developing the passage, the author relies mainly on

(A) statistics to demonstrate that air pollution has serious health consequences
(B) examples to show that air pollution is a long-standing problem
(C) first-hand accounts to refute claims that air pollution is worse now than it was a century ago
(D) inferences from historical records to track the increase in air pollution
(E) opinions from expert authorities to document the significance of air pollution

Item 11 is based on the following passage.

For too many years, communities have been losing public spaces that provide people with an opportunity to meet and exchange ideas. Today, the
Line privately owned shopping mall is often the only
5 remaining gathering space to be found in a community; however, public assembly, speeches, and leafleting can all be legally prohibited by the owners of private property.

11. The author of the passage is primarily concerned with explaining which of the following?

(A) Private places are more convenient than public ones.
(B) Speeches and leafleting are commercial activities.
(C) Freedom of speech is essential to a viable democracy.
(D) Shopping malls are gradually replacing public spaces.
(E) Privately owned shopping malls are not true public spaces.

GO ON TO THE NEXT PAGE

Item 12 is based on the following passage.

The cleaning and restoration of Michelangelo's frescoes on the ceiling of the Sistine Chapel were undertaken by some of the world's finest art restorers under the close supervision of an international team of art experts and historians. Nonetheless, the result produced a storm of controversy. Most modern viewers, it seemed, had become accustomed to seeing the frescoes with their colors dulled by layers of yellowing glue and varnish and with the contours of the figures obscured by centuries' accumulation of grime. These viewers thought the restored frescoes no longer looked like "serious art."

12. The author implies that

   (A) Michelangelo's frescoes contain subject matter that the public finds objectionable

   (B) some people who viewed the restored frescoes thought that they should be restored to their pre-cleaning status

   (C) most art works should be cleaned every few years to remove the dirt and grime that accumulates on their surfaces

   (D) some viewers expect that high art will be somber to reflect the seriousness of its artistic purpose

   (E) the art experts and historians who supervised the cleaning of the frescoes failed to protect the frescoes

Item 13 is based on the following passage.

Protectionists argue that an excess of exports over imports is essential to maintaining a favorable balance of trade. The value of the excess can then be converted to precious metals by demanding gold or silver from the nation or merchants owing the balance. This means, however, that the most favorable of all trade balances would occur when a country exported its entire national output and, in turn, imported only gold and silver. Since one cannot eat gold and silver, the protectionists must surely be incorrect.

13. The author develops the passage primarily by showing that

   (A) proponents of protectionism are not completely candid

   (B) most economists prefer trade to protectionism

   (C) arguments for protectionism lead to an absurd result

   (D) economic theories cannot be proved right or wrong

   (E) statistics can be manipulated to support any position

GO ON TO THE NEXT PAGE

Item 14 is based on the following passage.

In 1851, the United States established the Puget Sound District of the Bureau of Customs. American settlers, used to the duty-free woolens offered by the
Line British, feared that imposition and enforcement of
5 tariffs would not only increase the cost of woolens imported from the British side of the border but would result in the loss of British markets for American products. Consequently, American and British traders smuggled into the San Juan Islands British wool that
10 was then later sold as domestic wool by American sheepherders. This practice was so widespread and so successful that one naïve textbook writer, dividing the total "domestic" wool production of the islands by the reported number of sheep, credited San Juan's sheep
15 with the world's record for wool production: 150 pounds per sheep per year.

14. It can be inferred that the author refers to the textbook writer as "naïve" (line 12) because the writer

(A) failed to realize that the total given for domestic wool production included wool that had been smuggled into the islands
(B) relied on official statistics to determine the number of sheep raised in a particular region of the San Juan islands
(C) believed that American markets in British territory would not be jeopardized by the imposition of tariffs
(D) was aware of the possibility of smuggling arrangement but did not investigate further
(E) refused to believe that San Juan's sheep had actually set a world's record for wool production

GO ON TO THE NEXT PAGE

Items 15-24 are based on the following passage.

What we expect of translation is a reasonable facsimile of something that might have been said in our language. However, there is debate among critics as to what constitutes a reasonable facsimile. Most of us, at heart, belong to the "soft-line" party: A given translation may not be exactly "living language," but the facsimile is generally reasonable. The "hard-line" party aims only for the best translation. The majority of readers never notice the difference, as they read passively, often missing stylistic integrity as long as the story holds them. Additionally, a literature like Japanese may even be treated to an "exoticism handicap."

Whether or not one agrees with Roy A. Miller's postulation of an attitude of mysticism by the Japanese toward their own language, it is true that the Japanese have special feelings toward the possibilities of their language and its relation to life and art. These feelings impact what Japanese writers write about and how they write. Many of the special language relationships are not immediately available to the non-Japanese (which is only to say that the Japanese language, like every other, has some unique features). For example, in my own work on Dazai Osamu, I have found that his writing closely mimics the sense of the rhythms of spoken Japanese, and that such a mimicking is difficult to duplicate in English. Juda's cackling hysterically, "Heh, heh, heh" (in *Kakekomi uttae*), or the coy poutings of a schoolgirl (in *Joseito*) have what Masao Miyoshi has called, in *Accomplices of Silence*, an "embarrassing" quality. It is, however, the embarrassment of recognition that the reader of Japanese feels. The moments simply do not work in English.

Even the orthography of written Japanese is a resource not open to written English. Tanizaki Jun'ichiro, who elsewhere laments the poverty of "indigenous" Japanese vocabulary, writes in *Bunsho tokuhon* of the contribution to literary effect—to "meaning," if you will—made simply by the way a Japanese author chooses to "spell" a word. In Shiga Naoya's *Kinosaki nite*, for example, the onomatopoeic "bu—n" with which a honeybee takes flight has a different feeling for having been written in *hiragana* instead of *katakana*. I read, and I am convinced. Arishima Takeo uses onomatopoeic words in his children's story *Hitofusa no budo*, and the effect is not one of baby talk, but of gentleness and intimacy that automatically pulls the reader into the world of childhood fears, tragedies, and consolations, memories of which lie close under the surface of every adult psyche.

This, of course, is hard to reproduce in translation, although translators labor hard to do so. George Steiner speaks of an "intentional strangeness," a "creative dislocation," that sometimes is invoked in the attempt. He cites Chateaubriand's 1836 translation of Milton's *Paradise Lost*, for which Chateaubriand "created" a Latinate French to approximate Milton's special English as an example of such a successful act of creation. He also laments what he calls the "'moon in pond like blossom weary' school of instant exotica," with which we are perhaps all too familiar.

15. The author is primarily concerned with

   (A) criticizing translators who do not faithfully reproduce the style of works written in another language
   (B) suggesting that Japanese literature is more complex than English literature
   (C) arguing that no translation can do justice to a work written in another language
   (D) demonstrating that Japanese literature is particularly difficult to translate into English
   (E) discussing some of the problems of translating Japanese literature into English

16. It can be inferred that *Accomplices of Silence* is

   (A) an English translation of Japanese poetry
   (B) a critical commentary on the work of Dazai Osamu
   (C) a prior publication by the author on Japanese literature
   (D) a text on Japanese orthography
   (E) a general work on the problem of translation

17. In line 35, the word "orthography" means

   (A) poetry
   (B) vocabulary
   (C) spelling
   (D) translation
   (E) literature

GO ON TO THE NEXT PAGE

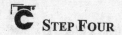

18. By the phrase "The moments simply do not work in English" (lines 33-34), the author means that

(A) English speakers are not able to comprehend the Japanese experience
(B) the Japanese descriptions do not translate well into English
(C) English is inferior to Japanese for describing intimate occurrences
(D) stock characters are more familiar to Japanese readers than to English readers
(E) "hard line" translators work more diligently at rendering texts than do "soft line" translators

19. The author cites Shiga Naoya's *Kinosaki nite* in order to

(A) illustrate the effect that Japanese orthography has on meaning
(B) demonstrate the poverty of indigenous Japanese vocabulary
(C) prove that it is difficult to translate Japanese into English
(D) acquaint the reader with an important work of Japanese literature
(E) impress upon the reader the importance of faithfully translating a work from one language into another

20. With which of the following statements would the author most likely agree?

(A) The Japanese language is the language that is best suited to poetry.
(B) English is one of the most difficult languages into which to translate any work written in Japanese.
(C) It is impossible for a person not fluent in Japanese to understand the inner meaning of Japanese literature.
(D) Most Japanese people think that their language is uniquely suited to conveying mystical ideas.
(E) Every language has its own peculiar potentialities that present challenges to a translator.

21. It can be inferred that the Japanese word "bu—n" (line 43) is most like which of the following English words?

(A) bee
(B) honey
(C) buzz
(D) flower
(E) moon

22. The author uses all of the following EXCEPT

(A) examples to prove a point
(B) citation of authority
(C) analogy
(D) personal knowledge
(E) contrasting two viewpoints

23. It can be inferred that the "exoticism handicap" (lines 12-13) mentioned by the author is

(A) the tendency of some translators of Japanese to render Japanese literature in a needlessly awkward style
(B) the attempt of Japanese writers to create for their readers a world characterized by mysticism
(C) the lack of literal, word-for-word translational equivalents for Japanese and English vocabulary
(D) the expectation of many English readers that Japanese literature can only be understood by someone who speaks Japanese
(E) the difficulty a Japanese reader encounters in trying to penetrate the meaning of difficult Japanese poets

24. The author's attitude toward the school of "instant exotica" (line 62) is one of

(A) endorsement
(B) disapproval
(C) confidence
(D) confusion
(E) courage

IF YOU FINISH BEFORE TIME IS CALLED, YOU MAY CHECK YOUR WORK ON THIS TEST ONLY. DO NOT WORK ON ANY OTHER TEST SECTION.

STOP

5 5 5 5 5 5 5 5 5 5 5 5

Time—25 Minutes **20 Items**	In this section, solve each item, using any available space on the page for scratchwork. Then, decide which is the best of the choices given and fill in the corresponding oval on the answer sheet.

Notes: The figures accompanying the items are drawn as accurately as possible unless otherwise stated in specific items. Again, unless otherwise stated, all figures lie in the same plane. All numbers used in these items are real numbers. Calculators are permitted for this test.

Reference:

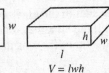
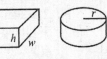

Circle: Rectangle: Rectangular Solid: Cylinder: Triangle:

$C = 2\pi r$ $A = lw$ $V = lwh$ $V = \pi r^2 h$ $A = \frac{1}{2}bh$ $a^2 + b^2 = c^2$

$A = \pi r^2$

- The measure in degrees of a straight angle is 180.
- The number of degrees of arc in a circle is 360.
- The sum of the measure of the angles of a triangle is 180.

---

1. $121{,}212 + (2 \cdot 10^4) =$

   (A) 321,212
   (B) 141,212
   (C) 123,212
   (D) 121,412
   (E) 121,232

2. If $6x + 3 = 21$, then $2x + 1 =$

   (A) 2
   (B) 3
   (C) 8
   (D) 6
   (E) 7

3. At a recreation center, it costs \$3 per hour to rent a Ping Pong table and \$12 per hour to rent a lane for bowling. For the cost of renting a bowling lane for two hours, it is possible to rent a Ping Pong table for how many hours?

   (A) 4
   (B) 6
   (C) 8
   (D) 18
   (E) 36

4. Jack, Ken, Larry, and Mike are j, k, l, and m years old, respectively. If $j < k < l < m$, which of the following could be true?

   (A) $k = j + l$
   (B) $j = k + l$
   (C) $j + k = l + m$
   (D) $j + k + m = l$
   (E) $j + m = k + l$

GO ON TO THE NEXT PAGE

5. The solution set for x in the equation $-|x| = -x$ is

(A) $\{x: x$ is a positive integer$\}$
(B) $\{x: x$ is either 0 or a positive integer$\}$
(C) $\{x: x > 0\}$
(D) $\{x: x \geq 0\}$
(E) $\{x: x$ is a real number$\}$

6. Out of a group of 360 students, exactly 18 are on the track team. What percent of the students are on the track team?

(A) 5%
(B) 10%
(C) 12%
(D) 20%
(E) 25%

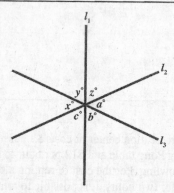

7. In the figure above, three lines intersect as shown. Which of the following must be true?

I. $a = x$
II. $y + z = b + c$
III. $x + a = y + b$

(A) I only
(B) II only
(C) I and II only
(D) I and III only
(E) I, II, and III

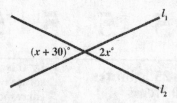

8. In the figure above, $x =$

(A) 15
(B) 30
(C) 45
(D) 60
(E) 90

9. The sum of the digits of a three-digit number is 11. If the hundreds digit is 3 times the units digit and 2 times the tens digit, what is the number?

(A) 168
(B) 361
(C) 632
(D) 641
(E) 921

10. The average (arithmetic mean) height of four buildings is 20 meters. If three of the buildings have a height of 16 meters, what is the height, in meters, of the fourth building?

(A) 32
(B) 28
(C) 24
(D) 22
(E) 18

11. If x is an odd integer, all of the following expressions are odd EXCEPT

(A) $x + 2$
(B) $3x + 2$
(C) $2x^2 + x$
(D) $2x^3 + x$
(E) $3x^3 + x$

GO ON TO THE NEXT PAGE

12. What is the sum of the areas of two squares with sides of 2 and 3, respectively?

   (A) 1
   (B) 5
   (C) 13
   (D) 25
   (E) 36

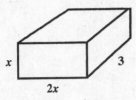

Note: Figure not drawn to scale.

13. In the figure above, the rectangular solid has a volume of 54. What is the value of x?

   (A) 2
   (B) 3
   (C) 6
   (D) 9
   (E) 12

14. If x is 80% of y, then y is what percent of x?

   (A) $133\frac{1}{3}\%$
   (B) 125%
   (C) 120%
   (D) 90%
   (E) 80%

15. From which of the following statements can it be deduced that $m > n$?

   (A) $m + 1 = n$
   (B) $2m = n$
   (C) $m + n > 0$
   (D) $m - n > 0$
   (E) $mn > 0$

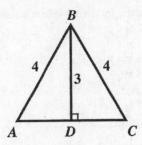

16. If $\sin \angle ABD = \dfrac{\sqrt{7}}{4}$ in the figure above, what is the length of $\overline{AC}$?

   (A) 5
   (B) 7
   (C) $2\sqrt{7}$ (approximately 5.29)
   (D) $4\sqrt{3}$ (approximately 6.93)
   (E) $3\sqrt{7}$ (approximately 7.93)

17. If $x \neq 0$, then $\dfrac{8^{2x}}{2^{4x}} =$

   (A) 2^{2x}
   (B) 4^{-x}
   (C) 4^{2x}
   (D) 4^{1-x}
   (E) 8^{-x}

18. If functions f, g, and h are defined as $f(x) = \frac{x}{2}$, $g(x) = x - 2$, and $h(x) = x^2$, then $f(g(h(2))) =$

   (A) -1
   (B) 0
   (C) 1
   (D) 4
   (E) 8

19. If $f(3) = 12$ and $f(-2) = 2$, which of the following could represent $f(x)$?

   (A) $\frac{1}{2}x$
   (B) $x + 9$
   (C) $2x + 6$
   (D) $3x + 8$
   (E) $4x + 10$

GO ON TO THE NEXT PAGE

20. Which of the following is true for all x and y such
    that $x > 0$ and $y < 0$?

    (A) $|xy| < x + y$
    (B) $|xy| < xy$
    (C) $xy < |xy|$
    (D) $|x| > |y|$
    (E) $|y| > |x|$

6 6 6 6 6 6 6 6 6 6 6 6

**Time—25 Minutes
24 Items**

For each item in this section, choose the best answer and blacken the corresponding space on the answer sheet.

Each item below has one or two blanks, each blank indicating that something has been omitted. Beneath the sentence are five lettered words or sets of words. Choose the word or set of words that **best** fits the meaning of the sentence as a whole.

Example:

Although its publicity has been ----, the film itself is intelligent, well acted, handsomely produced, and altogether ----.

(A) tasteless..respectable
(B) extensive..moderate
(C) sophisticated..amateur
(D) risqué..crude
(E) perfect..spectacular   ● Ⓑ Ⓒ Ⓓ Ⓔ

---

1. The millionaire was such a --- that any appearance he made in public was ----.

   (A) philistine..negligible
   (B) recluse..noteworthy
   (C) gourmand..distorted
   (D) lecher..unexpected
   (E) traitor..protracted

2. Because of the ---- of acupuncture therapy in China, Western physicians are starting to learn the procedure.

   (A) veracity
   (B) manipulation
   (C) liquidity
   (D) effectiveness
   (E) inflation

3. Being a celebrity has its ----, one of which is the almost complete lack of ----.

   (A) delusions..repression
   (B) presumptions..income
   (C) drawbacks..privacy
   (D) frustrations..notoriety
   (E) confrontations..intimacy

4. The program concluded with a modern symphony that contained chords so ---- that the piece produced sounds similar to the ---- one hears as the individual orchestra members tune their instruments before a concert.

   (A) superfluous..melody
   (B) pretentious..roar
   (C) melodious..applause
   (D) versatile..harmony
   (E) discordant..cacophony

5. The king was a haughty aristocrat, but he was not a ----; he ruled his country ---- with genuine affection for his people.

   (A) sycophant..benevolently
   (B) diplomat..complacently
   (C) monarch..stringently
   (D) despot..magnanimously
   (E) tyrant..superciliously

6. Although some critics interpret *The Aeneid* as a Christian epic, this interpretation is totally ----, since the epic predates Christianity.

   (A) infallible
   (B) acceptable
   (C) convincing
   (D) anachronistic
   (E) conventional

GO ON TO THE NEXT PAGE

7. Black comedy is the combination of that which is humorous with that which would seem ---- to humor: the ----.

   (A) apathetic..ignoble
   (B) heretical..salacious
   (C) inferior..grandiose
   (D) extraneous..innocuous
   (E) antithetical..macabre

8. The original British cast was talented and energetic, while the Broadway cast lacks the ---- of the original players; in fact, the performance is ----.

   (A) calmness..scintillating
   (B) splendor..fallow
   (C) verve..insipid
   (D) flexibility..meticulous
   (E) intractability..quaint

GO ON TO THE NEXT PAGE

Each passage below is followed by items based on its content. Answer the items following the passage on the basis of what is <u>stated</u> or <u>implied</u> in the passage..

Item 9 is based on the following passage.

Line
5

10

For nearly 250 years, public libraries have afforded patrons, regardless of their economic circumstances, a mind-boggling collection of materials that represent 50 centuries of human thought. Plato and Santayana, Shakespeare and Hemingway, and Bacon and Darwin all stand shoulder to shoulder on its shelves. The library is also a place to learn English, look for a job, read to children, write a term paper, or simply oil a squeaky day. The public library is an American institution older than the American flag; however, this great democratic institution is struggling to survive. This struggle is nothing short of a national calamity.

9. The author of the passage relies extensively on

    (A) statistics
    (B) authority
    (C) examples
    (D) deduction
    (E) quotations

GO ON TO THE NEXT PAGE

Items 10-24 are based on the following passages.

As long ago as the fifth century B.C., Greek physicians noted that people who had recovered from the "plague" would never get it again—they had acquired immunity. Modern scientists understand that the human immune system is a complex network of specialized cells and organs that protects the body against bacteria, viruses, fungi, and parasites.

Have you ever wondered why you become feverish when you are suffering from the flu? Your body's immune system is simply doing its job. Because
Line the presence of certain organisms in the body is
5 harmful, the immune system will attempt to bar their entry or, failing that, to seek out and destroy them.

At the heart of the immune system is the ability to distinguish between self and non-self. The body's defenses do not normally attack tissues that exhibit a
10 self-marker†. Rather, immune cells and other body cells coexist peaceably. But when immune defenders encounter cells or organisms carrying molecules that say "foreign," the immune troops muster quickly to eliminate the intruders.
15 Any substance that is capable of triggering an immune response is called an antigen. An antigen can be a virus, a bacterium, a fungus, or a parasite; tissues or cells from another individual, except an identical twin, also act as antigens; even otherwise harmless
20 substances such as ragweed pollen or cat hair can set off a misguided response known as an allergy, in which case the substance is called an allergen. An antigen announces its foreignness by means of intricate and characteristic shapes called epitopes, which protrude
25 from its surface.

The immune system controls the production, development, and deployment of white cells called lymphocytes and includes the bone marrow, the thymus (a multi-lobed organ behind the breastbone),
30 and the blood and lymphatic vessels. Like all other blood cells, cells destined to become immune cells are produced in the bone marrow and are called stem cells. Some stem cells develop into lymphocytes while others develop into phagocytes.
35 The two most important classes of lymphocytes are B cells, so called because they mature in the bone marrow, and T cells, which migrate to the thymus. T cells directly attack their targets, which include body cells that have been commandeered by virus or warped
40 by malignancy. (This is called cellular immunity.) B cells, in contrast, work chiefly by secreting antibodies into the body's fluids. (This is known as humoral immunity.)

The other group of stem cells is the phagocytes;
45 they are large white cannibal cells. A special group of phagocytes, called macrophages (literally, "big eaters"), also have the ability to "display" the antigen after it has been digested.

To fend off the threatening horde, the body has
50 devised astonishingly intricate defenses. Microbes attempting to enter the body must first find a chink in its armor. The skin and the mucous membranes that line the body's portals not only interpose a physical barrier, but they are also rich in scavenger cells and
55 antibodies. Next, invaders must elude a series of non-specific defenses—cells and substances equipped to tackle infectious agents without regard to their antigenic peculiarities. Many potential infections are stopped when microbes are intercepted by patrolling
60 scavenger cells or disabled by enzymes.

Microbes that breach the non-specific barriers are then confronted by weapons that are specifically designed to combat their unique characteristics. This immune system response includes both cellular and
65 humoral components.

The cellular response is initiated by a macrophage. The macrophage digests an antigen and then displays antigen fragments on its own surface. This gives the T cells their marching orders. Some
70 T cells become killer cells and set out to track down body cells that have become infected. Other T cells become communications cells and secrete substances that call other kinds of immune cells, such as fresh macrophages, to the site of the infection. Others
75 coordinate the movements of the various groups of cells once they arrive on the scene. Still others secrete substances that stimulate the production of more T cell troops.

Humoral immunity is primarily the function of
80 B cells, although some help from T cells is almost always needed. B cells, like macrophages, eat antigens. Unlike macrophages, however, a B cell can bind only to an antigen that specifically fits its antibody-like receptor, so the B cell exhibits an antigen fragment that
85 attracts the attention of a T cell. The B cell and T cell interact, and the helper T cell stimulates the B cell to produce clones of itself—each with the highly specific antibody-like receptor. These clones then differentiate into plasma cells and begin producing vast quantities of
90 identical antigen-specific antibodies. Released into the bloodstream, the antibodies lock onto their matching antigens. The antigen-antibody complexes are then cleansed from the circulatory system by the liver and the spleen.

GO ON TO THE NEXT PAGE

95 These seemingly chaotic but actually very well-orchestrated maneuvers continue until the attack has been repulsed. At that point, specialized T cells, called suppressors, halt the production of antibodies and bring the immune response to a close.

100 When viewed from a clinical perspective, this process manifests itself in the three classic symptoms of redness, warmth, and swelling. Redness and warmth develop when small blood vessels in the vicinity of the infection become dilated and carry more blood. 105 Swelling results when the vessels, made leaky by yet other immune secretions, allow soluble immune substances to seep into the surrounding tissue. But all of this subsides as the controller T cells begin their mop-up activities. And with that, your illness has run 110 its course.

†Distinctive molecules that are carried by virtually every body cell

10. The passage can best be described as a

   (A) refutation of an ancient medical idea
   (B) definition of a biological concept
   (C) description of a biological process
   (D) technical definition of a medical term
   (E) treatment for a particular disease

11. According to the third paragraph, an "allergen" differs from "antigens" in that an allergen

   (A) does not trigger an immune response
   (B) does not exhibit unique epitopes
   (C) is not ordinarily harmful
   (D) does not announce its foreignness
   (E) carries a unique self marker

12. The passage implies that without the ability to distinguish self from non-self cells, the immune system would

   (A) function effectively except against the most powerful threats
   (B) still be able to identify various epitopes
   (C) no longer require both T cells and B cells
   (D) rely exclusively on macrophages for defense against infection
   (E) be rendered completely ineffective

13. Which of the following best explains why tissue that is transplanted from an identical twin is not attacked by the immune system?

   (A) The transplanted tissue has the same self-identifying molecules as the body.
   (B) The transplanted tissue triggers an allergic, not antigenic, reaction.
   (C) The transplanted tissue has no unique identifying self or non-self markers.
   (D) The body's immune system recognizes the transplanted tissue as foreign but ignores it.
   (E) The body's immune system is unable to recognize the self/non-self markers.

14. According to lines 31-43, all of the following statements are true of T cells and B cells EXCEPT

   (A) They are two different types of lymphocytes.
   (B) B cells mature in the bone marrow, T cells in the thymus.
   (C) Both classes of cells are produced by the bone marrow.
   (D) Either class can differentiate into a macrophage.
   (E) T cells attack other cells; B cells secrete antibodies.

15. As used in this context, "humoral" (line 43) means

   (A) comical
   (B) latent
   (C) fluid
   (D) dangerous
   (E) infectious

16. The author refers to phagocytes as "cannibal cells" (line 45) because they

   (A) are large in size
   (B) digest human tissue
   (C) display antigen
   (D) eat other cells
   (E) commandeer viruses

GO ON TO THE NEXT PAGE

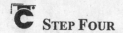

17. According to the passage, the body's first line of defense against microbes is

    (A) enzymes
    (B) scavenger cells
    (C) skin and mucous membranes
    (D) macrophage cells
    (E) T cells

18. The body's "non-specific defenses" (lines 55-56) ignore

    (A) antigenic epitopes
    (B) foreign substances
    (C) physical antibodies
    (D) scavenger cells
    (E) potential infections

19. According to paragraphs 9 and 10, cellular and humoral responses are similar in that both

    (A) require the presence of a macrophage
    (B) commence with one cell's digesting another
    (C) are carried out exclusively by one type of cell
    (D) necessitate the presence of B cells
    (E) result in the production of antibodies

20. The passage mentions all of the following as functions of the T cells EXCEPT

    (A) directing cellular activity
    (B) communicating with other cells
    (C) terminating an immune response
    (D) producing other T cells as needed
    (E) secreting antibodies into the blood

21. In line 96, "orchestrated" most nearly means

    (A) effective
    (B) desperate
    (C) musical
    (D) coordinated
    (E) prolonged

22. It can be inferred that without the presence of suppressor T cells,

    (A) B cells would be unable to clone themselves
    (B) non-specific defenses would become ineffective
    (C) immune reactions would continue indefinitely
    (D) macrophages would not respond to an infection
    (E) defenses to infection could not begin

23. Which of the following best describes the function of the final paragraph?

    (A) It alerts the reader to the topic that will follow.
    (B) It provides further details on functions of immune cells.
    (C) It highlights issues that need further research.
    (D) It answers the question raised in the first paragraph.
    (E) It recapitulates the most important points of the passage.

24. The passage relies upon an extended metaphor of an immune response as a

    (A) transaction between business partners
    (B) battle between warring camps
    (C) struggle against oppressive rule
    (D) debate between political candidates
    (E) concert by a large group of musicians

IF YOU FINISH BEFORE TIME IS CALLED, YOU MAY CHECK YOUR WORK ON THIS TEST ONLY. DO NOT WORK ON ANY OTHER TEST SECTION.

STOP

8 8 8 8 8 8 8 8 8 8 8 8

| Time—20 Minutes
16 Items | In this section, solve each item, using any available space on the page for scratchwork. Then, decide which is the best of the choices given and fill in the corresponding oval on the answer sheet. |

Notes: The figures accompanying the items are drawn as accurately as possible unless otherwise stated in specific items. Again, unless otherwise stated, all figures lie in the same plane. All numbers used in these items are real numbers. Calculators are permitted for this test.

Reference:

Circle: Rectangle: Rectangular Solid: Cylinder: Triangle:

$C = 2\pi r$ $A = lw$ $V = lwh$ $V = \pi r^2 h$ $A = \frac{1}{2}bh$ $a^2 + b^2 = c^2$

$A = \pi r^2$

- The measure in degrees of a straight angle is 180.
- The number of degrees of arc in a circle is 360.
- The sum of the measure of the angles of a triangle is 180.

1. If p, q, r, s, and t are whole numbers and the expression $2(p(q + r) + s) + t$ is even, which of the numbers *must* be even?

(A) p
(B) q
(C) r
(D) s
(E) t

2. If the area of a square is $9x^2$, what is the length of its side expressed in terms of x?

(A) $\frac{x}{3}$
(B) $3x$
(C) $9x$
(D) $\frac{x^2}{3}$
(E) $3x^2$

3. The sum, the product, and the average (arithmetic mean) of three different integers are equal. If two of the integers are x and $-x$, the third integer is

(A) $\frac{x}{2}$
(B) $2x$
(C) x
(D) 0
(E) -1

GO ON TO THE NEXT PAGE

4. The perimeter of the square above is

(A) 1
(B) $\sqrt{2}$
(C) 4
(D) $4\sqrt{2}$
(E) 8

5. A triangle has one side of length 4 and another side of length 11. What are the greatest and least possible integer values for the length of the remaining side?

(A) 7 and 4
(B) 11 and 4
(C) 14 and 8
(D) 15 and 7
(E) 16 and 7

6. If $2x + 3y = 19$, and x and y are positive integers, then x could be equal to which of the following?

(A) 3
(B) 4
(C) 5
(D) 6
(E) 7

7. The scores received by eleven students on a midterm exam are as follows: 45, 57, 75, 80, 80, 81, 83, 88, 91, 93, and 98. What is the median score?

(A) 75
(B) 79
(C) 80
(D) 80.5
(E) 81

8. If $a^2 b^3 c < 0$, then which of the following must be true?

(A) $b^3 < 0$
(B) $b^2 < 0$
(C) $b < 0$
(D) $c < 0$
(E) $bc < 0$

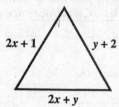

9. In the figure above, what is the perimeter of the equilateral triangle?

(A) 1
(B) 3
(C) 9
(D) 12
(E) 15

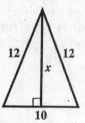

10. In the figure above, what is the value of x?

(A) 5
(B) 7.5
(C) $\sqrt{119}$
(D) 11
(E) 17

GO ON TO THE NEXT PAGE

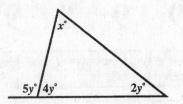

11. In the figure above, what is the value of *x*?

(A) 15
(B) 20
(C) 30
(D) 45
(E) 60

12. In the figure above, what is the length of $\overline{PQ}$?

(A) 0.12
(B) 0.16
(C) 0.13
(D) 0.11
(E) 0.09

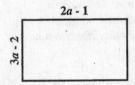

13. In the figure above, what is the perimeter of the rectangle?

(A) $10a - 6$
(B) $10a - 3$
(C) $6a - 2$
(D) $5a - 6$
(E) $5a - 3$

14. If the average (arithmetic mean) of *x*, *x*, *x*, 56, and 58 is 51, then *x* =

(A) 43
(B) 47
(C) 49
(D) 51
(E) 53

15. For how many integers *x* is $-2 \le 2x \le 2$?

(A) 1
(B) 2
(C) 3
(D) 4
(E) 5

16. If for any number *n*, ⭐*n* is defined as the least integer that is greater than or equal to n^2, then

⭐-1.1 =

(A) -2
(B) -1
(C) 0
(D) 1
(E) 2

IF YOU FINISH BEFORE TIME IS CALLED, YOU MAY CHECK YOUR WORK ON THIS TEST ONLY. DO NOT WORK ON ANY OTHER TEST SECTION.

STOP

9 9 9 9 9 9 9 9 9 9 9 9 9

Time—20 Minutes 19 Items	For each item in this section, choose the best answer and blacken the corresponding space on the answer sheet.

Each item below has one or two blanks, each blank indicating that something has been omitted. Beneath the sentence are five lettered words or sets of words. Choose the word or set of words that <u>best</u> fits the meaning of the sentence as a whole.

Example:

Although its publicity has been ----, the film itself is intelligent, well acted, handsomely produced, and altogether ----.

(A) tasteless..respectable
(B) extensive..moderate
(C) sophisticated..amateur
(D) risqué..crude
(E) perfect..spectacular

1. The judge, after ruling that the article had unjustly ---- the reputation of the architect, ordered the magazine to ---- its libelous statements in print.

   (A) praised..communicate
   (B) injured..retract
   (C) sullied..publicize
   (D) damaged..disseminate
   (E) extolled..produce

2. The fact that the office was totally disorganized was one more indication of the ---- of the new manager and of the ---- of the person who had hired him.

   (A) indifference..conscientiousness
   (B) ignorance..diligence
   (C) incompetence..negligence
   (D) tolerance..viciousness
   (E) propriety..confidence

3. Since the evidence of the manuscript's ---- is ----, its publication will be postponed until a team of scholars has examined it and declared it to be genuine.

   (A) authenticity..inconclusive
   (B) truthfulness..tarnished
   (C) veracity..indubitable
   (D) legitimacy..infallible
   (E) profundity..forthcoming

4. The press conference did not clarify many issues since the President responded with ---- and ---- rather than clarity and precision.

   (A) sincerity..humor
   (B) incongruity..candor
   (C) fervor..lucidity
   (D) animation..formality
   (E) obfuscation..vagueness

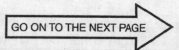
GO ON TO THE NEXT PAGE

5. Although the novel was not well written, it was
   such an exciting story that I was completely ----
   and could not put it down.

   (A) disenchanted
   (B) enthralled
   (C) indecisive
   (D) disgruntled
   (E) skeptical

Items 6-7 are based on the following passage.

Fifth Avenue and Forty-fourth Street swarmed
with the noon crowd. The wealthy, happy sun glittered
Line in transient gold through the thick windows of the
5 smart shops, lighting upon mesh bags and purses and
strings of pearls in gray velvet cases; upon gaudy
feather fans of many colors; upon the laces and silks of
expensive dresses; upon the bad paintings and the fine
period furniture in the elaborate show rooms of interior
10 decorators.
  Young working women, in pairs and groups and
swarms, loitered by these windows, choosing their
future boudoirs from some resplendent display that
included even a man's silk pajamas laid domestically
15 across the bed. They stood in front of the jewelry stores
and picked out their engagement rings, and their
wedding rings and their platinum wrist watches, and
then drifted on to inspect the feather fans and opera
cloaks; meanwhile digesting the sandwiches and
sundaes they had eaten for lunch.

6. It can be inferred that the women (line 10) are

   (A) planning elaborate weddings
   (B) window-shopping on their lunch break
   (C) eating lunch in the shops in the area
   (D) waiting to meet their husbands for lunch
   (E) walking briskly as a form of exercise

7. In context, "smart" (line 4) means

   (A) intelligent
   (B) inexpensive
   (C) busy
   (D) simple
   (E) stylish

GO ON TO THE NEXT PAGE

The two passages below are followed by items based on their content and the relationship between the two passages. Answer the items on the basis of what is <u>stated</u> or <u>implied</u> in the passages and in any introductory material that may be provided.

Items 8-9 are based on the following pair of passages.

Passage 1

The history of Earth has been punctuated by catastrophic events. Valleys were formed by dramatic plunges of fragments of the Earth's crust; mountains
Line rose in gigantic upheavals of land; rocks formed when
5 one worldwide ocean precipitated out great masses of different materials. The mix of observed animal and plant fossils can be explained only by events such as massive fires or floods that wiped out living forms that were then replaced by other species.

Passage 2

10 Great changes result from gradual processes over long periods of time. Valleys form as constantly flowing water from streams cuts through the sides and bottom of the land. Rocks and mountains are formed, destroyed, and reformed by on-going volcanic processes and weathering. Different fossil types in
15 successive rock layers represent changes that occur among related organisms due long-term evolutionary processes.

8. The use of the word "punctuated" in line 1 suggests events that are

(A) observable but gradual
(B) powerful but controlled
(C) known but mysterious
(D) sudden and well-defined
(E) concise and logical

9. The two passages develop differing viewpoints about the

(A) observable features of the Earth
(B) time that is spanned by Earth's history
(C) forces that have shaped the Earth
(D) importance of studying geology
(E) nature of scientific inquiry

GO ON TO THE NEXT PAGE

The two passages below are followed by items based on their content and the relationship between the two passages. Answer the items on the basis of what is <u>stated</u> or <u>implied</u> in the passages and in any introductory material that may be provided.

Items 10-19 are based on the following pair of passages.

Passage 1 is adapted from Henry David Thoreau's Walden *(1854) in which the author discusses his life of solitude in the New England woods. Passage 2 is adapted from* Public Opinion, *published in 1922 by Walter Lippman, a noted journalist and commentator.*

Passage 1

I am sure that I never read any memorable news in a newspaper. If we read of one man robbed, or murdered, or killed by accident, or one house burned, Line or one vessel wrecked, or one steamboat blown up, or
5 one cow run over on the railroad, or one mad dog killed, or one lot of grasshoppers in the winter—we never need read of another. One is enough. If you are acquainted with the principle, what do you care for a myriad instances and applications? All news, as it is
10 called, is gossip, even though many people insist on hearing it. If I should pull the bell-rope of the local church to sound a fire alarm, almost everyone in the entire area would stop everything and come running, not mainly to save property from the flames, but to see
15 the blaze, especially if it were the parish church itself on fire.

After a night's sleep the news is as indispensable to most people as breakfast: "Pray tell me everything important that has happened anywhere on this globe."
20 They read over coffee and rolls that a man has had his eyes gouged out the previous evening on the Wachito River. There was such a rush the other day at the railway office to learn the foreign news by the last arrival, that several large squares of plate glass were
25 broken—news that I seriously think a ready wit might have written a year or twelve years earlier with surprising accuracy. As for Spain, for instance, if you know how to throw in Don Carlos and the Infanta or Don Pedro and Seville and Granada from time to time
30 in the right proportions—they may have changed the names a little since I last saw the papers—and serve up a bull-fight when other entertainments fail, it will be true to the letter and give as good an idea of the exact state of ruin of things in Spain as the most succinct and
35 lucid reports under this head in the newspapers. And as for England, almost the last significant scrap of news from that quarter was the revolution of 1649; and if you have learned the history of her crops for an

average year, you never need attend to that thing again,
40 unless your speculations are of a merely pecuniary character. If one may judge who rarely looks into the newspapers, nothing new does ever happen in foreign parts, a French revolution not excepted.

Passage 2

There is an island in the ocean, where in 1914 a
45 few Englishmen, Frenchmen, and Germans lived. The island was not served by telegraph, and the British mail steamer came once every sixty days. By September, it had not yet come, and the islanders were still talking about the latest newspaper, which told about the
50 approaching trial of Madame Caillaux for the shooting of Gaston Calmette. It was, therefore, with more than usual eagerness that the whole colony assembled at the quay on a day in mid-September to hear from the captain what the verdict had been. Instead, they learned
55 of the start of the war and that for over six weeks those of them who were English and those of them who were French had acted as if they were friends with those of them who were Germans, when in fact they were enemies.

60 Their plight was not so different from that of most of the population of Europe. They had been mistaken for six weeks; on the continent, the interval may have been only six days or six hours, but there was an interval. There was a moment when the picture
65 of Europe on which business was conducted as usual, and it did not correspond in any way to the Europe that was about to make a jumble of so many lives. There was a time for which each person was still adjusted to an environment that no longer existed. All over the
70 world as late as July 25th people were making goods that they would not be able to ship, and buying goods that they would not be able to import. Careers were planned, enterprises were contemplated, and hopes and expectations were entertained, all in the belief that the
85 world as known was the world as it was. Authors were writing books describing that world. They trusted the picture in their heads. Then, over four years later, on a Thursday morning, came the news of an armistice, and people gave vent to their unutterable relief that the
90 slaughter was over. Yet, in the five days before the real

GO ON TO THE NEXT PAGE

armistice came, though the end of the war had been celebrated, several thousand young men died on the battlefields.

95 Looking back, we can see how indirectly we know the environment in which we live. We can see that the news of it comes to us sometimes quickly, sometimes slowly, but whatever we believe to be a true picture, we treat as if it were the environment itself. It is harder to remember that about the beliefs upon
100 which we are now acting, but in respect to other peoples and other ages, we flatter ourselves that it is easy to see when they were in deadly earnest about ludicrous pictures of the world. We insist, because of our superior hindsight, that the world as they needed to
105 know it, and the world as they did know it, were often two quite contradictory things. We can see, too, that while they governed and fought, traded and reformed in the world as they imagined it to be, they produced results, or failed to produce any, in the world as it was.
110 They started for the Indies and found America.

10. The newspaper report that a man has had his eyes gouged out is included by the author of Passage 1 as an example of

(A) a local event that affects people's lives directly
(B) an insignificant incident that does not affect the reader
(C) an unusual occurrence that merits special coverage
(D) an international incident that warrants detailed description
(E) a major event that merits national news coverage

11. The author mentions Don Carlos and the Infanta in order to

(A) demonstrate a thorough familiarity with current events in Spain
(B) familiarize the reader with recent events that occurred in Spain
(C) explain how events in Europe affect people all over the world
(D) illustrate the point that news from Spain repeats itself
(E) suggest that events in Spain should be reported in greater detail

12. The attitude of the author of Passage 1 towards the news is

(A) ridicule
(B) admiration
(C) indifference
(D) confidence
(E) caution

13. As used in this context, "attend to" (line 39) means

(A) be present at
(B) be ignorant of
(C) be concerned with
(D) grow weary of
(E) explain about

14. The author adds "especially if it were the parish church" (line 15) in order to

(A) emphasize that people are fascinated by the bizarre
(B) prove that citizens do not care about public property
(C) show that residents take an interest in local events
(D) stress the importance of the church to community
(E) refute the notion that more people do not read the news

15. According to the author of Passage 2, the people on the island "acted as if they were friends" (line 57) because they

(A) originally came from European countries
(B) were isolated from the rest of the world
(C) disagreed over the outcome of the trial
(D) shared an accurate view of the world
(E) did not realize that war had started

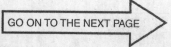
GO ON TO THE NEXT PAGE

16. The "plight" to which the author refers in line 60 was

   (A) incorrect reporting about the progress of the war
   (B) lack of accurate information about current conditions
   (C) an inability to obtain reports on a regular basis
   (D) slanted war news from the European front
   (E) need for more details about important events

17. In line 100, the author implies that people of another time

   (A) accomplished something significant based upon wrong information
   (B) failed to realize that the information available was wrong
   (C) could have foreseen that America lay between Europe and India
   (D) realized only in hindsight that they had landed in America
   (E) appear silly in light of what is now known about the world

18. Which of the following best summarizes the different points of view of the two passages?

   (A) The author of Passage 2 believes that news is important while the author of Passage 1 believes it is irrelevant.
   (B) The author of Passage 1 believes that news is unreliable while the author of Passage 2 believes that it is accurate.
   (C) The author of Passage 1 believes that newspapers provide critical information while the author of Passage 2 believes newspapers are too slow.
   (D) The author of Passage 1 believes that news coverage could be improved while the author of Passage 2 believes that it is already adequate.
   (E) The author of Passage 2 believes that newspaper should cover important international events while the author of Passage 1 believes local news is more important.

19. If the two authors had been able to write about the internet, they likely would

   (A) say that their points apply to the news content on the world wide web
   (B) acknowledge that the new media makes reporting more relevant and more reliable
   (C) insist that newspapers remain a better source of information than electronic media
   (D) conclude that global news coverage gives readers a more accurate view of the world
   (E) argue the quality of news reporting has declined with the development of the web

IF YOU FINISH BEFORE TIME IS CALLED, YOU MAY CHECK YOUR WORK ON THIS TEST ONLY. DO NOT WORK ON ANY OTHER TEST SECTION.

STOP

10 **10** **10** **10** **10** **10** **10** **10** **10**

Time—10 Minutes 14 Items	For each item in this section, choose the best answer and blacken the corresponding space on the answer sheet.

Directions: The following sentences test correctness and effectiveness of expression. In choosing answers, follow the requirements of standard written English; that is, pay attention to grammar, choice of words, sentence construction, and punctuation.

In each of the following sentences, part of the sentence or the entire sentence is underlined. Beneath each sentence you will find five ways of phrasing the underlined part. Choice A repeats the original; the other four are different.

Choose the answer that best expresses the meaning of the original sentence. If you think the original is better than any of the alternatives, choose it; otherwise choose one of the others. Your choice should produce the most effective sentence—clear and precise, without awkwardness or ambiguity.

Example: Answer

Allen <u>visiting</u> his cousin in France last summer.

(A) visiting
(B) visited
(C) does visit
(D) a visit
(E) is visiting   Ⓐ ● Ⓒ Ⓓ Ⓔ

1. In no field of history has the search for logical explanation been so diligent <u>so much as</u> the study of the decline and fall of the Roman Empire.

   (A) so much as
   (B) as in
   (C) for
   (D) due to
   (E) like

2. <u>Letters were received by the editor of the newspaper that complained of its editorial policy.</u>

   (A) Letters were received by the editor of the newspaper that complained of its editorial policy.
   (B) Letters were received by the editor of the newspaper that complains of its editorial policy.
   (C) Letters were received by the editor of the newspaper complaining of their editorial policy.
   (D) The editor of the newspaper received letters that were complaining of the paper's editorial policy.
   (E) The editor of the newspaper received letters complaining of the paper's editorial policy.

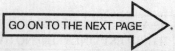
GO ON TO THE NEXT PAGE

3. Washington Irving's German-influenced stories were profoundly moving to Americans, <u>knowing more than most</u> Britons what it was like to feel the trauma of rapid change, and Americans found in the lazy Rip a model for making a success of failure.

    (A) knowing more than most
    (B) who knew more then most
    (C) knowing more then most
    (D) most who knew more about what
    (E) who knew more than most

4. <u>By law, a qualified physician can only prescribe medicine, protecting the public.</u>

    (A) By law, a qualified physician can only prescribe medicine, protecting the public.
    (B) By law, only a qualified physician can prescribe medicine, protecting the public.
    (C) By law, only a qualified physician can prescribe medicine that protects the public.
    (D) In order to protect the public, by law a qualified physician only can prescribe medicine.
    (E) In order to protect the public, by law only a qualified physician can prescribe medicine.

5. Improvements in economic theory and data gathering <u>today makes possible more accurate to forecast than was</u> possible even 20 years ago.

    (A) today makes possible more accurate to forecast than was
    (B) have made possible more accurate forecasts than were
    (C) have made possible more accurate forecasts than was
    (D) today make possible more accurate forecasts than was
    (E) today make possible more accurate forecasting that were

6. The viola, the alto member of the violin <u>family, having</u> four strings tuned C, G, D, and A, upward from the C below middle C (a fifth lower than the violin's strings).

    (A) family, having
    (B) family, had
    (C) families, having
    (D) family, having had
    (E) family, has

7. <u>In order to make skiing smoother, safer, and more enjoyable, a number of resorts have hired consultants</u> to design and sculpt the trails.

    (A) In order to make skiing smoother, safer, and more enjoyable, a number of resorts have hired consultants
    (B) In order to make skiing smoother, safer, and more enjoyable a number of consultants have been hired by resorts
    (C) In the interest of making skiing smoother, safer, and able to be enjoyed, a number of resorts have hired consultants
    (D) To make skiing smoother, safer, so that you can enjoy it, a number of resorts have hired consultants
    (E) To make skiing smoother, also safer and enjoyable, a number of resorts will have hired consultants

8. It is reported that some tribes in Africa used to eat the livers of their slain <u>enemies which they believed allowed them to ingest their courage</u>.

    (A) enemies which they believed allowed them to ingest their courage
    (B) enemies which they believed allowed them to ingest their enemies' courage
    (C) enemies which would, they believed, allow them to ingest their enemies' courage
    (D) enemies, a process they believed allowed them to ingest the courage of their enemies
    (E) enemies, a process they believed allowed them to ingest the enemy courage

GO ON TO THE NEXT PAGE

9. Horatio Greenough, <u>considering by many to be the first American to become a professional sculptor</u>, executed a bust of then President John Quincy Adams.

(A) considering by many to be the first American to become a professional sculptor
(B) considered by many to be the first American to become a professional sculptor
(C) considering by many to be the first American to have become a professional sculptor
(D) considered by many to be the first professional American sculptor
(E) considered by many to have become the first American professional sculptor

10. Her dissertation was interesting and well-researched, <u>but she lacked the organizational skills to make a convincing argument</u>.

(A) but she lacked the organizational skills to make a convincing argument
(B) lacking the organizational skills making a convincing argument
(C) but she also was lacking in organizational skills which would serve to make her arguments more convincing
(D) but having lacked the organizational skills of a convincing argument
(E) but without a convincing argument as a result of organizational skills

11. Credit card payments are now accepted in exchange for many goods and services around the world and in some countries, <u>like the Americans, is used even more widely than</u> cash.

(A) like the Americans, is used even more widely than
(B) like that of America, is used even more widely than
(C) as in America, are used even more widely than
(D) such as America, are used even more widely than
(E) such as America, are used even more widely as

12. Leprosy is not a highly contagious disease, yet it <u>has always and will continue to be feared until a vaccine will have been developed</u>.

(A) has always and will continue to be feared until a vaccine will have been developed
(B) is and always will continue to be feared until a vaccine is developed
(C) continues being feared and will be feared by people until the development of a vaccine
(D) has always been and will continue to be feared until a vaccine is developed
(E) is always feared and until a vaccine is developed, will continue to be so

13. <u>The delivery in large volume of certain welfare services are costly on account of the large number of public contact employees that are required by this.</u>

(A) The delivery in large volume of certain welfare services are costly on account of the large number of public contact employees that are required by this.
(B) The delivery of a large volume of certain welfare services are costly on account of the large number of public contact employees that this requires.
(C) The delivery in large volume of certain welfare services is costly because of the large number of public contact employees that is required.
(D) The delivery of certain welfare services in large volume is costly on account of the large numbers of public contact employees that is required.
(E) To deliver certain welfare services in large volume is costly on account of that this requires a large number of public service employees.

GO ON TO THE NEXT PAGE

14. To prove that acridines kill bacteria through asphyxiation rather than starvation (as is the case with sulfa drugs), <u>Dr. Martin nearly spent ten years building an artificial chemical wall around the bacteria</u> that deprives them of essential food.

(A) Dr. Martin nearly spent ten years building an artificial chemical wall around the bacteria
(B) building an artificial chemical wall around the bacteria was nearly Dr. Martin's task for ten years
(C) Dr. Martin spent nearly ten years building an artificial chemical wall around the bacteria
(D) nearly spending ten years, Dr. Martin built an artificial chemical wall around the bacteria
(E) ten years were nearly spent by Dr. Martin building an artificial chemical wall around the bacteria

IF YOU FINISH BEFORE TIME IS CALLED, YOU MAY CHECK YOUR WORK ON THIS TEST ONLY. DO NOT WORK ON ANY OTHER TEST SECTION.

STOP

Practice Test IV

EDUCATORS' #1 CHOICE FOR SCHOOL IMPROVEMENT

Cambridge Course Concept Outline
PRACTICE TEST IV

When completing Practice Test IV, use the Essay Response and Bubble Sheets beginning on page 797, unless otherwise directed by your instructor.

Name: _____   Date: _____

Student ID Number: _____

PRACTICE TEST IV

Section 1

Begin your essay on this page. If you need more space, continue on the next page.

_____

_____

_____

_____

_____

_____

_____

_____

_____

_____

_____

_____

_____

_____

_____

_____

_____

_____

_____

_____

_____

_____

_____

Name: _____   Date: _____

Student ID Number: _____

PRACTICE TEST IV

Start with number 1 for each new section. If a section has fewer questions than answer spaces, leave the extra answer spaces blank. Be sure to erase any errors or stray marks completely.

Section 2

1 Ⓐ Ⓑ Ⓒ Ⓓ Ⓔ	10 Ⓐ Ⓑ Ⓒ Ⓓ Ⓔ	19 Ⓐ Ⓑ Ⓒ Ⓓ Ⓔ	28 Ⓐ Ⓑ Ⓒ Ⓓ Ⓔ
2 Ⓐ Ⓑ Ⓒ Ⓓ Ⓔ	11 Ⓐ Ⓑ Ⓒ Ⓓ Ⓔ	20 Ⓐ Ⓑ Ⓒ Ⓓ Ⓔ	29 Ⓐ Ⓑ Ⓒ Ⓓ Ⓔ
3 Ⓐ Ⓑ Ⓒ Ⓓ Ⓔ	12 Ⓐ Ⓑ Ⓒ Ⓓ Ⓔ	21 Ⓐ Ⓑ Ⓒ Ⓓ Ⓔ	30 Ⓐ Ⓑ Ⓒ Ⓓ Ⓔ
4 Ⓐ Ⓑ Ⓒ Ⓓ Ⓔ	13 Ⓐ Ⓑ Ⓒ Ⓓ Ⓔ	22 Ⓐ Ⓑ Ⓒ Ⓓ Ⓔ	31 Ⓐ Ⓑ Ⓒ Ⓓ Ⓔ
5 Ⓐ Ⓑ Ⓒ Ⓓ Ⓔ	14 Ⓐ Ⓑ Ⓒ Ⓓ Ⓔ	23 Ⓐ Ⓑ Ⓒ Ⓓ Ⓔ	32 Ⓐ Ⓑ Ⓒ Ⓓ Ⓔ
6 Ⓐ Ⓑ Ⓒ Ⓓ Ⓔ	15 Ⓐ Ⓑ Ⓒ Ⓓ Ⓔ	24 Ⓐ Ⓑ Ⓒ Ⓓ Ⓔ	33 Ⓐ Ⓑ Ⓒ Ⓓ Ⓔ
7 Ⓐ Ⓑ Ⓒ Ⓓ Ⓔ	16 Ⓐ Ⓑ Ⓒ Ⓓ Ⓔ	25 Ⓐ Ⓑ Ⓒ Ⓓ Ⓔ	34 Ⓐ Ⓑ Ⓒ Ⓓ Ⓔ
8 Ⓐ Ⓑ Ⓒ Ⓓ Ⓔ	17 Ⓐ Ⓑ Ⓒ Ⓓ Ⓔ	26 Ⓐ Ⓑ Ⓒ Ⓓ Ⓔ	35 Ⓐ Ⓑ Ⓒ Ⓓ Ⓔ
9 Ⓐ Ⓑ Ⓒ Ⓓ Ⓔ	18 Ⓐ Ⓑ Ⓒ Ⓓ Ⓔ	27 Ⓐ Ⓑ Ⓒ Ⓓ Ⓔ	36 Ⓐ Ⓑ Ⓒ Ⓓ Ⓔ

Section 3

1 Ⓐ Ⓑ Ⓒ Ⓓ Ⓔ	10 Ⓐ Ⓑ Ⓒ Ⓓ Ⓔ	19 Ⓐ Ⓑ Ⓒ Ⓓ Ⓔ	28 Ⓐ Ⓑ Ⓒ Ⓓ Ⓔ
2 Ⓐ Ⓑ Ⓒ Ⓓ Ⓔ	11 Ⓐ Ⓑ Ⓒ Ⓓ Ⓔ	20 Ⓐ Ⓑ Ⓒ Ⓓ Ⓔ	29 Ⓐ Ⓑ Ⓒ Ⓓ Ⓔ
3 Ⓐ Ⓑ Ⓒ Ⓓ Ⓔ	12 Ⓐ Ⓑ Ⓒ Ⓓ Ⓔ	21 Ⓐ Ⓑ Ⓒ Ⓓ Ⓔ	30 Ⓐ Ⓑ Ⓒ Ⓓ Ⓔ
4 Ⓐ Ⓑ Ⓒ Ⓓ Ⓔ	13 Ⓐ Ⓑ Ⓒ Ⓓ Ⓔ	22 Ⓐ Ⓑ Ⓒ Ⓓ Ⓔ	31 Ⓐ Ⓑ Ⓒ Ⓓ Ⓔ
5 Ⓐ Ⓑ Ⓒ Ⓓ Ⓔ	14 Ⓐ Ⓑ Ⓒ Ⓓ Ⓔ	23 Ⓐ Ⓑ Ⓒ Ⓓ Ⓔ	32 Ⓐ Ⓑ Ⓒ Ⓓ Ⓔ
6 Ⓐ Ⓑ Ⓒ Ⓓ Ⓔ	15 Ⓐ Ⓑ Ⓒ Ⓓ Ⓔ	24 Ⓐ Ⓑ Ⓒ Ⓓ Ⓔ	33 Ⓐ Ⓑ Ⓒ Ⓓ Ⓔ
7 Ⓐ Ⓑ Ⓒ Ⓓ Ⓔ	16 Ⓐ Ⓑ Ⓒ Ⓓ Ⓔ	25 Ⓐ Ⓑ Ⓒ Ⓓ Ⓔ	34 Ⓐ Ⓑ Ⓒ Ⓓ Ⓔ
8 Ⓐ Ⓑ Ⓒ Ⓓ Ⓔ	17 Ⓐ Ⓑ Ⓒ Ⓓ Ⓔ	26 Ⓐ Ⓑ Ⓒ Ⓓ Ⓔ	35 Ⓐ Ⓑ Ⓒ Ⓓ Ⓔ
9 Ⓐ Ⓑ Ⓒ Ⓓ Ⓔ	18 Ⓐ Ⓑ Ⓒ Ⓓ Ⓔ	27 Ⓐ Ⓑ Ⓒ Ⓓ Ⓔ	36 Ⓐ Ⓑ Ⓒ Ⓓ Ⓔ

Section 4/5

1 Ⓐ Ⓑ Ⓒ Ⓓ Ⓔ	10 Ⓐ Ⓑ Ⓒ Ⓓ Ⓔ	19 Ⓐ Ⓑ Ⓒ Ⓓ Ⓔ	28 Ⓐ Ⓑ Ⓒ Ⓓ Ⓔ
2 Ⓐ Ⓑ Ⓒ Ⓓ Ⓔ	11 Ⓐ Ⓑ Ⓒ Ⓓ Ⓔ	20 Ⓐ Ⓑ Ⓒ Ⓓ Ⓔ	29 Ⓐ Ⓑ Ⓒ Ⓓ Ⓔ
3 Ⓐ Ⓑ Ⓒ Ⓓ Ⓔ	12 Ⓐ Ⓑ Ⓒ Ⓓ Ⓔ	21 Ⓐ Ⓑ Ⓒ Ⓓ Ⓔ	30 Ⓐ Ⓑ Ⓒ Ⓓ Ⓔ
4 Ⓐ Ⓑ Ⓒ Ⓓ Ⓔ	13 Ⓐ Ⓑ Ⓒ Ⓓ Ⓔ	22 Ⓐ Ⓑ Ⓒ Ⓓ Ⓔ	31 Ⓐ Ⓑ Ⓒ Ⓓ Ⓔ
5 Ⓐ Ⓑ Ⓒ Ⓓ Ⓔ	14 Ⓐ Ⓑ Ⓒ Ⓓ Ⓔ	23 Ⓐ Ⓑ Ⓒ Ⓓ Ⓔ	32 Ⓐ Ⓑ Ⓒ Ⓓ Ⓔ
6 Ⓐ Ⓑ Ⓒ Ⓓ Ⓔ	15 Ⓐ Ⓑ Ⓒ Ⓓ Ⓔ	24 Ⓐ Ⓑ Ⓒ Ⓓ Ⓔ	33 Ⓐ Ⓑ Ⓒ Ⓓ Ⓔ
7 Ⓐ Ⓑ Ⓒ Ⓓ Ⓔ	16 Ⓐ Ⓑ Ⓒ Ⓓ Ⓔ	25 Ⓐ Ⓑ Ⓒ Ⓓ Ⓔ	34 Ⓐ Ⓑ Ⓒ Ⓓ Ⓔ
8 Ⓐ Ⓑ Ⓒ Ⓓ Ⓔ	17 Ⓐ Ⓑ Ⓒ Ⓓ Ⓔ	26 Ⓐ Ⓑ Ⓒ Ⓓ Ⓔ	35 Ⓐ Ⓑ Ⓒ Ⓓ Ⓔ
9 Ⓐ Ⓑ Ⓒ Ⓓ Ⓔ	18 Ⓐ Ⓑ Ⓒ Ⓓ Ⓔ	27 Ⓐ Ⓑ Ⓒ Ⓓ Ⓔ	36 Ⓐ Ⓑ Ⓒ Ⓓ Ⓔ

Section 5/6

1 Ⓐ Ⓑ Ⓒ Ⓓ Ⓔ	10 Ⓐ Ⓑ Ⓒ Ⓓ Ⓔ	19 Ⓐ Ⓑ Ⓒ Ⓓ Ⓔ	28 Ⓐ Ⓑ Ⓒ Ⓓ Ⓔ
2 Ⓐ Ⓑ Ⓒ Ⓓ Ⓔ	11 Ⓐ Ⓑ Ⓒ Ⓓ Ⓔ	20 Ⓐ Ⓑ Ⓒ Ⓓ Ⓔ	29 Ⓐ Ⓑ Ⓒ Ⓓ Ⓔ
3 Ⓐ Ⓑ Ⓒ Ⓓ Ⓔ	12 Ⓐ Ⓑ Ⓒ Ⓓ Ⓔ	21 Ⓐ Ⓑ Ⓒ Ⓓ Ⓔ	30 Ⓐ Ⓑ Ⓒ Ⓓ Ⓔ
4 Ⓐ Ⓑ Ⓒ Ⓓ Ⓔ	13 Ⓐ Ⓑ Ⓒ Ⓓ Ⓔ	22 Ⓐ Ⓑ Ⓒ Ⓓ Ⓔ	31 Ⓐ Ⓑ Ⓒ Ⓓ Ⓔ
5 Ⓐ Ⓑ Ⓒ Ⓓ Ⓔ	14 Ⓐ Ⓑ Ⓒ Ⓓ Ⓔ	23 Ⓐ Ⓑ Ⓒ Ⓓ Ⓔ	32 Ⓐ Ⓑ Ⓒ Ⓓ Ⓔ
6 Ⓐ Ⓑ Ⓒ Ⓓ Ⓔ	15 Ⓐ Ⓑ Ⓒ Ⓓ Ⓔ	24 Ⓐ Ⓑ Ⓒ Ⓓ Ⓔ	33 Ⓐ Ⓑ Ⓒ Ⓓ Ⓔ
7 Ⓐ Ⓑ Ⓒ Ⓓ Ⓔ	16 Ⓐ Ⓑ Ⓒ Ⓓ Ⓔ	25 Ⓐ Ⓑ Ⓒ Ⓓ Ⓔ	34 Ⓐ Ⓑ Ⓒ Ⓓ Ⓔ
8 Ⓐ Ⓑ Ⓒ Ⓓ Ⓔ	17 Ⓐ Ⓑ Ⓒ Ⓓ Ⓔ	26 Ⓐ Ⓑ Ⓒ Ⓓ Ⓔ	35 Ⓐ Ⓑ Ⓒ Ⓓ Ⓔ
9 Ⓐ Ⓑ Ⓒ Ⓓ Ⓔ	18 Ⓐ Ⓑ Ⓒ Ⓓ Ⓔ	27 Ⓐ Ⓑ Ⓒ Ⓓ Ⓔ	36 Ⓐ Ⓑ Ⓒ Ⓓ Ⓔ

Section 6/7

1 Ⓐ Ⓑ Ⓒ Ⓓ Ⓔ	10 Ⓐ Ⓑ Ⓒ Ⓓ Ⓔ	19 Ⓐ Ⓑ Ⓒ Ⓓ Ⓔ	28 Ⓐ Ⓑ Ⓒ Ⓓ Ⓔ
2 Ⓐ Ⓑ Ⓒ Ⓓ Ⓔ	11 Ⓐ Ⓑ Ⓒ Ⓓ Ⓔ	20 Ⓐ Ⓑ Ⓒ Ⓓ Ⓔ	29 Ⓐ Ⓑ Ⓒ Ⓓ Ⓔ
3 Ⓐ Ⓑ Ⓒ Ⓓ Ⓔ	12 Ⓐ Ⓑ Ⓒ Ⓓ Ⓔ	21 Ⓐ Ⓑ Ⓒ Ⓓ Ⓔ	30 Ⓐ Ⓑ Ⓒ Ⓓ Ⓔ
4 Ⓐ Ⓑ Ⓒ Ⓓ Ⓔ	13 Ⓐ Ⓑ Ⓒ Ⓓ Ⓔ	22 Ⓐ Ⓑ Ⓒ Ⓓ Ⓔ	31 Ⓐ Ⓑ Ⓒ Ⓓ Ⓔ
5 Ⓐ Ⓑ Ⓒ Ⓓ Ⓔ	14 Ⓐ Ⓑ Ⓒ Ⓓ Ⓔ	23 Ⓐ Ⓑ Ⓒ Ⓓ Ⓔ	32 Ⓐ Ⓑ Ⓒ Ⓓ Ⓔ
6 Ⓐ Ⓑ Ⓒ Ⓓ Ⓔ	15 Ⓐ Ⓑ Ⓒ Ⓓ Ⓔ	24 Ⓐ Ⓑ Ⓒ Ⓓ Ⓔ	33 Ⓐ Ⓑ Ⓒ Ⓓ Ⓔ
7 Ⓐ Ⓑ Ⓒ Ⓓ Ⓔ	16 Ⓐ Ⓑ Ⓒ Ⓓ Ⓔ	25 Ⓐ Ⓑ Ⓒ Ⓓ Ⓔ	34 Ⓐ Ⓑ Ⓒ Ⓓ Ⓔ
8 Ⓐ Ⓑ Ⓒ Ⓓ Ⓔ	17 Ⓐ Ⓑ Ⓒ Ⓓ Ⓔ	26 Ⓐ Ⓑ Ⓒ Ⓓ Ⓔ	35 Ⓐ Ⓑ Ⓒ Ⓓ Ⓔ
9 Ⓐ Ⓑ Ⓒ Ⓓ Ⓔ	18 Ⓐ Ⓑ Ⓒ Ⓓ Ⓔ	27 Ⓐ Ⓑ Ⓒ Ⓓ Ⓔ	36 Ⓐ Ⓑ Ⓒ Ⓓ Ⓔ

Section 7/8

1 Ⓐ Ⓑ Ⓒ Ⓓ Ⓔ	6 Ⓐ Ⓑ Ⓒ Ⓓ Ⓔ	11 Ⓐ Ⓑ Ⓒ Ⓓ Ⓔ	16 Ⓐ Ⓑ Ⓒ Ⓓ Ⓔ
2 Ⓐ Ⓑ Ⓒ Ⓓ Ⓔ	7 Ⓐ Ⓑ Ⓒ Ⓓ Ⓔ	12 Ⓐ Ⓑ Ⓒ Ⓓ Ⓔ	17 Ⓐ Ⓑ Ⓒ Ⓓ Ⓔ
3 Ⓐ Ⓑ Ⓒ Ⓓ Ⓔ	8 Ⓐ Ⓑ Ⓒ Ⓓ Ⓔ	13 Ⓐ Ⓑ Ⓒ Ⓓ Ⓔ	18 Ⓐ Ⓑ Ⓒ Ⓓ Ⓔ
4 Ⓐ Ⓑ Ⓒ Ⓓ Ⓔ	9 Ⓐ Ⓑ Ⓒ Ⓓ Ⓔ	14 Ⓐ Ⓑ Ⓒ Ⓓ Ⓔ	19 Ⓐ Ⓑ Ⓒ Ⓓ Ⓔ
5 Ⓐ Ⓑ Ⓒ Ⓓ Ⓔ	10 Ⓐ Ⓑ Ⓒ Ⓓ Ⓔ	15 Ⓐ Ⓑ Ⓒ Ⓓ Ⓔ	20 Ⓐ Ⓑ Ⓒ Ⓓ Ⓔ

Section 8/9

1 Ⓐ Ⓑ Ⓒ Ⓓ Ⓔ	6 Ⓐ Ⓑ Ⓒ Ⓓ Ⓔ	11 Ⓐ Ⓑ Ⓒ Ⓓ Ⓔ	16 Ⓐ Ⓑ Ⓒ Ⓓ Ⓔ
2 Ⓐ Ⓑ Ⓒ Ⓓ Ⓔ	7 Ⓐ Ⓑ Ⓒ Ⓓ Ⓔ	12 Ⓐ Ⓑ Ⓒ Ⓓ Ⓔ	17 Ⓐ Ⓑ Ⓒ Ⓓ Ⓔ
3 Ⓐ Ⓑ Ⓒ Ⓓ Ⓔ	8 Ⓐ Ⓑ Ⓒ Ⓓ Ⓔ	13 Ⓐ Ⓑ Ⓒ Ⓓ Ⓔ	18 Ⓐ Ⓑ Ⓒ Ⓓ Ⓔ
4 Ⓐ Ⓑ Ⓒ Ⓓ Ⓔ	9 Ⓐ Ⓑ Ⓒ Ⓓ Ⓔ	14 Ⓐ Ⓑ Ⓒ Ⓓ Ⓔ	19 Ⓐ Ⓑ Ⓒ Ⓓ Ⓔ
5 Ⓐ Ⓑ Ⓒ Ⓓ Ⓔ	10 Ⓐ Ⓑ Ⓒ Ⓓ Ⓔ	15 Ⓐ Ⓑ Ⓒ Ⓓ Ⓔ	20 Ⓐ Ⓑ Ⓒ Ⓓ Ⓔ

Section 10

1 Ⓐ Ⓑ Ⓒ Ⓓ Ⓔ	6 Ⓐ Ⓑ Ⓒ Ⓓ Ⓔ	11 Ⓐ Ⓑ Ⓒ Ⓓ Ⓔ	16 Ⓐ Ⓑ Ⓒ Ⓓ Ⓔ
2 Ⓐ Ⓑ Ⓒ Ⓓ Ⓔ	7 Ⓐ Ⓑ Ⓒ Ⓓ Ⓔ	12 Ⓐ Ⓑ Ⓒ Ⓓ Ⓔ	17 Ⓐ Ⓑ Ⓒ Ⓓ Ⓔ
3 Ⓐ Ⓑ Ⓒ Ⓓ Ⓔ	8 Ⓐ Ⓑ Ⓒ Ⓓ Ⓔ	13 Ⓐ Ⓑ Ⓒ Ⓓ Ⓔ	18 Ⓐ Ⓑ Ⓒ Ⓓ Ⓔ
4 Ⓐ Ⓑ Ⓒ Ⓓ Ⓔ	9 Ⓐ Ⓑ Ⓒ Ⓓ Ⓔ	14 Ⓐ Ⓑ Ⓒ Ⓓ Ⓔ	19 Ⓐ Ⓑ Ⓒ Ⓓ Ⓔ
5 Ⓐ Ⓑ Ⓒ Ⓓ Ⓔ	10 Ⓐ Ⓑ Ⓒ Ⓓ Ⓔ	15 Ⓐ Ⓑ Ⓒ Ⓓ Ⓔ	20 Ⓐ Ⓑ Ⓒ Ⓓ Ⓔ

Student-Produced Responses

Only answers entered in the circles in each grid will be scored. You will not receive credit for anything written in the boxes above the circles.

9   10   11   12   13

14   15   16   17   18

1 1 1 1 1 1 1 1 1 1 1 1 1

Time—25 Minutes 1 Essay	Think carefully about the issue presented in the following excerpt and the assignment below.

DIRECTIONS: You have 25 minutes to plan and write an essay on the topic assigned below. DO NOT WRITE ON ANY OTHER TOPIC. AN ESSAY ON ANOTHER TOPIC IS NOT ACCEPTABLE. Think carefully about the issue presented in the following excerpt and the assignment below.

> The image of America as a "melting pot" is false and outdated. The United States absorbed millions of immigrants at the turn of the last century who, over time, lost their cultural heritage to become "American." This melting away of cultures into one larger "American" culture that took on some specific cultural influences of its new citizens can largely be attributed to the fact that many of these new immigrants were of European descent and could physically "fit in" with their neighbors. Today, immigrants from all corners of the globe tend to hold onto their cultural legacy, making modern American society closer to a "salad bowl" than a "melting pot."

Assignment: Is the United States more of a cultural "Melting Pot" or "Salad Bowl"? Plan and write an essay in which you develop your point of view on this issue. Support your position with reasoning and examples taken from your reading, studies, experience, and observations.

IF YOU FINISH BEFORE TIME IS CALLED, YOU MAY CHECK YOUR WORK ON THIS TEST ONLY. DO NOT WORK ON ANY OTHER TEST SECTION.

STOP

2 2 2 2 2 2 2 2 2 2 2 2

Time—25 Minutes 18 Items	In this section, solve each item, using any available space on the page for scratchwork. Then, decide which is the best of the choices given and fill in the corresponding oval on the answer sheet.

Notes: The figures accompanying the items are drawn as accurately as possible unless otherwise stated in specific items. Again, unless otherwise stated, all figures lie in the same plane. All numbers used in these items are real numbers. Calculators are permitted for this test.

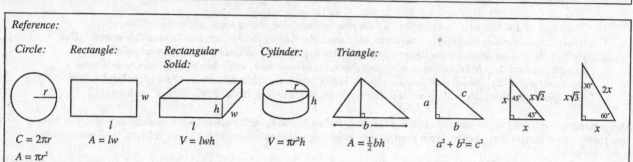

Reference:

Circle:
$C = 2\pi r$
$A = \pi r^2$

Rectangle:
$A = lw$

Rectangular Solid:
$V = lwh$

Cylinder:
$V = \pi r^2 h$

Triangle:
$A = \frac{1}{2}bh$
$a^2 + b^2 = c^2$

• The measure in degrees of a straight angle is 180.
• The number of degrees of arc in a circle is 360.
• The sum of the measure of the angles of a triangle is 180.

1. If $x^3 > x^2$, then which of the following could be the value of x?

(A) -2
(B) -1/2
(C) 1/2
(D) 1
(E) 3/2

2. A researcher has determined the following about the ages of three individuals:

The sum of Tom and Herb's age is 22.
The sum of Herb and Bob's age is 17.
The sum of Bob and Tom's age is 15.

How old is Herb?

(A) 5
(B) 7
(C) 10
(D) 12
(E) 15

GO ON TO THE NEXT PAGE

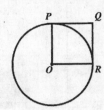

$$|x-2|=6$$
$$|y+8|=10$$

3. If $x<0$ and $y<0$, what is the value of $x-y$?

    (A)   3
    (B)   6
    (C)   9
    (D)   10
    (E)   14

4. The sum of three consecutive even integers is 154. If n is the least of the three integers, which one of the following equations represents the information given in the statement above?

    (A) $n+3=154$
    (B) $3n+2=154$
    (C) $3n+3=154$
    (D) $3n+4=154$
    (E) $3n+6=154$

5. The figure above shows nine tiles with single-digit numbers painted on them. If xy is the product of the value of any two tiles selected at random, how many different possible values for xy are there?

    (A)   4
    (B)   7
    (C)   10
    (D)   12
    (E)   16

6. In the figure above, if the area of the square $OPQR$ is 2, what is the area of the circle with center O?

    (A) $\frac{\pi}{4}$

    (B) $\pi\sqrt{2}$

    (C) 2π

    (D) $2\sqrt{2}\pi$

    (E) 4π

7. How many positive integers less than 30 are equal to 3 times an odd integer?

    (A)   10
    (B)   7
    (C)   5
    (D)   4
    (E)   3

GO ON TO THE NEXT PAGE

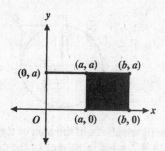

8. In the figure above, what is the area of the shaded portion, expressed in terms of a and b?

(A) $a(b-a)$
(B) $a(a-b)$
(C) $b(a-b)$
(D) $b(b-a)$
(E) ab

GO ON TO THE NEXT PAGE

Directions for Student-Produced Responses Items

Items 9-18 each require you to solve an item and mark your answer on a special answer grid. For each item, you should write your answer in the boxes at the top of each column and then fill in the ovals beneath each answer you write. Here are some examples.

Answer: 3/4 or .75
(show answer either way)

Answer: 325

Note: A mixed number such as $3\frac{1}{2}$ must be gridded as 7/2 or as 3.5. If gridded as "31/2," it will be read as "thirty-one halves."

Note: Either position is correct.

9. $\sqrt{(43-7)(29+7)} =$

10. A certain concrete mixture uses 4 cubic yards of cement for every 20 cubic yards of grit. If a contractor orders 50 cubic yards of cement, how much grit (in cubic yards) should he order if he plans to use all of the cement?

GO ON TO THE NEXT PAGE

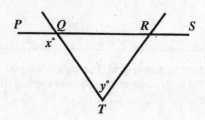

11. In the figure above, $\overline{QT} = \overline{QR}$. If $x = 120$, then $y =$

12. If $\frac{x}{y} = -1$, then $x + y =$

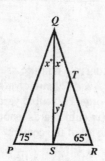

Note: Figure not drawn to scale.

13. In triangle $\triangle PQR$ above, if $\overline{PQ} \parallel \overline{ST}$, then $y =$

14. The average of seven different positive integers is 12. What is the greatest that any one of the integers could be?

15. A drawer contains four green socks, six blue socks, and ten white socks. If socks are pulled out of the drawer at random and not replaced, what is the minimum number of socks that must be pulled out to guarantee that two of every color have been selected?

16. On a trip, a motorist drove 10 miles at 20 miles per hour, 10 miles at 30 miles per hour, and 10 miles at 60 miles per hour. What fraction of her total driving time was spent driving 60 miles per hour?

GO ON TO THE NEXT PAGE

17. In Company A, 50% of the employees are women. In Company B, 40% of the employees are women. If Company A has 800 employees, and Company B has half that number, how many more women are employed at Company A than at Company B?

18. In the country of Zzyzyyx, $\frac{2}{5}$ of the population has blue eyes. How many people would you have to look at to find 50 with blue eyes, assuming that your sample has blue-eyed people in the same ratio as the general population?

3 3 3 3 3 3 3 3 3 3 3 3

Time—25 Minutes 35 Items	For each item in this section, choose the best answer and blacken the corresponding space on the answer sheet.

Directions: The following sentences test correctness and effectiveness of expression. In choosing answers, follow the requirements of standard written English; that is, pay attention to grammar, choice of words, sentence construction, and punctuation.

In each of the following sentences, part of the sentence or the entire sentence is underlined. Beneath each sentence you will find five ways of phrasing the underlined part. Choice A repeats the original; the other four are different.

Choose the answer that best expresses the meaning of the original sentence. If you think the original is better than any of the alternatives, choose it; otherwise choose one of the others. Your choice should produce the most effective sentence—clear and precise, without awkwardness or ambiguity.

Example: Answer

Allen visiting his cousin in France last summer.

(A) visiting
(B) visited
(C) does visit
(D) a visit
(E) is visiting

Ⓐ ● Ⓒ Ⓓ Ⓔ

1. Surprised by the enemy, the general's pursuit of total victory was abruptly halted.

(A) the general's pursuit of total victory was abruptly halted
(B) the pursuit of total victory by the general was abruptly halted
(C) the pursuit of the general of total victory was halted abruptly
(D) the general abruptly halted his pursuit of total victory
(E) then the general's pursuit of total victory halted abruptly

2. Larkspur High is only the tenth largest school in the district in terms of student enrollment but wins regional championships in many sports year after year.

(A) but wins
(B) though wins
(C) while wins
(D) still winning
(E) yet a winner of

GO ON TO THE NEXT PAGE

3. Rene Descartes, the 17th century French thinker, who is as famous as the mathematician who introduced Cartesian geometry.

   (A) who is as famous as
   (B) who is as famous than
   (C) is as famous as
   (D) being as famous as
   (E) as famous as

4. The new findings on the genetic causes of various diseases provide at once answers for researchers who have gone before and pose questions for future generations of thinkers who must use this information for the good of humanity.

   (A) and pose
   (B) but pose
   (C) and posing
   (D) while posed
   (E) and posed

5. If one compares the number of SUVs sold annually in this country with the compact car, we see clearly how much Americans admire large, ungainly vehicles.

   (A) If one compares the number of SUVs sold annually in this country with the compact car
   (B) If we compare the number of SUVs sold annually in this country with the compact car
   (C) Upon comparing the number of SUVs sold annually in this country with the compact car
   (D) When we compare the number of SUVs sold annually in this country with the number of compact cars
   (E) Comparing the number of SUVs sold annually in this country and the compact car

GO ON TO THE NEXT PAGE

Directions: The following sentences test your knowledge of grammar, usage, diction (choices of words) and idiom.

    Some sentences are correct.
    No sentence contains more than one error.

You will find that the error, if there is one, is underlined and lettered. Elements of the sentence that are not underlined will not be changed. In choosing answers, follow the requirements of standard written English.

If there is an error, select the <u>one underlined part</u> that must be changed to make the sentence correct and fill in the corresponding oval on your answer sheet.

If there is no error, fill in answer oval (**E**).

Example: **Answer**

    The principal <u>asked</u> ten of <u>we</u> students
                 A   B

    <u>to enter</u> the <u>public speaking</u> contest. <u>No error</u>   Ⓐ ⬤ Ⓒ Ⓓ Ⓔ
      C   D   E

---

6. <u>Her</u> and <u>the other</u> members of the team <u>spoke</u> to
   A   B   C

   the press after <u>their</u> final victory. <u>No error</u>
               D   E

7. Andre Breton <u>started</u> the Surrealist movement
              A

   <u>with</u> a manifesto <u>that</u> included the theories of
   B   C

   Freud <u>as well as</u> his own. <u>No error</u>
          D   E

8. In early America <u>there</u> <u>has been</u> very little
               A   B

   <u>to read</u> <u>except</u> for the books sent from Europe.
   C   D

   <u>No error</u>
   E

9. After <u>having took</u> the entrance exam, she <u>was</u>
        A   B

   <u>absolutely</u> sure that she <u>would be admitted</u> to the
   C   D

   college. <u>No error</u>
             E

10. <u>Although</u> the average person <u>watches</u> a news
    A   B

   program every day, <u>they do</u> not always
                C

   <u>understand</u> the issues discussed. <u>No error</u>
   D   E

GO ON TO THE NEXT PAGE ➡

11. Being that black bears are large and powerful,
    A   B

    many people fear them even though the bears are
                    C   D

    really quite shy. No error
                      E

12. The review of the concert mentioned that the
                              A   B

    soloist was a very promising talent and that the
                       C

    orchestra played capable. No error
                     D   E

13. The point of the coach's remarks were clearly
                     A   B

    to encourage the team and to restore its
    C   D

    competitive spirit. No error
                         E

14. The professor deals harshly with students who are
                  A   B

    not prepared, and he is even more severe with
                                 C

    those who plagiarize. No error
    D   E

15. When Mozart wrote "The Marriage of Figaro,"
                A

    the Emperor was shocked at him using mere
                    B   C

    servants in important roles. No error
             D   E

16. For a young woman who is ready to join the
    A   B

    work force, there now exists many more
                          C

    opportunities than existed for her mother.
                     D

    No error
    E

17. If he had known how difficult law school
           A   B

    would be, he would of chosen a different
    C   D

    profession. No error
                 E

18. The museum required that all people
                 A

    with an umbrella leave them at the door before
    B   C

    entering the exhibit. No error
    D   E

19. Americans used to go to the movies
             A

    as often as they watched television; but now
    B

    that they can watch movies in their homes,
         C

    they are doing less of it. No error
         D   E

20. When automobiles get designed and manufactured,
                     A

    corporations are often more concerned about cost
                 B   C

    than safety. No error
    D   E

21. Most people do not realize that some white
               A

    wines are actually made from red grapes.
         B   C   D

    No error
    E

22. Travel to countries with less than ideal sanitary
    A   B

    conditions increases the amount of victims of
               C   D

    hepatitis. No error
                E

GO ON TO THE NEXT PAGE

23. Movie fans <u>claim</u> there is <u>no greater</u> director than
                A   B

    <u>him,</u> although most critics <u>would cite</u> Bergman or
      C   D

    Kurosawa.   <u>No error</u>
               E

24. Economists <u>have established</u> a <u>correlation</u>—<u>albeit</u>
                 A   B   C

    an indirect one—<u>between</u> the sale of oil and the
                   D

    number of traffic accidents.   <u>No error</u>
                           E

25. The duckbill platypus, unlike other

    <u>mammal,</u> <u>does</u> not bear live young but
      A   B

    instead <u>reproduces</u> by <u>laying</u> eggs. <u>No error</u>
            C   D   E

GO ON TO THE NEXT PAGE

Directions: The following passages are early drafts of essays. Some parts of the passages need to be rewritten.

Read the passages and answer the items that follow. Some items are about particular sentences or parts of sentences and ask you to improve sentence structure and word choice. Other items refer to parts of the essays or the entire essays and ask you to consider organization and development. In making your decisions, follow the conventions of standard written English. After you have chosen your answer, fill in the corresponding oval on your answer sheet.

Items 26 - 31 refer to the following passage.

(1) My first real job was working at the Burger Barn. (2) Before that, I did odd jobs for neighbors such as mowing lawns and shoveling snow and was paid by them. (3) The Burger Barn is a typical fast food restaurant. (4) It serves food such as hamburgers and french fries. (5) The only experience that most people have with a fast food restaurant is as a customer. (6) They order and pay for it and then either sit down or go home to eat. (7) A lot more goes on behind the counter.

(8) There are rules for everything. (9) The oil for the french fries must be exactly 375 degrees, and the fries must cook until the timer sounds. (10) The patties must be cooked until they are well-done. (11) All counters, floors, and utensils must be cleaned and disinfected every evening.

(12) There must be so many orders of fries under the warming lamp and a certain number of burgers on the grill. (13) Paper products and condiments must be restocked every half hour, and employees receive 5 minute breaks every 2 hours with 20 minutes for lunch during a six-hour shift. (14) To outsiders, these rules may seem silly. (15) They are necessary to make sure that the food we serve is safe to eat and that during evening rush we can serve as many as 150 people. (16) The evening rush is from 5:30 pm to 7:00 pm.

26. In context, which is the best version of the underlined portion of sentence 2 (reproduced below)?

    Before that, I <u>did odd jobs for neighbors such as mowing lawns and shoveling snow and was paid by them</u>.

    (A) (As it is now.)
    (B) did odd jobs for neighbors such as mowing lawns and shoveling snow who paid me for them
    (C) was paid by neighbors for doing odd jobs such as mowing lawns and shoveling snow
    (D) received pay by neighbors for odd jobs such as mowing lawns and shoveling snow
    (E) mowed lawns and shoveled snow and did odd jobs for neighbors who paid me for them

27. In context, which is the best way to revise and combine the underlined portions of sentences 3 and 4 (reproduced below)?

    <u>The Burger Barn is a typical fast food restaurant. It serves</u> food such as hamburgers and french fries.

    (A) The Burger Barn is a typical fast food restaurant, serving
    (B) The Burger Barn is a typical fast food restaurant in that it serves
    (C) Typically, a fast food restaurant such as the Burger Barn serves
    (D) A fast food restaurant such as your typical Burger Barn serves
    (E) At the Burger Barn, the food that is typically served is

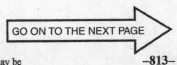

GO ON TO THE NEXT PAGE

28. Which of the following is the most logical replacement for the word "it" in sentence 6?

   (A) experience
   (B) restaurant
   (C) food
   (D) people
   (E) Burger Barn

29. In context, which of the following would be the best phrase to insert at the beginning of sentence 13?

   (A) However,
   (B) In addition,
   (C) Therefore,
   (D) Perhaps,
   (E) For example,

30. In context, which is the best version of the underlined portions of sentences 14 and 15 (reproduced below)?

   To outsiders, these rules may seem silly. They are necessary to make sure that the food we serve is safe to eat and that during evening rush we can serve as many as 150 people.

   (A) may seem silly, but they are necessary to make sure
   (B) may seem silly, since they are necessary to make sure
   (C) are necessary to make sure, even though they may seem silly,
   (D) are necessary, even though they may seem silly, and make sure
   (E) could be silly except that they are necessary to make sure

31. In context, which of the following would be the most appropriate revision of sentence 16?

   (A) Delete it because it does not contribute to the development of the essay.
   (B) Delete it because definitions are not appropriate in an essay.
   (C) Place it in quotation marks because it is a definition.
   (D) Move it to the beginning of the final paragraph.
   (E) Place it between sentences 5 and 6.

GO ON TO THE NEXT PAGE

Items 32 - 35 refer to the following passage.

(1) In the past several years, lawyers have increasingly been in the negative public spotlight. (2) A group of students hires a lawyer to sue their school because they don't like the mascot. (3) A driver sues a take-out restaurant because he was scalded by the hot coffee he spilled while driving. (4) A prison inmate goes all the way to the Supreme Court because the jail uses the wrong kind of peanut butter.

(5) All of these examples make lawyers seems like publicity-hungry, money-grubbing parasites. (6) Seemingly outrageous cases, are often incorrectly reported by the media.

(7) Take the famous "peanut butter case" as an example (8) Since inmates aren't permitted to have cash, they have accounts with the prison commissary where they buy items like soap, stationery, and snacks. (9) An inmate ordered a jar of crunchy-style peanut butter but got creamy-style instead. (10) Then the commissary repeatedly refused to fix the mistake. (11) The inmate properly returned the merchandise, but the commissary didn't credit his account. (12) So the inmate sued the commissary for the price of the peanut butter. (13) The inmate won, so the prison appealed and lost.

(14) When you hear the actual facts of the "peanut butter case," you can see that the inmate had a legitimate beef. (15) This is true of most of the other cases you hear about as well.

32. Which of the following would be the most suitable sentence to insert immediately after sentence 1?

   (A) Lawyers go to school for an additional three years after graduating from college.
   (B) Every night, the news has stories of how people have been hurt or injured that day.
   (C) I have often thought about becoming a lawyer after I graduate from college.
   (D) It seems as though every day we hear of another frivolous lawsuit.
   (E) Of course, not all lawyers are bad; a few are morally responsible.

33. To best connect paragraph two with the rest of the essay, which is the best word or phrase to insert after the underlined portion of sentence 6 (reproduced below)?

   Seemingly outrageous cases, are often incorrectly reported by the media.

   (A) certainly,
   (B) more or less,
   (C) however,
   (D) fortunately,
   (E) in a word,

34. Which of the following changes in the organization of paragraph three is most needed?

   (A) (As it is now.)
   (B) Start a new paragraph with sentence 9.
   (C) Put sentence 10 after sentence 11.
   (D) Start a new paragraph with sentence 12.
   (E) Put sentence 12 after sentence 13.

35. Which of the following would be most appropriate for the writer to do in a fifth paragraph to be added to the essay?

   (A) Explain why the media gets the facts of cases wrong.
   (B) Analyze the legal arguments in the "peanut butter case."
   (C) Refute the contention that prison inmate's have legal rights.
   (D) Present cases where people falsely claimed to be seriously injured.
   (E) Encourage the reader to consult with a lawyer.

IF YOU FINISH BEFORE TIME IS CALLED, YOU MAY CHECK YOUR WORK ON THIS TEST ONLY. DO NOT WORK ON ANY OTHER TEST SECTION.

STOP

4 4 4 4 4 4 4 4 4 4 4 4

| Time—25 Minutes 24 Items | For each item in this section, choose the best answer and blacken the corresponding space on the answer sheet. |

Each item below has one or two blanks, each blank indicating that something has been omitted. Beneath the sentence are five lettered words or sets of words. Choose the word or set of words that <u>best</u> fits the meaning of the sentence as a whole.

Example:

Although its publicity has been ----, the film itself is intelligent, well acted, handsomely produced, and altogether ----.

(A) tasteless..respectable
(B) extensive..moderate
(C) sophisticated..amateur
(D) risqué..crude
(E) perfect..spectacular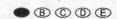

---

1. Although for centuries literature was considered something that would instruct as well as entertain, many modern readers have little patience with ---- works and seek only to be ----.

   (A) epic..demoralized
   (B) didactic..distracted
   (C) bawdy..absorbed
   (D) superficial..enlightened
   (E) ambiguous..misled

2. Because the poet was restless and uneasy in society, he sought a ---- existence and a life of ----.

   (A) stable..pleasure
   (B) claustrophobic..frivolity
   (C) materialistic..urbanity
   (D) conservative..squalor
   (E) nomadic..solitude

3. Because he was ---- and the life of the party, his friends thought that he was happy; but his wife was ---- and shy and was thought to be unhappy.

   (A) melancholy..sympathetic
   (B) philanthropic..conciliatory
   (C) vitriolic..sophomoric
   (D) garrulous..taciturn
   (E) inimical..gregarious

4. His offhand, rather ---- remarks ---- a character that was really rather serious and not at all superficial.

   (A) flippant..masked
   (B) pernicious..betrayed
   (C) bellicose..belied
   (D) controversial..revealed
   (E) shallow..enlivened

5. Although the faculty did not always agree with the chairperson of the department, they ---- her ideas mostly in ---- her seniority and out of respect for her previous achievements.

   (A) scoffed at..fear of
   (B) harbored..defense of
   (C) implemented..deference to
   (D) marveled at..lieu of
   (E) ignored..honor of

6. Although his work was often ---- and ----, he was promoted anyway, simply because he had been with the company longer than anyone else.

   (A) forceful..extraneous
   (B) negligent..creative
   (C) incomplete..imprecise
   (D) predictable..careful
   (E) expeditious..concise

7. Shopping malls account for 60 percent of the retail business in the United States because they are controlled environments, which ---- concerns about the weather.

(A) eliminate
(B) necessitate
(C) foster
(D) justify
(E) maintain

8. An oppressive ----, and not the festive mood one might have expected, characterized the gathering.

(A) senility
(B) capriciousness
(C) inanity
(D) solemnity
(E) hysteria

9. In order to ---- museums and legitimate investors, and to facilitate the ---- of pilfered artifacts, art magazines often publish photographs of stolen archaeological treasures.

(A) perpetuate..return
(B) protect..recovery
(C) encourage..excavation
(D) undermine..discovery
(E) confuse..repossession

GO ON TO THE NEXT PAGE

The two passages below are followed by items based on their content and the relationship between the two passages. Answer the items on the basis of what is <u>stated</u> or <u>implied</u> in the passages and in any introductory material that may be provided.

Items 10-17 are based on the following passage.

The following selection is an excerpt from a history text. It talks about athletic games in ancient Greece.

Perhaps the best-known of the ancient Greek religious festivals are the panhellenic gatherings at Olympia, in honor of Zeus, where the Olympics
Line originated in 776 B.C. These and other festivals in
5 honor of Zeus were called "crown festivals" because the winning athletes were crowned with wreaths, such as the olive wreaths of Olympia. Yet, in ancient Greece there were at least 300 public, state-run religious festivals that were celebrated at more than 250
10 locations in honor of some 400 deities. Most of these were held in the cities, in contrast to the crown festivals, which were held in rural sanctuaries. In Athens, for example, four annual festivals honored Athena, the city's divine protectress, in addition to
15 those for other gods. In all, some 120 days were devoted annually to festivals.

By far, the largest event of the Athenian religious calendar, rivaling the crown gatherings in prestige, was the Great Panathenaic festival. The development of the
20 Panathenaic festival—the ritual embodiment of the cult of Athena—evolved from a purely local religious event into a civic and panhellenic one. This transformation, and that of the image of Athena from an aggressively martial goddess to a more humane figure of victory,
25 parallels the great political change that occurred in Athens from 560 B.C. to 430 B.C., as it evolved from a tyranny to a democracy.

Athenian reverence for Athena originated in a myth that recounts a quarrel between Poseidon and
30 Athena over possession of Attica. In a contest arranged by Zeus, Athena was judged the winner and made the patron goddess of Athens, to which she gave her name. The origin of the Panathenaia, however, is shrouded in mystery. Perhaps it was founded by Erichthonius, a
35 prehistoric king of Athens. According to legend, after having been reared by Athena on the Acropolis, he held games for his foster mother and competed in the chariot race, which he reputedly invented. The first archaeological evidence for the festival is a
40 Panathenaic prize vase from 560 B.C. depicting a horse race, so scholars infer that equestrian events were part of the festival.

Much more is known about the Panathenaia after 566 B.C., when the festival was reorganized under the
45 tyrant Peisistaros. At that time, the festival, in addition to its annual celebration, was heightened every fourth year into the Great Panathenaia, which attracted top athletes from all over the region to compete for valuable prizes—such as 140 vases of olive oil for
50 winning the chariot race—rather than for honorific wreaths.

Every four years, some 1,300 painted amphorae were commissioned and filled with olive oil to be used as prizes. The accouterments of Athena—helmet,
55 spear, and shield—figured prominently in the iconic representations of the goddess on these vases, and served to identify the stylized figure and to associate the festival with the goddess. So far as is known, none of the crown games commissioned any art for their
60 festivals. From the mid-sixth century B.C. until the end of antiquity when the Christian emperors suppressed the pagan religions, the high point of Athenian religious life was the Great Panathenaia, held at a time that falls in our month of July.

GO ON TO THE NEXT PAGE →

10. The selection is mainly concerned with

    (A) identifying the origins of the modern Olympic games
    (B) describing the development of athletic games at Athens
    (C) contrasting religious practices in honor of Zeus and Athena
    (D) tracing the growth of democracy in ancient Greece
    (E) presenting a picture of the pageantry and art of ancient Greece

11. Which of the following is NOT mentioned as a characteristic of the games at Olympia?

    (A) The games were held in honor of Zeus.
    (B) Winners were crowned with wreaths.
    (C) The games originated in 776 B.C.
    (D) The games were held in or near cities.
    (E) Winners did not receive valuable prizes.

12. The author regards the suggestions that the Panathenaia originated under Erichtonius as

    (A) conclusively proved
    (B) a theoretical possibility
    (C) historically impossible
    (D) a hoax perpetrated by Athenians
    (E) a simple myth of ancient times

13. The word "equestrian" (line 41 refers to

    (A) weapons
    (B) gods
    (C) horses
    (D) tyrants
    (E) slaves

14. Which of the following is NOT mentioned as a characteristic of the Great Panathenaia?

    (A) It was held every four years.
    (B) It inspired the modern Olympic games.
    (C) It began at the time of Peisistaros.
    (D) It was held during our month of July.
    (E) It died out under the Christian emperors.

15. What word has most nearly the same meaning as "amphorae" (line 52)?

    (A) vases
    (B) wreaths
    (C) representations
    (D) games
    (E) crowns

16. "Iconic" (line 55) most nearly means

    (A) stylized depiction
    (B) religious statue
    (C) religious festival
    (D) assorted weapons
    (E) legendary figures

17. With which of the following statements would the author probably agree about any new evidence that art was commissioned for some crowned games?

    (A) The evidence disproves the theory that the crown games were held in honor of Zeus.
    (B) The evidence tends to show that Athena and Zeus were actually the same ancient Greek deity.
    (C) The evidence suggests that some crown games offered prizes but does not require a major reevaluation of current theories.
    (D) The evidence is irrelevant to what is known about ancient games because the most important were the Panathenaia and not the crown games.
    (E) The evidence reinforces the distinction between the crown games as amateur games and the Panathenaia as a contest for professional athletes.

GO ON TO THE NEXT PAGE

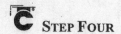

Items 18-24 are based on the following passage.

The following is an excerpt from a report that was prepared by an engineering firm on the feasibility of electric cars. The excerpt focuses on the uses of electro mechanical batteries as a power source.

Except that their output is alternating current rather than direct current, electromechanical batteries, or EMBs, would power an electric car in the same way
Line as a bank of electrochemical batteries. The modular
5 device contains a flywheel that is stabilized by nearly frictionless magnetic bearings integrated with a special ironless generator motor and housed in a sealed vacuum enclosure. The EMB is "charged" by spinning its rotor to maximum speed with an integral
10 generator/motor in its "motor mode." It is "discharged" by slowing the rotor of the same generator/motor to draw out the kinetically stored energy in its "generator mode." Initial research focused on the possibility of using one or two relatively large EMBs, but subsequent
15 findings point in a different direction.

Compared to stationary EMB applications such as with wind turbines, vehicular applications pose two special problems. Gyroscopic forces come into play whenever a vehicle departs from a straight-line course,
20 as in turning. The effects can be minimized by vertically orienting the axis of rotation, and the designer can mount the module in limited-excursion gimbals to resist torque. By operating the EMB modules in pairs—one spinning clockwise and the
25 other counterclockwise—the net gyroscopic effect on the car would be nearly zero.

The other problem associated with EMBs for vehicles is failure containment. Any spinning rotor has an upper speed limit that is determined by the tensile
30 strength of the material from which it is made. On the other hand, at a given rotation speed, the amount of kinetic energy stored is determined by the mass of the flywheel. It was originally thought that high-density materials such as metals were optimal for flywheel
35 rotors, and a metal flywheel does store more energy than an equivalent-size flywheel made of low-density material and rotating at the same speed. However, a low-density wheel can be spun up to a higher speed until it reaches the same internal tensile stresses as the
40 metal one, where it stores the same amount of kinetic energy at a much lower weight. Lightweight graphite fiber, for example, is more than ten times more effective per unit mass for kinetic energy storage than

steel. Plus, tests show that a well-designed rotor made
45 of graphite fibers that fails turns into an amorphous mass of broken fibers. This failure is far more benign than that of metal flywheels, which typically break into shrapnel-like pieces that are difficult to contain.

Not only is the uncontrolled energy that can be
50 released by each unit reduced, but the danger posed by a failed rotor is very small compared to that of rotors just two or three times larger. Thus, an array of small EMB modules offers major advantages over one or two large units.

18. The author's primary concern is to

(A) describe technological advances that make possible containment of uncontrolled kinetic energy discharge due to cataclysmic rotor failure

(B) report on new technologies that will make electric cars competitive with vehicles employing conventional internal combustion engines

(C) argue that an array of small EMB modules mounted in an electric car is more energy efficient than a single large EMB

(D) construct field tests that will prove whether or not mobile EMBs can be arranged so as to minimize unwanted torque

(E) demonstrate how a group of small EMB modules for use in an electric car can avoid technological problems that are associated with a single large EMB

19. It can be inferred that a non-metallic, low-density flywheel that has stored kinetic energy equivalent to that of a metallic, high-density flywheel is

(A) operating in its "motor mode" and discharging energy as it spins

(B) oriented vertically to the axis of rotation of the metallic flywheel

(C) spinning in the opposite direction of the metallic flywheel

(D) rotating at a higher speed than the metallic fly-wheel

(E) made of graphite fibers that disintegrate into harmless fragments upon failure

GO ON TO THE NEXT PAGE

20. With which of the following statements would the author of the passage LEAST likely agree?

    (A) Gyroscopic forces in applications such as wind turbines are not relevant factors because wind turbines remain in one place.
    (B) Lightweight non-metallic flywheels made of materials such as graphite fiber are less likely to fail at maximum stress than non-metallic flywheels.
    (C) An array of small EMB modules can provide the same amount of energy to the system of an electric car as one or two relatively large EMBs.
    (D) The amount of kinetic energy that can be stored by a flywheel is a function of the weight of its constituent materials and its maximum rotational speed.
    (E) Technological innovations such as frictionless bearings can help to make electromechanical batteries sufficiently efficient for use in electric cars.

21. In line 46, the phrase "more benign" means

    (A) less dangerous
    (B) more reliable
    (C) equally stable
    (D) less expensive
    (E) less efficient

22. The author regards the new EMB technology as

    (A) overrated
    (B) unattainable
    (C) promising
    (D) untested
    (E) impractical

23. The author states that the gyroscopic effect of EMB modules operating in pairs can be minimized if they are

    (A) constructed of high-density metal
    (B) rotated in opposite directions
    (C) operating in their "motor" mode
    (D) stabilized by frictionless bearings
    (E) spinning at high speeds

24. Which of the following best describes the logical development of the selection?

    (A) It mentions some technological challenges and describes some possible solutions.
    (B) It identifies some technological problems and dismisses attempts to solve them.
    (C) It outlines technological demands of an engineering application and minimizes their significance.
    (D) It presents a history of a technological question but offers no answers.
    (E) It examines some new approaches to an engineering problem and rejects them.

IF YOU FINISH BEFORE TIME IS CALLED, YOU MAY CHECK YOUR WORK ON THIS TEST ONLY. DO NOT WORK ON ANY OTHER TEST SECTION.

STOP

5 5 5 5 5 5 5 5 5 5 5 5

| Time—25 Minutes 20 Items | In this section, solve each item, using any available space on the page for scratchwork. Then, decide which is the best of the choices given and fill in the corresponding oval on the answer sheet. |

Notes: The figures accompanying the items are drawn as accurately as possible unless otherwise stated in specific items. Again, unless otherwise stated, all figures lie in the same plane. All numbers used in these items are real numbers. Calculators are permitted for this test.

Reference:

    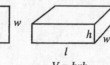

Circle: Rectangle: Rectangular Solid: Cylinder: Triangle:

$C = 2\pi r$ $A = lw$ $V = lwh$ $V = \pi r^2 h$ $A = \frac{1}{2}bh$ $a^2 + b^2 = c^2$
$A = \pi r^2$

• The measure in degrees of a straight angle is 180.
• The number of degrees of arc in a circle is 360.
• The sum of the measure of the angles of a triangle is 180.

1. A barrel contained 5.75 liters of water and 4.5 liters evaporated. How many liters of water remain in the barrel?

(A) 0.75
(B) 1.25
(C) 1.75
(D) 2.25
(E) 13.25

2. The expression "3 less than the product of 4 times x" can be written as

(A) $4x - 3$

(B) $3x - 4$

(C) $4(x - 3)$

(D) $3(4x)$

(E) $\frac{4x}{3}$

3. If $\frac{3}{4}$ of x is 36, then $\frac{1}{3}$ of x is

(A) 9
(B) 12
(C) 16
(D) 24
(E) 42

4. In the figure above, what is the value of $x + y$?

(A) 45
(B) 60
(C) 75
(D) 90
(E) 120

GO ON TO THE NEXT PAGE

5. If n is a multiple of 3, which of the following is also a multiple of 3?

(A) $2 + n$
(B) $2 - n$
(C) $2n - 1$
(D) $2n + 1$
(E) $2n + 3$

6. Which of the following is NOT equal to the ratio of two whole numbers?

(A) $\left(\frac{1}{5}\right)^2$

(B) $\frac{1}{5}$

(C) 0.20

(D) 5%

(E) $\sqrt{\frac{5}{1}}$

7. If the area of a square is 16, what is the perimeter?

(A) 2
(B) 4
(C) 8
(D) 16
(E) 32

8. If $12 + x = 36 - y$, then $x + y =$

(A) −48
(B) −24
(C) 3
(D) 24
(E) 48

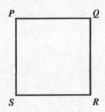

9. Two security guards, Jane and Ed, patrol the perimeter of the square area shown above. Starting at corner P at 8:00 p.m., Jane walks around the outside of the fence in a clockwise direction while Ed walks around the inside in a counterclockwise direction. If it takes exactly 10 minutes for each guard to walk from one corner to the next, where will they be two hours later, at 10 p.m.?

(A) Both at corner P
(B) Both at corner R
(C) Jane at corner P and Ed at corner R
(D) Ed at corner P and Jane at corner Q
(E) Ed at corner P and Jane at corner R

10. Depending on the value of k, the expression $3k + 4k + 5k + 6k + 7k$ may or may not be divisible by 7. Which of the terms, when eliminated from the expression, guarantees that the resulting expression is divisible by 7 for every positive integer k?

(A) $3k$
(B) $4k$
(C) $5k$
(D) $6k$
(E) $7k$

11. If $\frac{1}{3} < x < \frac{3}{8}$, which of the following is a possible value of x?

(A) $\frac{1}{2}$

(B) $\frac{3}{16}$

(C) $\frac{17}{48}$

(D) $\frac{9}{24}$

(E) $\frac{5}{12}$

GO ON TO THE NEXT PAGE

12. If $x^2 - y^2 = 3$ and $x - y = 3$, then $x + y =$

    (A) 0
    (B) 1
    (C) 2
    (D) 3
    (E) 9

13. If n is a positive integer, which of the following must be an even integer?

    (A) $n + 1$
    (B) $3n + 1$
    (C) $3n + 2$
    (D) $n^2 + 1$
    (E) $n^2 + n$

14. If the area of a square inscribed in a circle is 16, what is the area of the circle?

    (A) 2π
    (B) 4π
    (C) 8π
    (D) 16π
    (E) 32π

15. In a certain group of 36 people, only 18 people are wearing hats and only 24 people are wearing sweaters. If 6 people are wearing neither a hat nor a sweater, how many people are wearing both a hat and a sweater?

    (A) 30
    (B) 22
    (C) 12
    (D) 8
    (E) 6

16. $|-3| \cdot |2| \cdot \left|\frac{1}{2}\right| + (-4) =$

    (A) -1
    (B) 0
    (C) 1
    (D) $\frac{3}{2}$
    (E) 4

17. What are the values for which $\frac{x(x + 3)}{(x - 1)(x + 2)}$ is undefined?

    (A) -3 only
    (B) -2 only
    (C) 1 only
    (D) -2 and 1 only
    (E) -3, -2, and 1

GO ON TO THE NEXT PAGE

18. Which of the following graphs in the standard (x,y) coordinate plane correctly shows the points on the graph of $y = |x^2 - 3|$ for $x = -1, 0,$ and 1?

(A)

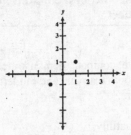

(B)

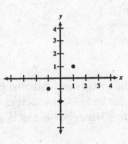

(C)

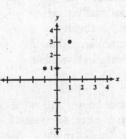

(D)

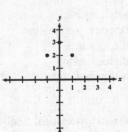

(E)

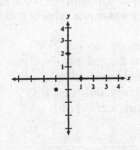

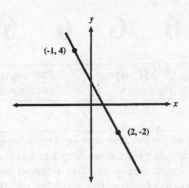

19. The figure above is a graph of which of the following equations?

(A) $y = -3x + 5$

(B) $y = -2x + 2$

(C) $y = -\frac{3}{2}x - 2$

(D) $y = \frac{2}{3}x + 3$

(E) $y = x + 2$

20. The relation defined by the set of ordered pairs $\{(0, 3), (2, 1), (3, 0), (-1, 2), (0, 5),$ and $(-2, 5)\}$ is NOT a function. Deleting which of the ordered pairs will make the resulting set a function?

(A) $(0, 3)$

(B) $(2, 1)$

(C) $(3, 0)$

(D) $(-1, 2)$

(E) $(-2, 5)$

IF YOU FINISH BEFORE TIME IS CALLED, YOU MAY CHECK YOUR WORK ON THIS TEST ONLY. DO NOT WORK ON ANY OTHER TEST SECTION.

STOP

6 6 6 6 6 6 6 6 6 6 6 6

Time—25 Minutes
24 Items

For each item in this section, choose the best answer and blacken the corresponding space on the answer sheet.

Each items below has one or two blanks, each blank indicating that something has been omitted. Beneath the sentence are five lettered words or sets of words. Choose the word or set of words that <u>best</u> fits the meaning of the sentence as a whole.

Example:

Although its publicity has been ----, the film itself is intelligent, well acted, handsomely produced, and altogether ----.

(A) tasteless..respectable
(B) extensive..moderate
(C) sophisticated..amateur
(D) risqué..crude
(E) perfect..spectacular

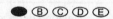

1. Despite the millions of dollars that are spent on improvements, the telephone system in India remains ---- and continues to ---- the citizens who depend on it.

(A) primitive..inconvenience
(B) bombastic..upset
(C) suspicious..connect
(D) outdated..elate
(E) impartial..vex

2. Contrary to popular opinion, bats are not generally aggressive and rabid; most are shy and ----.

(A) turgid
(B) disfigured
(C) punctual
(D) innocuous
(E) depraved

3. The ballet company demonstrated its ---- by putting both classical and modern works in the repertoire.

(A) versatility
(B) mollification
(C) treachery
(D) dignity
(E) obtrusiveness

4. Unlike the images in symbolist poetry, which are often vague and ----, the images of surrealist poetry are startlingly ---- and bold.

(A) extraneous..furtive
(B) trivial..inadvertent
(C) obscure..concrete
(D) spectacular..pallid
(E) symmetrical..virulent

5. A good trial lawyer will argue only what is central to an issue, eliminating ---- information or anything else that might ---- the client.

(A) seminal..amuse
(B) extraneous..jeopardize
(C) erratic..enhance
(D) prodigious..extol
(E) reprehensible..initiate

6. When the real estate agent finally suggested a property that the young couple could ----, they were shocked to see a ---- house that seemed as though it was on the verge of collapse.

(A) renovate..modern
(B) purchase..galling
(C) afford..ramshackle
(D) diversify..dilapidated
(E) envision..reserved

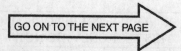
GO ON TO THE NEXT PAGE

7. Psychologists agree that human beings have a
   strong need to ---- their time; having too much
   idle time can be as stressful as having none at all.

   (A) threaten
   (B) annihilate
   (C) structure
   (D) punctuate
   (E) remand

8. While scientists continue to make advances in the
   field of ----, some members of the clergy continue
   to oppose the research arguing that it is ---- for
   human beings to tamper with life.

   (A) psychology..imperative
   (B) astronomy..fallacious
   (C) genetics..immoral
   (D) geology..erroneous
   (E) botany..unethical

GO ON TO THE NEXT PAGE

Each passage below is followed by one or more items based on its content. Answer the items following each passage on the basis of what is stated or implied in the passage.

Items 9-10 are based on the following passage.

Some scientists have theorized that the initial explosion of the dying star generates the high energy particles observed in supernova remnants, but these *Line* particles would quickly lose their energy as they cool
5 in the expanding cloud or escape from the remnant altogether. Instead, the acceleration of particles to high energies must be associated with the shockwave produced by the supernova explosion. The particles are accelerated to very high energies through collisions
10 with fragments in a process analogous to that of a ping-pong ball bouncing through a collection of randomly moving bowling balls. Over the course of many collisions, the ping-pong ball would be accelerated to a very high speed. It is too soon to say definitely that the
15 size and number of fragments associated with the shockwave are adequate to generate the high-energy electrons but a preliminary analysis looks promising.

9. The author regards the conclusion stated in the final sentence as

    (A) unproved but likely
    (B) unsubstantiated and doubtful
    (C) conclusively demonstrated
    (D) true by definition
    (E) unfounded speculation

10. The author develops the passage primarily by

    (A) raising an issue and discussing both pros and cons
    (B) logically deducing conclusions from a premise
    (C) explaining a known sequence of events
    (D) providing a list of examples to illustrate a principle
    (E) criticizing one theory and offering an alternative explanation

Item 11 is based on the following passage.

Chicory is a perennial wildflower, two to three feet high, with a taproot like the Dandelion. The flowers are somewhat like those of the Dandelion *Line* though they have a delicate tint of blue. You'll find it
5 growing throughout the summer along roadsides. Chicory, or Cichorium, is a word of Egyptian origin, and the Arab physicians called it "Chicourey." Cichorium is mentioned by Theophrastus as it was used amongst the ancient Greeks, and the names by
10 which the wild plant is known in all the languages of modern Europe are merely corruptions of the original Greek word. The root is roasted and ground for blending with coffee, though Chicory itself is totally lacking in caffeine.

11. The author assumes that

    (A) readers are familiar with the Dandelion
    (B) Chicory originated in the Middle East
    (C) modern European languages derive mainly from Greek
    (D) ancient Greeks preferred caffeine-free beverages
    (E) dandelions do not grow along roadsides

GO ON TO THE NEXT PAGE

Item 12 is based on the following passage.

To one unaccustomed to it, there is something inexpressibly lonely in the solitude of a prairie. The loneliness of a forest seems nothing compared to it. In
Line a forest, the view is shut in by trees, and the
5 imagination is left free to picture a livelier scene beyond. However, in the case of a prairie, there is an immense extent of landscape without signs of human existence; one is struck by the feeling of being far beyond the bounds of human habitation. It is a lonely
10 waste bounded by undulating swells of land, naked and uniform, and due to the deficiency of landmarks and distinct features, an inexperienced traveler may become lost as readily as upon the wastes of the ocean.

12. The author states that the prairie seems lonelier than the forest because

   (A) it is possible for a traveler to become lost more easily on the prairie
   (B) the forest is marked by paths that show routes to various destinations
   (C) the prairie is larger and more open than the ocean itself
   (D) trees of the forest resemble people who keep a traveler from feeling alone
   (E) the unobstructed view on the prairie shows the absence of other people

Item 13 is based on the following passage.

Every ten years, the federal government conducts a comprehensive census of the entire population, and the data gathered are published by the Bureau of
Line Census. By studying census data, demographers are
5 able to identify counties and communities throughout the country with populations that have specific characteristics, for example: high or low median age, large numbers of families with children, a high percentage of two-career couples, or particularly
10 affluent households. Characteristics such as these are often associated with particular viewpoints on important political issues.

13. The author is most likely leading up to a proposal to

   (A) require the census to be conducted more frequently
   (B) use census data to advise candidates on political issues
   (C) expand the scope of the census to gather more detailed data
   (D) maintain the confidentiality of census records
   (E) discontinue the practice of conducting the census

GO ON TO THE NEXT PAGE

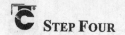

Item 14 is based on the following passage.

"Locks," says the old saw, "are installed to keep out honest people." In fact, most locks do not present much of a challenge to lock pickers, whether amateur or professional. The one on your front door probably consists of a cylinder held in place by a series of spring-loaded pins. When you insert the serrated key, the sharp edges of the key push the pins out of the way allowing you to turn cylinder with the key, thereby operating the bolt. The same result can be accomplished by inserting a pick and wrench, both small wire-like tools, and manipulating them in the right way. Gently turn the wrench to keep a constant rotational force on the cylinder while using the pick to push the pins out of the way one at a time. When the last pin is cleared, the wrench will naturally turn the cylinder and the lock will open for you. After a little practice, anyone with larceny in the heart can open your front door in less than 30 seconds.

14. Which of the following best describes the relationship between the last sentence of the passage and the first sentence?

(A) The first sentence states a hypothesis that is disproved by the passage and summarized by the last sentence.

(B) The first sentence makes a generalization that is then illustrated by examples referenced by the last sentence.

(C) The last sentence summarizes the development of the passage and notes that the first sentence makes a false statement.

(D) The last sentence shows that the development of the passage proves the point made in the first sentence.

(E) The last sentence uses details from the passage to contradict the assertion of the first sentence.

GO ON TO THE NEXT PAGE

Items 15-24 are based on the following passage.

Is the Constitution of the United States a mechanism or an organism? Does it furnish for the American community a structure or a process? The
Line Constitution is Newtonian in that it establishes a set of
5 forces and counter-forces. These confer power and impose limitations on power, and one of the great virtues of the Newtonian model is that correctives can be self-generated. They do not have to be imposed from without. The homely illustration is the cutting of
10 a pie into two pieces so that brother and sister will have equal shares. Rather than setting up a system of judicial review under an equal-protection clause—a device that might not work until the pie has become stale—you simply let one sibling cut the pie and the other choose a
15 piece.

The Newtonian system assumes that each branch has a capacity to act that is commensurate with its authority to act and to improve its ability to discharge its constitutional responsibilities. For example, on the
20 Congressional side, this means a rationalizing of the legislative process to improve its capability to formulate and carry through a legislative program that is coherent in policies and technically proficient. The goal involves better access to disinterested information
25 through better research staffs and facilities, as well as the selection of committee chairs most likely on a basis other than simple seniority. Other devices might alleviate the overburdened executive branch: a strengthened Cabinet, with a smaller, executive
30 Cabinet of respected statesmen to serve as a link between the White House and the departments, and between the President and the Congress. No constitutional impediment stands in the way of any of the structural changes on either the legislative or the
35 executive side.

In a Newtonian constitution, extraordinary force in one direction is likely to produce extraordinary, and sometimes excessive, force in another direction. In the early years of the New Deal, the Supreme Court,
40 generally over the dissent of its most respected members, engaged in a series of judicial vetoes that reflected an unjudicial approach to the function of judging. The President, on his part, countered with the Court reorganization plan, which seriously threatened
45 the independence of the judiciary. A Newtonian system demands constitutional morality. It would be possible, by excessive use of legal power, to bring the system to a standstill. Congress might refuse to appropriate for executive departments. The President might ignore
50 Supreme Court decisions. The Court might declare unconstitutional all laws that a majority of its members

would not have voted for. Without constitutional morality, the system breaks down.

The constitution is also Darwinian and stresses
55 process and adaptation. Justice Holmes remarked that "the provisions of the Constitution are not mathematical formulas having their essence in their form; they are organic living institutions." Growth and adaptation, to be sure, have sometimes been seen as
60 mutations, threatening the constitutional order. Chief Justice Marshall, near the close of his life, viewing with despair the developments of the Jacksonian era, confided to Justice Story, "The Union has been preserved thus far by miracles. I fear they cannot
65 continue."

It must be admitted that we have all too readily assigned responsibility for the Darwinian constitutional evolution to the Supreme Court. Congress has too often either neglected its opportunities and responsibilities or
70 has acted tentatively. When Congress does legislate, it is apt to regard its own constitutional judgment as only provisional, to await as a matter of course a submission to the Supreme Court. A striking example is the recent campaign finance law. But in the final analysis, is the
75 Constitution a mechanism or an organism? If light can be viewed as both wave and particles, depending on which analysis is the more serviceable for a given problem, why cannot the Constitution be seen as both a mechanism and an organism, a structure and a process?

15. The main purpose of the selection is to

(A) discuss two models of constitutional law
(B) criticize Congress and the executive branch for inaction
(C) suggest a new role for the Supreme Court
(D) challenge the validity of Supreme Court rulings
(E) call for a revised Constitution

16. In the first paragraph, the author makes use of

(A) circular reasoning
(B) authority
(C) analogy
(D) generalization
(E) ambiguity

GO ON TO THE NEXT PAGE

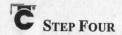

17. The author mentions the possibility of better research staffs for Congress (lines 24-25) as a method of

   (A) weakening the executive branch of government
   (B) improving the ability of the legislature to act
   (C) encouraging the judiciary to be independent
   (D) illegally increasing the workload of Congress
   (E) curtailing the power of the government

18. It can be inferred that the author's attitude toward the Supreme Court's decisions during the early years of the New Deal is one of

   (A) reflection
   (B) acceptance
   (C) support
   (D) indifference
   (E) disapproval

19. The author regards the President's attempt to reorganize the Supreme Court as

   (A) understandable but wrong
   (B) ineffective but correct
   (C) impractical but well-intentioned
   (D) necessary but misguided
   (E) half-hearted but moral

20. The author means for the word "Darwinian" (line 54) to echo the meaning of

   (A) self-generated (line 8)
   (B) homely (line 9)
   (C) proficient (line 23)
   (D) unjudicial (line 42)
   (E) organic (line 58)

21. With which of the following statements would the author most likely agree?

   (A) The Darwinian model and the Newtonian model produce almost identical interpretations of the Constitution.
   (B) A constitutionally permissible action might still be constitutionally immoral.
   (C) One branch of government is morally obligated not to criticize the actions of another.
   (D) The Newtonian model of the Constitution is superior to the Darwinian model.
   (E) The Supreme Court should have primary responsibility for evolving a Darwinian model of government.

22. In the final sentence, the author

   (A) poses a question for future research
   (B) introduces a new problem of constitutional theory
   (C) rejects the Darwinian model
   (D) suggests ways for improving governmental efficiency
   (E) asks a rhetorical question

23. The passage implies that

   (A) Congress is more important than either the executive or the judiciary
   (B) branches of government may have more constitutional authority than they use
   (C) the earliest Supreme Court justices were more sincere than today's justices
   (D) the Constitution sets up a very simple system for governmental decisions
   (E) constitutionally created hurdles block needed improvements in governmental efficiency

24. The author is primarily concerned with

   (A) creating a dilemma
   (B) evading a question
   (C) answering a question
   (D) pointing out a contradiction
   (E) reporting on a development

IF YOU FINISH BEFORE TIME IS CALLED, YOU MAY CHECK YOUR WORK ON THIS TEST ONLY. DO NOT WORK ON ANY OTHER TEST SECTION.

STOP

8 8 8 8 8 8 8 8 8 8 8 8

| Time—20 Minutes 16 Items | In this section, solve each item, using any available space on the page for scratchwork. Then, decide which is the best of the choices given and fill in the corresponding oval on the answer sheet. |

Notes: The figures accompanying the items are drawn as accurately as possible unless otherwise stated in specific items. Again, unless otherwise stated, all figures lie in the same plane. All numbers used in these items are real numbers. Calculators are permitted for this test.

Reference:

  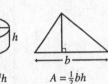

Circle: Rectangle: Rectangular Solid: Cylinder: Triangle:

$C = 2\pi r$ $A = lw$ $V = lwh$ $V = \pi r^2 h$ $A = \frac{1}{2}bh$ $a^2 + b^2 = c^2$

$A = \pi r^2$

- The measure in degrees of a straight angle is 180.
- The number of degrees of arc in a circle is 360.
- The sum of the measure of the angles of a triangle is 180.

Fabric	Cost
A	3 yards for $8
B	2 yards for $6
C	4 yards for $9
D	5 yards for $7
E	6 yards for $5

1. According to the table above, which fabric costs the <u>least</u> per square yard?

(A) A
(B) B
(C) C
(D) D
(E) E

2. $\dfrac{10^3(10^5 + 10^5)}{10^4} =$

(A) 10^4
(B) 10^6
(C) $2(10^2)$
(D) $2(10^4)$
(E) $2(10^9)$

3. If $x = b + 4$ and $y = b - 3$, then in terms of x and y, $b =$

(A) $x + y - 1$

(B) $x + y + 1$

(C) $x - y - 1$

(D) $\dfrac{x + y + 1}{2}$

(E) $\dfrac{x + y - 1}{2}$

GO ON TO THE NEXT PAGE

4. If $5x = 3y = z$, and x, y, and z are positive integers, all of the following must be integers EXCEPT

(A) $\frac{x}{zy}$

(B) $\frac{z}{5}$

(C) $\frac{z}{3}$

(D) $\frac{z}{15}$

(E) $\frac{x}{3}$

5. What is the width of a rectangle with an area of $48x^2$ and a length of $24x$?

(A) 2
(B) $2x$
(C) $24x$
(D) $2x^2$
(E) $2x^3$

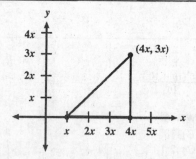

6. In the figure above, if the area of the triangle is 54, then $x =$

(A) $3\sqrt{3}$

(B) 3

(C) $2\sqrt{3}$

(D) 2

(E) $\sqrt{3}$

7. If $x = \frac{1}{y+1}$ and $y \neq 1$, then $y =$

(A) $x + 1$

(B) x

(C) $\frac{x+1}{x}$

(D) $\frac{x-1}{x}$

(E) $\frac{1-x}{x}$

8. If $\blacktriangle(x) = x + 1$ and $\blacktriangledown(x) = x - 1$, then which of the following is equal to $\blacktriangle(3) \cdot \blacktriangledown(5)$?

(A) $\blacktriangle 8$
(B) $\blacktriangle 12$
(C) $\blacktriangle 14$
(D) $\blacktriangledown 17$
(E) $\blacktriangledown 20$

9. If $x + y = 14$, then $\frac{x}{2} + \frac{y}{2} =$

(A) 4
(B) 5
(C) 6
(D) 7
(E) $\frac{y}{2}$

10. If the average of ten numbers—1, 2, 3, 4, 5, 6, 7, 8, 9, and x—is 6, what is x?

(A) 5
(B) 6
(C) 10
(D) 12
(E) 15

11. A certain mixture of gravel and sand consists of 2.5 kilograms of gravel and 12.5 kilograms of sand. What percent of the mixture, by weight, is gravel?

(A) 10%

(B) $16\frac{2}{3}\%$

(C) 20%

(D) 25%

(E) $33\frac{1}{3}\%$

GO ON TO THE NEXT PAGE

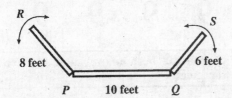

8 feet   6 feet

P   10 feet   Q

12. The figure above is the top view of a folding room divider, hinged at P and Q. If sections PR and QS are moved as shown until R and S meet, what will be the area, in square feet, enclosed? (Ignore the thickness of the hinges and the screen's sections.)

(A) 6
(B) 12
(C) 6π
(D) 24
(E) 12π

13. Motorcycle X averages 40 kilometers per liter of gasoline while Motorcycle Y averages 50 kilometers per liter. If the cost of gasoline is $2 per liter, what will be the difference in the cost of operating the two motorcycles for 300 kilometers?

(A) $3
(B) $6
(C) $12
(D) $15
(E) $20

14. For all positive integers, $\triangle n = \frac{n}{2}$ if n is even, and $\triangle n = n + 1$ if n is odd. $\triangle 2 \cdot \triangle 7 =$

(A) 4
(B) 5
(C) 6
(D) 7
(E) 8

15. For a positive integer k, which of the following equals $6k + 3$?

(A) $\frac{k+1}{2}$
(B) $\frac{1}{k} + 4$
(C) $2k + 1$
(D) $3(k + 1)$
(E) $3(2k + 1)$

16. To mail a letter costs x cents for the first ounce and y cents for every additional ounce or fraction of an ounce. Which of the following equations can be used to determine the cost, C, in cents to mail a letter that weighs a whole number of ounces, w?

(A) $C = w(x + y)$
(B) $C = x(w - y)$
(C) $C = x(w - 1) + y(w - 1)$
(D) $C = x + wy$
(E) $C = x + y(w - 1)$

IF YOU FINISH BEFORE TIME IS CALLED, YOU MAY CHECK YOUR WORK ON THIS TEST ONLY. DO NOT WORK ON ANY OTHER TEST SECTION.

STOP

9 9 9 9 9 9 9 9 9 9 9 9 9 9 9

| Time—20 Minutes | For each item in this section, choose the best answer and blacken the |
| 19 Items | corresponding space on the answer sheet. |

Each item below has one or two blanks, each blank indicating that something has been omitted. Beneath the sentence are five lettered words or sets of words. Choose the word or set of words that **best** fits the meaning of the sentence as a whole.

Example:

Although its publicity has been ----, the film itself is intelligent, well acted, handsomely produced, and altogether ----.

(A) tasteless..respectable
(B) extensive..moderate
(C) sophisticated..amateur
(D) risqué..crude
(E) perfect..spectacular

1. Large corporations use advertising not to liberate consumers with information about freedom of choice but to ------- them, holding them captive to the company's particular brand.

   (A) enslave
   (B) attract
   (C) enlighten
   (D) aid
   (E) secure

2. Hoping to impress his professor, Eugene did the work required for the course with -------, submitting all of the assignments on or before their due dates.

   (A) reluctance
   (B) alacrity
   (C) insouciance
   (D) fortitude
   (E) lassitude

3. John was bright but lazy and because of his ---- was never promoted to senior partner.

   (A) novelty
   (B) perjury
   (C) zeal
   (D) indemnity
   (E) indolence

4. The film was completely devoid of plot or character development: It was merely a ---- of striking images.

   (A) renouncement
   (B) montage
   (C) calumny
   (D) carnage
   (E) premonition

5. Though the concert had been enjoyable, it was overly ---- and the three encores seemed ----.

   (A) extensive..curtailed
   (B) protracted..gratuitous
   (C) inaudible..superfluous
   (D) sublime..fortuitous
   (E) contracted..lengthy

GO ON TO THE NEXT PAGE

Each passage below is followed by one or more items based on its content. Answer the items following each passage on the basis of what is stated or implied in the passage.

Items 6-7 are based on the following passage.

On one of those sober and melancholy days in the latter part of autumn, when the shadows of morning and evening almost mingle together and throw a gloom
Line over the decline of the year, I passed several hours
5 rambling about Westminster Abbey. It seems as if the awful nature of the place presses down upon the soul, and hushes the beholder into noiseless reverence. We are surrounded by the congregated bones of great men of past times, who have filled history with their deeds,
10 and the earth with their renown.† Yet, it provokes a smile at the vanity of human ambition to see how they are crowded together and jostled in the dust; what parsimony is observed in doling out a scanty nook, a gloomy corner, and a little portion of earth, to those,
15 whom, when alive, kingdoms could not satisfy. I passed some time in Poet's Corner, which occupies an end of one of the transepts or cross aisles of the abbey. The monuments are generally simple; for the lives of literary men afford no striking themes for the sculptor.
20 Shakespeare and Addison have statues erected to their memories; but the greater part have busts, medallions, and sometimes mere inscriptions.

†Over 3,000 famous people are buried in Westminster Abbey.

6. As used in this context, the word "awful" (line 6) means

   (A) frightening
   (B) impressive
   (C) terrible
   (D) unlit
   (E) dilapidated

7. The author finds it amusing that

   (A) people would be buried inside a structure like Westminster Abbey
   (B) only Shakespeare and Addison have statues erected to them
   (C) famous people are buried in relatively modest circumstances
   (D) even the powerful and famous eventually die
   (E) writers are buried in a remote part of the building

GO ON TO THE NEXT PAGE

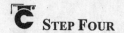

Item 8 is based on the following passage.

By the 1870s, several manufacturers were offering for sale prefabricated houses and other structures using a variety of building systems.
Line Prefabricated units were used extensively as army
5 barracks, field hospitals, railway stations, storehouses, fruit stands, and summer cottages. When the Klondike gold rush began, a New York company immediately began loading a vessel to carry houses to Seattle via Cape Horn, all of them ready-made in sections so that
10 they could be carried easily in boats up the Yukon or packed on sleds. However, these early experiments with prefabricated houses did not revolutionize the building industry. Carpenters and builders organized to resist the adoption of a method that threatened to
15 deprive many of their jobs. Architects, who had the weight and prestige of tradition behind them, also quietly did all that they could to discourage people from buying mass-produced products that threatened the integrity of their craft.

8. The author states that the main reason that prefabricated building did not succeed was

   (A) shipping cost of transporting components to remote building sites
   (B) organized opposition by important sectors of the building trade
   (C) limited number of applications for prefabricated structures
   (D) reluctance of large buyers to purchase prefabricated units
   (E) lack of sufficiently precise manufacturing processes

Item 9 is based on the following passage.

The beginning of the United States was characterized by two competing philosophies: the humanitarian philosophy of the French Enlightenment
Line and the English philosophy of laissez-faire. The
5 humanitarian strain espoused the notion of human perfectibility and had as its goal an equalitarian democracy in which the state would promote the welfare of all. The laissez-faire variation stressed the needs of an abstract "economic man" and saw the
10 state's main function as ensuring free markets. The first of these antagonistic philosophies was accepted by the agrarian leaders and came to be associated with Jefferson; the second came to dominate the thinking of the mercantile, capitalistic America and took form in
15 Hamiltonian Federalism.

9. The word "antagonistic" in line 11 means

   (A) incompatible
   (B) abstract
   (C) formal
   (D) uncivil
   (E) irreverent

GO ON TO THE NEXT PAGE

Items 10-19 are based on the following passage.

Passage 1

In 1893, Frederick Jackson Turner presented a paper to a group of historians convening in Chicago during the Columbian Exposition. Entitled "The
Line Significance of the American Frontier in History,"
5 Turner's paper drew little immediate reaction. Yet, no theory of history has had a greater influence on the direction and methodology of inquiry and the issues of debate in American history. Later historians took issue with some of Turner's interpretations; even some of his
10 own students were among those whose research proved some of his views to be wrong. Yet, these debates merely serve to illustrate the importance of Turner's hypothesis.

Turner's argument was a grand hypothesis about
15 how the settlement of the frontier had shaped the American experience and character. As with all general hypotheses in any field of study, it gave a coherent interpretation to many facts that had been largely ignored by historians up to that time.
20 Turner used statistical evidence from the 1880 census as the basis for a startling conclusion: Prior to 1880 there had been a frontier to be settled. By 1890, Turner pointed out, there was no longer any area of wilderness completely untouched by settlements. The
25 frontier had disappeared. The passing of the frontier, Turner concluded, was a historic moment.

Turner further claimed that the frontier experience had produced a distinctively American character, which was not explainable simply as the
30 predictable behavioral traits molded by English political institutions. Frontier settlers developed inquisitiveness, inventiveness, energy, and a great passion for freedom. These attributes defined a new American character—one evidenced in nationalism,
35 independence, and democracy. This new sense of national identity derived from the fact that people from every section of the country mixed at the Western frontier. Economic independence could be traced to the fact that the settlers no longer depended on England for
40 goods but had become self-sufficient. In addition, the frontier settlers, whose basic social unit was the family, enjoyed freedom from direct governmental interference. Frontier life thus reinforced the fundamental ideals of populist democracy.
45 In addition, Turner argued that the frontier fostered democracy in the cities of the East. The availability of free land at the frontier provided a "safety-valve" against possible social unrest: those discontented with social inequities and economic
50 injustice could strike out and settle the free land that was available in frontier territories.

Turner's thesis was thus original in both what it said and in the methodology that Turner used in formulating it. Up to the time of Turner's essay, history had been
55 essentially the history of politics. A Midwesterner, Turner challenged this traditional approach of Eastern historians by incorporating techniques of the social sciences, showing how factors of geography, economics, climate, and society influenced the
60 development of the American West. Although now common among historians, at the time this interdisciplinary approach was novel.

Passage 2

Three years before Turner put forth the frontier thesis, the U.S. Census Bureau had announced the
65 disappearance of a contiguous frontier line. For Turner, the significance of the frontier was its effect on the American character. According to Turner, uniquely American traits were developed by the frontier culture, including a can-do problem-solving attitude, a nervous
70 energy, and rugged individualism.

Turner's essay reached triumphalist heights in his belief that the promotion of individualistic democracy was the most important consequence of the frontier. Individuals, forced to rely on their own wits and
75 strength, were necessarily skeptical of hierarchies and fearful of centralized authority.

Turner's thesis that the frontier is the key to American history as a whole has rightfully been abandoned. There is too much evidence for the critical
80 influence of factors like slavery and the Civil War, immigration, and the development of industrial capitalism. But even as an account of the West and frontier, Turner's thesis was lacking.

Turner's formulation of "free land" ignored the
85 presence of the numerous Indian peoples whose subjugation was required by the nation's westward march. The many Indian wars started by American expansion belie Turner's argument that the American frontier, in sharp contrast to European borders between
90 nation-states, was "free land."

More fundamentally, the very concept of a frontier is dubious, because it applies to too many disparate places and times to be useful. How much do Puritan New England and the California of the
95 transcontinental railroad really have in common? Many such critics have sought to replace the idea of a moving frontier with the idea of the West as a distinctive region, much like the American South.

GO ON TO THE NEXT PAGE

Additionally, cooperation and communities of
100 various sorts, not isolated individuals, made possible
the absorption of the West into the United States. Most
migrant wagon trains, for example, were composed of
extended kinship networks. Moreover, the role of the
federal government and large corporations grew
105 increasingly important. Corporate investors built the
railroads; government troops defeated Indian nations;
even cowboys, enshrined in popular myth as rugged
loners, were generally low-level employees of cattle
corporations.

10. According to Passage 1, Turner's methodology
was original in its

(A) reliance on the history of politics to explain
the American experience
(B) use of an interdisciplinary approach to study
a historical question
(C) reliance on a presentation at a professional
conference to announce a theory
(D) suggestion that key terms like "frontier" have
to be more clearly defined
(E) insistence that historical theories be
supported by statistical evidence

11. The phrase "even some of his own students"
(lines 9-10) implies that students are

(A) not necessarily familiar with the most recent
scholarly work
(B) ordinarily sympathetic to the views of one of
their professors
(C) not likely to accept a theory until it has been
studied for some time
(D) disposed to propose new theories that have
little merit
(E) inclined to accept a new theory just because
of its novelty

12. The attitude of the author of Passage 1 toward
Turner's work can best be described as

(A) suspicious
(B) condescending
(C) undecided
(D) approving
(E) irreverent

13. In this context, "grand" (line 14) means

(A) incorrect
(B) comprehensive
(C) lavish
(D) tentative
(E) formal

GO ON TO THE NEXT PAGE

14. The author of Passage 2 lists the "factors" in lines 80-82 in order to show that

(A) Turner's thesis did not adequately explain the history of the frontier
(B) historians prior to Turner had tended to focus on only a single explanatory factor
(C) the frontier was only one of many important factors in American history
(D) different regions of America had different experiences of the frontier
(E) westward expansion occurred contemporaneously with other important historical events

15. The author of Passage 2 mentions wagon trains (line 102) in order to show that

(A) frontier land had previously been inhabited by indigenous peoples
(B) groups were as important in the westward expansion as individuals
(C) government army troops were needed to secure the safety of settlers
(D) groups from different regions came into contact at the frontier
(E) the frontier constituted a permanent region rather than moving line

16. It can be inferred that the author of Passage 2 believes that Turner's thesis

(A) is still generally valid
(B) had very limited usefulness
(C) was intellectually dishonest
(D) intentionally ignored evidence
(E) was not serious scholarship

17. In context, "belie" (line 88) means

(A) tell an untruth about
(B) conceal a flaw in
(C) prove to be false
(D) retract a point
(E) support strongly

18. Both passages mention all of the following as elements of Turner's view regarding the American character EXCEPT

(A) practical inventiveness
(B) pro-democracy attitude
(C) skepticism toward authority
(D) nationalistic feelings
(E) energetic life-style

19. The evidence that frontier land was not free (lines 84-90) most undermines what aspect of Turner's thesis as explained in Passage 1?

(A) safety-valve theory
(B) census data of 1880
(C) claim of self-sufficiency
(D) mixing at the frontier
(E) influence of English institutions

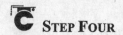

10 10 10 10 10 10 10 10 10

| Time—10 Minutes 14 Items | For each item in this section, choose the best answer and blacken the corresponding space on the answer sheet. |

Directions: The following sentences test correctness and effectiveness of expression. In choosing answers, follow the requirements of standard written English; that is, pay attention to grammar, choice of words, sentence construction, and punctuation.

In each of the following sentences, part of the sentence or the entire sentence is underlined. Beneath each sentence you will find five ways of phrasing the underlined part. Choice A repeats the original; the other four are different.

Choose the answer that best expresses the meaning of the original sentence. If you think the original is better than any of the alternatives, choose it; otherwise choose one of the others. Your choice should produce the most effective sentence—clear and precise, without awkwardness or ambiguity.

Example: Answer

Allen visiting his cousin in France last summer.

(A) visiting
(B) visited
(C) does visit
(D) a visit
(E) is visiting   Ⓐ ● Ⓒ Ⓓ Ⓔ

1. The paintings by Frederic Remington depict the American West and romanticized it.

   (A) depict the American West and romanticized it
   (B) was depicting the American West and also romanticizing it
   (C) depicted the American West and romanticized it
   (D) having depicted the American West also romanticized it
   (E) depicts and romanticizes the American West

2. To succeed in business dealings you must have a thorough knowledge of the market, be aggressive, and also the will to win.

   (A) you must have a thorough knowledge of the market, be aggressive, and also the will to win
   (B) one must have a thorough knowledge of the market, you must be aggressive, and have the will to win
   (C) you must have a thorough knowledge of the market, the willingness to win and be aggressive
   (D) requires being aggressive, knowing the market, and to have the will to win
   (E) requires that you have a thorough knowledge of the market, be aggressive, and have the will to win

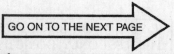
GO ON TO THE NEXT PAGE

3. There is new evidence to suggest that a child's personality is <u>developed more by everyday interactions rather than by</u> traumatic events.

   (A) developed more by everyday interactions rather than by
   (B) developed more by everyday interactions than by
   (C) developed more by everyday interactions and not by
   (D) being developed more by everyday interactions instead of
   (E) developing more by everyday interactions than by

4. <u>Hopelessly addicted to alcohol, the writings of Edgar Allan Poe are often</u> about death and the supernatural.

   (A) Hopelessly addicted to alcohol, the writings of Edgar Allan Poe are often
   (B) Edgar Allan Poe's being hopelessly addicted to alcohol and he often wrote
   (C) Hopelessly addicted to alcohol, Edgar Allan Poe often wrote
   (D) In that he was hopelessly addicted to alcohol, Edgar Allan Poe often wrote
   (E) The writings of Edgar Allan Poe, with his hopeless addiction to alcohol, are often

5. <u>With the writing of *Huckleberry Finn*, it marked the first time that the American vernacular was used in a novel.</u>

   (A) With the writing of *Huckleberry Finn* it marked the first time that the American Vernacular was used in a novel.
   (B) Marking the first time that the American vernacular was used in a novel was the writing of *Huckleberry Finn*.
   (C) The writing of *Huckleberry Finn* was the first time that the American vernacular was used in a novel.
   (D) The writing of *Huckleberry Finn* marked the first time that the American vernacular was used in a novel.
   (E) For the first time the American vernacular was used in a novel was *Huckleberry Finn*.

6. Parents and civic leaders are concerned about <u>protecting the children and the drugs that are available</u>.

   (A) protecting the children and the drugs that are available
   (B) the protection of the children and the drugs that are available
   (C) protecting the children and about the drugs that are available
   (D) protecting the children and the availability of drugs to them
   (E) protecting the children and the availability of drugs

7. Before this century, young girls were not expected to participate in <u>sports, so</u> they were never seriously trained to be athletes.

   (A) sports, so
   (B) sports that
   (C) sports and so
   (D) sports and
   (E) sports, and so consequently

8. Teachers of the old Italian school taught nothing but breathing, <u>believing that the better the breath support, the more beautiful the tone</u>.

   (A) believing that the better the breath support, the more beautiful the tone
   (B) believing it to be the case that the better the breath support would result in a more beautiful tone
   (C) in the belief that better breath support would result in that the tone would be more beautiful
   (D) believing the better breath support to be resulting in more beautiful tones
   (E) believing there to be a relationship between breath support and the more beautiful tone

GO ON TO THE NEXT PAGE

9. In European countries where socialism is a dominant force, <u>they often strike for political rather than for economic reasons</u>.

   (A) they often strike for political rather than for economic reasons
   (B) they often strike on account of political rather than for economic reasons
   (C) strikes are often called for political reasons rather than for economics
   (D) strikes are called by them for political reasons rather than for economic ones
   (E) strikes are often called for political rather than for economic reasons

10. James Fenimore Cooper was the first author <u>who writes</u> about truly American themes.

    (A) who writes
    (B) having written
    (C) to write
    (D) who had been writing
    (E) who has written

11. To be a successful musician requires extensive training, practice, and <u>you should also love performing</u>.

    (A) you should also love performing
    (B) loving to perform
    (C) one should love to perform
    (D) to love to perform
    (E) a love of performing

12. After the American Revolution, most of <u>those who had been loyal to the crown having gone</u> to Canada, where they settled.

    (A) those who had been loyal to the crown having gone
    (B) those who had been loyal to the crown have gone
    (C) them who have been loyal to the crown went
    (D) them having been loyal to the crown went
    (E) those who had been loyal to the crown went

13. Although it is cost effective to make perfumes from synthetic ingredients, in France <u>they used to make the classic fragrances using only flowers and natural essences</u>.

    (A) they used to make the classic fragrances using only flowers and natural essences
    (B) the classic fragrances used to be made by them using only flowers and natural essences
    (C) the classic fragrances used to be made using only flowers and natural essences
    (D) it used to be that the classic fragrances were made only with flowers and natural essences
    (E) the classic fragrances used to be made with flowers and natural essences only

14. Although the stock market seems to offer the possibility of great personal gain, you must understand that to invest in stocks <u>is accepting the risk of financial ruin as well</u>.

    (A) is accepting the risk of financial ruin as well
    (B) is to accept the risk of financial ruin as well
    (C) is to accept the risk as well of financial ruin
    (D) are accepting the risk of financial ruin as well
    (E) are to accept the risk of financial ruin as well

IF YOU FINISH BEFORE TIME IS CALLED, YOU MAY CHECK YOUR WORK ON THIS TEST ONLY. DO NOT WORK ON ANY OTHER TEST SECTION.   **STOP**

5

Step Five: Post-Assessment and Review

See how far you have come and measure your improvement with this second, official test.

Put into action all of the content knowledge and test-taking strategies you've learned.

Redirect your study plan with a new snapshot of your performance.

Make sure that you're able to work through the test quickly without losing accuracy.

Step Five Overview:

It's time to measure your progress. You will put into action everything that you've learned during this second "dress rehearsal." After taking this final exam, you will be able to compare your pre- and post-test scores and see how much you have improved. You will have a chance to identify any remaining areas of weakness so that you know where to focus your studies prior to the actual test.

EDUCATORS' #1 CHOICE FOR SCHOOL IMPROVEMENT

Cambridge Course Concept Outline
POST-ASSESSMENT AND REVIEW

The Essay Response and Bubble Sheets on pages 849-852 are for use when taking the SAT Post-Test.

Name: _____   Date: _____

Student ID Number: _____

SAT POST-TEST

Section 1

Begin your essay on this page. If you need more space, continue on the next page.

_____
_____
_____
_____
_____
_____
_____
_____
_____
_____
_____
_____
_____
_____
_____
_____
_____
_____
_____
_____
_____
_____
_____
_____
_____

Name: _____   Date: _____

Student ID Number: _____

SAT POST-TEST

Start with number 1 for each new section. If a section has fewer questions than answer spaces, leave the extra answer spaces blank. Be sure to erase any errors or stray marks completely.

Section 2

1 Ⓐ Ⓑ Ⓒ Ⓓ Ⓔ	10 Ⓐ Ⓑ Ⓒ Ⓓ Ⓔ	19 Ⓐ Ⓑ Ⓒ Ⓓ Ⓔ	28 Ⓐ Ⓑ Ⓒ Ⓓ Ⓔ
2 Ⓐ Ⓑ Ⓒ Ⓓ Ⓔ	11 Ⓐ Ⓑ Ⓒ Ⓓ Ⓔ	20 Ⓐ Ⓑ Ⓒ Ⓓ Ⓔ	29 Ⓐ Ⓑ Ⓒ Ⓓ Ⓔ
3 Ⓐ Ⓑ Ⓒ Ⓓ Ⓔ	12 Ⓐ Ⓑ Ⓒ Ⓓ Ⓔ	21 Ⓐ Ⓑ Ⓒ Ⓓ Ⓔ	30 Ⓐ Ⓑ Ⓒ Ⓓ Ⓔ
4 Ⓐ Ⓑ Ⓒ Ⓓ Ⓔ	13 Ⓐ Ⓑ Ⓒ Ⓓ Ⓔ	22 Ⓐ Ⓑ Ⓒ Ⓓ Ⓔ	31 Ⓐ Ⓑ Ⓒ Ⓓ Ⓔ
5 Ⓐ Ⓑ Ⓒ Ⓓ Ⓔ	14 Ⓐ Ⓑ Ⓒ Ⓓ Ⓔ	23 Ⓐ Ⓑ Ⓒ Ⓓ Ⓔ	32 Ⓐ Ⓑ Ⓒ Ⓓ Ⓔ
6 Ⓐ Ⓑ Ⓒ Ⓓ Ⓔ	15 Ⓐ Ⓑ Ⓒ Ⓓ Ⓔ	24 Ⓐ Ⓑ Ⓒ Ⓓ Ⓔ	33 Ⓐ Ⓑ Ⓒ Ⓓ Ⓔ
7 Ⓐ Ⓑ Ⓒ Ⓓ Ⓔ	16 Ⓐ Ⓑ Ⓒ Ⓓ Ⓔ	25 Ⓐ Ⓑ Ⓒ Ⓓ Ⓔ	34 Ⓐ Ⓑ Ⓒ Ⓓ Ⓔ
8 Ⓐ Ⓑ Ⓒ Ⓓ Ⓔ	17 Ⓐ Ⓑ Ⓒ Ⓓ Ⓔ	26 Ⓐ Ⓑ Ⓒ Ⓓ Ⓔ	35 Ⓐ Ⓑ Ⓒ Ⓓ Ⓔ
9 Ⓐ Ⓑ Ⓒ Ⓓ Ⓔ	18 Ⓐ Ⓑ Ⓒ Ⓓ Ⓔ	27 Ⓐ Ⓑ Ⓒ Ⓓ Ⓔ	36 Ⓐ Ⓑ Ⓒ Ⓓ Ⓔ

Section 3

1 Ⓐ Ⓑ Ⓒ Ⓓ Ⓔ	10 Ⓐ Ⓑ Ⓒ Ⓓ Ⓔ	19 Ⓐ Ⓑ Ⓒ Ⓓ Ⓔ	28 Ⓐ Ⓑ Ⓒ Ⓓ Ⓔ
2 Ⓐ Ⓑ Ⓒ Ⓓ Ⓔ	11 Ⓐ Ⓑ Ⓒ Ⓓ Ⓔ	20 Ⓐ Ⓑ Ⓒ Ⓓ Ⓔ	29 Ⓐ Ⓑ Ⓒ Ⓓ Ⓔ
3 Ⓐ Ⓑ Ⓒ Ⓓ Ⓔ	12 Ⓐ Ⓑ Ⓒ Ⓓ Ⓔ	21 Ⓐ Ⓑ Ⓒ Ⓓ Ⓔ	30 Ⓐ Ⓑ Ⓒ Ⓓ Ⓔ
4 Ⓐ Ⓑ Ⓒ Ⓓ Ⓔ	13 Ⓐ Ⓑ Ⓒ Ⓓ Ⓔ	22 Ⓐ Ⓑ Ⓒ Ⓓ Ⓔ	31 Ⓐ Ⓑ Ⓒ Ⓓ Ⓔ
5 Ⓐ Ⓑ Ⓒ Ⓓ Ⓔ	14 Ⓐ Ⓑ Ⓒ Ⓓ Ⓔ	23 Ⓐ Ⓑ Ⓒ Ⓓ Ⓔ	32 Ⓐ Ⓑ Ⓒ Ⓓ Ⓔ
6 Ⓐ Ⓑ Ⓒ Ⓓ Ⓔ	15 Ⓐ Ⓑ Ⓒ Ⓓ Ⓔ	24 Ⓐ Ⓑ Ⓒ Ⓓ Ⓔ	33 Ⓐ Ⓑ Ⓒ Ⓓ Ⓔ
7 Ⓐ Ⓑ Ⓒ Ⓓ Ⓔ	16 Ⓐ Ⓑ Ⓒ Ⓓ Ⓔ	25 Ⓐ Ⓑ Ⓒ Ⓓ Ⓔ	34 Ⓐ Ⓑ Ⓒ Ⓓ Ⓔ
8 Ⓐ Ⓑ Ⓒ Ⓓ Ⓔ	17 Ⓐ Ⓑ Ⓒ Ⓓ Ⓔ	26 Ⓐ Ⓑ Ⓒ Ⓓ Ⓔ	35 Ⓐ Ⓑ Ⓒ Ⓓ Ⓔ
9 Ⓐ Ⓑ Ⓒ Ⓓ Ⓔ	18 Ⓐ Ⓑ Ⓒ Ⓓ Ⓔ	27 Ⓐ Ⓑ Ⓒ Ⓓ Ⓔ	36 Ⓐ Ⓑ Ⓒ Ⓓ Ⓔ

Section 4/5

1 Ⓐ Ⓑ Ⓒ Ⓓ Ⓔ	10 Ⓐ Ⓑ Ⓒ Ⓓ Ⓔ	19 Ⓐ Ⓑ Ⓒ Ⓓ Ⓔ	28 Ⓐ Ⓑ Ⓒ Ⓓ Ⓔ
2 Ⓐ Ⓑ Ⓒ Ⓓ Ⓔ	11 Ⓐ Ⓑ Ⓒ Ⓓ Ⓔ	20 Ⓐ Ⓑ Ⓒ Ⓓ Ⓔ	29 Ⓐ Ⓑ Ⓒ Ⓓ Ⓔ
3 Ⓐ Ⓑ Ⓒ Ⓓ Ⓔ	12 Ⓐ Ⓑ Ⓒ Ⓓ Ⓔ	21 Ⓐ Ⓑ Ⓒ Ⓓ Ⓔ	30 Ⓐ Ⓑ Ⓒ Ⓓ Ⓔ
4 Ⓐ Ⓑ Ⓒ Ⓓ Ⓔ	13 Ⓐ Ⓑ Ⓒ Ⓓ Ⓔ	22 Ⓐ Ⓑ Ⓒ Ⓓ Ⓔ	31 Ⓐ Ⓑ Ⓒ Ⓓ Ⓔ
5 Ⓐ Ⓑ Ⓒ Ⓓ Ⓔ	14 Ⓐ Ⓑ Ⓒ Ⓓ Ⓔ	23 Ⓐ Ⓑ Ⓒ Ⓓ Ⓔ	32 Ⓐ Ⓑ Ⓒ Ⓓ Ⓔ
6 Ⓐ Ⓑ Ⓒ Ⓓ Ⓔ	15 Ⓐ Ⓑ Ⓒ Ⓓ Ⓔ	24 Ⓐ Ⓑ Ⓒ Ⓓ Ⓔ	33 Ⓐ Ⓑ Ⓒ Ⓓ Ⓔ
7 Ⓐ Ⓑ Ⓒ Ⓓ Ⓔ	16 Ⓐ Ⓑ Ⓒ Ⓓ Ⓔ	25 Ⓐ Ⓑ Ⓒ Ⓓ Ⓔ	34 Ⓐ Ⓑ Ⓒ Ⓓ Ⓔ
8 Ⓐ Ⓑ Ⓒ Ⓓ Ⓔ	17 Ⓐ Ⓑ Ⓒ Ⓓ Ⓔ	26 Ⓐ Ⓑ Ⓒ Ⓓ Ⓔ	35 Ⓐ Ⓑ Ⓒ Ⓓ Ⓔ
9 Ⓐ Ⓑ Ⓒ Ⓓ Ⓔ	18 Ⓐ Ⓑ Ⓒ Ⓓ Ⓔ	27 Ⓐ Ⓑ Ⓒ Ⓓ Ⓔ	36 Ⓐ Ⓑ Ⓒ Ⓓ Ⓔ

Section 5/6

1 Ⓐ Ⓑ Ⓒ Ⓓ Ⓔ	10 Ⓐ Ⓑ Ⓒ Ⓓ Ⓔ	19 Ⓐ Ⓑ Ⓒ Ⓓ Ⓔ	28 Ⓐ Ⓑ Ⓒ Ⓓ Ⓔ
2 Ⓐ Ⓑ Ⓒ Ⓓ Ⓔ	11 Ⓐ Ⓑ Ⓒ Ⓓ Ⓔ	20 Ⓐ Ⓑ Ⓒ Ⓓ Ⓔ	29 Ⓐ Ⓑ Ⓒ Ⓓ Ⓔ
3 Ⓐ Ⓑ Ⓒ Ⓓ Ⓔ	12 Ⓐ Ⓑ Ⓒ Ⓓ Ⓔ	21 Ⓐ Ⓑ Ⓒ Ⓓ Ⓔ	30 Ⓐ Ⓑ Ⓒ Ⓓ Ⓔ
4 Ⓐ Ⓑ Ⓒ Ⓓ Ⓔ	13 Ⓐ Ⓑ Ⓒ Ⓓ Ⓔ	22 Ⓐ Ⓑ Ⓒ Ⓓ Ⓔ	31 Ⓐ Ⓑ Ⓒ Ⓓ Ⓔ
5 Ⓐ Ⓑ Ⓒ Ⓓ Ⓔ	14 Ⓐ Ⓑ Ⓒ Ⓓ Ⓔ	23 Ⓐ Ⓑ Ⓒ Ⓓ Ⓔ	32 Ⓐ Ⓑ Ⓒ Ⓓ Ⓔ
6 Ⓐ Ⓑ Ⓒ Ⓓ Ⓔ	15 Ⓐ Ⓑ Ⓒ Ⓓ Ⓔ	24 Ⓐ Ⓑ Ⓒ Ⓓ Ⓔ	33 Ⓐ Ⓑ Ⓒ Ⓓ Ⓔ
7 Ⓐ Ⓑ Ⓒ Ⓓ Ⓔ	16 Ⓐ Ⓑ Ⓒ Ⓓ Ⓔ	25 Ⓐ Ⓑ Ⓒ Ⓓ Ⓔ	34 Ⓐ Ⓑ Ⓒ Ⓓ Ⓔ
8 Ⓐ Ⓑ Ⓒ Ⓓ Ⓔ	17 Ⓐ Ⓑ Ⓒ Ⓓ Ⓔ	26 Ⓐ Ⓑ Ⓒ Ⓓ Ⓔ	35 Ⓐ Ⓑ Ⓒ Ⓓ Ⓔ
9 Ⓐ Ⓑ Ⓒ Ⓓ Ⓔ	18 Ⓐ Ⓑ Ⓒ Ⓓ Ⓔ	27 Ⓐ Ⓑ Ⓒ Ⓓ Ⓔ	36 Ⓐ Ⓑ Ⓒ Ⓓ Ⓔ

Section 6/7

1 Ⓐ Ⓑ Ⓒ Ⓓ Ⓔ	10 Ⓐ Ⓑ Ⓒ Ⓓ Ⓔ	19 Ⓐ Ⓑ Ⓒ Ⓓ Ⓔ	28 Ⓐ Ⓑ Ⓒ Ⓓ Ⓔ
2 Ⓐ Ⓑ Ⓒ Ⓓ Ⓔ	11 Ⓐ Ⓑ Ⓒ Ⓓ Ⓔ	20 Ⓐ Ⓑ Ⓒ Ⓓ Ⓔ	29 Ⓐ Ⓑ Ⓒ Ⓓ Ⓔ
3 Ⓐ Ⓑ Ⓒ Ⓓ Ⓔ	12 Ⓐ Ⓑ Ⓒ Ⓓ Ⓔ	21 Ⓐ Ⓑ Ⓒ Ⓓ Ⓔ	30 Ⓐ Ⓑ Ⓒ Ⓓ Ⓔ
4 Ⓐ Ⓑ Ⓒ Ⓓ Ⓔ	13 Ⓐ Ⓑ Ⓒ Ⓓ Ⓔ	22 Ⓐ Ⓑ Ⓒ Ⓓ Ⓔ	31 Ⓐ Ⓑ Ⓒ Ⓓ Ⓔ
5 Ⓐ Ⓑ Ⓒ Ⓓ Ⓔ	14 Ⓐ Ⓑ Ⓒ Ⓓ Ⓔ	23 Ⓐ Ⓑ Ⓒ Ⓓ Ⓔ	32 Ⓐ Ⓑ Ⓒ Ⓓ Ⓔ
6 Ⓐ Ⓑ Ⓒ Ⓓ Ⓔ	15 Ⓐ Ⓑ Ⓒ Ⓓ Ⓔ	24 Ⓐ Ⓑ Ⓒ Ⓓ Ⓔ	33 Ⓐ Ⓑ Ⓒ Ⓓ Ⓔ
7 Ⓐ Ⓑ Ⓒ Ⓓ Ⓔ	16 Ⓐ Ⓑ Ⓒ Ⓓ Ⓔ	25 Ⓐ Ⓑ Ⓒ Ⓓ Ⓔ	34 Ⓐ Ⓑ Ⓒ Ⓓ Ⓔ
8 Ⓐ Ⓑ Ⓒ Ⓓ Ⓔ	17 Ⓐ Ⓑ Ⓒ Ⓓ Ⓔ	26 Ⓐ Ⓑ Ⓒ Ⓓ Ⓔ	35 Ⓐ Ⓑ Ⓒ Ⓓ Ⓔ
9 Ⓐ Ⓑ Ⓒ Ⓓ Ⓔ	18 Ⓐ Ⓑ Ⓒ Ⓓ Ⓔ	27 Ⓐ Ⓑ Ⓒ Ⓓ Ⓔ	36 Ⓐ Ⓑ Ⓒ Ⓓ Ⓔ

Section 7/8	1 Ⓐ Ⓑ Ⓒ Ⓓ Ⓔ	6 Ⓐ Ⓑ Ⓒ Ⓓ Ⓔ	11 Ⓐ Ⓑ Ⓒ Ⓓ Ⓔ	16 Ⓐ Ⓑ Ⓒ Ⓓ Ⓔ
	2 Ⓐ Ⓑ Ⓒ Ⓓ Ⓔ	7 Ⓐ Ⓑ Ⓒ Ⓓ Ⓔ	12 Ⓐ Ⓑ Ⓒ Ⓓ Ⓔ	17 Ⓐ Ⓑ Ⓒ Ⓓ Ⓔ
	3 Ⓐ Ⓑ Ⓒ Ⓓ Ⓔ	8 Ⓐ Ⓑ Ⓒ Ⓓ Ⓔ	13 Ⓐ Ⓑ Ⓒ Ⓓ Ⓔ	18 Ⓐ Ⓑ Ⓒ Ⓓ Ⓔ
	4 Ⓐ Ⓑ Ⓒ Ⓓ Ⓔ	9 Ⓐ Ⓑ Ⓒ Ⓓ Ⓔ	14 Ⓐ Ⓑ Ⓒ Ⓓ Ⓔ	19 Ⓐ Ⓑ Ⓒ Ⓓ Ⓔ
	5 Ⓐ Ⓑ Ⓒ Ⓓ Ⓔ	10 Ⓐ Ⓑ Ⓒ Ⓓ Ⓔ	15 Ⓐ Ⓑ Ⓒ Ⓓ Ⓔ	20 Ⓐ Ⓑ Ⓒ Ⓓ Ⓔ

Section 8/9	1 Ⓐ Ⓑ Ⓒ Ⓓ Ⓔ	6 Ⓐ Ⓑ Ⓒ Ⓓ Ⓔ	11 Ⓐ Ⓑ Ⓒ Ⓓ Ⓔ	16 Ⓐ Ⓑ Ⓒ Ⓓ Ⓔ
	2 Ⓐ Ⓑ Ⓒ Ⓓ Ⓔ	7 Ⓐ Ⓑ Ⓒ Ⓓ Ⓔ	12 Ⓐ Ⓑ Ⓒ Ⓓ Ⓔ	17 Ⓐ Ⓑ Ⓒ Ⓓ Ⓔ
	3 Ⓐ Ⓑ Ⓒ Ⓓ Ⓔ	8 Ⓐ Ⓑ Ⓒ Ⓓ Ⓔ	13 Ⓐ Ⓑ Ⓒ Ⓓ Ⓔ	18 Ⓐ Ⓑ Ⓒ Ⓓ Ⓔ
	4 Ⓐ Ⓑ Ⓒ Ⓓ Ⓔ	9 Ⓐ Ⓑ Ⓒ Ⓓ Ⓔ	14 Ⓐ Ⓑ Ⓒ Ⓓ Ⓔ	19 Ⓐ Ⓑ Ⓒ Ⓓ Ⓔ
	5 Ⓐ Ⓑ Ⓒ Ⓓ Ⓔ	10 Ⓐ Ⓑ Ⓒ Ⓓ Ⓔ	15 Ⓐ Ⓑ Ⓒ Ⓓ Ⓔ	20 Ⓐ Ⓑ Ⓒ Ⓓ Ⓔ

Section 10	1 Ⓐ Ⓑ Ⓒ Ⓓ Ⓔ	6 Ⓐ Ⓑ Ⓒ Ⓓ Ⓔ	11 Ⓐ Ⓑ Ⓒ Ⓓ Ⓔ	16 Ⓐ Ⓑ Ⓒ Ⓓ Ⓔ
	2 Ⓐ Ⓑ Ⓒ Ⓓ Ⓔ	7 Ⓐ Ⓑ Ⓒ Ⓓ Ⓔ	12 Ⓐ Ⓑ Ⓒ Ⓓ Ⓔ	17 Ⓐ Ⓑ Ⓒ Ⓓ Ⓔ
	3 Ⓐ Ⓑ Ⓒ Ⓓ Ⓔ	8 Ⓐ Ⓑ Ⓒ Ⓓ Ⓔ	13 Ⓐ Ⓑ Ⓒ Ⓓ Ⓔ	18 Ⓐ Ⓑ Ⓒ Ⓓ Ⓔ
	4 Ⓐ Ⓑ Ⓒ Ⓓ Ⓔ	9 Ⓐ Ⓑ Ⓒ Ⓓ Ⓔ	14 Ⓐ Ⓑ Ⓒ Ⓓ Ⓔ	19 Ⓐ Ⓑ Ⓒ Ⓓ Ⓔ
	5 Ⓐ Ⓑ Ⓒ Ⓓ Ⓔ	10 Ⓐ Ⓑ Ⓒ Ⓓ Ⓔ	15 Ⓐ Ⓑ Ⓒ Ⓓ Ⓔ	20 Ⓐ Ⓑ Ⓒ Ⓓ Ⓔ

Student-Produced Responses

Only answers entered in the circles in each grid will be scored. You will not receive credit for anything written in the boxes above the circles.

9   10   11   12   13

14   15   16   17   18

Step Six: Personal Study Plan

Step Six Highlights:

With the post-test data, create a focused study plan with the help of your instructor so you know where to review.

Don't waste time on areas you've already mastered; target the remaining areas of weakness to maximize your SAT score.

See what parts of the textbook you need to spend more time on: skills review, test-taking strategies, or pacing with practice tests.

Make sure you understand all the SAT-specific information on guessing, item-types, and content before the real test.

Step Six Overview:

Based on the results of the post-test, you will collaborate with your instructor to develop a personalized study plan. While each plan is different, you may be asked to return to items you've already reviewed but have not yet mastered in Steps Two, Three, or Four. If there are any items you have not yet completed, this is the time to return to those areas. You may need to review specific test-taking strategies; to focus on pacing, timing, and guessing; or to focus on other weaknesses. This plan will target your weaknesses in order to help you reach your true potential and ability.

EDUCATORS' #1 CHOICE FOR SCHOOL IMPROVEMENT

Cambridge Course Concept Outline
PERSONAL STUDY PLAN

In this step, you will design a study plan to maximize your performance on the official exam. Between the date that your course ends and the date of the official exam, you will want to maintain your skills, target a final set of challenging concepts, and all around ready yourself for victory on the SAT or PSAT.

On the pages that follow, you will find some useful tips for planning the final segment in your SAT or PSAT study.

PERSONAL STUDY PLAN

Up until this point, you have spent a great deal of time preparing for the test both in class and on your own. After receiving the results of your final assessment (Step Five) and finishing your SAT • PSAT preparation course, you will most likely have some spare time before the day of the official test. Spend this time wisely to make the best effort in preparation for the exam. This Personal Study Plan section is included as a short guide on how to use that remaining time to your best advantage.

A personal study plan is critical in order to reinforce and maintain the skills that you have learned throughout the course. Depending on whether several weeks or several days remain before the official exam date, you will want to plan your study differently. If there are several weeks remaining before the day of the test, you should plan to review more material than if there are only a few days remaining. If only a few days remain, a quick summary review is a better choice.

Many topics that are related to creating your personal study plan have already been covered in the Overcoming Test Anxiety section (Step One) of this textbook. It is important for you to review the material in that section when designing your study plan. In particular, you should balance a plan that will leave you confident of your preparation, but also calm and rested for the day of the exam.

The largest problem that most students face on the official exam is not a lack of subject knowledge but poor management of time. If you have not yet done so, take the four practice tests included in Step Four of this book. These practice tests not only serve to reinforce skills and strategies, but they also emphasize the importance of time management since they are to be administered with time restrictions. These time restrictions are put in place to simulate the experience of the actual test. Therefore, when taking the practice tests, hold rigorously to the allotted times. It is always worthwhile to return to a practice test to address skipped or unfinished items, but you should do so only at the conclusion of the allotted time.

Besides helping your pacing and preparedness, the practice tests are also an excellent guide to targeting your study plan. Look out for things that you know you could do better if you had the opportunity to peek at your notes. These are likely targets for review as you approach the day of the exam. Listing a few concrete topics for review sets a firm starting ground for your study plan.

The most significant aspect of a personal study plan is that it is a written plan. A written study plan is more concrete than one that you simply draw on from memory. So, when creating a personal study plan, write out a day-by-day schedule for reviewing all of the materials that are necessary to succeed on the test. This written format will provide a clear and dependable guide for study. The schedule should be prioritized according to the time that you will devote to each of the different subject areas based on the amount of time that you have remaining before the day of the official exam. Plan to review all of the materials equally several weeks before test day. Then, when the test date approaches, start focusing on the subject areas that are giving you the most difficulty. Divide your time proportionally among the test sections based on your assessment of the difficulty of the subject areas. Although subject area preparation is extremely important, the amount of time that you have remaining before the exam will determine how strongly you should focus on reviewing certain subject area material. In the final days before the test, you will not be able to learn a great deal of new material. Therefore, unless there is a long span of time between the end of your review course and the date of the exam, you should focus on practicing the skills that you have already learned (*e.g.*, time management, use of calculators, the process of elimination strategy, *etc.*).

The following sample schedules are provided for your reference. Remember that these schedules are only examples and that you should devise your own schedule to target the areas that you find most challenging. After you have designed a basic study plan, ask your teacher for insight. Your teacher may be able to suggest further strategies or a subtle re-allotment of your time.

If you are satisfied with your writing scores but have not attained your goals for the mathematics section, you might consider designing a study plan that emphasizes mathematics. Your plan for the week might appear as follows:

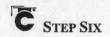

DAY OF THE WEEK	ASSIGNMENT	WHERE TO FIND IT
SATURDAY	Last class day. Formulate your study plan with your instructor.	
SUNDAY	Review coordinate geometry rules and memorize volume formulas.	Math Skills Review
MONDAY	Revisit punctuation rules, especially the use of colons, semicolons, and dashes.	Grammar and Mechanics Skills Review
TUESDAY	Review the Algebra formulas in the Math Express Skills Review	Math Express Skills Review
WEDNESDAY	Take a Math quiz or practice test	Step Three or Step Four
THURSDAY	Review Math explanations for Practice Tests III and IV.	Answers and Explanations
FRIDAY	Day off. Relax. Use test anxiety reduction strategies. Get a good night's sleep	Overcoming Test Anxiety (Step One)
SATURDAY	Test day. Eat a healthy breakfast	

On the other hand, if you are more comfortable with the mathematics portions of the test, you may want to review both the grammar and reading portions. While you may consider returning to vocabulary that you have already learned, it is probably too late to begin memorizing new word lists. Rather, a focus on concepts is a better use of your time. A plan that emphasizes reading and writing might appear as follows:

DAY OF THE WEEK	ASSIGNMENT	WHERE TO FIND IT
SATURDAY	Last class day. Formulate your study plan with your instructor.	
SUNDAY	Review coordinate geometry rules and memorize volume formulas.	Math Skills Review
MONDAY	Revisit punctuation rules, especially the use of colons, semicolons, and dashes.	Grammar and Mechanics Skills Review
TUESDAY	Review vocabulary and word roots.	Reading Skills Review
WEDNESDAY	Take a Writing quiz or practice test	Step Three or Step Four
THURSDAY	Review Critical Reading explanations for Practice Tests III and IV.	Answers and Explanations
FRIDAY	Day off. Relax. Use test anxiety reduction strategies. Get a good night's sleep	Overcoming Test Anxiety, Step One
SATURDAY	Test day. Eat a healthy breakfast	

Once you have determined your rubric for study, stick to it without fail. Such discipline will surely reward you on the day of the test. However, do not study too much. An hour or two of studying each day will be more productive than a severe study schedule that leaves you physically and mentally exhausted when the time comes to take the actual exam. Think of this process as training for a sport. While it is necessary to practice every day, it is counterproductive to overexert yourself and to practice too much.

Answers and Explanations

Answers and Explanations:
Step Two

READING SKILLS REVIEW

EXERCISE 1—CAREFUL READING OF CRITICAL READING: PASSAGES ITEM STEMS (p. 40)

1. **(A)** (A) is correct because the original asks for the main idea, which is the central theme, or primary focus, of the passage.

    (B) is wrong because the original asks for the main idea, which is the overarching theme, entailing much more than just a specific detail. Also, without any additional information, it is not possible to know whether the main idea is found in the first sentence.

    (C) is wrong because the main idea isn't necessarily found in the last sentence of the passage; it could be found anywhere in the passage.

    (D) is wrong because the original asks for the main idea, not a supporting detail. A supporting detail is usually a specific detail that supports the main idea.

2. **(D)** (A) is wrong because the author's statement regarding words and art does not necessarily involve how the two subjects relate to one another.

    (B) is wrong because the original does not simply ask for a statement that pertains to both words and art but asks for a statement that the author holds to be true regarding both words and art.

    (C) is wrong because the original asks for a statement that the author would hold to be true regarding both words and art, not just words.

    (D) is correct because, as stated above, the original asks for a statement that the author would hold to be true regarding both words and art.

3. **(C)** (A) is wrong because the original asks for a contextual definition of "address," not the most common definition.

    (B) is wrong because the original asks for a contextual definition of "address," not the only definition ("address" has more than one definition).

    (C) is correct because the original asks for the definition of "address" as it is used in the context of the passage.

    (D) is wrong because the original does not ask for who the author addresses in the passage; it asks for the meaning of the word "address."

4. **(D)** (A) is wrong because the original asks for the primary (central) purpose of the passage, not the primary (first) specific detail mentioned in the passage.

    (B) is wrong because the original asks for the primary purpose of the passage, not the author's tone.

    (C) is wrong because the original does not ask for how the passage makes you feel as a reader.

    (D) is correct because the original asks for the primary purpose, or main objective, of the passage.

5. **(C)** (A) is wrong because the original asks for the main point of the storyteller's interpretation, not the storyteller's interpretation of the main point.

    (B) is wrong because the original asks for the main point of the storyteller's interpretation, not for one of many potential interpretations made by the storyteller.

    (C) is correct because the original asks for the main point, or central focus, of the storyteller's interpretation.

    (D) is wrong because the original asks for the main point of an interpretation, not for one of many potential interpretations made by the storyteller.

6. **(A)** (A) is correct because the original asks for a meaning, or definition, of the term "Monocrats."

    (B) is wrong because the original asks the reader to make an inference about the meaning of the term; it does not ask for the author's interpretation of the term.

    (C) is wrong because the original does not ask for the reason why the author uses the term "Monocrats" in the passage.

    (D) is wrong because the original asks for a definition, not the location of the term in the passage.

7. **(B)** (A) is wrong because the original asks for what can be inferred about the author, not for why the author refers to something.

   (B) is correct because the original asks for the reader to infer how the author regards, or feels about, the Hudson Bay Company.

   (C) is wrong because the original does not ask about the author's association with the Hudson Bay Company.

   (D) is wrong because the original asks for what can be inferred about the author, not for what the reader can infer about the Hudson Bay Company.

8. **(B)** (A) is wrong because the original asks for why it is difficult to formulate a general historical law about revolution, not why it is difficult for the author to formulate plans.

   (B) is correct because the original asks for why it is difficult to formulate a general historical law about revolution.

   (C) is wrong because the original does not ask for why the author of Passage 1 formulates a general law.

   (D) is wrong because the original does not state that it is easy to formulate a general law.

9. **(C)** (A) is wrong because the original asks for a contextual, not a general, meaning of the phrase.

   (B) is wrong because the original asks for a meaning of the phrase "adequately articulated," not for a phrase that adequately articulates a line in the passage.

   (C) is correct because the original asks for a contextual meaning of the phrase "adequately articulated."

   (D) is wrong because the original does not ask for a specific phrase that is adequately articulated in the passage.

10. **(C)** (A) is wrong because the original does not ask for specific laws but for the cause of disappointment.

   (B) is wrong because the original states that general laws fail to explain historical events.

   (C) is correct because the original asks for the cause of disappointment at the failure of laws to explain events.

   (D) is wrong because the original asks for the cause of disappointment at the failure, not for the cause of the failure itself.

11. **(B)** (A) is wrong because the original asks for something that can be studied by means of a certain technique, not for a person (historian) who can explain this technique.

   (B) is correct because the original asks for something that can be studied by means of the Verstehen technique.

   (C) is wrong because the original does not ask for something that cannot be studied by means of the Verstehen technique.

   (D) is wrong because the original does not ask for a particular technique. The technique is known; the object of study is unknown.

12. **(B)** (A) is wrong because the original does not state that the author of Passage 1 necessarily refers to the "inside" of a historical event.

   (B) is correct because the original asks for something that the author of Passage 1 would refer to in order to account for the "inside" of a historical event.

   (C) is wrong because the original simply states that the author of Passage 2 refers to the "inside" of a historical event; it does not ask why the author of Passage 2 makes this reference.

   (D) is wrong because the original asks for something that would be referred to by the author of Passage 1, not the author of Passage 2.

13. **(B)** (A) is wrong because the original asks for an assumption that can be made by virtue of the list, not for a reason as to the list's contents.

   (B) is correct because the original asks for an assumption that can be made by virtue of the author's list of regions.

   (C) is wrong because the original asks for an assumption that can be made by virtue of the list of regions, not for a specific region that is included on the list.

   (D) is wrong because the original asks for an assumption that can be made by virtue of the list of regions, not for an assumption that can be made about the cultivation of maize.

14. **(D)** (A) is wrong because the original does not ask for what wheat and barley exemplify; it asks for a reason as to why the author mentions wheat and barley.

(B) is wrong because the original does not ask for the author's sequence of reference.

(C) is wrong because the original does not ask for where the author refers to wheat and barley in the passage but why the author refers to them in the passage.

(D) is correct because the original asks for a reason as to why the author mentions wheat and barley in the passage.

15. **(D)** (A) is wrong because the original asks for the author's primary (main or chief) purpose, not for the purpose that is mentioned in the first sentence.

(B) is wrong because the original asks for the author's primary, not secondary, purpose.

(C) is wrong because the original asks for the author's main purpose, not for the purpose that the reader first detects when reading the passage.

(D) is correct because the original asks for the author's primary purpose in (reason for) writing the passage.

EXERCISE 2—CAREFUL READING OF CRITICAL READING: PASSAGES ITEM STEMS (p. 42)

1. **(B)** (A) is wrong because the original asks for the contextual meaning of a certain word, not the tacit (unspoken) meaning of a certain line in the passage.

(B) is correct because the original asks for the meaning of the word "tacitly" in the context of a certain line in the passage.

(C) is wrong because the original does not ask for the meaning of the word "tacit."

(D) is wrong because the original asks for the contextual meaning of a certain word, not the tacit (unspoken) meaning of the first word in a certain line in the passage.

2. **(A)** (A) is correct because the original asks for how Stanton's tone changes between two paragraphs.

(B) is wrong because the original does not ask for Stanton's initial tone but for how Stanton's tone changes.

(C) is wrong because the original states that Stanton's tone changes but does not specify the quality of the tone (positive or negative).

(D) is wrong because the original states that Stanton's tone changes, not that it remains unchanged.

3. **(D)** (A) is wrong because the original asks for a way in which Madame de Staël and Dante are not alike.

(B) is wrong because the original asks for a way in which Madame de Staël is different from Dante, not a way in which she dislikes Dante.

(C) is wrong because the original does not ask whether Madame de Staël likes or dislikes Dante .

(D) is correct because the original asks for a way in which Madame de Staël and Dante are not alike.

4. **(B)** (A) is wrong because the original does not ask whether Sun Yat-sen is from Hong Kong.

(B) is correct because the original asks for something that Sun Yat-sen uses Hong Kong to exemplify.

(C) is wrong because the original asks for something that Sun Yat-sen uses Hong Kong to exemplify; it does not state that Sun Yat-sen uses Hong Kong to exemplify Chinese culture.

(D) is wrong because the original states that Sun Yat-sen uses Hong Kong as an example; it does not ask for an example of Sun Yat-sen's relationship to Hong Kong.

5. **(D)** (A) is wrong because the original does not ask whether Gandhi's charges are "on the level" (legitimate); it asks how Gandhi feels about the charge leveled (directed) against him.

(B) is wrong because the original does not state whether Gandhi exhibited any opposition to the charges leveled against him.

(C) is wrong because the original asks how Gandhi feels about the charge leveled against him, not how he would feel about leveling charges against others.

(D) is correct because the original asks how Gandhi feels about the charge leveled against him.

6. **(C)** (A) is wrong because the original does not ask for a reason why Rousseau complains to Madame d'Épinay.

   (B) is wrong because the original does not ask for how Rousseau feels about Madame d'Épinay's complaints but vice versa.

   (C) is correct because the original asks for how Madame d'Épinay feels about Rousseau's complaints.

   (D) is wrong because the original does not qualify whether Rousseau's complaints are or are not similar to Madame d'Épinay's complaints.

7. **(B)** (A) is wrong because the original does not ask about Rousseau's feelings toward Madame d'Épinay's philosophy.

   (B) is correct because the original asks for a summary of the difference (distinction) between Rousseau's and Madame d'Épinay's philosophies of friendship.

   (C) is wrong because the original asks for the difference, not similarity, between Rousseau's and Madame d'Épinay's philosophies of friendship.

   (D) is wrong because the original does not ask about a philosophy of rivalry.

8. **(A)** (A) is correct because the original asks for Galileo's reason behind including the second paragraph.

   (B) is wrong because the original does not ask about the relationship between the second paragraph and the remainder of the passage.

   (C) is wrong because the original does not ask about the order (sequence) in which the lines are arranged in the second paragraph; it asks about why Galileo includes the second paragraph.

   (D) is wrong because the original does not state whether or not Galileo is mentioned in the passage; Galileo wrote the passage.

9. **(C)** (A) is wrong because the original asks about Chekhov's opinions (views), not unsubstantiated conclusions that are not based on fact.

   (B) is wrong because the original asks for a point on which Chekhov does not express a definite opinion.

   (C) is correct because the original asks for a point on which Chekhov does not express a definite opinion.

   (D) is wrong because the original asks about Chekhov's opinions (views), not unsubstantiated conclusions that are not based on fact.

10. **(D)** (A) is wrong because the original asks about slaveholders' cruelty, not Sojourner Truth's cruelty.

    (B) is wrong because the original does not suggest that the slaveholders are Sojourner Truth's.

    (C) is wrong because the original asks about the basis of slaveholders' cruelty, not the basis for the justification of that cruelty.

    (D) is correct because the original asks about the basis of slaveholders' cruelty.

11. **(D)** (A) is wrong because the original does not ask whether Sojourner Truth actually approved of the Declaration of Sentiments.

    (B) is wrong because the original asks for what the reader would expect, not for what Sojourner Truth would have expected.

    (C) is wrong because the original does not ask about the Declaration of Sentience but about the Declaration of Sentiments. (Note: Pay careful attention to the spelling of words that are phonetically similar.)

    (D) is correct because the original asks about whether the reader would expect Sojourner Truth to have approved of the Declaration of Sentiments.

12. **(B)** (A) is wrong because the original does not ask for the main point of only the second paragraph but asks for the main point of the entire passage, which may or may not also be the main point of the second paragraph.

    (B) is correct because the original asks for the main point, or main idea, of the passage.

    (C) is wrong because the original asks for an overarching purpose of the passage, not for a specific detail that is mentioned in the passage.

    (D) is wrong because the original asks for a point that is necessarily important to an understanding of the passage. A point that is not mentioned in the passage would not necessarily be important to such an understanding.

13. **(C)** (A) is wrong because the original states that Vignes and Wolfskill are two names for one and the same site, not two different sites.

(B) is wrong because the original does not imply that the author values the Vignes/Wolfskill site more or less than any other site.

(C) is correct because the original asks for the primary reason why the author values the Vignes/Wolfskill site.

(D) is wrong because the original does not imply that the author values the Vignes/Wolfskill site more or less than any other site.

14. **(D)** (A) is wrong because the original asks for the meaning of a vocabulary word: "appropriate"; it does not ask about the appropriateness of a quote.

(B) is wrong because the original asks about the word "appropriate" in line 52; it does not ask about another word in that line.

(C) is wrong because the original does not ask about the appropriateness of line 52 in the context of the passage; it asks about the meaning of a word in the context of line 52.

(D) is correct because the original asks about the meaning of the word "appropriate" in the context of line 52.

15. **(A)** (A) is correct because the original asks for the chief characteristic (main quality) of Lady Bertram that is exposed in the excerpt.

(B) is wrong because the original does not ask whether Lady Bertram is a main character in the excerpt but asks about her main characteristic.

(C) is wrong because the original asks whether Lady Bertram's chief characteristic is exposed, not whether she exposes a different character's chief characteristic.

(D) is wrong because the original asks for the chief characteristic of Lady Bertram that is exposed in the excerpt.

16. **(C)** (A) is wrong because the original asks about an analogy (comparison), not a contrast.

(B) is wrong because the original asks about what the author of Passage 1 makes analogous to a novel, not about what the author of Passage 2 makes analogous to a novel.

(C) is correct because the original asks about what the author of Passage 1 makes analogous to a novel.

(D) is wrong because the original does not specify what is made analogous to a novel; the analogy is not necessarily made between two novels.

17. **(B)** (A) is wrong because the original asks for a statement with which both, not neither, authors would agree.

(B) is correct because the original asks for a statement with which both authors would agree.

(C) is wrong because the original asks for a statement with which both authors would agree, not only one of the two authors.

(D) is wrong because the original asks for a statement with which both authors would agree, not disagree.

18. **(D)** (A) is wrong because the original asks for a characteristic of an "allergen" that makes it different from "antigens." Although the difference is the same, the answer would be a representative trait of an "allergen," not "antigens."

(B) is wrong because the original does not ask about how "antigens" and an "allergen" are similar.

(C) is wrong because the original does not ask about similarity but about difference. Also, the original refers to "allergen" in the singular form and "antigens" in the plural form, not vice versa.

(D) is correct because the original asks for a characteristic of an "allergen" that makes it different from "antigens." Although the difference is the same, the answer would be a representative trait of an "allergen," not "antigens."

19. **(D)** (A) is wrong because the original refers to Mrs. Norris's many occupations, not Austen's many occupations.

(B) is wrong because the original asks about how Austen depicts Mrs. Norris, not about one of Mrs. Norris's many occupations.

(C) is wrong because the original asks about how Austen depicts Mrs. Norris, not about Mrs. Norris's many occupations.

(D) is correct because the original asks about how Austen depicts Mrs. Norris in describing her many occupations.

20. **(A)** (A) is correct because the original asks for something that is metaphorically associated with an immune response.

    (B) is wrong because the original does not ask for a contextual definition of an immune response.

    (C) is wrong because the original states that the passage relies upon an extended metaphor, which means that it most likely extends throughout more than one paragraph. However, the original does not ask about the number of paragraphs through which this metaphor might extend.

    (D) is wrong because the original asks about an immune response, not about the author's response to a metaphor.

21. **(B)** (A) is wrong because the original does not ask about what would convince a child that television violence is real but about what would deter a child from regarding such violence as real.

    (B) is correct because the original asks about what would deter (prevent) a child from regarding television violence as real.

    (C) is wrong because the original does not ask about a specific type of television violence.

    (D) is wrong because the original does not ask about what would deter a child from actually watching television violence but about what would deter a child from regarding it as real.

22. **(C)** (A) is wrong because the original asks about the function of the final paragraph, not about the content of the final paragraph. Function and content are not necessarily the same thing.

    (B) is wrong because the original asks about the function of the final paragraph, not about the function of the paragraph that precedes it.

    (C) is correct because the original asks about the function (purpose) of the final paragraph.

    (D) is wrong because the original asks about the function of the final paragraph, not about the function of the first paragraph.

23. **(D)** (A) is wrong because the original asks for a statement about dialogue in novels, not about dialogue in general.

    (B) is wrong because the original asks for a statement with which the author of Passage 2 would agree, not disagree.

    (C) is wrong because the original asks for a statement with which the author of Passage 2, not Passage 1, would agree.

    (D) is correct because the original asks for a statement about dialogue in novels with which the author of Passage 2 would agree. This answer choice is more specific than (A): dialogue in novels rather than dialogue in general. If (D) were not one of the given answer choices, then (A) would be considered the best restatement of the question that is being asked.

24. **(C)** (A) is wrong because the original states that Austen undercuts her description of the Miss Bertrams, not vice versa.

    (B) is wrong because the original states that Austen undercuts her own description; it does not state that the Miss Bertrams undercut Austen's description.

    (C) is correct because the original asks how Austen undercuts (undermines) her own description of the Miss Bertrams.

    (D) is wrong because the original states that the description is made of the Miss Bertrams, not of Austen.

25. **(D)** (A) is wrong because the original asks for the meaning of a vocabulary term: "asserting"; it does not ask about a particular statement that is asserted in the context of the passage.

    (B) is wrong because the original asks for the contextual meaning of a word, not the most common meaning of a word.

    (C) is wrong because the original asks about the implicit meaning of a word as it relates to the context of line 30; it does not ask about an explicit meaning that is actually provided in line 30.

    (D) is correct because the original asks for the contextual meaning of the word "asserting."

26. **(C)** (A) is wrong because the original asks for the meaning behind someone's use of a saying, not for the meaning behind the actual saying itself.

    (B) is wrong because the original refers to a saying made by Gertrude Stein, not Dolores Hayden.

    (C) is correct because the original asks for the meaning behind Dolores Hayden's use of Gertrude Stein's saying.

    (D) is wrong because the original refers to a saying made by Gertrude Stein, not Dolores Hayden.

27. **(B)** (A) is wrong because the original asks for the author's primary (chief) concern; in this case, "primary" is not intended to refer to the primacy of the first paragraph.

(B) is correct because the original asks for the author's primary (chief) concern (regard) in the passage.

(C) is wrong because although the word "concern" is used with the same general intent, the original provides no evidence that the author's concern is necessarily directed toward a dilemma.

(D) is wrong because the original asks for the author's primary (chief) concern, not the author's primary (first) topic of reference.

EXERCISE 3—CAREFUL READING OF MATH: MULTIPLE-CHOICE ITEM STEMS (p. 46)

1. **(D)** (A) is wrong because the original asks for how many minutes that it takes to make 30, not 270, thingamabobs at a particular per-hour rate. (A) is distracting because it simply adds together the two values given in the item stem.

(B) is wrong because the original does not ask for how many minutes that it takes to produce 8 sets of 30 thingamabobs, or 240 thingamabobs.

(C) is wrong because the original does not ask for how many minutes that it takes to produce 240 thingamabobs at a particular rate. (C) is also distracting because it switches the two values given in the item stem.

(D) is correct because the original asks for how many minutes that it takes to produce 30 thingamabobs at a rate of 240 thingamabobs per hour.

2. **(A)** (A) is correct because the original asks for the price of the item before the decrease, which is the same as the original price of the item.

(B) is wrong because the original refers to a 20-percent decrease in price, not to an 80-percent decrease.

(C) is wrong because the original asks for the price of the item before the decrease, not for the price after the decrease.

(D) is wrong because the original asks for the price of the item before the 20-percent decrease, not for the price before an 80-percent increase.

3. **(C)** (A) is wrong because the original asks for how much less candy that can be purchased for $3.50 at the new price, not at the old price.

(B) is wrong because the original does not ask for how much total candy that can be purchased for $3.50 at the new price but for how much less candy.

(C) is correct because the original asks for how much less candy that can be purchased for $3.50 at the new price.

(D) is wrong because the original does not ask for how much total candy that can be purchased for $3.50 at the old price but for how much less candy that can be purchased for $3.50 at the new price.

4. **(D)** (A) is wrong because the original asks for the percentage of marbles in the jar that are black, not white.

(B) is wrong because the original does not ask for the difference between black and white marbles in the jar. The original asks for a percentage.

(C) is wrong because the original does not ask for the percentage of marbles in the jar that are not black (white).

(D) is correct because the original asks for the percentage of the marbles in the jar that are black (not white).

5. **(C)** (A) is wrong because the original asks for the ratio (expressed in percent) of Tuesday's total number of students to Monday's total number of students, not for the ratio of the combined total number of students to Monday's total number of students.

(B) is wrong because the original does not ask for the ratio of the combined total number of students to Tuesday's total number of students.

(C) is correct because the original asks for the ratio (expressed in percent) of Tuesday's total number of students to Monday's total number of students.

(D) is wrong because the original does not ask for the ratio of Monday's total number of students to Tuesday's total number of students.

6. **(C)** (A) is wrong because although the mode is a type of average, unless specified, the term "average" refers to the mean average.

(B) is wrong because the mode of a series of values is that which occurs most frequently, not least frequently.

(C) is correct because the mode of a series of values is that which occurs most frequently.

(D) is wrong because the median of a series of values is not the same as the mode. The median is the middle value in a series of numbers.

7. **(C)** (A) is wrong because the original asks for how much chocolate that can be purchased for $12 at the given price, not for the difference between how much that can be purchased for $12 and how much that can be purchased for $10.

(B) is wrong because the original asks for how much chocolate that can be purchased for $12, not for the cost of 12 pounds of chocolate.

(C) is correct because the original asks for how much chocolate that can be purchased for $12 at the given price.

(D) is wrong because the original does not ask for how much chocolate that can be purchased for $10.

8. **(B)** (A) is wrong because the original asks for how many students that did not buy a yearbook, not for how many students that did buy a yearbook.

(B) is correct because the original asks for how many students that did not buy a yearbook based on the fact that 45%, or 540, did buy a yearbook.

(C) is wrong because the original states that 540 students bought yearbooks, not that a percentage of 540 students bought yearbooks.

(D) is wrong because the original states that 540 students bought yearbooks, not that a percentage of 540 students did not buy yearbooks.

9. **(C)** (A) is wrong because the original states that it takes Jill 1 hour to walk home at 4 miles per hour, not that it takes 4 hours to walk home at a rate of 5 miles per hour.

(B) is wrong because the original states that it takes Jill 1 hour to walk home at 4 miles per hour, not that it takes 1 hour to walk home at a rate of 5 miles per hour.

(C) is correct because the original states that it takes Jill 1 hour to walk home at 4 miles per hour.

(D) is wrong because the original states that it takes Jill 1 hour to walk home at 4 miles per hour, not that it takes 4 hours to walk home at a rate of 1 mile per hour.

10. **(D)** (A) is wrong because the original asks for the smallest integer of 5 consecutive integers totaling 40, and (A) does not specify that these integers must be consecutive.

(B) is wrong because the original asks for the smallest of 5 consecutive integers, not for the smallest of 10 consecutive integers.

(C) is wrong because the original asks for the smallest of 5 consecutive integers, not for the largest of 5 consecutive integers.

(D) is correct because the original asks for the smallest integer of 5 consecutive integers totaling 40.

11. **(A)** (A) is correct because the original asks for an equation that best describes, or expresses, the relationship between x and y in the table.

(B) is wrong because the original asks for an equation, not for a value that expresses how much y is greater than x.

(C) is wrong because the original asks for an equation, not for a value that expresses how much x is greater than y.

(D) is wrong because the original does not ask about the relationship between x and z; z is not even mentioned in the item stem.

12. **(C)** (A) is wrong because the original asks for the complete solution to the equation $x^2 - 3x = 4$, not to the equation $x^2 - 4x = 3$. (A) rearranges the values in the original equation.

(B) is wrong because the original asks for the complete solution to the given quadratic equation, not for the complete solution to the quadratic formula. There is no solution to the quadratic formula; it is used to solve quadratic equations.

(C) is correct because the original asks for the complete solution to the equation $x^2 - 3x = 4$.

(D) is wrong because the original asks for the complete solution to the given equation, not for a partial solution to the given equation. The complete solution would include two values for x, not just one value for x.

13. **(D)** (A) is wrong because the original asks for how many points that were scored on the first, not the fifth, turn.

(B) is wrong because the original does not ask for how many points that were scored after the fifth turn (total points). That information is already given: 465 total points were scored after five turns.

(C) is wrong because the original asks for how many points that were scored on the first turn, not after the first turn. The correct answer to (C) would be the total number of points scored from the second, third, fourth, and fifth turns.

(D) is correct because the original asks for how many points that the player scored on the first turn.

14. **(C)** (A) is wrong because the original asks for a number of days, not for a number of trucks. Also, the original uses the variable d to represent gallons of fuel needed per day for each truck, not to represent actual days.

(B) is wrong because the original asks for how many days that g gallons of fuel will supply t trucks, not for how many days that d gallons of fuel will supply t trucks.

(C) is correct because the original asks for how many days that g gallons of fuel will supply t trucks.

(D) is wrong because the original does not ask for how many days that both g and d gallons combined will supply t trucks. Both variables do not represent total gallon amounts: g represents a rate and d represents the total.

15. **(C)** (A) is wrong because the original states that the $25 price is increased and then the resulting price is decreased, not the other way around.

(B) is wrong because the original states that there is one item, not ten items.

(C) is correct because the original states that the $25 price is increased and then the resulting price is decreased.

(D) is wrong because the original asks for a final price after an increase and decrease, not for a percentage of the original price. (D) is distracting because it inappropriately adds the two 10% values together.

16. **(D)** (A) is wrong because the original asks for an average speed, not for a length of time.

(B) is wrong because the original uses m to represent miles and h to represent hours, not the other way around.

(C) is wrong because the original uses the value 45 to specify time (minutes), not distance (miles). Also, the original uses m to represent miles, not minutes.

(D) is correct because the original asks for an average speed based on a rate of m miles in h hours and 45 minutes.

17. **(B)** (A) is wrong because the original specifically asks for the hypotenuse of a right isosceles triangle, not for the hypotenuse of a right triangle. A right triangle does not necessarily have two equal sides, as does an isosceles triangle.

(B) is correct because the original asks for the hypotenuse of a right isosceles triangle, or a right triangle in which two sides are equal.

(C) is wrong because the original does not ask for the hypotenuse of an isosceles triangle in which all three sides are equal, or an equilateral triangle. In such a triangle, all three angles would measure 60° each. A right triangle, by definition, has one 90° angle.

(D) is wrong because the original does not ask for the hypotenuse of a 30°-60°-90° triangle. In such a triangle, each of the three sides would be of a different length.

18. **(D)** (A) is wrong because the original asks for the slope of one line, not for two slopes of two lines. Also, to find the slope of a given line, two points on that line must be given. (A), however, provides only one point for each of its two referenced lines.

(B) is wrong because the original asks for the slope of a line with four positive coordinates, not for the slope of a line with three positive coordinates and one negative coordinate. This negative coordinate would position the line in a different quadrant on the graph.

(C) is wrong because it reverses the x and y coordinates for each of the given points. With these points reversed, a different line is created.

(D) is correct because the original asks for the slope of a line with specific x and y coordinates: (3, 6) and (7, 9).

19. **(B)** (A) is wrong because the original does not ask for the average of 8 numbers. This information is already given. The original, rather, asks for the average of 14 numbers.

(B) is correct because the original asks for the average of all 14 numbers: the additive total of 8 numbers, plus the additive total of the other 6 numbers, divided by 14.

(C) is wrong because the original asks for the average of all 14 numbers, not for the average of 8 numbers plus the average of the other 6 numbers. These two formulations would produce different results.

(D) is wrong because the original does not ask for the average of the other 6 numbers. This information is already given. The average of the other 6 numbers is 8.

20. **(B)** (A) is wrong because the original asks about a geometric sequence, not a periodic sequence.

    (B) is correct because the original asks for a value that is represented by the second (between first and third) term in a geometric sequence.

    (C) is wrong because the original asks for a term (which represents a value) in a geometric sequence; it does not ask for a geometric term (geometric terminology) such as "isosceles triangle" or "supplementary."

    (D) is wrong because the original asks for a value that is represented by the second term in a geometric sequence that possesses the values 3,125 and 125; the original does not ask for the difference between these two given values.

EXERCISE 4—CAREFUL READING OF MATH: STUDENT-PRODUCED RESPONSES ITEM STEMS
(p. 49)

1. **(C)** (A) is wrong because the original asks about a number that is increased by 25, not about a number that is twice 25.

   (B) is wrong because the original asks about a number that is increased by 25, not about a number that is half of 25.

   (C) is correct because the original asks about a number that yields the same result when either increased by 25 or multiplied by 2.

   (D) is wrong because the original asks about a number that yields the same result when either increased by 25 or multiplied by 2, not vice versa.

2. **(B)** (A) is wrong because the original asks for a fraction of a fraction, which would require the multiplication, not division, of those two given fractions.

   (B) is correct because the original asks for a fraction of a fraction, which would require the multiplication of those two given fractions.

   (C) is wrong because the original asks for a fraction of a fraction, which would require the multiplication, not division, of those two given fractions.

   (D) is wrong because the original asks for a fraction of a fraction, which would require the multiplication, not addition, of those two given fractions.

3. **(C)** (A) is wrong because the original does not include the variable y in the group of values that is to be averaged.

   (B) is wrong because the original states that the average of a given group of values is 11, not 15.

   (C) is correct because the original asks for the value of x in a group of values that yields 11 when averaged; the group of values in (C), while arranged in a different order, are the same group of values that is provided in the original. Remember, the sequence of values in a group to be averaged is of no consequence.

   (D) is wrong because the original does not include the value 11 in the group of values that is to be averaged.

4. **(A)** (A) is correct because the original asks for Jane's age when Hector was twice her age; when Hector was 12, Jane was 6.

   (B) is wrong because the original does not ask for Jane's future age but for Jane's past age.

   (C) is wrong because this information is given in the original: When Hector was 36, Jane was 30.

   (D) is wrong because the original does not ask for Hector's age but for Jane's age.

5. **(D)** (A) is wrong because the original asks for the percent increase in price of a book, not the percent decrease in price of a book; also, the book originally cost $10.00 and now costs $12.50, not vice versa.

   (B) is wrong because the original states that the book now costs $12.50, not $22.50.

   (C) is wrong because the original asks for the percent increase in price, which requires determining a percentage of the original price, not the new price.

   (D) is correct because the original asks for the percent increase in price, which requires determining a percentage of the old price (original price).

6. **(B)** (A) is wrong because the original states that there are 36 people in the club, not 51 people.

   (B) is correct because the original states that there are 15 girls in a club with 36 people, which means that there are 21 boys; the original also asks for the fraction of the club (in lowest terms) that is boys (not girls).

   (C) is wrong because the original asks for the fraction of the club that is boys, not girls.

   (D) is wrong because the original asks for the fraction of the club that is boys, not girls.

7. **(A)** (A) is correct because the original asks for the least (smaller) of two consecutive integers that when added together total 29.

(B) is wrong because the original is concerned with two consecutive integers, not two non-consecutive integers.

(C) is wrong because the original is concerned with the smaller of two consecutive integers, not the larger of two consecutive integers.

(D) is wrong because the original is concerned with two consecutive integers that when added together total 29, not 92.

8. **(B)** (A) is wrong because the original asks for the percentage of marbles that is black, not white. (If there are 300 total black and white marbles in the jar and there are 156 white marbles, then there are 144 black marbles.)

(B) is correct because the original asks for the percentage of marbles that is black. (144 of the 300 marbles are black.)

(C) is wrong because the original states that there are 300 total marbles in the jar, not 456 total marbles.

(D) is wrong because the original states that there are 300 total marbles in the jar, not 456 total marbles.

9. **(D)** (A) is wrong because the original asks for the number of digits that change when a given decimal is rounded off to the nearest hundredth, not to the nearest tenth.

(B) is wrong because the original asks for the number of digits that change when a given decimal is rounded off to the nearest hundredth, not to the nearest thousandth. Also, the given decimal is 0.129914, not 0.129414.

(C) is wrong because in the original, the given decimal is 0.129914, not 0.129941.

(D) is correct because the original asks for the number of digits that change when 0.129914 is rounded off to the nearest hundredth.

10. **(B)** (A) is wrong because the original asks for how old Cindy is now, not for how old she will be 8 years from now.

(B) is correct because the original asks for how old Cindy is now (current age).

(C) is wrong because the original states that Ray is currently 10 years older than Cindy, not 8 years older.

(D) is wrong because the original asks for how old Cindy is now, not for old she will be in the future.

11. **(A)** (A) is correct because the original states that the "JOSH" of a particular number is defined as 3 less than 3 times that number. If x were to represent the number, then the original would be asking for the value of x that is equal to $3x - 3$.

(B) is wrong because the original states that the "JOSH" of a particular number is defined as 3 less than 3 times that number, not 3 more than 3 times that number.

(C) is wrong because the original states that the "JOSH" of a particular number is defined as 3 less than 3 times that number, not 3 more than 3 times another number. (The variables on either side of the equation must be the same.)

(D) is wrong because the original states that the "JOSH" of a particular number is defined as 3 less than 3 times that number, not 3 less than 3 times another number. (The variables on either side of the equation must be the same.)

12. **(B)** (A) is wrong because in the original, O represents the center point of the circle, not the circle itself.

(B) is correct because the original asks for the area of a circle with center O.

(C) is wrong because the original does not ask for the area of the center point. A point is one-dimensional and therefore does not have an area.

(D) is wrong because the original asks for the area of a circle, not for the circumference of a circle. Remember that although the circumference would be sufficient information to solve for the area, that is not the objective of this exercise.

13. **(C)** (A) is wrong because the original asks for the number of globs that is equivalent to 2 glops, not for the number of globs that is equivalent to 4 glips; that information is given in the original: 4 glips are 5 globs.

(B) is wrong because the original asks for the number of globs that is equivalent to 2 glops, not a particular number of glups. (Glup is the name of the country, not the name of one of the given quantifiable things.)

(C) is correct because the original asks for the number of globs that is equivalent to 2 glops.

(D) is wrong because the original does not ask for the number of globs that is equivalent to 3 glips.

14. **(C)** (A) is wrong because the original asks for the result of $\frac{4}{5}$ subtracted from its reciprocal (inverted fraction), not for the result of the given fraction's reciprocal $\left(\frac{5}{4}\right)$ subtracted from the given fraction $\left(\frac{4}{5}\right)$.

(B) is wrong because the original does not ask for the result of $\frac{4}{5}$ subtracted from itself.

(C) is correct because the original asks for the result of $\frac{4}{5}$ subtracted from its reciprocal (inverted fraction), $\frac{5}{4}$.

(D) is wrong because the original asks for the result of $\frac{4}{5}$ subtracted from its reciprocal. (The reciprocal is not defined as the difference between 1 and the given fraction.)

15. **(B)** (A) is wrong because the original asks for the difference between two fractions but it does not specify that the answer must necessarily be in decimal form.

(B) is correct because the original asks for the value of $\frac{2}{3} - \frac{5}{8}$ ($\frac{5}{8}$ subtracted from $\frac{2}{3}$).

(C) is wrong because the original does not ask for the value of $\frac{5}{8} - \frac{2}{3}$ ($\frac{2}{3}$ subtracted from $\frac{5}{8}$).

(D) is wrong because the original asks for the value of $\frac{5}{8}$ subtracted from $\frac{2}{3}$, not for the value of $\frac{8}{5}$ subtracted from $\frac{3}{2}$. ($\frac{8}{5}$ and $\frac{3}{2}$ are the reciprocals of the original given fractions.)

16. **(D)** (A) is wrong because the original asks for the average of three numbers, not the median average of three numbers.

(B) is wrong because in the original, 7.5 is not one of the given numbers.

(C) is wrong because the original asks for the average of three numbers, which requires dividing the sum total of those three numbers by 3, not multiplying the sum total by 3.

(D) is correct because the original asks for the average of three numbers (8.5, 7.8, and 7.7), which requires dividing the sum total of those numbers by 3. When adding numbers, sequence is of no consequence; the result will always be the same.

17. **(D)** (A) is wrong because the original asks for the area of a square with four points P, Q, R, and S that trace the square in that particular order. Based on this sequence, square $QSPR$ would not be the same figure as square $PQRS$.

(B) is wrong because the original asks for the area of a given square, not for the area of a given parallelogram. Although both shapes are quadrilaterals, only the square has four equal sides and four right angles.

(C) is wrong because the original asks for the area of a given square, not for the area of a given rectangle. Although both shapes are quadrilaterals, only the square has four equal sides.

(D) is correct because the original asks for the area of a square with four points P, Q, R, and S that trace the square in that particular order. Based on this sequence, only square $SRQP$ (traced in reverse order) would be the same figure as square $PQRS$.

18. **(A)** (A) is correct because the original asks for the result of $z - y$ given two different averages of two different groups of values. Remember that when adding numbers, sequence is of no consequence; the result will always be the same.

(B) is wrong because the original states that the average of 4, 5, x, and y is 6 and that the average of x, z, 8, and 9 is 8, not vice versa.

(C) is wrong for the same reason that (B) is wrong. (C) is slightly more confusing because the values in each group are rearranged.

(D) is wrong because the original asks for the result of $z - y$, not for the result of $y - z$.

19. **(C)** (A) is wrong because the original states that 0.01 is the resultant ratio of 0.1 to another value, not that 0.1 is the resultant ratio of 0.01 to another value.

(B) is wrong because the original asks for an unknown value that is determined by dividing 0.1 by 0.01, not vice versa.

(C) is correct because the original states that 0.01 (or .01) is the resultant ratio of 0.1 (or .1) to another value.

(D) is wrong because in the original, .001 is not one of the given values.

20. **(D)** (A) is wrong because the original states that line segment *CB* is equal, not parallel, to line segment *CA* and that line segment *DE* is parallel, not equal, to line segment *BA*. Remember that the two points in a line can be in either order.

(B) is wrong because the original states that ∠*BED* = 50°, not that ∠*EDB* = 50°. ∠*BED* and ∠*EDB* are not the same angle.

(C) is wrong because the original does not state either that line segment *AB* is parallel to line segment *AC* or that line segment *ED* is equal to line segment *BC*.

(D) is correct because the original asks for a value based on all of the same conditions that are provided in this answer choice. ∠*DEB* and ∠*BED* are the same angle.

EXERCISE 5—CAREFUL READING OF WRITING ITEM STEMS (p. 52)

1. **(D)** (A) is wrong because the original asks for something that would be inserted at the beginning of sentence 9, thereby being part of that particular sentence; it does not ask for something that would be inserted before sentence 9 (presumably between sentences 8 and 9).

(B) is wrong because the original does not ask for something that would be inserted after sentence 9 but for something that would be inserted at the beginning of (as part of) sentence 9.

(C) is wrong because the original does not ask for something that would be inserted as part of the eighth sentence, or sentence 8.

(D) is correct because the original asks for something that would be inserted at the beginning of sentence 9 (the ninth sentence) of the passage.

2. **(B)** (A) is wrong because the original asks for a description of the actual organization of the passage, not a hypothetical description of how the passage should be organized.

(B) is correct because the original asks for a description of how the passage is organized.

(C) is wrong because the original does not ask about a particular passage's description of how to best organize something; it asks for the best description of how a given passage is organized.

(D) is wrong because the original asks about the organization of a given passage; it does not ask the reader to make a further determination as to the sequence of a proceeding passage.

3. **(A)** (A) is correct because the original asks for an answer choice (word or phrase) that could be substituted for (used in place of) the word "this" in sentence 9 (the ninth sentence) of the passage.

(B) is wrong because the original does not state whether the noun to be substituted can be found in the same sentence as the pronoun "this."

(C) is wrong because the original does not ask about the location of the word "this" in sentence 9.

(D) is wrong because the original asks about a substitution for a particular word, not for an entire sentence.

4. **(C)** (A) is wrong because the original asks for the least appropriate (worst) revision (replacement) for the underlined portion of sentence 11 (the eleventh sentence) in the passage.

(B) is wrong because the original asks for the revision that *would* be the worst.

(C) is correct because the original asks for the least appropriate (worst) revision of the underlined part of sentence 11 in the passage.

(D) is wrong because the original does not ask about sentence 7 (the seventh sentence) in the passage; it asks about sentence 11 (the eleventh sentence).

5. **(C)** (A) is wrong because the original asks for the one technique that is not used in the passage. The word EXCEPT indicates that this item is a "thought-reverser."

(B) is wrong because the original uses EXCEPT to indicate that one of the four answer choices is not something that is used in the passage; the wording of (B) indicates just the opposite.

(C) is correct because the original asks for the one technique that is not used in the passage.

(D) is wrong because the original uses EXCEPT to indicate that one of the four answer choices is not something that is used in the passage; the wording of (D) indicates that there are three correct answers, which is not possible.

6. **(C)** (A) is wrong because the original does not ask the writer to use someone else's experience; the original also asks for one way in which technology benefits humankind, not two ways in which technology does not benefit humankind.

   (B) is wrong because the original asks the writer to take examples from literature in order to develop a response; it does not ask the writer to show how literature benefits humankind but how technology benefits humankind.

   (C) is correct because the original asks the writer to show how technology benefits (aids) humankind by taking examples from these four given areas.

   (D) is wrong because the original does not necessarily ask the writer to show how his or her experience reflects how technology benefits humankind.

7. **(D)** (A) is wrong because the original asks the writer to make an assessment based on the last 125 years, not the last 100 years (century); it also asks for the writer's opinion, not fact.

   (B) is wrong because the original does not ask about the advances upon a particular technological achievement but about the particular technological achievement itself; it also asks for the writer's opinion, not fact.

   (C) is wrong because the original does not ask about the advances upon a particular technological achievement; it uses the word "advancement" synonymously with "achievement."

   (D) is correct because the original asks the writer to give an opinion about what he or she considers to be the greatest technological advancement of the last 125 years (one and one-quarter centuries).

8. **(D)** (A) is wrong because the original does not refer to harmless violence, which is an oxymoron.

   (B) is wrong because the original does not refer to harmless violence, which is an oxymoron; it also does not try to draw a connection between two different types of media violence.

   (C) is wrong because the original asks whether media violence leads to (propagates) more violence, not whether it leads to harmless activity.

   (D) is correct because the original asks whether media violence leads to (propagates) more violence or whether it is harmless in its effect.

9. **(A)** (A) is correct because the original asks whether cultures in America merge (blend) into one as do the ingredients in a melting pot or whether they are mixed and distinct as are the ingredients in a salad bowl.

   (B) is wrong because the original proposes two metaphors regarding different cultures in America in which a melting pot represents merging and a salad bowl represents distinction, not vice versa.

   (C) is wrong because the original does not ask about the developmental relationship between an initially distinct society of cultures and a subsequently amalgamated society of cultures.

   (D) is wrong because the original does not ask about the developmental relationship between an initially amalgamated society of cultures and a subsequently distinct society of cultures.

10. **(B)** (A) is wrong because the original asks the writer to compare a past quality of life with the present quality of life; it does not ask the writer to compare or even to make the distinction between two separate past qualities of life (30 years ago vs. 40 years ago).

    (B) is correct because the original asks the writer to compare a past quality of life (30 to 40 years ago) with the present quality of life.

    (C) is wrong because the original does not ask the writer to compare two separate past qualities of life; (C) also uses the word "compelling" to modify a proposed difference between qualities of life, whereas the original uses the word "compelling" to inquire as to the writer's opinion regarding two different beliefs.

    (D) is wrong because the original does not ask the writer to compare two separate past qualities of life with the present quality of life.

EXERCISE 6—CODING OF ITEM STEMS (p. 56)

1. **SP** This is a Specific Points (Explicit Detail) item. The item stem asks you for an explicit detail that is made by the author regarding certain locator material ("tears and laughter"), as indicated by the phrase "According to the passage." Also, the word "EXCEPT" indicates that this is a "thought-reverser" item.

2. **E** This is an Evaluation (Implied Idea) item. The item stem asks you for an implied idea that is made by the author regarding a specific detail (an ability that animals lack).

3. **SP** This is a Specific Points (Vocabulary) item. The item stem asks you for the meaning of a vocabulary word ("ludicrous") as it is used in the context of the passage ("line #").

4. **SP** This is a Specific Points (Development) item. The item stem asks you for the manner with which the author develops the overall structure of the passage.

5. **SP** This is a Specific Points (Explicit Detail) item. The item stem asks you for an explicit detail regarding something specifically mentioned by the author in the second paragraph of the passage.

6. **GT** This is a General Theme (Main Idea) item. The item stem asks you for a description that summarizes the overall content, or central theme, of the passage.

7. **GT** This is a General Theme (Main Idea) item. The item stem asks you for a description of the author's primary concern, or central focus, in the passage.

8. **SP** This is a Specific Points (Explicit Detail) item. The item stem asks you for an explicit detail that is made by the author regarding certain locator material ("the open government statute is intended to accomplish"), as indicated by the phrase "The passage states." Also, the word "EXCEPT" indicates that this is a "thought-reverser" item.

9. **E** This is an Evaluation (Application) item. The item stem asks you to draw a conclusion about something ("a decision") that is supported by the details of the passage. To answer this item, you must apply those details to a new situation.

10. **SP** This is a Specific Points (Explicit Detail) item. The item stem asks you for an explicit detail regarding something that is specifically mentioned by the author in the final paragraph of the passage.

11. **SP** This is a Specific Points (Explicit Detail) item. The item stem asks you for an explicit detail that is made by the author regarding certain locator material ("the rules governing the commission"). Also, the word "EXCEPT" indicates that this is a "thought-reverser" item.

12. **E** This is an Evaluation (Implied Idea) item, as indicated by the phrase "It can be inferred from the passage." It asks you to identify an implied idea that is made by details in the passage.

13. **E** This is an Evaluation (Implied Idea) item as indicated by the structure of the item stem: "Which of the following statements...can be inferred." Specifically, the item stem asks you to identify an implied idea that is made by the author regarding "a 'review and comment' session."

14. **SP** This is a Specific Points (Explicit Detail) item. The item stem asks you for an explicit detail that is made by the author regarding certain locator material ("metamorphic rock"), as indicated by the phrase "According to the passage." Also, the word "EXCEPT" indicates that this is a "thought-reverser" item.

15. **SP** This is a Specific Points (Explicit Detail) item. The item stem asks you for an explicit detail that is made by the author regarding certain locator material ("the sequence of events leading to the present landscape"), as indicated by the phrase "As described by the selection."

16. **E** This is an Evaluation (Application) item. The item stem asks you to determine how the author regards his own explanation for something. To answer this item, you must further assess the details presented in the passage.

17. **SP** This is a Specific Points (Explicit Detail) item. The item stem asks you for a particular term that can be defined by explicit information that is provided by the author of the passage.

18. **E** This is an Evaluation (Application) item. The item stem asks you to choose a statement with which the author would most likely agree. In order to answer this item, you must have an understanding of the author's position and be able to extrapolate that information to determine the author's view on related issues.

19. **E** This is an Evaluation (Application) item. The item stem asks you to draw a conclusion about something ("the writings of Yevgeny Zamyatin") that is supported by the details of the passage. To answer this question, you must apply those details to a new situation.

20. **E** This is an Evaluation (Voice) item. The item stem asks you to determine the author's attitude toward something ("James Burnham's writing"), as indicated by the phrase "The author's treatment of."

21. **E**   This is an Evaluation (Implied Idea) item. The item asks you to determine the implicit meaning of a statement made by the author, "Burham inverted the logical priority of the individual over the state."

22. **SP**   This is a Specific Points (Explicit Detail) item. The item stem asks you for an explicit detail regarding something that is specifically mentioned by the author in the passage (the nature of his or her criticism of Burnham).

23. **SP**   This is a Specific Points (Explicit Detail) item. The item stem asks you for an explicit detail regarding something that is specifically mentioned by the author in the passage (why Burnham thinks that history will come to an end in a completely autocratic state). Notice that the phrase "According to Burnham" is interchangeable with either "According to the author" or "According to the passage."

24. **E**   This is an Evaluation (Implied Idea) item. The item stem asks you for an implied idea that is made by the author regarding a specific detail, as indicated by the phrase "It can be inferred from the passage."

25. **E**   This is an Evaluation (Implied Idea) item. The item stem asks you for an implied idea that is made by the author regarding a specific detail (the nature of "currently accepted theories on galaxy formation").

26. **SP**   This is a Specific Points (Explicit Detail) item. The item stem asks you for an explicit detail that is made by the author regarding certain locator material ("a cluster with a central, supergiant galaxy"), as indicated by the phrase "According to the passage."

27. **SP**   This is a Specific Points (Explicit Detail) item. The item stem asks you for an explicit detail that is made by the author regarding certain locator material ("the outcome of a collision between galaxies"), as indicated by the phrase "According to the passage."

28. **SP**   This is a Specific Points (Explicit Detail) item. The item stem asks you for an explicit detail that is made by the author regarding certain locator material ("a galaxy falls inward toward the center of a cluster"), as indicated by the phrase "According to the passage."

29. **SP**   This is a Specific Points (Explicit Detail) item. The item stem asks you for an explicit detail that is made by the author regarding certain locator material ("our Sun would probably not be found in a cluster such as Virgo"), as indicated by the phrase "According to the passage."

30. **E**   This is an Evaluation (Application) item. The item stem asks you to determine the meaning of a quote by Emerson based on what you have learned from the rest of the passage. Therefore, you are making a further assessment based on given details.

31. **E**   This is an Evaluation (Implied Idea) item. The item stem asks you for an implied idea that is made by the author regarding a specific detail ("the difference between farms and the landscape").

32. **SP**   This is a Specific Points (Vocabulary) item. The item stem asks you to determine the meaning of the vocabulary word "property" as it is used in the context of the phrase, "property in the horizon", in the passage (line #).

33. **E**   This is an Evaluation (Implied Idea) item. The item stem asks you for the meaning of a phrase ("color of the spirit") as it used in the context of the passage (line #). Whereas a Vocabulary item asks for the specific meaning of a term, this item asks for the implied meaning of a phrase as it used by the author.

34. **GT**   This is a General Theme (Main Idea) item. The item stem asks you for a description of the author's main purpose, or central theme, of the passage.

35. **E**   This is an Evaluation (Application) item. The item asks you to determine the difference between things that are described in the passage ("a life circumstance and a life event"). To answer this question, you must further assess the details presented in the passage.

36. **SP**   This is a Specific Points (Development) item. The item stem asks you to recognize a technique that the author does not use to develop the overall structure of the passage. The word "EXCEPT" indicates that this is a "thought-reverser" item.

37. **SP**   This is a Specific Points (Development) item. The item stem asks you to recognize the relationship between two consecutive paragraphs in the passage, which in turn indicates how the author develops the overall structure of the passage.

38. **SP** This is a Specific Points (Explicit Detail) item. The item stem asks you for a particular term that can be defined by explicit information that is provided by the author of the passage.

39. **SP** This is a Specific Points (Explicit Detail) item. The item stem asks you for an explicit detail that is made by the author regarding certain locator material (geographical features of Wineland), as indicated by the phrase "According to the passage."

40. **E** This is an Evaluation (Implied Idea) item. The item stem asks you for an implied idea that is made by the author regarding a specific detail, as indicated by the phrase "It can be inferred from the passage." The word "EXCEPT" indicates that this is a "thought-reverser" item.

41. **SP** This is a Specific Points (Development) item. The item stem asks you for the logical role played by a specific part of the passage (the author's mention of "the two high mountains"), as indicated by the structure "The author mentions…in order to."

42. **SP** This is a Specific Points (Explicit Detail) item. The item stem asks you for an explicit detail that is made by the author regarding certain locator material (similarities between Leif Erikson's voyage and Biarni's voyage), as indicated by the phrase "All of the following are mentioned." Also, the word "EXCEPT" indicates that this is a "thought-reverser" item.

43. **E** This is an Evaluation (Implied Idea) item. The item stem asks you for an implied idea that is made by the author regarding a specific detail (the historicity of the Biarni narrative), as indicated by the phrase "It can be inferred that the author."

EXERCISE 7—VOCABULARY: PASSAGES (p. 76)

1. **(E)** (A), (B), (C), and (D) are all possible meanings of the word "heartily"; however, (E) is the only answer choice that is appropriate in this context. Thomas Jefferson was "completely" tired from the daily conflicts, leading to his resignation from office.

2. **(C)** The "public" life that is the subject of this passage is a life in politics or government—an "official" life.

3. **(E)** The word "final" has many related meanings, including "last" (*e.g.*, "final" day), "closing" (*e.g.*, "final" statement), "ultimate" (*e.g.*, "final" offer), "eventual" (*e.g.*, "final" home), and "conclusive" (*e.g.*, "final" authority). In this context, the appropriate meaning is "conclusive." Jefferson insisted that his retirement would conclude his participation in public life.

4. **(B)** The word "allowed" can be used to mean "permitted" (*e.g.*, The manager "allowed" them to enter the store.) in this context, however, "allowed" means "admitted." Jefferson "admitted" that he had been forced to examine his true feelings on the subject of his retirement.

5. **(B)** The word "anticipating" can be used to mean "expecting," or "looking forward to" (*e.g.*, The boy was "anticipating" the arrival of his father.); in this context, however, "anticipating" means "presaging," or "predicting." The Republican party presaged the campaign tactics of the opposing party.

6. **(B)** The word "uniform" can be used to mean "standard" (*e.g.*, her "uniform" response to a question); in this context, however, the intended meaning of "uniform" is "unchanging." The newspapers presented Jefferson as "unchanging" in his advocacy of equal rights.

7. **(E)** The word "champion" can be used to mean "victor" (*e.g.*, the "champion" at the Olympics); in this context, however, the intended meaning of "champion" is "advocate," or "defender." The newspapers portrayed Adams as an "advocate" for, or a "defender" of, rank, titles, heredity, and distinctions.

8. **(B)** The word "senior" can be used to mean "older in age" (*e.g.*, He is four years my "senior."); in this context, however, "senior" means "higher in rank." The phrase "in public office" clarifies the intended meaning of the author. With regard to public office, Adams had always been a person of higher rank than Jefferson.

9. **(B)** A "luminary" is literally a bright object in the sky, but the word is also used to refer to a famous person. In this context, the extremely famous George Washington is compared to a less "famous person."

10. **(E)** The primary meaning of "diminution" is "a lessening in size" (*e.g.*, the "diminution" of the crowd); in this context, however, the concept is extended to mean "a lessening in esteem," or "degradation." Jefferson believed that Adams had never suffered a "lessening in esteem."

EXERCISE 8—VOCABULARY: SENTENCE COMPLETIONS (p. 78)

1. **C**	3. **E**	5. **A**	7. **C**	9. **D**	11. **A**
2. **B**	4. **D**	6. **B**	8. **D**	10. **C**	12. **B**

13. exceed, surpass

14. climax, high point, zenith

15. boring, dull, uninspiring

16. serious, severe, large-scale

17. complete, comprehensive

18. complete, total, authoritarian

19. hides, camouflages, conceals

20. wanted, infamous, notorious

21. dazed, confused, disoriented

22. generate, spark, increase

23. **TR** The survivors had been drifting for days in the lifeboat, and in their weakness, they appeared to be _____ rather than living beings.

This item is a "thought-reverser," as indicated by the phrase clue "rather than" in conjunction with the phrase clue "living beings." The blank must be filled with a word that means the opposite of something that is alive. "Dead," "spirits," and "ghosts" are possible completions. Notice that the missing word can either be an adjective (*e.g.*, "dead"), modifying the noun "beings," or a noun (*e.g.*, "spirits"), paralleling the phrase "living beings."

24. **TE** The guillotine was introduced during the French Revolution as a(n) _____, an alternative to other less humane means of execution.

This item is a "thought-extender," as indicated by the phrase clues "alternative to" and "less humane." The blank must be filled with a noun that extends the idea of something that is an "alternative to" a "less humane" practice. "Reform" and "improvement" are possible completions.

25. **TE** Because of the _____ nature of the chemical, it cannot be used near an open flame.

This item is a "thought-extender," as indicated by the conjunction clue "Because" and the phrase clue "cannot be used near an open flame." The blank must be filled with an adjective that extends the idea of a chemical that "cannot be used near an open flame." "Flammable," which means "easily capable of burning," is one obvious completion.

26. **CR** The Mayor's proposal for a new subway line, although a(n) _____, is not a final solution to the city's transportation needs.

This is a "combined reasoning" item because it is characterized by a "thought-extender," as indicated by the word clues "proposal" and "new," and a "thought-reverser," as indicated by the conjunction clue "although" and the word clue "final." The blank must be filled with a noun that both extends the idea of something that is "new" and reverses the idea of something that is "final." "Start" and "beginning" are possible completions.

27. **TE** In a pluralistic society, policies are the result of compromise, so political leaders must be _____ and must accommodate the views of others.

This item is a "thought-extender," as indicated by the conjunction clue "and" and the word clues "compromise" and "accommodate." The blank must be filled with an adjective that extends the idea of a "compromise" and parallels the idea of accommodation. "Tolerant" and "understanding" are possible completions.

28. **TR** The committee report vigorously expounded the bill's strengths but also acknowledged its _____.

This item is a "thought-reverser," as indicated by the conjunction clue "but" in association with the word clue "strengths." The blank must be filled with a plural noun that means the opposite of "strengths." "Weaknesses" and "shortcomings" are possible completions.

29. **TR** Because there is always the danger of a power failure and disruption of elevator service, high-rise buildings, while suitable for younger persons are not recommended for _____.

This item is a "thought-reverser," as indicated by the conjunction clue "while" and the phrase clue "younger persons." The sentence suggests that high-rise buildings are suitable for "younger persons" but not for a different group of people. So, the blank must be filled with a word or phrase that means the opposite of "younger persons." "The elderly" and "senior citizens" are possible completions.

30. **CR** For a child to be <u>happy</u>, his day must be very <u>structured</u>; when his routine is _____, he becomes <u>nervous and irritable.</u>

This is a "combined reasoning" item as indicated by both the "if-then" "thought-extender" structure and the "thought-reverser" word clues. The "if-then" logical structure of the sentence indicates that if the child is to be happy, his day must be structured. However, the word clue, nervous and irritable, after the semicolon suggests that the parallel structure in the second clause of the sentence must be the reverse of the first. If "structured" activity makes a child "happy," then unstructured activity would make a child "nervous and irritable." So, the blank must be filled with a verb that suggests the idea of unstructured activity. "Disrupted" and "interrupted" are possible completions.

31. **TE** The current spirit of _____ among different religions <u>has led to</u> a number of meetings that their leaders hope will lead to better <u>understanding</u>.

This item is a "thought-extender," as indicated by the phrase clue "has led to" and the word clue "understanding." The blank must be filled with a noun that satisfies the following construction: The spirit of _____ has led to understanding. "Cooperation" and "accord" are possible completions.

32. **TE** Our modern industrialized societies have been responsible for the greatest <u>destruction of nature and life</u>; indeed, it seems that more civilization <u>results in greater</u> _____. (annihilation, death)

This item is a "thought-extender," as indicated by the semicolon (punctuation clue) in conjunction with the "if-then" logical structure of the sentence. The blank must be filled with a noun that extends the idea of the "destruction of nature and life," thereby satisfying the following construction: If "modern industrialized societies" are "responsible for" the "destruction of nature and life," then "more civilization" "results in greater" _____. "Annihilation" and "death" are possible completions.

MATH SKILLS REVIEW

EXERCISE 1—WHOLE NUMBERS (p. 95)

1. **(B)** In order to solve this problem, you must find the thousands column in 12,345. To subtract one thousand, take away one digit from the number in the thousands column of 12,345, which is 2.

2. **(B)** First find the ten thousands column in 736,124. Then, add three to the number in the ten thousands column to increase the value of 736,124 by 30,000. The number in the ten thousands column is 3.

3. **(B)** Adding 1 to each digit of 222,222 is the same as 222,222 + 111,111. Therefore, adding 1 to each digit of 222,222 will increase the value of the number by 111,111.

4. **(C)** $(1 \cdot 10,000) + (2 \cdot 1,000) + (3 \cdot 100) + (4 \cdot 10) + (5 \cdot 1) = 10,000 + 2,000 + 300 + 40 + 5 = 12,345$. Another way to approach this problem is to realize that the question is given in the form of the column system. So, there is a 1 in the ten thousands place, a 2 in the thousands place, a 3 in the hundreds place, a 4 in the tens place, and a 5 in the unit place. This can be written as 12, 345.

5. **(C)** $(1 \cdot 1) + (1 \cdot 10) + (1 \cdot 100) + (1 \cdot 1,000) + (1 \cdot 10,000) = 1 + 10 + 100 + 1,000 + 10,000 = 11,111$. The fastest way to solve this problem is to see that it is given in the form of the column system, only inverted, starting with the unit place and moving up to the ten thousands place. So, there is a 1 in the ten thousands place, a 1 in the thousands place, a 1 in the hundreds place, a 1 in the tens place, and a 1 in the unit place. This can be written as 11,111.

6. **(D)** $(1 \cdot 100,000) + (2 \cdot 10,000) + (3 \cdot 1,000) = 100,000 + 20,000 + 3,000 = 123,000$. This problem is also given with the form of the column system in mind. To solve this quickly, note that there is a 1 in the hundred thousands place, a 2 in the ten thousands place, and a 3 in the thousands place. This can be written as 123,000.

7. **(C)** $(2 \cdot 1,000) + (3 \cdot 100) + (1 \cdot 10,000) + (2 \cdot 10) + 1 = 2,000 + 300 + 10,000 + 20 + 1 = 12,321$. To solve this quickly, note that there is a 1 in the ten thousands place, a 2 in the thousands place, a 3 in the hundreds place, a 2 in the tens place, and a 1 in the unit place. This can be written as 12,321.

8. **(E)** $(9 \cdot 10,000) + (9 \cdot 100) = 90,000 + 900 = 90,900$. To solve this quickly, note that there is a 9 in the ten thousands place, and a 9 in the hundreds place. This can be written as 90,900.

9. **(E)** $(2 \cdot 10,000) + (8 \cdot 1,000) + (4 \cdot 10) = 20,000 + 8,000 + 40 = 28,040$. Note that there is a 2 in the ten thousands place, an 8 in the thousands place, and a 4 in the tens place. This can be written as 28,040.

10. **(B)** $2 + 3 = 5$.

11. **(C)** $5 + 7 + 8 = 12 + 8 = 20$.

12. **(D)** $20 + 30 + 40 = 50 + 40 = 90$.

13. **(D)** $8 - 3 = 5$.

14. **(C)** $28 - 14 = 14$.

15. **(D)** $2 \cdot 8 = 16$.

16. **(C)** $20 \cdot 50 = 1,000$.

17. **(C)** $12 \cdot 10 = 120$.

18. **(B)** $(5 + 1) + (2 + 3) = 6 + 5 = 11$.

19. **(B)** $(5 + 2) - (3 \cdot 2) = 7 - 6 = 1$.

20. **(C)** $(2 + 3) \cdot (3 + 4) = 5 \cdot 7 = 35$.

21. **(C)** $(2 \cdot 3) + (3 \cdot 4) = 6 + 12 = 18.$

22. **(C)** $(3 \cdot 4) - (2 \cdot 3) = 12 - 6 = 6.$

23. **(E)** $12 \div 7 = 1$ with a remainder of 5.

24. **(A)** $18 \div 2 = 9$ with a remainder of 0.

25. **(A)** $50 \div 2 = 25$ with a remainder of 0.

26. **(D)** $15 \div 8 = 1$ with a remainder of 7.

27. **(B)** $15 \div 2 = 7$ with a remainder of 1.

28. **(B)** $8 \div 5 = 1$ with a remainder of 3. $13 \div 5 = 2$ with a remainder of 3. To solve this problem, first subtract 3 from both 8 and 13. You will get 5 and 10, respectively. Then, figure out if 5 and 10 can be divided by any of the answer choices without yielding a remainder. Both 5 and 10 are evenly divisible by 5.

29. **(A)** $33 \div 4 = 8$ with a remainder of 1. $37 \div 4 = 9$ with a remainder of 1. To solve this problem, first subtract 1 from both 33 and 37. You will get 32 and 36, respectively. Then, figure out if 32 and 36 can be divided by any of the answer choices without yielding a remainder. Both 32 and 36 are evenly divisible by 4.

30. **(D)** $12 \div 7 = 1$ with a remainder of 5. $19 \div 7 = 2$ with a remainder of 5. To solve this problem, first subtract 5 from both 12 and 19. You will get 7 and 14, respectively. Then, figure out if 7 and 14 can be divided by any of the answer choices without yielding a remainder. Both 7 and 14 are evenly divisible by 7.

31. **(D)** $(4 \cdot 3) + 2 = 12 + 2 = 14.$

32. **(C)** $(2 \cdot 3) \div (2 + 1) = 6 \div 3 = 2.$

33. **(C)** $[2 \cdot (12 \div 4)] + [6 \div (1 + 2)] = (2 \cdot 3) + (6 \div 3) = 6 + 2 = 8.$

34. **(E)** $[(36 \div 12) \cdot (24 \div 3)] \div [(1 \cdot 3) - (18 \div 9)] = (3 \cdot 8) \div (3 - 2) = 24 \div 1 = 24.$ Remember to work inside out.

35. **(B)** $[(12 \cdot 3) - (3 \cdot 12)] + [(8 \div 2) \div 4] = (36 - 36) + (4 \div 4) = 0 + 1 = 1.$ Solve the inside parentheticals first; then work outwards.

36. **(A)** $(1 \cdot 2 \cdot 3 \cdot 4) - [(2 \cdot 3) + (3 \cdot 6)] = 24 - (6 + 18) = 24 - 24 = 0.$

37. **(D)** Solve I, II, and III to see if the left side of the equation is equal to the right side.
I: $(4 + 3) - 6 = 4 + (6 - 2) \Rightarrow 7 - 6 = 4 + 4 \Rightarrow 1 \neq 8.$ II: $3(4 + 5) = (3 \cdot 4) + (3 \cdot 5) \Rightarrow 3(9) = 12 + 15 \Rightarrow 27 = 27.$
III: $(3 + 5) \cdot 4 = 4 \cdot (5 + 3) \Rightarrow 8 \cdot 4 = 4 \cdot 8 \Rightarrow 32 = 32.$ II and III are true statements.

38. **(B)** You can factor out 12 from 12, 24, and 36 to get $12(1 + 2 + 3).$

39. **(D)** You can factor out 25 from 25, 50, and 100 to get $25(1 + 2 + 4).$

40. **(B)** Factor out the 99 in the numerator; then, simplify. $\frac{99(121) - 99(120)}{33} = \frac{99(121 - 120)}{33} = \frac{99(1)}{33} = 3.$

41. **(A)** Factor out 1,234; then, simplify. $1,234(96) - 1,234(48) = 1,234(96 - 48) = 1,234 \cdot 48.$

42. **(C)** There are two numbers between 20 and 30 that are not divisible by any number other than themselves and one. They are 23 and 29.

43. **(C)** There are two numbers between 50 and 60 that are not divisible by any number other than one and themselves: 53 and 59.

44. **(A)** 11 is not divisible by any number other than 1 and itself. 111 is divisible by 3. 1,111 is divisible by 11. So, only I is prime.

45. **(E)** 12,345 is divisible by 5. 999,999,999 is divisible by 3. 1,000,000,002 is divisible by 2. None of the three Roman numerals are prime.

46. **(A)** First, list all the prime factors of each number. Then, multiply together the common prime factors from both numbers. This will be the greatest common factor between the two numbers. $25 = 5 \cdot 5$. $40 = 2 \cdot 2 \cdot 2 \cdot 5$. 5 is the greatest common factor of 25 and 40.

47. **(B)** First, list all the prime factors of each number. The product of the common prime factors will be the greatest shared factor: $6 = 2 \cdot 3$. $9 = 3 \cdot 3$. 3 is the greatest common factor of 6 and 9.

48. **(A)** First, list all the prime factors of each number. Then, multiply together the common prime factors from both numbers. This will be the greatest common factor between the two numbers. $12 = 2 \cdot 3 \cdot 3$. $18 = 2 \cdot 3 \cdot 3$. $2 \cdot 3 = 6$ is the greatest common factor of 12 and 18.

49. **(A)** First, list all the prime factors of each number. Then, multiply together the common prime factors from all the numbers. This will be the greatest common factor among the three numbers. $18 = 2 \cdot 3 \cdot 3$. $24 = 2 \cdot 2 \cdot 2 \cdot 3$. $36 = 2 \cdot 2 \cdot 3 \cdot 3$. $2 \cdot 3 = 6$ is the greatest common factor of 18, 24, and 36.

50. **(B)** First, list all the prime factors of each number. Then, multiply together the common prime factors from all the numbers. This will be the greatest common factor among the three numbers. $7 = 7$. $14 = 2 \cdot 7$. $21 = 3 \cdot 7$. 7 is the greatest common factor of 7, 14, and 21.

51. **(B)** The smallest multiple of two numbers is the smallest number that shares all of the prime factors of those two numbers. Since 5 and 2 are both prime, their product, 10 is the smallest common multiple.

52. **(A)** First, list all the prime factors of each number. Then, multiply all the prime factors that occur in either list. $12 = 2 \cdot 2 \cdot 3$. $18 = 2 \cdot 3 \cdot 3$. The prime factors that occur in either list are 2, 2, 3 and 3. So, the lowest common multiple of 12 and 18 is $2 \cdot 2 \cdot 3 \cdot 3 = 36$.

53. **(C)** Even numbers are evenly divisible by 2. 12 can be evenly divided by 2 twice. 36 can be evenly divided by 2 twice. Only 101 cannot be evenly divided by 2. Therefore, only I and II are even.

54. **(C)** According to the principles of odd and even numbers, when you multiply an even number with an odd number, you get an even number. But, if you multiply an odd number with another odd number, you will get an odd number. Therefore, only III results in an odd number.

55. **(C)** According to the principles of odd and even numbers, when you multiply an even number with an odd number, you get an even number. Also, if you add an odd number with another odd number, you will get an even number. But, if you multiply an odd number with another odd number, you will get an odd number. Therefore, both I and II will yield even numbers.

56. **(E)** There are no rules in the principles of odd and even numbers for division, therefore it is highly likely that answer choice (E) may not always be even. Test this out by substituting an even number for n, 2: $\frac{2}{2} = 1$, which is odd. Furthermore, the product of two even numbers is even, the sum of two even numbers is even, and the product of an even number and an odd number is even.

57. **(C)** I may be even if n is odd. II may be even if n is even. III is the only one that must be odd no matter what n, because any number times two will be even, and any even number minus an odd number, in this case one, will result in an odd number.

58. **(C)** Start by defining the question. It asks for the first number in a series of three consecutive whole numbers, where the third is equal to 8. So, you have three variables: n, $n + 1$, and $n + 2$. $n + 2 = 8 \Rightarrow n = 8 - 2 = 6$. The first of the three consecutive whole numbers is n, and n is equal to 6. Or, just count backwards twice from 8.

59. **(D)** Start by defining the question. It asks for the third number in a series of five consecutive odd numbers, where the fifth is equal to 15. So, you have five variables: n, $n + 2$, $n + 4$, $n + 6$, and $n + 8$. $n + 8 = 15 \Rightarrow n = 15 - 8 = 7$. The third of the five consecutive whole numbers is $n + 4$, and that is equal to 11, $7 + 4 = 11$. Alternatively, count backwards from 15.

60. **(C)** Start by defining the question. It asks for the largest of three consecutive whole numbers, where the total of all three numbers is equal to 15. So, you have three variables: n, $n + 1$, and $n + 2$, which is also your m, n, and o, respectively. $n + (n + 1) + (n + 2) = 15 \Rightarrow 3n + 3 = 15 \Rightarrow n = \frac{15 - 3}{3} = 4$. The largest of the three consecutive whole numbers is $n + 2$, and that is equal to 6, $4 + 2 = 6$.

61. **(A)** First, find the exponents of each of the prime factors in the equation. Then add one to each and multiply them together. The exponents of 2, 3, and 7 are 2, 1, and 1, respectively. $(2+1)(1+1)(1+1) = 3 \cdot 2 \cdot 2 = 12$. A has 12 positive factors including 1 and 84.

62. **(D)** First, find the exponents of each of the prime factors in the equation. Then add one to each and multiply them together. The exponents of 5, $(2)^3$, and 11 are 1, 3, and 1, respectively. $(1+1)(3+1)(1+1) = 2 \cdot 4 \cdot 2 = 16$. B has 16 positive factors including 1 and 440. The above is a method of finding all of the possible combinations of the prime factors of a number. Including the exponent zero, 5 can be taken to two powers, 0 and 1, 2 to 4 powers, 0, 1, 2, 3, and 4, and 11 to 2 powers, 0 and 1. Thus, the total number of combinations will be equal to the product of the number of possibilities for each prime.

63. **(A)** Since you perform all the operations inside the parenthesis first, you will multiply ab with the result from the parenthesis last. If either a or b is 0 then the whole equation would also be 0. Therefore, neither a nor b can be since the right side of the equation is not 0 but -6.

64. **(E)** Since you perform all the operations inside the brackets first, you will multiply e with the result from the brackets last. If e is 0 then the whole equation would also be 0. And since the right side of the equation is 3, e cannot be 0.

EXERCISE 2—FRACTIONS (p. 104)

1. **(E)** $\frac{(5 \cdot 8)+3}{8} = \frac{40+3}{8} = \frac{43}{8}$.

2. **(D)** $\frac{(2 \cdot 3)+3}{4} = \frac{8+3}{4} = \frac{11}{4}$.

3. **(B)** $\frac{(3 \cdot 12)+1}{12} = \frac{36+1}{12} = \frac{37}{12}$.

4. **(C)** $\frac{(1 \cdot 65)+1}{65} = \frac{65+1}{65} = \frac{66}{65}$.

5. **(C)** $\frac{(5 \cdot 7)+2}{7} = \frac{35+2}{7} = \frac{37}{7}$.

6. **(D)** Divide 12 by 8 to get 1 with a remainder of 4. The whole number part of the mixed number is 1 and the fraction is the remainder 4 over 8, which can be reduced to 1 over 2: $\frac{12}{8} = 12 \div 8 = 1\frac{4}{8} = 1\frac{1}{2}$.

7. **(A)** Divide 20 by 6 to get 3 with a remainder of 2. The whole number part of the mixed number is 3 and the fraction is the remainder 2 over 6, which can be reduced to 1 over 3: $\frac{20}{6} = 20 \div 6 = 3\frac{2}{6} = 3\frac{1}{3}$.

8. **(C)** Divide 23 by 13 to get 1 with a remainder of 10. The whole number part of the mixed number is 1 and the fraction is the remainder 10 over 13: $\frac{23}{13} = 23 \div 13 = 1\frac{10}{13}$.

9. **(E)** Divide 25 by 4 to get 6 with a remainder of 1. The whole number part of the mixed number is 6 and the fraction is the remainder 1 over 4: $\frac{25}{4} = 25 \div 4 = 6\frac{1}{4}$.

10. **(C)** Divide 201 by 100 to get 2 with a remainder of 1. The whole number part of the mixed number is 2 and the fraction is the remainder 1 over 100: $\frac{201}{100} = 201 \div 100 = 2\frac{1}{100}$.

11. **(B)** Divide both the numerator and denominator by the common factor of 3 to get 1 over 4. $\frac{3 \div 3}{12 \div 3} = \frac{1}{4}$.

12. **(C)** Divide both the numerator and denominator by the common factor of 27 to get 1 over 3. $\frac{27 \div 27}{81 \div 27} = \frac{1}{3}$.

13. **(B)** Divide both the numerator and denominator by the common factor of 125 to get 1 over 5: $\frac{125 \div 125}{625 \div 125} = \frac{1}{5}$.

14. **(E)** Divide both the numerator and denominator by the common factor of 13 to get 3 over 4: $\frac{39 \div 13}{52 \div 13} = \frac{3}{4}$.

15. **(E)** Divide both the numerator and denominator by the common factor of 11 to get 11 over 12: $\frac{121 \div 11}{132 \div 11} = \frac{11}{12}$.

16. **(A)** For each answer, determine the number that the numerator, four, of $\frac{4}{25}$ would have to be multiplied by to equal the numerators of the answer fractions. Then, multiply 25 by that number to see if it equals the denominators. Luckily, the first is the answer: $4 \cdot 2 = 8 \Rightarrow 25 \cdot 2 = 50$.

17. **(C)** All of the answer choices, except for C, can be reduced to 3 over 8. Because 31 is prime, $\frac{31}{81}$ is irreducible. $\frac{6}{16} = \frac{3}{8}$, $\frac{15}{40} = \frac{3}{8}$, $\frac{31}{81} \neq \frac{3}{8}$, $\frac{33}{88} = \frac{3}{8}$, and $\frac{120}{320} = \frac{12}{32} = \frac{3}{8}$.

18. **(C)** All of the answer choices, except for C, can be reduced to 3 over 4. $\frac{6}{8} = \frac{3}{4}$, $\frac{12}{16} = \frac{3}{4}$, $\frac{20}{24} = \frac{5}{6} \neq \frac{3}{4}$, $\frac{36}{48} = \frac{9}{12} = \frac{3}{4}$, and $\frac{300}{400} = \frac{3}{4}$.

19. **(B)** All of the answer choices, except for B, can be reduced to 5 over 6: $\frac{25}{30} = \frac{5}{6}$, $\frac{45}{50} = \frac{9}{10} \neq \frac{5}{6}$, $\frac{50}{60} = \frac{5}{6}$, $\frac{55}{66} = \frac{5}{6}$, and $\frac{100}{120} = \frac{50}{60} = \frac{5}{6}$.

20. **(E)** All of the answer choices, except for E, can be reduced to 1 over 6: $\frac{2}{12} = \frac{1}{6}$, $\frac{3}{18} = \frac{1}{6}$, $\frac{4}{24} = \frac{1}{6}$, $\frac{5}{30} = \frac{1}{6}$, and $\frac{6}{40} = \frac{3}{20} \neq \frac{1}{6}$.

21. **(B)** $\frac{1}{7} + \frac{2}{7} = \frac{1+2}{7} = \frac{3}{7}$.

22. **(B)** $\frac{5}{8} + \frac{1}{8} = \frac{5+1}{8} = \frac{6}{8} = \frac{3}{4}$.

23. **(D)** $\frac{12}{13} + \frac{12}{13} = \frac{12+12}{13} = \frac{24}{13}$.

24. **(B)** $\frac{3}{8} + \frac{5}{8} = \frac{3+5}{8} = \frac{8}{8} = 1$.

25. **(C)** $\frac{1}{11} + \frac{2}{11} + \frac{7}{11} = \frac{1+2+7}{11} = \frac{10}{11}$.

26. **(C)** Use the flying-X method to solve this problem. Remember to reduce the result. $\frac{3}{8} + \frac{5}{6} = \frac{3 \cdot 6}{8 \cdot 6} + \frac{5 \cdot 8}{6 \cdot 8} = \frac{18+40}{48} = \frac{58}{48} = \frac{29}{24}$.

27. **(E)** Use the flying-X method to solve this problem: $\frac{1}{8} + \frac{1}{7} = \frac{1 \cdot 7}{8 \cdot 7} + \frac{1 \cdot 8}{7 \cdot 8} = \frac{7+8}{56} = \frac{15}{56}$.

28. **(A)** Use the flying-X method to solve this problem: $\frac{1}{12} + \frac{1}{7} = \frac{1 \cdot 7}{12 \cdot 7} + \frac{1 \cdot 12}{7 \cdot 12} = \frac{7+12}{84} = \frac{19}{84}$.

29. **(B)** Use the flying-X method to solve this problem: $\frac{3}{5} + \frac{2}{11} = \frac{3 \cdot 11}{5 \cdot 11} + \frac{2 \cdot 5}{11 \cdot 5} = \frac{33+10}{55} = \frac{43}{55}$.

30. **(C)** Use the flying-X method to solve this problem. You only need to apply this to the first two fractions, because the third is a common multiple of the first two. $\frac{1}{2} + \frac{1}{3} + \frac{1}{6} = \frac{1 \cdot 3}{2 \cdot 3} + \frac{1 \cdot 2}{3 \cdot 2} = \frac{1}{6} = \frac{3+2+1}{6} = \frac{6}{6} = 1$.

31. **(D)** The common denominator for this problem is 6. Multiply the first fraction by $\frac{2}{2}$ to achieve a common denominator for the whole problem: $\frac{2}{3} + \frac{3}{6} + \frac{4}{6} = \frac{2 \cdot 2}{3 \cdot 2} + \frac{3}{6} + \frac{4}{6} = \frac{4+3+4}{6} = \frac{11}{6}$.

32. **(B)** $\frac{2}{3} - \frac{1}{3} = \frac{2-1}{3} = \frac{1}{3}$.

33. **(D)** $\frac{5}{7} - \frac{4}{7} = \frac{5-4}{7} = \frac{1}{7}$.

34. **(A)** The common denominator for this problem is 10. Multiply the second fraction by $\frac{2}{2}$ to achieve a common denominator for the whole problem: $\frac{9}{10} - \frac{1}{5} = \frac{9}{10} - \frac{1 \cdot 2}{5 \cdot 2} = \frac{9-2}{10} = \frac{7}{10}$.

35. **(A)** The common denominator for this problem is 4. Multiply the first fraction by $\frac{2}{2}$ to achieve a common denominator for the whole problem: $\frac{3}{2} - \frac{1}{4} = \frac{3 \cdot 2}{2 \cdot 2} - \frac{1}{4} = \frac{6-1}{4} = \frac{5}{4}$.

36. **(C)** Convert the mixed fraction into an improper fraction: $2\frac{1}{2} = \frac{(2 \cdot 2)+1}{2} = \frac{5}{2}$. Then, multiply the first fraction by $\frac{4}{4}$ to achieve a common denominator for the whole problem: $\frac{5 \cdot 4}{2 \cdot 4} = \frac{20}{8}$. $\frac{20}{8} - \frac{7}{8} = \frac{20-7}{8} = \frac{13}{8}$.

37. **(C)** Convert the mixed fractions into improper fractions: $2\frac{2}{3} = \frac{(2 \cdot 3)+2}{3} = \frac{8}{3}$, and $1\frac{1}{6} = \frac{(1 \cdot 6)+1}{6} = \frac{7}{6}$. Then, multiply the first fraction by $\frac{2}{2}$ to achieve a common denominator for the whole problem: $\frac{8 \cdot 2}{3 \cdot 2} = \frac{16}{6}$. Solve: $\frac{16}{6} - \frac{7}{6} = \frac{9}{6} = 1\frac{3}{6} = 1\frac{1}{2}$.

38. **(B)** Simplify the problem by canceling the 2s: $\frac{1}{2} \cdot \frac{2}{3} = \frac{1}{3}$.

39. **(B)** Simplify the problem by dividing the 2 in the numerator of the first fraction and the 4 in the denominator of the second fraction by 2: $\frac{2}{7} \cdot \frac{1}{4} = \frac{2 \cdot 1}{7 \cdot 4} = \frac{2}{28} = \frac{1}{14}$.

40. **(A)** $\frac{1}{3} \cdot \frac{1}{3} = \frac{1 \cdot 1}{3 \cdot 3} = \frac{1}{9}$.

41. **(B)** $\frac{1}{2} \cdot \frac{1}{2} \cdot \frac{1}{2} = \frac{1 \cdot 1 \cdot 1}{2 \cdot 2 \cdot 2} = \frac{1}{8}$.

42. **(A)** Simplify the problem by dividing the 3 in the denominator of the first fraction and the 3 in the numerator of the second fraction by 3. Simplify further by dividing the 4 in the denominator of the second fraction and the 4 in the numerator of the third fraction by 4: $\frac{2}{3} \cdot \frac{3}{4} \cdot \frac{4}{5} = \frac{2}{5}$.

43. **(A)** $\frac{1}{4} \cdot \frac{1}{8} \cdot 3 = \frac{1 \cdot 1 \cdot 3}{4 \cdot 8} = \frac{3}{32}$.

44. **(B)** Simplify the problem by dividing the 6 in the denominator of the second fraction and 12 by 6: $\frac{1}{3} \cdot \frac{1}{6} \cdot 12 = \frac{1}{3} \cdot 1 \cdot 2 = \frac{2}{3}$.

45. **(A)** Dividing by a fraction is the same by multiplying by its reciprocal, so invert the divisor, the second fraction, and then multiply. Simplify by dividing the 8 in the denominator of the first fraction and the 4 in the numerator of the second fraction by 4: $\frac{7}{8} \div \frac{3}{4} = \frac{7}{8} \cdot \frac{4}{3} = \frac{7}{2} \cdot \frac{1}{3} = \frac{7}{6}$.

46. **(C)** Invert the divisor, the second fraction, and then multiply. Simplify by dividing the 7 in the denominator of the first fraction and the 7 in the numerator of the second fraction by 7: $\frac{5}{7} \div \frac{1}{7} = \frac{5}{7} \cdot \frac{7}{1} = 5$.

47. **(B)** Dividing by a fraction is the same by multiplying by its reciprocal, so invert the divisor, the second fraction, and then multiply. Simplify by dividing the 12 in the denominator of the first fraction and the 12 in the numerator of the second fraction by 12: $\frac{1}{12} \div \frac{1}{12} = \frac{1}{12} \cdot \frac{12}{1} = \frac{12}{12} = 1$.

48. **(A)** Invert the divisor, the second fraction, and then multiply: $2 \div \frac{1}{11} = 2 \cdot 11 = 22$.

49. **(A)** Invert the divisor, the second fraction, and then multiply: $\frac{8}{9} \div \frac{7}{8} = \frac{8}{9} \cdot \frac{8}{7} = \frac{64}{63}$.

50. **(A)** Invert the divisor, the second fraction, and then multiply. Simplify by dividing the 10 in the denominator of the first fraction and the 5 in the numerator of the second fraction by 5: $\frac{1}{10} \div \frac{3}{5} = \frac{1}{10} \cdot \frac{5}{3} = \frac{1}{2} \cdot \frac{1}{3} = \frac{1}{6}$.

51. **(D)** $\left(\frac{1}{4}+\frac{2}{3}\right) \cdot \left(\frac{3}{2}+\frac{1}{4}\right) = \left(\frac{1 \cdot 3}{4 \cdot 3}+\frac{2 \cdot 4}{3 \cdot 4}\right) \cdot \left(\frac{3 \cdot 4}{2 \cdot 4}+\frac{1 \cdot 2}{4 \cdot 2}\right) = \frac{3+8}{12} \cdot \frac{12+2}{8} = \frac{11 \cdot 14}{12 \cdot 8} = \frac{11 \cdot 7}{12 \cdot 4} = \frac{77}{48}$.

52. **(C)** $\left(\frac{2}{3} \cdot \frac{1}{6}\right) \div \left(\frac{1}{2} \cdot \frac{1}{4}\right) = \frac{2}{18} \div \frac{1}{8} = \frac{1}{9} \cdot \frac{8}{1} = \frac{8}{9}$.

53. **(A)** $\left[\left(\frac{1}{3}+\frac{1}{2}\right) \cdot \left(\frac{2}{3}-\frac{1}{3}\right)\right] \cdot 18 = \left[\left(\frac{1 \cdot 2}{3 \cdot 2}+\frac{1 \cdot 3}{2 \cdot 3}\right) \cdot \left(\frac{1}{3}\right)\right] \cdot 18 = \left[\frac{5}{6} \cdot \frac{1}{3}\right] \cdot 18 = \frac{5}{6} \cdot 6 = 5$. Note that this problem is no harder than the others you have done. It is just longer. Solve from the inside out, one step at a time.

54. **(A)** $\left[\left(\frac{1}{3} \div \frac{1}{6}\right) \cdot \left(\frac{2}{3} \div \frac{1}{3}\right)\right] \cdot \left(\frac{1}{2}+\frac{3}{4}\right) = \left[\left(\frac{1}{3} \cdot 6\right) \cdot \left(\frac{2}{3} \cdot 3\right)\right] \cdot \left(\frac{1 \cdot 2}{2 \cdot 2}+\frac{3}{4}\right) = [2 \cdot 2] \cdot \frac{5}{4} = 5$. Do not panic at the side of this gargantuan problem. It is really just composed of many smaller problems that you can do. Solve each of those first, one at a time, and then combine the answers and solve them.

55. **(E)** $8\left(\frac{1}{3}+\frac{3}{4}\right) = 8\left(\frac{1 \cdot 4}{3 \cdot 4}+\frac{3 \cdot 3}{4 \cdot 3}\right) = 8 \cdot \frac{4+9}{12} = \frac{2 \cdot 13}{3} = \frac{26}{3}$.

56. **(C)** Use the flying-X method to solve this problem: $\frac{1}{4}-\frac{1}{5} = \frac{1 \cdot 5}{4 \cdot 5}-\frac{1 \cdot 4}{5 \cdot 4} = \frac{5-4}{20} = \frac{1}{20}$.

57. **(E)** Invert the divisor, the bottom fraction, and then multiply. Simplify by dividing the 4 in the numerator of the first fraction and the 2 in the denominator of the second fraction by 2: $\frac{4}{9} = \frac{4}{9} \cdot \frac{5}{2} = \frac{2}{9} \cdot 5 = \frac{10}{9} = 1\frac{1}{9}$.

58. **(A)** $\left(-\frac{1}{2}\right)^2+\left(\frac{1}{4}\right)^2+(-2)\left(\frac{1}{2}\right)^2 = \left(-\frac{1}{2}\right)\left(-\frac{1}{2}\right)+\left(\frac{1}{4}\right)\left(\frac{1}{4}\right)+(-2)\left(\frac{1}{2}\right)\left(\frac{1}{2}\right) = \frac{1}{4}+\frac{1}{16}-\frac{2}{4} = \frac{1}{16}-\frac{1}{4} = \frac{1-4}{16} = -\frac{3}{16}$.

59. **(D)** The fastest way to solve this problem is to convert all the fractions into decimals, and then compare them. $\frac{9}{16} = 0.5625$, $\frac{7}{10} = 0.7$, $\frac{5}{8} = 0.625$, $\frac{4}{5} = 0.8$, and $\frac{1}{2} = 0.5$. The largest fraction in this list is (D), $\frac{4}{5} = 0.8$.

60. **(D)** Jughead eats $\frac{2}{5}$ of a pound cake each day, and he eats this amount each day for three weeks, which is 21 days. $\frac{2}{5}$ lb./day • 21 days $= 21 \cdot \frac{2}{5}$ lb. $= \frac{42}{5}$ lb. $= 8\frac{2}{5}$ lb.

61. **(E)** Chompa eats $\frac{3}{8}$ of a bag of candy each day, which means he eats $\frac{21}{8}$ bags/week. If we invert that equation, we understand that every 8 weeks, Chompa eats 21. Since 42 is twice 21, 42 bags would last 16 weeks.

62. **(A)** Chiquita eats $2\frac{1}{2} = \frac{(2 \cdot 2)+1}{2} = \frac{5}{2}$ bananas each day, which means he eats $\frac{35}{2}$ bananas/week. So, Chinquita can eat 70 bananas in 4 weeks: $\frac{35}{2} \cdot 4 = 35 \cdot 2 = 70$.

63. **(B)** $3\frac{5}{16} + 2\frac{3}{4} = \frac{3 \cdot 16+5}{16} + \frac{2 \cdot 4+3}{4} = \frac{53}{16} + \frac{11}{4} = \frac{53}{16} + \frac{11 \cdot 4}{4 \cdot 4} = \frac{53+44}{16} = \frac{97}{16} = 6\frac{1}{16}$.

64. **(E)** $10\frac{1}{2} \div \frac{1}{2} = \frac{21}{2} \div \frac{1}{2} = \frac{21}{2} \cdot \frac{2}{1} = 21$.

65. **(D)** $5\frac{3}{4} \cdot 3 = \frac{23}{4} \cdot \frac{3}{1} = \frac{69}{4} = 17\frac{1}{4}$.

66. **(A)** The lowest common denominator for the first week is 24. Thus, $3\frac{1}{2} = 3\frac{12}{24}$, $1\frac{1}{4} = 1\frac{6}{24}$, $1\frac{1}{6} = 1\frac{4}{24}$, and $2\frac{3}{8} = 2\frac{9}{24}$. The total miles traveled in the first week is $3\frac{12}{24} + 1\frac{6}{24} + 1\frac{4}{24} + 2\frac{9}{24} = 7\frac{31}{24} = 8\frac{7}{24}$. The least common denominator for the second week is 16. Thus, $\frac{1}{4} = \frac{4}{16}$, $\frac{3}{8} = \frac{6}{16}$, $\frac{9}{16} = \frac{9}{16}$, $3\frac{1}{16} = 3\frac{1}{16}$, $2\frac{5}{8} = 2\frac{10}{16}$, $3\frac{3}{16} = 3\frac{3}{16}$. The total miles traveled in the second week is $\frac{4}{16} + \frac{6}{16} + \frac{9}{16} + 3\frac{1}{16} + 2\frac{10}{16} + 3\frac{3}{16} = 8\frac{33}{16} = 10\frac{1}{16}$. The common denominator for the first and second weeks is 48. Thus, $10\frac{1}{16} = 10\frac{3}{48}$ and $8\frac{7}{24} = 8\frac{14}{48}$. The difference between the second and the first weeks is $10\frac{3}{48} - 8\frac{14}{48} = 2\frac{3-14}{48} = 1\frac{51-14}{48} = 1\frac{37}{48}$.

67. **(C)** The best way to approach this problem is to compare the answers. Each 6-ft. board yields one $5\frac{1}{2}$-ft. board with $\frac{1}{2}$-ft. waste. Each 12-ft. board yields two $5\frac{1}{2}$-ft. boards with 1ft. waste. Each 22-ft. board yields four $5\frac{1}{2}$-ft. boards, with no waste. Each 24-ft. board yields four $5\frac{1}{2}$-ft. boards with two feet of waste. No 26-ft. boards are sold.

68. **(D)** $\frac{15}{16} = \frac{\$7,500}{x} \Rightarrow 15x = 16 \cdot \$7,500 = \$120,000 \Rightarrow x = \frac{\$120,000}{15} = \$8,000$.

69. **(D)** $increase = \frac{2}{3} \cdot 54,000 = 2 \cdot \frac{54,000}{3} = 2 \cdot 18,000 = 36,000$. Thus, the present population is $54,000 + 36,000 = 90,000$.

70. **(C)** Let x equal the final amount of liquid: $x = original \cdot \left(1 - \frac{1}{3}\right) \cdot \left(1 - \frac{3}{4}\right) = original \cdot \frac{2}{3} \cdot \frac{1}{4} = original \cdot \frac{1}{6}$.

71. **(C)** $\frac{7}{8}$ of capacity is 14 gallons. Thus, the tank's total capacity is $14 \div \frac{7}{8} = 14 \cdot \frac{8}{7} = 16$ gallons.

EXERCISE 3—SIGNED NUMBERS (p. 112)

1. **(E)** $3 + 1 = 4$. The original position is 3. Moving it 1 unit in the positive direction would result in 4.

2. **(D)** $5 - 2 = 3$. The original position is 5. Moving it 2 units in the negative direction would result in 3.

3. **(D)** $5 + (-2) = 5 - 2 = 3$. The original position of the counter is 5. Moving it 2 units in the negative direction would result in 3.

4. **(A)** $3 + 2 + (-7) = 5 - 7 = -2$. The original position of the counter is 3. Moving it 2 units in the positive direction would result in a 5. Moving the counter 7 units from the 5 in a negative direction would result in -2.

5. **(B)** $2 + (-4) = 2 - 4 = -2$. The original position of the counter is 2. Moving it 4 units in the negative direction would result in -2.

6. **(A)** $-2 + (-2) = -2 - 2 = -4$. The original position of the counter is -2. Moving it 2 units in the negative direction would result in -4.

7. **(C)** $4 + (-2) + (-2) = 4 - 2 + (-2) = 2 - 2 = 0$. The original position of the counter is 4. Moving it 2 units in the negative direction would result in a 2. Moving it 2 more units in the negative direction would result in 0.

8. **(A)** $-4 + (-1) + (-1) = -4 - 1 + (-1) = -5 - 1 = -6$. The original position of the counter is -4. Moving it 1 unit in the negative direction would result in a -5. Moving it 1 more unit in the negative direction would result in -6.

9. **(D)** $-4+8=8-4=4$. The original position of the counter is -4. Moving it 8 units in the positive direction would result in 4.

10. **(D)** $-2+2+(-1)=0-1=-1$.

11. **(E)** $2-(-1)=2+1=3$.

12. **(E)** $5-(-2)=5+2=7$.

13. **(D)** $0-(-4)=0+4=4$.

14. **(C)** $-2-(-1)=-2+1=1-2=-1$.

15. **(D)** $-3-(-1)-(-2)=-3+1-(-2)=-2+2=0$.

16. **(C)** $5+8+(-2)+(-1)=13-2+(-1)=11-1=10$.

17. **(C)** $12-7+6+(-1)=5+6+(-1)=11-1=10$.

18. **(C)** $3+(-3)=3-3=0$.

19. **(A)** $0+(-12)=0-12=-12$.

20. **(B)** $-3+1=1-3=-2$.

21. **(A)** $-2+(-6)=-2-6=-8$.

22. **(B)** $-2+(-3)+(-4)=-2-3+(-4)=-5-4=-9$.

23. **(D)** $100+(-99)=100-99=1$.

24. **(A)** $14-(-2)=14+2=16$.

25. **(A)** $2-(-5)=2+5=7$.

26. **(D)** $0-(-4)=0+4=4$.

27. **(D)** $-2-(-3)=-2+3=1$.

28. **(B)** $-5-(-1)-1=-5+1-1=-5$.

29. **(C)** $(5-1)+(1-5)=4+(-4)=4-4=0$.

30. **(E)** $[2-(-6)]-[-2+(-1)]=(2+6)-(-2-1)=8-(-3)=8+3=11$.

31. **(A)** $1 \cdot (-2)=-2$. An odd number of negatives will result in a negative answer.

32. **(A)** $-8 \cdot 6=-48$. An odd number of negatives will result in a negative answer.

33. **(E)** $-10 \cdot (-10)=100$. An even number of negatives will result in a positive answer.

34. **(D)** $-2 \cdot (-1) \cdot 1=2$. An even number of negatives will result in a positive answer.

35. **(A)** $-10 \cdot (-10) \cdot (-10)=-1,000$. An odd number of negatives will result in a negative answer.

36. **(D)** $-2 \cdot (-2) \cdot (-2) \cdot (-2)=16$. An even number of negatives will result in a positive answer.

37. **(D)** $-1 \cdot (-1) \cdot (-1) \cdot (-1) \cdot (-1) \cdot (-1) \cdot (-1) \cdot (-1) \cdot (-1) \cdot (-1)=1$. An even number of negatives will result in a positive answer.

38. **(B)** $4 \div (-2) = -2$ An odd number of negatives will result in a negative answer.

39. **(B)** $-12 \div 4 = -3$. An odd number of negatives will result in a negative answer.

40. **(C)** $-12 \div -12 = 1$. An even number of negatives will result in a positive answer.

41. **(C)** $[7 - (-6)] + [3 \cdot (2 - 4)] = (7 + 6) + (3 \cdot (-2)) = 13 + (-6) = 13 - 6 = 7$.

42. **(A)** $[2 \cdot (-3)][1 \cdot (-4)][2 \cdot (-1)] = (-6)(-4)(-2) = -48$.

43. **(C)** $(6 \cdot (-2)) \div (3 \cdot (-4)) = -12 \div (-12) = 1$.

44. **(B)** $\{[4 - (-3)] + [7 - (-1)]\}[-3 - (-2)] = [(4 + 3) + (7 + 1)](-3 + 2) = (7 + 8)(-1) = 15 \cdot (-1) = -15$.

45. **(D)** $[(2 \cdot (-1)) + (4 \div -2)][(-6 + 6) - (2 - 3)] = [-2 + (-2)][0 - (-1)] = (-2 - 2)(0 + 1) = -4 \cdot 1 = -4$.

46. **(B)** $(2 - 3)(3 - 2)(4 - 3)(3 - 4)(5 - 4)(4 - 5) = (-1)(1)(1)(-1)(1)(-1) = -1$.

47. **(D)** $[2(3 - 4)] + [(125 \div -25)(1 \cdot (-2))] = [2(-1)] + [(-5)(-2)] = -2 + 10 = 8$.

48. **(C)** $-\frac{1}{2} \cdot 2 \cdot (-\frac{1}{2}) \cdot 2 \cdot (-\frac{1}{2}) \cdot 2 = -1 \cdot (-1) \cdot (-1) = -1$.

49. **(B)** $[(2 \cdot 3) \div (-6 \cdot 1)][(21 \div 7) \cdot \frac{1}{3}] = (\frac{6}{-6})(\frac{3}{3}) = -1$.

50. **(A)** $(-5 \cdot (-2)) - (-2 \cdot (-5)) = 10 - 10 = 0$.

51. **(A)** $6 \div -\frac{1}{3} = 6 \cdot (-3) = -18$.

52. **(C)** $[-3 - (-3)] - [-2 - (-2)] - [-1 - (-1)] = (-3 + 3) - (-2 + 2) - (-1 + 1) = 0$.

53. **(A)** I is correct, since adding a negative number with another negative number must result in a negative number. II is incorrect, since an even number of negatives multiplied together results in positive answer. III is incorrect because it must equal 0: $n - n = 0$.

54. **(A)** I is correct, since an odd number of negatives multiplied together will result in a negative answer. II is incorrect, since an even number of negatives multiplied together results in a positive answer. III is incorrect because it must equal 0: $-n + n = 0$.

55. **(C)** I is correct, since an odd number of negatives multiplied together will result in a negative answer. II is correct because two negative numbers added together will result in a negative answer. III is incorrect, since it is an addition of two positive numbers, which must result in a positive number.

56. **(E)** I is incorrect because it must equal 0: $-n - (-n) = -n + n = 0$. II is correct, since an even number of negatives multiplied together will result in a positive answer. III is correct, since an even number of negatives multiplied together will result in a positive answer.

57. **(B)** I is incorrect because it is equal to n^6: $-n \cdot (-n) \cdot (-n) \cdot (-n) \cdot (-n) \cdot (-n) = (-n)^6 = n^6$, but $n \neq 0$. II is correct because it is equal to 0: $[(n - n) - n] - [(n - n) - n] = (0 - n) - (0 - n) = -n - (-n) = -n + n = 0$. II is incorrect because it is equal to n^2: $n \div [(n \div n) \div n] = n \div (1 \div n) = n \div \frac{1}{n} = n \cdot n = n^2, n \neq 0$.

58. **(D)** Point x between A and B is two times as far from A as from B. This means that $x - A$ is twice the distance of $B - x$. Solve the equation for x: $x - A = 2(B - x) \Rightarrow x - (-10) = 2(41 - x) \Rightarrow x + 10 = 82 - 2x \Rightarrow x + 2x = 82 - 10 \Rightarrow 3x = 72 \Rightarrow x = \frac{72}{3} = 24$.

59. **(B)** Point x between A and B is three times as far from A as from B. This means that $x - A$ is 3 times the distance of $B - x$. Solve the equation for x: $x - A = 3(B - x) \Rightarrow x - (-12) = 3(28 - x) \Rightarrow x + 12 = 84 - 3x \Rightarrow x + 3x = 84 - 12 \Rightarrow 4x = 72 \Rightarrow x = \frac{72}{4} = 18$.

60. **(E)** $|1| + |-2| + |3| + |-4| + |5| + |-6| + |7| + |-8| + |9| + |-10| + |11| + |-12| = 1 + 2 + 3 + 4 + 5 + 6 + 7 + 8 + 9 + 10 + 11 + 12 = 78$.

EXERCISE 4—DECIMALS (p. 121)

1. **(C)** $\frac{7}{10} = 0.7$.

2. **(C)** For each zero in the denominator, move the decimal one place to the left in the numerator: $\frac{73}{100} = 0.73$

3. **(B)** For each zero in the denominator, move the decimal one place to the left in the numerator: $\frac{21}{1,000} = 0.021$.

4. **(B)** Start to the right of the numerator, 557, and count one digit to the left for each zero in the denominator, 3. $\frac{557}{1,000} = 0.557$.

5. **(B)** Start to the right of the numerator, 34, and count one digit to the left for each zero in the denominator, 4. $\frac{34}{10,000} = 0.0034$.

6. **(E)** Start to the right of the numerator, 1, and count one digit to the left for each zero in the denominator, 6. $\frac{1}{1,000,000} = 0.000001$.

7. **(B)** Start to the right of the numerator, 30, and count one digit to the left for each zero in the denominator, 2. $\frac{30}{100} = 0.3$. Note that you can also reduce it first before converting it to a decimal. $\frac{30}{100} = \frac{30 \div 10}{100 \div 10} = \frac{3}{10} = 0.3$.

8. **(A)** $\frac{1,000}{4,000} = \frac{1,000 \div 1,000}{4,000 \div 1,000} = \frac{1}{4} = 0.25$.

9. **(E)** $\frac{1}{10} = 0.1$. I does not have the decimal in the right place. It has the decimal place one unit to the right of 1. II is correct, since the decimal point is one decimal place to the left of 1. III is also correct, since the decimal point is in the accurate position relative to the numerator number, one decimal place to the left of 1. The trailing zeros do not affect the value of the number.

10. **(A)** $\frac{25}{100} = 0.25$. Only I has the decimal in the correct position.

11. **(B)** $\frac{257}{100} = 2.57$.

12. **(B)** $\frac{57}{10} = 5.7$.

13. **(B)** First, convert the fraction so that the denominator is a multiple of ten. Since it is often difficult to determine what that number should be, use several steps: $\frac{5}{8} = \frac{5}{8} \cdot \frac{5}{5} = \frac{25}{40} \cdot \frac{5}{5} = \frac{125}{200} \cdot \frac{5}{5} = \frac{625}{1,000} = 0.625$. We multiply each time by the smallest number possible to put another zero at the end of the denominator, until the denominator is a multiple of ten, and no other number: $8 \rightarrow 40 \rightarrow 200 \rightarrow 1,000$.

14. **(C)** Convert the fraction so that the denominator is a multiple of ten, then reduce: $\frac{4}{5} = \frac{4}{5} \cdot \frac{2}{2} = \frac{8}{10} = 0.8$.

15. **(A)** Convert the fraction so that the denominator is a multiple of ten, then reduce: $\frac{1}{20} = \frac{1}{20} \cdot \frac{5}{5} = \frac{5}{100} = 0.05$.

16. **(B)** Convert the fraction so that the denominator is a multiple of ten, then reduce: $\frac{1}{50} = \frac{1}{50} \cdot \frac{2}{2} = \frac{2}{100} = 0.02$.

17. **(B)** Convert the fraction so that the denominator is a multiple of ten, then reduce: $\frac{3}{200} = \frac{3}{200} \cdot \frac{5}{5} = \frac{15}{1,000} = 0.015$.

18. **(D)** Convert the fraction so that the denominator is a multiple of ten, then reduce: $\frac{9}{500} = \frac{9}{500} \cdot \frac{2}{2} = \frac{18}{1,000} = 0.018$.

19. **(B)** Convert the fraction so that the denominator is a multiple of ten, then reduce: $\frac{17}{500} = \frac{17}{500} \cdot \frac{2}{2} = \frac{34}{1,000} = 0.034$.

20. **(A)** Convert the fraction so that the denominator is a multiple of ten, then reduce: $\frac{123}{200} = \frac{123}{200} \cdot \frac{5}{5} = \frac{615}{1,000} = 0.615$.

21. **(C)**
$$\begin{array}{r} 0.1 \\ +\ 0.1 \\ \hline 0.2 \end{array}$$

22. **(E)**
$$\begin{array}{r} 0.27 \\ 0.13 \\ +\ 0.55 \\ \hline 0.95 \end{array}$$

23. **(A)**   0.528
             0.116
         +   0.227
             0.871

24. **(A)**   0.700
             0.013
         +   0.028
             0.741

25. **(C)**   1.23000
         +   0.00001
             1.23001

26. **(B)**   57.100
             23.300
         +   35.012
             115.412

27. **(D)**   0.01000
             0.00100
             0.00010
         +   0.00001
             0.01111

28. **(A)**   0.9000
             0.0900
             0.0090
         +   0.0009
             0.9999

29. **(B)**   0.27000
             0.36000
             2.11170
             3.77777
         +   1.42000
             7.93947

30. **(D)**   12,279.10
              3,428.01
          +   3,444.99
             19,152.1

31. **(E)**   0.7
          −   0.3
              0.4

32. **(C)**   0.75
          −   0.25
              0.50

33. **(A)**   1.35
          −   0.35
              1.00

34. **(A)**   25.125
          −   5.357
              19.768

35. **(E)**

$$\begin{array}{r} 1.00000 \\ -\ 0.00001 \\ \hline 0.99999 \end{array}$$

36. **(D)** First, multiply as if the decimals are whole numbers: $0.2 \cdot 0.1 \Rightarrow 2 \cdot 1 = 2$. Then, count the total number of decimal places in the numbers that are being multiplied, 0.2 and 0.1. There is one place in each number, so move the decimal in the result of 2, to the right by two places: $: 2 \Rightarrow 0.02$.

37. **(D)** Multiply as if the decimals are whole numbers: $0.1 \cdot 0.1 \cdot 0.1 \Rightarrow 1 \cdot 1 \cdot 1 = 1$. Then, count the total number of decimal places in the numbers that are being multiplied, 0.1, 0.1, and 0.1. There are 3 decimal places. So, place the decimal three units to the left in the answer, starting from the right side of the last digit: 0.001.

38. **(A)** First, multiply as if the decimals are whole numbers: $1.1 \cdot 1.1 \cdot 1.1 \Rightarrow 11 \cdot 11 \cdot 11 = 1,331$. Then, count the total number of decimal places in the numbers that are being multiplied, 1.1, 1.1, and 1.1. There is a total of 3 decimal places in the problem. So, place the decimal point three units to the left in the answer, starting from the right side of the last digit: 1.331.

39. **(B)** Multiply as if the decimals are whole numbers: $0.11 \cdot 0.33 \Rightarrow 11 \cdot 33 = 363$. Count the total number of places in the numbers that are being multiplied, 0.11, 0.33. There is a total of 4 decimal places in the problem. Place the decimal four units to the left in the answer, starting from the right side of the last digit: 0.0363.

40. **(B)** First, multiply as if the decimals are whole numbers: $0.2 \cdot 0.5 \cdot 0.2 \cdot 0.5 \Rightarrow 2 \cdot 5 \cdot 2 \cdot 5 = 100$. Then, count the total number of decimal places in the numbers that are being multiplied, 0.2, 0.5, 0.2 and 0.5. There is a total of 4 decimal places in the problem. So, place the decimal point four units to the left in the answer, starting from the right side of the last digit: 0.01.

41. **(A)** First, multiply as if the decimals are whole numbers: $5 \cdot 0.25 \Rightarrow 5 \cdot 25 = 125$. Then, count the total number of decimal places in the numbers that are being multiplied, 5 and 0.25. There is a total of 2 decimal places in the problem. So, place the decimal point two units to the left in the answer, starting from the right side of the last digit: 1.25.

42. **(A)** First, multiply the numbers that have decimal components by a multiple of ten large enough that no numbers remain to the right: $0.000001 \cdot 1,000,000 = 1$. Remember the number you used. Now, multiply the numbers as normal: $10 \cdot 1 = 10$. Now, divide by the multiple of ten you used: $\frac{10}{1,000,000} = 0.00001$.

43. **(B)** First, multiply as if the decimals are whole numbers: $100 \cdot 0.00052 \Rightarrow 100 \cdot 52 = 5,200$. Then, count the total number of decimal places in the numbers that are being multiplied, 100 and 0.00052. There is a total of 5 decimal places in the problem. So, place the decimal point five units to the left in the answer, starting from the right side of the last digit: 0.052.

44. **(B)** First, multiply as if the decimals are whole numbers: $1.2 \cdot 1.2 \Rightarrow 12 \cdot 12 = 144$. Then, count the total number of decimal places in the numbers that are being multiplied, 1.2 and 1.2. There is a total of 2 decimal places in the problem. So, place the decimal point two units to the left in the answer, starting from the right side of the last digit: 1.44.

45. **(A)** None of the numbers right of the decimals are significant: $1.000 \cdot 1.000 \cdot 1.000 \cdot 1.000 = 1 \cdot 1 \cdot 1 \cdot 1 = 1$.

46. **(D)** $6 \div 0.2 = 60 \div 2 = 30$.

47. **(B)** $0.2 \div 5 = 2 \div 50 = 4 \div 100 = 0.04$.

48. **(B)** $1 \div 0.001 = 1 \div \frac{1}{1,000} = 1 \cdot \frac{1,000}{1} = 1,000$.

49. **(B)** $25.1 \div 2.51 \Rightarrow 25.1 = 2.51 \cdot 10 \Rightarrow \frac{25.1}{2.51} = 10$.

50. **(C)** $0.25 \div 8 = \frac{0.25}{8} \cdot \frac{4}{4} = \frac{1}{32} \cdot \frac{5}{5} = \frac{5}{160} \cdot \frac{5}{5} = \frac{25}{800} \cdot \frac{5}{5} = \frac{125}{4,000} \cdot \frac{5}{5} = \frac{625}{20,000} \cdot \frac{5}{5} = \frac{3,125}{100,000} = 0.03125$.

51. **(A)** That numbers are fractional does not change the fact that a number divided by itself will equal 1.

52. **(C)** $2 \div 2.5 = 20 \div 25 = \frac{20}{25} \cdot \frac{4}{4} = \frac{80}{100} = 0.8$.

53. **(E)** It is clear that the second number is the same as the first, except with the decimal point moved three places to the left. Thus, if we were to multiply 0.111 by 1,000, we would arrive at 111.

54. **(B)** Note that the second number is the same as the first, but with an extra zero before the decimal point. Thus, they differ by a factor of 10.

55. **(A)** $(0.002 \div 0.00002) \cdot 1{,}000 = 2 \div 0.02 = 20 \div 0.2 = 200 \div 2 = 100$.

56. **(C)** First, add the fractions together using the flying-x method: $\frac{3}{5} + \frac{5}{8} = \frac{3 \cdot 8}{5 \cdot 8} + \frac{5 \cdot 5}{8 \cdot 5} = \frac{24}{40} + \frac{25}{40} = \frac{49}{40} \cdot \frac{5}{5} \cdot \frac{5}{5} = \frac{1{,}225}{1{,}000} = 1.225$.

57. **(C)** An average of two numbers is the sum of the two numbers divided by two. Since the answer choices are all given in fractions, start by converting 0.75 into a fraction: $0.75 = \frac{3}{4}$. Then, add the two fractions: $\frac{2}{3} + \frac{3}{4} = \frac{2 \cdot 4}{3 \cdot 4} + \frac{3 \cdot 3}{4 \cdot 3} = \frac{8+9}{12} = \frac{17}{12}$. Next, divide by 2: $\frac{17}{12} \div 2 = \frac{17}{24}$.

58. **(B)** An average of three numbers is the sum of the three numbers divided by three. Since all of the answer choices are given in decimals, start by converting $\frac{1}{4}$ into a decimal: $\frac{1}{4} = 0.25$. Then, add the three decimals together: $0.1 + 0.01 + 0.25 = 0.36$. Next, divide by 3: $0.36 \div 3 \Rightarrow 36 \div 3 = 12 \Rightarrow 12 \div 100 = 0.12$.

59. **(D)** Convert the mixed number numerator into an improper fraction and the decimal denominator into a fraction: $12\frac{1}{3} = \frac{(12 \cdot 3)+1}{3} = \frac{37}{3}$ and $0.2 = \frac{2}{10} = \frac{1}{5}$. So, $\frac{37}{3} \div \frac{1}{5} = \frac{37}{3} \cdot \frac{5}{1} = \frac{185}{3}$.

60. **(B)** $0.1 = \frac{1}{10}$. Starting with the parenthesis, solve the equation following basic orders of operations: $\frac{1}{10}\left[\frac{1}{3} - 2\left(\frac{1}{2} - \frac{1}{4}\right)\right] = \frac{1}{10}\left[\frac{1}{3} - 2\left(\frac{1 \cdot 2}{2 \cdot 2} - \frac{1}{4}\right)\right] = \frac{1}{10}\left[\frac{1}{3} - \frac{2}{4}\right] = \frac{1}{10}\left[\frac{1 \cdot 4}{3 \cdot 4} - \frac{2 \cdot 3}{4 \cdot 3}\right] = \frac{1}{10}\left[-\frac{2}{12}\right] = -\frac{2}{120} = -\frac{1}{60}$.

61. **(D)** Add together the savings for each month: $\$4.56 + \$3.82 + \$5.06 = \$13.44$.

62. **(C)** The range of measurements for a rod of diameter 1.51 ± 0.015 inches is $1.510 - 0.015 = 1.495$ inches to $1.510 + 0.015 = 1.525$ inches.

63. **(C)** Add to find the total deductions: $\$3.05 + \$5.68 = \$8.73$. Subtract the total deductions from the salary to determine the check amount: $\$190.57 - \$8.73 = \$181.84$.

64. **(B)** The outer radius minus the inner radius is equal to the thickness of the metal: $2.84 - 1.94 = 0.90$.

65. **(C)** Add the daily earnings to find the total earnings: $\$20.56 + \$32.90 + \$20.78 = \$74.24$. Divide the total earnings by 2 to find out what Pete has left: $\$74.24 \div 2 = \$37.12$.

66. **(C)** Find the cost of $3\frac{1}{2}$ pounds of meat: $\$1.69 \cdot 3.5 \approx \$5.92$. Find the cost of 20 lemons: $\$0.60 \div 12 = \$0.05$ for 1 lemon and $\$0.05 \cdot 20 = \$1.00$ for 20 lemons. Add the cost of meat and the cost of lemons: $\$5.92 + \$1.00 = \$6.92$.

67. **(A)** Subtract the weight of the empty reel from the total weight to find the weight of the cable: $1{,}279$ lb. $- 285$ lb. $= 994$ lb. Each foot of cable weighs 7.1 lb. Therefore, to find the number of feet of cable on the reel, divide 994 by 7.1: $994 \div 7.1 = 9{,}940 \div 71 = 140$.

68. **(D)** Each fastener costs: $\$4.15 \div 100 = \$0.0415$. Thus, 345 fasteners cost: $345 \cdot 0.0415 = \$14.32$.

EXERCISE 5—PERCENTS (p. 128)

1. **(E)** To express a decimal as a percent, move the decimal point two units to the right and add a percent sign at the right of the number: $0.79 = 79\%$.

2. **(A)** To express a decimal as a percent, move the decimal point two units to the right and add a percent sign at the right of the number: $0.55 = 55\%$.

3. **(B)** To express a decimal as a percent, move the decimal point two units to the right and add a percent sign at the right of the number: $0.111 = 11.1\%$.

4. **(B)** To express a decimal as a percent, move the decimal point two units to the right and add a percent sign at the right of the number: $0.125 = 12.5\%$.

5. **(C)** To express a decimal as a percent, move the decimal point two units to the right and add a percent sign at the right of the number: $0.5555 = 55.55\%$.

6. **(A)** To express a decimal as a percent, move the decimal point two units to the right and add a percent sign at the right of the number: $0.3 = 30\%$.

7. **(C)** To express a decimal as a percent, move the decimal point two units to the right and add a percent sign at the right of the number: $0.7500 = 75\%$.

8. **(B)** To express a decimal as a percent, move the decimal point two units to the right and add a percent sign at the right of the number: $2.45 = 245\%$.

9. **(A)** To express a decimal as a percent, move the decimal point two units to the right and add a percent sign at the right of the number: $1.25 = 125\%$.

10. **(A)** To express a decimal as a percent, move the decimal point two units to the right and add a percent sign at the right of the number: $10 = 1,000\%$.

11. **(B)** To express a decimal as a percent, move the decimal point two units to the right and add a percent sign at the right of the number: $0.015 = 1.5\%$.

12. **(B)** To express a decimal as a percent, move the decimal point two units to the right and add a percent sign at the right of the number: $0.099 = 9.9\%$.

13. **(A)** To express a decimal as a percent, move the decimal point two units to the right and add a percent sign at the right of the number: $0.0333 = 3.33\%$.

14. **(A)** To express a decimal as a percent, move the decimal point two units to the right and add a percent sign at the right of the number: $0.001 = 0.1\%$.

15. **(A)** To express a decimal as a percent, move the decimal point two units to the right and add a percent sign at the right of the number: $0.0100 = 1\%$.

16. **(C)** To express a percent as a decimal, remove the percent sign and move the decimal point two units to the left: $25\% = 0.25$.

17. **(B)** To express a percent as a decimal, remove the percent sign and move the decimal point two units to the left: $56\% = 0.56$.

18. **(D)** To express a percent as a decimal, remove the percent sign and move the decimal point two units to the left: $10\% = 0.1$.

19. **(C)** To express a percent as a decimal, remove the percent sign and move the decimal point two units to the left: $100\% = 1$.

20. **(C)** To express a percent as a decimal, remove the percent sign and move the decimal point two units to the left: $250\% = 2.5$.

21. **(C)** To express a percent as a decimal, remove the percent sign and move the decimal point two units to the left: $1,000\% = 10.0$.

22. **(D)** To express a percent as a decimal, remove the percent sign and move the decimal point two units to the left: $0.25\% = 0.0025$.

23. **(E)** To express a percent as a decimal, remove the percent sign and move the decimal point two units to the left: $0.099\% = 0.00099$.

24. **(D)** To express a percent as a decimal, remove the percent sign and move the decimal point two units to the left: $0.0988\% = 0.000988$.

25. **(D)** To express a percent as a decimal, remove the percent sign and move the decimal point two units to the left: $0.00100\% = 0.00001$.

26. **(B)** To solve this problem, first, convert the fraction into a decimal number. Then, move the decimal point two units to the right and add a percent sign at the end of the number: $\frac{1}{10} = 0.1 = 10\%$.

27. **(C)** To solve this problem, first, convert the fraction into a decimal number. Then, move the decimal point two units to the right and add a percent sign at the end of the number: $\frac{3}{100} = 0.03 = 3\%$.

28. **(A)** To solve this problem, first, convert the fraction into a decimal number. Then, move the decimal point two units to the right and add a percent sign at the end of the number: $\frac{99}{100} = 0.99 = 99\%$.

29. **(C)** To solve this problem, first, convert the fraction into a decimal number. Then, move the decimal point two units to the right and add a percent sign at the end of the number: $\frac{100}{1,000} = \frac{1}{10} = 0.1 = 10\%$.

30. **(A)** To solve this problem, first, convert the fraction into a decimal number. Then, move the decimal point two units to the right and add a percent sign at the end of the number: $\frac{333}{100} = 3.33 = 333\%$.

31. **(B)** To solve this problem, first, convert the fraction into a decimal number. Then, move the decimal point two units to the right and add a percent sign at the end of the number: $\frac{9}{1,000} = 0.009 = 0.9\%$.

32. **(E)** To solve this problem, first, convert the fraction into a decimal number. Then, move the decimal point two units to the right and add a percent sign at the end of the number: $\frac{3}{4} = 0.75 = 75\%$.

33. **(D)** To solve this problem, first, convert the fraction into a decimal number. Then, move the decimal point two units to the right and add a percent sign at the end of the number: $\frac{4}{5} = 0.8 = 80\%$.

34. **(B)** To solve this problem, first, convert the fraction into a decimal number. Then, move the decimal point two units to the right and add a percent sign at the end of the number: $\frac{3}{50} = 0.06 = 6\%$.

35. **(D)** To solve this problem, first, convert the fraction into a decimal number. Then, move the decimal point two units to the right and add a percent sign at the end of the number: $\frac{3}{75} = 0.04 = 4\%$.

36. **(C)** To solve this problem, first, convert the fraction into a decimal number. Then, move the decimal point two units to the right and add a percent sign at the end of the number: $\frac{6}{500} = 0.012 = 1.2\%$.

37. **(D)** To solve this problem, first, convert the fraction into a decimal number. Then, move the decimal point two units to the right and add a percent sign at the end of the number: $\frac{111}{555} = 0.2 = 20\%$.

38. **(B)** To solve this problem, first, convert the fraction into a decimal number. Then, move the decimal point two units to the right and add a percent sign at the end of the number: $\frac{8}{5,000} = 0.0016 = 0.16\%$.

39. **(A)** To solve this problem, first, convert the fraction into a decimal number. Then, move the decimal point two units to the right and add a percent sign at the end of the number: $1\frac{1}{10} = 1.1 = 110\%$.

40. **(A)** To solve this problem, first, convert the fraction into a decimal number. Then, move the decimal point two units to the right and add a percent sign at the end of the number: $9\frac{99}{100} = 9.99 = 999\%$.

41. **(D)** To solve this problem, first, convert the fraction into a decimal number. Then, move the decimal point two units to the right and add a percent sign at the end of the number: $3\frac{1}{2} = 3.5 = 350\%$.

42. **(A)** To solve this problem, first, convert the fraction into a decimal number. Then, move the decimal point two units to the right and add a percent sign at the end of the number: $1\frac{3}{4} = 1.75 = 175\%$.

43. **(E)** To solve this problem, first, convert the fraction into a decimal number. Then, move the decimal point two units to the right and add a percent sign at the end of the number: $10\frac{1}{5} = 10.2 = 1,020\%$.

44. **(A)** To solve this problem, first, convert the fraction into a decimal number. Then, move the decimal point two units to the right and add a percent sign at the end of the number: $3\frac{1}{50} = 3.02 = 302\%$.

45. **(B)** To solve this problem, first, convert the fraction into a decimal number. Then, move the decimal point two units to the right and add a percent sign at the end of the number: $\frac{111}{100} = 1.11 = 111\%$.

46. **(D)** To solve this problem, first, convert the fraction into a decimal number. Then, move the decimal point two units to the right and add a percent sign at the end of the number: $\frac{7}{2} = 3.5 = 350\%$.

47. **(A)** To solve this problem, first, convert the fraction into a decimal number. Then, move the decimal point two units to the right and add a percent sign at the end of the number: $\frac{13}{5} = 2.6 = 260\%$.

48. **(B)** To solve this problem, first, convert the fraction into a decimal number. Then, move the decimal point two units to the right and add a percent sign at the end of the number: $\frac{9}{8} = 1.125 = 112.5\%$.

49. **(A)** To solve this problem, first, convert the fraction into a decimal number. Then, move the decimal point two units to the right and add a percent sign at the end of the number: $\frac{22}{5} = 4.4 = 440\%$.

50. **(A)** To solve this problem, first, convert the fraction into a decimal number. Then, move the decimal point two units to the right and add a percent sign at the end of the number: $\frac{33}{6} = 5.5 = 550\%$.

51. **(C)** First, convert the percent to a fraction. Remember that a percent just means that the denominator is 100: $18\% = \frac{18}{100}$.

52. **(C)** Convert the percentage into a decimal number by removing the percent sign and moving the decimal point two units to the left: $80\% = 0.8$.

53. **(B)** First, convert the percent to a fraction. Remember that a percent just means that the denominator is 100: $45\% = \frac{45}{100}$. Then, simplify the fraction: $\frac{45}{100} = \frac{45 \div 5}{100 \div 5} = \frac{9}{20}$.

54. **(B)** Convert the percentage into a decimal number by removing the percent sign and moving the decimal point two units to the left: $7\% = 0.07$.

55. **(B)** Convert the percentage into a decimal number by removing the percent sign and moving the decimal point two units to the left: $13.2\% = 0.132$.

56. **(B)** Convert the percentage into a decimal number by removing the percent sign and moving the decimal point two units to the left: $1.111\% = 0.01111$.

57. **(C)** Convert the percentage into a decimal number by removing the percent sign and moving the decimal point two units to the left: $10.101\% = 0.10101$.

58. **(B)** Convert the percent to a fraction. Remember that a percent just means that the denominator is 100: $33\% = \frac{33}{100}$.

59. **(C)** First, convert the percent to a fraction. Remember that a percent just means that the denominator is 100: $80.1\% = \frac{80.1}{100} = \frac{80.1 \cdot 10}{100 \cdot 10} = \frac{801}{1,000}$. Then, convert it to a decimal number: $80.1\% = 0.801$. Only answer choice C is an equivalent form of 80.1%.

60. **(D)** First, convert the percent to a fraction. Remember that a percent just means that the denominator is 100: $0.02\% = \frac{0.02}{100} = \frac{0.02 \cdot 100}{100 \cdot 100} = \frac{2}{10,000}$. Then, simplify the fraction: $\frac{2}{10,000} = \frac{2 \div 2}{10,000 \div 2} = \frac{1}{5,000}$.

61. **(D)** First, convert the percent to a fraction. Remember that a percent just means that the denominator is 100: $250\% = \frac{250}{100}$. Then, convert it to a decimal number: $250\% = 2.5$. Only answer choice D is an equivalent form of 250%.

62. **(C)** First, convert the percent to a fraction. Remember that a percent just means that the denominator is 100: $1,000\% = \frac{1,000}{100}$. Then, convert it to a decimal number: $1,000\% = 10$. Only answer choice C is an equivalent form of 1,000%.

63. **(B)** Add the percents as if they are regular numbers. Remember to add the percent sign at the end of the answer: $37\% + 42\% = 79\%$.

64. **(B)** Add the percents as if they are regular numbers. Remember to add the percent sign at the end of the answer: $210\% + 21\% = 231\%$.

65. **(B)** Add the percents as if they are regular numbers. Remember to add the percent sign at the end of the answer: $8\% + 9\% + 10\% + 110\% = 137\%$.

66. **(B)** Add the percents as if they are regular numbers. Remember to add the percent sign at the end of the answer: $254\% + 166\% + 342\% = 762\%$.

67. **(E)** Add the percents as if they are regular numbers. Remember to add the percent sign at the end of the answer: $0.02\% + 0.005\% = 0.025\%$.

68. **(C)** Subtract the percents as if they are regular numbers. Remember to add the percent sign at the end of the answer: $33\% - 25\% = 8\%$.

69. **(D)** Subtract the percents as if they are regular numbers. Remember to add the percent sign at the end of the answer: $100\% - 0.99\% = 99.01\%$.

70. **(B)** Subtract the percents as if they are regular numbers. Remember to add the percent sign at the end of the answer: $222\% - 22.2\% = 199.8\%$.

71. **(B)** This is an addition word problem, just add the percentages of the pages he read on Monday and Tuesday together: $15\% + 25\% = 40\%$.

72. **(D)** This is an addition word problem. Add the percentages of the lawn she mowed from 9-12 and 12-3 together: $35\% + 50\% = 85\%$.

73. **(C)** On Monday, 8% of the project is scheduled to be completed. On Tuesday, another 17% is scheduled to be completed. And, on Wednesday, another 25% is scheduled to be completed. The combined percentages of the project scheduled to be completed for these three days is 50%: $8\% + 17\% + 25\% = 50\%$. So, by the end of Wednesday one half, 50%, of the work is scheduled to be completed.

74. **(C)** This is an addition problem. Add the percent of the project scheduled to be completed Monday with the percent of the project scheduled to be completed Tuesday to arrive at the answer: $8\% + 17\% = 25\%$.

75. **(D)** You know that at the end of Wednesday one half of the project is scheduled to be completed: $8\% + 17\% + 25\% = 50\%$. And, at the end of Thursday, 83% of the project is scheduled to be completed: $8\% + 17\% + 25\% + 33\% = 83\%$. This means that, if the production is on schedule, $\frac{2}{3}$, 66.6%, of the work will be completed sometime Thursday.

76. **(D)** This is an addition problem. First, convert the added amount of water, $\frac{1}{4}$ of the bucket's capacity, into a percent: $\frac{1}{4} = 0.25 = 25\%$. Next, add the amount of water already in the bucket to the amount of water just added: $33\% + 25\% = 58\%$.

77. **(D)** First, find the amount of allowance that Edward spent: $15\% + 25\% = 40\%$. Next, subtract this amount from his total allowance to find out how much allowance he has left. Since we are working with percentages, the total amount of allowance Edward has is equal to 100%. Thus, $100\% - 40\% = 60\%$.

78. **(C)** To multiply percentages, first, convert the percents to decimals. Multiply the decimals together and then convert the answer back into a percent. $50\% \cdot 50\% = 0.5 \cdot 0.5 = 0.25 = 25\%$.

79. **(C)** To multiply percentages, first, convert the percents to decimals. Multiply the decimals together and then convert the answer back into a percent. $1\% \cdot 100\% = 0.01 \cdot 1 = 0.01 = 1\%$.

80. **(C)** This is a "What is X Percent of Some Quantity" question. Set up the equation. Remember that "of" indicates multiplication. $66\% \cdot 100 = 0.66 \cdot 100 = 66$. So, 66 of the marbles in the jar are red.

81. **(D)** This is a "What is X Percent of Some Quantity" question. Set up the equation. Remember that "of" indicates multiplication. $75\% \cdot 240 = 0.75 \cdot 240 = 180$. So, there are 180 sedans in this particular parking lot.

82. **(C)** This is a "What is X Percent of Some Quantity" question. Set up the equation. Remember that "of" indicates multiplication. $0.1\% \cdot 100 = 0.001 \cdot 189,000 = 189$. So, 189 of the names have the initials B.D.

83. **(C)** This is a "What Percent Is This of That" question. Note that $of = 10$ and $is = 1$. Set up the "is and of" equation to solve: $\frac{is}{of} = \frac{\%}{100} \Rightarrow \frac{1}{10} = 0.1 = \frac{\%}{100} \Rightarrow \% = 100 \cdot 0.1 = 10\%$.

84. **(C)** This is a "What Percent Is This of That" question. Note that $of = 12$ and $is = 3$. Set up the "is and of" equation to solve: $\frac{is}{of} = \frac{\%}{100} \Rightarrow \frac{3}{12} = \frac{1}{4} \Rightarrow .25 = \frac{\%}{100} \Rightarrow \% = .25 \cdot 100 = 25\%$.

85. **(A)** This is a "What Percent Is This of That" question. Note that $of = 40$ and $is = 50$. Set up the "is and of" equation to solve: $\frac{is}{of} = \frac{\%}{100} \Rightarrow \frac{50}{40} = 1.25 = 125\%$.

86. **(D)** This is a "What Percent Is This of That" question. Note that $of = 100$ and $is = 10$. Set up the "is and of" equation to solve: $\frac{is}{of} = \frac{\%}{100} \Rightarrow \frac{is}{100} = \frac{10}{100} \Rightarrow is = 100 \cdot 0.1 = 10$.

87. **(D)** This is a "What Percent Is This of That" question. Note that $of = 12$ and $is = 250$. Set up the "is and of" equation to solve: $\frac{is}{of} = \frac{\%}{100} \Rightarrow \frac{is}{12} = \frac{250}{100} \Rightarrow is = 12 \cdot 2.5 = 30$.

88. **(C)** This is a "What Percent Is This of That" question. Note that $of =$ Patty's age $= 48$ and $is =$ Al's age $= 36$. Set up the "is and of" equation to solve: $\frac{is}{of} = \frac{\%}{100} \Rightarrow \frac{36}{48} = \frac{3}{4} = 0.75 = \frac{\%}{100} \Rightarrow \% = 0.75 \cdot 100 = 75\%$.

89. **(D)** First, find out the total number of employees at the bank: $25 + 15 = 40$. This question can be simplified to "What percent is 25 women out of 40 employees?" Set up the "is and of" equation and solve. Note that $of =$ total number of employees $= 40$ and $is =$ number of women employees $= 25$. $\frac{is}{of} = \frac{\%}{100} \Rightarrow \frac{25}{40} = \frac{5}{8} = 0.625 = 62.5\%$.

90. **(E)** This is a "What Percent Is This of That" question. Note that $of =$ old price $= 5$ and $is =$ new price $= 8$ Set up the "is and of" equation to solve: $\frac{is}{of} = \frac{\%}{100} \Rightarrow \frac{8}{5} = 1.6 = \frac{\%}{100} \Rightarrow \% = 1.6 \cdot 100 = 160\%$.

91. **(C)** This is a "What Percent Is This of That" question. Note that $of =$ new price $= 8$ and $is =$ old price $= 5$ Set up the "is and of" equation to solve: $\frac{is}{of} = \frac{\%}{100} \Rightarrow \frac{25}{40} = \frac{5}{8} = 0.625 = 62.5\%$.

92. **(D)** This is a "What Percent Is This of That" question. Note that $of =$ old price $= 200$ and $is =$ new price $= 160$. Set up the "is and of" equation to solve: $\frac{is}{of} = \frac{\%}{100} \Rightarrow \frac{160}{200} = \frac{4}{5} = 0.8 = \frac{\%}{100} \Rightarrow \% = 0.8 \cdot 100 = 80\%$.

93. **(E)** This is a "What Percent Is This of That" question. Note that $of =$ new price $= 160$ and $is =$ old price $= 200$ Set up the "is and of" equation to solve: $\frac{is}{of} = \frac{\%}{100} \Rightarrow \frac{200}{160} = \frac{4}{5} = 0.8 = \frac{\%}{100} \Rightarrow \% = 1.25 \cdot 100 = 125\%$.

94. **(A)** This is a percent change word problem. Set up the equation: $\frac{change}{original} = \frac{200-160}{200} = \frac{40}{200} = \frac{20}{100} = 20\%$.

95. **(B)** This is a "What Percent Is This of That" question. Note that $of =$ enrollees for week $2 = 25$ and $is =$ enrollees for week $1 = 10$ Set up the "is and of" equation to solve: $\frac{is}{of} = \frac{\%}{100} \Rightarrow \frac{10}{25} = \frac{2}{5} = 0.4 = 40\%$.

96. **(C)** This is a "What Percent Is This of That" question. Note that $of =$ enrollees for week $5 = 30$ and $is =$ enrollees for week $4 = 15$. Set up the "is and of" equation to solve: $\frac{is}{of} = \frac{\%}{100} \Rightarrow \frac{15}{30} = \frac{1}{2} = 0.5 = 50\%$.

97. **(E)** This is a "What Percent Is This of That" question. Note that $of =$ enrollees for week $4 = 15$ and $is =$ enrollees for week $5 = 30$. Set up the "is and of" equation to solve: $\frac{is}{of} = \frac{\%}{100} \Rightarrow \frac{30}{15} = 2 = 200\%$.

98. **(D)** This is a percent change word problem. Set up the equation: $\frac{change}{original} = \frac{25-10}{10} = \frac{15}{10} = 1.5 = 150\%$.

99. **(A)** This is a percent change word problem. Set up the equation: $\frac{change}{original} = \frac{20-15}{20} = \frac{5}{20} = \frac{1}{4} = 0.25 = 25\%$.

100. **(D)** This is a "What is X Percent of Some Quantity" question. This question can be reworded as "What is 8% of $30?" Set up the equation. Remember that "of" indicates multiplication. $8\% \cdot 35 = 0.08 \cdot 35 = 2.8$. So, the sales tax on the textbook is $2.80.

101. **(D)** This is a "What is X Percent of Some Quantity" question. Set up the equation. First, find the cost of an 8.5% sales tax. Then, add that tax to the textbook cost. $8.5\% \cdot 30 = 0.085 \cdot 30 = 2.55$. So, the sales tax on the textbook is $2.55. Therefore, the total cost of this one textbooks is $32.55, $30 + $2.55 = 32.55.

102. **(C)** This is a "What is X Percent of Some Quantity" question. Remember that "of" indicates multiplication. $25\% \cdot 80 = 0.25 \cdot 80 = 20$.

103. **(B)** This is a "What is X Percent of Some Quantity" question. Remember that "of" indicates multiplication. $2.3\% \cdot 90 = 0.023 \cdot 90 = 2.07$.

104. **(A)** First, find out how many questions Gertrude got right on the entire test. This would be 80% of 50 questions, which is a "What is X Percent of Some Quantity" question. Then, find the difference between how many questions she answered correctly on the first 40 questions of the test to how many questions she answered correctly on the entire test to find out how many of the last 10 questions she answered correctly. $80\% \cdot 50 = 0.8 \cdot 50 = 40$. $40 - 34 = 6$.

105. **(C)** This is a "What Percent Is This of That" question. Note that $of = 1,000$ and $is = 105$. Set up the "is and of" equation to solve: $\frac{is}{of} = \frac{\%}{100} \Rightarrow \frac{105}{1000} = 0.105 = 10.5\%$.

106. **(C)** This is a "What Percent Is This of That" question. Note that $of = 50$ and $is = 40$. Set up the "is and of" equation to solve: $\frac{is}{of} = \frac{\%}{100} \Rightarrow \frac{40}{50} = \frac{4}{5} = 0.8 = 80\%$.

107. **(E)** This is a "What Percent Is This of That" question. Note that $of = 20$ and $is = 80$. Set up the "is and of" equation to solve: $\frac{is}{of} = \frac{\%}{100} \Rightarrow \frac{80}{20} = 4 = 400\%$.

108. **(C)** First, find the total number of students in the junior class: $300 + 500 = 800$. Then, set up the "is and of" equation and solve. Note that this question can be reworded to say "What percent is 500 out of 800 students?" Note that $of = 800$ and $is = $ number junior class students who didn't enroll in test prep $= 500$. $\frac{is}{of} = \frac{\%}{100} \Rightarrow \frac{500}{800} = \frac{5}{8} = 0.625 = 62.5\%$.

109. **(E)** This is a percent change word problem. Set up the equation: $\frac{change}{original} = \frac{0.05 - 0.02}{0.02} = \frac{0.03}{0.02} = \frac{3}{2} = 1.5 = 150\%$.

110. **(D)** First, find the number of students who did not receive A's: $30 - 6 = 24$. Then, set up the "is and of" equation and solve. Note that this question can be reworded to say "What percent is 24 out of 30 students in the class?" Note that $of = 30$ and $is = 24$. $\frac{is}{of} = \frac{\%}{100} \Rightarrow \frac{24}{30} = \frac{4}{5} = 0.8 = 80\%$.

111. **(D)** This is a "What Percent Is This of That" question. This question can be reworded as "What is 10 out of 12 games?" Note that $of = $ total number of games $= 12$ and $is = $ number of games the Wildcats won $= 10$. Set up the "is and of" equation to solve: $\frac{is}{of} = \frac{\%}{100} \Rightarrow \frac{10}{12} = \frac{5}{6} = 0.833\cdots = 83\%$.

112. **(E)** Find the total number of free throws attempted and the total number of free throws made. Divide the number of those made by those attempted: $\frac{86 + 46}{100 + 50} = \frac{132}{150} = 88\%$.

113. **(D)** This question can be simplified into "$256 is 80% of what?" Note that since it is discounted by 20%, the discounted price is the same as 80% of the original price: $100\% - 20\% = 80\%$. Set up a "This is X Percent of What" equation. Note that $\% = 80$ and $is = $ discounted price of stereo $= \$256$. Set up the "is and of" equation to solve: $\frac{is}{of} = \frac{\%}{100} \Rightarrow \frac{256}{x} = \frac{80}{100} \Rightarrow 80x = 256 \cdot 100 = 25,600 \Rightarrow x = \frac{25,600}{80} = 320$. The original price of the stereo was \$320.

114. **(B)** This question can be simplified into "136 is equal to 85% of the total number of jellybeans." Since the bag contains only red and black jellybeans, if 15% are red, then, 85% must be black: $100\% - 15\% = 85\%$. Set up a "is and of" equation and solve. Note that $\% = 85$ and $is = $ number of red jellybeans $= 136$. $\frac{is}{of} = \frac{\%}{100} \Rightarrow \frac{136}{x} = \frac{85}{100} \Rightarrow 85x = 136 \cdot 100 = 13,600 \Rightarrow x = \frac{13,600}{85} = 160$. There is a total of 160 jellybeans in the bag.

115. **(D)** $\$118.80 \cdot 0.20 = \$23.76$. $\$118.80 - \$23.76 = \$95.04$. Alternatively, $\$118.80 \cdot 0.80 = \$95.04$.

116. **(E)** Add the figures given for housing, food, clothing, and taxes: $26.2\% + 28.4\% + 12.0\% + 12.7\% = 79.3\%$. Subtract this total from 100% to find the percent for miscellaneous items: $100.0\% - 79.3\% = 20.7\%$.

117. **(C)** price of shuttlecocks $= 24 \cdot \$0.35 = \$8.40$. price of rackets $= 4 \cdot \$2.75 = \$11.00$. total price $= \$8.40 + \$11.00 = \$19.40$. Because the discount is 30% of the total, the actual cost is $100\% - 30\% = 70\%$ of the total. Thus, the actual cost is $70\% \cdot \$19.40 = 0.7 \cdot \$19.40 = \$13.58$.

118. **(E)** Subtract weight of wood after drying from original weight of wood to find amount of moisture in wood: $10 - 8 = 2$ ounces of wood. moisture content $= \frac{2\ ounces}{10\ ounces} = 0.2 = 20\%$.

119. **(A)** Find the number of each kind of coin: there are $10\% \cdot 800 = 0.1 \cdot 800 = 80$ dimes, $30\% \cdot 800 = 0.3 \cdot 800 = 240$ nickels, and $(100\% - 10\% - 30\%) \cdot 800 = 60\% \cdot 800 = 0.6 \cdot 800 = 480$ quarters. Thus, there are $80 \cdot 0.10 + 240 \cdot .05 + 480 \cdot 0.25 = 8.00 + 12.00 + 120.00 = 140.00$ dollars in the bag.

120. **(C)** The first solution contains 20% of 6 quarts of alcohol; the alcohol content $= 0.20 \cdot 6 = 1.2$ quarts. The second solution contains 60% of 4 quarts of alcohol; the alcohol content $= 0.60 \cdot 4 = 2.4$ quarts. The mixture contains: $1.2 + 2.4 = 3.6$ quarts of alcohol; $6 + 4 = 10$ quarts of liquid. The mixture's alcoholic strength of mixture $= 3.6 \div 10 = 36\%$.

121. **(D)** $2\frac{1}{2}\%$ of insured value $= \$348$. insured value $= \$348 \div 2\frac{1}{2}\% = \$348 \div 0.025 = \$13,920$. $\$13,920$ is 80% of the total value, so the total value is $\frac{\$13,920}{80\%} = \frac{\$13,920}{0.8} = \$13,920 \div \frac{4}{5} = \$13,920 \cdot \frac{5}{4} = \$13,920 \cdot 1.25 = \$17,400$.

122. **(D)** $\frac{1}{5} \cdot 35 = 7$ hours sorting mail; $\frac{1}{2} \cdot 35 = 17\frac{1}{2}$ hours filing; $\frac{1}{7} \cdot 35 = 5$ hours reception. Thus, $29\frac{1}{2}$ hours are accounted for, leaving $5\frac{1}{2}$ hours spend on messenger work. % messenger work $= 5\frac{1}{2} \div 35 = \frac{11}{2} \div \frac{35}{1} = \frac{11}{2} \cdot \frac{1}{35} = \frac{11}{70} = 0.15\frac{5}{7} = 15\frac{5}{7}\%$.

123. **(C)** $\frac{1,152 \text{ boys}}{80\%} = \frac{1,152}{0.8} = 1,152 \div \frac{4}{5} = 1,152 \cdot \frac{5}{4} = 1,440$ boys are enrolled. Thus, total students $= \frac{1,440}{40\%} = 1,440 \div \frac{2}{5} = 1,440 \cdot \frac{5}{2} = 3,600$.

124. **(B)** % raise $= \frac{\$27,500 - \$25,000}{\$25,000} = \frac{\$2,500}{\$25,000} = 0.1 = 10\%$.

125. **(B)** % population increase $= \frac{100,000 - 80,000}{80,000} = \frac{20,000}{80,000} = .25 = 25\%$.

126. **(D)** % decrease $= \frac{\$25 - \$21}{\$25} = \frac{\$4}{\$25} = \frac{16}{100} = 16\%$.

127. **(A)** This item can be answered without any calculation. Whenever something is doubled, the percent increase is 100%.

128. **(A)** % decrease $= \frac{200 - 150}{200} = \frac{50}{200} = 0.25 = 25\%$.

EXERCISE 6—MEAN, MEDIAN, AND MODE (p. 137)

1. **(A)** This is a basic average problem; just take the sum of all the numbers and divide that by the number of quantities involved: $\frac{8 + 6 + 16}{3} = \frac{30}{3} = 10$.

2. **(D)** This is a basic average problem; just take the sum of all the numbers and divide that by the number of quantities involved: $\frac{0 + 50}{2} = \frac{50}{2} = 25$.

3. **(C)** This is a basic average problem; just take the sum of all the numbers and divide that by the number of quantities involved: $\frac{5 + 11 + 12 + 8}{4} = \frac{36}{4} = 9$.

4. **(B)** This is a basic average problem; just take the sum of all the numbers and divide that by the number of quantities involved: $\frac{25 + 28 + 21 + 30 + 36}{5} = \frac{140}{5} = 28$.

5. **(C)** This is a basic average problem; just take the sum of all the numbers and divide that by the number of quantities involved: $\frac{\frac{1}{4} + \frac{3}{4} + \frac{2}{8} + \frac{1}{2} + \frac{3}{8}}{5} = \frac{\frac{2}{8} + \frac{6}{8} + \frac{2}{8} + \frac{4}{8} + \frac{3}{8}}{5} = \frac{\frac{20}{8}}{5} = \frac{20}{40} = \frac{1}{2}$.

6. **(E)** This is a basic average problem; just take the sum of all the numbers and divide that by the number of quantities involved: $\frac{\$0.78 + \$0.45 + \$0.36 + \$0.98 + \$0.55 + \$0.54}{6} = \frac{\$3.66}{6} = \$0.61$.

7. **(A)** This is a basic average problem; just take the sum of all the numbers and divide that by the number of quantities involved: $\frac{0.03 + 0.11 + 0.08 + 0.5}{4} = \frac{0.72}{4} = 0.18$.

8. **(C)** This is a basic average problem; just take the sum of all the numbers and divide that by the number of quantities involved: $\frac{1,001 + 1,002 + 1,003 + 1,004 + 1,005}{5} = \frac{5,015}{5} = 1,003$.

9. **(E)** This is a basic average problem; just take the sum of all the numbers and divide that by the number of quantities involved: $\frac{(-8) + (-6) + (-13)}{3} = -\frac{27}{3} = -9$.

10. **(A)** This is a basic average problem; just take the sum of all the numbers and divide that by the number of quantities involved: $\frac{79+85+90+76+80}{5} = \frac{410}{5} = 82$.

11. **(E)** This is a basic average problem; just take the sum of all the numbers and divide that by the number of quantities involved: $\frac{\$4.51+\$6.25+\$3.32+\$4.48+\$2.19}{5} = \frac{\$20.75}{5} = \$4.15$.

12. **(B)** This is a basic average problem; just take the sum of all the numbers and divide that by the number of quantities involved: $\frac{8.5+9.3+8.2+9.0}{4} = \frac{35}{4} = 8.75$.

13. **(B)** This is a basic average problem; just take the sum of all the numbers and divide that by the number of quantities involved: $\frac{44+33+45+44+29}{5} = \frac{195}{5} = 39$.

14. **(A)** The sum of all staff hours need to process 120 building permit applications is 360, so the average time it takes to process these 120 building permit applications is just the sum of all the staff hours divided by the quantity of permit applications: $\frac{360}{120} = 3$. The average processing time for each application is 3 hours.

15. **(C)** This is a basic average problem; just take the sum of all the numbers and divide that by the number of quantities involved: $\frac{84\%+89\%+87\%+90\%+80\%}{5} = \frac{430\%}{5} = 86\%$.

16. **(D)** This question asks for a missing element in an average. First, set up the equation for finding the average, then solve for x: $\frac{21+23+x}{3} = 24 \Rightarrow \frac{44+x}{3} = 24 \Rightarrow 44+x = 72 \Rightarrow x = 28$.

17. **(E)** This question asks for a missing element in an average. First, set up the equation for finding the average, then solve for x: $\frac{0+0+x}{3} = 5 \Rightarrow x = 15$.

18. **(A)** This question asks for a missing element in an average. First, set up the equation for finding the average, then solve for x: $\frac{150+200+180+x}{4} = 166 \Rightarrow 530+x = 664 \Rightarrow x = 134$.

19. **(D)** This question asks for a missing element in an average. First, set up the equation for finding the average, then solve for x: $\frac{81+79+85+90+x}{5} = 83 \Rightarrow 335+x = 415 \Rightarrow x = 80$.

20. **(D)** This question asks for a missing element in an average. First, set up the equation for finding the average, then solve for x: $\frac{\$30+2x}{10} = \$3.60 \Rightarrow \$30+2x = \$36 \Rightarrow 2x = \$6 \Rightarrow x = \$3$.

21. **(D)** First, find the total weight of the twelve books: $\frac{total\ weight}{12} = 2.75$ lbs. $\Rightarrow total\ weight = 33$ lbs. Second, find the total weight of the eleven books: $\frac{total\ weight}{11} = 2.70$ lbs. $\Rightarrow total\ weight = 29.7$ lbs. Third, find the difference between the two, this will be the weight of the removed book: 33 lbs. $-$ 29.7 lbs $=$ 3.3 lbs..

22. **(E)** First, find the sum of the seven scores: $\frac{total\ scores}{7} = 80 \Rightarrow total\ scores = 560$. Second, find the sum of the scores after the lowest and highest have been removed: $\frac{total\ scores}{5} = 78 \Rightarrow total\ scores = 390$. Thus, the sum of the lowest and highest scores is $560 - 390 = 170$. Their average is then, $average = \frac{170}{2} = 85$.

23. **(E)** This is a weighted average problem. Solve by setting up the average equation for a weighted problem. Note that the quantities contributing to the average is the total number of children in the group: $12+8 = 20$. $\frac{(12 \cdot 10)+(8 \cdot 15)}{20} = \frac{120+120}{20} = \frac{240}{20} = 12$ years.

24. **(B)** This is a weighted average problem. Note that the quantities contributing to the average is the total number of deposits Robert made in his savings account: $4+2+4 = 10$. Solve by setting up the average equation for a weighted problem. $\frac{(4 \cdot \$15)+(2 \cdot \$20)+(4 \cdot \$25)}{10} = \frac{\$60+\$40+\$100}{10} = \frac{\$200}{10} = \$20$.

25. **(B)** First, find the total weight of the six people: $\frac{total\ weight}{6} = 145 \Rightarrow total\ weight = 870$ lbs. Second, find the total weigh of all seven people: $\frac{total\ weight}{7} = 147 \Rightarrow total\ weight = 1029$ lbs. Third, find the weigh of the seventh person by taking the difference of the two totals: $1029 - 870 = 159$ lbs.

26. **(C)** This is a basic average problem. Remember that mean is a synonym for average. So, to solve, just take the sum of all the numbers and divide that by the number of quantities involved: $\frac{2+3+13+15+1}{5} = \frac{34}{5} = 6.8$.

27. **(B)** This is a basic average problem. Remember that mean is a synonym for average. So, to solve, just take the sum of all the numbers and divide that by the number of quantities involved: $\frac{-3+2+6+5+2+0}{6} = \frac{12}{6} = 2$.

28. **(E)** This question asks for a missing element in an average. First, set up the equation for finding the average, then solve for x: $\frac{-3+5+6+13+17+x}{6} = 10 \Rightarrow 38 + x = 60 \Rightarrow x = 22$.

29. **(B)** First, find the sum of the five numbers: $\frac{sum_1}{5} = 56 \Rightarrow sum_1 = 280$. Second, find the sum of the seven numbers: $\frac{sum_2}{7} = 58 \Rightarrow sum_2 = 406$. The sum of the two added numbers is the difference between the two totals: $406 - 280 = 126$. Their average is that number divided by two. Thus, their average is 63.

30. **(B)** This question is a variation of the basic average problem. First, set up the average equation. Then solve for x: $\frac{(3x+1)+(2x+4)+(x+10)}{3} = 13 \Rightarrow 6x + 15 = 39 \Rightarrow 6x = 24 \Rightarrow x = 4$.

31. **(C)** This is a weighted average problem. Note that the quantities contributing to the average is the total number of female corporate officers interviewed, 100. Solve by setting up the average equation for a weighted problem. $\frac{(34 \cdot 55)+(28 \cdot 45)+(26 \cdot 35)+(12 \cdot 25)}{100} = \frac{1870+1260+910+300}{100} = \frac{4340}{100} = 43.4$ years.

32. **(D)** To find the median for this problem, first list the numbers in ascending order. Then, since there is an even number of data points, average the two middle values. {26, 29, 30, 33, 33, 35, **37**, **38**, 40, 42, 42, 42, 47, 51} $\frac{37+38}{2} = \frac{75}{2} = 37.5$.

33. **(D)** To find the mode for this problem, first list the numbers in ascending order. Then, look for the number that occurs with the most frequency. For this problem, it is 42, and it occurs 3 times in the set. {26, 29, 30, 33, 33, 35, 37, 38, 40, **42**, **42**, **42**, 47, 51}

34. **(A)** This question asks for a missing element in an average. First, set up the equation for finding the average, then solve for x: $\frac{26+29+30+33+33+35+37+38+40+42+42+42+47+51+x}{15} = 37 \Rightarrow \frac{525+x}{15} = 37 \Rightarrow 525 + x = 555 \Rightarrow x = 30$.

35. **(C)** To find the median for this problem, first list the numbers in ascending order. Then, since there is an odd number data points, the middle value is the median. {1, 2, **3**, 7, 8}. The median is 3.

36. **(C)** To find the median for this problem, first list the numbers in ascending order. Then, since there is an odd number data points, the middle value is the median. {-16, -3, 0, 1, 2, **2**, 4, 4, 8, 9, 12}. The median is 2.

37. **(D)** To find the median for this problem, first list the numbers in ascending order. Then, since there is an even number data points, average the two middle values. {-16, -3, 2, 2, **4**, **4**, 8, 8, 9, 12} $\frac{4+4}{2} = 4$. The median is 4.

38. **(B)** To find the mode for this problem, first list the numbers in ascending order. Then, look for the number that occurs with the most frequency. For this problem, it is 8, and it occurs 2 times in the set. {4, **8**, **8**, 10, 15}

39. **(D)** To find the mode for this problem, first list the numbers in ascending order. Then, look for the number that occurs with the most frequency. For this problem, it is 2: {-2, **2**, **2**, **2**, 4, 6, 8, 8, 10}.

40. **(C)** In order for the mode to be a negative even number, then at least two of the three unknown values must be equal as well as being negative even numbers. Therefore, set each unknown number equal to another, solve for x (thus producing a mode—at least the two numbers of interest are equal, creating a mode), and then plug x back into to the unknowns to determine if the result really is a negative even number. $2x + 8 = x - 4 \Rightarrow x = -12$; $2x + 8 = 7x - 4 \Rightarrow 5x = 12 \Rightarrow x\frac{12}{5}$; $x - 4 = 7x - 4 \Rightarrow 6x = 0 \Rightarrow x = 0$. Thus, the three combinations of equations yield three possibilities for x. Now, we find which one makes at least two of the equations equal a negative, even number: Of the three values of x, only zero appears as an answer. Check your answer by evaluating the three equations with $x = 0$: $2x + 8 = 2(0) + 8 = 8$; $x - 4 = (0) - 4 = -4$; $7x - 4 = 7(0) - 4 = -4$. Thus, zero does indeed produce two values that are negative and even.

41. **(B)** $100 + 55 + 75 + 80 + 65 + 65 + 95 + 90 + 80 + 45 + 40 + 50 + 85 + 85 + 85 + 80 + 80 + 70 + 65 + 60 = 1450 \Rightarrow \frac{1450}{20} = 72.5$.

42. **(B)** $\frac{75 \cdot 0.15 + 100 \cdot 0.30 + 50 \cdot 0.72}{75+100+50} = \frac{11.25+30+36}{225} = \frac{77.25}{225} = 34\frac{1}{3}$ cents.

43. **(E)** Multiply the grade in each course by the weight given to it in the final average: $(90 \cdot 4) + (84 \cdot 3) + (75 \cdot 3) + (76 \cdot 1) = 360 + 252 + 225 + 76 = 913$. The total weight is $4 + 3 + 3 + 1 = 11$. The average is therefore $\frac{913}{11} = 83$.

44. **(D)** average $= \frac{3+4+4+0+1+2+0+2+2}{9} = \frac{18}{9} = 2$.

45. **(B)** Arrange the numbers in order: 0, 0, 1, 2, 2, 2, 3, 4, 4. Of the nine numbers, the fifth (middle) number is two.

46. **(C)** The most frequent data value in the set is two.

EXERCISE 7—RATIOS AND PROPORTIONS (p. 143)

1. **(B)** There are 3 blue marbles and 8 red marbles; thus, the ratio between them is 3:8, or $\frac{3}{8}$.

2. **(A)** The ratio between the teachers and the students is $\frac{24}{480} = \frac{6 \cdot 4}{10 \cdot 6 \cdot 4 \cdot 2} = \frac{1}{20}$, or 1:20.

3. **(D)** The ratio between works of fiction and works of non-fiction is $\frac{12,000}{3,000} = \frac{12}{3} = \frac{4 \cdot 3}{3} = \frac{4}{1}$, or 4:1.

4. **(C)** Since we want to find fractions equivalent to 1:3, ask yourself in which ratio, I – III, is the denominator three times as large as the numerator. I: $120 = 3 \cdot 40$; II: $100 \neq 3 \cdot 75$; III: $360 = 3 \cdot 120$. Thus, I and III are both equivalent to 1:3.

5. **(A)** There are 90 seventh-grade girls and a total of $90 + 80 = 170$ girls in Tyler Junior High. Thus, the ratio of seventh-grade girls to the total number of girls in Tyler Junior High is $\frac{90}{170} = \frac{9}{17}$.

6. **(A)** There are 80 eight-grade girls and a total of $90 + 85 + 80 + 75 = 330$ students in Tyler Junior High. The ratio between the eighth-grade girls and the total number of students in Tyler Junior High is then $\frac{80}{330} = \frac{8}{33}$.

7. **(D)** The question asks for the average mileage per gallon of an airplane that flies 275 miles on 25 gallons of fuel. Our goal, then, is to find, from the information given, the distance the plane flies on a single gallon of fuel. $\frac{miles}{gallon} = \frac{275}{25} = \frac{11 \cdot 25}{25} = 11 \frac{miles}{gallon}$.

8. **(B)** The ratio of chocolates to caramels to mints is 12:6:9. These are all divisible by three; the ratio can be simplified to 4:2:3.

9. **(B)** Let Lucy's money $= x$; Ricky's money $= y$; Ethel's money $= z$. The problem gives us the following ratios: $x : 2y$ and $y : 3z$. We substitute $3z$ for y in the first ratio, leaving us with $x : 2 \cdot (3z) \Rightarrow x : 6z$. Lucy has 6 times as much money as Ethel. So, the ratio of the amount of money Ethel has to the amount of money Lucy has is 1:6.

10. **(D)** 3 farkels : 2 kirns and 3 kirns : 5 pucks. First, we need to find a common element: kirns. Second, we must relate farkels and pucks to the same number of kirns. The lowest number that captures both ratios is 6 kirns. Then, 9 farkels : 6 kirns : 10 pucks. So, 9 farkels buy 10 pucks.

11. **(D)** First, set up the equations: $X : 2Y$; $Y : \frac{4}{3}Z$. Then, multiply the second equation by 2 to relate the first equation to the second equation. Now, we have $X : 2Y : \frac{4}{3}Z$. Thus, the ratio of the rate of operation of machine X to that of machine Z is $1 : \frac{4}{3}$ or $\frac{1}{\frac{4}{3}} = \frac{3}{4}$.

12. **(C)** First, we find the total number of 'parts' into which the marbles need to be divided. We can think of Bill as having 3 parts, and Carl as having 5 parts. Thus, there are 8 total parts. Second, we divide 48 into 8 equal parts to obtain 6 marbles per part. Since Bill has 3 parts, he should have 18 marbles, $3 \cdot 6 = 18$.

13. **(B)** We can express the division of shares between Nelix and Janeway as $J : 4N$. Thus, we see that there is a total of five parts. $\frac{\$10.00}{5} = \$2.00$. Janeway's share is 4 parts, so $\$2.00 \cdot 4 = \$8.00$.

14. **(C)** To divide something into unequal parts, we must first express those parts as fractions of a single whole. We can use the imagery of a pie. If the pie is distributed in a ratio of 2:3:5, we can add the parts, $2 + 3 + 5 = 10$. Next, we can cut the pie into ten equal pieces and give each person his or her share of the pie, one piece of pie for each part of the ratio. Thus we give 2 pieces, 3 pieces, and 5 pieces of pie. Now, applying that to the problem at hand, we divide $1000 by 10; each part of the 'pie' equals $100. The recipient of the largest "piece of the pie", will receive $5 \cdot \$100 = \$500$.

15. **(D)** $\frac{6}{8} = \frac{x}{4} \Rightarrow x = 4 \cdot \frac{6}{8} \Rightarrow x = \frac{6}{2} = 3$.

16. **(D)** $\frac{14}{x} = \frac{2}{7} \Rightarrow x \cdot \frac{14}{x} = x \cdot \frac{2}{7} \Rightarrow 14x = x\frac{2}{7} \Rightarrow 14 \cdot \frac{7}{2} = x = 49$.

17. **(E)** $\frac{3}{4}=\frac{4}{x} \Rightarrow \frac{4}{3}=\frac{x}{4} \Rightarrow x = 4 \cdot \frac{4}{3} = \frac{16}{3}$.

18. **(D)** $\frac{240 \text{ widgets}}{180 \text{ widgets}} = \frac{\$36}{x}$. Note that it is easier to determine x when it is the numerator of a fraction; therefore, invert both sides of the equation: $\frac{180 \text{ widgets}}{240 \text{ widgets}} = \frac{x}{\$36} \Rightarrow \$36 \cdot \frac{10 \cdot 6 \cdot 3}{10 \cdot 6 \cdot 4} = \$36 \cdot \frac{3}{4} = \$27 = x$.

19. **(D)** $\frac{450 \text{ grams}}{1 \text{ kilogram}=1000 \text{ grams}} = \frac{x}{\$9.60} \Rightarrow \$9.60 \cdot \frac{10 \cdot 9 \cdot 5}{10 \cdot 10 \cdot 5 \cdot 2} = \$9.60 \cdot \frac{9}{20} = \$0.48 \cdot 9 = \$4.32$.

20. **(E)** $\frac{z}{\$10.80} = \frac{50 \text{ feet}}{\$4.80} \Rightarrow z = \$10.80 \cdot \frac{5 \text{ feet}}{\$0.48} = 22.5 \cdot 5 \text{ feet} = 112.5 \text{ feet}$.

21. **(C)** If one quarter of a population has red hair, then three quarters do not: people with red hair : 3 people without red hair. Let z signify those without red hair. Then, $\frac{1}{1} = \frac{z}{100} \Rightarrow 100 \cdot 3 = 300 = z$.

22. **(B)** Let x be the amount raised when 50% of the goal has been reached: $\frac{x}{50} = \frac{\$12,000}{20} \Rightarrow 50 \cdot \$600 = \$30,000 = x$.

23. **(C)** $\frac{y}{50 \text{ kilograms}} = \frac{72 \text{ liters}}{48 \text{ liters}} = \frac{6 \cdot 4 \cdot 3 \text{ liters}}{6 \cdot 4 \cdot 2 \text{ liters}} \Rightarrow y = 50 \text{ kilograms} \cdot \frac{3}{2} = 75 \text{ kilograms}$.

24. **(C)** Be careful with this problem. You might be tempted to do the following: $\frac{x}{5 \text{ m/hr}} = \frac{2 \text{ hours}}{4 \text{ m/hr}} \Rightarrow x = 5 \text{ m/hr} \cdot \frac{1 \text{ hour}}{2 \text{ m/hr}} = 2.5 \text{ hours}$. But, reflection will show that the first relationship is incorrect. The way it is set up above, the hours will *increase* in proportion to the increase in speed; however, if the rate increases the trip should take less time. Note that this is answer A. A clear pitfall. When dealing with inverse proportions, group like objects, in this case hours and miles per hour, and invert one side of the proportion. Now lets try: $\frac{x}{2 \text{ hours}} = \frac{4 \text{ m/hr}}{5 \text{ m/hr}} \Rightarrow x = 2 \text{ hours} \cdot \frac{4}{5} = 1.6 \text{ hours}$.

25. **(B)** This is an inverse relationship problem. Group like terms: $\frac{x}{200 \text{ gallons/hr}} = \frac{5 \text{ hours}}{8 \text{ hours}}$. Now, invert the right side: $\frac{x}{200 \text{ gallons/hr}} = \frac{8 \text{ hours}}{5 \text{ hours}}$. Then, solve for x: $x = 200 \text{ gallons/hr} \cdot \frac{8}{5} = 40 \text{ gallons/hr} \cdot 8 = 320 \text{ gallons/hr}$.

26. **(C)** $\frac{3}{8} = 0.375$.

27. **(D)** $\frac{3}{4} = \frac{15}{x} \Rightarrow \frac{4}{3} = \frac{x}{15} \Rightarrow x = 15 \cdot \frac{4}{3} = 5 \cdot 4 = 20$.

28. **(B)** Let x be the number of problems Annika can solve in 48 minutes: $\frac{x}{10} = \frac{48}{30} \Rightarrow x = 10 \cdot \frac{48}{30} = 16$ problems.

29. **(E)** Let x signify the number of stairs Seung can mount in 18 minutes: $\frac{x}{18} = \frac{6}{4} \Rightarrow x = \frac{18 \cdot 6}{4} = \frac{108}{4} = 27$ steps. There is another way to think about the problem: 4 goes 4.5 times into 18. If Seung can ascend 6 stairs in 4 minutes, in 18 he should be able to ascend $4.5 \cdot 6 = 27$.

30. **(C)** Let x represent the cost of 6 candy bars: $\frac{x}{6} = \frac{\$1.04}{4} \Rightarrow x = 6 \cdot \$.26 = \$1.56$.

31. **(D)** Let x represent the number of steps Baby Andrew takes to walk 5 yards: $\frac{x}{8} = \frac{5}{2} \Rightarrow x = \frac{40}{2} = 20$ steps.

32. **(C)** 3:5 implies 8 parts. $\frac{40}{8} = 5$ and $5 \cdot 3 = 15$.

33. **(B)** Let x represent the number of ounces popped from 5 bags of popcorn: $\frac{28}{3} = \frac{x}{5} \Rightarrow x = \frac{5 \cdot 28}{3} = \frac{140}{3} = 46\frac{2}{3}$.

34. **(A)** $\frac{x}{60,000,000} = \frac{420}{1,000} = \frac{42}{100} = \frac{21}{50} \Rightarrow x = \frac{60,000,000 \cdot 21}{50} = 1,200,000 \cdot 21 = 25,000,000$ people.

35. **(D)** Think of this in terms of growth, not of total length. Thus, for the first four days, we want to use $12-5=7$ in the ratio: $\frac{x}{6} = \frac{7}{4} \Rightarrow x = \frac{6 \cdot 7}{4} = \frac{3 \cdot 7}{2} = 10.5$ cm. Now, we must remember to add this to the length after four days: $10.5 + 12 = 22.5$ cm.

36. **(C)** Let x be the time in minutes Elan needs to mow 5 lawns: $\frac{x}{85} = \frac{5}{3} \Rightarrow \frac{85 \cdot 5}{3} = \frac{425}{3} = 141$ minutes 40 seconds.

37. **(B)** Let x signify the fraction of a job Sarah does in 10 minutes: $\frac{x}{10} = \frac{1}{6} \Rightarrow 10 \cdot \frac{1}{30} = \frac{1}{3}$.

38. **(B)** $\frac{2\frac{1}{2}}{4} = \frac{1\frac{7}{8}}{s} \Rightarrow s = \frac{4 \cdot 1\frac{7}{8}}{2\frac{1}{2}} = \frac{1 \cdot \frac{15}{2}}{2\frac{1}{2}} = \frac{15}{2} \cdot \frac{2}{3} = 3$ inches.

39. **(C)** Let p equal the cost per dozen handkerchiefs: $\frac{3}{12} = \frac{\$2.29}{p} \Rightarrow p = \frac{12 \cdot \$2.29}{3} = \frac{4 \cdot \$2.29}{1} = \$9.16$.

40. **(A)** Let f equal the height of the first pole: $\frac{f}{24} = \frac{3}{4} \Rightarrow f = \frac{24 \cdot 3}{4} = \frac{6 \cdot 3}{1} = 18$ ft.

41. **(D)** Let y equal the unknown length: $\frac{3\frac{1}{2}}{\frac{1}{8}} = \frac{y}{1} \Rightarrow y = \frac{3\frac{1}{2} \cdot 1}{\frac{1}{8}} = 3\frac{1}{2} \div \frac{1}{8} = \frac{7}{2} \cdot \frac{8}{1} = \frac{7}{1} \cdot \frac{4}{1} = 28$ ft.

42. **(B)** If only two parts of a proportion are known, the problem must be solved by the ratio method. The ratio 10:1 means that if the alloy were separated into equal parts, 10 of those parts would be copper and 1 would be aluminum, for a total of $10 + 1 = 11$ parts. $77 \div 11 = 7$ lb. per part. The alloy contains 1 part aluminum. $7 \cdot 1 = 7$ lb. aluminum.

43. **(C)** The cost, c, is proportional to the number of square feet: $\frac{\$0.31}{c} = \frac{1}{180} \Rightarrow c = \frac{\$0.31 \cdot 180}{1} = \$55.80$.

44. **(B)** The amount earned is proportional to the number of days worked: $\frac{\$352}{a} = \frac{16}{117} \Rightarrow a = \frac{\$352 \cdot 117}{16} = \$2,574$.

45. **(D)** Let n equal the unknown length: $\frac{\frac{1}{8}}{3\frac{3}{4}} = \frac{12}{n} \Rightarrow n = \frac{12 \cdot 3\frac{3}{4}}{\frac{1}{8}} = 45 \div \frac{1}{8} = 45 \cdot \frac{8}{1} = 360$.

46. **(B)** The ratio of investment is: $9,000:7,000:6,000$ or $9:7:6$. $9 + 7 + 6 = 22$. $\$825 \div 22 = \$37.50$ for each share of the profit. James' share of the profit is $7 \cdot \$37.50 = \$262.50$. James spends $\$230$, so he is left with $\$262.50 - \$230.00 = \$32.50$.

47. **(A)** $\frac{1\frac{5}{8} \text{ inches}}{10 \text{ miles}} = \frac{2.25 \text{ inches}}{x \text{ miles}} \Rightarrow x = 2.25 \text{ inches} \cdot \frac{10 \text{ miles}}{1\frac{5}{8} \text{ inches}} = 2\frac{1}{4} \cdot \frac{10}{\frac{13}{8}} \text{ miles} = 2\frac{1}{4} \cdot \frac{80}{13} \text{ miles} = \frac{9}{4} \cdot \frac{80}{13} \text{ miles} = \frac{9 \cdot 20}{13} \text{ miles} = \frac{180}{13} \text{ miles}$.

48. **(C)** $\frac{72 \text{ inches tall}}{48 \text{ inches shadow}} = \frac{66 \text{ inches tall}}{x \text{ inches shadow}} \Rightarrow x = 66 \text{ inches tall} \cdot \frac{48 \text{ inches shadow}}{72 \text{ inches tall}} = \frac{66 \cdot 2}{3} \text{ inches shadow} = 44 \text{ inches shadow}$.

49. **(B)** $\frac{1 \text{ inch}}{12 \text{ feet}} = \frac{7 \text{ inches}}{x \text{ yards}} \Rightarrow x \text{ yards} = 7 \text{ inches} \cdot \frac{12 \text{ feet}}{1 \text{ inch}} \cdot \frac{1 \text{ yard}}{3 \text{ feet}} = \frac{7 \cdot 4}{1} \text{ yards} = 28 \text{ yards}$. Note that if 1 inch represents 12 feet, it also represents 4 yards. All we need to do now is to multiply the ratio 1 inch : 4 yards by seven. 7 inches : 28 yards.

50. **(E)** $\frac{4 \text{ units}}{7 \text{ inches}} = \frac{5 \text{ units}}{x \text{ inches}} \Rightarrow x \text{ inches} = 5 \text{ units} \cdot \frac{7 \text{ inches}}{4 \text{ units}} = \frac{35}{4} \text{ inches} = 8\frac{3}{4} \text{ inches} = 8.75 \text{ inches}$.

EXERCISE 8—EXPONENTS AND RADICALS (p. 154)

1. **(E)** $3^3 = 3 \cdot 3 \cdot 3 = 9 \cdot 3 = 27$.

2. **(D)** $2^4 = 2 \cdot 2 \cdot 2 \cdot 2 = 4 \cdot 2 \cdot 2 = 8 \cdot 2 = 16$.

3. **(E)** Any number taken to the first power is equal to itself: $x^1 = x$. Thus, $1,000,000^1 = 1,000,000$.

4. **(B)** Any number taken to the power of zero is equal to 1: $x^0 = 1$. Thus, $100^0 = 1$.

5. **(C)** $2^3 \cdot 2^2 = 2^{3+2} = 2^5$. When two numbers with the same base are multiplied, the result is equal to that base taken to the sum of the original exponents.

6. **(E)** I: $3^{10} \cdot 10^3 = 3^3 \cdot 3^7 \cdot 10^3 = 3^7 \cdot (3^3 \cdot 10^3) = 3 \cdot (3 \cdot 10)^3 = 3^7 \cdot 30^3$. We have manipulated the equation, so that we can compare like quantities. To accomplish this, we separated out the number of times 30 occurs in the base expression. Now, we compare it to the figure in I: $3^7 \cdot 30^3 = 30^{30} \Rightarrow 3^7 = \frac{30^{30}}{30^3} = 30^{30-3} = 30^{27}$. Clearly, $3^7 \neq 30^{27}$, so I is not true. As for II, $3^{10} \cdot 10^3 = 300 \cdot 1000 \Rightarrow 3^{10} = 300 \Rightarrow 3^9 = 100$. But, 3 doesn't further divide 100, so II is false. III: Since $10^3 = 1000 > 30 + 30 = 60$, III is also false.

7. **(C)** Use the product rule of exponents; add the exponents of like terms: $5^4 \cdot 5^9 = 5^{4+9} = 5^{13}$.

8. **(A)** Use the product rule of exponents; add the exponents of like terms: $2^3 \cdot 2^4 \cdot 2^5 = 2^{3+4+5} = 2^{12}$.

9. **(A)** $(2+3)^{20} = (5)^{20} = 5^{20}$.

10. **(A)** $\frac{2^5}{2^3} = 2^{5-3} = 2^2$. The quotient of two numbers with the same base is equal to that base taken to the difference of the exponent of the numerator and the exponent of the denominator.

11. **(B)** Use the quotient rule of exponents; subtract the exponents of like terms: $\frac{3^{10}}{3^8} = 3^{10-8} = 3^2$.

12. **(C)** Use the quotient rule of exponents; subtract the exponents of like terms: $\frac{5^2}{5^2} = 5^{2-2} = 5^0 = 1$. Thus, II and III are true.

13. **(C)** Use the quotient rule of exponents; subtract the exponents of like terms: $\frac{3^2}{3^3} = 3^{2-3} = 3^{-1} = \frac{1}{3^1} = \frac{1}{3}$. Thus, I and II are both true.

14. **(B)** Use the power rule of exponents; multiply the exponents: $(2^2)^3 = 2^{2 \cdot 3} = 2^6$.

15. **(B)** Use the power rule of exponents; multiply the exponents: $(5^2)^6 = 5^{2 \cdot 6} = 5^{12}$.

16. **(C)** Use the power rule of exponents; multiply the exponents: $(7^7)^7 = 7^{7 \cdot 7} = 7^{49}$.

17. **(E)** $(3 \cdot 2)^2 = 3^2 \cdot 2^2 = 3 \cdot 3 \cdot 2 \cdot 2 = 36$. So, I, II, and III are true.

18. **(D)** Look at I and III. They cannot both be true: $15^2 \neq 8^2$ Now, $(5 \cdot 3)^2 = 5^2 \cdot 3^2 = 15^2$. Thus, I and II are true.

19. **(C)** $\left(\frac{8}{3}\right)^2 = \frac{8^2}{3^2} = \frac{64}{9} \neq 11^2$. I and II only are true.

20. **(C)** $\left(\frac{4}{9}\right)^2 = \frac{4^2}{9^2} = \frac{16}{81}$.

21. **(C)** Use the product rule and the power rule: $(2 \cdot 2^2 \cdot 2^3)^2 = \left(2^{1+2+3}\right)^2 = (2^6)^2 = 2^{6 \cdot 2} = 2^{12}$.

22. **(A)** Use the quotient rule, then the power rule: $\left(\frac{2^4 \cdot 5^4}{2^2 \cdot 5^2}\right)^2 = \left(2^{4-2} \cdot 5^{4-2}\right)^2 = \left(2^2 \cdot 5^2\right)^2 = 2^{2 \cdot 2} \cdot 5^{2 \cdot 2} = 2^4 \cdot 5^4$. It is usually easier in the long run to first simplify the inside of a fraction before operating on it.

23. **(E)** Use the quotient rule: $\frac{3^6 \cdot 5^3 \cdot 7^9}{3^4 \cdot 5^3 \cdot 7^8} = 3^{6-4} \cdot 5^{3-3} \cdot 7^{9-8} = 3^2 \cdot 5^0 \cdot 7^1 = 3^2 \cdot 1 \cdot 7 = 3^2 \cdot 7$

24. **(A)** Use the quotient rule, then the power rule: $\left(\frac{5^{12} \cdot 7^5}{5^{11} \cdot 7^5}\right)^2 = \left(5^{12-11} \cdot 7^{5-5}\right) = \left(5^1 \cdot 7^0\right)^2 = 5^{1 \cdot 2} \cdot 7^{0 \cdot 2} = 5^2 \cdot 7^0 = 5^2 \cdot 1 = 25$.

25. **(D)** Use the quotient rule, then the power rule: $\left(\frac{12^{12} \cdot 11^{11} \cdot 10^{10}}{12^{12} \cdot 11^{11} \cdot 10^9}\right)^2 = \left(\frac{10^{10}}{10^9}\right)^2 = \left(10^{10-9}\right)^2 = \left(10^1\right)^2 = 10^{1 \cdot 2} = 100$.

26. **(A)** $\sqrt{36} = x \Rightarrow x^2 = 36$. We can immediately eliminate II, because the radical sign always denotes a positive number unless preceded by $\pm$. Now, we try placing I and III into x: $6^2 = 36$; $(-6)^2 = 36$; $\left(3\sqrt{3}\right)^2 = 9 \cdot 3 = 27$. Thus, only I is true.

27. **(C)** Remember, you can't add the insides of radicals when the radicals are added: $\sqrt{81} + \sqrt{4} \neq \sqrt{85}$. $\sqrt{81} + \sqrt{4} = 9 + 2 = 11$. Only III is true.

28. **(B)** Factor out perfect squares: $\sqrt{27} = \sqrt{9 \cdot 3} = 3\sqrt{3}$.

29. **(C)** Try to think of the number inside a radical as a composite containing a perfect square: $\sqrt{52} = \sqrt{13 \cdot 4} = 2\sqrt{13}$.

30. **(C)** $\sqrt{\frac{9}{4}} = \frac{\sqrt{9}}{\sqrt{4}} = \frac{3}{2}$.

31. **(A)** Rewriting this problem is the easiest way to solve it: $\frac{\sqrt{81}}{\sqrt{27}} = \sqrt{\frac{81}{27}} = \sqrt{3}$.

32. **(A)** $2\sqrt{2} = \sqrt{8} \Rightarrow \sqrt{4} < \sqrt{8} < \sqrt{9} \Rightarrow 2 < \sqrt{8} < 3$. But, $\sqrt{8}$ is much closer to 3 since 8 is much closer to 9. Thus, 2.8 is the best answer. Alternatively, you could use a calculator.

33. **(D)** $\sqrt{25} < \sqrt{27} < \sqrt{36} \Rightarrow 5 < \sqrt{27} < 6$. Because 27 is closer to 25 than to 36, $\sqrt{27}$ is closer to 5 than to 6. The only answer that fits these criteria is 5.1; check by using a calculator.

34. **(B)** 12 is closer to 9 than to 16, so $\sqrt{12}$ is closer to $\sqrt{9}=3$ than to $\sqrt{16}=4$. Since, $3<\sqrt{12}<4$, 3.4 is the best answer. The best way to approach these types of problems is to find the nearest two perfect squares, one above and one below, in this case 9 and 16. By taking their square roots we can wedge the unknown root between two known values. Then, we can determine which the unknown root is closer to by how close it is to the perfect squares we chose.

35. **(B)** $\sqrt{16}<\sqrt{23}<\sqrt{25}\Rightarrow 4<\sqrt{23}<5$. Considering that $\sqrt{23}$ is much closer to $\sqrt{25}$ than to $\sqrt{16}$, 4.8 is the best answer. Remember, if you have a calculator, by all means use it to solve these problems.

36. **(C)** $\sqrt{36}<\sqrt{45}<\sqrt{49}\Rightarrow 6<\sqrt{45}<7$. Since 45 is closer to 49 than to 36, $\sqrt{45}$ is closer to 7 than to 6. Thus, 6.6 is the best answer.

37. **(D)** For these types of problems, use the foil method: $\left(7+\sqrt{5}\right)\left(3-\sqrt{5}\right)=7\cdot 3-7\sqrt{5}+3\sqrt{5}-\left(\sqrt{5}\right)^{2}=21-4\sqrt{5}-5=16-4\sqrt{5}$.

38. **(B)** Use the foil method: $\left(5-\sqrt{2}\right)\left(3-\sqrt{2}\right)=15-5\sqrt{2}-3\sqrt{2}+\left(\sqrt{2}\right)^{2}=15-8\sqrt{2}+2=17-8\sqrt{2}$.

39. **(C)** Use the foil method: $\left(\sqrt{3}+1\right)\left(2-\sqrt{3}\right)=2\sqrt{3}-\left(\sqrt{3}\right)^{2}+2-\sqrt{3}=\sqrt{3}-3+2=-1+\sqrt{3}$.

40. **(E)** $\sqrt{2}\cdot 2\sqrt{3}=2\sqrt{3\cdot 2}=2\sqrt{6}$.

41. **(D)** $\sqrt{8}+\sqrt{50}=\sqrt{4\cdot 2}+\sqrt{25\cdot 2}=2\sqrt{2}+5\sqrt{2}=7\sqrt{2}$.

42. **(B)** $\sqrt{3^{2}+5^{2}}=\sqrt{9+25}=\sqrt{34}$.

43. **(D)** $\sqrt{\left(2\sqrt{3}\right)^{2}+2^{2}}=\sqrt{\left(2^{2}\cdot 3\right)+4}=\sqrt{12+4}=\sqrt{16}=4$. Don't be intimidated by these big problems; just solve from the inside out.

44. **(A)** Simplify to find out if the expression is rational: $\left(5+\sqrt{2}\right)\left(5-\sqrt{2}\right)=25-5\sqrt{2}+5\sqrt{2}-\left(\sqrt{2}\right)^{2}=25-2=23$. Note that because the two expressions in the parenthesis are of the form $\left(a+b\right)\left(a-b\right)=a^{2}-b^{2}$, the $\sqrt{2}$ will be squared and will equal 2, so there will be no radicals left in the expression.

45. **(B)** Because $\sqrt{2}$ is irrational, and we know that the sum or difference of a rational number and an irrational number is also irrational, we know that we are dealing with the quotient of two irrational numbers. Such a quotient is always irrational.

46. **(A)** Use the distributive law: $\frac{\sqrt{2}}{2}\left(\sqrt{6}+\frac{\sqrt{2}}{2}\right)=\frac{\sqrt{12}}{2}+\frac{\sqrt{4}}{4}=\frac{\sqrt{4\cdot 3}}{2}+\frac{1}{2}=\frac{2\sqrt{3}}{2}+\frac{1}{2}=\sqrt{3}+\frac{1}{2}$.

47. **(D)** $\frac{15\sqrt{96}}{5\sqrt{2}}=3\sqrt{48}=3\sqrt{16\cdot 3}=12\sqrt{3}$.

48. **(C)** In order to take the square root of a decimal, it must have an even number of decimal places so that its square root will have exactly half as many. In addition, the digits must form a perfect square (*e.g.* $\sqrt{0.09}=0.3$).

49. **(B)** $\left(-\frac{1}{3}\right)^{4}=\left(-\frac{1}{3}\right)\left(-\frac{1}{3}\right)\left(-\frac{1}{3}\right)\left(-\frac{1}{3}\right)=\frac{1}{81}$.

50. **(A)** $-4^{4}=-(4)(4)(4)(4)=-256$.

51. **(D)** $\sqrt[12]{x^{6}}=x^{\frac{6}{12}}=x^{\frac{1}{2}}$.

52. **(E)** $\sqrt[k]{6^{2km}}=6^{\frac{2km}{k}}=6^{2m}$. If m is any non-negative integer such as 0, 1, 2, *etc.*, then 6^{2m} must be a positive integer.

EXERCISE 9—ALGEBRAIC OPERATIONS (p. 165)

1. **(A)** Like terms are terms that contain exactly the same variable taken to the same power. Thus, while II contains x and xy, and III contains x^3 and x, I contains only one variable type: x.

2. **(E)** When two terms have the same variables taken to the same powers, they are said to be like terms. I contains only the variable x. II contains no variables, thus the terms are like. If you like, you could think of II as containing the variable x^0. III contains a single variable as well: x^2.

3. **(C)** Combine like terms by adding and subtracting the coefficients: $x + 2x + 3x = (1+2+3)x = 6x$.

4. **(C)** Combine like terms by adding and subtracting the coefficients: $2x + 3x - x + 4x = (2+3-1+4)x = 8x$.

5. **(E)** Because none of the terms a^3, a^2, or a are like terms, the expression cannot be reduced. Thus, $a^3 + a^2 + a$.

6. **(B)** Combine like terms by adding and subtracting the coefficients: $z^2 + 2z^2 - 5z^2 = (1+2-5)z^2 = -2z^2$.

7. **(A)** Combine like terms by adding and subtracting the coefficients: $a^3 - 12a^3 + 15a^3 + 2a^3 = (1-12+15+2)a^3 = 6a^3$.

8. **(E)** Combine like terms by adding and subtracting the coefficients: $3c + 2a - 1 + 4c - 2a + 1 = (3+4)c + (2-2)a - 1 + 1 = 7c$.

9. **(B)** Combine like terms by adding and subtracting the coefficients:
   $-7nx + 2nx + 2n + 7x = (-7+2)nx + 2n + 7x = -5nx + 2n + 7x$.

10. **(B)** Combine like terms by adding and subtracting the coefficients: $c^2 + 2c^2d^2 - c^2 = 2c^2d^2$.

11. **(C)** Combine like terms by adding and subtracting the coefficients: $2x^2 + 2x^2 + 2x^2 = (2+2+2)x^2 = 6x^2$.

12. **(C)** Combine like terms by adding and subtracting the coefficients: $3xy + 3x^2y - 2xy + y = 3x^2y + xy + y$.

13. **(E)** Don't let the length of this problem intimidate. It is no harder; it only requires more steps to complete. Combine like terms by adding and subtracting the coefficients: $x^2 + 2xy - 3x + 4xy - 6y + 2y^2 + 3x - 2xy + 6y$
   $= x^2 + 2y^2 + (2+4-2)xy + (-3+3)x + (-6+6)y = x^2 + 2y^2 + 4xy$.

14. **(A)** Combine like terms by adding and subtracting the coefficients:
   $8p + 2p^2 + pq - 4p^2 - 14p - pq = (2-4)p^2 + (1-1)pq + (8-14)p = -2p^2 - 6p$.

15. **(E)** Because no term shares a variable with any of the other terms, there is no way to simplify the given expression.

16. **(D)** Use the product rule of exponents: $(x^2)(x^3) = x^{2+3} = x^5$.

17. **(D)** Use the product rule of exponents: $(a)(a^2)(a^3)(a^4) = a^{1+2+3+4} = a^{10}$.

18. **(D)** Use the quotient rule of exponents: $y^5 \div y^2 = \frac{y^5}{y^2} = y^{5-2} = y^3$.

19. **(B)** Use the product rule of exponents: $(x^2y)(xy^2) = x^{2+1}y^{1+2} = x^3y^3$.

20. **(C)** Use the product rule of exponents: $(abc)(a^2bc^2) = a^{1+2}b^{1+1}c^{1+2} = a^3b^2c^3$.

21. **(C)** $(xy^2)(x^2z)(y^2z) = (x^{1+2}y^2z)(y^2z) = (x^3y^{2+2}z^{1+1}) = x^3y^4z^2$ or $(xy^2)(x^2z)(y^2z) = x^{1+2}y^{2+2}z^{1+1} = x^3y^4z^2$.

22. **(B)** Use the quotient rule of exponents: $\frac{x^2 y^4}{xy} = x^{2-1} y^{4-1} = xy^3$.

23. **(A)** Use the quotient rule of exponents: $\frac{a^3 b^4 c^5}{abc} = a^{3-1} b^{4-1} c^{5-1} = a^2 b^3 c^4$.

24. **(C)** Use the power rule of exponents: $\left(x^2 y^3\right)^4 = x^{2 \cdot 4} y^{3 \cdot 4} = x^8 y^{12}$.

25. **(B)** Use the power rule of exponents: $\left(\frac{a^2}{b^3}\right)^3 = \frac{a^{2 \cdot 3}}{b^{3 \cdot 3}} = \frac{a^6}{b^9}$.

26. **(C)** Use the quotient rule of exponents: $\frac{x^3 y^4 z^5}{x^4 y^2 z} = x^{3-4} y^{4-2} z^{5-1} = x^{-1} y^2 z^4 = \frac{y^2 z^4}{x}$.

27. **(C)** Use the quotient rule of exponents; then use the power rule: $\left(\frac{c^4 d^2}{c^2 d}\right)^3 = \left(c^{4-2} d^{2-1}\right)^3 = \left(c^2 d\right)^3 = c^{2 \cdot 3} d^{1 \cdot 3} = c^6 d^3$.

28. **(C)** Use the quotient rule of exponents; then use the product rule: $\left(\frac{x^2 y^3}{xy}\right)\left(\frac{x^3 y^4}{xy}\right) = \left(xy^2\right)\left(x^2 y^3\right) = x^{1+2} y^{2+3} = x^3 y^5$.

29. **(C)** Use the quotient rule of exponents; then use the product rule: $\left(\frac{abc^2}{abc^3}\right)\left(\frac{a^2 b^2 c}{ab}\right) = c^{-1}(abc) = ab$.

30. **(C)** Use the quotient rule of exponents; then use the product rule: $\left(\frac{x^3 y^2 z^2}{x^2 y^2 z}\right)^2 \left(\frac{x^3 y^2 z^4}{x^2 y z^4}\right)^3 = (xyz)^2 (xyz)^3 = (xyz)^{2+3} = (xyz)^5 = x^5 y^5 z^5$.

    Remember, this problem isn't harder, just longer. Work from the inside out; complex problems will always be composed of smaller problems you know how to do.

31. **(B)** $\frac{a}{c} + \frac{b}{c} = \frac{a+b}{c}$.

32. **(A)** $\frac{x}{2} + \frac{y}{2} + \frac{z}{2} = \frac{x+y+z}{2}$.

33. **(C)** $\frac{ab}{x} + \frac{bc}{x} + \frac{cd}{x} = \frac{ab+bc+cd}{x}$. The numerator cannot be combined any further. Recall that only like terms can be combined.

34. **(D)** $\frac{x^2}{k} + \frac{x^3}{k} + \frac{x^4}{k} = \frac{x^2 + x^3 + x^4}{k}$. Because the denominators are equal, the terms can be added. However, since the numerator does not contain like terms, each containing the same variable, but taken to different powers, they cannot be more closely combined.

35. **(A)** $\frac{2x}{z} - \frac{y}{z} = \frac{2x-y}{z}$.

36. **(E)** Multiply to find a common denominator: $\frac{x}{y} + \frac{y}{x} = \left(\frac{x}{x}\right)\left(\frac{x}{y}\right) + \left(\frac{y}{y}\right)\left(\frac{y}{x}\right) = \frac{x^2}{xy} + \frac{y^2}{yx} = \frac{x^2 + y^2}{xy}$.

37. **(E)** Multiply to find a common denominator: $\frac{a}{b} - \frac{b}{a} = \left(\frac{a}{a}\right)\left(\frac{a}{b}\right) - \left(\frac{b}{b}\right)\left(\frac{b}{a}\right) = \frac{a^2 - b^2}{ab}$.

38. **(E)** Multiply to find a common denominator: $\frac{x^2}{y} + \frac{x^2}{z} = \left(\frac{z}{z}\right)\left(\frac{x^2}{y}\right) + \left(\frac{y}{y}\right)\left(\frac{x^2}{z}\right) = \frac{x^2 z + x^2 y}{yz}$.

39. **(C)** Multiply to find a common denominator: $\frac{x}{a} + \frac{y}{b} + \frac{z}{c} = \left(\frac{b}{b}\right)\left(\frac{c}{c}\right)\left(\frac{x}{a}\right) + \left(\frac{a}{a}\right)\left(\frac{c}{c}\right)\left(\frac{y}{b}\right) + \left(\frac{a}{a}\right)\left(\frac{b}{b}\right)\left(\frac{z}{c}\right) = \frac{xbc + yac + zab}{abc}$.

40. **(D)** Multiply to find a common denominator: $\frac{x^2}{y^2} - \frac{y^2}{x^3} = \left(\frac{x^3}{x^3}\right)\left(\frac{x^2}{y^2}\right) - \left(\frac{y^2}{y^2}\right)\left(\frac{y^2}{x^3}\right) = \frac{x^5 - y^4}{x^3 y^2}$.

41. **(B)** Distribute: $2(x+y) = 2x + 2y$.

42. **(B)** Distribute: $a(b+c) = ab + ac$.

43. **(C)** Distribute: $3(a+b+c+d) = 3a + 3b + 3c + 3d$.

44. **(D)** Distribute: $2x(3x + 4x^2) = 6x^2 + 8x^3$.

45. **(D)** Distribute: $3a^2(ab+ac+bc)=3a^3b+3a^3c+3a^2bc$.

46. **(E)** FOIL and simplify: $(x+y)(x+y)=x^2+xy+yx+y^2=x^2+2xy+y^2$. This form occurs so frequently it should be memorized.

47. **(E)** FOIL and simplify: $(a+b)^2=(a+b)(a+b)=a^2+ab+ba+b^2=a^2+2ab+b^2$. This form occurs so frequently it should be memorized.

48. **(C)** FOIL and simplify: $(x-y)^2=(x-y)(x-y)=x^2-xy-yx+y^2=x^2-2xy+y^2$. This form occurs so frequently it should be memorized.

49. **(A)** FOIL and simplify: $(a+b)(a-b)=a^2-ab+ba-b^2=a^2-b^2$. This form occurs so frequently it should be memorized.

50. **(D)** FOIL and simplify: $(x-2)^2=(x-2)(x-2)=x^2-2x-2x+4=x^2-4x+4$.

51. **(D)** FOIL and simplify: $(2-x)^2=(2-x)(2-x)=4-2x-2x+x^2=x^2-4x+4$.

52. **(A)** FOIL and simplify: $(ab+bc)(a+b)=a^2b+ab^2+abc+b^2c=a^2b+ab^2+b^2c+abc$.

53. **(D)** FOIL and simplify: $(x-y)(x+2)=x^2+2x-yx-2y=x^2-xy+2x-2y$.

54. **(D)** FOIL and simplify: $(a+b)(c+d)=ac+ad+bc+bd$.

55. **(E)** FOIL and simplify: $(w+x)(y-z)=wy-wz+xy-xz$.

56. **(B)** FOIL and simplify: $(x+y)(w+x+y)=xw+x^2+xy+yw+yx+y^2=x^2+y^2+wx+wy+2xy$.

57. **(D)** FOIL and simplify: $(2+x)(3+x+y)=6+2x+2y+3x+x^2+xy=x^2+xy+5x+2y+6$.

58. **(C)** FOIL and simplify: $(x+y)^3=(x+y)(x^2+2xy+y^2)=x^3+2x^2y+xy^2+x^2y+2xy^2+y^3=x^3+3x^2y+3xy^2+y^3$.

59. **(A)** FOIL and simplify: $(x-y)^3=(x-y)(x^2-2xy+y^2)=x^3-2x^2y+xy^2-x^2y+2xy^2-y^3=x^3-3x^2y+3xy^2-y^3$.

60. **(D)** FOIL and simplify: $(a+b)(a-b)(a+b)(a-b)=(a^2-b^2)(a^2-b^2)=a^4-a^2b^2-a^2b^2+b^4=a^4-2a^2b^2+b^4$.

61. **(A)** Find the common factor: $2a+2b+2c=2(a+b+c)$.

62. **(D)** Find the common factor: $x+x^2+x^3=x(1+x+x^2)$.

63. **(A)** Find the common factor: $2x^2+4x^3+8x^4=2x^2(1+2x+4x^2)$.

64. **(D)** Find the common factor: $abc+bcd+cde=c(ab+bd+de)$.

65. **(D)** Find the common factor: $x^2y^2+x^2y+xy^2=xy(xy+x+y)$.

66. **(B)** $p^2+2pq+q^2=(p+q)(p+q)$. Know this backwards and forwards.

67. **(B)** $144^2 - 121^2 = (144 + 121)(144 - 121)$. Remember, $(a+b)(a-b) = a^2 - ab + ba - b^2 = a^2 - b^2$.

68. **(A)** $x^2 - y^2 = x^2 - xy + xy - y^2 = (x+y)(x-y)$.

69. **(B)** $x^2 + 2x + 1 = (x+1)(x+1)$.

70. **(C)** $x^2 - 1 = (x+1)(x-1)$.

71. **(B)** First ask yourself, what are the factors that will produce x^2? x times x. Then, what factors will produce 2? 2 and 1. Finally, what factors when added together through FOIL will produce $3x$? 2 times x and 1 times x. Thus, $x^2 + 3x + 2 = (x+2)(x+1)$.

72. **(B)** What factors will produce a^2? a times a. What factors will yield -2? $(+1,-2)$ and $(-1,+2)$. Finally, which of those terms when added together through FOIL will create $-a$? $+1$ and -2. Thus, we have $a^2 - a - 2 = (a-2)(a+1)$.

73. **(A)** p times p equals p^2. The last term, 3, can be produced from either $(+3,+1)$ or $(-3,-1)$. The middle term, $4p$, however, can only be the sum of $+3p$ and $+1p$. Thus, $p^2 + 4p + 3 = (p+3)(p+1)$.

74. **(A)** Given a quadratic, find two numbers, m and n such that their sum is equal to the coefficient of the middle term, in this case 6, and their product is equal to the last term. $c^2 + 6c + 8 = c^2 + 4c + 2c + 8 = (c+2)(c+4)$.

75. **(A)** $x^2 + x - 20 = x^2 + 5x - 4x - 20 = (x+5)(x-4)$.

76. **(C)** $p^2 + 5p + 6 = p^2 + 2p + 3p + 6 = (p+2)(p+3)$.

77. **(E)** We find two numbers, m and n such that their product is equal to 16 and their sum is equal to 8. $x^2 + 8x + 16 = x^2 + 4x + 4x + 16 = (x+4)(x+4)$.

78. **(D)** $x^2 - 5x - 6 = x^2 - 6x + x - 6 = (x-6)(x+1)$.

79. **(A)** $a^2 - 3a + 2 = a^2 - 2a - a + 2 = (a-2)(a-1)$.

80. **(C)** We find two numbers, m and n such that their product is equal to -12 and their sum is equal to 1. $x^2 + x - 12 = x^2 + 4x - 3x - 12 = (x+4)(x-3)$.

81. **(D)** $x^2 - 8x + 16 = x^2 - 4x - 4x + 16 = (x-4)(x-4) = (x-4)^2$.

82. **(D)** We solve the following equation: $x^2 + 12x + a^2 = (x+a)^2$. Now, since $2ax = 12x$, $a = 6$. Thus, $a^2 = 36$.

83. **(C)** A quadratic is a perfect square when it has only one root. The quadratic equation give us $x = \frac{-b \pm \sqrt{b^2 - 4ac}}{2a}$. Now, this will yield only one number only when the square root is equal zero. Thus, we need to solve $b^2 = 4ac$ where, in this case, $a = 4$, and $b = 12$. Thus, $12^2 = 4(4)c \Rightarrow 144 = 16c \Rightarrow c = 9$.

84. **(D)** $x^2 - 8x + 15 = x^2 - 5x - 3x + 15 = (x-5)(x-3)$.

85. **(B)** For this problem, note that the first term is $2x^2$. Thus, one of the first terms of our factors is x and the other is $2x$ (or they could be the negatives of the same terms). That alone lets us eliminate A, D, and E. Since the last terms of both B and C are

each equal to -3, the decisive factor will be the middle term: $+5x$. For C, we have $-6x + x = -5x$. Thus, B has to be the correct answer through process of elimination. Also, $-x + 6x = +5x$.

86. **(A)** First, re-arrange the expression: $10x^2 + 21x - 10$. The factors that will produce the first term, $10x^2$, are (10x,x), (5x,2x), and those terms in the negative. Similarly, the factors that will produce the last term, -10, are (10,-1), (-10,1),(5,-2), and (-5,2). We can get $21x$ by choosing (5x,2x) to produce the first terms and (5,-2) to produce the last terms: $10x^2 + 21x - 10 = (5x - 2)(2x + 5)$.

87. **(C)** Find the common factor: $ax^2 + 3ax = ax(x + 3)$.

88. **(B)** $2x^2 - 8x + 3 - (x^2 - 3x + 9) = x^2 - 5x - 6 = x^2 - 6x + x - 6 = (x - 6)(x + 1)$.

89. **(C)** $15x^2 + ax - 28 = (5x - 4)(3x + 7) = 15x^2 + 35x - 12x - 28 = 15x^2 + 23x - 28$. Thus, $a = 23$.

90. **(D)** $x^2 - 9 = (x + 3)(x - 3)$. This is one of the fundamental factors. Memorize it.

91. **(A)** Whenever you see the difference of two squared terms, you can always factor it as follows:
$x^2 - 9y^4 = x^2 + 3xy^2 - 3xy^2 - 9y^4 = (x + 3y^2)(x - 3y^2)$.

92. **(E)** $x^2 + 6x - 27 = x^2 + 9x - 3x - 27 = (x + 9)(x - 3)$.

93. **(D)** $\frac{8x^{-4}}{2x} = \frac{4}{x^{1+4}} = \frac{4}{x^5}$.

94. **(B)** $\frac{3^{-1}x^5y^2}{2xy} = \frac{x^{5-1}y^{2-1}}{3^1 \cdot 2} = \frac{x^4y}{6}$.

95. **(D)** $\frac{6x^{-5}y^2}{3^{-1}x^{-4}y} = \frac{6y^2}{3^{-1}x^{-4+5}y} = \frac{3^1 \cdot 6y}{x^1} = \frac{18y}{x}$.

96. **(A)** $\frac{9^2x^3y}{3^{-1}x^{-4}y} = 3^1 \cdot 81x^{3+4} = 243x^7$.

97. **(B)** $(-2)^2 = (-2)(-2) = 4$.

98. **(C)** $(-3)^2 \cdot 5 = 9 \cdot 5 = 45$.

99. **(C)** $(-2)^2 - 4(-2)(-3) - (-2) = 4 - 24 + 2 = -18$.

100. **(A)** $(x - y)(x^2 - 2x + 5) = x^3 - 2x^2 + 5x - x^2y + 2xy - 5y$.

101. **(E)** $\left(2x + \sqrt{3}\right)^2 = \left(2x + \sqrt{3}\right)\left(2x + \sqrt{3}\right) = 4x^2 + 4x\sqrt{3} + 3$.

102. **(C)** $2(-2)^2 - (-2)(3) = 8 + 6 = 14$.

103. **(E)** $\left(\frac{x^2y^3x^5}{2^{-1}}\right)^2 = \left(2x^7y^3\right)^2 = 4x^{14}y^6$.

104. **(C)** Choose any two low numbers to test this, say 1 and 1. $\sqrt{1^2 + 1^2} = \sqrt{2} \neq 1 + 1 = 2$. Thus, it could be no. Now, consider 0 and 0: $\sqrt{0^2 + 0^2} = 0 + 0 = 0$. Thus, it could be yes. So, we can't determine the answer from the information given.

105. **(A)** Remember, that we can square both sides of an equation and still preserve the equality of the equation. Since the square roots do not matter, it is obvious that this is our well known basic foil: $(x+y)(x+y) = x^2 + xy + yx + y^2 = x^2 + 2xy + y^2$.

106. **(C)** $\frac{x}{\sqrt{2x-y}} = x\sqrt{2x+y} \Rightarrow \frac{x}{x} = \sqrt{2x-y}\sqrt{2x+y} \Rightarrow 1 = \sqrt{4x^2-y^2} \Rightarrow 1^2 = 4x^2 - y^2$. Let $x = 1$. Then $1 = 4 - y^2 \Rightarrow -3 = -y^2 \Rightarrow y^2 = 3 \Rightarrow y = \sqrt{3}$. Thus, it can be true, for at least one pair (x,y). Now, consider $x = 3, y = 4$. Then, $1 = 4 \cdot 9 - 16 = 20$; this is obviously false.

107. **(A)** $\frac{6}{\sqrt{2a-3c}} = \frac{6\sqrt{2a-3c}}{(2a-3c)} \Rightarrow \frac{6}{6} = \frac{\sqrt{2a-3c}\sqrt{2a-3c}}{(2a-3c)} = \frac{\left(\sqrt{2a-3c}\right)^2}{(2a-3c)} = \frac{2a-3c}{2a-3c} = 1$. Thus, for all a and b, the expression is true.

108. **(D)** $\frac{n}{6} + \frac{2n}{5} = \frac{5n+12n}{30} = \frac{17n}{30}$.

109. **(B)** $\frac{1}{1} - \frac{x}{y} = \frac{y-x}{y}$.

110. **(B)** $\frac{x-y}{x+y} \div \frac{y-x}{y+x} = \frac{x-y}{x+y} \cdot \frac{y+x}{y-x}$. Since addition is commutative, you can cancel $x+y$ with $y+x$, as they are the same quantity. However, subtraction is not commutative, so you cannot cancel $x-y$ with $y-x$, as they are not the same quantity. Change the form of $y-x$ by factoring out -1. Thus, $y-x = (-1)(x-y)$. In this form, cancel $x-y$, leaving $\frac{1}{-1} = -1$.

111. **(A)** Simplify by multiplying every term in the fraction by x: $\frac{1+\frac{1}{x}}{\frac{2}{x}} \cdot \frac{x}{x} = \frac{x+1}{y}$.

112. **(E)** $\frac{2x^2}{y} \cdot \frac{2x^2}{y} \cdot \frac{2x^2}{y} = \frac{8x^6}{y^3}$.

113. **(D)** Simplify by multiplying every term of the fraction by xy: $\frac{\frac{1}{x}+\frac{1}{y}}{3} \cdot \frac{xy}{xy} = \frac{y+x}{3xy}$.

114. **(C)** $\frac{\sqrt{32b^3}}{\sqrt{8b}} = \sqrt{4b^2} = 2b$ if $b \geq 0$.

115. **(B)** $\sqrt{\frac{16x^2+9x^2}{144}} = \sqrt{\frac{25x^2}{144}} = \frac{5x}{12}$.

116. **(E)** The terms cannot be combined, and it is not possible to take the square root of separated terms.

117. **(D)** $\sqrt{\frac{100x^2-64x^2}{6,400}} = \sqrt{\frac{36x^2}{6,400}} = \frac{6x}{80} = \frac{3x}{40}$.

118. **(A)** $\sqrt{\frac{9y^2-y^2}{18}} = \sqrt{\frac{8y^2}{18}} = \sqrt{\frac{4y^2}{9}} = \frac{2y}{3}$.

119. **(E)** It is not possible to find the square root of separate terms.

120. **(A)** Since $x < 0$ and $y < 0$, $|x| = -x$ and $|xy| = xy$. Thus, $\frac{x}{|x|} + \frac{xy}{|xy|} = \frac{x}{-x} + \frac{xy}{xy} = -1 + 1 = 0$.

121. **(D)** $16x^4 - 81y^{16} = \left(4x^2 + 9y^8\right)\left(4x^2 - 9y^8\right) = \left(4x^2 + 9y^8\right)\left(2x + 3y^4\right)\left(2x - 3y^4\right)$.

EXERCISE 10—ALGEBRAIC EQUATIONS AND INEQUALITIES (p. 180)

1. **(C)** Divide by the coefficient of the variable x: $3x = 12 \Rightarrow x = \frac{12}{3} = 4$.

2. **(C)** Combine like terms, and divide by the coefficient of the variable: $2x + x = 9 \Rightarrow 3x = 9 \Rightarrow x = \frac{9}{3} = 3$.

3. **(C)** Combine like terms, and divide by the coefficient of the variable: $7x - 5x = 12 - 8 \Rightarrow 2x = 4 \Rightarrow x = 2$.

4. **(B)** Combine like terms, and divide by the coefficient of the variable: $3x + 2x = 15 \Rightarrow 5x = 15 \Rightarrow x = 3$.

5. **(E)** Combine like terms, and divide by the coefficient of the variable: $a - 8 = 10 - 2a \Rightarrow a + 2a = 10 + 8 \Rightarrow 3a = 18 \Rightarrow a = 6$.

6. **(E)** Combine like terms, and divide by the coefficient of the variable: $p - 11 - 2p = 13 - 5p$

$$p - 2p + 5p = 13 + 11 \Rightarrow 4p = 24 \Rightarrow p = 6$$

7. **(D)** Combine like terms, and divide by the coefficient of the variable: $12x + 3 - 4x - 3 = 8 \Rightarrow 8x = 8 \Rightarrow x = 1$.

8. **(B)** Combine like terms, and divide by the coefficient of the variable: $5x - 2 + 3x - 4 = 2x - 8 + x + 2$.

$$2x - 6 = 3x - 6 \Rightarrow 0 = x$$

9. **(D)** Combine like terms, and divide by the coefficient of the variable: $a + 2b - 3 + 3a = 2a + b + 3 + b$

$$4a - 2a = 2b - 2b + 3 + 3 \Rightarrow 2a = 6 \Rightarrow a = 3$$

10. **(C)** Combine like terms, and divide by the coefficient of the variable: $4y + 10 = 5 + 7y + 5$

$$4y - 7y = 10 - 10 \Rightarrow -3y = 0 \Rightarrow y = 0$$

11. **(A)** Combine like terms, and divide by the coefficient of the variable: $-4 - x = 12 + x \Rightarrow -16 = 2x \Rightarrow -8 = x$.

12. **(D)** Combine like terms, and divide by the coefficient of the variable: $\frac{x}{2} + x = 3 \Rightarrow \frac{3x}{2} = 3 \Rightarrow x = \frac{2}{3}3 = 2$.

13. **(D)** Combine like terms, and divide by the coefficient of the variable: $\frac{2x}{3} + \frac{x}{4} + 4 = \frac{x}{6} + 10 \Rightarrow \frac{2x}{3} + \frac{x}{4} - \frac{x}{6} = 6$.

$$\frac{4 \cdot 2x + 3x - 2x}{12} = 6 \Rightarrow 9x = 72 \Rightarrow x = 8$$

14. **(E)** Combine like terms, and divide by the coefficient of the variable: $\frac{a}{2} - \frac{a}{4} = 1 \Rightarrow \frac{2a - a}{4} = 1 \Rightarrow \frac{a}{4} = 1 \Rightarrow a = 4$.

15. **(E)** Combine like terms, and divide by the coefficient of the variable: $\frac{1}{p} + \frac{2}{p} + \frac{3}{p} = 1 \Rightarrow \frac{6}{p} = 1 \Rightarrow 6 = p$.

16. **(D)** Combine like terms, and divide by the coefficient of the variable: $\frac{2x-6}{3} = 8 \Rightarrow 2x - 6 = 24 \Rightarrow 2x = 30 \Rightarrow x = 15$.

17. **(C)** Combine like terms, and divide by the coefficient of the variable: $\frac{5-x}{5} = 1 \Rightarrow 5 - x = 5 \Rightarrow -x = 0 \Rightarrow x = 0$.

18. **(A)** Combine like terms, and divide by the coefficient of the variable: $\frac{2-x}{10} = 1 \Rightarrow 2 - x = 10 \Rightarrow -x = 8 \Rightarrow x = -8$.

19. **(B)** Combine like terms, and divide by the coefficient of the variable: $\frac{5}{x+1} + 2 = 5 \Rightarrow \frac{5}{x+1} = 3$

$$5 = 3(x+1) = 3x + 3 \Rightarrow 3x = 2 \Rightarrow x = \frac{2}{3}$$

20. **(C)** A moment's reflection will serve to convince you that $x = 1$. Note that the right side of the equation looks exactly like the left side, but with 1 in place of x.

21. **(B)** When given two equations with two unknowns, first solve for one unknown in terms of the other: $x + y = 6 \Rightarrow y = 6 - x$. Then, substitute that into the other equation: $3x + (6 - x) = 10 \Rightarrow 3x + 6 - x = 10 \Rightarrow 2x = 4 \Rightarrow x = 2$. Make sure to use both equations. If you substitute the results of the first equation back into the first equation, you will always get $0 = 0$.

22. **(B)** Solve for x in terms of y: $2x + y = 10 \Rightarrow x = \frac{10-y}{2}$. Now, substitute that into the other equation: $\left(\frac{10-y}{2}\right) + y = 7 \Rightarrow 10 - y + 2y = 14 \Rightarrow y = 4$.

23. **(A)** Solve for y in terms of x: $2x - y = 3 \Rightarrow -y = 3 - 2x \Rightarrow y = 2x - 3$. Now, replace the y in the first equation with the result from the first equation: $x + 3y = 5 \Rightarrow x + 3(2x - 3) = 5 \Rightarrow x + 6x - 9 = 5 \Rightarrow 7x = 14 \Rightarrow x = 2$.

24. **(C)** Here we will add the two equations together: $\begin{matrix} x + y = 2 \\ +x - y = 2 \end{matrix} \Rightarrow 2x = 4 \Rightarrow x = 2$. Now, replace x in one of the given equations with the numeric value of x: $(2) + y = 2 \Rightarrow y = 0$. Another way to approach this problem is to look and note that it doesn't matter whether we add or subtract y, both equations equal 2. This suggests that $y = 0$.

25. **(B)** Solve for a in terms of b: $a + b = 5 \Rightarrow a = 5 - b$. Plug that result into the second equation: $2(5 - b) + 3b = 12 \Rightarrow 10 - 2b + 3b = 12 \Rightarrow b = 2$.

26. **(A)** Solve for x: $2x = 4 \Rightarrow x = 2$. Insert that result into the first equation: $5(2) + 3y = 13 \Rightarrow 3y = 3 \Rightarrow y = 1$.

27. **(E)** Whenever the two given equations contain terms that are exactly opposite each other, it is easiest to add the two equations: $\begin{aligned} k - n &= 5 \\ +2k + n &= 16 \end{aligned} \Rightarrow 3k = 21 \Rightarrow k = 7$.

28. **(C)** We can easily manipulate the first equation so that it contains $(-t)$: $t = k - 5 \Rightarrow 5 = k - t \Rightarrow k - t = 5$. Now, we can add the two equations together to cancel out the t variables: $\begin{aligned} k - t &= 5 \\ +k + t &= 11 \end{aligned} \Rightarrow 2k = 16 \Rightarrow k = 8$.

29. **(B)** Use the second equation to solve for b in terms of a: $a - b = 3 \Rightarrow a - 3 = b$. Now, plug that result into the first equation: $a + 5(a - 3) = 9 \Rightarrow a + 5a - 15 = 9 \Rightarrow 6a = 24 \Rightarrow a = 4$.

30. **(B)** The first equation is already a solution of y in terms of x. Thus, we can enter that directly into the second equation to solve for x: $2(8 + x) + x = 28 \Rightarrow 16 + 2x + x = 28 \Rightarrow 3x = 12 \Rightarrow x = 4$.

31. **(D)** If we multiply the first equation by 2, we get an equation which will, when added to the second equation, cancel out the y terms: $\left(\frac{x+y}{2} = 4\right) \cdot 2 \Rightarrow x + y = 8 \Rightarrow \begin{aligned} x + y &= 8 \\ +x - y &= 4 \end{aligned} \Rightarrow 2x = 12 \Rightarrow x = 6$.

32. **(D)** If we multiply the first equation by 2 and the second by 3, we get two equations that, when added together, will yield an equation without y terms. We can then easily solve for x: $\left(\frac{x+y}{2} = 7\right) \cdot 2 \Rightarrow x + y = 14$; $\left(\frac{x-y}{3} = 2\right) \cdot 3 \Rightarrow x - y = 6 \Rightarrow \begin{aligned} x + y &= 14 \\ +x - y &= 6 \end{aligned} \Rightarrow 2x = 20 \Rightarrow x = 10$.

33. **(D)** Don't let the extra variable distract you: $\begin{aligned} x + y + z &= 10 \\ +x - y - z &= 4 \end{aligned} \Rightarrow 2x = 14 \Rightarrow x = 7$.

34. **(C)** Since the equations have two terms that are opposites of each other, solve by linear combination. To do this, add the equations and solve for x: $\begin{aligned} x + 2y - z &= 4 \\ +2x - 2y + z &= 8 \end{aligned} \Rightarrow 3x = 12 \Rightarrow x = 4$.

35. **(C)** Note that the first two equations have opposite terms: $\pm z$. Thus, we can add the first two equations together to produce an equation with just x and y terms. We can then use that equation with the third equation to solve for x: $\begin{aligned} x + y + z &= 6 \\ +x + y - z &= 4 \end{aligned} \Rightarrow 2x + 2y = 10 \Rightarrow x + y = 5 \Rightarrow \begin{aligned} x + y &= 5 \\ +x - y &= 3 \end{aligned} \Rightarrow 2x = 8 \Rightarrow x = 4$.

36. **(B)** Approach these types of questions by first factoring and then finding the two values of x, such that each factor equals 0: $x^2 - 5x + 4 = 0 \Rightarrow x^2 - 4x - x + 4 = (x - 4)(x - 1) = 0$. The left side will equal zero when $x = 4$ or $x = 1$.

37. **(D)** Use the quadratic formula: $x = \frac{-b \pm \sqrt{b^2 - 4ac}}{2a} = \frac{-(-3) \pm \sqrt{(-3)^2 - 4(1)(-4)}}{2(1)} = \frac{3 \pm \sqrt{9 + 16}}{2} = \frac{3 \pm 5}{2} = \{4, -1\}$. Or, simply factor: $x^2 - 3x - 4 = 0 \Rightarrow x^2 - 4x + x - 4 = (x - 4)(x + 1) = 0$. The left side will equal zero when $x = 4$ or $x = -1$.

38. **(A)** Factor to solve: $x^2 + 5x + 6 = 0 \Rightarrow x^2 + 3x + 2x + 6 = (x + 3)(x + 2) = 0$. Thus, $x = -3$ or $x = -2$.

39. **(C)** Use the quadratic formula: $x = \frac{-b \pm \sqrt{b^2 - 4ac}}{2a} = \frac{-(-3) \pm \sqrt{(-3)^2 - 4(1)(2)}}{2(1)} = \frac{3 \pm \sqrt{9-8}}{2} = \frac{3 \pm 1}{2} = \{1, 2\}$. Or, simply factor:
$x^2 - 3x + 2 = 0 \Rightarrow x^2 - 2x - x + 2 = (x-2)(x-1) = 0$. The left side will equal zero when $x = 2$ or $x = 1$.

40. **(E)** When given a list of choices, it is still wisest to factor the equation, as it is more accurate. If that is impossible, then substitute the values from the list back into the equation. $x^2 + 3x + 2 = 0 \Rightarrow x^2 + 2x + x + 2 = (x+2)(x+1)$. Thus, $x = -1$ or $x = -2$. So, I is false, and II and III are true.

41. **(A)** This problem is simply a quadratic problem with the form $ax^2 + bx + c = 0$. So, solve by factoring and equating both factors to zero: $x^2 + 5x = -4 \Rightarrow x^2 + 5x + 4 = 0 \Rightarrow x^2 + 4x + x + 4 = (x+4)(x+1) = 0$. Thus, $x = -1$ or $x = -4$.

42. **(C)** This is just a reformulation of a quadratic problem with the form $ax^2 + bx + c = 0$. So, first reorganize the equation to conform to the standard quadratic form, then factor and solve each set of factors by setting them equal to zero: $x^2 - 8 = 7x \Rightarrow x^2 - 7x - 8 = 0 \Rightarrow x^2 - 8x + x - 8 = (x-8)(x+1) = 0$. Thus, $x = -1$ or $x = 8$.

43. **(E)** Factor to solve: $k^2 - 10 = -3k \Rightarrow k^2 + 3k - 10 = 0 \Rightarrow k^2 + 5k - 2k - 10 = (k+5)(k-2) = 0$. Thus, $k = 2$ or $k = -5$.

44. **(B)** Factor to solve: $x^2 = 12 - x \Rightarrow x^2 + x - 12 = 0 \Rightarrow x^2 + 4x - 3x - 12 = (x+4)(x-3) = 0$. So, $x = -4$ or $x = 3$.

45. **(B)** Clearly, $x = 0$ would satisfy the equation. We search for a second value: $3x^2 = 12x \Rightarrow 3x = 12 \Rightarrow x = 4$.

46. **(A)** $4(5-x) = 2(10-x^2) \Rightarrow \frac{4(5-x) = 2(10-x^2)}{2} \Rightarrow 2(5-x) = (10-x^2) \Rightarrow 10 - 2x = 10 - x^2 \Rightarrow x^2 = 2x \Rightarrow x = 0$ or $x = 2$.

47. **(C)** $3 + 4x < 28 \Rightarrow 4x < 25 \Rightarrow x < \frac{25}{4} = 6.25$.

48. **(A)** $5(3x-2) \geq 50 \Rightarrow (3x-2) \geq \frac{50}{5} \Rightarrow 3x - 2 \geq 10 \Rightarrow 3x \geq 12 \Rightarrow x \geq 4$.

49. **(D)** $8 - 3x > 35 \Rightarrow -3x > 27 \Rightarrow 3x < -27 \Rightarrow x < -9$. Remember to reverse the direction of the inequality when dividing by a negative number, in this case negative 1.

50. **(D)** Factor to solve: $x^2 = 6x - 8 \Rightarrow x^2 - 6x + 8 = 0 \Rightarrow x^2 - 4x - 2x + 8 = (x-4)(x-2) = 0$. So, $x = 2$ or $x = 4$.

51. **(D)** The equation is true when either $(x-8)$ or $(x+2)$ equals 0. Thus, $x = 8$ or $x = -2$.

52. **(E)** $9 - 3(6-x) = 12 \Rightarrow 9 - 18 + 3x = 12 \Rightarrow 3x = 21 \Rightarrow x = 7$. It is worth noting that you can eliminate A and B, since an equation will have two solutions *only* if x is squared.

53. **(C)** Combine like terms, and divide by the coefficient of the variable: $\frac{x+5}{4} = 17 \Rightarrow x + 5 = 4 \cdot 17 \Rightarrow x = 68 - 5 = 63$.

54. **(B)** Combine like terms, and divide by the coefficient of the variable: $\frac{x}{2} - \frac{x-2}{3} = .4 \Rightarrow 2 \cdot 3\left(\frac{x}{2} - \frac{x-2}{3} = 0.4\right)$.
$3x - 2x + 4 = 2.4 \Rightarrow x = -1.6$

55. **(A)** Combine like terms, and divide by the coefficient of the variable:
$0.02x + 1.44 = x - 16.2 \Rightarrow 1.44 + 16.2 = x - 0.02x \Rightarrow 0.98x = 17.64 \Rightarrow x = \frac{17.64}{0.98} = 18$.

56. **(C)** Combine like terms, and divide by the coefficient of the variable: $3 - 2(x-5) = 3x + 4 \Rightarrow 3 - 2x + 10 = 3x + 4$
$13 - 4 = 3x + 2x \Rightarrow 5x = 9 \Rightarrow x = \frac{9}{5}$

57. **(D)** Factor to solve: $x^2 - 9x - 22 = 0 \Rightarrow x^2 - 11x + 2x - 22 = (x-11)(x+2) = 0$. Thus, $x = 11$ or $x = -2$.

58. **(E)** $(x+8)(x+1)=78 \Rightarrow x^2+9x+8=78 \Rightarrow x^2+9x-70=0 \Rightarrow x^2+14x-5x-70=(x+14)(x-5)$. Thus, $x=-14$ or $x=5$. We now test those two values in the second equation: $(5)^2+9(5)=25+45=70$; $(-14)^2+9(-14)=196-126=70$.

59. **(C)** Replace x in the equation by -6 and solve for y: $2(-6)+3y=12 \Rightarrow -12+3y=12 \Rightarrow 3y=24 \Rightarrow y=8$.

60. **(D)** When a line intersects the x-axis, $y=0$. Thus, replace y in the equation by 0: $5x+2(0)=20 \Rightarrow 5x=20 \Rightarrow x=4$. So, the point is $(4,0)$.

61. **(E)** $3x+5y=10 \Rightarrow 5y=10-3x \Rightarrow y=-0.6x+2$.

62. **(B)** $x=ay+3 \Rightarrow ay=x-3 \Rightarrow y=\frac{x-3}{a}$.

63. **(A)** $8x+16=(x+2)(x+5) \Rightarrow 8(x+2)=(x+2)(x+5)$. If $x=-2$, both sides will equal zero. But, we can also divide each side by $(x+2)$: $8=(x+5) \Rightarrow x=3$. Or, you can solve this equation formally: $8x+16=(x+2)(x+5)$ $8(x+2)=(x+2)(x+5) \Rightarrow 8(x+2)-(x+2)(x+5)=0 \Rightarrow (x+2)[8-(x+5)] \Rightarrow (x+2)(3-x)$. So, $x=-2$ or $x=3$.

64. **(C)** $\frac{x+5}{0.2}=\frac{x+5}{\frac{1}{5}}=5(x+5)=0.3x \Rightarrow 5x+25=0.3x \Rightarrow 4.7x=-25 \Rightarrow 47x=-25\cdot 10=-250 \Rightarrow x=-\frac{250}{47}$.

65. **(D)** Combine like terms, and divide by the coefficient of the variable: $\frac{0.2+x}{3}=\frac{\frac{5}{6}}{4}=\frac{5}{6\cdot 4} \Rightarrow 0.2+x=3\cdot\left(\frac{5}{24}\right)=\frac{5}{8}$

$x=\frac{5}{8}-\frac{1}{5}=\frac{5\cdot 5-1\cdot 8}{40}=\frac{17}{40}$.

66. **(C)** The statements $6<x$ and x is an integer imply that x is an integer equal to or greater than 7. The additional statement $x<8$ says that x is an integer equal to or smaller than 7. The three statements taken together show that $x=7$.

67. **(E)** $5\leq x\leq 7$ is true for 5, 6, and 7. The inequality can be broken down into three relationships: $5=x$, $5<x<7$, and $x=7$.

68. **(C)** Since x and y are integers, we know from the two inequalities that $x=3$ and $y=7$. Thus, $xy=3\cdot 7=21$.

69. **(A)** The minimum value of xy will equal the product of the smallest possible values of each x and y. From the first inequality, we see that $x=2$ is the smallest possible x. From the second, we see that $y=7$ is the smallest possible y. Thus, $xy=2\cdot 7=14$ is the minimum value of xy.

70. **(D)** $\frac{5}{2}=2.5$, $\frac{7}{2}=3.5$, and $\frac{3}{2}=1.5$. Thus, only I and III are true.

71. **(E)** $3^{8x+4}=27^{2x+12} \Rightarrow 27=3\cdot 3\cdot 3 \Rightarrow 27^{2x+12}=3^{2x+12}\cdot 3^{2x+12}\cdot 3^{2x+12}=3^{3(2x+12)}=3^{6x+36}$. Now, $3^{8x+4}=3^{6x+36}$, so $8x+4=6x+36$, and $2x=32 \Rightarrow x=16$.

72. **(D)** $(3+x)x=2x+x+16 \Rightarrow (3+x)x=3x+x^2=2x+x+16 \Rightarrow x^2=16 \Rightarrow x=\pm 4$.

73. **(A)** $10x^2=30 \Rightarrow x^2=3$ and $(6+y)y=6y+52 \Rightarrow 6y+y^2=6y+52 \Rightarrow y^2=52$. Thus, $2x^2+2y^2=2\cdot 3+2\cdot 52=110$.

74. **(B)** $|x|=5 \Rightarrow |-5|=5 \Rightarrow |5|=5$. Thus, $x=\pm 5$.

75. **(B)** The key to this problem is in the wording of the question: the authors define commutativity, and then ask about it in relation to *addition*. Only two of the answers have anything to do with addition, so you can eliminate the others. The definition of commutatitvity is that the order of objects doesn't matter in a 2-variable function. Addition is a 2-variable function: $a+b$. The commutative property merely states that $a+b=b+a$. But, it only holds for terms that are the same. Thus, $2a+b\neq 2b+a$ for all a and b.

76. **(C)** There is a total of 8 digits, and there are 2 digits that equal 4. Thus, the probability of Helen selecting a 4 is $\frac{\text{digits that equal four}}{\text{total digits}} = \frac{2}{8} = \frac{1}{4}$.

77. **(C)** $P = 6s = 6 \cdot 3 = 18$. The key to solving this problem it to realize that a regular hexagon (or polygon in general) has equal sides. Thus, knowing the length of one side is to know the length of all the sides of the hexagon. The perimeter can then be calculated.

78. **(D)** $I = prt = \$1,000 \cdot 0.06 \cdot 2 = \$120$. Remember here to convert the percentage to a decimal. Thus, $6\% = 0.06$.

79. **(B)** Just replace x with $3a$ in the second equation: $y = 5(3a) + 6 = 15a + 6$.

80. **(A)** Solve for x in terms of a: $2(x+3) = 18a + 10 \Rightarrow 2x + 6 = 18a + 10 \Rightarrow 2x = 18a + 4 \Rightarrow x = 9a + 2$.

81. **(A)** $F = 1.8C + 32 \Rightarrow 41° = 1.8C + 32 \Rightarrow 9° = \frac{9}{5}C \Rightarrow \frac{5}{9}9° = C \Rightarrow C = 5°$.

82. **(E)** Using the second equation, substitute x^4 for y: $x^5 = 8x^4 \Rightarrow x = 8$. Alternatively, you could divide the first equation by the second to directly obtain the answer: $\frac{x^5 = 8y}{x^4 = y} \Rightarrow x = 8$.

83. **(C)** You can set this up as the product of two ratios expressed in fractional terms: $\left(\frac{1}{6}\right)\left(\frac{1}{5}\right) = \frac{1}{30}$. George can choose from 6 pencils and 5 pens, which results in 30 possible combinations.

84. **(A)** This is asking about commutativity with respect to multiplication. Thus, only those answers that involve multiplication should be considered. This leaves us with answer choices A and C. The answer in C, $2a + b = 2b + a$, is false in general, since the two objects are different $2b \neq 2a$. Thus, the correct answer is $xy = yx$. Note that this expresses exactly the defined property: the order of the procedure, multiplication, doesn't affect the result.

85. **(D)** To find the constant, divide any term in the sequence by the term before it, so $\frac{8}{2} = \frac{128}{32} = 4$. To find the next term, multiply 128 by 4: $128 \cdot 4 = 512$.

86. **(E)** We are given the following sequence, $\left\{ \begin{matrix} 1,2,3, & 4 \\ 1,9,31,73 \end{matrix} \right\}$, and the equation that defines it, $x^3 + x^2 - 2x + 1$. The next term in the bottom sequence is determined by taking the next term in the top sequence, 5, and entering it into the given equation: $(5)^3 + (5)^2 - 2(5) + 1 = 125 + 25 - 10 + 1 = 141$.

87. **(D)** $\frac{\text{letters equal to 'D'}}{\text{total letters}} = \frac{2}{5}$.

88. **(A)** From the quadratic formula, $x = \frac{-b \pm \sqrt{b^2 - 4ac}}{2a}$, we know that the nature of the values of x depends most fundamentally on the terms inside the square root. For there to be two real solutions for x, the difference inside the square root must be positive. If it is zero there will be only one real solution. If it is negative, the solutions will be imaginary. Thus, $b^2 - 4ac > 0 \Rightarrow b^2 > 4ac \Rightarrow (8)^2 > 4(1)c = 4c \Rightarrow 64 > 4c \Rightarrow 16 > c \Rightarrow c < 16$. Only -10 fulfills that criterion.

89. **(A)** From the quadratic formula, $x = \frac{-b \pm \sqrt{b^2 - 4ac}}{2a}$, it is evident that there will be two distinct real values of x only when $b^2 - 4ac$ is positive. If that term is zero, there will only be one value for x: $\frac{-b}{2a}$. If it is negative, the values will be imaginary. So, $b^2 - 4ac > 0 \Rightarrow b^2 > 4ac \Rightarrow b^2 > 4(1)(8) = 32 \Rightarrow b^2 > 32 \Rightarrow b > \sqrt{32} = 4\sqrt{2}$. Only 6 fulfills that requirement.

90. **(D)** An inch is one thirty-sixth of a yard, so cost of x yards and y inches $= xk + \frac{yk}{36}$.

91. **(E)** $\frac{\pi r^2 h}{3} \Rightarrow \frac{\pi(3)^2 12}{3} = 36\pi$.

92. **(B)** $x^2 - 14k^2 = 5kx \Rightarrow x^2 - 5kx - 14k^2 = x^2 - 7kx + 2kx - 14k^2 = (x - 7k)(x + 2k)$. Thus, the two solutions for x in terms of k are $x = -2k$ and $x = 7k$.

93. **(E)** There is a general formula for the nth term of an arithmetic sequence: $a_n = a_1 + (n-1)c$, where a_n is the value of the nth term in the series, a_1 is the value of the first term in the series, and c is the constant designating the common difference between consecutive terms. Thus, with $n = 9$, $a_1 = 1$, and $c = 3$, we get $a_9 = 1 + (9-1)3 = 1 + 8 \cdot 3 = 25$.

94. **(B)** $\dfrac{\text{number of distinct letters in word the 'MATHEMATICS'}}{\text{number of letters in the alphabet}} = \dfrac{8}{26} = \dfrac{4}{13}$.

95. **(D)** $\frac{1}{a^2} - \frac{1}{b^2}$ is equivalent to $\left(\frac{1}{a} + \frac{1}{b}\right)\left(\frac{1}{a} - \frac{1}{b}\right)$. Therefore, $\frac{1}{a^2} - \frac{1}{b^2} = (7)(3) = 21$.

96. **(D)** Solve for x: $\frac{3x}{4} = 1 \Rightarrow 3x = 4 \Rightarrow x = \frac{4}{3}$. Substitute this value for x in the expression $\frac{2x}{3}$: $\frac{2x}{3} = \frac{2}{3}x = \frac{2}{3} \cdot \frac{4}{3} = \frac{8}{9}$.

97. **(D)** Substitute $\frac{y}{7}$ for x in the second equation: $7x = 12 \Rightarrow 7 \cdot \frac{y}{7} = 12 \Rightarrow y = 12$.

98. **(E)** Two equations are actually given: $x = k + \frac{1}{2}$ and $k + \frac{1}{2} = \frac{k+3}{2}$. Solve for k: $k + \frac{1}{2} = \frac{k+3}{2} \Rightarrow 2k + 1 = k + 3 \Rightarrow k = 2$. Substitute 2 for k and solve for x: $x = k + \frac{1}{2} = 2 + \frac{1}{2} = \frac{5}{2}$.

99. **(C)** Solve for x in the first equation: $7 - x = 0 \Rightarrow x = 7$. Substitute 7 for x in the second equation: $10 - x = 10 - 7 = 3$.

100. **(D)** $xy = \left(7 - \sqrt{3}\right)\left(7 + \sqrt{3}\right) = 49 + 7\sqrt{3} - 7\sqrt{3} - 3 = 49 - 3 = 46$. Therefore, (I) is rational. (II) is also rational: $\left(7 - \sqrt{3}\right) + \left(7 + \sqrt{3}\right) = 14$.

101. **(E)** $\dfrac{2^{x+4} - 2(2^x)}{2(2^{x+3})} = 1 - 2^{-3} = 1 - \frac{1}{2^3} = 1 - \frac{1}{8} = \frac{7}{8}$.

102. **(A)** $w = 8^x = 2y$, so $8^x = 2(2^x)$. Since $8^x = (2 \cdot 2 \cdot 2)^x = 2^{3x}$ and $2(2^x) = 2^{x+1}$, $2^{3x} = 2^{x+1} \Rightarrow 3x = x + 1 \Rightarrow 2x = 1 \Rightarrow x = \frac{1}{2}$.

103. **(B)** Using the provided formula for decay of a radioactive substance, substitute the given values and solve for t: $y = kc^{\frac{t}{i}}$
$1 = 7.68(0.5)^{\frac{t}{9}} \Rightarrow \frac{1}{7.68} = (0.5)^{\frac{t}{9}} \Rightarrow \ln\left(\frac{1}{7.68}\right) = \left(\frac{t}{9}\right)\ln(0.5) \Rightarrow t = 9 \cdot \frac{\ln\left(\frac{1}{7.68}\right)}{\ln(0.5)}$. Using a calculator, $t = 26.47$. Therefore, after 27 days, there is less than 1 gram left of the original radioisotope. Note: You may be able to find the solution more directly by using the "solve" key on a calculator.

104. **(D)** 105 months $= \frac{105}{12} = \frac{35}{4}$ years. Therefore, $16\left(2^{\frac{2x}{5}}\right) = 16\left(2^{\frac{2(35/4)}{5}}\right) = 16\left(2^{\frac{70/2}{5}}\right) = 16\left(2^{\frac{70}{20}}\right) = 16\left(2^{3.5}\right) \approx 181$.

105. **(E)** The equality holds true for all values in the set: $\frac{1+2+\cdots+n}{2+4+\cdots+2n} = \frac{\frac{n(n+1)}{2}}{n(n+1)} = \frac{n(n+1)}{2} \cdot \frac{1}{n(n+1)} = \frac{1}{2}$. Alternatively, substitute values from the set for n. Only a few substitutions are necessary to demonstrate that the equality is true for all values in the set.

106. **(B)** Eliminate (A) by substituting $x = -1$ or any value such that $-1 < x < 0$. Eliminate (C) by multiplying the right side of the equation to obtain $x^3 + 8$. Eliminate (D), since $36 < 72$. Eliminate (E), since $\frac{2^x}{2^{x-1}} = 2^{x-(x-1)} = 2^1 = 2$.

107. **(A)** 3^3 is odd, as are 5^5, 7^7, and 11^{11}. Since the sum of four odd numbers is an even number, and an even number is divisible by 2, 2 is the smallest prime number that the divides the sum of $3^3 + 5^5 + 7^7 + 11^{11}$.

108. **(A)** This problem is solved most quickly by using a calculator. If $x = 1$, $3^{\frac{1}{4}} < 2^1$. If $x = 3$, $3^{\frac{1}{4} + \frac{3}{4}} < 2^3$. If $x = 5$, $3^{\frac{1}{4} + \frac{3}{4} + \frac{5}{4}} = 3^{\frac{9}{4}} < 2^5$. If $x = 7$, $3^{\frac{1}{4} + \frac{3}{4} + \frac{5}{4} + \frac{7}{4}} = 3^4 < 2^7$. If $x = 9$, $3^{\frac{1}{4} + \frac{3}{4} + \frac{5}{4} + \frac{7}{4} + \frac{9}{4}} = 3^{\frac{25}{4}} > 2^9$. $x = 9$, which is a multiple of three.

109. **(C)** $x^{128} = 16^{32} = 8^{64} = 4^{128} \Rightarrow x = \pm 2$

110. **(C)** $8^0 = 1$; $9^{-2} = \frac{1}{9^2} = \frac{1}{81}$; $\left(\frac{1}{9}\right)^{-2} = \frac{1}{\left(\frac{1}{9}\right)^2} = \frac{1}{\frac{1}{81}} = 81$; $\left(\frac{1}{8}\right)^{\frac{2}{3}} = \left(\sqrt[3]{\frac{1}{8}}\right)^2 = \left(\frac{1}{2}\right)^2 = \frac{1}{4}$; $\left(\frac{1}{16}\right)^{-\frac{1}{4}} = \frac{1}{\sqrt[4]{\frac{1}{16}}} = \frac{1}{\frac{1}{2}} = 2$. Therefore, three of the given numerical expressions represent whole numbers.

111. **(D)** $3^{x+2} = 3^x \cdot 3^2 = y \cdot 9 = 9y$.

112. **(B)** $x = \sqrt{x} + 20 \Rightarrow x - 20 = \sqrt{x} \Rightarrow x^2 - 40x + 400 = x \Rightarrow x^2 - 41x + 400 = 0 \Rightarrow (x-25)(x-16) = 0 \Rightarrow x = 25$ or $x = 16$. Since this reduction required taking the square of each side of the equation, check both values for x in the equation. Let $x = 25$: $25 - 20 = x = \sqrt{25} \Rightarrow 5 = 5$. Let $x = 16$: $16 - 20 = x = \sqrt{16} \Rightarrow -4 \neq 4$. Therefore, x is equal to only one value, 25.

113. **(E)** Since $x = 3k$, and k is an integer, the values of x that must be tested are: $-6, -3, 0, 6,$ and 12. If $x = -6, \sqrt{2x+8} = \sqrt{-4}$; this equality is invalid for any value of y. If $x = -3, \sqrt{2x+8} = \sqrt{2}$, which is valid for $y = 2$. If $x = 0, \sqrt{2x+8} = \sqrt{8}$, which is valid for $y = 8$. If $x = 6, \sqrt{2x+8} = \sqrt{14}$, which is valid for $y = 14$. If $x = 12, \sqrt{2x+8} = \sqrt{28}$, which is valid for $y = \sqrt{28}$. The sum of the valid values for y is: $-3 + 0 + 6 + 12 = 15$.

114. **(B)** If $k = 12$, $\sqrt{8x} + 12 = 18 \Rightarrow 8x = 36 \Rightarrow x = 4.5$. If $k = 13$, $\sqrt{8x} + 13 = 18 \Rightarrow 8x = 25 \Rightarrow x = \frac{25}{8}$. If $k = 14$, $\sqrt{8x} + 14 = 18 \Rightarrow 8x = 16 \Rightarrow x = 2$. Therefore, only one value of k meets the stated requirements.

EXERCISE 11—GEOMETRY (p. 199)

1. **(C)** There are $360°$ in a circle. Thus, $x = 360° - 270° = 90°$.

2. **(D)** A circle possesses at all times $360°$. Thus, $x = 360° - (2 \cdot 120°) = 120°$.

3. **(C)** Every circle has $360°$. Thus, $x = 360° - 240° = 120$.

4. **(B)** A line has $180°$. Thus, when met by another line, the sum of the two new angles is $180°$. $x = 180° - 150° = 30°$.

5. **(E)** A straight line measures $180°$ on each side. $x = 180° - 60° = 120°$.

6. **(A)** The sum of the angles around a given point is always $360°$. So, the sum of the degrees of two angles created by two lines emanating from a given point will always equal $360°$. Thus, $x = 360° - 150° = 210°$.

7. **(E)** The little box in the figure indicates a $90°$ angle. Since a line measures $180°$ to a side, $x = 180° - 90° = 90°$. This is such a common calculation and shorthand for representing right angles that it should be memorized. It is also the basis for many of the more advanced calculations that will be required for this test.

8. **(D)** l_1 and l_2 are perpendicular, thus the angles they form are each $90°$. Now, $x = 90° - 30° = 60°$.

9. **(B)** When two lines intersect, the opposite angles are congruent, or equal. Thus, we have four angles, two measuring $120°$ and two measuring $x°$. The sum of these angles is equal to $360°$. $2x = 360° - (2 \cdot 120°) = 120° \Rightarrow x = 60°$. Alternatively, recognize that line 2 is $180°$ on both sides. Therefore, $x = 180° - 120° = 60°$.

10. **(A)** Opposite angles created by the intersection of two lines are equal. Thus, $x = 30°$.

11. **(B)** The statement $\overline{AB} \cong \overline{BC}$ means that the lengths of these two sides are the same. Because two angles of the triangle in question are equal, the triangle is isosceles. In such a case, the sides opposite the angles are equal in length. Thus, II is true. For a special class of isosceles triangle, the equilateral triangle, where all three angles are equal, the measure of all three sides is the same. For such a triangle, however, since the sum of the three angles must equal $180°$, each angle must be $60°$. Since that is not the case for this triangle, we can conclude that I and III are false.

12. **(B)** The diagram given shows two parallel lines, intersected by a third line. In the special case when that intersecting line is perpendicular to the parallel lines, all of the eight angles created are equal. That is not true generally. However, it is always true for cases represented by the diagram that each angle falls into one of two categories, and there are four angles for each intersection point.. On the diagram, all of the opposite angles are equal. Thus, $a° = d° = e° = h°$ and $b° = c° = f° = g°$. Only II is true.

13. **(A)** $a° = d° = e° = h°$ and $b° = c° = f° = g°$ since this is the general case of the intersection of two parallel lines by another line. Thus, only I is true.

14. **(C)** As always, if two angles lie on the same side of an intersected line, then their sum is $180°$. So, I and II are true. As for III, $b°$ and $g°$ are similar and thus, except for the exceptional case of a perpendicular intersecting line, unequal.

15. **(A)** $g = 180° - 120° = 60°$.

C ANSWERS AND EXPLANATIONS

16. **(A)** $h°$ and $d°$ are similar, thus $d = 60°$.

17. **(C)** In a triangle, two angles are equal if and only if their opposite sides are equal. Thus, $z° = x°$.

18. **(E)** The measure of two sides of a triangle are equal if and only if their opposite angles are equal. Thus, $\overline{PQ} \cong \overline{QR} \cong \overline{PR}$. Also, since all the internal angles of this triangle are congruent, $60°$, this must be an equilateral triangle. Therefore, all the sides must be congruent.

19. **(E)** Because the sides of this triangle are all equal, all of the angles are equal as well: $x° = y° = z°$.

20. **(C)** The perimeter of any closed polygon (e.g. a triangle) is equal to the sum of its sides: $P = 3 + 5 + 7 = 15$.

21. **(A)** The perimeter of a triangle is the sum of its three sides. In this instance: $P = 4 + 8 + 8 = 20$.

22. **(C)** The perimeter of the given triangle is the sum of the lengths of its sides: $P = 3 \cdot 6 = 18$.

23. **(C)** The area of a triangle is equal to one-half the product of its width and its height. The width can be the length of any side, while the height is not necessarily the length of a side, but the length of a perpendicular line originating from the triangle's vertex. This line is called the altitude. In this instance, $A = \dfrac{3 \cdot 8}{2} = 12$.

24. **(E)** A triangle's area is equal to one-half of the product of its altitude and its width. Thus, $A = \dfrac{5 \cdot 10}{2} = 25$.

25. **(D)** The area of a triangle is equal to the one-half the product of its altitude and its width. Thus, $A = \dfrac{4 \cdot 9}{2} = 18$.

26. **(B)** For right triangles, the sum of the squares of the lengths of the two legs adjacent to the right angle is equal to the square of the length of the hypotenuse. Thus, $\overline{RS}^2 = 3^2 + 4^2 = 9 + 16 = 25 \Rightarrow \overline{RS} = 5$. This is a 3-4-5 right triangle. It shows up often on the test, so memorize it.

27. **(B)** $\overline{AB}^2 + \overline{BC}^2 = \overline{AC}^2 \Rightarrow \overline{AB}^2 + 6^2 = 10^2 \Rightarrow \overline{AB}^2 + 36 = 100 \Rightarrow \overline{AB}^2 = 64 \Rightarrow \overline{AB} = 8$, by the Pythagorean theorem.

28. **(A)** $\overline{PR}^2 + \overline{PQ}^2 = \overline{QR}^2 \Rightarrow \overline{PR}^2 + 5^2 = 13^2 \Rightarrow \overline{PR}^2 = 169 - 25 = 144 \Rightarrow \overline{PR} = 12$, by the Pythagorean theorem.

29. **(D)** This problem can be approached in two ways. First, you can remember that for a 45°-45°-90° isosceles triangle, the length of the hypotenuse is equal to the length of a side (the two sides besides the hypotenuse are equal) times $\sqrt{2}$. Thus, we can arrive immediately at $\overline{AC} = 4\sqrt{2}$. This is certainly worth committing to memory. Second, you can just use the Pythagorean theorem to arrive at the same result: $\overline{AC}^2 = 4^2 + 4^2 = 16 + 16 = 32 \Rightarrow \overline{AC} = \sqrt{32} = \sqrt{16 \cdot 2} = 4\sqrt{2}$.

30. **(E)** Using the theorem of Pythagoras, $\overline{JL}^2 = 3^2 + 5^2 = 9 + 25 = 34 \Rightarrow \overline{JL} = \sqrt{34}$.

31. **(B)** This problem is a good example of how test-writers place 'noise' in the problem. Noise is information that isn't actually required to solve the problem. For example, in this problem the test-writers give you the length of the right side of the parallelogram; it is additional information that is not needed to solve the problem. The area of a parallelogram is equal to the product of its base (the length of its bottom (or top) side) and its height, as obtained by an altitude line. The line that makes a right angle with the base of the parallelogram is the altitude. Thus, $A = 20 \cdot 6 = 120$.

32. **(B)** This problem requires two steps. First, we must determine the length of the altitude that forms the right side of the triangle in the parallelogram. This can easily be computed by using a calculator to solve $\sin 30° = \frac{x}{10}$, so $x = 10\sin 30° = 5$. Otherwise, it can be done by relying on a basic fact about $30° - 60° - 90°$ triangles: the length of the side opposite to the 30° angle is equal to one-half the length of the hypotenuse. Thus, $l = $ length of the altitude $= \frac{10}{2} = 5$. Second, we multiply the length of the altitude by the length of the base to acquire the area: $A = 5 \cdot 16 = 80$.

33. **(C)** First, we need to find the length of the parallelogram's altitude. We start by finding the angle of the triangle formed by drawing an altitude through the left side of the diagram. The angle opposite to that is equal to $135°$; therefore, since this is a

parallelogram, the angle encompassing the altitude line is also $135°$. We can also see that the part of that angle inside the triangle will be equal to $135° - 90° = 45°$. Since the triangle is a right triangle, we know now that both of its non-right angles are $45°$. A property of such triangles that should certainly be memorized both legs of the triangle are equal to one-half the product of the length of the hypotenuse and $\sqrt{2}$. Thus, $l =$ length of the altitude $= 8\sqrt{2}\frac{\sqrt{2}}{2} = \frac{8 \cdot 2}{2} = 8$. Knowing the length of the altitude, we can now compute the area: $A = l \cdot b = 8 \cdot 16 = 128$, with $b =$ the length of the base.

34. **(C)** $\angle ABO = \angle ABD = 70°$. $\angle ABD$ is an *inscribed angle*. The number of degrees of such an angle is equal to the half of the degrees of the arc it intercepts, in this case, $\measuredangle AD$, which is the perimeter of the circle from point A to point D. The measure of that arc is thus $\measuredangle AD = 2 \cdot \angle ABD = 2 \cdot 70° = 140°$. Now, since BD is a diameter, $\measuredangle BD = 180°$. But, $\measuredangle BD = \measuredangle BA + \measuredangle AD$. Thus, $\measuredangle BA = 180° - 140° = 40°$. $\measuredangle BA$ is an arc intercepted by $\angle BOA$, which is similar to its opposite angle, $\angle COD$. Thus, $\angle COD = 40°$.

35. **(B)** That $\overline{AC}$ and $\overline{DE}$ bisect each other, implies that $\overline{AB} \cong \overline{BC}$ and $\overline{EB} \cong \overline{BD}$. Since we know additionally that $\angle ABE = \angle DBC$, we can conclude that $\overline{AE} \cong \overline{DC}$. Therefore, the two triangles are similar. Thus, $\angle C = \angle A = 20°$. So, $\angle DBC + \angle D + \angle C = 180° \Rightarrow \angle DBC = 180° - 86° - 20° = 74°$.

36. **(A)** The longest side of a triangle is always opposite the triangle's largest angle. To compare, we need to find the measure of $\angle C$: $\angle C = 180° - \angle A - \angle B = 180° - 23° - 84° = 73°$. Therefore, $\angle B$ is the largest angle. The side opposite $\angle B$ is the side that connects the other two points. Thus, the longest side is $\overline{AC}$.

37. **(D)** $\angle C = 180° - \angle A - \angle B = 180° - 40° - 70° = 70°$. The longest side is the angle opposite the largest angle, but here we do not have a largest angle. We only have two longer angles that are equal to each other. So, in this instance, the two longer sides are the ones opposite those two angles: $\overline{AC} \cong \overline{AB}$.

38. **(C)** The smallest angle of a triangle is the angle opposite its shortest side. $\overline{AB}$ is the shortest side, thus $\angle C$ is the smallest angle.

39. **(B)** The edges of the square's sides will also be edges of the cube. Since $A_s =$ area of side $= 49 = l^2 \Rightarrow l = 7$. Now, $A_c =$ area of the cube $= l^3 = 7^3$.

40. **(D)** A cube has six surfaces, each a square, all equal in dimensions. Therefore, $SA =$ surface area of the cube $= 54 = 6 \cdot A_s \Rightarrow A_s = 9$, where A_s is the area of each surface square. Each side of the squares, and thus the cube itself, has a length of 3 inches. So, $V = 3^3 = 27$.

41. **(D)** To solve this equation, we can divide the trapezoid into three sections, by dropping two perpendicular lines from the top two vertices of the trapezoid to the base. Because they are perpendicular to the base, and the base and the top are parallel, they are identical in length to the given altitude. Now, to find the length of the bottom edge of the right triangle, we use the Pythagorean theorem: $x^2 + 6^2 = 10^2 \Rightarrow x^2 = 64 \Rightarrow x = 8$. Since the upper and lower edges are parallel, the bottom edge of the left triangle is thus $26 - 8 - 12 = 6$. So, $A_t =$ total area $= A_{left\triangle} + A_{right\triangle} + A_{rect.} = \frac{6 \cdot 6}{2} + \frac{6 \cdot 8}{2} + 6 \cdot 12 = 18 + 24 + 72 = 114$. Alternatively, use the equation $A_t = \frac{h(b_1 + b_2)}{2} = \frac{6(12+26)}{2} = 114$.

42. **(B)** We can create two triangles and a rectangle within the trapezoid by dropping altitudes from the upper vertices of the trapezoid. These altitudes are perpendicular to the lower side. Thus, they are equal in length to the given altitude. To determine the length of the bottom side of the left triangle, use the Pythagorean theorem: $l^2 = 20^2 - 16^2 = 400 - 156 = 144$ $l = 12$. The equation would be no different for the triangle on the right, so the upper base is $b_2 = 30 - 12 - 12 = 6$. Thus, $P = 30 + 20 + 20 + 6 = 76$.

43. **(D)** To solve this problem, you must know the formula for the surface area of a sphere: $SA_{sphere} = 4\pi r^2$, where r is the radius of the sphere. So, $SA = 324\pi = 4\pi r^2 \Rightarrow r^2 = \frac{324\pi}{4\pi} = 81 \Rightarrow r = 9$. Use this radius in the equation given for the volume of a sphere: $V = \frac{4}{3}\pi r^3 = \frac{4}{3}\pi 9^3 = \frac{4 \cdot 81 \cdot 9}{3}\pi = 4 \cdot 81 \cdot 3\pi = 972\pi$ cm^2.

44. **(D)** $P = 2s_1 + 2s_2 = 2 \cdot 2 + 2 \cdot 4 = 4 + 8 = 12$, where s_1 and s_2 are two different, non-parallel sides of the rectangle.

45. **(E)** $P = 2s_1 + 2s_2 = 2 \cdot 3 + 2 \cdot 5 = 6 + 10 = 16$, where s_1 and s_2 are two different, non-parallel sides of the rectangle.

46. **(E)** $A = s_1 \cdot s_2 = 4 \cdot 5 = 20$, where s_1 and s_2 are two different, non-parallel sides of the rectangle.

47. **(C)** $A = s_1 \cdot s_2 = 3 \cdot 4 = 12$, where s_1 and s_2 are two different, non-parallel sides of the rectangle.

48. **(C)** $A = s_1 \cdot s_2 = 2 \cdot 7 = 14$, where s_1 and s_2 are two different, non-parallel sides of the rectangle.

49. **(D)** $A = s^2 = 5^2 = 25$, where s is the length of one of the square's sides.

50. **(D)** The diameter of a circle is twice its radius. Thus, the diameter of a circle with a radius of 2 is 4.

51. **(B)** A circle's radius is equal to one-half the length of the circle's diameter. Thus, for a circle with a diameter of 10, the radius is 5.

52. **(C)** $C = 2\pi r = 2\pi(3) = 6\pi$, where r is the radius.

53. **(B)** $C = 2\pi r = 2\pi(5) = 10\pi$, where r is the radius.

54. **(A)** $C = \pi d = \pi(8) = 8\pi$, where d is the diameter of the circle.

55. **(D)** $A = \pi r^2 = \pi(3)^2 = 9\pi$, where r is the radius of the circle.

56. **(A)** $A = \pi r^2 = \pi(5)^2 = 25\pi$, where r is the radius of the circle.

57. **(A)** $r = \frac{d}{2} = \frac{8}{2} = 4 \Rightarrow A = \pi r^2 = \pi(4)^2 = 16\pi$, where r and d are the radius and the diameter of the circle, respectively.

58. **(E)** $r = \frac{d}{2} = \frac{12}{2} = 6 \Rightarrow A = \pi r^2 = \pi(6)^2 = 36\pi$, where r and d are the radius and the diameter of a circle, respectively.

59. **(B)** A special property of 30°-60°-90° triangles is that the side opposite the 30° angle is equal to one half the length of the hypotenuse. Thus, $2 = \frac{b}{2} \Rightarrow b = 4$. Another special property of this type of triangle is that the side adjacent to the 30° angle is equal to the length of the hypotenuse multiplied by $\frac{\sqrt{3}}{2}$. Thus, $a = 4\frac{\sqrt{3}}{2} = 2\sqrt{3}$.

60. **(C)** Because this is a 30°-60°-90° triangle, $c = \frac{8}{2} = 4$ and $d = \frac{8\sqrt{3}}{2} = 4\sqrt{3}$.

61. **(E)** Since this is a 30°-60°-90° triangle, $7\sqrt{3} = f\frac{\sqrt{3}}{2} \Rightarrow f = 7\sqrt{3} \cdot \frac{2}{\sqrt{3}} = 14$. Now, $e = \frac{f}{2} = \frac{14}{2} = 7$.

62. **(C)** In a 30°-60°-90° triangle, the side adjacent to the 30° angle is equal to the hypotenuse times $\frac{\sqrt{3}}{2}$. Thus, $6 = h\frac{\sqrt{3}}{2} \Rightarrow h = \frac{12}{\sqrt{3}} = 12 \cdot 3^{-\frac{1}{2}} = 4 \cdot 3^1 \cdot 3^{-\frac{1}{2}} = 4 \cdot 3^{\frac{1}{2}} = 4\sqrt{3}$. Now, in such a triangle, the side opposite the 30° angle is equal to half the length of the hypotenuse. Therefore, $g = \frac{h}{2} = \frac{4\sqrt{3}}{2} = 2\sqrt{3}$.

63. **(B)** The lengths of the three sides of an equilateral triangle with $P = 24$ are each 8. If we drop an altitude from one point to the opposite side, we will have bisected the triangle, creating two 30°-60°-90° triangles (note that the top angle was split into two, so it is 30°). Now, the side adjacent to the 30° angle is equal to the length of the hypotenuse, 8, times $\frac{\sqrt{3}}{2}$. Thus, $a = 8\frac{\sqrt{3}}{2} = 4\sqrt{3}$.

64. **(A)** This is a 45°-45°-90° triangle. It is also isosceles. Thus, the sides equal to the two right angles are equal. Thus, $i = 3$. Now, using the Pythagorean theorem, we can arrive at the length of the hypotenuse: $j^2 = 3^2 + 3^2 = 18 \Rightarrow j = \sqrt{18} = 3\sqrt{2}$. The last equation demonstrates a result worth remembering. That is, if i is the length of one leg of a 45°-45°-90° triangle, then the hypotenuse is equal to the length of that side times $\sqrt{2}$.

65. **(D)** We use a general result: $k = m = 9\sqrt{2}\frac{\sqrt{2}}{2} = 9$. This is evident from a general property of 45°-45°-90° triangles: $s = \frac{h\sqrt{2}}{2}$, where h is the length of the hypotenuse, and s is the length of one of the sides.

66. **(B)** There are two ways to do this. First, use the Pythagorean theorem:
$AC^2 = AB^2 + BC^2 = \left(\sqrt{6}\right)^2 + \left(\sqrt{6}\right)^2 = 6 + 6 = 12 \Rightarrow AC = \sqrt{12} = 2\sqrt{3}$. Second, note that since $AB = BC$, the triangle ABC is a 45°-45°-90° triangle. A general property of such triangles is that $h = s\sqrt{2}$, where h is the hypotenuse, and s is one of the sides. Thus, $AC = \sqrt{6}\sqrt{2} = \sqrt{12} = 2\sqrt{3}$.

67. **(A)** $P = 40 = 4s \Rightarrow s = 10$. The diagonal divides the square into two similar, 45°-45°-90° isosceles triangles. The diagonal is the hypotenuse of those triangles, so $d = h = s\sqrt{2} = 10\sqrt{2}$.

68. **(E)** Here we must use properties of both 30°-60°-90° triangles and 45°-45°-90° triangles. The hypotenuse of the lower triangle is equal to twice the length of the side opposite to the 30° angle. Thus, $h = 12 \cdot 2 = 24$. Now, $p = s\sqrt{2} = 24\sqrt{2}$.

69. **(D)** Divide the circle into minutes: $\frac{360}{60} = 6$. Thus, each minute measures 6°. Twenty minutes after is 120°. There are 30° between each hour. Since it is one-third past the hour, the hour hand is one-third of the way to three. It thus measures: $(2 \cdot 30) + \left(\frac{1}{3} \cdot 30\right) = 70$. The difference between the two is 50°.

70. **(C)** $A = \pi r^2 = 49 \Rightarrow r^2 = \frac{49}{\pi} \Rightarrow r = \frac{7}{\sqrt{\pi}}$.

71. **(B)** $C = \frac{22\pi}{3} = 2\pi r \Rightarrow r = \frac{11}{3} \Rightarrow A = \pi r^2 = \pi \left(\frac{11}{3}\right)^2 = \frac{121\pi}{9}$.

72. **(B)** $A = \pi r^2 = 36\pi^3 \Rightarrow r^2 = 36\pi^2 \Rightarrow r = 6\pi$.

73. **(E)** $C = 2\pi r = 2\pi(8) = 16\pi$.

74. **(A)** The coordinates indicate that the radius is 8. Thus, $A_{shaded} = \frac{A}{4} = \frac{\pi r^2}{4} = \frac{\pi(8)^2}{4} = 16\pi$.

75. **(B)** $A = A_B - A_A = \pi r_B^2 - \pi r_A^2 = \pi\left(3^2 - 2^2\right) = 5\pi$.

76. **(A)** First, we find the radius of the circle. The lengths of the sides of the square will be twice that radius.
$A_C = 144\pi = \pi r^2 \Rightarrow r = 12$. $A_S = (2 \cdot 12)^2 = 576$. The area of the shaded area is $A_{shaded} = A_S - A_C = 576 - 144\pi$.

77. **(A)** Each side of the first square measures 10. We must find the diameter of the inscribed circle:
$A = 64\pi = \pi r^2 \Rightarrow r = 8 \Rightarrow d = 2r = 16$. The ratio of the first square to the second is $\frac{10}{16} = \frac{5}{8}$.

78. **(A)** $A = s^2 = 64x^2 y^{16} \Rightarrow s = \sqrt{64x^2 y^{16}} = 8xy^8$.

79. **(B)** Use the theorem of the venerable Pythagoras: $A = l^2 = 4^2 - 3^2 = 16 - 9 = 7$. Therefore, each side of the square is equal to $\sqrt{7}$, and the area of the square is $\sqrt{7} \cdot \sqrt{7} = 7$.

80. **(B)** $A = \frac{l_1 l_2}{2} = \frac{4 \cdot 5}{2} = 10$, where l_1 and l_2 are the legs of the triangle.

81. **(D)** While it is drawn to look like a 90° triangle, it is not a foregone conclusion. To prove that it is a 90° triangle, first, extend the line $\overline{AO}$ down to the other side of the circle to a new point, say C. Since $\overline{AC}$ is a diameter, arc $\measuredangle AC$ measures 180°. $\angle OAB$ is an inscribed angle. Hence it is half as large as the arc it intercepts, $\measuredangle BC$. Thus, $\measuredangle BC$ measures 90°. But, $\measuredangle AB + \measuredangle BC = 180° \Rightarrow \measuredangle AB = 180° - 90° = 90°$. The angle $\angle AOB$ is a central angle. Therefore possesses the same number of degrees as the arc it intercepts, $\measuredangle AB$. Thus, $\angle AOB$ is indeed a right angle. Now we know too that OAB is a 45°-45°-90° triangle. Thus, $OA = OB = 4\sqrt{2}$. So, $A_{shaded} = \frac{A}{4} - A_T = \frac{\pi\left(4\sqrt{2}\right)^2}{4} - \frac{\left(4\sqrt{2}\right)^2}{2} = 8\pi - 16$.

82. **(C)** $A = 15 = AB \cdot BC = 6 \cdot BC \Rightarrow BC = \frac{15}{6} \Rightarrow AC^2 = 6^2 + \left(\frac{3 \cdot 5}{3 \cdot 2}\right)^2 = 36 + \left(\frac{5}{2}\right)^2 = 36 + \frac{25}{4} = \frac{144+25}{4} \Rightarrow AC = \sqrt{\frac{169}{4}} = \frac{13}{2} = 6.5$.

83. **(D)** Only D is a true statement of the Pythagorean theorem. Don't get tripped up because they rearranged the usual order of variables.

84. **(A)** $41^2 - 40^2 = x^2 \Rightarrow x = \sqrt{1681 - 1600} = 9$. Thus, $A = 9 \cdot 40 = 360 \Rightarrow Cost = 360 \cdot \frac{12}{100} = 12 \cdot 3.6 = \$43.20$.

85. **(B)** $BD^2 = 23 + 13 \Rightarrow BD = \sqrt{36} = 6$. So, $BC^2 = 6^2 - \left(4\sqrt{2}\right)^2 = 36 - 32 = 4 \Rightarrow BC = 2$.

86. **(C)** The diagonal of a square is the hypotenuse of the two $45°$-$45°$-$90°$ triangles created inside the square by the presence of the diagonal. Thus, $s = \frac{h\sqrt{2}}{2} = \frac{5\sqrt{2}\sqrt{2}}{2} = 5$, where s is one of the square's sides and h is the length of the diagonal. Therefore, $A = s^2 = 5^2 = 25$.

87. **(E)** $x^2 = 13^2 - 12^2 = 139 - 144 = 25 \Rightarrow x = 5$. Thus, $A = s_1 s_2 = 5 \cdot 12 = 60$.

88. **(D)** $x^2 = \left(\sqrt{29}\right)^2 - 5^2 = 29 - 25 = 4 \Rightarrow x = 2$.

89. **(A)** $s^2 + s^2 = 2s^2 = \left(2\sqrt{3}\right)^2 = 12 \Rightarrow s^2 = 6 \Rightarrow s = \sqrt{6} \Rightarrow P = 4s = 4\sqrt{6}$.

90. **(C)** $\frac{P_{ABC}}{P_{DEF}} = \frac{3 \cdot 10}{2 \cdot 10 + 12} = \frac{30}{32} = \frac{15}{16}$, or 15:16.

91. **(D)** $A = \pi r^2 = \pi \left(2\sqrt{5}\right)^2 = 20\pi$.

92. **(C)** $A = 12\pi = \pi r^2 \Rightarrow r^2 = 12 \Rightarrow r = 2\sqrt{3}$.

93. **(D)** $C = 2 \cdot \sqrt{6}\pi = 2\pi\sqrt{6} = 2\pi r \Rightarrow r = \sqrt{6}$.

94. **(B)** $h^2 = l_1^2 + l_2^2 = 2^2 + 5^2 = 4 + 25 = 29 \Rightarrow h = \sqrt{29}$.

95. **(C)** $h^2 = l_1^2 + l_2^2 \Rightarrow 37^2 = 35^2 + l_2^2 \Rightarrow l_2^2 = 1369 - 1225 = 144 \Rightarrow l_2 = 12$.

96. **(C)** $V = l_1 \cdot l_2 \cdot l_3 = 2\sqrt{12} \cdot 3\sqrt{6} \cdot 4\sqrt{3} = 24\sqrt{12 \cdot 6 \cdot 3} = 24\sqrt{2 \cdot 2 \cdot 3 \cdot 2 \cdot 3 \cdot 3} = 24 \cdot 2 \cdot 3\sqrt{6} = 144\sqrt{6}$.

97. **(B)** $C = \sqrt{128}\pi = 2\pi r \Rightarrow r = \frac{\sqrt{128}}{2} = \frac{2\sqrt{32}}{2} = \sqrt{32} = 4\sqrt{2} \Rightarrow V = Ah = \pi r^2 h = \pi \left(4\sqrt{2}\right)^2 10 = 320\pi$.

98. **(C)** Let the third angle in the triangle on the right be $y°$. Now, we set up a system of equations: $x° + y° + 50 = 180 \Rightarrow x° + y° = 130°$. The third angle in the left triangle must be $180° - y°$. Thus,

$x° + 60° + \left(180 - y°\right) = 180° \Rightarrow x° - y° = -60°$. Now, we add these equations together, $\begin{array}{r} x + y = 130 \\ +x - y = -60 \end{array} \Rightarrow 2x = 70° \Rightarrow x = 35°$.

99. **(A)** Since $\sqrt{3}$ and 2 are both more than one, as we move right in the three-part ratio, the terms increase in size. Thus, x is the smallest side. So, the largest side is $2x$, or 10.

100. **(C)** The hypotenuse of a $30°$-$60°$-$90°$ triangle is equal to twice the length of the side opposite to the $30°$ degree angle. Thus, $JK = 12m$.

101. **(C)** In a right isosceles triangle, the two legs are equal. Thus, $DF^2 = FE^2 \Rightarrow 2DF^2 = DE^2 = \left(\sqrt{6}\right)^2 = 6$

$$DF = \frac{\sqrt{6}}{\sqrt{2}} = \sqrt{6} \cdot 2^{-\frac{1}{2}} = \sqrt{3 \cdot 2 \cdot 2^{2 \cdot \frac{-1}{2}}} = \sqrt{3 \cdot 2^{-1+1}} = \sqrt{3}$$

102. **(C)** The longest side of any right triangle is the hypotenuse. Thus, the legs are equal to one-half the hypotenuse and the hypotenuse times $\frac{\sqrt{3}}{2}$. Thus, $A = \frac{s_1 \cdot s_2}{2} = \frac{\frac{h}{2} \cdot \frac{h\sqrt{3}}{2}}{2} = \frac{h^2\sqrt{3}}{8} = \frac{\left(2\sqrt{3}\right)^2 \cdot \sqrt{3}}{8} = \frac{12\sqrt{3}}{8} = 1.5\sqrt{3}$.

103. **(B)** $AD^2 = 2 \cdot 4^2 = 32 \Rightarrow AC^2 = 2AD^2 = 2 \cdot 32 = 64 \Rightarrow AD = 8$.

104. **(C)** $\angle ABC$ is an interior angle. Such angles are equal in degrees to one half of the arc they intercept, in this instance $\overset{\frown}{BC}$. Therefore, $\angle ABC = 30°$. So, $BC = \frac{AC}{2} = 4$ and $AB = \frac{AC\sqrt{3}}{2} = 4\sqrt{3}$. Thus, $A = \frac{AB \cdot BC}{2} = \frac{4 \cdot 4\sqrt{3}}{2} = 8\sqrt{3}$.

105. **(D)** The angle opposite to $2x°$ is also equal to $2x°$. Therefore, $x° + 2x° + 60° = 180° \Rightarrow x° = 40° \Rightarrow 2x° - 60° = 20°$.

106. **(E)** Since a is opposite to y, $a° = y°$. Next, $a° + 30° + x° = 180° \Rightarrow a° = 150° - x°$. Similarly, $c° = 30°$, so $a° + b° + c° = 180° \Rightarrow a° = 180° - b° - c° = 150° - b°$. Since, A through D are true, E must be false.

107. **(C)** Because $\overline{EC} \parallel \overline{AB}$, $\angle EAB \cong x$ and $\angle CBA \cong y$. $\angle BCE + \angle A + \angle B = 180° - y° + x° + y° = 180° + x°$.

108. **(D)** $\overline{AD} \parallel \overline{BD}$. Thus, $\angle DBC° = \angle DCB = 80°$. So, $\angle BDC° = 180° - 80° - 80° = 20°$.

109. **(A)** When a line intersects a parallel line, there are two sets of four angles, each angle in the set is congruent. Those angles are opposite each other. The angles opposite to 7 are 1, 3, and 5.

110. **(B)** $3y° + y° = 180° \Rightarrow y° = \frac{180°}{4} = 45°$. Since x and y are opposite each other, $x° = y° = 45°$.

111. **(A)** $\angle BAC° = 37° \Rightarrow \angle ABC = 180° - 90° - 37° = 53°$. Given two sides of a triangle, the larger side will be opposite the larger angle. Thus, $AC > BC$.

112. **(B)** $\angle CGM° = \angle GHJ° = 126° \Rightarrow \angle CGO° = 180° - 126° = 54° \Rightarrow \angle EGC° = \angle EGF° + \angle FGC° = \frac{54°}{3} + \frac{54°}{3} = 36°$.

113. **(D)** This is a ratio problem. Since the smaller triangle is similar to the larger triangle, $\frac{AC}{AB} = \frac{CD}{BE} \Rightarrow \frac{6}{2} = \frac{CD}{5} \Rightarrow CD = 15$.

114. **(B)** The smallest perimeter will occur when the triangle is smallest. In this problem, 40 should be set as the largest length. Since the ratio between the two triangles is 1:2, the other two sides will have lengths 24 and 28. Thus, the smallest possible perimeter that can be obtained under the constraints of the problem is 92.

115. **(E)** $V = Ah = \pi \left(\frac{8x}{2}\right)^2 3y = 48x^2 y\pi$.

116. **(E)** perimeter $= 2(length) + 2(width) = 68$ yards. $width = 48$ feet $= 16$ yards. Thus, 68 yards $= 2(length) + 2(16) = 2(length) + 32 \Rightarrow 36$ yards $= 2(length) \Rightarrow length = 18$ yards.

117. **(E)** perimeter $= 2l + 2w = 2(46) + 2(34) = 92 + 68 = 160$ feet $= \frac{160}{3}$ yards $= 53\frac{1}{3}$ yards.

118. **(E)** The umbrella would be the hypotenuse of a right triangle whose legs are the dimensions of the trunk.

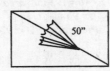

From the Pythagorean theorem, the sum of the dimensions of the trunk squared must at least equal the length of the umbrella squared, which is 50^2 or $2,500$. Only (E) works: $40^2 + 30^2 = 1,600 + 900 = 2,500$.

119. **(A)** The new road is the hypotenuse of a right triangle, and the legs are the old road.

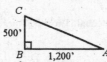

Use the Pythagorean theorem: $AC^2 = 500^2 + 1200^2 = 250,000 + 1,440,000 = 1,690,000 = 1,300^2 \Rightarrow AC = 1,300$ feet. The old road was 1,700 feet. Thus, the difference is $1,700 - 1,300 = 400$ feet.

120. **(C)** Since $6^2 + 8^2 = 10^2$, the triangle is a right triangle. The area of the triangle is $\frac{6 \cdot 8}{2} = \frac{48}{2} = 24$ in.². Therefore, the area of the rectangle is 24 in.². If the width of the rectangle is 3 inches, the length is $\frac{24}{3} = 8$ inches. The perimeter of the rectangle is $2(3+8) = 2 \cdot 11 = 22$ inches.

121. **(C)** The ladder forms a right triangle with the wall and the ground.

First, find the height that the ladder reaches when the lower end of the ladder is 25 feet from the wall: $25^2 + x^2 = 65^2$ $x^2 = 3,600 \Rightarrow x = 60$. The ladder reaches 60 feet up the wall when its lower end is 25 feet from the wall. If the upper end is moved down 8 feet, the ladder will reach a height of $60 - 8 = 52$ feet. The new triangle formed has a hypotenuse of 65 feet and one leg of 52 feet. Find the length of the other leg: $52^2 + x^2 = 65^2 \Rightarrow x^2 = 1,521 \Rightarrow x = 39$. The lower end of the ladder is now 39 feet from the wall. This $39 - 25 = 14$ feet farther than it was before.

122. **(C)** Convert the dimensions of the bin to inches: 4 feet = 48 inches, 3 feet = 36 inches, and 2 feet = 24 inches. Thus, *volume* $= 48 \cdot 36 \cdot 24 = 41,472$ in.³ The *volume per brick* $= 8 \cdot 4 \cdot 2 = 64$ in.³ Note that the bricks' dimensions evenly divide the dimensions of the bin. Thus, the *number of bricks* $= \frac{41,472}{64} = 648$ bricks.

123. **(D)** The trench contains 2 yd. $\cdot$ 5 yd. $\cdot$ 4 yd. $= 40$ yd.³ $\Rightarrow 40 \cdot \$2.12 = \$84.80$.

124. **(C)** Find the dimensions of the square: if the area of the square is 121 square inches, each side is $\sqrt{121} = 11$ inches, and the perimeter is $4 \cdot 11 = 44$ inches. Next, find the dimensions of the rectangle: the perimeter of the rectangle is the same as the perimeter of the square, since the same length of wire is used to enclose either figure. Therefore, the perimeter of the rectangle is 44 inches. If the two lengths are each 13 inches, their total is 26 inches, and $44 - 26$ inches, or 18 inches, remain for the two widths. Each width is equal to $18 \div 2 = 9$ inches. Thus, the area of a rectangle with length 13 in. and width 9 in. is $13 \cdot 9 = 117$ in.²

125. **(B)** area of walk = area of large rectangle – area of small recangle $= (34 \cdot 24) - (30 - 20) = 816 - 600 = 216$ ft.²

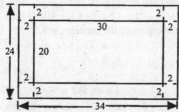

126. **(A)** If the area of a circle is 49π, its radius is $\sqrt{49} = 7$. The circumference is equal to $2 \cdot 7 \cdot \pi = 14\pi$.

127. **(D)** In one hour, the minute hand rotates through 360°. In two hours, it rotates through $2 \cdot 360° = 720°$.

128. **(C)** Find the area of each surface: *area of top* $= 12 \cdot 16 = 192$ in.²; *area of bottom* $= 12 \cdot 16 = 192$ in.²; *area of front* $= 6 \cdot 16 = 96$ in.²; *area of back* $= 6 \cdot 16 = 96$ in.²; *area of right side* $= 6 \cdot 12 = 72$ in.²; *area of left side* $= 6 \cdot 12 = 72$ in.² Therefore, total *surface area* $= 2 \cdot 192 + 2 \cdot 96 + 2 \cdot 72 = 720$ in.²

129. **(A)** For a cube, $V = e^3$. If the volume is 64 in.³, each edge is $\sqrt[3]{64} = 4$ inches. A cube has 12 edges. If each edge is 4 inches, the sum of the edges is $4 \cdot 12 = 48$ inches.

130. **(C)** The unlabeled angle inside the triangle is equal to x: $(x+15) + (x+15) + x = 180 \Rightarrow 3x + 30 = 180 \Rightarrow 3x = 150 \Rightarrow x = 50$.

131. **(C)** The question asks for: "Area of square with side 5" minus "Area of square with side 4" $= (5 \cdot 5) - (4 \cdot 4) = 25 - 16 = 9$.

132. **(D)** A triangle with sides of 4, 6, and 8 has a perimeter of $4 + 6 + 8 = 18$. An equilateral triangle with the same perimeter has three sides of length $18 \div 3 = 6$.

133. **(B)** Since $\overline{AB} \cong \overline{BC}$, $\triangle ABC$ is a 45°-45°-90° triangle. $\angle BAD = 45° + 15° = 60°$, so $x = 180 - 90 - 60 = 30$.

134. **(C)** $A_{rectangle} = l \cdot w \Rightarrow 1 = l \cdot \frac{3}{4} \Rightarrow l = \frac{4}{3}$.

135. **(C)** The three arcs together are a semicircle, or half the perimeter length of the entire circle. Since $P = 2\pi r$, the sum of the three arcs equals $\frac{P}{2} = \pi r$. Thus, $2\pi + 6\pi + 14\pi = \pi r \Rightarrow r = 2 + 6 + 14 = 22$.

136. **(B)** The unmarked angle plus the 120° angle form a straight line: $120° + x = 180° \Rightarrow x = 60°$. Then, since the unmarked angle is part of a right triangle, $90° + 60° + y = 180° \Rightarrow y = 30°$.

137. **(C)** If two angles of a triangle are congruent, then the two sides of the triangle that are opposite those two angles are also congruent. $\overline{BC}$ is opposite $\angle A$, and $\overline{AC}$ is opposite $\angle B$, so $\overline{AC} \cong \overline{BC}$.

138. **(C)** A ray extends infinitely in one direction: in the figure, $\overrightarrow{AB}$ is incomplete. As $\overrightarrow{AB}$ is extended through B, the ray will intersect the circle at two points.

139. **(C)** Since both pairs of opposite angles of $ABCD$ are congruent, $ABCD$ is a parallelogram. In a parallelogram, the opposite sides must be congruent. Thus, $\overline{AB} \cong \overline{DC}$ and $\overline{AD} \cong \overline{DC}$.

140. **(A)** Let $\angle A = x°$:, so $\angle AFB = x°$. An exterior angle of a triangle is equal to the sum of the two remote interior angles, From $\triangle ABF$, $\angle CBF = 2x°$; and $\overline{BF} \cong \overline{CF}$, so $\angle BCF = 2x°$. From $\triangle AFC$, $\angle CFE = 3x°$, and $\overline{CF} \cong \overline{CE}$, so $\angle CEF = 3x°$. From $\triangle ACE$, $\angle DCE = 4x°$; $\overline{CE} \cong \overline{DE}$, so $\angle CDE = 4x°$; and $\overline{AD} \cong \overline{AE}$, so $\angle DEA = 4x°$. Thus, in $\triangle ADE$, $4x + 4x + x = 180 \Rightarrow x = 20$.

141. **(D)** Use the Pythagorean theorem to find the length of the base $\overline{BC}$ and the length of the altitude $\overline{AB}$. Let $BC = b$ and $AB = h$: $b + h = 3\sqrt{38} \Rightarrow (b + h)^2 \Rightarrow b^2 + h^2 + 2bh = 9(38) = 342$. Since $AC = 10\sqrt{2}$, $b^2 + h^2 = \left(10\sqrt{2}\right)^2 = 200$. Thus, $b^2 + h^2 + 2bh = 342 - 200$ $b^2 + h^2 + 2bh = 342 \Rightarrow 2bh = 342 - 200 = 142 \Rightarrow bh = 71$. $A_{triangle} = \frac{bh}{2} = \frac{(AB)(BC)}{2} = \frac{71}{2} = 35.5$.

142. **(C)** Based on the properties of tangents, the radius of a circle at the point of tangency is perpendicular to the tangent line. Use the Pythagorean theorem to find the length of the radius: $(AO)^2 + 8^2 = 10^2 \Rightarrow AO = 6$. Thus, $A_{circle} = \pi r^2 = \pi(6)^2 = 36\pi$.

143. **(E)** A radius is perpendicular to a tangent at the point of tangency; thus, both $\angle OBC$ and $\angle OAC$ are right angles. Thus, $\angle AOB$ must be a right angle. Since $\overline{OA} \cong \overline{OB}$, $OACB$ is a square. The area of the shaded region is the area of the square minus one-fourth of the area of the circle: $A_{shaded\ region} = \left(S_{square}\right)^2 - \frac{\pi r^2}{4} = 10^2 - \frac{\pi \cdot 10^2}{4} = 100 - 25\pi$.

144. **(C)** Draw a line from P to $\overline{AO}$ intersecting $\overline{AO}$ at C so that $\overline{PC} \parallel \overline{AB}$:

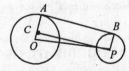

Since a tangent and a radius are perpendicular to each other, $\angle OBC$ and are right angles. Because of the parallel lines, $ABPC$ must be a rectangle. Thus, $AC = 3$ and $OC = 10$. $\angle OCP$ is a right angle, so use the Pythagorean theorem to find the length of $\overline{PC}$ in $\triangle PCO$: $10^2 + PC^2 = 26^2 \Rightarrow PC = 24$. Since $ABPC$ is a rectangle, $AB = 24$.

145. **(E)** A radius is perpendicular to a tangent at the point of tangency, so a right triangle is formed. Use the Pythagorean theorem to find the length of the hypotenuse of this right triangle: $h^2 = x^2 + y^2 = 12^2 + 16^2 = 144 + 256 = 400 \Rightarrow h = 20$.

146. **(A)** Draw perpendicular lines from T and R to $\overline{PA}$. $\overline{PA}$ is then divided into three lengths, from left to right, of 16, 12, and 16:

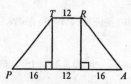

Given the properties of a 45°-45°-90° triangle, the altitude of the trapezoid (perpendicular line from T to $\overline{PA}$) is 16. Therefore, the area of the trapezoid is $\frac{h}{2}(b_1 + b_2) = \frac{16}{2}(12 + 44) = 448$.

147. **(D)** Since the length of $\overline{BC}$ is equal to one-half the length of $\overline{CD}$, $\angle BDC = 30°$. Alternatively, since $\sin\angle BDC = \frac{10}{20}$, $\angle BDC = 30°$. Thus, $\angle C = 60°$. Furthermore, since $\overline{BC} \cong \overline{ED}$, $BEDC$ is an isosceles trapezoid, and $\angle EDC = 60°$. The sum of the interior angles of any triangle is 180°; thus, $\angle A = 60°$, and $\triangle ACD$ is equilateral. Thus, $AC = AD = DC$, and $AB = AE = 10$. From the properties of parallel lines, $\angle ABE = 60°$. Thus, $\triangle ABE$ is also an equilateral triangle. The area of an equilateral triangle can be given as: $A = \frac{s^2\sqrt{3}}{4} = \frac{10^2\sqrt{3}}{4} = 25\sqrt{3}$.

148. **(C)** $\tan\angle ACB = 1$, so $\frac{AB}{BC} = 1 \Rightarrow \frac{10}{BC} = 1 \Rightarrow BC = 10$. Since both legs of the triangle are equal in length, $\angle BAC = \angle ACB = 45°$. Therefore, using the properties of a 45°-45°-90° triangle or the Pythagorean theorem, $AC = 10\sqrt{2}$.

149. **(D)** $AF + FE = 9 + 1 = 10$. Since $ACDE$ is a square, $AB = AC - BC = 10 - 8 = 2$. $A_{\text{rectangle}} = AF \cdot AB = 9 \cdot 2 = 18$. $A_{\text{square}} = (AC)^2 = 10^2 = 100$. Therefore, the probability of a point chosen at random in the interior of the square also being in the interior of the rectangle is $\frac{A_{\text{rectangle}}}{A_{\text{square}}} = \frac{18}{100} = \frac{9}{50}$.

150. **(E)** Label the given angles A, B, C, D, and E. Write a list of all possible combinations created using two angles: AB, AC, AD, AE, BC, BD, BE, CD, CE, and DE. Therefore, there are ten possible combinations. Only AB, AC, and BC are combinations resulting in acute angles. Thus, the probability of the new angles being acute is: $\frac{3}{10}$.

151. **(C)** Let d equal the time of Dave's arrival. Let k equal the time of Kathy's arrival. Since they agreed to wait 15 minutes for each other to arrive before leaving, $|d - k| \leq \frac{15}{60} = \frac{1}{4}$. The following graph represents this equation for the two hours between 10:00 PM and midnight in units of hours:

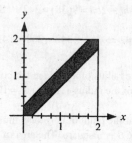

Based on this figure, the probability that Dave and Kathy were at Pizza Palace at the same time is equal to the area of the shaded region divided by the area of the square. $A_{\text{square}} = s^2 = 2^2 = 4$. To determine the area of the shaded region, subtract the area of the two triangles on either side of the shaded region from the area of the square: $A_{\text{shaded}} = 4 - 2(\frac{1}{2} \cdot \frac{7}{4} \cdot \frac{7}{4}) = \frac{15}{16}$. Thus, the probability of Dave and Kathy being at Pizza Palace together is $\frac{A_{\text{shaded}}}{A_{\text{square}}} = \frac{\frac{15}{16}}{4} = \frac{15}{64}$.

EXERCISE 12—FUNCTIONS, GRAPHS, AND COORDINATE GEOMETRY (p. 224)

1. **(D)** The numerator, $x - 2$, is less than zero whenever $x < 2$ and the denominator, $2x - 13$, is less than zero whenever $x < 6.5$. However, for $f(x) < 0$, the numerator must be positive and the denominator must be negative. Therefore, $2 < x < 6.5$, and so 6 is the largest whole number that x can be, (D). Alternatively, simply substitute the answer choices into the function to find the largest value of x for which $f(x) < 0$: $\frac{x-2}{2x-13} = \frac{6-2}{2(6)-13} = -4$.

2. **(C)** To generate two equations with two unknowns, substitute the given values for x into $f(x)$: $f(x) = kx + w$ $f(2) = 8 = 2k + w$ and $f(6) = 20 = 6k + w$. To eliminate w, subtract $f(2)$ from $f(6)$: $20 - 8 = 12 = (6k + w) - (2k + 2) = 4k$

$k = 3$. To determine w, substitute $k = 3$ into either equation and solve for w: $8 = 2k + w \Rightarrow w = 8 - 2(3) = 2$. Thus, $k + w = 3 + 2 = 5$.

3. **(B)** The absolute value of any real number k is k if $k \geq 0$ and $-k$ if $k < 0$. Since $-5 < x < -1$, $1 + 2x < 0$. Therefore, $|1 + 2x| = -1 - 2x$. $f(x) = |14 - |1 + 2x|| = |14 - (-1 - 2x)| = |15 + 2x|$. Finally, $15 + 2x > 0$, so $|15 + 2x| = 15 + 2x$.

4. **(E)** If $f(f(x)) = x$, then $f(x)$ is its own inverse. This means that if $y = \frac{kx}{3x+5}$ is solved for x as a function of y, then $x = f(y)$: $y = \frac{kx}{3x+5} \Rightarrow 3xy + 5y - kx = 0 \Rightarrow x(3y - k) = -5y \Rightarrow x = \frac{-5y}{3y-k}$. $f(y) = \frac{ky}{3y+5}$, and since $x = f(y)$, $\frac{ky}{3y+5} = \frac{-5y}{3y-k}$. Thus, $k = -5$.

5. **(B)** $f(2) + g(3) = (3 + 2^2) + (2 + 3)^3 = 3 + 4 + 5^3 = 7 + 125 = 132$.

6. **(B)** (B) is the only graph in which x can be any real number, and y can be any real number that is equal to or greater than zero.

7. **(A)** The range is the set of all values for y, and the domain is the set of all values for x. If $y = 0$, $4x = 0 \Rightarrow x = 0$. If $y = 9$, $4x = 9^2 \Rightarrow x = \frac{81}{4} = 20.25$. If $y = 16$, $4x = 16^2 \Rightarrow 4x = 256 \Rightarrow x = 64$. Thus, the domain is $\{0, 20.25, 64\}$.

8. **(D)** The domain is $\{0, 1, 2, 3, 4, 5, 6, \ldots\}$. Substitution of the first six numbers yields the values 1, 3, 5, 7, 9, and 11 for y. Therefore, the range for y is the set of all positive odd integers.

9. **(E)** $7x + 4y = 218 \Rightarrow 4y = 218 - 7x \Rightarrow y = \frac{218-7x}{4}$. Beginning with 1, substitute consecutive whole numbers for x until two whole number values for y are generated. If $x = 1$, then $y = \frac{218-7}{4}$, which is not a whole number. If $x = 2$, then $y = \frac{218-7(2)}{4} = 51$, which is the largest value for y. The next largest value for y is for $x = 6$, $y = \frac{218-7(6)}{4} = 44$. Thus, the answer is $51 + 44 = 95$.

10. **(B)** Since dividing by zero is not possible, if $x^2 - 11x + 30 = 0$, then $(x - 5)(x - 6) = 0$, and $x = 5$ or $x = 6$. Therefore, 5 and 6 are the only whole numbers not in the domain of values for x.

11. **(A)** To find which letter is a possible value of $\frac{F}{X}$, determine the range of possible values. X might be any value between -3 and -2, and F appears to be 4. Therefore, if $X = -3$, $\frac{F}{X} = \frac{4}{-3} = -1\frac{1}{3}$, and if $X = -2$, $\frac{F}{X} = \frac{4}{-2} = -2$. A is the only letter that lies between the values of -2 and $-1\frac{1}{3}$.

12. **(A)** Find the midpoint of $\overline{AB}$ by averaging the x-coordinates and averaging the y-coordinates: $\left(\frac{6+2}{2}, \frac{2+6}{2}\right) = (4, 4)$.

13. **(C)** O is the midpoint of $\overline{AB}$. $\frac{x+4}{2} = 2 \Rightarrow x + 4 = 4 \Rightarrow x = 0$. $\frac{y+6}{2} = 1 \Rightarrow y + 6 = 2 \Rightarrow y = -4$. Therefore, (x, y) is $(0, -4)$.

14. **(A)** $d = \sqrt{(8-4)^2 + (6-3)^2} = \sqrt{4^2 + 3^2} = \sqrt{16 + 9} = \sqrt{25} = 5$.

15. **(D)** Sketch the triangle. $A_{\text{triangle}} = \frac{b \cdot h}{2} = \frac{3 \cdot 4}{2} = 6$.

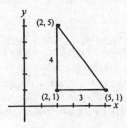

16. **(A)** Since the area of a circle is πr^2, $16\pi = \pi r^2 \Rightarrow r = 4$. The points in (B), (C), (D), and (E) are all 4 units from the origin, so the circle passes through each of these points. Only (A), (4, 4), is not on a circle of radius 4 centered on the origin.

17. **(A)** $slope = m = \frac{y_2 - y_1}{x_2 - x_1} = \frac{27 - (-5)}{8 - 0} = \frac{32}{8} = 4$.

18. **(E)** $slope = \frac{1}{3} = \frac{y - 7}{12 - 3} \Rightarrow y - 7 = 3 \Rightarrow y = 10$.

19. **(B)** From the slope-intercept form of a line equation, we know that the coefficient on the variable x, 5, is the slope.

20. **(C)** $slope = m = \frac{y_2 - y_1}{x_2 - x_1} = \frac{2k - 8}{w - 3}$.

21. **(C)** Lines that are parallel have the same slope and point $(0, y)$ corresponds to the y-intercept. Write the given equation in slope-intercept form: $4x + 2y = 17 \Rightarrow y = \frac{-4x + 17}{2} = -2x + \frac{17}{2}$. Therefore, $m = -2$ for the two parallel lines. The given y-intercept point is $(0, 13)$, so $b = 13$. The equation is: $y = -2x + 13$.

22. **(B)** Perpendicular lines have reciprocal slopes with opposite signs. The slope of the given line is $-\frac{1}{2}$, so the perpendicular line has a slope of 2. The y-intercept point given for the perpendicular line is $(0, -5)$, so $b = -5$. The line equation is $y = 2x - 5$.

23. **(B)** Since no drawing is provided, sketch the coordinate system and enter points P and Q:

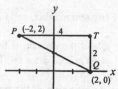

Find the distance between the two points by using the Pythagorean theorem: $PT^2 + QT^2 = PQ^2 \Rightarrow 4^2 + 2^2 = 16 + 4 = 20$. Therefore, $PQ = \sqrt{20} = \sqrt{4 \cdot 5} = 2\sqrt{5}$. Alternatively, the distance formula may be used: $d = \sqrt{(x_2 - x_1)^2 + (y_2 - y_1)^2} = \sqrt{(2 - (-2))^2 + (0 - 2)^2} = \sqrt{4^2 + (-2)^2} = \sqrt{20} = 2\sqrt{5}$.

24. **(A)** Use the distance formula: $d = \sqrt{(x_2 - x_1)^2 + (y_2 - y_1)^2} = \sqrt{(x + 1 - x)^2 + (y + 1 - y)^2} = \sqrt{1^2 + 1^2} = \sqrt{2}$.

25. **(C)** A quick sketch of the information provided in the problem shows that we need to employ the Pythagorean theorem:

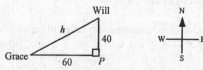

The shortest distance from Will to Grace is the hypotenuse of this right triangle: $h^2 = 60^2 + 40^2 = 3,600 + 1,600 = 5,200$. $h = \sqrt{5,200} = \sqrt{4 \cdot 1,300} = \sqrt{4 \cdot 4 \cdot 325} = \sqrt{16 \cdot 25 \cdot 13} = 20\sqrt{13}$.

26. **(A)** Use the distance formula to determine the distance between the two points $(5, 6)$ and $(6, 7)$: $d = \sqrt{(x_2 - x_1)^2 + (y_2 - y_1)^2} = \sqrt{(6 - 5)^2 + (7 - 6)^2} = \sqrt{1^2 + 1^2} = \sqrt{2}$.

27. **(A)** The coordinates of point A are (x, y). Regardless of the y-coordinate of point B, it is 7 units to the left, or in the negative direction, of point A. Therefore, the x-coordinate of point B is that of point A, minus 7 units, or $x - 7$.

28. **(E)** The x-coordinate of point S is the same as that of point R, x, while the y-coordinate is three times that of point R, $3y$. Thus, point S has the coordinates $(x, 3y)$.

29. **(C)** To move 7 units to the right on the coordinate plane, add 7 to the original x-coordinates; to move 5 units downward, subtract 5 from the original y-coordinates.

30. **(E)** Since the graph is of a straight line, plug the values given in the question into the straight line equation, $y = mx + b$ (m is the slope and b is the y-intercept when x is zero), and solve for y. One point on the graph is $(0, 0)$, so the y-intercept, b, is 0. A second point on the graph is $(2, 3)$, so $m = \frac{3 - 0}{2 - 0} = \frac{3}{2}$. Thus, $y = \frac{3x}{2}$. Substitute 4.2 for x: $y = \frac{3(4.2)}{2} = 6.3$.

31. **(B)** If $(x, -4)$ is in Quadrant III, then x is negative. If $(-1, y)$ is in Quadrant II, then y is positive. Therefore, (x, y) or $(-, +)$ is in Quadrant II.

32. **(E)** Since a figure is not provided, draw one:

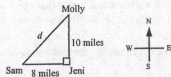

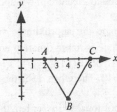

Use the Pythagorean theorem to find the approximate distance between Molly's house and Sam's house: $d = \sqrt{8^2 + 10^2} = \sqrt{64 + 100} = \sqrt{164}$. Since $\sqrt{144} = 12$ and $\sqrt{169} = 13$, $\sqrt{164}$ is between 12 and 13. Therefore, the approximate difference between the two paths is: 18 miles − 12 miles = 6 miles, or 18 miles − 13 miles = 5 miles. Since 5 miles is the largest answer choice, (E) is the correct choice. You may also use a calculator.

33. **(D)** Since the figure provided is not complete, fill it in. Use $\overline{AC}$ as the base of $\triangle ABC$ because it lies on the x-axis. $A = \frac{bh}{2} = \frac{4 \cdot 4}{2} = 8$.

34. **(C)** Use the distance formula to determine the distance between the two points $(-1, 4)$ and $(2, 8)$: $d = \sqrt{(x_2 - x_1)^2 + (y_2 - y_1)^2}$ $d = \sqrt{(2 - (-1))^2 + (8 - 4)^2} = \sqrt{3^2 + 4^2} = \sqrt{25} = 5$.

35. **(B)** $slope = m = \frac{rise}{run} = \frac{y}{18} \Rightarrow y = 18m$.

36. **(B)** $midpoint = \left(\frac{x_1 + x_2}{2}, \frac{y_1 + y_2}{2}\right) = \left(\frac{-2 + 8}{2}, \frac{15 + 17}{2}\right) = \left(\frac{6}{2}, \frac{32}{2}\right) = (3, 16)$.

37. **(D)** Use a form of the midpoint formula: $\frac{3 + x}{2} = 7$ (the x-coordinate of the center of the circle); $\frac{2 + y}{2} = 5$ (the y-coordinate of the center of the circle). Then, solve for the missing coordinates: $\frac{3 + x}{2} = 7 \Rightarrow 3 + x = 14 \Rightarrow x = 11$; $\frac{2 + y}{2} = 5 \Rightarrow 2 + y = 10 \Rightarrow y = 8$. The answer is (D): $(11, 8)$

38. **(A)** $f(x) = 17x + 14 \Rightarrow f(2) = 17(2) + 14 = 48$; $f(3) = 17(3) + 14 = 65$; $f(4) = 17(4) + 14 = 82$. Therefore, $f(2) + f(3) + f(4) = 48 + 65 + 82 = 195$.

39. **(C)** The first, fourth, and fifth graphs are each part or all of a non-vertical line, so each represents a linear function. Both the second and third graphs represent parts of two lines, so they do not represent a linear function. The correct answer is (C).

40. **(E)** If $x = 2$, then $g(2) = 3(2) + 8 = 14$. Thus, two points that belong to $f(x)$ are represented by $(1, 5)$ and $(2, 14)$. Since $f(x)$ is linear, $f(x) = mx + b$. Substitute $(1, 5)$ and $(2, 14)$ into $f(x) = mx + b$: $f(1) = 5 = m + b$ and $f(2) = g(2) = 14 = 2m + b$. From these two equations, $m = 9$. Substitute $b = 5 - m = 5 - 9 = -4$. Thus, $f(x) = 9x - 4$. Therefore, $f(4) = mx + b = (9)(4) - 4 = 32$.

41. **(C)** The four equations for the four sets can be found using the equation for the slope of a line, $m = \frac{y_2 - y_1}{x_2 - x_1}$ and the form of a linear equation, $y = mx + b$: $y = 2x + 1$, $y = -10x + 2$, $y = 3x - 11$, and $y = 4x - 7y$. Substituting the y-value from each of the ordered pairs in which x is unknown into the respective equation returns the following values for x: $-\frac{1}{2}$, -1, 3, 5. Therefore, x is less than zero for two of the sets of ordered pairs.

42. **(D)** Substitute the given values for (x, y) into the linear equation, $y = mx + b$. For $(5, 20)$, $20 = 5m + b$; for $(9, 32)$, $32 = 9m + b$. Determine the value for m by subtracting the first equation from the second equation: $32 - 20 = 12 = (9m + b) - (5m + b) = 4m \Rightarrow m = 3$. Determine the value for b by substitute $m = 3$ into either of the two equations: $20 = 5m + b \Rightarrow b = 20 - 5(3) = 5$. Therefore, $m + b = 5 + 3 = 8$.

43. **(D)** For both of the given equations, $y = 0$ for $x = 0$. Therefore, $(0, 0)$ must lie on both of the plotted functions—eliminate (A), (B), and (E). Since neither of the two equations yields multiple y-values for a given value of x, eliminate (C). (D) must be the correct choice.

44. **(C)** Equations with both y and x^2 terms represent parabolas that open up or down. The general equation for such parabolas is $y = a(x-h)^2 + k$, where the vertex is located at (h, k). To determine the vertex coordinates, rewrite the given equation in the standard form by completing the square: $y = -2x^2 + 16x - 1 = -2(x^2 - 8x + 16) - 1 + 32 = -2(x-4)^2 + 31$. Therefore, the vertex, or highest point on the curve, is $(4, 31)$. Alternatively, the maximum value of y can be determined by entering the function into a graphing calculator.

45. **(C)** This problem is solved directly by setting the two equations equal to one another and solving for x: $4x^2 = x^2 + 3x$ $4x^2 - x^2 - 3x = 0 \Rightarrow 3x^2 - 3x = 0 \Rightarrow 3x(x-1) = 0$. Therefore, $x = 1$ or $x = 0$. Substitute these values for x into either of the two given equations to find the value of y at these points: $y = 4(1)^2 = 4$ and $y = 4(0)^2 = 0$. Therefore, the two graphs intersect at two points: $(1, 4)$ and $(0, 0)$. Alternatively, use a graphing calculator to plot the two functions.

46. **(B)** Substitute the given x-values to determine which equation returns the closest approximation for the y-value. If $x = 2$: (A) $y = x^2 + 6 = 10$; (B) $y = x^2 + 3x + 2 = 12$; (C) $y = 2x^2 + x + 4 = 14$; (D) $y = x^2 - x + 8 = 10$; (E) $y = 2x^2 + x + 4 = 16$. If $x = 5$, the y-values for (A), (B), (C), (D), and (E) are 31, 42, 59, 28, and 64, respectively. Therefore, (B) is the correct equation for the curve. Alternatively, use the quadratic regression feature of a graphing calculator.

47. **(A)** Using the given order pairs, determine the approximate value of the slope $(m = \frac{y_2 - y_1}{x_2 - x_1})$: $m_{21} = \frac{23-18}{2-1} = 5$; $m_{32} = \frac{27-23}{3-2} = 4$; $m_{43} = \frac{32-27}{4-3} = 5$; $m_{54} = \frac{38-32}{5-4} = 6$. Thus, the slope is approximately equal to 5, and $y = 5x + b \Rightarrow b = y - 5x$. Substitute the ordered pairs into this equation to determine b: $b(1,18) = y - 5x = 18 - 5 = 13$; $b(2,23) = 23 - 10 = 13$; $b(3,27) = 27 - 15 = 12$; $b(4,23) = 32 - 20 = 12$; $b(5,38) = 38 - 25 = 13$. Therefore, 13 is the best approximation of b.

48. **(D)** The distance traveled is directly proportional to insect length; thus, for the shapes in (A), (B), (C), (D), and (E), a 1-inch long insect would travel 4 inches, 3 inches, 3.14 inches, 1.57 inches, and 5 inches, respectively. Only (D) comes close to the observed distances traveled.

49. **(A)** Parallel lines have equal slopes. Since $\frac{0-(-2)}{4-0} = \frac{2}{4} = \frac{1}{2}$, the slope of each line is $\frac{1}{2}$.

50. **(C)** The center of the circle is also the midpoint of the diameter. This allows for solutions determining the x and y points of the second end of the diameter. Solving for x: $19 = \frac{4+x}{2} \Rightarrow 38 = 4 + x \Rightarrow x = 34$. Solve for y: $7 = \frac{6+y}{2} \Rightarrow 14 = 6 + y \Rightarrow y = 8$. The second end of the diameter is located at $(34, 8)$.

51. **(D)** Each corner of a square is a right angle. Since $\angle FGH \cong \angle A$, $\angle FGH = 90°$. Thus, the slope of $\overline{FG}$ must be the opposite reciprocal of the slope of $\overline{GH}$. The slope of $\overline{FG}$ is $\frac{8-4}{3-5} = \frac{4}{-2} = -2$. Therefore, the slope of $\overline{GH}$ is $\frac{1}{2}$. Alternatively, substitute the four given points to determine the slope of $\overline{GH}$. (8, 6): $m = \frac{6-4}{8-5} = \frac{2}{3}$; (9, 6): $\frac{6-4}{9-5} = \frac{1}{2}$; (11, 7): $m = \frac{7-4}{11-5} = \frac{1}{2}$; (13, 8): $m = \frac{8-4}{13-5} = \frac{1}{2}$. Thus, three of the four ordered pairs could represent point H.

52. **(E)** Parallel lines have equal slopes. The slope of the first line is: $\frac{17-5}{-2-1} = \frac{12}{-3} = -4$. Thus, $\frac{y-6}{13-17} = -4 \Rightarrow y = (-4)(-4) + 6 = 22$.

53. **(C)** Solve using the distance formula: $d = \sqrt{(7-(-2))^2 + ((-7)-5)^2} = \sqrt{9^2 + (-12)^2} = \sqrt{81+144} = \sqrt{225} = 15$.

54. **(D)** $A_{\text{circle}} = \pi r^2 = 9\pi \Rightarrow r = 3$. Thus, the center of the circle is at $(0, 3)$, and the constant function, $y = k$, intersects the circle at $(0, 6)$. Therefore, $k = 6$.

55. **(A)** Since y is equal to a constant value divided by something, $y \neq 0$. Complete the square: $x^2 + 6x + 7 = (x+3)^2 - 2$. Thus, the part of the graph below the x-axis reaches a peak or maximum at $(-3, -2)$ and $y \neq -1$. Therefore, there are two integer values for y that are not a part of the graph: 0 and -1.

56. **(B)** The lowest point on the upper function plot occurs when $x = 1$: $(1, 4)$. The highest point on the bottom function plot occurs when $x = -5$: $(-5, 2)$. Thus, $2 < y < 4$ are the values for y that are not on plot of the function.

57. **(E)** The equation of the transformed graph is: $y = (x-2+4)^2 + 3 = (x+2)^2 + 3$. To find the point of intersection, set the two equations equal to each other: $(x+2)^2 + 3 = (x-2)^2 + 3 \Rightarrow x^2 + 4x + 4 = x^2 - 4x + 4 \Rightarrow 8x = 0 \Rightarrow x = 0$. By substitution, $y = 3$. Therefore, the point of substitution is $(0, 3)$.

58. **(A)** Complete the square for $y = 2x^2 = 12x + 1$: $y = 2(x^2 + 6x + 9) + 1 - 2(9) = 2(x + 3)^2 - 17$. From this last equation, the three transformations can be determined: (1) vertical stretch by a factor of two; (2) horizontal shift of three units to the left; and (3) vertical shift of 17 units down.

59. **(B)** The point (0, 0) is the center of the original circle, so (4, 2) must be the center of the transformed circle. This eliminates (A), (C), and (E). The point (0, −4) is on the original circle, so (0 + 4, −4 + 2) = (4, −2) must be on the transformed circle— eliminate (D). Therefore, the correct answer must be (B). In general, solve this type of problem by moving a few key coordinate points in accordance with the transformation(s).

60. **(B)** The points in the scatter plot in (B) are the only ones that generally represent a curvilinear relationship.

61. **(D)** (A) and (B) can be immediately eliminated since for these equations each y-value is more than the corresponding value for x. The residuals (actual y-values minus the y-values as predicted by a possible line) for (C), (D), and (E), respectively, are: {6, 4, 0, −22, −38, −33, −45}, {2, 5, 5, −6, −7, 8, 6}, and {−6, −18, −24, −74, −120, −135, −167}. The set with the smallest variance is the second from last, (D). Alternatively, use a graphing calculator to perform the least squares regression line of best fit calculations: the resulting equation is $y \approx 2.04x + 3.15$.

EXERCISE 13—SOLVING STORY PROBLEMS (p. 238)

1. **(A)** The amount of the discount is $12. The rate of discount is figured on the original price: $\frac{12}{80} = \frac{3}{20} \Rightarrow \frac{3}{20} \cdot 100 = 15\%$.

2. **(C)** Lilian spent $\frac{1}{3}$ of $60, or $20, at the supermarket, leaving her with $40. Of the $40 she spent $\frac{1}{2}$, or $20, at the drugstore, leaving her with $20 when she returned home.

3. **(A)** The segment $\overline{OP}$ is made up of the radius of circle O and the radius of circle P. To find the length of $\overline{OP}$, you need to know the lengths of the two radii. Since the length of the radius is equal to one-half the length of the diameter, the radius of the circle O is $\frac{8}{2} = 4$, and the radius of circle P is $\frac{6}{2} = 3$. Thus, $OP = 3 + 4 = 7$.

4. **(C)** $70 represents 80% of the marked price: $70 = 0.80x \Rightarrow 700 = 8x \Rightarrow \$87.50 = x$.

5. **(B)** Let x = number of quarters; $2x$ = number of nickels; and $35 - 3x$ = number of dimes. Convert the money values to cents: $25(x) + 5(2x) + 10(35 - 2x) = 400 \Rightarrow 25x + 10x + 350 - 30x = 400 \Rightarrow 5x = 50 \Rightarrow x = 10$.

6. **(E)** $r\% = \frac{r}{100}$. The commission is $\frac{r}{100} \cdot = \frac{rs}{100}$.

7. **(D)** Let x = first integer; $x + 2$ = second integer; $x + 4$ = third integer. $3(x) = 3 + 2(x + 4) = 3 + 2x + 8 \Rightarrow x = 11$. Therefore, the third integer is $11 + 4 = 15$.

8. **(B)** $273 represents 130% of the cost: $1.30x = \$273 \Rightarrow 13x = \$2,730 \Rightarrow x = \$210$. Thus, the cost is $210. To yield 10% profit on the cost, the refrigerator should be sold for: $1.10 \cdot \$210 = \$231$.

9. **(B)** The more feet, the more pounds—this is a *direct variation*: $\frac{60 \text{ feet}}{80 \text{ lbs.}} = \frac{6 \text{ feet}}{x \text{ lbs.}} \Rightarrow \frac{3}{4} = \frac{6}{x} \Rightarrow 3x = 24 \Rightarrow x = 8$.

10. **(D)** Work with a simple figure, such as $100: first sale price is 90% of $100, or $90; final sale price is 85% of $90, or $76.50; total discount was $100 - \$76.50 = \$23.50$. Therefore, *percent of discount* $= \frac{\$23.50}{\$100} = .235 = 23.5\%$.

11. **(C)** Let: b = Stan's age now; $b + 15$ = Robert's age now; $b - y$ = Stan's age y years ago; $b + 15 - y$ = Robert's age y years ago. Therefore, $b + 15 - y = 2(b - y) \Rightarrow b + 15 - y = 2b - 2y \Rightarrow 15 = b - y$.

12. **(B)** Let: marked price = m, first sale price = $0.85m$, and net price = $0.90(0.85m) = 0.765m$. Therefore, $0.765m = \$306 \Rightarrow m = \$400$. In this case, it would be easy to work from the answers: 15% of $400 is $60, making a first sale price of $340; 10% of this price is $34, making the net price $306. (A), (C), and (D) would not give a final answer in whole dollars.

13. **(D)** The larger the gear, the fewer revolutions per time period—this is an *inverse variation*: (50 inches)(15 revolutions) = (30 inches)(x revolutions) $\Rightarrow 750 = 30x \Rightarrow x = 25$.

14. **(C)** Let $100 be the selling price. If the profit is 20% of the selling price, or $20, then the cost is $80. Thus, the profit based on cost is: $\frac{20}{80} = \frac{1}{4} = 25\%$.

15. **(B)**

	No. of oz.	×	$\frac{\% \text{ acid}}{100}$	=	Amount of Acid
Original	20		0.05		1
Added	x		1.00		x
Mixture	$20 + x$		0.24		$0.24(20 + x)$

$1 + x = 0.24(20 + x)$. Multiply by 100 to eliminate the decimals: $100 + 100x = 480 + 24x \Rightarrow 76x = 380 \Rightarrow x = 5$.

16. **(B)** The more men, the less days—this is an *inverse variation*: $(x \text{ men})(h \text{ days}) = (y \text{ men})(? \text{ days}) \Rightarrow ? \text{ days} = \frac{xh}{y}$.

17. **(C)** If profit is to be 20% of selling price, cost must be 80% of selling price: $\$72 = 0.80x \Rightarrow \$720 = 8x \Rightarrow x = \$90$.

18. **(A)** The a lbs. of nuts are worth a total of ab cents. The c lbs. of nuts are worth a total of cd cents. The value of the mixture is $ab + cd$ cents. Since there are $a + c$ pounds, each pound is worth $\frac{ab + cd}{a + c}$ cents. Since the dealer wants to add 10 cents to each pound for profit, and the value of each pound is in cents, add 10 to the value of each pound: $\frac{ab + cd}{a + c} + 10$.

19. **(A)** The more days, the more oil—this is a *direct variation*: $\frac{40 \text{ gallons}}{7 \text{ days}} = \frac{x \text{ gallons}}{10 \text{ days}} \Rightarrow 7x = 400 \Rightarrow x = 57\frac{1}{7}$.

20. **(E)** If Nell invests x additional dollars at 8%, her total investment will amount to $\$2,400 + x$ dollars. $0.05(2,400) + 0.08(x) = 0.06(2,400 + x) \Rightarrow 5(2,400) + 8x = 6(2,400 + x) = 12,000 + 8x = 14,400 + 6x$ $2x = 2,400 \Rightarrow x = \$1,200$.

21. **(B)** The team must win 75%, or $\frac{3}{4}$, of the games played during the entire season. With 60 games played and 32 more to play, the team must win $\frac{3}{4} \cdot 92 = 69$. Since 40 games have already been won, the team must win 29 additional games.

22. **(D)** The more sugar, the more flour—this is a *direct variation*: $\frac{13 \text{ oz. sugar}}{18 \text{ oz. flour}} = \frac{10 \text{ oz. sugar}}{x \text{ oz. flour}} \Rightarrow 13x = 180 \Rightarrow x = 13\frac{11}{13}$.

23. **(B)** Total time elapsed is $5\frac{1}{2}$ hours. However, one hour was used for dinner. Therefore, Ivan drove at 30 m.p.h. for $4\frac{1}{2}$ hours, covering 135 miles.

24. **(E)** Let *original price* $= p$, and the *original sales* $= s$; *original gross receipts* $= ps$. Let the *new price* $= 0.75p$, and *new sales* $= 1.20s$; *new gross receipts* $= 0.90ps$. Gross receipts are only 90% of what they were. Therefore, they decrease by 10%.

25. **(A)** The more miles, the more gasoline—this is a *direct variation*: $\frac{25 \text{ miles}}{2 \text{ gallons}} = \frac{150 \text{ miles}}{x \text{ gallons}} \Rightarrow 25x = 300 \Rightarrow x = 12$.

26. **(B)** $time = \frac{distance}{rate} = \frac{30}{60} = \frac{1}{20}$ hour, or 3 minutes. Therefore, the arrival time is 5:01 p.m.

27. **(B)** 5% of sales between $200 and $600 is $0.05(\$600 - \$200) = \$20$. 8% of sales over $600 is $0.08(\$200) = \$16$. Therefore, the total commission is: $\$20 + \$16 = \$36$.

28. **(E)** The more children, the fewer days—this is an *inverse variation*: $(30 \text{ children})(4 \text{ days}) = (40 \text{ children})(x \text{ days}) \Rightarrow 120 = 40x \Rightarrow x = 3$.

29. **(C)** Dave takes 30 minutes to wash the car alone. $\frac{x}{15} + \frac{x}{30} = 1 \Rightarrow 2x + x = 30 \Rightarrow 3x = 30 \Rightarrow x = 10$.

30. **(D)** The larger the quantity of salami, the greater the cost—this is an *inverse variation*: $\frac{c \text{ cents}}{16 \text{ oz. salami}} = \frac{x \text{ cents}}{a \text{ oz. salami}} \Rightarrow x = \frac{ac}{16}$.

31. **(C)** The more miles, the more kilometers—this is a *direct variation*: $\frac{3 \text{ miles}}{4.83 \text{ kilometers}} = \frac{x \text{ miles}}{11.27 \text{ kilometers}} \Rightarrow 4.83x = 33.81 \Rightarrow x = 7$.

32. **(C)** The increase is by 9,000. Find the percent of increase by dividing the change (increase) in enrollment by the original enrollment: $\frac{9,000}{3,000} = 3 = 300\%$.

33. **(B)** By paying attention to how the units cancel so as to leave the desired value, it is easy to find the necessary equation: $\frac{6 \text{ papers}}{s \text{ seconds}} \cdot m \text{ machines} \cdot x \text{ seconds} = 18,000 \Rightarrow x = \frac{18,000s}{6m} = \frac{3,000s}{m} \text{ seconds} = \frac{50s}{m}$.

34. **(B)** The more pencils, the greater the cost—this is a *direct variation*: $\frac{p \text{ pencils}}{d \cdot 100 \text{ cents}} = \frac{x \text{ pencils}}{c \text{ cents}} \Rightarrow x = \frac{pc}{100d}$.

35. **(D)** Write two equations based on the given information. *discount price = list price − 20% discount*: $d = l - 0.20l$. *discount price = profit + cost*: $d = p + c$. Since the cost is \$4,800, and the profit is equal to 25% of the cost, or $0.25c$, $d = 0.25c + c$. $.80l = 1.25c \Rightarrow l = \frac{1.25 \cdot \$4,800}{.80} = \$7,500$.

36. **(A)** The variable m varies directly as t^2: $\frac{m_1}{t_1^2} = \frac{m_2}{t_2^2} \Rightarrow \frac{7}{(1)^2} = \frac{m}{(2)^2} \Rightarrow m = 28$.

37. **(D)** $16\frac{2}{3}\% = \frac{16\frac{2}{3}}{100} = \frac{\frac{(16 \cdot 3)+2}{3}}{100} = \frac{\frac{50}{3}}{100} = \frac{50}{300} = \frac{1}{6}$. Thus, since $16\frac{2}{3}\%$ of x equals 6: $6 = \frac{x}{6} \Rightarrow x = 36$. Therefore, the number of students who passed the course is: $36 - 6 = 30$.

38. **(D)** To solve the problem directly, turn the story into algebraic equations: $value_2 = value_1 - (0.10 \cdot value_1) \Rightarrow v_2 = 0.90v_1$; $rate_2 = rate_1 + (0.10 \cdot rate_1) \Rightarrow r_2 = 1.10r_1$. Since $tax = value \cdot tax\ rate$, $tax_2 = value_2 \cdot rate_2 = 0.90v_1 \cdot 1.10r_1 = (0.90 \cdot 1.10) \cdot tax_1 = 0.99 \cdot tax_1$, or a 1% decrease.

39. **(B)** The variable m varies jointly as r and l: $\frac{m_1}{r_1 l_1} = \frac{m_2}{r_2 l_2} \Rightarrow \frac{8}{(1)(1)} = \frac{m}{(2)(2)} \Rightarrow m = 32$.

40. **(E)** $40\% = \frac{2}{5} \Rightarrow \frac{2}{5} \cdot 95\% = 38\%$.

41. **(C)** Create a formula. Anna was born three years after $1980 - x$, so she was born in $1980 - x + 3$. 20 years later the year will be $1980 - x + 3 + 20 = 2003 - x$.

42. **(B)** $500 + 0.05x = \$2,400 \Rightarrow 0.05x = \$1,900 \Rightarrow 5x = \$190,000 \Rightarrow x = \$38,000$.

43. **(B)** The correct answer must be smaller than the shortest time given, for no matter how slow a helper may be, he does do part of the job and therefore it will be completed in less time. $\frac{time\ spent}{total\ time\ needed\ to\ do\ job\ alone} = \frac{x}{3} + \frac{x}{5} = 1$. Multiply by 15 to eliminate fractions: $5x + 3x = 15 \Rightarrow 8x = 15 \Rightarrow x = 1\frac{7}{8}$ hours.

44. **(C)** This problem is easily solved by using a Venn diagram. Use circles to represent students taking the SAT and students taking the ACT. The overlap of the two circles represents students taking both tests; students not taking either test are represented outside of the circles.

Thus, the total number of students is: $88 + 80 + 95 + 27 = 290$.

45. **(C)** Count the subsets that meet the requirements: {3}, {5}, {7}, {9}, {3, 5}, {3, 6}, {3, 7}, {3, 9}, {5, 6}, {5, 7}, {5, 9}, {6, 7}, {6, 9}, {7, 9}, {3, 5, 6}, {3, 5, 7}, {3, 5, 9}, {3, 6, 7}, {3, 6, 9}, {3, 7, 9}, {5, 6, 7}, {5, 6, 9}, {5, 7, 9}, {6, 7, 9}, {3, 5, 6, 7}, {3, 5, 6, 9}, {3, 5, 7, 9}, {3, 6, 7, 9}, and {5, 6, 7, 9}. Therefore, there are 29 possible subsets of 1, 2, 3, or 4 elements containing one or more odd numbers.

46. **(D)** Draw a Venn diagram of the information provided. The four unlabeled parts of the circles in the Venn diagram must total to 14 (51 − 10 − 12 − 15 = 14). Notice that the unlabeled parts of the circles can be assigned various numbers, as the following two extreme cases indicate.

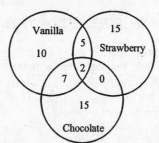
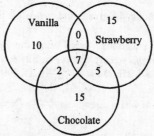

In the first of the two extreme cases above, two students liked both chocolate and strawberry. In the second of the two extreme cases above, twelve students liked both chocolate and strawberry. Thus, the answer is (D).

47. **(D)** The least common multiple of 6 and 8 is 24. The intersection is {24, 48, 72, 96, 120, ...}, which is the set of all positive integral multiples of 24.

48. **(D)** If y varies directly as x, then $\frac{y}{x}$ is always the constant of variation. In the example, $\frac{12.3}{4.1} = 3$, so 3 is the constant of variation. In this case, the constant of variation is: $\frac{6.72}{4.2} = 1.6$.

49. **(C)** Direct variation relationships are expressed as $y = kx$, and inverse variation relationships are expressed as $xy = k$; in both cases, k is a constant real number. The first equation in (C) relates a direct variation: $x = \frac{y}{3} \Rightarrow y = 3x$. The second equation, $xy = 7$, relates an inverse variation. Finally, the third equation, $x^2 + y^2 = \frac{x}{5}$ is neither direct nor inverse variation. Therefore, (C) is the correct answer.

50. **(C)** Let R, x, and d represent the wire's resistance, length, and diameter, respectively. The question states that the resistance of a wire is expressed as $R = \frac{kx}{d^2}$. The proportional constant, k, is determined from the information provided for the first wire: $R = \frac{kx}{d^2} \Rightarrow k = \frac{Rd^2}{x} = \frac{(0.1 \text{ ohm})(0.1 \text{ in.})^2}{50 \text{ feet}} = \frac{(0.1)^3}{50}$. Therefore, the resistance for the second wire is: $R = \frac{kx}{d^2} = \frac{0.1^3 \cdot 9{,}000}{50 \cdot 0.3^2} = 2$.

51. **(C)** $y = kx \Rightarrow 10 = k(1.25) \Rightarrow k = 8$; thus, $y = 8x$. $w = cx^2 \Rightarrow 8 = c\left(\sqrt{2}\right)^2 \Rightarrow c = 4$; thus, $y = 4x^2$. $4x^2 = 8x \Rightarrow 4x^2 - 8x = 0 \Rightarrow 4x(x-2) = 0$; thus, $x = 0$ or $x = 2$.

52. **(B)** The formula for the circumference of a circle is: $C = 2\pi r$, where r is the radius of the circle. Therefore, the constant of variation is 2π.

53. **(D)** The graphs in (A), (B), (C), and (E) all have at least one point for which either x or y is zero, and thus at these points, $xy = 0$, whereas $xy \neq 0$ at all other points where neither x nor y are zero. Therefore, xy is not a constant value for these four graphs. Only (D) represents a possible inverse variation relationship.

54. **(E)** Substitute 1, 2, 4, 6, and 12, respectively, for n to find the approximate values after 1 year: $10,416$, $10,420.33$, $10,422.53$, $10,423.28$, and $10,424.02$. Trying the other years also indicates that n is approximately 12.

GRAMMAR AND MECHANICS SKILLS REVIEW

EXERCISE 1—PARTS OF SPEECH (p. 273)

1. ambulance = noun
   traffic = noun
   it = pronoun
   hurried = verb
   hospital = noun
2. movers = noun
   unloaded = verb
   and = conjunction
   it = pronoun
   in = preposition
3. dark = modifier
   clouds = noun
   blocked = verb
   our = pronoun
   and = conjunction
4. dinner = noun
   cleared = verb
   table = noun
   and = conjunction
   sat = verb
5. room = noun
   was filled = verb
   with = preposition
   authors = noun
   Polish = modifier

6. first = modifier
   shows = noun
   were = verb
   earlier = modifier
   programs = noun
7. waiter = noun
   arrived = verb
   Victor = noun
   ordered = verb
   and = conjunction
8. inspector = noun
   finally = modifier
   approved = verb
   and = conjunction
   allowed = verb
9. notified = verb
   in = preposition
   water = noun
   would be = verb
   hours = noun
10. band = noun
    finished = verb
    crowd = noun
    burst = verb
    loud = modifier

11. telephoned = verb
    her = pronoun
    would be = verb
    their = pronoun
    date = noun
12. cat = noun
    was sleeping = verb
    warmth = noun
    of = preposition
    sun = noun
13. train = noun
    pulled = verb
    called = verb
    name = noun
    and = conjunction
14. we = pronoun
    children = noun
    were = verb
    in = preposition
    rear = noun
15. they = pronoun
    leave = verb
    teach = verb
    hikers = noun
    and = conjunction

16. covered = verb
    steaming = modifier
    melted = modifier
    sticky = modifier
    syrup = noun
17. weekend = noun
    made = verb
    special = modifier
    brilliant = modifier
    beautiful = modifier
18. eventful = modifier
    wrote = verb
    but = conjunction
    his = pronoun
    unopened = modifier
19. barely = modifier
    make out = verb
    bus = noun
    as = conjunction
    it = pronoun
20. offered = verb
    us = pronoun
    or = conjunction
    were = verb
    delicious = modifier

21. **(C)** When stating that one thing is different from another, the correct phrase is "different from." (A) is wrong because "different than" is used only when comparing a difference in degree (*e.g.*, "She is more difficult than Derek."). (B) is wrong because the phrase "different of" is not idiomatic. Finally, (D) is wrong because the resulting construction is grammatically incorrect.

22. **(D)** A sentence should not end with a preposition, so "to" should be omitted. (A), (B), and (C) are wrong because the resulting sentences still end with prepositions.

23. **(B)** "To take advantage of" is an appropriate idiomatic expression, so (B) is the correct answer choice. (A), (C), and (D) are wrong because the resulting sentences are not idiomatic.

24. **(A)** The original is correct. (B), (C), and (D) are wrong because the sentence requires a preposition to be idiomatic.

25. **(A)** The original is correct. When sales decline, a company's management department will sometimes "lay off," or fire, workers. "Laid off" is the past tense form of this idiomatic expression. (B), (C), and (D) are wrong because the resulting sentences are not idiomatic.

26. **(B)** In this context, the words "in to" should be spelled as one word ("into"). The idiomatic expression is "to look into" something. "In to" would be idiomatic in a different context (*e.g.*, "I gave in to their demands."). (C) and (D) are wrong because the resulting sentences are not idiomatic.

27. **(C)** "To take upon" a responsibility is another way of saying "to undertake" a responsibility. (A), (B), and (D) are wrong because the resulting sentences are not idiomatic.

28. **(B)** If a person finds a task to be "beneath her," then she believes that she is too good to perform the task. That is the intended meaning of this sentence, so (B) is the correct answer choice. The original is wrong because it incorrectly implies that the task is physically, or spatially, below her. (C) and (D) are wrong because the resulting sentences are grammatically incorrect.

29. **(B)** In this context, the word "sometime" means that the store will open at an indefinite time over the course of the next half hour. Another way to say that something will happen by a certain time is to say that it will happen "within" a certain time. It is possible to say that something will happen "inside" a half hour, but that expression is colloquial and should be avoided in formal writing.

30. **(A)** The original is correct. Another way to say that you are not feeling well is to say that you are "under the weather." (B), (C), and (D) are wrong because the resulting sentences are not idiomatic.

31. **(B)** In this context, "waiting for" is the correct expression. The original is wrong because it implies that the students are "waiting on," or acting as servants for, the instructor. (C) and (D) are wrong because the resulting sentences are grammatically incorrect.

32. **(B)** To save energy, you would "turn off" a light. The original is wrong because it is grammatically incorrect; "of" is a word, but it is a preposition, not an adjective. (C) is wrong because the resulting sentence implies that you would return the lights to some unspecified place. Finally, (D) is wrong because it implies that you would rotate the lights to save energy.

33. **(C)** "To swing into motion" means "to start moving." When the music started playing, the dancers started moving. (A), (B), and (D) are wrong because the preposition "into" is required to create the appropriate idiomatic expression.

34. **(B)** The bank is located "on the corner," or at the intersection, of Main and Packard. The original is wrong because it implies that the bank is somehow located inside the corner, which is physically impossible. (C) could be a correct answer choice if the bank were located around the corner from Main and Packard. However, the sentence uses the phrase "of Main and Packard." Finally, (D) is wrong because the resulting sentence lacks a preposition that locates the corner.

35. **(B)** When a person objects to, or offers an objection to, something, he or she is speaking out against that thing. (A) and (C) are wrong because the resulting sentences are not idiomatic. (D) is wrong because the resulting sentence is grammatically incorrect.

36. **(C)** When a person has difficulty getting to sleep, he or she remains awake "until," or up to the time of, actually falling asleep. So, (C) is the best answer choice. "Till" is a colloquial way of shortening the word "until, and a more formal word should be preferred. (B) is wrong because the resulting sentence does not make sense. (D) is wrong because it implies that Ralph had trouble sleeping when it was very late at night. That is not the intended meaning of the sentence.

EXERCISE 2—COMMON GRAMMATICAL ERRORS (p. 287)

1. **(A)** The adjective "harsh" is intended to modify the verb "deals." However, an adjective cannot be used to modify a verb. So, the adverb "harshly" should be used instead.

2. **(D)** "Them" is intended to be a pronoun substitute for "advertising," but "advertising" is singular, not plural. "It" should replace "them."

3. **(D)** "You" is intended to refer to "one," but "one" is in the third person while "you" is in the second person. The sentence could be corrected simply by omitting the underlined portion altogether: "…and read a book."

4. **(C)** "That" has no clear referent. "That" might refer either to "horrifying conditions" or to "English boarding schools." The ambiguity could be avoided by rewording the sentence: "…about the horrifying conditions in the English boarding schools, conditions that he learned about…."

5. **(C)** "It" has no clear referent. "It" might refer either to "movement" or to "manifesto." The sentence can be corrected by including an appropriate noun to clarify the speaker's meaning: "…of a manifesto, a work that incorporated…."

6. **(D)** "Capable" is intended to modify "played," a verb. Thus, the adverb form must be used: "…played capably."

7. **(B)** "Who" and "whom" are the correct pronouns to use for people: "…countryside who sheltered…."

8. **(B)** "We" cannot be used as the object of "to." The correct choice of pronoun is "us."

9. **(A)** When a pronoun is used to modify a gerund, the pronoun must be in the possessive case: "Your taking the initiative…."

10. **(C)** "Which" has no clear antecedent. Had the speaker hoped to avoid the conference or just being selected to be the representative of the group at the conference? To avoid the ambiguity, the sentence will have to be substantially revised: "…at the conference, and I had hoped to avoid the conference altogether."

11. **(C)** "Whom" should be used here instead of "which," since the pronoun refers to a person.

12. **(D)** The subject of the main clause is "few," a plural pronoun, so the verb should be "are" rather than "is."

13. **(B)** The subject of the sentence is "differences," a plural noun, so the verb should be "help" rather than "helps."

14. **(B)** "Hardly no" is a double negative. The sentence should read "hardly any."

15. **(B)** The subject of the sentence is "diaries," a plural noun. The verb should be "provide" rather than "provides."

16. **(D)** "Its" intends to refer to "whales," so the sentence should use the plural pronoun "their."

17. **(A)** A pronoun used to modify a gerund must be in the possessive case: "His being at the rally…."

18. **(D)** "Satisfactory" is intended to modify "system." Therefore, another verb is required: "…and is more than satisfactory."

19. **(B)** "Who" is intended to be the object of the verb "recommended," so the objective case pronoun "whom" is required.

20. **(B)** "Recent" is intended to modify "constructed," an adjective. However, an adjective cannot be used to modify another adjective. Here the adverb "recently" should be used.

21. **(D)** "Which" does not have a clear referent. It is unclear whether the faculty was angry because the resolution passed or because it passed with few dissenting votes. The sentence must be rewritten to clarify the speaker's intention. One acceptable rewrite is as follows: "Many faculty members grew angry when the student senate passed the resolution banning smoking in the cafeteria with scarcely any dissenting votes."

22. **(D)** "Your" is intended to refer to "one's," so you need some kind of third person pronoun, for example, "his or her."

23. **(D)** "It" lacks a referent. "It" seems to refer to something like "insurance," but there is no such noun in the sentence. The sentence could be corrected by using the noun "insurance" in place of the pronoun "it."

24. **(C)** "Candid" is intended to modify the verb "wrote," so the sentence must use the adverb "candidly."

25. **(A)** The sentence commits the error of the "ubiquitous they." The sentence can be corrected by using a noun such as "the team" or "the management" in place of "they." Note that changing the plural noun to a singular noun, such as "the team," requires that the verb also be singular.

26. The adverb "slowly" is the correct answer choice. The verb "does" is being modified, and verbs are modified by adverbs.

27. The adverb phrase "really well" is the correct answer choice. The verb "understand" is being modified, and verbs are modified by adverbs.

28. The adjective "polite" is the correct answer choice. "Be" is a linking verb, and linking verbs are modified by adjectives. Although the blank follows the verb, the sense of "polite" more clearly qualifies the subject. Since nouns are qualified by adjectives, "polite" is the correct choice.

29. The adverb "well" is the correct answer choice. The verb "doing" is being modified, and verbs are modified by adverbs.

30. The adjective "good" is the correct answer choice. The pronoun "it" is being modified, and pronouns (like nouns) are modified by adjectives. In this sentence, the sense of goodness qualifies the noun, not the verb. Therefore, the adjective "good" is the correct completion.

31. The adjective "terrible" is the correct answer choice. The noun "mess" is being modified, and nouns are modified by adjectives.

32. The adjective "awful" is the correct answer choice. "Felt" is a linking verb, and linking verbs are modified by adjectives. When describing the subject, and not the manner in which some action is being undertaken, adjectives are used.

33. The adverb "terribly" is the correct answer choice. The adjective "exciting" is being modified, and adjectives are modified by adverbs.

34. The adverb "well" is the correct answer choice. The verb "doing" is being modified, and verbs are modified by adverbs.

35. The adverb "well" is the correct answer choice. The verb "smell" is being modified, and verbs are modified by adverbs.

36. This item primarily tests diction. Both "hard" and "hardly" are adverbs, however "hard" expresses effort, while "hardly" means "barely." Mrs. Chang would not be proud of her son because he hardly worked in class.

37. The adverb "fast" is the correct answer choice. The verb "biked" is being modified, and verbs are modified by adverbs. This question is tricky because "fast" can function either as an adjective or an adverb. In this context, it functions as an adverb. On the other hand, "quick" can only function as an adjective. The adverb "quickly" would also be acceptable in this context, but that is not one of the answer choices.

38. The adjective "near" is the correct answer choice. The noun "college" is being modified, and nouns are modified by adjectives.

39. The adverb "slowly" is the correct answer choice. The verb "appeared" is being modified, and verbs are modified by adverbs.

40. The adjective "healthy" is the correct answer choice. "Remain" is a linking verb, and linking verbs are followed by adjectives. When attempting to ascribe a characteristic to a subject, an adjective is used, even if it follows a verb.

41. The adjective "heavy" is the correct answer choice. "Felt" is a linking verb, and linking verbs are followed by adjectives. The quality of weight is more applicable to the subject, thus an adjective is appropriate.

EXERCISE 3—ANALYZING SENTENCE STRUCTURE (p. 298)

1. The plural subject "many people" requires the plural form "receive."

2. The plural subject "books" requires the plural form "were." The plural subject is modified by a prepositional phrase that contains a singular noun ("on the top shelf"). However, the object of a prepositional phrase ("shelf") cannot serve as the subject of the sentence.

3. The plural subject "stores" requires the plural form "offer." The plural subject is modified by a prepositional phrase that contains a singular noun ("in the downtown sector's newly renovated mall"). However, the object of a prepositional phrase ("mall") cannot serve as the subject of the sentence.

4. The plural subject "bottles" requires the plural form "remain." The plural subject is modified by a prepositional phrase that contains a singular noun ("of the vintage wine"). However, the object of a prepositional phrase ("wine") cannot serve as the subject of the sentence.

5. The singular subject "tourist" requires the singular form "is." The singular subject is modified by a clause that contains a plural noun ("who visits the caverns"). However, this is not the subject of the main clause.

6. The plural subject "several different species" requires the plural form "were." This is a tricky sentence because it uses an inverted structure in which the verb ("were") precedes the subject ("several different species"). In addition, the sentence begins with a prepositional phrase that contains a singular noun ("Underneath the leaf covering"). However, the object of a prepositional phrase ("leaf covering") cannot serve as the subject of the sentence.

7. The plural subject "young boys" requires the plural form "were." This is a tricky sentence because the subject and verb are separated by a long clause ("who had never before been in trouble with the law"). In addition, the last word of this clause ("law") is a singular noun, which could easily be misinterpreted as the subject of the sentence. However, this is not the subject of the main clause.

8. The plural subject "several barrels" requires the plural form "have." Again, the subject and verb are separated by intervening material ("containing a highly toxic liquid"), and the last word of this intervening material is a singular noun ("liquid"), which could easily be misinterpreted as the subject of the sentence. However, this is not the subject of the main clause.

9. The plural subject "sponsors" requires the plural form "hope." The plural subject is modified by a prepositional phrase that contains a singular noun ("of the arts and crafts fair"). However, the object of a prepositional phrase ("fair") cannot serve as the subject of the sentence.

10. The plural subject "Dawn, Harriet, and Gloria" requires the plural form "are." This is a tricky sentence because the subject is a compound subject made up of singular elements. Remember that a compound subject consists of two or more elements that are joined together by the conjunction "and." Compound subjects always require plural forms, even when each of the elements is singular.

11. The singular subject "the mayor" requires the singular form "worries." The subject and verb are separated by intervening material that contains a plural noun ("whose administration has been rocked by several crises"). However, this is not the subject of the main clause.

12. The plural subject "acts" requires the plural form "have been." This sentence is difficult for two reasons. First, it uses an inverted structure in which the verb ("have been") precedes the subject ("several acts") Remember that "here" and "there" do not typically act as the subjects of sentences. Second, the plural subject is modified by a prepositional phrase that contains a singular noun ("of vandalism"). However, the object of a prepositional phrase ("vandalism") cannot serve as the subject of the sentence.

13. The plural subject "rock musicians" requires the plural form "lose."

14. This sentence contains a long prepositional phrase: "from the branches of the tree that hang over the fence." When attempting to determine the correct agreement for a sentence, ignore prepositional phrases. The remaining sentence is "the leaves fall into the neighbor's yard," where it is clear that we need the plural form "fall" to agree with "the leaves."

15. The plural subject "The computer and the printer" requires the plural form "have." This sentence is difficult for two reasons. First, the subject of the sentence is a compound subject made up of singular elements ("the computer" and "the printer"). Even though this compound subject consists of singular subjects, a compound subject always requires a plural form. Second, the subject and verb are separated by a modifying clause ("which are sitting on James' desk"), and the last word in this clause is a singular noun ("desk"). However, this is not the subject of the main clause.

16. The singular subject "Theresa" requires the singular form "was." The subject and verb are separated by a qualifying phrase that contains a plural noun ("waders"). However, this is not the subject of the main clause.

17. Attention should not be paid to prepositional clauses. They in no way affect subject-verb agreement. Eliminating the prepositional phrase, the sentence reads: "the film critic writes that the film is very funny and entertaining." At this point, the correct verb-choice is clear.

18. This sentence contains a clause introduced by "that", which can be ignored. The new sentence becomes "several of the ingredients have to be prepared in advance."

19. The singular subject "The computer" requires the singular form "was." This sentence is difficult because the subject and verb are separated a large group of words that modifies the subject of the sentence ("The computer").Focus only on those parts of the sentence that are required to have a complete sentence, since clauses and phrases do not enter into subject-verb agreement considerations.

20. The singular subject "support" requires the singular form "has." This sentence is difficult because it uses an inverted structure in which the verb ("has been") precedes the subject ("support"). This inverted structure can make subject-verb agreement more difficult to understand. Remember that "here" and "there" do not typically act as the subjects of sentences.

21. The plural subject "Bill and Jean" requires the plural form "are." "Bill and Jean" is a compound subject. Even though this compound subject consists of singular elements ("Bill" and "Jean"), a compound subject always requires a plural form.

22. The plural subject "several students" requires the plural form "were." This sentence uses an inverted structure (as noted by the word "there"), which can make subject-verb agreement more difficult to understand. However, a plural subject always requires a plural form.

23. The singular pronoun "his or her" is the correct answer choice. A pronoun must always agree with its antecedent: If the antecedent is singular, then the pronoun must be singular. The antecedent in this sentence is the singular "no one."

24. The singular pronoun "her" is the correct answer choice. A pronoun must always agree with its antecedent: If the antecedent is singular, then the pronoun must be singular. In this sentence, the antecedent is the singular "each," not the plural noun "sisters." "Sisters" is part of the prepositional phrase that modifies "each." Ignore phrases and clauses; they do not affect subject-verb agreement.

25. The singular subject "music" requires the singular form "is." This sentence might be confusing because the singular subject is modified by a prepositional phrase that contains a plural noun ("of Verdi's operas"). Secondary phrases and clauses should not be considered in subject-verb agreement items.

26. The plural pronoun "their" is the correct choice. The antecedent ("All the musicians") is plural. So, the pronoun must be plural.

27. The subject of this sentence ("Either Mrs. Martinez or Carlos") is a disjunctive subject. Disjunctive subjects consist of multiple elements that are introduced by the pronoun "either." When a disjunctive subject is used, the verb in the sentence must agree with the last element in the disjunctive subject. The last element in this disjunctive subject is the singular "Carlos." So, the singular form "goes" is required.

28. "Have" is the correct answer choice. "Have had" would imply that the speaker wanted the tasks done before she asked. But, the stipulation "by the time I got home from work" puts the actions that the speaker desires after she asks, but before she returns from work.

29. "Could" is the correct answer choice. It correctly establishes the sequence of events. First, the storekeeper lost most of his business to a conglomerate retail store. As a result, he "could" not pay his bill last month. It is important to recognize that the entire sequence of events took place and concluded in the past. The present tense auxiliary verb "can" is wrong because it incorrectly suggests that the storekeeper is still unable to pay his monthly rent bill. "Can" should also arouse suspicion because the resulting "can not" is low-level; "cannot" is always preferred.

30. "Became" is the correct answer choice. It correctly establishes the sequence of events. First, the weather "became" cold. Then, Jim "could" not ride his bicycle to work. Both events took place in the past, and the change in weather preceded Jim's inability to ride his bicycle. The present tense verb "becomes" is wrong because it suggests that the future condition of the weather will affect Jim's past ability to ride.

31. **(D)** (C) is wrong because the correct verb must agree with the singular, 3rd person subject "gentleman." (B) and (E) are wrong because the correct verb must also be in the present tense since the activity is happening in the present. Finally, (A) is wrong because the correct verb must also complement the auxiliary verb "is." (D) is the only answer choice that satisfies all of these conditions.

32. **(B)** The correct verb must be in the past tense since the activity happened last night. Therefore, (B) "supposed" is the correct answer choice. (A), (C), (D), and (E) can all be eliminated since none of these answer choices are in the past tense.

33. **(E)** The correct verb must be in the past tense since the "My friend has…to" construction indicates past activity. So, (A), (C), and (D) can be eliminated. As for (B), although "began" is a past tense verb, it creates an incorrect present perfect construction ("has began"). (E) creates a correct present perfect construction ("has begun").

34. **(B)** The correct verb must be in the past tense since "He has" indicates past activity. So, (C), (D), and (E) can be eliminated. (A) appears to be a past tense verb. However, "catched" is not a correct conjugation of "catch" in any circumstance. "Caught" is the past tense form of "catch."

35. **(A)** The correct verb must be in the present tense, since "he could" suggests something that is based on a condition ("if he were asked"). "Sing" is the correct verb form.

36. **(C)** The correct verb must be in the past tense since "she has" indicates past activity. So, (A) and (E) can be eliminated. (D) can be eliminated because it is an incorrect attempt to form the past tense of "sing". As for (B), although "sang" is a past tense verb, it creates an incorrect present perfect construction ("has sang"). (C) creates a correct present perfect construction ("has sung").

37. **(D)** The correct verb must be in the past tense since "They have already" indicates past activity. Therefore, (A), (B), (C), and (E) can be eliminated.

38. **(E)** The correct verb must be in the past tense since "He has" indicates past activity. So, (A) and (D) can be eliminated. (C) can be eliminated because it is an incorrect attempt to form the past tense of "give"; "gived" is not a word. As for (B), although

"gave" is a past tense verb, it creates an incorrect present perfect construction ("has gave"). (E) creates a correct present perfect construction ("has given").

39. **(C)** (A) and (D) are wrong because they suggest an object that does not exist in the sentence. What is he "to devote" to his parents? What is he "devoting" to his parents? (B) and (E) are wrong because they cannot be used after "He is"; they result in sentences that are grammatically incorrect. Therefore, (C) is the correct answer choice.

40. **(D)** The correct verb must parallel the verb that already exists in the sentence ("designed"). So, (A), (B), (C), and (E) can be eliminated. Therefore, (D) is the correct answer choice.

41. **(C)** The correct verb must indicate past activity since this activity happened at the same time as when "he ran onto the stage." So, (A), (B), and (D) can be eliminated. As for (E), although "had laughed" does indicate past activity, it is the past perfect form of "laugh." The past perfect is used to describe activity that was undertaken and completed before another past activity. In this sentence, the two activities happened at the same time. Therefore, (C) is the correct answer choice.

42. **(E)** The correct verb must indicate past activity since this activity allowed her to make the upcoming Olympics. So, (B), (C), and (D) can be eliminated. As for (A), although "had jumped" does indicate past activity, it is the past perfect form of "jump." The past perfect is used to describe activity that was undertaken and completed before another past activity. In this sentence, the Olympics are still in the future. So, the past perfect "had jumped" is incorrect. Therefore, (E) is the correct answer choice.

43. **(A)** The correct verb must indicate past activity since the cause of the pain is in the past ("she continued to blame me"). (E) is wrong because it suggests that the cause of the pain is in the future. (D) is wrong because the resulting sentence is grammatically incorrect. (A), (B), and (C) all sound like they might be correct answer choices. However, (B) is ultimately wrong because the resulting sentence suggests that the pain is ongoing; there is no concrete evidence in the sentence to confirm that this is the case. (C) is wrong because the resulting sentence suggests that the pain fluctuates (e.g., "It has hurt. Then it did not hurt. Weeks later, though, it hurt again."); there is no concrete evidence in the sentence to confirm that this is the case either. Therefore, (A) is the correct answer choice.

44. **(E)** The correct verb must include a subjunctive because the second half of the sentence ("if he had really...") describes a condition that is either known or supposed to be contrary to fact. So, (A), (B), and (D) can be eliminated. Finally, (C) is wrong because the past participle of "see" is "seen," not "saw." Therefore, (E) is the correct answer choice.

45. **(B)** (A) and (D) are wrong because the correct verb must agree with the singular, 3rd person subject "child." (C) and (E) are wrong because they distort the sequence of events. First, the child learned how to stand. Then, she walked. The word "now" indicates present activity, as well as parallelism with "is able".

46. **(E)** The correct verb must be in the future tense since the activity will take place "tomorrow morning." So, (A), (B), (C), and (D) can be eliminated. Therefore, (E) is the correct answer choice.

47. **(B)** The first part of the sentence includes a past perfect construction ("After she had completed her investigation"). A past perfect construction describes activity that was undertaken and completed before another past activity. So, the correct answer choice must also indicate past activity. Accordingly, (A), (D), and (E) can be eliminated. As for (C), "has written" indicates something that happened before the moment of speech, but fails to place the event after the investigation. Only (B) follows the logic of the sentence.

48. **(E)** The correct verb must indicate past activity since this activity happened at the same time as "When I was growing up." (A) and (B) are wrong because they indicate present and future activity, respectively; they distort the sequence of events. (C) is wrong because a present perfect construction describes activity that was undertaken but not concluded in the past; however, the speaker describes something that is firmly set in the past, not an ongoing activity. Finally, (D) is wrong because it too fails to indicate that the past activity has concluded. Therefore, (E) is the correct answer choice: The past tense "spent" indicates something that is firmly set in the past.

49. **(A)** The correct verb will be parallel to "get," which is a present form. Only "order" is also in the present tense.

50. **(C)** The correct verb must indicate past activity since the activity has happened "for years now." So, (A), (B), and (D) can be eliminated. (E) is wrong because the word "now" also indicates that the activity is ongoing. Therefore, (C) is the correct answer choice.

51. **(A)** "We were just leaving" indicates past activity, so the correct verb must also indicate past activity. (B) is wrong because it incorrectly suggests that the telephone has not yet rung. (C) is wrong because it distorts the sequence of events; in other words, it fails to establish the fact that they first tried to leave and then the telephone started to ring. (D) is wrong because it uses a

present perfect construction, which describes activity that started but did not finish in the past; there is no evidence in the sentence to suggest that the telephone is still ringing. Finally, (E) is wrong because it uses a past perfect construction, which describes an activity that started and finished before another past activity. In this sentence, though, the activity (the telephone ringing) does not start and finish before some other past activity. Rather, the telephone prevents the other activity in the sentence (leaving) from happening. Therefore, (A) is the correct answer choice.

52. **(E)** "We arrived at the house" indicates past activity, so the correct verb must also indicate past activity. (A) and (B) are wrong because they indicate present and future activity, respectively. (C) is wrong because it uses a past perfect construction, which describes activity that started and finished before another past activity. However, this sentence does not identify another past activity that occurred prior to the wedding. Finally, (D) is wrong because it uses a present perfect construction, which describes activity that started but did not finish in the past; there is no evidence in the sentence to suggest that the wedding was not entirely finished. Therefore, (E) is the correct answer choice.

53. **(C)** (A), (B), and (D) can be eliminated because they distort the sequence of events. The resulting sentences suggest that first the car stalled and then the plans were made. (E) is wrong because it uses a present perfect construction, which describes activity that occurred anterior to the present. But, we need a form that expresses anteriority to a past event. Therefore, (C) is the correct answer choice.

54. **(B)** The word "while" indicates that the events described by two clauses were happening simultaneously. Only "was" testing agrees with "were putting."

55. **(D)** Because this sentence describes a simple sequence of events, the verbs should be in the same tense. Only "flew" agrees with "landed."

56. **(C)** (B) and (E) are wrong because they are plural forms that do not agree with the singular noun "baby." (A) and (D) are wrong because they incorrectly imply that the baby has not yet arrived. Therefore, (C) is the correct answer choice.

57. **(E)** (A) and (B) are wrong because they distort the fact that the desire to drive from Wisconsin to Washington preceded the fact that they were late. In other words, the resulting sentences do not accurately reflect the sequence of events; a present activity cannot precede a past activity ("we were late"). (D) is incorrectly conjugated. (C) is wrong because the sentence requires an active verb construction ("We wanted"), but (C) results in an incomplete passive verb construction ("We were wanted") that never answers who wanted them. Therefore, (E) is the correct answer choice.

58. **(C)** The condition "if it doesn't rain" is in the present tense, so the completion should also be in the present tense. So, (A), (B), (D), and (E) can all be eliminated because they indicate either past or future activity.

59. **(C)** The sentence commits an error of logical expression, because it implies that all the people coming into the museum have but a single camera. It could be corrected by changing "a camera" to "cameras."

60. **(B)** The sentence is flawed by faulty parallelism. It could be corrected by changing "to maintain" to "maintaining."

61. **(A)** The sentence contains the incorrect form of the irregular verb "to lay" and is corrected by changing "laying" to "lying."

62. **(D)** The final phrase is out of place. As written, the sentence implies that the cockroach is unlike destructive garden pests, but the speaker means to say that the cockroach is not like the praying mantis. The sentence can be corrected by relocating the phrase closer to the noun it modifies: "The praying mantis, unlike the cockroach, which serves no useful function, is welcomed by homeowners...."

63. **(C)** The incorrect form of the verb "to hang" is used. Instead, the sentence should read: "...picture was hung...."

64. **(D)** Unlike in the previous item in which the correct sentence read: "...picture was hung...," when one is talking about the hanging of a person, the correct verb form is "hanged," not "hung."

65. **(B)** The original sentence is a run-on sentence. It can be corrected by adding end-stop punctuation: "We spent an exhausting day shopping. We could hardly wait to get home."

66. **(A)** The sentence is flawed by a lack of parallelism, an error that can be corrected by substituting the adjective "charismatic" for the phrase "has charisma."

67. **(A)** This item is a sentence fragment that lacks a conjugated verb. The fragment can be changed into a complete sentence by substituting "displayed" for "displaying."

68. **(C)** The improper form of "to sew" is used. The sentence should read: "The woman…has sewn the hem.…"

69. **(B)** The use of the subjunctive "would have been" is illogical. The use of the subjunctive incorrectly implies that the loss of lives and money is contingent upon some event, but no such event is mentioned in the sentence. The sentence can be corrected by substituting "will have been."

70. **(C)** This is a run-on sentence. It should read: "The house on the corner was completely empty. No one came to the door."

71. **(C)** The sentence suffers from a lack of parallelism. This deficiency can be corrected by changing "taking" to "to take." (In any event, the use of the gerund "taking" instead of the infinitive "to take" is not idiomatic.)

72. **(C)** The incorrect verb tense of "to freeze" is used. The sentence can be corrected by substituting "frozen" for "froze."

73. **(D)** The tense of the first verb is not sequentially consistent with the tense of the second verb. The sentence can be corrected by substituting "experiences" for "experienced."

74. **(C)** This is a run-on sentence. It can be corrected by adding a question mark: "Where had everyone gone? All the lights were off."

75. **(B)** The original sentence contains an incorrect verb form. The sentence should read: "Rather than declare bankruptcy.…"

76. **(D)** The use of the present tense "loses" is illogical and inconsistent with the use of the past tense "was" earlier in the sentence. The error can be corrected by substituting "lost" for "loses."

77. **(B)** This is a run-on sentence. The sentence is correct if a comma is added between "slowly" and "almost." The correct sentence reads: "We entered the cave very slowly, almost afraid of what we might find there."

78. **(C)** The original sentence contains the incorrect form of the verb "to drink." The corrected sentence reads: "…he drank all of the poison from the vial."

79. **(C)** The elements of the sentence are not parallel. It would be correct if "cross-checking" were changed to "cross-checked."

80. **(B)** The sentence contains an incorrect form of the verb "to fling." It can be corrected by changing "flinged" to "flung."

81. **(C)** The sentence is a run-on sentence. The sentence may be corrected in one of two ways, both changes occurring between "happen" and "my." First, end-stop punctuation may be added: "…was going to happen. My heart.…" Second, an exclamation mark could be used instead of a period: "…was going to happen! My heart.…"

82. "When at school, he studies, goes to the library, and works on the computer."

    In the original, the final element in the series incorrectly begins with the word "he," which disrupts the parallelism of the sentence. In the corrected sentence, each element in the series agrees with the pronoun "he," but it is not necessary to repeat that pronoun at any point.

83. "In order to get eight hours of sleep, the student prefers sleeping in late in the morning to going to bed early in the evening."

    In the corrected sentence, the two verbs that follow "prefers" are both gerunds ("sleeping…going"). As a result, the sentence is parallel.

84. "I still need to pass Math 252 and English 301 and return two overdue books before I am allowed to graduate."

    In the corrected sentence, the two verbs that describe what the student needs to do are parallel ("pass…return"). Pass, in turn, has a parallel construction containing two nouns. These two levels of parallelism should not be mixed.

85. The original is correct. The objects of "either" are correctly paralleled.

86. The original is correct. The subject-verb agreement across the main and subordinate clauses is correctly paralleled.

87. The original is correct. The original exhibits the correct parallelism of verb-subject agreement between the two clauses joined by "either…or.…"

88. "Our instructor suggested that we study the assignment carefully, go to the library to research the topic extensively, and conduct a survey among 20 subjects."

In the original, the final element in the series incorrectly begins with the words "we should." These words disrupt the parallelism of the sentence. In the corrected sentence, each element of the series begins with a parallel verb form ("study...go...conduct"). It is unnecessary to repeat the subject at any point in such a series. In fact, such a repetition is ungrammatical.

89. "The increase of attrition among community college students is caused by a lack of family support and a limited income while attending school."

The original not only suffers from faulty parallelism, but its second element is a complete sentence unto itself ("students have a limited income while attending school"). In the corrected sentence, the causes of increased attrition are parallel noun forms ("a lack of family support...a limited income").

90. "Many non-smokers complained about the health risks associated with second-hand smoke; as a result, smoking is banned in the library and the cafeteria, and smokers have to leave the building to light a cigarette."

In the original, the first and second elements in the series suggest a parallel series. The third element, however, disrupts the parallelism. The corrected sentence simply eliminates the series to create the needed parallelism.

91. "After talking to financial aid and seeing your advisor, return to the registrar's office."

In the corrected sentence, the two tasks detailed at the beginning of the sentence are now expressed in parallel gerund verb forms ("talking...seeing").

92. "Professor Walker helped not only me, but many of my classmates as well."

In the corrected sentence, "not only" is moved to its proper place. As a result, what is intended to be parallel is made clear (Professor Walker's help to "me" and Professor Walker's help to "my classmates").

93. "In his communications class, he can work either in groups or in pairs."

In the corrected sentence, "either" is moved to its proper place. As a result, what is intended to be parallel is made clear (a choice to work "in groups" or a choice to work "in pairs").

94. "I prefer that other geography class because of the clear explanations and numerous exercises in the textbook, as well as Mrs. Patrick's vivid teaching style."

The original suffers from faulty parallelism; as a result, it incorrectly implies that "Mrs. Patrick's vivid teaching style" was a feature of the geography textbook. The correct sentence makes clear that the textbook and Mrs. Patrick's teaching style are both features of the preferred geography class.

95. "The question is whether to study tonight or to get up earlier tomorrow morning."

In the original, the second element incorrectly begins with the words "should I." These words disrupt the parallelism of the sentence. Specifically, the second element is a complete sentence unto itself (Should I get up earlier tomorrow morning?). In the corrected sentence, both elements have parallel verb forms ("to study" and "to get up").

96. "Reasons for the latest tuition increase are the upgraded computers, the new library, and the 6.5% inflation."

The original not only suffers from faulty parallelism, but the third element in the series is a complete sentence unto itself (Inflation has increased to 6.5%.). In the corrected sentence, the three causes for the tuition increase are parallel noun forms ("the upgraded computers...the new library...the 6.5% inflation").

EXERCISE 4—PROBLEMS OF LOGICAL EXPRESSION (p. 310)

1. **(C)** The original suffers from faulty parallelism. "Would return" creates the necessary parallelism ("would go...would return"). Also, it firmly establishes the correct sequence of events—first, she "would go"; then, she "would return." (A), (B),

(D), and (E) do not create the necessary parallelism. They place the grandmother's actions in different and unconnected time frames.

2. **(B)** The original has a problem of pronoun-antecedent agreement. Remember that a pronoun must agree in number with its antecedent, or referent. According to this sentence, the canning jars preserve "the food." "Food" is a singular noun. Singular pronouns refer to singular nouns, so the plural pronoun "them" should be replaced by the singular pronoun "it." (C) and (D) are wrong because they do not solve the problem of pronoun-antecedent agreement. (E) solves the problem of pronoun-antecedent agreement, but it incorrectly substitutes the singular form "preserves" for the plural form "preserve"; the singular form "preserves" does not agree with the plural noun "jars." (B) is the only answer choice that uses the correct pronoun and provides a plural form for the plural noun "jars" ("would preserve it").

3. **(C)** "By late fall" indicates activity that is complete, so the correct verb must be in the past tense. (A), (B), and (E) can therefore be eliminated. As for (D), although "was lined" is in the past tense, the singular "was" does not agree with the plural subject "shelves." (C) is the correct answer choice because it is a past tense verb, and it agrees in number with the subject.

4. **(E)** This item requires the use of contextual information. Sentence 6 describes something that contrasts what is stated in sentence 5. As a result, sentence 6 needs to begin with a word that signals such a contrast. "However" accomplishes this task. The other answer choices do not suggest contrast; in fact, they suggest that sentence 6 will offer a logical continuation of the idea that is expressed in sentence 5.

5. **(B)** The original has a problem of pronoun-antecedent agreement. According to this sentence, "the produce" is at risk of spoiling. "Produce" is a singular noun. Singular pronouns refer to singular nouns, so the plural pronoun "they" should be replaced by the singular pronoun "it." (A) and (C) are wrong because they do not solve the problem of pronoun-antecedent agreement. (D) and (E) fail to use the conditional "would." (B) is the only answer choice that both maintains the conditional parallel and solves the problem of pronoun-antecedent agreement.

6. **(A)** The original is correct. (B), (D), and (E) are wrong because they incorrectly introduce the present tense into a sentence that clearly describes past activity ("during the winter months"). (C) is wrong because it uses a present perfect construction. A present perfect construction describes activity anterior to the moment of speech. What the speaker wants to express here, however, is that the preservation of food was important at the same time as the past winter months. (C) does not express that subtlety.

7. **(B)** The original has a problem of subject-verb agreement. The singular noun "nothing" requires a singular form. So, (A) and (D) can be eliminated. (C) and (E) solve the problem of subject-verb agreement, but they incorrectly indicate past activity. In the third paragraph, the discussion of home-canning takes place in the present tense. (B) is the only answer choice that supplies a singular form and keeps the discussion in the present tense.

8. **(E)** The original suffers from faulty parallelism. The three elements in the series are not expressed in the same form ("packed...fitted...you submerge them"). In order to solve this problem, the final verb in the series must be made parallel with the preceding verbs ("packed...fitted...submerged"). (E) accomplishes this task.

9. **(C)** The original implies that the killing of dangerous organisms causes food to spoil. (B) and (E) indicate that the organisms had already caused spoilage at the time of the heating. Finally, (D) incorrectly asserts that the goal of the killing is spoilage.

10. **(E)** As written, the original incorrectly implies that the vacuum does the cooling. (C) and (D) are wrong for the same reason; they incorrectly imply that the vacuum gradually cools. (B) is wrong because it begins the sentence with a pronoun that has no clear antecedent. (E) is correct because it provides a noun and correctly asserts that jars, not a vacuum, are being cooled.

11. **(A)** The original is correct. (C), (D), and (E) are wrong because they indicate that the organisms already have entered, or are in the process of entering. They incorrectly imply that organisms can enter the jar prior to the breaking of the seal. (B) is wrong because it suggests current activity rather than conditional activity.

12. **(B)** The original suffers from a problem of subject-verb agreement. The singular form "seems" does not agree with the plural subject of the sentence ("jams and jellies"). (C) is wrong for the same reason. The last paragraph takes place in the present tense, so (D) and (E) are wrong because they incorrectly introduce future and past activity, respectively. (B) is the only answer choice that solves both the problem of subject-verb agreement and the discrepancy of tense.

13. **(B)** The last paragraph is descriptive. It describes home-canning, homemade jams and jellies, and how you will enjoy giving these homemade preserves as gifts. The original is wrong because it incorrectly indicates present activity and implies that "you" already enjoy the practice of giving homemade preserves as gifts. However, the last paragraph actually assumes that you have not yet made preserves (Sentence 17 suggests finding a book about home-canning.). In fact, you first need to make the

preserves before you can give them away; so, the future tense is required. (C), (D), and (E) are wrong because they do not indicate future activity.

14. **(C)** The original suffers from a shift in pronoun case. The last paragraph establishes that the author is addressing a 2nd person audience ("when you have made them yourself" and "You also enjoy"). However, the original unnecessarily switches from addressing "you" to addressing "one." (B) is wrong because it creates a grammatically incorrect sentence without a proper subject. (D) and (E) are wrong for the same reason as the original.

15. **(A)** The sentence has a dangling modifier. As written, the sentence implies that Emily Dickinson herself was written. To correct this error, it would have to be rewritten to bring the introductory modifier closer to the noun it modifies (poems): "Emily Dickinson's poems, written in almost total isolation from the world, spoke of love and death."

16. **(D)** The use of the perfect tense "had given up" is not consistent with the use of the past tense "entertained," for the use of the perfect tense implies that the pianist gave up his attempt to become a composer before he even entertained the idea of becoming one. The sentence can be corrected by substituting "gave up" for "had given up."

17. **(B)** The sentence commits an error of illogical expression, for, as written, it implies that the fans' leaving the stadium would ordinarily be sufficient to halt a game and reschedule it for later. The problem of illogical expression can be corrected by substituting the conjunction "but" for "even though."

18. **(A)** The sentence has a dangling modifier. It implies that the bank president is highly qualified for the position. The sentence needs major revision: "The bank president will conduct a final interview of the new candidate tomorrow. Since the candidate is highly qualified for the position, the president will make her a job offer after the interview."

19. **(C)** The sentence commits an error of logical expression by implying that the "reason" is an effect of some other cause, when the speaker really means to say that the reason and the cause are the same thing, the explanation for the phenomenon. The error can be corrected by substituting "that" for "because." (Note: This use of "because" to introduce a noun clause can also be considered an example of an expression that is not acceptable in English usage.)

20. **(A)** The sentence contains a dangling modifier. As written, it implies that the police officer is listening in broken English (not listening to broken English). The sentence can be corrected by relocating the modifier: "The police officer patiently listened to the tourist ask in broken English for directions to Radio City Music Hall,...."

21. **(C)** The choice of "since" is illogical, because "since" implies that there is a causal or explanatory connection between Hemingway's view of bullfighting and the fact that bullfighting is a controversial sport that repulses some people. The problem of illogical subordination can be corrected by substituting "but" for "since."

22. **(D)** The sentence contains a misplaced modifier. As written, it implies that Peter hopes to learn how to protect his investments from the threat posed by a well-known investment banker. The sentence must be rewritten: "...in order to learn from a well-known investment banker methods to protect his investments."

23. **(D)** The sentence makes an error of logical expression, for it seems to compare our space program to the Soviet Union. The error is eliminated by using the phrase "to that of" instead of "to" after "superior."

24. **(B)** The sentence contains a misplaced modifier. The placement of "only" seems to imply a restriction on the verb rather than on the subject. The sentence is easily corrected by moving "only" and placing it just before "licensed lawyers."

25. **(A)** The sentence contains a dangling modifier and seems to compare ballerinas of the romantic ballet with the movement of Judith Jamison. To correct this error, the sentence would have to be substantially rewritten: "Judith Jamison's movement seems more African than European-American, and her physical appearance, which is unlike that of the pale and delicately built ballerinas of romantic ballet, reinforces the contrast."

26. **(D)** The sentence contains an error of logical expression. It attempts to compare an amount of decaffeinated coffee with coffee containing caffeine. The sentence can be corrected by inserting clarifying phrases: "...the number of tons of coffee containing caffeine consumed by Americans."

27. **(D)** The sentence contains a misplaced modifier. As written, it implies that the workers are illiterate because they do not know how to read on the job. The sentence can be corrected by relocating the offending phrase so that it is closer to the noun it modifies: "... many mistakes are made on the job by workers...."

28. **(D)** The sentence makes an illogical statement. It attempts to compare "men" and "branch of the service." The sentence can be corrected by inserting a clarifying phrase: "...than do men in any other branch...."

29. **(A)** The sentence contains a dangling modifier. It implies a comparison between A.J. Ayer, the person, and the writings of Gilbert Ryle. The error can be corrected in the following way: "Like the writing of A.J. Ayer, much of...."

30. "The life of my generation is easier than that of my parents."

    The original suffers from a faulty comparison. It attempts to compare "The life of my generation" with "my parents." However, unlike items cannot logically be compared; a comparison can only be made between like items. In the corrected sentence, the phrase "that of" is inserted before "my parents" in order to make a logical comparison. Now, one life (of a generation) is compared to another life (of parents).

31. "My two daughters enjoy different TV shows; the older one watches game shows, while the younger one prefers talk shows."

    The original is wrong because it incorrectly uses the superlative forms of the adjectives "old" and "young" ("oldest" and "youngest"). The superlative form is only used when three or more items are compared. In the original, however, only two items (two daughters) are compared. In the corrected sentence, the comparative forms of the adjectives "old" and "young" ("older" and "younger") are used.

32. "Her present instructor is the best of all the ones she has had so far."

    The original is wrong because it incorrectly uses the comparative form of the adjective "good" ("better"). The comparative form is only used when two items are compared. In the original, however, the "present instructor" is compared to all previous instructors. In other words, at least three items are compared. In the corrected sentence, the superlative form of the adjective "good" ("best") is used.

33. "In the technology lab, I choose the computer with the greatest memory."

    The original is wrong for two reasons. First, it incorrectly uses two techniques to express a comparison when only technique is required. Two items can either be compared by adding "-er" to the adjective or by placing "more" before the adjective. "More greater" is grammatically incorrect. Second, the original incorrectly uses the comparative form. The comparative form is used when two items are compared. However, it is logical to assume that there are more than two computers in the technology lab. In the corrected sentence, the superlative form of the adjective "great" ("greatest") is used in place of "more greater."

34. "According to the counselor, taking these classes in this order is much more beneficial than the other way around."

    In the original, two items are compared (taking classes "in this order" and taking classes "the other way around," or in the opposite order). When two items are compared using an adjective, the comparative form of that adjective is required. However, the original fails to use the comparative form. Since "beneficialer" is not a word, the word "more" must be used. In the corrected sentence, "more" is placed before "beneficial."

35. "Our school is unique in many aspects."

    The original is wrong because it unnecessarily uses an adverb to modify the adjective "unique." "Unique" already expresses the highest degree of individuality; there are no comparative or superlative forms of this adjective. In the corrected sentence, the adverb "very" is omitted.

36. "The fraternity he joined is better than all other fraternities."

    The original is wrong because it illogically compares a "fraternity" to itself. When the comparative form of an adjective ("better") is used in an expression to compare one item to any other item of that kind, an adjective such as "other" or "else" is required to separate the initial item from the rest of the items. For example, the statement "Tom is better than any boy" is illogical because it incorrectly implies that Tom is also better than himself. However, the statement "Tom is better than any other boy" makes a logical comparison between Tom and other boys. In the corrected sentence, the adjective "other" is placed before "fraternities."

37. The original is correct. Two items are compared, and they are expressed as like items ("Professor Baker's explanations" and "Professor Thomas' explanations").

38. The original is correct. Two experiences are compared (learning "online" and learning "in a regular classroom"), and the sentence correctly uses the comparative form of "many/much" ("more").

39. "Which of these three sections is best?"

The original is wrong because it uses the comparative form ("better") when the superlative form ("best") should be used. Three items are compared ("three sections"). When more than two items are compared, the superlative form of the adjective is required. In the corrected sentence, "better" is replaced with "best."

40. "I am spending more time on the assignments in my management class than on those in all my other classes combined."

The original suffers from a faulty comparison. It attempts to compare "assignments in my management class" with "all my other classes combined." However, unlike items cannot logically be compared; a comparison can only be made between like items. In the corrected sentence, the phrase "those in" is inserted before "all my other classes combined" in order to make a logical comparison. Now, assignments (in management class) are compared to other assignments (in all other classes combined).

41. "You will receive your grades no later than tomorrow at 2 p.m."

The original is wrong because it uses the superlative form of "late" ("latest") when the comparative form ("later") should be used. Two items are compared (an unspecified time when grades will be issued and the specific time of 2 p.m. tomorrow). When two items are compared, the comparative form of the adjective is required. In the corrected sentence, "latest" is replaced with "later."

42. "There is no need for further negotiation."

The original uses the wrong comparative form of the adjective "far." "Farther" is the form that is typically used to describe distance (e.g., "farther down the road"). "Further" is the form that is typically used to describe extent or degree (e.g., "further negotiations" or "further studies"). In the original, the extent of current negotiations is discussed. Therefore, the comparative form "further" is required.

43. "She is doing so badly in her art class that she could not do any worse."

The original is wrong because it uses the superlative form of "bad" ("worst") when the comparative form ("worse") should be used. Two items are compared (the woman's current performance in art class and her possible performance in art class). When two items are compared, the comparative form of the adjective is required. In the corrected sentence, "worst" is replaced with "worse."

44. "This exercise seems more difficult than all of the others."

The original is wrong because it illogically compares an "exercise" to itself. When the comparative form of an adjective ("more difficult") is used in an expression to compare one item to any other item of that kind, an adjective such as "other" or "else" is required to separate the initial item from the rest of the items. In the corrected sentence, "more difficult than all of them" is changed to "more difficult than all of the others."

45. "Going to school, he tripped on a crack in the pavement."

The original suffers from a misplaced modifier ("going to school"). Remember that a modifier should be placed as close as possible to what it modifies. Otherwise, the modifier might appear to modify some other element in the sentence. In the original, "going to school" is intended to modify "tripped." However, these two elements appear at opposite ends of the sentence. As a result, it sounds as though the pavement is going to school. In the corrected sentence, "going to school" is placed at the beginning of the sentence.

46. "Only Mary failed the test; everyone else in her class passed."

Simply by its placement, the word "only" can drastically change the entire meaning of a sentence. In the original, "only" is placed before "failed." As a result, it sounds as though Mary failed the test but did not fail anything else. However, the second half of the sentence clearly states that all of her classmates passed the test. Therefore, the original intends to say that Mary was the only student in her class who failed the test. In the corrected sentence, "only" is placed before "Mary" so that the intended meaning is made clear.

47. "Did you see the film on television about the five people on the boat?"

The original suffers from a misplaced modifier ("on television"). Remember that a modifier should be placed as close as possible to what it modifies. Otherwise, the modifier might appear to modify some other element in the sentence. In the original, "on television" is intended to modify "see" (the film is actually being shown on television). However, these two elements appear nearly at opposite ends of the sentence. As a result, it sounds as though the film is about a television program involving five people on a boat. In the corrected sentence, "on television" is placed immediately after "the film."

48. "The police officer, in his patrol car, ordered the man to stop."

The original suffers from a misplaced modifier ("in his patrol car"). In the original, "in his patrol car" is intended to modify "the police officer." However, these two elements appear at opposite ends of the sentence. As a result, it sounds either as though "the man" (rather than "the police officer") is in his own patrol car or he is in the police officer's patrol car. In the corrected sentence, "in his patrol car" is placed after "the police officer."

49. "When you picked up the phone, the noise became muted."

The original is unclear because the modifier ("Upon picking up the phone") modifies a subject that does not actually appear in the sentence. Who picked up the phone? As a result of this absence, the modifier incorrectly modifies the noun that is closest to it ("the noise"). In the corrected sentence, an actual subject ("you") is introduced, indicating that a person picked up the phone.

50. "While I was swimming, a fish nibbled on my toe."

The original is unclear because the modifier ("While swimming") modifies a subject that does not actually appear in the sentence. Who was swimming? As a result of this absence, the modifier incorrectly modifies the noun that is closest to it ("a fish"). Of course, we can be quite certain that the fish was swimming when it bit the toe; after all, fish are always swimming. Also, the possessive pronoun "my" indicates that the toe belongs to a person. Therefore, the modifier could not have been intended to modify "a fish." In the corrected sentence, an actual subject ("I") is introduced, indicating that a person was swimming.

51. The original is correct, unless the author intends to say that the church is on Cemetery Hill. The proximity of "on Cemetery Hill" to "people" suggests that the people are on Cemetery Hill, not the church.

52. "Of all his admirers, only his wife loved him."

Simply by its placement, the word "only" can drastically change the entire meaning of a sentence. In the original, "only" is placed before "loved." As a result, it sounds as though the wife had limited affection for her husband (she only loved him). However, "Of all his admirers" makes it clear that this is not the intended meaning. The original intends to say that although he had many admirers, only his wife actually loved him. In the corrected sentence, "only" is placed before "his wife" so that the intended meaning is made clear.

53. "When we entered the class, the blackboard came into view."

The original is unclear because the modifier ("Upon entering the class") modifies a subject that does not actually appear in the sentence. Who entered the class? As a result of this absence, the modifier incorrectly modifies the noun that is closest to it ("the blackboard"). In the corrected sentence, an actual subject ("we") is introduced, indicating that a group of persons entered the class.

54. "The baby was in a stroller pushed by his mother."

The original suffers from a misplaced modifier ("in a stroller"). In the original, "in a stroller" is intended to modify "the baby." However, these two elements are separated by the phrase "was pushed by his mother." As a result, it sounds as though the mother was in the stroller. In the corrected sentence, "in a stroller" is placed closer to "the baby," indicating that the baby is in the stroller.

55. "She likes tennis, golf, and swimming."

The original suffers from faulty parallelism. The three elements in the series are not expressed in the same form ("tennis...golf...to go swimming"). The first two items are nouns ("tennis" and "golf"), but the third item is a verb ("to go swimming"). In the corrected sentence, the verb "to go swimming" is replaced by the noun "swimming."

56. "He could not deliver the supplies because the roads had not yet been plowed."

The original is wrong because it treats a dependent clause ("because the roads had not yet been plowed") as an independent clause. A dependent clause cannot stand by itself. By definition, a dependent clause depends on another clause for its meaning and completeness. In the original, "because the roads had not yet been plowed" does not have any clear meaning as a separate sentence. What was the result of the roads not being plowed? In the corrected version, the period between "supplies" and "Because" is omitted, forming two separate sentences. Now, the dependent clause "because the roads had not yet been plowed" functions properly.

57. "If you want to succeed, you must be willing to work hard."
"If one wants to succeed, one must be willing to work hard."

The original suffers from a shift in pronoun case. It switches from addressing "you" to addressing "one." Pronoun case should remain consistent.

58. "Jeff is taller than any other boy in his class."

The original is wrong because it illogically compares "Jeff" to himself. When the comparative form of an adjective ("taller") is used in an expression to compare one item to any other item of that kind, an adjective such as "other" or "else" is required to separate the initial item from the rest of the items. The original intends to say that Jeff is taller than any other boy in his class. In the corrected sentence, the adjective "other" is simply placed before "boy."

59. "To get to school, we walked nearly two miles."

The original suffers from a misplaced modifier ("nearly"). Remember that a modifier should be placed as close as possible to what it modifies. Otherwise, the modifier might appear to modify some other element in the sentence. In the original, "nearly" is intended to modify "two miles." However, these two elements are separated by the verb "walked." As a result, it sounds as though they nearly, but did not actually, walk. In the corrected sentence, "nearly" is placed before "two miles," indicating how far they walked.

60. "The heroine was unbelievably naive."

The original is wrong because it uses an adjective ("unbelievable") to modify another adjective ("naïve"). Adverbs should be used to modify adjectives. In the corrected sentence, the adjective "unbelievable" is replaced by the adverb "unbelievably."

61. The original is correct. The adverb "carefully" is used to modify the verb "drive." Also, the two independent clauses are punctuated as two separate sentences.

62. "Leaning out the window, she could see the garden below."

The original is unclear because the modifier ("leaning out the window") modifies a subject that does not actually appear in the sentence. Who leaned out the window? As a result of this absence, the modifier incorrectly modifies the noun that is closest to it ("the garden"). In the corrected sentence, an actual subject ("she") is introduced, indicating that a female person leaned out the window.

63. "The hotel room that we had reserved was clean and comfortable."

The original suffers from a misplaced modifier ("that we had reserved"). In the original, "that we had reserved" is intended to modify "The hotel room." However, these two elements are separated by the clause "was clean and comfortable." As a result, "that we had reserved" modifies the adjective "comfortable," but this relationship makes no sense and the resulting sentence is grammatically incorrect. In the corrected sentence, "that we reserved" is placed after "The hotel room," indicating that they had reserved the hotel room.

64. "This book is heavier than that one."

The original is needlessly wordy. The comparative form of "heavy" ("heavier") clearly indicates that the weights of two books are compared. Therefore, the phrase "in weight" is redundant. In the corrected sentence, the phrase "in weight" is omitted.

EXERCISE 5—IDIOMS AND CLARITY OF EXPRESSION (p. 326)

1. The adjective "principal" is the correct answer choice. "Principal" means "chief" or "main," which is the intended meaning in this context. ("He is the main backer of the play.") The noun "principle" means "truth" or "rule." Since an adjective is required to successfully complete the sentence, the noun "principle" is the wrong word choice in this context because it is not an adjective.

2. The verb "accept" is the correct answer choice. "Accept" means "to agree to," which is the intended meaning in this context. ("I hope your company will agree to our offer.") The verb "except" means "to leave out" or "to object to." However, someone does not typically hope that another company will object to their offer. The preposition "except" means "other than," but since a verb is required to successfully complete the sentence, the preposition "except" is the wrong word choice in this context.

3. The noun "weather" is the correct answer choice. "Weather" means "atmospheric conditions," which is the intended meaning in this context. The conjunction "whether" means "if." Since a noun is required to successfully complete the sentence, the conjunction "whether" is the wrong word choice in this context because it cannot be modified by the adjective "good."

4. The preposition "into" is the correct answer choice. "Into" indicates something that moves from one place to the inside or interior of another place. The sentence intends to say that the rabbit moves from outside of the hat back "into" the hat. The preposition "in" does not indicate the necessary facet of movement.

5. The verb "advise" is the correct answer choice. "Advise" means "to offer advice," which is the intended meaning in this context. The noun "advice" means "information about what should be done in a particular situation." Furthermore, a verb is required to successfully complete the sentence, the noun "advice" is the wrong word choice in this context.

6. The conjunction "than" is the correct answer choice. "Than" is used after comparative adjectives or adverbs in order to introduce the second item in a comparison. The sentence intends to make a comparison between someone's actual height and her imagined height. The adverb "then" is used to indicate when something happened or the result/consequence of an event (*e.g.*, "If you knock, then I will enter."). Since a conjunction is required to successfully complete the sentence, the adverb "then" is the wrong word choice in this context.

7. The phrase "all ready" is the correct answer choice. As a self-contained phrase, this noun ("all") and adjective ("ready") combination means "completely prepared." As two separate words, the phrase "all ready" means "all of them are prepared." In either case, the phrase expresses the intended meaning and properly modifies "they." The adverb "already" means "by a certain time." Since an adverb cannot modify a pronoun ("they"), "already" is the wrong word choice in this context.

8. The noun "stationery" is the correct answer choice. "Stationery" means "writing paper," which is the intended meaning in this context. ("She answered the letter on shocking pink writing paper.") The adjective "stationary" means "standing still." Since a noun is required to successfully complete the sentence, the adjective "stationary" is the wrong word choice in this context.

9. The noun "effect" is the correct answer choice. As a noun, "effect" means "result," which is the intended meaning in this context. ("What is the result you are trying to achieve?") The verb "affect" means "to produce an effect in." Since a noun is required to successfully complete the sentence, the verb "affect" is the wrong word choice in this context.

10. The verb "sit" is the correct answer choice. "Sit" means "to seat oneself," which is the intended meaning in this context. ("I want to seat myself next to my grandfather.") The verb "set" means "to place something down," and it is the wrong word choice in this context. The speaker does not want to set something next to his or her grandfather.

11. The verb "lie" is the correct answer choice. As a verb, "lie" means "to recline," which is the intended meaning in this context. The verb "lay" means "to put," and it is the wrong word choice in this context.

12. The adverb "altogether" is the correct answer choice. "Altogether" means "entirely," which is the intended meaning in this context. The speaker says that he or she is entirely tired of someone else's excuses. The phrase "all together" is used to describe a group that is acting in unison. Since an adverb is required to successfully complete the sentence, the phrase "all together" is the wrong word choice in this context.

13. The past tense verb "passed" is the correct answer choice. "Pass" means "to move past something," which is the intended meaning in this context. The adjective "past" means "at an earlier time." Since a verb is required to successfully complete the sentence, the adjective "past" is the wrong word choice in this context.

14. The noun "dessert" is the correct answer choice. "Dessert" means "the final course of a meal," which is the intended meaning in this context. Since a noun is required to successfully complete the sentence, the verb "desert," which means "to abandon," is

the wrong word choice in this context. The noun "desert" means "an arid area," but that is not the intended meaning in this context.

15. The verb "lose" is the correct answer choice. "Lose" means "to misplace" or "to be unable to keep," and "to be unable to keep," which is the intended meaning in this context. The adjective "loose" means "not fastened or restrained." Since a verb is required to successfully complete the sentence, the adjective "loose" is the wrong word choice in this context.

16. The verb "affect" is the correct answer choice. "Affect" means "to change" or "to influence," which is the intended meaning in this context. The speaker wants to know how much the final examination will influence his or her grade. "Effect" can function as either a verb or a noun, and a verb is required to successfully complete the sentence. However, the verb "effect" means "to cause" or "to bring about," and neither of these meanings is intended in this context.

17. The contraction "you're" is the correct answer choice. "You're" is a shortened version of the phrase "you are," and it successfully completes the sentence. The possessive pronoun "your" is the wrong word choice in this context because it results in a sentence without a verb.

18. "Used" is the correct answer choice. "Used to" is an idiomatic expression that means "accustomed to," which is the intended meaning in this context. ("She's not accustomed to such cold weather.") "Use" can function as either a verb or a noun. The verb "use" means "to employ" or "to put into service," and the noun "use" means "the manner of using, or usage." "Use to," however, is a the correct idiomatic expression.

19. The verb "rise" is the correct answer choice. "Rise" means "to increase," which is the intended meaning in this context. The verb "raise" means "to lift" or "to erect." The cost of the coat will increase; however, the sentence does not emphasize anyone acting to "raise" the price.

20. "Supposed" is the correct answer choice. "Supposed to" is an idiomatic expression that means "ought to" or "should"; in this context, "supposed" successfully completes the sentence. The verb "suppose" means "to assume" or "to guess." "Suppose to," however, is not a correct idiomatic expression.

21. The possessive pronoun "its" is the correct answer choice. A possessive pronoun is used before a noun to indicate that the noun belongs to someone or something else. In this context, the pronoun "its" indicates that the bowl belongs to the cat. The contraction "it's" is a shortened version of the phrase "it is," which is the wrong word choice in this context.

22. The adjective "conscious" is the correct answer choice. "Conscious" means "aware," which is the intended meaning in this context. ("Are you aware of what you are doing?") The noun "conscience" means "the ability to recognize the difference between right and wrong." Since an adjective is required to successfully complete the sentence, the noun "conscience" is the wrong word choice in this context because it is not an adjective.

23. The verb "seem" is the correct answer choice. "Seem" means "to appear," which is the correct meaning in this context. The past participle "seen" does not work grammatically in this sentence. A correct sentence could be formed with "be seen", but that is not an answer choice.

24. The plural noun "allusions" is the correct answer choice. "Allusions" means "references," which is the intended meaning in this context. "Literary allusions" are references to other works of literature. The plural noun "illusions" means "wrong ideas" or "wrong perceptions," and it is the wrong word choice in this context. While an entirely possible word choice, "literary allusions" is an idiomatic expression, and thus should be preferred.

25. The noun "complement" is the correct answer choice. "Complement" means "a completing part," which is the intended meaning in this context. The noun "compliment" means "an expression of praise or admiration," and it is the wrong word choice in this context. While a bottle of wine might be worthy of a compliment, a bottle of wine itself cannot be a compliment.

26. The adjective "later" is the correct answer choice. "Later" is a comparative adjective that compares two times, in this instance the time of speech and the time thought. The adjective "latter" means "the second of two," which is the wrong word choice in this context. "Latter" incorrectly implies that the sentence is about two things, two choices, or two persons. Furthermore, it cannot be used in conjunction with the comparative "than." Something cannot be more "latter" than something else.

27. The noun "build" is the correct answer choice. As a noun, "build" means "physical makeup" or "body," which is the intended meaning in this context. ("My cousin has a swimmer's body.") As a verb, "build" means "to construct," and "built" is the past tense form of this verb. Since a noun is required to successfully complete the sentence, the verb "built" is the wrong word choice in this context.

28. The past tense verb "knew" is the correct answer choice. "Know" means "to be familiar with" or "to understand," and "to be familiar with," which is the intended meaning in this context. ("I was never familiar with him before today.") The adjective "new" means "of recent origin." Since a verb is required to successfully complete the sentence, the adjective "new" is the wrong word choice in this context.

29. The adjective "personal" is the correct answer choice. "Personal" means "of or relating to a person's character, conduct, or affairs," which is the intended meaning in this context. The noun "personnel" means "an organized body of individuals," and it is the wrong word choice in this context. While it is possible to ask a "personnel question," or a question regarding personnel, "personal question" is idiomatic, and thus should be preferred.

30. The noun "course" is the correct answer choice. "Course" means "path," and a "golf course" is a place where people play golf. The adjective "coarse" means "vulgar" or "harsh," which is the wrong word choice in this context.

31. The adjective "cloth" is the correct answer choice. The noun "cloth" means "a type of fabric used for a specific purpose." The verb "clothe" means "to put on clothes" or "to dress," and it is the wrong word choice in this context.

32. The verb "elude" is the correct answer choice. "Elude" means "to escape from" or "to avoid," which is the intended meaning in this context. ("The ball carrier was trying to avoid the tacklers.") The verb "allude" means "to make reference to," which is the wrong meaning in this context.

33. The adverb "no" is the correct answer choice. "No" is a negative that indicates denial, refusal, absence, or lack. The sentence intends to say that there was a lack of exhibitions. The verb "know" means "to have knowledge" or "to understand." Since an adverb is required to successfully complete the sentence, the verb "know" is the wrong word choice in this context.

34. The prefix "ante" is the correct answer choice. "Ante" means "before." An "anteroom" is a room that is located before, or in front of, another room. The prefix "anti" means "against." However, there is no such room as an "anti room."

35. The noun "morale" is the correct answer choice. "Morale" means "spirit," which is the intended meaning in this context. Since a noun is required to successfully complete the sentence, the adjective "moral," which means "ethical," is the wrong word choice in this context. The noun "moral" means "lesson," but that is not the intended meaning in this context.

36. The adjective "capital" is the correct answer choice. "Capital" can function as either a noun or an adjective. As a noun, "capital" means "place of government" or "wealth." As an adjective, "capital" means "upper case," which is the intended meaning in this context. The noun "capitol" means "a building where government or legislatures are located." Since an adjective is required to successfully complete the sentence, the noun "capitol" is the wrong word choice in this context.

37. The verb "faze" is the correct answer choice. "Faze" means "to worry" or "to disturb," which is the intended meaning in this context. "Phase" can function as either a verb or a noun, and a verb is required to successfully complete the sentence. However, the verb "phase" means "to carry out in stages," which is not the intended meaning in this context.

38. "Excess" is the correct answer choice. "In excess of" means "a state surpassing specified limits," which is the intended meaning in this context; therefore, "excess" successfully completes the sentence. "Access" can function as either a noun or a verb. The noun "access" means "availability," and the verb "access" means "to get at." However, neither of these meanings successfully completes the sentence.

39. The verb "proceed" is the correct answer choice. "Proceed" means "to go ahead" or "to continue," which is the intended meaning in this context. ("Now, may we continue with the debate?") The verb "precede" means "to come or go before," and it is the wrong word choice in this context.

40. The noun "forte" is the correct answer choice. "Forte" means "strength," which is the intended meaning in this context. ("Her strength is writing lyrics for musical comedy.") The noun "fort" means "a fortified place," which is an incorrect word choice in this context.

41. The verb "disperse" is the correct answer choice. "Disperse" means "to scatter," which is the intended meaning in this context. ("They wondered how they were going to scatter the huge crowd.") The verb "disburse" means "to pay out," and it is the wrong word choice in this context. While it is possible to disburse something (*e.g.*, money) to a huge crowd, the sentence as it stands implies that the payment would be comprised of the crowd, which is unlikely.

42. The adverb "formally" is the correct answer choice. "Formally" means "in a formal way." The sentence intends to say that everyone was wearing formal attire for the dinner party. So, everyone was most likely dressed in tuxedos, evening gowns, *etc.*

The adverb "formerly" means "before" or "at an earlier time;" placed before "dressed", "formerly" could be idiomatic, but at the insertion point, it would not be.

43. The adjective "averse" is the correct answer choice. "Averse" means "having a feeling of opposition or dislike," which is the intended meaning in this context; it is used to describe a person or group of persons. ("I am not opposed to continuing the discussion at another time.") The adjective "adverse" means "serving to oppose" or "unfavorable," and it is the wrong word choice in this context; it is used to describe circumstances (*e.g.*, "they fought the battle under adverse conditions").

44. The noun "incidence" is the correct answer choice. "Incidence" means "the frequency of occurrence," which is the intended meaning in this context. The speaker asks if something can be done to diminish the frequency with which influenza occurs. The plural noun "incidents" means "events," but it does not make sense for events to be diminished.

45. The adjective "dual" is the correct answer choice. "Dual" means "double, " which is the intended meaning in this context. The speaker says that seeing the film in class will serve two purposes. The noun "duel" means "a contest between two persons or groups," and it is the wrong word choice in this context.

46. The verb "expend" is the correct answer choice. "Expend" means "to use up," which is the intended meaning in this context. ("I'm not sure I want to use up so much energy on that project.") The verb "expand" means "to spread out," which is the wrong word choice in this context.

47. The noun "discomfort" is the correct answer choice. "Discomfort" means "lack of ease," which is the intended meaning in this context. ("Imagine my lack of ease when she showed up at the party too!) The verb "discomfit" means "to upset." Since a noun is required to successfully complete the sentence, "discomfit" is the wrong word choice in this context.

48. The noun "idol" is the correct answer choice. "Idol" means "image or object of worship," which is the intended meaning in this context, as indicated by the adjective "famous." The adjective "idle" means "unemployed or unoccupied." Since a noun is required to successfully complete the sentence, "idle" is the wrong word choice in this context.

49. The verb "emigrate" is the correct answer choice. "Emigrate" means "to leave a country," which is the intended meaning in this context. The verb "immigrate" means "to enter a country," and it is the wrong word choice in this context. The position of the preposition "from" in relationship to the verb "emigrate" indicates the intended meaning of the sentence. If the two prepositions were inverted, then "immigrate" would be the correct answer choice.

50. The noun "clique" is the correct answer choice. "Clique" means "an exclusive group of people," which is the intended meaning in this context. ("I think she is part of an exclusive group of snobs and creeps.") The noun "click" means "a brief, sharp sound," and it is the wrong word choice in this context.

51. The noun "prophecy" is the correct answer choice. "Prophecy" means "prediction, which is the intended meaning in this context. ("She paid little attention to the fortune-teller's prediction.") The verb "prophesy" means "to predict." "Prophecy" and "prophesy" have similar meanings; however, since a noun is required to successfully complete the sentence, "prophesy" is the wrong word choice in this context.

52. The noun "lightning" is the correct answer choice. "Lightning" means "the electric discharge in the atmosphere that precedes or accompanies rain." The sentence intends to say that the lights go out when the house is struck by an electric bolt or discharge. The progressive verb "lightening" means "making less heavy." Since a noun is required to successfully complete the sentence, the verb "lightening" is the wrong word choice in this context.

53. The adjective "whatever" is the correct answer choice. "Whatever" means "any or anything," which is the intended meaning in this context. The speaker offers to provide any assistance that is required. "What ever" is simply a misspelled version of "whatever."

54. The adjective "imminent" is the correct answer choice. "Imminent" means "impending" or "immediate," which is the intended meaning in this context. ("We are in immediate danger of losing our reservations.") The adjective "eminent" means "prominent" or "outstanding," and it is the wrong word choice in this context. It would not be idiomatic to describe the loss of reservations as a prominent or outstanding danger.

55. The verb "adapt" is the correct answer choice. "Adapt" means "to change" or "to adjust," which is the intended meaning in this context. ("Will she be able to adjust to our way of performing the operation?") The verb "adopt" means "to take in as one's own," and it is the wrong word choice in this context.

56. The noun "epitaphs" is the correct answer choice. "Epitaph" means "an inscription on a tombstone," which is the intended meaning in this context. ("As we went through the old cemetery, we were fascinated by some of the inscriptions on the tombstones." The noun "epithet" means "a term used to describe or characterize the nature of a thing or person," and it is the wrong word choice in this context. While it is quite possible for an epithet (*e.g.*, "The Great Emancipator") to be part of an epitaph, the noun "cemetery" indicates that "epitaphs" is the better word choice in this context.

57. The preposition "among" is the correct answer choice. "Among" is used when referring to three or more people or things. The sentence intends to say that he shared the riches with three people ("Laura," "Millie," and "Ernestine"). The preposition "between" is used when referring to either two people or two things, which is not the case in this context.

58. The noun "benefit" is the correct answer choice. As a noun, "benefit" means "an advantage." Interestingly enough, the noun "advantage" means "benefit." However, "for his advantage" is not an idiomatic expression. The correct idiomatic expression is "for his benefit." The preposition "for" indicates the intended meaning of the sentence. If the preposition "for" were changed to the preposition "to," then "advantage" would be the correct answer choice ("to his advantage").

59. The adverb "a lot" is the correct answer choice. "A lot" means "a great number of" or "much," which is the intended meaning in this context. ("Much of the time, he falls asleep at nine o'clock.") "Alot" is simply a misspelled version of "a lot."

60. The noun "number" is the correct answer choice. "Number" is used when describing things that can be counted accurately, which is the intended meaning in this context since people can be counted accurately. The noun "amount" is used when describing things that cannot be counted accurately (*e.g.*, "the amount of pain" or "the amount of effort"), and it is the wrong word choice in this context.

61. The adverb "almost" is the correct answer choice. "Almost" means "nearly," which is the intended meaning in this context. ("I see him in the park nearly every day.") The adjective "most" means "the majority of," and it is the wrong word choice in this context. "Most every day" is not an idiomatic expression.

62. The adjective "all right" is the correct answer choice. "All right" means "fine," which is the intended meaning in this context. ("Are you sure that he is fine now?") "Alright" is simply a misspelled version of "all right."

63. The verb "annoy" is the correct answer choice. "Annoy" means "to bother," which is the intended meaning in this context. ("She is just beginning to bother her mother.") The verb "aggravate" means "intensify an already troublesome situation." Because we cannot assume that the situation is already vexing, "annoy" is a more fitting choice.

64. The singular noun "alumnus" is the correct answer choice. "Alumnus" means "a graduate of a school," which is the intended meaning in this context. ("He is the school's oldest living graduate.") The plural noun "alumni" is the wrong word choice in this context because only one person is mentioned in the sentence.

65. The adverb "alongside" is the correct answer choice. "Alongside" means "to the side," which is the intended meaning in this context. ("He spotted the riverbank and then guided the canoe up to the side.") In this case, "alongside" properly modifies "guided." The preposition "alongside of" means "side by side with." Since an adverb is required to successfully complete the sentence, the preposition "alongside of" is the wrong word choice in this context; a sentence cannot end with a preposition.

66. The conjunction "since" is the correct answer choice. As a conjunction, "since" is another way to say "because," which is the intended meaning in this context. ("Because it is Wednesday, we are going to a Broadway matinee.")

67. The adjective "eager" is the correct answer choice. "Eager" means "having a great interest in" or "enthusiastic," and it is used when describing a thing that is desired. The sentence intends to say that he has a great desire to be finished with his dental treatment. The adjective "anxious" means "worried," and it is used when describing a thing that is not desired. We can be certain that he desires the conclusion of his dental treatment.

68. The verb "meet" is the correct answer choice. "Meet" means "to come into the presence of someone or something," which is the intended meaning in this context. "Meet at" is an example of low-level (informal) usage that might appear in casual conversation. It is the wrong word choice in this context because it creates a sentence that ends with a preposition.

69. The adverb "awhile" is the correct answer choice. "Awhile" means "for a short time," which is the intended meaning in this context. ("My aunt just went inside to rest for a short time.") "A while" is the proper form only when preceded by a preposition. Thus, "my aunt just went inside to rest for a while."

70. The adverb "about" is the correct answer choice. "About" means "approximately," which is the intended meaning in this context. ("It was approximately noon when we met for lunch.") As an adverb, "around" also means "approximately," but it is more suited for describing movement and position.

71. "Couple of" is the correct answer choice because it creates the appropriate adjective ("a couple of") to modify "books." The noun "couple" means "two persons or things." Since an adjective is required to successfully complete the sentence, the noun "couple" is the wrong word choice in this context.

72. "You and me" is the correct answer choice. Since both pronouns in this context are objects of the preposition "between," they should be in the objective case ("you" and "me"). The pronoun "I" is an example of the nominative (or subjective) case, so "you and I" is the wrong word choice in this context.

73. The adjective "continuous" is the correct answer choice. "Continuous" means "non-stop" or "proceeding without stopping," which is the intended meaning in this context. ("The non-stop ticking of the clock was very disconcerting.") The adjective "continual" means "at frequent intervals," and it is the wrong word choice in this context. The clock does not tick at frequent intervals (with breaks in-between); instead, it ticks without any breaks at all.

74. "Seems unable" is the correct answer choice. The verb "seems" means "appears," which is the intended meaning in this context. ("She appears unable to get up early enough to eat breakfast with him.") "Cannot seem" is the wrong word choice in this context because the resulting sentence is vague and confusing. The verb "seem" means "appear." How can it be impossible for her to appear to get up early?

75. The verb "assume" is the correct answer choice. "Assume" means "to suppose," which is the intended meaning in this context. ("I suppose that you really earned your salary today.") The verb "expect" can also mean "to suppose," but it is an example of low-level (informal) usage that might appear in casual conversation; therefore, it is less acceptable in standard written English.

76. The adjective "uninterested" is the correct answer choice. "Uninterested" means "to have no interest," and that is the intended meaning in this context. The speaker has no interest in seeing the movie. The adjective "disinterested" means "unbiased by personal interest or advantage," and it is the wrong word choice in this context

77. "Just as" is the correct answer choice. "Just as" means "in the same way as," which is the intended meaning in this context. "Every bit as" is an example of low-level (informal) usage that might appear in casual conversation; therefore, it is less acceptable in standard written English. "Every bit as" is also needlessly wordy.

78. The conjunction "that" is the correct answer choice. As a conjunction, "that" is used to introduce a relative clause. In this context, "that" introduces "it will snow today." The conjunction "whether" is typically used to introduce the first of two or more alternatives, and it is incorrect in this context because the sentence is not about two or more alternatives.

79. The pronoun "one another" is the correct answer choice. "One another" is used when describing the relationship among three or more people. The sentence intends to say that four people ("Sam," "Joe," "Lou," and "Artie") worked together. The pronoun "each other" is used when describing the relationship between two people.

80. The conjunction "whether" is the correct answer choice. "Whether" is typically used to introduce the first of two or more alternatives. The sentence intends to introduce two alternatives ("to have lunch with her or to have lunch with her sister"). Interestingly enough, the conjunction "if" means "whether," but it is the wrong word choice in this context because it cannot be used to introduce the first of two or more alternatives. If "if" were used, the response to the question would be "yes" or "no." It would not present the choice between the sisters correctly.

81. The plural noun "human beings" is the correct answer choice. "Humans" can function as a plural noun, but the word "human" typically functions as an adjective rather than a singular noun. Therefore, "human beings" is the best word choice in this context.

82. The verb "finalize" is the correct answer choice. "Finalize" means "to agree on final details" or "to put into final form," which is the intended meaning in this context. ("We hope to put the deal into final form this month.") The verb "conclude" means "to end." However, someone does not typically hope to end a business deal; he or she typically hopes to begin a deal once the final details have been resolved. Therefore, "conclude" is the wrong word choice in this context.

83. The past tense verb "flouted" is the correct answer choice. "Flout" means "to disregard in a disrespectful way," which is the intended meaning in this context. ("We were upset when she disregarded her mother's orders.") The verb "flaunt" means "to show off" or "to display in an ostentatious manner," it would be unlikely to see someone showing off his or her mother's orders.

84. The adjective "healthful" is the correct answer choice. "Healthful" means "conducive to good health." The sentence intends to say that she eats foods that are conducive to (or likely to produce) good health. The adjective "healthy" means "possessing good health," and it is the wrong word choice in this context. Foods are typically not said to be in good health; instead, people or animals are said to be in good health.

85. The noun "slander" is the correct answer choice. "Slander" means "the attack of someone's reputation with spoken words," which is the intended meaning in this context ("He said such terrible things about her"). The noun "libel" means "the attack of someone's reputation with written words," and it is the wrong word choice in this context.

86. "Regard" is the correct answer choice. "In regard to" is an idiomatic expression that means "about," which is the intended meaning in this context. ("I would like to see you about the apartment you plan to rent.") "Regards" can function as either a plural noun or a singular verb. The plural noun "regards" means "sentiments of esteem or affection," and the singular verb "regards" means "observes" or "looks upon." "In regards to," however, is not an idiomatic expression.

87. The adverb "regardless" is the correct answer choice. "Regardless" means "without regard" or "in spite of." The sentence intends to say that she is always late for work in spite of the fact that she wakes up early in the morning. "Irregardless" is considered non-standard or low-level usage, and it is the wrong word choice in this context. It is redundant to add the negative prefix "ir-" to the root word "regardless."

88. The verb "lend" is the correct answer choice. "To lend a hand" is an idiomatic expression that means "to help." The sentence intends to say that he will help carry the groceries. "To loan a hand" is not an idiomatic expression.

89. The singular verb "is" is the correct answer choice. "Media" can function as either a plural noun or a singular noun. "Media" is the plural form of the singular noun "medium." However, the singular noun "media" means "a group of people who make up the communications industry," which is the intended meaning in this context. A group is singular; thus, the plural verb "are" is the wrong word choice in this context.

90. The preposition "off" is the correct answer choice. As a preposition, "off" means "so as to be removed from," which is the intended meaning in this context. "Off of" is an example of low-level (informal) usage that might appear in casual conversation; therefore, it is less acceptable in standard written English.

91. The verb "stop" is the correct answer choice. "To stop sending" is the correct idiomatic expression. "To quit sending" is not an idiomatic expression.

92. The conjunction "that" is the correct answer choice. As a conjunction, "that" can be used to introduce a noun clause ("she is hungry"). The conjunction "because" should not be used to introduce a noun clause.

93. The verb "manage" is the correct answer choice. "Manage" means "to direct," which is the intended meaning in this context. ("Does he direct the department efficiently?") The verb "run" has several definitions, one of which is "to operate" (*e.g.*, "run a lawnmower"). However, the verb "run" cannot be used in this manner to describe people ("the department"). In this context, "run" is an example of low-level (informal) usage that might appear in casual conversation; therefore, it is less acceptable in standard written English.

94. The singular pronoun "his or her" is the correct answer choice. The antecedent, or referent, in this sentence is the singular "anyone." The plural pronoun "their" does not agree in number with the singular antecedent, and it is the wrong word choice in this context.

95. "Any other" is the correct answer choice. When comparing someone to the rest of a group, a word such as "other" or "else" is required to separate that person from the other members of the group. The sentence intends to say that she scored more points than every player on the team (except, of course, herself). In this context, the use of "any" would imply that she scored more points than herself, a logical impossibility.

96. The conjunction "but" is the correct answer choice. "But" is used to indicate the contrast between two things. The sentence intends to say that his very neat room stands in contrast to her very messy room. The conjunction "while" is also used to indicate contrast; however, it further suggests a causal connection between the two things (*e.g.*, The reason for the neatness is in some way related to the reason for the messiness.). This causal connection, however, is not justified in this context.

97. "Try to" is the correct answer choice. "Try to" makes clear the fact that he will undertake only one activity ("being more pleasant to his sister"). On the other hand, "try and" incorrectly suggests that he will undertake two separate activities ("he will try" and "he will be more pleasant to his sister"). What will he try?

98. "Whoever" is the correct answer choice. This is a very difficult question. At first, it would appear that "whomever" is the correct answer choice since it comes after the verb and is the object of the preposition "to." Both of these reasons would typically justify using the objective case ("whomever"). However, in this instance, the object of the preposition "to" is the entire clause that follows. This clause requires a subject, and subjects are always expressed in the nominative case ("whoever").

99. The preposition "for" is the correct answer choice. The preposition "on" inadvertently creates the verb phrase "wait on." This verb phrase is used when talking about service or servants (*e.g.*, "I will wait on your table tonight."), and it is the wrong word choice in this context.

100. **(C)** Either the gerund "lecturing" or the infinitive "to lecture" successfully completes the sentence.

101. **(A)** The meaning of the verb "forgot" changes, depending on whether it is followed by an infinitive or a gerund. In the case of the infinitive ("he forgot to meet me"), the sentence implies that he neglected to meet the speaker. In the case of the gerund ("he forgot meeting me"), the sentence implies that he failed to remember meeting the speaker. Since he reintroduced himself to the speaker, the gerund is required in this context.

102. **(B)** The meaning of the verb "remember" changes, depending on whether it is followed by an infinitive or a gerund. In the case of the infinitive ("please remember to arrive"), the sentence implies that the day of the test is in the future. In the case of the gerund ("please remember arriving"), the sentence implies that the day of the test is in the past. However, it is unlikely that a teacher would ask his or her students to remember when they arrived five minutes early to a test that they took in the past. Therefore, the infinitive is required in this context.

103. **(B)** The verb "hesitate" is almost always followed by an infinitive.

104. **(B)** The verb "proceed" is almost always followed by an infinitive.

105. **(C)** Either the gerund "accepting" or the infinitive "to accept" successfully completes the sentence.

106. **(A)** The verb "tolerate" is almost always followed by a gerund.

107. **(C)** Either the gerund "writing" or the infinitive "to write" successfully completes the sentence.

108. **(C)** Either the gerund "preparing" or the infinitive "to prepare" successfully completes the sentence.

109. **(A)** The meaning of the verb "tried" changes, depending on whether it is followed by an infinitive or a gerund. In the case of the infinitive ("The applicant tried to ask"), the sentence implies that applicant attempted but failed to ask for an extension. In the case of the gerund ("The applicant tried asking"), the sentence implies that the applicant asked for an extension but was rejected. Since the sentence says that the applicant's request was turned down, the gerund is required in this context.

110. **(B)** The verb "warn" is almost always followed by an infinitive.

111. **(A)** The verb "anticipate" is almost always followed by a gerund.

112. **(B)** The verb "force" is almost always followed by an infinitive.

113. **(C)** Either the gerund "hearing" or the infinitive "to hear" successfully completes the sentence.

114. **(A)** The verb phrase "spend time" is almost always followed by a gerund.

115. **(B)** The noun "relation" means "family member." The noun "relationship" means "connection," which is the intended meaning in this context; there is a connection between the amount of imported oil and the number of traffic accidents. Therefore, "relation" should be replaced with "relationship."

116. **(D)** The verb "lay" means "to put." The verb "lie" means "to recline," which is the intended meaning in this context; Westminster Abbey is a place where English notables and royalty are buried. Therefore, "lay" should be replaced with "lie."

117. **(B)** The verb "adopt" means "to take in as one's own." The verb "adapt" means "to change," which is the intended meaning in this context; the speaker is unsure whether the script can be changed to meet certain requirements. Therefore, "adopted" should be replaced with "adapted."

118. **(B)** The phrase "would of" is not acceptable in standard written English. This phrase is commonly confused with the contraction of "would have" ("would've") because they sound the same as one another. Therefore, "would of chosen" should be replaced with "would have chosen."

119. **(A)** "Get built" is low-level, or informal, usage that might appear in casual conversation. However, it is not acceptable in standard written English. The correct verb phrase is "are built."

120. **(C)** The expression "as much than" is not idiomatic. The correct idiomatic expression is "as much as." Therefore, "than" should be replaced with "as."

121. **(D)** The expression "neither...or..." is not idiomatic. When a negative statement is made about two separate things, the correct idiomatic expression is "neither...nor...." Therefore, "or" should be replaced with "nor."

122. **(D)** The original is wrong for two reasons. First, it suggests that Helen Walker's willingness to sing pleases the audience. While her willingness most certainly contributes to the audience's pleasure, the sentence intends to say specifically that Helen Walker's songs please the audience; an audience typically demands encores when it enjoys the actual performance. The infinitive "to please" would make it perfectly clear that it is her songs (rather than her willingness) that please the audience. Second, the original is incorrectly punctuated; there should be a comma between "song" and "which." Therefore, "which pleases" should be replaced with "to please."

123. **(C)** The original is needlessly wordy. The phrase "as to whether" should be replaced with "whether." The resulting sentence is more concise and less vague.

124. **(D)** The expression "not of the same...with..." is not idiomatic. The correct idiomatic expression is "not of the same...as...." Therefore, "with" should be replaced with "as."

125. **(D)** The expression "so long that" is not idiomatic. The correct idiomatic expression is "so long as." Therefore, "that" should be replaced with "as."

126. **(D)** The original is awkward and needlessly wordy. The phrase "less of a sentence" should be replaced with "a lesser sentence." The resulting sentence is less awkward and more concise.

127. **(C)** The verb "allows" is almost always followed by an infinitive. Therefore, "attaching" should be replaced with "to attach."

128. **(C)** The expression "an earlier time as" is not idiomatic. The correct idiomatic expression is "an earlier time than." Therefore, "as" should be replaced with "than."

129. **(C)** The verb "raise" means "to lift" or "to erect." The verb "rise" means "to increase," which is the intended meaning in this context. Unemployment is not something that can be physically lifted; however, it is quantifiable and therefore subject to both increase and decrease. So, "raise" should be replaced with "rise."

EXERCISE 6—PUNCTUATION (p. 342)

1. He was not aware that you had lost your passport.

   A period is required after "passport" since the sentence is an independent clause and a statement.

2. Did you report the loss to the proper authorities?

   A question mark is required after "authorities" since the sentence is an independent clause and a direct request for information. A sentence that asks a question is an interrogative sentence.

3. I suppose you had to fill out many forms.

   A period is required after "forms" since the sentence is an independent clause and a statement. Do not be distracted by the nature of uncertainty in this statement, as indicated by the word "suppose"; this sentence is not a direct request for information (interrogative).

4. What a nuisance!

An exclamation mark is required after "nuisance" since the statement is an expression of strong emotion, as indicated by the "What a..." structure.

5. I hate doing so much paper work!

An exclamation mark is required after "work" since the statement is an expression of strong emotion, as indicated by the verb "hate."

6. Did you ever discover where the wallet was?

A question mark is required after "was" since the sentence is an independent clause and a direct request for information. A sentence that asks a question is an interrogative sentence.

7. I imagine you wondered how it was misplaced.

A period is required after "misplaced" since the sentence is an independent clause and a statement Do not be distracted by the nature of uncertainty in this statement, as indicated by the word "imagine"; this sentence is not a direct request for information (interrogative).

8. Good for you!

An exclamation mark is required after "you" since the statement is an expression of strong emotion.

9. At least you now have your passport.

A period is required after "passport" since the sentence is an independent clause and a statement. A comma is not required after the phrase "At least"; it would introduce an awkward and unnecessary pause. Read the sentence aloud to double-check this pause.

10. What will you do if it happens again?

A question mark is required after "again" since the sentence is an independent clause and a direct request for information. A sentence that asks a question is an interrogative sentence.

11. I don't know if they are coming, though I sent them an invitation weeks ago.

The original is missing three pieces of punctuation. First, a period is required after "ago" since the sentence is a combination of two independent clauses that are statements. Second, a comma is required before "though." Remember that a comma is required before a coordinating conjunction (*e.g.*, "and," "or," "but," "though") that joins two independent clauses. Finally, in the first independent clause, an apostrophe is required to create the contraction of "do not"; the apostrophe should be inserted between the letter "n" and the letter "t" ("don't"). Note that the apostrophe is properly located in place of the letter that was contracted.

12. Neurology is the science that deals with the anatomy, physiology, and pathology of the nervous system.

The original is missing two pieces of punctuation. First, a period is required after "nervous system" since the sentence is an independent clause and a statement. Second, two commas are required to set off the three elements in the series ("anatomy," "physiology," and "pathology"). Remember that commas are always used to separate elements in a series (as long as there are three or more elements in the series).

13. Nursery lore, like everything human, has been subject to many changes over long periods of time.
Nursery lore—like everything human—has been subject to many changes over long periods of time.

The original is missing two pieces of punctuation. First, a period is required after "time" since the sentence is an independent clause and a statement. Second, either two commas or two dashes are required (one before "like" and the other after "human") to set off the non-restrictive element ("like everything human"). Remember that a non-restrictive element contains non-essential information and can therefore be removed (as indicated by either commas or dashes) without changing the meaning of the original. When choosing between commas and dashes, remember that dashes are for stronger breaks and are less formal.

14. Bob read Joyce's Ulysses to the class; everyone seemed to enjoy the reading.

The original is missing three pieces of punctuation. First, a period is required after "reading" since the sentence is a combination of two independent clauses that are statements. Second, in the first independent clause, a possessive apostrophe is required to indicate that Joyce wrote *Ulysses*; the apostrophe should be inserted between the letter "e" and the letter "s" ("Joyce's"). Finally, "end-stop" punctuation is required after "class" to separate the two independent clauses that make up the sentence ("Bob read Joyce's *Ulysses* to the class" and "everyone seemed to enjoy the reading"). Either a period or a semicolon could be used to separate these clauses; however, if a period were used, "everyone" would need to be capitalized. Remember that this exercise does not test capitalization; therefore, a semicolon is required. A semicolon also emphasizes the connection between the two closely related independent clauses.

15. In order to provide more living space, we converted an attached garage into a den.

The original is missing two pieces of punctuation. First, a period is required after "den" since the sentence is an independent clause and a statement. Second, a comma is required after "living space" to more clearly set off short introductory phrase ("In order to provide more living space").

16. Because he is such an industrious student, he has many friends.

The original is missing two pieces of punctuation. First, a period is required after "friends" since the sentence is an independent clause and a statement. Second, a comma is required after "student" to more clearly set off the introductory subordinate clause ("Because he is such an industrious student"). Remember that if the subordinate clause were to follow the main clause, then a comma would not be required ("He has many friends because he is such an industrious student.").

17. I don't recall who wrote *A Midsummer Night's Dream*.

The original is missing three pieces of punctuation. First, an apostrophe is required in the title of the play to indicate the possessive case; the apostrophe should be inserted between the letter "t" and the letter "s" ("*Night's*"). Second, a period is required after "*A* Midsummer *Night's Dream*" since the sentence is an independent clause and a statement. Finally, an apostrophe is required to create the contraction of "do not"; the apostrophe should be inserted between the letter "n" and the letter "t" ("don't").

18. In the writing class, students learned about coordinating conjunctions—and, but, so, or, yet, for, and nor.

The original is missing several pieces of punctuation. First, a period is required after "nor" since the sentence is an independent clause and a statement. Second, a comma is required after "class" to more clearly set off the short introductory phrase ("In the writing class"). Third, a dash is required after "conjunctions" to set off the explanatory group of words that follows. Finally, six commas are required to set off the seven elements in the series (the list of coordinating conjunctions). Remember that commas are always used to separate elements in a series (as long as there are three or more elements in the series). Also, be careful not to confuse the functional coordinating conjunction in the sentence ("and") with the coordinating conjunction "and" that occurs as an element of the series.

19. "Those who do not complain are never pitied" is a familiar quotation by Jane Austen.

The original is missing two pieces of punctuation. First, a period is required after "Jane Austen" since the sentence is an independent clause and a statement. Second, quotation marks are required around the words written by Jane Austen ("Those who do not complain are never pitied"). Remember that quotation marks are used to enclose the actual words of a speaker or writer.

20. Howard and his ex-wife are on amicable terms.

The original is missing two pieces of punctuation. First, a period is required after "terms" since the sentence is an independent clause and a statement. Second, a hyphen is required between "ex" and "wife" to create the compound noun "ex-wife."

21. Her last words were, "call me on Sunday," and she jumped on the train.

The original is missing several pieces of punctuation. First, a period is required after "train" since the sentence is a combination of independent clauses that are statements. Second, in the first independent clause, quotation marks are required around the words that are spoken by the woman ("call me on Sunday"). Third, in the first independent clause, a comma is required after "were" to set off this brief quotation. Finally, a comma is required before "and." Remember that a comma is required before a coordinating conjunction (*e.g.*, "and," "or," "but," "though") that joins two independent clauses. However, remember to insert the comma before the second inserted quotation mark.

22. He is an out-of-work carpenter.

   The original is missing two pieces of punctuation. First, a period is required after "carpenter" since the sentence is an independent clause and a statement. Second, two hyphens are required (one before and one after "of") to create the compound adjective "out-of-work."

23. This is what is called a "pregnant chad."

   The original is missing two pieces of punctuation. First, a period is required after "pregnant chad" since the sentence is an independent clause and a statement. Second, quotation marks are required (one before "pregnant" and the other after the inserted period) to emphasize words that are used in a special or unusual way ("pregnant chad"); the chad is not literally pregnant.

24. "Come early on Monday," the teacher said, "to take the exit exam."

   The original is missing three pieces of punctuation. First, a period is required after "exam" since the sentence is an independent clause and a statement. Second, quotation marks are required around both sets of words that are spoken by the teacher ("Come early on Monday" and "to take the exit exam"). Remember that the fourth quotation mark should appear after the inserted period. Finally, two commas are required (one before the second inserted quotation mark and the other after "said") to set off the teacher's spoken words.

25. The dog, man's best friend, is a companion to many.
   The dog—man's best friend—is a companion to many.

   The original is missing three pieces of punctuation. First, a period is required after "many" since the sentence is an independent clause and a statement. Second, an apostrophe is required to indicate the possessive case of "man"; the apostrophe should be inserted between the letter "n" and the letter "s" ("man's"). Finally, either two commas or two dashes are required (one before "man's" and the other after "friend") to set off the non-restrictive element ("man's best friend"). Remember that a non-restrictive element contains non-essential information and can therefore be removed (as indicated by either commas or dashes) without changing the meaning of the original. When choosing between commas and dashes, remember that dashes are for stronger breaks and are less formal.

26. The winner of the horse race is, to the best of my knowledge, Silver.
   The winner of the horse race is—to the best of my knowledge—Silver.

   The original is missing two pieces of punctuation. First, a period is required after "Silver" since the sentence is an independent clause and a statement. Second, either two commas or two dashes are required (one before "to" and the other after "knowledge") to set off the non-restrictive element ("to the best of my knowledge").original Remember that a non-restrictive element contains non-essential information and can therefore be removed (as indicated by either commas or dashes) without changing the meaning of the original. When choosing between commas and dashes, remember that dashes are for stronger breaks and are less formal.

27. Every time I see him, the dentist asks me how often I floss.

   The original is missing two pieces of punctuation. First, a period is required after "floss" since the sentence is an independent clause and a statement. Second, a comma is required after "him" to more clearly set off the introductory clause ("Every time I see him").

28. The officer was off-duty when he witnessed the crime.

   The original is missing two pieces of punctuation. First, a period is required after "crime" since the sentence is an independent clause and a statement. Second, a hyphen is required between "off" and "duty" to create the compound modifier "off-duty."

29. *Anna Karenina* is my favorite movie.

   A period is required after "movie" since the sentence is an independent clause and a statement.

30. Red, white, and blue are the colors of the American flag.

   The original is missing two pieces of punctuation. First, a period is required after "flag" since the sentence is an independent clause and a statement. Second, two commas are required to set off the three elements in the series ("Red," "white," and "blue"). Remember that commas are always used to separate elements in a series (as long as there are three or more elements in the series).

31. Stop using "stuff" in your essays; it's too informal.

The original is missing several pieces of punctuation First, a period is required after "informal" since the sentence is a combination of two independent clauses that are statements. Second, in the first independent clause, quotation marks are required around the word that is recurring in the essays ("stuff") since it is a direct quotation from the essays. Third, in the second independent clause, an apostrophe is required to create the contraction of "it is"; the apostrophe should be inserted between the letter "t" and the letter "s" ("it's"). Finally, "end-stop" punctuation is required after "essays" to separate the two independent clauses that make up the sentence ("Stop using 'stuff' in your essays" and "it's too informal"). Either a period or a semicolon could be used to separate these clauses; however, if a period were used, "it's" would need to be capitalized. Remember that this exercise does not test capitalization; therefore, a semicolon is required. A semicolon also emphasizes the connection between the two closely related independent clauses.

32. She was a self-made millionaire.

The original is missing two pieces of punctuation. First, a period is required after "millionaire" since the sentence is an independent clause and a statement. Second, a hyphen is required between "self" and "made" to create the compound modifier "self-made."

33. The Smiths, who are the best neighbors anyone could ask for, have moved out.
    The Smiths—who are the best neighbors anyone could ask for—have moved out.

The original is missing two pieces of punctuation. First, a period is required after "out" since the sentence is an independent clause and a statement. Second, either two commas or two dashes are required (one before "who" and the other after "for") to set off the non-restrictive element ("who are the best neighbors anyone could ask for"). Remember that a non-restrictive element contains non-essential information and can therefore be removed (as indicated by either commas or dashes) without changing the meaning of the original. When choosing between commas and dashes, remember that dashes are for stronger breaks and are less formal.

34. My eighteen-year-old daughter will graduate this spring.

The original is missing two pieces of punctuation. First, a period is required after "spring" since the sentence is an independent clause and a statement. Second, two hyphens are required (one before and one after "year") to create the compound modifier "eighteen-year-old."

35. Dracula lived in Transylvania.

A period is required after "Transylvania" since the sentence is an independent clause and a statement.

36. The students were told to put away their books.

A period is required after "books" since the sentence is an independent clause and a statement.

37. Begun while Dickens was still at work on *Pickwick Papers*, *Oliver Twist* was published in 1837 and is now one of the author's most widely read works.

The original is missing three pieces of punctuation. First, a period is required after "works" since the sentence is an independent clause and a statement. Second, a possessive apostrophe is required to indicate that Dickens wrote *Pickwick Papers*; the apostrophe should be inserted between the letter "r" and the letter "s" ("author's"). Finally, a comma is required after "*Pickwick Papers*" to more clearly set off the introductory clause ("Begun while Dickens was still at work on *Pickwick Papers*").

38. Given the great difficulties of making soundings in very deep water, it is not surprising that few such soundings were made until the middle of this century.

The original is missing two pieces of punctuation. First, a period is required after "century" since the sentence is an independent clause and a statement. Second, a comma is required after "deep water" to set off the introductory clause ("Given the great difficulties of making soundings in very deep water").

39. Did you finish writing your thesis prospectus on time?

    A question mark is required after "time" since the sentence is an independent clause and it is a direct request for information (interrogative).

40. The root of modern Dutch was once supposed to be Old Frisian, but the general view now is that the characteristic forms of Dutch are at least as old as those of Old Frisian.

    The original is missing two pieces of punctuation. First, a period is required after "Old Frisian" since the sentence is a combination of independent clauses that are statements. Second, a comma is required before "but." Remember that a comma is required before a coordinating conjunction (*e.g.*, "and," "or," "but," "though") that joins two independent clauses.

41. Moose, once scarce because of indiscriminate hunting, are protected by law, and the number of moose is once again increasing. Moose—once scarce because of indiscriminate hunting—are protected by law, and the number of moose is once again increasing.

    The original is missing three pieces of punctuation. First, a period is required after "increasing" since the sentence is a combination of independent clauses that are statements. Second, in the first independent clause, either two commas or two dashes are required (one before "once" and the other after "hunting") to set off the non-restrictive element ("once scarce because of indiscriminate hunting"). Remember that a non-restrictive element contains non-essential information and can therefore be removed (as indicated by either commas or dashes) without changing the meaning of the original. Finally, a comma is required before "and." Remember that a comma is required before a coordinating conjunction (*e.g.*, "and," "or," "but," "though") that joins two independent clauses. "End-stop" punctuation is not an option in this case since "and" can neither be capitalized (in the case of a period) nor removed (in the case of a semicolon).

42. He ordered a set of books, several records, and a film almost a month ago.

    The original is missing two pieces of punctuation. First, a period is required after "ago" since the sentence is an independent clause and a statement. Second, two commas are required to set off the three elements in the series ("a set of books," "several records," and "a film"). Remember that commas are always used to separate elements in a series (as long as there are three or more elements in the series).

43. Perhaps the most interesting section of New Orleans is the French Quarter, which extends from North Rampart Street to the Mississippi River.

    The original is missing two pieces of punctuation. First, a period is required after "Mississippi River" since the sentence is an independent clause and a statement. Second, a comma is required before "which" for the sake of clarity. Without a comma, the sentence implies that the most interesting section of New Orleans is the part of the French Quarter between North Rampart Street and the Mississippi River. However, the sentence intends to say that the French Quarter, in its entirety, extends from North Rampart Street to the Mississippi River.

44. Writing for a skeptical and rationalizing age, Shaftesbury was primarily concerned with showing that goodness and beauty are not determined by revelation, authority, opinion, or fashion.

    The original is missing three pieces of punctuation. First, a period is required after "fashion" since the sentence is an independent clause and a statement. Second, a comma is required after "age" to more clearly set off the introductory clause ("Writing for a skeptical and rationalizing age"). Finally, three commas are required to set off the four elements in the series ("revelation," "authority," "opinion," and "fashion"). Remember that commas are always used to separate elements in a series (as long as there are three or more elements in the series).

45. We tried our best to purchase the books, but we were completely unsuccessful even though we went to every bookstore in town.

    The original is missing two pieces of punctuation. First, a period is required after "town" since the sentence is a combination of independent clauses that are statements. Second, a comma is required before "but." Remember that a comma is required before a coordinating conjunction (*e.g.*, "and," "or," "but," "though") that joins two independent clauses.

46. A great deal of information regarding the nutritional requirements of farm animals has been accumulated over countless generations by trial and error; however, most recent advances have come as the result of systematic studies at schools of animal husbandry.

The original is missing three pieces of punctuation. First, a period is required after "animal husbandry" since the sentence is a combination of independent clauses that are statements. Second, in the second independent clause, a comma is required after the parenthetical expression "however." Finally, "end-stop" punctuation is required after "trial and error" to separate the two independent clauses that make up the sentence ("A great deal of information regarding the nutritional requirements of farm animals has been accumulated over countless generations by trial and error" and "however, most recent advances have come as the result of systematic studies at schools of animal husbandry"). Either a period or a semicolon could be used to separate these clauses; however, if a period were used, "however" would need to be capitalized. Remember that this exercise does not test capitalization; therefore, a semicolon is required. A semicolon also emphasizes the connection between the two closely related independent clauses.

47. *Omoo*, Melville's sequel to *Typee*, appeared in 1847 and went through five printings in that year alone.
Omoo—Melville's sequel to *Typee*—appeared in 1847 and went through five printings in that year alone.

The original is missing three pieces of punctuation. First, a period is required after "alone" since the sentence is an independent clause and a statement. Second, a possessive apostrophe is required to indicate that Melville wrote *Omoo* and *Typee*; the apostrophe should be inserted between the letter "e" and the letter "s" ("Melville's"). Finally, either two commas or two dashes are required (one before "Melville's" and the other after "*Typee*") to set off the non-restrictive element ("Melville's sequel to *Typee*"). Remember that a non-restrictive element contains non-essential information and can therefore be removed (as indicated by either commas or dashes) without changing the meaning of the original. When choosing between commas and dashes, remember that dashes are for stronger breaks and are less formal.

48. "Go to Florence for the best gelato in all of Italy," said the old man to the young tourist.

The original is missing three pieces of punctuation. First, a period is required after "tourist" since the sentence is an independent clause and a statement. Second, quotation marks are required around the words that are spoken by the old man ("Go to Florence for the best gelato in all of Italy"). Finally, a comma is required after "Italy" to set off the quotation.

49. Although the first school for African Americans was a public school established in Virginia in 1620, most educational opportunities for African Americans before the Civil War were provided by private agencies.

The original is missing two pieces of punctuation. First, a period is required after "private agencies" since the sentence is an independent clause and a statement. Second, a comma is required after "1620" to more clearly set off the introductory clause ("Although the first school for African Americans was a public school established in Virginia in 1620").

50. As the climate of Europe changed, the population became too dense for the supply of food obtained by hunting, and other means of securing food, such as the domestication of animals, were necessary.
As the climate of Europe changed, the population became too dense for the supply of food obtained by hunting, and other means of securing food—such as the domestication of animals—were necessary.

The original is missing several pieces of punctuation. First, a period is required after "necessary" since the sentence is a combination of independent clauses that are statements. Second, in the first independent clause, a comma is required after "changed" to more clearly set off the introductory clause ("As the climate of Europe changed"). Third, in the second independent clause, either two commas or two dashes are required (one before "such" and the other after "animals") to set off the non-restrictive element ("such as the domestication of animals"). Remember that a non-restrictive element contains non-essential information and can therefore be removed (as indicated by either commas or dashes) without changing the meaning of the original. Finally, a comma is required before "and." Remember that a comma is required before a coordinating conjunction (*e.g.*, "and," "or," "but," "though") that joins two independent clauses. "End-stop" punctuation is not an option in this case since "and" can neither be capitalized (in the case of a period) nor removed (in the case of a semicolon). When choosing between commas and dashes, remember that dashes are for stronger breaks and are less formal.

51. In Faulkner's poetic realism, the grotesque is somber, violent, and often inexplicable; in Caldwell's writing, it is lightened by a ballad-like, humorous, sophisticated detachment.

The original is missing several pieces of punctuation. First, a period is required after "detachment" since the sentence is a combination of independent clauses that are statements. Second, two apostrophes are required (one to indicate the possessive case of "Faulkner" and the other to indicate the possessive case of "Caldwell"); the first apostrophe should be inserted between the letter "r" and the letter "s" ("Faulkner's"), and the second apostrophe should be inserted between the letter "l" and the letter "s" ("Caldwell's"). Third, in the second independent clause, a hyphen is required between "ballad" and "like" to create the compound modifier "ballad-like." Fourth, in the first independent clause, a comma is required after "poetic realism" to more clearly set off the introductory clause ("In Faulkner's poetic realism"). Fifth, in the second independent clause, a comma is required after "writing" to more clearly set off the introductory clause ("in Caldwell's writing"). Sixth, two commas are required to set off the three elements in the series that describes Faulkner's concept of the grotesque ("somber," "violent," and "often inexplicable"). Seventh, two commas are required to set off the three elements in the series that describes Caldwell's concept of the grotesque ("ballad-like," "humorous," and "sophisticated"). Note that this series of three adjectives modifies the noun "detachment." Finally, "end-stop" punctuation is required after "inexplicable" to separate the two independent clauses that make up the sentence ("In Faulkner's poetic realism, the grotesque is somber, violent, and often inexplicable" and "in Caldwell's writing, it is lightened by a ballad-like, humorous, sophisticated detachment"). Either a period or a semicolon could be used to separate these clauses; however, if a period were used, "in" would need to be capitalized. Remember that this exercise does not test capitalization; therefore, a semicolon is required. A semicolon also emphasizes the connection between the two closely related independent clauses.

52. The valley of the Loire, a northern tributary of the Loire at Angers, abounds in rock villages; they occur in many other places in France, Spain, and northern Italy.
    The valley of the Loire—a northern tributary of the Loire at Angers—abounds in rock villages; they occur in many other places in France, Spain, and northern Italy.

    The original is missing several pieces of punctuation. First, a period is required after "northern Italy" since the sentence is a combination of independent clauses that are statements. Second, in the first independent clause, either two commas or two dashes are required (one before "a" and the other after "Angers") to set off the non-restrictive element ("a northern tributary of the Loire at Angers"). When choosing between commas and dashes, remember that dashes are for stronger breaks and are less formal. Third, in the second independent clause, two commas are required to set off the three elements in the series ("France," "Spain," and "northern Italy"). Finally, "end-stop" punctuation is required after "rock villages" to separate the two independent clauses that make up the sentence ("The valley of the Loire, a northern tributary of the Loire at Angers, abounds in rock villages" and "they occur in many other places in France, Spain, and northern Italy"). Either a period or a semicolon could be used to separate these clauses; however, if a period were used, "they" would need to be capitalized. Remember that this exercise does not test capitalization; therefore, a semicolon is required. A semicolon also emphasizes the connection between the two closely related independent clauses.

53. The telephone rang several times; as a result, his sleep was interrupted.

    The original is missing three pieces of punctuation. First, a period is required after "interrupted" since the sentence is a combination of independent clauses that are statements. Second, in the second independent clause, a comma is required after "result" to more clearly set off the introductory clause ("as a result"). Finally, "end-stop" punctuation is required after "times" to separate the two independent clauses that make up the sentence ("The telephone rang several times" and "as a result, his sleep was interrupted"). Either a period or a semicolon could be used to separate these clauses; however, if a period were used, "as" would need to be capitalized. Remember that this exercise does not test capitalization; therefore, a semicolon is required. A semicolon also emphasizes the connection between the two closely related independent clauses.

54. He has forty-three thousand dollars to spend; however, once that is gone, he will be penniless.

    The original is missing several pieces of punctuation. First, a period is required after "penniless" since the sentence is a combination of independent clauses that are statements. Second, a hyphen is required between "forty" and "three" because every whole number from twenty-one to ninety-nine (even when it is used as part of a larger number) is always hyphenated. Third, in the second independent clause, a comma is required after the parenthetical expression "however." Fourth, in the second independent clause, a comma is required after "gone" to more clearly set off the clause ("once that is gone") that precedes the main clause ("he will be penniless"). Finally, "end-stop" punctuation is required after "spend" to separate the two independent clauses that make up the sentence ("He has forty-three thousand dollars to spend" and "however, once that is gone, he will be penniless"). Either a period or a semicolon could be used to separate these clauses; however, if a period were used, "however" would need to be capitalized. Remember that this exercise does not test capitalization; therefore, a semicolon is required. A semicolon also emphasizes the connection between the two closely related independent clauses.

55. Before an examination, do the following: review your work, get a good night's sleep, eat a balanced breakfast, and arrive on time to take the test.

    The original is missing several pieces of punctuation. First, a period is required after "test" since the sentence is a command. Second, a comma is required after "examination" to more clearly set off the introductory clause ("Before an examination"). Third, a colon is required after "following" to precede the list of items that follows. Fourth, an apostrophe is required to indicate the possessive case of "night"; the apostrophe should be inserted between the letter "t" and the letter "s" ("night's"). Finally, three commas are required to set off the four elements in the series ("review your work," "get a good night's sleep," "eat a balanced breakfast," and "arrive on time to take the test"). Remember that commas are always used to separate elements in a series (as long as there are three or more elements in the series).

EXERCISE 7—CAPITALIZATION AND SPELLING (p. 348)

1. You should capitalize "Thanksgiving." The names of holidays are always capitalized.

2. You should not capitalize "flower." Common nouns are not capitalized unless they are the first word in a sentence or they are part of a title.

3. You should not capitalize "airplane." Common nouns are not capitalized unless they are the first word in a sentence or they are part of a title.

4. You should capitalize "Ohio." The names of states are always capitalized.

5. You should capitalize "France." The names of countries are always capitalized.

6. You should capitalize "Muhammad Ali." Proper names (proper nouns) are always capitalized.

7. You should not capitalize "magician." Common nouns are not capitalized unless they are the first word in a sentence or they are part of a title.

8. You should not capitalize "tin can." Common nouns are not capitalized unless they are the first word in a sentence or they are part of a title.

9. You should capitalize "Rocky Mountains." Proper names (proper nouns) are always capitalized.

10. You should capitalize "Governor Davis." Proper names (proper nouns) are always capitalized, and titles are always capitalized when used in conjunction with proper names.

11. You should not capitalize "pine tree." Common nouns are not capitalized unless they are the first word in a sentence or they are part of a title.

12. You should not capitalize "overcoat." Common nouns are not capitalized unless they are the first word in a sentence or they are part of a title.

13. You should not capitalize "television." Common nouns are not capitalized unless they are the first word in a sentence or they are part of a title.

14. You should capitalize "Michael Jordan." Proper names (proper nouns) are always capitalized.

15. You should not capitalize "arsonist." Common nouns are not capitalized unless they are the first word in a sentence or they are part of a title.

16. You should not capitalize "uncle." Titles are not capitalized unless they are used in conjunction with proper names (*e.g.*, "Uncle Jim").

17. You should not capitalize "token." Common nouns are not capitalized unless they are the first word in a sentence or they are part of a title.

18. You should not capitalize "hamburger." Common nouns are not capitalized unless they are the first word in a sentence or they are part of a title.

19. You should not capitalize "Halloween." The names of holidays are always capitalized.

20. You should not capitalize "morning." Common nouns are not capitalized unless they are the first word in a sentence or they are part of a title.

21. You should capitalize "Central Park." Proper names (proper nouns) are always capitalized.

22. You should not capitalize "ten o'clock." Days are capitalized, but times of day are not capitalized.

23. You should capitalize "January." The names of months are always capitalized.

24. You should not capitalize "afternoon." Common nouns are not capitalized unless they are the first word in a sentence or they are part of a title.

25. You should capitalize "Monday." The names of days of the week are always capitalized.

26. The correct spelling is "field." (See the "i" before "e" rule.)

27. The correct spelling is "conceit." (See the "i" before "e" rule.)

28. The correct spelling is "sleigh." (See the "i" before "e" rule.)

29. The correct spelling is "vein." (See the "i" before "e" rule.)

30. The correct spelling is "ceiling." (See the "i" before "e" rule.)

31. The correct spelling is "niece." (See the "i" before "e" rule.)

32. The correct spelling is "scientific." (See the "i" before "e" rule.)

33. The correct spelling is "seizure." (See the "i" before "e" rule.)

34. The correct spelling is "conscientious." (See the "i" before "e" rule.)

35. The correct spelling is "ancient." (See the "i" before "e" rule.)

36. The correct spelling is "fibbing." You must double the final consonant ("b") of a one-syllable root word if the final consonant is preceded by a single vowel ("i").

37. The correct spelling is "begging." You must double the final consonant ("g") of a one-syllable root word if the final consonant is preceded by a single vowel ("e").

38. The correct spelling is "controllable." You must double the final consonant ("l") of a two-syllable root word if the accent is on the second syllable and the final consonant is preceded by a single vowel ("o").

39. The correct spelling is "commitment." If the suffix begins with a consonant ("-ment"), then you do not double the last letter of the root word ("commit").

40. The correct spelling is "colorful." If the suffix begins with a consonant ("-ful"), then you do not double the last letter of the root word ("color").

41. The correct spelling is "stopping." You must double the final consonant ("p") of a one-syllable root word if the final consonant is preceded by a single vowel ("o").

42. The correct spelling is "biggest." You must double the final consonant ("g") of a one-syllable root word if the final consonant is preceded by a single vowel ("i").

43. The correct spelling is "quitting." You must double the final consonant ("t") of a one-syllable root word if the final consonant is preceded by a single vowel ("i").

44. The correct spelling is "robbing." You must double the final consonant ("b") of a one-syllable root word if the final consonant is preceded by a single vowel ("o").

45. The correct spelling is "gladly." If the suffix begins with a consonant ("-ly"), then you do not double the last letter of the root word ("glad").

46. The correct spelling is "bridal." If the suffix begins with a vowel ("-al") and the root word ends with a vowel ("e"), then you drop the last letter of the root word.

47. The correct spelling is "forcible." If the suffix begins with a vowel ("-ible") and the root word ends with a vowel ("e"), then you drop the last letter of the root word.

48. The correct spelling is "forceful." If the suffix begins with a consonant ("-ful"), then you do not double the last letter of the root word ("force").

49. The correct spelling is "imaginary." If the suffix begins with a vowel ("-ary") and the root word ends with a vowel ("e"), then you drop the last letter of the root word.

50. The correct spelling is "hopeless." If the suffix begins with a consonant ("-less"), then you do not double the last letter of the root word ("hope").

51. The correct spelling is "truly." If the suffix begins with a consonant ("-ly"), then you do not double the last letter of the root word ("true").

52 The correct spelling is "removing." If the suffix begins with a vowel ("-ing") and the root word ends with a vowel ("e"), then you drop the last letter of the root word.

53. The correct spelling is "lifelike." If the suffix begins with a consonant ("-like"), then you do not double the last letter of the root word ("life").

54. The correct spelling is "likely." If the suffix begins with a consonant ("-ly"), then you do not double the last letter of the root word ("like").

55. The correct spelling is "serviceable." "Serviceable" is an exception to the rule regarding a suffix that begins with a vowel ("-able") and a root word that ends with a vowel ("e"). (See explanation #52 in this exercise for the specific rule.)

56. The misspelled word is "consceince." "Conscience" is the correct spelling. (See the "i" before "e" rule.)

57. The misspelled word is "aviater." The correct spelling is "aviator."

58. The misspelled word is "alltogether." The correct spelling is "altogether."

59. The misspelled word is "desireable." The correct spelling is "desirable." If the suffix begins with a vowel ("-able") and the root word ends with a vowel ("e"), then you drop the last letter of the root word.

60. The misspelled word is "independance." The correct spelling is "independence."

61. The misspelled word is "billian." The correct spelling is "billion."

62. The misspelled word is "naturaly." The correct spelling is "naturally." "Naturally" does not represent an instance of consonant doubling; rather, it is the mere concatenation of a word, which ends with a consonant, and a suffix, which begins with one.

63. The misspelled word is "speach." The correct spelling is "speech."

64. The misspelled word is "transfered." The correct spelling is "transferred." You must double the final consonant ("r") of a two-syllable root word if the accent is on the second syllable and the final consonant is preceded by a single vowel ("e"). Note that "transfer" can either be pronounced with the accent on the first syllable or the second syllable.

65. The misspelled word is "reciept." The correct spelling is "receipt." (See the "i" before "e" rule.)

66. The misspelled word is "calender." The correct spelling is "calendar."

67. The misspelled word is "affidavid." The correct spelling is "affidavit."

68. The misspelled word is "diptheria." The correct spelling is "diphtheria."

69. The misspelled word is "prevelent." The correct spelling is "prevalent."

70. The misspelled word is "bookeeper." The correct spelling is "bookkeeper." Compound words are made up of two words, and "bookkeeper" is a compound word ("book" and "keeper").

71. The misspelled word is "repetetious." The correct spelling is "repetitious."

72. The misspelled word is "donkies." The correct spelling is "donkeys." When the root word ends with a "y" ("donkey"), and the "y" is preceded by a vowel ("e"), then you simply add "s" to form the plural.

73. The misspelled word is "wirey." The correct spelling is "wiry."

74. The misspelled word is "propagander." The correct spelling is "propaganda."

75. The misspelled word is "specificaly." The correct spelling is "specifically."

76. The misspelled word is "innoculate." The correct spelling is "inoculate."

77. The misspelled word is "amethist." The correct spelling is "amethyst."

78. The misspelled word is "laringytis." The correct spelling is "laryngitis."

79. The misspelled word is "cinamon." The correct spelling is "cinnamon."

80. The misspelled word is "resind." The correct spelling is "rescind."

81. The misspelled word is "irresistably." The correct spelling is "irresistibly."

82. The misspelled word is "brocoli." The correct spelling is "broccoli."

83. The misspelled word is "mayonaise." The correct spelling is "mayonnaise."

84. The misspelled word is "jeoperdy." The correct spelling is "jeopardy."

85. The misspelled word is "mocassin." The correct spelling is "moccasin."

WRITING SKILLS REVIEW

EXERCISE 1—SAMPLE ESSAY 1 (p. 364)

Essay 1—Below Average Response

> Residents of rural areas insist that their life is better. People living in urban city areas prefer the lively life that they lead. Each has a viewpoint, but I feel that the city life is much better. Urban areas have good streets and roads and many things to do.
>
> A city is closer together than rural areas. Everything can be reached pretty quickly by car, bus, or even bicycle. The streets are maintained by the city in winter and summer. My Aunt in the mountains is snowed in each winter for days at a time. Sometimes traffic is a problem in urban areas, but that's the price you pay.
>
> The urban areas have so many activities to do. Lots of movies, concerts, and sports events are always going on. Because the urban areas have more people and money, more famous artists visit and perform there.
>
> Some really important things in cities include good hospitals and healthcare. With lots of people there is a need for specialist doctors and great hospitals, even for children. I feel that I can find people in the city that share my interests whatever I decide on.
>
> In conclusion, urban areas are the best places to live. Americans, and people around the world are moving from rural areas more each day to get to the excitement and opportunity of urban areas.

Writing skill and position on issue:

This essay demonstrates developing writing skills. Although the writer's position on the issue is clear, he or she fails to provide an adequate introduction to the issue. The writer does discuss both sides of the argument, but he or she is unsuccessful in describing the relationship between the two sides. The writer's thesis is not broad enough to sufficiently cover the point raised in the fourth paragraph regarding "hospitals and healthcare."

Development of ideas and organization of essay:

The ideas presented are good but lack sufficient elaboration. The writer does not include clear topic sentences in any of the three body paragraphs, and there are random statements that are not organized in any coherent pattern throughout the essay. This lack of coherence distracts the reader from obtaining a clear understanding of the argument. For example, the writer mentions that he or she "can find people in the city that share my interests" in the same paragraph (fourth) that he or she discusses "hospitals and healthcare"; however, no logical connection is made between these two ideas. Since the essay prompt asks the writer to compare two living conditions, the development of such an essay would require the use of comparisons and contrasts. However, the writer does not adequately use either of these tools to support his or her thesis. Overall, the writer presents a list of the qualities that he or she prefers in cities but does not explain why this list adds up to a higher quality of life.

Structure of essay, paragraphs, and transitions:

The writer has a grasp of the basic structure of an essay: an introduction, a body, and a conclusion. However, the paragraphs are too short; they are not supported or expanded sufficiently; and they become unfocused. The essay also lacks transitions; its content is presented in a choppy fashion, with random introductions of the writer's main points. The only transitional phrase ("In conclusion"), which appears in the last paragraph, is contrived and low-level usage.

Language usage, sentence structure, and punctuation:

The essay is understandable, but it contains many errors in grammar and mechanics that distract the reader from its content. In the first paragraph, for example, the writer states that "Urban areas have…many things to do." However, "areas" cannot "have things to do." The proper phrase would be "There are many things to do in urban areas." Also, in the second paragraph, the writer omits the word "living" from the sentence "My Aunt in the mountains…." Overall, an excess of low-level language (e.g., "pretty quickly," "that's the price you pay", and "Lots of") mars the quality of the essay. In the last paragraph, the comma after "Americans" is unnecessary. Stylistically, the writer does not vary the sentence structure and resorts to simple sentences and lists.

Summary and conclusions:

The essay would likely receive a grade of below average to average (4 - 6).

Essay 2—Above Average Response

The question of the quality of the rural life versus the life of a city dweller is an interesting one that faces each adult making a decision about their life activities. Plainly, United States citizens "voted with their feet" and have flocked to the cities in the 20th century. But recently there has been some movement back to rural areas and the "simple life" that they represent. I feel that a more rural area offers the best quality of life in the beginning of the 21st century. This opinion is based on the issues of emotional health, community involvement and opportunity, and best usage of my time.

Life in urban areas can be very stressful and difficult. Noise and traffic go on 24 hours a day. "Street people" who may need intervention may be outside your door in a downtown area. Traffic may make your voyage to work or entertainment difficult and lengthy. In rural areas the noise level is lessened, the roads less crowded, and more humane contact is likely.

In a more rural area, each person can have more of an impact within the community. The problems and challenges may be shared community wide and not just in your own neighborhood as in a large city. You can more easily be known and make a difference in a rural area. A contrary view contends that newcomers are sometimes not part of the "community family" in a small town. Gaining acceptance can be harder than in cities used to an influx of new people.

A rural area places less demands on my personal time: less traffic, less commuting, and fewer lines of people waiting to get services. I could get home faster from work and pursue my own interests.

In conclusion, I prefer rural areas. Keeping in communication and accessing healthcare used to be a problem there. But the Internet and satellite dishes helped alleviate the first concern. Regional health centers and rapid transportation have helped make "big city" healthcare available to rural areas.

Writing skill and position on issue:

This essay shows good facility with written English, clear organization, and mostly consistent writing skills. The writer's position on the issue is presented clearly and the thesis is well developed. In the third paragraph, the writer presents a contrary viewpoint, which is a strong and persuasive technique. However, he or she fails to refute this opposing viewpoint, which is important when presenting evidence that is contrary to the thesis.

Development of ideas and organization of essay:

The initial paragraph effectively details both sides of the issue. Reference to social trends gives the writer a voice of authority. Examples are well presented and elaborated upon with sufficient detail. The arguments are laid out in a logical order and structured closely after the thesis statement. Each supporting paragraph begins with an organizing topic sentence and continues with an in-depth discussion of the writer's major points.

Structure of essay, paragraphs, and transitions:

In the introduction, the writer previews the evidence that he will use to support his or her thesis, and the structural set-up in the opening paragraph is closely followed throughout the essay. The supporting paragraphs are appropriate, and each deals with an argument or position of the writer. The transition that is used to move from the second paragraph to the third paragraph ("In a more rural area") is very effective; however, transition usage in general is low. For example, "In conclusion" is a low-level usage transitional phrase.

Language usage, sentence structure, and punctuation:

The analogy "voted with their feet" is effective in this essay, and the supporting details hold the reader's interest. Minor errors in grammar and mechanics do not distract the reader from understanding the essay and are likely present due to time restrictions that are placed on the writer.

Summary and conclusions:

The essay is clearly written and demonstrates a firm command of the language. It would likely receive a grade of average to above average (8 - 10).

EXERCISE 2—SAMPLE ESSAY 2 (p. 366)

Essay 1—Below Average Response

The Internet is used daily by millions of citizens and businesses around the world. However, I feel that the Internet has invaded people's lives and our society. It has caused bad effects on business, people in smaller countries, and on home life in the USA.

The first problem the Internet is the expense and the need for knowledge to use it. If you do not know how to effectively use a computer. Or, if you don't have the money for the computer, the software and the Internet support, then you are considered backward. Many people and families do not have these resources or the money needed. Airlines are now even charging more to call them for reservations, than if you use the Internet.

If you do have the computer, and have Internet access, then there is the problem of the content. Just a few people with prejudice can have their writings accessed all over the world. There is no fact checking or editing of information, as there is for newspapers or magazines. Also some content is gross and suited only for adults. Parents have a problem watching out for what their children access.

Home life is hurt when family members get addicted to using the Internet. Games and chat rooms can take up many hours each day. Online shopping can easily run up large debts. And worse, you can connect with dangerous people who mask their identity and planned activities.

I agree that controlled Internet activity can be useful and a valuable information resource. But the Internet has mainly caused problems that are worse than its usefulness.

Writing skill and position on issue:

The essay illustrates developing skills. The writer's position is clearly, though awkwardly, presented in the introductory paragraph. The introduction, though adequate in presenting a thesis statement, does not introduce the topic effectively, mentioning only briefly the proliferation of the Internet. The writer fails to address the scope of the issue by providing both sides of the argument.

Development of ideas and organization of essay:

The thesis statement in the initial paragraph attempts to set up the structure that is to be followed in the essay. However, only one of its three claims is actually developed. Neither injury to "business" nor injury to "people in smaller countries" is elaborated upon in the paragraphs that follow. The negative impact of the Internet on "home life in the USA" is the only point that is developed. Unfortunately, each of its supporting paragraphs lacks a consistent internal structure. In the second paragraph, for example, the writer begins by discussing how people are unable to afford Internet access (as well as resources, support, and training for such a service) but then lapses into an example about airlines charging more for non-Internet reservation assistance. There may be a connection between these two ideas, but the writer fails to make this connection. The essay wanders, introducing several new, non-supportive points. Finally, the conclusion is too brief and fails to summarize the major points of the essay.

Structure of essay, paragraphs, and transitions:

The basic three-part essay structure (an introduction, a body, and a conclusion) is present but weak. Only the second paragraph flows smoothly from the introduction because of the use of a transitional phrase ("The first problem…."). Transition usage is absent in the remainder of the essay. Only the fourth paragraph has a clear topic sentence; the other body paragraphs lack structure and focus.

Language usage, sentence structure, and punctuation:

The sentence fragment in the second paragraph needs repair. Low-level language usage, such as "bad," "hurt," and "gross," detract from the quality of the writing. The writer needs to work on making better word choices to increase the readability and interest of the essay.

Summary and conclusions:

This essay lacks the necessary qualities of an effective essay. The essay would likely receive a grade of below average to average (5 - 7).

Essay 2—Above Average Response

The usage of the Internet is increasing daily. Citizens in most countries have daily access to a vast array of information. Much of the information and the usage is valuable, and I feel this outweighs the problems. What are some of the significant beneficial uses of the Internet to you and me, to businesses, and for government agencies?

The Internet provides us with instant access to almost infinite arrays of information. This access can be used for education, entertainment, or even our daily shopping. Challenges include spurious sites, gross inappropriate content and actual criminal stealing of personal information. The Internet has given us a direct contact with businesses. I help my parents make travel plans, and book affordable plane trips and hotels using travel sites on the Internet.

Businesses are able to reach out directly to consumers and to other business via the Internet. This gives both a much wider range of choice in products and services. However, the Internet has also had its downside with Internet based businesses blazing and then failing like a shooting star. These failures cost investors billions of dollars, and lost the workers their jobs.

Governmental agencies using the Internet can offer residents faster services such as license renewals, at lower cost to the agencies. The democratic governmental goals of "transparency" and "public access" can be better met if we can read every document and attend every meeting using the Internet.

The value of the Internet is increased if all citizens can have access to it, not just the well-off. Therefore, computers and access from libraries and other public sites is essential, and some cities are pursuing this goal.

I feel the Internet is valuable and will increase in usefulness as we learn more about the best uses for it.

Writing skill and position on issue:

This essay illustrates solid writing skills, and the writer's position is made very clearly. The introduction adequately presents the topic in an interesting way, employing an atypical inversion of the thesis statement into a question. The overall flow and structure of the essay is consistent and logical. Instances that are opposed to the writer's position are presented appropriately and add interest.

Development of ideas and organization of essay:

Ideas are generally presented and developed effectively; appropriate examples are used and explored in detail. A couple of minor points are misplaced and confusing, such as when the writer recommends that we all "read every document and attend every meeting using the Internet." However, these errors do not detract from the overall strength of the essay. The writer effectively introduces opposing arguments; however, he or she does not explicitly refute these claims. This slight oversight undermines the writer's argument, but it is permissible since the writer presents an essay in which the "pros" outweigh the "cons."

Structure of essay, paragraphs, and transitions:

The initial paragraph is clear and provides an atypical thesis in the form of a question. The supporting paragraphs are appropriate, and they are integral to the writer's argument. Each supporting paragraph is predicated upon its own topic sentence as well as the thesis. The examples are compelling and varied. The closing paragraph offers an appropriate and conclusive summary but could use further development.

Language usage, sentence structure, and punctuation:

The essay shows varied and strong language usage. The few errors noted will not distract the reader and are likely due to the time restrictions placed on the writer. The sentences vary in length and style and are effective in presenting the writer's arguments.

Summary and conclusions:

The writer successfully makes an intelligent point of social commentary regarding the need for free Internet access to all. The essay would likely receive a grade of average to above average. Replace with numerical grading system (9 - 11).

EXERCISE 3—SAMPLE ESSAY 3 (p. 368)

Essay 1—Below Average Response

My position is that bio-engineered foods should be accepted and not be called "Frankenfoods." An insulting term like that causes conflict and I feel is incorrect. Sure there are concerns that bio-engineered foods could change other natural foods. But there are advantages to bio-engineered foods.

With the growing populations around the world, more food will be needed each year. But the land is going away due to new houses and businesses being built. Bio-engineered crops can produce more in a given field. So food production can meet our appetites.

The fresh water is getting more salty in the San Francisco Bay area. Bio-engineered crops could be made resistant to some salt problems and let crops still be grown.

What if food scientists could add vitamins, or other helpful components to crops such as corn? Then some illnesses from deficiencies of vitamins would be lower in the country. Many of the bio-engineered crops are being developed in the USA. Our agriculture businesses could really be helped by increased trade in these seeds and plants.

Sure, scientific progress must watched for dangers. But I think bio-engineered foods can help us like so many other scientific developments have in the past.

Writing skill and position on issue:

The essay illustrates some developing skills. A restatement of the essay prompt and an introduction to the issue would be more effective than beginning the essay with "My position…." The writer's position is stated in a roundabout way, arguing about language more than substance. The writer fails to provide a thesis statement that explains his or her position and how the rest of the essay is to be organized.

Development of ideas and organization of essay:

The essay should be better focused; supporting paragraphs should include transitions and topic sentences. Most of the points are valid and supportive of the writer's position; however, they are not well developed and require further elaboration. Specific examples, rather than hypothetical ones ("What if…."), would strengthen the writer's overall argument.

Structure of essay, paragraphs, and transitions:

The supporting paragraphs are generally appropriate for the ideas expressed in them, but the essay would flow better if transitions were used. The writer moves abruptly from one idea to the next. The essay does possess the basic structural elements: an introduction, a body, and a conclusion. However, the concluding paragraph is too short and requires more development.

Language usage, sentence structure, and punctuation:

Low-level language usage and a number of language errors detract from the essay's overall readability and presentation. How does "food production meet our appetites"? It would be better to write: "Food production can meet the nutritional needs of a growing population." Rather than write "let crops be grown," write "enable crops to be grown." "Going away" is a poor choice of words. The land is not "going away"; the use of the land is just "changing" from agricultural to other uses. Grammatical errors, such as "must watched for dangers" instead of "must watch for dangers," distract the reader from the content of the essay. Some sentences are too brief, not completing their ideas effectively for the reader. The use of "sure" in the introduction and conclusion is colloquial and inappropriate for an essay such as this one.

Summary and conclusions:

More information on the ideas listed would better support the writer's position. The essay would likely receive a grade of below average to average. Replace with numerical grading system (5-7).

Essay 2—Above Average Response

Bio-engineered foods have been discussed frequently in the media in the last few years. The European community and the USA have even had major trade disputes over the issue. The term "Frankenfood" fits the opinion of many activists in the USA and Europe. The activists fear the effects of bio-engineering on the world's food supply. I agree with the concerned activists, and contend that the effects can be negative. We and our food supply will suffer, as will world trade and people in less developed countries.

As "Frankenfoods" with their altered genetics are planted widely, they may crossbreed with native plants. For example, the genetic changes could proliferate through all wheat plants starting from a small number of bio-engineered wheat fields. If the genetic change proves to be injurious to some people, or bad for crop survival, then farmers could not "back-out" the genetic changes.

When I visited a relative's farm in the Midwest, I learned that bio-engineered crops resistant to weed killer has caused a problem. The weed killer resistance has passed into some weeds, and now they are facing "Frankenweeds." These weeds cannot be controlled by the chemicals that were previously effective. This leads to more chemicals being used to eliminate even more hardy weeds.

Bio-engineered crops may be patented and owned by large companies. These companies can charge high fees for the seeds. Less-developed countries will be at even more of an economic disadvantage as more crops are bio-engineered. If the European community continues to resist American bio-engineered foods, our trade in farm goods with them will suffer greatly.

Looking at the contrary argument, a strong case has been made by scientists for the advantages of bio-engineered crops. Scientists note increased production, resistance to pests, and added nutrients. Useful drugs may even be produced by these bio-engineered crops. But the problems of crossbreeding and contamination of the food supply are very important. Therefore I believe bio-engineered crops must be strongly controlled and tested over a few years before widespread usage is allowed.

Writing skill and position on issue:

This essay shows solid and strong expression and writing skills. Each side of the issue is presented well in the beginning of the essay. The essay could be improved with a better thesis statement, detailing the major points that the writer intends to cover throughout the rest of the essay. The writer presents his or her opinion clearly and even offers a standard for qualifying the use of bio-engineered crops.

Development of ideas and organization of essay:

Ideas introduced in the initial paragraph are clearly presented and supported with arguments. Good personal experience examples and scientific explanations are used to support the writer's position. The essay could be improved with better explanations in some of the supporting paragraphs. For example, in the fourth paragraph, the writer could explain how increased costs for bio-engineered seeds would lead to an economic disadvantage for less-developed countries. Overall, the development of ideas is logical and consistent with the subject matter. The writer even presents a contrary position and refutation to this position, which add to the richness of content and argument.

Structure of essay, paragraphs, and transitions:

The essay has a clear structure, and good transitions help the reader to understand the positions that are argued. The supporting paragraphs are appropriate, and each paragraph deals with an argument or position of the writer. The fourth paragraph is the only paragraph that lacks a transition. This lapse is probably due to the time restrictions that are placed on the writer. The concluding paragraph is effectively introduced by referencing the contrary argument.

Language usage, sentence structure, and punctuation:

Language usage is appropriate and the vocabulary is sophisticated (e.g., "contend," "proliferate," and "injurious"). The few punctuation errors do not distract the reader and are likely due to the time restrictions that are placed on the writer.

Summary and conclusions:

The writer's control of language usage is strong. The few language errors do not detract significantly from the presentation of the ideas. The essay would likely receive a grade of average to above average. Replace with numerical grading system (9 - 11).

Answers and Explanations:
Step Three

CRITICAL READING: PASSAGES

CRITICAL READING: PASSAGES—CORE LESSON (p. 377)

1. C	8. C	15. C	22. D	29. C	36. C	43. A	50. D
2. A	9. E	16. A	23. E	30. B	37. B	44. A	51. B
3. A	10. D	17. C	24. C	31. E	38. B	45. C	52. D
4. D	11. A	18. D	25. C	32. A	39. B	46. C	53. E
5. B	12. D	19. D	26. A	33. D	40. A	47. A	54. C
6. E	13. A	20. E	27. D	34. C	41. C	48. A	55. D
7. C	14. C	21. A	28. E	35. B	42. A	49. B	56. A

CRITICAL READING: PASSAGES—EXTENDED LESSON (p. 392)

1. D	9. A	17. B	25. B	33. D	41. A	49. D	57. A
2. B	10. D	18. A	26. A	34. B	42. E	50. A	
3. A	11. A	19. E	27. B	35. A	43. E	51. B	
4. B	12. E	20. D	28. E	36. D	44. D	52. E	
5. C	13. C	21. C	29. C	37. B	45. A	53. B	
6. A	14. B	22. B	30. D	38. A	46. C	54. B	
7. A	15. B	23. B	31. A	39. A	47. C	55. E	
8. A	16. B	24. D	32. B	40. B	48. A	56. E	

CRITICAL READING: PASSAGES—CHALLENGE ITEMS (p. 408)

1. C	9. C	17. B	25. E	33. D	41. E	49. A	57. E
2. C	10. D	18. D	26. C	34. E	42. C	50. E	58. C
3. A	11. A	19. B	27. C	35. C	43. E	51. C	59. E
4. A	12. A	20. A	28. A	36. B	44. A	52. D	60. B
5. E	13. C	21. C	29. C	37. E	45. D	53. B	
6. C	14. D	22. A	30. B	38. C	46. A	54. B	
7. E	15. D	23. B	31. E	39. E	47. D	55. A	
8. B	16. B	24. B	32. A	40. A	48. D	56. B	

CRITICAL READING: PASSAGES—TIMED-PRACTICE QUIZZES (p. 430)

QUIZ I

1. A	2. C	3. A	4. B	5. A	6. C	7. D	8. D

QUIZ II

1. D	2. B	3. B	4. C	5. A	6. E	7. C

QUIZ III

1. C	2. B	3. E	4. A	5. B	6. B	7. C	8. A

QUIZ IV

1. B	3. E	5. B	7. B	9. C
2. A	4. D	6. E	8. A	10. B

QUIZ V

1. D	3. D	5. A	7. B	9. D
2. A	4. B	6. A	8. E	10. E

QUIZ VI

1. A	3. C	5. A	7. D	9. E
2. A	4. B	6. B	8. B	10. A

CRITICAL READING: SENTENCE COMPLETIONS

CRITICAL READING: SENTENCE COMPLETIONS—CORE LESSON (p. 457)

1. C	6. B	11. A	16. D	21. B	26. B	31. B
2. D	7. A	12. C	17. B	22. B	27. D	32. C
3. D	8. A	13. E	18. C	23. B	28. A	33. B
4. E	9. D	14. B	19. E	24. A	29. E	
5. E	10. E	15. C	20. E	25. B	30. E	

CRITICAL READING: SENTENCE COMPLETIONS—CHALLENGE ITEMS (p. 462)

1. C	9. B	17. B	25. D	33. C	41. C	49. B	57. C
2. A	10. E	18. A	26. B	34. A	42. B	50. C	
3. B	11. A	19. C	27. B	35. C	43. A	51. E	
4. C	12. D	20. D	28. B	36. D	44. A	52. D	
5. A	13. A	21. B	29. D	37. D	45. A	53. B	
6. E	14. B	22. D	30. B	38. E	46. A	54. A	
7. C	15. D	23. C	31. D	39. C	47. B	55. B	
8. A	16. B	24. D	32. A	40. C	48. D	56. B	

CRITICAL READING: SENTENCE COMPLETIONS—TIMED-PRACTICE QUIZZES (p. 470)

QUIZ I

1. B	3. A	5. B	7. D	9. E	11. B
2. C	4. E	6. C	8. B	10. C	12. E

QUIZ II

1. E	3. D	5. E	7. E	9. A	11. C
2. D	4. A	6. D	8. B	10. C	12. B

QUIZ III

1. B	3. E	5. D	7. C	9. D	11. B
2. B	4. E	6. D	8. C	10. C	12. D

MATH: MULTIPLE-CHOICE

MATH: MULTIPLE-CHOICE—CORE LESSON (p. 485)

1. C	18. C	35. E	52. A	69. B	86. A	103. A	120. B
2. C	19. B	36. A	53. A	70. B	87. D	104. A	121. A
3. D	20. D	37. D	54. D	71. D	88. E	105. E	122. D
4. D	21. C	38. C	55. D	72. A	89. D	106. A	123. B
5. C	22. B	39. D	56. C	73. C	90. D	107. A	124. C
6. A	23. C	40. B	57. A	74. D	91. B	108. B	125. B
7. E	24. D	41. D	58. E	75. D	92. E	109. D	126. D
8. B	25. E	42. E	59. B	76. D	93. C	110. C	127. C
9. C	26. E	43. E	60. E	77. E	94. C	111. D	128. E
10. D	27. C	44. D	61. C	78. D	95. D	112. D	129. C
11. D	28. D	45. C	62. C	79. C	96. C	113. C	130. E
12. D	29. C	46. D	63. A	80. C	97. A	114. B	131. B
13. D	30. A	47. B	64. A	81. D	98. A	115. C	132. B
14. E	31. C	48. E	65. C	82. E	99. E	116. B	133. B
15. D	32. B	49. D	66. E	83. B	100. D	117. C	134. A
16. C	33. C	50. C	67. B	84. D	101. A	118. A	135. B
17. E	34. D	51. C	68. D	85. D	102. C	119. E	136. E

137. A	149. D	161. E	173. E	185. D	197. C	209. A	221. B
138. E	150. D	162. A	174. C	186. E	198. D	210. B	222. C
139. D	151. B	163. A	175. C	187. C	199. B	211. B	223. C
140. C	152. C	164. A	176. C	188. E	200. B	212. B	224. E
141. C	153. C	165. C	177. C	189. E	201. C	213. D	225. B
142. B	154. E	166. D	178. A	190. A	202. C	214. D	226. E
143. C	155. D	167. C	179. B	191. E	203. D	215. A	
144. B	156. B	168. D	180. C	192. C	204. C	216. E	
145. C	157. C	169. E	181. C	193. C	205. D	217. A	
146. A	158. E	170. C	182. A	194. D	206. D	218. D	
147. D	159. E	171. D	183. C	195. C	207. B	219. E	
148. C	160. B	172. E	184. E	196. D	208. B	220. A	

MATH: MULTIPLE-CHOICE—CHALLENGE ITEMS (p. 530)

1. B	5. D	9. C	13. C	17. B	21. B	25. B	29. C
2. C	6. D	10. D	14. E	18. B	22. B	26. A	
3. C	7. B	11. A	15. B	19. C	23. A	27. E	
4. E	8. D	12. D	16. E	20. C	24. B	28. C	

MATH: MULTIPLE-CHOICE—TIMED-PRACTICE QUIZZES (p. 537)

QUIZ I

1. A	3. D	5. D	7. E	9. B	11. D	13. D	15. A
2. E	4. C	6. D	8. D	10. C	12. C	14. A	

QUIZ II

1. C	4. B	7. B	10. C	13. D	16. C	19. E
2. A	5. C	8. D	11. D	14. E	17. E	20. D
3. C	6. C	9. A	12. D	15. E	18. C	

QUIZ III

1. C	5. D	9. D	13. A	17. C	21. C	25. E
2. C	6. B	10. D	14. A	18. B	22. B	
3. E	7. B	11. D	15. C	19. E	23. D	
4. B	8. A	12. A	16. B	20. B	24. B	

MATH: STUDENT-PRODUCED RESPONSES

MATH: STUDENT-PRODUCED RESPONSES—CORE LESSON (p. 557)

1. 25	5. 650	9. 12	13. .25	17. 90	21. 12	25. 8/15	29. 48
2. 13.6	6. 3/8	10. 8	14. 25	18. 7.5	22. 180	26. 45	30. 3/8
3. 1/32	7. 50	11. 30	15. 7/12	19. 11	23. 2664	27. 50	31. 1.25
4. 1/24	8. 2	12. 75	16. 16.8	20. 6	24. 4	28. 14	32. 60

MATH: STUDENT-PRODUCED RESPONSES—CHALLENGE ITEMS (p. 567)

1. 45	3. 9	5. 13	7. 72	9. 8	11. 60	13. 5
2. 6	4. 2	6. 70	8. 7	10. 8	12. 30	

MATH: STUDENT-PRODUCED RESPONSES—TIMED-PRACTICE QUIZZES (p. 573)

QUIZ I

1. 4 or 5	3. 3/2 or 1.5	5. 5	7. 0	9. 8
2. 2	4. 30	6. 5	8. 3	10. 2

QUIZ II

1. 5	3. 3/2 or 1.5	5. 10	7. 1800	9. 72
2. 10	4. 0	6. 80	8. 15	10. 50

QUIZ III

1. 9	3. 7.5	5. 45	7. 65	9. 9/20
2. 5/9	4. 1.71	6. 9	8. 20	10. 1.3

MATH: STUDENT-PRODUCED RESPONSES—CALCULATOR EXERCISE (p. 582)

1. 1	3. 2	5. 1	7. 3	9. 3
2. 2	4. 3	6. 2	8. 3	10. 3

WRITING

WRITING—CORE LESSON (p. 589)

1. A	15. D	29. B	43. C	57. C	71. E	85. C	99. D
2. B	16. B	30. B	44. C	58. C	72. E	86. D	100. A
3. B	17. D	31. D	45. D	59. E	73. E	87. C	101. A
4. C	18. C	32. C	46. B	60. A	74. A	88. A	102. E
5. D	19. C	33. A	47. C	61. A	75. E	89. A	103. B
6. B	20. D	34. D	48. B	62. D	76. B	90. B	104. A
7. C	21. C	35. B	49. C	63. A	77. C	91. D	105. E
8. C	22. D	36. D	50. B	64. A	78. A	92. B	106. B
9. B	23. A	37. D	51. E	65. B	79. C	93. B	107. E
10. A	24. A	38. D	52. E	66. B	80. B	94. D	108. A
11. A	25. D	39. B	53. C	67. A	81. C	95. B	109. A
12. E	26. B	40. B	54. D	68. A	82. E	96. E	110. D
13. E	27. D	41. C	55. B	69. C	83. E	97. E	
14. A	28. A	42. D	56. D	70. B	84. B	98. –	

WRITING—CHALLENGE ITEMS (p. 607)

1. A	6. C	11. C	16. D	21. A	26. A	31. B	36. E
2. E	7. B	12. B	17. B	22. E	27. B	32. D	37. A
3. D	8. D	13. B	18. D	23. E	28. A	33. C	
4. D	9. A	14. A	19. B	24. C	29. D	34. B	
5. A	10. A	15. E	20. E	25. C	30. C	35. E	

WRITING—TIMED-PRACTICE QUIZZES (p. 616)

QUIZ I

1. C	3. E	5. D	7. E	9. A	11. D	13. C	15. E
2. D	4. B	6. D	8. E	10. D	12. A	14. B	16. C

QUIZ II

1. D	3. E	5. A	7. B	9. C	11. B	13. E	15. A
2. A	4. D	6. B	8. B	10. C	12. A	14. B	16. B

QUIZ III

1. B	3. B	5. A	7. D	9. E	11. C	13. D	15. C
2. D	4. B	6. C	8. A	10. C	12. B	14. A	16. D

Answers and Explanations:
Step Four

PRACTICE TEST I

SECTION 2—MATHEMATICS (p. 642)

1. D	4. C	7. A	10. 12.5	13. 2	16. 45
2. A	5. B	8. B	11. 8	14. 72	17. 30
3. A	6. B	9. 0	12. 8	15. 15.5	18. 2/9

SECTION 3—WRITING (p. 646)

1. E	6. D	11. B	16. D	21. A	26. B	31. C
2. B	7. E	12. B	17. B	22. B	27. B	32. A
3. C	8. C	13. C	18. E	23. A	28. E	33. C
4. C	9. D	14. A	19. E	24. D	29. D	34. E
5. E	10. C	15. D	20. D	25. B	30. E	35. B

SECTION 4—CRITICAL READING (p. 655)

1. B	4. C	7. D	10. C	13. D	16. C	19. D	22. E
2. C	5. B	8. B	11. C	14. A	17. E	20. E	23. C
3. B	6. B	9. B	12. A	15. A	18. A	21. C	24. A

SECTION 5—MATHEMATICS (p. 663)

1. A	4. E	7. B	10. E	13. C	16. E	19. A
2. B	5. C	8. C	11. C	14. A	17. A	20. B
3. D	6. C	9. D	12. E	15. C	18. D	

SECTION 6—CRITICAL READING (p. 667)

1. B	4. E	7. A	10. B	13. E	16. C	19. B	22. B
2. C	5. C	8. E	11. A	14. B	17. E	20. A	23. E
3. A	6. A	9. B	12. D	15. A	18. C	21. E	24. B

SECTION 8—MATHEMATICS (p. 673)

1. E	4. D	7. C	10. B	13. E	16. C
2. E	5. E	8. E	11. B	14. E	
3. E	6. C	9. A	12. D	15. D	

SECTION 9—CRITICAL READING (p. 677)

1. C	4. A	7. C	10. B	13. D	16. E	19. A
2. A	5. A	8. B	11. B	14. A	17. E	
3. B	6. E	9. C	12. E	15. E	18. B	

SECTION 10—WRITING (p. 682)

1. B	3. A	5. B	7. A	9. E	11. D	13. D
2. C	4. E	6. B	8. D	10. E	12. A	14. C

PRACTICE TEST II

SECTION 2—MATHEMATICS (p. 694)

1. B	4. A	7. C	10. 35	13. 1	16. 6
2. A	5. C	8. D	11. 10	14. 15	17. 3
3. D	6. D	9. 0	12. 30	15. 9	18. 5

SECTION 3—WRITING (p. 699)

1. D	6. A	11. A	16. D	21. B	26. A	31. A
2. C	7. D	12. D	17. C	22. D	27. A	32. B
3. A	8. C	13. D	18. A	23. B	28. C	33. C
4. B	9. E	14. D	19. B	24. E	29. C	34. A
5. A	10. E	15. D	20. D	25. D	30. C	35. A

SECTION 4—CRITICAL READING (p. 707)

1. B	4. C	7. E	10. C	13. A	16. E	19. C	22. B
2. E	5. D	8. B	11. C	14. B	17. D	20. E	23. C
3. B	6. D	9. E	12. E	15. A	18. C	21. A	24. B

SECTION 5—MATHEMATICS (p. 714)

1. C	4. E	7. D	10. E	13. E	16. A	19. C
2. D	5. B	8. E	11. A	14. A	17. B	20. B
3. C	6. D	9. A	12. B	15. B	18. E	

SECTION 6—CRITICAL READING (p. 719)

1. A	4. C	7. B	10. C	13. E	16. C	19. D	22. E
2. D	5. B	8. A	11. C	14. C	17. B	20. A	23. A
3. A	6. B	9. E	12. B	15. C	18. B	21. C	24. A

SECTION 8—MATHEMATICS (p. 726)

1. C	3. E	5. B	7. C	9. D	11. C	13. C	15. D
2. A	4. E	6. D	8. D	10. C	12. A	14. E	16. E

SECTION 9—CRITICAL READING (p. 730)

1. E	4. E	7. B	10. A	13. E	16. C	19. A
2. A	5. E	8. D	11. D	14. B	17. B	
3. B	6. C	9. C	12. D	15. C	18. E	

SECTION 10—WRITING (p. 735)

1. C	3. D	5. A	7. C	9. B	11. A	13. A
2. A	4. C	6. C	8. C	10. E	12. B	14. E

PRACTICE TEST III

SECTION 2—MATHEMATICS (p. 748)

1. C	4. B	7. D	10. 500	13. 30	16. 108
2. B	5. E	8. A	11. 25	14. 120	17. 10
3. C	6. D	9. 12	12. 784	15. 15.7	18. 0

SECTION 3—WRITING (p. 753)

1. A	6. D	11. C	16. A	21. C	26. A	31. E
2. B	7. E	12. D	17. E	22. D	27. C	32. C
3. C	8. D	13. B	18. C	23. A	28. D	33. C
4. E	9. C	14. A	19. D	24. B	29. C	34. D
5. A	10. B	15. C	20. B	25. B	30. C	35. A

SECTION 4—CRITICAL READING (p. 761)

1. A	4. B	7. B	10. B	13. C	16. B	19. A	22. C
2. B	5. D	8. A	11. E	14. A	17. C	20. E	23. A
3. C	6. C	9. E	12. D	15. E	18. B	21. C	24. B

SECTION 5—MATHEMATICS (p. 769)

1. B	4. E	7. C	10. A	13. B	16. C	19. C
2. E	5. D	8. B	11. E	14. B	17. A	20. C
3. C	6. A	9. C	12. C	15. D	18. C	

SECTION 6—CRITICAL READING (p. 773)

1. B	4. E	7. E	10. C	13. A	16. D	19. B	22. C
2. D	5. D	8. C	11. C	14. D	17. C	20. E	23. D
3. C	6. D	9. C	12. E	15. C	18. A	21. D	24. B

SECTION 8—MATHEMATICS (p. 779)

1. E	3. D	5. C	7. E	9. C	11. E	13. A	15. C
2. B	4. C	6. C	8. E	10. C	12. B	14. B	16. E

SECTION 9—CRITICAL READING (p. 782)

1. B	4. E	7. E	10. B	13. C	16. B	19. A
2. C	5. B	8. D	11. D	14. A	17. A	
3. A	6. B	9. C	12. A	15. E	18. A	

SECTION 10—WRITING (p. 788)

1. B	3. E	5. B	7. A	9. B	11. D	13. C
2. E	4. E	6. E	8. D	10. A	12. D	14. C

SECTION 1—WRITING (p. 747)

Sample Essay 1—Below Average Response

The study hall time I have each day is very important to me. Some schools have cut it out to add another subject to school. We only have so much time in the evening, and without study hall, students might never get their homework done. Study hall really helps students who need to work harder and students with part-time jobs, lots of chores, or athletics.

Students that have to put in a lot of extra work in subjects, really welcome study hall. They may have a poor environment for class work at home. Sometime help is available in study hall for problem subjects. Study hall has reference books not always available in the home. If you have study hall, you at least don't get more homework at that time. Some students just rest in study hall, and don't work on school. That is their choice if they want to waste time.

If you have a part-time job you really need study hall to do at least some of your homework. This also applies to athletes. They have hours of practice each evening and may be too tired afterwards to study well. Study hall provides a good break in the hard day at school, and lets students keep up better in the classroom subjects.

Writing skill and position on issue:

This essay demonstrates developing skill. The writer's position is understood, but the essay lacks a clear thesis statement. The essay is simply not sophisticated enough to present the complexity of the issue; it is written with an abrupt and conversational tone that is not appropriate for this type of formal presentation.

Development of ideas and organization of essay:

The essay is mostly written from a personal point of view and uses personal experiences to support its position. The ideas that are presented in the one body paragraph (the second paragraph) are not structured in any particular order and do not follow any organizational scheme; they distract the reader with their choppiness. For example, the second paragraph randomly discusses different points of the argument without giving any consideration to further development or general cohesiveness of thought; the writer discusses both the help that is available during study sessions and the advantage of not being assigned any other homework in study hall. These two ideas do not flow together and should not be included in the same paragraph. The essay could be improved by presenting the opposing viewpoint and its refutation in order to contrast and in turn reinforce the writer's position. Also, the last paragraph essentially serves as another body paragraph because it simply discusses several other benefits of study hall.

Structure of essay, paragraphs, and transitions:

The structure is too simple. The body of the essay should consist of more than one paragraph. The paragraphs lack good topic sentences and transitions are not used. Since the last paragraph does not adequately provide a conclusion that summarizes the writer's major points, the essay is missing one of its three essential structural elements.

Language usage, sentence structure, and punctuation:

The writer shifts between the subjective and objective point of view. This inconsistent voice detracts from the readability of the essay. Low-level language usage and some language errors are present in the essay. For example, "don't work on school" is ambiguous. The writer most likely intends to say that students do not do their schoolwork. "Lots of" is low-level usage.

Summary and conclusions:

Major structural and organizational flaws and language usage errors signify a seriously limited essay. The essay would likely receive a grade of below average to average (5 - 7).

Sample Essay 2—Above Average Response

Study hall is beneficial to many students and should therefore not be eliminated from school. It provides the extra time needed to complete homework, review for a test, or even prepare ahead for future assignments. Since students are given the opportunity to take elective classes throughout the school day, study hall should be integrated into their schedule so that they may better manage their studies. Study hall especially helps students in the areas of time management, outside activities, and improved performance in subject areas.

Students under the strains of time management may require study hall to just keep up with their studies. Extracurricular activities, athletics, and after-school jobs can be very time-consuming and tend to distract students from their studies. In order to accommodate these activities, many students deprive themselves of sleep due to late hours of study at home. To a student who works after school to earn some extra spending money, or to help support his or her family, study hall may be the only chance to complete course work.

By allowing for some free time, study hall enables a student to broaden his or her skills and grow as a well-rounded person. Extracurricular activities and after-school jobs provide the necessary outlet for students to relax and socialize with their peers. Many students are even able to apply to their studies new skills learned in other environments.

Study hall is an elective that actually supports the required curriculum. Although many electives may be fun and interesting, students who take study hall can actually devote more time to math, science, and English. Study hall also provides a supportive educational environment that may not be available in every home due to the living arrangements.

In summary, study hall has many more benefits compared to those of having just another subject class. Students under oppressive time pressures can catch up with studies, expand their horizons with reading, and keep up in the face of outside activity demands with the help of study hall.

Writing skill and position on issue:

This essay shows good facility with written English and clear organization. The writer offers a great introduction into the subject and presents a strong thesis. His or her position is clearly stated in the opening sentence, and it is supported throughout the essay.

Development of ideas and organization of essay:

The overall development of ideas and structure is logical and consistent, going from general to specific; however, some of the generalizations could be improved with more supporting details. The third paragraph, in particular, would benefit from added examples that connect the ideas and make them more effective. The relationship between free time, study hall, and extracurricular activities should be made explicit. Further improvements could be made by presenting an opposing viewpoint and its refutation in order to contrast and in turn reinforce the writer's position.

Structure of essay, paragraphs, and transitions:

All of the essential structural elements of an essay are present: an introduction, a body, and a conclusion. The initial paragraph expresses strong ideas and introduces the topic of each of the following paragraphs. The supporting paragraphs are appropriate, each paragraph deals with an argument or position of the writer, and each argument/paragraph is presented in an order that reflects the writer's organizational scheme.

Language usage, sentence structure, and punctuation:

Overall, the language usage is appropriate for this type of essay. However, in the second and fifth paragraphs, the word "just" is low-level usage. "In summary" is low-level usage as a transitional phrase for the concluding paragraph.

Summary and conclusions:

Overall, the essay is strong in structure and content The essay would likely get a grade of average to above average (10 - 12).

SECTION 2—MATHEMATICS (p. 748)

1. **(C)** Solve for x:

$$5,454 = 54(x+1)$$
$$\frac{5,454}{54} = x+1$$
$$101 = x+1$$
$$x = 100$$

2. **(B)** This question tests your understanding of exponents. Use the basic operations of exponents to solve for x and y, and then compute their difference. Multiplying two similar items, k, with differing exponents is the same as adding the exponents together. So, $x+9 = 21; x = 12$. Then, raising an exponent to a power is the same as multiplying both exponents. So, $y \cdot 3 = 18$; $y = 6$. And $x - y = 12 - 6 = 6$.

3. **(C)** You can reason verbally to a solution here: The two machines can seal and stuff a total of 500 envelopes per minute: $150 + 350 = 500$. So, it will take a minute and a half to do 750: $500 + 250 = 750$; 250 is half of 500. Or, you could set up a proportion: $\frac{500 \text{ envelopes}}{1 \text{ minute}} = \frac{750 \text{ envelopes}}{x \text{ minutes}} \Rightarrow x = \frac{750}{500} = 1.5 \text{ minutes}$.

4. **(B)** You can reason through this problem: Because y is squared, doubling y results in a four fold increase, while doubling z halves the original value. So, the net result is a doubling of x. It is easier, however, just to pick a couple of values and see what happens. Let $y = 2$ and $z = 3$. The value of x is originally 4: $x = \frac{3(2)^2}{3} = 4$. And when y is doubled to 4, and z is doubled to 6, x becomes 8: $x = \frac{3(4)^2}{6} = 8$. And, 8 is twice as large as 4.

There is another way to approach this problem: $x_0 = \frac{3y^2}{z}$ and $x_1 = \frac{3(2y)^2}{2z} = \frac{12y^2}{2z} = \frac{2 \cdot 3y^2}{z}$.

5. **(E)** First, find the area of the circle: $\pi r^2 = \pi(2)^2 = 4\pi$. Since the shaded area is equal to 3π, it accounts for $\frac{3\pi}{4\pi} = \frac{3}{4}$ of the circle. Thus, the unshaded area accounts for $\frac{1}{4}$ of the circle. This means that angle x plus the angle vertically opposite x are equal to $\frac{1}{4}$ of $360° = 90°$. Thus, $2x = 90$, and $x = 45$. Alternatively, since the figure is drawn to scale, and $x°$ is clearly an acute angle, (E) must be the correct answer since it is the only one that is less than 90°.

6. **(D)** Use the "*is-over-of*" strategy: $\frac{this\ is}{of\ that} = \frac{\%}{100} \Rightarrow \frac{tin}{entire\ bar} = \frac{x}{100} \Rightarrow x = 100 \cdot \frac{100}{100 + 150} = 100 \cdot \frac{100}{250} = \frac{200}{5} = 40\%$.

7. **(D)** Rewrite the equation: $\frac{1}{x} + \frac{1}{y} = \frac{1}{z}$. Add the fractions using the "flying-x" method: $\frac{x+y}{xy} = \frac{1}{z}$. Multiply both sides by z: $z \cdot \frac{x+y}{xy} = 1$. Multiply both sides by $\frac{xy}{x+y}$: $z = \frac{xy}{x+y}$. Alternatively, assume some values. If $x = 1$ and $y = 1$, $z = \frac{1}{2}$. Then, substitute 1 for x and 1 for y into the choices. Only (D) generates the value $\frac{1}{2}$.

8. **(A)** Set up a table to show the possibilities:

	Imported	Not Imported	Totals
$100 or more			
Less than $100			
Totals			

Now, fill in the numbers that are given:

	Imported	Not Imported	Totals
$100 or more			20%
Less than $100			
Totals	60%		

Since the total must equal 100%:

	Imported	Not Imported	Totals
$100 or more			20%
Less than $100			80%
Totals	60%	40%	100%

Next, 40% of the total articles priced at $100 or more are imported, and 40% of 20% = 8%.

	Imported	Not Imported	Totals
$100 or more	8%		20%
Less than $100			80%
Totals	60%	40%	100%

And by adding and subtracting you can complete the table:

	Imported	Not Imported	Totals
$100 or more	8%	12%	20%
Less than $100	52%	28%	80%
Totals	60%	40%	100%

Or, you can reach the same conclusion by assuming some numbers.

9. **(12)** Just solve for x: $3x + 2 = 8 \Rightarrow 3x = 6 \Rightarrow x = 2$. So, $6(2) = 12$.

10. **(500)** The profit on each box of candy is $2 - $1 = $1. To earn a total profit of $500, it will be necessary to sell $500 ÷ $1 = 500 boxes.

11. **(25)** This is a simple percent question. Use the "*is*-over-*of*" strategy: $\frac{\text{seniors}}{\text{total}} = \frac{90}{360} = \frac{1}{4} = 25\%$

12. **(784)** If the floor were a perfect rectangle, it would have a width of 4 • 5 = 20 meters, a length of 8 • 5 = 40 meters, and a total area of 20 • 40 = 800 square meters. But the floor is not a perfect rectangle. Its actual area is smaller. Subtract the area of the missing corner. It has dimensions of 0.8 • 5 = 4. So, its area is 16. The actual area is 800 − 16 = 784.

13. **(30)** The angles labeled $3w$ and $(5w + 20)$ form a straight angle: $3w + (5w + 20) = 180$. Solve for w:

$$8w + 20 = 180 \Rightarrow 8w = 160 \Rightarrow w = 20$$

Then, find the measure of the angle that is labeled

$(5w + 20)°$: $5(20) + 20 = 120°$. Since this angle is a vertical angle to the angle that is labeled $4x$, $4x$ must also equal $120°$. Therefore, $4x = 120 \Rightarrow x = 30$.

Alternatively, once you have solved for w, solve for x since the angles labeled $3w$ and $4x$ also form a straight angle:

$3w + 4x = 180 \Rightarrow 3(20) + 4x = 180$
$60 + 4x = 180 \Rightarrow 4x = 120 \Rightarrow x = 30$

You can also guestimate the value of x. The angle labeled $4x$ appears to be $120°$, so x must be about $30°$.

14. **(120)** If the club spent $\frac{2}{5}$ of the budget on the first project, it was left with $\frac{3}{5}$ of $300 = 180. If it spent $\frac{1}{3}$ of 180, it was left with $180 - $60 = 120.

15. **(15.7)** It is easy enough to figure that for six numbers to average 16, they must add up to

$6 \cdot 16$, or 96. The numbers given add up to

$10 + 12 + 15.1 + 15.2 + 28 = 80.3 \Rightarrow$

$96 - 80.3 = 15.7$, which must be the missing x.

16. **(108)** This problem has multiple steps, but the arithmetic is simple. The only amount you have to work with is 12 geese, so start there.

12 geese = 20% of birds

$12 = \frac{20}{100}x \Rightarrow 12 = \frac{1}{5}x \Rightarrow x = 12 \cdot 5 = 60$

Now, you know that there are 60 birds in all. If 25% of the animals are birds, 60 birds = 25% of the animals.

$60 = \frac{25}{100}y \Rightarrow 60 = \frac{1}{4}y \Rightarrow y = 60 \cdot 4 = 240$

This is still not the answer—remember that you want a number representing mammals. You must find what part of this 240-animal total is mammals.

% of mammals = 100% − (25% + 30%) = 45% 45% (240) = 108 mammals

17. **(10)** First convert Jerry's final height to inches:

$5 \cdot 12 = 60 \Rightarrow 60 + 10 = 70$

Jerry's 7-inch growth is 10% of 70 inches.

18. **(0)** If you can't picture it in your head, draw it on paper:

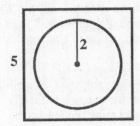

A circle with a radius of 2 has a diameter of 4, so when it is superimposed on a square with sides of 5, it never intersects that square, assuming that the centers are the same.

SECTION 3—WRITING (p. 753)

1. **(A)** The underlined portion is correct. It is best, however, to check the other answer choices to be sure that none of them improve the original sentence. (B) is incorrect because the sentence requires the simples past tense, not the present perfect tense. (C) is incorrect because it results in a sentence fragment without a conjugated verb. (D) is wrong because it is not logical to use the present tense to refer to what is obviously a past event. (E) is not idiomatic English and changes the intended meaning of the original sentence.

2. **(B)** The original suffers from a shifting verb tense. The underlined portion ("will pose") is in the future tense; however, the other verbs in the sentence ("determined" and "postponed") indicate that the events took place in the past. Since muddy conditions existed, and the director postponed the game because of the potential for injury, the subjunctive "would" is required to indicate that these injuries may or may not actually happen. Therefore, (B) is the correct answer choice. (C) is wrong because it eliminates the main verb of the sentence. (D) is wrong because it uses a past participle instead of the subjunctive. Finally, (E) is wrong because it uses a present participle instead of the subjunctive.

3. **(C)** The original has a word usage problem. In the underlined portion, "if" is not idiomatic. In this context, "whether" would be the appropriate word choice. Therefore, (C) is the correct answer choice because it simply replaces "if" with "whether." (B) is wrong because it does not address the problem of the original. Also, "instruction as college program" is grammatically incorrect. (D) is wrong because it distorts the intended meaning of the original by implying that there are doubts in terms of the program's merits, rather than doubts in terms of student interest in the program. Finally, (E) is an interesting choice; it simply eliminates "if" altogether, and the resulting sentence makes clear that the doubt is about the viability of the program. However, like (B), (E) is wrong because "instruction as college program" is grammatically incorrect.

4. **(E)** The original suffers from the infamous "dangling modifier." As written, the phrase "In a panicked tone" modifies the first important noun that follows it ("the duty nurse"). However, the sentence intends to say that the mother (not the duty nurse) was speaking in a panicked tone. Therefore, "In a panicked tone" should be repositioned so that it is closer to the phrase that it is intended to modify ("the mother"). (E) makes the needed correction. (B) is wrong because it incorrectly implies that the child was speaking in a panicked tone. (C) is wrong because it incorrectly implies that there was some sort of cause and effect relationship between the mother's plea and her tone; however, the mother does not ask for help *because* her tone is panicked. Finally, (D) is wrong for the same reason as the original; the modifying phrase ("in a panicked tone") still seems to apply to "The duty nurse."

5. **(A)** The original is correct. The use of "with" before "sexual harassment" is important because it makes clear that there were two separate and distinct charges against the CEO. (B) is wrong because it eliminates "with," thereby creating an ambiguous sentence; (B) incorrectly implies that the CEO diverted company funds and diverted sexual harassment. (C) is wrong because it unnecessarily changes the main verb to the past progressive tense ("was being accused"). (D) is wrong because it too creates an ambiguous sentence; its use of "both" incorrectly implies that the CEO diverted both funds and sexual harassment. Finally, (E) is wrong for two reasons. First, it incorrectly implies that the CEO diverted company funds and sexual harassment. Second, it uses the passive voice in a weak manner, making the sentence awkward and confusing.

6. **(D)** The problem with the original sentence is that "river" is supposed to refer to both the Blue Nile and the White Nile, so you need the plural: "of the Blue Nile and White Nile rivers." As for (A), "capital" is the correct word (compared with "capitol").. As for (B), "is" correctly agrees with its subject, Khartoum. As for (C), the preposition "at" is the correct one to use here.

7. **(E)** The original sentence is correct as written. As for (A), the compound subject "hieroglyphics and the alphabet" is plural and needs the plural verb "are." As for (B), "that" correctly connects the first two clauses. As for (C), "though" is correctly used to introduce a subordinate clause. And as for (D), "only developing" completes the second verb of the subordinate clause.

8. **(D)** The original sentence includes an incomplete split construction: graduates or teachers at the University of Chicago. The problem is that some words have been omitted: graduates . . . at the University of Chicago. What the sentence should say is: graduates of or teachers at the University of Chicago. As for (A), "most influential" correctly describes the economists who are very influential. As for (B), "economists" says exactly what the sentence intends. And as for (C), "are" correctly agrees with "economists."

9. **(C)** The use of the present tense "establishes" is inconsistent with the other verb in the sentence, "drew." Since "drew" is the past tense, (C) should be "established." As for (A), "during" is here a preposition that introduces a phrase to modify the verb sequence in the main clause: When did Penn do all of this? As for (B), "only" correctly shows that this was the one trip made. And as for (D), "with" has an appropriate meaning in this context.

10. **(B)** The subject of the sentence is the singular "dynamite," so the verb should be the singular "was" rather than the plural "were." As for (A), "made from" is an appropriate idiom, and "made" introduces the phrase that modifies "explosive." As for (C), "who" is the correct choice when referring to people, in this case the chemist named Nobel. And as for (D), "endowed" is correctly in the past tense.

11. **(C)** The problem in the original sentence is its shifting point of view. The sentence switches from second person to the third person. This could be corrected by changing "one" to "you." As for (A), "when" is a subordinate conjunction that introduces an adverbial clause to tell the reader "when" the reader will be able to hear these elements: when you are listening to Khachaturian. As for (B), "heritage" is used idiomatically. And as for (D), "can hear" is an appropriate verb form.

12. **(D)** The original sentence exhibits faulty parallelism. The elements in the series should have similar forms: can use, refine, and produce. As for (A), "improvement" functions as an appositive and refers to "open-hearth process." As for (B), "producing" is the right verb form. And as for (C), the adjective "high" correctly modifies "content."

13. **(B)** The problem in the original sentence is "feeds." "Feeds" is a conjugated verb, that is, it shows person and tense: The salamander feeds every night. But in this sentence, the verb "feed" is not intended to be the main or conjugated verb. Rather, the main verb is "is found." "Usually . . . insects" is a long adjective that modifies salamander, so "feeds" should be changed to "feeding," an adjective. As for (A), "usually" is an adverb that correctly modifies the adjective "nocturnal." As for (C), "is found" is the right number to agree with singular "salamander." And finally, as for (D), "damp" has a meaning that is appropriate here.

14. **(A)** The problem with the original sentence is that "law" should be "laws." Your "ear" should tell you that, but you can also reason that "first" implies others to follow, so "law" needs to be plural. As for (B), "that" correctly introduces a dependent clause to act as the object of "states." As for (C), "each" is properly to used here to indicate "every one of them." And (D) is correct, since "is" agrees with "orbit."

15. **(C)** The problem with the original sentence is that the pronoun "their" does not agree with "each." "Their" should be replaced with "its." As for (A), the preposition "for" introduces an adjective phrase that modifies "New York City." As for (B), "offers" correctly agrees with the singular subject. As for (D), "own" is needed to attribute the flavors to each different cuisine.

16. **(A)** The original sentence includes a misplaced modifier. "While rowing" seems to modify "direction and speed," but "direction and speed" do not row. The sentence could be completely rewritten to position "rowers" closer to "while rowing," or "while rowing" could be made a prepositional phrase such as "In rowing." As for (B), "are" correctly agrees with the compound subject "direction and speed." As for (C), "who" is correctly to refer to the person who is the coxswain. And as for (D), "strokes" correctly refers to the use of the oars by the rowers.

17. **(E)** The original sentence is correct as written. "One" is an appositive that modifies "rayon." "Fibers" is correctly in the plural. "Made from" is idiomatic. And as for (D), "chiefly" is an adverb that properly modifies "derived."

18. **(C)** The original sentence contains an incorrect verb tense. The main verb of the sentence ("was") is in the past tense, so everything else has to be built around that time frame. "Writes" should be "wrote." As for (A), "popular" appropriately modifies speaker. As for (B), "who" correctly refers to "speaker," a person. As for (D), "music" can be an adjective as well as a noun, and this usage is appropriate here.

19. **(D)** The original sentence contains an instance of low-level usage. (D) must use either the infinitive (started to write) or the gerund (started writing) but not a combination of the two. As for (A), the past tense "traveled" correctly puts the action in the past and makes it consistent with the other verbs in the sentence. As for (B), "where" introduces a subordinate clause that modifies France. As for (C), "some of" is an idiom that is used correctly here.

20. **(B)** The original sentence contains a non-idiomatic usage of a preposition. The idiomatic phrasing for this context is "aim at" not "aim to." ("Aim to" is sometimes used to mean "intend to.") As for (A), the phrasing is idiomatic. As for (C), "which" is a relative pronoun that introduces and functions as the subject of the relative clause. And as for (D),"itself" correctly refers to "weapons." ("Itself" here is used to stress that it is the weapon that receives the reflected signal.)

21. **(C)** The problem with the original sentence is that the pronouns do not agree. "Their" is intended to refer to "system" and so must be singular, "its." As for (A), "was" is correctly in the past tense and agrees with the singular "chivalry." As for (B), "grew out of" is an idiomatic phrase that has an appropriate meaning in this context. And as for (D), the plural "centuries" is correct since there are two centuries mentioned.

22. **(D)** The problem with the original sentence is one of diction (word choice). The correct word is "conquered." As for (A), "that" is a relative pronoun that refers to "area" and that introduces the clause about Portugal. As for (B), "added to" is the correct idiom. And as for (C), "around," meaning "about" in this case, has the right meaning for this context.

23. **(A)** The three elements in the series should have parallel forms: valedictorian, gold medalist, and internationally renowned singer. The sentence could be corrected by deleting "he was." As for (B), you need the adverb "internationally" to modify the adjective "renowned." As for (C), "was" correctly agrees with "Paul Robeson." And as for (D), "many" is used idiomatically.

24. **(B)** The original sentence contains a subject-verb error. The singular "is covered" needs to be plural in order to agree with the plural subject, "cavities." As for (A), "which" is a relative pronoun that refers to "nose." As for (C) and (D), the use of both prepositions is idiomatic.

25. **(B)** The problem with the original sentence is that the three elements in the series should be in similar form: sight, hearing, smell. (A) correctly conveys the notion of time or sequence. As for (C), "seriously" is an adverb that is correctly used to modify "is degraded." And as for (D), "more" is the proper adjective because the two abilities are being compared: normal and more acute.

26. **(A)** Sentence 2 asks "Why?" And the rest of the passage answers that question: The writer likes the idea of struggling artists living in picturesque circumstances. (B) is wrong because the writer intends to answer the question. As for (C), while the writer certainly seems confident, expressing that confidence is not the logical function of sentence 2. (D) is an interesting point, but ahs no place in this essay. Finally, as for (E), although this is a question, it is not intended to raise doubts. Instead, the author intends to provide an answer.

27. **(C)** Inserting the information as a parenthetical expression helps to preserve the flow of the first paragraph. In addition, the information must accurately and effectively refer to "Left Bank." So, (C) is the best choice. The other choices suggest complete sentences, and inserting a whole sentence into the paragraph is likely to be distracting to the reader and give too much importance to a fairly minor detail.

28. **(D)** The problem with the original sentence is that "they" does not have a referent. Only (D) addresses this issue. But there is another reason to prefer (D). Sentence 6 is not very well integrated into the rest of the paragraph. The reader will likely have trouble understanding the significance of the tragic romance. So, a good revision would make the connection clear, and (D) does.

29. **(C)** The problem with the original sentence is that the future tense "will make" is inconsistent with the past tense verbs throughout the rest of the paragraph. (C) solves this problem. As for (A), eliminating "but" results in a comma splice—two sentences jammed together, separated by only a comma without a conjunction. As for (B), there is no reason for this change ("they" has a clear antecedent), and the change does not solve the problem just outlined. As for (D), starting a new sentence will not solve the original problem, and creating a new sentence will disrupt the flow of the paragraph. Finally, as for (E), "and" doesn't send the same signal to the reader that "but" does.

30. **(C)** One problem with the original sentence is that "being that" is low-level usage. Those words should be deleted. Additionally, sentence 16 could be tightened up a bit by making the final phrase an appositive: Murger, the struggling writer. (C) makes both of these revisions. As for (A), "In point of fact" would normally be used to add emphasis to the sentence, but it doesn't appear that any additional emphasis is appropriate here. As for (B), eliminating "story" leaves just the "this," a word that is ambiguous in its reference. As for (D), a semicolon would signal to the reader that a clause is to follow; but no clause comes and that would be confusing. And as for (E), though it would not be wrong to speak of Murger in the past tense, this change will not address the two problems that are mentioned above.

31. **(E)** The focus of the essay is on giving the reader some general rules of flag etiquette and then encouraging the reader to look for more information on the topic. Sentence 18 best summarizes this development. Sentence 1, though it is the opening sentence, is not the main point. The reference to the convention is a kind of jumping-off point to get the essay started, but the idea that is stated in sentence 1 is a relatively minor detail. As for (B) and (C), these are relatively minor details. (D) marks the lead-up to the writer's conclusion, but sentence 16 itself does not restate the main point.

32. **(C)** The first paragraph actually should be two paragraphs, separated between sentences 4 and 5. The first four sentences provide background for the reader. Starting with sentence 5, the writer gives the reader specific rules for displaying the flag. (A) and (B) are wrong because this would break apart the information about the Flag Code. And (D) and (E) are wrong because this would break apart the information about the general rules for displaying the flag.

33. **(C)** The difficulty with the original sentence is the inconsistent use of the plural and singular versions of flag. The rest of the paragraph talks about "the flag," using that term to refer to all U.S. flags in general. So this sentence needs to be rewritten to conform to the singular. Therefore, (B) is definitely wrong. As for (A), deleting "unless" just runs two thoughts together and ignores the fact that the second is subordinate to the first—"unless." As for (D), while it would not be incorrect to remove "when" from the sentence, there is no good reason for doing so, and (D) fails to address the real problem with sentence 8. Finally, as for (E), replacing the comma with a semicolon will signal to the reader that another independent clause is coming after the semicolon—but the second idea, as noted, is a subordinate or dependent thought.

34. **(D)** The original sentence is in need of revision because the "when raising the flag" doesn't have anything to modify. The phrase can't modify "it," because "it" refers to "flag," and you'd have a sentence that illogically says: When raising the flag, the flag should be hoisted briskly. (D) solves this problem by making it clear that "you" or the "reader" is the one raising the flag. (B), (C), and (E) don't address this problem and actually introduce phrasings that are even more awkward.

35. **(A)** The problem with the original sentence is that it does not clearly express the relationship between the two ideas that are mentioned. (A) solves the problem by stating directly: The other points may surprise you. (B) is wrong because the result is a dependent clause that is introduced by "because" instead of a complete sentence. (C) is wrong because this version confuses the connection between the ideas that are mentioned in the original passage. It is the various points of etiquette in the Flag Code that may surprise you—not the fact that the Code contains many points. As for (D), this is pretty weak choice that doesn't clarify matters. And (E) uses the passive voice, making that choice needlessly indirect when compared with (A).

SECTION 4—CRITICAL READING (p. 761)

1. **(A)** The sentence gives you a very strong adverb clue with the word "unfairly." You can eliminate (B) since something that is unfair could not be objective. You can also eliminate (C) and (D) because they do not create meaningful sentences. (A), "biased," is the best word to convey the idea that the book blamed unfairly.

2. **(B)** This sentence features combined reasoning. The first blank extends the thought that "the universe was well-ordered," as indicated by the coordinate conjunction thought-extender, "and." You can eliminate (A) since it is not logical that something would be well-ordered and baffling. (C), (D), and (E) are not words that you would use to describe the universe. This leaves (B). There is a "but" or "yet" understood in this sentence, so the next blank will be something opposite to "harmonious." The second element of (B) works because "chaotic" is the opposite of "harmonious."

3. **(C)** The key here is the thought-extender, "because." The blank extends the first half of the sentence by explaining why hot milk has been a cure for insomnia. If you know that something that cures insomnia is a soporific, this is a quick and easy item. However, even if you don't know the word soporific, all of the other answers are easily eliminated.

4. **(B)** "Since" is a thought-extender that links the two blanks, which helps eliminate (A) and (D). Also, given that there is a body of research already existing, the results of the new experiment can only be irrelevant to it, consistent with it, or inconsistent with it. Therefore, eliminate choice (C). Then, substitute both words of the remaining choices in order to determine the correct answer. (A) cannot be correct since results would not be speculative if they were similar to the research already done. (D) is not possible because the body of research would not be "dispelled by" convincing results. (E) makes no sense because if the results were redundant, then they would not contradict the existing research. This leaves you with (B), which works very well. Results might be considered anomalous if they were inconsistent with the research already done.

5. **(D)** The logical clue here is a thought-extender, "because," but the order in which the ideas are presented in the sentence makes this extender difficult to see. The idea that follows "because" specifies the cause of the first idea: The ---- of traditional values causes modern life to ---- neurosis. Substitute each of the choices into this new sentence. Only (D) produces a sentence that fits the logical structure.

6. **(C)** The overall structure of this sentence depends on a thought-extender. The first blank must complete a phrase that is set off by commas that explains why Peter does what he does. Also, the word in the first blank must describe an emotional reaction that is an appropriate response to the phrase clue, "repeated rejections." On this ground, eliminate (A), (B), and (D), since it is not logical for anyone to be encouraged, elated, or inspired by rejection. (C) and (E) are both possible reactions to rejection, but (E) does not provide the overall logical continuity that is needed.

7. **(B)** This sentence hinges on the second blank. The sentence sets up a contrast "between" (key word) how artists view their own talent and their knowledge that few will succeed. Eliminate (A), (C), and (E), since they fail to provide a contrast. It would not be surprising that an artist who neglected, was indifferent to, or disregarded his talent would not succeed. Eliminate (D), since the phrase "dissolution of their own talent" is not meaningful.

8. **(A)** This is a Development item. Remember that an assumption is most often an unstated premise that underlies the structure of a passage. For example: "Betsy would be the best choice for Student Council President because

she is the only candidate with public speaking experience." This line of reasoning assumes, though it does not say so explicitly, that public speaking experience is a good qualification for the office. In this test item, the author assumes, without saying so explicitly, that the first written references to balls would have coincided with the introduction of balls to the region. After all, if writers were likely to mention balls only 500 years after they first appeared, then there would be no reason for the author to date the events in the way they have been dated. The other choices are ideas that are related to the topic of the passage, but they do not function as underlying assumptions in the way that (A) does.

9. **(E)** This is a Main Idea item. The author starts by saying that some commentators see the novel as romantic, and then immediately says this is incorrect. The rest of the passage explains why the novel is actually realistic. (E) best describes this development. Now, it is worth looking at the incorrect answers as well. (A) is incorrect because it was Dickens, not the author of this passage, who hoped to expose conditions in the boarding houses. (B) is incorrect because the author does not necessarily believe that this distinction exhausts the possibilities. Rather, the author takes this distinction as a starting point because commentators have tended to regard Nicholas Nickleby as romantic rather than realistic. (C) is similar to (E) but it is too broad and severe in scope: The author wants to correct a misunderstanding, but the author is not trying to revise extensive literary criticism. Finally, while the author is advancing a theory of Nicholas Nickleby, that is not equivalent to proposing a new literary theory of the novel in general.

10. **(B)** This is a Development item. The author relies mainly on examples (Nottingham, bronchitis, art, Sherlock Holmes, buildings) to show that air pollution is not a recent phenomenon. As for (A), the author mentions the figure "30%," but that does not make the whole passage a discussion of statistics. Similarly, the author mentions the Queen and an art critic, who presumably saw things first hand, but the passage also refers to other evidence as well—so, eliminate (C). (D) is incorrect because there is only one mention of historical records, and (E) is incorrect because the only expert mentioned is the art critic.

11. **(E)** This is a Main Idea item. The author says that public spaces are disappearing and that shopping malls are all that remain. Shopping malls, however, are privately owned properties where freedom of speech is subject to the restrictions of the property owners. So, the shopping mall is not actually a public space. Therefore, (E) is the correct answer choice. (A) is wrong because the author does not mention the idea of convenience.(B) is wrong because the author does not refer to speeches and leafleting as "commercial" activities. (C) is perhaps the second-best answer choice, because this passage might be used in an argument about the importance of public spaces and free speech; however, the passage does not address the issue of democracy or even attempt to characterize freedom of speech as a condition of its viability. Finally, (D) is wrong because it is too narrow: the author merely mentions how shopping malls are gradually replacing public spaces in order to support the main argument that these malls themselves are not true public spaces.

12. **(D)** This is an Implied Idea item. According to the passage, some people who looked at the cleaned frescoes thought that the bright colors were not suitable for serious art. So we can infer that these people think that high art should be dark and serious to reflect the purpose of art. (That may be a silly expectation, but it is a fair inference about those viewers.) As for (A), it is not the subject matter but appearance of the frescoes that caused controversy. As for (B), though some people apparently objected to the appearance of the cleaned frescoes, nothing in the passage suggests that they thought the dirt should be replaced. As for (C), the author does not discuss when or how often art in general should be cleaned. And as for (E), the author doesn't say that it was a mistake to clean the frescoes nor that the job was done badly—even thought some people found the result a little surprising.

13. **(C)** This is a Development item. The writer uses what is called, in technical logical terminology, a *reductio ad absurdum*, or *reductio*. A *reductio* is an argument that shows that the premises or assumptions of a position lead to an absurd result. In this case, the writer shows that protectionism leads to the absurd result of having nothing but gold and silver—no food, no clothes, no heat—just precious metal. (A) describes an attempt to discredit an opponent: We should reject protectionism because the people who support it stand to make a lot of money themselves. In other words, the protectionists have a hidden motive. But that is not what the writer does here. As for (B), the author doesn't say what most economists think. As for (D), while some of us may believe this

contention, this particular passage does not address this issue. And we may feel the same way about statistics,. but this particular author doesn't make that argument.

14. **(A)** This is an Implied Idea item. The textbook writer must have looked at the total wool production reported for the area and the total number of sheep. On dividing "production" by "sheep," the writer determined that production was a record-setting 150 pounds per sheep. The problem with the statistic is that the total wool reported as produced in the islands included a large quantity of smuggled wool that was relabeled "domestic" wool. The textbook writer uncritically accepted the information as reported and announced that these were record-setting sheep. (B) is incorrect because the number of sheep is not the figure that caused the odd result. It was probably accurate. What caused the figure to be so high was the inflated production figure, a figure that included smuggled as well as domestically produced wool. (C) is incorrect because the affect on other markets did not affect the calculation of the bogus number. (D) takes the assumption too far: The implication of the passage is that the writer simply was not aware of the possibility that the production figure included smuggled wool. (E) is incorrect because the writer did accept the figure and was for that very reason considered naïve.

15. **(E)** This is a Main Idea item. (A) is not correct because although the author discusses the difficulty of translation, he does not criticize translators. In fact, he seems sympathetic to their problems since he is a translator himself. (B) is not correct since he mentions the fact that all languages have their particular difficulties and uses the poetry of Milton—an English poet—as an example of a text that is difficult to translate. (C) is wrong because although the author says it is difficult to do justice to a work in another language, he refers to some translations that are successful—those that please the "hard-liners," for instance. He also mentions Chateaubriand's translation of *Paradise Lost* as a successful translation. (D) is incorrect because although the author mentions some of the difficulties of translating Japanese into English, the point of the passage is not that Japanese is particularly difficult—just that it is difficult in some particular ways.

16. **(B)** This is an Implied Idea item. The author mentions the fact that he has translated some work by Dazai Osamu. He then mentions another book, *Accomplices of Silence*, which discusses certain aspects of Osamu's work. We may infer, then, that the book mentioned is a critical commentary on the work of Osamu. It is certainly not an English translation of Japanese poetry since it is clear that this book talks *about* the literature. It is not a prior publication by the author of the passage because he or she names another author—Masao Miyoshi; thus, (C) is incorrect. (D) is wrong because the author gives examples of the things mentioned in Miyoshi's book, and they have nothing to do with orthography. Finally, (E) is wrong because it is clear that Miyoshi's comments as quoted by the author are about Osamu's effects in Japanese, not in English; therefore, the author is not talking about the problems of translation.

17. **(C)** This is a Vocabulary item. In the third paragraph, the author discusses the effect of spelling on Japanese literature, and that is what "orthography" means.

18. **(B)** This is an Explicit Detail item. In paragraph two, the author develops the point that Japanese has some special features that make translation into English difficult. The author offers a couple of examples, concluding that "the moments do not work in English." This means that it is impossible to translate them exactly. (A) is incorrect because it overstates the case. Some aspects of the text cannot be fully rendered, but the author doesn't say that the Japanese experience is completely unavailable to people who do not speak Japanese. As for (C), the author simply says that languages are different, not that one is necessarily superior to the other. As for (D), there is no indication that these are stock characters. And (E) represents a confused reading of the preceding paragraph.

19. **(A)** This is a Development item. The author uses an example taken from *Kinosaki nite* to illustrate the onomatopoeic effect of writing a word in one system of orthography rather than another. (B) is incorrect because although the author mentions that a Japanese writer laments the poverty of indigenous Japanese vocabulary, this fact is not the point of his example. In fact, the example actually demonstrates a certain richness of the Japanese language. (C) is incorrect because the example has nothing to do with translation. It is an example of an effect that is rendered in Japanese. (D) is not correct since the reader actually learns nothing at all about this work of literature except that this literary device appears in it. Finally, (E) is wrong because, again, the example has nothing to do with translation.

20. **(E)** This is an Application item. (A) is incorrect because although the author says that the Japanese people have special feelings about the possibilities of their language, he does not say that he shares these feelings. (B) is wrong because although the author discusses the difficulties of translating Japanese, he says that the difficulty stems from the peculiarities of the Japanese language, not from the limitations of the English. There is no reason to assume that the author thinks it would be easier to translate Japanese into any other language. (C) is wrong because it overstates the case: The author might say that it is difficult, but not necessarily impossible, for someone not fluent in Japanese to understand Japanese literature. (D) is wrong because the author specifically brackets the question of the truth of this hypothesis. (E) is correct because the author states that although Japanese has "special language relationships," he just means that like any other language, it has unique features. Thus, the author seems to feel that all languages have special qualities and they all present special challenges to a translator.

21. **(C)** This is an Implied Idea item. Since the author cites this word as an example of onomatopoeia (a poetic device in which the word that is used to describe an action *sounds* like the action itself), the answer can only be (C): buzz. In English, the word "buzz" sounds like the flight of a bee.

22. **(C)** This is a Development item. The author uses many examples to illustrate points: onomatopoeia in *Kinosaki nite*, for instance. The author also cites the particular effects that are difficult to translate in the work of Osamu. The author cites several authorities: Miyoshi on the subject of Osamu, and George Steiner on the subject of translation. As for (D), the author discusses personal experience in translating the work of Osamu. Finally, as for (E), the author also contrasts the entry barriers for business

23. **(A)** This is an Implied Idea item. (B) cannot be correct since the "handicap" is the result of translating the poetry, not the result of the Japanese writer's intention. (C) is incorrect because although there may be no word-for-word equivalents, that is a general problem of translation, not just a problem of translating Japanese into English. (D) is incorrect because the handicap is not related to the expectations of the reader. (E) is obviously incorrect since the problem is related to translation and has nothing to do with the problems of a Japanese reader reading in Japanese. The example quoted by the author is obviously a translator's attempt to make the English sound "oriental," or what a Western audience thinks "oriental" sounds like. So, (A) is the correct response.

24. **(B)** This is a Voice item. The author cites Steiner in the final paragraph as "lamenting" or regretting the "instant exotica," and then the author adds: "with which we are perhaps all too familiar." So, the author agrees that the "instant exotica" is a silly way of translating Japanese. Since the author's attitude is negative, (B) is the right response, and the other choices have to be incorrect.

SECTION 5—MATHEMATICS (p. 769)

1. **(B)** $2 \cdot 10^4 = 20{,}000$, and $121{,}212 + 20{,}000 = 141{,}212$.

2. **(E)** Solve for x: $6x + 3 = 21 \Rightarrow 6x = 18 \Rightarrow x = 3$. Thus: $2x + 1 = 2(3) + 1 = 7$.
   Alternatively, recognize that dividing the left side of the first equation by 3 gives you the left side of the second equation: $\frac{6x+3}{3} = 2x + 1$. Therefore, all you have to do to determine the right side of the second equation is divide the right side of the first equation by 3: $\frac{21}{3} = 7$.

3. **(C)** There is no trick to this question. Just use "supermarket math." Find out how much the one thing would cost. Then, using that cost, find out how much of the other you can buy. The cost of renting a bowling lane for two hours is $2 \cdot \$12 = \$24$. For $24, you can rent a Ping Pong table for $\$24 \div \$3 = 8$ hours.

4. **(E)** You can reason in general terms to the correct answer. As for (A), since k is less than l, k cannot be equal to l plus j. The same reasoning applies to (B), (C), and (D). (E), however, could be true. For example, if Jack is 5, Ken is 10, Larry is 15, and Mike is 20, then $5 + 20 = 10 + 15$.

5. **(D)** For all x, $|x| \geq 0$. Therefore, $-|x| \leq 0$. Since $-x = -|x|$, $-x \leq 0$. So, the solution set is $\{x : x \geq 0\}$.

6. **(A)** Use the "*is-over-of*" strategy: $\dfrac{this\ is}{of\ that} = \dfrac{\%}{100} \Rightarrow \dfrac{\text{students on track team}}{\text{total students}} = \dfrac{x}{100} \Rightarrow \dfrac{18}{360} = \dfrac{x}{100} \Rightarrow x = 5\%$.

7. **(C)** (I) must be true because a and x are vertical angles. Similarly, (II) must be true because y and b are equal and z and c are equal. (III), however, is not necessarily true. x and a are equal, y and b are equal, but you do not have information on which to base a conclusion about the relationship between x and y or the relationship between a and b.

8. **(B)** Set up an equation: $x + 30 = 2x \Rightarrow x = 30$. Alternatively, just "guestimate" the size of the right-hand angle: It is about 60°, so half would be about 30°.

9. **(C)** Simply test-the-test. Only (C) fits the specified conditions: $6 + 3 + 2 = 11$; $6 = 3 \cdot 2$; and $6 = 2 \cdot 3$.

10. **(A)** Use the method for finding the missing element of an average. Since the average height of all four buildings is 20, the sum of the heights of all four is $4 \cdot 20 = 80$. The three known heights total $3 \cdot 16 = 48$, so the missing value is: $80 - 48 = 32$.

11. **(E)** Use the properties of odd and even numbers to answer this question. Alternatively, substitute a number for x. If $x = 1$, an odd number:

    (A) $x + 2 = 1 + 2 = 3$ (Odd)
    (B) $3x + 2 = 3(1) + 2 = 5$ (Odd)
    (C) $2x^2 + x = 2(1)^2 + 1 = 2 + 1 = 3$ (Odd)
    (D) $2x^3 + x = 2(1)^3 + 1 = 2 + 1 = 3$ (Odd)
    (E) $3x^3 + x = 3(1)^3 + 1 = 3 + 1 = 4$ (Even)

12. **(C)** One square has an area of $2 \cdot 2 = 4$, and the other has an area of $3 \cdot 3 = 9$. The sum of their areas is: $4 + 9 = 13$.

13. **(B)** Set up an equation: $x \cdot 2x \cdot 3 = 54 \Rightarrow 2x^2 = 18 \Rightarrow x^2 = 9 \Rightarrow x = \sqrt{9} = 3$. Alternatively, test-the-test. Try each answer choice as the value of x until you find one that generates a volume of 54.

14. **(B)** Since x is 80% of y, $x = 0.8y$, and $y = \dfrac{x}{0.8} = 1.25x$. Thus, y is 125% of x. Alternatively, assume some values. If $y = 100$, then $x = 80\%$ of y, or 80. Finally, find what percent y is of x: $\dfrac{100}{80} = \dfrac{5}{4} = 1.25 = 125\%$.

15. **(D)** Rewrite $m - n > 0$ by adding n to both sides: $m > n$. As for (A), this proves that $m < n$. As for (B), this proves nothing about m and n, since m and n might be either negative or positive. The same is true of (C), which is equivalent to $m > -n$. Finally, as for (E), you have neither relative values for m and n nor their signs.

16. **(C)** You can use the Pythagorean Formula to find $\overline{AD}$ and $\overline{DC}$: $\overline{BD}^2 + \overline{AD}^2 = \overline{AB}^2 \Rightarrow 3^2 + \overline{AD}^2 =$

    $4^2 \Rightarrow \overline{AD}^2 = 7 \Rightarrow \overline{AD} = \sqrt{7}$. So, the base of the triangle $= 2 \cdot \sqrt{7} = 2\sqrt{7}$. You can also use the trigonometry information that is provided:

    $$\sin \angle ABD = \dfrac{\overline{AD}}{\overline{AB}} \Rightarrow \sin \angle ABD = \dfrac{\overline{AD}}{4}$$
    $$\dfrac{\sqrt{7}}{4} = \dfrac{\overline{AD}}{4} \Rightarrow \overline{AD} = \sqrt{7}.$$

17. **(A)** Remember that the rules of exponents can be applied only to terms of like bases. Here, the numerator has a base of 8 and the denominator has a base of 2. Before we can manipulate the expression, it will be necessary to change one or the other term. There are several different routes that are available to us. For example:

$$8^{2x} = (8)^{2x} = (2 \cdot 2 \cdot 2)^{2x} = (2^{2x})(2^{2x})(2^{2x}) = 2^{2x+2x+2x} = 2^{6x}$$

Now, we can complete our division:

$$2^{6x} \div 2^{4x} = 2^{6x-4x} = 2^{2x}$$

Or:

$$(8)^{2x} = (2^3)^{2x} = (2)^{(3)(2x)} = 2^{6x}$$

And complete the division as shown above. Or, you could choose to work with the denominator. We think, however, that the best approach to this problem is just to assume a value for x. Say $x = 1$:

$$\frac{8^{2(1)}}{2^{4(1)}} = \frac{8^2}{2^4} = \frac{64}{16} = 4.$$

If we substitute 1 for x into the answer choices, the correct choice will generate the value 4:

A. $2^{2(1)} = 4$ (Right!)
B. $4^{-1} = \frac{1}{4}$ (Wrong.)
C. $4^{2(1)} = 16$ (Wrong.)
D. $4^{1-1} = 4^0 = 1$ (Wrong.)
E. $8^{-1} = \frac{1}{8}$ (Wrong.)

18. **(C)** Here we have a group of nested functions. Just perform the indicated operations, working from the inside to the outside: $h(2) = (2)^2 = 4 \Rightarrow g(4) = 4 - 2 = 2 \Rightarrow f(2) = \frac{2}{2} = 1$.

19. **(C)** The easiest way to solve this problem is just to plug in numbers. Since the answers are arranged in order of ascending value, try (C) first: $2(3) + 6 = 6 + 6 = 12$. And: $2(-2) + 6 = -4 + 6 = 2$. (C) is correct.

20. **(C)** This question tests properties of numbers. Examine each expression. (A) is not necessarily true. $|xy|$ is always a positive number, but $x + y$ could be a negative number—depending on the relative size of x and y. Nor is (B) true. $|xy|$ is always positive, but xy is always negative. For this reason, however, (C) is true. Since $|xy|$ is always positive and xy negative, $|xy|$ is always greater than xy. Finally, (D) and (E) might or might not be true depending on the relative magnitudes of x and y.

SECTION 6—CRITICAL READING (p. 773)

1. **(B)** This sentence does not have a logical structure that will help you select the correct answer. The first blank merely asks that you supply an adjective. The first elements of each answer choice are possible descriptions of a millionaire. The second part of the sentence, however, has a key phrase that tells you that something about his public appearances is an issue. The only word among the first possibilities that has anything to do with going out is "recluse." So, start with that choice and see if it works. If he is a recluse, then his public appearances will indeed be noteworthy. If you check the other possibilities, it is clear that the second word of each choice does not create a meaningful sentence when substituted into the blank.

2. **(D)** The key clue here is the thought-extender, "because." This clue tells you that Western physicians are learning a procedure as a result of "the _____ of the acupuncture therapy in China." Logically, they are doing so because the

procedure is desirable, so you should look for a noun that has a positive connotation. This eliminates (B) and (E). If you substitute (A) or (C), the sentence is meaningless. So, the answer must be (D).

3. **(C)** This sentence really depends on the second blank. You can eliminate (A), (B), and (E). The phrases "Being a celebrity has its presumptions" (or confrontations or delusions) is extremely unlikely. The second part of the sentence tells you to look for a "lack of" (key phrase) something that would create the situation described in the first blank. (D) does not work because a celebrity does not lack notoriety (fame is part of the definition of celebrity). Thus, the correct choice is (C).

4. **(E)** The second blank is an extension of the idea in the first part of the sentence. We know from the key phrase, "sounds similar to the ____ one hears as the individual members tune their instruments before a concert," that this sound will be negative. The only logical answer, even without considering the second blank, is (E). Confirming this, you can eliminate (A) because the idea of hearing a melody does not explain why a chord is superfluous. You can eliminate (B) because the idea of hearing a roar does not explain why a chord might be pretentious. You can eliminate (C) because the idea of hearing applause does not explain why a chord might be melodious. Eliminate (D), because the idea of hearing harmony does not explain why a chord might be versatile. (E) preserves the sense and logic of the sentence. Hearing cacophony explains that the chord is discordant.

5. **(D)** This sentence features combined reasoning. The key to the first half of the sentence is "but." The king was not something that is like "a haughty aristocrat." You can eliminate (A) and (C). "Sycophant" does not provide a logical contrast. Putting "monarch" into the first blank results in a contradiction because by definition a king is a monarch). The second blank must be filled by a word that can later be extended by the phrase "genuine affection." Of the remaining choices, only (D) has a second element with the positive overtones needed to complete that extension. Students can also focus on the extending nature of the semicolon, which indicates that the king would rule positively, or "magnanimously."

6. **(D)** The key to this sentence is the subordinate conjunction thought-reverser, "although." The blank would have to be something that connotes falseness or being out of proper order. Only (D), "anachronistic," which means something that is not in chronological order, fits this sentence.

7. **(E)** The best way to attack this item is to substitute each pair until you find one that works, keeping in mind that the colon indicates that the second blank extends the first blank. You can immediately eliminate (A) on the grounds of usage as "apathetic to humor" makes no sense. Next, the salacious is not "heretical to humor," so eliminate (B). The grandiose is not "inferior to humor," so eliminate (C). The innocuous is not "extraneous to humor," so eliminate (D). (E) remains, which does make sense. The macabre might be "antithetical to humor."

8. **(C)** This item features combined reasoning. The key word clue in the first part of the sentence is the word "while." This word tells you that the Broadway cast was the opposite of the British cast. The first blank extends the idea of what the British cast was. Look for a word that goes with "energy" and "talent." (B) and (C) are possibilities; the others do not extend the idea. The word in the second blank must be the opposite of the description of the British cast and extend the faults of the Broadway case, as the semicolon clue indicates. (D), "meticulous," makes no sense, so the correct answer must be (C).

9. **(C)** This is a Development question. One of the most striking features in this passage is the extensive use of "examples." The author of the passage lists several writers whose books can be found on the shelves of a public library; the author also lists several library activities that might be undertaken by its patrons. (A) and (B) are wrong because the author of the passage neither provides "statistics" nor cites an "authority." As for (D), the author does not engage in any form of logical "deduction." Finally, (E) is wrong because the author does not actually quote from any of the sources that he or she gives as examples; in fact, the author provides no "quotations" at all.

10. **(C)** Use the "two-part answers" strategy, as each choice has two parts: the first word and the rest of the answer. (A) and (E) can be eliminated because "refutation" and "treatment" do not really describe the passage. Then (C) must be the right answer since the passage is a description of a biological process. The passage mentions the

concept "immune system," but it is primarily concerned with describing how the immune system works and not simply with defining the term.

11. **(C)** This is an Explicit Detail item. In the third paragraph, the author states that any substance capable of triggering an immune response is called an antigen, and gives some examples. The author adds that some "otherwise harmless" substances can trigger an immune reaction—things such as pollen or pet hair—and are called allergens.

12. **(E)** This is an Application question. The very basis of the immune system, according to the passage, is the ability to distinguish non-self from self cells. It is only when the body detects an outsider that the immune system is activated; presumably, without this ability, the system might attack the body itself. In any case, the result would be a real mess. So, the other choices, insofar as they suggest that some part or parts of the system might continue to work, have to be incorrect.

13. **(A)** Since the answer to this question is not specifically stated in the passage, it must be inferred. In the third paragraph, the author states that foreign tissue will trigger an immune reaction unless it comes from an identical twin. Couple this idea with information about self-markers. According to the footnote, the self-marker is a distinctive series of molecules that allow the cells of the immune system to distinguish cells that belong to the body from those that do not. Since an identical twin's tissue is not treated as foreign, you can infer that it must carry the same molecular markers as the body itself.

14. **(D)** (D) is the only answer choice that is not a true statement. (A), (B), (C), and (E) are all mentioned in lines 31-42.

    (A) Lines 35-37: "The two most important classes of lymphocytes are B cells…and T cells…."
    (B) Lines 36-38: "B cells…mature in the bone marrow, and T cells…migrate to the thymus.
    (C) Lines 31-37: "…[stem] cells are produced in the bone marrow…Some…develop into lymphocytes…lymphocytes are B cells…and T cells…."
    (E) Lines 39-42: "T cells directly attack…body cells….B cells, in contrast, work chiefly by secreting antibodies…."

15. **(C)** This is a Vocabulary item, and in the referenced line, the author explains that "humoral" immunity works by way of antibodies in the body's fluids. You know that (A) has to be incorrect since such a connection could not possibly be the key to this kind of question. And the other words have meanings that do not connect to the idea of the fluids and immunity.

16. **(D)** This is a Vocabulary item. The obvious meaning of cannibal is "eats humans," so (B) cannot be right. However, the idea of "eating" is half right; the phagocytes eat other cells.

17. **(C)** This is an Explicit Detail item. In the seventh paragraph, the author talks about the body's "astonishingly intricate defenses" and notes that the first line of defense is the body's armor, or skin and mucous membranes. The other mechanisms do not come into play until a microbe has managed to penetrate the first line of defense.

18. **(A)** According to lines 55-57, the nonspecific defenses attack infectious agents without regard to their antigenic peculiarities. That idea is almost enough to get the answer to this question. However, it is necessary to look back earlier in the passage to where the author discusses what gives an antigen its particular characteristics. In the third paragraph, the author explains that an antigen is what it is because of epitopes, intricate and characteristic shapes on the surface of the cell.

19. **(B)** The first sentence of the ninth paragraph states that the cellular immune response is started by a macrophage. The first sentence of the tenth paragraph states that a B cell eating some other cell starts not by a macrophage, but by the humoral immune response. Therefore, (A) is close but doesn't quite get it right. The correct answer is (B): Both processes begin with one cell gobbling up another.

20. **(E)** To answer this question, determine which answer is the exception by verifying which answers are true. Lines 69-75 specifically mention (A), (B), and (D) as functions of the T cells, and lines 94-96 mention (C). Thus, all of those choices are true. However, secreting antibodies (lines 85-87) is not a function of T cells. Therefore, (E) is not true and is the right answer.

21. **(D)** This is a Vocabulary item, so "musical," (C), cannot be the right substitute for "orchestrated." Instead, the author has been describing the incredibly complex interactions of the various cells of the immune system. Therefore, the best substitute is "coordinated."

22. **(C)** In lines 97-99, the author states that suppressor T cells end the body's immune reaction. Without the T cells, what would happen? Apparently, the immune reaction, with all the various cells doing their jobs, would just keep going on. Without the referee to blow the whistle to signal that the game is over, the process would not stop.

23. **(D)** In the first paragraph, the author poses the question: "Have you ever wondered why you become feverish when you are suffering from the flu?" Then, in the last paragraph, the author answers the question: "When viewed from a clinical perspective, this process [the reaction of the immune system] manifests itself in the three classic symptoms [of feverishness]." Now, it may seem as though the last paragraph does something else, such as conclude the essay. However, that is not an answer choice. Even if (D) is not really a good description, it is the best of the available answer choices.

24. **(B)** One of the most striking literary features of the passage is the author's extensive reliance on a metaphor of warring camps: The immune cells are the defenders and the infectious agents are the attackers; the body has defenses against the attackers; the immune cells are troops that are assembled to fight the aliens. The author clearly uses images such as troops and battle, *etc.*, so (B) is the best answer choice.

SECTION 8—MATHEMATICS (p. 779)

1. **(E)** The expression $2(p(q + r) + s)$ will be an even number regardless of the values of p, q, r, or s. But whether the whole expression is even depends on t. If t is even, then the whole expression is even; if t is odd, then the whole expression is odd.

2. **(B)** Use the formula for finding the area of a square: area = side • side. $s \cdot s = 9x^2 \Rightarrow s^2 = 9x^2 \Rightarrow s = \sqrt{9x^2} = 3x$. Or, you can assume some values. If $x = 1$, the area of the square is 9, and its side is 3. Substitute 1 for x in the choices. Both (B) and (E) yield the value 3. So, pick another number, say 3. If $x = 3$, the area of the square is 81, and its side is 9. Substitute 3 for x in both (B) and (E); only (B) yields the correct value 9.

3. **(D)** You can arrive at the correct answer in several ways. First, you can reason that if the product of three different integers is 0, one of the integers is 0. Of x and $-x$, one is positive and the other negative, so they cannot be 0. The missing number must be 0. You can also set up equations, but that seems unnecessarily complicated. You would be better off using a third method, just substituting some values for x. You'll find that the missing number must be 0.

4. **(C)** The diagonal of a square creates an isosceles right triangle. Use the Pythagorean Theorem, and let the length of each side be s: $s^2 + s^2 = (\sqrt{2})^2 \Rightarrow 2s^2 = 2 \Rightarrow s^2 = 1 \Rightarrow s = 1$. Since the side has a length of 1, the perimeter of the square is $4(1) = 4$.

5. **(C)** The sum of the lengths of any two sides of a triangle must be greater than the length of the third side. So, in this case, the third side must be greater than 7 but less than 15. The difference between 11 and 4 is 7, so 7 marks the limit of the shorter side of a triangle with sides of 11 and 4. But the side must be an integer, so the shortest possible side is 8. Conversely, the sum of 4 and 11 is 15. So, 15 marks the limit of the longer side. Since the longer side must have an integral value, its maximum length is 14.

6. **(C)** You might reason that the only permissible values for x are those which, when multiplied by 2 and subtracted from 19, yield a number that is divisible by 3. That's a lot of reasoning. Just test-the-test. Try (A). If x is 3, then $2x$ is 6, and $3y = 13$. But then y cannot be an integer, so (A) is wrong. The correct answer is (C). If x is 5, then $3y = 9$, and $y = 3$, an integer.

7. **(E)** The median is defined as the value of the center-most number, when arranged numerically. In this case, the numbers are already arranged numerically, and the median is the center number, 81.

8. **(E)** Since the expression is less than zero, either one or three of the factors must be negative. The inequality can be rewritten as $a^2b^2bc < 0$ (since $b^3 = b^2b$). Both $a^2 b^2$ are greater than 0. Therefore, $bc < 0$, and (C) must be true. Alternatively, reason as follows: a^2 cannot be negative, so either b^3 is negative, or c is negative, but not both. This means that either b or c is negative but not both, so, bc must be negative. You can eliminate (A), (B), (C), and (D) since they might be, but are not necessarily, true.

9. **(C)** Since this is an equilateral triangle, the sides are equal. Set up equations:

$$2x + 1 = 2x + y \Rightarrow y = 1$$

And

$$2x + y = y + 2$$

Since one of the sides is $y + 2$, stop after solving the first equation for y. The length of the side $= 1 + 2 = 3$. Then, since the three sides are equal in length, the perimeter is $3 \cdot 3 = 9$

10. **(C)** Do not be fooled by the answer "13": This is not a 5-12-13 right triangle. In that case, the side of length 12 would be the second longest leg, not the hypotenuse. You know that in a right triangle, $a^2 + b^2 = c^2$, in which c is the length of the hypotenuse. By plugging in the numbers that you have, you see that $5^2 + b^2 = 12^2$, or $25 + b^2 = 144$. Since $144 - 25 = 119$, b must be the square root of 119.

11. **(E)** First, find the value of y: $5y + 4y = 180 \Rightarrow 9y = 180 \Rightarrow y = 20$. Next, find the value of x: $4y + 2y + x = 180 \Rightarrow 6y + x = 180$. $6(20) + x = 180 \Rightarrow 120 + x = 180 \Rightarrow x = 60$.

12. **(B)** The trick here is to recognize that each of the marks between the numbered marks is $\frac{1}{5}$ of the distance between the numbered marks. The distance between each numbered mark is 0.1, so each of the others is worth $0.1 \div 5 = 0.02$. And, given that there are 8 marks between P and Q,

$$\overline{PQ} = 8(0.02) = 0.16.$$

13. **(A)** The perimeter is: $2(3a - 2) + 2(2a - 1) =$ $6a - 4 + 4a - 2 = 10a - 6$. Alternatively, assume a value for a. If $a = 2$, then the length of the figure is $3(2) - 2 = 4$, and the width of the figure is $2(2) - 1 = 3$. The perimeter would be: $4 + 4 + 3 + 3 = 14$. Thus, substituting 2 for a into the correct formula will return a value of 14.

14. **(B)** Use the technique for finding the missing elements of an average. The average of the five numbers is 51, so their sum is $5 \cdot 51 = 255$. The two known values total 114, so the remaining three numbers total $255 - 114 = 141$. Thus, the missing value is $141 \div 3 = 47$.

15. **(C)** x could be -1, 0, or 1.

16. **(E)** Do the operation indicated in the defined function: $(-1.1)^2 = 1.21$, and the smallest integer greater than that is 2.

SECTION 9—CRITICAL READING (p. 782)

1. **(B)** There are several ways of analyzing this item. First, the overall structure depends on a thought-extender. The second blank must explain the results or consequence of the first blank. Additionally, you can rely on key words such as "unjustly" and "libelous" to help you deduce that the action of the magazine was wrong. On this basis, eliminate (A) and (E); there is nothing wrong with praising or extolling. Eliminate (C) and (D) because they do not explain the natural consequences of the judge's ruling. (C), however, does the job. The judge ruled that the article had wrongly damaged the architect's reputation, so he or she ordered the magazine to make amends by retracting what it had printed.

2. **(C)** This sentence contains a coordinate conjunction thought-extender, "and." The blanks must explain why the operation was so "disorganized" (key word). Additionally, the two blanks describe the same kind of behavior and must be a parallel. Eliminate (A) and (B), because those word pairs are opposites, not parallels. Eliminate (D) and (E), since they do not supply the needed parallel; they are not related at all. (C) is the choice that supports the overall logical structure of the sentence while providing the parallel between the blanks.

3. **(A)** "Since" signals a thought-extender. The blanks must set up the explanation that is given in the part of the sentence following the comma. Why would the publication need to be "postponed" (key word), until further study? Something is missing—the two blanks together must provide it. (A) is the best choice.

4. **(E)** This entire sentence is a thought-reverser. The President responded with something other than "clarity and precision." You should immediately look for a pair of words that conveys a meaning that is opposite to "clarity and precision." In addition, the two words in the correct answer choice will be parallel as the coordinate conjunction "and" joins the two blanks. (E) does the job.

5. **(B)** The sentence contains a subordinate conjunction thought-reverser, "although," and a thought-extender. First, the reader's reaction to the novel is opposite to what would be expected if the book were not well-written. Also, you must extend the thought of the exciting story that the reader "could not put down" (key phrase). Eliminate (A), (D), and (E) because the reader would have put the book down had he or she been any of those things. (C) makes no sense at all, so you are left with (B), which completes the thought perfectly.

6. **(B)** This is an Implied Idea item. The passage doesn't specifically say that the young women are window-shopping, but you reach that conclusion by reading carefully. The young women are looking at very expensive merchandise through the shop windows. The passage does not say that the women actually buy anything, so you can infer that they are window-shopping. As for (A), the young women are not really planning anything specific; they are having fun. As for (C) and (D), the passage states that they have already eaten lunch. As for (E), while some people might exercise on their lunch breaks, these young women are digesting their lunches as they window-shop in expensive stores.

7. **(E)** This is a Vocabulary item. Since "smart" is a common word, you can pretty much bet that (A) is not the correct answer. Instead, "smart" in this context refers to the fancy stores with their expensive merchandise, so the best choice available is "stylish." As for (B), the stores are expensive, not inexpensive; and as for (D), they are elaborate and not simple. As for (C), the stores are busy, but "smart" in this context refers to the kind of merchandise that the store carries.

8. **(D)** This is a Vocabulary item, but notice that it also seems like an Implied Idea item. That is not surprising since a Vocabulary item is really a special kind of Implied Idea item: Can you figure out the meaning of the word based upon the context? The author of Passage 1 emphasizes dramatic and sudden forces as the agents of change. "Punctuated" is a word that is related to "punctual" and "point" and so conveys the idea of something that happens suddenly—starts and then stops. This definition is consistent with the author's idea of change as a series of sudden events. (A) is incorrect because the author of Passage 1 emphasizes sudden, not gradual, change. As for (B), while the events are powerful, they are not controllable. As for (C), though the whole story has perhaps not yet been told, there is nothing mysterious about it. As for (C), "concise" and "logical" just do not describe physical events.

9. **(C)** This is an Explicit Detail item that asks you to synthesize information from the two passages. Passage 1 argues that change is dramatic; Passage 2 argues that it is gradual; and (C) summarizes that difference. As for (A), the authors apparently agree on the observable features but disagree on how to explain them. As for (B), the authors may or may not agree entirely on the time that is involved, but they do not disagree about the length of historical time—though they do disagree about the events that fill up that time. As for (D) and (E), both apparently agree that geology and science are important.

10. **(B)** This is a Development item. The author is arguing that most of the stories in the newspaper are not really worth reading. He includes this report as an example to show just how silly some news coverage is. It is an odd occurrence that does not really affect the person who reads about it—except insofar as it functions as idle gossip. The other choices must be wrong because the event is not significant.

11. **(D)** This is a Development item, as signaled by the "in order to." In the second paragraph, the author of Passage 1 is making the point that the foreign news is not really news and mentions the examples of Spain, England, and France. He writes that it is possible just to toss in some generic information about Spain, and the resulting report will be accurate. (D) best summarizes how the author uses this example. The other choices are wrong because the author is not offering real news, only a parody of the news.

12. **(A)** This is a Voice item, and the whole point of Passage 1 is that the reports contained in the newspaper are really worthless, covering all kinds of events that ultimately have no significance. At key points in the passage, the author pokes fun at the news: People would come running in response to a fire alarm in the hope of seeing a good fire, even if it were the church that was burning. Since the author's attitude is negative, you can eliminate (B), (C), and (D). As for (E), while the author might caution readers against the news, his attitude toward the news itself is not mistrust or wariness but ridicule.

13. **(C)** This is a Vocabulary item, so you can be pretty sure that the correct answer is not going to be the most common meaning of "attend." As a result, (A) is wrong. In this context, "attend" means to "pay attention to," and (C) is a good match. The other choices do not fit the meaning of the sentence.

14. **(A)** This is a Voice item. The author says that people would respond to the fire alarm not because they want to help save property from destruction but because they want to watch a fire. The author adds that this is particularly true if the church itself is on fire. The author is adding emphasis to the point by saying that people would show up to watch their own church burn. As for (B), while it seems that these people might not care enough about property to put out the fire, this is not the point that the author wants to prove. He wants to prove that they would enjoy watching the church burn. (C) is wrong because the point is not that people are legitimately interested in local affairs but that in this case they are fascinated by something unusual. (D) has to be wrong because the point is that people are less interested in the church than in watching a fire. Finally, (E) is wide of the mark.

15. **(E)** This is an Explicit Detail item. The author states that the people on the island had continued to act as friends even though they were enemies (meaning that the countries from which they originally came were at war). (A) and (B) are ideas mentioned in the selection but do not respond to the question asked. (C) is not discussed in that paragraph, and (D) belongs to another part of the passage altogether.

16. **(B)** This is an Explicit Detail item. The "plight" that both the islanders and the residents of Europe shared was the delay in the news reporting. Though the delay may have been longer (in the case of the islander) or shorter (in the case of Europeans nearer to the events), there was a still a delay during which people were in the position of acting on outdated and wrong information. As for (A), the reporting was not wrong; it was just delayed. As for (C), even regular reports can be outdated. As for (D), the problem was not biased news but late news. As for (E), it was not partial information but lack of current information that was the problem.

17. **(A)** This is an Implied Idea item. In the final paragraph, the author states that from our perspective we can see that results were achieved even though people were working with outdated or wrong information. The author offers overseas exploration as an example; with the backing of the Spanish government, Columbus set sail for India only to land in what is now the Americas, and to be credited with a significant achievement. As for (B), while the Spanish government and Columbus worked with wrong information, this is not the author's point—the results are

what matters. As for (C) and (E), the author talks about hindsight and does not fault those who made errors because their information was limited. (D) represents a misunderstanding of the final paragraph.

18. **(A)** This is an Application item. The author of Passage 1 thinks that the news is only so much gossip. The author of Passage 2 thinks that news is important, even if it arrives a little late. As for (B), the author of Passage 1 does not really care whether news is accurate or not; it's just gossip. As for (C), again, the author of Passage 1 insists that the news has no value at all. As for (D), the author of Passage 2 really does not hold out much hope for the news, though author two might allow that faster reporting is better than slower reporting. As for (E), while it is true that Passage 1 mentions some local events, the author does not say that one type of event is more suitable for coverage than the other is. Similarly, while author two talks about international events, he does not say that reporting on international events is particularly suited to all newspapers.

19. **(A)** This is an Application item. We do not know what the authors would have said about the web because they obviously died before it was invented, but we can make a good guess. The author of Passage 1 would probably just say, "See I told you so, more and faster junk." (And you have to admit that there is some merit in that point; a lot of the stuff on the web is garbage.) Figure out author two is a little harder. The point of the second passage is that no matter how fast the news comes, there is always some delay between the event and the report, and during that time, we are operating on wrong information. That point is nicely summarized by the first sentence of paragraph three: how indirectly we know the environment. Thus, the second author would probably say that while the web closes the gap somewhat, it does not eliminate it. As for (B), there is no way that author one is going to buy into this point. As for (C), surely author two would allow that the web is faster and therefore at least a little better. In any event, author one is going to say that both sources are terrible. The same reasoning applies to (D) and (E).

SECTION 10—WRITING (p. 788)

1. **(B)** The underlined portion is not idiomatic. The correct expression is "so…as in…." Only (B) conforms to this: "so diligent as in the study…." (A), (C), (D), and (E) all use faulty expressions that do not represent standard English usage.

2. **(E)** The original sentence is incorrect because the modifier "that complained of its editorial policy" is too far removed from the word it modifies, "letters." As written, the sentence seems to imply that the newspaper complained of its editorial policy. (C) fails to eliminate this ambiguity. (B) introduces an error of subject-verb agreement. (D) eliminates the ambiguity but is needlessly wordy. The best choice is (E). (E) corrects the error of the original sentence and has two additional points in its favor. First, the thought is rendered directly with the active voice instead of indirectly with the passive voice. Second, (E) uses the noun "paper's" instead of the pronoun "its," which makes the sentence clearer.

3. **(E)** (A) is wrong because there is no noun to refer to "Americans." (B) corrects that error but introduces the non-idiomatic phrase "more then" instead of "more than." (C) combines the errors of the first two choices. (D) is hopelessly awkward and non-idiomatic. (E) is correct and precise.

4. **(E)** The original sentence contains two ambiguities. First, the placement of the modifier "only" implies that the only legal action that a physician can take is prescribing medicine, when the sentence really means to say that it is only physicians who can prescribe medicine. Second, placing the modifier "protecting the public" so close to *medicine* implies that the medicine, not the law, is intended to protect the public. Only (E) corrects both of these errors.

5. **(B)** The underlined portion contains three errors. First, the verb "makes" does not agree with its subject, which is "improvements." Second, "today" introduces a possible ambiguity, because its placement implies that the sentence is talking about data that is gathered on a particular day. In any event, "today" is superfluous. Third, the use of the infinitive "to forecast" is not idiomatic. Only (B) eliminates all three of the errors.

6. **(E)** The original sentence is wrong because it is a sentence fragment—there is no main verb. (B) is incorrect because there is no need to use the past tense. (C) commits the same error as (B) does and commits an additional

error by making "family" plural. (The resulting phrase is not logical because there is only one violin family.) (D) is wrong because it too is a fragment. (E) is the correct choice because it has a conjugated verb in the correct tense.

7. **(A)** The underlined portion is correct. The sentence maintains parallel structure and the subject agrees with the verb. (B) is incorrect for two reasons. First, (B) switches to the passive voice. As a result, (B) is not as concise as the underlined portion. Second, (B) changes the intended meaning of the original sentence. (C) and (D) are wrong because the resulting sentences would lack a parallel structure. (E) also introduces an error of parallelism and compounds the problem by using the future perfect tense.

8. **(D)** The original sentence is incorrect because the relative pronoun "which" lacks a clear referent. "Which" ought to refer to something like "eating," but there is no such noun in the sentence. (B) and (C) fail to correct this error. (D) and (E) both correct the error, but (E), by changing "enemies" to an adjective, creates a non-idiomatic expression. Additionally, (D) is better than the underlined portion because by using the noun "enemies" instead of the pronoun "their," it avoids a potential ambiguity. (Did the people hope to ingest their own courage or that of the enemy?)

9. **(B)** The use of "considering" in the underlined portion is not idiomatic. (B), (D), and (E) attempt to correct the error, but (D) and (E) make the intended meaning of the original sentence ambiguous. Neither the phrase "first professional American sculptor" nor the phrase "first American professional sculptor" makes clear which of the two elements, American or professional, the speaker considers more important.

10. **(A)** The underlined portion is correct. (B) fails to make a logical statement by omitting the conjunction "but," which shows the relationship between the clauses. (C) is wordy, the use of the word "also" is illogical, and (C) changes the intended meaning of the original sentence by introducing the word "more" ("more convincing"). (D) creates an illogical sentence. It is not clear what lacks the organizational skills, and the resulting sentence implies that it is the convincing argument that has organizational skills rather than the person who is making the argument. (E) is also illogical. It implies that it was because of organizational skills that there was no convincing argument. (A) makes it clear that the person doing the writing lacked organizational skills.

11. **(D)** The original sentence commits two errors. First, it sets up an illogical comparison between "countries" and "Americans." Second, the verb "is" fails to agree with its subject, "cards." (B) fails to correct the second error. Additionally, (B) is incorrect because "like" is non-idiomatic here and "that" doesn't refer to anything. (C) corrects the problem of agreement, but "as" is not idiomatic. (The "as" implies a similarity between two activities, but the sentence means to create a contrast between America, where credit cards are frequently used, and some other countries.) Finally, (E) implies that credit cards are used as cash more widely in America than in other countries, but the original sentence means to say that in America, credit cards are used more widely than cash.

12. **(D)** The underlined portion is incorrect because it includes an incomplete construction: "has always…to be feared." Also, the future perfect tense is inappropriate. (B) is incorrect because it has the same incomplete construction as the underlined portion does. (C) is wrong because it is awkward and not idiomatic. (E) changes the meaning of the original sentence: Leprosy is not continually being feared. (E) is also awkwardly worded. (D) is the best choice because the construction is complete and the verb tense is appropriate.

13. **(C)** The original sentence contains three errors. First, "on account of" is not acceptable in standard written English as a substitute for "because." Second, the verb "are" does not agree with the subject of the sentence, "delivery." Third, "this" does not have a clear referent.

14. **(C)** The underlined portion is incorrect because of a misplaced modifier. The sentence says that Dr. Martin "nearly spent" ten years doing something. This construction implies that he did not actually embark on the task. (Look closely at the difference between the statements "I nearly spent $10" and "I spent nearly $10.") The sentence means to say that he spent *nearly* ten years on the task. (B) is wrong because it changes the meaning of the sentence. Here, "nearly" refers to his task and not the length of time he took to accomplish it. (D) is incorrect because it is susceptible to misreading. (D) implies that the process of asphyxiation took almost ten years. Additionally, the placement of the phrase "nearly spending ten years" is awkward. Finally, (E) is wrong because it switches to the passive voice, and like the underlined portion, it implies that Dr. Martin did not actually begin the task. (C) is correct because it makes it clear that the doctor spent nearly ten years building the artificial wall.

PRACTICE TEST IV

SECTION 2—MATHEMATICS (p. 802)

1. E	4. E	7. C	10. 250	13. 20	16. 1/6
2. D	5. B	8. A	11. 60	14. 63	17. 240
3. E	6. C	9. 36	12. 0	15. 18	18. 125

SECTION 3—WRITING (p. 808)

1. D	6. A	11. A	16. C	21. E	26. C	31. A
2. A	7. E	12. D	17. D	22. D	27. A	32. D
3. C	8. B	13. B	18. B	23. C	28. C	33. C
4. A	9. A	14. E	19. D	24. E	29. B	34. C
5. D	10. C	15. C	20. A	25. A	30. A	35. A

SECTION 4—CRITICAL READING (p. 816)

1. B	4. A	7. A	10. B	13. C	16. A	19. D	22. C
2. E	5. C	8. D	11. D	14. B	17. C	20. B	23. B
3. D	6. C	9. B	12. B	15. A	18. E	21. A	24. A

SECTION 5—MATHEMATICS (p. 822)

1. B	4. D	7. D	10. B	13. E	16. A	19. B
2. A	5. E	8. D	11. C	14. C	17. D	20. A
3. C	6. E	9. A	12. B	15. C	18. D

SECTION 6—CRITICAL READING (p. 826)

1. A	4. C	7. C	10. E	13. B	16. C	19. A	22. E
2. D	5. B	8. C	11. A	14. D	17. B	20. E	23. B
3. A	6. C	9. A	12 E	15. A	18. E	21. B	24. C

SECTION 8—MATHEMATICS (p. 833)

1. E	3. E	5. B	7. E	9. D	11. B	13. A	15. E
2. D	4. A	6. C	8. D	10. E	12. D	14. E	16. E

SECTION 9—CRITICAL READING (p. 836)

1. A	4. B	7. C	10. B	13. B	16. B	19. A
2. B	5. B	8. B	11. B	14. C	17. C
3. E	6. B	9. A	12. D	15. B	18. D

SECTION 10—WRITING (p. 842)

1. C	3. B	5. D	7. A	9. E	11. E	13. C
2. E	4. C	6. C	8. A	10. C	12. E	14. B

SECTION 1—WRITING (p. 801)

Sample Essay 1—Below Average Response

I feel America continues to be a "Melting Pot" for immigrants coming to America. People come here with their own language and ideas. But they come here for the benefits of our country. They want free speech, and the choice of where they live and what they do in life. Sure some immigrants keep to their own stores and business services such as lawyers and doctors. And they watch television for news and events in their former countries. But most want what they came here for, a better life for them and their kids. You can see evidence of the "Melting Pot" idea versus the "Salad Bowl" in the schools and in the daily newspaper.

I have seen students from many backgrounds playing well on our schools athletic teams. Immigrant students I know work very hard to improve their language skills. We all listen to some of the same tunes, and like popular bands. Their parents get on them to study harder just as mine do. The common experience we share is trying to do OK in school and get out afterwards to succeed in America.

The community newspaper has ads for many of the businesses owned by recent immigrants. They have to compete hard against more traditional businesses to make money. So over time established businesses will have to appeal to the new immigrants, and the new immigrant businesses will have to appeal to more of us. Over time we will become more alike.

The "Melting Pot" will continue to simmer in America, and with time immigrants will adapt and become more like immigrants have in the past, that is "Americans."

Writing skill and position on issue:

The essay illustrates some developing skills. The writer's position is presented clearly but ineffectively. The introductory paragraph is not structured in any logical fashion; it rambles on about the reasons why people immigrate to America without relating these reasons to the topic of America as a "Melting Pot." Additionally, this paragraph raises the opposing point of view (America as a "Salad Bowl") without first establishing the writer's thesis statement. The opposing argument would be better positioned in one of the later body paragraphs, with an organized and structured refutation of every one of its points. An explication of the difference between a "Melting Pot" and a "Salad Bowl" would also be helpful in order to clarify the use of these metaphors.

Development of ideas and organization of essay:

The organization of the introduction lacks a clear structure. The introductory paragraph tries to address too many varied points when it should only introduce the topic and present the writer's position and thesis statement. Although the writer does present some interesting examples throughout the essay, these examples are not fully developed and supported. For example, the second paragraph does not explain how these certain common experiences lead to a "Melting Pot" society in which the constituents lose their cultural identity. The third paragraph is better at explaining this connection, but the paragraph would be improved if it made explicit the connection between becoming "more alike" and losing cultural identity.

Structure of essay, paragraphs, and transitions:

The writer simply and clearly sets up the structure of the essay. The essay is rather short, and could have been more effective with further expansion of some of the arguments. There is no use of transitions throughout the essay, and the third paragraph lacks a topic sentence. The concluding paragraph is brief, but the metaphor of the "Melting Pot" is nicely reinforced.

Language usage, sentence structure, and punctuation:

Low-level language usage and some language errors distract from the presentation. Starting a sentence with "Sure some immigrants…" is low-level usage. The term "OK" should not be used in an essay such as this one. There are minor punctuation errors.

Summary and conclusions:

Additional information on the ideas listed would more ably support the writer's position. The essay would likely receive a grade of below average to average (6 - 8).

Sample Essay 2—Above Average Response

Is the image of America as a "Melting Pot" false and outdated, or is it alive and vital? People of many cultures and backgrounds populated the country from the beginning. Thus, the term the great "Melting Pot" for America. I feel that the people who have arrived in recent years have not assimilated, and have made our country more of a "Salad Bowl." The separateness is especially seen in recent immigrant commercial and business areas, and in their media. Other major evidence of the "Salad Bowl" effect is seen in the public school system.

In our major cities, there are areas of services, restaurants, grocery stores and clubs completely oriented to particular immigrant populations and their language and customs. As these areas expand, the immigrants have little need to adapt their language or life activities to the larger "American" culture. This is in contrast to earlier immigrant influxes, where they were immersed in the life of the cities with varied cultures and interests.

Thousands of immigrants from a particular country have settled in some rural cities in the Midwest areas of the USA, such as where my Grandparents live. Here again their culture, language and traditions are imported with them, and they live in these small towns as separate islands. The public schools are especially challenged to educate in the face of varied language backgrounds, clothing requirements, and expectations of male/female differences.

The widespread availability of hundreds of channels of television on cable and satellite has increased the "Salad Bowl" effect. The major networks were watched by most Americans in the recent past, and this helped assimilate them into a set of common ideas and norms. With a channel for every major national group or language, the media can be viewed as encouraging the lack of assimilation.

A contrary view to the "Salad Bowl" idea can be expressed. The contention is that as the children of immigrants grow up in America, they will help bring their families and communities into the mainstream. This has occurred with many immigrant populations in the past, including the Irish, the Italians and people from the Middle East. However, I feel that the "Salad Bowl" prevails over the "Melting Pot" now because of the issues detailed above.

Writing skill and position on issue:

This essay shows good facility with written English and clear organization. The writer takes a clear stance on the topic with a strong thesis statement. The writer introduces the topic clearly and effectively, and each of the following paragraphs elaborates upon the writer's main points and builds on the idea of cultural separateness in America ("Salad Bowl").

Development of ideas and organization of essay:

A strong position on the issue is presented. Overall, the writer adheres to the organizational scheme that is introduced in the first paragraph. The only discrepancy occurs in the third and fourth paragraphs. In the thesis statement, the writer refers to the "media" before the "public school system"; and, in the body, he or she refers to the "public school system" in the third paragraph and the "media" in the fourth paragraph. However, this alteration does not detract from the overall development of the essay. In the last paragraph, the writer cleverly presents the opposing argument (America as a "Melting Pot"), only to explicitly refute its claims by referring to the points presented in the body paragraphs of the essay.

Structure of essay, paragraphs, and transitions:

The initial paragraph expresses strong ideas, and introduces the topics of the supporting paragraphs. The supporting paragraphs are appropriate, and each deals with an argument or position of the writer. The writer elaborates on the ideas presented but fails in most cases to provide specific examples. Such examples would make the argument more difficult to refute.

Language usage, sentence structure, and punctuation:

Sophisticated vocabulary (*e.g.*, "assimilated," "oriented," and "contention") and the effective use of metaphor (*e.g.*, "small towns as separate islands") strengthen the essay. Some lengthy sentences might slow the reader slightly, but they communicate the argument effectively. The few minor punctuation errors will not distract the reader from understanding the essay and are likely the result of the time restrictions placed on the writer.

Summary and conclusions:

The writer uses vivid examples that pertain to his or her position and to the subject matter in general. Personal experience and historical experience are both cited effectively. The essay would likely receive a grade of average to above average (10 - 12).

SECTION 2—MATHEMATICS (p. 802)

1. **(E)** One way of solving this problem is to reason abstractly about the properties of the terms used. A negative number cubed is negative, but squared it is positive. Thus, x is not less than 0. A positive fraction grows smaller each time it is multiplied by itself. For example: $\left(\frac{1}{2}\right)^2 = \frac{1}{4} \Rightarrow \left(\frac{1}{4}\right)^2 = \frac{1}{16}$. Thus, the fewer times it is multiplied by itself, the larger it is. Therefore, x cannot be a positive number less than 1. Finally, x cannot be 1, because $x^3 > x^2 \Rightarrow (1)^3 > (1)^2 \Rightarrow 1 > 1$, which is false. Only (E) remains.

2. **(D)** You can set up a system of equations to solve this problem:

   $T + H = 22;\ H + B = 17;\ B + T = 15$

   Using the first two equations:

   $$\begin{array}{r} T + H = 22 \\ -(H + B = 17) \\ \hline T - B = 5 \end{array}$$

   Couple the result with the third equation:

   $$\begin{array}{r} T - B = 5 \\ +(B + T = 15) \\ \hline 2T = 20 \end{array}$$

   $2T = 20 \Rightarrow T = 10$

   Since $T + H = 22\,T + H = 22$, and Tom is 10, Herb must be 12.

3. **(E)** Solve using absolute value conventions:

   $|x - 2| = 6$

   Either $x - 2 = 6$ or $x - 2 = -6$. So, $x = 8$ or $x - 2 = -4$.

   $|y + 8| = 10$

Either: $y + 8 = 10$ or $y + 8 = -10$. Thus, $y = 2$ or $y - 2 = -18$ So, since x and y are both negative, $x - y = -4 - (-18) = 14$.

4. **(E)** If n is the least of the three integers, then the other two can be represented as $n + 2$ and $n + 4$, so the sum of the three integers must be $n + (n + 2) + (n + 4) = 154 \Rightarrow 3n + 6 = 154$.

5. **(B)** The best way to solve the problem is just to test for the different values. The seven possibilities are 0, 2, 3, 4, 6, 8, and 12.

6. **(C)** Here we have another composite figure. The side of the square is also the radius of the circle. Since the square has an area of 2, its side is:

    $s \cdot s = 2 \Rightarrow s^2 = 2 \Rightarrow s = \sqrt{2}$. And $\sqrt{2}$ is the radius of the circle. So, the area of the circle is $\pi r^2 = \pi(\sqrt{2})^2 = 2\pi$.

7. **(C)** You can solve this problem mathematically by reasoning that the eligible integers must meet two requirements. They must be between 0 and 30, and they must equal 3 times an odd integer. So, the eligible numbers are 3 multiplied by the sequence of odd numbers, with the last eligible number being the one before the one which, when multiplied by 3, generates a product greater than 30. But why reason that way? Just start counting. The first such number is 3 (3 • 1). The next eligible number is 9 (3 • 3). The next is 15 (3 • 5). The next is 21 (3 • 7). And the last is 27 (3 • 9). So, there are 5 of them.

8. **(A)** The coordinates establish that this figure is a rectangle. The width of the rectangle is a, and the length is $b - a$. So, the area is $a(b - a)$. You can also assume values and get the same result. Assume that $a = 2$ and $b = 4$. The rectangle has a width of 2, a length of $4 - 2 = 2$, and an area of $2 \cdot 2 = 4$. Substitute 2 for a and 4 for b into the formulas in the answer choices and the correct formula will yield 4.

9. **(36)** Perform the indicated operations: $\sqrt{(43 - 7)(29 + 7)} = \sqrt{(36)(36)} = 36$

10. **(250)** Set up a direct proportion:

    $$\frac{\text{Cement } X}{\text{Cement } Y} = \frac{\text{Grit } X}{\text{Grit } Y}$$
    $$\frac{4}{50} = \frac{20}{x}$$

    Cross-multiply:

    $$4x = (20)(50)$$
    $$x = \frac{(20)(50)}{4} = 250$$

11. **(60)** Label the other two angles in the triangle:

    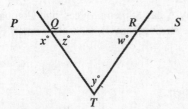

    $$x + z = 180$$
    $$120 + z = 180$$
    $$z = 60$$

Next: $z + w + y = 180$

And since $\overline{QT} = \overline{QR}$, $y = w$

So, $60 + y + y = 180$

$2y = 120$
$y = 60$

12. **(0)** You have only one equation but two variables, so you cannot solve for x and y individually. Instead, look for a way to rewrite the first equation to give you the information that you need:

$\frac{x}{y} = -1$

$x = -y$

$x + y = 0$

13. **(20)** Since $\overline{PQ} \parallel \overline{ST}$, the "big angle/little angle" theorem establishes that $x = y$. So, if we find the value of x, we have found the value of y.

$75 + 65 + x + x = 180$

$2x + 140 = 180$

$2x = 40$

$x = 20$

So, $y = 20$.

14. **(63)** Use the method for finding the missing element of an average. The smallest possible sum for six different positive integers is $1 + 2 + 3 + 4 + 5 + 6 = 21$. The sum of all 7 integers is $7 \cdot 12 = 84$. So, with the average of the 7 numbers still being 12, the largest the seventh number could be is $84 - 21 = 63$.

15. **(18)** This question is a little tricky, but it doesn't require any advanced mathematics. If the room were completely dark and you were in a hurry to make sure that you got at least one pair of each color, how many socks would you need to pull from the drawer? Well, what's the worst thing that might happen? You might pull all ten white socks on the first ten tries, then all six blue socks on the next six tries. So far, you have only white socks and blue socks, and you have pulled sixteen socks. Now, there is nothing left in the drawer but green socks. Two more picks and you'd have two green socks. So, on the worst assumption, eighteen picks will guarantee you a pair of each color.

16. **(1/6)** Time can be expressed as distance/rate. In this case, then, time $= \frac{10}{20} + \frac{10}{30} + \frac{10}{60}$. Giving the fractions a common denominator, you find that time $= \frac{3}{6} + \frac{2}{6} + \frac{1}{6}$, or $\frac{6}{6}$. She spent $\frac{1}{6}$ of $\frac{6}{6}$ time driving 60 miles per hour, so $\frac{1}{6}$ of her total driving time was spent at that rate.

17. **(240)** This is a simple problem with multiple steps. You know that Company A has 800 employees, and Company B has half that, or 400 employees. Of those at Company A, 50% are women. At Company B, 40% are women.

Company A: $0.50(800) = 400$ women
Company B: $0.40(400) = 160$ women
Company A has $400 - 160$ more women than Company B, or 240 more women.

18. **(125)** Use a direct proportion to solve:

$$\frac{2}{5} = \frac{50}{x}$$

Cross multiply: $2x = 250$

$x = 125$

SECTION 3—WRITING (p. 808)

1. **(D)** Since it is the general who was surprised by the enemy, "general" should be placed as close to the modifying phrase as possible. Since the modifying phrase is the introductory part of the sentence, this means making "general" the subject of the sentence.

   (A) The original sentence contains a misplaced modifier. As written, the sentence implies that the pursuit (not the general) was surprised by the enemy.
   (B) This choice fails to correct the placement of the modifier.
   (C) This choice not only fails to correct the error in the original sentence, but it introduces a new error. The use of "of" changes the meaning of the original sentence.
   (E) This choice not only fails to correct the error in the original sentence, but it introduces a gratuitous "then."

2. **(A)** The original is correct. In this context, "but" is the appropriate conjunction because it joins two verbs ("is" and "wins"), thereby creating the necessary contrasting structure (the school is *this* but does *that*). (B) and (C) are wrong because they incorrectly introduce subordinate conjunctions ("though" and "while," respectively). A subordinate conjunction is used to introduce a clause with a subject; however, the second clause in this sentence lacks a subject. (D) is wrong because "winning" is a participle that does not clearly modify a noun. Finally, (E) is wrong because it eliminates the verb in the second clause.

3. **(C)** The problem with the original is that it lacks a main verb. The relative pronoun "who" should be eliminated to fix the problem. (C) is the correct answer choice because it eliminates the relative pronoun. As a result, "is" becomes the main verb of the sentence, with "Rene Descartes" as its subject. (B) fails to solve the problem of the original, and it introduces a new problem; "as famous than" is not an idiomatic expression. Finally, (D) and (E) are wrong because they do not solve the problem of the original; in each case, the resulting sentence lacks a main verb.

4. **(A)** The original is correct. The phrase "at once" indicates that the findings simultaneously possess two qualities. In the underlined portion, the use of the conjunction "and" creates a structure that appropriately demonstrates this simultaneity (the findings provide something *and* pose something else). In addition, the verb "pose" correctly parallels the verb "provide." (B) is wrong because the conjunction "but" distorts the intended meaning of the original—that the findings simultaneously possess two qualities. Finally, (C), (D), and (E) are wrong because they destroy the parallelism between the two verbs.

5. **(D)** There are two problems with the original sentence. First, it suffers from a shifting point of view. The underlined portion is written from the 3rd person point of view ("one"). However, the second part of the sentence arbitrarily shifts to the 1st person point of view ("we"). Remember that point of view must always remain consistent. Second, the original suffers from a faulty comparison; it attempts to make a comparison between the number of SUVs sold and the actual concept of a compact car. However, the sentence intends to make a comparison between the number of SUVs sold and the number of compact cars sold. (D) is the only answer choice that corrects both of these problems. (B), (C), and (E) all fail to address the faulty comparison.

6. **(A)** "Her" is an objective case pronoun. It cannot function as the subject of a sentence. The sentence should read "She and...."

   (B) "The other" correctly and logically modifies "members."
   (C) "Spoke" is a logical verb tense in this context and indicates that the action is in the past.
   (D) "Their" correctly agrees with the plural subject.

7. **(E)** The sentence is correct as written.

    (A) The verb correctly indicates a past action.
    (B) The phrase "started...with a..." is an acceptable English idiom.
    (C) "That" is a correctly used relative pronoun that refers to "manifesto."
    (D) "As well as" is an acceptable English construction that is used to connect two ideas of equal importance.

8. **(B)** The verb "has been" is used when an action that started in the past continues into the present. But the action in the sentence is already completed and is entirely in the past. A correct sentence might use the verb "was" instead.

    (A) "There" is correctly used to connect "In America" with the rest of the sentence.
    (C) "To read" should be used here rather than any other noun form of the verb. It would be incorrect, for example, to use the construction "was very little reading."
    (D) "Except" is a logical choice of preposition for the content of the sentence.

9. **(A)** "Took" is the past tense of the verb "to take." The construction "having..." requires the past participle of the verb, having taken.

    (B) "Was" is a logical choice of verb tense to indicate that the action belongs to the past, and the verb correctly agrees with its subject, "she."
    (C) "Absolutely" correctly modifies the adjective "sure." It would be incorrect to use the adjective form "absolute sure."
    (D) "Would be admitted" is the correct choice of verb to show speculation or a contrary-to-fact condition. The verb "would" indicates that admission to the school either has not yet occurred or did not occur.

10. **(C)** "They" is a plural pronoun, but its antecedent is singular, "person." So, the correct choice of pronouns is "he," "she," or "he or she." Notice also that the verb "do" is underlined as well. This is because the verb must also be changed to conform to the correct choice of pronoun: "he or she does."

    (A) The "although" is a conjunction that is correctly used to join the subordinate idea that is expressed in the first clause with the more important idea that is expressed in the main clause.
    (B) "Watches" is a correct choice of verb. It agrees with its singular subject, "person," and its tense is consistent with the tenses of the other verbs in the sentence.
    (D) "Understand" is the correct form of the verb to complete construction the "do...understand."

11. **(A)** "Being that" is low-level usage and is not acceptable in standard written English. The sentence could be corrected by substituting "since" for "being that."

    (B) "Are" is a correctly used verb. Its tense is consistent with the tense of the other verbs in the sentence, and it agrees with its plural subject, "bears."
    (C) "Them" is a correctly used pronoun. It is the object of the verb *fear*, and it correctly agrees in number with its plural antecedent, "bears."
    (D) "Even though" is a conjunction that is correctly used to introduce an idea that is less important than the idea in the main clause.

12. **(D)** "Capable" is an adjective and cannot be used to modify the verb "played." The correct choice is the adverb *capably*.

    (A) "Mentioned" correctly describes an action that was completed in the past.
    (B) "That" is correctly used to introduce the noun clause that is the object of the verb "mentioned."
    (C) The use of "promising" to modify "talent" is idiomatic.

13. **(B)** The subject of the sentence is "point," not "remarks," so the verb should be singular, "was."

(A) "Coach's" is a possessive form of the noun "coach," which correctly modifies "remarks" to establish the source of the remarks.
(C) "To encourage" is the proper and idiomatic choice of verb form.
(D) "Its" is a possessive pronoun that modifies "spirit." The antecedent of "its" is "team," and "team" can be either singular or plural depending on the intent of the speaker. In this case, the speaker refers to the team as a whole, which is singular.

14. **(E)** The sentence is correct as written.

(A) The use of the present-tense verb, "deals," is consistent with the other verbs in the sentence, and the verb agrees with its subject, "professor."
(B) "Who" is the correct choice of pronouns to refer to people ("students"), and "are" correctly reflects the fact that "who" refers to a plural noun.
(C) "More severe" is the comparative form of "severe." And it is correct to use an adjective, because it is the pronoun "he" ("professor") that is modified.
(D) Again, "who" is the correct pronoun to refer to people. And "those" is a pronoun that can be used instead of the construction "those people."

15. **(C)** "Him" is an objective case pronoun. It cannot be used to modify the "-ing" form (gerund) of a verb. The correct choice of pronoun is "his."

(A) The verb *wrote* correctly describes action that was completed in the past. And it is consistent with the other verb in the sentence, "was shocked," which is also in the past.
(B) *Was shocked* is consistent with the other verb in the sentence. And "was" correctly agrees with its subject, "Emperor," which is singular.
(D) "In" is an acceptable choice of preposition for the sentence.

16. **(C)** The sentence has an inverted structure; that is, the subject follows the verb. The subject of the sentence is "opportunities," which is plural. The verb should be "exist."

(A) "For" is an acceptable choice of preposition.
(B) "To join" is the correct verb form. It would be incorrect to use the "-ing" form: "… ready in joining…."
(D) "Than existed" correctly sets up a comparison between two like situations: "than existed for her mother." ("Opportunities" is understood.)

17. **(D)** "Would of chosen" is low-level usage. The correct construction is "would have chosen."

(A) "Had known" correctly indicates an action that was completed in the past and placed in time before some other action ("would have chosen").
(B) "Difficult" is an adjective that is correctly used to modify "law school."
(C) "Would be" is a correct choice of verb to indicate that the difficulty did not become manifest until after the person was already in law school.

18. **(B)** There is no agreement between the subject, the object, and the object's pronoun; they should all be plural: "people," "umbrellas," "them." The sentence intends to refer to several people, each with an umbrella. As written, however, it implies that several people jointly possess a single umbrella. The sentence can be corrected by changing "an umbrella" to "umbrellas."

(A) The verb "required" correctly describes an action that was completed in the past.
(C) "Them" is a correctly chosen pronoun. It will agree with the corrected version of underlined part (B).
(D) "Entering" is correctly used as the object of the preposition "before."

19. **(D)** The pronoun "it" lacks a clear antecedent. It wants to refer to something like "movie-going," but there is no such expression in the sentence. The sentence can be corrected by replacing "it" with "are going to the movies less frequently."

 (A) "Used to go" is correctly used to show repeated past actions extending over a period of time.
 (B) "As often as" correctly sets up a comparison of the frequency of two actions.
 (C) "They can watch" is correct. "They" agrees in number with its antecedent, "Americans," and "can watch" provides the needed contrast between what used to be the case and what is now the case.

20. **(A)** "Get designed" is low-level usage. The sentence should read "are designed."

 (B) "Are" is the correct choice. Its tense conveys the idea that the problem described is ongoing, and it agrees in number with its subject, "corporations."
 (C) "More concerned" is the correct way to make a comparison here.
 (D) The comparison is correctly completed by "than": "…more concerned with this than that."

21. **(E)** The sentence is correct as written.

 (A) The verb "do not realize" is correctly used to describe a present and ongoing state of affairs, and it agrees in number with its plural subject, "people."
 (B) The use of the "-ing" form of the verb "to include" is idiomatic.
 (C) "Are" is consistent in tense with the other verb in the sentence (part A), and it correctly agrees with its subject, "wines."
 (D) "From" is the correct choice of prepositions here.

22. **(D)** "Amount" is the wrong choice of word in this context. When used correctly, it describes bulk quantities, like air, water, and sand, that are not measured out in units. Here, the correct word is "number," because each victim is a separate entity.

 (A) "Travel" is a noun with a meaning that is appropriate in this context.
 (B) "Less than" correctly sets up a comparison between those countries that have ideal conditions and those that do not.
 (C) "Increases" describes an action that is present and ongoing, and it agrees in number with the subject, "travel."

23. **(C)** "Him" is the wrong choice of pronoun. The construction "no greater…than" means "no greater…than he is." The "is" is understood, but the correct choice of pronouns is a subject pronoun. The sentence should read "than he."

 (A) The verb "claim" correctly describes action in the present, and it agrees with its subject, "fans."
 (B) "No greater" correctly sets up a comparison between one director and the other two directors.
 (D) The use of "would" correctly indicates a conditional event. The fans would, if given a chance, mention the names of the others. And the word "cite" is correctly chosen because it means "to mention."

24. **(E)** The sentence is correct as written.

 (A) The verb "have established" refers to action in the past, and "have correctly" agrees with its subject, "economists."
 (B) "Correlation" has an appropriate meaning in this context.
 (C) "Albeit" has an appropriate meaning in this context.
 (D) "Between" is a correct choice of preposition to show the needed connection.

25. **(A)** The word "other" implies more than one, so the singular "mammal" should be replaced with the plural "mammals."

 (B) The singular verb "does" agrees with the singular subject "platypus."

(C) The singular verb "reproduces" agrees with the singular subject "platypus."
(D) The gerund, or "-ing" form, is correctly used in this context to convey the sense of an ongoing action: "by laying."

26. **(C)** The original sentence is incorrect—the pronoun "them" does not have a clear antecedent. (C) corrects this error by clarifying who did the paying: "Before that, I was paid by neighbors for doing odd jobs such as mowing lawns and shoveling snow." Choices (B) and (E) fail to correct this error. (D) is not correct because "received pay by" is not idiomatic English (correct usage is "received pay from").

27. **(A)** This question asks you to combine two related sentences. Choice (A) is the correct answer: "The Burger Barn is a typical fast food restaurant, serving food such as hamburgers and french fries." Choices (B) and (E) are needlessly wordy and choices (C) and (D) change the intended meaning of the original sentences.

28. **(C)** The question asks you to replace "it" in sentence 6. Since the Burger Barn serves food and the "they" in sentence 6 refers to Burger Barn customers, the logical choice is (C), "food."

29. **(B)** The last paragraph of this essay gives several examples of rules that the Burger Barn employees must follow in order to ensure adequate amounts of safe food. Sentence 12 states "There must be so many orders of fries under the warming lamp and a certain number of burgers on the grill." Sentence 13 continues to give additional rules. Therefore, the best answer is choice (B): "In addition, paper products and condiments must be restocked every half hour...." None of the remaining choices are logical in the context of the paragraph.

30. **(A)** This question asks you to combine two related sentences. Sentences 14 and 15 represent a thought-reverser—while the "rules may seem silly" to outsiders, there are reasons for these rules. Choice (A) is the best answer: "To outsiders, these rules may seem silly, but they are necessary to make sure...."

31. **(A)** This questions asks you for the best revision of sentence 16. Choices (B) and (C) are nonsensical: Definitions are appropriate if they contribute to the essay's development and definitions need not be in quotation marks. Moving the sentence (choices (D) and (E)) does nothing to further the essay development. The best choice is (A), to delete the sentence, because it does not contribute to the development of the essay.

32. **(D)** In order for a sentence to be inserted, it must not only be generally relevant to the topic, but it needs to make sense when inserted at the particular point. In this case, the writer has started off by saying generally that lawyers get bad press and then has followed up with three specific examples. Therefore, a sentence that provides a transition would be appropriate, and (D) does this by introducing the three examples that follow. (A) introduces a topic that is out of place in the overall essay. (A) would be appropriate if the author were talking about education requirements, but it does not fit into the passage as written. (B) is somewhat like (D), but the point of the focus of the passage is not injuries but the behavior of lawyers. (C) is irrelevant to the topic of the passage, even though it mentions lawyers. As for (E), it is consistent with the idea of the passage (those horror stories are not necessarily true), but (E) doesn't fit in between (1) and (2).

33. **(C)** The question asks you to choose a word or phrase that will integrate the second paragraph into the overall development. Sentence 6 is intended to signal a shift from the discussion of the three initial examples, which seem outrageous, to a more careful examination of one of the examples to show that the case was not as crazy as it was reported to be. "However" is a good word to signal this shift. (A) and (D) don't signal a change of direction. (B) and (D) do not have appropriate meanings in this context.

34. **(C)** The third paragraph tells the story of the "peanut butter case." As written, sentences 10 and 11 are out of order. In the sequence of events, the commissary's failure to credit the account comes before its repeated refusal to fix the mistake. (C) makes the needed change. As for (E), the other sentences are presented in the right order. And as for (B) and (D), paragraph three properly hangs together as a paragraph because it discusses a single topic.

35. **(A)** Thus far, the author has shown that the crazy cases you hear about in the news may not be so crazy after all. At least, that's what the peanut butter case is supposed to show. And in paragraph four, the writer says that "this is true of most other cases as well." The writer needs to back up that claim, and a good approach would be to

explain how it is that the media manage to get this so wrong—as (A) suggests. (B) is incorrect because the legal arguments would be technical and beyond the scope of the essay. As for (C), the writer seems to think that inmates have some legal rights, as demonstrated by the peanut butter case. As for (D), the essay is going in the wrong direction for this choice. The writer doesn't want to discuss those cases where people made false claims but cases where legitimate claims were ridiculed by the press. Finally, as for (E), while the writer wants to show that lawyers have been given a bad rap (those silly cases really aren't so silly), (E) goes too far. Nothing in the passage suggests that the writer believes that everyone should go see a lawyer.

SECTION 4—CRITICAL READING (p. 816)

1. **(B)** The logical key to this question is a double reversal. "Although," a subordinate conjunction thought-reverser, seems to indicate that the positive overtones of the description in the first clause will contrast with those of the description in the second clause. However, the second clause contains the key phrase "little patience," which functions as a negative. This double reversal implies that the blanks will actually extend the thought that is expressed in the first clause. The first blank extends the concept of literature that instructs as well as entertains, so you should look for an adjective that describes this type of literature. All of the first choices might describe literature, so unless you know that "didactic" means "instructive," you have to look at the second blank. "Only" sets up a contrast between the second blank and the first. You are now looking for something that is more or less opposite to "instructive." Again, all of the second elements make some sense when substituted into the blanks, but only one reverses the idea of "instructive," and that is "distracted," meaning pleasure or entertainment.

2. **(E)** This question is basically a thought-extender, set up with "because." The blanks are further indications of the poet's restlessness and uneasiness in society. Also, the coordinate conjunction "and" indicates that the two blanks will parallel each other. You can eliminate (B) on the grounds of usage, because it makes no sense to say that someone seeks a claustrophobic existence. You can eliminate (C) because someone who is uneasy in society would hardly seek a life of urbanity. Although (A) and (D) create meaningful sentences, they do not extend the logic of the first part of the sentence. The poet would not seek a conservative nor a stable existence as a result of his restlessness, nor would he seek a life of pleasure or squalor as a result of his uneasiness in society. (E) is the only choice that logically completes the idea: The poet became nomadic because he felt restless in society.

3. **(D)** This question contains a thought-extender, the coordinate conjunction "and," and a thought-reverser, the subordinate conjunction "although." The first blank must parallel the idea that someone was the life of the party. We can immediately eliminate (A), because someone who is melancholy is not likely to be the life of a party. (B) makes no logical sense. You can eliminate (C) and (E) on the same grounds. This is largely a matter of vocabulary since you must know that "garrulous" means "talkative," "inimical" means "hostile," and *vitriolic* means *nasty*. Only (D) makes any sense. His wife must be the opposite of "the life of the party." The second element of (D), "taciturn," which means "silent," works very nicely.

4. **(A)** This sentence begins with a thought-extender and then reverses the idea. The first blank needs an adjective that is related to the key word "offhand" that could also be applied to "remarks." This becomes a vocabulary question because you must know the meanings of all five of the first elements. All five answers make some sense, so it is a matter of substituting each pair to make sure that the logic of the sentence is maintained. If you know what "flippant" means, you don't have to look any further. He was flippant, but this attitude masked a serious nature. This nicely maintains the logic of the sentence: "He seemed *x* but was really *y*."

5. **(C)** This question starts with a subordinate conjunction thought-reverser, "although." (A) does not reverse the idea. The same is true of (D) and (E). (B) and (C) remain possibilities, so test the second elements. The faculty might harbor her ideas, but they can't be doing it in defense of her seniority. That makes no sense. (C) works well. Because they respect her seniority, the faculty implements her ideas although they do not always agree with her. This makes a perfectly logical and idiomatic sentence.

6. **(C)** The "although," a subordinate conjunction thought-reverser, sets up a contrast between the idea of a promotion and the quality of the person's work: The work must be bad, even though the person was promoted.

Additionally, the two blanks must themselves be parallel since both describe the poor quality of the work and are connected with a coordinate conjunction thought-extender, "and."

7. **(A)** The blank is a thought-extender, indicated by "because," that explains the result of a controlled environment. The result of a controlled environment would be that you do not have to worry about the weather.

8. **(D)** The thought-reverser "not" introduces a contrast. The blank requires a word that means the opposite of a "festive mood" (key phrase). Also, the key adjective "oppressive" clues students to try "solemnity," which is a good fit.

9. **(B)** The logical structure of this sentence is defined by a thought-extender. The information that comes before the comma must explain why art magazines publish photos of stolen property. Additionally, the two blanks must create a parallel, because of the coordinate conjunction thought-extender, "and." Publishing the photos must do roughly the same thing for museums and "legitimate investors" (key phrase) that is done for stolen property. In this case, the result must be good. The museums and investors are protected and the stolen property is recovered.

10. **(B)** This question has the unmistakable identifying feature of a Main Idea question: "mainly concerned." If you summarize the development of the passage, the correct answer should be evident. (A) is too narrow because the modern Olympic games go back to the crown festivals—a different set of games than the Panathenaic games. (C) is too broad because the passage focuses almost exclusively on games, not on religious practices in general. (D) must be wrong since there is only a passing mention of democracy. Finally, (E) is incorrect since the discussion of art is incidental to the main topic: the development of the games.

11. **(D)** The word "mentioned" tags this as an Explicit Detail item, and it has a thought-reverser: NOT. Four of the five choices are mentioned in the selection. The one idea that is not mentioned is the right answer. (D) is the correct answer because the author does not mention this idea. In fact, the author says that the crown games were rural festivals. The other ideas are mentioned in the selection as characteristics of the crown games.

12. **(B)** This is a Voice item. The author says that the origin of the Panathenaia is "shrouded in mystery," so nothing is definite. But the author also says that the identification of the games with the prehistoric king Erichthonius is "perhaps" correct. (B) is the best description of this attitude.

13. **(C)** This is a Vocabulary item. And the reference to chariots and horse races makes it clear that "equestrian" must relate to horses. In fact, that is the primary definition of the word. When you have a word that is unusual, the correct answer is usually the primary meaning. It's only when the word is a common one that the Vocabulary-in-Context question refers to an uncommon meaning.

14. **(B)** This is an Explicit Detail item. Remember that these are the questions most like the ones you are usually asked on a test and that the correct answer is in the selection—or in this case, the correct answer is the only one out of the five choices that is NOT in the text. The author does not say that the Great Panathenaia inspired the modern games. Rather, the author says that the games at Olympia in honor of Zeus inspired the modern games.

15. **(A)** This is a Vocabulary item. "Amphorae" is an unusual word, so the correct answer will likely be the standard meaning, vase. If you knew in advance the meaning of amphora, then this was an easy question. Even if you did not know the meaning before reading the paragraph, you can infer the meaning from the context. The author is talking about vases filled with olive oil as prizes and refers to decorated amphorae filled with oil. So, you can infer that amphorae means vase.

16. **(A)** This is another Vocabulary item, and you may have seen the word "icon" before in connection with the graphical interface of a computer: click on the icon to do something. That is not the meaning intended here, but it is related. The iconic representations are stylized representations with features that enable the viewer to associate the icon with a concept, in this case, with the goddess Athena.

17. **(C)** This is an Application item. (The "probably agree" is the clue.) So, the question is: What would new evidence do to the author's analysis? Not much. Remember that the author draws a distinction between the rural, crown,

and Panathenaic games. One of the minor points in the analysis is that the rural games did not offer grand prizes. If it turned out that a couple did, that wouldn't really require a complete revision of the analysis.

18. **(E)** This is a Main Idea item. The first and last sentences of the selection effectively provide the answer that you are looking for. (A) is too narrowly drafted because the author discusses not just the containment issue (the second issue). (B) goes beyond the explicit scope of the selection because "competitiveness" is not mentioned. (C) likewise is wide of the mark. The author focuses on physical forces not energy efficiency. And finally, (D) is incorrect because the author does not suggest any new experiments.

19. **(D)** This is an Implied Idea item. In paragraph three, the author explains that the energy stored by a flywheel is a function of its weight and speed and that a lighter-weight flywheel would have to spin faster in order to store the same energy as a heavier one. So, you can infer that if the weights are different but the stored energy is the same, the lighter wheel is spinning faster—and that's choice (D). (A) is a confused reading of the first paragraph, and that information doesn't help answer the question that is asked. Similarly, (B) and (C) come out of paragraph two and aren't relevant here. Finally, (E) bears on the issue of safety, not on the physics by which energy is stored.

20. **(B)** This is an Application item. The author says that lighter weight flywheels cause less damage when they fail, but does not say that they are less likely to fail. In fact, in paragraph three the author talks of spinning a light-weight wheel until it "reaches the same internal tensile stresses" as the heavier one. At this point it is just as likely to break; the consequences are just not so horrendous. The author would probably agree with (A) since windmills are stationary. And the author would probably agree with (C) since the opening sentence says that EMBs would power an electric car. (D) is based upon the third paragraph. (E) finds adequate support in the first paragraph.

21. **(A)** This is a Vocabulary item. The author is discussing what happens when one of these rapidly spinning wheels breaks up. If it's made of heavy metal, the result is a lot of shrapnel flying everywhere. But if it's made of graphite fiber, then the result is a tangled bunch of threads—much less dangerous than the alternative.

22. **(C)** This is a Voice item. Remember that you can often arrange the attitudes on a scale form negative to positive. The author's attitude in this case is positive. So, you can eliminate every choice but (C).

23. **(B)** This is an Explicit Detail item, so the correct answer must satisfy two criteria: be explicitly stated (though perhaps not in the same words) in the passage and respond to the question that is asked. The answer to this question is specifically given in the second paragraph: The net effect is zero when they are spinning in opposite directions.

24. **(A)** This is a Development item. The author introduces the idea of EMBs for use in cars and describes generally how they would work. Then, in paragraph two, the author states that they pose "two special problems." The author describes those problems and explains how they are minimized by using different technological solutions.

SECTION 5—MATHEMATICS (p. 822)

1. **(B)** Perform the indicated operation: $5.75 - 4.5 = 1.25$.

2. **(A)** Translate the expression into "algebrese." The product of 4 times x is written as $4x$, and 3 less than that would be $4x - 3$.

3. **(C)** This question really just tests fractions. If $\frac{3}{4}$ of x is 36, then: $(\frac{3}{4})(x) = 36 \Rightarrow x = 36 (\frac{4}{3}) = 48$. And $\frac{1}{3}$ of 48 is 16.

4. **(D)** The measure of the unlabeled angle in the triangle on the top is 90°. The angle vertically opposite it in the triangle on the bottom is therefore also equal to 90°. Thus, $x + y + 90 = 180 \Rightarrow x + y = 90$.

5. **(E)** There are two ways to attack this question. One is to reason that:

(A) $2 + n$ cannot be a multiple of 3. Since n is a multiple of 3, when $2 + n$ is divided by 3, there will be a remainder of 2;
(B) $2 - n$ cannot be a multiple of 3 for the same reason that $2 + n$ cannot be a multiple of 3;
(C) $2n - 1$ cannot be a multiple of 3. Since n is a multiple of 3, $2n$ will also be a multiple of 3, and $2n - 1$ cannot be a multiple of 3;
(D) $2n + 1$ cannot be a multiple of 3 for the same reason that $2n - 1$ cannot be a multiple of 3; and finally,
(E) $2n + 3$ is a multiple of 3. $2n$ is a multiple of 3; 3 is a multiple of 3; so, $2n + 3$ is a multiple of 3.

You can reach the same conclusion just by substituting an assumed value that is a multiple of 3 into the choices. Assume that $n = 3$.

(A) $2 + n = 2 + 3 = 5$, not a multiple of 3.
(B) $2 - n = 2 - 3 = -1$, not a multiple of 3.
(C) $2n - 1 = 2(3) - 1 = 6 - 1 = 5$, not a multiple of 3.
(D) $2n + 1 = 2(3) + 1 = 6 + 1 = 7$, not a multiple of 3.
(E) $2n + 3 = 2(3) + 3 = 6 + 3 = 9$, a multiple of 3.

6. **(E)** Remember that a ratio is just another way of writing a fraction. So, just inspect each of the answer choices. As for (A), $(\frac{1}{5})^2$ is equal to $\frac{1}{25}$, and both 1 and 25 are whole numbers. As for (B), $\frac{1}{5}$ is the ratio of 1 to 5, so (B) is not the correct choice. As for (C), 0.20 is equal to $\frac{1}{5}$, the ratio of two whole numbers. And 5% can be written as $\frac{5}{100}$, or $\frac{1}{20}$. Finally, $\sqrt{5}$ is not a whole number, so the expression in (E) is not the ratio of two whole numbers.

7. **(D)** If you know the area of a square, you can find its perimeter, and vice versa.

Area = side • side
side • side = 16
$s^2 = 16 \Rightarrow s = 4$ (Remember, distances are always positive, never negative.)

So, the perimeter is equal to $4s$, or $4 • 4 = 16$.

8. **(D)** Here, you have one equation with two variables. It's not possible to solve for x or y individually, but you don't need to. Just rewrite the equation so that you have it in the form $x + y$. $12 + x = 36 - y \Rightarrow x + y = 36 - 12 = 24$.

9. **(A)** One way of analyzing this question is to reason that the square has four sides and each guard requires ten minutes to walk the distance of a side. In two hours, or 120 minutes, each guard will walk $120 \div 10 = 12$ sides. So, each guard will make three complete trips around the lot ($12 \div 4 = 3$), bringing each back to his or her original starting point. That's a big explanation for something that is not really that complicated. Why not just let your finger do the walking? Trace the route that each guard will follow. At 8:10, Jane is at point Q; at 8:20, she is at point R; at 8:30, she is at point S; and so on. Not very elegant, but effective.

10. **(B)** Again, here is a problem for which there is a standard math approach and a test prep approach. You can analyze the problem as follows. The sum of $3k$, $4k$, $5k$, $6k$, and $7k$ is $25k$, a number that will be divisible by 7 only if k is divisible by 7. If, however, the coefficient of k were divisible by 7, then that number would be divisible by 7 regardless of the value of k. It we drop the term $4k$ from the group, the sum of the remaining terms is $21k$. Since 21 is divisible by 7, $21k$ will be divisible by 7 regardless of the value of k. Now, the test prep approach assumes a value for k, say $k = 1$. Then, the total of the five terms is $3 + 4 + 5 + 6 + 7 = 25$. Getting rid of which one will yield a number divisible by 7? The answer is to get rid of the 4, because 21 is divisible by 7.

11. **(C)** It would be a mistake to try to convert each of these fractions to decimals to find the value that lies between $\frac{1}{3}$ and $\frac{3}{8}$. Instead, find an escape route. Use a benchmark, approximate, or do whatever else is available. First, eliminate (A), because $\frac{1}{2}$ is more than $\frac{3}{8}$. Next, eliminate (B). $\frac{3}{15}$ is equal to $\frac{1}{5}$, so $\frac{3}{16}$ is smaller than $\frac{1}{5}$ (a larger denominator makes for a smaller fraction, given the same numerator). (C) is close to and slightly less than $\frac{18}{48}$, which is $\frac{3}{8}$. So, (C) is the correct choice. But let's finish the line of reasoning. As for (D), $\frac{9}{24}$ is equal to $\frac{3}{8}$, not less than $\frac{3}{8}$. Finally, $\frac{5}{12}$ is equal to $\frac{10}{24}$, and $\frac{3}{8}$ is equal to $\frac{9}{24}$.

12. **(B)** By this point in your study, you should almost automatically factor the expression $x^2 - y^2$ into $(x+y)(x-y)$. Since $(x-y) = 3$, $(x+y)(3) = 3$, so $x + y = 1$.

13. **(E)** You can reason this out mathematically. As for (A), whether $n + 1$ is odd or even will depend on whether n is odd or even. The same is true for (B) and (C), because whether $3n$ is odd or even will depend on whether n is odd or even. As for (D), n^2 could be odd or even. If n^2 is even, then the expression $n^2 + 1$ is equal to an odd number. And if n^2 is odd, the expression is equal to an even number. Or, you can just assume some numbers.

14. **(C)** No figure is provided, so sketch one:

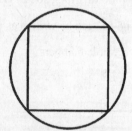

Since the square has an area of 16, it has a side of 4 and a diagonal $4\sqrt{2}$. The diagonal of the square is also the diameter of the circle. So, the circle has a diameter of $4\sqrt{2}$ and a radius of $2\sqrt{2}$. Finally, a circle with a radius of length $2\sqrt{2}$ has an area of $\pi(2\sqrt{2})^2 = \pi(8) = 8\pi$.

15. **(C)** We can use the overlapping circles diagram:

$$\text{Hats} = 18 \quad \text{Sweaters} = 24$$

$$18 - x \quad x \quad 24 - x$$

The twist here is that the diagram is not intended to represent all 36 people in the group. 6 of the 36 are wearing neither a hat nor a sweater. So, the total represented by the diagram is $36 - 6 = 30$.

$$18 - x + x + 24 - x = 30$$
$$-x + x - x + 18 + 24 = 30$$
$$-x + 42 = 30 \implies -x = -12 \implies x = 12.$$

16. **(A)** Just do the calculation. Since $|-3| = 3$:

$$|-3| \cdot |2| \cdot \left|\frac{1}{2}\right| + (-4) = 3 \cdot 2 \cdot \frac{1}{2} - 4 =$$

$3 - 4 = -1.$

17. **(D)** When $x = 1$, $x - 1 = 0$, so the entire expression is undefined. Similarly, when $x = -2$,

   $x + 2$ is 0, and the expression is undefined. When $x = -3$, then $x + 3$ is equal to 0, so the value of the expression is 0.

18. **(D)** Find the corresponding values for y:

   $y = |(-1)^2 - 3| = |1 - 3| = |-2| = 2$
   $y = |(0)^2 - 3| = |-3| = 3$
   $y = |(1)^2 - 3| = |1 - 3| = |-2| = 2$

   (D) is the correct plotting of the points (-1, 2),

   (0, 3), and (1, 2).

19. **(B)** We want to create an equation of the form

   $y = mx + b$, in which m is the slope of the line and b is the y-intercept. Begin by calculating the slope:
   $m = \frac{(-2) + (-4)}{(2) - (-1)} = \frac{-6}{3} = -2.$

   Therefore: $y = -2x + b$.

   Now use one of the pairs of coordinates provided in the graph:

   $4 = -2(-1) + b \Rightarrow 4 = 2 + b \Rightarrow b = 2.$

20. **(A)** To be a function, a relation can have only one output for each input. In other words, for all ordered pairs (x, y), for any value x there can be only one y. Inspecting the relation defined by the given set, either (0, 3) or (0, 5) must be eliminated to make the relation a function. Only (0, 3) is given as a possible answer.

SECTION 6—CRITICAL READING (p. 826)

1. **(A)** The sentence starts with a thought-reverser, "despite," so we know that the correct choice will describe something unexpected given the amount of money that is invested. The second blank will be a logical continuation of the first blank, as the verb "continues" indicates. (B), (C), and (E) can be eliminated immediately because they do not create meaningful phrases when substituted into the first blank. (A) and (D) are possibilities because a phone system can be both primitive and outdated. Next, we eliminate (D) because an outdated phone system would hardly elate those who depend on it. (A) creates a logical sentence: The system is primitive, despite the money spent on it, and it continues to inconvenience those who use it.

2. **(D)** This sentence starts with a thought-reverser, so we know that bats are going to be something that is the opposite of "aggressive" and "rabid." The blank would have to be filled with a word that parallels "shy," as indicated by the coordinate conjunction thought-extender, "and." We can eliminate (A), (B), and (C) because they are not things one would say about bats and are not opposites for "aggressive" and "rabid." We can also eliminate (E) because a bat would probably not be described as "depraved." (D), "innocuous," which means "harmless," is the opposite of "aggressive" and goes nicely with "shy."

3. **(A)** This is basically a vocabulary question. You need to know what noun means "the ability to do more than one thing well," as indicated by the key phrase, "both Classical and modern works." Only "versatility" completes the sentence. (B), (C), (D) and (E) create meaningless sentences.

4. **(C)** In this sentence, a thought-extender and a thought-reverser are the logical keys. The first blank needs a word that continues the idea of "vagueness," as indicated by the coordinate conjunction thought-extender, "and". The second blank is "unlike" the first and must therefore be something close to an opposite. Also, the second blank would be close to "bold" because of the coordinate conjunction thought-extender, "and." All of the choices make sense since they can all be used to describe images, but only one parallels "vague" and that is "obscure." The second element of (C), "concrete," is an opposite of "obscure" and completes the sentence nicely. The second elements of (A), (B), (D), and (E) are not things that could be said of images and make no sense when substituted in the sentence.

5. **(B)** This sentence contains both a thought-reverser and a thought-extender. The sentence says that the lawyer argues only what is central, eliminating something. Students should focus on the key word "eliminated" for the first blank. Logically, when something is eliminated, it is not central, so you should look for a word that means not central. (A) and (B) are both possibilities. Eliminate (C), (D), and (E) because they do not make sense in this context. The second element is the deciding factor here. The lawyer would not want to jeopardize her client, therefore (B) is the best answer. It makes no sense to say that the lawyer would not want to amuse her client.

6. **(C)** This item is a matter of vocabulary. By focusing on the second blank and the key word "collapse," it is clear that the only two possible answers are (C) or (D). We can eliminate (D) on the basis of usage because one does not diversify a house. The second element of (A) disqualifies that answer. A modern house would not look as if it were about to collapse. A house can be neither galling nor reserved, so that eliminates (B) and (E). Ramshackle, the second word of choice (C), means "broken down or about to collapse" and completes the sentence perfectly.

7. **(C)** This item contains a type of thought-reverser. Before looking at the choices, you already know that you need a word that describes something you can do with time so that it is not idle, which is reinforced by the extending nature of the semicolon. Eliminate all choices except (C) because they not only say nothing useful about time, but they create meaningless sentences.

8. **(C)** You cannot eliminate any of the choices on the grounds of usage, since each, when substituted into the sentence, will create a meaningful idiomatic phrase. The key to the sentence is the word "life." The field of study that completes the first blank must be a science that not only studies but directs the course of life, as indicated by the word "tamper." This eliminates (B), (D), and (E). Although one might say that psychology tampers with life, it makes no sense to say that the clergy oppose it and think that it is imperative. By the process of elimination, this leaves only (C).

9. **(A)** This is a Voice item. The words "unproved but likely" do not appear specifically in the passage, but you can infer that this is the author's attitude. The author says that it is "too soon" to say definitely that the theory is correct but adds that it "looks promising." (B) is incorrect because the author does not regard the theory as "doubtful." (C) overstates the case in the other direction: "promising" does not mean "conclusively demonstrated." (D) is simply a bad description of the passage: The author is not defining terms. (E) is incorrect because the author believes that there is evidence for the theory.

10. **(E)** This is a Development item. The author begins by citing one theory: The particles come from the initial explosion. Then, the author says this theory cannot be right: No, the particles would run out of energy. Finally, the author offers a different explanation: The particles are bounced around by fragments in the shockwave. (A) is a distracting answer choice because recognizes that the author seems to debate, but the author doesn't discuss pros and cons of an issue; the author compares two theories. (B) is incorrect because there is no logical deduction. (C) is incorrect because there is no sequence outlined. (D) is incorrect because there is no list of examples.

11. **(A)** This is an Implied Idea item. In the first two sentences, the author describes the appearance of chicory by comparing it to dandelions, but this assumes that the reader is familiar with the dandelion. As for (B), the fact that the plant was known in the Middle East does not mean that it originated there. In addition, the fact that there are Greek words in modern European languages doesn't mean that Greek is the main influence, so (C) is incorrect. As for (D), the fact that the Greeks knew of chicory does not mean that they brewed it nor that they knew it lacked caffeine. And finally, (E) at least has the merit of mentioning dandelions, but there is nothing in the passage to support the suggestion that dandelions do not grow on roadsides.

12. **(E)** This is an Explicit Detail item. The author states that the prairie seems lonelier than the forest because the lines of sight are longer, making it clear that there is no one else around. At least with the forest, according to the author, one can always imagine that just around the next group of trees there might be others; but on the prairie, one can see that there is no one else. (E) summarizes this notion. (A) is incorrect because the idea of getting lost is found in the comparison of the prairie to the ocean; this question is asking about the feeling of loneliness that is caused by the lack of other people. (B) is incorrect because the author never mentions any paths. (C) is incorrect because the comparison of ocean and prairie is not used to explain the feeling of loneliness. (D) has no support in the passage.

13. **(B)** This is an Application item. The author states that the census data are useful in identifying certain characteristics that seem to determine thinking about some political issues. It seems likely that the author would elaborate on this statement by discussing exactly how the data could be used: in choosing candidates or advising candidates in light of what the voters likely believe, (B). (A) is incorrect because the "ten years" is just a bit of background. The remainder of the passage does not refer to the frequency of the census. As for (C), while a political advisor might like to have more detailed data, no such proposal is suggested by the passage. It is not that (C) is impossible; rather, it is just that (B) is a much easier conclusion to reach. You should always prefer the easier or safer conclusion for a problem like this. (D) is incorrect because confidentiality is never mentioned. Finally, (E) is incorrect because it goes well beyond the passage. There is absolutely nothing to suggest that the author opposes the census. Again, (B) is a much easier conclusion to reach.

14. **(D)** This is a Development item. The author begins by saying that locks only keep out honest people and then goes on to talk about how easy it is to pick a lock. The last sentence then says, "See, it really is easy." So the last sentence is a summary of the development of the passage (the instructions on how to pick a lock), and this development shows that locks are not much use against anyone but an honest person. Since the last sentence ties the passage together in a consistent whole, (A), (C), and (E) have to be incorrect. (E) is incorrect because it just misses the point that the examples are supposed to prove: Crooks are not deterred by locks.

15. **(A)** This is a Main Idea item. The author begins by asking which of two models better describes the Constitution. The selection then examines both models. The author ends by creating an analogy between constitutional theory and physics that suggests that both models are useful. (A) provides the best description of this development. (B) is too narrow to be a correct description of the main idea of the selection. The author also criticizes the judiciary, and the main emphasis of the passage is theoretical. (C) is also too narrow. The author suggests obliquely that the Supreme Court has perhaps taken too much responsibility for evolving constitutional doctrine, but that is not the main point of the passage. Finally, (E) is surely wrong because the author is concerned about how to interpret the existing Constitution.

16. **(C)** This is a Development item. In the first paragraph, the author likens a certain view of the Constitution to dividing a pie between two siblings. The best description of this technique is "analogy."

17. **(B)** This is an Explicit Detail item. In the referenced lines, the author mentions a couple of ways to strengthen the ability of Congress to act, and one of these is getting better information. This change would presumably make Congress more efficient and therefore would not just increase the workload, so (D) is incorrect. Since the suggestion is aimed specifically at the legislature, (A), (C), and (E) are incorrect.

18. **(E)** This is a Voice item, and there are two very strong clues: "respected" and "unjudicial." According to the author, the Supreme Court overrode its most respected members and acted unjudicially. So, the author disapproves strongly of those decisions. Since the other choices are at worst neutral, all of the other choices are incorrect.

19. **(A)** This is a Voice item. In the third paragraph, the author notes that in a Newtonian model, extraordinary action may trigger excessive reaction. And the author uses the Court reorganization plan as an example. Since the plan was an excessive reaction, we know the author would condemn it. Further, the author uses terms such as "unjudicial" and "seriously threatened." (A) provides the best description of this attitude: The author understands why the President acted as he did but disagrees with the policy. The remaining choices are incorrect because the author thinks the policy was wrong.

20. **(E)** This is a Vocabulary item that works a little like a logical structure question since you are supposed to connect the word "Darwinian" back to something earlier in the passage. In the first sentence, the author distinguishes two views of the Constitution: mechanistic and organic. The discussion of the Newtonian view analyzes the Constitution in terms of mechanisms; *e.g.,* force, counterforce, *etc.* Then, paragraph four marks a shift: The Constitution is also Darwinian—this would be the organic view. The other choices must be incorrect because they don't preserve the parallelism: Newton:Darwin::mechanistic:organic.

21. **(B)** This is an Application item. In the third paragraph, the author states that a Newtonian system requires "constitutional morality" or restraint. He explains that a branch of government might well have the legal authority to do acts that would interfere with the proper functioning of government. Thus, the author would likely agree with statement (B). Conversely, the author would almost surely reject (A). In the final paragraph, the analogy between constitutional theory and physics implies that both models are useful—one has advantages that the other lacks and vice versa. (C) represents a misreading of the phrase "constitutional morality." The "morality" that is called for in the third paragraph is restraint, but not restraint from criticism. "Constitutional morality" is restraint from legal but counterproductive actions. (D) makes the same type of mistake that (B) makes. The author states that both models have their advantages and that both should be used. Finally, (E) directly contradicts by the first sentence of the final paragraph; the author states that it is unfortunate that the Court has had so much responsibility for the Darwinian model.

22. **(E)** In the final paragraph, having discussed the merits of the two models, the author draws an analogy between physics and constitutional theory. A physicist might, suggests the author, use either of two models to understand light depending on the need. With the analogy, the author implies that the same is true of constitutional theory. So, the author asks a question in the final sentence that he believes has already been answered. (A) is wrong because the author apparently believes the analogy disposes of the problem introduced in the first paragraph. (B) is wrong because the problem that is addressed by the selection was introduced in the first paragraph. (C) is wrong because the author regards both models as useful. And (D) is a description of some of the other paragraphs in the selection—but not of the final sentence.

23. **(B)** This is an Implied Idea item. In the second paragraph, the author suggests some things that the executive and legislative branches might do to make government better—things that are constitutionally permissible. Thus, we can infer that the branches of government may have more authority than they are using. (A) is incorrect because the author seems to regard all three branches as equally important. (That is part of the Newtonian model.) (C) is wrong because the only part of the passage that even hints that judges might be "insincere" is the discussion about the New Deal decisions—and that compares members of the same Court. (D) must be incorrect because the author implies that the constitutional process is sufficiently complex that it cannot be explained by a single model. Finally, our analysis of the correct choice shows that (E) is wrong; the author believes that governmental efficiency can be improved by taking constitutionally permissible action.

24. **(C)** This is a Main Idea item. Our analysis for the previous questions shows that the author's main purpose is to answer the questions posed at the beginning of the selection. As for (A), a dilemma occurs when a person finds herself in an "either/or" situation and neither alternative is particularly attractive. Here, rather than creating a dilemma, the author avoids one by arguing that it is not necessary to embrace one model to the exclusion of the other: You can use both models. As for (B), the author does not explicitly answer the question that is posed in the last sentence because it is rhetorical. This is not because the author wishes to evade the question; the author does not answer because he or she thinks that the answer is obvious. As for (D), the author discusses two different models, but does not examine points of inconsistency between them. Finally, as for (E), though the author does state that the Darwinian model talks of "process," it would be incorrect to say that the author is reporting on a development.

SECTION 8—MATHEMATICS (p. 833)

1. **(E)** Set up the cost of each fabric as a fraction and compare the fractions directly using a benchmark.

   (A) $\frac{8}{3}$

   (B) $\frac{6}{2} = 3$

   (C) $\frac{9}{4}$

   (D) $\frac{7}{5}$

   (E) $\frac{5}{6}$

   $\frac{5}{6}$, (E), is less than 1. The other fractions are greater than 1, so (E) is the smallest value.

2. **(D)** Obviously, you cannot do the calculation, so look for an escape route. Cancel and factor:

   $$\frac{10^3(10^5 + 10^5)}{10^4} = \frac{10^3[2(10^5)]}{10^4} = \frac{2(10^8)}{10^4} = 2(10^4)$$

3. **(E)** To find b in terms of x and y, you will first need to set b equal to x and equal to y:

   $x = b + 4 \qquad y = b - 3$
   $x - 4 = b \qquad y + 3 = b$

   Now, combine the two equations by adding:

   $b = x - 4$
   $+ (b = y + 3)$
   $\overline{\quad 2b = x + y - 1}$

   So, $b = \frac{(x + y - 1)}{2}$.

   You can arrive at the same conclusion by substituting some numbers. Let $b = 1$. Then, $x = 1 + 4 = 5$, and $y = 1 - 3 = -2$. Substitute 5 for x and -2 for y into the answer choices. The correct choice will yield the value 1.

4. **(A)** Since $z = 5x = 3y$, and x, y, and z are integers, z is a multiple of both 3 and 5, so z is evenly divisible by 5, 3, and 15. And z is divisible by both x and y individually, but z is not necessarily divisible by the product of x and y. Finally, since $5x = 3y$, and x and y are integers, x is a multiple of 3 (and evenly divisible by 3). You can reach the same conclusion by substituting some numbers. The most natural assumption is to let $z = 15$, so $x = 3$ and $y = 5$. But on that assumption, every answer choice is an integer. So, try the next multiple of 15. Let $z = 30$, so $x = 6$ and $y = 10$. Now, (A) is no longer an integer: $30 \div (6 \cdot 10) = \frac{1}{2}$.

5. **(B)** You can solve the problem by using the formula for finding the area of a rectangle:

   Area of rectangle = width • length

   $$48x^2 = w(24x) \Rightarrow w = \frac{48x^2}{24x} = 2x.$$

   You can reach the same conclusion by substituting numbers. Assume that $x = 2$. Then, the area of the rectangle is $48(2^2) = 48(4) = 192$, and the length is 48. So, 48 times the width is equal to 192, and the width is $192 \div 48 = 4$. So, if $x = 2$, the correct choice will yield the value 4. Only choice (B) works.

6. **(C)** You can deduce the value for x in the following way. The length of the base of the triangle is $4x - x = 3x$, and the length of the altitude is $3x - 0 = 3x$ (the difference between the y coordinates). Now, use the formula for finding the area of a triangle:

$$\frac{1}{2}(3x)(3x) = 54 \implies (3x)(3x) = 108$$
$$9x^2 = 108 \implies x^2 = 12$$
$$x = \sqrt{12} = 2\sqrt{3} \quad (x \text{ is a distance, so } x \text{ must be positive.})$$

7. **(E)** Rewrite the equation: $x = \frac{1}{y+1} \implies x(y+1) = 1 \implies y+1 = \frac{1}{x} \implies y = \frac{1}{x} - 1 \implies y = \frac{1-x}{x}$ You can arrive at the same conclusion by assuming some numbers. Assume that $y = 1$. On that assumption, $x = \frac{1}{2}$. Then, substitute $\frac{1}{2}$ for x in the formulas in the answer choices; the correct choice will yield the value 1.

8. **(D)** Here we have a defined function. First, do ▲ to 3 and ▼ to 5:

$$\blacktriangle(3) = 3 + 1 = 4$$
$$\blacktriangledown(5) = 5 - 1 = 4$$

So, $\blacktriangle(3) \cdot \blacktriangledown(4) = 16$. Now, test-the-test. Work backwards from the choices:

(A) $\blacktriangle(8) = 8 + 1 = 9$ (Wrong)
(B) $\blacktriangle(12) = 12 + 1 = 13$ (Wrong)
(C) $\blacktriangle(14) = 14 + 1 = 15$ (Wrong)
(D) $\blacktriangledown(17) = 17 - 1 = 16$ (Correct)
(E) $\blacktriangledown(20) = 20 - 1 = 19$ (Wrong)

9. **(D)** You may be able to figure this out without doing any arithmetic by thinking $\frac{1}{2}x + \frac{1}{2}y = \frac{1}{2}(14)$. Another easy way is to try any numbers that fit in place of x and y.

$$4 + 10 = 14 \qquad \frac{1}{2}(4) + \frac{1}{2}(10) = 7$$

$$6 + 8 = 14 \qquad \frac{1}{2}(6) + \frac{1}{2}(8) = 7$$

10. **(E)** If the average of ten numbers is 6, then the total of the numbers must be 60 since $60 \div 10 = 6$.

$$1 + 2 + 3 + 4 + 5 + 6 + 7 + 8 + 9 = 45$$
$$60 - 45 = 15, \text{ so } x \text{ must be equal to } 15.$$

11. **(B)** Use the "*is*-over-*of*" formula. The "*of* that," that forms the denominator of the fraction, is the mixture. How much of the mixture is there? $2.5 + 12.5 = 15$. So, 15 is the denominator of the fraction, and the other number in the problem ("*is* this") is the numerator: $\frac{2.5}{15} = \frac{1}{6}$. And $\frac{1}{6}$ is one of the common fraction/decimal equivalents that you were encouraged to memorize. Don't divide; just convert by memory: $\frac{1}{6} = 0.1666 = 16\frac{2}{3}\%$

12. **(D)** Complete the sketch:

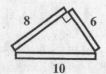

The triangle has sides of 6, 8, and 10, which you should recognize as multiples of 3, 4, and 5. So, the triangle is a right triangle. The sides of 6 and 8 form the right angle, so they can be used as altitude and base for finding the area:

$$\text{Area} = \frac{1}{2} \cdot \text{altitude} \cdot \text{base} = \frac{1}{2} \cdot 6 \cdot 8 = 24$$

13. **(A)** Proportions make this calculation easy. First, do the calculation for Motorcycle X.

$$\frac{\text{Fuel Used } X}{\text{Fuel Used } Y} = \frac{\text{Miles Driven } X}{\text{Miles Driven } Y}$$

(The X and Y here refer to the two different situations, not the motorcycles.)

$\frac{1}{x} = \frac{40}{300}$. Cross-multiply and solve for x:

$$300 = 40x \Rightarrow 40x = 300 \Rightarrow x = 7.5$$

So, Motorcycle X uses 7.5 liters of fuel for the 300-mile trip. Now, do the same for Motorcycle Y: $\frac{1}{x} = \frac{50}{300} \Rightarrow 300$ $= 50x \Rightarrow 50x = 300 \Rightarrow x = 6$. So, Motorcycle Y uses 6 liters of fuel for the trip. Since Motorcycle X uses $7.5 - 6$ $= 1.5$ liters more than Motorcycle Y, the fuel for Motorcycle X costs $1.5 \cdot \$2 = \$3$ more.

14. **(E)** Here, we have a defined function problem. Just do the indicated operations.

$$\boxed{2} = \frac{2}{2} = 1$$

$\boxed{7} = 7 + 1 = 8$, and $1 \cdot 8 = 8$.

15. **(E)** You can factor $6k + 3$: $6k + 3 = 3(2k + 1)$, which is choice (E). If you miss that insight, you can assume some numbers to substitute into the choices. Assume that $k = 1$. Then, $6k + 3 = 6(1) + 3 = 6 + 3 = 9$. Now, substitute 1 for k into the choices. The correct one will yield the value 9.

16. **(E)** You can devise the formula as follows. The formula will be x, the cost for the first ounce, plus some expression to represent the additional postage for weight over x ounces. The postage for the additional weight is y cents per ounce, and the additional weight is w minus the first ounce, or $w - 1$. So, the additional postage is $y(w - 1)$, and the total postage is $x + y(w - 1)$. You can reach the same conclusion by assuming some numbers to be substituted into the answer choices. Make the ridiculous assumption that the first ounce costs 1 cent and every additional ounce is free. If $x = 1$ and $y = 0$, then a letter of 10 ounces ($w = 10$) will cost 1 cent. Substitute 1 for x, 0 for y, and 10 for w into the choices. The correct formula will generate the value 1. Even on these silly assumptions, you can eliminate every choice but (D) and (E). Make another set of assumptions, and you'll have the correct answer.

SECTION 9—CRITICAL READING (p. 836)

1. **(A)** The logical structure of this sentence provides two context clues. First, the "*not this but that*" structure in the first part of the sentence indicates that the blank must be filled in with a word that means the opposite of "liberate." So, (C), (D), and (E) can safely be eliminated. Second, the clause that follows the comma is a further explanation of the missing word, so the blank must be filled in with a word that has the same meaning as "hold captive." (B) is wrong because it is a "distractor" answer choice; you should not confuse "hold captive" with "captivate," and you should also recognize that "attract" does not mean the opposite of "liberate." Therefore, (A) is the correct answer choice.

2. **(B)** This Sentence Completions item primarily focuses on vocabulary. The clause that follows the comma is a further explanation of the missing word, so the blank must be filled in with a word that describes speed and efficiency. (B) is the only answer choice that satisfies this meaning; "alacrity" means "speed, or quickness."

3. **(E)** This is a straightforward vocabulary question. The word substituted in the blank must continue the idea of "lazy," as indicated by the thought-extender, "because." In fact, since the blank refers to "lazy," the substituted word will be a synonym. Only (E), which means "slothfulness" or "laziness," does the job.

4. **(B)** As with the previous item, this item is also primarily a vocabulary question. The colon signals that the second clause extends the thought in the first clause. You can eliminate (A), (C), (D), and (E) because they are not things that could be said of images and therefore fail on the grounds of usage. This leaves you with the correct answer, (B). A montage is a series of rapid images in film.

5. **(B)** The thought-reverser word "though" sets up a contrast. The concert was enjoyable, but it suffers from some defect. Eliminate (D) since to be sublime is not to have a defect. Additionally, the two blanks themselves are parallel since they complete similar thoughts and are joined by "and," a coordinate conjunction thought-extender. (A) and (E) contain words that are opposite in meaning, so they must be wrong. Finally, the words in (C) are unrelated, so they cannot provide the needed contrast.

6. **(B)** This is a Vocabulary item, so you should stay away from the most common meanings of the word such as those suggested by (A) and (C). A good clue to the author's use is "reverence" (line 7), and in fact, the word means aw-ful or full of awe. (D) and (E) are ideas found in the passage but not in connection with "awful."

7. **(C)** This is an Explicit Detail item, and the only mention of anything amusing is the reference to the observation that the bones of famous and powerful people are jammed together into small corners and plots—as (C) indicates. As for (A), while you might find this fact amusing, the author does not say that he finds it amusing, so (A) cannot be the answer to this Explicit Detail question. (B), (D), and (E) seem to be true, according to the author, but these ideas do not respond to the question that is asked.

8. **(B)** This is an Explicit Detail item, and the author explicitly says the reason that pre-fabricated building did not succeed was opposition by carpenters, builders, and architects, (B). As for (A), the author mentions that the components had to be shipped to building sites but does not indicate that the cost was prohibitive. As for (C), the author seems to think that there were quite a few uses for the units. (D) must be incorrect since railroads and the army, both large organizations, bought such units. Finally, the author does not mention (E).

9. **(A)** This is a Vocabulary item, and as a matter of test-taking strategy you should be ready to eliminate any choices that have overly negative overtones, so eliminate (D) and (E). The correct choice is (A). The organizing principle of the passage is the division between the two philosophies: humanitarianism and laissez-faire economics. These philosophies are built on different assumptions and reach drastically different conclusions. Hence, they are incompatible with each other. As for "abstract" and "formal," philosophy can be both of those things, but that is not the meaning of "antagonistic" in this context.

10. **(B)** This is an Explicit Detail item. In the last paragraph, and the last sentence in particular, the author of the first passage states that the interdisciplinary approach used by Turner was a new technique. (B) best captures this idea. As for (A), the same paragraph states specifically that the reliance on political history was characteristic of history prior to Turner. As for (C), although Turner made the original presentation at a conference, the passage does not say that presenting was a technique of study. It just happens that Turner used the opportunity to present his new theory, but Turner could equally well have published an article or made an informal presentation to colleagues. As for (D), the first passage doesn't enter into such a debate, though you will find some mention of this in the second passage. But because the information appears in the second passage, it cannot be an answer to this Explicit Detail item about the first passage. Finally, as for (E), while Turner did use statistics from the Census, the author does not say that Turner insisted that everything be supported by statistics.

11. **(B)** This is an Implied Idea item. The first passage notes even some students of Turner demonstrated that some of his points were wrong. There would have been no reason to use the "even" unless one would ordinarily expect for

students to support the work of a professor. And in the development of the passage, the author is pointing out that even though Turner's thesis was criticized by some scholars who might otherwise have been supporters, the thesis still remains important. As for (A), the passage implies that the students did scholarly work on the thesis, not that they were ignorant of it. As for (C), the passage actually implies that students are likely to embrace the work of a professor. As for (D), there is no support for this conclusion in the text. (E) is wrong because there is nothing to support such a conclusion. While students might be inclined to embrace the work of a professor, that is not equivalent to accepting a new theory just because it is new.

12. **(D)** The author of Passage 1 evidently approves of Turner's work. The passage says that it had great influence, that it was original, and that it used a novel approach. That's pretty good review. As for (A), while the author allows that Turner's thesis was not immune to debate or even criticism, this does not mean that the author was "suspicious" of the work itself. After all, it could turn out to be that Turner's conclusions are ultimately false; but the groundbreaking approach and radical theory would still have value. As for (B), the thesis is not treated negatively. (E) is wrong for the same reason that (B) is wrong. Finally, as for (C), the author takes a pretty strong position, so "undecided" is not a good description.

13. **(B)** This is a Vocabulary item. Because "grand" is a word with some common meanings, you can pretty much discount any choices that use these more common synonyms. That would certainly eliminate (C) and (E). Instead, the author is using the word "grand" in a derivative sense to mean large or great or overall. Turner's thesis did try to be comprehensive, accounting for the uniquely American character. As for (A), though the author allows that Turner's thesis was not perfect, line 15 is not where that discussion occurs. And (D) must be wrong since Turner's thesis was not tentative.

14. **(C)** This is a Development item. The author of Passage 2 discusses the limitations of Turner's theory, and one of the most important of these is its attempt to explain everything American in terms of the frontier. At the referenced lines, the author lists some other very important historical factors in order to show that the frontier could not have been the entire story. As for (A), this is the topic introduced at the end of that paragraph and developed in the following paragraphs, but it is not an answer to this question. As for (B), even granting that this statement is correct, it is not an answer to this question. For example, the author mentions the Civil War in order to show that Turner's thesis was too limited, not that traditional histories were too limited. As for (D), this is a point that is raised in paragraph five, so it is not an answer to the question asked about paragraph three. As for (E), while this statement is true (Westward expansion lasted for years during which time other important events took place.), it doesn't give the reason that the author has in mind. The author doesn't intend to show that these events occurred but that the events were important.

15. **(B)** This is a Development item. At the end of paragraph three, the author of Passage 2 states that Turner's thesis, in addition to failing as a comprehensive theory of American history, does not do an adequate job of explaining the frontier. The next three paragraphs are the specific points to support this argument: (i) land wasn't free, (ii) frontier is a dubious concept, and (iii) groups as well as individuals were important. The information about wagon trains supports this last point: It was groups, not loners, who moved into the westward regions and stayed. As for (A), (C), (D), and (E), these are ideas that are mentioned here and there, but they do not explain the significance of the wagon trains.

16. **(B)** This is a Voice item. The author of Passage 2 is critical of the frontier thesis, but you'll notice that the criticisms all deal with Turner's ideas. For example, Turner thought that the frontier offered free land, but the author of Passage 2 argues that he was wrong because the land was already used by indigenous peoples. So, while the passage criticizes Turner's idea, it doesn't criticize Turner himself. Thus, (C), (D), and (E) are wrong and (B) is correct. As for (A), the author says that the thesis has "rightfully" been abandoned because of its weaknesses.

17. **(C)** This is a Vocabulary item. You get the information you need to answer the question from the discussion about the significance of the Indian Wars. Turner claimed that the land was free, but in reality, it was necessary to pursue a policy of military aggression to secure the land. So, when the author writes that the wars "belie" the free land theory, the author means "give the lie to" or "prove false." (A) is a distracting choice, but don't be mislead by the superficial connection between "lie" and "untruth." In this context, the phrase is "give the lie to," not "lie

about." As for (B), (C), and (E), while these are phrases that relate generally to the idea of debating the merits of a theory, they don't focus on the connection between the wars and the free land thesis.

18. **(D)** This is an Explicit Detail item. If you review the texts, you find that both authors mention (A), (B), (C), and (E). However, you'll find reference to "nationalism" only in the first passage.

19. **(A)** This is an Application item. To a certain extent, any weakening of Turner's theory would have implications for all aspects of the theory. So, you might argue that the referenced evidence, in some way, tends to show that people from different regions did not mix at the frontier because the frontier was not quite as well-defined as Turner thought. But that's a pretty feeble point, and so (D) is wrong. You can apply similar reasoning to (B), (C), and (E). The best answer here is (A). The "safety valve" point, as explained in Passage 1, maintained that people who were dissatisfied with life in the urban areas could simply pack up and move to the country because there was land for the claiming. If the "free land" thesis is false, then the "safety valve" thesis must also be false.

SECTION 10—WRITING (p. 842)

1. **(C)** This choice corrects the errors in the original sentence. It places both verbs in the past, a change which conforms the verbs to the logic of the sentence.

(A) The underlined portion is characterized by an illogical choice of verbs. "Depict," which shows present action, clashes with "romanticized," which shows past action.
(B) This choice introduces a new error. "Was" does not agree with the subject, "paintings." And in any event, the choice of verb tense is not improved. "Was depicting" shows an ongoing action in the past, a verb tense which is not appropriate here.
(D) This choice does not reflect the logic of the sentence. The act of painting by the artist accomplished both a depiction and a romanticization at the same time. The choice of tenses here suggests that the effects were separate in time.
(E) This choice is almost correct. It is possible to use present-tense verbs here because the paintings still exist and continue to depict the American West. But the verbs do not agree with their subject.

2. **(E)** This choice provides the needed parallelism. Three verbs follow the subject "you": "must have," "be," and "have."

(A) The original sentence is characterized by a lack of parallelism. The elements in the series "knowledge," "be aggressive," and "also the will" must have parallel forms.
(B) This choice does not correct the faulty parallelism and introduces the additional error of shifting subjects ("One…you.").
(C) This choice does not correct the faulty parallelism. "Be aggressive" is a verb, but the other two similar elements are nouns ("knowledge" and "willingness").
(D) "To have" is not parallel with "being" and "knowing."

3. **(B)** This choice uses the correct construction "more…than."

(A) The construction "more…rather than" is not idiomatic.
(C) This choice makes an error in logic. The construction "more…and not by" is illogical. The "more" shows that something has what the other thing has, just more so. But the "not" indicates that something completely lacks what the other thing has.
(D) This choice makes two errors. First, it makes the same kind of logical mistake that (C) makes. Additionally, the phrase "is being developed" changes the logic of the sentence. As changed, the sentence seems to describe the development of a single child.
(E) This choice also changes the meaning of the sentence. The original sentence (which uses the passive voice) states that the child's personality is being acted upon by outside forces. This choice makes the child's personality the source of the action.

4. **(C)** This choice solves the problem of the misplaced modifier and clearly renders the meaning of the sentence.

(A) The original sentence commits the error of the misplaced or dangling modifier. As written, the sentence implies that the writings (of Poe) have the bad habit.
(B) This choice avoids the problem of the misplaced modifier but introduces two new errors. First, the construction "Poe's being" turns a verb phrase into a noun phrase where one is not appropriate. Second, the sentence lacks a clear division between the ideas of addiction and writing (and is a run-on sentence).
(D) "In that" is low-level usage and is not acceptable in standard written English.
(E) The phrase "with his…alcohol" should not be used here. If a phrase is set off like this following the subject, it is usually intended to modify the subject, for example, "The writings of Poe, with their vivid descriptions, …." To refer to Poe himself at this point in the sentence requires a clause: "Poe, who was hopelessly addicted to alcohol often wrote, …."

5. **(D)** This choice corrects both the errors in the original sentence.

(A) The original sentence is characterized by two problems. The "with" construction is not idiomatic, and the "it" has no antecedent.
(B) This choice does not have enough subjects for its verbs. If you read "was" as having "marking" for its subject, then the other verb, "was used," has no subject, and vice versa.
(C) This choice introduces a logic error. The sentence means to say that the novel was the first one in which the American vernacular was used. This choice asserts, however, that it was the author's act of writing that was the first time the vernacular was used.
(E) This choice has the same problem as answer choice (B): not enough subjects for its verbs. If you read "was used" to have the subject "first time," then the other verb "was" has no subject, and vice versa.

6. **(C)** This choice eliminates the ambiguity by defining the scope of the "about protecting".

(A) The original sentence contains an ambiguity. The scope of the phrase "about protecting" is not clearly defined. As originally written, the sentence implies that the parents and civic leaders are protecting the drugs.
(B) This choice does not eliminate the error and introduces the awkward construction "concerned about the protection."
(D) This choice introduces a new error. The phrase "to them," tacked on to the end of this choice, is not necessary and is not idiomatic.
(E) This choice has the same problem as (A): The scope of the "about protecting" is still not clearly defined. This choice implies that people wish to protect the availability of drugs.

7. **(A)** The original sentence is correct. The "so" shows the logical connection between the first idea and the second. The second idea is a consequence of the first. Additionally, the underlined portion is correctly punctuated. You need a comma to keep the two ideas from running together.

(B) This choice obscures the connection between the two ideas.
(C) This choice is incorrectly punctuated. You can't use "and" to do the job of a comma here.
(D) This choice is incorrect because a comma is needed. Additionally, it obscures the connection between the ideas that is clearly stated in the original sentence.
(E) This choice is correctly punctuated, but it is packed with unnecessary conjunctions. You don't need "and," "so," and "consequently."

8. **(A)** The sentence as originally written is correct.

(B) This choice puts the phrase "it to be the case that" where it isn't needed, disrupting the logic of the sentence.
(C) This choice begins correctly, but the inclusion of the second "that" disrupts the logic of the sentence.
(D) This is just a variation of (B) and (C). The result is an awkward rendering of the idea in the original sentence.
(E) This choice makes the same sort of mistake as (D) makes. It begins correctly, but then the use of "more beautiful" distorts the meaning of the sentence.

9. **(E)** This choice succeeds where (C) fails. It corrects the error in the original sentence, and the thought is properly completed: "political reasons rather than for economic reasons."

(A) The original sentence commits the error of using the "ubiquitous they." "They" doesn't have a clear antecedent.
(B) This choice fails to eliminate the "ubiquitous they" and introduces another error: "On account" is low-level usage.
(C) This choice almost succeeds. It corrects the error in the original sentence, but the phrase is never completed.
(D) This choice, too, almost succeeds, but it substitutes a "ubiquitous them" for the "ubiquitous they."

10. **(C)** This choice corrects the original problem by using the infinitive. Since the infinitive doesn't show time (past, present, or future), it doesn't conflict with the other verb.

(A) The original sentence contains an illogical choice of verb tense. Cooper was the first author to do something (an action completed in the past). If there is to be a second main verb in the other clause, it must also show a completed past action.
(B) "Having written" indicates past action, but it is not a verb form that can be the main verb in a clause.
(D) "Had been writing" indicates an action that was completed in the past, but it implies an action that ended before another action in the past, for example, "Cooper had been writing at his desk when the butler announced dinner."
(E) "Has written" does not indicate a completed past action, but implies that the action continues into the present. For example, "Cooper, who will be here tomorrow, has written …."

11. **(E)** This choice provides the necessary parallelism. The noun "love" is parallel to the other two nouns: "training," "practice," and "love."

(A) The original sentence suffers from faulty parallelism. "Training" and "practice" are nouns, so the third element in the series should also be a noun.
(B) This choice attempts to introduce a noun, but the noun form of the verb (the "-ing" form) is not idiomatic here. The sentence now reads "requires…loving to perform."
(C) This choice merely repeats the error with a different subject.
(D) This choice makes the same kind of mistake made by (B), above. The noun form of the verb (this time, the "to" form) does not create an idiomatic phrase. The choice now reads "requires…to love to perform."

12. **(E)** This choice corrects the problem of tense. The "had been" signals an action that took place in the past before another action took place in the past. Then "went" refers to the other past action.

(A) The choice of verb tense in the original sentence is incorrect. The logic of the sentence shows a sequence of events. People were loyal to the crown; the loyalist side was defeated; the loyalists went to Canada. The "having gone" implies that the flight to Canada came before the defeat.
(B) This choice changes the incorrect tense, but "have gone" is itself incorrect. "Have gone" is used to show past action in reference to the present. But the other action in the sentence is a completed past action.
(C) This choice incorrectly changes "had been" to "have been" which does not reflect that the action is a completed past action. Additionally, the phrase "them who" is not acceptable.
(D) This choice combines the weakest aspects of (B) and (C).

13. **(C)** This choice corrects the problem in the original sentence, and it does not introduce any new errors. This may not be the absolutely best way of rendering the thought, but it is the best of the five answer choices.

(A) Here is another example of the "ubiquitous they."
(B) This choice substitutes the "ubiquitous them" for the "ubiquitous they," a substitution which does not improve the sentence.
(D) This choice is difficult to eliminate. It contains no glaring grammatical error, but it is awkward; "it used to be that" is unnecessarily wordy.

(E) This is the second best choice. In what way does it differ from choice (C)? "Using" versus "with." What the sentence means to state is that the fragrances were made "from" or "using" natural ingredients, not "with" natural ingredients.

14. **(B)** The original sentence suffers from faulty parallelism: "to invest…is accepting…." (B), (C), and (E) make the necessary correction, and (D) does not. (C), however, changes the meaning of the original sentence, so (C) cannot be correct. (E) introduces an error of subject-verb agreement by changing "is" to "are." The subject of "is" is "to invest," which requires a singular verb.